THE BRITISH YEAR BOOK OF
INTERNATIONAL LAW

THE
BRITISH YEAR BOOK OF
INTERNATIONAL LAW
1996

SIXTY-SEVENTH YEAR OF ISSUE

OXFORD
AT THE CLARENDON PRESS
1997

Oxford University Press, Great Clarendon Street, Oxford OX2 6DP

Oxford New York
Athens Auckland Bangkok Bogota Bombay
Buenos Aires Calcutta Cape Town Dar es Salaam
Delhi Florence Hong Kong Istanbul Karachi
Kuala Lumpur Madras Madrid Melbourne
Mexico City Nairobi Paris Singapore
Taipei Tokyo Toronto Warsaw
and associated companies in
Berlin Ibadan

Oxford is a trade mark of Oxford University Press

The British Year Book of International Law is an annual
publication, starting with Volume 52 (1981). Orders for
subscriptions or for individual volumes can be placed through
a bookseller or subscription agent. In case of difficulty please
write to the Retail Services Dept., Oxford University Press
Distribution Services, Saxon Way West, Corby, Northants
NN18 9ES, UK

British Library Cataloguing in Publication Data

The British year book of international law.
1996; sixty-seventh year of issue
I. International law—Periodicals
341'.05 JX1
ISBN 0–19–825883–6

Computerset by
Interactive Sciences Ltd, Gloucester.

Printed in Great Britain
on acid-free paper
by Biddles Ltd.
Guildford and King's Lynn

Editorial Communications should be addressed as follows:

Articles and Notes:
Professor Ian Brownlie
All Souls College, Oxford, OX1 4AL
Books for Review:
Professor J. G. Merrills
University of Sheffield Faculty of Law,
Crookesmoor Building, Conduit Road,
Sheffield, S10 1FL.

The Editors and members of the Editorial Committee do not make themselves in any way responsible for the views expressed by contributors, whether the contributions are signed or not.

The British Year Book of International Law is indexed in *Current Law Index*, published by Information Access Company, and in *Legal Journals Index*, published by Legal Information Resources Limited.

CONTENTS

THE LAW AND PROCEDURE OF THE
INTERNATIONAL COURT OF JUSTICE
1960–1989*

PART EIGHT

By HUGH THIRLWAY‡

III. POINTS OF SUBSTANTIVE LAW, 1960–1989 (*continued*)

Division D: *International Organizations*

Introduction

* © Hugh Thirlway, 1996.
‡ Professor of International Law, Graduate Institute of International Studies, Geneva; formerly Principal Legal Secretary, International Court of Justice.

INTRODUCTION

The present section of these articles follows on from the observations
made by Sir Gerald Fitzmaurice, commenting on the earlier case law of
the Court, in earlier *Year Books*;[1] but it has proved convenient to depart
slightly from the structure of his treatment of the subject. Initially he

[1] This *Year Book*, 29 (1952), pp. 1–37; 34 (1958), pp. 1–5; *Collected Edition*, I, pp. 70–106; II,
pp. 428–32.

found it appropriate to deal, in one chapter, with 'International Organizations and Tribunals', of which the first section was addressed to 'International organizations, with particular reference to the United Nations and the Charter', and the second to 'Questions of competence and procedure', which dealt solely with such questions in relation to tribunals, and specifically the Court itself. Subsequently, 'Questions of jurisdiction, competence and procedure' became a distinct chapter, of which one section was addressed to questions relating to resolutions of the General Assembly.

During the period now under consideration, questions of jurisdiction, competence and procedure have bulked so large in the work of the Court that their allocation to a separate chapter seems inescapable, and that chapter is reserved to a subsequent *Year Book*. In dealing with international organizations, it has seemed useful to try to extract from the various dicta of the Court in this field such principles and rules as may be of general application, to all international organizations, or at least to all 'open' or universal organizations, before dealing with decisions of the Court related to the specific provisions of the Charter, or relations solely between organs of the United Nations. The distinction is not a sharp one, as will become apparent, but it none the less seems helpful to try to make it. A final chapter will group and summarize the various points decided, including decisions relating to other organizations (IMO, ICAO, WHO).

The various advisory opinions resulting from decisions of the United Nations Administrative Tribunal, delivered on requests from the Committee on Applications for Review of Administrative Tribunal Judgments,[2] will be examined to the extent that they may throw light on general questions of law relating to international organizations, or to the United Nations in particular. However, these opinions also touch on questions of the internal administrative law of the United Nations, the status, rights and obligations of United Nations staff, etc., but such questions will, in these articles be left aside.[3] A number of judges have indicated the view that these matters do not properly form part of the work of the Court as principal judicial organ of the organization, and the procedure which led to their coming before the Court is in the process of being abolished.

It is perhaps not superfluous to recall that the purpose of the present article is not to survey the whole field of the law of international

---

[2] *Application for Review of Judgment No. 158 of the United Nations Administrative Tribunal (Fasla)*, ICJ Reports, 1973, p. 166; *No. 273 (Mortished)*, ICJ Reports, 1982, p. 325; *No. 333 (Yakimetz)*, ICJ Reports, 1987, p. 18.

[3] The reader is referred to the excellent study of the Court's handling of these matters by Amerasinghe, 'Cases of the International Court of Justice relating to Employment in International Organizations', *Fifty Years of the International Court of Justice (Mélanges Jennings)*, p. 193, as well as to Ruzie, 'La CIJ et la fonction publique internationale', *International Law at a Time of Perplexity (Mélanges Rosenne)*, p. 679; 'Tendances récentes de la fonction publique internationale', *Perspectives du droit international et européen (Mélanges Apollis)*, p. 47.

organizations in general, or of the United Nations in particular, but to note and comment on the decisions of the Court in which questions falling within this field have arisen.

Chapter I

International Organizations in General

1. *The Legal Personality of International Organizations*[4]

Did you ever expect a corporation to have a conscience, when it has no soul to be damned, and no body to be kicked?

Attributed to Lord Thurlow (1731–1806)

The law relating to the legal personality of international organizations owes much to the jurisprudence of the Court in the 1949 *Reparation for Injuries* advisory opinion. In the period now under review, no case has arisen before the Court requiring quite such a radical examination of the matter,[5] but the Court has had occasion to contribute further to the law in this field.

(1) *Legal personality as a fact, opposable to third States*

A most important element in the *Reparation for Injuries* decision was of course the finding by the Court that

fifty States, representing the vast majority of the members of the international community, had the power, in conformity with international law, to bring into being an entity possessing objective international personality, and not merely personality recognized by them alone, together with the capacity to bring international claims.[6]

The last phrase of this passage was the essential element in 1949, but, as Fitzmaurice observed,[7] the Court's underlying reasoning is quite general. There is no doubt that non-member States could not object, specifically in the context of claims made by the organization, that for

---

[4] See Fitzmaurice, this *Year Book*, 29 (1952), pp. 2–8; *Collected Edition*, I, pp. 71–7.

[5] That period has of course seen the litigation and academic controversy over the collapse of the International Tin Council, which raised acute problems of the effects of international legal personality; but the ICJ has not been in any way concerned in that affair. See Greenwood in this *Year Book*, 60 (1989), pp. 461–75, 477–9; UKMIL, this *Year Book*, 49 (1978), pp. 346–8.

[6] *ICJ Reports*, 1949, p. 185.

[7] This *Year Book*, 29 (1952), p. 4, footnote; *Collected Edition*, I, p. 73, footnote. In his general course at the Hague Academy in 1957, Sir Gerald observed that recognition of the international personality of an organization by its member States usually suffices for its functioning, and expressed the view that any non-member State which has dealings or relations with the organization thereby extends a sort of recognition of its international personality, which however is declaratory and not constitutive: 'The General Principles of Law Considered from the Standpoint of the Rule of Law', *Recueil des cours*, 92 (1957-II), p. 33.

them it had no legal existence; but was the impact of international legal personality on them limited to the mere fact that 'the United Nations' meant something more than, and different from, the mere association of a number of States? Specifically, can a non-member State treat as non-existent an act done by the United Nations as an entity, and thus in the exercise of its legal personality?[7a]

In the *Namibia* case, the United Nations Security Council had adopted Resolution 276, by which it declared the continued presence of South Africa in Namibia to be illegal, and called upon States to act accordingly. The Court was asked to say in its advisory opinion what were the legal consequences 'for States' (not 'for member-States') of the continued presence of South Africa in Namibia notwithstanding that resolution, and thus had to determine the legal position as regards third States. Its view on this aspect was stated as follows:

> In the view of the Court, the termination of the Mandate and the declaration of illegality of South Africa's presence in Namibia are opposable to all States in the sense of barring *erga omnes* the legality of a situation which is maintained in violation of international law: in particular, no State which enters into relations with South Africa concerning Namibia may expect the United Nations or its Members to recognize the validity or effects of such relationship, or the consequences thereof. The Mandate having been terminated by decision of the international organization in which the supervisory authority over its administration was vested, and South Africa's presence in Namibia having been declared illegal, it is for non-Member States to act in accordance with those decisions.[8]

The interesting part of this reasoning for our purposes is the last sentence. The question there is not the powers of the General Assembly or the Security Council, but the effects of an act of the organization as an entity. Although no specific reference is made to the question of international legal personality, the existence of such personality, opposable to all States (*erga omnes*), underlies the Court's reasoning. The point is lucidly put by Judge de Castro:

> These [non-member] States have no obligations under the Charter. Nonetheless they should respect a declaration of the forfeiture of the legal title to possess the territory pronounced by a legitimate authority, against a State which received the territory in order to administer it in the name of the international organization.[9]

[7a] A more doubtful case is that of a State which has been a member of an organization, but then withdraws from it; the suggestion has been made that such State could then, as it were, withdraw its recognition of the personality of the organization. See Seidl-Hohenveldern, 'Responsibility of Member States of an Organization for Acts of that Organization', *Le droit international à l'heure de sa codification (Mélanges Ago)*, vol. 3, p. 417, quoting Gidel on the analogous problem of France's attitude to the Vatican, 'Quelques idées sur la condition internationale de la Papauté', *Revue générale de droit international public*, 18 (1911), p. 610.

[8] *ICJ Reports*, 1971, p. 56, para. 126.

[9] Separate opinion, *ICJ Reports*, 1971, p. 219.

The legal *existence* of the authority is a precondition of its legitimacy.

It is however not sufficient, for third States to be obligated, that an international entity act as such: it must so act in a context in which it has, as an entity, a recognized role to play: hence the emphasis by the Court on the possession by the United Nations of the supervisory authority over the administration of the Mandate (It is worth recalling that the question put to the Court concerned, not the legal effects for States of Security Council Resolution 276 (1970), but the legal effects of South Africa's continued presence in Namibia notwithstanding that resolution—the distinction may possibly not be trivial). This of course raises, in the context of Namibia, the difficult problem of succession of international organizations, already examined by Fitzmaurice in relation to the earliest stage of the Court's involvement with the territory of South West Africa,[10] and to which he had, as a judge, to return in the later stages of that involvement; this aspect will be examined below.

In his 1952 article Fitzmaurice drew attention to the distinction between capacity to bring an international claim for breach of an obligation owed to an international organization, and the existence of an obligation capable of being enforced by such a claim; as he pointed out, the Court in the *Reparation for Injuries* case had carefully disclaimed any intention of going into the circumstances in which such an obligation might exist.[11] Fitzmaurice in fact asserted the non-existence, in general international law, of obligations owed to international organizations by non-member States, in the absence of specific circumstances, such as the existence of a treaty concluded with the organization. This latter exception is self-evident: in the *Headquarters Agreement (PLO)* case, the obligations incumbent upon the United States under the Headquarters Agreement would, *mutatis mutandis*, have been incumbent upon Switzerland under the Agreement for the European Office at Geneva (the Ariana site); and the fact that Switzerland is not a UN member would be irrelevant.

Some doubt may however be felt, after more than forty years, whether Fitzmaurice's view as to the absence of obligations in general law owed by non-member States to international organizations is still correct; and those doubts are confirmed by the approach of the Court in the *WHO/Egypt* case. The question of the position of international organizations in relation to general international law is the subject of section 2(1) below; it may however be observed here that if international organizations can participate in practices which give rise to customary rules binding on them, such rules must equally be binding on the States concerned in those practices (or, possibly, on all States, as a matter of general customary law), whether or not such States are members of the particular

---

[10] This *Year Book*, 29 (1952), pp. 8 ff.; *Collected Edition*, I, pp. 77 ff.
[11] This *Year Book*, 29 (1952), p. 21; *Collected Edition*, I, p. 90.

organization concerned. For example, at least in the field of relations with host States, the principles discerned in the *WHO/Egypt* case must be taken to be opposable to Switzerland in its capacity of host State to numerous international organizations of which it is not a member, and to impose on it certain obligations toward those organizations. More generally, the more that the United Nations (in particular) is called upon to establish relationships[12] with States as an actor on the international scene, on equal terms as it were,[13] the more it must be bound by, and entitled to take advantage of, customary law applicable to such relationships.[14] This conclusion may however be obscured by the procedural fact that neither the United Nations nor any other international organization can appear as a party before the Court, so that the actual enforcement of a claim must be by other means.

Also indicative in this sense is the advisory opinion in the *Namibia* case, and specifically its reliance on the customary rules concerning termination of a treaty relationship on account of breach, as justifying the action of the United Nations, through the General Assembly, terminating the Mandate for South West Africa.[15] It has to be conceded that the context is one of treaty law, or, to be more precise, of the customary law rules governing treaty relationships; and if an international organization concludes, or succeeds to, a treaty, it can hardly be excluded from reliance on, or subjection to, customary rules of this kind.[16] It is however striking to observe that Fitzmaurice, in his dissenting opinion, disagreed with this finding on the grounds (*inter alia*) that 'the position in regard to private law contracts and *ordinary* international treaties' (italics added)

[12] On the assumption always that the establishment of such relationships falls within the competences conferred on the organization concerned; there is thus no conflict here with the *principe de spécialité* regarded by legal writers as applicable to international organizations in the light of the *Reparation for Injuries* decision: cf. Nguyen Quoc Dinh, *Droit international public* (5e. éd par Daillier et Pellet), paras. 390, 396.

[13] It remains true that, as the Court observed in 1949, international personality of the UN 'is not the same thing as saying that [the organization] is a State, which it certainly is not, or that its legal personality and rights and duties are the same as those of a State' (*ICJ Reports*, 1949, p. 179).

[14] The 1982 UN Convention on the Law of the Sea reserves the possibility for ships to sail under the flag of the United Nations (Art. 93); in the event of injury to, or unlawful treatment of, such a ship by a non-member State, then (apart from claims under the Convention itself—non-members Nauru and Switzerland have signed but not ratified the Convention), it would seem that a claim could be brought by the United Nations against the offender, in the exercise of the capacity recognized in 1949 for breach of a customary law obligation.

[15] See further on this below, sub-section (3).

[16] It would be interesting to speculate whether an international organization which had concluded a treaty with a non-member State could bring a claim, not for breach of the treaty, but for breach of the obligation not to defeat its object and purpose, an obligation which, as the Court found in the *Nicaragua* case, if it exists in relation to a particular treaty, finds its basis in customary law, not in the treaty itself: see *ICJ Reports*, 1986, p. 135, para. 270, and the present writer's comments in this *Year Book*, 63 (1992), pp. 48–54. The obligation stated in Article 18 of the Vienna Convention on the Law of Treaties, that of a State which has signed but not ratified a treaty, not to defeat its object and purpose, is paralleled in Article 18 of the 1986 Convention on Treaties between States and International Organizations; but that Convention is of course not in force, and the obligation is not identical with the one found to exist in the *Nicaragua* case.

was different from an 'institutional' situation;[17] for him, in the institutional context, it would have been necessary that the appropriate powers 'should have been given concrete expression in what are the governing instruments', it being not possible to rely on 'any theory of implied or inherent powers'.[18] He also observed (perhaps with more justification) that if the rules applicable to treaties or contracts were to be applied to the relationship between the UN and the Mandatory, then they should all be applied; and in his view it would follow from those rules that the disappearance of the League put an end to the relationship, which could only have been restored by a novation.

At all events, it would seem to be a mistake to apply too rigorously what is known as the *principe de spécialité*,[19] so as to recognize an international organization as having only those rights (and obligations) provided for in its constituent instrument, or required for the discharge of its functions. The nature of the relationships into which it enters may, as in the case of the rules applicable to treaties, necessarily cause certain customary law rules to attach; and even if an organization is not a State, if and so far as it legitimately behaves like a State, the appropriate legal rules applicable to States should operate in relation to it.

(2) *Attributes of international personality*

It is unclear what powers, if any, are automatically and necessarily implied by the possession of international personality. In the *Reparation for Injuries* case, when discussing the question whether the United Nations had capacity to bring an international claim, the Court observed that

Whereas a Sate possesses the totality of international rights and duties recognized by international law, the rights and duties of an entity such as the [United Nations] Organization must depend upon its purposes and functions as specified or implied in its constituent documents and developed in practice,[20]

and went on to find that the organization did have the capacity to make an international claim because this was necessary for the discharge of its functions.[21] This suggests that the matter is wholly governed by the constitutive instrument coupled with practice: that an international

---

[17] *ICJ Reports*, 1971, pp. 266–7, para. 68.
[18] *ICJ Reports*, 1971, p. 267, para. 70.
[19] See below, section 2, sub-section (3); p. 32 and n. 117.
[20] *ICJ Reports*, 1949, p. 80; cf. Fitzmaurice, this *Year Book*, 29 (1952), p. 4; *Collected Edition*, I, p. 83.
[21] These functions 'could not be effectively discharged if they involved the concurrent action, on the international plane, of fifty-eight or more Foreign Offices' (ibid.); the prospect of this bureaucratic nightmare suggests that there can be virtually no international organization beyond a certain minimum size which would *not* be held to have capacity to bring international claims. It may be doubted whether, even so, such capacity should be regarded as an automatic attribute of international personality.

organization comes naked into the world except in so far as its progenitors have chosen to make provision for it in the constitutive treaty.

On the other hand, in the *WHO/Egypt* case, the Court thought it necessary

to underline at the outset that the question before it is not whether, in general, an organization has the right to select the location of the seat of its headquarters or of a regional office. On that question there has been no difference of views in the present case, and there can be no doubt that an international organization does have such a right.[22]

Is every international organization therefore born clutching at least this equivalent of the proverbial silver spoon—the right to choose the location of, as it were, its cradle? It must be supposed that this cannot be more than a presumption, if a strong one: there are numerous examples of organizations whose seat is predetermined in the constitutive instrument,[23] a provision which must presumably be taken to prevail over, or pre-empt, the right referred to in the *WHO/Egypt* case. Yet in practice if the appropriate organ of the infant organization, or even the initial members thereof by unanimous agreement, decided to override the constitutional provision and establish the seat of the organization elsewhere (with the consent of the State concerned[24]), it does not appear that this decision could be objected to as illicit and void.

(3) *Succession of international organizations*[25]

The question of succession between international organizations has not attracted much doctrinal attention,[26] save in the very special case of the claim of the United Nations General Assembly to have inherited the powers of the League of Nations in relation to the Mandate for South West Africa, with which the Court was concerned in 1950, 1955, 1956 and 1971. Fitzmaurice emphasized in his 1952 article that the 1950 *South West Africa* advisory opinion turned largely on the effect of particular instruments, but nevertheless advanced the following two

---

[22] *ICJ Reports*, 1980, p. 89, para. 37.

[23] An obvious example is the International Court itself (though it is an organ, not an organization): see Article 22 of the Statute.

[24] Kelsen (*The Law of the United Nations* (1964), p. 98) suggested that there might be an obligation on States to offer hospitality to organizations of which they are members; but in practice the point is academic.

[25] This was the rubric used by Fitzmaurice (and of course other scholars) under which to treat the question of the demise of the League of Nations and its replacement by the United Nations in relation to South West Africa/Namibia; but the Court itself did not use the expression until, in the 1971 *Namibia* advisory opinion, it referred to the United Nations as the 'successor' of the League (*ICJ Reports*, 1971, p. 49, para. 102). Individual judges had however used the expression in opinions: see *ICJ Reports*, 1950, pp. 172–3 (Judge Read), 159–61 (Judge McNair).

[26] The International Law Commission in 1971 considered that the scope for codification and progressive development of the law on the subject was limited: *ILC Yearbook*, 1971, vol. 2, part 2, pp. 79–80; and generally on the subject, cf. Myers, *Succession between International Organizations* (1993).

general propositions as supported by the Court's findings in that opinion:

(i) There *can* be an automatic devolution of functions from one international organization on to another in the event of the extinction of the former.
(ii) There is a presumption that such a devolution occurs whenever the following conditions are fulfilled:
a. a given organization becomes extinct, but another organization intended generally to take its place comes or has come into being, having essentially the same purposes and principles, with a similar or analogous constitution and institutions, and carrying out broadly the same functions, in the same field;
b. the constitutive instrument of the new organization specifically authorizes or enables it to assume and carry out the functions in question.[27]

When the matter came before the Court in 1971 in the context of the request by the Security Council for an advisory opinion on the *Legal Consequences for States of the Continued Presence of South Africa in Namibia*, Judge Fitzmaurice dissented from the majority view, *inter alia*, inasmuch as he held that there had been no legal successorship between the United Nations and the League of Nations. In his view,

there are only three ways in which the United Nations could, upon the dissolution of the League, have become invested with the latter's power in respect of mandates as such: namely (*a*) if specific arrangement to that effect had been made,—(*b*) if such a succession must be implied in some way,—(*c*) if the mandatory concerned . . . could be shown to have consented to what would in effect have been a *novation* . . . [28]

The first and third possibilities were rejected by Judge Fitzmaurice on the facts: they do not concern the general point now under discussion. He rejected also any application in the specific case of the second possibility,[29] thereby differing from the view of the Court in the 1950 advisory opinion on which he had been commenting in 1952,[30] essentially on the grounds that the Council of the League, to which Mandatories were bound to report, and the United Nations General Assembly, which had, it was argued, inherited the supervisory functions of the League Council, were too different from each other in size, composition, powers, functions and method of deciding. His conclusion was thus:

For these reasons it seems to me to be juridically impossible to postulate such a metamorphosis as taking place automatically or unless by consent. *To do so would not merely be to change the identity of the organ entitled to supervise the*

---

[27] This *Year Book*, 29 (1952), pp. 8–10; *Collected Edition*, I, pp. 77–9 (italics original).
[28] Dissenting opinion, *ICJ Reports*, 1971, p. 227, para. 11 (italics original).
[29] As Fitzmaurice had noted in 1952 (this *Year Book*, 29 (1952), pp. 10–11, footnote; *Collected Edition*, I, pp. 79–80, footnote), in 1950 even the theoretical possibility of an implied succession had been rejected by some judges—McNair and Read: see *ICJ Reports*, 1950, pp. 159, 172.
[30] In fairness it should be added that Fitzmaurice in 1952 regarded 'the whole question of succession and devolution between international organizations' as 'controversial and still unsettled': see the 1952 footnote referred to in the immediately preceding footnote to the present article.

implementation of the obligation but, by reason of this change, to change also the nature of the obligation itself.[31]

He did not discuss the matter in terms of a presumption, but would presumably have contended that these considerations were such as to exclude any presumption of the kind envisaged in the 1952 article.

The Court itself in the 1971 opinion hardly touched on the specific question of succession, being apparently content to take it for granted that the view taken in the 1950 advisory opinion was, on this as on other points, to be regarded as sound. Its emphasis was much more on the survival of the Mandate for South West Africa as an institution, with the consequence that the obligation of the Mandatory to report to *somebody* also survived; and who else could that be but the United Nations?[32] It recalled the very cogent observation made in the 1950 advisory opinion that if the Mandate lapsed, South Africa's authority over the territory, derived from the Mandate, would also have lapsed: 'To retain the rights derived from the Mandate and to deny the obligations thereunder could not be justified'.[33]

The Court did however have to deal, against the wishes of some of its members, with the question of the effect of a succession between the League of Nations and the United Nations, as regards the possibility of termination of mandates. It was apparently accepted on all sides that as a matter of principle a successor organization cannot succeed to more in the way of powers than were possessed by the organization succeeded to.[34] To the objection that no provision was made in the Mandates system for unilateral termination of a Mandate by the League Council, the Court, as noted above, replied by appealing to the 'general principles of international law regulating the termination of a treaty relationship on account of breach': the Mandate was 'an international agreement having the character of a treaty or convention', and the General Assembly had declared the existence of a material breach of the Mandate. Resolution 2145, terminating the Mandate,

is therefore to be viewed as the exercise of the right to terminate a relationship in case of a deliberate and persistent violation of obligations which destroys the very object and purpose of that relationship.[35]

---

[31] *ICJ Reports*, 1971, p. 233, para. 19 (italics original).

[32] Fitzmaurice in his dissenting opinion challenged this assumption also, suggesting that a special body could have been set up by the Mandatory itself, possibly in conjunction with other Mandatories: *ICJ Reports*, 1971, pp. 230–1, para. 16.

[33] *ICJ Reports*, 1950, p. 133, quoted in *ICJ Reports*, 1962, p. 333, and in *ICJ Reports*, 1971, p. 42, para. 81.

[34] This was clearly recognized in the 1950 advisory opinion when it was stated that 'The degree of supervision to be exercised by the General Assembly should not therefore exceed that which applied under the Mandates System', (*ICJ Reports* 1950, p. 138), a finding that rendered necessary the two subsequent requests for advisory opinion on *Voting Procedure* and *Hearing of Petitioners*. The principle is stated forcibly in Fitzmaurice's dissenting opinion: *ICJ Reports*, 1971, p. 264, para. 65.

[35] *ICJ Reports*, 1971, pp. 46–7, paras. 94–5, quoting *ICJ Reports*, 1962, p. 330.

Fitzmaurice disagreed, on the basis that such principle, applicable to simple contractual relationships, could not be transposed to an institutional system, where express provision would be required for such a unilateral right to exist;[36] this is a matter already examined above.

Fitzmaurice's tentative statement of the general law on succession of international organizations, contained in his 1952 article and quoted above, can be regarded as confirmed by the Court's decision in the *Namibia* case; to it can be added the further (fairly self-evident) general rule that a succession does not confer on the successor organization any powers additional to or wider than those enjoyed by the predecessor organization. These powers are however not limited to those specifically provided for in the relevant instruments, but will include those read in by necessary implication or conferred by general international law on any entity in a position, in relation to some other subject of international law, equivalent or analogous to that of the predecessor organization. The inclusion of these non-explicit powers will however of course be subject to any exclusion or limitation contained in the governing texts themselves.

2. *The Law Applicable to International Organizations*

(1) *International organizations and general international law*

There is of course no doubt that, in their relations with each other and with sovereign States, international organizations are subject to general international law in the same way (in principle) as are States themselves.[37] This was stated in round terms by the Court in its advisory opinion on the *Interpretation of the Agreement of 25 March 1951 between the WHO and Egypt*:

International organizations are subjects of international law and, as such, are bound by any obligations incumbent upon them under general rules of international law, under their constitutions or under international agreements to which they are parties.[38]

So far as concerns the latter category of obligations, those under treaty law, an international organization which has power to make treaties[39]

---

[36] *ICJ Reports*, 1971, pp. 266–7, para. 68.

[37] On this and generally, see Llanos Mansilla, 'Las organizaciones internationales come sujetos de derecho internacional', *Anuario hispano-luso-americano de derecho internacional*, 8 (1987), p. 97; Menon, 'International Organizations as Subjects of International Law', *Revue de droit international, de sciences diplomatiques et politiques*, 70 (1992), p. 61.

[38] *ICJ Reports*, 1980, pp. 89–90, para. 37.

[39] Which probably means any international organization other than one declared by its constitutive instrument not to have such powers: cf. the 1973 resolution of the *Institut de droit international, Annuaire de l'institut*, 1973, p. 797, and Art. 6 of the 1986 Vienna Convention on the Law of Treaties between States and International Organizations. Cf. also Art. 6 of the Draft Articles presented to the ILC on Relations between States and International Organizations: *ILC Yearbook*, 1990, vol. 2, part 2, p. 86.

must necessarily be bound by the provisions of a treaty to which it is a party, as a matter of *pacta sunt servanda*. This is of course stated in Article 26 of the 1986 Vienna Convention on the Law of Treaties between States and International Organizations or between International Organizations, which, though not yet in force, may on this point at least be regarded as codifying existing law. General principles of law as part of international law must, by virtue of their generality, be applicable to all subjects of international law, including international organizations.

As for customary law, the content of such law derives primarily from the practice of States; but in principle it would seem that in any field in which international organizations are called upon to act alongside States, the practice of organizations may also contribute to the formation or the maintenance in existence of a custom. *A fortiori* must this be the case where the matters to be regulated by the law are matters directly related to the existence and operation of particular international organizations; a good example is that of United Nations responsibility, in the context of peace-keeping operations, for unlawful acts of its officials or members of a peace-keeping force.[40] As was observed, for example, by Eli Lauterpacht in 1965, unlawful acts by international organizations are not limited to such matters as *ultra vires* acts, but include 'acts which even though committed by international organizations are nevertheless of a kind which could be committed by States'.[41] There are of course limitations on the extent to which rules of law impinge, in practical terms, on an international organization; as was pointed out by Judge Ago in his separate opinion in the *WHO/Egypt* case,

An international organization is, like a State, a subject of international law, but it is one which enjoys limited international legal capacity, and in particular, unlike a State, it is a subject of law which lacks all territorial basis,[42]

at least until it has concluded a host agreement with some State.

The Court took the opportunity to declare the existence of such rules of law applicable to international organizations—though it did not *expressis verbis* refer to them as rules of customary law—in its advisory opinion in that case. The questions put to it for opinion were, according to their terms, simply matters of treaty law:

---

[40] See Rousseau in *Revue générale de droit international public*, 73 (1969) p. 1110, and the Report of the International Law Commission on State Responsibility, *ILC Yearbook*, 1975, vol. 2, part 2, pp. 88–90. Questions have also arisen as to responsibility of organizations concerned with outer space for objects launched into outer space: see Galicki, 'Liability of International Organizations for Space Activities', *Polish Yearbook of International Law*, 5 (1972–3), p. 199.

[41] They include denial of justice, misuse of territory, failure to recognize the effects of nationality, or breach of treaty obligations': E. Lauterpacht, 'The Legal Effects of Illegal Acts of International Organizations', in Jennings (ed.), *Essays in Honour of Lord McNair*, p. 89.

[42] *ICJ Reports*, 1980, p. 155.

1. Are the negotiation and notice provisions of Section 37 of the Agreement of 25 March 1951 between the World Health Organization and Egypt applicable in the event that either party to the Agreement wishes to have the [WHO] Regional Office transferred from the territory of Egypt?
2. If so, what would be the legal responsibilities of both the World Health Organization and Egypt, with regard to the Regional Office in Alexandria, during the two-year period between notice and termination of the Agreement?[43]

The background to the case 'was a falling-out between Egypt and the other Arab States owing to the former's rapprochement with Israel; a majority decision was taken in the WHO Regional Committee to transfer the Regional Office from Alexandria to the territory of another State in the Region, and this was viewed by Egypt, among others, as a political decision designed to penalize Egypt, and not inspired by any motives related to health or the working of the Organization.

In the WHO Assembly the question was however raised whether any transfer of the Regional Office would be covered by section 37 of the 1951 Agreement, which constituted the host agreement relating to that Office; that section provided:

The present Agreement may be revised at the request of either party. In this event the two parties shall consult each other concerning the modifications to be made in its provisions. If the negotiations do not result in an understanding within one year, the present Agreement may be denounced by either party giving two years' notice.[44]

The matter was therefore referred to the Court for advisory opinion, in the terms set out above; the Court however, emphasizing the importance of ascertaining 'what are the legal questions really in issue in questions formulated in a request',[45] decided that the 'true legal question under consideration in the World Health Assembly' was:

What are the legal principles and rules applicable to the question under what conditions and in accordance with what modalities a transfer of the Regional Office from Alexandria may be effected?[46]

The effect of this re-definition of the question was to involve considerations of law deriving from sources other than the 1951 Agreement, i.e. from customary law and, if appropriate, general principles of law. It was in this context that the Court made the statement quoted above that international organizations, as subjects of international law, are bound by any obligations incumbent upon them 'under general rules of inter-

---

[43] *ICJ Reports*, 1980, p. 74.
[44] *ICJ Reports*, 1980, p. 88, para. 34.
[45] *ICJ Reports*, 1980, p. 88, para. 35, referring to the opinions in the *Admissibility of Hearing of Petitioners by the Committee on SW Africa, ICJ Reports*, 1956, p. 26, and *Certain Expenses of the UN, ICJ Reports*, 1962, pp. 156–8.
[46] *ICJ Reports*, 1980, p. 88, para. 35.

national law'.[47] Furthermore, after setting out the various views as to the applicability and interpretation of section 37, it concluded that

Whatever view may be held on the question whether the establishment and location of the Regional Office in Alexandria are embraced within the provisions of the 1951 Agreement, and whatever view may be held on the question whether the provisions of Section 37 are applicable to the case of a transfer of the Office from Egypt, the fact remains that certain legal principles and rules are applicable in the case of such a transfer.[48]

These principles and rules, being independent of the correct interpretation of the 1951 Agreement, could only be rules of customary law (or conceivably general principles of law). If, however, they were rules of customary law, it would have to be possible to show that they derived from a practice coupled with an *opinio juris*, on the part of States, or of international organizations, or both.

As already noted above, the Court began by declaring that 'an organization has the right to select the location of the seat of its headquarters or of a regional office',[49] and did not see any need to indicate what the source of that right might be; it is reasonable to regard it as a necessary element of the existence of international personality. It is not difficult to see a *power* to select the location of its seat as an implied power of an international organization, one of those referred to by the Court, in relation to the United Nations, in the *Reparation for Injuries* case as being

those powers which, though not expressly provided in the Charter, are conferred upon it by necessary implication as being essential to the performance of its duties.[50]

International personality is however not itself a source of law in the classic sense, but the creation of law. If a source is required for the concept of international personality of organizations and the implications of the concept, it must surely be the general principles of law, either by municipal analogy to corporations, or simply as one of the class of general principles entailed in international legal relations.[51]

When examining the legal rules and principles applicable to the case of a transfer of the Regional Office, the Court directed its attention to

a considerable number of host agreements of different kinds, concluded by States with various international organizations and containing varying provisions regarding the revision, termination or denunciation of these agreements,[52]

---

[47] *ICJ Reports*, 1980, pp. 89–90, para. 37.
[48] *ICJ Reports*, 1980, p. 92, para. 42.
[49] *ICJ Reports*, 1980, p. 89, para. 37.
[50] *ICJ Reports*, 1950, p. 182; see Fitzmaurice, this *Year Book*, 29 (1952), p. 5; *Collected Edition*, I, p. 74.
[51] Cf. Mosler in Bernhardt (ed.), *Encyclopedia of Public International Law*, vol. 2, pp. 522–4.
[52] *ICJ Reports*, 1980, p. 94, para. 45.

and concluded that

despite their variety and imperfections,[53] the provisions of host agreements regarding their revision, termination or denunciation are not without significance in the present connection.[54]

The Court explained immediately that that significance was twofold:

In the first place, they confirm the recognition by international organizations and host States of the existence of mutual obligations incumbent upon them to resolve the problems attendant upon a revision, termination or denunciation of a host agreement.[55]

The thrust of this is not entirely clear. Obviously a revision, termination or denunciation of a host agreement will raise problems, and these will have to be resolved, either by means foreseen in the agreement itself, or by *ad hoc* arrangements agreed between the parties. There is an 'obligation' to resolve the problems in the sense that, if not resolved, they will remain problems; but does this imply the existence of some *legal* obligation, and if so, to do what?[56]

The Court however continues:

But they [sc. the provisions referred to] do more, since they must be presumed to reflect the views of organizations and host States as to the implications of those obligations in the contexts in which those provisions are intended to apply. In the view of the Court, therefore, they provide certain general indications of what the mutual obligations of organizations and host States to co-operate in good faith may involve in situations such as the one with which the Court is here concerned.[57]

Putting the matter in simpler, if cruder, terms, we may say that the provisions quoted show the ways in which States and organizations tackle, in advance, the problems which are expected to result from a termination or revision of a host agreement; and this, for the Court, is clearly a practice which may be creative of a customary rule. But what of the *opinio juris*? It is this requirement which makes clear what the point

---

[53] The Court felt 'bound to observe' in this connection 'that in future closer attention might with advantage be given to their drafting' (*ICJ Reports*, 1980, p. 94, para. 46). There is some illogicality in this patronizing remark: if treaties are being examined as evidence of a practice, they must surely be taken as they stand; one cannot in the same breath criticize them for not saying adequately what one would have preferred, *a priori*, to see them express.

[54] *ICJ Reports*, 1980, p. 94, para. 46.

[55] Ibid.

[56] If the problems amount to, or result in, a dispute, there will of course be an obligation to settle it by peaceful means, on the lines of Article 33 of the Charter, but this does not seem to be what is meant.

[57] *ICJ Reports*, 1980, p. 94, para. 46.

of the Court's first deduction was: the practice had to be shown to result from, and be the practical implementation of, a perceived duty to act.

Two problems may be noted. In the first place, while it is well recognized that the conclusion of similar treaties may amount to State practice constitutive of a customary rule,[58] yet to deduce the existence of a custom from similar provisions in a number of treaties is always open to the objection that the existence of such treaties might, in many instances, equally well be taken to point to a conviction on the part of the States concerned that there was no customary rule to the effect suggested, since if such rule had existed, the treaty provisions might have been thought unnecessary. Secondly, where the specific dispute under examination is one in which such a treaty exists, that treaty must be given effect, and the customary rule, if it is found to exist, can only be invoked to supplement the treaty, not to contradict it.[59] In the *WHO/Egypt* case there was, as we have seen, a deliberate widening by the Court of the question put to it, for reasons which were, no doubt, excellent in themselves. This could not, however, justify the Court in applying to the dispute rules of customary law which were more general than, and ousted by, a specific treaty.

In this connection, the Court observed toward the end of its opinion:

the Court takes as its starting point the mutual obligations incumbent upon Egypt and the Organization to co-operate in good faith with respect to the implications and effects of the transfer of the Regional Office from Egypt. The Court does so the more readily as it considers those obligations to be the very basis of the legal relations between the Organization and Egypt under general international law, under the Constitution of the Organization and under the agreements in force between Egypt and the Organization.[60]

In what sense could such obligations be 'the very basis' of the legal relations referred to? So far as the Constitution of the Organization and the various agreements concluded with Egypt were concerned, the 'basis', in the sense of the principle from which those relations acquired legal force, was simply the principle of *pacta sunt servanda*. Mutual obligations to co-operate in good faith could flow from the existence of a

---

[58] Cf. *SS Lotus, PCIJ*, Series A, No. 10 (1927), p. 27.

[59] This is not the place to go further into the question of the possible hierarchy of sources of international law; in such a case as the one here examined, the treaty must surely prevail over custom, either on the basis that Article 38 of the ICJ Statute enumerates a hierarchical order; or as a matter of logic, one of the purposes of treaties being to create a legal order diverging from the customary law situation (and as an implication *a contrario* from the recognition of the existence of *jus cogens*); or by application of the principles of *lex posterior* and *lex specialis*. A qualification may be noted for the *lex posterior* principle: did the WHO agreement antedate the growth of a customary rule, and indeed contribute to its creation?

[60] *ICJ Reports*, 1980, p. 95, para. 48.

treaty relationship;[61] and the desirability of regulating planned intentions to co-operate might well underlie the provisions included in a treaty instrument. Such mutual obligations might exist as part of 'general international law', and in a sense form the basis of it; but, considerations of *jus cogens* apart, there is no room for the application of 'general international law' if the point in issue is directly regulated by a treaty in force between the parties. The passage quoted must be seen therefore as a somewhat rhetorical justification of the decision of the Court to re-define the question submitted to it, a decision inspired by concern to contribute to the defusing of the political situation behind the submission of the request.

An earlier case relating to an international organization in which the Court appeared ready to look beyond the specific provisions of constitutive instruments to what it saw as underlying general principles, though in a different field, was that concerning the *Appeal relating to the Jurisdiction of the ICAO Council*. The question under examination was whether the provisions in Article 84 of the Chicago Convention on Civil Aviation, and section 2 of Article II of the related International Air Services Transit Agreement, concerning appeals to the Court from decisions of the ICAO Council, applied only to decisions on the merits of a dispute or also to decisions on interlocutory matters, or at least to decisions on jurisdiction. The Court supported its finding, in favour of the latter view, not on textual considerations, or other considerations of the kind referred to in Articles 31 and 32 of the Vienna Convention on the Law of Treaties (themselves regarded by the Court as generally declaratory of customary law on the subject[62]), but on general considerations as to the nature of (in particular) interlocutory decisions on jurisdiction, jurisdictional objections, and the appeal process.[63] It is possible, to put it no higher, that the Court was influenced by the fact that it was dealing with the constitutive instrument of an international organization (and an instrument closely related thereto) to place more stress on such general and 'institutional' considerations rather than on the intention of the parties and the object and purpose of the treaties taken each as a whole.

To return to the *WHO/Egypt* case, what were the obligations of general law which the Court found to be incumbent upon the WHO and Egypt? They may be summarized as: 'a duty to consult together in good

---

[61] At the time of the *WHO/Egypt* opinion, the Court had not yet had occasion to develop the idea of an extra-conventional obligation not to defeat the object and purpose of a treaty, which formed a controversial element in its decision in the *Nicaragua* case: see n. 16, above, and the previous article in this series, this *Year Book*, 63 (1992), pp. 48 ff.

[62] *Land, Island and Maritime Frontier Dispute (El Salvador/Honduras)*, *ICJ Reports*, 1992, pp. 582–3, para. 373; *Territorial Dispute (Libya/Chad)*, *ICJ Reports*, 1994, p. 21, para. 41.

[63] *ICJ Reports*, 1972, pp. 55–7, para. 18.

faith', in advance, as to the 'conditions' and 'modalities' of a transfer of the Regional Office; in the event of a decision to transfer, a duty 'to consult together and negotiate regarding the various arrangements needed to effect the transfer' in an orderly manner and with a minimum of prejudice to the work of the WHO; and a 'duty upon the party which wishes to effect the transfer to give a reasonable period of notice . . . taking account of all practical arrangements needed'.[64] The Court could give only general indications as to the periods of consultation and the reasonable notice, but quoted in this context both the 1951 Agreement itself[65] (one year for negotiations; two years' notice) and Article 56 of the Vienna Convention on the Law of Treaties (twelve months' notice).

The essential point to be brought out here is however that the Court recognized that the relationships between States and international organizations may involve practices which give rise to a customary rule peculiar to those relationships, and binding on both the States and the organizations directly concerned in the practices, as well as (*semble*) other States and organizations involved in analogous relationships. Demonstration of an *opinio juris* may present difficulties, and this is perhaps a weak point of the *WHO/Egypt* opinion, which does not really tackle the problem. Accordingly, there is not a lot which can be said by way of comment, except to draw attention to one particularity of the potential custom-forming actions of international organizations. It is axiomatic that such organizations do not have the plenitude of powers and functions attributable to sovereign States, but only those specifically conferred on each organization by its constitution or by necessary implication;[66] and the practical implications of the absence of other attributes of statehood, such as territory, may also be material. Accordingly the essential element of *choice*, in the background to any discussion of the establishment of the *opinio juris*, may be limited or lacking. In examining whether a State acted as it did because it regarded itself as under a customary law obligation, it is normally material to consider what other courses might have been open to it. In the specific case of the law relating to the seat of an international organization, it should not be overlooked that an organization, having no territory,[67] must have a seat, if only a provisional one, in the territory of some State willing to receive

---

[64] *ICJ Reports*, 1980, pp. 95–6, para. 49. Some of these indications may be regarded as a form of soft law, in their flexibility and dependence on circumstances.

[65] An interesting example of a sort of *renvoi* from one source to another and back again!

[66] See the *Reparation for Injuries* case and Fitzmaurice in this *Year Book*, 29 (1952), pp. 14 ff.; *Collected Edition*, I, pp. 83 ff.

[67] Cf. the observations of Judge Ago, quoted above (text and n. 42). For present purposes we may leave out of account such historically interesting but ultimately irrelevant entities as the Sovereign Order of the Knights of Malta.

it, if it is to enjoy any effective existence at all. Accordingly, its actions to that end can hardly be associated with an *opinio juris*, showing a sense of *legal* compulsion, if they were dictated by a purely practical compulsion.[68]

(2) *Constitutive and other instruments of international organizations and their interpretation*[69]

(a) *The Charter and analogous instruments*

In the *Reparation for Injuries* case, the Court observed that 'the rights and duties of an entity such as the [United Nations] Organization must depend upon its purposes as specified or implied in its constituent documents and developed in practice',[70] and it must also be there that one must look to regulate any question of the rights, duties and operation of the organs of the organization. The constitutive instrument of an international organization is by definition an international treaty, and the Court's approach to the interpretation of, in particular, the UN Charter, was restated in the *Certain Expenses* case:

On the previous occasions when the Court has had to interpret the Charter of the United Nations, it has followed the principles and rules applicable in general to the interpretation of treaties, since it has recognized that the Charter is a multilateral treaty, albeit a treaty having certain special characteristics.[71]

In that case, the Court applied general rules of treaty interpretation, for example in determining whether, with reference to the word 'expenses' and the word 'budget' in Article 17 of the Charter, 'the qualifying adjective "regular" or "administrative" should be understood to be implied':

Since no such qualification is expressed in the text of the Charter, it could be read in, only if such qualification must necessarily be implied from the provisions of the Charter read as a whole, or from some particular provision

---

[68] This is effectively an application of the approach adopted by the Court in the *North Sea* cases to maritime delimitations effected by States already parties to the 1958 Geneva Convention on the Continental Shelf: see *ICJ Reports*, 1969, p. 43, para. 76. and the present writer's comments in this *Year Book*, 61 (1990), p. 44.

[69] This section deals only with questions of principle, as exemplified by interpretations by the Court of the UN Charter and other instruments; certain specific questions of interpretation of those instruments will be examined below, in Chapter III.

Generally on the subject of the interpretation of constitutional instruments, see Amerasinghe, 'Interpretation of Texts in Open International Organizations', this *Year Book*, 65 (1994), pp. 175 ff.

[70] *ICJ Reports*, 1949, p. 180.

[71] *ICJ Reports*, 1962, p. 157.

thereof, which makes it unavoidable to do so in order to give effect to the Charter.[72]

This is clearly an application as much of Fitzmaurice's Principle of Integration and Principle of Effectiveness as of the corresponding provisions of the Vienna Convention on the Law of Treaties.[73]

The Court made an interesting observation in this connection in the *ICAO Appeal* case, when dealing with the question whether appeal to the Court lay, under the relevant provisions of the Chicago Convention establishing ICAO (and the related International Air Services Transit Agreement), solely against a final decision on the merits, or also against a preliminary decision by the ICAO Council as to its jurisdiction.

The case is presented to the Court in the guise of an ordinary dispute between States (and such a dispute underlies it). Yet in the proceedings before the Court, it is the act of a third entity—the Council of ICAO—which one of the Parties is impugning and the other defending. In that aspect of the matter, the appeal to the Court contemplated by the Chicago Convention and the Transit Agreement must be regarded as an element of the general regime established in respect of ICAO. In thus providing for the judicial recourse by way of appeal to the Court against decisions of the Council concerning interpretation and application . . . the Chicago Treaties gave member States, and through them the Council, the possibility of ensuring a certain measure of supervision by the Court over those decisions. To this extent, the Treaties enlist the support of the Court for the good functioning of the Organization, and therefore the first reassurance for the Council lies in the knowledge that means exist for determining whether a decision as to its own competence is in conformity or not with the provisions of the treaties governing its action. If nothing in the text requires a different conclusion, an appeal against a decision of the Council as to its own jurisdiction must be receivable, since from the standpoint of the supervision by the Court of the validity of the Council's acts, there is no ground for distinguishing between supervision as to jurisdiction, and supervision as to merits.[74]

This amounts to a special application of the principle of effectiveness, regarded as referable to the effectiveness of the organization, as a whole, created by the treaty being interpreted.

The Charter is however a treaty said, in the *Certain Expenses* case, to have 'special characteristics'. What those 'special characteristics' are, and whether they are peculiar to the Charter or a feature of all treaties by

---

[72] *ICJ Reports*, 1962, p. 159. Similarly the Court looked first at 'the text of Article 17' and then at 'its place in the general structure and scheme of the Charter': ibid., p. 162.

[73] See the previous article in this series, this *Year Book*, 62 (1991), pp. 37–48. Cf. also the interpretation from context in the Court's treatment of Article 25 of the Charter in the *Namibia* case: *ICJ Reports*, 1971, p. 53, para. 114.

[74] *ICJ Reports*, 1972, pp. 60–1, para. 26; cf. below, p. 49.

which an international organization is brought into being, is not specifically indicated in the advisory opinion;[74a] the text however continues first by referring to consideration of 'the structure of the Charter' and 'the relations established by it between the General Assembly and the Security Council', and secondly by recalling that in the *Competence of the General Assembly* case, the Court had 'sustained its interpretation . . . by considering the manner in which the organs concerned "have consistently interpreted the text" in their practice'.[75] This is of course a technique of interpretation not available in the case of treaties in general; it may be regarded as a logical extension of the recognized role of the subsequent practice *of the parties* in determining interpretation, as contemplated by Article 31(3)(*b*) of the Vienna Convention.[76]

Specifically, in the *Certain Expenses* case the Court had (*inter alia*) to determine the meaning of the word 'action' in Article 11, paragraph 2, of the Charter, which provides that any question relating to the maintenance of international peace and security 'on which action is necessary' has to be referred by the General Assembly to the Security Council. The Court read 'action' as signifying 'coercive or enforcement action', and found that 'The practice of the Organization throughout its history bears out' this interpretation.[77] Another example in the same advisory opinion, not presented specifically as an appeal to practice, was in relation to the meaning of the word 'budget' in Article 17, paragraph 1, of the Charter: was this to be read as meaning only the regular or administrative budget? One of the Court's reasons for rejecting this limitation was that the Constitution of the International Refugee Organization, drawn up by the General Assembly, had provided for separate budget headings, 'but no such distinctions were introduced into the Financial Regulations of the United Nations which were adopted by unanimous vote in 1950, and which, in this respect, remain unchanged'.[78] The IRO Constitution was relevant only as showing what might have been, or as indicating

---

[74a] The recent advisory opinion on *Legality of the Use by a State of Nuclear Weapons in Armed Conflict* should be mentioned, although it falls outside the period considered; on this point the opinion states:

'the constituent instruments of international organizations are also treaties of a particular type; their object is to create new subjects of law endowed with a certain autonomy, to which the parties entrust the task of realizing common goals. Such treaties can raise specific problems of interpretation owing, *inter alia*, to their character which is conventional and at the same time institutional; the very nature of the organization created, the imperatives associated with the effective performance of its functions, as well as its own practice, are all elements which may deserve special attention when the time comes to interpret these constituent treaties.'

(*ICJ Reports*, 1996, para. 19 of the advisory opinion.)

[75] Ibid., quoting *ICJ Reports*, 1950, pp. 8–9.

[76] Some comment has already been made on this matter in a previous article: this *Year Book*, 62 (1991), pp. 49–50.

[77] *ICJ Reports*, 1962, pp. 164–5. The Court did not spell out the nature of the 'practice of the Organization' which it had in mind. Counsel for the UK refuted the contrary argument on different grounds: *Pleadings*, pp. 341–2.

[78] *ICJ Reports*, 1962, p. 159.

consciousness of a potential distinction; what mattered was the unanimous practice exemplified by the adoption of the financial Regulations. On this same point, the Court then went on to examine what was more evidently 'practice'—the details of what had in fact been included regularly in the 'budget' of the Organization, and was able to conclude that 'the practice of the Organization is entirely consistent with the plain meaning of the text'.[79]

An example of this interpretation technique outside the Charter context is afforded by the *IMCO (Maritime Safety Committee)* case. The question before the Court was the interpretation of Article 28(*a*) of the Convention establishing IMCO, whereby 'not less than eight' of the member States elected to the Maritime Safety Committee were to be 'the largest ship-owning nations'; was this to be judged simply by gross registered tonnage, in which case the member States were bound to elect the major flags-of-convenience States, Panama and Liberia, or could the member States take into account, as it was argued, 'the realities' or 'the true situation'?[80] One of the arguments used by the Court in deciding that Panama and Liberia had to be elected was that 'The practice followed by the [IMCO] Assembly in relation to other Articles [of the Convention] reveals the reliance placed upon registered tonnage' in determining, for example, 'nations having a substantial interest in providing international shipping services'.[81]

However, the use of subsequent practice in interpreting treaties may raise delicate problems. Does such practice, even of the parties, necessarily indicate what had been their intention at the time of concluding the treaty, or may it not be equally referable to a subsequent recognition of the most convenient method of acting under the treaty, a matter in short of application rather than interpretation? In the case of the United Nations, in view of the original intention that the organization would ultimately comprise all peace-loving States, Judge Sir Percy Spender was ready to hold, in the *Certain Expenses* case, that

the intention of the framers of the Charter appears less important than intention in many other treaties where the parties are fixed and constant and where the nature and subject-matter of the treaty is different.[82]

If intention is irrelevant, then practice deemed to show it is also irrelevant; and Judge Spender in fact preferred a textual approach. A further problem, noted by Judge Sir Gerald Fitzmaurice in the same case, is that some kinds of apparent 'practice' may consist of acts which were carried out purely voluntarily, and without any intention of

---

[79] *ICJ Reports*, 1962, p. 160.
[80] *ICJ Reports*, 1960, p. 166.
[81] *ICJ Reports*, 1960, p. 167.
[82] Separate opinion, *ICJ Reports*, 1962, p. 185.

complying with what might have been seen as an obligation under the treaty; this he found relevant to the argument regarding the significance of United Nations practice as to the financing by members of certain operations.[83]

If the practice was universal among the parties, the question whether it pointed to an interpretation or an application of the treaty is purely academic; but if the practice is not directly that of the parties, but that of organs created under the treaty in which the parties are represented, the situation is less clear.

In the *IMCO* case the Court had no doubts on this aspect:

This reliance [by the IMCO Assembly] upon registered tonnage in giving effect to different provisions of the Convention, and the comparison which has been made of the texts of Articles 60 and 28(a), persuade the Court to the view that it is unlikely that when the latter Article was drafted and incorporated into the Convention it was contemplated that any criterion other than registered tonnage should determine which were the largest ship-owning nations.[84]

Inasmuch as the practice was that of the Assembly, in which all member States were represented, it could be argued that the practice was equivalent to a practice universally adopted by all parties, and therefore properly indicative of their original intent; though even in the case of such an organ of universal membership, if the organization is an 'open' one, the situation may be complicated by the possible presence of States which were not original parties to the relevant instrument, and took no part in its drafting.[85]

The analysis of practice of an organ as revelatory of the original intention of the parties becomes more difficult if the organ in question is of limited membership.[86] Such is clearly the case of the Security Council; and in the *Namibia* case the Court had to determine the legal effect of the established practice of treating the abstention of a permanent member of the Council as not impeding the adoption of a resolution, despite the requirement of Article 27(3) that the proposal receive 'the concurring votes of the permanent members'. The Court's ruling that a resolution adopted over the abstention of a permanent member was valid is probably to be read as a finding that there had been an agreed modification of the Charter requirements by subsequent practice;[87] but

---

[83] Separate opinion, *ICJ Reports*, 1962, p. 201.

[84] *ICJ Reports*, 1960, p. 169.

[85] A point made forcibly by South Africa in the *Namibia* case: see *Pleadings* vol. 1, p. 395, para. 33; vol. 2, pp. 207–8.

[86] For example, the 1961 Working Group of Fifteen relied on in the *Certain Expenses* case: *ICJ Reports*, 1962, p. 161.

[87] See previous articles in this series, this *Year Book*, 61 (1990), p. 77; 62 (1991), pp. 48–9.

its wording is not wholly unambiguous.[88] It had been argued on behalf of the Secretary-General (as an alternative to the preferred view that there had been a modification of the Charter by practice) that 'the development relating to voluntary abstentions' could be 'looked upon as an interpretation of the Charter by subsequent practice',[89] and the representative of the OAU appeared to prefer this approach, citing in support Article 31(3)(*b*) of the Vienna Convention.[90] South Africa did not fail to point out the legal difficulties in this approach, including that of assimilating the practice of a limited organ to the practice of the parties who had concluded the Charter; and while the Court was undoubtedly right to override South Africa's objection, a teasing legal conundrum remains.

In the same case, an even more curious appeal to 'practice' is to be found in the Court's treatment of the question of interpretation of Article 24 of the Charter. In support of its interpretation, the Court quotes a statement presented to the Security Council by the Secretary-General on 10 January 1947, in which he expressed the view which the Court was to uphold in the *Namibia* case.[91] This had been brought to the Court's attention by the representative of the Secretary-General in the case; but he had described the circumstances in 1947 in which the statement had been presented, and had concluded by relying, not on the statement itself, but on the fact that '10 out of 11 members of the Security Council, including the 5 permanent members, rejected the restrictive interpretation of Article 24'.[92] It is not apparent why the Court chose to refer only to the Secretary-General's statement, and not to its endorsement by the Security Council.

The difficulty referred to above becomes perhaps more significant if it is desired to appeal, in support of an interpretation of the constituent instrument of an international organization, to the practice of an organ of that organization composed, not of the representatives of member States, but of (for example) experts participating in their personal capacity, or indeed to the practice of the Secretariat, since it then becomes impossible to assimilate such practice to practice *of the parties* to the instrument. This is a point which was perhaps overlooked in the case concerning the *Applicability of the Privileges and Immunities Convention* (the *Mazilu*

---

[88] The matter is dealt with in a single short paragraph: *ICJ Reports*, 1971, p. 22, para. 22. The Court laid some emphasis on the fact that a permanent member desiring to prevent the adoption of a resolution could always do so by casting a negative vote; since this is true even if the text is read literally, it seems to be an argument pointing toward interpretation rather than modification. It seems however that the Court probably regarded the objection based on Article 27(3) as untenable—almost frivolous—in view of the general acceptance of the Security Council practice, and saw no need to spell out the exact legal basis of that practice. Note however the view of Judge Bustamante in the *Certain Expenses* case that, despite the established practice, the 'intrinsic legality' of a resolution so adopted could be challenged by a member if it chose: *ICJ Reports*, 1962, p. 305.

[89] *Namibia* case, *Pleadings*, vol. 2, p. 39 (Mr Stavropoulos).

[90] *Namibia* case, *Pleadings*, vol. 2, pp. 91–2 (Mr Elias).

[91] *ICJ Reports*, 1971, p. 52, para. 110.

[92] *Namibia* case, *Pleadings*, vol. 2, pp. 45–7 (Mr Stavropoulos).

case). In fact in that case the instrument to be interpreted was not the constituent instrument of an international organization but a separate convention, namely the Convention on the Privileges and Immunities of the United Nations; but in view of the close relationship between the Charter and that Convention it was probably in principle legitimate to appeal to something which might be referred to as the 'practice of the United Nations'. The issue was the meaning of the term 'experts on mission' in section 22 of the Convention. In its examination of this question, the Court referred to information supplied by the Secretary-General, showing that 'the United Nations has had occasion to entrust missions' to various persons in various circumstances; but it was not shown what organ of the UN, other than the Secretariat, had entrusted such persons with missions.[93] The Secretary-General referred specifically to a number of 'committees, commissions or similar bodies whose members serve, not as representatives of States, but in a personal capacity',[94] but it was not clear whether the practice relied on was a practice of those bodies, or whether in all cases a particular interpretation of 'experts on missions' could be traced back, if only through subsidiary bodies, to the General Assembly.

Practice, of whatever organ of an international organization, must presumably have a considerable degree of consistency to be convincing as a subsidiary means of interpretation. On the other hand, if variations in practice can be explained by tangential circumstances, not affecting the significance of the prevailing practice, such variations can apparently be disregarded.[95]

In the specific context of the United Nations, it is of course also the case that the Court itself is an organ of the organization; could its own practice serve to support an interpretation of the Charter (or of its own Statute, which is an integral part of the Charter)? If a practice of the Court could be pointed to, independent of its actual decisions, which implied a particular interpretation of the Charter, what value, if any, should be attached to it? The hypothesis might seem to be far-fetched; but it could be suggested that the Court has acted as though it did not consider that provisional measures indicated under Article 41 of the Statute are binding on the parties to the case; is this material to the controversial question whether or not such measures are binding?[96] If so, it cannot be on the basis that an interpretation of the Statute is being

---

[93] See *ICJ Reports*, 1989, p. 194, para. 48, based on the section of the Secretary-General's Written Statement entitled 'Relevant Practice under the Convention', *Pleadings*, pp. 186–8.

[94] *ICJ Reports*, 1989, p. 194, para. 48.

[95] See the discussion of UN budgetary practices in relation to unforeseen and extraordinary expenses in the *Certain Expenses* case, where adverse votes in the General Assembly were attributed to a special, irrelevant, circumstance: *ICJ Reports*, 1962, p. 161.

[96] See the present writer's observations in Bernhardt (ed.), *Interim Measures Indicated by International Courts* (Max-Planck-Institut für ausländisches öffentliches Recht und Völkerrecht, Heidelberg, 1994), p. 151.

given by practice attributable indirectly to the parties to that instrument.[97]

A further nuance, if no more, differentiating the interpretation of the constitutive instrument of an international organization from other treaties is, it is suggested, that the Court has shown itself ready to give slightly more weight to teleological considerations:[98] to ensure the effective performance of the objects and functions of an organization may be a more influential consideration than the simple test of the 'object and purpose' of the treaty mentioned in Article 31(1) of the Vienna Convention. The object and purpose of the treaty will be to establish the organization contemplated, and to confer on it certain powers and functions; that it should function effectively according to those powers and functions is a secondary objective, normally implied rather than stated. Thus in the *Fasla (UNAT Judgment No. 158)* case, the question was raised whether the Committee on Applications for Review of Administrative Tribunal Judgments could be regarded as an 'organ of the United Nations' for purposes of Article 96 of the Charter. The Court referred to the provisions for principal and subsidiary organs in Articles 7 and 22 of the Charter, and continued:

The object of both those Articles is to enable the United Nations to accomplish its purposes and to function effectively. Accordingly, to place a restrictive interpretation on the power of the General Assembly to establish subsidiary organs would run contrary to the clear intention of the Charter. Article 22, indeed, specifically leaves it to the General Assembly to appreciate the need for any particular [subsidiary] organ, and the sole restriction placed by that Article on the General Assembly's power to establish subsidiary organs is that they should be 'necessary for the performance of its functions'.[99]

The first part of the argument is superfluous: if the General Assembly, on the face of the text, is the sole judge of the necessity for the performance of its functions of any particular organs, that is the end of the matter. Unless the General Assembly is to be regarded as infallible, it does not follow that the decision to establish any particular organ will 'enable the United Nations to accomplish its purposes and to function effectively'; it could happen that in the view of some observers, and indeed of the Court, if it were allowed to substitute its own judgment for

---

[97] The question of the effect of provisional measures will be examined in a later article on 'Questions of competence, jurisdiction and procedure'.

[98] Though, as observed in a previous article in this series (this *Year Book*, 62 (1991), pp. 18–19), the general trend in the last 35 years has been toward giving teleological considerations more weight than in the periods discussed by Fitzmaurice, and this notwithstanding the priority given in the Vienna Convention to the text, to be interpreted 'in the light of' the object and purpose.

[99] *ICJ Reports*, 1973, pp. 172–3, para. 16.

that of the Assembly, such organ might be unnecessary or even detrimental to the functioning of the Organization.

(b) *Subsidiary legislation; resolutions*

(i) *Validity.* In the *Mortished (UNAT Judgment No. 273)* case, the Court observed that

all valid regulations and rules adopted by a United Nations organ must derive their validity from the provisions of the Charter,[100]

and this bears the hallmark of an observation of general law, applicable *mutatis mutandis* to all international organizations. What, however, is the meaning of 'validity'? It is clear that regulations and rules made by an organ of an international organization will have no validity unless the constitutive instrument, explicitly or by necessary implication, confers power to make such regulations and rules. Under Article 101 of the Charter, the staff regulations for the Secretariat are adopted by the General Assembly: accordingly, if the Secretary-General purported to make such regulations,[101] these would have no validity. But what if the General Assembly made regulations including a provision in conflict with the Charter: if, say, during the McCarthyite period of pressure by the US Government on the Secretary-General, the Assembly had included in the regulations a requirement that staff members were subject to security clearance by their own governments, or even by the host government? Such a provision could be argued to be in conflict with Article 100, paragraphs 1 and 2, of the Charter: but would it follow that it was invalid?

The decision in the *Mortished* case seems to recognize this distinction, and even to imply that a regulation regularly made would not necessarily be 'invalid' simply on the ground that its *content* was inconsistent with the Charter. The question before the Court was whether UNAT had committed 'an error on a question of law relating to the provisions of the Charter' for the purposes of Article 11 of the Tribunal's Statute, which opened the possibility of a request for advisory opinion on the point; after making the observation quoted above, the Court went on to say that

It does not follow, however, that every question of the interpretation or application of those regulations or rules is a question of law relating to the provisions of the Charter. . . . Accordingly, it would be quite mistaken to suppose that, because the law applied by the Tribunal, or indeed the law applied by any organ of the United Nations, derives its ultimate validity from the Charter, the ground of Article 11 now under examination means that an

---

[100] *ICJ Reports*, 1982, p. 358, para. 65.
[101] As distinct from the Staff Rules which the Secretary-General makes under powers delegated to him through the Staff Regulations.

objection to any interpretation by the Tribunal of staff rules and regulations is a matter for advisory opinion of the Court.[102]

In due course in its advisory opinion, the Court considered whether UNAT *had* erred on a question of law relating to the provisions of the Charter, and found that it had not. The question was the consistency of the Tribunal's ruling, not with the Charter as such, but with a resolution of the General Assembly, binding (apparently) on the basis of Article 101 of the Charter. The Tribunal had given effect to what it found to be an 'acquired right' of a staff member, which right could no longer be implemented because of the terms of the Assembly resolution referred to, with the result that the staff member should be compensated for the injury thus suffered.

(ii) *Interpretation*. It is unclear to what extent, if any, the rules as to interpretation of treaties may be applied, by extension, to the interpretation of the resolutions or decisions of international organizations. In one sense, a resolution represents, like a treaty, a meeting of wills, a coming-together of the (possibly opposing) aspirations of the States whose representatives have negotiated its drafting. In another sense, it is a unilateral act, an assertion of the will of the organ adopting it, or a statement of its collective view of a situation. In the latter spirit, Judge de Castro emphasized the need to treat a resolution (*in casu*, one requesting an advisory opinion), as a whole.

It seems clear that, in order to interpret a resolution of the United Nations General Assembly, as when interpreting a law or with [*sic*] any unilateral declaration in general, it is necessary to enquire into its purpose and the reason for its existence. It is not therefore permissible to isolate the questions asked from the body of the resolution in which they are inserted.[103]

The same result would of course be achieved by applying the recognized rule as to interpretation in context.

One practical question which has arisen in this respect is the significance of *travaux préparatoires*. In the *Certain Expenses* case, it was sought to interpret the resolution requesting the advisory opinion in the light of the rejection, at the meeting at which it had been adopted, of an amendment (the 'French amendment') which had been proposed to its text. The Court did not find it necessary

to expound the extent to which the proceedings of the General Assembly antecedent to the adoption of a resolution, should be taken into account in interpreting that resolution.[104]

---

[102] *ICJ Reports*, 1982, p. 358, para. 65.
[103] *Western Sahara*, separate opinion, *ICJ Reports*, 1975, p. 132.
[104] *ICJ Reports*, 1962, p. 156.

Since the question of interpretation concerned the scope of the question submitted to the Court, it applied a presumption that the General Assembly would not 'seek to fetter or hamper the Court in the discharge of its judicial functions'. It did however reject one argument based on the rejection of the French amendment with the observation that

If any deduction is to be made from the debates on the point, the opposite conclusion would be drawn from the clear statements of sponsoring delegations that they took it for granted the Court would consider the Charter as a whole.[105]

The same question—the possible significance of a rejected proposal—arose in the *Namibia* case: South Africa argued that since, at the final Assembly of the League of Nations, the Chinese delegation had introduced a proposal contemplating express provision for the transfer of supervisory functions over Mandates from the League of Nations to United Nations organs, and the proposal was not adopted, no such transfer was then envisaged, and therefore did not occur.[106] In rejecting this argument, the Court made a useful general statement as to its attitude to deductions of this kind from 'the incident of the dog in the night-time':[107]

The Court is unable to accept the argument advanced. The fact that a particular proposal is not adopted by an international organ does not necessarily carry with it the inference that a collective pronouncement is made in a sense opposite to that proposed. There can be many reasons determining rejection or non-approval.[108]

The Court explained the reasons why the adoption of the Chinese proposal 'could have raised difficulties'.

Judge Fitzmaurice disagreed, and (in a different context—that of the possible revocability of the Mandate) offered his own 'Applicable Principle of Interpretation' in his dissenting opinion:

Where a particular proposal has been considered but rejected, for whatever reason, it is not possible to interpret the instrument or juridical situation to which the proposal related as if the latter had in fact been adopted.[109]

---

[105] *ICJ Reports*, 1962, p. 157. Judge Spiropoulos made a declaration indicating his disagreement with the Court on this point: in his view, rejection of the French amendment did signify the desire of the Assembly that the Court should not examine the question of the 'conformity' of the various resolutions; *ICJ Reports*, 1962, pp. 180–1.

[106] There was in fact also a proposal to the same effect by the Executive Committee to the United Nations Preparatory Commission: see *ICJ Reports*, 1971, p. 36, para. 68.

[107] Sherlock Holmes in A. Conan Doyle, *Silver Blaze*.

[108] *ICJ Reports*, 1971, p. 36, para. 69. Cf. also the question of relevance of the records of a multilateral conference at which a convention was adopted: *Border and Transborder Armed Actions, ICJ Reports*, 1988, p. 86, para. 37, and this *Year Book*, 62 (1991), p. 37. It appears however that it is legitimate, when interpreting a treaty, to argue from what is not in the treaty but might have been: cf. the reference, in the *Certain Expenses* case, to the constitution of the International Refugee Organization, above, text and n. 78.

[109] *ICJ Reports*, 1971, p. 275.

It is suggested that the expression 'for whatever reason' makes the principle too wide; if a proposal is rejected as unnecessary, as merely spelling out what it is intended to achieve, and what it is thought has been achieved, by the existing text, then its rejection changes nothing. On the other hand, Fitzmaurice's formulation is (correctly, it is suggested) cautious, in that he does not go so far as to suggest that the rejection of a proposal automatically implies acceptance of its opposite.

In the *Western Sahara* case, the Court examined, among other things, 'the preparatory work and context of resolution 3292 (XXIX)', by which the General Assembly had requested an advisory opinion.[110] This however was not with a view to ascertaining the meaning of the text of that resolution, but in order to deal with an objection by Spain to the giving of the opinion requested. Spain contended that to give a reply would be 'devoid of purpose', because the method of decolonization of the territory of Western Sahara had already been settled by the General Assembly; thus the purported reason for the request (which related to the status of the territory before colonization), namely, to assist the General Assembly in its future decisions on decolonization of the territory, did not justify it. Spain claimed that 'the questions put to the Court are therefore irrelevant, and the answers cannot have any practical effect'.[111] In form, therefore, the question was not one of interpretation; but it may be noted that, in order to say whether the Spanish objection was correct, the Court had, essentially, to ascertain the object of the request; and this could primarily be done by interpreting its text.

(3) *Powers of international organizations and of their organs*[112]

It was already well established, and recognized in the *Reparation for Injuries* case, in relation to the United Nations Organization, that the powers of an international organization comprise both the powers expressly conferred on it by its constituent instrument, and

> those powers which, though not expressly provided in the Charter, are conferred upon it by necessary implication as being essential to the performance of its duties.[113]

This is in effect a qualification of the rigidity of the *principe de spécialité*, laid down by the Permanent Court in the *European Commission of the Danube* case, that an international organization has in principle only the powers conferred on it by its constituent instrument.[113a] Commenting on

[110] *ICJ Reports*, 1975, p. 31, para. 53.
[111] *ICJ Reports*, 1975, p. 29, para. 48.
[112] For comment on the Court's findings as to the powers specifically of the United Nations General Assembly and Security Council, see Chapter II, section 4, below.
[113] *ICJ Reports*, 1949, p. 182.
[113a] *PCIJ*, Series B, No. 14, p. 64. On the principle, see the advisory opinion on *Legality of the Use by a State of Nuclear Weapons in Armed Conflict*, *ICJ Reports*, 1996, para. 25 of the advisory opinion.

this decision, Fitzmaurice[114] drew attention to the fact that the Court's view took the middle ground between the extreme teleological approach of Judge Alvarez in the *Admissions* case,[115] that an organization must be able to develop 'in accordance with the requirements of international life', and the more restrictive view of Judge Hackworth in the *Reparation for Injuries* case, that 'implied powers flow from a grant of express powers and are limited to those that are "necessary" to the exercise of powers expressly granted',[116] thus not extending so far as powers necessary for the achievement of the *purposes* of the organization. The Court had the opportunity of re-examining the question in the *Certain Expenses* case in 1962; and it again found that the measure of implied powers was the achievement of the purposes of the organization. After enumerating the purposes of the United Nations in Articles 1 and 2 of the Charter, the Court said:

These purposes are broad indeed, but neither they nor the powers conferred to effectuate them are unlimited. Save as they have entrusted the Organization with the attainment of these common ends, the Member States retain their freedom of action. But when the Organization takes action which warrants the assertion that it was appropriate for the fulfilment of one of the stated purposes of the United Nations, the presumption is that such action is not *ultra vires* the Organization.[117]

The Court speaks here only of a presumption; but it is not apparent in what circumstances such a presumption could be rebutted. All that is required is that the action should be deemed (by whom?) appropriate for fulfilment of a purpose of the organization, regardless of its relationship with the extent of the specific powers conferred on the organization. In fact, it may be inappropriate to refer to the *powers* conferred on the organization by its constituent instrument, since it is much more in the nature of such an instrument, as demonstrated by the Charter, to speak of the *purposes* to be achieved.

What of powers conferred, not by the constituent instrument, but *ab extra*, by some other instrument or provision of law? This possibility was a key element in the Court's opinion in the *Namibia* case. On the basis that the United Nations had succeeded to the position of the League of Nations in relation to the Mandate for South West Africa, the powers of the League could be exercised by the United Nations in that context, independently of the purposes and powers stated in the Charter. So far, so good; this had already been established in the 1950 opinion on the

[114] This *Year Book*, 29 (1952), pp. 5–6, *Collected Edition*, I, pp. 74–5.

[115] Separate opinion, *ICJ Reports*, 1948, p. 68.

[116] Separate opinion, *ICJ Reports*, 1950, p. 198.

[117] *ICJ Reports*, 1962, p. 168. The second sentence of this passage states the so-called 'principle of speciality', already adumbrated in the *Reparation for Injuries* case: *ICJ Reports*, 1949, p. 179. Cf. Chaumont, 'La signification du principe de spécialité dans les organisations internationales', *Mélanges Rolin*, 1964, p. 55. See p. 8, above.

International Status of South West Africa.[118] The termination of the Mandate was, however, seen as the exercise of a power conferred by general international law, wherever there existed a treaty relationship. This power was therefore also derived from outside the Charter.

Such externally derived powers still have to be exercized by an organ of the organization receiving them; and they will therefore run in parallel to the constitutionally conferred powers of the organs. As shown by the 1955 and 1956 opinions on the *Voting Procedure* and *Hearing of Petitioners*[119] in relation to South West Africa, this may involve questions of harmonization of powers derived from different sources.

A specific grant of powers in the constitution of an organization is to be expected in relation to the organs of the organization as distinct from the organization as an entity; and the Court, in the *Certain Expenses* case, emphasized the difference between questions of *vires* in relation to the organization and such questions in relation to a particular organ.

If it is agreed that the action in question is within the scope of the functions of the Organization but it is alleged that it has been initiated or carried out in a manner not in conformity with the division of functions among the several organs which the Charter prescribes, one moves to the internal plane, to the internal structure of the Organization. If the action was taken by the wrong organ, it was irregular as a matter of that internal structure, but this would not necessarily mean that the expense incurred was not an expense of the Organization [i.e., that the action was not that of the Organization]. Both national and international law contemplate cases in which the body corporate or politic may be bound, as to third parties, by an *ultra vires* act of an agent.[120]

The Court does not say that internal competence is irrelevant; it leaves open the possibility of situations in which the violation by the organ of an organization of the distribution of powers and functions within the organization is so flagrant that the decision has to be treated as a nullity, for all purposes. The presumption, one may take it, is however in favour of the validity of decisions as far as third parties are concerned. Indeed, the Court stated in the *Certain Expenses* case that

when the Organization takes action which warrants the assertion that it was appropriate for the fulfilment of one of the stated purposes of the United Nations, the presumption is that such action is not *ultra vires* the Organization.[121]

---

[118] *ICJ Reports*, 1950, p. 128.

[119] *ICJ Reports*, 1955, p. 67; 1956, p. 23.

[120] *ICJ Reports*, 1962, p. 168; note the reference to the *functions* of the Organization rather than to its *powers*. The reference to international law in the last sentence presumably contemplates those situations in which State responsibility is incurred by the act of an 'organ of the State' acting in that capacity, even though that organ was acting irregularly or *ultra vires*: cf. the *Youmans* case, *Reports of International Arbitral Awards*, vol. 4, p. 116, and the ILC Draft Articles on State Responsibility, Art. 10, and the commentary in *ILC Yearbook*, 1975, vol. 2, pp. 61–70.

[121] *ICJ Reports*, 1962, p. 168.

This will presumably be so, *a fortiori*, where any alleged invalidity is of a purely formal nature (arising from irregularities in voting, etc.). Thus in the *Namibia* case, the Court, when dealing with South Africa's objections to the formal validity of the resolution requesting the advisory opinion, stated that

A resolution of a properly constituted organ of the United Nations which is passed in accordance with that organ's rules of procedure, and is declared by its President to have been so passed, must be presumed to have been validly adopted.[122]

Neither of these dicta however serves to remove all doubt. The presumption in either case must be a rebuttable one,[123] since otherwise the Court would not have gone into questions of validity of resolutions at all. (In the case of the *Namibia* dictum, the reference both to passage of the resolution in accordance with the rules of procedure, and to the presidential statement, lead one to suppose that the ruling of the president of the organ concerned is decisive; but this would produce an irrebuttable presumption which, as just observed, is inconsistent with the Court's approach to the question.) How is it to be established, prior to or in the absence of a ruling by the Court, whether the assertion that an action was 'appropriate for the fulfilment of one of the stated purposes' of an organization is or is not warranted; or whether or not a resolution was in fact passed in accordance with the rules of procedure, if the president's statement is not conclusive?

The impact of procedural irregularities has been considered by the Court in two cases during the period under review. In the *Appeal relating to the Jurisdiction of the ICAO Council*, India argued (*inter alia*) that the decision of the ICAO Council in the dispute between itself and Pakistan, against which India was appealing to the Court under provisions of the Chicago Convention on Civil Aviation and Air Transit Agreement, 'was vitiated by various procedural irregularities, and should, accordingly, on that ground alone, be declared null and void'.[124] The Court declined to go into the matter, 'particularly as the alleged irregularities do not prejudice in any fundamental way the requirements of a just procedure'; its main justification for inaction was however:

The Court's task in the present proceedings is to give a ruling as to whether the Council had jurisdiction in the case. This is an objective question of law, the answer to which cannot depend on what occurred before the Council. Since the Court holds that the Council did and does have jurisdiction, then, if there were in fact procedural irregularities, the position would be that the Council would have reached the right conclusion in the wrong way. Nevertheless it would have

---

[122] *ICJ Reports*, 1971, p. 22, para. 20; referred to below, p. 50.
[123] In this sense E. Lauterpacht, 'The Legal Effect of Illegal Acts of International Organizations', in Jennings (ed.), *Essays in Honour of Lord McNair*, p. 117.
[124] *ICJ Reports*, 1972, p. 69, para. 44.

reached the right conclusion. If, on the other hand, the Court had held that there was and is no jurisdiction, then, even in the absence of any irregularities, the Council's decision to assume it would have stood reversed.[125]

This decision, which is not above criticism,[126] could only take this form because the Court was sitting by way of appeal, and is somewhat unhelpful as to the position of third parties in face of a decision which may be vitiated by procedural irregularities.

Nor is the other case in which the Court has dealt with such irregularities of much greater help. In the *Application for Review of UNAT Judgment No. 273 (Mortished)*, the proceedings of the Committee on Applications for Review, from which the request for an advisory opinion had come, had, as the Court found, involved a series of serious procedural irregularities. The relevance of these to the Court's decision was however not seen as possibly leading to the conclusion that the request for opinion was invalidated, so that there was nothing for the Court to decide, but rather that the Court might, in the exercise of its recognized discretion under Article 65 of the Statute, decline to give an opinion.[127] In contrast, in the *Namibia* case, the objections raised by South Africa to the formal validity of the Security Council resolution requesting the opinion were treated at the outset of the advisory opinion as matters of competence, not of the exercise of discretion; the reason being, of course, that South Africa had clearly presented them as such. The implication is clearly that, had any of South Africa's objections been upheld, the resolution would have been ineffective as against third parties, in which category the Court itself would be placed.

The distinction between action in excess of the powers of an *organization*, and action *ultra vires* an *organ* of an organization, made by the Court in the *Certain Expenses* case, is clearly a valid one. What effect does the distinction however have in practice? In particular, is a third party concerned to enquire whether an action affecting him was or was not within the *vires* of the organization, but entitled to disregard questions of distribution of powers within the organization, and to treat as valid a decision taken by the wrong organ, or a decision preceded by procedural irregularities? From the passage quoted above from the *Certain Expenses* opinion, this would seem the correct conclusion as to the Court's view. It has been pointed out that in later passages of the opinion, the Court seems not to respect the distinction it has itself made, and to regard as material evidence which would point to the action of the General Assembly having been an encroachment on the prerogatives of the

---

[125] *ICJ Reports*, 1972, pp. 69–70, para. 45.

[126] It was dissented from by Judges Jiménez de Aréchaga and Morozov: *ICJ Reports*, 1972, pp. 153–4, 158–9. See the present writer's comments, 'Procedural law and the International Court of Justice', *Fifty Years of the International Court of Justice (Mélanges Jennings)*, pp. 400 ff.

[127] It was the view of Judge El-Khani that it should so decline: *ICJ Reports*, 1982, pp. 447 ff.

Security Council.[128] However, the dictum quoted above relates to a body corporate or politic being bound 'as to third parties' by an *ultra vires* act of an agent or organ; whereas the question at issue in the *Certain Expenses* case was the effect of decisions of the General Assembly for dissident member States. In short, the suggestion that third parties may rely on, and treat as valid, *ultra vires* acts of organs of international organizations, provided such acts are within the powers, as being appropriate to the purposes, of the organization, is probably to be regarded strictly as an *obiter dictum*—but not the less welcome for that.

(4) *Privileges and immunities of international organizations and their staff*

Two requests for advisory opinion during the period under review have arisen out of problems related to the question of privileges and immunities, but in one the question submitted to the Court was purely procedural, and did not authorize it to enter into the substance of the matter, and in the other the request was, as the Court found, deliberately circumscribed so as to require from the Court only a decision of principle. The request of the General Assembly for an opinion on the *Applicability of the Obligation to Arbitrate under Section 21 of the United Nations Headquarters Agreement of 26 June 1947* was, as its title indicates, limited to the effect of the compromissory clause in the Headquarters Agreement. The case arose out of legislation introduced in Congress under which, *inter alia*, it would become unlawful to maintain any office in the United States for the Palestine Liberation Organization, and it was evident that the Observer Mission of the PLO to the United Nations was aimed at. The Secretary-General had pointed out that the members of the Mission were invitees of the United Nations, and therefore covered by sections 11, 12 and 13 of the Headquarters Agreement with the United States. The Court was requested to give an advisory opinion simply on the question whether the arbitration clause in the Head-quarters Agreement had become applicable,[129] and, as the Court found, it was

not called upon to decide whether the measures adopted by the United States in regard to the Observer Mission of the PLO to the United Nations do or do not run counter to the Headquarters Agreement.[130]

It had no difficulty in finding that a dispute concerning the interpretation

[128] E. Lauterpacht, 'The Legal Effect of Illegal Acts of International Organizations', in Jennings (ed.), *Essays in Honour of Lord McNair*, pp. 110–12.

[129] The matter was not open-and-shut, even though the State Department had taken the view that the legislation would be a breach of the obligations of the United States under the Headquarters Agreement; Congress had paid no attention and gone ahead, but the legislation had not been implemented at the time the Court was seised.

[130] *ICJ Reports*, 1988, p. 26, para. 33.

or application of the Agreement had arisen, so as to bring the arbitration clause into play.

The request of the Economic and Social Council for an opinion on the *Applicability of Article VI, Section 22, of the Convention on the Privileges and Immunities of the United Nations* concerned a Romanian national, Mr Dumitru Mazilu, who had been entrusted by a Sub-Commission of the Commission on Human Rights with the preparation of a report. Subsequent conduct by the Romanian Government amounted, it was suggested, to interference with Mr Mazilu's role as an 'expert on mission' within the meaning of section 22 of the Privileges and Immunities Convention, and thus to breaches of that Convention. The Court limited its findings to a statement that

In these circumstances Mr Mazilu continues to have the status of special rapporteur, and as a consequence must be regarded as an expert on mission within the meaning of Section 22 of the General Convention. That Section is accordingly applicable in the case of Mr Mazilu.[131]

The expression 'in the case of' was that used in the request for opinion, and the Secretary-General in his written statement to the Court had suggested that the Court had not been asked 'about the consequences of that applicability, that is about what privileges and immunities Mr Mazilu might enjoy as a result of his status and whether or not these had been violated'.[132]

The practical interest of the advisory opinion is thus essentially in its interpretation of the concept of 'expert on mission' as used in the Privileges and Immunities Convention, i.e., as a matter of treaty interpretation rather than as one of general law relating to the immunities of the staff of international organizations. More relevant however is the Court's finding on the question 'whether experts on missions can invoke these privileges and immunities against the States of which they are nationals or on the territory of which they reside'.[133]

In this connection the Court notes that Section 15 of the General Convention provides that the terms of Article IV, Sections 11, 12 and 13, relating to the representatives of Members 'are not applicable as between a representative and the authorities of the State of which he is a national or of which he is or has been the representative'. Article V, concerning officials of the Organization, and Article VI, concerning experts on missions for the United Nations, do not, however, contain any comparable rule. This difference of approach can readily be explained. The privileges and immunities of Articles V and VI are conferred with a view to ensuring the independence of international officials and experts in the interests of the Organization. This independence must be respected by all States including the State of nationality and the State of residence.[134]

[131] *ICJ Reports*, 1989, p. 198, para. 60.
[132] *ICJ Reports*, 1989, p. 187, para. 27.
[133] *ICJ Reports*, 1989, p. 195, para. 51.
[134] Ibid.

The reasoning rests on the same principles as that in the *Reparation for Injuries* case, while relating to the opposite situation to that there presented: in 1949 the Court found that if a staff member had to rely on his national State for protection, his independence might well be compromised;[135] but his independence might equally, or more forcibly, be compromised if his own national State were not bound to respect the privileges and immunities devised to enable him to discharge his duties to the Organization.

Judge Shahabuddeen, in his separate opinion, pursued a similar philosophy to resolve an aspect of the case not dealt with in the advisory opinion itself. The Romanian Government had contended that

an expert is not accorded such privileges and immunities anywhere and everywhere, but only in the country to which he is sent on mission, and also in the countries to [*sic*] which he must transit when travelling to meet the requirements of the mission. In the same way, the privileges and immunities only come into existence from the expert's time of departure, when he travels to accomplish the mission. In so far as the expert's journey to carry out the mission for the United Nations has not begun, for reasons entirely unconnected with his activity as an expert, there is no legal basis upon which to lay claim to privileges and immunities under the Convention.[136]

Judge Shahabuddeen drew attention to the curious result of this argument:

not having begun his journey, the expert has no privileges and immunities, and, not having any privileges and immunities, he cannot enforce a right to begin the journey. Locked within this system, the expert may well be unable to perform the mission which the privileges and immunities were intended to enable him to perform.[137]

Although the discussion proceeded on the discrete basis that the point arose in whatever country the expert happened to be when he contemplated beginning his journey, Mr Mazilu in fact complained of the obstacles put in his way by his own Government, and it would clearly be the State of nationality or of residence which would be most likely to refuse privileges and immunities on the ground asserted by Romania. Thus it was again the independence of international officials, extended in this respect to 'experts' as a class of, as it were, temporary *ad hoc* officials, which was in question.

In this context, Judge Shahabuddeen's conclusion seems absolutely right: that the provisions of the Convention

must . . . be construed as extending to afford protection against all acts which

---

[135] *ICJ Reports*, 1949, p. 182; see Fitzmaurice, this *Year Book*, 29 (1952), pp. 11–12; *Collected Edition*, I, pp. 80–1.
[136] Romania's written statement, English translation quoted in separate opinion of Judge Shahabuddeen, *ICJ Reports*, 1989, p. 218 (for French original see *Pleadings*, p. 203).
[137] *ICJ Reports*, 1989, p. 219.

could frustrate their operation or empty them of real content, with the consequence of effectively preventing the expert from embarking on or resuming his mission. The dangers which proverbially lurk in the use of maxims do not seem to forbid recourse in this case to the well-known words *quando lex aliquid alcui concedit concedere videtur et id sine quo res ipsa non potest*—when the law gives a man anything, it gives him that also without which the thing itself cannot exist.[138]

CHAPTER II

THE UNITED NATIONS

1. *Relations between United Nations Organs*

In the multitude of counsellors there is safety.

Proverbs, xi. 14

The relationship between the various principal organs of the United Nations to some extent results from the Charter, not so much in the sense that it is there stated (except to a limited extent and by implication), but rather in the sense that the absence of such organizational dispositions points to the absence of any hierarchical order, each organ being independent in its own sphere.[139] This signifies, not that it is impossible for one organ to encroach on the exclusive domain of another, but that, as the Court observed in the *Certain Expenses* case, 'As anticipated in 1945, . . . each organ must, in the first place at least, determine its own jurisdiction'.[140] Questions of the interaction between, in particular, the Security Council and the General Assembly have arisen before the Court,[141] as have questions of the relationship of the Court itself to those two organs, in particular the Security Council.

(1) *Relationship between the Security Council and the General Assembly*

In the *Certain Expenses* case, one of the arguments advanced in support of the view that the General Assembly's resolutions authorizing the Congo and UNEF operations were ineffective to render the consequent expenditure 'expenses of the Organization' was that those operations fell within the category of the maintenance of international peace and security.

---

[138] *ICJ Reports*, 1989, p. 220.
[139] Cf. Fitzmaurice in this *Year Book*, 29 (1952), pp. 33–4; *Collected Edition*, I, pp. 102–3.
[140] *ICJ Reports*, 1962, p. 168.
[141] In previous periods, the *Admissions* case (*ICJ Reports*, 1947–48, p. 57) and the *Competence of the General Assembly* case (*ICJ Reports*, 1950, p. 4), commented on by Fitzmaurice in this *Year Book* (see n. 139, above).

The argument rests in part on the view that when the maintenance of international peace and security is involved, it is only the Security Council which is authorized to decide on any action relative thereto. It is argued further that since the General Assembly's power is limited to discussing, considering, studying and recommending, it cannot impose an obligation to pay the expenses which result from its recommendations. This argument leads to an examination of the respective functions of the General Assembly and of the Security Council under the Charter, particularly with respect to the maintenance of international peace and security.

Article 24 of the Charter provides:
'In order to ensure prompt and effective action by the United Nations, its Members confer on the Security Council primary responsibility for the maintenance of international peace and security . . . '
The responsibility conferred is 'primary', not exclusive. This primary responsibility is conferred upon the Security Council, as stated in Article 24, 'in order to ensure prompt and effective action'. To this end, it is the Security Council which is given a power to impose an explicit obligation of compliance if for example it issues an order or command to an aggressor under Chapter VII. It is only the Security Council which can require enforcement by coercive action against an aggressor.

The Charter makes it abundantly clear, however, that the General Assembly is also to be concerned with international peace and security.[142]

The Court went on to quote Article 14 of the Charter, and to point out that the only limitation is that stated in Article 12, that the Assembly is not to recommend measures while the Security Council is dealing with the same matters, unless requested by the Council.

(2) *Relationship between the Court and the other principal organs*

The question of the relationship of the Court itself with the other organs[143] can arise in two ways. It has been argued before the Court on occasion that it could not or should not decide a particular matter because to do so would encroach on the functions of, in particular the Security Council; and in other circumstances it has been contended that a decision already taken by a principal organ of the United Nations cannot be reviewed by the Court. It is of course possible for both issues to arise in relation to the same circumstances brought before the Court; but the distinction is clear, and was well expressed by the Court in its judgment on jurisdiction in the *Nicaragua* case. The United States had appealed to the primary responsibility of the Security Council in matters of international peace and security as a reason why the Court should find

---

[142] *ICJ Reports*, 1962, p. 163.

[143] 'By virtue of its judicial independence, the ICJ, as the "principal judicial organ" of the UN (Art. 92), clearly stands outside any hierarchical order, if indeed there is any, among the principal organs of the UN': Jaenicke in Simma (ed.), *The Charter of the United Nations*, sub. Art. 7, p. 196. For the possible implication of subordination of the Court's having adopted the practice of submitting a report to the General Assembly, see Engel, 'Annual Reports of the International Court of Justice to the General Assembly?', this *Year Book*, 44 (1970), p. 193.

Nicaragua's claims inadmissible; but since Nicaragua had not obtained satisfaction from the Council, it was argued also that the proceedings before the Court were 'objectionable as being in effect an appeal to the Court from an adverse decision of the Security Council'. The Court did not accept this:

> The Court is not asked to say that the Security Council was wrong in its decision, nor that there was anything inconsistent with law in the way in which the Members of the Council employed their right to vote. The Court has been asked to pass judgment on certain legal aspects of a situation which has also been considered by the Security Council, a procedure which is entirely consonant with its position as the principal judicial organ of the United Nations.[144]

(a) *Separation of functions*

In the case concerning the *United States Diplomatic and Consular Staff in Tehran*, the attack on the United States Embassy had been the subject of decisions of the Security Council, and, as the Court found, the Council was 'actively seised of the matter' when the Court took a decision to indicate provisional measures. These measures were brought to the attention of the Council; and

> it does not seem to have occurred to any Member of the Council that there was or could be anything irregular in the simultaneous exercise of their respective functions by the Court and the Security Council. Nor is there in this any cause for surprise. Whereas Article 12 of the Charter expressly forbids the General Assembly to make any recommendation with regard to a dispute or situation while the Security Council is exercising its functions in respect of that dispute or situation, no such restriction is placed on the functioning of the Court by any provision either of the Charter or the Statute of the Court. The reasons are clear. It is for the Court, the principal judicial organ of the United Nations, to resolve any legal questions that may be in issue between parties to a dispute; and the resolution of such legal questions by the Court may be an important, and sometimes decisive, factor in promoting the peaceful settlement of the dispute.[145]

The Court is therefore not obliged to admit a sort of objection of litispendence if the matter before it is also before the Security Council; nor would it normally be possible for it to disseise itself, or decline to decide, as a matter of discretion, on such a ground.[146] In the exercise of any power, however, in which the Court does possess a discretion (i.e.

---

[144] *ICJ Reports*, 1984, p. 436, para. 98.

[145] *ICJ Reports*, 1980, pp. 21–2, para. 40, with a reference to Article 36, para. 3, of the Charter.

[146] But cf. the decision in the *Northern Cameroons* case, commented on below. Attention has also been drawn to the recognition by the PCIJ in the *Minority Schools* case (*PCIJ*, Series A, No. 15, p. 23) that there might be 'exceptional cases in which the dispute which States might desire to refer to the Court would fall within the exclusive jurisdiction reserved to some other authority'; there might, it is argued, be such cases reserved exclusively to the Security Council. See Skubiszewski, 'The International Court of Justice and the Security Council', *Fifty Years of the International Court of Justice (Mélanges Jennings)*, pp. 619–21.

excluding the power and duty to decide the case before it), the Court may well take into account the existence of activity in the Security Council.

This is illustrated by the decision on the request for the indication of provisional measures in the *Aegean Sea Continental Shelf* case. In addition to requesting measures to protect what it claimed to be its rights, Greece in that case also requested the indication of measures in order to prevent the aggravation or extension of the dispute; at the time it was unsettled whether or not the Court had power to indicate measures solely for that purpose.[147] In connection with this request, the Court indicated that it had 'cognizance of the fact that' the Security Council had simultaneously been seised of the dispute between Greece and Turkey, and had adopted a resolution (Resolution 395 (1976)) which *inter alia* called on the parties to resume direct negotiations, and appealed to them 'to do everything within their power to ensure that this results in mutually acceptable solutions'.[148] The Court took note of the reactions of Greece and Turkey to this resolution, which in its view amounted to express recognition of the responsibility of the Security Council for international peace and security; it observed that the Council had recalled the parties' obligations under the Charter with regard to the peaceful settlement of disputes, which obligations, in the Court's view, were 'clearly imperative in regard to their present dispute concerning the continental shelf in the Aegean'; and added:

it is not to be presumed that either State will fail to heed its obligations under the Charter of the United Nations or fail to heed the recommendations of the Security Council addressed to them with respect to their present dispute.[149]

The Court's conclusion was that it was not necessary for it to decide whether it could indicate provisional measures 'for the sole purpose of preventing the aggravation or extension of a dispute',[150] i.e. that there was no need to indicate provisional measures of this kind.

Clearly, if the Court had been satisfied, simply on the basis of the conduct of the parties, and in the absence of any approach to the Security Council, that there was no risk of aggravation or extension of the dispute, its decision would have been the same;[151] yet the references to the action of the Council do add an extra dimension. In this context, it is interesting to observe that the Court found that there had been express recognition

---

[147] Such a power would not appear to fall within the actual terms of Article 14 of the Court's Statute; however, it was claimed and exercised by the Chamber seised of the *Frontier Dispute* between Burkina Faso and Mali: *ICJ Reports*, 1986, p. 9, para. 18, and that jurisprudence has since been followed by the full Court in the case concerning the *Land and Maritime Boundary between Cameroon and Nigeria, ICJ Reports*, 1996, p. 22, para. 41.

[148] *ICJ Reports*, 1976, p. 12, paras. 37, 38.

[149] *ICJ Reports*, 1976, p. 13, para. 41.

[150] *ICJ Reports*, 1976, p. 13, para. 42.

[151] Cf. the PCIJ decision in the case of the *South Eastern Territory of Greenland*, that the declarations of the two parties 'taken together are indicative of the existence in responsible circles in both countries of a state of mind and of intentions which are eminently reassuring', so that no measures were necessary: *PCIJ*, Series A/B, No. 48, p. 286.

by the parties of 'the responsibility of the Security Council for the maintenance of international peace and security', not—as in Article 24, paragraph 1, of the Charter—*primary* responsibility. The Court may be taken to have been discreetly underlining the fact that the Court itself also had such responsibility; this is confirmed by the separate opinion of Judge Lachs, who there observed:

The Court does not, to my way of thinking, arrogate any powers excluded by its Statute when, otherwise than by adjudication, it assists, facilitates or contributes to the peaceful settlement of disputes between States, if offered the occasion at any stage of the proceedings,[152]

and inclusion of the word 'primary' might have raised questions as to the meaning of that adjective, and the contention that the Court not merely did not need to indicate measures, but was actually debarred from indicating them when the Security Council had been seised and had taken action.[153]

In the *Nicaragua* case, the problem was raised not only of the primary responsibility of the Security Council for the maintenance of international peace and security, but also of the relevance of a Charter provision referring to procedures for dispute settlement which were to prevail even over the competence of the Security Council in this domain. The United States asserted that the Court should not indicate provisional measures in view of the existence of the system of negotiation for peace in Central America known as the Contadora Process. In the United States' contention,

In the circumstances of this case, where the United Nations and the Organization of American States have approved the Contadora process, such questions [as raised by Nicaragua] regarding the use of force during hostilities are more properly committed to resolution by the political organs of the United Nations and of the Organization of American States.[154]

The United States relied on the 'primary responsibility' of the Council, and Chapter VIII of the Charter on regional arrangements; it also drew attention particularly to Article 52 of the Charter, 'as a result of which . . . Nicaragua is bound by a commitment to regional agencies and arrangements for the pacific settlement of local disputes';[155] it will be

---

[152] *ICJ Reports*, 1976, p. 20.
[153] Turkey in its observations on the request for provisional measures went no further than suggesting that the request was 'premature having regard to the Security Council proceedings': *Pleadings*, p. 69. The Court itself raised the matter during the oral proceedings, when a question was put on behalf of the Court as a whole (not a common proceeding), asking whether in the view of Greece the Security Council resolution was 'a circumstance to be taken into consideration by the Court for the purposes of the present proceedings' (*Pleadings*, p. 135); the answer of Greece was (appropriately) laconic: in the view of Greece, 'les deux procédures, au Conseil de sécurité et à la Cour, sont distinctes l'une de l'autre' (ibid., p. 137).
[154] Quoted at *ICJ Reports*, 1984, p. 185, para. 37.
[155] *ICJ Reports*, 1984, p. 185, para. 36.

recalled that paragraph 2 of that Article requires members to have recourse to local agencies for settlement of disputes 'before referring them to the Security Council'.

Unfortunately the Court, in its order on provisional measures, did not deal with these arguments specifically: it simply recorded the contention of the Nicaraguan Agent that previous decisions of the Court established the principle 'that the Court is not required to decline to take cognizance of one aspect of a dispute merely because that dispute has other aspects, and that the Court should not decline an essentially judicial task merely because the question before the Court is intertwined with political questions', before going on to find that 'the circumstances require [the Court] to indicate provisional measures'.[156]

The matter was dealt with more extensively at the stage of the Court's judgment on jurisdiction and admissibility. The United States had argued that the proceedings were inadmissible because essentially Nicaragua was simply arguing that the United States was

engaged in an unlawful use of armed force, or breach of the peace, or acts of aggression against Nicaragua, a matter which is committed by the Charter and by practice to the competence of other organs, in particular the United Nations Security Council,[157]

and reference was of course made to Article 24 of the Charter.

The Court first dealt with this contention as follows:

The United States is thus arguing that the matter was essentially one for the Security Council since it concerned a complaint by Nicaragua involving the use of force. However, having regard to the *United States Diplomatic and Consular Staff in Tehran* case, the Court is of the view that the fact that a matter is before the Security Council should not preclude it being dealt with by the Court and that both proceedings could be pursued *pari passu*,[158]

and the Court quoted the passages from the judgment in that case already referred to above. This dictum does not however meet the real gravamen of the United States objection, since the matter was not one that the Security Council just happened to be dealing with at the same time as the Court, but one, in the United States contention, that was in the exclusive competence of the Security Council. This however depends on the characterization of the dispute before the Court as being 'a charge of aggression and armed conflict envisaged in Article 39 of the United Nations Charter, which can only be dealt with by the Security Council in accordance with the provisions of Chapter VII of the Charter, and not in accordance with the provisions of Chapter VI';[159] and the Court did not accept that characterization, in particular because no notification had

---

[156] *ICJ Reports*, 1984, p. 186, paras. 38, 39.
[157] *ICJ Reports*, 1984, p. 431, para. 89.
[158] *ICJ Reports*, 1984, p. 433, para. 93.
[159] *ICJ Reports*, 1984, p. 434, para. 94.

been given to the Council in accordance with Chapter VII. Had the Court stopped there, it would have been possible to regard it as at least open to question whether, if the full panoply of Chapter VII procedure had clearly been invoked, the Court would have been bound to accept the contention of the United States that it should not encroach on the peculiar of the Security Council.

The Court however proceeded to examine the wider question of principle, in terms recalling its findings in the *Certain Expenses* case, quoted above: after citing the terms of Article 24 of the Charter, it pointed out that

The Charter accordingly does not confer *exclusive* responsibility upon the Security Council for the purpose [of maintenance of international peace and security]. While in Article 12 there is a provision for a clear demarcation of functions between the General Assembly and the Security Council, . . . there is no similar provision anywhere in the Charter with respect to the Security Council and the Court. The Council has functions of a political nature assigned to it, whereas the Court exercises purely judicial functions. Both organs can therefore perform their separate but complementary functions with respect to the same event.[160]

The structure of the argument is slightly puzzling, and still leaves certain doubts as to the Court's precise intentions. The general dictum just quoted appears to make it unnecessary to determine whether Nicaragua's claim was or was not a twin brother of a matter being dealt with by the Security Council under Chapter VII; and the transition from the Court's rejection of this characterization to the general point runs as follows:

It is clear that the complaint of Nicaragua is not about an ongoing armed conflict between it and the United States, but one requiring, and indeed demanding, the peaceful settlement of disputes between two States. Hence, it is properly brought before the principal judicial organ of the Organization for settlement.[161]

If the complaint *had* been about an ongoing armed conflict, could it have been properly brought before the Court for settlement?

(b) *Review by the Court of the decisions of the political organs*[162]

The question whether the Court is bound by decisions of the political organs, and specifically the Security Council, of the United Nations may be regarded as an aspect of the problem of the powers of organs of international organizations, and the consequences of exceeding those

---

[160] *ICJ Reports*, 1984, pp. 434–5, para. 95.

[161] *ICJ Reports*, 1984, p. 434, para. 94, *in fine*.

[162] This is a question which has been the subject of intense discussion in recent years: for an excellent overview of the subject from the standpoint of the effectiveness of the United Nations as a whole, with an extensive bibliography, see Alvarez, 'Judging the Security Council', *American Journal of International Law*, 90 (1996), p. 1.

powers, already examined in Chapter I, section 2(3), above. It presents, however, a special character because of the Court's judicial status, and has thus sometimes been bedevilled by misplaced analogies with munici- pal constitutional structures. The Court dismissed such an approach in its advisory opinion in the *Certain Expenses* case:

In the legal systems of States, there is often some procedure for determining the validity of even a legislative or governmental act, but no analogous procedure is to be found in the structure of the United Nations. Proposals made during the drafting of the Charter to place the ultimate authority to interpret the Charter in the International Court of Justice were not accepted; the opinion which the Court is in the course of rendering is an *advisory* opinion. As anticipated in 1945, therefore, each organ must, in the first place, at least, determine its own jurisdiction.[163]

This however does not answer the question: what is the Court to do if the validity of a decision of the Security Council is challenged in a case before it, and the decision in the case will turn on whether or not that validity can be upheld, or presumed?

In the *Namibia* case, the Court was asked to indicate the 'legal consequences for States' of a resolution of the Security Council declaring South Africa's presence in Namibia illegal, and that resolution was in turn based on an earlier resolution of the General Assembly terminating, or purporting to terminate, South Africa's Mandate over the territory. Was it open to the Court to examine the legality and legal effect of these resolutions? South Africa in particular argued that it was, and that the General Assembly resolution had been ineffective to terminate the Mandate, with evident consequences for the effectiveness of the Security Council resolution. Other States appearing in the case, and the Secre- tary-General, argued that 'the Court was not authorized by the terms of the request, in the light of the discussions preceding it, to go into the validity of these resolutions', and that 'the Court should not assume powers of judicial review of the action taken by other principal organs of the United Nations without specific request to that effect, nor act as a court of appeal from their decisions'.[164]

The difficulty of this approach was that it is only tenable if the principal organs of the organization are sole judges of the extent of their powers;[164a] for if the hypothesis be once admitted that a given resolution might be, objectively speaking (whatever that may mean), invalid or *ultra vires*, the Court could not be expected to act as though it were not.[165] The

---

[163] *ICJ Reports*, 1962, p. 168, emphasis original.

[164] *ICJ Reports*, 1971, p. 45, para. 88.

[164a] i.e. that, as Chief Justice Holt said of an Act of Parliament, it 'can do no wrong, though it may do several things that look pretty odd': *City of London* v. *Wood* (1701).

[165] As Judge Gros put it in the *WHO/Egypt* case, 'A decision [of an international organization] which is contrary to international law does not become lawful because a majority of States has voted in favour of it . . . ': *ICJ Reports*, 1980, p. 104.

question is not strictly whether the Court has powers of judicial review:[166] if the case were such that a resolution of another principal organ was the whole basis of the question put to the Court, it must be open to the Court to find that such resolution was illegal or ineffective, since otherwise it would either have to refuse an opinion, or give an opinion based on what it considered to be a false premiss—hardly a desirable state of affairs.[167] Furthermore, the fact that the issue arose on a request for an advisory opinion tended to obscure the real point: the function of the Court being 'to decide in accordance with international law', it could not give a decision which was not so in accordance; and thus if the validity of a resolution of a United Nations organ was a key element in a legal dispute between States, brought before it as such, it could not evade reviewing the resolution in question.[168] This problem has in fact arisen in a very direct form in the Bosnian case concerning *Application of the Genocide Convention* and in the two cases brought by Libya arising out of the *Lockerbie* incident, the orders in which on the question of provisional measures will be briefly examined below.[169]

In the *Namibia* case, it was apparently conceded by those favouring a limitation on the powers of the Court that it could review a decision of another principal organ if specifically asked to do so—presumably by that organ, since such consensual jurisdiction could hardly permit, for example, the General Assembly to obtain an advisory opinion on the validity of a resolution of the Security Council. The Court apparently endorsed this view, since after first stating that

Undoubtedly, the Court does not possess powers of judicial review or appeal in respect of the decisions taken by the United Nations organs concerned,

it continued:

[166] It is perhaps worth noting in passing that a recognized power to review, by way of advisory opinion, decisions of the Security Council would not still all controversy, first because opinions are not binding and secondly because States persist in rejecting binding judgments if their interests are sufficiently engaged: cf. Frowein, 'The Internal and External Effects of Resolutions by International Organizations', *Zeitschrift für ausländisches öffentliches Recht und Völkerrecht*, 49 (1989), p. 783.

[167] Cf. the recent decision of the International Criminal Tribunal for the Former Yugoslavia that in the exercise of *la compétence de la compétence* it was entitled to review the legality of the actions of the Security Council in establishing it: *Prosecutor v. Tadic, International Legal Materials*, 35 (1996), p. 32.

[168] As Alvarez observes, 'ICJ judges may find it increasingly difficult to avoid "reviewing" Council action . . . because the law they may be asked to review relates to or relies on Council determinations . . . . As the Council generates more law, ICJ judges, elected to decide the law, will find it difficult to avoid re-examining some of that Council-generated law': loc. cit. above (n. 162), p. 20.

[169] See *ICJ Reports*, 1992, p. 14, para. 36, p. 15, para. 40; ibid., p. 126, paras. 39, 43. In view of the nature of the Security Council resolutions attacked in these cases, the seriousness of the consequences of a decision by the Court that, for the purposes of its judgment, the resolution was ineffective must not be under-estimated (see Alvarez, loc. cit. above (n. 162), pp. 5–6); but, it is submitted, the Court's obligation must be to declare the law as it sees it.

The question of the validity or conformity with the Charter of General Assembly resolution 2145 (XXI) or of related Security Council resolutions does not form the subject of the request for advisory opinion,[170]

with the clear indication that such a specific request would have been honoured.[171]

There seems to be no clear example of this procedure being followed. At first sight, it might seem as though this was in effect what was done in the case of *Certain Expenses of the United Nations*.[172] However, by asking whether certain expenditure which had been authorized by a number of General Assembly resolutions did or did not constitute 'expenses of the Organization' for the purposes of Article 17, paragraph 2, of the Charter, the Assembly was really asking whether that expenditure could be compulsorily apportioned and imposed on member States under that article; but if the Court had replied that the expenditure was not 'expenses of the Organization', this would not have invalidated the resolutions which had authorized it. A similar interpretation must be given to what occurred in the case concerning *South West Africa—Voting Procedure* in 1955.[173] The General Assembly there requested an advisory opinion on the question whether a specific rule on voting procedure in the Assembly on questions relating to reports and petitions concerning South West Africa was a correct interpretation of the Court's 1950 advisory opinion on the status of the territory. It was clearly, if impliedly, accepted that if the rule were *not* such a correct interpretation, then its implementation would be unlawful at least *vis-à-vis* South Africa as Mandatory; and the rule had been adopted by a General Assembly resolution. If the Court had found (as it did not) that the rule was not a correct interpretation, and therefore legally incorrect, it would however not have been effectively declaring the resolution which adopted the rule to have been unlawful, or *ultra vires*; it would simply have been warning the Assembly that to apply the rule would be legally incorrect.

In one case before the Court, the possibility of review of the decision of an organ of an international organization was envisaged in the constitutive instrument, though not by way of request for advisory

---

[170] *ICJ Reports*, 1971, p. 45, para. 89.

[171] Contrariwise, it would seem that an organ requesting an advisory opinion could expressly indicate that it did not intend the Court to look behind a given resolution, or question its validity. This, in the view of Judge Koretsky, was what was done in the *Certain Expenses* case (dissenting opinion, *ICJ Reports*, 1962, pp. 253–4). The Court in such circumstances might well decline to give an opinion: see the observation of the majority opinion in that case that 'The Court must have full liberty to consider all relevant data available to it in forming an opinion': *ICJ Reports*, 1962, p. 157.

[172] *ICJ Reports*, 1962, p. 151.

[173] *ICJ Reports*, 1955, p. 67. The 1956 opinion on *Admissibility of Hearings of Petitioners by the Committee on South West Africa, ICJ Reports*, 1956, p. 23, is of less interest, since in that case no decision had yet been taken by the General Assembly, the Court's advice being sought beforehand. These cases fall outside the period indicated by the title of these articles, but were not fully examined by Fitzmaurice in the previous series: see this *Year Book*, 60 (1989), p. 5.

opinion. The *Appeal relating to the Jurisdiction of the ICAO Council* was brought on the basis of provisions in (*inter alia*) the Chicago Convention establishing ICAO, whereby disputes as to the interpretation or application of the Convention were to be decided by the Council at the request of a party, but with possibility of appeal to the Court. The Court noted in its judgment that the Convention enlisted 'the support of the Court for the good functioning of the Organization', and regarded it as a 'reassurance' for the Council that it knew 'that means exist for determining whether a decision'—*in casu* a decision as to its own jurisdiction—'is in conformity or not with the provisions of the treaties governing its action'.[174] While there may be some doubt whether the members of the Council would necessarily feel this as a reassurance rather than a hindrance, it is clear that, the matter being constitutionally provided for, the question of the consent of the Council to a re-examination of its decision by the Court does not arise.

In any event, for the reason already stated, the question of consent, authorization or request by the body which had taken the decision seems to be something of a red herring: if the question arose in a contentious case, it would have to be resolved independently of any consent of the organ concerned, so that it does not appear that the fact that the matter was raised in advisory proceedings would make any difference. However, recognition of the possibility that the Court might be specifically *asked* to review a decision of another principal organ, and might, following such a request, find that the decision was invalid, suggests that such decisions are not to be conclusively presumed to be valid and validly adopted; unless one argues that the organ in question is sole judge of the question, or that the decision benefits from an absolute presumption of validity, but that presumption yields if the deciding organ itself has doubts, and refers those doubts to the Court. This is however a somewhat artificial argument.

At all events, in the *Namibia* case, despite having asserted, as noted above, that it had no powers of 'judicial review or appeal in respect of the decisions taken by the United Nations organs concerned', the Court did proceed to examine the validity of General Assembly Resolution 2145 (XXI). Its explanation was as follows:

However, in the exercise of its judicial function and since objections have been advanced the Court, in the course of its reasoning, will consider these objections before determining any legal consequences arising from those resolutions.[175]

The use of the expression 'in the course of its reasoning' suggests that the Court was alive to the point referred to above, that not to question a possibly false premiss, on the ground that it was constituted by a United Nations resolution, might lead the Court to a conclusion which was false

[174] *ICJ Reports*, 1972, pp. 60–1, para. 26; cf. above, p. 21.
[175] *ICJ Reports*, 1971, p. 45, para. 89.

as a matter of law. On the other hand, the reference to the objections which had been raised might be read as implying that the Court would not feel it right to raise a question of validity of a resolution *proprio motu*, even if some of its Members had doubts on the point.

A similar appeal was taken earlier in the *Namibia* advisory opinion, when the Court was concerned with an objection by South Africa to the *formal* validity of the Security Council resolution regarding the Court's opinion. The Court first stated resoundingly that

A resolution of a properly constituted organ of the United Nations which is passed in accordance with that organ's rules of procedure, and is declared by its President to have been so passed, must be presumed to have been validly adopted;

but nevertheless went on to say that

However, since in this case the objections made concern the competence of the Court, the Court will proceed to examine them.[176]

It is thus difficult to see what is the force of the presumption of validity in the case of a matter concerning the Court's competence; and the distinction between matters of competence and matters of merits is difficult to discern.

In fact the Court was able to dismiss the objections made, and uphold the validity of the various decisions; but the fact that it was ready to examine the objections must signify that it would be ready, in a proper case, to uphold such objections if it were satisfied that they were well-founded. What, in that case, becomes of the assertion, that the Court has no powers of judicial review of decisions of other principal organs? What does 'judicial review' mean? In the words of Judge Schwebel, in his dissenting opinion in the *Mortished* case,

To posit an authority of the Administrative Tribunal to set aside or overrule decisions of the General Assembly is to invest the Tribunal with a power of judicial review vis-à-vis the Assembly. But the Tribunal does not enjoy that extraordinary power,[177]

and this is a definition which appears to correspond to the anxieties of those commentators who oppose the existence of any power of review. However, what we are discussing is not, as already observed, a power of 'review' in the sense of power to 'overrule or set aside' decisions, but rather a power to say, if the nature of the issues before the Court requires it, that a given decision did not have the effect which its authors intended it to have, and thought that it did have. Ultimately, the absence of a power of 'review' seems to mean no more than this: that the Court has no

---

[176] *ICJ Reports*, 1971, p. 22, para. 20.
[177] *Application for Review of Judgment No. 273 of the United Nations Administrative Tribunal, ICJ Reports*, 1982, p. 544, para. 144.

initiative in the matter. If requested by a principal organ to say whether a given decision, to be taken by that organ or already taken, is valid, it may give a reply; and if the question of the validity of a decision arises as a necessary part of the chain of reasoning required to arrive at a decision in a contentious case—or on a request for advisory opinion, as in the *Namibia* case—, then the Court is bound to satisfy itself of such validity. But the Court obviously has no power to call in a suspect decision, and of its own motion declare it invalid. Nor can it—or at least it should not—question the validity of a resolution which forms part of the subject-matter of the case before it if the parties accept that validity.[178]

In the *Northern Cameroons* case, there had been a General Assembly Resolution (1608 (XV)) rejecting the plea of the Republic of Cameroon that the plebiscite held in the Trust Territory of the Northern Cameroons should be declared null and void. The Court observed in the course of its reasoning that 'there is no doubt—*and indeed no controversy*—that the resolution had definitive legal effect'.[179] This observation was preceded by the reservation that the Court had not found it 'necessary to consider here whether or not the General Assembly based its action on a correct interpretation of the Trusteeship Agreement'; and later in the same paragraph it was recorded that

The Applicant here has expressly said it does not ask the Court to revise or to reverse those conclusions of the General Assembly or those decisions as such, and it is not therefore necessary to consider whether the Court could exercise such an authority.[180]

Although the Court declined to exercise jurisdiction in the *Northern Cameroons* case, on the grounds that the case was 'moot', that the decision asked for would have no 'forward reach', the observations quoted are not merely an indication of the nature of the case such as would have no particular authority in view of the interlocutory decision not to act: they are part of the reasoning underlying that decision.

It is however important to note that neither the question whether the Court had power to review the General Assembly decision, nor that of the validity of Resolution 1608 (XV), were relevant to the jurisdictional question: that question was determined solely by what the applicant was asking the Court to do. Thus if a judge—or even the Court as a whole—had taken the prima facie view that it did have power to review a resolution, and that Resolution 1608 (XV) was invalid, this would have been irrelevant. A decision invalidating the resolution would have been one having a 'forward reach', unlike the decision which Cameroon was in

---

[178] This would seem to be clear in a contentious case, where the parties are free to waive objections of this kind; the position is perhaps less clear in advisory proceedings, in view of the presence in the background of other States affected by the resolution.

[179] *ICJ Reports*, 1963, p. 32, emphasis added.

[180] *ICJ Reports*, 1963, p. 32. In fact the applicant expressed the view that the Court 'would not be competent' to annul the resolution terminating the trusteeship; ibid., p. 33.

fact asking for, but no such decision could be taken, because to do so would be to act *ultra petita*. It follows that the *Northern Cameroons* decision is no authority on the question whether or not the Court may raise *proprio motu* a question of validity of a resolution if such validity is seen as an essential element in the reasoning of the judgment that the Court will have to deliver. On the other hand, the Court did not feel it necessary to state categorically, as it did in the *Namibia* and *Mortished*[181] cases, that it had no power of judicial review in respect of General Assembly decisions.

So long as there has been no ruling by the Court on the validity of a decision of a political organ, are States which opposed the decision free to argue that it is invalid, and decline to give effect to it? This was what occurred in the *Certain Expenses* case; and there is some encouragement to be found for such an attitude in the dissenting opinion of President Winiarski in that case:

In the international legal system, . . . there is, in the absence of agreement to the contrary, no tribunal competent to make a finding of nullity. It is the State which regards itself as the injured party which itself rejects a legal instrument vitiated, in its opinion, by such defects as to render it a nullity. Such a decision is obviously a grave one and one to which resort can be had only in exceptional cases, but one which is nevertheless sometimes inevitable and which is recognized as such by general international law.

A refusal to pay, as in the case before the Court, may be regarded by a Member State, loyal and indeed devoted to the Organization, as the only means of protesting against a resolution of the majority which, in its opinion, disregards the true meaning of the Charter and adopts in connection with it a decision which is legally invalid; . . . [182]

Judge Gros took a similar view in the *WHO/Egypt* case:

A decision of the WHO which is contrary to international law does not become lawful because a majority of States has voted in favour of it. The WHO and, in particular, its Assembly were created by the member States in order to carry out that which they had decided to do together, and that alone; member States are not bound to implement an unlawful act if that is what they hold it to be, and the practice of international organizations has shown that recourse is had in such circumstances to a refusal to carry out such act. Consequently, nothing is settled by a decision taken by a majority of member States in matters in which a specialized agency oversteps its competence. Numbers cannot cure a lack of constitutional competence.[183]

Looking at the problem of 'judicial review' in a wider context, much of the discussion has focused on the need to ensure the stability of the United Nations system, in particular the role of the Security Council in

---

[181] *ICJ Reports*, 1982, p. 363, para. 76.
[182] *ICJ Reports*, 1962, p. 232.
[183] *ICJ Reports*, 1980, p. 104.

the maintenance of international peace and security, a consideration which the Court is entitled to take into account, but which, it is suggested, must take second place to the need to do justice in the case before it. An analogy may perhaps be drawn with a problem which arose before the Court in a case which falls just outside the strict period the subject of these articles. In the case concerning the *Arbitral Award of 31 July 1989 (Guinea-Bissau/Senegal)*, the Court was asked to say that the award in question was 'inexistent' or 'absolutely null and void', but both parties agreed that the proceedings before the Court 'were not intended by way of appeal from the Award or as an application for revision of it'.[184] In the Court's view it followed, on the authority of the case concerning the *Arbitral Award made by the King of Spain*,[185] that the Court was not 'called upon to pronounce on whether the arbitrator's decision was right or wrong'. On this basis, the Court declined to go into a question, raised by Guinea-Bissau, whether the arbitrators had correctly interpreted the *compromis* determining their jurisdiction.[186] The award of 31 July 1989 was addressed to the question whether a Franco-Portuguese Agreement of 26 April 1960, determining a maritime boundary, had the force of law between Guinea-Bissau and Senegal. If the proceedings before the Court had been framed as a request that the Court determine the maritime boundary between the two States, Senegal would have raised the jurisdictional objection that this was a matter 'in regard to which the parties have agreed to have recourse to some other method of settlement', the subjection of a reservation in Senegal's acceptance of jurisdiction; but in any event, Senegal could have argued that the maritime boundary should be declared to be what it had been decided to be by the arbitration award. At that point, the problem would have arisen whether, in order to arrive at a correct conclusion in law as to the position of the maritime boundary, the Court could or should have reviewed the correctness of the arbitrators' decision. Should the parties be held to have accepted, by their *compromis*, that the decision of the arbitrators should be final, even if it appeared flawed by errors of law or jurisdiction? There is a lucid discussion of the problem in the separate opinion of Judge Shahabuddeen in the *Arbitral Award* case.[187] Similarly, does becoming a Member of the United Nations imply acceptance that a decision of the Security Council enjoys an absolute presumption of formal and substantive validity?

The Orders on provisional measures in the two *Lockerbie* cases, though they fall outside the period now under examination, should be briefly

---

[184] *ICJ Reports*, 1991, p. 62, paras. 24, 25.
[185] *ICJ Reports*, 1960, at p. 214.
[186] *ICJ Reports*, 1991, p. 69, para. 47.
[187] *ICJ Reports*, 1991, at pp. 110 ff. Se also the remarks of the present writer, 'Reflections on the Articulation of International Judicial Decisions and the Problem of "Mootness" ', in Macdonald (ed.), *Essays in Honour of Wang Tieya*, pp. 792-7.

noticed. In those cases there was an explicit contention by Libya that Security Council Resolution 748 (1992), calling upon Libya to hand over the alleged terrorist bombers, was 'contrary to international law',[188] but the Court declined to go into that question *at the stage of provisional measures*. On the assumption that the Security Council resolution was valid and binding under Article 24 of the Charter, then it was an obligation under the Charter for the purposes of Article 102 thereof, and as such prevailed over any obligations under the 1971 Montreal Convention relied on by Libya. The Court's wording was however cautious: it did not regard itself as debarred from examining the validity of the resolution.

Whereas the Court, while thus not at this stage called upon to determine definitively the legal effect of Security Council resolution 748 (1992), considers that, whatever the situation previous to the adoption of that resolution, the rights claimed by Libya under the Montreal Convention cannot now be regarded as appropriate for protection by the indication of provisional measures;[189] . . .

The reference to non-examination of the validity of the resolution 'at this stage', while non-committal, is more suggestive of an asserted power to carry out such an examination at the appropriate stage than of a disavowal of such power. At the same time, the Court takes care not to rule, even prima facie, that Libya's rights under the Convention have been cancelled out by the Security Council decision; all it says is that those rights are not 'appropriate for protection' by provisional measures. If there is a large question mark over the continuing existence or validity of rights, which cannot be removed in the course of the *summaria cognitio* available in provisional measure proceedings, it is difficult to see what other course was open to the Court.

A final question to be briefly noted is the impact of a decision by the Court that a given decision, let us say of the Security Council, cannot be upheld. Strictly, as we have seen, the only effect given to such a finding by the Court itself is the appropriate legal conclusion for the decision of the case before it; unless, of course, it is giving an advisory opinion, at the request of the organ concerned, on the very question of the validity of the decisions. Yet, as was observed thirty years ago in a study of this somewhat neglected subject, there is general recognition that 'as a matter of principle illegal acts ought not to give rise to valid and permanently effective consequences in law'.[190] It has been suggested that there may be degrees of invalidity, or that a finding by the Court of invalidity could

[188] *ICJ Reports*, 1992, p. 14, para. 36; p. 126, para. 39.
[189] *ICJ Reports*, 1992, p. 15, para. 40; pp. 126–7, para. 43.
[190] Eli Lauterpacht, 'The Legal Effect of Illegal Acts of International Organizations', in Jennings (ed.), *Essays in Honour of Lord McNair*, at p. 115.

render the decision voidable at the discretion of the organ concerned.[191] The Court has never been called upon to determine the point; but Judge Morelli, in his separate opinion in the *Certain Expenses* case, regarded any such idea as a false analogy with municipal legal systems, where there exist 'means of recourse . . . against the illegitimacy of administrative acts':

In the case of acts of international organizations, and in particular the acts of the United Nations, there is nothing comparable to the remedies existing in domestic law in connection with administrative acts. The consequence of this is that there is no possibility of applying the concept of voidability to the acts of the United Nations. If an act of an organ of the United Nations had to be considered as an invalid act, such invalidity could constitute only the *absolute nullity* of the act.[192]

He went on to say, however, that 'It is only in exceptionally serious cases that an act of the Organization could be regarded as invalid, and hence an absolute nullity';[193] which suggests that a considerable degree of unauthorized action might go totally unsanctioned.

(3) *Subsidiary organs of the United Nations*

Article 7, paragraph 2, and Article 22 of the Charter contemplate the possibility for the General Assembly to create 'subsidiary organs'. When the first case came before the Court by way of request for advisory opinion by the Committee on Applications for Review of Administrative Tribunal Judgments,[194] namely the *Fasla* case in 1973,[195] it was questioned by some judges whether, first of all, that body was an 'organ' of the United Nations and therefore able to benefit from the provisions of Article 96, paragraph 2, of the Charter and to enjoy an authorization from the General Assembly to request advisory opinions. Judge Gros in particular[196] observed that

This Committee, devoid as it is of permanence and of continuity in its composition, and not accumulating any experience, is merely a kind of occasional panel meeting at irregular intervals, or a conference of member States, but certainly not an organ in the proper, institutional sense of the word.[197]

The Court however regarded the word 'organ' as much more flexible in its possible signification:

[191] Alvarez, 'Judging the Security Council', *American Journal of International Law*, 90 (1996), pp. 6–7, citing Lauterpacht (previous note) '*passim*'.
[192] *ICJ Reports*, 1962, p. 222 (emphasis original).
[193] Ibid., p. 223.
[194] Established by the General Assembly by Resolution 957 (X), amending the Statute of the United Nations Administrative Tribunal.
[195] *Application for Review of Judgment No. 158 of the United Nations Administrative Tribunal, ICJ Reports*, 1973, p. 166.
[196] The other dissenter on this point was Judge Morozov, but his opinion is not fully argued: *ICJ Reports*, 1973, p. 298.
[197] *ICJ Reports*, 1973, p. 259, para. 19.

Nor does it appear to the Court that there is substance in the suggestion that the particular constitution of the Committee would preclude it from being considered an 'organ' of the United Nations. As provided in paragraph 4 of Article 11, the Committee is composed of 'the Member States the representatives of which have served on the General Committee of the most recent regular sessions of the General Assembly'. But this provision is no more than a convenient method of establishing the membership of the Committee, which was set up as a separate committee invested with its own functions separate from those of the General Committee. Paragraph 4, indeed, underlined the independent character of the Committee by providing that it should establish its own rules . . . . Accordingly, the Court sees no reason to deny to the Committee the character of an organ of the United Nations which the General Assembly clearly intended it to possess.[198]

While rejecting Judge Gros' view that the Committee was too 'flimsy' to be an organ, the Court does seem here to insist on an essential characteristic of a subsidiary organ, not raised by the dissenters: that the organ be 'independent'. The case concerning the *Effect of UNAT Awards* had established that the General Assembly can establish a subsidiary organ which is so independent that the General Assembly itself cannot refuse to implement its decisions; but that was in the special context of the creation of a judicial organ. Generally, there must be limits on the independence of a subsidiary organ, if it is to remain subsidiary.[199] It is therefore surprising to see the Court apparently saying, not merely that a subsidiary organ can be created to be independent, but that such independence is a defining characteristic. Mention is however specifically made of the Committee's independence from the General Committee, which goes really to the effective existence of the Review Committee, rather than to its independence of the General Assembly.

Consideration of the nature of a subsidiary organ in the *Fasla* case also raised another question: is it open to the General Assembly to establish an organ with functions going beyond those entrusted to the General Assembly itself? A very clear view on this was expressed by Judge Onyeama:

I am of the opinion that the General Assembly cannot legally establish a subsidiary body to perform functions which were not specifically assigned to the Assembly itself, or within the range of its functions.[200]

This view however raised an evident difficulty in the light of the *Effect of Awards* case, since in that case the Court expressly rejected the view that

[198] *ICJ Reports*, 1973, para. 18.

[199] At the San Francisco Conference, the term 'auxiliary organ' was used until a late stage in the drafting, when 'subsidiary organ' was substituted. It has been suggested that this change was unfortunate: 'The term "subsidiary organ" suggests a body on the same level which discharges its responsibilities independently from the main organ, whereas the term "auxiliary organ " hints at a dependent and more subordinated position': Hilf in Simma (ed.), *The Charter of the United Nations*, sub. Art. 22, p. 382.

[200] *ICJ Reports*, 1973, p. 226.

in establishing the Administrative Tribunal 'the General Assembly was establishing an organ which it deemed necessary for the purpose of its own functions'. However, the Court's interpretation in 1954 of what had occurred was that 'By establishing the Administrative Tribunal, the General Assembly was not delegating the performance of its functions: it was exercising a power which it had under the Charter to regulate staff relations'.[201] Judge Onyeama explained that he understood the 1954 opinion

to mean that the General Assembly, in establishing the United Nations Administrative Tribunal, could not have been acting under Article 22 of the Charter as the Charter does not confer judicial functions on the General Assembly, but that it was exercising a power to regulate staff relations under Chapter XV of the Charter.[202]

Judge Onyeama was able to accept this view, not only as applicable to the Tribunal itself, as found in the 1954 opinion, but also as applicable to the Committee on Applications for Review; he was therefore able to recognize that the Committee had power to request advisory opinions as being an 'organ' of the United Nations, even though for him it was not a 'subsidiary organ' set up under Article 22.

It might at first sight be questioned whether an organ established by the General Assembly can be anything other than a 'subsidiary organ' as contemplated by Article 22; if it is not, from whence does the Assembly derive the power to establish it? Yet the Court seems in 1962 to have recognized that bodies may be established by the General Assembly which are not 'subsidiary organs': in the *Certain Expenses* case, it referred to the setting-up, as a 'normal feature of the functioning of the United Nations', by the Assembly of 'commissions or other bodies' which 'constitute, *in some cases*, subsidiary organs established under the authority of Article 22 of the Charter'.[203]

The Court itself did not express a specific view on the point which worried Judge Onyeama, but the wording of the advisory opinion suggests that the majority did not share his view. After recalling the provisions of Articles 7 and 22 of the Charter, the Court stated:

The object of both those Articles is to enable the United Nations to accomplish its purposes, and to function effectively. Accordingly, to place a restrictive interpretation on the power of the General Assembly to establish subsidiary organs would run contrary to the clear intention of the Charter. Article 22, indeed, specifically leaves it to the General Assembly to appreciate the need for any particular organ, and the sole restriction placed by that Article on the General Assembly's power to establish subsidiary organs is that they should be 'necessary for the performance of its functions'.[204]

[201] *ICJ Reports*, 1954, p. 61.
[202] *ICJ Reports*, 1973, p. 227.
[203] *ICJ Reports*, 1962, p. 165 (emphasis added).
[204] *ICJ Reports*, 1973, pp. 172–3, para. 16.

The Court, in its usual diplomatic or sibylline fashion, does not indicate what particular 'restrictive interpretation' it is rejecting, but it is likely to be that espoused by Judge Onyeama; though in such case it must be said that the texts are rather in favour of the restrictive interpretation, since Article 22 refers to the condition that the subsidiary organ be necessary 'for the performance of *its* functions', i.e. the functions of the General Assembly, not those of the Organization as a whole.[205] Nevertheless, in the next paragraph of the 1973 opinion, the Court refers to the 1954 opinion in terms which suggest that it shared Judge Onyeama's interpretation of that opinion, and continues:

From the above reasoning it necessarily follows that the General Assembly's power to regulate staff relations also comprises the power to provide machinery for initiating the review by the Court of the judgments of such a tribunal,[206]

and Judge Onyeama in his opinion explained that it was this passage which enabled him to support the Court's findings.

It is therefore difficult to regard the point as settled by the 1973 opinion, one way or the other, and it must be conceded that there is much force in Judge Onyeama's view that one organ can only create a subsidiary organ to discharge some part of the functions of the higher organ.[207] In the case of the General Assembly, the problem probably only arises in relation to the judicial function, in view of the wide remit of the Assembly: for example, it could presumably create a subsidiary organ which would have functions of maintenance of international peace and security, even though it would be in competition with the Security Council, since such functions are shared by the Assembly. Judge de Castro saw the difficulty, but got round it by treating the creation of the Committee as a delegation, not of a judicial function which the Assembly lacked, but of the function of requesting advisory opinions;[208] this view of the matter was however rejected by the Court, since it would cast doubt on the existence of any separate 'activities' of the Committee for the purposes of Article 96 of the Charter.[209]

2. *Effect of Resolutions and Decisions of United Nations Organs*

Great actions are not always true sons
Of great and mighty resolutions.

Samuel Butler, *Hudibras*, Pt. 1, c.1, 885

---

[205] A point taken by Judge Morozov in his dissent: *ICJ Reports*, 1973, p. 298.

[206] *ICJ Reports*, 1973, p. 173, para. 17.

[207] The principle is apparently recognized in practice that 'the GA cannot transfer more powers to subsidiary organs than it possesses under the Charter': Hilf in Simma (ed.), *The Charter of the United Nations*, sub Art. 22, p. 385.

[208] *ICJ Reports*, 1973, p. 277.

[209] 'This is not a delegation by the General Assembly of its own power to request an advisory opinion; . . .': *ICJ Reports*, 1973, p. 174, para. 20.

The question whether the acts of international organizations, and in particular, United Nations General Assembly resolutions, might constitute an independent source of law, and that of their possible contribution to the development of customary law, have been examined earlier in this series of articles.[210] It was there noted that the Court has not lent its support to any idea that General Assembly resolutions may, of their own force, be binding on all States as a matter of general international law. The jurisprudence of the Court now to be examined is that addressed to the question of the extent to which decisions of the Security Council, and the resolutions of the General Assembly, have binding or other authoritative effects for States, both members and non-members, and for subsidiary organs of the organization.[211]

(1) Decisions of the Security Council[212]

(a) Effect for member States

Until the *Namibia* case in 1971, the Court had not had occasion to examine the interpretation of Article 25 of the Charter, and the effect of 'decisions' of the Security Council by virtue of that article. It had therefore had nothing to say on the controversy whether the 'decisions' referred to in Article 25 are solely those taken under Chapter VII, when the Court is acting in relation to threats to the peace, or also include other decisions. This question was however directly in point in the *Namibia* case, since the intention of the Security Council decision declaring the presence of South Africa in Namibia to be unlawful was clearly that it should be binding and effective for member States; but that decision was not adopted following the procedure of Chapter VII. What provisions of the Charter could be regarded as serving as a basis for the Security Council's action? Article 24 was relied on in argument, and the question was therefore raised by South Africa

whether, as has sometimes been maintained, Article 24 constitutes 'a residuary source of authority which can be drawn upon to meet situations which are not covered by the more detailed provisions in the succeeding Articles'. To put the

---

[210] This *Year Book*, 61 (1990), pp. 80 ff.; see also the exhaustive study by Blaine Sloan, 'General Assembly Resolutions Revisited (Forty Years After)', this *Year Book*, 58 (1987), pp. 39ff.; and Economides, 'Les actes institutionnels internationaux et les sources du droit international', *Annuaire français de droit international*, 34 (1988), p. 131.

[211] The question of the effect of such decisions for the Court itself has been examined in the previous section. The two questions are obviously closely interconnected; but the previous section was addressed essentially to the question whether the Court can invalidate a resolution, and the present section to the question of the effect of resolutions which have not been successfully challenged before the Court.

[212] During the period covered by Fitzmaurice's articles, few questions had arisen as to the effect of Security Council resolutions, so that he only had occasion to refer briefly to the point: this *Year Book*, 29 (1952), pp. 1–34; 34 (1958), pp. 1–5; *Collected Edition*, I, pp. 70–106; II, pp. 428–32.

question another way, does Article 24 confer upon the Security Council not only the powers laid down in Chapters VI, VII, VIII, and XII, but also such *further* powers, consistent with the Purposes and Principles of the United Nations, as are necessary to enable it to maintain international peace and security?[213]

South Africa naturally contended that it did not; but the Court rejected this view:

As to the legal basis of the resolution [276 (1970)], Article 24 of the Charter vests in the Security Council the necessary authority to take action such as that taken in the present case. The reference in paragraph 2 of this Article to specific powers of the Security Council under certain chapters of the Charter does not exclude the existence of general powers to discharge the responsibilities conferred in paragraph 1.[214]

There remained the question whether such a decision, taken under the general powers of Article 24, constituted a 'decision' which members had undertaken to accept and carry out under Article 25. The Court's view on this virtually followed as a necessary consequence from its interpretation of Article 25; the general power which the Court found had been conferred by that Article would be of little use if it did not produce a binding decision.

It would be an untenable interpretation [presumably of Article 24] to maintain that, once such a declaration [that a certain situation was illegal] had been made by the Security Council under Article 24 of the Charter, on behalf of all member States, those Members would be free to act in disregard of such illegality or even to recognize violations of law resulting from it. When confronted with such an internationally unlawful situation, Members of the United Nations would be expected to act in consequence with the declaration made on their behalf.[215]

The philosophy of this reading of the Charter is interesting. One would have thought it sufficient to establish that the signatories of the Charter had had the intention of conferring upon the Security Council certain powers of action in certain circumstances, and that in consequence States subsequently becoming members of the United Nations had similarly accepted that situation. The matter being a simple question of a treaty commitment, the idea that action taken under the power so conferred by agreement should be treated as having been taken 'on behalf of' the members seems supererogatory. There is nothing wrong with a theory of delegated powers of this kind, but does it add anything? Rhetorically, it makes more apparently convincing the idea that member States should abide by what has been done on their behalf; but it is only in a purely

---

[213] *Namibia, Pleadings*, vol. 1, p. 502 (original emphasis), quoting *Repertory of United Nations Practice*, vol. 2, p. 19.

[214] *ICJ Reports*, 1971, p. 52, para. 110. In support of this view the Court quoted a statement made by the Secretary-General to the Security Council on 10 January 1947; see p. 25, above.

[215] *ICJ Reports*, 1971, p. 52, para. 112.

formal and theoretical sense that Resolution 276 (1970) could have been said to have been adopted 'on behalf of' South Africa.

It may be that the Court was endeavouring to base the binding character of Resolution 276 (1970) on two distinct arguments. If Article 25 applied to that resolution as a 'decision', then member States were bound to apply it. But if it were thought that Article 25 did not apply, it would still (on the Court's argument) be impossible for member States to disown what had been done on their behalf. Some support for this interpretation is given by the structure of the argument. It is only after making the finding quoted above, with its reference to a declaration made 'on behalf of' member States, that the Court moves on to Article 25:

The question *therefore* arises as to the effect of this decision of the Security Council for States Members of the United Nations in accordance with Article 25 of the Charter.[216]

The use of the link 'therefore' is puzzling: the effect of Article 25 would be a relevant question whether or not the theory of delegated powers were adopted. Another reading might of course be that the Court, in the first passage quoted above, is saying that it would be to be expected that Article 25 would apply to a decision of this type; and then goes on to find, much to its satisfaction, that it does so apply.

At all events, the Court's position as to the effect of Article 25 is unequivocal:

It has been contended that Article 25 of the Charter applies only to enforcement measures adopted under Chapter VII of the Charter. It is not possible to find in the Charter any support for this view. Article 25 is not confined to decisions in regard to enforcement action but applies to 'the decisions of the Security Council' adopted in accordance with the Charter. Moreover that Article is placed, not in Chapter VII, but immediately after Article 24 in that part of the Charter which deals with the functions and powers of the Security Council. If Article 25 had referred solely to decisions of the Security Council concerning enforcement action under Articles 41 and 42 of the Charter, that is to say, if it were only such decisions which had binding effect, then Article 25 would be superfluous, since this effect is secured by Articles 48 and 49 of the Charter.[217]

One inconspicuous consequence for member States of a binding decision of the Security Council, which was not mentioned specifically in the advisory opinion (but noted in the separate opinion of Judge Ammoun[218]), was to take on importance twenty years later in the *Lockerbie* cases. Under Article 103 of the Charter, obligations of the members of the United Nations under the present Charter are to prevail over 'their obligations under any other international agreement'; and the

---

[216] *ICJ Reports*, 1971, p. 52, para. 112, *in fine* (emphasis added).
[217] *ICJ Reports*, 1971, pp. 52–3, para. 113.
[218] *ICJ Reports*, 1971, p. 99.

former category must include the obligation under Article 25 to 'accept and carry out' Security Council decisions.[219]

(b) *Effect for non-member States*

The dicta in the *Namibia* advisory opinion as to the effect of the Court's findings on non-members of the United Nations have already been discussed above, in the context of the impact on third States of acts *of the organization*, as distinct from acts of this or that organ. This is not however an interpretation universally accepted; and it must be conceded that the manner in which the Court expressed itself lends itself to alternative interpretations. The paragraph in question begins with the qualification: 'As to non-member States, although not bound by Articles 24 and 25 of the Charter', and then continues by noting that 'they have been called upon in paragraphs 2 and 5 of resolution 276 (1970) to give assistance in the action which has been undertaken by the United Nations in regard to Namibia'.[220] This reference recalls the provision of Article 2, paragraph 6, of the Charter that 'The Organization shall ensure that States which are not members of the United Nations shall act in accordance with these Principles so far as may be necessary for the maintenance of international peace and security'. According to one school of thought, on the basis of this text, 'the binding force of decisions of the SC under Art. 25 may extend to non-Members'.[221] The *Namibia* decision, it is suggested, lends no support to this view, which was apparently espoused before it only by one speaker in the oral proceedings.[222]

(c) *Effects for other international organizations*

It seems clear that even decisions of the Security Council are not binding on the specialized agencies or other organizations as such. As Fitzmaurice observed of the specialized agencies, 'These Agencies may be affiliated to the United Nations, but they are separate international entities, and can only be bound by their own decisions'.[223] In the *Namibia* case, the question put to the Court only concerned the legal effects 'for States' of South Africa's presence in Namibia, coupled with Security Council Resolution 276 (1970). Judge Ammoun, however, reviewed the conduct of the specialized agencies, and criticized the World Bank group (IBRD, IDA, IFC) for action inconsistent with the illegality of South Africa's presence.[224] A Security Council resolution certainly has, and normally should have, an impact on other organiza-

---

[219] *Lockerbie, Provisional Measures, ICJ Reports*, 1992, p. 15, para. 39; p. 126, para. 42.

[220] *ICJ Reports*, 1971, p. 56, para. 126.

[221] Delbrück in Simma (ed.), *The Charter of the United Nations*, sub. Art. 25, §19, p. 414.

[222] Mr Elias, representing the OAU: *Pleadings*, vol. 2, p. 105.

[223] This *Year Book*, 34 (1958), p. 6; *Collected Edition*, vol. 2, p. 433.

[224] Separate opinion, *ICJ Reports*, 1971, pp. 94–5.

tions, to the extent that United Nations members would be in breach of Article 25 of the Charter if they voted in favour of action by the other organization flagrantly in contradiction with a binding Security Council decision.

(2) *Decisions of the General Assembly*

As already noted, the starting point for discussion of resolutions of the General Assembly must be that in general they are recommendations only, without binding effect even for United Nations members; nor has the Court in its decisions cast any doubt on this general principle. Fitzmaurice had earlier emphasized the fundamental nature of the recognized distinction, as regards legal effect, between Security Council decisions, under Article 25 of the Charter, and General Assembly resolutions, and had expressed the view that only an amendment of the Charter could affect the position.[225] At the same time, he drew attention to certain kinds of resolution which do in effect have an obligatory force, and distinguished a number of classes, which will, slightly adjusted, be used for the purpose of the present discussion.

(a) *Decisions of the Assembly relating to its own domestic procedures or economy*

In his article in the 1958 *Year Book*, Fitzmaurice included in this category 'resolutions . . . in which [the Assembly] takes a decision affecting its own internal economy or action, e.g., . . . decides . . . to include a certain item in its budget', and in a footnote he added that 'If a certain item is voted into the budget, it becomes part of the budget of the organization, to which Members are already bound by Article 17 of the Charter to contribute their share as apportioned by the Assembly'.[226] Four years later he was called upon to sit in the *Certain Expenses* case, which required a more profound examination of this simple statement.

The question put to the Court by the General Assembly for advisory opinion was also essentially simple in form, though made lengthy by the need to enumerate by their reference numbers a quantity of Assembly and Security Council resolutions: shorn of these specificities, it was: 'Do the expenditures authorized in the General Assembly resolutions enumerated, relating to the Congo operations and to the operations of UNEF in the Middle East, constitute "expenses of the Organization" within the meaning of Article 17, paragraph 2, of the Charter?'.[227] Article 17, paragraph 2, it will be recalled, provides that 'The expenses of the Organization shall be borne by the Members as apportioned by the General Assembly'. The reply of the Court was that they did constitute such expenses; but what is here of interest is the question of the effect, for

[225] This *Year Book*, 34 (1958), p. 2; *Collected Edition*, vol. 2, p. 429.
[226] This *Year Book*, 34 (1958), p. 3; *Collected Edition*, vol. 2, p. 430.
[227] For the full text, see *ICJ Reports*, 1962, p. 152.

members of the organization, of the resolutions in question on the basis of the Court's finding. As is frequently the case, the Court was careful to limit its reply to what it understood to be the narrow question put. It identified three possible questions which could arise on the interpretation of Article 17: that of identifying what are the 'expenses of the Organization'; that of their apportionment by the General Assembly; and that of the interpretation of the phrase 'shall be borne by the Members'.[228] In its resolution adopting the request for an advisory opinion, the Assembly had recognized 'its need for authoritative legal guidance' on the obligations of members in the matter of financing the Congo and UNEF operations,[229] and the Court noted that it was the second and third questions identified by it which directly involved 'the financial obligations of the Members'; nevertheless, it limited itself to the first question, so avoiding, even by implication, stating that members were bound to pay their apportioned share of the expenses in question.[230] In line with this approach, it is nowhere stated specifically in the opinion that the decisions of the General Assembly authorizing the contested expenditures were binding on member States.

Nevertheless, the explicit statement of the position in the separate opinion of Judge Sir Percy Spender is implicit also in the Court's advisory opinion:

Once the General Assembly has passed upon what are the expenses of the Organization, and it is apparent that the expenditure incurred and to be incurred on behalf of the Organization is in furtherance of its purposes, their character as such and any apportionment thereof made by the General Assembly under Article 17(2) of the Charter cannot legally be challenged by any Member State. Its decision cannot be impugned and becomes binding upon each Member State. It would be anarchic of any interpretation of the Charter were each Member State its own interpreter of whether this or that particular expense was an expense of the Organization, within the meaning of Article 17(2), and could, by its own interpretation, be free to refuse to comply with the decisions of the General Assembly.[231]

There is perhaps some inconsistency in including the precautionary condition that the expenditure is in furtherance of the organization's purposes, since it opens up the question of who is to judge whether this is so: if any member State is free to disagree on the point, an equally anarchic situation would result.

Judge Sir Gerald Fitzmaurice was ready to go further than the Court; he held, first that an Assembly resolution of this kind was in any event

---

[228] *ICJ Reports*, 1962, pp. 157–8.

[229] Resolution 1731 (XVI), quoted at *ICJ Reports*, 1962, pp. 152–3.

[230] Later in the opinion it reiterated that the General Assembly could follow any one of several alternative courses of action to meet the obligations of the organization, of which apportionment under Article 17, paragraph 2, was only one: *ICJ Reports*, 1962, pp. 169–70.

[231] *ICJ Reports*, 1962, p. 183.

binding on any State that did not vote against it, since its action could be taken to imply, if not acceptance of an obligation to participate in the action authorized by the resolution, at least 'willingness to contribute to the expenses of carrying it out'.[232] Secondly, his interpretation of the *travaux préparatoires* was that there had been an intention—in this departing from the voting system of the League—that Member States were to be obliged to pay their apportioned shares, 'irrespective of how their votes were cast on any given occasion, at all events as regards all the essential activities of the Organization'. If the resolution voted on were one solely directed to the making of a payment or contribution, then it would follow that the resolution would be of a binding nature, even for those States which did not vote in favour of it.[233]

(b) *Other Assembly decisions*

The Mandate for South West Africa was, as the Court found in the *Namibia* advisory opinion, terminated by Resolution 2145 (XXI) of the United Nations General Assembly. The objection was however taken by South Africa that the powers and functions of the General Assembly do not include the power to take decisions, but merely to make recommendations, as indicated in Article 10 of the Charter. Furthermore, it was contended that by adopting that resolution, the Assembly was purporting to effect a transfer of territory, which is also not within its powers; and it was under the heading of the latter objection that the Court dealt also with the former.

The Court had already found that the effect of Resolution 2145(XXI) was a determination that South Africa was in breach of the Mandate, that it 'has, in fact disavowed the mandate', and had repudiated it.[234] This amounted in itself to an answer to the suggestion that the Assembly had effected a transfer of territory, but in addition, 'This is not a finding on facts, but the formulation of a legal situation'. The Court then dealt in effect with the argument that the Assembly had no powers of decision in the following sentence of the opinion:

For it would not be correct to assume that, because the General Assembly is in principle vested with recommendatory powers, it is debarred from adopting, in specific cases within the framework of its competence, resolutions which make determinations or have operative design.[235]

Now it is of course true that the General Assembly can adopt resolutions which 'have operative design' within the field of, for example, internal and budgetary matters (the point treated in the preceding section). But it remains true that in the political field the powers of the

---

[232] *ICJ Reports*, 1962, p. 210.
[233] Ibid., pp. 211–12.
[234] *ICJ Reports*, 1971, p. 45, para. 95, quoting the resolution.
[235] *ICJ Reports*, 1971, p. 50, para. 105.

Assembly are purely recommendatory: that is, the powers which it enjoys under the Charter. The analysis of the situation which seems to underlie the Court's thinking is that the organization, as such, inherited certain powers from the League of Nations; the General Assembly was the United Nations body corresponding to the League Council;[236] thus when it was a question of the organization exercising the inherited powers, it was for the General Assembly to exercise them; and that had nothing to do with the limitations in the Charter on the Assembly's role in the organization, since the relevant powers were derived *ab extra*,—unless, that is, it were argued that the nature of the Assembly was such that it *could not* take operative decisions, whatever the alleged source of the power to do so. The question was complicated by the fact that it was not contended that the Assembly was exercising a power of revocation contained within the Mandate, and therefore inherited with the Mandate from the League Assembly. It was found that the power to terminate a treaty relationship on account of breach was a power existing in general law, exercisable by any party to a treaty; the United Nations had succeeded to the treaty relationship constituted by the Mandate; and accordingly the appropriate organ of the United Nations could terminate that relationship, whatever its powers under the Charter.

An interpretation expressly made on these lines would have left open the question whether, within the United Nations context, or the Charter context, there was room for an effective decision-making power of the General Assembly outside the category of internal and budgetary matters. As it is, the dictum of the Court leaves a wide field for speculation on the context in which, or the extent to which, the General Assembly may adopt resolutions which 'make determinations or have operative design'.

If, in the *Namibia* case, the General Assembly had been exercising a power of revocation of the Mandate expressly stated in the text of that instrument, the situation would have been simpler: it would be a case of a treaty attributing to a resolution of the General Assembly an effect going beyond that conferred on such a decision by the Charter; and if the Mandate had been a post-war document referring to the United Nations rather than the League, the case would be clearer still. It is however also possible that a decision taken, not by reference to a special treaty, but in the normal course of the work of the Assembly, may acquire such exceptional or additional effect as a result of the operation of a treaty. A case in point is the situation which arose in the case concerning the *Applicability of the Obligation to Arbitrate under Section 21 of the United Nations Headquarters Agreement of 26 June 1947*. The question in respect of which arbitration was sought was whether the United States was in breach of the Headquarters Agreement by closing, or threatening to

---

[236] See *International Status of South West Africa*, advisory opinion, *ICJ Reports*, 1950, p. 137.

close, the Permanent Observer Mission of the Palestine Liberation Organization. Under section 11 of the Agreement, the United States had undertaken not to 'impose any impediments to transit to or from the Headquarters District' of 'persons invited to the Headquarters District by the United Nations'. By General Assembly Resolution 3237 (XXIX) the PLO had been 'invited' to participate in the sessions and work of the Assembly. Thus it was the contention of the Secretary-General (which was not disputed by the United States) that the PLO was entitled to the protection of section 11.[237] The same point could be expressed by saying that Resolution 3237 (XXIX) was binding on the United States, and had an obligatory effect not normally attached to a resolution; and that would have been so even if the United States had voted against the resolution.

(c) *Effect as regards other UN organs and the specialized agencies*

It is generally accepted that in any given international organization, resolutions of the principal policy-making or executive organs are binding on all subordinate organs.[238] In the *Mortished* case,[239] a request for advisory opinion from the Committee on Applications for Review of Administrative Tribunal Judgments, the central question (as the Court found) was whether the Tribunal had 'erred on a question of law relating to the provisions of the Charter of the United Nations'; the contention of the United States in the case was that the Tribunal had so erred by failing to apply a General Assembly resolution which had amended the United Nations Staff Regulations so as to suppress the right of retiring staff members to receive a so-called 'repatriation grant' even if they elected to remain, after retirement, in the country of their duty station. It was unquestioned in the case that the Tribunal, as a subordinate (if not 'subsidiary'[240]) organ was obliged to apply decisions of the General Assembly, and the Court emphasized the point:

Certainly the Tribunal must accept and apply the decisions of the General Assembly made in accordance with Article 101 of the United Nations Charter.[241]

The only slightly unexpected aspect of this dictum is that it is, in terms, limited to decisions taken under Article 101 of the Charter, concerning the appointment of staff. This is, no doubt, the context in which the

---

[237] See *ICJ Reports*, 1988, pp. 15–16, paras. 8–11. The Court was in fact not seised of the merits of the dispute, and therefore made no finding on the point; but it serves to illustrate the point as to the possibility of an extended effect, conferred *ab extra*, of an Assembly resolution.

[238] Cf. Frowein, 'The Internal and External Effects of Resolutions by International Organizations', *Zeitschrift für ausländisches öffentliches Recht und Völkerrecht*, 49 (1989), p. 780.

[239] *Application for Review of Judgment No. 273 of the United Nations Administrative Tribunal, ICJ Reports*, 1982, p. 325.

[240] See the discussion of this point above, pp. 56 ff.

[241] *ICJ Reports*, 1982, p. 363, para. 76.

Assembly will most frequently adopt decisions which will be relevant to cases before the Tribunal; but does that mean that if some resolution of the General Assembly adopted outside the field of staff relations nevertheless was relevant to the legal analysis of a case before the Tribunal, it could, if not disregard the resolution, at least permit itself to re-examine it? It would seem not; but the Court's specific statement that

Certainly there can be no question of the Tribunal possessing any 'powers of judicial review or appeal in respect of the decisions' taken by the General Assembly, powers which the Court itself does not possess[242]

directly follows the first statement quoted above, as though it were a consequence of that statement, and consequently a conclusion confined to the limited field of that statement.[243]

As regards the specialized agencies, it is clear that if Security Council decisions are not, as such, binding upon them, *a fortiori* decisions or recommendations of the General Assembly also lack binding force. It is however to be noted that the termination of the Mandate for South West Africa was the act of the General Assembly; and if that act had been ineffective *vis-à-vis* the specialized agencies (for example), would the Security Council's decision consequent on the Assembly's resolution have had any effect for them?[244] This is essentially the reason for treating the termination as the act *of the organization.*

CHAPTER III

SUMMARY OF DECISIONS RELATING TO INTERNATIONAL
ORGANIZATIONS

The purpose of the present section is to bring together various findings of the Court in the course of the period examined relating to the operation of the United Nations, and of other international organizations, a number of which have already been commented on in the analyses of the major questions in the preceding sections.

1. *The United Nations*

(1) *Self-defence and Article 51 of the Charter*

In the *Nicaragua* case, the Court found itself in the curious position of having to decide a dispute on the basis solely of customary law, even

---

[242] *ICJ Reports*, 1982, p. 363, para. 76, quoting *ICJ Reports*, 1971, p. 45, para. 89.

[243] It is also relevant to note that the declared absence of any 'powers of judicial review or appeal' for the Court itself in respect of decisions of other principal organs probably does not prevent the Court from examining the formal or substantive validity of such decisions if this is necessary for the determination of the case before it. See above, pp. 46–7.

[244] Cf. the criticism of Judge Ammoun, cited in n. 224, above.

though it was recognized and indeed urged by both parties that provisions of multilateral treaties, and in particular of the United Nations
Charter, were very much in point.[245] One of the relevant issues in the
case was the exercise of the right of self-defence, and the Court had to
refer to Article 51 of the Charter, even though it was jurisdictionally
debarred from applying it. (Its task was simplified by a finding that that
article was little more than a *renvoi* to customary law.)[246] Although the
case thus involved questions of interpretation of the Charter, the issues
involved were no part of the law of international organizations, but
matters of general law, to be treated elsewhere in these articles.

(2) *Powers of decision of the Security Council*

The Court's finding, in the *Namibia* case, that the Security Council
has power to take a decision, binding on member States under Article 25
of the Charter, not only when acting in relation to threats to the peace
under Article VII, but also when acting under other Chapters of the
Charter, has already been examined above,[247] but is noted here also for
completeness of the present section.

(3) *Powers of decision of the General Assembly*

Similarly, it is recalled here that, as already noted above, the Court in
the *Namibia* case explained that

it would not be correct to assume that, because the General Assembly is in
principle vested with recommendatory powers, it is debarred from adopting, in
specific cases within the framework of its competence, resolutions which make
determinations or have operative design.[248]

(4) *The 'expenses' and the 'budget' of the organization*

It has been stated in an authoritative quarter that the Court's answer
to the question put to it in the *Certain Expenses* case 'was entirely
predictable, and made virtually no difference to the entrenched positions
of the opponents of the powers assumed by the General Assembly as
regards military peacekeeping'.[249] It should however perhaps be
recorded that in the case the Court upheld the power of the General
Assembly to treat as 'expenses', to be included in the 'budget' of the
organization, and therefore (though the Court did not venture to say so)
payable by apportionment among member States, the cost of peace-
keeping activities in the Congo and the Middle East, adopted by

---

[245] For further details and comment, see the first article in this series in this *Year Book*, 60 (1989), pp. 154 ff.

[246] *ICJ Reports*, 1986, p. 94, para. 176.

[247] *ICJ Reports*, 1971, p. 52; above, section 3(1).

[248] *ICJ Reports*, 1971, p. 50, para. 105; above, section 3(2).

[249] D. W. Bowett, 'The Court's Role in relation to International Organizations', *Fifty Years of the International Court of Justice (Mélanges Jennings)*, at p. 185.

resolutions bitterly opposed by certain States, which regarded them as encroachments on the prerogatives of the Security Council.[250]

(5) Trusteeship: effects of termination

In the *Northern Cameroons* case, the Court had occasion to comment on the legal effects of the termination by the General Assembly, with the consent of the Administering Authority, of a Trusteeship established under Chapter XIII of the Charter.

[F]rom the point of view of a Member of the United Nations, other than the Administering Authority itself, it is clear that any rights which may have been granted by the Articles of the Trusteeship Agreement to other Members of the United Nations or their nationals came to an end. This is not to say that, for example, property rights which might have been obtained in accordance with certain Articles of the Trusteeship Agreement and which might have vested before the termination of the Agreement, would have been divested by the termination.[251]

This careful proviso may be compared with the Court's indications, in the *Namibia* case, of the effects of the termination of South Africa's entitlement to remain in Namibia effected by General Assembly Resolution 2145, and the subsequent Security Council resolution. After referring to the duty of States of non-recognition of South Africa's administration of Namibia, stated in the Security Council resolution, the Court added this qualification:

In general, the non-recognition of South Africa's administration of the territory should not result in depriving the people of Namibia of any advantages derived from international co-operation. In particular, while official acts performed by the Government of South Africa on behalf of or concerning Namibia after the termination of the Mandate are illegal and invalid, this invalidity cannot be extended to those acts, such as, for instance, the registration of births, deaths and marriages, the effects of which can be ignored only to the detriment of the inhabitants of the Territory.[252]

The *Northern Cameroons* decision was invoked by Australia in the case (in fact falling outside the period now under consideration) concerning *Certain Phosphate Lands in Nauru*, in which Nauru sought to claim against Australia, one of the three States which had jointly administered the Territory under a Trusteeship Agreement, for rehabilitation of phosphate lands on the island worked out during the trusteeship period. Quoting the *Northern Cameroons* case, the Court accepted that the Trusteeship had been terminated and was no longer in force; and added:

[250] For a recent survey of the case in its context, see Kouassi, 'Roles respectifs du Conseil de sécurité et de l'Assemblée générale dans le traitement des opérations de maintien de la paix', *Colloque de l'Académie de droit international*, 1992, p. 427.

[251] *ICJ Reports*, 1963, p. 34.

[252] *ICJ Reports*, 1971, p. 56, para. 125.

In the light of these considerations, it might be possible to question the admissibility of an action brought against the Administering Authority on the basis of the alleged failure by it to comply with its obligations with respect to the administration of the Territory.[253]

It nevertheless rejected Australia's objection on the facts, finding that at the time of termination of the Trusteeship, 'everyone was aware of subsisting differences of opinion' on the matter of rehabilitation, and that although the relevant resolution did not expressly reserve Nauru's rights, 'the Court cannot view that resolution as giving a discharge to the Administering Authority with respect to such rights'.[254]

(6) *Voting in the Security Council: abstention*

Mention has already been made a number of times, in various contexts, in these articles of the ruling in the *Namibia* case[255] that a resolution may be validly adopted by the Security Council over the abstention of one or more of the permanent members, despite the reference in Article 27 of the Charter to the 'concurring votes of the permanent members'; but that decision is recorded here also, *pro memoria*, in its own right as a decision on the interpretation of the Charter.

(7) *Regional arrangements under Chapter VIII of the Charter*

In the *Nicaragua* case, one of the objections by the United States to the admissibility of the application was that the political process of negotiation in Central America known as the 'Contadora Process' constituted a 'regional arrangement' for the maintenance of peace or for the settlement of disputes. It contended that the maintenance of international peace was a matter for the Security Council, but that under Article 52, paragraph 2, of the Charter, there was a prior obligation to submit disputes to regional arrangements or agencies.[256] It deduced that accordingly Nicaragua was under an obligation to exhaust such regional processes before seising the Court (and was also under a similar obligation under Articles 20 and 21 of the Charter of the OAS).[257] One of the grounds mentioned by the Court for rejecting the United States objection was simply that

---

[253] *ICJ Reports*, 1992, p. 251, para. 23.

[254] *ICJ Reports*, 1992, p. 253, para. 30. After rejection of the Australian preliminary objections, the case was the subject of a friendly settlement and proceedings were withdrawn: *ICJ Reports*, 1993, p. 322.

[255] *ICJ Reports*, 1971, p. 22, para. 22.

[256] See above, pp. 43–4.

[257] *ICJ Reports*, 1984, pp. 432, 438, paras. 89, 102. As regards the OAS, the question of the effect of Articles II and IV of the Pact of Bogotá, and the significance in this connection of the Contadora Process, was examined in the judgment on jurisdiction and admissibility in the case of *Border and Transborder Armed Actions (Nicaragua v. Honduras)*, *ICJ Reports*, 1988, p. 69; that decision will be analysed in a future article on 'Questions of competence, jurisdiction and procedure'.

The Court does not consider that the Contadora process, whatever its merits, can properly be regarded as a 'regional arrangement' for the purposes of Chapter VIII of the Charter of the United Nations.[258]

It did not explain its reasons for taking this view; but it was pointed out by Nicaragua in its pleadings that the members of the Security Council itself were 'well aware of the work of the Contadora Group and approved and applauded it. But they saw in it no bar to the Security Council addressing the problem.'[259] It may be deduced from this that the Council itself did not regard the Process as a 'regional arrangement' taking priority over its own involvement; such a view could not bind the Court, but would have persuasive force.

2. *Other Organizations*

(1) *IMCO (IMO): the* Maritime Safety Committee *case*

The essence of the Court's 1960 advisory opinion in this case was that the IMCO Maritime Safety Committee which had been elected on 15 January 1959, and which did not include either Liberia or Panama as members, was not constituted in accordance with the relevant provisions of the 1948 Convention establishing the organization. The facts of the matter have been outlined in a previous article,[260] as has the text to be interpreted (Article 28 of the IMCO Convention), but for convenience the latter will be repeated here:

The Maritime Safety Committee shall consist of fourteen Members elected by the Assembly from among the Members, governments of those nations having an important interest in maritime safety, of which not less than eight shall be the largest ship-owning nations . . . [261]

The Court interpreted the final words of this provision as having 'a mandatory and imperative sense', so that, despite the use of the word 'elect', the IMCO Assembly was bound to include 'the largest ship-owning nations' in the Committee. It further found that the test to establish which were 'the largest ship-owning nations' was simply that of registered tonnage, as contended by Panama and Liberia.[262]

---

[258] *ICJ Reports*, 1984, p. 440, para. 107.

[259] Nicaraguan memorial on jurisdiction and admissibility, para. 222. The pleadings in the case have not yet been published in the Court's series of *Pleadings, Oral Arguments, Documents*.

[260] This *Year Book*, 62 (1991), p. 29.

[261] *ICJ Reports*, 1960, p. 154.

[262] At the 1961 session of the IMCO Assembly, Liberia was duly elected to the Committee, but Panama had in the meantime fallen back to eleventh place in the table of registered tonnage, and was therefore no longer able to insist on inclusion.

(2) *The International Civil Aviation Organization: the* Appeal relating to the Jurisdiction of the ICAO Council

As a matter of interpretation of the 1944 Chicago Convention on Civil Aviation and International Air Services Transit Agreement, the decision in this case resolved two fairly straightforward points. Under Article 84 of the Convention, a 'disagreement between two or more contracting States relating to the interpretation or application' of the Convention could be decided by the ICAO Council; and any contracting State could appeal from that decision to the Court.[263] Under section 2 of Article II of the Transit Agreement, the same procedure for dispute settlement applied to disputes concerning the interpretation or application of that text. Pakistan had brought before the Council a dispute with India, alleged to involve the interpretation or application of the Convention and the Agreement; and the Council had given a preliminary decision upholding its jurisdiction to deal with the application. India appealed to the Court; and the essential questions for decision were, first whether appeal lay against a decision other than a final decision on the merits; and if so, whether the Council had been correct in finding that it had jurisdiction.

On the first question, the Court found that, while purely procedural or interlocutory decisions were not intended to be the subject of appeal, a decision on jurisdiction was not within the same category, being 'although, in the purely temporal sense, a preliminary question', yet 'in its essence, a substantial question crucially affecting the position of the parties relative to the case'.[264] On the second question, the issues involved had little to do with the actual text, and correct interpretation of the Convention and Agreement, but more to do with the circumstances of the case, in particular an alleged suspension of the two treaties as between the parties. Accordingly, examination of the Court's treatment of this part of the case will be reserved for a later article on 'Questions of jurisdiction, competence and procedure'.

---

[263] More precisely 'to an *ad hoc* arbitral tribunal agreed upon with the other parties to the dispute or to the Permanent Court of International Justice'; by virtue of Article 37 of the Statute, the reference to the PCIJ was to be read, as between India and Pakistan, the parties to the dispute, as being to the ICJ.

[264] *ICJ Reports*, 1972, p. 56, para. 18.

THE HERITAGE OF STATES: THE PRINCIPLE OF UTI POSSIDETIS JURIS TODAY*

By MALCOLM N. SHAW‡

I. INTRODUCTION

The territorial definition of States is a matter of the first importance within the international political system. It expresses in spatial terms the dimensions and sphere of application of authority of States and provides the essential framework for the operation of an international order that is founded upon strict territorial division. In terms of international law specifically, the territorial delineation raises and determines issues ranging from the nationality of inhabitants to the application of particular legal norms and it is the essential framework within which the vital interests of States are expressed and with regard to which they interact and collide.[1] Many of the fundamental norms of both classical and modern international law are predicated upon, and defend, such spatial division. The law relating to territory remains of the highest importance for the international system. This is so despite the growth both of transnational structures, whether by inter-governmental or by non-governmental operation, and of developing international concern with the conduct of affairs within the territorial jurisdiction of States. Such developments clearly impact upon territorial sovereignty, but the essential structure remains firmly in place.

Since the territorial definition of States is the spatial context for the application of State competence, particular problems are generated with

---

* © Professor Malcolm N. Shaw, 1997.

‡ Barrister; Sir Robert Jennings Professor of International Law, University of Leicester.

[1] See generally Jennings, *The Acquisition of Territory in International Law* (1963); Verzijl, *International Law in Historical Perspective* (1970), vol. 3, p. 297; Shaw, *Title to Territory in Africa: International Legal Issues* (1986); Hill, *Claims to Territory in International Law and Relations* (1945); Gottman, *The Significance of Territory* (1973); Schoenborn, 'La nature juridique du territoire', *Recueil des cours*, 30 (1929–V), p. 85; Delbez, 'Le territoire dans ses rapports avec l'état', *Revue générale de droit international public*, 39 (1932), p. 705; Dembinski, 'Le territoire et le développement du droit international', *Annuaire suisse de droit international*, 31 (1975), p. 71; Bastid, 'Les problèmes territoriaux dans la jurisprudence de la CIJ', *Recueil des cours*, 107 (1962–III), p. 361; De La Pradelle, *La Frontière* (1928); De Visscher, *Problèmes de confins en droit international public* (1969); Sharma, *International Boundary Disputes and International Law* (1976); Munkman, 'Adjudication and Adjustment—International Decision and the Settlement of Territorial and Boundary Disputes', this *Year Book*, 46 (1972–3), p. 1; Bardonnet, 'Les frontières terrestres et la relativité de leur tracé', *Recueil des cours*, 153 (1976–V), p. 9; Société française pour le droit international, *La Frontière* (1980); Jennings and Watts (eds.), *Oppenheim's International Law*, vol. 1 (9th edn., 1992), chapter 5, and Nguyen Quoc Dinh, Daillier and Pellet, *Droit international public* (5th edn., 1994), p. 444.

regard to the transmission of State sovereignty from one entity to another and the consequential creation of new States. Specifically, the international system needs to provide rules for the transmission of territorial limits in relation to such changes in sovereignty. This is for a variety of reasons ranging from the basic requirements of international stability and minimization of the possibilities of conflict to the need for internationally accepted principles of jurisdictional application and structures of authority and responsibility.

Rules have emerged over the last century and a half concerning the transmission of territorial competence in the context of what might generically be termed 'colonialism'. Such rules have only gradually been clarified and analysed. One key question is to determine whether these rules possess an application beyond the strictly colonial framework, or in other words to establish whether such rules constitute a package of rights and obligations that might be termed an 'heritage' for newly established States, however created. Secondly the nature of such rights and obligations requires attention. The principle of *uti possidetis juris* developed as an attempt to obviate territorial disputes by fixing the territorial heritage of new States at the moment of independence and converting existing lines into internationally recognized borders, and can thus be seen as a specific legal package, anchored in space and time, with crucial legitimating functions. It is also closely related to the principle of the stability of boundaries and both draws upon and informs a variety of other principles of international law, ranging from consent and acquiescence to territorial integrity and the prohibition of the use of force against States.

II. BOUNDARIES AND TERRITORIES

The term 'heritage' as employed in this article is based upon the phrase 'colonial heritage' as used by international tribunals.[2] It refers to what the Chamber of the International Court in the *Burkina Faso/Mali* case has called 'the photograph of the territory' at the critical date of independence.[3] Although in that case the discussion was within the context of the colonial model because of the factual circumstances, the analysis can be extended to other independence situations. The debate concerning 'heritage' raises a series of issues that are of great importance in an international system that operates upon the foundation of sovereign, independent States. Such entities are territorially defined, that is, they are created and function and draw their sustenance within a specific

---

[2] See, e.g., Judge Bedjaoui's dissenting opinion in the *Guinea-Bissau* v. *Senegal* case, 83 ILR 61–2.

[3] *ICJ Reports*, 1986, pp. 554, 568.

spatial setting. States have no meaning outside this context. Judge Huber noted in the *Island of Palmas* case that:

Territorial sovereignty is, in general, a situation recognized and delimited in space, either by so-called natural frontiers as recognized by international law or by outward signs of delimitation that are undisputed, or else by legal engagements entered into between interested neighbours, such as frontier conventions, or by acts of recognition of States within fixed boundaries.[4]

Boundaries evidence the extent of State sovereignty and form the limits of the operations of the domestic legal system. They demarcate the territorial framework within which jurisdiction is established and exercised.[5] Acts of State sovereignty are, therefore, territorially entrenched and, save in a few exceptional cases, so restricted. Boundaries both legitimize and demarcate the exercise of territorial sovereignty of States. There is thus a close relationship between boundaries and territorial sovereignty. As the Chamber of the International Court noted, 'to "define" a territory is to define its frontiers',[6] and the reverse is also true.

The protection of the inviolability of boundaries has assumed a crucial role in the international system. As the International Court emphasized in the *Corfu Channel* case, 'between independent States, respect for territorial sovereignty is an essential foundation of international relations',[7] and international instruments abound reinforcing the territorial integrity of States.[8] Of course, there are important differences between the concepts of territorial integrity and the inviolability of boundaries, but for present purposes the point is sustained that the function of boundaries lies essentially in determining the extent of the physical expression of the State and thus serving to preserve the territorial integrity of States. Violation of the boundaries of a State will prima facie fall within the definition of aggression.[9]

Boundaries are invariably the product of political events and thus human action, and as such are all in a sense artificial. Oppenheim defines boundaries as the imaginary lines on the surface of the earth which separate the territory of one State from that of another or from

---

[4] *Reports of International Arbitral Awards*, vol. 2, pp. 829, 838.
[5] See the *Guinea-Bissau* v. *Senegal* case, 83 ILR 1, 36.
[6] *ICJ Reports*, 1994, pp. 6, 26.
[7] *ICJ Reports*, 1949, p. 35.
[8] See, for example, Article 2(4) of the United Nations Charter; Article 17 of the Charter of the Organization of American States, 1948; Article 9 of the Draft Declaration on Rights and Duties of States, 1949; Articles 2 and 3 of the Charter of the Organization of African Unity, 1963; General Assembly Resolutions 1514 (XV) (the Colonial Declaration) and 2625 (XXV) (the Declaration on Principles of International Law Concerning Friendly Relations and Co-operation among States).
[9] See General Assembly Resolution 3314 (XXIX) on the Definition of Aggression. See generally Dinstein, *War, Aggression and Self-Defence* (2nd edn., 1994); Cassese, *Violence and Law in the Modern Age* (1988); Damrosch and Scheffer (eds.), *Law and Force in the New International Order* (1991), and Brownlie, *International Law and the Use of Force by States* (1963).

unappropriated territory or from the open sea,[10] while the Arbitration Tribunal in the *Guinea-Bissau* v. *Senegal* case emphasized that 'an international frontier is a line formed by the successive extremities of the area of validity in space of the norms of the legal order of a particular State'.[11]

The perception of artificiality is simply that the boundaries as existing do not conform with certain indicia of distinctions between groups of peoples or in some way are inconsistent with natural phenomena. In fact, the development of the boundary as such in the sense of a strict, linear division is a relatively modern conception. In earlier centuries, the concept of the border zone predominated over that of fixed-line frontiers.[12] The need for defined borders really only arose as States developed in the post-Westphalian world and populations expanded into border areas and cross-boundary communication thereby increased significantly. Exact boundaries, however, could only really develop when map-making and geographic techniques were sufficiently advanced to facilitate such delimitation and demarcation.[13]

To some extent, the doctrine of natural frontiers had been an attempt to achieve precise boundaries in earlier centuries. It was founded upon the assertion that certain natural features such as mountain ranges, forests, water and deserts were preferable to artificial boundaries. But natural boundaries in this strict geographic sense could not be taken to imply that such a division might be the best line of differentiation between peoples of dissimilar languages and traditions. It was and is not unknown for there to be no natural boundary between peoples of differing traditions and origins and conversely for natural features such as rivers and mountain ranges not to mark lines of division between different peoples. The crest of a mountain range would therefore not constitute a 'natural frontier' where people of the same tradition and language inhabited both sides of the mountain.

In fact, the notion of a natural boundary beyond strict geographical characterization is primarily a political assertion, and it is extraordinary how many States claiming a natural frontier required the annexation to their national territories of additional lands belonging to other States and how few were prepared to contemplate ceding territory to others in order to effect a more 'natural' frontier.[14] As Prescott has powerfully written, 'the idea of "natural boundaries" has been discredited for decades . . . all political boundaries are artificial because they require the selection of a specific line within a zone where change in the physical characteristics of

---

[10] Op. cit. above (n. 1), p. 661. See also Bothe, 'Boundaries', *Encyclopedia of Public International Law*, vol. 1 (1992), pp. 443, 444.

[11] 83 ILR 36.

[12] See, for example, Reeves, 'International Boundaries', *American Journal of International Law*, 38 (1944), p. 533.

[13] Hill, op. cit. above (n. 1), p. 23.

[14] See Verzijl, op. cit. above (n. 1), p. 516, and Schoenborn, loc. cit. above (n. 1), pp. 126–35.

the landscape may be more or less rapid'.[15] Thus even as a strictly geographical term, it is uncertain and ambiguous. How much more so when human factors obtrude.

Just as boundaries are distinct from territories in that the former constitute lines defining the limits of territorial sovereignty and jurisdiction while the latter are those areas over which such rights are exercised, so there are significant differences between boundary and territorial disputes.[16] Boundary disputes are primarily concerned with either written or verbal or geographic uncertainties, while territorial disputes involve relatively large areas of land and claims to title. Title imports rules of international law that deal with acquisition of territorial sovereignty, such as occupation, prescription and cession, with assertions of self-determination and historical continuity often being additionally voiced. In the case of boundary disputes, the usual situation concerns ambiguities inherent in the instruments creating the boundaries[17] or problems in fixing the alignment on the ground.[18]

Boundary problems in general concern disputes between adjacent States over the line to be drawn between their areas of sovereignty, whereas territorial disputes involve one State claiming to remove another from an area of its sovereignty on the basis of a better title. As the International Court noted in the *North Sea Continental Shelf* cases, 'the appurtenance of a given area, considered as an entirety, in no way governs the precise delimitation of its boundaries, any more than uncertainty as to boundaries can affect territorial rights'.[19]

A good example of the different approaches to a dispute taken on the basis of either a territorial or a boundary question is afforded by the *Libya/Chad* case. Libya claimed that the problem concerned the attribution of territory, whereas Chad asserted that the problem centred upon the location of a boundary. Libya based its claim upon a coalescence of rights and titles, including those of the indigenous inhabitants, those of the Senoussi Order (an influential religious confraternity) and those of a succession of sovereign States, namely the Ottoman Empire, Italy and Libya. Various geographical and climatic and security considerations were also stated to be relevant considerations. Chad claimed a boundary

---

[15] *Boundaries and Frontiers* (1978), p. 106.

[16] See, for example, Bardonnet, loc. cit. above (n. 1), pp. 48–52, and Oppenheim, op. cit. above (n. 1), pp. 668–9.

[17] See, for example, the false assumption enshrined in a Treaty of 1881 dealing with the Argentine–Chile boundary that the line of the highest peaks and the continental water-parting dividing rivers flowing into the Pacific from those flowing into the Atlantic coincided along the whole boundary: see the *Argentine/Chile* award of 1902, *Reports of International Arbitral Awards*, vol. 9, p. 29, and the *Argentine–Chile Frontier* award of 1966, 38 ILR 10.

[18] See, for example, Cukwurah, *The Settlement of Boundary Disputes in International Law* (1967), p. 78. Some delimited boundaries have not been demarcated at all, and others have been demarcated but because of poor maintenance the demarcation line has disappeared: see Shaw, op. cit. above (n. 1), pp. 260 ff.

[19] *ICJ Reports*, 1969, p. 32.

upon the basis of a 1955 Franco-Libyan Treaty. Alternatively, it based its claim upon a range of prior instruments referred to in the 1955 Treaty and maintained that even without such treaty provisions, it could rely on *effectivités* or the actual exercise of sovereign authority.[20] In the event, the Court determined the issue upon the application of the 1955 Treaty.

However, one cannot push this distinction too far since both kinds of dispute ultimately concern the question of sovereignty over a defined piece of land and many of the same kinds of State activity are relevant both to the question of title to territory and to the correct determination of a boundary line. In practice, treaties are likely to be relevant in both cases, as would be the actual display of sovereign activity and the attitudes adopted by the parties and by third States. As the Chamber noted in the *El Salvador/Honduras* case,

the location of boundaries seemed often, in the arguments of the Parties, to be incidental to some 'claim', or 'title', or 'grant', respecting a parcel of territory, within circumambient boundaries only portions of which are now claimed to form an international boundary. It is rather as if the disputed boundaries must be constructed like a jig-saw puzzle from certain already cut pieces so that the extent and location of the resulting boundary depend upon the size and shape of the fitting piece.[21]

The best approach therefore would be to regard boundary disputes as a particular kind of territorial dispute, one that has evolved some special rules.[22] Indeed, the Chamber of the International Court took the view in the *Burkina Faso/Mali* case that the difference between the two types of dispute was in the great majority of cases not so much a difference of kind as a difference of degree as to the way in which the operation in question is carried out. It was noted that

the effect of any delimitation, no matter how small the disputed area crossed by the line, is an apportionment of the areas of land lying on either side of the line . . . [and] . . . the effect of any judicial decision rendered either in a dispute as to attribution of territory or in a delimitation dispute is necessarily to establish a frontier.[23]

This is essentially correct. Territorial and boundary disputes cannot exist as totally separate categories, free from the impact of considerations pertinent to each of them. Many of the same factors would need to be weighed in determining the issue, although the way in which the issues may be oriented and the particular technical rules that may be applicable

[20] *ICJ Reports*, 1994, pp. 4, 15.
[21] *ICJ Reports*, 1992, pp. 351, 388.
[22] See Jennings, op. cit. above (n. 1), pp. 12–13, and Sharma, op. cit. above (n. 1), pp. 4–7.
[23] *ICJ Reports*, 1986, pp. 7, 563. See also the view expressed in the *Aegean Sea Continental Shelf* case that 'it would be difficult to accept the broad proposition that delimitation is entirely extraneous to the notion of territorial status. Any disputed delimitation of a boundary entails some determination of entitlement to the areas to be delimited': *ICJ Reports*, 1978, pp. 3, 35.

may vary depending upon the characterization of the essential nature of the dispute.

III. THE PRINCIPLE OF THE STABILITY OF BOUNDARIES[24]

Jennings has written that the problem of the legal ordering of territorial stability and territorial change lies at the heart of the whole problem of the legal ordering of international society.[25] An international system founded upon the co-existence and co-operation of some two hundred independent and sovereign States all characterized by the supremacy of the internal legal order within determined territorial limits cannot but be oriented towards territorial certainty. Change may take place but not in an arbitrary nor an unpredictable fashion. Despite the encouraging growth of international standards in, for example, human rights[26] and environmental law,[27] and notwithstanding the evolution of international organizations[28] and functional cross-border jurisdictional provisions,[29] it simply cannot be denied that the fundamental orientation of international law still focuses upon territorial sovereignty. Accordingly, the principle of the stability of boundaries constitutes an overarching postulate of the international legal system and one that both explains and generates associated legal norms.

The establishment of a boundary proceeds upon the basis of the consent of the relevant States, for, as the International Court noted, 'the fixing of a frontier depends on the will of the sovereign States directly concerned'.[30] It also follows that such States are free to determine for themselves how this operation may be conducted.[31] The most logical and

---

[24] See in particular Kaikobad, 'Some Observations on the Doctrine of Continuity and Finality of Boundaries', this *Year Book*, 54, (1983), p. 119; Bardonnet, loc. cit. above (n. 1), p. 9, and Kohen, 'Le règlement des différends territoriaux à la lumière de l'arrêt de la C.I.J. dans l'affaire Libye/Tchad', *Revue générale de droit international public*, 99 (1995), pp. 301, 320 ff.

[25] Op. cit. above (n. 1), p. 87.

[26] See, for example, Meron (ed.), *Human Rights in International Law* (1986), 2 vols; Sieghart, *The International Law of Human Rights* (1983); Robertson and Merrills, *Human Rights in the World* (4th edn., 1996), and Henkin and Hargrove (eds.), *Human Rights: An Agenda for the Next Century* (1994).

[27] See, for example, Birnie and Boyle, *International Law and the Environment* (1992), and Sands, *Principles of International Environmental Law* (1995).

[28] See, for example, Bowett, *The Law of International Institutions* (4th edn., 1982), and Schermers and Blokker, *International Institutional Law* (3rd edn., 1995).

[29] See, for example, the Anglo–French Protocol concerning Frontier Controls and Policing, Co-operation in Criminal Justice, Public Safety and Mutual Assistance relating to the Channel Fixed Link, 1991, which provides for elements of jurisdiction to be exercised by the officials of one country in specific areas of the territory of the other (Cm 1802 and this *Year Book*, 62 (1991), p. 623), and the Israel–Jordan Treaty of Peace, 1994, which permits Israeli acts of jurisdiction within specific areas of Jordan (*International Legal Materials*, 34 (1995), p. 43).

[30] *ICJ Reports*, 1994, pp. 4, 25.

[31] Unless, of course, the Security Council determines otherwise in the interests of international peace and security. See, e.g., Security Council Resolutions 687 (1991) and 833 (1993). See below, p. 148.

the easiest method is usually for the States themselves to reach agreement enshrined in a treaty describing the relevant boundary line. This may be done either by re-confirming an existing boundary line or by deciding to recognize a particular line whatever its previous status as a boundary line. In this case, the agreement so to recognize it 'invests it with a legal force which it had previously lacked'.[32] The purpose of such agreements is manifestly to entrench and render certain a particular territorial situation. As the Arbitration Tribunal in the *Guinea-Bissau* v. *Senegal* case noted, 'in all cases, the purpose of the relevant [delimitation] treaties is the same: to determine in a stable and permanent manner the area of validity in space of the legal norms of States'.[33]

This act of recognition may itself be accomplished in a variety of ways and is not restricted to express incorporation in an international treaty. For example, in the *Temple of Preah Vihear* case, a line had been drawn upon a map and this was intended to represent the frontier agreed by a delimitation commission under a treaty which had provided that the frontier should follow a watershed. As it happened the line drawn did not follow the watershed. Nevertheless, the International Court upheld the map line on the basis that 'both the Parties, by their conduct, recognized the line and thereby in effect agreed to regard it as being the frontier line'.[34] The same point was made by the Arbitration Tribunal in the *Taba* case, when it was concluded that even if the 'Parker pillar' (a masonry pillar which constituted the first masonry pillar of the boundary between Egypt and Palestine under the delimitation agreement of 1 October 1906) had not been placed during the demarcation process at the site of the relevant provisional telegraph pole as required, 'the parties to the Agreement of 1906 had, by their conduct, agreed to the boundary as it was demarcated by masonry pillars in 1906–07 and to the location of the Parker pillar as the final pillar of the boundary line at that time'.[35] Thus, considerations of stability militate in favour of the accepted status quo.

Once created in accordance with international law, a boundary is protected and assumes finality and permanence. What is established on the basis of the consent of the States concerned can only be undone or modified by the exercise of such consent. As the Court declared in the *Temple* case,

when two countries establish a frontier between them, one of the primary objects is to achieve stability and finality. This is impossible if the line so established

---

[32] *ICJ Reports*, 1994, p. 23.
[33] 83 ILR 36.
[34] *ICJ Reports*, 1962, pp. 6, 33.
[35] 80 ILR 224, 303–5. See also the *Rann of Kutch* case, 50 ILR 1, 475, where it was noted by the Chairman of the Tribunal that it was 'not open to the Tribunal to disturb a boundary settled in this manner by the British Administration and accepted and acted upon by it, as well as the State of Kutch, for nearly a quarter of a century'.

can, at any moment, and on the basis of a continuously available process, be called in question, and its rectification claimed, whenever any inaccuracy by reference to a clause in the parent treaty is discovered. Such a process could continue indefinitely, and finality would never be reached so long as possible errors still remained to be discovered. Such a frontier, so far from being stable, would be completely precarious.[36]

The point was repeated in the *Beagle Channel* case, where the Tribunal noted that 'a limit, a boundary, across which the jurisdictions of the respective bordering States may not pass, implies definitiveness and permanence'.[37]

The question arises immediately as to why this should be so. Why should the establishment of boundaries be automatically cloaked with an assumption of permanence to a greater degree than is the case with other international obligations? The answer can only be found deeper within the international system. The international system is rooted in and is nourished by the notion of independent sovereign States. Despite the growth in norms specifically requiring international co-operation, the essential headstone for the system is that of the equality of States. And since States are the territorial expression of individual political and legal orders, the institution of boundaries has to lie at the core of current international law. The stability of the international territorial order is crucial.

As Jennings has emphasized, 'some other kinds of legal ordering need to be capable of constant change to meet new needs of a developing society; but in a properly ordered society, territorial boundaries will be among the most stable of all institutions'.[38] Indeed, one may observe that a properly ordered society can hardly be instituted without the require-ment of territorial stability. Not that change cannot happen, but that it can only take place in a clear, secure and regulated manner. In addition, it is important that such change cannot be too easily accomplished even within the afore-mentioned guidelines, for territorial change tends to bring with it political disruption which one should be loath to accept too glibly or in too facile a manner. As pointed out by the Court of Arbitration in the *Dubai/Sharjah* case, 'the re-opening of the legal status of the boundaries of a State may give rise to very grave consequences, which may endanger the life of the State itself',[39] while the letter of the United Nations Secretary-General transmitting the Final Report of the UN Iraq-Kuwait Boundary Demarcation Commission to the Security

---

[36] *ICJ Reports*, 1962, p. 34. See also Kaikobad's comment that 'a continuously available process which allows States to question an established and respected alignment should be denied them in the interests of stability': loc. cit., above (n. 24), pp. 119, 122.

[37] HMSO, 1977, p. 11. See also the *Aegean Sea Continental Shelf* case, *ICJ Reports*, 1978, pp. 3, 35–6, and the *Tunisia/Libya* case, *ICJ Reports*, 1982, pp. 18, 66.

[38] Op. cit. above (n. 1), p. 70.

[39] 91 ILR 543, 578. See also Bowett, 'The Dubai/Sharjah Boundary Arbitration of 1981', this *Year Book*, 65 (1994), p. 103.

Council emphasized that 'the certainty and stability of the boundaries are in the best interest of Iraq and Kuwait'.[40]

Stability can never be the sole or even the dominant principle in international affairs, since the push for change is a constant in contemporary conditions, not least because of the revolution in technology generally. New principles arise and old principles develop in response to new challenges which affect the balance of the international system. In addition, the principle of the territorial stability of States is subject to the need to preserve or restore international peace and security as this has developed under the United Nations system.[41] Nevertheless for present purposes it suffices to underline that the principle of territorial stability is a key precept in the conduct of international life and will remain so until such time as the international system ceases to be founded upon the concept of sovereign States.

This requirement of the territorial stability of States involves a consideration of several associated principles.

1. *Consent*

The best means to ensure stability in general is to rely upon the consent of the parties themselves, so that once the relevant parties have by whatever means agreed upon a boundary line, that agreement constitutes a binding obligation. It cannot be overturned by reference to earlier materials. It is a proposition of fundamental importance that demonstrates that the key to boundary delimitation lies in the consent of the relevant States. This consent may be manifested in a variety of ways, of which express agreement through a binding treaty is but the most apparent. Recognition may be demonstrated by conduct also, and this point is illustrated in the *Temple* and *Taba* cases discussed above.[42] Reference may also be made to the award in the *Dubai/Sharjah* case, where the Court emphasized that:

the principle of the stability of boundaries—boundaries established here by administrative decisions and not arising by Treaty or in consequence of an arbitral award—depends precisely upon their recognition and effective application in subsequent practice.[43]

The Court analysed the status and effect of a series of decisions made by Mr Tripp, the British Political Agent at the time, as to the boundary between the two Emirates in question in 1956 and 1957. These decisions were binding decisions, but did not amount to arbitral awards. The Court put the essential situation as follows:

[40] S/25811. See further below, p. 148.
[41] See below, p. 147.
[42] Above, p. 82.
[43] 91 ILR 543, 584.

if the boundary established in the Tripp decisions was in fact recognised and effectively applied by the Parties in subsequent years then the Court would be required to apply those decisions even were they to have been at variance with the legal position in the disputed areas at the time they were taken. But if, on the contrary, the boundary was either in whole or in part rejected by one Party or the other as contrary to an existing legal title at the time of the decisions, and was neither recognised nor effectively applied in practice by both of the Parties, then this Court would have the right to set aside those decisions to the extent of the non-application.[44]

Thus the fundamental test is that of the attitude adopted by the parties, so that an acceptance of a modification in the title established by a legal decision earlier would in the interests of stability be sanctioned. There is one point worth commenting upon here. The Court appeared to require both recognition and effective application in practice of the modification in question. This may not always be the case, depending on the circumstances, but it does underline the essential proposition that modifications of existing legal boundary lines will need to be demonstrated by firm evidence. In addition, the roles of acquiescence and estoppel may clearly be relevant in this context since the failure to contest a territorial claim concretized by actual possession could well be decisive in the circumstances. Of course, requirements of stability as well as respect for binding agreements necessitate that modification of the provisions of the latter by the parties concerned must be shown to have been actually agreed by those parties. Such modification cannot lightly be presumed.[45] This proposition also applies where the instrument in question is not an international agreement but an internal administrative act. One would expect the burden of proof to be slightly less onerous here, although the award in the *Dubai/Sharjah* case would appear to suggest otherwise.[46] Much, however, will depend upon the particular circumstances.

Thus, as well as express conduct, assertion by one side coupled with 'negative conduct—that is to say failure to act, react or speak, in circumstances where failure so to do must imply acquiescence or acceptance'[47]—may indeed suffice for the purpose in the situation at hand.[48] Once proved, such subsequent alteration will bind the parties. One may even go beyond this to note that even where the consent of the parties, expressly or impliedly formulated, is founded upon an error, this may not suffice to challenge the modified situation accepted by the

---

[44] Ibid., 585.

[45] See Judge Fitzmaurice's separate opinion in the *Temple* case, *ICJ Reports*, 1962, p. 55. See also the *Argentine–Chile Frontier* case, 38 ILR 10, 76–9, and the *Frontier Land* case, *ICJ Reports*, 1959, pp. 209, 227–30.

[46] 91 ILR 568–85.

[47] Judge Fitzmaurice's separate opinion in the *Temple* case, *ICJ Reports*, 1962, p. 55.

[48] See the dissenting opinion by Judge Bebler in the *Rann of Kutch* case, 50 ILR 409–15. See further below, p 144.

parties.[49] As Brownlie concluded in the context of the Tanzania-Uganda boundary, 'legal and other considerations dictate a principle of finality and stability: the actual alignment acquiesced in by the States concerned should prevail'.[50]

One may note the key reason adduced by the International Court for such an approach. It was specifically emphasized in the *Temple* case, in the context of Thailand's acceptance of the modified boundary line, that 'she has, for fifty years, enjoyed such benefits as the Treaty of 1904 conferred on her, if only the benefit of a stable frontier'.[51] In other words, the maintenance of a stable boundary constitutes a crucial element within the international system and will itself play a key role in the question of title. However, consent may be vitiated by coercion. Article 52 of the Vienna Convention on the Law of Treaties 1969 provides that where the conclusion of a treaty has been procured by the threat or use of force in violation of the principles of international law embodied in the Charter of the United Nations, such a treaty is void.[52] This provision cannot, however, be projected back to a period before which such coercion actually constituted a vitiating factor. The principle of intertemporal law provides that a claim has to be examined in the light of the law in existence at the time such a claim is made,[53] and a treaty validly made at the time cannot be deemed null and void by the development of subsequent norms relating to the use of force, otherwise many of the colonial treaties establishing the international territorial order would be regarded as avoided. It is particularly to be noted that the Declaration on Principles of International Law Concerning Friendly Relations and Co-operation among States (General Assembly Resolution 2625 (XXV)) provides that the principle of the non-acquisition of territory by force is not to be affected *inter alia* by any international agreement made prior to the Charter and valid under international law.[54]

Similarly, the provisions regarding *jus cogens* cannot be regarded as affecting colonial territorial settlements.[55] Article 53 of the Vienna Convention provides that 'a treaty is void if, *at the time of its conclusion*, it conflicts with a peremptory norm of international law' (emphasis

---

[49] The *Taba* case, 80 ILR 306.

[50] *African Boundaries* (1979), pp. 1015–16. See also McEwan, *International Boundaries of East Africa* (1971), pp. 50–1 and 281–2.

[51] *ICJ Reports*, 1962, p. 32.

[52] See generally McNair, *The Law of Treaties* (1961), pp. 206–11, and Brownlie, op. cit. above (n. 9), pp. 404–5. See also *Yearbook of the International Law Commission*, 1966, vol. 2, pp. 246–7, and Sinclair, *The Vienna Convention on the Law of Treaties* (2nd edn., 1984), pp. 177–9.

[53] See further below, p. 129.

[54] See also *Yearbook of the International Law Commission*, 1964, vol. 1, p. 34.

[55] See generally Sztucki, *Jus Cogens and the Vienna Convention on the Law of Treaties* (1974); Sinclair, op. cit. above (n. 52), p. 203; Virally, 'Réflexions sur le *jus cogens*', *Annuaire français de droit international*, 12 (1966), p. 1; Rozakis, *The Concept of Jus Cogens in the Law of Treaties* (1976); Gomez Robledo, 'Le *jus cogens* international', *Recueil des cours*, 172 (1981–III), p. 17; Gaja, '*Jus Cogens* beyond the Vienna Conventions', ibid., p. 279, and Hannikainen, *Peremptory Norms (Jus Cogens) in International Law* (1988).

added), while Article 64 stipulates that 'if a new peremptory norm of general international law emerges, any *existing treaty* which is in conflict with that norm becomes void and terminates' (emphasis added). In other words, a valid colonial treaty establishing a territorial situation will not be avoided as a consequence, for example, of the emergence long after the conclusion of the treaty of any rule of *jus cogens* to the effect that colonialism is unlawful. Article 71(2)(*b*) emphasizes the point by stating that the termination of a treaty under Article 64 'does not affect any right, obligation or legal situation of the parties created through the execution of the treaty prior to its termination'. This element of execution is, of course, at the heart of boundary treaties.

2. *The Objectivization of Boundary Treaties*

The second consequential principle that one may draw from the overarching precept of stability is that once boundaries have been established or confirmed in an international agreement, an objective reality has been created which will survive the demise of the treaty itself. The point was noted in the *Free Zones of Upper Savoy and the District of Gex* case, where it was emphasized that the Manifesto of the Royal Sardinian Court of Accounts of 9 September 1829, marking in effect the acceptance of a request of the Canton of Valois under Article 3 of the Treaty of Turin 1816, 'confers on the delimitation of the zone of Saint-Gingolph the character of a treaty stipulation which France must respect as Sardinia's successor in the sovereignty over the territory in question'.[56]

The International Court recently reaffirmed the principle in the context of the 1955 Treaty between Libya and France concerning the boundary between the former and Chad claiming through the latter. The Court declared that

the establishment of this boundary is a fact which, from the outset, has had a legal life of its own, independently of the fate of the 1955 Treaty. Once agreed the boundary stands, for any other approach would vitiate the fundamental principle of the stability of boundaries, the importance of which has been repeatedly emphasised by the Court (*Temple of Preah Vihear, ICJ Reports, 1962*, p. 34; *Aegean Sea Continental Shelf, ICJ Reports, 1978*, p. 36).

A boundary established by treaty thus achieves a permanence which the treaty itself does not necessarily enjoy. The treaty can cease to be in force without in any way affecting the continuance of the boundary . . . This is not to say that two States may not by mutual agreement vary the border between them; such a result can of course be achieved by mutual consent, but when a boundary has been the subject of agreement, the continued existence of that boundary is not

[56] *PCIJ*, Series A/B, No. 46, pp. 96, 145.

dependent upon the continued life of the treaty under which the boundary is agreed.[57]

This principle of the objectivization of boundary treaties is, of course, a curious one for it allows for provisions of a treaty in effect to continue beyond the treaty itself and it can really only be justified on the basis of the underlying rule as to the stability of boundaries. The manner by which this objectivization occurs is open to debate. One approach declares that upon ratification the boundary agreement is deemed to be executed and it thereafter acts as a kind of conveyance;[58] another approach is by way of application of the principle *nemo dat quod non habet*, that is, the predecessor State may transfer to the successor State only the territorial extent of its own competence. O'Connell, for example, writes that 'since a State can acquire from another only so much territory as that other possessed, the latter's boundary treaties with neighbouring States delimit the extent of the territory absorbed'.[59] The point was also made by the Chamber of the International Court in the *Burkina Faso/Mali* case, where it was noted that 'by becoming independent, a new State acquires sovereignty with the territorial base and boundaries left to it by the colonial power'.[60]

The basic principle is buttressed by two further principles. The first relates to the *rebus sic stantibus* rule. This provides that a party to a treaty may unilaterally invoke as a ground for terminating or suspending the operation of the treaty the fact that there has been a fundamental change of circumstances from those which existed at the time of the conclusion of the treaty.[61] The doctrine was enshrined in Article 62 of the Vienna Convention on the Law of Treaties 1969, which was accepted by the International Court in the jurisdictional phase of the *Fisheries Jurisdiction* cases as a codification of existing customary international law.[62] The

---

[57] *ICJ Reports*, 1994, p. 37.

[58] See, for example, Lester, 'State Succession to Treaties in the Commonwealth', *International and Comparative Law Quarterly*, 12 (1963), pp. 475, 492; Keith, *Theory of State Succession* (1907), p. 22, and Castrén, 'Aspects récents de la succession d'états', *Recueil des cours*, 78 (1951–I), pp. 385, 437. See also Resolution No. 8 of the 53rd Conference of the International Law Association, which noted that 'when a treaty which provides for the delimitation of a national boundary between two States has been executed in the sense that the boundary has been delimited and no further action needs to be taken, the treaty has spent its force and what is succeeded to is not the treaty but the extent of national territory so delimited': *Report of the 53rd Conference* (1968), pp. 589 ff. See generally Waldock's Fifth Report on Succession of States in respect of Treaties, *Yearbook of the International Law Commission*, 1972, vol. 2, pp. 2, 44 ff.

[59] *State Succession in Municipal Law and International Law* (1967), vol. 2, p. 273.

[60] *ICJ Reports*, 1986, p. 568.

[61] See, for example, McNair, *The Law of Treaties* (1961), pp. 681–91; Elias, *The Modern Law of Treaties* (1974), p. 119; Sinclair, op. cit. above (n. 52); Lissitzyn, 'Treaties and Changed Circumstances (*Rebus Sic Stantibus*)', *American Journal of International Law*, 61 (1967), p. 895; De Caviedes, 'De La clause "rebus sic stantibus" à la clause de révision dans les conventions internationales', *Recueil des cours*, 118 (1966–II), p. 109, and Haraszti, 'Treaties and the Fundamental Change of Circumstances', *Recueil des cours*, 146 (1975–III), p. 1.

[62] *ICJ Reports*, 1974, pp. 3, 18.

test elucidated by the Court was whether there had been a radical transformation in the extent of obligations imposed by the treaty in question.[63] However, it was stipulated in Article 62(*a*) of the Vienna Convention that the doctrine would not be invoked 'if the treaty establishes a boundary',[64] and it is clear from the International Law Commission's Commentary that such treaties should constitute an exception to the general rule permitting termination or suspension, since otherwise the rule might become a source of dangerous frictions.[65]

The second buttressing principle relates to State succession.[66] Article 16 of the Vienna Convention on Succession of States in respect of Treaties 1978[67] provides that 'a newly independent State[68] is not bound to maintain in force or to become a party to any treaty by reason only of the fact that at the date of the succession of States the treaty was in force in respect of the territory to which the succession of States relates'. This adoption of the so-called 'clean slate' principle immediately raises the issue of boundary treaties.

However, there is no doubt at all that the predominant view has been in favour of the proposition that the 'clean slate' approach does not apply to boundary treaties. Waldock, for example, noted in his first report on Succession of States and Governments in Respect of Treaties that

the weight both of opinion and practice seems clearly to be in favour of the view that boundaries established by treaties remain untouched by the mere fact of a succession. The opinion of jurists seems, indeed, to be unanimous on the point even if their reasoning may not always be exactly the same. In State practice the unanimity may not be quite so absolute; but the State practice in favour of continuance in force of boundaries established by treaty appears to be such as to justify the conclusion that a general rule of international law exists to that effect.[69]

[63] Ibid.

[64] See also Article 62(2) of the Vienna Convention on the Law of Treaties between States and International Organizations, 1986.

[65] *Yearbook of the International Law Commission*, 1966, vol. 2, p. 259.

[66] See in general O'Connell, op. cit. above (n. 59); O'Connell, 'Recent Problems of State Succession in Relation to New States', *Recueil des cours*, 130 (1970–II), p. 95; Bardonnet, *La succession d'états à Madagascar* (1970); International Law Association, *The Effect of Independence on Treaties* (1965); Zemanek, 'State Succession after Decolonization', *Recueil des cours*, 116 (1965–III), p. 180; Bedjaoui, 'Problèmes récents de succession d'états dans les états nouveaux', *Recueil des cours*, 130 (1970–II), p. 455; Udokang, *Succession of New States to International Treaties* (1972); Makonnen, *International Law and the New States of Africa* (1983); Shaw, 'State Succession Revisited', *Finnish Yearbook of International Law*, 5 (1994), p. 34, and UN *Materials on Succession of States* (1967) and supplement, A/CN.4/263, 1972.

[67] As at the end of 1994 this convention had 20 signatories and 13 States parties: see *Multilateral Treaties Deposited with the Secretary-General, Status as at 31 December 1994*, ST/LEG/SER. E/13, p. 82. By Article 49 of the convention, it will come into force on the thirtieth day following the date of deposit of the fifteenth instrument of ratification or accession.

[68] Defined in Article 2(1)(f) of the convention as 'a successor State the territory of which immediately before the date of succession of States was a dependent territory for the international relations of which the predecessor State was responsible'.

[69] *Yearbook of the International Law Commission*, 1968, vol. 2, pp. 92–3 (footnotes omitted). See also Bedjaoui, ibid., p. 112.

This approach was in essence accepted by the International Law Commission and by governments and ultimately in Article 11 of the Vienna Convention on Succession of States in Respect of Treaties. This provides that 'a succession of States does not as such affect: (*a*) a boundary established by a treaty . . . '. The wording used is instructive. The reference, of course, is to a boundary established by a treaty and not to the treaty itself as such, and it is important to differentiate between the instrument and the objective reality it creates or recognizes. In this sense, the treaty is constitutive. However, the wording of Article 11 is negative rather than positive. It does not, as does the principle of *uti possidetis*, assert that a given boundary situation at a given time subsists and thus imposes a positive obligation upon successor States. Article 11, rather, negatively provides that a succession of States as such does not affect a boundary established by a treaty. In other words, the boundary in question may be affected by legal grounds other than that of succession and thus challenged upon bases other than succession *simpliciter*.[70] No obligation to accept existing boundaries is posited in overt terms. Article 11 is formulated in preservative terms, simply conserving an existing situation, whose legality may be attacked upon any appropriate grounds. There is no presumption that the existing situation is the correct or valid one, to be supported by the international community or the relevant parties, whether as a matter of strict law or international policy, but merely a statement preventing the fact of succession as such from being used as a challenge to the status, whatever that may be, of the existing boundary in question. Again, Article 11 applies only to boundaries established by treaty, so that boundaries established by other means are not covered. This would include not only recognition or acquiescence, but also boundaries established by virtue of municipal legal action.

This textual analysis of Article 11 would appear to demonstrate that the effect of the provision as such is not extensive. However, there are factors which militate against this minimalist view. First, the negative position in fact masks a positive statement. To declare that a succession of States does not affect a boundary established by a treaty means in effect that such an existing boundary continues to exist notwithstanding the succession, so that the change in sovereignty is powerless to undermine such a boundary settlement. Secondly, subsequent opinion has in fact illustrated a tendency to interpret Article 11 in a positive manner, as requiring respect for treaty-based boundary settlements. The International Court of Justice in the *Tunisia/Libya* case expressly stated that 'this rule of continuity *ipso jure* of boundary and territorial treaties was later embodied in the 1978 Vienna Convention on Succession of States in Respect of Treaties',[71] while the Arbitration Commission

---

[70] See, for example, Report of the International Law Commission, 26th Session, pp. 201–2.

[71] *ICJ Reports*, 1982, pp. 18, 66. See also the *Burkina Faso/Mali* case, *ICJ Reports*, 1986, pp. 554, 563, and Judge Ajibola's separate opinion in the *Libya/Chad* case, *ICJ Reports*, 1994, pp. 6, 64.

established by the International Conference on Yugoslavia[72] stated in Opinion No. 3 that 'all external frontiers must be respected in line with the principle stated in the United Nations Charter, in the Declaration on Principles of International Law concerning Friendly Relations and Co-operation among States in accordance with the Charter of the United Nations (General Assembly Resolution 2625 (XXV)) and in the Helsinki Final Act, a principle which also underlies Article 11 of the Vienna Convention of 23 August 1978 on the Succession of States in Respect of Treaties'.[73]

Thirdly, the basis for this exception to the 'clean slate' rule was generally accepted to lie in the requirements of the international community with regard to the maintenance of international peace and security. Sir Francis Vallat, the Special Rapporteur in 1974, declared, for example, that acceptance of the idea that a bilateral boundary treaty could be swept aside by a succession of States 'would result in chaos' and was 'unthinkable'.[74] It was pointed out that 'the disturbance of existing boundaries is much more likely to create chaos than their maintenance'.[75] This view was also put by a number of members of the International Law Commission[76] and by a number of governments.[77] In other words, the policy issue standing behind Article 11 expresses the community interest in preserving territorial stability, thus reflecting a rather wider approach than the wording taken on its own might otherwise tend to suggest. Many International Law Commission members[78] and governments[79] also took the position that the exception was already part of customary international law, and this reinforces the general policy approach.

This principle cannot be taken to mean that either an unsettled or a contested boundary can be converted into an agreed line simply by way of succession, nor may it preclude subsequent alteration with the consent of the parties concerned.[80] However, it does mean that an agreed boundary established or confirmed in a treaty cannot be challenged

---

[72] See below, p. 106.

[73] 92 ILR 170, 171.

[74] *Yearbook of the International Law Commission*, 1974, vol. 1, p. 204.

[75] Ibid., p. 83.

[76] See, for example, ibid., pp. 210 (Moreno); 213 (Ago); 216 (Tsuruoka); 219 (Yasseen) and 221 (Ustor).

[77] See, for example, *UN Conference on Succession of States in respect of Treaties* (1977), Comments of Governments (A/Conf.80/5), pp. 143–4 (Australia); 150 (German Democratic Republic); 152–3 (Indonesia) and 166 (the Philippines).

[78] See, for example, *Yearbook of the International Law Commission*, 1974, vol. 1, pp. 206 (Sette-Camara); 210 (Ushakov); and 213 (Ago). The Special Rapporteur stressed that the basis of his proposal was to be found in long-established customary law: ibid., p. 222.

[79] See, for example, *UN Conference on Succession of States in respect of Treaties* (1977), Comments of Governments (A/Conf.80/5), pp. 150 (German Democratic Republic); 172 (USSR) and 175 (USA).

[80] Whether it means that the boundary can be challenged upon the basis of the invalidity of the treaty concerned is open to question. Waldock expressed the view that it could: *Yearbook of the International Law Commission*, 1972, vol. 1, pp. 259–60.

simply on the grounds of a succession, and it does in reality and in practice reinforce the principle of territorial stability.

3. *Interpreting Boundary Treaties*

The third consequential axiom that may be drawn from the principle of stability is that the interpretation of boundary treaties will be influenced and guided by it. As the Permanent Court noted in the *Treaty of Lausanne* case,

the very nature of a frontier and of any conventions designed to establish frontiers between two countries imports that a frontier must constitute a definite boundary line throughout its length . . . [and] . . . it is . . . natural that any article designed to fix a frontier should, if possible, be so interpreted that the result of the application of its provisions in their entirety should be the establishment of a precise, complete and definitive frontier.[81]

This approach was supported in the *Frontier Land* case[82] and the *Libya/Chad* case.[83] In the latter case, the Court noted that the relevant 1955 Franco-Libyan Treaty had to be taken to have determined a permanent frontier. It was stated that 'there was nothing in the 1955 Treaty to indicate that the boundary agreed was to be provisional or temporary; on the contrary it bears all the hallmarks of finality'.[84] In other words, in the absence of any indication to the contrary, one must presume that a boundary treaty is intended to be conclusive and determinative. This was a point that had also been made in the analogous context of a boundary award in the *Argentine-Chile Frontier* case, where the Tribunal had emphasized that 'since the 1902 Award was a valid Award, it must be assumed to have settled the entire boundary between Argentina and Chile in the area covered by it'.[85] And as the International Court went on to declare in the *Libya/Chad* case, 'once agreed, the boundary stands, for any other approach would vitiate the fundamental principle of the stability of boundaries'.[86]

The presumption can only apply in the absence of evidence to the contrary, so that where an agreement manifests an intention that it should not be complete or final, or where the agreement itself does not establish or recognize an international boundary, it cannot apply. One cannot utilize the presumption, for example, in order to determine that a boundary has been established where the treaty itself does no such

---

[81] *PCIJ*, Series B, No. 12, p. 20. See also the *Jaworzina* case, *PCIJ*, Series B, No. 8, p. 32, and Bardonnet, loc. cit. above (n. 1), pp. 25–31.

[82] *ICJ Reports*, 1959, pp. 221–2.

[83] *ICJ Reports*, 1994, pp. 23–4.

[84] Ibid., p. 37.

[85] 38 ILR 81. See also the *Jaworzina* case, *PCIJ*, Series B, No. 8, p. 32.

[86] *ICJ Reports*, 1994, p. 37.

thing. This was the point argued unsuccessfully by Libya in its litigation with Chad.[87] As Judge Shahabuddeen concisely and clearly put it,

the principle of the stability of boundaries, as it applies to a boundary fixed by agreement, hinges on there being an agreement for the establishment of a boundary; it comes into play only after the existence of such an agreement is established and is directed to giving proper effect to the agreement. It does not operate to bring into existence a boundary agreement where there was none.[88]

However, where such a treaty does exist, Judge Shahabuddeen notes, 'the principle of stability of boundaries is a valuable one . . . [and] . . . its proper use is in the interpretation and application of the treaty',[89] or as Judge Ajibola put it in the same case, 'the special rule of interpretation of treaties regarding boundaries is that it must, failing contrary evidence, be supposed to have been concluded in order to ensure peace, stability and finality'.[90] Thus, there is a presumption that courts will favour an interpretation of a treaty creating a boundary that holds that a permanent, definite and complete boundary has been established.[91]

4. *The Principle of Stability as a Balancing Norm*

The principle of stability plays an important role in a further significant manner. It can act as a balancing or testing principle in order to determine which of competing norms may be the applicable one in any given situation. In other words, it may be regarded as a hierarchically superior proposition. This has become particularly apparent with regard to the possibilities of conflict between the norms of self-determination and territorial integrity (as expressing and protecting the boundary established in accordance with the principle of *uti possidetis juris*).

This was particularly addressed by the Chamber of the International Court in the *Burkina Faso/Mali* case, which declared that:

the essential requirement of stability in order to survive, to develop and gradually to consolidate their independence in all fields, has induced African States judiciously to consent to the respecting of colonial frontiers, and to take account of it in the interpretation of the principle of self-determination of peoples.[92]

---

[87] *ICJ Reports*, 1994, pp. 22–3.
[88] Ibid., p. 45.
[89] Ibid., p. 50.
[90] Ibid., p. 64, and see also ibid., p. 65.
[91] See Crawford, 'The General Assembly, the International Court and Self-determination', in Lowe and Fitzmaurice (eds.), *Fifty Years of the International Court of Justice* (1996), pp. 585, 601.
[92] Ibid., p. 567.

It was noted that, although *uti possidetis* appeared to conflict with self-determination,

> the maintenance of the territorial status quo in Africa is often seen as the wisest course, to preserve what has been achieved by peoples who have struggled for their independence, and to avoid a disruption which would deprive the continent of the gains achieved by much sacrifice.[93]

In other words, the criterion or demand of stability has required that the choice between the principles of territorial integrity and self-determination should be determined upon the basis of the priority of the former. This accords with State practice. Thus in the confrontation between the requirement to maintain the territorial integrity of a colony and the desire to permit the widest application of the principle of the self-determination of the colonial people, a confrontation of particularly marked sensitivity, the pull of stability has produced a response in favour of the former.[94]

5. *Stability and Equity*

The principle of stability also impacts upon the application of equity[95] in territorial disputes. Clearly, it would offend all notions of stability if a boundary dispute could be resolved by a court on the basis of equity in

---

[93] Ibid. See also Judge Ajibola in the *Libya/Chad* case, *ICJ Reports*, 1994, p. 91.

[94] See below, p 119.

[95] See generally Degan, *L'équité en droit international* (1970); Akehurst, 'Equity and the General Principles of Law', *International and Comparative Law Quarterly*, 25 (1976), p. 801; Cheng, 'Justice and Equity in International Law', *Current Legal Problems*, 8 (1955), p. 185; De Visscher, *De l'équité dans le règlement arbitral ou judiciaire des litiges de droit international public* (1972); Bardonnet, 'Equité et Frontières Terrestres', in *Mélanges offerts à Paul Reuter* (1981), p. 34; E. Lauterpacht, 'Equity, Evasion, Equivocation and Evolution in International Law', *Proceedings of the American Branch of the ILA* (1977–8), p. 33, and *Aspects of the Administration of International Justice* (1991), pp. 117–52; Jennings, 'Equity and Equitable Principles', *Annuaire suisse de droit international*, 42 (1986), p. 38; Oppenheim, op. cit. above (n. 1), p. 43; Higgins, *Problems and Process* (1994), chapter 13; Miyoshi, *Considerations of Equity in the Settlement of Territorial and Boundary Disputes* (1993); Rosenne, 'Equitable Principles and the Compulsory Jurisdiction of International Tribunals', *Festschrift für Rudolf Bindschedler* (1980), p. 410, and 'The Position of the International Court of Justice on the Foundations of the Principle of Equity in International Law', in Bloed and Van Dijk (eds.), *Forty Years International Court of Justice: Jurisdiction, Equality and Equity* (1988), p. 108; Pirotte, 'La notion d'équité dans la jurisprudence récente de la CIJ', *Revue générale de droit international public*, 77 (1973), p. 131; Chattopadhyay, 'Equity in International Law: Its Growth and Development', *Georgia Journal of International and Comparative Law*, 5 (1975), p. 381; Lapidoth, 'Equity in International Law', *Israel Law Review*, 22 (1987), p. 161; Schachter, *International Law in Theory and Practice* (1991), p. 49; Lowe, 'The Role of Equity in International Law', *Australian Yearbook of International Law*, 12 (1992), p. 54, and Thirlway, 'The Law and Procedure of the International Court of Justice 1960–1989', this *Year Book*, 60 (1989), p. 49. Note also Judge Weeramantry's separate opinion in the *Jan Mayen (Denmark v. Norway)* case, *ICJ Reports*, 1993, pp. 38, 211.

its widest sense of *ex aequo et bono*,[96] in the absence of such a direction by the parties. Equity in a broad sense (although always *infra legem*) has played an important part in the development of international maritime delimitation,[97] focusing upon the need to arrive at an equitable solution in the particular circumstances upon the basis of the existing rules of international law.[98] Such application of equity is in order to mitigate certain inequities and cannot be extended to the refashioning of nature to the detriment of legal rules.[99] It entails a detailed and broad consideration of relevant factors and, as the International Court has emphasized, there is 'no legal limit to the considerations which States may take account of for the purpose of making sure that they apply equitable procedures'.[100] What really counts, however, is the achievement of an equitable result in the light of all relevant considerations.[101] This, of course, begs a whole raft of questions that cannot be tackled in the context of this particular enquiry.[102]

What is important to note is the fact that the evolution of equity to its greatest extent has taken place with regard to maritime delimitations. Territorial issues, however, fall into a different category altogether.[103] In the case of maritime delimitations, the key issue is not which delimitation line the parties have already agreed to and thus remain bound by, nor is it whether they have established title effectively over the maritime spaces up to the claimed lines. It is rather a question of determining the line on the basis of a weighing of a range of relevant considerations with a view to attaining an equitable result in the circumstances. In the case of territorial delimitations, the former issues define and constitute the legal framework for the resolution of the dispute. Equity follows the law. And

[96] Under Article 38(2) of the Statute of the International Court of Justice 1945, the Court may decide a case *ex aequo et bono* if the parties so agree. This provision has not been used. See, for example, Rosenne, *The Law and Practice of the International Court* (1965), vol. 1, pp. 323–6. See also Judge Weeramantry, loc. cit. above (n. 95), pp. 226–30. For further discussion of the concept, see E. Lauterpacht, loc. cit. above (n. 95), p. 45 and *Aspects of the Administration of International Justice* (1991), pp. 117–52; Jennings, loc. cit. above (n. 95), p. 27, and Thirlway, loc. cit. above (n. 95), pp. 50–62.

[97] See, for example, the *North Sea Continental Shelf* cases, *ICJ Reports*, 1969, p. 3; the *Anglo-French Continental Shelf* case, 54 ILR 6; the *Tunisia/Libya* case, *ICJ Reports*, 1982, p. 18; the *Gulf of Maine* case, *ICJ Reports*, 1984, p. 246; the *Guinea–Guinea-Bissau Maritime Delimitation* case, 77 ILR 636; the *Libya/Malta* case, *ICJ Reports*, 1985, p. 13, and the *Denmark* v. *Norway (Jan Mayen)* case, *ICJ Reports*, 1993, p. 38.

[98] See, for example, the *North Sea Continental Shelf* cases, *ICJ Reports*, 1969, p. 47, and the *Fisheries Jurisdiction* cases, *ICJ Reports*, 1974, p. 33.

[99] See, for example, the *North Sea Continental Shelf* cases, *ICJ Reports*, 1969, pp. 49–50; the *Anglo-French Continental Shelf* case, 54 ILR 123–4; the *Tunisia/Libya Continental Shelf* case, *ICJ Reports*, 1982, p. 60, and the *Gulf of Maine* case, *ICJ Reports*, 1984, pp. 313–14.

[100] The *North Sea Continental Shelf* cases, *ICJ Reports*, 1969, p. 50.

[101] See the *Tunisia/Libya Continental Shelf* case, *ICJ Reports*, 1982, p. 59, and the *Libya/Malta Continental Shelf* case, *ICJ Reports*, 1985, pp. 38–9. See also Higgins, op. cit. above (n. 95), pp. 219 ff.

[102] See, for example, Weil, *The Law of Maritime Delimitations—Reflections* (1989); Lowe, loc. cit. above (n. 95), and Brown, *The International Law of the Sea* (1994), vol. 1, pp. 155 ff.

[103] See Munkman, loc. cit. above (n. 1), pp. 55–6.

the law is clear at least as to how to tackle terrestrial disputes. Legal title and the effective display of sovereign authority (coupled with the operation of the principle of acquiescence) are the two key tools, long accepted in international jurisprudence.[104] There is thus no room for equity in its expansive role here. A court would not be required to take into account a wide range of relevant factors affecting the dispute in general in order to balance them out to produce an equitable result in the circumstances. It would be required to examine closely and carefully the issue of legal title, that is, applicable treaties and any relevant unilateral commitments and effective display of sovereignty.

As the Chamber noted in the *Burkina Faso/Mali* case,

to resort to the concept of equity in order to modify an established frontier would be quite unjustified. Especially in the African context, the obvious deficiencies of many frontiers inherited from colonisation, from the ethnic, geographical or administrative standpoint, cannot support an assertion that the modification of these frontiers is necessary or justifiable on the ground of considerations of equity.[105]

This position was reiterated clearly in the *El Salvador/Honduras* case, where it was stated that 'even equity *infra legem*, a recognized concept in international law, could not be resorted to in order to modify an established frontier inherited from colonisation whatever its deficiencies'.[106] And the Chamber was very decisive in rejecting the relevance of unequal population density and inequality of natural resources in such circumstances.[107]

The same point had in effect been made by the Court in the *Temple* case, where it was pointed out that 'frontier rectifications cannot in law be claimed on the ground that a frontier area has turned out to have an importance not known or suspected when the frontier was established'.[108] Equity cannot be utilized to revise a boundary once it has been established as a matter of legal title. This was emphasized by the International Court in the *Libya/Chad* case, where the Court, having found that the 1955 Franco-Libyan Treaty determined a permanent frontier, declared that no other factor was relevant. Thus, issues as to the history of the 'borderlands' claimed by Libya on the basis of title inherited from the indigenous people, the Senoussi Order, the Ottoman

---

[104] See, for example, the *Island of Palmas* case, *Reports of International Arbitral Awards*, vol. 2, p. 829; the *Clipperton Island* case, *American Journal of International Law*, 26 (1932), p. 390; the *Eastern Greenland* case, PCIJ, Series A/B, No. 53, p. 46, and the *Minquiers and Ecrehos* case, *ICJ Reports*, 1953, p. 47.

[105] *ICJ Reports*, 1986, p. 633.

[106] *ICJ Reports*, 1992, p. 396.

[107] Ibid. See also the *Tunisia/Libya* case, *ICJ Reports*, 1982, p. 77.

[108] *ICJ Reports*, 1962, p. 25. See also Bastid, loc. cit. above (n. 1), p. 469.

Empire and Italy fell away.[109] In addition, the dispute over effectiveness of occupation by the various States and entities in the past and questions as to *terra nullius* and spheres of influence, and indeed of rather more vague claims on the basis of security and geographical considerations, were all deemed explicitly or implicitly by the Court to be irrelevant.[110] As the Court forcefully and significantly concluded by a 16 to 1 majority,[111] 'the 1955 Treaty completely determined the boundary between Libya and Chad'.[112]

It is only if equitable principles are specifically imported into the decision-making process by an appropriate reference to a court that such issues may arise.[113] Equity in the narrow sense will be discussed later.[114]

IV. THE DOCTRINE OF *UTI POSSIDETIS JURIS*

The problems associated with the legitimacy of the territorial framework of newly independent States emerging out of colonialism led to the evolution of the doctrine of *uti possidetis*,[115] which has been slowly mutating over time. In essence, the doctrine provides that new States will come to independence with the same borders that they had when they were administrative units within the territory or territories of one colonial power and the fundamental aim of the doctrine is to underline the principle of the stability of State boundaries.[116] More than that, however, *uti possidetis* provides the new State with a territorial legitimation. It enables the State to proclaim the juridically acceptable nature of its territorial definition, both internally and externally. *Uti possidetis*, therefore, constitutes the adoption of a particular approach to statehood

[109] It was Libya's contention that the parties to the 1955 Treaty only intended to recognize the frontiers that had been previously fixed by international instruments and that this did not include the Libya–Chad frontier: *ICJ Reports*, 1994, pp. 6, 22.

[110] *ICJ Reports*, 1994, p. 39.

[111] Only Judge *ad hoc* Sette-Camara voted against.

[112] Ibid., p. 40.

[113] See, for example, the *Bolivia–Peru Boundary* case, *Reports of International Arbitral Awards*, vol. 11, p. 133.

[114] Below, p. 139.

[115] See, for example, Bardonnet, loc. cit. above (n. 1), pp. 13, 54 ff; Moore, 'Memorandum on *Uti Possidetis*: Costa Rica–Panama Arbitration 1911', *The Collected Papers of John Bassett Moore* (1944), vol. 3, p. 328; Tran Van Minh, 'Remarques sur le principe de l'intangibilité des frontières', in Fenet (ed.), *Peuples et états du tiers monde face à l'ordre international* (1976), p. 51; Blum, *Historic Titles in International Law* (1965), p. 341; Whiteman's *Digest of International Law*, vol. 2 (1968), p. 1086; Pinho Campinos, 'L'actualité de l' "uti possidetis" ', in Société française pour le droit international, *La Frontière* (1980), p. 95; Oppenheim, op. cit. above (n. 1), pp. 669 ff; Nguyen Quoc Dinh, Daillier and Pellet, op. cit. above (n. 1), p. 461; Cukwurah, *The Settlement of Boundary Disputes in International Law* (1967), p. 114; Hill, op. cit. above (n. 1), p. 154, and Sorel and R. Mehdi, 'L'*uti possidetis* entre la consécration juridique et la pratique: essai de réactualisation', *Annuaire français de droit international*, 40 (1994), p. 11.

[116] Oppenheim, op. cit. above (n. 1), p. 670.

and sovereignty. It focuses questions of legitimacy and recognition primarily (and perhaps it may be said, traditionally, exclusively) upon territorial factors and thus acts as a counter-weight to other legitimizing principles, such as ethnic, religious or historic affinities. The principle of *uti possidetis* functions in the context of the transmission of sovereignty and the creation of a new independent State and conditions that process.

1. *The Development of the Doctrine*

The doctrine of *uti possidetis* has its origins in Roman law, where it operated as an interdict of the Praetor by which the disturbance of the existing state of possession of immovables as between two individuals was forbidden.[117] *Uti possidetis ita possideatis.* It served thus to preserve the *status quo* even if the latter had been established as a consequence of the use of force. The doctrine appeared in international law initially as a principle of consolidation of the *de facto* situation following hostilities, so that the simple conclusion of peace would vest in the belligerents such territory as was actually under their control at that point.[118] It then materialized in the era of colonization in the form of a doctrine of actual possession with the aim of mitigating disputes between expanding powers.[119]

Finally, the doctrine emerged in Latin America as a principle for establishing or enshrining the control of the local authorities as against potential claimants on the basis of not so much actual as constructive possession. The focus shifted from effective occupation of areas to sanctification of the colonial administrative line. In this form, indeed, Reisman argues, 'it bestowed an aura of historical legality to the expropriation of the lands of indigenous peoples'.[120] In fact, the real thrust of the doctrine as developed in Latin America was external rather than internal. It was intended to prevent any renewal of European colonization on the basis that parts of the continent constituted *terrae nullius* and thus were open to acquisition of sovereignty by effective occupation by any State.[121] It was thus an assertion of constructive or fictional possession or occupation since many unexplored and uninhabited regions existed in Latin America.

[117] See Moore, op. cit. above (n. 115), p. 328. See also Judge Ajibola's separate opinion in the *Libya/Chad* case, *ICJ Reports*, 1994, p. 83, and Reisman, 'Protecting Indigenous Rights in International Adjudication', *American Journal of International Law*, 89 (1995), pp. 350, 352, n. 8.
[118] See Hall, *International Law* (8th edn., 1924), p. 673, and Bernhardt et al. (eds.), *Encyclopedia of Public International Law*, vol. 1 (1992), pp. 449–50.
[119] Moore, op. cit. above (n. 115), p. 332.
[120] Loc. cit. above (n. 117), p. 352.
[121] See, as to the use of *uti possidetis* as a counter to British claims to the Falkland Islands, Cohen-Jonathan, 'Les îsles Falkland (Malouines)', *Annuaire français de droit international*, 18 (1972), p. 235, and Sorel and Mehdi, loc. cit. above (n. 115), p. 19.

This approach was exemplified in the arbitral award of the Swiss Federal Council in the *Colombia-Venezuela* case,[122] in which it was declared that the consequence of the rule of *uti possidetis* would be that encroachments and attempts at colonization from across the borders as well as occupations in fact would be rendered pointless from a legal point of view.[123] It is particularly interesting to note that the intention of preventing boundary disputes as between the successor States of the former Spanish Empire was referred to almost in passing. The principle of *uti possidetis* would also have the advantage, it was noted, of suppressing frontier disputes between the new States.[124] The Chamber of the International Court understood this orientation and concluded in the *El Salvador/Honduras* case that 'the principle of *uti possidetis* is concerned as much with title to territory as with the location of boundaries; certainly a key aspect of the principle is the denial of the possibility of *terra nullius*'.[125] Thus, the doctrine moved from its original function of preserving the actual state of affairs, with its consequential emphasis upon actual possession however brought about, to an approach that forbade acquisition of title by occupation of territory deemed *terra nullius* or by conquest, the latter being at the time, of course, still a legitimate mechanism for territorial change.[126] Only in passing did it appear to concern itself with avoidance of boundary disputes as such.

In time, the subsidiary hope became the focus of the norm. Although some questioned the existence of *uti possidetis* as a principle of law,[127] primarily upon the basis of an exaggerated concern with regard to its uncertainty, it is beyond question that it has been established as a rule of international law. Practice in Latin America is to all intents and purposes unequivocal. A variety of treaties between Latin American States have referred specifically to the principle,[128] as have a number of State

[122] *Reports of International Arbitral Awards*, vol. 1, p. 223.
[123] Ibid., p. 228.
[124] Ibid.
[125] *ICJ Reports*, 1992, p. 387. Note Oppenheim's view that the doctrine 'conflates boundary and territorial questions by assuming as a governing principle that boundaries must be as they were in law at the declaration of independence: viz 1810 for former Spanish colonies in South America and 1822 for those in Central America': op. cit. above (n. 1), p. 669.
[126] See, for example, the *El Salvador/Honduras* case, *ICJ Reports*, 1992, p. 558.
[127] Fisher called it an 'indefinite and illusory concept' with a continuing uncertain meaning: 'The Arbitration of the Guatemalan-Honduran Boundary Dispute', *American Journal of International Law*, 27 (1933), pp. 403, 415. See also Waldock, 'Disputed Sovereignty in the Falkland Island Dependencies', this *Year Book*, 25 (1948), pp. 311, 325–6. The tribunal in the *Beagle Channel* case seemed a little unclear as to the precise status of the principle, accepting it as 'possibly, at least at first, a political tenet rather than a true rule of law . . . [although] . . . it undoubtedly constituted an important element in the inter-relationships of the continent': HMSO, 1977, pp. 4–5.
[128] See, for example, Moore, op. cit. above (n. 115), pp. 335 ff; the *Beagle Channel* case, HMSO, 1977, pp. 4 ff; the *Colombia–Venezuela* case, *Reports of International Arbitral Awards*, vol. 1, p. 223; the *Honduras Borders* case, *Reports of International Arbitral Awards*, vol. 2, p. 1307, and the *Arbitral Award of the King of Spain* case, *ICJ Reports*, 1960, pp. 191, 199. See also Tran Van Minh, loc. cit. above (n. 115), p. 61.

constitutions.[129] Judge *ad hoc* Torres Bernardez in his separate opinion in the *El Salvador/Honduras* case, for example, emphasized that 'from the start, the first Constitutions of the Central American Republics defined their respective "national territories" by a broad reference to the 1821 *uti possidetis juris*'.[130] Recent judgments and awards have also confirmed the principle,[131] not least the *El Salvador/Honduras* case itself where the Chamber emphasized in terms that 'there can be no doubt about the importance of the *uti possidetis juris* principle as one which has, in general, resulted in certain and stable frontiers throughout most of Central and South America'.[132]

In Latin America, the principle operated within a particular framework, that is, the succession of a variety of States to the former Spanish Empire. It did not as such deal with situations where the boundaries in question were those between sovereigns in international law. Thus the concept appears essentially in two manifestations. *Uti possidetis juris* referred to a legal line founded upon legal title as was the rule adopted by the successor States to the Spanish Empire, while *uti possidetis de facto* was an interpretation founded upon factual possession maintained by Brazil, which, of course, was the successor to the Portuguese colony on the continent.[133] It was an approach that emerged after the war of 1801 between Spain and France on the one side and Portugal on the other, which was seen by Brazil as having revoked the Spanish-Portuguese Treaty of 1777 delimiting the relevant boundaries. It thus marked a reversion to the original principle of *uti possidetis* in international law which simply accepted the territorial results of war and actual possession irrespective of how this was achieved.[134] However, this approach has been strongly contested by the other States of South America, and its application may be seen as confined to the particular circumstances of Brazil's claims.

From Latin America, the doctrine moved to Africa, where it was more clearly focused from the start. Part of the reason for this lies in the nature of colonial boundaries in Africa. Judge Ajibola in his separate opinion in the *Libya/Chad* case noted that the colonial penchant for geometric lines had left Africa with a high concentration of States whose frontiers were

---

[129] See, for example, the two parties in the *Colombia–Venezuela* case, *Reports of International Arbitral Awards*, vol. 1, pp. 223, 278.

[130] *ICJ Reports*, 1992, p. 631. See also Judge *ad hoc* Holguín's dissenting opinion, *Award of the King of Spain* case, *ICJ Reports*, 1960, pp. 192, 221 ff.

[131] See, for example, the *Rann of Kutch* case, 50 ILR 407 (Judge Bebler's dissenting opinion) and 470 (Chairman Lagergren); the *Dubai/Sharjah* case, 91 ILR 543, 578; the *Burkina Faso/Mali* case, *ICJ Reports*, 1986, p. 565; the *Guinea-Bissau* v. *Senegal* case, 83 ILR 35; the *El Salvador/Honduras* case, *ICJ Reports*, 1992, pp. 351, 386, and the *Libya/Chad* case, *ICJ Reports*, 1994, pp. 83 ff. (Judge Ajibola).

[132] *ICJ Reports*, 1992, p. 386.

[133] See Bardonnet, loc. cit. above (n. 1), p. 55.

[134] See *Encyclopedia of Public International Law*, op. cit. above (n. 118), p. 452, and Judge Caneiro's separate opinion in the *Minquiers and Ecrehos* case, *ICJ Reports*, 1953, pp. 47, 104–5.

drawn with little or no consideration for those factors of geography, ethnicity, economic convenience or reasonable means of communication that had played a part in boundary determinations elsewhere, so that boundaries on that continent were patently even more artificial than elsewhere in the world since most of them were 'merely straight lines traced on the drawing board with little relevance to the physical circumstances on the ground'.[135]

It is incontestable that in the process of the European colonization of Africa in particular, ethnic considerations were in general ignored and the various colonies and protectorates established included within their borders, with few exceptions, large numbers of different, often antagonistic, tribes, while dividing others between different jurisdictions.[136] The geometric method of establishing boundaries was indeed favoured, and ignorance of geographical features according to which many boundaries were drawn was marked. As Lord Salisbury declared in 1890,

We have been engaged . . . in drawing lines upon maps where no white man's feet have ever trod; we have been giving away mountains and rivers and lakes to each other, but we have only been hindered by the small impediment that we never knew exactly where those mountains and rivers and lakes were.[137]

However, it is true that many boundary delimitations did take some account of local conditions such as ethnic considerations and the structure and extent of African political entities. Several treaties incorporated provisions noting that account was to be taken of tribal groupings in the drawing of borders. The Anglo-French Treaty of 1890, for example, provided that the northern border of what was later to become Nigeria should be drawn 'in such a manner as to comprise in the sphere of action of the Niger Company all that fairly belongs to the Kingdom of Sokoto',[138] while a treaty between Britain and Portugal in 1891 provided that part of the border between their central African territories would follow the western boundary of the Barotse kingdom.[139] Other examples exist,[140] but they do not in all reality detract from the central issue. African boundaries were in the main arbitrarily drawn and, even more importantly, were and are perceived to have been established and entrenched in an historical context that many find alien and demeaning.

---

[135] *ICJ Reports*, 1994, pp. 6, 52–3.

[136] See, for example, Shaw, op. cit. above (n. 1), pp. 50 ff. See also Yakemtchouk, *L'Afrique en droit international* (1971), pp. 70–3; Allott, *Boundaries and the Law in Africa: African Boundary Problems* (1969); Anene, *The International Boundaries of Nigeria* (1970); Lindley, *The Acquisition and Government of Backward Territory in International Law* (1926); Alexandrowicz, *The European–African Confrontation* (1973), and Okoye, *International Law and the New African States* (1972).

[137] Cited by Judge Ajibola, *ICJ Reports*, 1994, p. 53.

[138] Anene, op. cit. above (n. 136), p. 13. See also Hertslet, *Map of Africa by Treaty* (3rd edn., 1909), vol. 2, p. 229.

[139] See Touval, 'Treaties, Borders and the Partition of Africa', *Journal of African History*, 7 (1966), pp. 279, 289.

[140] See Shaw, op. cit. above (n. 1), pp. 50 ff.

This approach has on occasion threatened to challenge the legitimacy of such borders, but despite indications in the immediate pre-independence period and a short while thereafter, such an approach has not been sustained.[141] On the contrary, it was precisely because of the precariousness of colonial boundaries in their geographic, historical and ethnic context that the principle of *uti possidetis* operating as a guarantee of devolved boundaries fell upon such fertile ground. The principle of the stability of boundaries operates within a particularly sensitive framework when one considers specifically colonial boundaries. The manner of their establishment by the colonial powers in an arbitrary and cavalier fashion has not failed to arouse hostility and opprobrium, and it is precisely because of this that the question of entrenching the rule of succession to colonial frontiers as a principle of international law has acquired such a resonance in the practice of the continent. Without a widely accepted norm of territorial stability based upon the colonial spatial heritage, other legitimating principles, ranging from historic to ethnic and geographic ties, would have been drawn into issues of territorial sovereignty and a dramatic re-ordering of the African territorial order would have been on the agenda, complete with all the ensuing hazards.

It is no longer disputed that colonial territories have a special status in international law. From being perceived simply as part of the sovereignty and territorial definition of the colonial power, such territories were at a certain stage accepted as constituting specific areas apart from the metropolitan States. The Declaration on the Granting of Independence to Colonial Countries and Peoples adopted on 14 December 1960[142] called for immediate steps to be taken in trust and non-self-governing territories and all territories which had not yet attained independence to transfer power to the people of those territories, while General Assembly Resolution 1541 (XV) adopted the next day declared that there was an obligation to transmit information to the UN under Chapter XI of the Charter regarding a territory 'which is geographically separate and is distinct ethnically and/or culturally from the country administering it'. The seminal Declaration on Principles of International Law concerning Friendly Relations and Co-operation among States adopted on 24 October 1970[143] emphasized that 'the territory of a colony or other non-self-governing territory has under the Charter a status separate and distinct from the territory of the State administering it', and that such status was to exist until the people of that territory had exercised the right to self-determination. Upon this basis, the adoption and development of the principle of *uti possidetis* in Africa was conditioned.

---

[141] Ibid., pp. 182 ff.
[142] General Assembly Resolution 1514 (XV).
[143] General Assembly Resolution 2625 (XXV).

The key document was Resolution 16(1) of the Organization of African Unity, adopted in Cairo in 1964. This stated that colonial frontiers existing at the moment of decolonization constituted a tangible reality, which all member States pledged themselves to respect.[144] It was a political statement of the highest order and one with important juridical associations. The issue was discussed in the leading case of *Burkina Faso/ Mali* by the Chamber of the International Court. Although both States had expressly requested that the Court settle the dispute on the basis of 'the principle of the intangibility of colonial frontiers',[145] the Chamber took the opportunity to consider the norm of *uti possidetis*.[146] It was declared in an important and now much quoted statement that

the principle [of *uti possidetis*] is not a special rule which pertains solely to one specific system of international law. It is a general principle, which is logically connected with the phenomenon of the obtaining of independence, wherever it occurs. Its obvious purpose is to prevent the independence and stability of new States being endangered by fratricidal struggles provoked by the challenging of frontiers following the withdrawal of the administering power.[147]

The Chamber noted that the fact that the new African States had agreed to respect the administrative boundaries and frontiers established by the colonial powers 'must be seen not as a mere practice contributing to the gradual emergence of a principle of customary international law, limited in its impact to the African continent as it had previously been to Spanish America, but as the application in Africa of a rule of general scope'.[148] In this context, the 1964 OAU Resolution 'deliberately defined and stressed the principle of *uti possidetis juris*'[149] rather than constituting the source of the principle itself, so that the application of that principle could not be challenged on the basis that in 1960 (the year when Burkina Faso and Mali became independent), the OAU did not yet exist.[150] The numerous affirmations of the intangibility of colonial borders made by African statesmen and by the OAU itself thus recognized and confirmed an existing principle and neither created a new rule nor extended to Africa

---

[144] OAU Doc. AHG/Res. 16(1). See *Africa Research Bulletin* (July 1964), pp. 122 ff., and Shaw, op. cit. above (n. 1), pp. 185–7.

[145] *ICJ Reports*, 1986, p. 565.

[146] See also Naldi, 'The Case Concerning the Frontier Dispute (Burkina Faso/Republic of Mali): *Uti Possidetis* in an African Perspective', *International and Comparative Law Quarterly*, 36 (1987), p. 893.

[147] *ICJ Reports*, 1986, p. 565.

[148] Ibid. See also Judge Moreno Quintana in his dissenting opinion in the *Frontier Land* case, *ICJ Reports*, 1959, pp. 209, 255.

[149] *ICJ Reports*, 1986, pp. 565–6.

[150] Ibid., p. 567.

a rule previously applied only in another continent.[151] It is also to be noted that the African approach, based simply upon the notion of the preservation of the pre-existing colonial borders, moved a step further from the original Latin American concept,[152] which had dealt with the consequences of the succession of a number of States from one colonial power and was oriented towards external threats.

It cannot be denied that the effect of establishing and accepting the *uti possidetis* principle is to entrench the boundaries that had been arbitrarily and often callously instituted by the colonial powers, a matter that is politically and emotionally difficult. But it is also true that while the colonial boundaries have aroused considerable ire for their arbitrary and alien character, such opposition rarely extends to challenging their legitimacy as distinct from emphasizing the associated political problems.[153] The Chamber in the *Burkina Faso/Mali* case concluded that

especially in the African context, the obvious deficiencies of many frontiers inherited from colonisation, from the ethnic, geographical or administrative standpoint, cannot support an assertion that the modification of these frontiers is necessary or justifiable on the ground of consideration of equity. These frontiers, however unsatisfactory they may be, possess the authority of the *uti possidetis* and are thus fully in conformity with contemporary international law.[154]

As Brownlie has noted, 'the general principle, that pre-independence boundaries of former colonial administrative divisions all subject to the same sovereign remain in being, is in accordance with good policy and has been adopted by governments and tribunals concerned with boundaries in Asia and Africa.'[155] Not to accept the territorial solution of statehood emerging from decolonization would require acceptance of another legitimizing principle, such as ethnic or historic affinity. The fact that this has not happened is testament to the fears associated with such solutions.

The principle of *uti possidetis* has been applied in the case law not only with regard to Latin America and Africa, but also in Asia. In the *Temple*

---

[151] Ibid., p. 566. See also Brownlie, *African Boundaries* (1979), pp. 10–12. See also, with regard to the independence of Eritrea, Goy, 'L'indépendance de l'Erythrée', *Annuaire français de droit international*, 39 (1993), p. 350.

[152] See to this effect the conclusion of the Arbitration Tribunal in the *Guinea-Bissau v. Senegal* case, 83 ILR 35; cf. Judge Bedjaoui's dissenting opinion, ibid., pp. 57–8.

[153] See, for example, Judge Bedjaoui's dissenting opinion in the *Guinea-Bissau v. Senegal* case, 83 ILR 62–3.

[154] *ICJ Reports*, 1986, p. 633.

[155] *Principles of Public International Law* (4th edn., 1990), p. 135, footnotes omitted. See also Brownlie, *African Boundaries* (1979) pp. 9–12.

of Preah Vihear case, the International Court was faced with a territorial dispute between Cambodia, as one of the successors to French Indo-China, and Thailand. The Court clearly explained that:

It is common ground between the Parties that the present dispute has its *fons et origo* in the boundary settlements made in the period 1904–1908, between France and Siam (as Thailand was then called) and, in particular, that the sovereignty over Preah Vihear depends upon a boundary treaty dated 13 February 1904, and upon events subsequent to that date.[156]

Pursuant to delimitation work undertaken within the context of the 1907 boundary treaty between the parties, maps were prepared by French topographical officers at the request of the Siamese Government. One of these maps related to the region in dispute. The Court found that the parties adopted the map in question over a period of fifty years as representing the outcome of the work of the delimitation of the frontier in the Temple region, thus conferring upon it a binding character. Cambodia had based its case upon this map, while Siam was held to have acquiesced. The situation was such as to have required a response or reaction from the Siamese authorities, both in the light of the circumstances of the public communication of the map and with regard to indications on the face of the map. This did not happen. Indeed, the map had been in use without Siamese objection for some fifty years.[157] Thus Siam was deemed to have accepted it and the delimitation line therein portrayed.[158] The Court considered that the acceptance by the parties of the map caused it to enter the treaty settlement and to become an integral part of it.[159] Although the principle of *uti possidetis* is not in terms referred to, it is clear that the Court and the parties operated on the basis of it. It was accepted that the boundary between the two States was that existing at the moment of independence of Cambodia (since Thailand had always been independent), and that that was based upon a series of Franco-Siamese treaties, as interpreted in the light of particular practice.

It can therefore not be denied that *uti possidetis* applies within the framework of decolonization in the accepted sense. The key question is whether the doctrine has an application in the context of independence from already independent States, that is, outside of the traditional decolonization process.

---

[156] *ICJ Reports*, 1962, pp. 6, 16.
[157] Ibid., p. 32.
[158] Ibid., pp. 22–5. See also ibid., pp. 28–9 and 32.
[159] Ibid., p. 33.

(a) *The former Yugoslavia*[160]

After a period of rising tension, the Yugoslav Republics of Croatia and Slovenia declared their independence on 25 June 1991,[161] following upon referenda held in Slovenia in December 1990 and in Croatia in May 1991. These declarations were suspended for three months and were confirmed on 8 October 1991. Slovenia and Croatia were recognized by the member States of the European Community on 15 January 1992.[162] A referendum on sovereignty was held in Macedonia in September 1991 in favour of a sovereign and independent Macedonia within an association of Yugoslav States.[163] A referendum was held in Bosnia-Herzegovina on 29 February and 1 March 1992 in favour of independence.

[160] See generally Silber and Little, *The Death of Yugoslavia* (1995); Glenny, *The Fall of Yugoslavia* (1995); Zametica, 'The Yugoslav Conflict', *Adephi Paper* (1992), p. 270; UN Department of Information, *The United Nations and the Situation in the Former Yugoslavia* (1995); Pellet, 'Note sur la commission d'arbitrage de la conference Européenne pour la paix en Yougoslavie', *Annuaire français de droit international*, 37 (1991), p. 229; Weller, 'The International Response to the Dissolution of the Socialist Federal Republic of Yugoslavia', *American Journal of International Law*, 86 (1992), p. 569; Blum, 'UN Membership of the "New" Yugoslavia: Continuity or Break?', *American Journal of International Law*, 86 (1992), p. 830, and Müllerson, *International Law, Rights and Politics* (1994).

[161] See Opinion No. 1 of the Arbitration Commission of the European Conference on Yugoslavia, 92 ILR 162, 165. The Conference was convened by the European Community and its member States acting within the framework of European Political Co-operation in a Declaration of 27 August 1991. The Conference was to bring together the Yugoslav Federal Presidency and Federal Government, the Presidents of the six Yugoslav Republics and representatives of the European Community and its member States. The Declaration also established an Arbitration Commission, consisting of five of the Presidents of Constitutional Courts in European Community countries. Two of its members were to be appointed unanimously by the Federal Presidency or, in the absence of agreement, by the three other members appointed by the Community and its member States. The Commission was chaired by M. Badinter. See Pellet, loc. cit. above (n. 160), and generally on the Arbitration Commission, Craven, 'The EC Arbitration Commission on Yugoslavia', this *Year Book*, 66 (1995), p. 333.

[162] See Weller, loc. cit. above (n. 160), p. 586, and EPC Press Release 9/92. The Arbitration Commission in Opinion No. 7, adopted on 11 January 1992, held that the Republic of Slovenia satisfied the tests laid down in the Guidelines on the Recognition of New States in Eastern Europe and in the Soviet Union and in the Declaration on Yugoslavia adopted on 16 December 1991 by the European Community and its member States: see Weller, loc. cit. above (n. 160), p. 593, and 92 ILR 179. Note that the recognition of Croatia was despite the view expressed by the Arbitration Commission in Opinion No. 5 on 11 January 1992 that Croatia's Consitutional Act did not fully incorporate all the guarantees on human rights and minority protection required by the Guidelines and the Declaration. On 4 July 1991, the Arbitration Commission adopted Observations on Croatian Constitutional Law, holding that this law satisfied the requirements of general international law regarding the protection of minorities: ibid., p. 209. The tests laid down in the Guidelines and the Declaration referred *inter alia* to respect for the provisions of the UN Charter and the Final Act of Helsinki and the Charter of Paris especially with regard to the rule of law, democracy and human rights; guarantees for the rights of ethnic and national groups and minorities in accordance with the commitments made in the framework of the Conference on Security and Co-operation in Europe, and acceptance of commitments made with regard to disarmament and nuclear non-proliferation: see text in 92 ILR 173–5.

[163] The Arbitration Commission in Opinion No. 6, adopted on 11 January 1992, held that the Republic of Macedonia satisfied the tests laid down in the Declaration on Yugoslavia and the Guidelines on the Recognition of New States in Eastern Europe and in the Soviet Union. Eventually this Republic was recognized under the provisional name of 'The Former Yugoslav Republic of Macedonia': see Craven, 'What's in a Name? The Former Yugoslav Republic of Macedonia and Issues of Statehood', *Australian Yearbook of International Law*, 16 (1995), p. 199.

Bosnia was recognized by the European Community and its member States on 6 April 1991.[164] On 22 May that year, the Republic of Slovenia, the Republic of Bosnia and Herzegovina and the Republic of Croatia were admitted to membership of the United Nations.[165] The remaining two Republics of the Former Yugoslavia, Serbia and Montenegro, decided on 27 April 1992 to establish a new entity called the Federal Republic of Yugoslavia.[166] 'The Former Yugoslav Republic of Macedonia' was admitted to the UN on 8 April 1993.[167]

In dealing with the consequences of the tragic collapse of the former Yugoslavia, the international community was obliged to address the issue of the status of the boundaries of the new entities. This was done in two ways: first, with regard to the international boundaries[168] of the former State. These borders with Italy, Austria, Hungary, Romania, Bulgaria, Albania and Greece were addressed by the Declaration on Yugoslavia adopted by the European Community and its member States on 16 December 1991, which specifically stated that:

The Community and its member States also require a Yugoslav Republic to commit itself, prior to recognition, to adopt constitutional and political guarantees ensuring that it has no territorial claims towards a neighbouring Community State.[169]

This provision, and subsequent activities, took place in the context of Greek fears that the former Yugoslav Republic of Macedonia, by adopting the name of 'Macedonia', was in fact asserting a territorial claim to parts of northern Greece.[170] The Arbitration Commission in Opinion No. 6 concluded, in the light of statements made by the Minister of

[164] See EPC Declaration on Yugoslavia, EPC Press Release 40/92, and Weller, loc. cit. above (n. 160), p. 593.
[165] See General Assembly Resolutions 46/236, 46/237 and 46/238.
[166] See Opinion No. 10 adopted by the Arbitration Commission on 4 July 1992: 92 ILR 206. This entity, however, claimed to be the continuation of the Socialist Federal Republic of Yugoslavia. The Arbitration Commission held that the Federal Republic of Yugoslavia was a new State and not a continuation of the former State: ibid., and Opinion No. 9, ibid., p. 203. See also Opinion No. 11, 96 ILR 719. Security Council Resolution 757 (1992) referred to 'The former Socialist Federal Republic of Yugoslavia' and noted that 'the claim by the Federal Republic of Yugoslavia (Serbia and Montenegro) to continue automatically the membership of the former Socialist Federal Republic of Yugoslavia in the United Nations has not been generally accepted', while Security Council Resolution 777 (1992) declared that 'the State formerly known as the Socialist Federal Republic of Yugoslavia has ceased to exist' and that 'the Federal Republic of Yugoslavia (Serbia and Montenegro) cannot continue automatically the membership of the former Socialist Federal Republic of Yugoslavia in the United Nations'. See also General Assembly Resolution 47/1 and the *Genocide Convention (Bosnia and Herzegovina* v. *Federal Republic of Yugoslavia (Serbia and Montenegro))* case, *ICJ Reports*, 1993, pp. 3, 13–4.
[167] See Security Council Resolution 817 (1993).
[168] See below, p. 112, with regard to international boundaries and *uti possidetis*.
[169] 92 ILR 174.
[170] See Craven, loc. cit. above (n. 63), and Keesing's Contemporary Archives, *Record of World Events*, 38 (1992), p. 38734.

Foreign Affairs of 'the Republic of Macedonia'[171] and in view of amendments made on 6 January 1992 to the Constitution of 17 November 1991,[172] that:

The Republic of Macedonia has, moreover, renounced all territorial claims of any kind in unambiguous statements binding in international law; that the use of the name 'Macedonia' cannot therefore imply any territorial claim against another State.[173]

The Arbitration Commission decided in Opinion No. 11 that the date upon which Macedonia became a sovereign State was on 17 November 1991 (the date of adoption of the Constitution).[174] The Foreign Ministers of the European Community issued a Declaration on the Former Yugoslav Republic of Macedonia on 2 May 1992, in which it was stated that the European Community and its member States 'are willing to recognize that State as a sovereign and independent State, within its existing borders, and under a name that can be accepted by all parties concerned'.[175]

Thus, and without entering into the question of recognition policy of third States, it is clear that no claim to alter the existing international boundary of the former Yugoslavia was internationally acceptable, so that the continuance of the existing international boundary was upheld. This point was firmly put by the Arbitration Commission in Opinion No. 3, in which it was stressed that:

All external frontiers must be respected in line with the principle stated in the United Nations Charter, in the Declaration on Principles of International Law concerning Friendly Relations and Co-operation among States in accordance with the Charter of the United Nations (General Assembly Resolution 2625 (XXV)) and in the Helsinki Final Act, a principle which also underlies Article 11 of the Vienna Convention of 23 August 1978 on the Succession of States in Respect of Treaties.[176]

---

[171] Renouncing all territorial claims of any kind and giving a formal undertaking to refrain from hostile propaganda against any State: see 92 ILR 184–5.

[172] Article 49 of the Macedonian Constitution of 1991 had provided that the Republic 'cares for the status and rights of those persons belonging to the Macedonian people in neighbouring countries': see Blaustein and Flanz (eds.), *Constitutions of the Countries of the World* (1993), p. 17. Amendment No. I stated that:

'1. The Republic of Macedonia has no territorial claim on neighbouring States.

2. The frontiers of the Republic of Macedonia shall not be altered except in accordance with the Constitution, by agreement between States and on the basis of the generally acknowledged rules of international law': see 92 ILR 186.

[173] Ibid., p. 187.

[174] 96 ILR 718, 721.

[175] 92 ILR 187.

[176] Ibid., 171.

Secondly, the question of those boundaries of the successor States *inter se*, being the former internal administrative divisions of the Socialist Federal Republic of Yugoslavia, raised fundamental issues of international policy. The European Guidelines on Recognition adopted on 16 December 1991 specifically and crucially called for 'respect for the inviolability of *all* frontiers which can only be changed by peaceful means and by common agreement'.[177] The reference was not restricted to existing international boundaries, but was to 'all frontiers'. This logically included all existing frontiers, whether international or internal by provenance, that had become or were to become international boundaries. The issue was specifically addressed by the Arbitration Commission. In Opinion No. 2, adopted on 11 January 1992, the Commission noted, in the context of a question as to whether the Serbian population in Croatia and Bosnia-Herzegovina possessed the right to self-determination, that:

it is well established that, whatever the circumstances, the right to self-determination must not involve changes to existing frontiers at the time of independence (*uti possidetis juris*) except where the States concerned agree otherwise.[178]

The matter was faced more directly in Opinion No. 3, in which the Commission was asked whether the internal boundaries between Serbia and Croatia and Bosnia-Herzegovina respectively constituted frontiers in terms of public international law. The Arbitration Commission, basing itself four-square upon the statement in the *Burkina Faso/Mali* case,[179] declared that:

Except where otherwise agreed, the former boundaries become frontiers protected by international law. This conclusion follows from the principle of respect for the territorial status quo and in particular from the principle of *uti possidetis*. *Uti possidetis*, though initially applied in settling decolonisation issues in America and Africa, is today recognized as a general principle, as stated by the International Court of Justice in its Judgment of 22 December 1986 in the case between *Burkina Faso and Mali* (*Frontier Dispute*, (1986) *ICJ Reports* 554 at 565).[180]

---

[177] Ibid., 174 (emphasis added).
[178] Ibid., 168.
[179] Above, p. 103.
[180] 92 ILR 171. Note further that Article X of the General Framework Agreement for Peace in Bosnia and Herzegovina (the Dayton Peace Agreement of 21 November 1995) provided that 'The Federal Republic of Yugoslavia and the Republic of Bosnia and Herzegovina recognise each other as sovereign independent States within their international borders'. Security Council Resolution 1038 (1996) reaffirmed the independence, sovereignty and territorial integrity of Croatia.

(b) *The former USSR*[181]

The Agreement establishing the Commonwealth of Independent States signed at Minsk on 8 December 1991,[182] linking together all of the former Republics of the USSR apart from the three Baltic States,[183] provided in Article 5 that 'the High Contracting Parties acknowledge and respect each other's territorial integrity and the inviolability of existing borders within the Commonwealth'. This was reinforced by the Alma Ata Declaration of 21 December 1991, signed by eleven of the former Republics (i.e. excluding the Baltic States and Georgia),[184] which referred to the States 'recognizing and respecting each other's territorial integrity and the inviolability of existing borders'. It should also be noted that the parties confirmed their adherence to the UN Charter and the Helsinki Final Act and undertook to 'discharge the international obligations incumbent upon them under treaties and agreements' entered into by the former USSR. While these instruments do not specifically differentiate between *uti possidetis* as turning internal boundaries into international boundaries and territorial integrity as the principle of international law protecting recognized international boundaries, it is clear that the intention was to assert a *uti possidetis* doctrine, not least since this would provide international and regional (as well as crucial national) legitimation for the new borders. In addition, and once established, the classical rules of international law would sustain those borders as existing, unless the relevant parties agreed to a change. Of course, the European Community guidelines on Recognition were intended to apply to the former USSR as well as the former Yugoslavia and thus provide important evidential support for international acceptance of the *uti possidetis* principle in this particular context.[185] The principle of *uti possidetis* derives additional support from subsequent State practice concerning the attempted secession of Abkhazia from the Republic of Georgia[186] and the fighting between Azerbaijan and Armenia

[181] See Müllerson, op. cit. above (n. 160); Sorel and Mehdi, loc. cit. above (n. 115), and Yakemtchouk, 'Les conflits de territoires et de frontières dans les Etats de l'ex-URSS', *Annuaire français de droit international*, 39 (1993), p. 393.

[182] Signed by the Republic of Belarus, the Russian Federation and the Ukraine, *International Legal Materials*, 31 (1992), p. 138. The Protocol of Alma Ata signed on 21 December 1991 added the Republics of Azerbaijan, Armenia, Kazakhstan, Kyrgyzstan, Moldova, Tajikistan, Turkmenistan and Uzbekistan: ibid., p. 147. The Republic of Georgia joined the CIS on 8 October 1993: see *International Legal Materials*, 34 (1995), p. 1298.

[183] As to which see Müllerson, op. cit. above (n. 160), pp. 119 ff.

[184] *International Legal Materials*, 31 (1992), p. 148.

[185] Note also that Article 6 of the Ukraine–Russian Federation Treaty of 19 November 1990 provided that both parties recognized and respected the territorial integrity of the former Russian and Ukrainian Republics of the USSR within the borders existing within the framework of the USSR.

[186] See, for example, Security Council Resolutions 876 (1993); 896 (1994); 906 (1994); 937 (1994); 977 (1995); 993 (1995) and 1036 (1996) reaffirming respect for the sovereignty and territorial integrity of Georgia faced with the attempted Abkhazian secession. See also Yakemtchouk, loc. cit. above (n. 181), pp. 426 ff. See also ibid., pp. 422 ff. with regard to the conflict between Georgia and the South Ossetian region.

concerning the Armenian populated Nagorny Karabakh area of Azerbaijan.[187] In each case, the territorial integrity of the States concerned, successors of the Republics of the former USSR, was reaffirmed in circumstances demonstrating that the definition of the territory concerned was that of the former Republic.

(c) *The former Czechoslovakia*[188]

On 1 January 1993, the Czech and Slovak Federal Republic ceased to exist and was succeeded by two new States, the Czech Republic and Slovakia. The frontiers of the former State had been established by the Peace Treaties of 1919.[189] By the Treaty on the General Delimitation of the Common State Frontiers of 29 October 1992, the boundary between the two new States was to be the administrative border existing between the Czech and Slovak parts of the former State.

The logic of this is clear. The essence of the adoption of the principle of *uti possidetis*, first in Latin America and then in Africa, was to minimize threats to peace and security, whether internal, regional or international, by establishing an acceptable rule of the appropriate territorial framework for the creation of new States and thus entrenching, at least, territorial stability at that critical moment. Precisely the same impulse can be taken to lie behind the recognition of the principle outside the purely colonial context where the same dangers resulting from the break-up of existing States are evident. There is little to suggest that the hazards resulting from the creation of new States out of parts or all of existing States and the perils of widespread disruption and ethnic violence are restricted to the traditional colonial situation or to the continents of Latin America and Africa. The same broad reasons impelling the establishment of the principle of *uti possidetis* as a specific regional norm, have led to the establishment of that principle as a general principle in international law.

2. *International and Administrative Boundaries*

The boundaries in question for a new State may be either former international boundaries or former internal, administrative boundaries. The situation is different with regard to each of them.

---

[187] See Security Council Resolutions 822 (1993); 853 (1993); 874 (1993) and 884 (1993) reaffirming respect for the sovereignty and territorial integrity of all States in the region including Azerbaijan and reaffirming also the inviolability of international borders and the inadmissibility of the use of force for the acquisition of territory. See also Yakemtchouk, loc. cit. above (n. 181), pp. 411 ff.

[188] See Malenovsky, 'Problèmes juridiques liées à la partition de la Tchécoslovaquie, y compris tracé de la frontière', *Annuaire français de droit international*, 39 (1993), p. 305.

[189] The Treaty of Versailles with Germany, the Treaty of St Germain with Austria, the Treaty of Trianon with Hungary and the Treaties of Versailles and Sèvres with Poland.

(a) *International boundaries*

International boundaries are established in brief and simple terms in order to mark the line beyond which the sovereignty and territorial jurisdiction of one international legal person turns into the sovereignty and territorial jurisdiction of another. Such boundaries arise by virtue of consent and are usually enshrined in international treaties, whether bilateral or multilateral, including peace treaties.[190] They are intended to create a permanent line, fixed both geographically and legally, with full effect within the international system. They constitute factual realities with important juridical consequences in the field of the exercise of sovereign authority and international responsibility.

In the case of those boundaries of a new State that were formerly an international boundary and established by international treaty, such boundaries *ipso facto* became objectivized at the time of the treaty in question and continue in time, irrespective of any changes of sovereignty on either side of the international line so drawn. This is also the case where the international boundary has become internationally recognized otherwise than by treaty, for example by way of recognition or acquiescence. The rules of State succession ensure that the lines in question simply continue in force and bind the new State. After all, in this situation, the interests and rights of at least two sovereigns are engaged and any unilateral change would invariably impact upon, and may constitute a violation of, the recognized rights of the other. An international boundary between colonial or other non-independent territories under the sovereignty of different States, or between an independent State and a colony or non-independent territory, established or recognized under the terms of an international treaty or otherwise under the rules of international law, is binding as from the coming into effect of that instrument and continues in effect until such time as the boundary is modified (if ever) by the consent of the parties concerned.

The argument was put forward by Guinea-Bissau in the *Guinea-Bissau* v. *Senegal* arbitration that the *uti possidetis* principle 'should only apply to treaties concluded a long way back', so that treaties concluded by the colonial powers once 'the process of liberation has begun' would be null and void if they related to 'essential elements of the right of peoples to self-determination'.[191] The Tribunal did not accept this approach and declared that

the agreements relating to boundaries signed by a colonial State before the process of liberation had an international impact do not have to fulfil any special condition of antecedence for them to be validly invoked against the successor State. Guinea-Bissau has not been able to establish in the course of the present

---

[190] See, for example, the view of the Committee of Jurists in the Aaland Islands dispute that boundaries established as part of a peace settlement create 'true objective law': *League of Nations Official Journal, Special Supplement* No. 3 (October 1920), p. 17.

[191] 83 ILR 38.

arbitration the existence of any norm of international law imposing such a condition.[192]

The basic principle must be correct, although the formulation by the Tribunal is perhaps rather unfortunate with regard to the phrase 'before the process of liberation had an international impact', since that might be interpreted to mean that once such a process had commenced then boundary agreements might not benefit from the rule. No doubt, were a colonial power on the eve of independence to seek without the clear consent of the population of the territory to alter the territorial configuration of the area concerned, this would have a serious political impact and would raise questions in the context of the application of the principle of self-determination, but any international legal repercussions would have to be carefully assessed, and there is little practice to suggest an 'exclusion zone' of time around the date of independence with regard to the behaviour of the legitimate sovereign. While it is clear that colonial territories have a 'separate and distinct status', they do not possess separate sovereignty, and the line that is protected is that in existence at the moment of independence not that existing at some unclear point in the past. Any other approach would import considerable instability into an already sensitive political situation. In any event, the better interpretation of the phrase 'before the process of liberation had an international impact' used by the Tribunal simply means before the process of liberation of the territory in question had been completed in accordance with international criteria and the territory had thus acquired independence.

Once an international boundary has been established or recognized by a treaty, the boundary provisions of that treaty take on a life of their own and continue irrespective of the status of the treaty itself. This principle is founded upon the objectivization of boundary treaties as manifested in the rules of State succession and supported by considerations of *nemo dat quod non habet* and by the recognized parameters of the norm of *rebus sic stantibus*. It may also be seen as falling under the umbrella of the principle of the stability of boundaries or what the Chamber of the International Court termed the 'essential requirement of stability'.[193]

The International Court certainly took this view in the *Libya/Chad* case. Having come to the conclusion that the 1955 Franco-Libyan Treaty 'must . . . be taken to have determined a permanent frontier'[194] and that nothing in the Treaty indicated that the boundary agreed was to be provisional or temporary, it followed that 'the establishment of this boundary is a fact which, from the outset, has had a legal life of its own,

---

[192] Ibid., 39.

[193] *ICJ Reports*, 1986, p. 567.

[194] *ICJ Reports*, 1994, p. 37. It should be noted that the debate with regard to the 1955 Treaty between the parties concerned the scope and meaning of the treaty itself. Libya was itself a party to this treaty and thus for it questions of State succession did not arise.

independently of the fate of the 1955 Treaty. Once agreed, the boundary stands.'[195] Indeed, the Court emphasized that the Treaty 'completely determined the boundary between Libya and Chad'.[196]

The fact that the new State succeeds to the internationally recognized boundary is well attested by State practice. In the *Tunisia/Libya* case, the Court examined the land boundary between the two States in the context of establishing the starting-point of the maritime boundary. It was noted that the Convention of 19 May 1910 between the Bey of Tunis and the Emperor of the Ottomans established the boundary as between the Regency of Tunis (a French protectorate) and the Vilayet of Tripoli (under the sovereignty of the Ottoman Empire, and which was ceded to Italy in 1911). This line became the boundary between the independent States of Libya and Tunisia. The Court emphasized that the 1910 Convention 'definitely established the land frontier between the two countries' and exemplified the principle declared in the 1964 Cairo Resolution of the OAU, according to which all member States pledged themselves to respect the borders existing on their achievement of national independence. The Court stated that 'this rule of continuity *ipso jure* of boundary and territorial treaties was later embodied in the 1978 Convention on Succession of States in respect of Treaties'.[197] In addition, the Chamber of the Court in the *Burkina Faso/Mali* case emphasized that 'there is no doubt that the obligation to respect pre-existing international boundaries in the event of a State succession derives from a general rule of international law, whether or not the rule is expressed in the formula *uti possidetis*'.[198]

The principle of the continuity of international boundaries extends beyond the *uti possidetis* concept. The latter is concerned only with the territorial aspects of the process of transition to independence of a new State; it does not apply where, for example, the rearrangements taking place do not result in the creation of a new State. However, the principle of the continuity of international boundaries will apply in this situation. For example, in the process of German unification (where in legal terms the Federal Republic of Germany simply extended its territorial jurisdiction and sovereignty over the area of the former German Democratic Republic so that no new State was created), it was clearly provided that the former took over the existing territory of the latter. Article 1(1) of the Unification Treaty[199] provided that:

Upon the accession of the German Democratic Republic to the Federal

[195] Ibid.
[196] Ibid., p. 40.
[197] *ICJ Reports*, 1982, pp. 18, 65–6.
[198] *ICJ Reports*, 1986, pp. 554, 566.
[199] Treaty on the Establishment of German Unity between the Federal Republic of Germany and the German Democratic Republic, 31 August 1991, *International Legal Materials*, 30 (1991), p. 457.

Republic of Germany . . . the Länder of Brandenburg, Mecklenburg-Western Pomerania, Saxony, Saxony-Anhalt and Thuringia shall become Länder of the Federal Republic of Germany. The establishment of these Länder and their boundaries shall be governed by the provisions of the Constitutional Act of 22 July 1990.

As far as the eastern boundary of the former German Democratic Republic was concerned, this had been established on the Oder-Neisse line by the Four Allied Powers (UK, USA, USSR and France) at the Conference of Potsdam 1945, although the finality of this was questioned.[200] The German Democratic Republic and Poland signed a treaty on 6 July 1950 agreeing that this line constituted 'the State frontier between Germany and Poland'.[201] However, the Four Allied Powers were not parties to this so that its ultimate legal value was questionable. In the Treaty of 12 August 1970 between the USSR and the Federal Republic of Germany, both parties declared that the existing frontiers of all States in Europe were inviolable, 'including the Oder-Neisse line which forms the western frontier of the People's Republic of Poland'.[202] In the Treaty between the Federal Republic of Germany and Poland of 7 December 1970,[203] it was accepted by both parties that the Oder-Neisse line constituted the western State frontier of Poland. The inviolability of the existing borders was confirmed, and absolute respect was pledged for the territorial integrity of both States.[204] In the Treaty on the Final Settlement with respect to Germany between the US, the UK, France, the USSR, and the Federal Republic of Germany and the German Democratic Republic of 12 September 1990, the Four Powers terminated their rights and responsibilities with regard to Berlin and Germany as a whole. Article 1(1) provided clearly that:

---

[200] This arrangement was 'pending the final determination of Poland's western frontier', and the area in question was to be 'under the administration of the Polish state': see Cmnd. 1552, Doc. no. 13, p. 57, para. VIII. Poland took the view that it obtained sovereignty over the area, not least because the Potsdam Conference referred to the territories as 'former German territories' and authorized the expulsion of Germans from the area in question: ibid., and para. XII, and see *L and JJ* v. *Polish State Railways*, 24 ILR 77. See also the *Federal Republic of Germany/German Democratic Republic* case, 78 ILR 150, and R. Piotrowicz, 'The Polish-German Frontier in International Law: The Final Solution', this *Year Book*, 63 (1993), p. 367. Note in particular Bernhardt (ed.), *Encyclopedia of Public International Law*, vol. 2 (1995), pp. 561 ff.

[201] *UN Treaty Series*, vol. 319, p. 93.

[202] See *International Legal Materials*, 9 (1970), p. 1026.

[203] Treaty concerning the Basis for Normalising Relations, *International Legal Materials*, 10 (1971), p. 127. The Treaty was ratified by the Federal Republic of Germany in 1972. The accompanying Resolution in the Bundestag of 17 May 1972 appeared to suggest that the Treaty did not create a legal basis for existing frontiers, although it was noted that 'the treaties [i.e. including the 1970 Treaty with the USSR] proceed from the frontiers as actually existing today, the unilateral alteration of which they exclude'. See, for a detailed analysis of this and the Treaty of 7 December 1970, Piotrowicz, loc. cit. above (n. 200), pp. 372 ff. See also Skubiszewski, 'Poland's Western Frontier and the 1970 Treaties', *American Journal of International Law*, 67 (1973), p. 23, and Frowein, 'Legal Problems of the German Ostpolitik', *International and Comparative Law Quarterly*, 23 (1974), p. 105.

[204] Article 1(2) and (3).

The united Germany shall comprise the territory of the Federal Republic of Germany, the German Democratic Republic and the whole of Berlin. Its external borders shall be the borders of the Federal Republic of Germany and the German Democratic Republic.

Germany and Poland agreed to recognize 'the existing border between them' in the Treaty of 14 November 1990 between them[205] in accordance with Article 1(2) of the Treaty on Final Settlement.[206]

It is instructive to note that Article 1(1) concludes that 'the confirmation of the definitive nature of the borders of the united Germany is an essential element of the peaceful order in Europe'.

(b) *Administrative boundaries*

Internal or administrative boundaries are boundaries established by municipal law in order to divide parts of the same sovereign territory for purely domestic purposes.[207] Such administrative divisions may alter widely over time. To take one example, the Sudan was created in 1890 as an administrative entity within French West Africa, but nine years later was dismembered and distributed amongst its neighbours. In 1902 the territory of Sénégambie and Niger was created. In 1904 the western part was renamed the French Sudan. In 1919 the *cercles* of Gaoua, Bobo-Dioulasso, Dédougou, Ouagadougou, Dori and Fada N'Gourma, part of Upper Senegal and Niger, were established as the separate colony of Upper Volta. In 1920, the remaining colonies of Upper Senegal and Niger were termed French Sudan and in 1922, Niger became an independent colony. The French Sudan achieved independence as the Federation of Mali in 1960. The decree of 1 March 1919 creating Upper Volta was rescinded in 1932 and the territory was incorporated in whole or in part into Niger and into French Sudan or the Ivory Coast. In 1947, Upper Volta was reconstituted and as such became independent in 1960,

---

[205] Agreement in relation to Ratification of the Border between them, *International Legal Materials*, 31 (1992), p. 1292. The boundary is laid down by reference to the agreement of 6 July 1950 between the German Democratic Republic and Poland and subsequent acts and agreements of 1951 and 1989 (which dealt with the maritime boundary) between these parties, and the agreement of 7 December 1970 between the Federal Republic of Germany and Poland.

[206] See also Schreuer, 'The Legal Status of the Polish Boundaries', in Vierdag, Fitzmaurice and Lefeber (eds.), *The Changing Political Structure of Europe* (1991), p. 79; Frowein, 'Germany Reunited', *Zeitschrift für ausländisches öffentliches Recht und Völkerrecht*, 51 (1991), p. 333, and 'Reunification of Germany', *American Journal of International Law*, 86 (1992), p. 152, and Czaplinski, 'The New Polish-German Treaties and the Changing Political Structure of Europe', ibid., p. 163.

[207] Note that such administrative lines established by one colonial power may also relate to divisions between colonies and mandates or trust territories. In such cases, consideration must be given to the nature of such arrangements, which created a special status *erga omnes*, so that any modification of boundaries required League or UN approval depending always upon the express terms of the mandate or trust agreement: see, for example, the *International Status of South West Africa* case, *ICJ Reports*, 1950, p. 128; Marston, 'Termination of Trusteeship', *International and Comparative Law Quarterly*, 18 (1969), p. 1. Administrative lines may also be established with regard to protectorates, but here it seems that the approval of the protected State is required: see the *Dubai/Sharjah* case, 91 ILR 543, 584–5.

becoming Burkina Faso in 1984.[208] While this is an extreme example,[209] it does serve to illustrate the fact that administrative boundaries as such are not intended to constitute permanent boundaries. Nor are they boundaries protected as such under international law. They are created and exist solely under municipal law.

Administrative boundaries may also be of various kinds. As the Chamber of the International Court noted in the *El Salvador/Honduras* case with regard to the former Spanish South American colonies, 'there were administrative boundaries of different kinds or degrees'.[210] The Chamber noted, for example, 'provinces' (a term itself with varying meanings over time), *Alcaldías Mayores*, *Corregimientos*, *Intendencias*, the territorial jurisdiction of the higher courts (*Audencias*), Captaincies-General and Vice-Royalties. In addition, the jurisdictions of general administrative bodies did not always coincide with those of particular or special jurisdictions, such as military commands. There were also ecclesiastical jurisdictions. Thus a range of differing boundaries were superimposed on one another in a veritable mosaic, varying in time and space. And as the Chamber pointed out significantly, 'it has to be remembered that no question of international boundaries could ever have occurred to the minds of those servants of the Spanish Crown who established administrative boundaries'.[211]

Thus, it must be accepted that the effect of the application of the principle of *uti possidetis* is to turn administrative boundaries into international boundaries in the context of the independence process and so invest those administrative boundaries with a significance and a purpose that they were never intended to have.[212] The Court in the *Dubai/Sharjah* case put this point clearly:

In the view of the Court one cannot attribute the same value to a boundary which has been settled under a treaty, or as the result of an arbitral or judicial proceeding, in which independent interested Parties have had a full opportunity to present their arguments, as to a boundary which has been established by way of an administrative decision emanating from an authority which could have failed to take account of the Parties' views and arising in a situation of inherent inequality. In the first hypothesis, except in a case of nullity, the principles of *pacta sunt servanda* or of *res judicata* could be invoked to prevent the boundary so settled being called again into question. In the second hypothesis, the

[208] Ibid., p. 569.
[209] But see Shaw, op. cit. above (n. 1), pp. 50 ff.
[210] *ICJ Reports*, 1992, p. 387.
[211] Ibid., pp. 387–8.
[212] Ibid., p. 388.

boundary would have been established in the majority of cases, in the interests of the administering authority, on the basis of other than legal criteria, and according to the needs of a particular political or economic context.[213]

Despite the clear and undeniable differences between international and administrative boundaries, the effect of *uti possidetis* is to turn the latter into the former. However, not all administrative boundaries turn into international boundaries. The problem is to determine in international law which administrative boundaries have this capacity.

The first thing to note for *uti possidetis* in the colonial context is that what count are the administrative units established by the colonial powers and not any pre-existing divisions. The Chamber noted in the *El Salvador/Honduras* case that 'it was the administrative boundaries between Spanish colonial administrative units, not the boundaries between Indian settlements as such, that were transformed, by the operation of the *uti possidetis juris*, into international boundaries in 1821'.[214] The temporal dimension is also crucial here. In other words, it is the administrative lines existing at a particular moment in time that may be transformed into international lines.[215] In some cases, the existing administrative line may have reflected an earlier international boundary, which then resumes its former status.[216]

In the case of Federal States, the administrative divisions that count are the lines between the federal components of the former State. Such has been the case with regard to the former Yugoslavia and the former USSR. In the former situation, recognition was given by the European Community and its member States and by other States and the United Nations in the framework of membership to the former Republics of that State within the administrative boundaries as existing at the time that the former Yugoslavia began to dissolve. No recognition was given to the Krajina region of Croatia inhabited, until hostilities in 1995, overwhelmingly by Serbs. In fact, the Arbitration Commission specifically noted in Opinion No. 2 that while the Serb populations in Croatia and Bosnia-Herzegovina were entitled to minority rights, including the right to identity and the right to choose their nationality, this did not extend to 'changes to existing frontiers at the time of independence' unless the

---

[213] 91 ILR 543, 579.

[214] *ICJ Reports*, 1992, p. 393.

[215] See below, p. 129.

[216] See, for example, with regard to Eritrea, Goy, loc. cit. above (n. 151), p. 350. The former international boundary between Eritrea and Ethiopia had been established by the Treaties of 10 July 1900 and 16 May 1908. See also Brownlie, *African Boundaries* (1979), p. 9.

States concerned otherwise agreed.[217] Again, claims by the majority Russian population in the Crimea (part of the Ukraine) to join the Russian Federation or to independence have not been accepted.[218]

Whether internal lines other than clear divisions between federal units outside the colonial situation have the capacity to become international boundaries is a question that can only truly be resolved within the context of specific situations. If the relevant parties within the context of a dismemberment of an existing State wish a particular administrative line of little real import to become an international boundary,[219] then there is nothing in international law to prevent this. Where the matter is contested, then much will turn upon the traditional processes of State creation, such as effectiveness and third party recognition or acquiescence. All that can be stated is that current practice in Europe demonstrates that there is a presumption in favour of federal units constituting the defined territory of new States.[220] The validity in this context of other administrative boundaries would depend upon the circumstances.

3. *Self-Determination, Territorial Integrity and* Uti Possidetis

It is important to differentiate the principles of self-determination, *uti possidetis* and territorial integrity. First mentioned in general terms in

[217] 92 ILR 167, 168.

[218] See, for example, Yakemtchouk, loc. cit. above (n. 181), pp. 398 ff. See also Lowe and Warbrick, 'Current Developments: Public International Law—Recognition of States', *International and Comparative Law Quarterly*, 41 (1991), pp. 473, 478. Similarly calls for independence by, for instance, Abhazia and South Ossetia in the Republic of Georgia and Chechnya in the Russian Federation have gone unsupported internationally: Yakemtchouk, loc. cit. above (n. 181), pp. 409 ff. On the contrary, the Security Council has adopted resolutions specifically reaffirming respect for the sovereignty and territorial integrity of Georgia, Azerbaijan and all the States in the region: see, for example, Security Council Resolutions 822 (1993); 853 (1993); 876 (1993); 884 (1993) and 896 (1994).

[219] See, for example, the legislative process whereby British India was partitioned into the independent States of India and Pakistan: see sections 2–4 of the Indian Independence Act of 1947. This provided that Pakistan was to consist of Sindh, British Baluchistan, the North-West Frontier Province, the Moslem majority areas of Punjab and Bengal and the Moslem majority areas of the district of Sylhet in the Province of Assam. The Provinces of Punjab and Bengal were divided into two each (East and West Punjab and East and West Bengal), while provision was made for the district of Sylhet to form part of the new Province of East Bengal. The Act also provided for the creation of Boundary Commissions.

[220] Note also that the constitutional status of such federal units, including their capacity, is of weight in the context of creation of statehood. See, for example, Arbitration Commission Opinion No. 3, where it was stated that 'the principle [of *uti possidetis*] applies all the more readily to the Republics since the second and fourth paragraphs of Article 5 of the Constitution of the SFRY [the Socialist Federal Republic of Yugoslavia] stipulated that the Republics' territories and boundaries could not be altered without their consent': 92 ILR 170, 172. See also Opinion No. 8, ibid., p. 194. See further Shaw, 'Peoples, Territorialism and Boundaries', *European Journal of International Law*, 8 (1997).

Articles 1(2) and 55 of the UN Charter, the principle of self-determination[221] proclaims that all peoples may 'freely determine their political status and freely pursue their economic, social and cultural development'.[222] The 1970 Declaration on Principles of International Law concerning Friendly Relations,[223] which can be regarded as constituting an authoritative interpretation of the seven Charter provisions it expounds, states *inter alia* that 'by virtue of the principle of equal rights and self-determination of peoples enshrined in the Charter of the United Nations, all peoples have the right freely to determine . . . their political status', while all States are under the duty to respect this right in accordance with the Charter.[224] The principle of self-determination evolved as the legal engine driving the process of decolonization. It constituted a vital norm, both obligating colonial powers to grant independence (or other acceptable form of political status) and endowing the colonial territory with a special status and consequently international legitimation.

The principle has also obtained judicial support. In the *Namibia* case, the International Court emphasized that 'the subsequent development of international law in regard to non-self-governing territories as enshrined in the Charter of the United Nations made the principle of self-determination applicable to all of them'.[225] This was reaffirmed in the *Western Sahara* case.[226] The Court moved one step further in the *East Timor (Portugal v. Australia)* case,[227] when it declared that 'Portugal's assertion that the right of peoples to self-determination, as it evolved from the Charter and from United Nations practice, has an *erga omnes* character, is irreproachable'. The Court emphasized that the right of peoples to self-determination was 'one of the essential principles of

---

[221] See in general Ofuatey-Kodjoe, 'Self Determination', in Schachter and Joyner (eds.), *United Nations Legal Order* (1995), vol. 1, p. 349; Umozurike, *Self-Determination in International Law* (1972); Rigo-Sureda, *The Evolution of the Right of Self-Determination* (1973); Shukri, *The Concept of Self-Determination in the United Nations* (1967); Pomerance, *Self-Determination in Law and Practice* (1982); Shaw, op. cit. above (n. 1), pp. 59–144; Tomuschat (ed.), *Modern Law of Self-Determination* (1993); Cassese, *Self-Determination of Peoples* (1995); Franck, *Fairness in International Law and Institutions* (1995), chapter 5; Higgins, op. cit. above (n. 95), chapter 7; Brölmann, Lefeber and Zieck (eds.), *Peoples and Minorities in International Law* (1993), and Koskenniemi, 'National Self-Determination Today: Problems of Legal Theory and Practice', *International and Comparative Law Quarterly*, 43 (1994), p. 241.

[222] See General Assembly Resolution 1514 (XV), the Declaration on the Granting of Independence to Colonial Countries and Peoples, adopted in 1960, and common Article 1 of the International Covenant on Civil and Political Rights 1966 and the International Covenant on Economic, Social and Cultural Rights 1966. See also Brownlie, *Principles of Public International Law* (4th edn., 1990), p. 595, and Asamoah, *The Legal Significance of the Declarations of the General Assembly of the United Nations* (1966), pp. 177–85.

[223] General Assembly Resolution 2625 (XXV).

[224] See Rosenstock, 'The Declaration of Principles of International Law Concerning Friendly Relations', *American Journal of International Law*, 65 (1971), pp. 111 and 115.

[225] *ICJ Reports*, 1971, pp. 16, 31.

[226] *ICJ Reports*, 1975, pp. 12, 31. See also the *Burkina Faso/Mali* case, *ICJ Reports*, 1986, pp. 554, 567, and the *Guinea-Bissau v. Senegal* case, 83 ILR 1, 24 ff.

[227] *ICJ Reports*, 1995, pp. 90, 102.

contemporary international law'.[228] These cases all concerned in one way or another decolonization situations. But the real question today is whether the principle of self-determination has an application beyond colonial territories and, if so, what the content of that principle may be. Practice demonstrates that self-determination has not been interpreted to mean that any group defining itself as such can decide for itself its own political status up to and including secession from an already independent State.[229] After all, the very UN instruments constituting the foundation of the development of self-determination also clearly opposed the partial or total disruption of the national unity and territorial integrity of States.[230] Regional instruments also emphasized the importance of the territorial integrity of States. Principle VIII of the Helsinki Final Act, for instance, noted that:

> The participating States will respect the equal rights of peoples and their right to self-determination, acting at all times in conformity with the purposes and principles of the Charter of the United Nations and with the relevant norms of international law, including those relating to territorial integrity of States.[231]

In addition, the Charter of Paris for a New Europe adopted by the Heads of State and Government of the Conference on Security and Co-operation in Europe in 1990 declared that the participating States 'reaffirm the equal rights of peoples and their right to self-determination in conformity with the Charter of the United Nations and with the relevant norms of international law, including those relating to territorial integrity of States'.[232]

In effect, the principle of self-determination in so far as it relates to existing independent States that do not possess overseas colonies has

[228] Ibid.

[229] See, for example, Ofuatey-Kodjoe, loc. cit. above (n. 221), p. 385; Hannum, *Autonomy, Sovereignty and Self-Determination* (1990), p. 469; Higgins, op. cit. above (n. 221), p. 121; Franck, op. cit. above (n. 221), pp. 149 ff., and Cassese, op. cit. above (n. 221), p. 122. Note, for example, the view of the UN Secretary-General that 'as an international organisation, the United Nations has never accepted and does not accept and I do not believe it will ever accept the principle of secession of a part of a member State': *UN Monthly Chronicle* (February 1970), p. 36, and see also the comment by the Minister of State, Foreign and Commonwealth Office, that 'it has been widely accepted at the United Nations that the right of self-determination does not give every distinct group or territorial sub-division within a State the right to secede from it and thereby dismember the territorial integrity or political unity of sovereign independent States': this *Year Book*, 54 (1983), p. 409.

[230] See, for example, paragraph 6 of the Declaration on the Granting of Independence to Colonial Countries and Peoples (General Assembly Resolution 1514 (XV) 1960) and the Declaration on Principles of International Law concerning Friendly Relations (General Assembly Resolution 2625 (XXV) 1970). Note also that the UN has adopted resolutions reaffirming the territorial integrity of States and criticizing secessionist activities: see, for example, Security Council Resolutions S/5002 (1961); 716 (1991) and the resolutions with regard to the Caucasian States noted above at note 186.

[231] Principle IV on the Territorial Integrity of States underlined respect for this principle, noting that the participating States 'will refrain from any action inconsistent with the purposes and principles of the Charter of the United Nations against the territorial integrity, political independence or the unity of any participating State': see Cmnd. 6198 (1975), pp. 3 and 5.

[232] See also Article III [3] of the OAU Charter, 1963.

been reoriented to focus upon internal human rights questions.[233] Its use, however, as a crucial principle of collective human rights[234] has been particularly analysed by the UN Human Rights Committee, established under the International Covenant on Civil and Political Rights 1966, in interpreting Article 1 of that instrument.[235] In its General Comment on Self-Determination adopted in 1984,[236] the Committee emphasized that the realization of the right was 'an essential condition for the effective guarantee and observance of individual human rights'.[237] The Committee takes the view, as Higgins has noted,[238] that 'external self-determination requires a State to take action in its foreign policy consistent with the attainment of self-determination in the remaining areas of colonial or racist occupation. But internal self-determination is directed to their own peoples.' In the context of the significance of the principle of self-determination within independent States, the Committee has encouraged States parties to provide in their reports details about participation in social and political structures,[239] and in engaging in dialogue with representatives of States parties, questions are regularly posed as to how political institutions operate and how the people of the State concerned participate in the governance of their State.[240] This necessarily links in

[233] The clause in the 1970 Declaration on Principles of International Law concerning Friendly Relations stating that nothing in the section on self-determination shall be construed as authorizing or encouraging the dismembering or impairing of the territorial integrity of States conducting themselves in compliance with the principle of self-determination 'as described above and thus possessed of a government representing the whole people belonging to the territory without distinction as to race, creed or colour' may be seen, first, as establishing the primacy of the principle of territorial integrity and, secondly, as indicating the content of self-determination within the territory. Whether it also can be seen as offering legitimacy to secession from an independent State in exceptional circumstances is the subject of much debate. Cassese, for example, concludes that 'a racial or religious group may attempt secession, a form of external self-determination, when it is apparent that internal self-determination is absolutely beyond reach. Extreme and unremitting persecution and the lack of any reasonable prospect for peaceful challenge may make secession legitimate': op. cit. above (n. 221), p. 120. See also Rosenstock, 'The Declaration on Principles of International Law', *American Journal of International Law*, 65 (1971), pp. 713, 732. It would appear that practice demonstrating the successful application of even this modest proposition is lacking.

[234] Note Brownlie's view that the principle of self-determination has a core of reasonable certainty and that this consists in 'the right of a community which has a distinct character to have this character reflected in the institutions of government under which it lives': 'The Rights of Peoples in International Law', in Crawford (ed.), *The Rights of Peoples* (1988), pp. 1, 5.

[235] See in particular McGoldrick, *The Human Rights Committee* (1994), chapter 5; Cassese, op. cit. above (n. 221), pp. 59 ff., and Nowak, *UN Covenant on Civil and Political Rights, CCPR Commentary* (1993), part 1.

[236] General Comment 12: see HRI/GEN/1/Rev. 1, p. 12 (1994).

[237] The principle is seen as a collective one and not one that individuals could seek to enforce through the individual petition procedures provided in the First Optional Protocol to the Covenant. See the *Kitok* case, Report of the Human Rights Committee, A/43/40, pp. 221, 228; the *Lubicon Lake Band* case, A/45/40, vol. 2, pp. 1, 27; *EP v. Colombia*, A/45/40, vol. 2, pp. 184, 187, and *RL v. Canada*, A/47/40, pp. 358, 365.

[238] 'Postmodern Tribalism and the Right to Secession', in *Peoples and Minorities in International Law*, op. cit. above (n. 221), p. 31.

[239] See, e.g., the Report of Colombia, CCPR/C/64/Add.3, pp. 9 ff. (1991).

[240] See, e.g., with regard to Canada, A/46/40, p. 12. See also A/45/40, pp. 120–1, with regard to Zaire.

with consideration of other articles of the Covenant concerning, for example, freedom of expression (Article 19), freedom of assembly (Article 21), freedom of association (Article 22) and the right to take part in the conduct of public affairs and to vote (Article 25). The right of self-determination provides the overall framework for the consideration of the principles relating to democratic governance.[241]

The principle of self-determination, therefore, applies beyond the colonial context, but within the territorial framework of independent States. It cannot be utilized as a legal tool for the dismantling of sovereign States.[242]

The relationship between self-determination and *uti possidetis* is clearly a crucial one for the international community. The former principle in general political terms constitutes one form of legitimacy for groups to acquire independence. It offers ethnic groups, for example, a principle of collective action. However, in terms of its definition in international law as relating to the right to establish a new State, it has been considerably constrained. It has in fact been restricted as a legal principle to the colonial situation. Self-determination does not provide groups outside of this context with the legal right to secede from existing independent States and create a new State. *Uti possidetis* provides an alternative basis of legitimation for independence. This focuses upon territoriality rather than upon personal attributes, such as ethnicity or religion or historic ties. The relationship between these two principles was discussed by the Chamber of the International Court in the *Burkina Faso/Mali* case.[243] The Court noted that at first sight *uti possidetis* conflicted with the right of peoples to self-determination.[244] However, it was emphasized that *uti possidetis* constituted a general principle, whose purpose was to prevent the independence and stability of new States from being endangered by fratricidal struggles provoked by the challenging of frontiers. This 'essential requirement of stability in order to

[241] See Franck, 'The Emerging Right to Democratic Governance', *American Journal of International Law*, 86 (1992), p. 46, and Thornberry, 'The Democratic or Internal Aspect of Self-Determination', in *Modern Law of Self-Determination*, op. cit. above (n. 221), p. 101.

[242] Note that UN resolutions calling for self-determination within South Africa focused upon the *apartheid* system and demanded majority rule based upon universal suffrage: see General Assembly Resolutions 2396 (XXIII) and 2671 (XXV) and Security Council Resolutions 282 (1970); 311 (1972) and 418 (1977). Note in particular that the establishment by South Africa of bantustans was seen as a violation of the principle of self-determination and prejudicial to the territorial integrity of the State and the unity of its people: see General Assembly Resolutions 2671 (XXV); 2775E (XXVI); 2923E (XXVII); 3151G (XXVIII); 3324E (XXIX) and 3411G (XXX). References to self-determination in UN resolutions have also been made with regard to Palestine: see, for example, General Assembly Resolutions 2672C (XXV) and 3236 (XXIX). However, such references need to be seen in the context of the military occupation by Israel of parts of the former British mandate of Palestine following the 1967 War and in the context of the recognition of Israel by the United Nations and most members of the international community. Self-determination for the Palestinians, therefore, cannot be taken to mean dismemberment of the State of Israel: see Cassese, op. cit. above (n. 221), p. 240.

[243] *ICJ Reports*, 1986, p. 554.

[244] Ibid., p. 567.

survive, to develop and gradually to consolidate their independence in all fields' had therefore induced African States 'judiciously to consent to the respecting of colonial borders, and to take account of it in the interpretation of the principle of self-determination of peoples'.[245] In other words, where the situation was such that a conflict appeared between the two principles, then that of *uti possidetis* would have precedence, and that for reasons relating to stability.

The point was underlined by the Arbitration Commission of the Conference on Yugoslavia, which emphasized in Opinion No. 2 that 'it is well established that, whatever the circumstances, the right to self-determination must not involve changes to existing frontiers at the time of independence (*uti possidetis juris*) except where the States concerned agree otherwise'.[246] The Yugoslav situation well illustrates the dominance of the territorial over the personal basis for independence.[247]

In fact, the conflict between the two principles in the field of international law is more apparent than real.[248] This is because self-determination has been interpreted in a way which restricts its full operation (in terms of allowing the target group the full choice of political status up to and including independence) to carefully constrained situations. It is limited to the colonial situation in this sense. Beyond this point, self-determination is transmuted into a principle relating to the internal governance of independent States.

The principle of territorial integrity sustains the territorial definition of sovereign independent States. The International Court in the *Corfu Channel* case declared that 'between independent States, respect for territorial sovereignty is an essential foundation of international relations'.[249] A variety of international norms protect the territorial integrity of States.[250] It is therefore uncontroversial to underline that the territorial delineation of independent States is safeguarded by the rules of international law. It would, however, be incorrect simply to fuse together the notions of territorial integrity and *uti possidetis*.[251] The former principle protects the territorial definition of independent States, while the latter constitutes a principle explaining how the territorial definition of States has arisen in particular situations. It is a principle of transition linked to the transmission of sovereignty from one entity to another and provides a bridging mechanism. Thus, once a new State has come into

---

[245] Ibid.

[246] 92 ILR 167, 168.

[247] See above, p. 106.

[248] But see Franck, op. cit. above (n. 221), pp. 146 ff.

[249] *ICJ Reports*, 1949, p. 35. See also the *Nicaragua v. US* case, *ICJ Reports*, 1986, p. 3. See also Bowett, *Self-Defence in International Law* (1958), p. 29.

[250] See, for example, Article 2(4) of the UN Charter; Article 11 of the Montevideo Convention on the Rights and Duties of States, 1933; Article 17 of the Charter of the Organization of American States, 1948; Article 3 of the OAU Charter, 1963, and Principles III and IV of the Helsinki Final Act, 1975.

[251] See, for example, Franck, op. cit. above (n. 221), p. 146.

existence, territorially defined in the light of *uti possidetis*, its territory as an independent State is protected by virtue of the principle of territorial integrity of States.

4. *The Essence of* Uti Possidetis

If *uti possidetis* can now be accepted as a rule of international law, as appears clearly to be the case, one needs to turn to the question of its essential meaning. The Chamber considered this in the *Burkina Faso/Mali* case and came to the following conclusion:

the essence of the principle lies in its primary aim of securing respect for the territorial boundaries at the moment when independence is achieved. Such territorial boundaries may be no more than delimitations between different administrative divisions or colonies all subject to the same sovereign. In that case, the application of the principle of *uti possidetis* resulted in administrative boundaries being transformed into international frontiers in the full sense of the term.[252]

This definition was declared in the *El Salvador/Honduras* case to constitute an authoritative statement,[253] and in that case the Chamber went on to emphasize that '*uti possidetis juris* is essentially a retrospective principle, investing as international boundaries administrative limits intended originally for quite other purposes'.[254]

The issue had been discussed in some detail in the *Honduras Borders* case. There, the Special Boundary Tribunal commenced by focusing upon possession as the test, but took this to mean the situation at the moment the colonial regime had been terminated, so that *uti possidetis* in fact and necessarily referred to the administrative control resting on the will of the Spanish Crown. Accordingly, administrative control contrary to such will would have constituted mere usurpation which would not have been able to confer any 'status of possession' as against the Crown's possession in fact and law. Administrative control exercised by the colonial entity in accordance with the will of the Crown constituted a 'juridical line'.[255] The key therefore, and despite some initial confusion regarding the use of the term 'possession', centred upon 'the administrative control held prior to independence pursuant to the will of the Spanish Crown'.[256]

As the Chamber put it in the *El Salvador/Honduras* case, 'it was the administrative boundaries between Spanish colonial administrative units . . . that were transformed by the operation of the *uti possidetis juris*,

---

[252] *ICJ Reports*, 1986, p. 566.
[253] *ICJ Reports*, 1992, p. 386.
[254] Ibid., p. 388.
[255] *Reports of International Arbitral Awards*, vol. 2, p. 1324.
[256] Ibid.

into international boundaries in 1821'.[257] The point was put in more detail by Judge *ad hoc* Torres Bernardez in his separate opinion. He emphasized that:

by virtue of the Spanish-American Republics' *uti possidetis juris* principle the colonial or administrative boundaries of Spanish *virreinatos, capitanías, intendencias* or *provincias* became international boundaries between neighbouring Spanish-American States as from the very date of independence. This also means that 'possession' was *not* defined in terms of effective possession or occupation but by reference to the former Spanish legislation . . . Thus the concept of 'possession' embodied in the *uti possidetis juris* principle of the Spanish-American Republics is the concept of the right to possess according to Spanish legislation ('title') and not a reflection of factual situations of usurpation by former Spanish colonial authorities, such as might have existed, or of the fact of occupation or control by this or that Spanish-American Republic following independence (the *de facto* situations).[258]

Thus neither actual possession nor reference to factors other than the administrative lines drawn by the former colonial power could impact upon the international boundary situation, and pre-colonial lines of division ceased to have any direct relevance.[259]

The question as to whether the doctrine of *uti possidetis* applies not only to land boundaries but also to maritime boundaries has also been raised. In the *Guinea – Guinea-Bissau* case in 1985,[260] the first question faced by the Arbitration Tribunal was to decide whether the 1886 boundary delimitation convention between France and Portugal established a maritime boundary also. The Tribunal noted that only if the answer to this question were positive would the issue arise as to whether the doctrine of *uti possidetis* applied.[261] In the event, since it was held that the 1886 treaty did not deal with the maritime boundary, the problem of a maritime *uti possidetis* did not arise.[262] The issue, however, did arise for discussion and decision in the *Guinea-Bissau v. Senegal* case in 1989.[263] In that case concerning the maritime boundaries of the two States, Guinea-Bissau argued that State succession (and thus by implication *uti possidetis*) did not apply to maritime frontiers. The majority of the Tribunal did not agree. It was pointed out that that State 'has not been able to invoke any precedent in which the *tabula rasa* rule was applied to a maritime boundary established in the colonial era', while on the

---

[257] *ICJ Reports*, 1992, p. 393.

[258] Ibid., p. 635 (emphasis original).

[259] Ibid., p. 393, and Judge *ad hoc* Torres Bernardez, ibid., at p. 636. See also Nelson, 'The Arbitration of Boundary Disputes in Latin America', *Netherlands International Law Review*, 20 (1973), at pp. 278–9. Note in particular Reisman's powerful criticism of this orientation, loc. cit. above (n. 117), at pp. 354 ff.

[260] 77 ILR 635.

[261] Ibid., 657.

[262] Ibid., 675.

[263] 83 ILR 1.

contrary a number of cases demonstrating succession to colonially established maritime lines were in evidence.[264] In addition, the Tribunal felt that Guinea-Bissau's own conduct had shown that it believed that succession of States operated in respect of maritime boundary treaties. The Tribunal also emphasized that the Arbitration Agreement signed between Guinea-Bissau and Guinea in 1983 in order to settle that particular dispute incorporated an express reference to the 1964 OAU resolution accepting colonial boundaries. Since that dispute was a maritime dispute, the Tribunal concluded that both parties had accepted that the principle of respect for colonial boundaries applied also to maritime boundaries.[265] Thus a rather mixed array of factors impelled the Tribunal to the view that State succession applied to maritime boundaries as it did to land boundaries generally, and with particular respect to Guinea-Bissau.

This view was the subject of a powerful riposte by Judge Bedjaoui in his dissenting opinion. He took the view contrary to the approach of the Tribunal that the absence of specific comment in the various relevant texts dealing with the *uti possidetis* principle (including the *travaux préparatoires* of the two Vienna Conventions on State succession) meant that the principle could not be extended to maritime boundaries.[266] Judge Bedjaoui concluded that '*there was simply no colonial heritage to preserve in the matter of maritime boundaries*' (emphasis in original).[267] However, the fact that many colonial maritime boundaries were not delimited cannot mean that those that were so delimited ceased to have effect. There are two issues here, and the principle of *uti possidetis* has never been taken to mean that an unsettled boundary becomes settled simply by succession.

The fact that instruments have not specifically referred to maritime boundaries cannot be understood as meaning that such agreed colonial boundaries ceased to operate. Lack of practice in fact works the other way since it is undeniable, as the Tribunal noted,[268] that there have been some maritime boundaries established during the period of colonialism, and while such practice was not extensive, what is striking is the absence of protests against such boundaries. Guinea-Bissau's assertions stand out in this respect. The basic principle of stability of boundaries applies in such situations also, and in this sense there is no essential difference between terrestrial and maritime boundaries. Both concern the delimitation of the spatial sovereignty of the State concerned.

[264] Ibid., 37.
[265] Ibid., 38.
[266] Ibid., 60.
[267] Ibid., 62.
[268] Ibid., 37.

Certainly the view taken, correctly it is submitted, by the Chamber in the *El Salvador/Honduras* case in dealing with the Gulf of Fonseca was that:

the rights in the Gulf of Fonseca of the present coastal States were thus acquired, like their land territories, by succession from Spain . . . accordingly, it is necessary to enquire into the legal situation of the waters of the Gulf in 1821 at the time of succession from Spain; for the principle of the *uti possidetis juris* should apply to the waters of the Gulf as well as to the land.[269]

The Chamber confirmed that the Gulf of Fonseca constituted an historic bay and that the waters of the Gulf outside the three-mile maritime belts were 'historic waters', and concluded that these waters were in the circumstances of the case 'subject to a joint sovereignty of the three coastal States'.[270] What is particularly interesting for present purposes is that the Chamber, while noting that these waters had not in the past been divided between the three States according to the principle of *uti possidetis*, concluded by emphasizing the role of that principle, since it took the view that 'a joint succession of the three States to the maritime areas seems in these circumstances to be the logical outcome of the principle of *uti possidetis juris* itself'.[271] In other words, the doctrine applied to what were in effect maritime boundaries, but in the special circumstances of that bay did so not in the form of a division of waters but rather by way of joint sovereignty over them by the three coastal States.

5. *Determining the* Uti Possidetis *Line*

It was noted in the *Burkina Faso/Mali* case that 'the principle of *uti possidetis* freezes the territorial title; it stops the clock but does not put back the hands'.[272] This immediately raises two particular issues, the applicable law determining the definition of the relevant line and the appropriate temporal framework. The applicable law in one sense is the constitutional law of the colonial power, for it is primarily with respect to the valid titles established under that system that one can identify the relevant administrative line, although once that line is identified the colonial law becomes merely one evidential fact among others. The Chamber in *Burkina Faso/Mali* noted that the determination of the relevant frontier line had to be appraised in the light of French colonial law, since the line in question had been an entirely internal administrative border within French West Africa. As such it was defined not by international law, but by the French legislation applicable to such

---

[269] *ICJ Reports*, 1992, p. 589.
[270] Ibid., p. 601.
[271] Ibid., pp. 601–2.
[272] *ICJ Reports*, 1986, p. 568.

territories. However, the essence of *uti possidetis* is the transmission of a particular territorial framework to the new State, and the precise identity of that line (as the existing administrative border) is a matter of fact. The Chamber emphasized, correctly, that the principle of *uti possidetis* is a rule of international law and not one of international plus internal law, so that the reasons underpinning the geographical location of the line also import considerations of fact as such. Colonial law, therefore, constitutes simply one fact among others in the process of determining the line.[273] Other relevant factors would include administrative practices and actual exercise of authority.

This approach was reinforced in the *El Salvador/Honduras* case, where the Chamber stated that 'when the principle of *uti possidetis juris* is involved, the *jus* referred to is not international law but the constitutional or administrative law of the pre-independence sovereign'.[274] However, it was also noted that where the law itself gave no clear and definite answer, it would be appropriate to examine the conduct of the new States during the period immediately after independence in an attempt to throw light on the contemporary appreciation of the situation. The Tribunal in the *Honduras Borders* case in particular underlined the importance of such activities, noting that the declarations and acts of the parties on attaining independence amounted to:

a virtually contemporaneous and solemn declaration of the extent of administrative authority deemed to have been enjoyed by the preceding colonial entity. The Constitutions of the new States, and the governmental acts of each, especially when unopposed, or when initial opposition was not continued, are of special importance.[275]

Thus, although the applicable law as such at the moment immediately prior to independence is that of the former sovereign, this needs to be tempered by the introduction of further elements should that law not clearly identify the line in question or where a dissonance between the law and actual practice at the appropriate time is demonstrated.

The appropriate temporal framework imports the issue of intertemporal law.[276] This provides that 'the law to be applied to a given situation must be the law in force at the time when it arose' and that 'a legal event must be assessed in the light of the law in force at the time of

---

[273] *ICJ Reports*, 1986, p. 568. See also the separate opinion of Judge Abi-Saab, who agreed with the Chamber's formulation, but disagreed with its application in the circumstances: ibid., p. 659.

[274] *ICJ Reports*, 1992, p. 559.

[275] *Reports of International Arbitral Awards*, vol. 2, p. 1325.

[276] See, for example, Elias, 'The Doctrine of Intertemporal Law', *American Journal of International Law*, 74 (1980), p. 285; Brownlie, op. cit. above (n. 222), pp. 129–30: Oppenheim, op. cit. above (n. 1), pp. 1281–2; Fitzmaurice, *The Law and Procedure of the International Court of Justice* (1986), vol. 1, p. 135; Jennings, *The Acquisition of Territory in International Law* (1963), pp. 28–31, and Thirlway, 'The Law and Procedure of the International Court of Justice 1960–1989', this *Year Book*, 60 (1989), pp. 4, 128. See also the *Western Sahara* case, *ICJ Reports*, 1975, pp. 12, 38–9.

its occurrence'.[277] Thus the question of the critical date is raised.[278] The critical date as a legal concept posits that there is a certain moment at which the rights of the parties crystallize, so that acts after that date cannot alter the legal position. It is a moment which is more decisive than any other for the purpose of the formulation of the rights of the parties in question. In some cases, there is self-evidently a 'critical date' in this sense. For example, if rights under a particular treaty are at issue, the date of the treaty assumes importance,[279] or if a claim is made for occupation of a territory on a specified date, then that date will generate a significance for the determination of the rights of the parties.[280] In many cases, there will be no such self-evident 'critical date', and one should be wary of searching for one in all cases and in all situations.[281]

The doctrine of *uti possidetis*, however, is clearly anchored in time. As the Chamber emphasized in the *Burkina Faso/Mali* case, *uti possidetis* 'applies to the new State (as a State) not with retroactive effect, but immediately and from that moment onwards. It applies to the State *as it is*, i.e. to the "photograph" of the territorial situation then existing. The principle of *uti possidetis* freezes the territorial title; it stops the clock, but does not put back the hands.'[282] It thus appears obvious that the moment of independence is the 'critical date'. However, the matter is not always that simple. Where there is more than one State involved, then logically it should be the date of first independence that will be important. But this may be of more apparent significance than real, since the date of independence may simply mark the date of succession to boundaries which have been established with binding force by earlier instruments.[283] To talk in such circumstances of the date of first independence being 'critical' may not always be helpful in the ascertainment of legal rights and obligations in dispute. Again, the moment of independence may not be 'critical' for these purposes for several possible reasons. There may be a dispute between the parties as to whether the date of independence or the date of the last exercise of jurisdiction for administrative organizational purposes by the former sovereign is the more appropriate date,[284] or the *uti possidetis* line may in some circumstances only be determined

---

[277] See the *Guinea-Bissau* v. *Senegal* case, 83 ILR 32 and 45. See also the *Island of Palmas* case, *Reports of International Arbitral Awards*, vol. 2, p. 845, and the *Aegean Sea Continental Shelf* case, *ICJ Reports*, 1978, pp. 3, 33–4.

[278] See the influential formulation by Fitzmaurice in the oral pleadings, the *Minquiers and Ecrehos* case, *ICJ Reports*, 1953, Memorials, vol. 2, pp. 62–4, and Fitzmaurice, 'The Law and Procedure of the International Court of Justice, 1951–4; Points of Substantive Law. Part II', this *Year Book*, 32 (1955–6), p. 20. See also the *Island of Palmas* case, *Reports of International Arbitral Awards*, vol. 2, p. 845, and the *Eastern Greenland* case, PCIJ, Series A/B, No. 53, p. 45.

[279] See, for example, the *Island of Palmas* case, *Reports of International Arbitral Awards*, vol. 2, p. 845. See also Jennings, op. cit. above (n. 1), pp. 31 ff.

[280] See, for example, the *Eastern Greenland* case, PCIJ, Series A/B, No. 53, p. 45.

[281] See Oppenheim, op. cit. above (n. 1), p. 711, and Jennings, op. cit. above (n. 1), pp. 31 ff.

[282] *ICJ Reports*, 1986, p. 568 (emphasis added).

[283] As in the *Libya/Chad* case, *ICJ Reports*, 1994, p. 6.

[284] See the *Burkina Faso/Mali* case, *ICJ Reports*, 1986, p. 570.

upon a consideration of materials appearing later than the date of independence,[285] or such a 'critical date' may have been moved to a later date than that of independence by a subsequent treaty[286] or by an adjudication award.[287] Indeed, the critical date may not be the same for all purposes in the same litigation,[288] and the situation may be such that more than one date may be seen as 'critical'.[289] Its importance then is relative and depends entirely upon the circumstances of the case.[290] More generalized references, however, to a 'critical period'[291] or to 'the temporal context'[292] are of value in establishing the appropriate framework of time in particular situations and in the light of the particular circumstances. In some cases, there may be multiple dates of juridical significance, and complicated issues *inter se* may not always be avoidable.[293]

More particular problems, however, may appear to arise in the event of an internal boundary, which was once an international boundary, being altered and then subsequently becoming transformed into an international boundary. This is the case with regard to the Baltic States, which were illegally annexed by the USSR in 1940. During the period of absorption into the USSR, the boundaries of these States were altered, so that the boundaries of the Republics which became again independent States in 1991[294] upon the demise of the Soviet Union do not conform with their boundaries as at the date of the annexations.[295] Thus, there appears to be a conflict of *uti possidetis* lines, those internationally accepted prior to the annexations and those consequential upon restoration of independence. The question is particularly sensitive since the

---

[285] See the *El Salvador/Honduras* case, *ICJ Reports*, 1992, pp. 56 ff.

[286] See the *Beagle Channel* case, HMSO, 1977, pp. 5–6.

[287] The *El Salvador/Honduras* case, *ICJ Reports*, 1992, p. 401. See also the *Burkina Faso/Mali* case, *ICJ Reports*, 1986, p. 570, and the separate opinion of Judge Ajibola, the *Libya/Chad* case, *ICJ Reports*, 1994, p. 91.

[288] See the *Argentine–Chile* case, 38 ILR 79–80.

[289] See the *Rann of Kutch* case, 50 ILR 470.

[290] See ibid. and the *Burkino Faso/Mali* case, *ICJ Reports*, 1986, p. 570, for examples where the concept was held to be of little or no practical value. A similar view was taken in the *Dubai/Sharjah* case, 91 ILR 590–4.

[291] See the *Taba* case, 80 ILR 284, 299 and 324.

[292] See the *Western Sahara* case, *ICJ Reports*, 1975, pp. 12, 38.

[293] See, for example, the determination of the Arbitration Commission of the Conference on Yugoslavia, in Opinion No. 11, that the dates of succession (and independence) of each of the successor States of the Former Yugoslavia were the following: 8 October 1991 for Croatia and Slovenia, 17 November 1991 for the Former Yugoslav Republic of Macedonia, 6 March 1992 for Bosnia-Herzegovina and 27 April 1992 for the Federal Republic of Yugoslavia (Serbia and Montenegro): 96 ILR 719, 722. This will prove a complicating factor in the eventual apportionment of the assets and debts of the Former Yugoslavia.

[294] The Declaration made at a European Community Extraordinary Ministerial Meeting on 27 August 1991 stated that: 'The Community and its member States warmly welcome the restoration of the sovereignty and independence of the Baltic States which they lost in 1940': this *Year Book*, 62 (1991), p. 558.

[295] See Müllerson, op. cit. above (n. 160), pp. 145 ff, and 'New Developments in the Former USSR and Yugoslavia', *Virginia Journal of International Law*, 33 (1993), p. 299.

annexations were in violation of international law, and indeed most Western States granted only *de facto* recognition to them.[296] Estonia and Latvia appear to be seeking a return to the 1940 borders, to which Russia objects.[297] Were it not for the illegality of the annexations, there would be no doubt that the borders of the Soviet Republics of 1991 would constitute the *uti possidetis* lines. Even so, it may very well be the case that considerations of international peace and security and territorial stability dictate acceptance of the 1991 boundaries as the existing international boundaries. The fact that the international community as a whole has afforded no support for such claims for restoration is particularly important.

The heart of the problem concerning the relevance and application of the principle of *uti possidetis* is to be able to determine the definitive location of the line of administrative control at the appropriate time. Several reasons have made this a particularly difficult enterprise.

First, many regions in South America (and indeed other analogous areas in the world) at the relevant time were simply unexplored by the authorities in question and thus geographically unknown. Many lines were drawn in ignorance of important geographical features or on the basis of mistaken views as to the location or existence of such geographical features as were referred to. To give but one example, the British claim to 'Mount Mfumbiro' as falling within the British sphere of influence by virtue of the 1890 Anglo-German Treaty was based upon agreements allegedly made by Stanley. In the event the claim was not contested, and it was only much later that it was discovered that no mountain of that name existed, and that Mfumbiro was rather the name of a plain located near where the imaginary mountain was supposed to have existed.[298] In addition, it was not unknown for tribal chiefs to give an exaggerated definition of the extent of their territory in negotiations with the colonial power in order to expand their own power base.[299] Even the use of science in the era of colonization gave rise to problems and as one colonial official noted despairingly in 1893, 'meridians move around Africa like mountains'.[300]

These difficulties led on to a second point: not only in many cases had the boundaries of jurisdiction not been fixed with precision by the colonial power, but there were in addition areas in which no effort had been made to assert any semblance of administrative authority.[301] Indeed, the law of the colonial power may simply not have provided for

---

[296] See, for example, the statement by the Minister of State at the Foreign and Commonwealth Office on 26 March 1991: this *Year Book*, 62 (1991), p. 564.

[297] See Müllerson, op. cit. above (n. 160), p. 148.

[298] See Hertslet, op. cit. (n. 138), p. 124.

[299] See Prescott, op. cit. above (n. 15), pp. 64–7 and 94–5.

[300] Ibid., p. 65.

[301] See, for example, the *Honduras Borders* case, *Reports of International Arbitral Awards*, vol. 2, p. 1325.

certain situations such as the appurtenance of marginal areas or sparsely populated areas of minimal economic significance.[302] To complicate the situation further, the actual exercise of administrative authority and control was not always consistent, and a variety of mechanisms and structures were in operation. For example, in Spanish Central America, one might need to consider provinces (a term whose meaning varied at different times), *alcaldías mayores* and *corregimientos*, and subsequently *intendencias* as well as the territorial jurisdictions of a higher court (*audiencias*), Captaincies-General and Vice-Royalties. Furthermore, the jurisdictions of such general administrative bodies did not necessarily coincide in territorial scope with certain bodies possessing special or particular jurisdictions. In addition, there existed various ecclesiastical jurisdictions which were supposed to be followed in principle by the territorial jurisdiction of the main civil administrative units in Spanish America, but did not always do so.[303] In other words, where the colonial administrative lines were not clearly and unambiguously defined, *uti possidetis* may speak 'with an uncertain voice'[304] and serious attempts may be required in order to determine where that line may be deemed to be.

The doctrine of *uti possidetis* originally commenced as a mechanism for defending actual possession regardless of how it came about.[305] In time, actual possession became transmuted into a fictional or constructive possession founded upon administrative lines,[306] but the focus upon administrative lines of necessity brought into consideration notions of actual possession in terms of the actual display of authority. This has led to debate as to the precise relationship between legal titles and display of authority (*effectivités*).

The Tribunal in the *Honduras Borders* case emphasized that the relevant test was that of administrative control prior to independence pursuant to the will of the Spanish Crown. In seeking the necessary evidence of such administrative control at the relevant time, one needed to take into account all manifestations of the will of the Crown, ranging from 'royal *cedulas* or rescripts, to royal orders, laws and decrees, and also, in the absence of precise laws or rescripts, to conduct indicating royal acquiescence in colonial assertions of administrative authority'. Indeed, the Tribunal felt that 'continued and unopposed assertion of administrative authority . . . not shown to be an act of usurpation because of conflict with a clear and definite expression of the royal will,

---

[302] See the *El Salvador/Honduras* case, *ICJ Reports*, 1992, p. 559.

[303] *ICJ Reports*, 1992, p. 387. See also the *Burkina Faso/Mali* case, *ICJ Reports*, 1986, pp. 569 ff.

[304] The *El Salvador/Honduras* case, *ICJ Reports*, 1992, p. 386.

[305] Above, p. 98.

[306] But see above, p. 100, with regard to the Brazilian approach to *uti possidetis*, stressing possession rather than right.

is entitled to weight and is not to be overborne by reference to antecedent provisions or recitals of an equivocal character'.[307]

It was emphasized in the *Burkina Faso/Mali* case that the concept of 'title' included not only documentary evidence, but also 'any evidence which may establish the existence of a right, and the actual source of that right'.[308] Thus, succession to the former colonial power would be regarded as a source of rights for successor States, with the territorial definition being provided by the principle of *uti possidetis*, while the legislative acts of the sovereign dealing with the constitution and extent of particular administrative units would constitute 'titles' in a slightly different sense. Private land grants to individuals or communities would not as such constitute 'titles', although they might have a role in a slightly different way in a confirmatory fashion.[309] Certainly, the Chamber in the *El Salvador/Honduras* case felt that such grants (or titles in a strictly domestic law sense) would be relevant as evidence of where the particular boundary was thought to be, and there would be a presumption that such grants would in the normal course of events avoid the straddling of existing lines between different administrative units. Indeed, it was also possible that where the line in question was doubtful, 'the common boundaries of two grants by different provincial authorities could well have become the provincial boundary'.[310]

Generally acts of sovereign authority or *effectivités* play a subsidiary role in the determination of the boundary line, but this depends on the circumstances. The Chamber defined 'colonial *effectivités*' as 'the conduct of the administrative authorities as proof of the effective exercise of territorial jurisdiction in the region during the colonial period'.[311] In considering the nature of such displays of authority, account may be taken of any particularist conceptions of sovereignty held in the territory in question. The International Court noted in the *Western Sahara* case that, 'where sovereignty over territory is claimed, the particular structure of a State may be a relevant element in appreciating the reality or otherwise of a display of State authority adduced as evidence of that sovereignty'. In that case, one needed to have regard to the fact that Morocco's special character consisted in the fact that it was founded on the common religious bond of Islam and on the personal allegiance of various tribes to the Sultan.[312] Similar consideration was given in the *Dubai/Sharjah* case to the fact that the key element in the social and political organization of the area in question was that the various tribes owed personal allegiance to particular sheikhs, and the control of the

[307] *Reports of International Arbitral Awards*, vol. 2, pp. 1324–5.
[308] *ICJ Reports*, 1986, p. 564.
[309] The *El Salvador/Honduras* case, *ICJ Reports*, 1992, pp. 388–9.
[310] Ibid., p. 394.
[311] The *Burkina Faso/Mali* case, *ICJ Reports*, 1986, p. 586.
[312] *ICJ Reports*, 1975, p. 44.

latter was through the tribal system. As such, the political boundaries in the area changed frequently.[313]

None the less, while note must be taken of the different forms of political organization in particular geographical contexts, this should not be understood as altering the fundamental principle of the law of territory that the test is that of 'effective display of authority' however that authority may be constituted or expressed.[314] In addition, in determining the impact of the display of authority, regard needs to be had to the nature of the territory in question and to the balance of competing claims in assessing the necessary standard of proof in the circumstances.[315]

In discussing the relationship between such acts and titles in the context of *uti possidetis*, the following conclusion was reached by the Chamber in the *Burkina Faso/Mali* case:

Where the act corresponds exactly to law, where effective administration is additional to the *uti possidetis juris*, the only role of *effectivité* is to confirm the exercise of the right derived from a legal title. Where the act does not correspond to the law, where the territory which is the subject of the dispute is effectively administered by a State other than the one possessing a legal title, preference should be given to the holder of the title. In the event that the *effectivité* does not co-exist with any legal title, it must invariably be taken into consideration. Finally, there are cases where the legal title is not capable of showing exactly the territorial expanse to which it relates. The *effectivités* can then play an essential role in showing how the title is interpreted in practice.[316]

In practice, such acts are of great importance. They may confirm existing titles, evidence the existence and scope of such titles, interpret such titles in situations of ambiguity and constitute a determinative means of resolving boundary disputes where no pertinent title exists.[317] But the notion of *effectivités* may extend beyond the colonial situation, and the action of States upon independence in formally describing the extent of their territorial boundaries, for example, may be highly significant, particularly where unopposed or where initial opposition is not maintained.[318] At the same time it is necessary to consider the role of post-independence *effectivités* in a wider context, and it will, of course, be realised that the Chamber in the *Burkina Faso/Mali* case slips from

[313] 91 ILR 543, 587–8.
[314] The *Western Sahara* case, *ICJ Reports*, 1975, p. 43. See also the *Dubai/Sharjah* case, 91 ILR 589–90.
[315] See the *Island of Palmas* case, *Reports of International Arbitral Awards*, vol. 2, p. 840; the *Eastern Greenland* case, *PCIJ*, Series A/B, No. 53, p. 46; the *Clipperton Island* case, *American Journal of International Law*, 26 (1932), p. 390; the *Minquiers and Ecrehos* case, *ICJ Reports*, 1953, p. 47; the *Western Sahara* case, *ICJ Reports*, 1975, p. 43, and the *Dubai/Sharjah* case, 91 ILR 589.
[316] *ICJ Reports*, 1986, pp. 586–7.
[317] See the *El Salvador/Honduras* case, *ICJ Reports*, 1992, p. 399.
[318] See the *Honduras Borders* case, *Reports of International Arbitral Awards*, vol. 2, p. 1325.

consideration of a clear *uti possidetis* situation to a more generalized situation of territorial title and the consequential relationship between acquisition of territory and effective occupation where no *uti possidetis* line exists for whatever reason.

It is interesting in this context to note the process adopted by the Chamber in the *El Salvador/Honduras* case with regard to the islands in the Gulf of Fonseca. It was stated that since the islands had been discovered by Spain in 1522 and remained under that State's sovereignty for some three centuries, the starting-point was the doctrine of *uti possidetis*. The next stage was consideration of relevant titles, and this proved fruitless since no land titles (utilized in the analysis of the land boundary between the parties) existed and the legislative and administrative texts were confused and conflicting.[319] The Chamber turned to colonial *effectivités* and concluded that they too were 'too fragmentary and ambiguous to be sufficient for any firm conclusion' to be based thereupon.[320] Thus, it was clear that neither title nor sovereign display of authority prior to independence could identify the *uti possidetis* line. In such circumstances, one is either left with deducing where such a line may have been by reference to other materials, or with trying to utilize such material in order to determine where such a line may be deemed to have been, or with reverting to the traditional methods of seeking to ascertain a boundary line.

The Chamber adopted a mixed approach. It sought to ascertain from the conduct of the parties in the period following independence where the *uti possidetis* line must have been. In addition, it took into account other international legal principles, independent of the *uti possidetis* doctrine, in particular the significance of the conduct of the parties as constituting acquiescence.[321] It was specifically declared that regard may be had to documentary evidence of such post-independence acts 'when it considers that they afford indications in respect of the 1821 *uti possidetis juris* boundary, providing a relationship exists between the *effectivités* concerned and the determination of that boundary'.[322]

Although the Chamber regarded acquiescence as separate from the principle of *uti possidetis* and as having a role primarily in the context of acquisition of territory by way of occupation of *terra nullius*, for example,

[319] *ICJ Reports*, 1992, pp. 558–9.
[320] Ibid., p. 563.
[321] Ibid.
[322] *ICJ Reports*, 1992, p. 399, and see ibid., pp. 572–3, for examples accepted as such *effectivités*, comprising records of appointment of justices of the peace; military appointments and/or orders; issue of licences; documents relating to the holding of elections; taxation records; national census records; registration of births and deaths; registrations of contracts of sale of land; civil proceedings before the courts; criminal proceedings records; municipal and other proceedings regarding the disposition of land; records relating to postal services; public works records; public health services documents and documents relating to the construction of schools and appointment of teachers. Note also the examples given in the *Argentine–Chile* case of 'material frequently employed for substantiating claims to territorial sovereignty': 38 ILR 88.

it nevertheless accepted that it could be of significance for the purposes of determining the *uti possidetis* line. The Chamber noted that the question was whether the exercise or display of sovereignty by the one party, particularly when accompanied by a lack of protest by the other, could indicate the presence of an *uti possidetis juris* title in the party thus exercising sovereignty, where the evidence on the basis of documentary title or colonial *effectivités* was ambiguous.[323] The Chamber concluded that:

Where the relevant administrative boundary was ill-defined or its position disputed, in the view of the Chamber the behaviour of the two newly independent States in the years following independence may well serve as a guide to where the boundary was, either in their shared view or in the view acted on by one and acquiesced in by the other.[324]

Of course, one would need to proceed cautiously here, since the two situations of determining a disputed or ambiguous *uti possidetis* line and establishing *de novo* a line founded upon effective display of sovereign authority are distinct. The former is retrospective, since evidence is sought as to the existence of a particular situation at the close of the colonial period, while the latter is continuous in seeking to demonstrate that title has been progressively established by a process of cumulative and overwhelming display of effective State authority in which the attitudes adopted by third States becomes a significant factor. In one case, the *uti possidetis* line is clarified, in the other it is in effect created by the concordance of assertion and acquiescence. Of course, the two processes may not easily be distinguishable in practice, and where consideration of both the relevant titles and colonial *effectivités* does not produce a clear boundary line, examination of the immediate post-independence practice of the new States would then become appropriate in order to determine what the situation at the moment of independence had been or should be taken to have been.[325] This may take the form either of elucidating a shared view or, probably more likely, of claims made by one State and acquiesced in by the other.[326] In fact, if the immediate post-independence practice is itself inconclusive, actual possession itself 'backed by the exercise of sovereignty may be taken as evidence confirming the *uti possidetis juris* title',[327] although it must be

---

[323] Ibid., p. 564.
[324] Ibid., p. 565. See also the *Honduras Borders* case, *Reports of International Arbitral Awards*, vol. 2, pp. 1324–5.
[325] Ibid., p. 559.
[326] Ibid., p. 565.
[327] Ibid., pp. 566 and 579. This would, of course, be buttressed by acquiescence. It was noted in the *Honduras Borders* case that 'priority in settlement in good faith would appropriately establish priority of right': *Reports of International Arbitral Awards*, vol. 2, p. 1359.

noted that the presence or absence of objections or protest is likely to prove especially important in such situations.[328]

There is therefore a grey area where the constructive search for an *uti possidetis* line merges or overlaps with the search for a line *de novo* and the same factors or indicia of confirmation or acquisition of sovereignty play a role. Essentially one is concerned with 'effective possession and control', coupled if at all possible with acquiescence.[329] The precise characterization of the process will depend in effect upon the assertions made by the parties in question, so that if both parties claim on the basis of the existence of an *uti possidetis* line, the Court would naturally focus upon seeking to determine that line directly or by implication or inference (as in the *El Salvador/Honduras* case itself[330]).

In its specific consideration of the situation concerning the islands in the Gulf of Fonseca, the Chamber, noting that evidence as to title and pre-independence *effectivités* was too ambiguous to establish the *uti possidetis* line, considered the conduct of the parties in the post-independence period, both in the context of where the parties assumed the *uti possidetis* line to be and more generally with regard to acquiescence. In so far as the island of Meanguera was concerned, the Chamber pointed to the intensification of the presence of El Salvador 'without objection or protest from Honduras', and that 'throughout the whole period covered by the documentation produced by El Salvador concerning Meanguera, there is no record of any protest made by Honduras to El Salvador'.[331] There was one exception to the absence of protest, however, but the Chamber declared that this protest by Honduras, 'coming after a long history of acts of sovereignty by El Salvador in Meanguera was made too late to affect the presumption of acquiescence on the part of Honduras. The conduct of Honduras vis-à-vis earlier *effectivités* reveals an admission, recognition, acquiescence or other form of tacit consent to the situation.'[332]

The Chamber concluded that in the light of the ambiguous position on the basis of colonial titles and *effectivités*, the assertion of El Salvador's claim to the island plus its effective possession and control over a long period were sufficient. If any doubt remained, it was noted, the position of El Salvador was 'made definitive by the acquiescence of Honduras'.[333]

The question of the subsequent conduct of the parties was touched upon by the International Court very briefly in the *Libya/Chad* case, without mentioning in terms the concept of acquiescence. The Court

---

[328] See for example, the comments in the *El Salvador/Honduras* case, *ICJ Reports*, 1992, pp. 572 and 574.

[329] Ibid., p. 579.

[330] *ICJ Reports*, 1992, p. 564.

[331] Ibid., pp. 572 and 574.

[332] Ibid., p. 577.

[333] Ibid., p. 579.

referred to a number of treaties made between the parties after the 1955 Treaty (which it held had determined the issue) and noted that there was 'support for the proposition that after 1955, the existence of a determined frontier was accepted and acted upon by the Parties'. It stated with regard to the 1966 Treaty, dealing *inter alia* with frontier questions, that 'if a serious dispute had indeed existed regarding frontiers, eleven years after the conclusion of the 1955 Treaty, one would expect it to have been reflected in the 1966 Treaty'.[334] The Court also examined the attitude of the parties in international fora and particularly noted that UN publications during the nine-year period between Libyan independence and Chad independence had continued to state a particular geographical dimension of Chad based upon French reports (1,284,000 square kilometres). This figure supported Chad's claim to the territory in dispute, since it clearly and expressly included the disputed BET region, but not Libya's claim. The Court briefly commented that 'Libya did not challenge the territorial dimensions of Chad as set out by France',[335] but refrained from drawing precise legal conclusions.

Of course, situations may arise where the *uti possidetis* line cannot be determined whether by reference to titles or to pre- or post-independence displays of authority, and a line *de novo* cannot be demonstrated by reference to the traditional principles of the acquisition of title to territory. In such cases, one is obliged to consider other factors. Equity in its broadest sense is clearly not appropriate in land boundary disputes,[336] but there would appear to be a role for equity in particular carefully constrained situations where a gap in the boundary line cannot otherwise be bridged.

In the special circumstances of the *Honduras Borders* case, for example, the Tribunal referred to a number of special situations which required particular consideration 'as equity and justice may require', such as the fact that a particular area had originally been part of the territory of Honduras and had been separated solely for the purpose of a special royal regime which had terminated.[337] The Treaty of 1830 had permitted the Tribunal to depart from the strict *uti possidetis* line where it saw fit and determine any necessary compensation, and this was interpreted as empowering the Tribunal to determine the definitive boundary 'as justice may require'. The Tribunal concluded that a definitive border could not be determined in an idealistic way 'without regard to the settlement of the territory and existing equities created by the enterprise of the respective parties'.[338] In this context, it is interesting

---

[334] *ICJ Reports*, 1994, p. 35.
[335] Ibid., p. 36.
[336] See above, p. 94.
[337] *Reports of International Arbitral Awards*, vol. 2, p. 1336.
[338] Ibid., p. 1352.

to note that the award provides that 'advances in good faith followed by occupation and development, unquestionably created equities'.[339]

In the *Rann of Kutch* case the view was taken that as far as two deep inlets were concerned:

> it would be inequitable to recognise these inlets as foreign territory. It would be conducive to friction and conflict. The paramount consideration of promoting peace and stability in this region compels the recognition and confirmation that this territory which is wholly surrounded by Pakistan territory, also be regarded as such.[340]

The tribunal also took the view that since a particular part of the boundary was 'jagged' it would be 'unsuitable and impracticable as an international boundary'. Accordingly, the line would be adjusted.[341]

In the *Burkina Faso/Mali* case, the Chamber concluded that as far as the pool of Soum was concerned, it was not possible to establish from colonial and post-colonial documentation which of two possible lines constituted the relevant administrative line, so it was felt appropriate to divide the pool in an equitable manner. This was done, in the absence of any special circumstances, equally.[342]

In the *El Salvador/Honduras* case, the Chamber took the view that topographical features would be relevant in certain circumstances. Where no definite line could be extracted from the relevant instruments, it was explained that the Chamber 'felt it right . . . to take some account of the suitability of certain topographical features to provide an identifiable and convenient boundary'.[343] Similarly, the Chamber was prepared to accept that in the case of a particular small uninhabited island, continuity with a larger island meant that it could be characterized as a dependency of the latter so that the issue of sovereignty would be resolved together.[344]

Of course, characterizing this process as one of equity at all may be seen as controversial, and one may simply regard the matter as one for the relevant tribunal to solve in such a way as to avoid a *non-liquet* or having to admit that a decision cannot be made. That would not be acceptable, particularly within the framework of the crucial principle of stability. However the process may be termed (and equity in its narrow sense does not appear inconsistent with decided case law), the need for a tribunal to reach a decision and uphold the stability of territorial settlements is essential.

---

[339] Ibid., p. 1359.

[340] 50 ILR 520.

[341] Ibid., p. 521.

[342] *ICJ Reports*, 1986, pp. 629–33.

[343] *ICJ Reports*, 1992, p. 390. Note that the Chamber was at pains to deny that an appeal was being made to the concept of 'natural frontiers': ibid.

[344] Ibid., pp. 570 and 579.

6. *Modification of the* Uti Possidetis *Line*

It is important not to overstate the import of the principle of *uti possidetis*. It does not posit that the boundaries existing at the moment of independence are immutable and incapable of change. That can happen. What it does say is that without evidence to the contrary, then the boundary that continues is the one that was in evidence at independence, and that any alteration thereto must be demonstrated and proved by acceptable evidence.

(a) *Modification by consent*

The territorial framework for the decolonization process has consistently been that of the colonially defined territory. Exceptions to the exercise of self-determination within this framework have been few indeed. In the case of the British administered Cameroons trust territory, self-determination resulted not in independence as a new State but in partition as between Nigeria and the Republic of Cameroun (the former French administered trust territory). The British Cameroons was administered in two parts, the northern part together with the northern Region of neighbouring Nigeria and the southern part, administered as a separate unit. This division was upheld as valid by a United Nations Trusteeship Visiting Mission in 1958, which noted that the inhabitants of the northern sector were closer to their northern Nigerian neighbours than to the population of the southern part, who resembled the inhabitants of the French Cameroons.[345] Accordingly, it was recommended that separate determinations of the wishes of the inhabitants be made.[346] This was accepted by the General Assembly.[347] In the event, the southern sector voted for unification with the former French Cameroons, while the northern sector voted for joining Nigeria.[348] General Assembly Resolution 1608(XV) specifically endorsed the results of the plebiscites, stated that the peoples of the two parts of the trust territory had freely and secretly expressed their wishes, and decided that the trusteeship should be terminated by northern Cameroons joining the Federation of Nigeria as a separate province of the northern region of that State and by southern Cameroons joining the Republic of Cameroun.[349] The justification given for this exceptional procedure in the context of decolonization was that of ethnic differences, and its basis was that of the consent of the three relevant parties in this trust territory situation, the administering power, the population and the United Nations.

---

[345] T/1446 and Add.1, para. 16.

[346] Ibid., para 170.

[347] Resolution 1350 (XIII).

[348] In fact, the first plebiscite in the north revealed a majority in favour of postponing a decision, and a second plebiscite was therefore held: see General Assembly Resolution 1473 (XIV). See Shaw, op. cit. above (n. 1), pp. 112–13.

[349] See also the *Northern Cameroons* case, *ICJ Reports*, 1963, pp. 15, 20–4.

It is clear that sovereign States have the capacity to alter their territorial configuration and thus modify existing boundaries by express consent.[350] This will invariably in practice be demonstrated by treaty provision. Such modifications may constitute merely modest changes to the boundary or they may constitute rather more significant changes in the nature of a territorial cession rather than a boundary rectification. Whatever the circumstances, the key determinant will be provided by proof of mutual consent and such consent is sufficient to replace the *uti possidetis* line. The Court in the *Beagle Channel* case, for example, noted that in the context of the 1881 Boundary Treaty between the parties (Argentina and Chile):

> the regime created by the 1881 Treaty whatever it was, superseded and replaced all previous territorial arrangements or understandings between the Parties, together with any former principles governing territorial allocation in Spanish-America.[351]

Accordingly, the Court took the view that:

> it is no part of its task to pronounce on what would have been the rights of the Parties on the basis of the *uti possidetis juris* of 1810 because, in the first place, these rights—whatever they may have been—are supposed to have been overtaken and transcended by the regime deriving from the 1881 Treaty.[352]

The point was also made by the Chamber in the *El Salvador/Honduras* case, where it was stated that:

> the Chamber does not consider that the effect of the application of the principle of the *uti possidetis juris* in Spanish America was to freeze for all time the provincial boundaries which, with the advent of independence, became the frontiers between the new States. It was obviously open to those States to vary the boundaries between them by agreement.[353]

Changes may also occur by way of multilateral treaty provision, such as the peace settlements that took place after the First World War.[354] These also may be seen in most cases as reflective of the consent of the relevant parties.[355] In addition, changes to the *uti possidetis* line may take place as a consequence of post-independence adjudication, which is perforce founded upon the consent of the parties. This may occur in two ways. The consequential award may either overtly modify the previous *uti possidetis* line or it may interpret it in a way that may be controversial. In the latter case, as the Chamber emphasized in the *El Salvador/*

---

[350] See the *Libya/Chad* case, *ICJ Reports*, 1994, p. 37. See also Kaikobad, loc. cit. above (n. 24), p. 120.

[351] HMSO, 1977, p. 4.

[352] Ibid., p. 5.

[353] *ICJ Reports*, 1992, p. 408.

[354] See the Report of the Committee of Jurists on the Aaland Islands, *League of Nations Official Journal*, Special Supplement No. 3, p. 17 (October 1920).

[355] See, for example, Crawford, *The Creation of States in International Law* (1979), pp. 308 ff.

Honduras case, 'The award's view of the *uti possidetis juris* position prevails and cannot now be questioned juridically, even it could be questioned historically'.[356]

It should also be noted in this context that the subsequent conduct of the parties may modify the provisions of a treaty establishing a boundary. In the *Temple* case, the International Court held that Thailand had in the circumstances accepted a particular map as representing the work of delimitation pursuant to boundary treaties between 1904 and 1907 and 'hence recognised the line on that map as being the frontier line', even though that line did not follow the watershed as required under the 1904 Treaty.[357] The parties by their conduct recognized the map line and, as a consequence, the Court found that the map became an integral part of the treaty settlement so that the parties had accepted an interpretation of the treaty settlement according to which, wherever the map line diverged from the watershed line, the former would prevail.[358] In the *Taba* case, the Tribunal stated that:

If a boundary line is once demarcated jointly by the parties concerned, the demarcation is considered as an authentic interpretation of the boundary agreement even if deviations may have occurred or if there are some inconsistencies with maps.[359]

The key is the acceptance by subsequent conduct of the parties of the modified line. In the *Taba* case, the Tribunal noted that Turkey had never complained about the placing of the first boundary pillar[360] and the demarcation line had been implicitly recognized in Ottoman documents of October 1911. Accordingly, the parties to the 1906 Treaty 'had, by their conduct, agreed to the boundary as it was demarcated by masonry pillars in 1906–07 and to the location of the Parker pillar as the final pillar of the boundary line at that time'.[361]

(b) *Modification by international recognition*

While cession of territory by a State is an attribute of sovereignty, secession is an act contrary to the will of the State. Both nevertheless involve a change to the territorial definition of the State and thus impact upon the territorial integrity of States and the inviolability of frontiers. Where the boundaries of an independent State are altered by the secession of part of that State and a third State is involved in circumstances amounting to intervention, then the principle of respect for the territorial integrity of States at least will be breached. The International

---

[356] *ICJ Reports*, 1992, p. 401.
[357] *ICJ Reports*, 1962, p. 32.
[358] Ibid., pp. 33–4.
[359] 80 ILR 297.
[360] Which Israel argued in the arbitration had not been placed in the location required by the relevant Treaty of 1906: ibid., p. 303.
[361] Ibid., p. 305.

Court declared in the *Corfu Channel* case that 'between independent States, respect for territorial sovereignty is an essential foundation of international relations',[362] while in the *Nicaragua* case, it was emphasized that:

the principle of non-intervention . . . forbids all States or groups of States to intervene directly or indirectly in internal or external affairs of other States. A prohibited intervention must accordingly be one bearing on matters in which each State is permitted, by the principle of State sovereignty, to decide freely.[363]

However, where no third State has intervened in the situation, no rule of international law as such is offended. International law is neutral with regard to secession. The international legal instruments dealing with respect for the territorial integrity of States bind States and not inhabitants within States. The inhabitants of an independent State do not possess an international legal right permitting them to secede. Similarly there is no international legal duty upon inhabitants forbidding them to secede.[364] It is a matter at this stage of domestic law. Should a secessionist effort succeed in the establishment of a new State as a matter of proven effectiveness, and should this be recognized by the international community,[365] then a new legal situation is created.[366] In such cases, the territorial definition of the original State is modified as a consequence of the interplay of the principles of effectiveness and recognition.

(c) *Modification by acquiescence*

The principle of acquiescence is a key principle in international law[367] and it has a general role with regard to the acquisition of territorial

---

[362] *ICJ Reports*, 1949, p. 35.

[363] *ICJ Reports*, 1986, p. 108.

[364] But under Article 29 of the African Charter on Human and Peoples' Rights 1981, 'Each individual shall also have the duty . . . 5. To preserve and strengthen the national independence and the territorial integrity of his country and to contribute to its defence in accordance with the law'. See, for example, Bello, 'The African Charter on Human and Peoples' Rights', *Recueil des cours*, 194 (1985-V), p. 5; Neff, 'Human Rights in Africa', *International and Comparative Law Quarterly*, 33 (1984), p. 331; Umozurike, 'The African Charter on Human and Peoples' Rights', *American Journal of International Law*, 77 (1983), p. 902, and Ramcharan, 'The *Travaux Préparatoires* of the African Commission on Human Rights', *Human Rights Law Journal*, 13 (1992), p. 307.

[365] i.e. third States, the State from which the secession has taken place and the United Nations. Recognition by all these persons is not essential, but that of third States is crucial.

[366] See the examples of Bangladesh (Oppenheim, op. cit. above (n. 1), p. 144) and Eritrea (Goy, loc. cit. above (n. 151)).

[367] See, for example, Lauterpacht, 'Sovereignty over Submarine Areas', this *Year Book*, 27 (1950), p. 376; MacGibbon, 'The Scope of Acquiescence in International Law', this *Year Book*, 31 (1954), p. 143; MacGibbon, 'Estoppel in International Law', *International and Comparative Law Quarterly*, 7 (1958), p. 468; Bowett, 'Estoppel before International Tribunals and its Relation to Acquiescence', this *Year Book*, 33 (1975), p. 176; Martin, *L'estoppel en droit international public* (1979); and Sinclair, 'Estoppel and Acquiescence', in Lowe and Fitzmaurice (eds.), *Fifty Years of the International Court of Justice* (1996), p. 104.

sovereignty.[368] As we have seen, acquiescence may be of importance in the process of seeking to demonstrate the location at any particular point of the *uti possidetis* line where this is not clear from other material.[369]

The second way in which acquiescence may be of relevance to *uti possidetis* is where it is applied in order to effect a modification of that line. In the *Honduras Borders* case, the Tribunal was expressly authorized to depart from the *uti possidetis* line 'in the interests of justice' and in order to take account of 'interests' acquired by either party beyond that line in the post-*uti possidetis* 1821 period.[370] But this type of provision is rare. In the *Temple* case, the Court analysed the situation with regard to the communication of the map in question to the Siamese authorities, particularly the circumstances surrounding the handing over to these authorities of the map, and concluded that:

It is clear that the circumstances were such as to call for some reaction, within a reasonable period, on the part of the Siamese authorities, if they wished to disagree with the map or had any serious question to raise in regard to it. They did not do so, either then or for many years, and thereby must be held to have acquiesced. *Qui tacet consentire videtur si loqui debuisset ac potuisset.*[371]

Acquiescence had taken place by virtue of an absence of response from Siam in circumstances in which a response should have been forthcoming had Siam not accepted the line on the map which deviated from the watershed line posited by the 1904 Treaty.[372] The Court concluded:

That the Siamese authorities by their conduct acknowledged the receipt, and recognised the character, of these maps, and what they purported to represent, is shown by the reaction of the Minister of the Interior, Prince Damrong, in thanking the French Minister in Bangkok for the maps, and in asking him for another fifteen copies of each for transmission to the Siamese provincial Governors.[373]

The Court also pointed to the fact that Prince Damrong (at this time no longer Minister of the Interior but President of the Royal Institute of Siam) paid in 1930 a quasi-official visit to the Temple, where he was received by French officials with the French flag flying. It was noted that the Prince could not possibly have failed to see the implications of such

---

[368] See, for example, the *Grisbadarna* case, *Hague Court Reports* (1916), p. 122; the *Eastern Greenland* case, *PCIJ*, Series A/B, No. 53, pp. 22, 46 and 54; and the *Anglo-Norwegian Fisheries* case, *ICJ Reports*, 1951, pp. 116, 139.

[369] See above, p. 136.

[370] Article V of the Special Agreement: *Reports of International Arbitral Awards*, vol. 2, p. 1322.

[371] *ICJ Reports*, 1962, p. 23.

[372] The Court also took into account the fact that there were indications on the face of the map which 'required a reaction if the Siamese authorities had any reason to contend that the map did not represent the outcome of the work of delimitation': ibid., p. 23.

[373] Ibid., pp. 23–4.

a reception and 'a clearer affirmation of title on the French Indo-Chinese side can hardly be imagined. It demanded a reaction. Thailand did nothing'.[374]

The Court in this case also appeared to be hinting that estoppel also may operate in the context of confirming or establishing a boundary, above and beyond treaty interpretation and acquiescence considerations. The Court drew particular attention to the fact that:

Thailand is now precluded by her conduct from asserting that she did not accept [the map]. She has, for fifty years, enjoyed such benefits as the Treaty of 1904 conferred on her, if only the benefit of a stable frontier.[375]

It is unclear whether the Court regarded this as a separate ground for supporting the Cambodian argument or whether it simply supported the striking evidence of Siamese acquiescence in French sovereignty over the Temple area. There is, of course, a clear theoretical distinction between acquiescence, where the State in question has accepted a particular position by its conduct, and estoppel, where the State has acted as though it has accepted such a position and thus misled the other party even though in reality this has not represented its true position.[376] However, in reality such a distinction is often difficult to maintain and much will depend upon how a particular set of facts is presented and argued.[377] Indeed in many cases claims as to acquiescence, estoppel and consideration of the subsequent conduct of the parties in the context of interpretation of a particular treaty will often be founded upon the same facts.[378] It would be unusual indeed for estoppel itself to constitute a decisive factor in the attribution of title to territory, not least because of its negative orientation and difficulties of proof.[379] Nevertheless, estoppel could well be of significance in the circumstances in providing supporting evidence of acquiescence claims and in the context of the subsequent conduct of the parties for treaty interpretation purposes.

The Court in the *Dubai/Sharjah* case also accepted that a binding boundary line (in this case a line founded upon an internal and not an international instrument) could be modified as a result of the recognition and effective application of another line.[380] The Court declared that:

[374] Ibid., p. 30.
[375] Ibid., p. 32.
[376] See Thirlway, loc. cit. above (n. 95), p. 29, and the separate opinion of Judge Fitzmaurice in the *Temple* case, *ICJ Reports*, 1962, p. 63. The Chamber of the International Court in the *Gulf of Maine* case stated that 'the concepts of acquiescence and estoppel, irrespective of the status accorded to them by international law, both follow from the fundamental principles of good faith and equity. They are, however, based on different legal reasoning, since acquiescence is equivalent to tacit recognition manifested by unilateral conduct which the other party may interpret as consent, while estoppel is linked to preclusion': *ICJ Reports*, 1984, p. 305.
[377] See, for example, the *El Salvador/Honduras* case, *ICJ Reports*, 1992, pp. 408–9.
[378] See the *Award of the King of Spain* case, *ICJ Reports*, 1960, p. 192; the *North Sea Continental Shelf* cases, *ICJ Reports*, 1969, p. 26, and the *Nicaragua* case, *ICJ Reports*, 1986, p. 414.
[379] See also Jennings, op. cit. above (n. 1), p. 51.
[380] 91 ILR 585.

if a State, on achieving independence, protests against a boundary established in this way [ie. by administrative decision] and subsequently behaves as if such a boundary never existed—for example, by acting as if it had sovereign authority in the disputed area—then the non-application of the decision by both of the interested States may deprive that decision of legal value.[381]

The role of acquiescence was further discussed by the Chamber in the *El Salvador/Honduras* case. After noting that the *uti possidetis juris* position could be qualified by adjudication and by treaty, the Chamber continued as follows:

the question then arises whether it can be qualified in other ways, for example, by acquiescence or recognition. There seems to be no reason in principle why these factors should not operate, where there is sufficient evidence to show that the parties have in effect clearly accepted a variation, or at least an interpretation, of the *uti possidetis juris* position.[382]

In examining the situation in the First Sector of the Land Boundary, the Chamber pointed out that while the *uti possidetis* line could be varied by agreement between the States concerned, 'some other forms of activity, or inactivity, might amount to acquiescence in a boundary other than that of 1821'.[383] Indeed, the Chamber concluded with regard to this sector of the boundary that:

the situation was susceptible of modification by acquiescence in the lengthy intervening period; and the Chamber finds that the conduct of Honduras from 1881 until 1972 may be regarded as amounting to such acquiescence in a boundary corresponding to the boundary between the Tepangüisir lands granted to Citalá and those of Ocoteopeque.[384]

In other words, acquiescence may play a crucial role both in the ascertainment of the *uti possidetis* line, where the titles and colonial *effectivités* are ambiguous, and in the modification of that line where this has in fact occurred. In addition, acquiescence is also important where no *uti possidetis* line could be determined, so that recourse to traditional principles of territorial acquisition, such as exercise of authority and acceptance of that by the other party, was required.

(d) *Modification in the interests of peace and security*

The principle of *uti possidetis* draws sustenance from the precept of the stability of boundaries as reflecting policy considerations with regard to stability of the international system as a whole. However, where the situation is such that the application of *uti possidetis* would itself seriously

---

[381] Ibid., 579.
[382] *ICJ Reports*, 1992, p. 401. See also Sinclair, loc. cit. above (n. 367), pp. 117 ff.
[383] Ibid., p. 408.
[384] Ibid., pp. 408–9.

threaten peace and security, the international community has been prepared to modify the presumptive boundary.

In the case of the British mandated territory of Palestine, for example, faced with irreconcilable differences and outbreaks of violence between the Jewish and Arab communities, the General Assembly took the view that since 'the present situation . . . is likely to impair the general welfare and friendly relations among nations', partition should be instituted and independent Jewish and Arab States created.[385] It should also be noted here that the Mandate for Palestine incorporated the Balfour Declaration with regard to the establishment of a 'Jewish National Home in Palestine'.

The case of the decolonization of the Belgian trust territory of Ruanda-Urundi is the second example of this rare process.[386] Following upon General Assembly pressures to grant the territory independence,[387] disturbances commenced between the rival Tutsi and Hutu tribes. A UN Visiting Mission was sent and as a result, the Trusteeship Council recommended independence for the territory as a single composite State.[388] This was endorsed by the General Assembly in Resolution 1579(XV) and confirmed in Resolutions 1605(XV) and 1743(XVI). A Commission was established by the General Assembly to reconcile the rival factions in the deteriorating situation. However, this reported that the territory was divided and reference was made to the 'psychosis of mutual distrust'.[389] This report convinced the UN Fourth Committee of the need to partition the territory.[390] Accordingly, the General Assembly adopted Resolution 1746(XVI), which noted that the efforts to maintain the unity of the trust territory of Ruanda-Urundi had failed and took account of the desires of Rwanda and Burundi to become separate and independent States on 1 July 1962. Thus the UN accepted that in the interests of peace and security the retention of the pre-independence territorial structure was not possible. The wishes of the two units were clearly of major importance here as were no doubt the fears that a repetition of events in the neighbouring Belgian Congo might be repeated. It is also to be noted that the two units had been separate kingdoms and had continued this way under both German and Belgian rule.

More intriguing is Security Council Resolution 687(1991) concerning

---

[385] Resolution 181(II). See generally Moore (ed.), *The Arab-Israel Conflict* (1974), 3 volumes, and Lauterpacht (ed.), *Oppenheim's International Law*, vol. 1 (8th edn., 1955), pp. 217–19.

[386] See Lemarchand, *Rwanda and Burundi* (1970), and Shaw, op. cit. above (n. 1), pp. 113–14.

[387] See in particular General Assembly Resolution 1413 (XIV).

[388] See T/1551; T/1538; T/L.985 and Add.1; T/L.1004 and T/L.1005.

[389] See A/5126 and Add.1.

[390] See *General Assembly Official Records*, 16th session, 4th Committee, 1305th meeting, para. 14, and ibid., 1307th–1327th meetings.

inter alia the Iraq-Kuwait boundary.[391] Acting specifically under Chapter VII and thus in a manner binding on all member States of the UN, the Security Council:

2. *Demands* that Iraq and Kuwait respect the inviolability of the international boundary and the allocation of islands set out in the 'Agreed minutes between the State of Kuwait and the Republic of Iraq Regarding the Restoration of Friendly Relations, Recognition and Related Matters', signed by them in the exercise of their sovereignty at Baghdad on 4 October 1963 and registered with the United Nations and published by the United Nations in document 7063, United Nations, *Treaty Series*, 1964;

3. *Calls upon* the Secretary-General to lend his assistance to make arrangements with Iraq and Kuwait to demarcate the boundary between Iraq and Kuwait, drawing on appropriate material, including the map transmitted by Security Council document S/22412 and to report back to the Security Council within one month;

4. *Decides* to guarantee the inviolability of the above-mentioned international boundary and to take all necessary measures to that end in accordance with the Charter of the United Nations.

The Iraq-Kuwait Boundary Demarcation Commission was duly established[392] and produced its Final Report on 20 May 1993.[393] The demarcation process did not reallocate territory between Iraq and Kuwait but 'simply carried out the technical task necessary to demarcate for the first time the precise coordinates of the international boundary reaffirmed in the 1963 Minutes'.[394] The UN Secretary-General in transmitting the Final Report to the Security Council specifically noted that:

I believe that the work performed by the Commission will have a beneficial effect on the restoration of international peace and security in the area concerned, in conformity with the purposes of Security Council Resolution 687(1991). The certainty and stability of the boundaries are in the best interest of Iraq and Kuwait and I expect the Governments of both countries to respect

---

[391] See Mendelson and Hulton, 'The Iraq-Kuwait Boundary', this *Year Book*, 64 (1993), p. 135, 'La revendication par l'Iraq de la souveraineté sur le Koweït', *Annuaire français de droit international*, 36 (1990), p. 195, and 'The Iraq-Kuwait Boundary: Legal Aspects', *Revue belge de droit international*, 23 (1990), p. 293. See also Lauterpacht, Greenwood, Weller and Bethlehem (eds.), *The Kuwait Crisis: Basic Documents* (1991), and Weller, (ed.), *Iraq and Kuwait, The Hostilities and Their Aftermath* (1993).

[392] See S/22558 and S/22620. See also Mendelson and Hulton, this *Year Book*, loc. cit. above (n. 391), pp. 141–2.

[393] The Final Report of the Demarcation of the International Boundary between the Republic of Iraq and the State of Kuwait, S/25811: 94 ILR 1.

[394] Ibid., p. 28. See also to the same effect Security Council Resolution 773 (1992); the statement of the President of the Security Council of 17 June 1992 issued on behalf of its members, S/24113; the letter of 21 May 1993 from the UN Secretary-General to the President of the Security Council transmitting the Final Report, S/25811; Security Council Resolution 833 (1993), preamble; and the statement of the President of the Security Council of 28 June 1993, S/26006.

the objective and impartial results achieved by the Iraq-Kuwait Boundary Demarcation Commission.[395]

The Security Council in Resolution 833(1993), again acting under Chapter VII, reaffirmed that the decisions of the Commission regarding the demarcation of the border were final and with particular emphasis:

Underlines and reaffirms its decision to guarantee the inviolability of the above-mentioned international boundary which has now been finally demarcated by the Commission and to take as appropriate all necessary measures to that end in accordance with the Charter, as provided for in paragraph 4 of resolution 687 (1991) and paragraph 4 of resolution 773 (1992).

It is certainly unusual to find the Security Council confirming in such a way an international boundary between two States who are in dispute as to that boundary. The competence of the Council in this situation no doubt flows from the general conditions of the Iraqi attack upon Kuwait and the UN response thereto up to and including the establishment of the cease-fire. It is also to be noted that both States accepted Resolution 687(1991) and the creation of the Commission.[396] However, Mendelson and Hulton conclude that the Commission in reality went somewhat beyond merely laying down on the ground the agreed international boundary. Certain parts of the boundary were either not defined by the relevant instruments or vaguely defined, while in the northern sector, the boundary was located further north than had previously been regarded as the correct position.[397]

More pertinently, the Council confirmed, and guaranteed, a boundary that in the view of one of the parties may have deviated from the *uti possidetis* line. Whether this was or was not the case is not examined here. The basic point for present purposes is that what seems to have happened is that the Security Council asserted the competence in principle to modify a *uti possidetis* line in the specific interests of international peace and security. Two provisos have, of course, to be made. First, that the whole Iraq-Kuwait situation was highly unusual, not least in the nature and dimensions of the UN actions, and secondly, that what was expressly stated to have happened was simply confirmation of an international boundary followed by its demarcation. In reality, rather more happened and a significant, if rather exceptional, door has been left ajar.

---

[395] S/25811.

[396] Although Iraq at times questioned and objected to it: see for example S/22457 and S/25905. See also Mendelson and Hulton, this *Year Book*, loc. cit. above (n. 391), pp. 140–1 and 195.

[397] This *Year Book*, loc. cit. above (n. 391), pp. 192–3.

V. Conclusion

The following comments may, on the basis of the foregoing discussion, be made:

(i) The principle of territorial sovereignty remains crucial in the international legal system and will continue so to do for the foreseeable future, despite developments emphasizing the inter-State, non-State and international co-operative aspects of the system. As a consequence, the precept of territorial stability, and thus the principle of the stability of boundaries, ranks highly within international law and generates a variety of norms that focus essentially upon continuity and certainty. Such norms seek to render the process of territorial definition and change as predictable and as deliberate as possible for international policy reasons.

(ii) Within this framework, a series of particular associated and consequential rules and principles have evolved that attempt to preserve the territorial *status quo* as much as possible at all stages. Accordingly, for example, provisions in treaties may be modified by subsequent conduct, including acquiescence, where clearly demonstrated, while boundary treaties will be interpreted in the light of a presumption of finality and stability and therefore in such a way as to minimize the possibilities of unpredictability and unilateral challenge.

(iii) The principle of *uti possidetis juris* constitutes that part of the concept of territorial stability that concerns the mechanism and process of the transmission of sovereignty to a new State. It acts to give a territorial dimension and definition to that process by positing the continuation of the territorial definition of the particular entity comprised within an earlier sovereignty, and is limited to that situation, both temporally and conceptually. As such, it is both a factual and a legal concept. It is not a principle of operation allocating territorial title of infinite application. Nor is it limited to the colonial situation. However, the role that it plays is variable.

(iv) *Uti possidetis* will play only a framework role where the boundary, or part of the boundary of the new State, already existed as an international boundary. Boundaries established by treaties constitute objective realities that exist above and beyond such treaties themselves, binding both the parties to the treaties and their successors in title. There is a presumption against change in these circumstances, although such boundaries may be modified by the subsequent practice of the parties, provided this is clearly demonstrated.

(v) The role of *uti possidetis* will become proportionately more important, however, where the previous boundary existed simply as an administrative line, for the element of international consent or recognition is inevitably absent. The process of location of this line will involve a consideration of a range of factors including the provisions of the relevant colonial (or previous) law, actual administrative practice, *effectivités* generally, both colonial (or previous) and post-independence, recognition and acquiescence.

(vi) The application of *uti possidetis* will not be overriden by the norm of self-determination. The latter has in practice been constrained by virtue of its cautious definition in international law. The adoption of a purely ethnic approach to self-determination as a legitimating principle for the territorial configuration of new States, which would be radical in demanding in reality extensive changes in previously accepted territorial limits, has not taken place within the international community. Apart from isolated examples, justified on the basis of special circumstances and the preservation or restoration of peace and security as determined by the organized international community, the accepted territorial framework for the decolonization process has been that of the colonially defined unit, while in the post-independence situation, no recognition or acceptance of an international legal right of secession has occurred. Self-determination in the post-independence situation has re-oriented itself into a principle of human rights applicable within the territorial framework of the sovereign State. It may, however, have an application within the context of consensual change.

(vii) The principle of *uti possidetis* is also consistent with the operation of the concept of territorial integrity. *Uti possidetis* relates to the transition from one sovereignty to another and thus is temporally constrained. Once a State is independent, the principle of territorial integrity takes over in order to protect and preserve as between the members of the international community the territorial definition, as provided by the application of *uti possidetis*, of that newly sovereign State. The two principles are connected, however, for recourse will inevitably be had to *uti possidetis* in order to determine the basis of the territorial definition of a State.

(viii) The *uti possidetis* line is not itself a line of actual possession as such, but rather the line (of whatever status at the time) established in law by the previous sovereign by virtue of a positive act of legislative or administrative authority or as a consequence of a series of relevant and authoritative acts. However, such a line may need to be demonstrated or proved by recourse to *effectivités*, including actual possession, or with regard to subsequent practice. It may indeed be an *ex post facto* rationalization in the light of activities undertaken or views expressed at various relevant times.

(ix) In addition to constituting the territorial dimension of the process of transmission of sovereignty to a new State, *uti possidetis* will constitute the inevitable starting-point in the process of determining the location of an inter-State boundary in dispute.

(x) There is a strong presumption in international law, for reasons of international policy, in favour of the existence of an *uti possidetis* line.

There are also strong presumptions that this line is both complete and permanent. Accordingly, for example, courts will seek to interpret treaties concerning boundaries as determining these boundaries and in as full and final a way as possible.

(xi) The presumptions of completeness and permanence may be rebutted by evidence to the contrary and may be of varying strength depending upon the situation. Where the lines are those established by an international treaty, then the presumption is to all intents and purposes unrebuttable, save by the proven subsequent practice of the parties to the treaty or of their successors in title. The presumption is particularly powerful in the colonial situation. In the case of new States arising by way of secession from, or dissolution of, already independent States, the strength of the presumption will depend *inter alia* upon the nature of the former entity. Where this was a Federal State, the presumption will clearly be that new States emerging out of it will bear the same boundaries as the federal units possessed. The more unitary a State, the less strong will become the presumption, for *uti possidetis* requires an accepted administrative line. It will, however, always depend upon the circumstances of the particular situation, including constitutional law and administrative practices as to the distribution of power and authority, and consent as variously expressed.

(xii) In pursuance of the presumptions surrounding *uti possidetis*, international tribunals will do their utmost to discover the *uti possidetis* line in both an actual and constructive fashion. The key factors will centre upon legal titles or the actual display of sovereignty coupled with acquiescence. Even if the colonial line cannot be determined in the light of contemporaneous titles and *effectivités*, courts are highly likely to resort to post-independence materials in an attempt to determine where that line was accepted or deemed by the parties to have been, or indeed where the court itself may deem such line to have been. Even where gaps appear in an otherwise determined line, resort will be had to equity in a minimalist fashion in order to maintain the coherence, and thus completeness, of the *uti possidetis* boundary. However, such gaps would need to be relatively inconsequential.

(xiii) The doctrine of *uti possidetis*, however, cannot resolve all problems. Where there simply was no *uti possidetis* line at any given part of the boundary in question as a matter of demonstrated fact (beyond relatively inconsequential gaps that can be linked by resort to equity), the principle as such ceases to be of use. Again, *uti possidetis* is of little value where there exists a genuine factual dispute as to where the line lay. In such circumstances, a court will have resort to the traditional mechanisms of territorial acquisition, which revolve around many of the techniques used in establishing the *uti possidetis* line such as the search for titles, *effectivités*, recognition and acquiescence, treaty interpretation, practice and estoppel.

(xiv) The *uti possidetis* line, once identified, is not immutable. It can be changed by consent, whether expressed by treaty or by an award or by virtue of contrary practice by one party coupled with acquiescence therein by the other. In exceptional situations, the *uti possidetis* line may be affected by action by the organized international community for reasons of peace and security.

(xv) Accordingly, *uti possidetis* subsists within the framework of the principle of territorial stability and in the context of the traditional principles of the acquisition of territory. The doctrine performs an important function within the international community of States, but it is not an absolute principle of invariable application which can of itself resolve all boundary disputes or provide an answer to all territorial conundrums. *Uti possidetis* does, however, constitute a vital starting-point, and from time to time the finishing-point also, in the phenomenon of territorial disputes.

BOSNIA AND HERZEGOVINA: CIVIL WAR OR INTER-STATE CONFLICT? CHARACTERIZATION AND CONSEQUENCES*

By CHRISTINE GRAY‡

Was the conflict in Bosnia and Herzegovina a civil war or an inter-State conflict? States and writers were fundamentally divided on this issue. Obviously the dichotomy is too simple; a third possible (and plausible) category would be a civil war with outside intervention, the most common type of conflict since the Second World War. And the nature of the conflict in Bosnia and Herzegovina changed over time with the dissolution of the former Yugoslavia. Also the conflict in Bosnia and Herzegovina cannot be adequately understood in isolation from the conflict in the rest of the former Yugoslavia. But the stark choice between civil war and inter-State conflict is one that was put forward forcefully by the parties involved. The government of Bosnia and Herzegovina and States sympathetic to it argued that the conflict was an inter-State war and that Yugoslavia (Serbia and Montenegro)[1] was the aggressor against Bosnia either directly or through the Bosnian Serbs and the Croatian Serbs. Yugoslavia (Serbia and Montenegro) insisted on the civil nature of the conflict.

This issue of the characterization of the conflict is important in many contexts. It is central to the case brought by Bosnia and Herzegovina against Yugoslavia (Serbia and Montenegro) in the International Court of Justice;[2] it affected the claim of Yugoslavia (Serbia and Montenegro) to recognition as the successor State of the former Yugoslavia and to a seat in the United Nations;[3] and it was raised in the *Tadic* case before the

---

* © Dr Christine Gray, 1997.

‡ Lecturer in Law, University of Cambridge; formerly Reader in Law, University of Oxford.

[1] The name 'Yugoslavia (Serbia and Montenegro)' has been used purely for convenience, because it was used by the International Court of Justice (see below, n. 2). The question of the name gave rise to considerable controversy. Yugoslavia (Serbia and Montenegro) itself used the name Federal Republic of Yugoslavia, as the successor State to the former Yugoslavia; Croatia and Bosnia and Herzegovina challenged its right to this name and referred to it as Serbia and Montenegro.

[2] *Application of the Convention on the Prevention and Punishment of the Crime of Genocide (Bosnia and Herzegovina v. Yugoslavia (Serbia and Montenegro))*, Request for the Indication of Provisional Measures, ICJ Reports, 1993, pp. 3, 325 (see note by Gray, *International and Comparative Law Quarterly*, 43 (1994), p. 704); *Jurisdiction and Admissibility*, ICJ Reports, 1996.

[3] Gray, loc. cit. above (n. 2), at p. 707; Blum, 'UN Membership of the New Yugoslavia — Continuity or Break', *American Journal of International Law*, 86 (1992), p. 830; Agora, ibid., 87 (1993), p. 240.

International Criminal Tribunal for the former Yugoslavia.[4] The characterization of the conflict was also central to the debate over the lifting of the arms embargo on Bosnia and Herzegovina and on Bosnia's right to self-defence, and it is on this issue that the second part of this article will focus, because of its continuing significance for United Nations practice on arms embargoes and for the interpretation of Article 51 of the United Nations Charter.[5]

'Threats to international peace and security'

The conflict began in 1991 as a civil war in Yugoslavia, but a civil conflict that the United Nations Security Council characterized as a 'threat to international peace and security'. The origin of the conflict lay in the determination of Slovenia and Croatia to secede from the Federal State of Yugoslavia and in the opposition of the Federal Government and the Croatian Serbs.[6] When fighting escalated between the Croats and the Serbs in Croatia, the Security Council passed its first resolution on Yugoslavia, Resolution 713, stating that it was 'concerned by the fighting in Yugoslavia . . . and by the consequences for the countries of the region, in particular in the border areas of neighbouring countries', and that it was also concerned 'that the continuation of the situation constitutes a threat to international peace and security'.[7] It accordingly called on the parties to respect the current ceasefire and decided under Chapter VII of the United Nations Charter to impose an arms embargo on the whole of Yugoslavia, as it then was.[8]

This willingness to find a threat to international peace and security on the basis of a civil war was nothing new in the practice of the Security Council[9] and, given the dangers of the Yugoslav conflict spreading to neighbouring States such as Albania, Greece, Russia and Turkey, the characterization of the situation as a threat to international peace and security was more obviously justified in the case of Yugoslavia than in cases such as Haiti.[10] In the debate leading up to the unanimous adoption of Resolution 713, Yugoslavia itself expressly consented to the Security

[4] *International Legal Materials*, 35 (1996), p. 32. In this case Tadic argued, *inter alia*, that the tribunal lacked subject-matter jurisdiction over his case. He said that the tribunal had jurisdiction only over international armed conflict; as this was an internal conflict, the tribunal had no jurisdiction. The tribunal did not pronounce on this question of the nature of the conflict. It said that it did not matter whether the conflict was internal or international; individual criminal responsibility could arise in both types of conflict.

[5] See below at n. 143.

[6] Keesing's *Record of World Events* (hereafter *Keesing's*), 1991, pp. 38019, 38204, 38274, 38373, 38502, 38513, 38559.

[7] Passed unanimously, 25 September 1991.

[8] On lifting the arms embargo, see below at n. 143.

[9] See T.M. Franck, *Fairness in International Law* (1995), p. 224; N.D. White, *Keeping the Peace* (1993), p. 44.

[10] Resolution 841, 16 June 1993, *UN Yearbook*, 1993, p. 334; see Franck, op. cit. above (n. 9), at p. 112.

Council putting the situation in Yugoslavia on its agenda.[11] For China, the USSR and Zaire this consent was crucial in legitimating action by the Security Council.[12] The United Kingdom took a more expansive line. It denied that it was premature to use the language of Chapter VII; the conflict had a strong international dimension. The patchwork of nationalities and minorities meant that a full-scale war might not be confined easily to a single territory.[13] The USA alone attributed blame at this stage. It said that a lot of parties bore responsibility but that in its opinion the Government of Serbia and the Yugoslav federal military bore a special and growing responsibility for the grim future facing Yugoslavia. The aim of Serbia was to create a greater Serbia, using force to establish control of territory outside Serbia. Therefore aggression within Yugoslavia was a direct threat to international peace and security. The USA was speaking with reference mainly to Croatia, but said that the fate of Bosnia and Herzegovina also was in the balance.[14] However, the Security Council in its Resolution 713 was not concerned with attributing blame at this stage and it treated the conflict as civil.

Similarly, when the fighting spread to Bosnia and Herzegovina in 1992,[15] the Security Council again used the language of Article 39 of the United Nations Charter with reference to Bosnia and Herzegovina in 'Determining that the situation in Bosnia and Herzegovina and in other parts of the former Socialist Federal Republic of Yugoslavia constitutes a threat to international peace and security'.[16] The Security Council subsequently maintained this pattern of referring only to 'threats to international peace and security' with regard to Bosnia and Herzegovina; it did not find 'breaches of the peace' or 'acts of aggression' under Article 39.[17] And it did not make references to 'threats to international peace and security' in every resolution, not even in every resolution under Chapter VII.[18] Rather it seems to have used this language as a mark of emphasis when it passed a resolution breaking new ground.

Thus, it referred to 'a threat to international peace and security' in Resolution 757, the first resolution imposing sanctions on Yugoslavia (Serbia and Montenegro);[19] in Resolution 770, the first resolution authorizing member States to use force in the former Yugoslavia, to

---

[11] UN Doc. S/PV 3009.

[12] Ibid.

[13] Ibid.

[14] Ibid.

[15] *UN Yearbook*, 1992, p. 344; *Keesing's*, 1991, pp. 38832, 38848, 38918, 38970, 39012, 39035, 39102, 39149, 39198.

[16] Resolution 757, 30 May 1992, passed 13–0–2 (China, Zimbabwe).

[17] This is typical of the Security Council's preference to avoid the more serious findings under Article 39. See, for example, White, op. cit. above (n. 9), at pp. 44–52.

[18] It is noteworthy that the Security Council often does not make express reference to Article 39, but simply uses its language or an approximation thereto.

[19] See n. 16, above.

secure the delivery of humanitarian assistance;[20] in Resolution 807, the first resolution on UNPROFOR to be passed under Chapter VII;[21] in Resolution 827 establishing the international criminal tribunal;[22] and also in Resolution 1021 welcoming the initialling of the general framework of peace at the end of the conflict but nevertheless reaffirming that the situation still constituted a threat to international peace and security.[23]

In considering the nature of this 'threat to international peace and security', the crucial underlying issue that divided States was whether the conflict in Bosnia and Herzegovina which started as a civil war subsequently became in inter-State conflict on the breakup of the former Yugoslavia and the admission of its former republics as members of the United Nations.[24] Clearly there was outside intervention in Bosnia and Herzegovina; what was the scope of this? Was it sufficient to make any other State an aggressor or guilty of an armed attack against the State of Bosnia and Herzegovina?

Civil war or inter-State conflict: the opposing views

The fundamental difference between States was obvious in communications to the Security Council and in Security Council debates on the conflict in the former Yugoslavia. Thus Bosnia and Herzegovina repeatedly wrote to the Security Council claiming that it was the victim of aggression. These claims were sometimes in general terms,[25] but Bosnia and Herzegovina also made specific statements that Yugoslavia (Serbia and Montenegro) was responsible. For example, in May 1992 Bosnia and Herzegovina wrote: 'By 15 May 1992, date of the Security Council resolution 752, the Republic of Bosnia-Herzegovina had already become the victim of the most naked and barbaric form of aggression of any sovereign State against another since the dark days of World War II . . . . We were hoping against our own worst suspicions that resolution 752 would have a real impact in deterring further aggression by the Belgrade regime and its tools, the 'Yugoslav' or Serbian National Army and their affiliated irregulars.'[26] Again, in June 1992, Bosnia and Herzegovina wrote that

For 11 weeks now, the sovereign nation of Bosnia-Herzegovina has suffered the brutal aggression of Serbian and Montenegran regular and paramilitary forces

---

[20] 13 August 1992, 12–0–3 (China, India, Zimbabwe).
[21] 19 February 1993, passed unanimously. See Gray, 'Host State Consent and United Nations Peacekeeping in Yugoslavia', *Duke Journal of International Law*, 7 (1996), p. 241.
[22] 25 May 1993, passed unanimously.
[23] 22 November 1995, passed 14–0–1 (Russia).
[24] Croatia, Slovenia and Bosnia and Herzegovina were admitted to the United Nations on 22 May 1992: *UN Yearbook*, 1992, p. 137.
[25] For example, UN Doc. S/24331.
[26] UN Doc. S/24024.

and extremists within the Serbian population of Bosnia-Herzegovina, who are armed, organized and supported by the former Yugoslav army and Serbia.

Overly cautious and ambiguous diplomatic language of international leaders and official reports have equated the two sides in this conflict. They are not the same. One is the aggressor, the other is the victim. Such obfuscation encourages aggression, not conciliation. It undermines the cause of justice and fails to differentiate between the two sides, let alone protect the victim.[27]

These and later claims of a war of aggression carried out by the Belgrade regime and its proxies[28] were backed by other States' communications to the Security Council. The EC, which was working through the Conference in Yugoslavia to secure a peaceful settlement, in its declarations on Yugoslavia first condemned the violence in Bosnia and Herzegovina, in particular that by the Yugoslav People's Army (JNA), and urged the Belgrade authorities to do all in their power to prevent violent activities by Serb irregulars.[29] It then issued a Declaration on Bosnia and Herzegovina on 11 May 1992, saying that all had contributed to the present situation but most of the blame lay on the Yugoslav People's Army (JNA) and the authorities in Belgrade.[30] Other states followed this line.[31] Australia's letter was more precise than most in its attribution of responsibility. It said: 'All the parties to the conflict carried some responsibility for its continuation but . . . Serbia and Montenegro carry the principal burden of responsibility. This is evidenced by the scale and inhumanity of the activities of the Yugoslav People's Army and of the irregular Serbian forces which are either under the direction of the authorities in Belgrade or over which those authorities have not attempted to assert effective control.'[32]

In the Security Council debates States repeated these views. Only a few states put the opposing view that the conflict was a civil one and that Yugoslavia (Serbia and Montenegro) was not the aggressor or responsible for the Bosnian Serbs. In the debates on sanctions, on lifting the arms embargo and on the role of UNPROFOR the divisions were clear. For example, in August 1992 Zimbabwe said that the situation in Bosnia and Herzegovina was essentially a civil war.[33] It also abstained on the imposition of sanctions on Yugoslavia (Serbia and Montenegro) under Resolutions 757 and 787.[34] In the same debate Morocco replied that it was not a question of civil war, but a question of the invasion of one State by another State. In another debate the USA spoke of the aggression of

[27] UN Doc. S/24137.
[28] UN Doc. S/24226, S/24331, S/24588, S/24601, S/24616.
[29] UN Doc. S/23830.
[30] UN Doc. S/23906.
[31] Egypt, Turkey, Hungary and Germany all sent letters to the Secretary-General (UN Doc. S/23975, 24446, 23845, 23805).
[32] UN Doc. S/24042.
[33] UN Doc. S/PV 3106.
[34] Resolution 787, 16 November 1992, passed 13–0–2 (China, Zimbabwe).

the Serbian regime and the United Kingdom said that responsibility was shared among many but that there was no doubt who bore the principal responsibility.[35]

Slovenia asserted in February 1994 in a debate on lifting the arms embargo on Bosnia and Herzegovina that 'The war in Bosnia and Herzegovina is neither a religious war nor an ethnic conflict, nor is it a three-way civil war as some observers tend to believe. That war started as a war of aggression against a United Nations member state and it has remained, in essence, a war for territorial expansion.'[36] Yugoslavia (Serbia and Montenegro) did not accept this characterization of the conflict; it said that conflict was a civil war.[37] In a debate in April 1994 it elaborated on this. It said: 'A civil, interethnic and religious war provoked by unconstitutional separatism and forceful secession has been treated as aggression by one indigenous and constituent nation of Bosnia and Herzegovina, the Bosnian Serbs, against the others.'[38] This does not even acknowledge the accusations directed against Yugoslavia (Serbia and Montenegro) itself.

The Secretary-General's reports

The Secretary-General produced a long series of reports to the Security Council on the progress of the conflict in the former Yugoslavia. These do not include any formal pronouncements by the Secretary-General as to the civil or inter-State nature of the conflict, but they do give a clear and objective picture of the scope of outside intervention.[39] His report in April 1992, in response to the Security Council's request to him to investigate the prospects for deployment of a peace-keeping force in Bosnia and Herzegovina, showed that not surprisingly there was no consensus among the parties as to the responsibility for the fighting.[40] Yugoslavia (Serbia and Montenegro) asserted that the President of Bosnia and Herzegovina was responsible and that hostilities had been initiated by units from Croatia. The President of Croatia said that the Croatian regular army was not fighting in Bosnia and the only Croatian forces present were irregulars. According to the President of Bosnia and Herzegovina, the excessive territorial claims by the Bosnian Serbs were the source of the conflict. The Secretary-General did not at this stage pronounce on responsibility; he stressed the need for a ceasefire.

---

[35] UN Doc. S/PV 3082.

[36] UN Doc. S/PV 3336; see also statement of Saudi Arabia: 'The statment that what is happening in Bosnia and Herzegovina is a civil war is an attempt to mislead world public opinion and to project the Serbs as parties to an internal dispute. What is happening in Bosnia and Herzegovina is a blatant act of aggression.'

[37] UN Doc. S/PV 3336.

[38] UN Doc. S/PV 3367; see also S/PV 3370, p. 33.

[39] From July 1993 the focus of the Secretary-General's reports shifted away from intervention to issues such as safe areas, the no-fly zone and the progress of the peace negotiations.

[40] UN Doc. S/23836.

The Secretary-General to some extent attributed responsibility to the Serbs, although not directly to Yugoslavia (Serbia and Montenegro). In his report of 12 May 1992 he said:

4. Intense hostilities are taking place elsewhere in the Republic, notably in Mostar and the Neretva valley (JNA versus Croat forces; Belgrade's claim that these are units of the Croatian Army is contested by Zagreb and has not been confirmed by UNPROFOR, but it is not disputed that individual members of the Croatian Army with their weapons, are extensively deployed in Bosnia and Herzegovina) . . .

5. All international observers agree that what is happening is a concerted effort by the Serbs of Bosnia and Herzegovina, with the acquiescence of, and at least some support from, JNA, to create 'ethnically pure' regions in the context of negotiations on the 'cantonization' of the Republic . . . . The techniques used are the seizure of territory by military force and intimidation of the non-Serb population. The conclusion of a partial cease-fire agreement between Croat and Serb leaders on 6 May 1992 has revived suspicions of a Croat-Serb carve up of Bosnia and Herzegovina, leaving minimal territory to the Muslim community. Further concern has been caused by the decision of the Belgrade authorities to withdraw from Bosnia and Herzegovina by 18 May 1992 all JNA personnel who were not citizens of that Republic. This will leave in Bosnia and Herzegovina, without effective political control, as many as 50,000 mostly Serb troops and their weapons. They are likely to be taken over by the Serb party.[41]

On 30 May, 6 June and 15 June 1992 the Secretary-General reported on the progress of the withdrawal of the JNA and the Croatian army from Bosnia and Herzegovina.[42] Both Yugoslavia (Serbia and Montenegro) and Croatia denied any interference in Bosnia and Herzegovina, claiming that the troops were Croatian and Serbian citizens of Bosnia not under their authority. The Secretary-General said that the JNA needed assistance to leave Bosnia and Herzegovina as the Bosnia and Herzegovina Government had blockaded some of the JNA forces. He reported that the Bosnian Serbs had proclaimed their own army; as to who controlled the Serb forces in Bosnia and Herzegovina, the Secretary-General said that there were different groups, but uncertainty about who exercised political control over them further complicated the situation. It had become clear that the word of the Belgrade authorities was not binding on the army of General Mladic of the 'Serbian Republic of Bosnia and Herzegovina'.[43]

The Secretary-General also said that no withdrawal of the Croatian Army from Bosnia and Herzegovina had taken place. The Croatian Government claimed that these forces were irregulars who had left the Croatian Army and were not subject to its authority, but international observers said that portions of Bosnia and Herzegovina were under the

[41] UN Doc. S/23900.
[42] UN Doc. S/24049, S/24075, S/24100.
[43] See contrary view of Lord Owen: UN Doc. S/25015.

control of Croatian military units, whether belonging to the local Territorial Defence, to paramilitary groups or to the Croatian Army. 'It none the less remains a matter of great concern that demobilized elements of the armies of both sides should have been permitted to retain control over their tanks, armoured personnel carriers, artillery, personal weapons and uniforms. There is also reason to believe that both Serb and Croat combatants continued to receive at least part of their financial and logistic support from outside.'[44] Again, in a report of 24 November 1992 the Secretary-General reported that the resolution calling for the withdrawal of foreign forces remained largely unimplemented. The Croatian Army was reliably reported to be engaged extensively in Bosnia and Herzegovina and the Serb forces in Bosnia and Herzegovina were receiving logistical support from Yugoslavia (Serbia and Montenegro).[45]

In General Assembly debates of August 1992 and January 1993 Croatia expressly admitted the presence of its troops in border areas of Bosnia and Herzegovina and justified this on the basis that they were there with the consent of the government under an agreement of June 1992 between the two States.[46] There was no debate on this question, and the Secretary-General did not examine this claim, but it is at least open to doubt whether the presence of the Croatian army in Bosnia and Herzegovina was compatible with Resolution 752, calling for the withdrawal of elements of the Croatian army in Bosnia and Herzegovina.[47]

At the end of 1992 the Security Council decided that it wanted to institute monitoring of the borders of Bosnia and Herzegovina, especially those with Yugoslavia (Serbia and Montenegro), in order to facilitate implementation of its resolutions on the arms embargo, non-intervention, and sanctions against Yugoslavia (Serbia and Montenegro).[48] Accordingly it asked the Secretary-General to make a report on the deployment of observers on the borders of Bosnia and Herzegovina.[49] The Security Council subsequently in June 1993 asked the Secretary-General to report further on options for the deployment of international observers on the borders of Bosnia and Herzegovina.[50] However, the Secretary-General could not at that time hold out any prospect of effective monitoring because of lack of UN resources, and in March 1994 he again said that resources did not allow monitoring.[51] Effective

[44] UN Doc. S/24100.
[45] UN Doc. S/24848; see also S/24748, S/24759.
[46] UN Doc. A/46/PV 89, A/47/PV 86.
[47] See below at n. 107.
[48] Resolution 787, above, n. 34, "considers that, in order to facilitate the implementation of the relevant Security Council resolutions, observers should be deployed on the borders of the Republic of Bosnia and Herzegovina, and requests the Secretary-General to present to the Council as soon as possible his recommendations on this matter'.
[49] The Secretary-General reported on 21 December 1992: UN Doc. S/25000.
[50] Resolution 838, 10 June 1993, passed unanimously.
[51] UN Doc. S/26018, confirmed UN Doc. S/1994/300.

monitoring was established only after the closure of the border between Yugoslavia (Serbia and Montenegro) and the Bosnian Serbs in August 1994.[52]

From mid-1993 to March 1994 the main fighting in Bosnia and Herzegovina took place between the forces of Bosnia and Herzegovina and those of Bosnian Croats, aided by Croatia.[53] However, the accusation by Yugoslavia (Serbia and Montenegro) of Croatian Army incursions into Bosnia and Herzegovina in May 1993[54] and the newspaper reports of further incursions in November 1993[55] were apparently not discussed in any report of the Secretary-General. As regards the May operations, five non-aligned members of the Security Council wrote a memorandum saying that the Security Council should consider the imposition of economic sanctions against Croatia if its offensive actions continued, particularly those against Bosnian Muslims in Mostar.[56] This was not pursued by the Security Council.

In January and February 1994 the Croatian army again went into Bosnia and Herzegovina. Bosnia and Herzegovina complained to the Security Council.[57] The Secretary-General described in a letter of 1 February 1994 to the Security Council the deployment by Croatia of elements of its army in central and southern Bosnia and Herzegovina.[58] The Security Council made a statement expressing deep concern that Croatia had deployed elements of its army in Bosnia and Herzegovina and strongly condemned Croatia. It then accordingly asked the Secretary-General to monitor closely the situation and to report to the Council within two weeks on progress towards the complete and full withdrawal of all elements of the Croatian army as well as military equipment from Bosnia and Herzegovina.[59] In his report the Secretary-General said that the ability of UNPROFOR to observe developments throughout Bosnia and Herzegovina was limited. UNPROFOR was not therefore in a position to verify in a systematic fashion whether all elements of the Croatian Army and the equipment concerned were being withdrawn. But the Secretary-General reported that UNPROFOR had observed one

---

[52] See below at n. 70.
[53] UN Doc. S/26066; *UN Yearbook*, 1993, pp. 460, 466. Bosnia and Herzegovina made the rather strange claim that 'This fighting is not a conflict based along ethnic lines. Rather, it is a consequence of the international community's arms embargo on Bosnia and Herzegovina, and the international community's failure to provide adequate humanitarian assistance to the besieged population in central Bosnia and Herzegovina. . . . If the two armies had adequate defence capabilities and if the population in central Bosnia were adequately assisted with humanitarian needs, conflict between local leaders would have never occurred': UN Doc. S/25646.
[54] UN Doc. S/25780; see also David Owen, *Balkan Odyssey* (1995), p. 178; *Keesing's*, 1993, p. 39471.
[55] *Keesing's*, 1993, p. 39743.
[56] UN Doc. S/25782.
[57] UN Doc. S/1994/95, *UN Yearbook*, 1994, p. 548, and *Keesing's*, 1994, p. 39827.
[58] UN Doc. S/1994/109; see also Human Rights Rapporteur report, UN Doc. S/1994/265, confirming the direct involvement of the Croatian army.
[59] UN Doc. S/PRST/1994/6.

convoy leaving Bosnia and Herzegovina. Despite Croatian statements
that other forces would also leave Bosnia and Herzegovina, no other
withdrawals had been observed. Therefore UNPROFOR continued to
assess that there could still be 5,000 Croatian Army troops in Bosnia and
Herzegovina, although no command posts nor any full brigades operating as formed units had been identified. It appeared that Croatian Army
troops were now being more circumspect and may have been removing
their insignia while in Bosnia and Herzegovina and replacing them with
those of the Bosnian Croats.[60] In response Croatia wrote that 'Croatian
volunteers' that had been situated in Bosnia and Herzegovina had now
returned to Croatia.[61] But the Secretary-General did not accept this
description of the troops; he wrote of 'the recent increase of outside
involvement in the Bosnian conflict, especially Croatian Army involvement in southern and central Bosnia and Herzegovina'.[62] The fighting in
Bosnia and Herzegovina between the Bosnian Croats and government
forces was ended by the Washington agreement of March 1994.[63] After
this agreement, the Secretary-General reported on joint actions in Bosnia
and Herzegovina by the Croatian army and Bosnian Government forces
against the Bosnian Serbs.[64]

Yugoslavia (Serbia and Montenegro) continued to express political
support for the Bosnian Serbs until August 1994, when the refusal of the
Bosnian Serbs to accept the latest peace plan led Yugoslavia (Serbia and
Montenegro) to announce that it was cutting off all but humanitarian
supplies to the Bosnian Serbs. It undertook:

(A) To break off political and economic relations with the Republika Srpska;
(B) To prohibit the stay of the members of the leadership of the Republika
Srpska (Parliament, Presidency and Government) in the territory of the Federal
Republic of Yugoslavia;
(C) As of today the border of the Federal Republic of Yugoslavia is closed for all
transport towards the Republika Srpska except food, clothing and medicine.[65]

This severing of relations led to the partial suspension of sanctions
against Yugoslavia (Serbia and Montenegro) by the Security Council in
Resolution 943.[66] Croatia and Bosnia and Herzegovina continued to
express reservations about this suspension, as they said that Yugoslavia

---

[60] UN Doc. S/1994/190.
[61] UN Doc. S/1994/197.
[62] UN Doc. S/1994/300.
[63] The Washington agreement is reproduced in UN Doc. S/1994/255; see also *UN Yearbook*,
1994, p. 549; *Keesing's*, 1994, pp. 39871, 39925; and see below at n. 105.
[64] UN Doc. S/1994/1389, S/1995/650, S/1995/666; see below at n. 106.
[65] UN Doc. S/1994/932. Yugoslavia (Serbia and Montenegro) had once before, in May 1993,
announced an end to its support for the Bosnian Serbs after their rejection of the Vance-Owen Peace
Plan (*UN Yearbook*, 1993, p. 475).
[66] Resolution 943, 23 September 1994, passed 11–2 (Djibouti, Pakistan) – 2 (Nigeria,
Rwanda).

(Serbia and Montenegro) was still helping the Bosnian Serbs.[67] The Security Council at the same time imposed sanctions directly on the Bosnian Serbs.[68] Following these resolutions, arrangements were made for the monitoring of the border between Bosnia and Herzegovina and Yugoslavia (Serbia and Montenegro).[69] Reports by the Secretary-General to the Security Council largely confirmed Yugoslavia (Serbia and Montenegro)'s compliance with its commitment to close the border and showed that the allegations of Bosnia and Herzegovina and Croatia were not well-founded. The monitors reporting to the Secretary-General stated that Yugoslavia (Serbia and Montenegro) was continuing to meet its commitment to close the border between it and the areas of Bosnia and Herzegovina under the control of the Bosnian Serb forces.[70]

Security Council resolutions

In contrast to the complex picture given by the Secretary-General's reports, the picture that emerges from the Security Council resolutions on Bosnia and Herzegovina is very much more one-sided. The impression given is that Yugoslavia (Serbia and Montenegro) was almost solely responsible for any intervention in Bosnia. The Security Council in its resolutions tended to criticize Yugoslavia (Serbia and Montenegro). It made far fewer and weaker criticisms of Croatia. These resolutions reflect the tenor of Security Council debates and communications to the Council; both show that almost every State held Yugoslavia (Serbia and Montenegro) to some extent responsible with almost no State willing to defend it or, more surprisingly, to criticize Croatia for its interventions.[71]

The Security Council began its involvement with Bosnia and Herzegovina by calling in Resolution 749 for a ceasefire.[72] It next made a general statement calling for the end of outside interference;

The Council demands that all forms of interference from outside Bosnia and Herzegovina cease immediately. In this respect, it specifically calls upon Bosnia and Herzegovina's neighbours to exercise all their influence to end such interference. The Council condemns publicly and unreservedly the use of force,

---

[67] UN Doc. S/PV 3428.

[68] Resolution 942, 23 September 1994, passed 14–0–1 (China).

[69] After Resolution 959, 19 November 1994, passed unanimously, expressed concern at violation of the border between Croatia and Bosnia and Herzegovina, the Security Council passed Resolution 970 and Resolution 988 reaffirming the duty on Yugoslavia (Serbia and Montenegro) not to allow material to pass through the Serb areas of Croatia to the Bosnian Serbs. See the Security Council debates, UN Doc. S/PV 3487, S/PV 3522.

[70] UN Doc. S/1994/1074, 1124, 1246, 1372; S/1995/6, 104, 175, 255, 302, 406, 510 confirmed the effectiveness of the closure, despite allegations by Croatia and Bosnia and Herzegovina in UN Doc. S/PV 3428, 3487, 3522. The Secretary-General reported in December 1994 that 'all verifiable information received up to December had proved inaccurate' (*UN Yearbook*, 1994, p. 558 at p. 559).

[71] See below at n. 93.

[72] Resolution 749, 7 April 1992, passed unanimously.

and calls upon all regular or irregular military forces to act in accordance with these principles.[73]

In its first resolution calling for an end to outside intervention in Bosnia and Herzegovina, Resolution 752,[74] the Security Council was even-handed. It said that, having considered the announcement in Belgrade on 4 May 1992 concerning the withdrawal of the JNA from republics other than Yugoslavia (Serbia and Montenegro), it

> Demands that all forms of interference from outside Bosnia-Herzegovina, including by units of the Yugoslav People's Army (JNA) as well as elements of the Croatian Army cease immediately, and that Bosnia-Herzegovina's neighbours take swift action to end such interference and respect the territorial integrity of Bosnia-Herzegovina;
>
> Demands that those units of the Yugoslav People's Army (JNA) and elements of the Croatian Army now in Bosnia-Herzegovina must either be withdrawn, or be subject to the authority of the Government of Bosnia-Herzegovina, or be disbanded and disarmed with their weapons placed under effective international monitoring, and requests the Secretary-General to consider without delay what international assistance could be provided in this connection.

This resolution was passed on 15 May 1992, that is before Bosnia and Herzegovina was admitted to membership of the United Nations but at a time when the process of admission was already well under way.

Subsequently, the Security Council moved away from its even-handed approach; from Resolution 757 until Resolution 943 in September 1994 it seemed to treat Yugoslavia (Serbia and Montenegro) as primarily responsible for breach of Resolution 752 and only rarely made reference to Croatian involvement. At the Security Council debate on Resolution 752 almost all the States that spoke held Yugoslavia (Serbia and Montenegro) responsible expressly or implicitly.[75] Only China and Zimbabwe did not take this line; they also abstained in the vote on Resolution 757 imposing sanctions on Yugoslavia (Serbia and Montenegro).[76] This resolution started by noting that 'in the very complex context of events in the former Socialist Federal Republic of Yugoslavia all parties bear some responsibility for the situation', but it nevertheless went on to impose sanctions only on Yugoslavia (Serbia and Montenegro). The relevant sections said:

> Deploring the fact that the demands in resolution 752 (1992) have not been complied with . . .
>
> Acting under Chapter VII of the Charter of the United Nations,
>
> 1. Condemns the failure of the authorities in the Federal Republic of Yugoslavia

---

[73] UN Doc. S/23842.
[74] Resolution 752, 15 May 1992, passed unanimously.
[75] UN Doc. S/PV 3082.
[76] Resolution 757: see n. 16, above.

(Serbia and Montenegro), including the Yugoslav's People's Army (JNA) to take effective measures to fulfil the requirements of resolution 752 (1992);

2. Demands that any elements of the Croatian Army still present in Bosnia and Herzegovina act in accordance with paragraph 4 of resolution 752 (1992) without delay;

3. Decides that all States shall adopt the measures set out below which shall apply until the Security Council decides that the authorities in the Federal Republic of Yugoslavia (Serbia and Montenegro), including the Yugoslav People's Army, have taken effective measures to fulfil the requirements of resolution 752 (1992).

That is, the Security Council condemned Yugoslavia (Serbia and Montenegro). Whereas the USA spoke of the Security Council sanctions as a response to the 'aggression of the Serbian regime',[77] European States and others in Security Council debates repeatedly insisted that the aim of sanctions was not to punish, but to achieve changes in policy by Yugoslavia (Serbia and Montenegro).[78] Cape Verde gave the most seductive version of this:

In voting for this draft resolution it is not our intention to endorse action against Serbia and Montenegro, nor to impose hardship on their people. Our only intention is to assist in the creation of an environment conducive to the restoration of peace and tranquillity in Bosnia and Herzegovina that will allow a peaceful and negotiated solution for the internal problems of that member of the United Nations to be worked out.[79]

But in imposing sanctions on Yugoslavia (Serbia and Montenegro) the Security Council was implicitly attributing to it responsibility for the conflict and acting as if pressure on Yugoslavia (Serbia and Montenegro) were the best way of ending or limiting the conflict. That is, it treated Yugoslavia (Serbia and Montenegro) as in some sense responsible for the JNA troops remaining in Bosnia and Herzegovina and Serb irregulars. Yugoslavia (Serbia and Montenegro) in rejecting this responsibility spoke of the sanctions as a 'policy of collective punishment'.[80] In contrast, the Security Council did not treat the continuing Croatian presence in Bosnia and Herzegovina as a violation of Resolution 752.

To strengthen the sanctions against Yugoslavia (Serbia and Montenegro) the Security Council passed Resolution 787 on 6 November 1992, thus appearing to confirm Yugoslavia (Serbia and Montenegro)'s responsibility.[81] The Security Council expressed deep concern at the threats to the territorial integrity of the Republic of Bosnia and Herzegovina, which, as a State member of the United Nations, enjoys the rights provided for in the Charter of the United Nations. It

---

[77] UN Doc. S/PV 3082.
[78] For example, UN Doc. S/PV 3487, S/PV 3522.
[79] UN Doc. S/PV 3082.
[80] UN Doc. S/PV 3522.
[81] See n. 34, above.

Condemns the refusal of all parties in the Republic of Bosnia and Herzegovina, in particular the Bosnian Serb paramilitary forces, to comply with its previous resolutions, and demands that they and all other concerned parties in the former Yugoslavia fulfil immediately their obligations under these resolutions.

This resolution was more specific than earlier resolutions in its references to the exact nature of the outside intervention and in its demands for an end to this. It did not, however, actually name Yugoslavia (Serbia and Montenegro) or expressly hold it responsible for allowing infiltration in this part of the resolution. It demanded that

all forms of interference from outside the Republic of Bosnia and Herzegovina, including infiltration into the country of irregular units and personnel, cease immediately, and reaffirms its determination to take measures against all parties and others concerned which fail to fulfil the requirements of resolution 752(1992) and its other relevant resolutions, including the requirement that all forces, in particular elements of the Croatian Army, be withdrawn, or be subject to the authority of the Government of the Republic of Bosnia and Herzegovina, or be disbanded or disarmed.

Despite the reference to the Croatian Army, the Security Council strengthened the sanctions against Yugoslavia (Serbia and Montenegro) but took no comparable measures against Croatia.

The Security Council was again one-sided and again specific in its call for an end to intervention in Resolution 819.[82] This noted the ICJ's indication of provisional measures against Yugoslavia (Serbia and Montenegro),[83] and condemned the Bosnian Serbs for violations of humanitarian law, interference with humanitarian aid, and action against UNPROFOR. It then demanded that Yugoslavia (Serbia and Montenegro) immediately cease the supply of military arms, equipment and services to the Bosnian Serb paramilitary units in Bosnia and Herzegovina. But it did not expressly hold Yugoslavia (Serbia and Montenegro) responsible for all the actions of the Bosnian Serbs or assert direct intervention by it.

The shift of focus away from Yugoslavia (Serbia and Montenegro) to the Bosnian Serbs continued in subsequent Security Council resolutions leading up to the imposition of sanctions on the Bosnian Serbs in 1994. First, Resolution 820 condemned the Bosnian Serbs for not accepting the peace plan for Bosnia and Herzegovina in April 1993. This resolution also strengthened the sanctions against Yugoslavia (Serbia and Montenegro) in order to stop goods reaching Serbian Croat areas in Croatia or the Bosnian Serbs.[84] Yugoslavia (Serbia and Montenegro) argued in the Security Council debate that it had co-operated to end the war in Bosnia and Herzegovina, it had repeatedly stated that it had no territorial claims

---

[82] Resolution 819, 16 April 1993, passed unanimously.
[83] See n. 2, above.
[84] Resolution 820, 17 April 1993, 13–0–2 (China, Russia).

on any of its neighbours and none of its army remained in Bosnia and Herzegovina. Nevertheless, the international community and the Security Council had persisted in treating it as party to the conflict and in calling for its punishment and isolation. The conviction that Yugoslavia (Serbia and Montenegro) could order the Bosnian Serbs to accept something that threatened their survival and that they were ready to obey orders from Belgrade was illusory and false. It was doing its utmost to advise the Bosnian Serbs but it could not order a people to capitulate who were dying and sacrificing all they had in order to survive on their land.[85] Later resolutions repeated the demands for non-intervention and for peaceful settlement of the conflict, the call for an end to arms supplies to the Bosnian Serbs and the concern at non-compliance with Security Council resolutions, especially by the Bosnian Serbs.[86]

Finally, in a major shift after Yugoslavia (Serbia and Montenegro) announced the end to co-operation with the Bosnian Serbs in August 1994,[87] the Security Council imposed sanctions directly on the Bosnian Serbs.[88] This followed the precedent of earlier Security Council measures against non-State entities that were not co-operating with UN peace efforts, such as the Khmer Rouge in Cambodia and UNITA in Angola.[89] As a reward to Yugoslavia (Serbia and Montenegro) for closing its border with the Bosnian Serbs, the Security Council partially suspended the sanctions on it.[90] Nevertheless, in the Security Council debates some States still pressed for the continuation of the sanctions and persisted in blaming Yugoslavia (Serbia and Montenegro) for the conflict. Thus the USA said: "My Government continues to believe that the Belgrade authorities have primary responsibility for what has happened in the former Yugoslavia during the past three years'.[91] In reply Yugoslavia (Serbia and Montenegro) argued that as the initial resolution on sanctions, Resolution 757, 'contains no demands on the Federal Republic of Yugoslavia that have not been realised', the Security Council should immediately lift all measures taken against it. Yugoslavia claimed that it had exerted permanent positive pressure on the Serb side in the former Bosnia-Herzegovina, including the severance of political and economic relations with the Republic of Srpska, in order to have it accept the offered solutions. However, just like the entire international community, the Federal Republic of Yugoslavia could not ensure a cessation of the civil war in the former Bosnia-Herzegovina since 'our country does not take part in that war nor has it any influence whatsoever on two out of the

[85] UN Doc. S/PV 3203, p. 26.
[86] Resolutions 824, 836, 838, 859, 913.
[87] See n. 65, above.
[88] Resolution 942: see n. 68, above.
[89] UN Yearbook, 1993, p. 255; UN Yearbook, 1992, p. 258; UN Chronicle, September 1993, p. 26.
[90] Resolution 943: see n. 66, above.
[91] UN Doc. S/PV 3428. Also Croatia and Bosnia and Herzegovina pressed for sanctions to continue (UN Doc. S/PV 3487, 3522).

three sides involved. All the units of the Army of Yugoslavia were withdrawn from the territory of the former Bosnia-Herzegovina prior to 21 May 1992 . . . . Following the decision of the Government of the Federal Republic of Yugoslavia of 4 August 1994, only humanitarian assistance is being delivered to this area from the Federal Republic of Yugoslavia.'[92]

This long sequence of resolutions clearly gives the impression that the Security Council regarded first Yugoslavia (Serbia and Montenegro) and then the Bosnian Serbs as responsible for the continuation of the conflict. There was very little reference to Croatian intervention in Bosnia. As we have seen, after the initial references to the presence of 'elements of the Croatian army' in Resolutions 752, 757 and 787, there were no subsequent references to Croatian intervention in Bosnia, in contrast to several resolutions containing condemnations of Croatia's violations of the United Nations peace plan in Croatia itself.[93]

In response to Croatian intervention in Bosnia and Herzegovina (and in its occasional criticisms of the Government of Bosnia and Herzegovina for violations of ceasefires and of humanitarian law[94]) the Security Council generally limited itself to *statements*, a less formal and therefore less serious form of condemnation than resolutions. Although the main fighting from mid-1993 to March 1994 was between the Government of Bosnia and Herzegovina and Bosnian Croats helped by Croatia, and although serious atrocities were committed by both sides,[95] the Security Council was reluctant to pass resolutions criticising Croatia, apparently because of German and United States support for Croatia.[96]

The outbreak of fighting in Bosnia and Herzegovina between the Bosnian Muslims and the Bosnian Croats in April 1993 led to a call by the Security Council for a ceasefire.[97] When the Bosnian Croats violated this ceasefire Croatia issued a public statement condemning them.[98] But the Security Council did not entirely take this condemnation at face value. It made a statement in May 1993 strongly condemning the major military offensive launched by the Bosnian Croat paramilitary unit.[99] It called upon Croatia to exert all its influence on the Bosnian Croat leadership and paramilitary units with a view to ceasing immediately their attacks. It also called on Croatia to adhere strictly to its obligations under Security Council Resolution 752(1992) including putting an end

[92] UN Doc. S/1994/1298.
[93] Croatia was condemned in Resolutions 762, 802, 807, 994, 1009.
[94] For example, UN Chronicle, June 1993, p. 8.
[95] UN Doc. S/25920, S/26146, S/26211, S/26342, S/26419, S/26437, S/26469, S/26617, S/26641, S/26742, S/26835, S/1994/78, S/1994/87, S/1994/154, S/PV 3276.
[96] For examples of US and German support, see Owen, op. cit. above (n. 54), at pp. 333, 386; Keesing's, 1993, p. 39564; 1995, p. 40692.
[97] UN Doc. S/25646.
[98] UN Doc. S/25748, S/25749.
[99] UN Doc. S/25746.

to all forms of interference and respecting the territorial integrity of the Republic of Bosnia and Herzegovina. The Security Council reaffirmed in the context of the Bosnian Croatian offensive the unacceptability of the acquisition of the territory by force and of the practice of ethnic cleansing. That is, the Security Council did not directly attribute responsibility for the invasion to Croatia, but the statement nevertheless implied that Croatia had violated Resolution 752.[100] In November 1993 there were newspaper reports of Croatian Army incursions into Bosnia and Herzegovina, but the Security Council issued only a general statement expressing concern about the situation in Bosnia and Herzegovina.[101]

In February 1994 the Security Council in another statement actually condemned Croatia for deploying its army in Bosnia and Herzegovina. It said that it was deeply concerned that the Republic of Croatia had deployed elements of the Croatian Army along with heavy military equipment in Bosnia and Herzegovina: 'The Security Council strongly condemns the Republic of Croatia for this serious hostile act against a Member State of the United Nations, which constitutes a violation of international law, the Charter of the United Nations and relevant Security Council resolutions, in particular resolution 752(1992), in which the Council demanded an immediate end to all forms of interference and full respect for the territorial integrity of the Republic of Bosnia and Herzegovina'. The Security Council demanded that Croatia withdraw forthwith all elements of the Croatian Army along with military equipment, and fully respect the territorial integrity of Bosnia and Herzegovina. It would consider other serious measures if Croatia failed to put an immediate end to all forms of interference in Bosnia and Herzegovina.[102]

Even in the face of this Croatian intervention in Bosnia and Herzegovina, very few States were willing openly to criticize it in the Security Council debates. In February 1994 only Pakistan criticized Croatia as well as Yugoslavia (Serbia and Montenegro);[103] and in March 1994 only the Czech Republic mentioned the Croatian invasion. It said: 'There still remains the vexing question of the involvement of troops of the Republic of Croatia in Bosnia and Herzegovina. The Czech Republic finds such involvement unacceptable under any circumstances and rejects any attempts to link their withdrawal with the political process underway. These troops must leave.'[104]

---

[100] See above at n. 56.
[101] UN Doc. S/26716.
[102] UN Doc. S/PV 3333; S/PRST/1994/6.
[103] UN Doc. S/PV 3336, p. 39; Pakistan said that it awaited the report on withdrawal of the Croatian army, and if the army did not withdraw there should be economic sanctions on Croatia.
[104] UN Doc. S/PV 3444, p. 7.

The Government of Bosnia and Herzegovina and the Bosnian Croats and Croatia subsequently ended the conflict between them by the Washington agreement in March 1994. This was welcomed by the Security Council in Resolution 908.[105] From that date, Croatia invoked the Washington agreement to justify the presence of its army in Bosnia and Herzegovina.[106] But, as in the early years of the conflict when Croatia had invoked an earlier agreement between itself and Bosnia and Herzegovina to justify stationing its troops in Bosnia and Herzegovina,[107] there is room for doubt as to whether this was compatible with Resolution 752 calling for an end to all forms of interference from outside Bosnia and Herzegovina. Yugoslavia (Serbia and Montenegro) wrote to the Security Council in December 1994 about the active involvement of the regular army of Croatia in Bosnia and Herzegovina; Croatia had confirmed that the Croatian forces had been deployed to the border region between itself and Bosnia and Herzegovina and had taken military activity in that area. It justified the presence of the Croatian army by the agreement between Croatia and Bosnia and Herzegovina and the relevant request from Bosnia and Herzegovina. Yugoslavia (Serbia and Montenegro) said that in doing so, the authorities of Croatia acted in flagrant violation of Security Council Resolutions 752, 757 and 787 which call upon the Croatian army to withdraw from Bosnia and Herzegovina.[108]

In so far as the Croatian army was intervening in a civil war, it is not obvious that even an invitation from the government would be enough to override the prohibition on intervention in Resolution 752. The Secretary-General raised this question early in the conflict in December 1992. He said:

The tasks arising from resolutions 752 and 787 are reasonably clear. They would require border observers to concern themselves with all movements of regular or irregular military personnel . . . from neighbouring countries into Bosnia and Herzegovina. The context of both these resolutions indicates that the Council was concerned with all forms of interference directed against the Government of Bosnia and Herzegovina. It could therefore be argued that United Nations border observers should not concern themselves with regular or irregular military personnel . . . destined for the forces of the Government of Bosnia and Herzegovina. The Council would wish to clarify this point if it decided to deploy border observers.[109]

However, the Secretary-General did not return to this argument in later reports, nor did the Security Council expressly pronounce on the issue.

---

[105] Resolution 908, 31 March 1994, passed unanimously, Bosnia and Herzegovina said: 'This agreement certainly brings to an end an unnatural combat between victims of fascism': UN Doc. S/PV 3344, p. 3.
[106] UN Doc. S/1994/1425.
[107] See above at n. 46.
[108] UN Doc. S/1994/1425.
[109] UN Doc. S/25000.

Other resolutions call for peaceful settlement of the dispute and therefore tend to support an interpretation of Resolution 752 that would prohibit intervention even to help the government of Bosnia and Herzegovina.[110] If this interpretation is adopted then Croatian intervention would be unequivocally lawful only if Croatia were acting in collective self-defence of Bosnia and Herzegovina under Article 51 of the United Nations Charter.[111] Croatia argued that troops from Serbia were taking part in the fighting but did not make any express claim of collective self-defence. It may, therefore, simply have been relying on the right to help a government in a civil war if there has been outside intervention against the government.[112] It did not address the issue of the application of Resolution 752. Yugoslavia (Serbia and Montenegro) denied any involvement and invoked United Nations reports in its support.[113]

In July 1995 Croatia and Bosnia and Herzegovina followed up their Washington agreement by making the Split Declaration;[114] this followed a cross-border offensive by the Krajina Serbs against Bihac in Bosnia and Herzegovina on 19 July 1995 and committed Croatia to assist Bosnian Government forces in the area around Bihac.[115] Bihac had been declared a safe area in 1993, it had not been demilitarized and was used as a base by Bosnia and Herzegovina forces.[116] It was the centre for many offensives and counter-offensives throughout the conflict, and was subjected to attack by the Krajina Serbs coming from over the Croatian border and also to Croatian army involvement.[117] Croatia maintained that the fall of Bihac to Serb forces would threaten its national security interests.[118]

In August 1995 the Croatian Army again entered Bosnia and Herzegovina, with the co-operation of the government. In combination with its major offensive in the territory of Croatia to retake the United Nations Protected Areas controlled by the Krajina Serbs, Croatia used its forces to relieve Bihac.[119] The Security Council in Resolution 1009[120] condemned Croatia for its offensive in violation of the United Nations peace plan in Croatia, but did not mention the action in Bihac. In the debate leading to Resolution 1009 Croatia said that its action in the territory of

---

[110] See n. 86, above.
[111] See below at n. 122.
[112] For a discussion of the law on intervention in civil wars, see L. Doswald Beck, 'The Legal Validity of Military Intervention by Invitation of the Government', this *Year Book*, 56 (1985), p. 189; for the UK government position, see this *Year Book*, 57 (1986), p. 614 at p. 616.
[113] UN Doc. S/1994/1425.
[114] *Keesing's*, 1995, p. 40689; *UN Chronicle*, December 1995, p. 7.
[115] UN Doc. S/1995/666.
[116] See the Secretary-General's report on safe areas: UN Doc. S/1994/555.
[117] *UN Yearbook*, 1994, pp. 522–31. The Security Council responded in Resolution 959 to border crossing by the Krajina Serbs; on Croatian involvement see UN Doc. S/1995/650.
[118] UN Doc. S/1995/666.
[119] UN Doc. S/1995/666; Owen, op.cit. above (n. 54), at p. 354.
[120] Resolution 1009, 10 August 1995, passed unanimously.

Bosnia and Herzegovina was carried out at the express request of that government: 'coming to the aid of a friendly government is fully consistent with the Charter of the United Nations'.[121] Again this is something less than a claim of collective self-defence. In order to make such a claim Croatia would have had to show an armed attack (or, more controversially, the threat of one) attributable to a third State.[122] But it did not explicitly do this. Instead it argued that it was not right to compare its actions in Croatia and in Bosnia and Herzegovina with the behaviour of Yugoslavia (Serbia and Montenegro): 'The earlier actions by Belgrade and its proxies were foreign aggression, pure and simple, against a legally declared and later, internationally recognized Member State. Any such comparison, therefore, not only breeds ill will in Croatia's public opinion but also calls into question well-established practice of international law and norms of international behaviour.'[123] Its justification implicitly was that it was helping a government by collective forcible counter-measures within its territory against a foreign use of force; it seems that this could come within the scope of permissible use of force although the issue was not addressed in the *Nicaragua* case.[124] But it is not clear that this would be compatible with Resolution 752. In the debate Bosnia and Herzegovina itself did not offer a legal justification of Croatia's action, and it is noteworthy that the USA expressly regretted the means used, thus implying a breach of Resolution 752, but recognized that the safe area of Bihac was now open to humanitarian relief.[125]

It was only in September 1995, when Croatia and Bosnia and Herzegovina undertook a joint offensive in Bosnia after Operation Deliberate Force by NATO forces against the Bosnian Serbs,[126] that the Security Council passed a *resolution* on Croatian intervention in Bosnia, and even that was in general terms[127] and was adopted without public debate in the Security Council.[128] Both Bosnia and Herzegovina and Croatia wrote to the Security Council to try to justify their use of force after they had accepted the 8 September 1995 Geneva agreement on the basic principles for a peace accord.[129] Croatia said that its army was operating in the territory of Bosnia and Herzegovina at the express

---

[121] UN Doc. S/PV 3563.

[122] Case concerning the *Military and Paramilitary Activities in and against Nicaragua (Nicaragua v. USA) (Merits), ICJ Reports*, 1986, p. 14, at para. 194.

[123] UN Doc. S/PV 3563.

[124] It seems that the discussion in the *Nicaragua* case of collective counter-measures not qualifying as collective self-defence left open the possibility that such forcible measures could be lawful if in response to a government invitation and not involving force against the territory of another State. See paras. 210 ff.

[125] UN Doc. S/PV 3563.

[126] *UN Chronicle*, December 1995, p. 9.

[127] Resolution 1016, 21 September 1995, passed unanimously.

[128] UN Doc. S/PV 3581.

[129] UN Doc. S/1995/780, Annex II; *Keesing's*, 1995, p. 40735.

request of the Government and consistently with international law and within the framework of the bilateral agreement signed between the two governments.[130] Yugoslavia (Serbia and Montenegro) again argued that the Croatian action was a violation of Resolution 752.[131] Bosnia and Herzegovina did not offer a clear legal justification.[132] Resolution 1016 said that the Security Council was gravely concerned about 'all offensive and hostile acts in the Republic of Bosnia and Herzegovina by the parties concerned, including those most recently undertaken', and noted the assurances given by the Governments of the Republic of Bosnia and Herzegovina and the Republic of Croatia regarding offensive actions in Western Bosnia. It called upon all parties to refrain from violence and reiterated that there could be no military solution to the conflict in Bosnia and Herzegovina. The ceasefire finally came into effect on 12 October 1995.[133]

The General Assembly

The tendency to treat Yugoslavia (Serbia and Montenegro) and then the Bosnian Serbs as the guilty party is even more marked in the resolutions of the General Assembly. The first of these was passed on 25 August 1992, Resolution 46/242; it simply called for an end to all outside intervention in Bosnia and for the withdrawal of the Croatian Army and the JNA,

Deploring the grave situation in Bosnia and Herzegovina and the serious deterioration of the living conditions of the people there, especially the Muslim and Croat populations, arising from the aggression against the territory of the Republic of Bosnia and Herzegovina, which constitutes a threat to international peace and security, . . .
2. Demands also that all forms of interference from outside the Republic of Bosnia and Herzegovina cease immediately.[134]

This does not expressly hold Yugoslavia (Serbia and Montenegro) responsible for the Bosnian Serbs; the nature of the 'aggression' against the territory of Bosnia and Herzegovina and the responsibility for it are left unclear. But preambular paragraph 11 said on 'ethnic cleansing':

Recalling the report of the Secretary-General of 12 May 1992, in which he states that 'all international observers agree that what is happening is a concerted effort by the Serbs of Bosnia and Herzegovina, with the acquiescence of, and at least some support from, the Yugoslav People's Army, to create ethnically pure regions in the context of negotiations on the cantonization of the Republic in the Conference of the European Community on Bosnia and Herzegovina' . . .

[130] UN Doc. S/1995/812.
[131] UN Doc. S/1995/831.
[132] UN Doc. S/1995/808.
[133] UN Chronicle, Spring 1996, p. 25; Keesing's, 1995, p. 40780.
[134] GA Resolution 46/242, 25 August 1992, passed 136–1–5.

Russia proposed an amendment to this, referring to the further statement in the Secretary-General's report that portions of Bosnia and Herzegovina were under the control of Croatian military or paramilitary units. But this amendment was rejected by 69–9–50. Yugoslavia (Serbia and Montenegro) repeated that the JNA had ceased to exist and that none of its soldiers remained in Bosnia and Herzegovina.[135]

The next resolution of the General Assembly on 18 December 1992, Resolution 47/121, did expressly hold Yugoslavia (Serbia and Montenegro) responsible as the aggressor in Bosnia.[136] It is striking that the General Assembly, unlike the Security Council, used the language of aggression. This resolution said:

Gravely concerned about the deterioration of the situation in Bosnia and Herzegovina owing to intensified aggressive acts by the Serbian and Montenegrin forces to acquire more territories by force, characterised by a consistent pattern of gross and systematic violations of human rights . . .

Strongly condemning Serbia and Montenegro and their surrogates in the Republic of Bosnia and Herzegovina for their continued non-compliance with all relevant United Nations resolutions,

Deeply regretting that the sanctions imposed by the Security Council have not had the desired effect of halting the aggressive acts by Serbian and Montenegrin irregular forces and the direct and indirect support of the Yugoslav People's Army for the aggressive acts in the Republic of Bosnia and Herzegovina . . .

2. Strongly condemns Serbia, Montenegro and Serbian forces in the Republic of Bosnia and Herzegovina for violation of the sovereignty, territorial integrity and political independence of the Republic of Bosnia and Herzegovina, and their non-compliance with existing resolutions of the Security Council and the General Assembly, as well as the London Peace Accords of August 1992.

3. Demands that Serbia and Montenegro and Serbian forces in the Republic of Bosnia and Herzegovina immediately cease their aggressive acts and hostility and comply fully and unconditionally with the relevant resolutions of the Security Council.

4. Demands that, in accordance with Security Council resolution 752(1992), all elements of the Yugoslav People's Army still in the territory of the Republic of Bosnia and Herzegovina must be withdrawn immediately, or be subject to the authority of the Government of the Republic of Bosnia and Herzegovina, or be disbanded and disarmed with their weapons placed under effective United Nations control.

Less strongly, the resolution in paragraph 5

Demands also that, in accordance with Security Council resolution 752(1992) all elements of the Croatian Army that *may be*[137] in the Republic of Bosnia and Herzegovina and that are not already operating in accord with the authority of the Government of the Republic of Bosnia and Herzegovina must be withdrawn

[135] *UN Yearbook*, 1992, p. 368.
[136] Passed 102–0–57.
[137] Emphasis added.

immediately or be subject to the authority of that Government or be disbanded and disarmed with their weapons placed under effective United Nations control.

The General Assembly's resolution on 20 December 1993, Resolution 48/88, was less strong than that of the previous year in its language on the role of Yugoslavia (Serbia and Montenegro).[138] Like the Security Council it shifted its main criticism to the Bosnian Serbs. It did not directly refer to Yugoslavia (Serbia and Montenegro) as responsible for aggressive acts or violation of the sovereignty of Bosnia, but used more general language in the preamble:

> Gravely concerned that the unprovoked armed hostilities and aggression continue against Bosnia and Herzegovina and that the relevant resolutions of the Security Council remain unimplemented . . .

It did, however, refer to a report of the Committee on the Elimination of Racial Discrimination noting with great concern that links existed between Serbia and Montenegro and Serbian militaries and paramilitary groups responsible for massive, gross and systematic violations of human rights in Bosnia and in Croatian territories controlled by Serbs. The resolution not only condemned the Bosnian Serbs for ethnic cleansing and 'aggression', but also expressed alarm at the hostilities by the Bosnian Croats; it referred at several points to aggressive acts against Bosnia and Herzegovina by extremist Bosnian Croat military elements and expressed alarm at the collusion between Serbian and Bosnian Croat forces to seek the dismemberment of Bosnia and Herzegovina. This was because, as described above,[139] from mid-1993 to March 1994 the most serious fighting in Bosnia and Herzegovina was between Bosnia and Herzegovina forces and Bosnian Croats, aided by Croatia. But in the *operative* paragraphs of Resolution 48/88 the General Assembly condemned expressly only 'Serbian forces', for 'continued violation of the international border between the Republic of Bosnia and Herzegovina and the Republic of Croatia'; it also called on 'the Republic of Serbia and Montenegro' to cease the supply of military arms, equipment and services to Bosnian Serb paramilitary units; also 'the Bosnian Serb party' was called on to lift the siege of Sarajevo; and the 'Republic of Serbia and Montenegro' and the 'Bosnian Serbs' together were condemned for violations of humanitarian law.

By November 1994, there was another shift of emphasis by the General Assembly, following the partial suspension of sanctions on Yugoslavia (Serbia and Montenegro) by the Security Council in September 1994. Although General Assembly Resolution 49/10 again referred to the armed hostilities and continued aggression against Bosnia

[138] Passed 109–0–57.
[139] See text at nn. 53 and 95, above.

and Herzegovina,[140] its condemnations were almost all of the Bosnian Serbs alone, and not of Yugoslavia (Serbia and Montenegro) except in operative paragraph 11, which 'condemns vigorously all violations of human rights and international humanitarian law committed by parties to the conflict, especially those violations committed as policy by Serbia and Montenegro and the Bosnian Serbs, who have done so systematically, flagrantly and on a massive scale against the people of Bosnia and Herzegovina'.

Paragraph 13 of Resolution 49/10 'Demands that the Federal Republic of Yugoslavia (Serbia and Montenegro) uphold its commitment and obligation to comply with resolution 752, and to cease any military and logistic support to the Bosnian Serbs'. This acknowledges the change of policy by Yugoslavia (Serbia and Montenegro) in August 1994, but the General Assembly indicated some continuing suspicion by saying that it supported the decisions of the Security Council to terminate automatically the partial suspension of sanctions in the event that Serbia and Montenegro were found not to implement effectively its decision to close the border with Bosnia and Herzegovina. The resolution also called upon 'all parties, in particular the Federal Republic of Yugoslavia, to comply fully with all Security Council resolutions regarding the situation in the Republic of Bosnia and Herzegovina and strictly to respect its territorial integrity, and in this regard concludes that their activities aimed at achieving integration of the occupied territories of Bosnia and Herzegovina into the administrative, military, educational, transportation and communication systems of the Federal Republic leading to a de facto state of occupation are illegal, null and void, and must cease immediately'.

Analysis

This fairly detailed survey of United Nations resolutions is intended to show the view taken by the international community of the nature of the conflict in the former Yugoslavia. The different organs of the United Nations give very different pictures of the conflict. The picture emerging from the Security Council's resolutions, and even more strongly from the General Assembly's resolutions, is one of Yugoslavia (Serbia and Montenegro)'s responsibility. But, despite the imposition of sanctions on Yugoslavia (Serbia and Montenegro), the careful language of the Security Council resolutions reflects a civil conflict; they accuse Yugoslavia (Serbia and Montenegro) of non-compliance with Resolution 752's demands to secure the withdrawal of the JNA and to stop intervention, and call on it to stop all forms of interference, including infiltration of irregular units (Resolution 787) and supply of arms, equipment and services (Resolution 819). That is, the Security Council avoided any

---

[140] Passed 97–0–61.

direct accusation of aggression or of armed attack; the statement of the duty to prevent infiltration did not necessarily imply that Yugoslavia (Serbia and Montenegro) was responsible for the irregular units in such a way as to amount to aggression or an armed attack. Its allegations are of intervention. In contrast the Security Council criticized Croatia only in statements. The General Assembly proved more critical of Yugoslavia (Serbia and Montenegro) and went further in accusing it of aggressive acts and also in saying that the Bosnian Serbs were surrogates of Yugoslavia (Serbia and Montenegro). It did not make any similar criticism of Croatia. That is, the General Assembly comes closer to determining an inter-State conflict.

In contrast to the Security Council and the General Assembly resolutions, an examination of the Secretary-General's reports to the Security Council during the conflict gives a rather different and more complex picture. The Secretary-General's reports describe logistical support by Yugoslavia (Serbia and Montenegro) to the Bosnian Serbs and intervention by the Croatian army into Bosnia and Herzegovina. They do not support a claim that the conflict was an inter-State war between Yugoslavia (Serbia and Montenegro) and Bosnia and Herzegovina.

It must be asked whether the one-sided approach in resolutions by the United Nations organs enhanced the authority of the Security Council or helped to secure the resolution of the conflict.[141] The dreadful abuses by the Bosnian Serbs, and the assistance to them by Yugoslavia (Serbia and Montenegro), led to a reluctance to condemn other parties and an approach that was less than even-handed. Allegations by Yugoslavia (Serbia and Montenegro) of intervention by Croatia, or of atrocities by parties other than the Serbs, were not debated in the Security Council, apparently because member States did not accept that Yugoslavia (Serbia and Montenegro) was in a position to make any accusations against others.[142] The conduct of this crisis by the United Nations organs shows yet again that failure to condemn particular behaviour is not necessarily good evidence of its legality.

The debate over lifting the arms embargo

The issue whether the conflict in the former Yugoslavia was a civil war or an inter-State conflict was central to the controversy over the lifting of the arms embargo on Bosnia and Herzegovina. This question of lifting the embargo created fundamental divisions; it split the USA and Europe; it divided the General Assembly and the Security Council; and the International Court of Justice was called on by Bosnia and Herzegovina

---

[141] C. Boyd, 'Making Peace with the Guilty', *Foreign Affairs*, 1995(5), p. 22.

[142] For some of Yugoslavia (Serbia and Montenegro)'s accusations, see UN Doc. S/1994/1172, S/1994/1286, S/1994/1425, S/1994/1429, S/1995/326, S/1995/382, S/1995/591, S/1995/632, S/1995/658, S/1995/732; S/24894, 25237, 25279, 25283, 25379, 25780, 26672, 26894.

in its application against Yugoslavia (Serbia and Montenegro) to pronounce on the interpretation and the validity of the Security Council
resolution that imposed the arms embargo.

The arms embargo had been imposed by Security Council Resolution
713 on 25 September 1991;[143] this was done with the consent of
Yugoslavia, as it then was. In the debate leading up to the adoption of the
resolution Yugoslavia said that 'we have to defend ourselves from
ourselves'.[144] It said that this was of concern to the Security Council
because the crisis threatened peace and security on a large scale.
Yugoslavia was in conflict with itself; the situation was complex and it
was not possible in the debate to deal with all the causes, but no factor
(*sic*) on the Yugoslav scene was completely free from guilt. At the
moment it was of no consequence who was the first to start and who to
escalate the crisis further. What mattered now was to break the vicious
circle.

Resolution 713 was adopted unanimously. The relevant paragraph
provides that the Security Council:

Decides, under Chapter VII of the Charter of the United Nations, that all States
shall, for the purpose of establishing peace and stability in Yugoslavia, immediately implement a general and complete embargo on all deliveries of weapons
and military equipment to Yugoslavia until the Security Council decides
otherwise following consultation between the Secretary-General and the Government of Yugoslavia.

This departs from earlier United Nations practice under Chapter VII.
The arms embargo was not intended as a sanction *against* Yugoslavia, as
in the cases of Security Council action against South Africa[145] and
Rhodesia,[146] and subsequently Libya.[147] Rather, it was designed to
prevent the escalation of the conflict, as with the later arms embargoes
against Somalia,[148] Liberia[149] and Rwanda,[150] imposed after Resolution
713.

Subsequently, in May 1992 Bosnia and Herzegovina was admitted as
a member State to the United Nations. At first the government of Bosnia
and Herzegovina sought the deployment of a UN force.[151] Later, when
it had become disappointed in what UNPROFOR could achieve because
UNPROFOR was not authorized, equipped or willing to take sides in the

---

[143] See n. 7, above.
[144] UN Doc. S/PV 3009.
[145] Security Council Resolution 418, 4 November 1977.
[146] Security Council Resolution 217, 20 November 1965.
[147] Security Council Resolution 748, 31 March 1992.
[148] Security Council Resolution 733, 23 January 1992.
[149] Security Council Resolution 788, 19 November 1992.
[150] Security Council Resolution 918, 17 May 1994.
[151] UN Doc. S/23363, 23836, 24137, 24226. See Gray, loc. cit. above (n. 21).

conflict,[152] Bosnia and Herzegovina began to seek the lifting of the arms embargo. Its first request to the Security Council for lifting the embargo was made in September 1992 and included detailed allegations of intervention by Yugoslavia (Serbia and Montenegro). It said that:

All week we have received reports about a massive troop and arms influx from Serbia and Montenegro along the eastern border of the country. These reinforcement troops are approaching the town of Visograd, burning and destroying everything in their way, and displacing the local non-Serb population. The aggressor is transferring all of its available manpower and weaponry across the border before the international observers are deployed along this border.[153]

Bosnia and Herzegovina argued that because of the arms embargo they could not defend themselves. If the international community was unwilling or unable to fulfil its pledges and promises to come to their defence before Sarajevo fell, then the only alternative for them was to exercise their right of self-defence and collective defence. Article 51 of the United Nations Charter granted them the absolute right to defend themselves. In order to exercise those rights, the arms embargo against Bosnia and Herzegovina must be lifted. If the Security Council refused to stop this latest onslaught from Serbia and Montenegro it must give them the tools to do the job. 'The United Nations cannot have it both ways. Enforcing the arms embargo means you must defend us. Failing to defend us means that you must lift the arms embargo.'

But the Security Council, although it met several times at the request of Bosnia and Herzegovina, did not in its several debates on Bosnia and Herzegovina in 1992 discuss lifting the arms embargo. Its response at this stage was to impose a ban on military flights over Bosnia and Herzegovina[154] and to strengthen the arms embargo and the sanctions against Yugoslavia (Serbia and Montenegro) by Resolution 787.[155] This latter resolution expressed the Council's concern 'at the threats to the territorial integrity of the Republic of Bosnia and Herzegovina, which as a State Member of the United Nations, enjoys the rights provided for in the Charter of the United Nations'. It then authorized States to use 'such measures as may be necessary to halt all inward and outward maritime

---

[152] *UN Yearbook*, 1992, p. 346; UN Doc. S/1994/555, para. 14; Bosnia and Herzegovina reply, S/1994/575.

[153] UN Doc. S/24588. See also UN Doc. S/24601. Earlier, Croatia and Bosnia and Herzegovina on 23 September 1992 had established a short-lived Joint Defence Committee. They said that the international community had failed to stop the aggression against them and they therefore requested that the arms embargo against them be lifted (*Keesing's*, 1992, p. 39103).

[154] Resolution 781, 9 October 1992, passed 14–0–1 (China); Resolution 786, 10 November 1992, passed unanimously; and also Resolution 816, 31 March 1993, passed 14–0–1 (China). The Secretary-General's reports on the no-fly ban were limited to a record of allegations of violations. He did not attribute blame to Yugoslavia (Serbia and Montenegro) or to Croatia (*UN Yearbook*, 1993, p. 463; *UN Yearbook*, 1994, p. 552).

[155] See n. 34, above.

shipping in order to inspect and verify their cargoes and destinations and to ensure strict implementation of the provisions of resolutions 713 and 757'.

The General Assembly's calls for lifting of the arms embargo and Article 12 of the United Nations Charter

However, the General Assembly did debate Bosnia and Herzegovina's request for lifting of the arms embargo in December 1992, and by 102 votes to 0 with 57 abstentions it passed Resolution 47/121.[156] As was described above, in this resolution the General Assembly expressly condemned Yugoslavia (Serbia and Montenegro) for aggression against Bosnia and Herzegovina.[157] It reaffirmed that the Republic of Bosnia and Herzegovina had the inherent right to individual or collective self-defence, until the Security Council had taken the measures necessary to maintain international peace and security. It urged the Security Council to consider certain measures on an urgent basis; these were:

(*a*) In the event that Serbian and Montenegrin forces fail to comply fully with all relevant resolutions of the Security Council, under the provisions of Chapter VII of the Charter of the United Nations, to authorize Member States, in cooperation with the Government of the Republic of Bosnia and Herzegovina, to use all necessary means to uphold and restore the sovereignty, political independence, territorial integrity and unity of the Republic of Bosnia and Herzegovina;

(*b*) To exempt the Republic of Bosnia and Herzegovina from the arms embargo as imposed on the former Yugoslavia under Security Council resolution 713.

Also in 1993 and 1994 the General Assembly passed similar resolutions calling on the Security Council to consider lifting the arms embargo on Bosnia and Herzegovina.[158]

These General Assembly resolutions raise questions about the separation of powers between the Security Council and the General Assembly: should the General Assembly intervene in this way in conflicts being dealt with by the Security Council? Article 12 of the United Nations Charter expressly provides for a separation of powers. It says:

While the Security Council is exercising in respect of any dispute or situation the functions assigned to it in the present Charter, the General Assembly shall not make any recommendation with regard to that dispute or situation unless the Security Council so requests.

[156] The USA voted for the resolution; most European States abstained.
[157] See n. 136, above.
[158] Resolution 48/88, 20 December 1993, passed by 109–0–57; Resolution 49/10, 3 November 1994, passed by 97–0–61. In resolution 49/10 the General Assembly noted the offer of the Government of Bosnia and Herzegovina to seek *de jure* lifting of the arms embargo with effective application deferred for up to six months, or as may be further deferred by the Security Council, especially in view of an acceptance and implementation of the Contact Group's peace plan by the Bosnian Serbs.

On the face of it, this is designed to preserve the primary role of the Security Council in maintaining international peace and security under Article 24 of the Charter. The aim of the drafters was to avoid the possibility of the General Assembly interfering with the work of the Security Council, or of the Security Council and the General Assembly coming to opposing conclusions on an issue.[159] Thus it might be expected that Article 12 would prohibit any General Assembly recommendation like that on the lifting of the arms embargo in Resolutions 47/121, 48/88 and 49/10.

However, Article 12 has been very narrowly interpreted in United Nations practice. Simma in his commentary on the United Nations Charter shows in detail how Article 12 has been undermined over time.[160] At first the Security Council held the view that 'the mere inclusion of a dispute or situation in the list of matters with which the Security Council was dealing barred the General Assembly from making recommendations on those affairs'. But subsequently the General Assembly adopted the practice of making recommendations on issues with which the Security Council was dealing actively. The United Nations Legal Counsel said that the General Assembly had not regarded itself as debarred from making a recommendation unless the Security Council was exercising its functions at that moment. Moreover the General Assembly has not regarded the Security Council as 'exercising its functions' if it has failed to pass a resolution because of the veto. And the General Assembly has regarded itself as free to make a recommendation as long as it did not directly contradict a Security Council resolution. It was acceptable for the Assembly to take a position which had been rejected in the Security Council.

As Simma concludes, this interpretation of Article 12 is 'hardly compatible with the wording, purpose, and origin of Article 12, but it is sustained by state practice'. Blum is even more critical; he speaks of the 'total erosion of the constitutional relationship between the General Assembly and the Security Council as envisaged by the Charter', and says that the practice should be seen as 'an impermissible violation of the Charter, rather than a legitimate and commonly accepted bona fide interpretation of its provisions'.[161]

The first General Assembly resolution calling for reconsideration of the arms embargo in Resolution 713 was passed before the Security Council had debated the question of lifting the embargo. It could be argued that this General Assembly resolution (and its successors) do not directly contradict Security Council Resolution 713, although clearly they are intended to secure the partial repeal of that resolution. But the

---

[159] See B. Simma (ed.), *The Charter of the United Nations: A Commentary* (1994), p. 254; and Y. Z. Blum, *Eroding the United Nations Charter* (1993), p. 103.

[160] Simma, op. cit. above (n. 159).

[161] Blum, op. cit. above (n. 159).

Security Council did pass several resolutions reaffirming Resolution 713 after Bosnia and Herzegovina had come to independence.[162] The General Assembly resolutions seem to have been carefully designed to avoid *direct* contradiction with these because they do not themselves purport to recommend the lift of the arms embargo but simply call on the Security Council to consider this. But they could be seen as, if not in direct contradiction with Security Council resolutions, at least designed to put pressure on the Security Council in a way that Article 12 was meant to avoid. The second General Assembly Resolution, 48/88, was passed *after* the Security Council had considered and rejected a draft resolution put forward in June 1993 to lift the embargo.[163] It was only because the General Assembly took a wide view of its own powers (on the basis of the narrow interpretation of Article 12 that has been adopted in United Nations practice) that it was possible for it to pass Resolution 48/88. The General Assembly resolution did not directly contradict a Security Council resolution, but it did in substance contradict the sense of the Security Council vote not to lift the embargo. Under United Nations practice this has not been treated as a violation of the Charter or unconstitutional.

It is very doubtful whether it is advisable for the General Assembly to play the type of role that it assumed in the Yugoslav conflict. The result of its resolutions was exactly what Article 12 was designed to avoid, a divided United Nations. The authority of the Security Council, and therefore its ability effectively to secure a negotiated solution to the complex dispute, was undermined. In the case of Bosnia and Herzgovina it can be argued that the General Assembly resolutions helped to give encouragement to the Government of Bosnia and Herzegovina to believe it could seek a military solution, and thus served to prolong the dispute.[164]

The Security Council debates on lifting the arms embargo

As was mentioned above, the Security Council debated the question of lifting the embargo in 1993. The issue first came up during the general debate on Bosnia and Herzegovina in April,[165] when a number of States called for a lift of the embargo, and a draft resolution proposing the lift of the embargo was put forward by 22 States for debate in June 1993.[166] Bosnia and Herzegovina in the debate drew attention to the legal significance of the characterization of the conflict and also to the reluctance of the Security Council openly to commit itself on this question. It said:

[162] See below, n. 173.
[163] See n. 166, below.
[164] See, for example, Owen, op. cit. above (n. 54), at pp. 239–40.
[165] UN Doc. S/PV 3201, 3202, 3203.
[166] UN Doc. S/PV 3247.

Genocide and aggression are two powerful words in any language or tone. They convey images that shock and frighten civilised mankind. These are the images of present-day Bosnia and Herzegovina. They also underlie powerful legal considerations. There is an obligation on the part of the community of nations to take concrete steps to halt immediately the actions those words represent. Obviously, that is the reason why certain members of the Council avoid the use of these two words.

Bosnia and Herzegovina called for a clarification that the arms embargo did not apply to its defence forces. It invoked Article 51 of the United Nations Charter and argued that as it was the victim of aggression it should be allowed to defend itself. The arms embargo in Resolution 713 did not apply to Bosnia and Herzegovina.[167] But the resolution failed to secure the necessary majority; the vote was 6–0–9. The USA was the only permanent member to support the resolution; China, Russia, the United Kingdom and France all abstained. Bosnia and Herzegovina responded by threatening to sue the United Kingdom for failure to prevent genocide and for having illegally maintained an arms embargo on Bosnia and Herzegovina in violation of Article 51 of the Charter. It withdrew the threat a month later.[168] The question of lifting the embargo came up repeatedly in later debates on Bosnia and Herzegovina and the General Assembly proposal for a resolution was discussed in November 1994.[169]

Those opposing the lifting of the arms embargo relied mainly on practical and political arguments. Thus, for example, in June 1993 the United Kingdom said that lifting the embargo would not ensure that the arms actually reached the Government of Bosnia and Herzegovina. Already those arms being sent in violation of Resolution 713 to the Government often fell into other hands. Moreover, a decision to lift the arms embargo would lead to an intensification of the conflict since the Bosnian Serbs and the Bosnian Croats would try to gain military advantage before the weapons could reach the Government.[170] In the same debate France, Japan and Russia all said that lifting the embargo would interfere with the negotiation process and reduce the chance of peaceful settlement. Also, lifting the embargo would endanger United Nations troops on the ground in Bosnia and Herzegovina and would jeopardize the humanitarian operation. The same arguments were made repeatedly in other Security Council debates in 1993 and 1994 and in the General Assembly, with increasing emphasis on the incompatibility of lifting the embargo with the continued presence of UNPROFOR and with the pursuit of a negotiated solution.

[167] UN Doc. S/PV 3454; see also S/PV 3336, S/PV 3370.
[168] *UN Yearbook*, 1993, p. 465.
[169] UN Doc. S/PV 3454.
[170] UN Doc. S/PV 3247. On the UK allegations that the arms embargo was being violated, see below at n. 214.

Arguments for lifting the arms embargo

Those arguing for lifting the embargo challenged the application of Resolution 713 to Bosnia and Herzegovina in diverse ways. The first Security Council debate that looked at this question did not contain much in the way of legal argument on Resolution 713,[171] but later debates produced a variety of legal challenges to the arms embargo. The main arguments were (1) that Resolution 713 had been superseded and was no longer in force, (2) that the resolution should not be interpreted to apply to Bosnia and Herzegovina, and (3) that Resolution 713 was invalid.

First, some States argued that events had overtaken this resolution; it had been passed before Bosnia and Herzegovina became an independent State and therefore it was now superseded and could not apply to prevent Bosnia and Herzegovina from exercising its right to self-defence under Article 51 of the United Nations Charter now that it had become a member of the United Nations. Thus, Iran said that Resolution 713 had been adopted under totally different circumstances and before the existence of Bosnia and Herzegovina.[172] But this argument is not convincing because many Security Council resolutions passed after Bosnia and Herzegovina joined the United Nations expressly reaffirmed Resolution 713.[173] From Resolution 757 onwards the Security Council often included in its resolutions a general formula reaffirming Resolution 713. As these resolutions were passed after Bosnia and Herzegovina became a member of the United Nations, it seems clear that the arms embargo was intended to continue to apply to the whole of the former Yugoslavia. This is confirmed by Resolution 777; in its operative part this resolution said that Yugoslavia (Serbia and Montenegro) could not continue automatically the membership of the former Socialist Federal Republic of Yugoslavia in the United Nations.[174] Unlike earlier resolutions, Resolution 777 actually expressly singled out Resolution 713 for reaffirmation. Thus it seems very clear that the arms embargo was intended to continue.

Another version of this argument was that subsequent developments had affected the interpretation of Resolution 713; it should not be interpreted to apply to Bosnia and Herzegovina. Bosnia and Herzegovina took this line itself and many other States followed this.[175] For example, Afghanistan claimed that the Security Council had never intended to extend Resolution 713 to be validly applicable with regard to Bosnia and

---

[171] UN Doc. S/PV 3247.
[172] UN Doc. S/PV 3370; see also Slovenia, S/PV 3367.
[173] Resolutions reaffirming 713 are 757, 758, 760, 761, 762, 764, 770, 771, 777, 780, 781, 787, 824, 827, 836.
[174] Resolution 777, 19 September 1992, passed 12–0–3 (China, India, Zimbabwe).
[175] UN Doc. S/PV 3454.

Herzegovina.[176] Also it was argued that Resolution 713 should not be interpreted to deny Bosnia and Herzegovina the right of self-defence. Alternatively, if Resolution 713 did deprive Bosnia and Herzegovina of its right to self-defence, then it was invalid.[177]

The case concerning Application of the Convention on the Prevention and Punishment of the Crime of Genocide

This pattern of interrelated arguments on Resolution 713 can be seen also in the *Genocide* case, brought by Bosnia and Herzegovina against Yugoslavia (Serbia and Montenegro) before the International Court of Justice.[178] As part of its application on the merits of the case, Bosnia and Herzegovina argued that Yugoslavia (Serbia and Montenegro) had used force against Bosnia and Herzegovina in violation of Articles 2(1), 2(2), 2(3), 2(4), and 33(1) of the United Nations Charter and in violation of customary international law. It asked for a declaration that Yugoslavia (Serbia and Montenegro) had violated the sovereignty of Bosnia and Herzegovina by armed attacks against Bosnia and Herzegovina by air and land, aerial trespass into Bosnian airspace, and efforts by direct and indirect means to coerce and intimidate the Government of Bosnia and Herzegovina. It also claimed that Yugoslavia (Serbia and Montenegro) had intervened in the internal affairs of Bosnia and Herzegovina, and that it had armed, equipped, financed, supplied and otherwise encouraged, supported, aided and directed military and paramilitary actions in and against Bosnia and Herzegovina by means of its agents and surrogates.

Under those circumstances, Bosnia and Herzegovina asked for a declaration that it had the sovereign right to defend itself and its people under United Nations Charter Article 51 and customary international law, including by means of immediately obtaining military weapons, equipment, supplies and troops from other States; and also to request the assistance of any other State to come to its defence. Bosnia and Herzegovina therefore challenged the application to it of Security Council Resolution 713. It put forward two interrelated arguments on this point. First, Resolution 713 should be construed in a manner that would not impair the inherent right of individual or collective self-defence under Article 51 and the rules of customary international law. And all subsequent Security Council resolutions that referred to or reaffirmed Resolution 713 must also be so construed. Second, Resolution 713 and all subsequent resolutions referring to it must not be construed to impose an arms embargo upon Bosnia and Herzegovina, 'as required by Articles 24(1) and 51 of the United Nations Charter and in accordance with the customary doctrine of *ultra vires*'. This cautiously worded

---

[176] UN Doc. S/PV 3336. The Secretary-General raised this issue in UN Doc. S/25000 (see above at n. 109).

[177] See below at n. 194.

[178] See n. 2, above.

request gave the Court a choice between, first, simply interpreting Resolution 713 in such a way as to exempt Bosnia and Herzegovina from the arms embargo and, second, the much more controversial (and unprecedented) option of declaring Resolution 713 *ultra vires* because it conflicted with the United Nations Charter.[179]

At the provisional measures stage it was clear that Bosnia and Herzegovina's primary concern was to escape the arms embargo. Thus, in its first application for provisional measures, Bosnia and Herzegovina sought declarations that Yugoslavia (Serbia and Montenegro) should cease supporting groups engaged in military or paramilitary activities against Bosnia and Herzegovina; should cease all military or paramilitary activities by its own officials or agents; and that Bosnia and Herzegovina had the right to obtain military weapons and to request and receive the assistance of any State to come to its defence.[180]

Underlying all these requests was the view that the conflict in Bosnia and Herzegovina was an inter-State conflict and that Yugoslavia (Serbia and Montenegro) was the aggressor, or at least an intervening State responsible for attacks on Bosnian Muslims. Bosnia and Herzegovina claimed in its application that the acts it was complaining of were committed by former members of the Yugoslav People's Army and by Serb military and paramilitary forces under the direction of, at the behest of, and with assistance from Yugoslavia, and that Yugoslavia was therefore fully responsible under international law for their activities. Yugoslavia (Serbia and Montenegro) disagreed with Bosnia and Herzegovina's characterization of the conflict. It argued that the situation was not one of aggression by one State against another, but a civil war, and asserted that it had no soldiers in the territory of Bosnia and Herzegovina and that it did not militarily support any side in the conflict.

The case therefore highlights the division as to the nature of the conflict. The central issue of responsibility is very similar to that in the *Nicaragua* case[181] where the USA was held responsible, not only for its own direct violations of the international prohibition on the use of force, but also for its breach of the principle of non-intervention through its support to the *contras*. The USA had committed a clear breach of the principle of non-intervention by its financial support, training, supply of weapons, intelligence and logistical support.[182] However, the Court found that the relation of the *contras* to the US Government was not so much one of dependence and control that it was right to equate the *contras*, for legal purposes, with an organ of the US Government or as acting on behalf of that Government. It said: 'The Court does not

---

[179] See J. E. Alvarez, 'Judging the Security Council', *American Journal of International Law*, 90 (1996), p. 1, and works cited therein.

[180] See n. 2, above.

[181] See n. 122, above.

[182] *ICJ Reports*, 1986, p. 14, para. 242.

consider that the assistance given by the United States to the *contras* warrants the conclusion that these forces are subject to the United States to such an extent that any acts they have committed are imputable to that State. It takes the view that the contras remain responsible for their acts, and that the United States is not responsible for the acts of the contras, but for its own conduct vis-a-vis Nicaragua, including conduct related to the acts of the *contras*.'[183]

In the *Genocide* case the Court was called on in the application of Bosnia and Herzegovina on the merits for similar determinations as to whether there was a direct breach by Yugoslavia (Serbia and Montenegro) of Article 2(4), on the relation between the Bosnian Serbs and Yugoslavia (Serbia and Montenegro), and as to the scope and nature of Yugoslavia (Serbia and Montenegro)'s intervention. But the Court did not pronounce on the crucial issue of the nature of the conflict at the provisional measures stage. Because its jurisdiction was prima facie based on the 1948 Genocide Convention, the claims by Bosnia and Herzegovina for provisional measures allowing it to obtain military weapons despite Resolution 713 went beyond the scope of that Convention and were therefore rejected. The Court at this stage and at the jurisdictional stage insisted on confining its jurisdiction to the compromissory clause in the Genocide Convention.[184] As regards the arguments about the nature of the conflict, the Court said that it could not make definitive findings of fact or imputability at that stage. It simply held that there was a grave risk of acts of genocide being committed and that, whether or not any such acts in the past could be legally imputable to Yugoslavia (Serbia and Montenegro) or to Bosnia and Herzegovina, both States were under an obligation to do all in their power to prevent the commission of any such acts in the future.[185]

However, in its Order the Court indicated that only Yugoslavia (Serbia and Montenegro) should take all measures within its power to prevent commission of the crime of genocide, and that Yugoslavia (Serbia and Montenegro) should in particular ensure that any military, paramilitary or irregular armed units which may be directed or supported by it, as well as any organization and persons which may be subject to its control, direction or influence, do not commit genocide.[186] That is, the order was one-sided; it implied Yugoslavia (Serbia and Montenegro)'s involvement in the conflict in Bosnia and Herzegovina. Again, in response to the second request for provisional measures, the Court simply reaffirmed its first order.[187] On the measures requested by Yugoslavia (Serbia and Montenegro) against Bosnia and Herzegovina, the Court briefly said that

---

[183] Ibid., paras. 109–16.
[184] *ICJ Reports*, 1993, p. 3 at para. 38. On the jurisdictional stage, see below at n. 190.
[185] Ibid., para. 44.
[186] Ibid., para. 52.
[187] *ICJ Reports*, 1993, p. 325.

circumstances were not such as to require an order addressed to Bosnia and Herzegovina parallel to that addressed to Yugoslavia (Serbia and Montenegro).[188]

This one-sided approach led Judge Tarassov to criticize the Court's orders and to dissent on the relevant parts. He said that the order requiring Yugoslavia (Serbia and Montenegro) 'to ensure' that units which *may* be directed or supported by it and that organizations or persons which *may* be subject to its control do not commit any acts of genocide could be interpreted as showing that the Court believed that Yugoslavia (Serbia and Montenegro) was indeed involved in such genocidal acts. These provisions were very close to a prejudgment of the merits, despite the Court's recognition that in an order indicating provisional measures it was not entitled to reach determinations of fact or law.[189]

The issues of the interpretation and validity of Resolution 713 were not before the Court at the next stage of the *Genocide* case; in 1996, the issues of jurisdiction and admissibility were decided by the Court.[190] But the question of the nature of the conflict did come up for examination by the Court at this stage because Yugoslavia (Serbia and Montenegro) argued that the Court did not have jurisdiction. It argued this on the ground that there was no international dispute under Article IX of the Genocide Convention on which the jurisdiction of the Court was based. Yugoslavia (Serbia and Montenegro) said also that the case was not admissible; there was no international dispute as the conflict in Bosnia and Herzegovina was of a domestic nature. The case referred to events that took place within the framework of a civil war. Yugoslavia was not a party to it and did not exercise jurisdiction over that territory, and there was consequently no international dispute. The Court rejected these arguments; it said rather cursorily and without any substantial explanation that irrespective of the nature of the conflict the obligations of prevention and punishment under the Genocide Convention remained identical. However, it could not at this stage settle the question whether Yugoslavia took part directly or indirectly in the conflict.[191]

The right of Bosnia and Herzegovina to self-defence, and the interpretation and validity of Resolution 713

The Court thus avoided the controversial issue of the scope of its powers of judicial review of Security Council action in these preliminary stages of the *Genocide* case.[192] It did not have to pronounce on the

---

[188] Ibid., para. 46.
[189] *ICJ Reports*, 1993, p. 3 at p. 26.
[190] *ICJ Reports*, 1996.
[191] Ibid., para. 31.
[192] See n. 179, above.

interpretation and validity of Resolution 713.[193] But these questions of interpretation and validity were important in the Security Council and General Assembly debates on lifting the arms embargo. The most extreme form of challenge to the arms embargo came from those States which argued that Resolution 713 was invalid. Few States expressly took this position, but Malaysia, Afghanistan and Iran did argue that the embargo was invalid and illegal.[194] Afghanistan said that no embargo remained valid in international law if its continuation would lead to the commission of genocide. And Afghanistan pursued this position to its logical conclusion that, because the Resolution was invalid, States were entitled to ignore it. It said that there could be no Security Council resolution that validly applied to Bosnia and Herzegovina when it called for an arms embargo against Bosnia and Herzegovina and 'every Member State, including those on the Security Council, is legally entitled to proceed individually or collectively to deliver arms to Bosnia and Herzegovina'.

However, most States took less extreme positions. Even those who argued most strongly for lifting the embargo either called for a new resolution by the Security Council expressly allowing lifting of the arms embargo against Bosnia and Herzegovina or called for a pronouncement by the Security Council on the proper interpretation of Resolution 713.[195] Many of the States seeking the lifting of the arms embargo did so because they said that Resolution 713 contradicted Article 51 of the United Nations Charter and denied Bosnia and Herzegovina its right to individual and collective self-defence. This was Bosnia and Herzegovina's own position and that of the USA. Bosnia and Herzegovina said: 'It is clear to us that the arms embargo imposed by Resolution 713 (1991) does not apply to the Government of the Republic of Bosnia and Herzegovina. We are a country under attack from a much better-armed aggressor bent on territorial conquest and genocide. It is clear that the aggression continues and that the Council still has not fully confronted the aggressor. Our rights under Article 51 of the Charter are clear and absolute.'[196] The USA said that the Bosnian Government should be

---

[193] And it may well again be able to avoid this question of the construction of Resolution 713 and the right of Bosnia and Herzegovina to defend itself when it comes to decide the merits of the case. The Court has insisted on confining its jurisdiction to compromissory clause of the Genocide Convention. The main issue on the merits, therefore, will be the accusation of genocide against Yugoslavia (Serbia and Montenegro), and it may be that the question of the interpretation and validity of Resolution 713 will be withdrawn or be found to have been overtaken by the end of the conflict. Therefore, although the Court may have to decide whether Bosnia and Herzegovina was the victim of a violation of Article 2(4), it may not have to decide whether it was a victim of an armed attack giving it the right to use force in self-defence.

[194] Malaysia, UN Doc. S/PV 3454; Afghanistan, UN Doc. S/PV 3336 and 3454; Iran, UN Doc. S/PV 3370.

[195] Those seeking a new resolution to repeal Resolution 713 included Pakistan, Nigeria, Malaysia, Egypt, Iran, Tunisia, Sudan, Kuwait, Estonia, USA. Those seeking reinterpretation of Resolution 713 included Senegal, Turkey, Iran.

[196] UN Doc. S/PV 3336, p. 14.

exempted from the arms embargo; the victims of aggression should be finally permitted to defend themselves and there were no grounds in justice or in law for denying the Government of Bosnia and Herzegovina the right to defend itself.[197]

Although Article 51 of the United Nations Charter preserves the right of self-defence only 'until the Security Council has taken the measures necessary to maintain international peace and security', no one seriously argued that this applied to the conflict in Bosnia and Herzegovina in such a way as to deprive Bosnia and Herzegovina of its right to self-defence.[198] Those States opposing lifting the arms embargo did not argue that Bosnia and Herzegovina's right to self-defence had been superseded by Security Council action.

The question of the interpretation of Article 51 has in the past given rise to some controversy as to what constitutes 'measures necessary to maintain international peace and security'.[199] Should this have the wide interpretation that any Chapter VII action by the Security Council would exclude the right of self-defence? Or should the narrow interpretation be preferred, that only effective action would amount to 'measures necessary to maintain international peace and security'? Best known are the disagreements with regard to the application of Article 51 to the Falklands conflict and to the Iraqi invasion of Kuwait.[200] In the latter, the Security Council, apparently in order to avoid the sort of challenge that had been made to the United Kingdom's claim to self-defence of the Falklands, expressly included in its resolution imposing economic sanctions on Iraq under Chapter VII of the United Nations

---

[197] UN Doc. S/PV 3367, p. 50, S/PV 3454. Within the USA, Congress voted for the Dole Bill providing for the unilateral end of the arms embargo (*Keesing's*, 1995, p. 40690). The Bill required the USA to lift the embargo after a withdrawal of UNPROFOR from Bosnia and Herzegovina or within 12 weeks of a request by the Bosnia and Herzegovina Government. It included a statement that the continued application of the arms embargo to the Government of Bosnia and Herzegovina contravened the right of self-defence and was therefore inconsistent with international law. President Clinton vetoed the Bill on 11 August 1995 and events in Bosnia and Herzegovina developed in such a way that the Bill was not brought back to Congress.

[198] Paradoxically, it was those States which supported lifting the arms embargo and which wanted to protect Bosnia and Herzegovina's right of self defence under Article 51 that sometimes seemed to assume that the Security Council had taken action to supersede Bosnia and Herzegovina's temporary right of self defence. Thus, for example, Malaysia said that 'While the Council decision has prevented the Government of Bosnia and Herzegovina from protecting its own people, at the same time the Council has not fully discharged its responsibility under Article 24 of the Charter to take proper and effective action to restore international peace and stability' (UN Doc. S/PV 3454). This seems to be designed to address the argument that while the Security Council was exercising its powers under Chapter VII Bosnia and Herzegovina had no right of self-defence. This was the line taken by Moor, 'The Republic of Bosnia and Herzegovina and Article 51: Inherent Rights and Responsibilities', *Fordham International Law Journal*, 18 (1995), p. 870.

[199] White, op. cit. above (n. 9), at p. 55; Greig, 'Self-Defence and the Security Council. What does Article 51 require?', *International and Comparative Law Quarterly*, 40 (1991), p. 366 at p. 389; Simma, op. cit. above (n. 159), at p. 676.

[200] Rostow, 'Until What? Enforcement Action or Collective Self-Defence', *American Journal of International Law*, 85 (1991), p. 506; Schacter, 'UN Law in the Gulf Conflict', ibid., p. 452; D. J. Harris, *Cases and Materials in International Law* (4th edn., 1991), at p. 854.

Charter a phrase 'Affirming the inherent right of individual or collective self-defence, in response to the armed attack by Iraq against Kuwait, in accordance with Article 51 of the Charter'. Thus, the Security Council spelled out that although it was undertaking action under Chapter VII, Kuwait retained its right to self-defence under Article 51.[201] No such express reference to Article 51 was included in the Security Council's resolutions on the Yugoslav conflict, but from Resolution 787 of 16 November 1992 onwards the Security Council included in certain resolutions the general statement that 'Bosnia and Herzegovina, . . . as a State Member of the United Nations, enjoys the rights provided for in the Charter of the United Nations'.[202] This would seem to be enough to preserve Bosnia and Herzegovina's legal right to self-defence under Article 51.

The much more controversial question was whether Resolution 713 illegally deprived Bosnia and Herzegovina of this right to self-defence. Did Resolution 713 violate Article 51? This was the claim of those seeking the lifting of the embargo, even though they almost all sought a new resolution reinterpreting or replacing Resolution 713 rather than mounting any direct challenge to the validity of the resolution. This argument that an arms embargo violated the right of self-defence under the Charter seems untenable and even dangerous. It is regrettable that those States opposing lifting the embargo did not actually address the legal arguments on this point in the Security Council and General Assembly debates. Both in the general debates and in those debates specifically on draft resolutions calling for the lifting of the embargo, the States opposing lifting the embargo either simply registered their opposition or put forward practical and political arguments.[203] They did not enter into any legal debate on Article 51.

But it is clear that there are strong arguments against any claim that an arms embargo violates Article 51 of the Charter. If an arms embargo is *inherently* inconsistent with Article 51, this would unduly limit the Council's discretion under Article 41 and deprive it of what it has seen as a useful tool, either to put pressure on a wrong-doing State or to try to limit the escalation of a conflict. All other States subject to arms embargoes could also challenge their application; Libya, Iraq, Somalia, Liberia and Rwanda[204] would all claim that their rights under the Charter prevailed over the arms embargo. It seems unlikely that Bosnia and Herzegovina and the other States calling for lifting the embargo were putting this argument that every arms embargo violated Article 51,

[201] Greenwood, 'New World Order or Old? The Invasion of Kuwait and the Rule of Law', *Modern Law Review*, 55 (1992), p. 153.
[202] Resolutions 787, 836, 859, 998.
[203] See above at n. 170.
[204] On Rwanda, see below at n. 205.

although the language they used was very vague and could easily be read to have this extreme meaning.

Even if Bosnia and Herzegovina was putting forward a less fundamental argument and was claiming merely that in the particular circumstances the arms embargo in Resolution 713 violated its right to self-defence, this seems a dangerous precedent and one that would undermine the freedom of the Security Council to maintain an arms embargo. The Government of Bosnia and Herzegovina was not overtly seeking support for itself in a civil war; rather it was arguing that the conflict was not purely civil and that it had the right of self-defence under Article 51. In putting this case, Bosnia and Herzegovina was necessarily applying to have the embargo lifted to enable it to use its right of self-defence to respond to future armed attacks. It therefore did not have to make clear whether it was alleging actual past armed attacks by Yugoslavia (Serbia and Montenegro) or lesser violations of Article 2(4) or intervention. Other States suffering civil wars and subject to arms embargoes, such as Somalia, Liberia and Rwanda, could also make plausible cases that they were under threat from outside and needed to exercise their right of self-defence. The better position is that an arms embargo may affect the exercise of the right to self-defence, but it does not actually deny the right. Although this distinction may seem formalistic, it is important. It preserves the right of the Security Council to choose to continue an arms embargo even on a State under possible threat from outside, in order to stop the escalation of a civil war.

But the impact of the controversy over the arms embargo on Bosnia and Herzegovina is apparent in the action taken by the Security Council with regard to Rwanda. The Security Council had imposed an arms embargo in 1994, against the wishes of the government then in power, to try to prevent the escalation of violence and to limit the widespread massacres.[205] But in 1995 the government that had come to power after the arms embargo claimed that there was a threat to it from outside, from refugee Hutus in Zaire. In response to a plea by the Government of Rwanda requesting urgent action to lift the restrictions on the sale or supply of arms and *matériel* to the Government in order to ensure the security of the Rwandan population,[206] the Security Council unanimously passed Resolution 1011.[207] This noted with great concern reports of military preparations and increasing incursions into Rwanda by elements of the former regime. It also recalled that the prohibition on the delivery of arms and *matériel* was originally aimed at stopping the use of

[205] Resolution 918, 17 May 1994, imposed a mandatory arms embargo strengthened by Resolution 997.
[206] UN Doc. S/1995/547.
[207] Resolution 1011, 16 August 1995, passed unanimously. See *UN Chronicle*, December 1995, p. 12; *Keesing's*, 1995, p. 40665. Following the precedent of Resolution 864, 15 September 1993, which allowed the supply of arms to the Government of Angola but not to UNITA, various safeguards designed to secure the delivery of the arms to the Government of Rwanda were included.

such arms and equipment in the massacres of innocent citizens. It therefore suspended the arms embargo for one year as far as supplies to the Government were concerned.

The Security Council was apparently influenced by its experience with Bosnia and Herzegovina and did not want again to appear to be denying a State the right to defend itself. Several States in the debate spoke of the need to allow Rwanda to secure arms in order to exercise its right of self-defence, including the USA which was a strong supporter of the resolution.[208] In contrast, others focused on the need for the Government of Rwanda to respond to destabilization and its internal security problem, and did not use the language of self-defence.[209] Just as was the case with Bosnia and Herzegovina, there is some doubt as to how far lifting the embargo would help one side in a civil war rather than enabling self-defence against an external aggressor. Some States in speaking for lifting the embargo expressed the pious hope that the arms would be used only for self-defence.[210] It is not clear how far the alleged threat from Zaire was a real one.[211]

Zaire expressed concern at the lifting of the embargo. It said:

By suspending the embargo on the supply of arms to Rwanda for a trial period of one year, the Security Council would authorize Rwanda to obtain military equipment and other modern, sophisticated war materiel at a time when it is barely concealing its warlike intentions and when it is threatening to attack refugee camps in Zaire. It is also a time when Rwanda is not promoting a climate of understanding and national reconciliation, but, rather, is encouraging new flows of refugees to Zaire, which has the appearance of the expulsion of Rwanda's own nationals for political, ethnic and tribal reasons.

In other words, even though the Security Council has included conditions in this text, adoption of the draft resolution will not contribute to easing tension in the region.[212]

Some States shared Zaire's concern over the need for Rwanda to act to encourage the return of the refugees and thereby to reduce any threat from Zaire's territory.[213] But the Security Council suspended the embargo and abandoned its policy of trying to limit the amount of arms in Rwanda. This precedent will make it more difficult for the Security Council to maintain against the wishes of the government of the State concerned an arms embargo imposed during a civil war.

---

[208] Botswana, Argentina, Nigeria and Oman argued this: UN Doc. S/PV 3566.

[209] Italy and Honduras, ibid.

[210] Indonesia and Nigeria said this, ibid.

[211] Nigeria argued that lifting the embargo would deter future attacks, and after the lifting of the embargo it is true that there were no significant incursions. However, it is impossible to determine whether this was really due to the lifting of the embargo or whether there was never any real danger. There was only a minor incursion from Zaire in May 1996 (*Keesing's*, 1996, p. 41130).

[212] UN Doc. S/PV 3566.

[213] France, Botswana and the Czech Republic, ibid.

Endnote

Bosnia and Herzegovina depicted itself as the victim, not only of the Bosnian Serbs, but also of aggression by Yugoslavia (Serbia and Montenegro). Yugoslavia (Serbia and Montenegro) replied that it was not a party to the conflict in Bosnia and Herzegovina and that none of its troops remained in Bosnia and Herzegovina after 18 May 1992; it denied involvement in what it described as a civil war. In part these claims as to the nature of the conflict are political rhetoric, designed to mask the more complex reality and to secure international support. The aim of this article is not to reach a final verdict on the characterization of the conflict in the former Yugoslavia, although a provisional conclusion that the conflict was a civil one with outside intervention seems justified. Rather the aim has been to set out the radically opposing positions of the various parties concerned, and of the different organs of the United Nations, in such a way as to make clear the legal consequences, if any, of the characterization.

It has turned out that in certain contexts the decision whether to characterize the conflict as civil war or inter-State conflict did not have to be made and the characterization was not decisive of the rights involved. Thus in the *Tadic* case before the International Criminal Tribunal for the former Yugoslavia and in the two stages of the *Genocide* case already decided by the International Court of Justice, the tribunal held that the nature of the conflict was not decisive of the case in the way claimed by Tadic and Yugoslavia (Serbia and Montenegro) respectively; crimes against humanity and genocide could be committed irrespective of the nature of the conflict. The International Court of Justice has still to pronounce on the merits of the *Genocide* case; but it may equally well be able to avoid the issue of characterization in the same way that it did at the provisional measures and jurisdictional stages. The crucial issues will be a mixture of fact and law, the questions of how far the actions of the Bosnian Serbs were imputable to Yugoslavia (Serbia and Montenegro) and of the extent of Yugoslavia (Serbia and Montenegros)'s intervention. Whether or not the Court itself addresses the issue of the nature of the conflict, a final verdict on this question will need to take account of the mass of conflicting evidence that will be submitted to the Court.

In contrast, the characterization of the conflict was of crucial significance in the debate over lifting the arms embargo. Bosnia and Herzegovina's claim for lifting the embargo was made on the basis that the embargo violated its right to self-defence under Article 51 of the United Nations Charter. This argument would not be available in a purely civil war, and accordingly Bosnia and Herzegovina needed to show that Yugoslavia (Serbia and Montenegro) had behaved or would behave in such a way as to make exercise of its rights under Article 51 necessary, either that Yugoslavia (Serbia and Montenegro) had committed an armed attack or that it would in the future commit such an attack. Intervention or an act of aggression not amounting to an armed attack would not be enough.

However, to put this long drawn-out controversy over lifting the embargo in perspective, the arms embargo did not in fact prevent the supply of arms to Bosnia and Herzegovina. It is now clear that Europe and the USA turned a blind eye to the delivery of weapons to Croatia, and through Croatia to Bosnia and Herzegovina. By the second half of 1992 the arms embargo hardly restricted Croatia's import of arms and Bosnia and Herzegovina could obtain arms at the discretion of Croatia. David Owen reported that Western Europe and the USA tolerated and condoned this practice; they did not impose any effective restrictions on Croatia building up its army, and allowed it to control the quantity and quality of arms reaching Bosnia and Herzegovina.[214]

On 22 November 1995, the Security Council as part of the peace settlement finally provided for the lifting of the arms embargo[215] and in June 1996, after the conclusion of an arms control agreement between the parties within Bosnia and Herzegovina as well as between Bosnia and Herzegovina, Croatia and Yugoslavia (Serbia and Montenegro), the embargo was finally lifted.[216]

[214] Owen, op. cit. above (n. 54), at pp. 23, 47–8, 73–4, 127, 271, 381–4; C. Boyd, loc. cit. above (n. 141), at pp. 30–1. On the USA's tolerance of Iranian supply of arms to Bosnia and Herzegovina, see *The Guardian*, 18 April 1996, 9 May 1996.

[215] Passed 14–0–1 (Russia).

[216] *Keesing's*, 1996, p. 41152.

THE INTERNATIONAL LEGAL REGULATION OF STRADDLING FISH STOCKS*

By PETER G. G. DAVIES *and* CATHERINE REDGWELL‡

INTRODUCTION

The post-war era has seen unprecedented developments in the international law of the sea. Perhaps the most striking has been the erosion of traditional high seas freedoms in consequence of the extension of coastal State jurisdiction over the living and non-living resources of the sea-bed, subsoil and water column to a distance of 200 nautical miles from the coast. The 1982 Law of the Sea Convention (LOSC)[1] established this *sui generis* concept of the exclusive economic zone (EEZ), and thereby significantly reduced the area of oceans freely open to exploitation by all States. A regime of common resources, freely exploited and consequently frequently overexploited, has been replaced in the 200-mile exclusive economic zone with coastal State sovereign rights and stewardship over resources.

The outer limit of the exclusive economic zone is determined solely by the geographic criterion of distance and does not correspond with any significant biological reality.[2] A number of coastal States, Canada and Argentina in particular, had sought at least the functional exercise of jurisdiction over fish stocks beyond the 200-mile zone.[3] To such so-called 'broad margineers', viz., States with a wide continental margin over which biological productivity extends well beyond 200 nautical miles, the 200-mile limit was an unsatisfactorily arbitrary limit to

* © Peter G. G. Davies and Catherine Redgwell, 1997.
‡ Lecturer in Law and Senior Lecturer in Law respectively, University of Nottingham. Particular thanks are due to Patricia Birnie, Stephen Weatherill and Jack Davies for their helpful comments and suggestions.

[1] Doc. A/CONF.62/122 and Corr. 1 to 11, reproduced in *International Legal Materials*, 21 (1982), p. 1261.

[2] This may be contrasted with Article 1 of the 1980 Convention on the Conservation of Antarctic Marine Living Resources, which uses the Antarctic Convergence as the limit of application of the Convention in recognition of the fact that biological productivity, indeed the Antarctic marine ecosystem as a whole, is influenced by this convergence where warmer northern waters meet colder southern waters.

[3] See further below, n. 219; see also the Canadian working paper submitted to the Sub-Committee II of the Committee on the Peaceful Uses of the Seabed and Ocean Floor Beyond the Limits of National Jurisdiction, A/AC.139/SC.II/L/8, 27 July 1972, which promotes a functional approach to the management of ocean living resources, recognizing different management regimes for different species groups.

coastal State jurisdiction over living resources.[4] However, given that the EEZ encompasses over 90% of commercially exploited fish stocks, it is perhaps unsurprising that the 1982 Law of the Sea Convention devoted comparatively little attention to the conservation and management of high seas fish stocks. The traditional high seas freedom of fishing, which had held sway since the seventeenth century, thus emerged relatively unscathed from the 1982 Convention in its substance, though reduced in its area of application.

Since 1982, however, there has been a rise in fishing effort outside the 200-mile zone as traditional distant water fishing nations (DWFN) seek new areas to exploit. This has been matched in some cases with mismanagement and overexploitation of resources within the 200-mile limit. These developments have caused renewed pressures on fish stocks which do not observe the 200-mile limit in their life cycle: so-called 'straddling fish stocks'.[5] In response to such pressures, both Canada and Argentina have legislated to provide for the exercise of jurisdiction beyond their 200-mile zone; in the Canadian case, the exercise of

---

[4] Whilst coastal States may, as part of their continental shelf jurisdiction, exercise sovereign rights over the sedentary species of the continental shelf beyond 200 miles to an outer limit defined in accordance with criteria set forth in Article 76 LOSC, this does not encompass the living resources of the superjacent water column beyond 200 miles. A senior Canadian Foreign Affairs official is reported recently to have 'dismissed as "totally irrelevant" the suggestion that control over the seabed beyond the 200-mile limit could help in fisheries disputes': *The Globe and Mail*, 23 December 1995, at p. A5.

[5] Stocks may straddle the boundary between two zones of national jurisdiction, e.g. the territorial sea of two States. This is referred to as a transboundary stock. 'Straddling stocks' cross a zone of national jurisdiction and the high seas. The boundary could be between the territorial sea, EEZ or EFZ and the high seas, or an 'enclave', which is a high seas pocket encircled by the maritime zone(s) of one or more States. Straddling stocks occur where continental shelves and slopes extend beyond 200 nautical miles, such as the high seas 'doughnut hole' between Russia and the United States (Alaskan pollock), the Grand Banks off the coast of Newfoundland (cod and halibut or turbot), the Patagonian shelf off the coast of Argentina (Patagonian hake), and the south-east Pacific off the coasts of Peru and Chile (horse mackerel). Since fish move to areas of lower population density, fishing beyond the EEZ can have a particularly adverse impact upon fish stocks which straddle the EEZ/ high seas boundary. For fuller discussion, see UN Division for Ocean Affairs and the Law of the Sea, *The Regime for High-Seas Fisheries: Status and Prospects* (1992), at pp. 21–2; Freestone, 'The Effective Conservation and Management of High Seas Living Resources: Towards a New Regime?', *Canterbury Law Review*, 5:3 (1994), p. 341 (the authors are indebted to Nigel Gravells for his assistance with this source); Miles and Burke, 'Pressures on the UN Convention on the Law of the Sea of 1982 Arising from New Fisheries Conflicts: The Problem of Straddling Stocks', *Ocean Development and International Law*, 20 (1989), p. 343; Applebaum, 'The Straddling Stock Problem: The Northwest Atlantic Situation, International Law, and Options for Coastal State Action', in Soons (ed.), *Implementation of the Law of the Sea Convention through International Institutions* (1990), Proceedings of the 23rd Annual Conference of the Law of the Sea Institute; Meltzer, 'Global Overview of Straddling and Highly Migratory Fish Stocks: The Nonsustainable Nature of High Seas Fisheries', *Ocean Development and International Law*, 25 (1994), p. 255; and Pfirter, 'Straddling Stocks and Highly Migratory Stocks in Latin American Practice and Legislation: New Perspectives in Light of Current International Negotiations', *Ocean Development and International Law*, 26 (1995), p. 127. See also Francalanci and Scovazzi, *Lines in the Sea* (1994), at pp. 182–3, where the Grand Banks are illustrated in map 84 as the paradigm example of 'straddling stocks'.

The Bering Sea is now regulated by a treaty concluded 16 June 1994 between the coastal States (USA, Russia) and active distant water fishing nations (DWFN) in the region (China, Japan, Korea

enforcement jurisdiction including the use of force is explicitly authorized by legislation in areas beyond Canada's 200-mile exclusive fishing
zone (EFZ).[6]

Force was used against a Spanish trawler, the *Estai*, arrested by
Canadian authorities in March 1995, which prompted Spain to bring
proceedings against Canada before the International Court of Justice
alleging, *inter alia*, infringement of its enjoyment of the freedom of the
high seas including the freedom of fishing.[7] It is the purpose of this
article to consider the general international law of the sea framework
within which the lawfulness or otherwise of Canada's actions against the
Estai,[8] and the resulting dispute between Canada and Spain,[9] will be
evaluated. The background to the dispute is outlined in Part I, followed
by an overview of the development this century of the international law
of the sea in respect of straddling fish stocks in Part II. Developments
since the 1982 LOSC was concluded are analysed in Part III, including
the recently concluded Agreement for the Implementation of the United
Nations Convention of the Law of the Sea of 10 December 1982 relating
to the Conservation and Management of Straddling Fish Stocks and
Highly Migratory Fish Stocks.[10] This Agreement was opened for
signature on 4 December 1995 and is likely to provide the framework
within which future straddling stock disputes will be settled.

This article will conclude with an analysis of the nature of the current
legal framework within which conservation and management measures
governing straddling stocks are now formulated, an assessment of the
extent to which the Straddling Stocks Agreement resolves previous
deficiencies in such regime, and an evaluation of the applicability of
certain general principles of international environmental law to those
issues which, it is submitted, remain as sources of contention between
States in the management of straddling fish stocks.

---

and Poland). For the text of the Convention on the Conservation and Management of Pollack
Resources in the Central Bering Sea, see *Law of the Sea Bulletin*, 27 (1995), pp. 84–93; *International
Legal Materials*, 34 (1995), p. 69. Lucchini holds this agreement up as an exemplary illustration of
the best solution for the resolution of straddling stocks conflicts, viz., negotiated settlement:
Lucchini, 'La loi canadienne du 12 mai 1994: la logique extrême de la théorie du droit préférential
de l'état côtier en haute mer au titre des stocks chevauchants', *Annuaire français de droit international*
40 (1994), p. 864, at pp. 874–5.

[6] See further discussion below, text accompanying nn. 63–77.

[7] See further below, nn. 97–105 and accompanying text.

[8] It is not the authors' intention to assess the compatibility of the Canadian action with the rules
and principles of general public international law. However, see Davies, 'The EC/Canadian
Fisheries Dispute in the Northwest Atlantic', *International and Comparative Law Quarterly*, 44
(1995), pp. 933–8, on the Canadian assertion that such action was a response to an emergency
situation and, as such, justified under the doctrine of necessity.

[9] And between Canada and the EC, since the EC exercises exclusive competence in fisheries
matters: see further below, n. 30.

[10] *International Legal Materials*, 34 (1995), p. 1542, hereinafter 'Straddling Stocks Agreement'
('SSA'). This article focuses on straddling fish stocks and will not consider highly migratory fish
stocks.

PART I: THE EC/CANADIAN FISHERIES DISPUTE

(a) *The Incident*

On 9 March 1995, a Spanish trawler, the *Estai*, whilst fishing in an area known as the Nose of the Grand Banks off Newfoundland, was approached by a Canadian patrol boat which proceeded to fire four 50mm rounds across its bows.[11] Canadian fisheries protection officers boarded the trawler and arrested its captain, Enrique Davila Gonzales, before seizing the vessel and towing it to the Canadian port of St John's, Newfoundland.

The incident had taken place some 245 nautical miles from the Canadian coast and outside Canada's exclusive fisheries zone ('EFZ') declared on 1 January 1977.[12] Noting that the incident took place in international waters, the European Community Fisheries Commissioner, Emma Bonino, was minded to refer to the incident as an 'act of organized piracy'.[13] In response, the Canadian Government indicated that the

---

[11] See *The Times*, 11 March 1995, p. 15.

[12] On 1 January 1977 Canada declared a 200-nautical-mile EFZ; see R. W. Smith, *Exclusive Economic Zone Claims: An Analysis and Primary Documents* (1986), p. 12. The UN Convention on the Law of the Sea (*International Legal Materials*, 21 (1982), p. 1261) ('the Law of the Sea Convention' or 'LOSC') indicates that coastal States have 'sovereign rights for the purpose of . . . exploiting, conserving and managing the natural resources, whether living or non-living' within their exclusive economic zones ('EEZ'): Article 56. The Law of the Sea Convention came into force on 16 November 1994 but, at the time of writing, neither Spain, Canada nor the EC are parties. However, the EEZ regime has obtained customary status; see *Continental Shelf Case (Libya v. Malta)*, *ICJ Reports*, 1985, p. 13. Canada has declared an EFZ rather than an EEZ but would enjoy similar rights in such an area concerning living resources as it would have enjoyed had it declared an EEZ; see Harris, *Cases and Materials on International Law* (4th edn., 1991), p. 426. On EEZs generally see Attard, *The Exclusive Economic Zone in International Law* (1987). See further discussion below, Part II.

[13] Loc. cit. above (n. 11), 11 March 1995. The UK Secretary of State for Agriculture, Fisheries and Food, William Waldegrave, criticized Ms Bonino's choice of words, describing them as 'intemperate and unwise': *The Times*, 29 March 1995, p. 1. Mr Waldegrave's remarks were characteristic of the British Government's conciliatory approach towards Canada following the incident. The Spanish Government dispatched two warships to the area and introduced visa restrictions for visiting Canadian nationals; it also received vocal support from the European Commission, as well as the French and German Governments (see *The Independent*, 7 April 1995, p. 11, and *The Times*, 14 March 1995, p. 12). However, the British Government urged a move to a negotiated settlement and appeared to have some sympathy with Canada's criticism of Spanish overfishing; Michael Jack, a UK Minister of State in the Ministry of Agriculture, Fisheries and Food indicated that 'Spain's past activities may have influenced Canada's view today, and it is hardly surprising that Canada is taking such a robust stance': HC Debs., vol. 256, col. 563 (13 March 1995). The British Government's unwillingness to discuss the imposition of EC trade sanctions against Canada received criticism from the Spanish Government; see *The Times*, 7 April 1995, p. 11.

Alleged overfishing by Spanish trawlers inside Community waters has attracted criticism from other EC member States including Ireland and the UK; see *The Times*, 12 April 1995, p. 1. The UK Government has been particularly critical of 'quota-hopping', the situation where a foreign-owned trawler sails under a UK flag and notes its catch against the UK annual catch quota determined

action was necessary to halt overfishing of Greenland halibut,[14] a straddling stock which migrates between Canada's EFZ and the adjacent international waters, by EC registered vessels. The Canadian Foreign Minister, Mr André Ouellet, defending his Government's action, indicated that 'Canada had no other choice but to take action at sea to put a stop to this practice'.[15]

(b) Background to the Dispute

The 1950s and 1960s had witnessed a dramatic increase in the total number of fish caught in the Northwest Atlantic area.[16] Modern, efficient fishing fleets, from as far afield as the USSR, East and West Germany, Spain, Portugal and Poland, competed with the Canadian and US fleets.[17] Fisheries management in the Northwest Atlantic region was the responsibility of the International Commission for the Northwest Atlantic Fisheries ('ICNAF') established by the International Northwest Atlantic Fisheries Treaty.[18] In the 1970s ICNAF began to regulate the total volume of fish catches by establishing total allowable catches ('TACs') for specific fish stocks.[19] Halliday, Peacock and Burke note that the 'stimulus for these ICNAF regulatory actions was the decline in abundance of groundfish stock . . . The Canadian industry reached the

under the CFP. It has been suggested that 'foreign-owned boats, mostly Spanish and Dutch, take over 40% of British quotas for hake and plaice': *The Independent*, 31 May 1996, p. 1.

From 1 January 1996 the Spanish and Portuguese fleets have access to most EC waters, although certain restrictions still apply; access to the 'Irish Box' area, for instance, 'is to be restricted to a maximum of 40 vessels at any one time. Furthermore, within the area of the Irish Box, the Irish Sea and the Bristol Channel continue to be no-go areas for Spanish fishing vessels': letter to co-author dated 11 May 1995 from A. P. Carroll, Ministry of Agriculture, Food and Fisheries.

[14] Greenland halibut is a type of 'groundfish' and is also known as turbot. The Canadian Government has indicated that its own research carried out in February 1994 'suggested a two-thirds decline from the biomass [of Greenland halibut stock off lower Labrador and Eastern Newfoundland] surveyed in 1991. An even greater reduction was found in the number of large fish. These surveys also indicated that the population was made up of an increased proportion of young fish, of ages three and four years. In order for these fish to contribute to the growth of the stock, they must be allowed to mature and reproduce. They reproduce at age 10 years or more': Canadian Ministry of Oceans and Fisheries, *Background Information on Greenland Halibut Issue*, Doc. B-HQ-95-3E, March 1995. Addressing the Canadian House of Commons on 13 March 1995, the Canadian Minister of Fisheries and Oceans, Brian Tobin, noted that '[c]oncerning the catches found aboard the *Estai*, we found that up to 70 per cent of all the fish caught were small and immature': HC Deb. (Can.), 1995, 13 March, at p. 10383.

[15] *The Times*, loc. cit. above (n. 11), p. 15.

[16] O'Reilly-Hinds notes that 'total landings from treaty areas increased from 1.8 million tonnes [in 1954] to a peak of nearly 4 million tonnes in 1966': 'Crisis in Canada's Atlantic Sea Fisheries', *Marine Policy*, 19(4) (1995), p. 273.

[17] See Juda, 'World Marine Fish Catch in the Age of Exclusive Economic Zones and Exclusive Fishery Zones', *Ocean Development and International Law*, 22 (1991), pp. 11–15. For brief analysis of the bilateral fisheries agreements concluded with such States upon the declaration of Canada's 200-mile EFZ, see below, n. 125 and accompanying text.

[18] International Convention for the Northwest Atlantic Fisheries, *United Nations Treaty Series*, vol. 157, p. 157.

[19] Halliday, Peacock and Burke, 'Development and Management Measures for the Groundfish Fishery in Atlantic Canada', *Marine Policy*, November 1992, p. 413.

brink of economic collapse in 1974 when steeply rising costs and poor markets coincided with a decline in fishing success, and substantial government assistance was required over the ensuing three years.'[20]

By declaring an EFZ in 1977, Canada assumed responsibility for the management of fish stocks within the 200-mile zone. However, like many coastal States, Canadian management of its own fishing industry has left much to be desired. Despite acknowledging the need to cut the size of its fishing industry as long ago as the late 1960s,[21] the Canadian Government heavily subsidized its rapidly expanding fishing industry in the late 1970s and early 1980s. Schrank has recently noted that the Canadian Government 'permitted the industry to grow completely out of control until it was too late. Canada is still paying the price because of the resultant overfishing and because the Government now has to support, at great expense, a large number of fishing families.'[22] He further notes that the Canadian Department of Fisheries and Oceans 'has suffered from a policy schizophrenia, never being able to determine whether its chief goal is to set and implement policy for the fishery as a viable industry or whether it is to maximize employment and save non-viable rural communities'.[23] In 1992 the Canadian Government was forced to impose a total ban on the fishing of cod in its EFZ, and its 1994 Groundfish Management Plan established a 1994 total allowable catch for groundfish equal to just a quarter of the catch in 1989.[24]

Canada has frequently acknowledged that its own fishing fleet has in the past contributed to the severe depletion of fish stocks in the Northwest Atlantic by overfishing both within its EFZ and in international waters.[25] The Canadian Government has now taken steps to address the issue at a domestic level by introducing measures since 1994 that have directly led to 40,000 workers leaving the fishing industry.[26] It is in this context that the management of Northwest Atlantic fish stocks *outside* Canada's EFZ should be assessed, particularly bearing in mind that conservation measures introduced by Canada to conserve stocks

---

[20] Ibid., p. 413.

[21] See Schrank, 'Extended Fisheries Jurisdiction: Origins of the Current Crisis in Atlantic Canada's Fisheries', *Marine Policy*, 19(4) (1995), pp. 287–91.

[22] Ibid., p. 290. See further below, n. 26 and accompanying text.

[23] Ibid., p. 291.

[24] Ibid., p. 285. Recently the Canadian Standing Senate Committee on Fisheries has noted that '[f]ishing closures are now in effect on some 11 groundfish stocks, and severe restrictions have been placed on fishing other stocks. The rebuilding of the resource has yet to begin; scientific assessments for 1995 reveal little sign of improvement. Northern cod, once the North Atlantic's largest cod stock, has continued to decline despite the moratorium in place since July 1992. The Department of Fisheries and Oceans suggests that it could take as long as 14 years for the stock to recover and for a diminished fishery to return': Report of the Standing Senate Committee on Fisheries, 'The Atlantic Groundfish Fishery: Its Future', First Session, Thirty-Fifth Parliament, December 1995, preface.

[25] See, for example, the statement by Tobin, HC Deb. (Can.), 1994, 11 May, at p. 4212.

[26] See *The Times*, 28 March 1995, p. 12; £430 million per year is currently paid to fishermen and fish plant workers displaced from the Atlantic groundfish industry.

within its EFZ would be severely undermined if the regulation of straddling stocks, which migrate between the EFZ and international waters, is inadequate.

(c) *Regulation of Straddling Stocks under the Convention on Future Multilateral Co-operation in the Northwest Atlantic Fisheries ('Northwest Atlantic Fisheries Convention')*[27]

The management of Northwest Atlantic fish stocks located in international waters has since 1979 been determined within the Northwest Atlantic Fisheries Organization ('NAFO'),[28] established by the Northwest Atlantic Fisheries Convention.[29] Both Canada and the EC are parties to this Convention.[30] NAFO's predecessor, ICNAF,[31] had been

[27] Cmnd. 7569; see also EC Council Regulation 3179/78 of 28 December 1978, *Official Journal* (hereinafter OJ) 1978, L378/1, where the text of the treaty is reproduced. There are fifteen parties to the treaty: Bulgaria, Canada, Cuba, Denmark, Estonia, European Community, Iceland, Latvia, Lithuania, Japan, Korea, Norway, Poland, Romania and Russia. The Northwest Atlantic Fisheries Convention came into force on 1 January 1979. See generally M. Dahmani, *The Fisheries Regime of the Exclusive Economic Zone* (1987), pp. 115–16, and Sand (ed.), *The Effectiveness of International Environmental Agreements* (1992), pp. 280–4.

[28] NAFO meets annually (Article IV(4)). It comprises four main institutions: the General Council, established *inter alia* 'to supervise and coordinate the organisational, administrative, financial and other internal affairs of [NAFO], including the relations among its constituent bodies' (Article III(a)); the Scientific Council, which may provide scientific advice to coastal States (Article VI(c)) and to the Fisheries Commission (Article VI(d)); the Fisheries Commission itself (see below, nn. 34–9 and accompanying text); and the Secretariat, which provides the necessary administrative support (Article XV).

[29] Northwest Atlantic Fisheries Convention, Article II(1).

[30] The EC acts on behalf of its member States within NAFO. It is well established that the EC has exclusive competence in the area of fisheries management and conservation including treaty-making capacity; see Churchill, 'EC Fisheries and an EZ-Easy!', *Ocean Development and International Law*, 23 (1992), p. 149, and Donoghue, 'EC Participation in Protection of the Marine Environment', *Marine Policy*, November 1993, pp. 515–18. See also Case 25/94, *Commission v. Council*, judgment of 19 March 1996, on the United Nations Food and Agriculture Organization's Agreement to Promote Compliance with International Conservation and Management Measures by Fishing Vessels on the High Seas.

The EC has acquired treaty-making capacity either by *express* provision in the EC Treaty, or *impliedly*; the European Court of Justice ('ECJ') has stipulated that EC competence to enter into international agreements 'arises not only from an express conferment by the Treaty . . . but may equally flow from other provisions of the Treaty and from measures adopted, within the framework of those provisions, by the Community institutions. In particular, each time the Community, with a view to implementing a common policy envisaged by the [EC] Treaty, adopts provisions laying down common rules, whatever form these may take, the Member States no longer have the right, acting individually or even collectively, to undertake obligations with third countries which affect those rules' (Case 22/70, *Commission v. Council*, [1971] ECR 263, at p. 274 ('ERTA case')). See also ECJ Opinion on the World Trade Organization, Opinion 1/94, [1994] ECR I–5267, and, generally, Emiliou, 'The Allocation of Competence between the EC and its Member States in the Sphere of External Relations', in Emiliou and O'Keefe (eds.), *The European Union and World Trade Law* (1996), pp. 31–41. The ECJ has subsequently confirmed that the EC has *implied* treaty-making capacity in the area of fisheries conservation and management by virtue of the fact that duties and powers have been given to the EC's institutions in such areas on an internal level (Joined Cases 3/76, 4/76 and 6/76, *Officier van Justitie v. Kramer*, [1976] ECR 1279); see Churchill, *EEC Fisheries Law* (1987), p. 169.

[31] See above, n. 18 and accompanying text.

widely regarded as ineffective,[32] and, as such, was a factor which led both Canada and the USA to declare their respective EFZ and EEZ in the 1970s.[33] The establishment of NAFO was at the urging of Canada who, according to Driver, 'made it clear to countries intending to fish in the Canadian E[F]Z, particularly those of the Eastern bloc, that access would not be granted unless they joined a new international agreement on fisheries outside 200 miles limits in the north-west Atlantic'.[34]

NAFO's Fisheries Commission is 'responsible for the management and conservation of the resources of the Regulatory Area'.[35] Only the Grand Banks' Nose and Tail are within the Northwest Atlantic Fisheries Convention's Regulatory Area ('NAFO's Regulatory Area'), the remainder of the Grand Banks falling within Canada's EFZ.[36] No part of that area forming part of Canada's EFZ falls within the NAFO's Regulatory Area.[37] NAFO's Fisheries Commission therefore only has authority to manage fish stocks outside Canada's EFZ.

In exercising its management and conservation duties, the Fisheries Commission 'may adopt proposals for joint action by the Contracting Parties designed to achieve the optimum of the fishery resources of the Regulatory Area'.[38] There is an interplay between national and international rules to the extent that the practice within NAFO is to ensure co-ordination between their proposals in respect of conservation and management of the high seas fishery and measures adopted by the coastal States within the adjacent EFZ and EEZ; NAFO's Fisheries Commission's proposals

shall seek to ensure consistency between:
(a) any proposal that applies to a stock or group of stocks occurring both within the Regulatory Area and within an area under the fisheries' jurisdiction of a coastal State, or any proposal that would have an effect through species interrelationships on a stock or group of stocks occurring in whole or in part within an area under the fisheries' jurisdiction of a coastal state,
and (b) any measures or decisions taken by the coastal state for the management and

---

[32] See Donaldson and Pontecorvo, 'Economic Rationalisation of Fisheries: the Problem of Conflicting National Interests on Georges Bank', Ocean Development and International Law Journal, 8 (1980), p. 163.

[33] See Fluharty and Dawson, 'Management of Living Resources in the Northeast Pacific and the Unilateral Extension of the 200 Mile Fisheries Zone', Ocean Development and International Law, 6 (1979), pp. 21–4.

[34] Driver, 'International Fisheries', in Barston and Birnie (eds.), The Maritime Dimension (1980), chapter 2, at p. 43. Access to the resources within the Canadian EFZ is regulated by bilateral treaty; see further below, text accompanying nn. 125–30.

[35] Northwest Atlantic Fisheries Convention, Article XI(1).

[36] Although the area within Canada's EFZ, as well as NAFO's Regulatory Area, form part of the 'Convention Area' as defined by Article I(1), within which NAFO is to 'contribute through consultation and cooperation to the optimum utilisation, rational management and conservation of fishing resources' (Article II(1)), NAFO is not responsible for the management of fisheries resources within Canada's 200-mile limit.

[37] Article I(2).

[38] Ibid., Article XI(2).

*concentration of that stock or group of stocks with respect to fishing activities
conducted within the area under its fisheries jurisdiction.*[39]

It is of importance to note that 'special consideration' should be given to
Canada in allocating catches from the Grand Banks in the light of their
coastal communities' dependency on the fishing of such stocks.[40] However, this practice of affording preferential treatment to Canada under
NAFO does not give rise to a 'subregional rule' within the Northwest
Atlantic conferring on Canada a special interest in the straddling stock
resources.[41]

Canada has become frustrated with NAFO, not so much because of a
perceived lack of consistency between its own conservation measures
within its EFZ and the nature of NAFO's Fisheries Commission's
proposals, but rather owing to NAFO's inability to enforce its own
proposals. Three main difficulties have been identified:

(i) *Use of objections*

NAFO proposals, such as catch quotas or measures regulating the size
of fish nets, will be binding[42] on a State party unless it formally objects
to the measure within a period of 60 days of its notification,[43] or gives
notice 'at any time after the expiration of one year from the date on which
a measure enters into force' that it withdraws its own prior acceptance of
a proposal.[44] It has become established practice that a State party
unilaterally sets its own catch quota if it has objected to a NAFO
measure; the text of the Northwest Atlantic Fisheries Convention makes
no reference to the legitimacy of such unilateral action.

---

[39] Ibid., Article XI(3) (emphasis added). Article XI(3)(b) notes that the 'appropriate State and the
[Fisheries] Commission shall accordingly promote the coordination of such proposals, measures and
decisions. Each coastal State shall keep the Commission informed of its measures and decisions for
the purposes of this Article.'

[40] Article XI(4):
'Proposals adopted by the Commission for the allocation of catches in the Regulatory Area shall
take into account the interests of Commission members whose vessels have traditionally fished
within that Area, and, in the allocation of catches from the Grand Banks and Flemish Cap,
Commission members *shall give special consideration to the Contracting Party whose coastal
communities are primarily dependent on fishing for stocks related to these fishing banks* and which has
undertaken extensive efforts to ensure the conservation of such stocks through such international
action, in particular, by providing surveillance and inspection of international fisheries on these
banks under an international scheme of joint enforcement' (emphasis added).
'Special consideration' to coastal communities is therefore dependent on such communities'
dependency on the fishing of such stocks *and* the coastal State's participation in conservation and
management measures.

[41] Kwiatkowska, *The 200 Mile Exclusive Economic Zone in the New Law of the Sea* (1989),
p. 80.

[42] Northwest Atlantic Fisheries Convention, Article XI(7).

[43] Ibid., Article XII(1).

[44] Ibid., Article XII(3); in these circumstances the State party giving notice will cease to be bound
by the proposal 'at the end of one year from the date of receipt of the notice by the Executive
Secretary [of NAFO]'.

Since Spain and Portugal became members of the EC in 1986, the EC has persistently utilized the objection procedure to object to fish quotas established by NAFO.[45] It has then proceeded to establish its own catch quotas.[46] Canada has consistently voiced strong disapproval of such action,[47] regarding such activity as a serious undermining of both its own and NAFO's conservation plans.

(ii) *Lack of enforcement*

Enforcement of NAFO measures is the responsibility of States parties, who 'agree to take such action, including the imposition of adequate sanctions for violations, as may be necessary to make effective the provisions of this Convention and to implement [NAFO measures]'.[48] A Scheme of Joint International Inspection[49] was adopted by NAFO on 10 February 1988. Under this Scheme as amended ('Joint Inspection Scheme'),[50] States parties are to nominate 'Special Inspection Vessels' and appoint inspectors to carry out inspection duties from such vessels. Only by mutual agreement would 'inspectors assigned by one party . . . be placed on board the special inspection vessels of another party

---

[45] Prior to Spain and Portugal's accession to the EC, the then EC member States were concerned that allowing open access to EC waters to the large Spanish and Portuguese fleets would seriously deplete fish stocks in such waters. As a result, such access was restricted; see Churchill, loc. cit. above (n. 30), pp. 138–9. Day notes that to 'offset this restriction, the [EC] has given priority in external fishing relations to finding overseas locations where Spain and Portugal could deploy their large fishing capabilities. The waters off Namibia, Morocco and in NAFO's Regulatory Area have provided some destinations for their distant water fleets': 'Tending the Achilles Heel of NAFO: Canada Acts to Protect the Nose and Tail of the Grand Banks', *Marine Policy*, 19(4) (1995), p. 268. The vast majority of EC vessels fishing in the NAFO Regulatory Area are Spanish and Portuguese. These vessels have now been excluded from fishing off the Namibian coast. The EC has seen fit to object to NAFO catch quotas to offset the Spanish and Portuguese fleets' restricted access to EC waters; see Day, ibid., p. 268.

[46] For instance, in December 1990 the EC established its own catch quotas for two fish stocks managed by NAFO (redfish and witch flounder) despite being denied a NAFO catch quota; see Government of Canada, *News Release*, Document HQ-NA-90-05ZE, 20 December 1990. Also the EC established its own quotas from 1986–8 for certain stocks of cod despite a NAFO moratorium which had been introduced for reasons of conservation; see Sullivan, 'Conflict in the Management of a Northwest Atlantic Transboundary Cod Stock', *Marine Policy*, April 1989, pp. 126–7. See also Fauteux, 'L'initiative juridique canadienne sur la pêche en haute mer', *Canadian Yearbook of International Law*, 8 (1995), pp. 42–7.

[47] Serge April, the Canadian Director General of the Legal Affairs Bureau in the Canadian Department of External Affairs, addressing the Fisheries Council of Canada's 44th Annual Convention, noted that the EC used the objection procedure 'to avoid the conservation measures adopted by the coastal state and all other Member States together. It used a legal loophole to defeat the object and purpose of the NAFO Treaty': paper delivered on 26 October 1989, p. 2. See also an address by the Canadian Minister for International Trade, J. C. Crosbie: 'Notes for an Address to Europe 1992 Seminar and the Fisheries Council of Canada', 18 October 1990, pp. 3–9.

[48] Northwest Atlantic Fisheries Convention, Article XVII.

[49] Reproduced in EEC Council Regulation 1956/88 of 6 July 1988, OJ, 1988, L175/1.

[50] Amended by Council Regulation No. 436/92 of 10 February 1992, OJ, 1992, L54/1, Council Regulation No. 761/94 of 6 April 1994, OJ, 1994, L90/7, and by Council Regulation No. 3067/95 of 21 December 1995, OJ, 1995, L329/1. On 13 September 1991 a modified scheme was adopted by NAFO; for full text, see Council Regulation No. 436/92 above.

assigned to the scheme'.[51] Inspections 'shall aim at ensuring equal treatment between all contracting parties with vessels operating in the Regulatory Area through an equal distribution of inspections'.[52] A NAFO inspector has the ability to cite an alleged infringement, take photographs to assist in collecting evidence,[53] and determine that the vessel ceases to fish in certain circumstances.[54]

It should be noted that it is the flag State alone which decides whether to proceed to prosecute an alleged infringement of NAFO conservation and management measures, the text of the treaty noting that its enforcement scheme provides for 'flag State prosecution and sanctions';[55] it has been documented that even though both Canadian and EC inspectors were active in the NAFO Regulatory Area in 1992 and 1993, the violations by Spanish and Portuguese vessels which they reported rarely led to prosecutions.[56]

Day notes that '[o]f all NAFO members, the only one to put large scale resources at [NAFO's] disposal for surveillance and monitoring purposes has been Canada'.[57] Moreover NAFO's Scientific Council are of the opinion that States parties deliver incorrect and inaccurate reports concerning catches.[58] These weaknesses apparent in enforcement of NAFO measures were borne in mind in the negotiations for the Straddling Stocks Agreement, to which NAFO formed the paradigmatic Regional Fisheries Organization ('RFO').[59]

(iii) *Fishing by non-parties to NAFO and the issue of re-flagging*

Not all fishing vessels active in the NAFO Regulatory Area are registered by States that are party to the Northwest Atlantic Fisheries Convention. Vessels from non-party States, such as the Bahamas, Belize,

---

[51] Joint Inspection Scheme, Article 1(iii).

[52] Joint Inspection Scheme, Article 2(i).

[53] Joint Inspection Scheme, Article 6(vi).

[54] If the fishing vessel concerned has for instance been active in a closed area or using prohibited gear, the NAFO inspector shall 'immediately attempt to communicate with an inspector of the contracting party for the inspected vessel' or the competent authority nominated by contracting parties to deal with such infringements (Article 6(iv)), and once the consent of such person or persons has been given to the continued presence on board the fishing vessel of the NAFO inspector, 'the master [of the fishing vessel] may not resume fishing until the [NAFO] inspector is reasonably satisfied, as a result of either the action taken by the vessel's master or the [NAFO] inspector's communication with an inspector or designated authority of the contracting party for the inspected vessel, that the apparent infringement will not be repeated' (Joint Inspection Scheme, Article 6(iv)(c)).

[55] Article XVIII.

[56] See *The Independent*, 18 March 1995, which notes that 'under NAFO rules, it is up to the vessels' home countries to prosecute. But in 1993, only 6 of the 49 vessels charged with violations were prosecuted': p. 8. Any enforcement vessel may issue a citation to any vessel registered in a party to NAFO. Details of citations will then be passed to the NAFO administrative centre in Dartmouth, Nova Scotia. Offending vessels' flag State will be informed by NAFO of the offence and it is up to the flag State to consider prosecution; see Senate Deb. (Can.), 1994, 12 May, at p. 467.

[57] Day, loc. cit. above (n. 45), p. 263.

[58] Ibid., p. 263.

[59] See discussion below, Part III.

Cayman Islands, Chile, Honduras, Mexico, Panama, Sierra Leone and the United States,[60] are not bound by NAFO conservation measures. In addition there is evidence that trawlers registered in NAFO countries are re-flagging by registering in non-NAFO States. Spanish and Portuguese crewed vessels represent a high percentage of reflagged trawlers.[61] During the course of 1993 thirty-three fishing vessels from non-NAFO States were active in the NAFO Regulatory Area.[62]

(d) *The Coastal Fisheries Protection Act*[63]

As a consequence of NAFO's inability to enforce its own conservation measures, Canada opted to take unilateral action to conserve straddling stocks in the NAFO Regulatory Area. On 12 May 1994 an amendment[64] was made to the Coastal Fisheries Protection Act, section 5.2 providing that

No person, being aboard a *foreign fishing vessel of a prescribed class*, shall, in the NAFO Regulatory Area, fish or prepare to fish for a straddling stock in contravention of any of *the prescribed conservation and management measures*.[65]

The Act as amended further provided that subsequent regulations could be enacted designating any fish stock 'that occurs both within Canadian fisheries waters and in an area beyond and adjacent to Canadian fisheries waters'[66] a straddling stock for the purposes of the Act. Implementing regulations could, if necessary, be introduced prescribing a type of foreign vessel for the purposes of section 5.2,[67] as well as to so prescribe

any measure for the conservation and management of any straddling stock to be complied with by persons aboard a foreign fishing vessel of a prescribed class in order to ensure that the foreign fishing vessel does not engage in any activity that undermines the effectiveness of conservation and management measures for any

---

[60] Miles and Burke, loc. cit. above (n. 5), p. 344.

[61] Day, loc. cit. above (n. 45), p. 262.

[62] Government of Canada Doc. B-HQ-94-13E of May 1994, which also notes: '[a]s of May 1994, there were 11 ocean trawlers in the area which were stateless or registered in flag-of-convenience countries. The current flag-of-convenience problem is largely caused by vessels from Panama, Honduras and Belize.'

[63] Coastal Fisheries Protection Act, RSC 1985, c. C–33, as amended by RSC 1985, c. 31 (1st supp.), c. 39 (2nd supp.); Statutes of Canada, 1990, c. 44; Statutes of Canada, 1992, c. 1; Statutes of Canada, 1994, c. 14. See Lucchini, loc. cit. above (n. 5), who considers the provisions of the Act not only contrary to international law but inopportune diplomatically in the light of the straddling stocks negotiations then under way.

[64] Statutes of Canada, 1994, c. 14. On 10 May 1994, Canada amended its declaration accepting the compulsory jurisdiction of the International Court of Justice: see further below, section (e).

[65] Coastal Fisheries Protection Act, section 5.2 (emphasis added).

[66] Ibid., section 6.b.1.

[67] Ibid., section 6.b.2.

straddling stock that are taken under the [Northwest Atlantic Fisheries Convention].[68]

The Canadian Minister of Fisheries and Oceans indicated that, following the amendment to the Coastal Fisheries Protection Act, '[a]ny vessel from any nation fishing at variance with good conservation rules could ... be subject to action by Canada'.[69] Importantly, fisheries protection officers were granted wide-ranging powers including the power to board and inspect any fishing vessel in the NAFO Regulatory Area.[70] Force could be used to disable a fishing vessel if a protection officer thought it necessary to do so in the course of arresting its captain.[71] In addition, any member of the offending crew could be fined if found guilty of fishing contrary to the provisions of section 5.2.[72] Neither the Northwest Atlantic Fisheries Convention nor the Law of the Sea Convention provides for the exercise of such extensive powers.[73]

In April 1994, a month before the amendment to the Coastal Fisheries Protection Act, Canadian authorities arrested the *Kristina Logos* which had been fishing 228 miles from the Canadian coast. This fishing vessel had been reflagged as Panamanian, but had in fact also retained its Canadian registration.[74] The crew were Portuguese. The vessel was arrested for fishing in the NAFO Regulatory Area contrary to NAFO conservation measures. This arrest, combined with the amendment to the Coastal Fisheries Protection Act and the subsequent implementing regulations[75] which prohibited the fishing of straddling stocks by vessels from Panama, Cayman Islands, Belize, St Vincent and the Grenadines, Honduras and Sierra Leone, effectively brought to an end fishing by vessels from non-NAFO States.[76]

---

[68] Ibid., section 6.b.3.i. In addition, regulations could prescribe 'any further measure for the conservation and management of any straddling stock to be complied with by persons aboard a foreign fishing vessel of a prescribed class': section 6.b.3.ii. The Coastal Fisheries Protection Act as amended therefore allowed for action to be taken if a prescribed vessel was engaged in activity which undermined not only NAFO conservation and management measures but also any other measure which may have been prescribed (such as conservation measures previously only of relevance to the Canadian fishing industry).

[69] Tobin, HC Deb. (Can.), 1994, 11 May, at p. 4216.

[70] Coastal Fisheries Protection Act, section 7.a.

[71] Ibid., sections 8.1.a and 8.1.b.

[72] Ibid., section 18.1.

[73] These points are explored further below.

[74] The Canadian Minister of Fisheries and Oceans regarded this arrest as an action against a Canadian vessel: 'Overfishing has occurred on the nose and tail of the Grand Banks, overfishing on occasion by Canadian fleets. Let us have the courage, the integrity and the honesty to admit that and stop that overfishing. We have demonstrated in the last few months that where a Canadian vessel breaks the rules Canada shall reach out the long arm of its enforcement power and impose proper conservation measures. A month ago we went out 300 miles to arrest the *Stephen B*, a Canadian tuna boat fishing against [International Commission for the Conservation of Atlantic Tuna] rules, to protect bluefin tuna, a highly migratory species. We went out 228 miles to arrest the *Kristina Logos*, a Canadian registered vessel catching ... cod. *We are not asking the world to accept a standard that we do not impose upon ourselves first*': Tobin, HC Deb. (Can.), 1994, 11 May, at p. 4213 (emphasis added).

[75] SOR/94–362.

[76] See Day, loc. cit. above (n. 45), p. 264.

The Canadian Government had hoped that any dispute between NAFO States parties could be resolved within NAFO.[77] However, if EC registered vessels were felt to be acting in a manner that undermined NAFO measures, it would always be possible to prescribe such vessels under the Coastal Fisheries Protection Act and curtail their fishing activities in the NAFO Regulatory Area.

(e) *Canada's Revised Declaration under Article 36(2) of the ICJ Statute*

On 10 May 1994, two days prior to the amendment of the Coastal Fisheries Protection Act allowing for action to be taken against prescribed vessels in international waters within the NAFO Regulatory Area, Canada gave notice of termination of its acceptance of the compulsory jurisdiction of the International Court of Justice made on 10 September 1985[78] under Article 36(2) of the Statute of the International Court of Justice. In its place a revised declaration was made, paragraph 2 of which accepted the Court's compulsory jurisdiction 'over all disputes arising after the present declaration with regard to situations or facts subsequent to this declaration' with the exception of

(a) disputes in regard to which the parties have agreed or shall agree to have recourse to some other method of peaceful settlement;[79]

---

[77] Moving the second reading of the bill to amend the Coastal Fisheries Protection Act, the Canadian Minister of Oceans and Fisheries indicated: 'The Government and I have said we will stop foreign overfishing, not foreign fishing forever but improper fishing practices. We have said we will do it by agreement where it is possible to reach agreement and by unilateral action where unilateral action is necessary. We believe we have the means. We hope we have the will and the measures within the NAFO regime for NAFO to police itself, for NAFO to take the steps required, and for NAFO member States to police their own vessels . . . We believe Canada can police Canadian vessels. We believe that all other NAFO member States can and should do the same. Our expectation is that they will do the same. If one is a party to an agreement one should want to see that the agreement is lived up to fully': Tobin, HC Deb. (Can.), 1994, 11 May, at p. 4216.

[78] *ICJ Yearbook*, 1992–3, pp. 79–80.

[79] It should be noted that neither the text of the Northwest Atlantic Fisheries Convention nor of the Agreed Minute (see below, n. 304 and accompanying text) provides for a dispute settlement procedure. The Joint Inspection Scheme (see above, n. 49 and accompanying text) does provide for such a procedure (clause 15), but would apply only in respect of the much narrower range of disputes which could arise under that scheme.

It is submitted that the Agreed Minute of 20 April 1995 between the EC and Canada should not in itself be regarded as the settling of the dispute, the Agreed Minute noting that 'The EC and Canada maintain their respective positions on the conformity of the amendment of 25 May 1994 to Canada's Coastal Fisheries Protection Act, and subsequent regulations, with customary international law and the NAFO Convention. Nothing in this Agreed Minute shall prejudice any multilateral convention to which the EC and Canada, or any Member State or Canada, are parties, or their ability to preserve and defend their rights in conformity with international law, and the views of either Party with respect to any question relating to the Law of the Sea': Agreed Minute, paragraph D.1. The reference to the Agreed Minute being without prejudice to 'their ability to preserve and defend their rights in conformity with international law' must surely allow for the bringing of an action by either party before the Court. Note that, in releasing the *Estai*, the Canadian Attorney-General indicated that such action was taken for reasons of public interest (see n. 302, below), and not because of any admission on Canada's part that its actions had been unlawful.

(b) disputes with the Government of any other country which is a member of the Commonwealth, all of which disputes shall be settled in such manner as the parties have agreed or shall agree;

(c) disputes with regard to questions which by international law fall exclusively within the jurisdiction of Canada;[80] and

(d) disputes arising out of or concerning conservation and management measures taken by Canada with respect to vessels fishing in the NAFO Regulatory Area, as defined in the Convention on Future Multilateral Cooperation in the Northwest Atlantic Fisheries, 1978, and the enforcement of such measures.[81]

The Canadian Minister of Foreign Affairs, André Ouellet, indicated that 'to protect the integrity of [the amendment of May 1994 to the Coastal Fisheries Protection Act], we registered a reservation to the International Court of Justice, explaining that this reservation would of course be temporary and would apply only during such time as we felt was necessary to take retaliatory action against those engaged in overfishing'.[82] Canada's revised declaration took immediate effect.[83]

This is not the first time Canada has included a reservation in its Article 36(2) declaration to offset the possibility of proceedings being brought before the Court concerning its activity taken pursuant to a Canadian Act of Parliament. In 1970 Canada passed the Arctic Waters Pollution Prevention Act[84] introducing anti-pollution measures in a 100-mile zone (approximately) around Canadian islands in the Arctic

---

[80] See further the text of Spain's application to the Court, which stipulates that Spain's action before the Court relates to the Coastal Fisheries Protection Act which it submits is 'in itself an internationally wrongful act' and, on that basis, does not fall 'exclusively within Canada's jurisdiction': below (text accompanying n. 97).

[81] *ICJ Yearbook*, 1993–94, p. 88.

[82] Senate Deb. (Can.), 1994, 12 May, at p. 463.

[83] Canada's previous declaration of 10 September 1985 noted that 'The Government of Canada . . . reserves the right at any time . . . *with effect as from the moment of such notification*, either to add to, amend or withdraw any of the foregoing reservations, or any that may hereafter be added': *ICJ Yearbook*, 1984–85, p. 79 (emphasis added).

It is important to note this aspect of Canada's 1985 declaration bearing in mind the Court's judgement in *Nicaragua v. USA, ICJ Reports*, 1984, p. 392; on the question of the Court's jurisdiction, the Court deliberated on the effect of the Secretary of State George Shultz's letter of 6 April 1984 which sought to exclude from the Court's jurisdiction disputes between the United States of America and 'any Central American State or arising out of or related to events in Central America'. This letter was deposited three days before Nicaragua filed an application commencing proceedings against the United States. As to the ability of the Shultz letter to exclude jurisdiction, the Court made reference to the United States of America's declaration under Article 36(2) dated 26 August 1946 (*ICJ Yearbook*, 1983–84, p. 91) which the Shultz letter intended to modify. In such declaration it had been stipulated that 'this declaration remains in force for a period of 5 years and *thereafter until the expiration of 6 months after notice may be given to terminate this declaration*' (emphasis added). The Court held that in so providing, 'the United States entered into an obligation which is binding upon it vis-à-vis other States parties to the Optional Clause system' (*ICJ Reports*, 1984, p. 392, at p. 419), and that 'the six months notice clause forms an important integral part of the United States Declaration and it is a condition that must be complied with in case of termination or modification': p. 421.

[84] *International Legal Materials*, 9 (1970), p. 543.

region.[85] Canada's declaration of 7 April 1970 under Article 36(2) excluded the Court's jurisdiction in 'disputes arising out of or concerning jurisdiction or rights claimed or exercised by Canada in respect of the conservation, management or exploitation of the living resources of the sea, or in respect of the prevention or control of pollution or contamination of the marine environment in marine areas adjacent to the coast of Canada'.[86] This declaration was withdrawn in 1985 with Canada widely perceived as having achieved *ex post facto* vindication of its action in Article 234 of the LOSC regarding protection of ice-covered areas.[87]

(f) *The EC's Objection to the Share-out of the Greenland Halibut TAC*

At its annual meeting from 19–23 September 1994, NAFO determined the TACs for eleven fish stocks. Following advice from NAFO's Scientific Committee, a TAC for Greenland halibut was established for the first time. No more than 27,000 tonnes of halibut were to be landed in 1995.[88] At a special meeting of NAFO from 30 January 1995 to 1 February 1995 the share-out of the 27,000 tonnes TAC was decided; 16,300 tonnes were allocated to Canada and 3,400 tonnes to the EC.[89] The EC had argued for 75% of the TAC being 'proportionate to its track record . . . in the most recent three-year period'.[90] Canada, on the other hand, believed that the EC should not be rewarded in this way for its previous overfishing of the halibut stock.

Dissatisfied with its allocation, the EC formally objected to its allocation of the TAC,[91] and proceeded to establish its own quota

---

[85] The Act provided for the control of shipping, the prescribing of vessel construction standards and, if necessary, restrictions on the free passage of shipping in an area which at that time fell within international waters. The then Canadian Prime Minister Trudeau was at pains to note that Canada was not asserting sovereign rights in this area, and made a 'distinction between the absolute claim of sovereignty which means you own everything, the land, the water, the resources in the water and so on . . . against the other aspect which is not an assertion of sovereignty, but an assertion of determination to control certain aspects of what is happening there': ibid., p. 602.

[86] Ibid., p. 599. See generally MacDonald, 'The New Canadian Declaration of Acceptance of the Compulsory Jurisdiction of the International Court of Justice', *Canadian Yearbook of International Law*, 8 (1970), p. 3.

[87] See Merrills, *International Dispute Settlement* (2nd edn., 1993), p. 235.

[88] The EC agreed to this TAC and passed legislation which noted such approval; see EC Council Regulation 3366/94 of 20 December 1994, OJ, 1994, L363/60. The European Parliament was of the opinion that the EC should have objected to the *27,000 tonnes* TAC as being too low, particularly bearing in mind that NAFO's Scientific Committee, although in favour of the establishment of a TAC, recommended that the halibut TAC should not exceed *40,000 tonnes*; see European Parliament Resolution B4–0430/94 of 18 November 1994, OJ, 1994, C341/262.

[89] The remainder of the TAC was distributed between Russia (3,200 tonnes), Japan (2,600 tonnes) and the other NAFO States (1,500 tonnes).

[90] Michael Jack, Minister of State, HC Debs., vol. 256, col. 561 (13 March 1995).

[91] See nn. 42–7 and accompanying text on the legitimate use of the objection procedure under the Northwest Atlantic Fisheries Convention.

amounting to 18,630 tonnes, equivalent to 69% of the established NAFO TAC for 1995.[92]

Two weeks prior to the EC's formal objection, the Canadian Minister of Fisheries and Oceans indicated that the Canadian Government had 'heard reports that the EC may object to the NAFO decision and set unilateral quotas. That is not acceptable to Canada. The last time the EC set unilateral quotas they destroyed flatfish stocks and northern cod. Canada will not stand by and see more stocks destroyed.'[93] On 3 March 1995, following the registering of the EC's formal objection, Canadian regulations[94] implementing the Coastal Fisheries Protection Act were amended to establish EC fishing vessels as a 'prescribed class' for the purposes of section 5.2. From such time any EC trawler deemed by Canadian authorities to be fishing in contravention of a NAFO conservation and management measure would be committing an illegal act under Canadian law. By March 1995 the Canadian authorities monitoring the EC fleet had concluded that EC registered trawlers had landed the 3,400 tonnes of halibut allocated to the EC for 1995 by NAFO.[95] Six days after EC vessels had been prescribed under the Coastal Fisheries Protection Act, the *Estai* had been seized and its captain arrested.[96]

(g) *International Court of Justice Proceedings:* Spain *v.* Canada

On 28 March 1995 Spain[97] began legal proceedings against Canada by filing an application at the Registry of the International Court of Justice.

---

[92] EC Council Regulation 850/95 of 6 April 1995, OJ, 1995, L86/1.

[93] Tobin, HC Deb. (Can.), 1995, 14 February, at p. 9605.

[94] See above, n. 75 and accompanying text. It is to be noted that these implementing regulations prescribe vessels under the Coastal Fisheries Protection Act by reference to such vessels' flag State status. It is submitted that such provisions could be regarded as being contrary to Article 119(3) of the Law of the Sea Convention, which stipulates that, with regard to the establishing of conservation measures concerning high seas living resources, 'States concerned shall ensure that conservation measures and their implementation do not discriminate in form or in fact against the fishermen of any State'; see further below, n. 181. Canada would presumably seek to counter this argument by indicating that similar enforcement action to that endorsed under the Coastal Fisheries Protection Act as amended, and its implementing regulations, was taken against its own fishing vessels; see above, n. 74 and accompanying text.

[95] See Day, loc. cit. above (n. 45), p. 266.

[96] The Canadian Government on 31 March 1995 indicated that 'charges have been laid against the master of the vessel and the vessel for fishing for a straddling stock in contravention of Canadian law. The master also has been charged with failing to stop when required to do so on signal of a government vessel; throwing overboard or destroying part of the vessel's equipment, namely its fishing gear; and wilfully obstructing a protection officer in the execution of the officer's duty': Canadian Department of Fisheries and Oceans, Doc. B-H-95-09E of 31 March 1995.

[97] It would not have been possible for the EC to institute proceedings before the Court as Article 34(1) of the Statute of the International Court of Justice stipulates that 'Only States may be parties in cases before the Court', although the Court may be minded to either ask for or receive any relevant information or evidence possessed by the EC if the case proceeds beyond the jurisdictional phase; Article 34(2) notes: 'The Court . . . may request of public international organizations information relevant to cases before it, and shall receive such information presented by such organizations on their own initiative'.

Spain's application specifically notes that Canada had, by amending the Coastal Fisheries Protection Act on 12 May 1994, endeavoured 'to impose on all persons on board foreign ships a broad prohibition on fishing in the NAFO Regulatory Area, that is, on the high seas, outside Canada's exclusive economic zone',[98] and that the Coastal Fisheries Protection Act as so amended 'expressly permits . . . the use of force against foreign fishing boats in the zones that Article 2.1 unambiguously terms the "high seas" '.[99] The application further makes reference to the fact that the regulations implementing the Coastal Fisheries Protection Act were amended on 3 March 1995 and allowed for the specific use of force against Spanish and Portuguese vessels. The Court has indicated that the 'Application of Spain alleges the violation of various principles and norms of international law and states that there is a dispute between the Kingdom of Spain and Canada which, *going beyond the framework of fishing, seriously affects the very principles of the freedom of the high seas and, moreover, implies a very serious infringement of the sovereign rights of Spain*'[100] and requests:

(*a*) that the Court find that the legislation of Canada, *in so far as it claims to exercise a jurisdiction over ships flying a foreign flag on the high seas, outside the exclusive economic [sic] zone of Canada*, is not opposable to the Kingdom of Spain;

(*b*) that the Court adjudge and declare that Canada is bound to refrain from any repetition of the reported acts, and to offer to the Kingdom of Spain the reparation that is due, in the form of an indemnity of which the amount must cover all the damages and injuries occasioned; and

(*c*) that, consequently, the Court declare also *that the boarding on the high seas, on 9 March 1995, of the ship Estai flying the flag of Spain, and the measures of coercion and the exercise of jurisdiction over that ship and over its captain, constitute a concrete violation of the aforementioned principles and norms of international law.* [Emphasis added.]

The Spanish action is therefore based on the submission that the Coastal Fisheries Protection Act as amended illegally establishes Canadian jurisdiction over foreign vessels in international waters and allows for unjustified use of force against such vessels. The Canadian Government has at all times stated that the amendment to the Coastal Fisheries

[98] ICJ Communiqué No. 95/8, 29 March 1995.
[99] Ibid.
[100] Ibid. (emphasis added). The Spanish application to the Court makes explicit reference to the breaches of international law committed by Canada in respect of, *inter alia*, the exclusivity of flag State jurisdiction, freedom of the high seas, freedom of fishing on the high seas, and the principle that the high seas cannot be subjected to the sovereignty of any State: Spanish Application, Part 2, paragraphs a-d in particular. The authors are grateful to Philippe Kirsch, QC, Agent for the Government of Canada, for supplying the text of this application.

Protection Act did not amount to an assertion of an extended EFZ jurisdiction beyond its 200-mile limit.[101]

Attempting to circumvent Canada's intended exclusion of the Court's jurisdiction,[102] the Spanish application stated:

the exclusion of the jurisdiction of the Court in relation to disputes which may arise from management and conservation measures taken by Canada with respect to vessels fishing in the NAFO Regulatory Area and the enforcement of such measures . . . *does not even partially affect the present dispute.* Indeed, the Application of the Kingdom of Spain does not refer exactly to the disputes concerning those measures, *but rather to their origin, to the Canadian legislation which constitutes their frame of reference.* The Application of Spain directly attacks the title invoked to justify the Canadian measures and their acts of enforcement, *a piece of legislation which, going a great deal further than the mere management and conservation of fishery resources, is in itself an internationally wrongful act of Canada, as it is contrary to the fundamental principles and norms of international law;* a piece of legislation which for that reason does not fall exclusively within the jurisdiction of Canada either, according to its own Declaration (paragraph 2(c) thereof).[103]

At the time of writing the written proceedings in the jurisdictional phase had been concluded[104] and the Court's decision is awaited as to whether it enjoys jurisdiction on the issues raised by Spain's application.[105]

---

[101] See Tobin, HC Deb. (Can.), 1994, 11 May, at p. 4213.

[102] For discussion of Canada's amended declaration under Article 36(2) of the Statute of the Court, see above, text following n. 78. Article 36(3) stipulates that Article 36(2) declarations '*may* be made *unconditionally* or *on condition of reciprocity* on the part of several or certain States, or for a certain time' (emphasis added). The Canadian notification is conditional (see below, nn. 79–81 and accompanying text) and is valid until such time as notice of termination is given. The concept of 'reciprocity' has been defined by the Court as enabling 'the State which has made the wider acceptance of the jurisdiction of the Court to rely on the reservations to the acceptance laid down by the other party': *Interhandel* case (*Switzerland* v. *USA*), *ICJ Reports*, 1959, p. 6, at p. 23. The terms of Spain's acceptance of the Court's jurisdiction in its declaration under Article 36(2) of 29 October 1990 (*ICJ Yearbook*, 1993–94, pp. 115–16) would not, it is submitted, restrict the Court from hearing the issues raised in these proceedings.

[103] ICJ Communiqué (above, n. 98) (emphasis added).

[104] See *Fisheries Jurisdiction* (*Spain* v. *Canada*), order of 8 May 1996, *ICJ Reports*, 1996, p. 58. The parties were awaiting notice from the Court as to when the oral hearings in the jurisdictional phase will be held: letter to co-author dated 12 August 1996 from Philippe Kirsch, QC, Agent for the Government of Canada.

[105] It is clear that the dispute between Spain and Canada involves discussion of various rules and principles of general international law, but also has a direct bearing on environmental rules and principles. With the consent of the parties the dispute could have been brought before the Chamber of the Court for Environmental Matters which was established under Article 26(1) of the Statute of the Court on 19 July 1993; see ICJ Communiqué No. 93/20, 19 July 1993, which notes that 'In view of the developments in the field of environmental law and protection which have taken place in the last few years, and considering that it should be prepared to the fullest possible extent to deal with an environmental case falling within its jurisdiction, the Court has now deemed it appropriate to establish a seven-member Chamber for Environmental Matters'. On the creation of the Environment Chamber and the Court's previous deliberations on matters relating to the environment see Fitzmaurice, 'Environmental Protection and the International Court of Justice', in Lowe and Fitzmaurice (eds.), *Fifty Years of the International Court of Justice* (1996), pp. 293–315.

PART II: STRADDLING FISH STOCKS UNDER THE INTERNATIONAL LAW OF THE SEA

(a) *Introduction*

The whole concept of 'straddling' stocks necessarily presupposes a boundary. Traditionally the international law of the sea knew only three zones—internal waters, the territorial sea and the high seas. Internal waters were subject to State sovereignty and not international in character. The territorial sea was also subject to the sovereignty of the coastal State, but with the well-recognized exception for the innocent passage of ships from third States. Beyond the territorial sea lay the high seas, over which no State exercised sovereignty and which belonged to no particular State. Within the territorial sea the coastal State enjoyed exclusive access to the fishery, while on the high seas the 'freedom of the high seas' prevailed, encompassing freedom of fishing. Thus high seas fisheries were open to all 'and subject to the control of no one save as each nation may enact legislation concerning its own fishermen'.[106] This doctrine was based on the concept that the resources of the sea were virtually inexhaustible,[107] and that the oceans did not lend themselves to effective occupation and possession and were considered as *res communis*.[108]

Since most major fishery resources exist beyond the narrow belt of the territorial sea, be it 3 or 12 miles in breadth,[109] fisheries regulation by the coastal State within the territorial sea 'does not offer any great potential for control and protection in regard to the major fishery resources'.[110]

[106] The *Bering Fur Seals* arbitration, Moore, *International Arbitrations* (1898), vol. 1, at p. 816 (British arguments).

[107] Carroz notes that as late as 1955—three years before the four Geneva Conventions on the Law of the Sea were concluded—most fish stocks, save for those in the north Atlantic and north Pacific, were under-exploited or not exploited at all: 'Les problèmes de la pêche a la conférence de droit de la mer et dans la pratique des états', *Revue générale de droit international public*, 84 (1980), p. 705, at p. 706. He further notes that, largely as a consequence of the development of fishing and vessel technologies, '[c]ette situation s'est modifiée radicalement, surtout depuis la première et la seconde Conférences des Nations Unies sur le droit de la mer en 1958 et 1960': ibid. See also the 1992 FAO Report, *The State of Food and Agriculture* (several developments not foreseen following the conclusion of the LOSC, notably investment in large-scale fishing vessels capable of fishing great distances from port).

[108] See Grotius, *Mare liberum* (1609); Leonard, *International Regulation of Fisheries* (1971), at p. 35; and Fulton, *The Sovereignty of the Sea* (1911), at pp. 344–7.

[109] It will be recalled that the 1958 Geneva Convention on the Territorial Sea and Contiguous Zone failed to stipulate the outermost limit of the territorial sea in consequence of States' failure to agree. Article 24(2) merely provides that the contiguous zone may not extend further than twelve miles from the baselines from which the breadth of the territorial sea is measured. In 1960 the Second United Nations Conference on the Law of the Sea was convened to consider, *inter alia*, the outer limit of the territorial sea and fishing zone. In the event a US proposal, supported *inter alios* by Canada, for a '6 + 6' formula, viz., a six-mile territorial sea and a six-mile fishing zone, was defeated by one vote. The Third United Nations Conference on the Law of the Sea (1973–82) finally saw agreement by States on an outer limit for the territorial sea of twelve miles: cf. Article 3 LOSC.

[110] Fleischer, 'Fisheries and Biological Resources', in Dupuy and Vignes (eds.), *A Handbook on the New Law of the Sea* (1991), vol. 2, at p. 997.

Thus the economic incentive to take conservation measures effective within the territorial sea, only to observe the fishery moving beyond coastal State jurisdiction on to the high seas, was minimal. On the high seas, while in theory flag State jurisdiction prevents a regulatory lacuna, the practice has been a *de facto* freedom of exploitation.[111] Without co-ordination of effort, the incentive for a flag State to impose more stringent standards on its fleet than those imposed by other States on their fleets was slight. Such difficulties stem in part from the common property characteristics of fisheries resources and the 'tragedy of the commons'[112] which may result from over-exploitation of a common property resource.[113]

State practice since the 1940s has seen a steady incursion by coastal States into high seas areas for a variety of functional purposes, including fisheries jurisdiction.[114] The 1945 Truman 'Proclamation Concerning the Policy of the United States with Respect to Coastal Fisheries in Certain Areas of the High Seas'[115] was designed to establish conservation zones beyond the territorial sea in areas traditionally fished by US nationals, for the purpose of the exercise of US authority over domestic

[111] In the International Law Commission's commentary to what became Article 1(1) of the 1958 Geneva Convention on Fishing and the Conservation of the Living Resources of the High Seas, recognizing the high seas freedom of fishing, the ILC noted that this did not preclude States from entering into treaty arrangements for the regulation of fishing. Such arrangements would, of course, only be binding on the States parties to them: *Yearbook of the International Law Commission*, 1956, vol. 2, p. 253 at p. 286. There is in fact abundant evidence of State practice showing co-operation through international agreements to regulate high seas fishing activities in areas of intense use to maintain the commercial viability of the stocks. One of the first international fishery agreements, and perhaps one of the most successful, was the 1911 Convention for the Preservation and Protection of Fur Seals concluded by Russia, Japan, the US, and Great Britain on behalf of Canada, replaced in 1957 but recently discontinued: *British Foreign and State Papers*, vol. 104, p. 175; Birnie and Boyle, *International Law and the Environment* (1992), at pp. 493–6. For analysis of more recent selected agreements, ranging from the 1946 International Convention for the Regulation of Whaling to the 1991 Dakar Convention on Fisheries Co-operation among West African States, see Székely and Kwiatkowska, 'Marine Living Resources', in Sand (ed.), *The Effectiveness of International Environmental Agreements* (1992).

[112] Hardin, 'The Tragedy of the Commons', in Hardin and Baden (eds.), *Managing the Commons* (1977).

[113] Churchill and Lowe identify four consequences flowing from the common property nature of marine living resources: (1) 'a tendency for fish stocks to be fished above biologically optimum levels'; (2) 'a tendency for more fishermen to engage in a fishery than is economically justified'; (3) 'a likelihood of competition and conflict between different groups of fishermen'; and (4) 'the necessity for any regulation of marine fisheries to have a substantial international component': *The Law of the Sea* (2nd rev. edn., 1988), at p. 224.

[114] One of the earliest controversies over a high seas fishery arose in the English Channel in joint use by English and French fishermen of the Channel fishery. The problem was viewed primarily as one of conflict resolution rather than resource conservation. For further discussion of fisheries conflicts of the late 19th and early 20th centuries, see Leonard, op. cit. above (n. 108).

[115] Presidential Proclamation No. 2668, 16 USC sec. 741; reproduced in the United Nations Legislative Series, *High Seas*, at pp. 112–13; see also McDougal and Burke, *The Public Order of the Oceans* (1962), at pp. 966–7. Perhaps better known is Presidential Proclamation No. 2667 which stated that the United States considered the natural resources of the sea-bed and subsoil of the continental shelf as appertaining to the United States and subject to its jurisdiction and control: *American Journal of International Law*, 40 (1946), at p. 45 (Supplement).

fishing activities and any new foreign entrants to the fishery. In the case of existing foreign fishing activity, bilateral agreements were to be entered into.[116] The impetus for this measure was the anticipated entry of Japan into the Alaskan salmon fishery.[117] In 1947 Peru and Chile, followed by Ecuador in 1952, claimed a 200-mile 'territorial sea' in order further to encompass the migration routes of the highly migratory tuna fishery.[118] The Icelandic extension of its exclusive fisheries jurisdiction first to 12 and then to 50 nautical miles, which provoked the 'Cod Wars', was soon overwhelmed by events at the Third United Nations Conference on the Law of the Sea, the negotiation of which lasted from 1973 to 1982.[119] Indeed, to a certain extent the development of the law of the sea in this regard has been fuelled by unilateral action, subsequently garnering more widespread international support.[120]

Thus, as the law of the sea has further developed, coastal State (national) jurisdiction over living resources has extended, first through

[116] Proclamation No. 2668, ibid.

[117] Eckert, *The Enclosure of Ocean Resources: Economics and the Law of the Sea* (1979), at p. 129.

[118] Since the freedom of navigation was recognized, this extension is not wholly consonant with the juridical status of a 'territorial sea'. For discussion of these and other regional developments which supported the extension of coastal State jurisdiction prior to the Third United Nations Conference on the Law of the Sea, see Division of Ocean Affairs and Law of the Sea, UN Office of Legal Affairs, *Exclusive Economic Zone: Legislative History of Articles 56, 58 and 59 of the United Nations Convention on the Law of the Sea* (1992), Part One; see also Njenga, 'Historical Background of the Evolution of the Exclusive Economic Zone and the Contribution of Africa', in Pontecorvo (ed.), *The New Order of the Oceans: The Advent of a Managed Environment* (1986).

[119] In the *Fisheries Jurisdiction* cases the International Court of Justice recognized the preferential rights of fishing in adjacent waters in favour of the coastal State in a situation of special dependence on its coastal fisheries, while rejecting Iceland's unilateral extension of its fishing zone to 50 nautical miles: *ICJ Reports*, 1974, p. 3 (*UK v. Iceland*) and 175 (*FRG v. Iceland*). For criticism of the Court's assertion that this rule of customary law had come into existence since the unsuccessful Second United Nations Conference on the Law of the Sea in 1960, see Churchill, 'The Fisheries Jurisdiction Case: The Contribution of the International Court of Justice to the Debate on Coastal States' Fisheries Rights', *International and Comparative Law Quarterly*, 24 (1975), p. 82, particularly at pp. 93 ff. Churchill analyses the difference between an EFZ regime and coastal States' preferential rights in adjacent waters and concludes that the 'great difference' between them is that 'under the latter the coastal State does not have exclusive jurisdictional rights, and possibly not even any kind of special jurisdictional right or competence. The preference relates to catch and not to jurisdiction, unlike an exclusive fisheries zone where the exclusiveness relates to jurisdiction and not necessarily to catch': ibid., at p. 87.

It will be recalled that Iceland first extended its fisheries jurisdiction to 12 miles in consequence of the failure in 1958 to establish an outer limit of the territorial sea 'or to establish any effective provisions in favour of coastal States particularly dependent on fisheries': Churchill, ibid., at p. 83. The further extension to 50 miles, announced in 1971 with effect from 1 September 1972, is roughly coterminous with the outer extent of Iceland's continental shelf and slope: ibid., at p. 84, n. 6.

[120] In 1958 the fishing limits of 57 of 79 then independent coastal States coincided with the territorial sea boundary, while 22 States claimed fishing zones beyond their territorial sea. Since 1958, 117 claims specifying fishing limits have been made, peaking in 1977/78 as EEZ claims picked up momentum. During the period from the commencement of the Third United Nations Conference on the Law of the Sea negotiations in 1972, and 1978, some 55 coastal States proclaimed a 200-mile EEZ or EFZ. See Smith, op. cit. above (n. 12), at p. 11. In consequence of Canada's proclamation of a 200-mile EFZ from 1 January 1977, a number of bilateral agreements were entered into recognizing the special interests of Canada in fish stocks beyond the 200-mile limit: see further text accompanying nn. 125–30, below.

fishing zones and then through recognition of the exclusive economic zone (EEZ). Detailed provisions on the EEZ are included in the 1982 Law of the Sea Convention, discussed further below, but the general concept is also clearly a part of customary international law.[121] Within the EEZ the coastal State enjoys sovereign rights over the living and non-living resources of the zone. Other States do not have access as of right to the resources of the EEZ. With an estimated 90% of commercially exploited living resources located within the 200-mile coastal belt,[122] this extension of coastal State jurisdiction had profound consequences for fisheries exploitation and conservation.

One 'knock-on effect' of the extension of exclusive economic or fisheries zones to 200 miles was the displacement of foreign fishing fleets from traditional fishing grounds. A 1982 Report by the Canadian Task Force on Atlantic Fisheries observed:

As a consequence of extended jurisdiction by coastal states, a number of 'distant water' fishing nations have been left with fleets of expensive, under-utilized vessels. These vessels, with few other fishing opportunities, create continuing conservation and allocation problems in stock overlapping the Canadian 200-mile zone or outside it.

Indeed, the Task Force suggests that overfishing beyond the 200-mile zone was a technique employed explicitly to exert pressure on the Canadian authorities to accord more favourable treatment to foreign vessels within the Canadian 200-mile zone.[123] Conversely, it has also been suggested that the desire of distant water fishing nations to have access to the surplus within the EEZ has provided coastal States with a lever to exact conservation measures in adjacent areas of the high seas.[124] This is certainly borne out by the treaty practice of Canada, which from the 1970s onwards has concluded a number of bilateral and multilateral agreements in which its special interest[125] in straddling stocks beyond

---

[121] See n. 12, above.

[122] Driver, loc. cit. above (n. 34), at p. 44.

[123] Report of the Task Force on Atlantic Fisheries (Canada), *Navigating Troubled Waters: A New Policy for the Atlantic Fisheries* (1982), at p. 71; see also McRae, 'Special Problems Relating to Fisheries in the EEZ: A Canadian Perspective', in Pharand and Leanza (eds.), *The Continental Shelf and the Exclusive Economic Zone: Delimitation and Legal Regime*, p. 309, at p. 314. The Task Force Report also indicated that trade barriers to Canadian fish products were also raised to force access to Canadian quotas:

'Expanded market access for Canadian groundfish products is important. The strategy of several European fishing nations appears to be to limit or deny that market access to force Canada to concede quotas inside the 200-mile zone. Once foreign fleets are re-admitted on a significant scale it would be more difficult to force them out again': ibid., at pp. 72–3.

[124] Fleischer, loc. cit. above (n. 110), at p. 1116.

[125] In 9 of the 10 agreements which Leger examines, the English words 'special interest' are translated as 'l'intérêt particulier' in the French: Leger, 'Les accords bilatéraux régissant la pêche étrangère dans les eaux canadiennes', *Canadian Yearbook of International Law*, 16 (1978), p. 116.

the 200-mile limit is recognized.[126] Indeed, the bilateral agreement which Canada concluded with Norway on 2 December 1975 'est le premier à être conclu entre deux pays portant sur le régime des 200 milles' elaborated during UNCLOS III.[127] As a consequence of the Canadian extension of its fishery zone to 200 nautical miles on 1 January 1977, bilateral agreements were concluded with distant water fishing nations active in Canadian waters and beyond, including vessels from Bulgaria, Romania, East Germany, and Cuba.[128] Common Article 3 of these agreements recognizes the special interest of Canada in the resources of the adjacent high seas area,[129] and requires the concordance of high seas conservation measures with measures taken by Canada within its national jurisdiction.[130]

(b) *The 1958 Regime*[131]

The 1958 Geneva Convention on the High Seas[132] recognizes the customary high seas freedom of fishing, subject to reasonable regard for the interests of other States in their exercise of the freedom of the high seas.[133] In principle it codifies customary international law in this respect.[134] Further elaboration of the exercise of this high seas freedom, and the duties attendant upon that exercise, are contained in the 1958

[126] See further Meseguer, 'Le régime juridique de l'exploitation de stocks communs de poissons au-delà des 200 milles', *Annuaire français de droit international*, 28 (1982), p. 885; Leger, loc. cit. above (n. 125); and De Mestral, 'Deux récents accords bilatéraux en matière de pêche en 1977', *Canadian Yearbook of International Law*, 15 (1977), p. 287. On NAFO, see further above, text accompanying nn. 27–62.

[127] Leger, loc. cit. above (n. 125).

[128] For extracts of the pertinent provisions of these and other bilateral agreements with Canada, see Applebaum, loc. cit. above (n. 5), pp. 309–17 (Annex 4).

[129] 'Les deux gouvernements confirment la nécessité de veiller à l'intérêt spécial de Canada, y compris les besoins de ses collectives côtières dan les ressources de ce secteur extérieur et immédiatement adjacent à la zone de pêche': Leger, loc. cit. above (n. 125), at p. 129, paraphrasing Article 3(1).

[130] Article 3(2) recognizes 'le besoin de concordance entre les mesures appliqués à l'intérieur de la zone et elles qui s'appliquent dans le secteur adjacent, ainsi que des principes énoncés au paragraphe 1', viz., the special interest of the coastal State: Leger, ibid.

[131] Comprising the four 1958 Geneva Conventions on the Law of the Sea on the High Seas (*United Nations Treaty Series*, vol. 450, p. 82), the Continental Shelf (*United Nations Treaty Series*, vol. 499, p. 311), the Territorial Sea and Contiguous Zone (*United Nations Treaty Series*, vol. 516, p. 205) and Fishing and Conservation of the Living Resources of the High Seas (*United Nations Treaty Series*, vol. 559, p. 285).

[132] *United Nations Treaty Series*, vol. 450, p. 82. The Convention entered into force on 30 September 1962 and had 62 parties as of 31 December 1995. Canada signed but has not ratified the High Seas Convention; Spain acceded to all four Geneva Conventions on 25 February 1971. Of these Canada has only ratified the Continental Shelf Convention (on 6 February 1970).

[133] Article 2, HSC.

[134] While the High Seas Convention is the only one of the four 1958 Geneva Conventions on the Law of the Sea which claims in its preamble to be 'generally declaratory of established principles of international law', it falls short of providing a comprehensive code for the regulation of high seas activities and its provisions have given rise to problems of application. See further Lucchini and Voeckel, *Droit de la mer*, tome 1 (1990), pp. 75–6 (1958 Geneva Conventions reflect Article 13 of the Statute of the International Law Commission, viz., codification and progressive development of international law).

Geneva Convention on Fishing and Conservation of the Living Resources of the High Seas.[135] This was the first convention to address global fisheries conservation, though of the four Geneva Conventions it attracted the smallest number of ratifications.[136] Spain has acceded to the Fishing Convention, while Canada has signed but not ratified it. This Convention entered into force on 20 March 1966 and, like the other Geneva Conventions, is replaced by the 1982 Law of the Sea Convention where a Contracting Party is party to both Conventions.[137] None the less it is necessary briefly to examine its provisions, if only to understand the backdrop against which the Law of the Sea Convention negotiations proceeded; indeed, some proposals in Committee Two[138] of UNCLOS III relied in part on the approach of the 1958 Fishing Convention.

Article 6(1) of the Fishing Convention explicitly recognizes that 'A coastal State has a special interest in the maintenance of the productivity of the living resources in any area of the high seas adjacent'[139] to its

[135] UN Doc. A/Conf.13/L.54; Misc. No. 15 (1958), Cmnd. 584; loc. cit. above (n. 131). The high seas freedom of fishing is not an absolute one. In addition to the reasonable regard provision of Article 2 of the High Seas Convention, Article 1 of the 1958 Fishing Convention provides:
'1. All States have the right for their nationals to engage in fishing on the high seas, subject (a) to their treaty obligations, (b) to the interests and rights of coastal States as provided for in this Convention, (c) to the provisions contained in the following Articles concerning conservation of the living resources of the high seas.
2. All States have the duty to adopt, or to co-operate with other States in adopting, such measures for their respective nationals as may be necessary for the conservation of the living resources of the high seas.'
Further discussion of the articles on living resources to which the high seas freedom of fishing is subject follows below.
[136] As of 31 December 1995 there were 37 parties to the Fishing Convention, namely: Australia*, Belgium, Bosnia and Herzegovina, Burkina Faso, Cambodia, Colombia, Denmark, Dominican Republic, Fiji*, Finland*, France*, Haiti*, Jamaica*, Kenya*, Lesotho, Madagascar, Malawi, Malaysia, Mauritius*, Mexico*, Netherlands*, Nigeria*, Portugal, Senegal*, Sierra Leone*, Soloman Islands, South Africa, Spain, Switzerland, Thailand, Tonga*, Trinidad and Tobago*, Uganda*, United Kingdom, USA, Venezuela and Yugoslavia*. Those States marked with an asterisk are also parties to the 1982 LOSC which entered into force on 16 November 1994. For discussion of the legal effect upon the 1958 Conventions of the entry into force of the 1982 LOSC, see further below, n. 156.
[137] See further below, n. 156. Spain and Canada are parties in common only to the 1958 Continental Shelf Convention which is of no relevance to the present discussion. Thus the provisions of the 1958 Fishing Convention and the 1982 LOSC will apply only to the extent that they reflect customary international law. As a signatory to both the 1958 Fishing Convention and the 1982 LOSC, Canada has the additional obligation not to act inconsistently with the object and purpose of these Conventions: Article 18, Vienna Convention on the Law of Treaties. This obligation has the temporal limitation of the timely entry into force of the treaty; it will also cease where a signatory indicates clearly its intention not to become bound.
[138] UNCLOS III negotiations were carried out in three committees, with Committee Two responsible for traditional law of the sea issues including questions regarding the limits of national jurisdiction which encompasses the EEZ and fisheries jurisdiction.
[139] There is no definition of 'adjacent' contained in the Fishing Convention. The International Law Commission, which prepared the draft articles on which the 1958 Geneva Conventions are based, considered but then abandoned the idea of a 100-mile area in which coastal State rights would be applied. A Spanish proposal that a depth criterion of 500 metres be employed to define the limits of adjacency was rejected by the Conference. For further discussion, see McDougal and Burke, op. cit. above (n. 115), at p. 989; and *1958 United Nations Conference on the Law of the Sea Official Records*, vol. 2: Plenary Meetings, A/CONF.13/38.

territorial sea'.[140] With a view to maintaining productivity, any coastal State may 'adopt unilateral measures of conservation appropriate to any stock of fish or other marine living resources in any area of the high seas adjacent to its territorial sea, provided that negotiations with other States concerned have not led to an agreement within six months'.[141] Other States have an obligation to enter into such negotiations with the coastal State at its request where their nationals are engaged in fishing in any area of the high seas adjacent to the territorial sea of the requesting coastal State.[142] Thus unilateral measures may only be taken when such negotiations have failed to lead to an agreement, and where the circumstances set forth in Article 7(2) are met, viz.:

—conservation measures are needed urgently;
—the measures adopted are based on scientific findings;[143] and
—such measures do not discriminate in form or in fact against foreign fishermen.

These requirements in Article 7(2) are designed to ensure that whilst unilateral measures may be taken by the coastal State, such measures must meet these objective preconditions and their implementation must be non-discriminatory. In the event of dispute, recourse is to be had to binding dispute settlement comprising a special five-member commission, as set forth in Articles 9–12 of the Fishing Convention. The Article 9 dispute settlement procedure is also available where two or more States are fishing the same stock or stocks of fish on the high seas and a State requests negotiation of a conservation agreement. If no conservation agreement is agreed within 12 months of such a request, then the Article

---

[140] De Mestral loc. cit. above (n. 126), at p. 291, argues that even before the extension of coastal State jurisdiction to 200 miles, by virtue of treaty practice and custom, Canada possessed a special interest in all of the fish stocks 'au large de ses côtes et ce droit fut reconnu expressément en 1958' in the Fishing Convention. De Mestral considers further support for the special or preferential right of the coastal State to have come from the ICJ judgment in the *Fisheries Jurisdiction* cases in 1974, discussed loc. cit. above (n. 119).

[141] Article 7(1). Oda argues that this 'should not be construed as enabling the coastal State to extend its control directly over nationals of other states. Rather, in certain circumstances, fishing states are obliged to apply the measures unilaterally adopted by the coastal state to their own nationals.' Thus he concludes that the 1958 Convention does not disturb the traditional rule of the freedom of the high seas with fishing vessels obliged to observe only the law of their own flag State there: 'Fisheries under the United Nations Convention on the Law of the Sea', *American Journal of International Law*, 77 (1983), p. 739 at p. 740.

[142] Article 6(3). Article 5 also addresses the problem of new entrants to a fishery where agreement has already been reached amongst States with existing fishing interests in the area. In essence these measures are opposable to the new entrant, subject to recourse to the compulsory dispute settlement procedures of Article 9 of the Convention.
The 1958 Geneva Conference adopted, at the 15th Plenary Meeting on 25 April 1958, a resolution on 'International Fishery Conservation Conventions' which encourages States to use regional fishery organizations (RFO) as the vehicle for achieving agreement in respect of conservation measures on the high seas: *Official Records*, loc. cit. above (n. 139), at p. 144.

[143] The requirement of urgency, linked to existing knowledge of the fishery, would appear to rule out the application of a precautionary approach: see further Article 10(1)(a)(i), which requires that 'scientific findings demonstrate the necessity of conservation measures'.

9 compulsory dispute settlement procedure may be invoked by any of the parties.[144]

The provisions of the 1958 Fishing Convention were relatively favourable for the coastal State. Not only is the special interest of the coastal State in adjacent high seas stocks recognized, but so is the power of the coastal State to adopt unilateral conservation measures[145] which remain in force and opposable to other States parties until any dispute regarding their validity has been settled under the Fishing Convention.[146] In addition, third States fishing adjacent areas of the high seas are to refrain from enforcing conservation measures there which are 'opposed to' those adopted by the coastal State, 'but may enter into negotiations with the coastal State with a view to prescribing by agreement the measures necessary for the conservation of the living resources of the high seas in that area'.[147] The importance of these provisions to the balance between coastal and distant water fishing interests which the Fishing Convention seeks to achieve is underscored by the fact that no reservations are permitted to Articles 6 or 7, nor to the dispute settlement provisions of Articles 9–12.[148]

As will be seen further below, in several key respects the 1958 Fishing Convention goes further than the 1982 LOSC in recognizing the special interests of the coastal State in stocks in adjacent areas of the high seas. For some States it may have gone too far:[149] the Fishing Convention has only received 37 ratifications to date,[150] and did not receive the support of distant water fishing nations so critical to the success of the balance

---

[144] Article 4.

[145] With the preconditions stipulated above of failure to agree with other States concerned and, where measures are taken, the need for urgency to be demonstrated, a sound scientific basis for the measures, and their non-discriminatory application: Article 7.

[146] Article 7(3). However, the special commission may determine that the measures in dispute should not be applied pending its award, provided that in the case of a dispute under Article 7 (unilateral measures) the special commission has found prima facie evidence that the need for the urgent application of such measures does not exist: Article 10(2).

[147] Article 6(4). If agreement on such conservation measures is not reached within twelve months, then any party may initiate the Article 9 dispute settlement procedure: Article 6(5).

[148] By virtue of Article 19(1). Indeed, such was the importance of agreeing to these provisions together—the recognition of the special interest of coastal States with the safeguard for distant water fishing nations of compulsory dispute settlement—that there was considerable debate regarding voting procedures in respect of these articles. Although the Continental Shelf Convention had been voted upon article-by-article, proposals were made that the Conference should consider these provisions of the Fishing Convention as a whole; a 'mini-package deal'. In the event, despite the protests of some delegates, Articles 49–60A of the International Law Commission's draft articles were voted upon en bloc: see further *Official Records*, loc. cit. above (n. 139), at pp. 43 ff.

[149] McDougal and Burke refer to the provisions of Articles 6 and 7 as having overemphasized coastal State interests and therefore 'highly undesirable', though redeemed to some extent by the counterbalance of the compulsory dispute settlement provisions: op. cit. above (n. 115), at p. 981.

[150] For a full list of ratifications see above, n. 136; the list includes the United Kingdom, the United States, France, Spain and Portugal. As noted above, Canada signed but did not ratify the Convention. The EC cannot become a party because Article 15 of the Fishing Convention does not provide for the participation of entities other than States.

between coastal and distant water fishing interests which the Convention sought to achieve. Nor is there evidence that the innovative remedy in Article 7 has ever actually been applied in a dispute.[151] Attempts to introduce a similar provision into the LOSC failed.[152] It may be that the approach of the 1958 Convention is inappropriate for application to straddling stocks across the new maritime zones generated under the 1982 LOSC.[153] What may have been appropriate for conditions prevailing when the relevant boundary was a territorial sea/high seas one may not be so in view of the recognition of not only the special interests but the sovereign rights of the coastal State to both the living and non-living resources in a zone 200 miles in breadth.[154]

(c) The 1982 LOSC[155]

The 1982 United Nations Convention on the Law of the Sea (LOSC) entered into force on 16 November 1994. For 18 of the parties to the 1958 Fishing Convention their obligations *inter se* have been replaced by the provisions of the LOSC regarding, *inter alia*, the EEZ (Part V) and

[151] Yonezawa, 'Some Thoughts on the Straddling Stock Problem in the Pacific Ocean', in Kuribayashi and Miles (eds.), *The Law of the Sea in the 1990s: A Framework for Further Cooperation* (1990), Proceedings of the 24th Annual Conference of the Law of the Sea Institute, at p. 133; Lagoni, Report of the ILA International Committee on the EEZ, 'Principles Applicable to Living Resources occurring both within and without the Exclusive Economic Zone or in Zones of Overlapping Claims', *Report of the Sixty-Fifth Conference of the International Law Association, Cairo 1992* (1993), at p. 267, n. 51 (the procedural solution of Article 7 'was apparently at no time of any practical relevance'); Burke, *The New International Law of Fisheries* (1994), at p. 13; and Oda, loc. cit. above (n. 141), at p. 755.

[152] Nandan and Rosenne, *United Nations Convention on the Law of the Sea 1982: A Commentary* (1993–5), 5 volumes; see also the US proposal to the Sea-Bed Committee: UN Doc. A/AC.138/SC.II/L.40, discussed in Lucchini, loc. cit. above (n. 5), at p. 872.

[153] Yonezawa, loc. cit. above (n. 151), at p. 133; Lagoni, loc. cit. above (n. 151), at p. 270, para. 46 ('exceptional jurisdiction' under Article 7 exercised 'in legally and factually different circumstances than in the case of the EEZ').

[154] See further Treves, 'La pêche en haute mer et l'avenir de la Convention des Nations Unies sur le droit de la mer', *Annuaire français de droit international*, 38 (1992), p. 888.

[155] Doc. A/CONF.62/122 and Corr. 1 to 11, reproduced in *International Legal Materials*, 21 (1982), p. 21. The 1982 Law of the Sea Convention ('LOSC') which resulted from negotiations in Three Committees between 1973–1982 at the Third United Nations Conference on the Law of the Sea ('UNCLOS III') has been the subject of a voluminous literature. See, generally, Churchill and Lowe, op. cit. above (n. 113); Dupuy and Vignes, op. cit. above (n. 110), 2 volumes; Lucchini and Voelckel, *Le droit de la mer* (1990), 2 volumes; O'Connell, *The International Law of the Sea* (1982), 2 volumes; Brownlie, *Principles of Public International Law* (4th edn., 1990), Part I. For a detailed commentary on the drafting history of the LOSC, see Nordquist (editor in chief), Nandan, Rosenne and Grandy, *United Nations Convention on the Law of the Sea 1982: A Commentary* (1993–95), 5 volumes. See also Platzöder, *Third United Nations Conference on the Law of the Sea: Documents* (1988), 18 volumes (series 1). A further valuable source of information is the publications of the UN Division for Ocean Affairs and the Law of the Sea, including the *Law of the Sea Bulletin* (1983–).

the high seas (Part VII).[156] To the extent that these provisions deal with the problem of straddling stocks, each part will be addressed in turn. At the time of writing, both Canada and Spain[157] have signed but not yet ratified the Convention, which as at 13 August 1996 had received 106 ratifications.[158] The extent of their treaty obligations in respect of the LOSC are therefore only to refrain from acting in a manner inconsistent

[156] See above, n. 136. Article 311 LOSC addresses its relationship with other Conventions, paragraph 1 of which provides: 'This Convention will prevail as between States Parties, over the Geneva Conventions on the Law of the Sea of 29 April 1958'. This is an application of the rule found in Article 30 of the Vienna Convention on the Law of Treaties ('VCLT') regarding the application of successive treaties relating to the same subject-matter, described by Sinclair as '[a] particularly obscure aspect of the law of treaties': Sinclair, *The Vienna Convention on the Law of Treaties* (2nd edn., 1984), at p. 93.
Rosenne and Sohn describe the effect of Article 311 thus:
'The formulation used is reasonably standard and it implies the concurrent existence of the two regimes. The 1982 Convention governs the relations of all parties to it, and to that extent the relevant Conventions of 1958 cease to have effect. As between States which are parties to any or all of the 1958 Conventions but not to the 1982 Convention, their relations will continue to be governed by the 1958 instruments. The same will apply as between a State which is a party to one or more of the 1958 Conventions and a State which is a party to the 1958 Conventions and has accepted the new Convention. This means that the 1958 Conventions are not directly or fully superseded by the 1982, as had originally been proposed':
Rosenne and Sohn (volume eds.), in Nordquist (ed.), *United Nations Convention on the Law of the Sea 1982: A Commentary* (1989), volume 5, at pp. 242–3.
Apparently Rosenne and Sohn would regard the 1958 Conventions as superseded only as between States party to the new Convention (and also party to any of the 1958 Conventions), a conclusion consonant with Article 30 VCLT. Applebaum has argued that the use of the word 'prevail' means that even as between States who are parties to the LOSC but also to one or more of the 1958 Conventions, those *provisions* of the 1958 Conventions which are not incompatible with the 1982 Convention will persist: Applebaum, loc. cit. above (n. 5), at p. 293. It is submitted that this is not consistent with the *travaux préparatoires* of Article 311, nor with the general approach of the residual rules contained in Articles 30 and 59 (termination or suspension of the operation of a treaty implied by conclusion of a later treaty) of the Vienna Convention on the Law of Treaties. It should be noted that the disputes regarding the interpretation or application of Article 311 fall under the dispute settlement procedures of Part XV LOSC. However, this is a good example of where a dispute arising under the LOSC may require the interpretation and application of other rules, viz., the Vienna Convention on the Law of Treaties and customary treaty law rules.
[157] Pursuant to Article 310 LOSC, Spain made a lengthy declaration on signature which states, *inter alia*, that '[i]t considers that, without prejudice to the provisions of Article 297 . . . Articles 51, 61 and 62 of the Convention preclude considering the powers of the coastal State to determine the allowable catch, its harvesting capacity and the allocation of surpluses'. For the text of the declaration, see *Multilateral Treaties desposited with the Secretary-General, Status as at 31 December 1995*, ST/LEG/SER.E/14, at p. 813. Whilst declarations to the LOSC are permitted, Article 309 prohibits reservations, unless expressly permitted by other articles of the Convention. This was to preserve the 'package deal' character of the Convention.
[158] With the accession of Mongolia. Nine of the fifteen member States of the EC are parties to the LOSC as of 13 August 1996, namely, Germany, Italy, Austria, Greece, France, Finland, Ireland, Sweden and the Netherlands. The EC has signed but not ratified the Convention. Whereas the EC's competence in fisheries matters is exclusive (see above, n. 30), the wide range of matters covered by the LOSC will require both the EC and its member States to ratify in order to give full force and effect to the LOSC within the EC: see, generally, McGoldrick, *International Relations Law of the European Union* (1997).
From 1 January to 13 August 1996 alone an additional 22 States have indicated their consent to be bound by the LOSC, an increase in activity partly explained by the desire to participate in the nomination and election of judges to the International Tribunal for the Law of the Sea: see further below, n. 255.

with the object and purpose of the Convention.[159] Thus it will be particularly important in the ensuing discussion to determine the extent to which the straddling stock provisions of the LOSC are reflective of customary international law.[160] Some attention will also be paid to the innovative dispute settlement provisions of the LOSC which, though not governing in the present dispute between Canada and Spain since neither has ratified the LOSC, may resolve future conflicts between States regarding the conservation and management of straddling stocks.[161]

(i) *High seas*

Article 87(1) LOSC provides that the freedom of the high seas is exercised under the conditions laid down by the Convention and by other rules of international law. All high seas freedoms must be exercised with due regard[162] for the interests of other States in their exercise of the freedom of the high seas.[163] Freedom of fishing is further subject to the conditions set forth in section 2 of Part VII, which contains five relatively brief articles (Articles 116–120) addressed to the 'conservation and management of the living resources of the high seas'.[164]

Article 116 stipulates that:

All States have the right for their nationals to engage in fishing on the high seas subject to:
(*a*) their treaty obligations;
(*b*) the rights and duties as well as the interests of the coastal States provided for, *inter alia*, in article 63, paragraph 2,[165] and articles 64 to 67;[166] and
(*c*) the provisions of this section.[167]

---

[159] Article 18 VCLT.

[160] As will become clearer below, the essential difficulty with the 1982 LOSC is not so much the extent to which its provisions on fisheries codify customary international law, but its failure fully to address the problems of management of high seas fisheries. The 1992 FAO State of Food and Agriculture Report, whilst acknowledging that the fisheries provisions of the LOSC are 'widely considered to be codifications of customary international law', notes that several developments were not foreseen, most notably continued investment in large-scale fishing vessels capable of extended distant water fishing, and the significant growth in fishing effort on the high seas beyond the 200-mile limit.

[161] This is even more likely since the 1995 Straddling Stocks Agreement was concluded, since it utilizes the dispute settlement procedures of the 1982 LOSC: see further below, Part III.

[162] 'Reasonable regard' in the 1958 High Seas Convention, Article 2.

[163] Article 87(2).

[164] For analysis of the negotiating background and resulting text of Articles 116–120, see Nandan, Rosenne and Grandy (eds.), op. cit. above (n. 155), vol. 3 (1995), at pp. 279–317.

[165] The only provision of the LOSC explicitly to address the problem of straddling stocks, considered in further detail in the next section.

[166] These are the provisions of the LOSC which address anadromous and catadromous stocks, highly migratory species and marine mammals. Articles 63–67 are contained in Part V on the EEZ, which is considered further in the next section. By operation of Article 120, the provisions of Article 65 regarding marine mammals in the EEZ also apply to the conservation and management of marine mammals on the high seas.

[167] i.e. section 2, 'Conservation and Management of the Living Resources of the High Seas', Articles 116–120.

This is substantially a repetition of the formula contained in Article 1(1) of the 1958 Fishing Convention.[168] Article 117 also repeats, with one minor drafting change,[169] the obligation contained in Article 1(2) of the 1958 Fishing Convention for all States 'to take, or to co-operate with other States in taking, such measures for their respective nationals as may be necessary for the conservation of the living resources on the high seas'. The duty to co-operate is further elaborated in Article 118[170] in respect of States whose nationals exploit the same resources, or different resources in the same area, with recognition of subregional or regional fisheries organizations as possible vehicles for such co-operation.[171] This goes further than the 1958 regime in its recognition of the interdependence of stocks, indicated by the concern for fishing effort in the same region but in respect of different stocks,[172] and in the recognition of subregional and regional fisheries organizations (RFOs) as a possible vehicle for co-operation.[173] However, there is no express obligation to negotiate until agreement is reached, nor are the consequences of a failure to reach agreement stipulated.[174]

---

[168] Above, n. 135.

[169] 'Adopt' has been replaced with 'take'.

[170] Article 118 provides;
'States shall co-operate with each other in the conservation and management of living resources in the areas of the high seas. States whose nationals exploit identical living resources, or different living resources in the same area, shall enter into negotiations with a view to taking the measures necessary for the conservation of the living resources concerned. They shall, as appropriate, co-operate to establish subregional or regional fisheries organizations to this end.'

[171] Hey appears to suggest that there is an obligation under Article 118 to enter into such arrangements: *The Regime for the Exploitation of Transboundary Marine Fisheries Resources* (1989), at p. 83, n. 2; *contra*, cf. Freestone, loc. cit. above (n. 5). If a coastal State is fishing straddling stocks in the high seas area adjacent to its EEZ or EFZ, it will be under an obligation to enter into co-operative arrangements with other States exploiting that stock or different stocks in the same area by virtue of Article 118. That is, a coastal State fishing straddling stocks on the adjacent high seas assumes concurrently the rights and duties of a fishing State under Article 63(2). (See further Lagoni, loc. cit. above (n. 151), at p. 265, para. 32.) In contrast, Hey argues that where the coastal State is not engaged in high seas exploitation, Article 63(2) leaves it the discretion whether to participate in the co-operative arrangement. States fishing on the high seas, on the other hand, do not have such discretion and will be obliged to co-operate unless the coastal State is satisfied that the duty of due diligence has been complied with: op. cit. above, p. 83. Presumably this obligation could be met through the demonstration of proper conservation measures applied by the third State to its vessels fishing on the high seas.

[172] Article 4(1) of the 1958 Convention simply provides that '[i]f the nationals of two or more States are engaged in fishing the same stock or stocks of fish or other marine living marine resources in any area or areas of the high seas, these States shall, at the request of any of them, enter into negotiations with a view to prescribing by agreement for their nationals the necessary measures for the conservation of the living resources affected'. Failure to agree within twelve months permits any party to invoke the compulsory dispute settlement procedures of Article 9 (Article 4(2)).

[173] Carroz notes the absence of reference to international organizations in the text of the 1958 Convention: loc. cit. above (n. 107), at p. 726. The 1958 Convention does recognize certain depositary and notification functions for the FAO, which also plays a consultative role in the default procedures for designating members of the special commission under Article 9: see Articles 5(1) and 9(2).

[174] *The Regime for High-Seas Fisheries*, op. cit. above (n. 5), at p. 26, para. 77.

Article 119[175] is potentially far-reaching in that it stipulates the measures that States shall take in determining the allowable catch of high seas resources and the criteria to be taken into account in establishing other conservation measures for high seas living resources.[176] It draws to a very considerable extent upon the principles set forth in Article 61 LOSC regarding conservation of the living resources of the EEZ.[177] Article 119(1) provides that States shall take measures to maintain *or restore*[178] harvested species at levels which can produce maximum sustainable yield of the resource, 'as qualified by environmental and economic factors'. These factors include: the special requirements of developing States; fishing patterns; interdependence of stocks; and 'any generally recommended international minimum standards, whether sub-regional, regional or global'.[179] Also required to be taken into consideration are the effects on dependent and associate species, with the requirement to maintain or restore such species above levels where

[175] Article 119 provides:
1. In determining the allowable catch and establishing other conservation measures for the living resources in the high seas, States shall:
(a) take measures which are designed, on the best scientific evidence available to the States concerned, to maintain or restore populations of harvested species at levels which can produce the maximum sustainable yield, as qualified by relevant environmental and economic factors, including the special requirements of developing States, and taking into account fishing patterns, the interdependence of stocks and any generally recommended international minimum standards, whether subregional, regional or global;
(b) take into consideration the effects on species associated with or dependent upon harvested species with a view to maintaining or restoring populations of such associated or dependent species above levels at which their reproduction may become seriously threatened.
2. Available scientific information, catch and fishing effort statistics, and other data relevant to the conservation of fish stocks shall be contributed and exchanged on a regular basis through competent international organizations, whether subregional, regional or global, where appropriate and with participation by all States concerned.
3. States concerned shall ensure that conservation measures and their implementation do not discriminate in form or in fact against the fishermen of any State.'
[176] In contrast, the 1958 Convention is very much a product of its time, defining 'conservation of the living resources of the high seas' as meaning 'the aggregate of the measures rendering possible the *optimum sustainable yield* from those resources so as to secure a *maximum supply of food* and other marine products. Conservation programmes should be formulated with a view to securing in the first place a supply of food for human consumption': Article 2, 1958 Fishing Convention (emphasis added). However, security of food supply is also an objective of the 1995 FAO Code on Responsible Fisheries; while the SSA refers to the conservation and sustainable use of straddling and highly migratory fish stocks. See further discussion of these instruments below, Part III.
[177] The Article 119 requirement that conservation measures and their implementation be non-discriminatory finds no parallel in Article 61. However, it should be noted that Article 62(4) requires the laws and regulations of the coastal State applicable to nationals fishing in the EEZ to be consistent with the LOSC, while Article 310 obliges all parties to implement the LOSC in good faith and not to exercise their rights, jurisdiction and freedoms in a manner which would constitute an abuse of right. See further Kwiatkowska, op. cit. above (n. 41), at p. 67.
[178] There is no obligation of restoration in the 1958 Convention, which is a reflection of the fact that few stocks were over-exploited at that time: see Carroz, loc. cit. above (n. 107).
[179] Article 119(1)(a). The use of 'include' indicates that this constitutes a non-exhaustive list of 'relevant environmental and economic factors'. These factors would permit a coastal State to depart from the MSY standard and set conservation measures designed, for example, to provide a greater abundance of the fishery for long-term economic reasons. See further discussion in Burke, op. cit. above (n. 151), at p. 112.

reproduction might seriously be threatened.[180] Finally, Article 119(2) imposes a weak obligation to exchange catch data and statistics 'on a regular basis, through competent international organizations . . . where appropriate and with participation of all States concerned', while Article 119(3) requires conservation measures *and* their implementation to be non-discriminatory.[181]

However, notable by its absence is any mention in Article 119 of the need to take into account conservation measures taken within a 200-mile zone in respect of conservation of the straddling stocks on the high seas beyond. It will be recalled that the 1958 Convention did address this point,[182] specifically prohibiting third States from enforcing conservation measures in areas adjacent to the coastal State's territorial waters where those measures are 'opposed to' the coastal State's measures.[183] The impression conveyed by the 1982 Convention is that, with the extension of coastal State jurisdiction to 200 nautical miles, the problem of high seas fisheries conservation was viewed as much less pressing, with the appropriate fora for such matters being the regional and subregional fisheries organizations which, in consequence of the 200-mile EEZs and EFZs, are of much reduced importance.

In addition to the compatibility criterion, the question remains whether, under the high seas provisions of the LOSC, a coastal State may exercise jurisdiction over living resources beyond its 200-mile zone. Certainly all States have the duty to take, and to co-operate with other States in taking, measures for the conservation of the living resources of the high seas. This duty is clearly spelled out in Article 117 LOSC and doubtless reflects current customary law on the point.[184] An important

---

[180] Article 119(1)(b).

[181] Thus a State establishing conservation measures cannot discriminate against the nationals of any State fishing on the high seas. What Article 119(3) does not make clear is which groups are to be compared: Burke, op. cit. above (n. 151), at p. 131. An obligation of equal treatment poses particular problems in connection with new entrants. Pannatier observes that 'toute tentative de tirer avantage des mesures de conservation afin de'exclure de nouveaux arrivants se heurterait à l'obligation générale de non-discrimination' in Article 119(3): *Le pillage des ressources biologiques de la haute mer* (forthcoming). Nandan, Rosenne and Grandy conclude that, where conservation and management measures have been established, a new entrant could not 'ignore or flaunt [*sic*] such measures simply in exercise of their rights or because they have not been able to obtain an allocation': op. cit. above (n. 55), vol. 3, at p. 313; see also Burke, op. cit. above (n. 151), at p. 131.

For an analysis of the Canadian measures in the light of this provision, see above, n. 94.

[182] See also Article XI(3) of NAFO: Burke, op. cit. above (n. 151), at p. 135, n. 144; and see further above, text accompanying nn. 125–30 (bilateral fishery agreements entered into by Canada with compatibility requirement).

[183] Article 6(4); see further above, text accompanying n. 147. This omission is not remedied in Part V LOSC, Article 63(2): see further below.

[184] See further *The Regime for High-Seas Fisheries*, loc. cit. above (n. 5), at pp. 25–9; see also Hey, op. cit. above (n. 171), particularly chapter 2.

caveat is that this duty extends only to measures for their respective nationals; thus Article 117 relies on the traditional basis for the exercise of jurisdiction on the high seas, namely, nationality. The 1982 Convention fails explicitly to provide a treaty basis on which a State might take, and enforce, fishery conservation measures beyond the 200-mile zone save in respect of its own nationals. This should not be surprising, given the resistance to 'creeping coastal State jurisdiction'[185] by the major maritime powers and the significant gain already achieved by coastal States with the EEZ provisions.[186]

But Miles and Burke argue that, to be effective, Article 116 *should* be interpreted so as to authorize the coastal State to take conservation measures in respect of straddling stocks with which other States would be required to comply. Implicitly, it is argued, Article 116 provides for the extension of coastal State conservation measures to the adjacent high seas area where straddling stocks are concerned. Otherwise, they suggest, '[t]he rights of the coastal state, expressly made superior to the high seas fishing state, would . . . be empty and the high seas state would have no meaningful obligation different from its obligation to any state'.[187] Ambassador Mansilla refers to the lack of effectiveness of coastal State conservation measures within the EEZ should the same stock be exempt from such measures beyond the 200-mile limit. He shares Miles and

[185] Oda concluded in 1983 that an extension of the jurisdiction to regulate the straddling stocks in the adjacent area would amount to creeping coastal State jurisdiction. The 'mere attempt' at exercising competence or jurisdiction over high seas fisheries by any particular State would be 'tantamount to a clear violation of the basic principle of the freedom of the high seas': Oda, loc. cit. above (n. 141). But cf. Orrego Vicuña, who refers to post-UNCLOS III steps to acknowledge the unity of straddling stocks and the special interest of coastal States in their conservation and management as, in fact, 'preventing a kind of reverse creeping jurisdiction in favour of distant water fishing nations': 'Toward an Effective Management of High Seas Fisheries and the Settlement of Pending Issues of the Law of the Sea', *Ocean Development and International Law*, 24:1 (1993), p. 81 at p. 86. However, unless it is successfully demonstrated that international law already recognizes the special interest of the coastal State in straddling stocks in adjacent high seas areas, it is difficult to characterize the enjoyment by distant water fishing nations (DWFN) of the freedom of fishing on the high seas as 'reverse creeping jurisdiction'. Indeed, since many DWFN did not become parties to the 1958 Fishing Convention, it would be necessary to demonstrate either that international law already recognizes such a special interest, or that it is recognized in the LOSC and binding on States parties, in order for coastal State interests to prevail over the high seas freedom of fishing.

[186] This is the view expressed by, *inter alios*, Yonezawa, loc. cit. above (n. 151), at p. 132. Unlike Miles and Burke, he does not consider that Article 116 confers any rights on coastal States additional to those found in Part V LOSC. See also Meseguer, who recalls the intervention of the Spanish delegation in 1979 on this point: loc cit. above (n. 126), at pp. 895–6 (by Ambassador Eduardo Ibañez, Committee Two, 21 August 1979).

[187] Miles and Burke, loc. cit. above (n. 5), at p. 352. In respect of this last point it may be observed that high seas States do have an additional obligation *vis-à-vis* coastal States in respect of mutually exploited straddling stocks, under Article 63(2). Whether this is a 'meaningful obligation' is another question, explored further in the next section which examines Article 63(2). As to whether the coastal States' rights are made 'superior' to those of high seas fishing States, see further below, text accompanying n. 240.

Burke's view of the potential scope of Article 116.[188] Such an approach would be more consistent with the objectives of sustainable development,[189] and with recognition of the unity of the resource notwithstanding the biologically artificial 200-mile limit.[190]

Even assuming that coastal State conservation measures may apply to straddling stocks beyond the 200-mile limit, a number of questions remain: would these measures be required to give effect to international standards? What if international standards do not exist? How are such standards to be enforced—by the coastal State, as provided for, *inter alia*, in the Canadian Coastal Fisheries Protection Act,[191] or by the flag State, as Oda suggests?[192] It will be recalled that the 1958 Convention permitted unilateral coastal State measures in the event of a failure of the coastal State and foreign high seas fishing State to agree, and where the preconditions set forth in Article 7(2) are met. However, should such measures be taken, the 1958 Convention further provides for compulsory third-party adjudication to ensure that any measures taken are urgently required and based on sound scientific evidence. The LOSC, despite suggestions from some quarters, does not follow this route. There is no provision for unilateral coastal State measures.[193] As we have seen, criteria are set forth in Article 119 for determining conservation and other measures for the living resources on the high sea, including taking

---

[188] Commentary, Ambassador Mansilla (Secretary General, Comision Permanente del Pacifico Sur) in Kuribayashi and Miles (eds.), op. cit. above (n. 151), at p. 146 (expressly disagreeing with Yonezawa, loc. cit. above (n. 151); see also Joyner and DeCola, 'Chile's Presential Sea Proposal: Implications for Straddling Stocks and the International Law of Fisheries', *Ocean Development and International Law*, 24:1 (1993), p. 99 at p. 106:
'Article 116 specifically acknowledges the interests of the coastal state in managing straddling stocks. The fact that this provision contains a direct reference to Article 63(2) indicates that coastal states' rights, duties, and interests with respect to straddling stocks *cannot be ignored*' (emphasis added).
Whilst 'cannot be ignored' is rather ambiguous, Joyner and DeCola unequivocally reject a 'present interpretation' of Article 116 giving 'the coastal state any special rights to take unilateral actions that would mitigate deleterious effects of unregulated fishing of straddling stocks on the high seas, beyond recognized zones of national jurisdiction': ibid.

[189] See further Sands, 'International Law in the Field of Sustainable Development', this *Year Book*, 65 (1994), at p. 303.

[190] See FAO Technical Paper No. 335, *Review of the State of World Fishery Resources: Marine Fisheries* (1994), updated in FAO Fisheries Circular No. 884 (1995), which criticizes the failure to appreciate the need to manage resources as population units 'whichever jurisdiction they fall into': introduction, para. 16. Both the FAO Code of Responsible Fisheries and the SSA recognize biological unity and other biological characteristics: see further discussion below, Part V.

[191] Above, text accompanying nn. 63–77. It will be recalled that the Canadian legislation provides for the implementation both of domestic and of NAFO measures, though in the case of the arrest of the *Estai* it was NAFO regulatory measures which Canada stated it was enforcing.

[192] Loc. cit. above (n. 141).

[193] Neither the LOSC nor the subsequent Straddling Stocks Agreement contains a counterpart to Article 7 of the 1958 Fishing Convention, which arguably would have upset the balance between coastal and distant water fishing States' interests achieved in the LOSC and carried through to the SSA. This point is returned to below, in Part III.

into account 'any generally recommended international minimum standards, whether subregional, regional or global'. Article 119 thus sets the parameters for 'conservation measures for the living resources in the high seas' which would apply to any conservation measures in respect of straddling stocks beyond the 200-mile limit. Thus even in the absence of further agreement the coastal State would not have *carte blanche* to legislate for the conservation of straddling stocks in adjacent high seas areas; and the non-discrimination obligation in Article 119(3) would apply.

In addition, whilst academic authority is divided on whether coastal States have a recognized special interest in straddling stocks beyond their 200-mile zone, and on the juridical nature of that interest,[194] there is little support for unilateral enforcement action by the coastal State against third States on the high seas for breach of coastal State and/or international conservation measures extended to straddling stocks in the adjacent area.[195] It will be recalled that the 1958 Convention, whilst recognizing the ability of coastal States in certain circumstances to extend conservation measures to stocks beyond their territorial sea, did not specifically address the issue of enforcement of such measures. Therefore general international law principles would apply.[196] The LOSC does not provide a basis upon which enforcement action might be taken on the high seas by one State against another for the failure to comply with the coastal State's conservation measures;[197] nor is there jurisdiction unilaterally to enforce multilaterally agreed standards in the absence of specific agreement.[198] Indeed, the exceptions to the exclusivity of flag State jurisdiction on the high seas are very narrowly circumscribed in Part VII of the LOSC, with the power to arrest on the high seas confined to instances of piracy and unauthorized broadcasting.[199] Nor would the present state of international law appear to contemplate

[194] In particular, whether it confers legislative and/or enforcement jurisdiction on the coastal State in respect of straddling stocks on the high seas.

[195] See further discussion below, section (iii), text accompanying nn. 240–8.

[196] Oda concludes that it is up to the flag State to do so: loc. cit. above (n. 141); see also Lagoni, loc. cit. above (n.151), at p. 270, para. 45 (lack of coastal State enforcement jurisdiction in the adjacent area unless otherwise agreed).

[197] Miles and Burke arrive at a similar conclusion: loc. cit. above (n. 5), at p. 351.

[198] The Straddling Stocks Agreement makes some significant innovations in this connection, considered further below, Part III.

[199] Articles 105 and 109. These are the only two cases under the LOSC of States other than the flag State enjoying both legislative and enforcement jurisdiction over ships on the high seas: Churchill and Lowe, op. cit. above (n. 113), at p. 171. Additional enforcement jurisdiction is conferred by Article 110, which embodies the right of visit and search of a foreign ship where there are reasonable grounds for suspecting that the ship is engaged in piracy, the slave trade, unauthorized broadcasting (and the enforcing State has jurisdiction under Article 109), or is a ship without nationality. For further discussion see Churchill and Lowe, ibid., at pp. 171–6.

unilateral enforcement of a general conservation obligation in areas beyond national jurisdiction.[200]

(ii) *EEZ*

Article 63 LOSC[201] addresses the problem of transboundary (Article 63(1))[202] and straddling (Article 63(2)) stocks.[203] In this brief article is found the only reference to these stocks in the Convention, prompting Churchill and Lowe to observe that '[t]he Law of the Sea Convention conveys the impression that most fish stocks confine themselves to the EEZ of a single coastal State'.[204]

Article 63(2) provides:

Where the same stock or stocks of associated species occur both within the exclusive economic zone and *in an area beyond and adjacent to the zone*, the coastal State and the States fishing for such stocks in the adjacent area *shall seek*, either directly or through appropriate subregional or regional organizations, to agree upon the measures necessary for the conservation of these stocks in the adjacent area.[205]

It could be argued that the obligation in Article 63(2) to 'seek' to agree measures on conservation of straddling stocks extends only to conservation of such stocks *beyond* the EEZ—'in the area beyond and adjacent to the zone'—and not to conservation of the stocks within their whole geographic range in areas of both national and international jurisdiction. Attard emphasizes this limitation, and notes that presumably this restriction was imposed so as not to appear to undermine coastal State

---

[200] Miles and Burke, loc. cit. above (n. 5), at p. 351, n. 24.

[201] For analysis of the negotiating background to and text of Article 63, see Nandan, Rosenne and Grandy (eds.), op. cit. above (n. 155), vol. 2 (1993), at pp. 639–47; see also Meseguer, loc. cit. above (n. 126), at pp. 888 ff. Fleischer refers to Article 63 as not belonging solely to Part V of the LOSC concerning the EEZ, since it lays down obligations which also apply to the high seas: loc. cit. above (n. 110), at p. 1121; on the same point, Oda, loc. cit. above (n. 141), at p. 753. Hey, op. cit. above (n. 171), at p. 55, concludes that States co-operating under Article 63(1) are concerned with implementing the EEZ regime whilst those co-operating under Article 63(2) are concerned with implementing the high seas regime.

[202] Article 63(1) provides:

'1. Where the same stock or stocks of associated species occur within the exclusive economic zones of two or more coastal States, then these States shall seek, either directly or through appropriate subregional or regional organizations, to agree upon the measures necessary to co-ordinate and ensure the conservation and development of such stocks without prejudice to the other provisions of this Part.'

Fleischer criticizes Article 63 for failing to address the problem of stocks crossing other boundaries, such as internal waters or territorial sea boundaries: 'The New Régime of Maritime Fisheries' *Recueil des cours*, 209 (1988–II), p. 95, at p. 176.

[203] Though Article 63(2) does not refer to 'straddling stocks' as such.

[204] Churchill and Lowe, op. cit. above (n. 113), at p. 234.

[205] Emphasis added.

rights within the EEZ.[206] The obligation is a very weak one: merely to 'seek' to agree. Indeed, Orrego Vicuña concludes that '[t]here is no obligation to enter into such agreements as evidenced by the expression "shall seek"'.[207] Like Attard, he is clearly influenced in this inter-pretation by the language of Article 63 and the sovereign rights which coastal States enjoy over living resources within the exclusive economic zone.[208]

Another weakness of Article 63(2) is the failure to provide any specific recourse in the event of inability to reach agreement,[209] unlike the 1958 Convention which not only addressed resolution of the conflict between States through the application of a compulsory dispute settlement procedure but also provided for the unilateral application by the coastal State of conservation measures pending the outcome of the dispute. Under the LOSC the failure to agree measures for the conservation of straddling fish stocks leads neither to a suspension of fishing nor to the provisional application of national or regional measures.[210] However, if the dispute settlement provisions of Part XV of the LOSC apply then there is the possibility of provisional measures, which might provide such a result.[211] But does the failure to agree *simpliciter* constitute a 'dispute' for the purposes of the application of Part XV LOSC?[212] The unsuccessful amendment to Article 63(2) proposed by Canada and seven other States in 1982 would have provided that a failure to agree under

---

[206] Op. cit. above (n. 12), at p. 184.

[207] Orrego Vicuña, *The Exclusive Economic Zone* (1989), at p. 61. Joyner and DeCola ambiguously assert that '[i]t is clear that Article 63(2) obligates both the coastal state and foreign fishing states to "seek agreement" on necessary measures to ensure the conservation of any straddling stocks': loc. cit. above (n. 188), at p. 106.

[208] Mfodwo, Tsaymeni and Blay clearly share this view, for they conclude that '[a]ll [the coastal State] is required to do is to "seek to agree" with the fishing state or states on the relevant measures. Should this search fail, the coastal state would be free to exercise its sovereign rights under Articles 61 and 62': 'The Exclusive Economic Zone: State Practice in the African Atlantic Region', *Ocean Development and International Law*, 20 (1989), p. 445 at p. 461. But see Fleischer, who argues that, in the case of transboundary and straddling stocks, 'it would seem advisable and even necessary for the States concerned to enter into negotiations and co-operate on suitable arrangements, including the use of regional commissions. The coastal State will also be *under obligations to do so* because of existing provisions and custom on conservation measures and because of the damage which might otherwise be done to the legitimate interests of other States': loc. cit. above (n. 110), at p. 1070 (emphasis added).

[209] Treves concludes that Article 63(2) 'reste fidèle au principe de la haute mer et ne prévoit pas de conséquences pour le cas où les ententes prévues n'étaient pas obtenues': 'Codification du droit international des états dans le droit de la mer', *Recueil des cours*, 223 (1990–IV), p. 9, at p. 231. Nor is any guidance given as to the substance of any agreement which should be reached, save for the general conservation obligations which are set out in the EEZ provisions of Article 61 and mirrored in the high seas provisions of Article 119.

[210] Lagoni notes that '[t]he right of all States for their nationals to engage in fishing in the area is neither suspended nor terminated in this case': loc. cit. above (n. 151), at p. 265, para. 39.

[211] Pursuant to Article 290 LOSC.

[212] Lagoni, loc. cit. above (n. 151), at p. 268, para. 40.

Article 63(2) constituted a dispute, and allowed a court or tribunal to apply provisional measures at the request of any of the interested States.[213]

There is no doubt that certain coastal States were disappointed by the wording of Article 63(2), which does little more than recognize a duty to co-operate with other States, directly[214] or through regional arrangements, in the conservation of straddling stocks. No special interest of the coastal State in straddling stocks is recognized. 'Bref, la conférence ne semble pas vouloir reconnaître l'intérêt spécial de l'état côtier au-delà de 200 milles',[215] at least in so far as straddling stocks are concerned. In respect of other fisheries more directly linked to the land domain, such as anadromous species,[216] coastal States have seen their special interest explicitly recognized.[217] Thus, as regards anadromous species, not only is the primary interest and responsibility of the State of origin acknowledged, but where the species is fished beyond the EEZ, Article 66(3)(a) LOSC stipulates that the 'States concerned shall maintain consultations with a view to achieving agreement on terms and conditions of such fishing giving due regard to the conservation requirements and the needs of the State of origin in respect of these stocks'.[218]

The failure of the LOSC explicitly to recognize the special interests of coastal States in respect of straddling stocks impacted in particular upon Argentina and Canada, both States with wide continental margins

[213] A/CONF.62/L.114, 13 April 1982, reproduced in Platzöder, op. cit. above (n. 155), vol. 15, at p. 25.

[214] Lagoni argues that where a State is not bound by the conservation measures adopted by a RFO, perhaps because an objection procedure has been invoked resulting in the non-application of these measures to the objecting State (for an example see NAFO Articles XI and XII), that State none the less has an obligation to seek *directly* to agree with the coastal State upon measures necessary for the conservation of straddling stocks: ILA 1992 Report, loc. cit. above (n. 151), at p. 267, para. 37. There is logic to this argument, viz., that the opt-out of a State from its obligations in pursuance of its rights under a regional arrangement does not *ipso facto* relieve the objecting State of its other treaty and customary law obligations such as those contained in Article 63(2).

[215] De Mestral, loc. cit. above (n. 126), at pp. 292 and 294, relying on A/CONF.62/W.P.10, 15 July 1977, Article 63(2), from which the final text adopted did not substantially depart.

[216] As Meseguer points out, Part V of the LOSC establishes not only a general regime but also five special fisheries regimes in respect of: highly migratory species (Article 64); marine mammals (Article 65); anadromous species, which originate in rivers but spend part of their life cycle at sea (Article 66); catadromous species, which are spawned at sea but spend part of their life cycle within areas of coastal State jurisdiction (Article 67); and sedentary species (Article 68): loc. cit. above (n. 126), at p. 886.

[217] Oda has expressed the view that, save in respect of anadromous stocks, the provisions of the LOSC have 'unnecessarily confused' the high seas freedom of fishing by making it subject in Article 116(b) to the rights and interests of the coastal State in Articles 63(2), and 64–47: *International Control of Sea Resources* (1989 reprint, with new introduction), at pp. xxi–xxii.

[218] In respect of both anadromous (Article 66) and catadromous (Article 67) species there is an obligation for the State of origin/State in whose waters the species spends the greater part of their life cycle, and another State in whose waters the species migrates, to reach agreement in respect of conservation and management of the species.

attracting foreign fishing fleets.[219] After early discussion in Committee Two, straddling stocks did not form the basis of significant substantive discussion between the adoption of the Evensen text in 1975[220] and the resumption by Canada and Argentina of their 'campaign' for recognition of the special interest of the coastal State in straddling stocks in 1980.[221] At the ninth session in 1980, commenced in the spring and resumed in the summer, Argentina and Canada made informal proposals for amendment of Article 63 to reflect the special interest of the coastal State, supported by Australia, Cape Verde, Colombia, Costa Rica, Guatemala, Iceland, New Zealand, Philippines, Portugal, Sao Tome and Principe, Senegal, Sierra Leone and Uruguay. According to Sanger, their 'campaign' was simply launched too late:

> It began in earnest only in 1980, after the 'margineers' group had won its tough battle for a broad definition of the continental shelf. This definition gave them sovereign rights over mineral resources and sedentary species to the edge of the margin, but not over fish swimming in the water-column above [beyond the 200-mile zone]; they could argue a lack of logic in this distinction. Their campaign on 'straddling stocks' consisted in negotiating an addition to Article 63 ... By 1981 some 16 countries were co-sponsoring an amendment, and as many again supported it. But important fishing states (Japan, the Soviet Union and Spain) opposed it;[222] and the United States and the European Community wanted to keep Article 63 at the level of simple co-operation.[223]

While support was obtained from, *inter alia*, Australia, Cape Verde, Iceland and New Zealand, there was also clear opposition to any recognition of a special interest of coastal States in straddling stocks from traditional distant water fishing States. Thus the *travaux préparatoires* of

---

[219] For the text of the informal proposals submitted by Argentina (1979, 1980), Canada (1980), and by a group of 15 coastal States comprising Argentina, Australia, Canada, Cape Verde, Colombia, Costa Rica, Guatemala, Iceland, New Zealand, Philippines, Portugal, Sao Tome and Principe, Senegal, Sierra Leone and Uruguay (1980), see Platzöder, op. cit. above (n. 155), vol. 5, at pp. 56–60. A formal proposal for amendment of Article 63(2) was submitted to the eleventh session of the Conference in April 1982 by 8 States, but the amendment was not pressed to the vote: see A/CONF.62/L.114 (1982) (Australia, Canada, Cape Verde, Iceland, Philippines, Sao Tome and Principe, Senegal and Sierra Leone), reproduced in Platzöder, ibid., vol. 16, at p. 25. Many delegations spoke against the amendment, including: Greece, Spain, Japan, Romania, German Democratic Republic, USSR, Korea, Belgium on behalf of the then 10 member States of the EEC, Bulgaria, Ukraine, Hungary, Mongolia, Byelorussia, and Pakistan: see further Meseguer, loc. cit. above (n. 126), at p. 897, n. 44.

[220] Even in 1975 it was clear that a number of States were opposed to wording in Article 63 recognizing any special interest of the coastal State in straddling stocks beyond their jurisdiction. Meseguer notes that Bulgaria, Japan, Romania, the German Democratic Republic, and the States of the EEC (which at that time did not include Spain or Portugal amongst its members, nor Austria, Sweden and Finland), had consistently opposed any such recognition in Committee Two negotiations: loc. cit. above (n. 126), at p. 893, n. 26.

[221] See the summary of negotiations in Nandan, Rosenne and Grandy, op. cit. above (n. 155), vol. 2, at pp. 641–6.

[222] Delegations from Spain, the Ukraine, Japan, Bulgaria, Cameroon, Poland, Portugal, Romania, Seychelles, USSR and Korea spoke against the amendment: Meseguer, loc. cit. above (n. 126), at p. 895, n. 38.

[223] C. Sanger, *Ordering the Oceans; The Making of the Law of the Sea* (1986), at p. 151.

the 1982 LOSC may not support an interpretation of Article 63(2) as embodying any special interest, and certainly a predominant interest, of the coastal State in straddling stocks, as this was fairly clearly rejected by the majority of States.[224] Such arguments are also undermined by the difference in wording between paragraphs 1 and 2 of Article 63, with paragraph 2 seemingly concerned with high seas fisheries with no requirement of compatibility with internal EEZ measures.

The formal amendment to Article 63(2) supported by Canada and seven other States was withdrawn at the final negotiating session of UNCLOS III in April 1982, apparently owing to a linkage with a quite unrelated dispute which flared up at the last minute—the innocent passage of warships through the territorial sea. An amendment was introduced which would have required at a minimum prior notification of such passage. A compromise was reached on the conditions for withdrawal of the amendment; the price of attaining Soviet consent for this compromise was the withdrawal of the straddling stocks amendment.[225]

Some of the States which had supported the amendment were not content to let the matter lie. On signing the Convention, Cape Verde, Sao Tome and Principe, and Uruguay[226] declared that States fishing straddling stocks in the adjacent area must reach agreement with the coastal State upon the measures necessary for conservation of such stocks.[227] Costa Rica declared on signing the Convention that States fishing straddling stocks in the area of the high seas adjacent to the Costa Rican

---

[224] It will be recalled that in the event of ambiguity or obscurity in the meaning of a treaty provision, '[r]ecourse may be had to supplementary means of interpretation, including the preparatory work of the treaty and the circumstances of its conclusion': Article 32, Vienna Convention on the Law of Treaties.

[225] Sanger, op. cit. above (n. 223), at pp. 151–2. There was also pressure from the President of the Conference to withdraw the amendment, which would have risked consensus on the overall 'package deal': Applebaum, loc. cit. above (n. 5), at p. 283; *The Regime for High-Seas Fisheries*, op. cit. above (n. 5), at p. 24, para. 69.

[226] Sao Tome and Principe and Cape Verde supported both the informal proposals and the formal amendment. Kwiatkowska cites the practice of these three States, the States sponsoring the formal amendment, and the developments within NAFO as contributing to the possible development of a new legal concept of a coastal State's special interest in straddling stocks: 'Creeping Jurisdiction beyond 200 Miles in Light of the Law of the Sea Convention and State Practice', *Ocean Development and International Law*, 22 (1991), at p. 169.

[227] *Law of the Sea Bulletin*, No. 5, reproduces the text of all 36 declarations made by States and entities upon signature of the Convention; see also *Multilateral Treaties deposited with the Secretary-General, Status as at 31 December 1995*, ST/LEG/SER.E/14, at p. 803 (Cape Verde), p. 813 (Sao Tome and Principe) and p. 814 (Uruguay). Both Cape Verde and Uruguay confirmed these declarations on ratification of the LOSC. Sao Tome ratified the LOSC on 3 November 1987, evidently without confirming its declaration; however, Article 310 does not require such confirmation, nor would Article 23(2) of the Vienna Convention on the Law of Treaties apply since this confirmation requirement applies only to reservations. None of these States appears to have reflected its declaration in EEZ legislation: see UN Division for Ocean Affairs and the Law of the Sea, *National Legislation on the Exclusive Economic Zone* (1993), which reproduces extracts from the EEZ legislation of, *inter alios*, Sao Tome and Principe (1978), Cape Verde (1977) and Costa Rica (1975). There is no entry for Uruguay.

exclusive economic zone 'have the obligation to agree with the coastal State on the appropriate conservation measures'. Does this wording significantly depart from the substance of the obligation contained in Article 63(2), or might it legitimately be viewed as an amplification or interpretation of the LOSC rather than an attempt to modify or suspend rights thereunder in their application to these States?[228] It is submitted that the wording of Article 63(2) comports not an obligation to agree but the obligation to seek agreement—there is no obligation to establish joint conservation measures nor to co-ordinate existing measures or scientific research. At best there is here an obligation to co-operate in the conservation of straddling stocks which may have the character of an emerging principle of customary law.[229]

Treves has pointed out that the particular danger to the LOSC lies not only in functional extensions of jurisdiction beyond the 200-mile limit for enforcement purposes—in essence, the Canadian approach—but in the extension beyond 200 miles of an EEZ/EFZ jurisdictional regime.[230] He cautions that '[d]es pressions fortes pourraient dériver d'idées portant sur une extension unilatérale de la jurisdiction des Etats côtiers sur des zones au-delà des 200 milles'.[231] Chile, for example, has declared a 'presential sea' [232] extending jurisdiction to a defined geographic area enclosing nearly two million square nautical miles from Antarctica to

[228] In other words, a declaration and not a reservation. There is no evidence that other States have objected to these declarations, in contrast to the controversial 'declaration' by the Philippines to which a number of States objected: see further *Multilateral Treaties*, op. cit. above (n. 227), at pp. 816–18, and at p. 821, n. 11 (Philippines response to Australia's objection to its declaration).

[229] Kwiatkowska, op. cit. above (n. 41), at p. 80. However, whilst willing to accept that requirements of consistency between coastal and fishing State measures would 'not appear to contradict the substance' of Article 63(2), she clearly rejects as incompatible with this provision any requirement of recognition of a special interest of the coastal State—and any subregional rule to this effect in the North-West Atlantic: ibid.; but for a slightly modified approach, willing to concede that this is an 'open question', see Kwiatkowska, loc. cit. above (n. 226), at p. 169. Under Article 311 LOSC it is of course always open to States to conclude bilateral or regional agreements modifying or suspending the operation of provisions of the LOSC, upon notice and within the constraints of certain stipulated safeguards (e.g. compatible with object and purpose of the LOSC, cannot affect third party rights or performance of their obligations). The provisions of Article 311 are mirrored in Article 44 of the SSA. It could be argued that an agreement contrary to Article 63(2) is not incompatible with the overall object and purpose of the Law of the Sea Convention; apart from the general constraints already mentioned it is only agreements derogating from Article 136 LOSC (common heritage of mankind principle) which are expressly prohibited (Article 311(6)).

[230] Treves, loc. cit. above (n. 209), at p. 233.

[231] Ibid. Lucchini also warns, in connection with the Canadian Coastal Fisheries Protection Act which he considers to be contrary to international law, of the increased risk of other States following Canada's unilateralist approach: loc. cit. above (n. 5), at p. 875.

[232] See Orrego Vicuña, 'The "Presential Sea": Defining Coastal States' Special Interests in High Seas Fisheries and other Activities', *German Yearbook of International Law*, 35 (1992), p. 264, and 'Coastal States' Competences over High Seas Fisheries and the Changing Role of International Law', *Zeitschrift für ausländisches und öffentliches Recht und Völkerrecht*, 55 (1995), p. 536, and loc. cit. above (n. 185); Joyner and DeCola, loc. cit. above (n. 188).

Easter Island.[233] Extended jurisdiction was one solution evidently suggested by the United States at a stage in its negotiations with the Soviet Union regarding the Bering Sea 'doughnut hole' straddling stocks problem.[234] Such unilateral action has been taken in the context of the omissions within the LOSC and the pressure on high seas stocks to which the extension of coastal State jurisdiction gave rise, much as Iceland responded to the failure of the Second United Nations Conference on the Law of the Sea in 1960 with the unilateral extension of its fisheries jurisdiction. In addition to Chile and Canada, Argentina has also adopted measures with effects beyond its national jurisdiction.[235]

The failure of the straddling stocks amendment has at least two legal consequences. Firstly, Article 63(2) fails explicitly to recognize a special interest (or preferential right)[236] of the coastal State in the conservation and management of straddling stock resources beyond the EEZ. A second and related consequence is that the assertion of any such special interest, certainly as the prevailing interest, may in fact be *contrary* to Article 63(2)[237] and to the general freedom of fishing which pursuant to Article 116 is subject only to the rights and obligations of the coastal State set forth in, *inter alia*, Article 63(2). In the end Article 63(2) may do no more than express a general obligation to co-operate, overlaid with an obligation of due diligence imposed on third States fishing straddling stocks on the high seas to co-operate with the adjacent coastal State in adopting conservation measures.[238] The essential tension between the high seas freedom of fishing, entailing the right to exploit a common property resource, and the sovereign rights of the coastal State, remains with 'each group of states [having] interests based on different types of rights'.[239] A balancing of rights is necessary, with neither set of rights necessarily predominant.

---

[233] Treves doubts whether the principle of the presential sea will operate at the juridical level, performing rather a geopolitical function (an 'océanopolitique' concept), but expresses concerns about the pressure extended jurisdiction places upon the fundamental boundary between EEZ and high seas agreed in the LOSC: loc. cit. above (n. 209), at p. 235.

[234] Treves, ibid., at p. 233, n. 639, citing Burke, 'Fishing in the Bering Sea Donut: Straddling Stocks and the New International Law of Fisheries', *Ecology Law Quarterly*, 16 (1989), p. 285 at p. 303.

[235] Article 5 of Act No. 23.968 of 14 August 1991 provides, *inter alia*:
'National provisions concerning the conservation of resources shall apply beyond the two hundred (200) nautical mile zone in the case of migratory species or species which form part of the food chain of species of the exclusive economic zone of Argentina':
reproduced in *EEZ: Legislative History*, op. cit. above (n. 118); see also Treves, loc. cit. above (n. 154), at p. 896.

[236] This is how Lugten characterizes it—Article 63 'is silent on the subject of whether the coastal State, or dwfn [distant water fishing nation] is to possess preferential rights over these fish': 'Fisheries War for the Halibut', *Environmental Policy and Law*, 25 (1995), nos. 4/5, at p. 225.

[237] Kwiatkowska so concludes: op. cit. above (n. 41), at p. 80.

[238] Hey, op. cit. above (n. 171), at p. 83.

[239] Ibid., at p. 82; see also *The Regime for High-Seas Fisheries*, op. cit. above in (n. 5), at p. 23, para. 66, which concludes that Articles 63 and 64 do not resolve the underlying conflict of rights which is at the heart of the conflict over straddling and highly migratory fish stocks.

(iii) *Article 63(2) and Article 116(b)*

While Article 63(2) fails explicitly to recognize any special interest of the coastal State in straddling stocks, it will be recalled that the high seas provisions of Article 116 do acknowledge that the high seas freedom of fishing is subject to the *rights, duties and interests* of the coastal State as provided for in, *inter alia*, Article 63(2). But the legal effect of this cross-referencing is far from clear, and there is a lack of consensus in the doctrine regarding the effect of Articles 63(2) and 116(b). A recent UN study concludes that, ultimately, a resolution of the controversy over straddling stocks will require 'an enhanced understanding of the nature of the "right" that States have for their nationals to fish on the high seas and the relationship of this right to the rights, duties and interests of the coastal State referred to in article 116'.[240]

Representing a widely accepted view of the consequences of the LOSC, Nandan and Rosenne conclude that the high seas freedom of fishing has been 'fundamentally altered' in the 1982 Convention from a regime with 'the flag State solely competent to determine the activities of its own vessels, subject to the general restrictions imposed by international law, and . . . under no obligation to recognise the rights of adjacent coastal States' to one where 'a coastal State has interests and rights where species and stocks spend part of their life both within and beyond the State's exclusive economic zone'.[241] It is regarding the content and scope of these rights and interests that scholars are most divided.

Those generally favouring the coastal State position argue for preferential or superior rights of the coastal State in management of straddling stocks. For example, Lugten concludes that coastal States' rights, interests and duties in respect of straddling stocks take precedence over freedom of fishing on the high seas,[242] while Applebaum argues that Article 116 grants coastal States the 'preferential right' to establish conservation measures even on the high seas in the absence of international agreement.[243] This latter analysis is seemingly shared by one of

---

[240] *The Regime for High-Seas Fisheries*, op. cit. above (n. 5), at p. 24, para. 70.

[241] Nandan, Rosenne and Grandy, op. cit. above (n. 155), vol. 3, at p. 287, para. 116.9(e); see also Kwiatkowska, loc. cit. above (n. 226), at p. 168.

[242] 'The clear intention of the LOSC is that international law requires all States engaged in high seas fishing to co-operate with the relevant coastal State for the conservation and management of the stocks concerned. Furthermore, as the right to fish on the high seas is *subject* to the rights, duties and interests of the relevant coastal State, there is a clear implication that the rights, duties and interests of the coastal State are to take precedence over the right to fish on the high seas': Lugten, loc. cit. above (n. 236), at p. 224 (emphasis added). Hey, on the other hand, states that neither the coastal State nor third States fishing straddling stocks on the high seas have a predominant interest in these stocks on the high seas: op. cit. above (n. 171), at p. 83. See also Mfodwo *et al.*, loc. cit. above (n. 208), at p. 462, who conclude that Articles 116(b) and 63(2) establish the priority for coastal State measures in the adjacent zone, but that this constraint on the high seas freedom of fishing is not reflected at customary international law: '[I]t is only state practice, including dispute settlement [under] the Convention . . . which will clarify the scope and content of this new rule'.

[243] Loc. cit. above (n. 5), and as quoted in Lagoni, loc. cit. above (n. 151), at p. 270, n. 65.

the few authors explicitly to address the problem of fisheries resources under international law in a recent monograph devoted to the law of the sea and fisheries law, William T. Burke. He concludes that:

article 116 means that the right to fish on the high seas is subject to the sovereign rights, as well as the interests, of coastal states as provided in the articles of Part V of the 1982 Convention. Accordingly, the 1982 Convention might be interpreted as providing that high seas fishing upon stocks that also occur within a coastal state's EEZ is subject to the *sovereign rights* of that coastal state.[244]

Fleischer would not go so far, suggesting that 'quasi-sovereign rights' may be acquired by the coastal State through bilateral agreements accessing the resources of the EEZ in return for concessions in connection with the high seas fishery.[245]

So controversial have straddling stocks proven that the section on straddling stocks of the Report prepared by the ILA EEZ Committee (R. Lagoni, Rapporteur) for the 1992 Cairo meeting is subject to the explicit dissent of two leading experts on fisheries on the Committee, Kwiatkowska and Burke.[246] The conclusion of the Report in connection with straddling stocks is that Articles 63(2) and 116(*b*) provide the basis for co-operation between coastal and fishing States, upon whom lies the obligation to negotiate in good faith 'with a view to agreeing on the necessary conservation measures for [straddling] stocks in the adjacent area'. It continues:

Pending or failing agreement, the fishing States concerned have to pay due regard to the interests of the coastal State in the conservation of the straddling stock (Art. 116(b) and *vice versa*. The costal [sic] State may not extend its jurisdiction beyond its EEZ.[247]

---

[244] Burke, op. cit. above (n. 151), at p. 133 (emphasis added); see also Miles and Burke, loc. cit. above (n. 5), at p. 352 ('If Article 116 is to be effective, it may need to be interpreted to authorize the coastal State to secure its superior right by prescribing conservation measures with which high seas fishing states are obliged to comply').

[245] 'Bilateral agreements on the right to fish inside the 200-mile zones may be used by the coastal State to gain a sort of *de facto* control or *quasi-sovereign rights* even in regard to activities which take place and resources which are found in the high seas beyond the 200-mile limit. In particular, this may be the case where foreign States granted rights in areas within the 200-mile zones do not have any clear-cut legal claim to such access, and therefore may be willing to accept certain limitations and regulations of their high seas fisheries in return for favours accorded by the coastal State':

loc. cit. above (n. 110), at p. 1116 (emphasis added). However, he continues with an explicit reservation regarding whether this form of coastal State (indirect) control beyond the 200-mile limit will generate a blurring of the national (EEZ)/international (HS) distinction, and recalls the prohibition on discrimination in form or in fact against fishermen from any State in respect of high seas fisheries conservation measures and their implementation contained in Article 119(3).

[246] Loc. cit. above (n. 151). No explanation for the dissent is provided in the published proceedings.

[247] Loc. cit. above (n. 151), at pp. 276–7.

Any disputes regarding these duties,[248] which the ILA Report considers to reflect customary international law, are subject to binding decision under section 2 of Part XV LOSC.

Since it is indeed likely that disputes regarding the scope and content of the obligations under Articles 63(2) and 116(*b*) could arise, the dispute settlement procedures of Part XV will be examined before turning to look at developments since the conclusion of the LOSC.

(d) *Dispute Settlement under the LOSC*

States are under a general obligation to resolve disputes regarding the interpretation or application of the LOSC by peaceful means, in accordance with Article 2(3) of the United Nations Charter.[249] Any dispute over high seas fisheries is subject to the general dispute settlement procedures contained in Part XV of the 1982 LOSC. These provisions apply *mutatis mutandis* to any dispute between States Parties to the Straddling Stocks Agreement, whether or not they are parties to the LOSC; in addition, these dispute settlement provisions apply to the interpretation or application of a global, regional or subregional fisheries agreement relating to straddling or highly migratory stocks, whether or not the States parties are also parties to the LOSC.[250] This would encompass NAFO, for example. Finally, it is pertinent in the context of the Canada/Spain dispute to observe that by operation of Article 7(2) of Annex IX of the LOSC, 'Part XV applies *mutatis mutandis* to any dispute between parties to this Convention, one or more of which are international organizations'.[251] Thus the EC, should it become a party to the LOSC and/or the SSA, could avail itself of the dispute settlement procedures set out in Part XV, with the exception of the International Court of Justice, recourse to which is only open to States.[252]

The innovative provisions of Part XV of the LOSC provide a menu of dispute settlement procedures ranging from 'compulsory' conciliation to binding dispute settlement by the International Court of Justice (ICJ), the International Tribunal for the Law of the Sea (ITLOS), arbitration or special arbitration. Section 1 of Part XV sets forth non-binding

---

[248] There is a reference to duties and to 'collateral duties', without elaboration.

[249] Article 279 LOSC.

[250] By virtue of Article 30 SSA. Balton considers that '[t]his element, perhaps more than any other in the agreement, may improve the effectiveness of regional fishery organizations', but with the import caveat that their members become party to the SSA: 'Strengthening the Law of the Sea: The New Agreement on Straddling Fish Stocks and Highly Migratory Fish Stocks', *Ocean Development and International Law*, 27 (1996), at p. 143.

[251] It will be recalled that Annex IX, Article 7 of which addresses settlement of disputes, permits participation in the LOSC by 'international organizations'. The EC signed the LOSC on 7 December 1994 but has not yet ratified. It would also have access to the dispute settlement procedures under the LOSC in respect of the SSA: see further below.

[252] This is confirmed by Article 7(1) of Annex IX of the LOSC.

dispute settlement—conciliation—which is applicable to all disputes, including fisheries. In addition, under Article 297(3) of the LOSC, any disputes over high seas fisheries may be referred to compulsory dispute settlement procedures under section 2 of Part XV of the LOSC. On signature, ratification, accession, or at any time thereafter, States[253] may choose one or more means of dispute settlement from the following list:

—the International Tribunal for the Law of the Sea;
—the International Court of Justice;
—an arbitral tribunal; and/or
—a special arbitral tribunal.[254]

In practice, therefore, States, may choose a variety of mechanisms for a variety of disputes. The International Tribunal for the Law of the Sea is a new institution created by the LOSC which came into being in late 1996; the closing date for nominations for membership of the tribunal was 17 June 1996 with election of the 21 members of the Tribunal at a meeting of the States parties on 1 August 1996.[255] The ICJ, which includes at the disposal of potential litigant States an environmental chamber,[256] is, as we have already seen, considering the jurisdictional phase of the Canada/Spain dispute.[257] Arbitration is the default dispute settlement procedure in Part XV, applicable where a dispute is either not covered by a declaration in force, or where the parties to a dispute have chosen different forms of dispute settlement.[258] Special arbitration, further elaborated in Annex VIII of the LOSC, is available for disputes arising from the interpretation or application of the LOSC regarding, *inter alia,* fisheries. This employs arbitrators with expertise in specified fields. For fisheries, a list of experts is drawn up and maintained by the United Nations Food and Agriculture Organization.

An important safeguard for coastal States in the application of the compulsory dispute settlement provisions of section 2 of Part V is contained in Article 297(3)(*a*), which provides:

Disputes concerning the interpretation or application of the provisions of this Convention with regard to fisheries shall be settled in accordance with section 2,

[253] Or international organizations, subject to Article 7(1) of Annex IX LOSC, which restricts their choice to arbitration, special arbitration, and the International Tribunal for the Law of the Sea.

[254] Article 287(1) LOSC. These procedures will apply to the settlement of disputes under Part VIII SSA unless another procedure has been accepted by a State party on signature, ratification, accession or at any time thereafter: Article 30(3) SSA. It is also open to non-parties to the LOSC to select Article 287 procedures under Article 30(4) SSA.

[255] See generally Rosenne, 'Establishing the Tribunal for the Law of the Sea', *American Journal of International Law*, 89 (1995), at p. 806.

[256] Above, n. 105.

[257] Above, text following n. 97.

[258] Article 287(3), (4). The parties may otherwise agree upon another form of dispute settlement under Article 287 in lieu of arbitration as the default dispute settlement procedure.

except that the coastal State shall not be obliged to accept the submission to such settlement of any dispute relating to its sovereign rights with respect to the living resources in the exclusive economic zone or their exercise, including its discretionary powers for determining the allowable catch, its harvesting capacity, the allocation of surpluses to other States and the terms and conditions established in its conservation and management laws and regulations.[259]

Thus while high seas fisheries may be subject to compulsory dispute settlement, conservation and management of EEZ stocks is not. This underscores both the unwillingness to trespass on coastal States' sovereign rights over their EEZ, and the inability to perceive fish as transboundary in character.[260]

In addition, Article 298 provides States with a further option to exclude certain disputes from the application of one or more of the dispute settlement procedures outlined above; this includes 'disputes concerning law enforcement activities in regard to the exercise of sovereign rights or jurisdiction excluded from the jurisdiction of a court or tribunal under article 297, paragraph 2 or 3'.[261] That is, disputes relating to law enforcement activities in respect of fisheries provisions, since they fall under the express exceptions within Article 297, may also be exempted from specified dispute settlement procedures under Article 298.[262] If, however, it is alleged that the coastal State has, *inter alia*, 'manifestly failed to comply with its obligations to ensure through proper

---

[259] This limitation is carried through to dispute settlement under the SSA: Article 32 SSA. See also the Spanish declaration on signature of the LOSC, op. cit. above (n. 157).

[260] How then would a dispute in respect of straddling stocks be characterized: an EEZ dispute under Article 63(2), or a high seas dispute under Article 116? If the dispute is one characterized as relating exclusively to fish stocks on the high seas, then this may tilt the balance in favour of high seas freedom of fishing subject to due regard and to the conservation criteria of Article 119. Even if the special interest of the coastal State is incorporated by virtue of one possible interpretation of Article 116, this is not of course as robust as the nature of that special interest within the EEZ. On the other hand, characterization of the dispute as one relating to the EEZ will not necessarily tilt the balance wholly in favour of the coastal State. Firstly, there is the view that Article 63(2) is a high seas and not an EEZ provision; secondly, Article 59 LOSC, which addresses the resolution of any conflict over the attribution of rights and jurisdiction *within* the EEZ, does not embody a presumption in favour of coastal State rights and jurisdiction. Indeed, Article 59 constitutes a derogation from the pre-existing freedom of fishing on the high seas, and as such may be interpreted restrictively. Therefore the juridical character of the zone in which the dispute is considered to arise will be of critical influence upon the balancing of interests.

[261] Alongside military and law enforcement activities, States may also exclude disputes relating to maritime boundary delimitations, historic bays or titles, and the maintenance of international peace and security where the Security Council is dealing with the matter: Article 298(1)(a)–(c) LOSC. An earlier draft also included 'disputes arising out of the discretionary rights by a coastal State pursuant to its regulatory and enforcement jurisdiction under this Convention, except in cases involving an abuse of power', but this was removed in the light of the more precise provisions contained in Article 297: Rosenne and Sohn (volume eds.), in Nordquist (ed.), *United Nations Convention on the Law of the Sea: A Commentary*, vol. 5 (1989), at p. 110, para. 298.3.

[262] The latter was included at the insistence of certain delegations which could not accept the submission of certain categories of disputes to compulsory dispute settlement, and which would not have the option of making a reservation to this effect upon signature, ratification or accession because Article 309 of the LOSC prohibits reservations unless expressly permitted by articles of the Convention.

conservation and management measures that the maintenance of the living resources in the exclusive economic zone is not seriously endangered', and no settlement has been reached under section 1 of Part XV (non-binding conciliation), then the dispute shall, at the request of any party to the dispute, be submitted to conciliation under section 2 of Annex V which provides for compulsory submission to conciliation.[263]

A weakness in this framework for dispute settlement under the LOSC lies in its adherence to the arbitrary geographic boundary of EEZ/high seas and the difficulty which this may create for the settlement of disputes requiring consideration of, for example, the compatibility of a high seas conservation measure with measures taken by the coastal State within its EEZ.[264] This dichotomy between straddling stocks as a high seas fisheries conservation problem, and conservation of those stocks within the EEZ, is reflected in the wording of the straddling stocks provisions, Article 63(2). There is no requirement for the co-ordination of measures taken within the EEZ and beyond the EEZ; as we have seen, Article 63(2) refers only to 'measures necessary for the conservation of the stocks *in the adjacent area*'.[265] As it stands, the compatibility of internal and external measures may only be assessed where a dispute calls both into question, and where the coastal State prima facie exhibits 'manifest failure'.[266] Whilst at first blush it might appear unlikely that a State would vigorously enforce stringent conservation measures outside its EEZ whilst manifestly failing to conserve resources within the EEZ, leading to protest by foreign fishing States, it is in fact a frequent complaint by distant water fishing nations that over-zealous regulation of the area outside the EEZ is a consequence of bad management within the EEZ and the depletion of stocks there, putting more pressure on straddling stocks.[267] Indeed, over-capacity is a frequently cited culprit for over-exploitation of coastal fish stocks,[268] as well as for the pressure put on straddling stocks.[269] However, the burden of proof will doubtless be heavy where manifest failure is alleged, with these dispute settlement

[263] Article 297(3)(b)(i).

[264] The unsuccessful amendment to Article 63(2) proposed by Canada *et al.* provided, *inter alia*, that in establishing definitive or provisional conservation measures for straddling stocks in the adjacent area, 'the tribunal shall take into account those measures applied to the same stocks by the coastal State within its exclusive economic zone and the interests of other States fishing those stocks': A/CONF.62/L.114, 13 April 1982, reproduced in Platzöder, op. cit. above (n. 155), vol. 16, at p. 25.

[265] Emphasis added; see further Carroz, loc. cit. above (n. 107), at p. 718. This may be contrasted with Article 63(1), which makes reference to 'measures necessary to coordinate and ensure conservation and development of such stocks': see Hey, op. cit. above (n. 171), at p. 55, n. 6.

[266] 'allowing' conciliation to proceed.

[267] For criticism of the expansion of coastal fisheries, see Yonezawa, loc. cit. above (n. 151), at pp. 127–35; see also the criticism of Canadian management, above, text accompanying n. 22.

[268] D. D. Huppert, Commentary, in Miles and Kuyabashi, op. cit. above (n. 151), at p. 141. This is a reference to over-capacity within the coastal fishing industry.

[269] Here over-capacity refers to global fishing capacity, and to pressure placed on straddling stocks by distant water fishing nations in particular. See, generally, FAO 1994 Report, loc. cit. above (n. 190).

procedures thus reaffirming the dominance of coastal States with respect to the living resources of the EEZ.[270]

(e) *Assessment*

Coastal States achieved recognition of their special interest in straddling stocks in the undersubscribed 1958 Fishing Convention, which also obliges high seas fisheries measures not to oppose coastal State measures and permits the high seas extension of coastal State measures in certain circumstances. None of this is provided for explicitly in the LOSC. There is no express requirement of compatibility between coastal State EEZ conservation measures and measures taken in respect of straddling stocks in the adjacent high seas area. Nor is there recognition of the special interest of the coastal State in Article 63(2). While Article 116 subjects the high seas freedom of fishing to the rights, duties and interests of the coastal State as provided for, *inter alia*, in Article 63(2), these rights, duties and interests are not well-defined and do not give rise to any special or priority right of the coastal State in the conservation and management of high seas straddling fish stocks.

Nor is there any basis under the 1982 LOSC for the unilateral extension of legislative or enforcement jurisdiction over vessels on the high seas save in respect of the traditional exercise of flag State jurisdiction. Whilst the Law of the Sea Convention does contain very limited exceptions to the exclusivity of that jurisdiction on the high seas, these do not apply to fisheries matters. Indeed, the impression conveyed by the LOSC is one of scant concern for the management of high seas fisheries, and for the enforcement of conservation measures on the high seas. This may be contrasted with the detailed provisions on enforcement of measures in respect of the protection and preservation of the marine environment in Part XII, for example. At best, therefore, the Law of the Sea Convention obliges coastal and high seas fishing States to seek agreement on the conservation measures applicable to straddling stocks, measures which must comport with generally recommended international standards. This obligation to co-operate exists at customary international law. However, there is no obligation actually to reach agreement and no consequences attach to the failure to agree save for recourse under the Law of the Sea Convention to the dispute settlement procedures of Part XV.

In the light of these omissions and weaknesses in the LOSC in respect of the balancing of the right to engage in the high seas freedom of fishing and the rights, duties and interests of the coastal State acknowledged in Article 116, it is perhaps not surprising that particularly affected coastal States have sought unilaterally to regulate straddling stocks on the high

---

[270] Hey, op. cit. above (n. 171), at p. 48.

seas. These unilateral measures have been combined with a renewed campaign for the recognition and elaboration of coastal State interests in straddling stocks adjacent to their zones in other international fora, including the follow-up to the 1972 Stockholm Conference on the Human Environment held in Rio de Janeiro in 1992, and within the specialized agency of the United Nations responsible, *inter alia*, for fisheries matters, the Food and Agriculture Organization (FAO). This pressure was successful, resulting in December 1995 in the conclusion of the Straddling Stocks Agreement. These developments will be discussed in turn.

PART III: POST-UNCLOS DEVELOPMENTS

(a) *UNCED*[271]

Meetings of the States particularly concerned to fill the lacuna in the Convention after the failure of proposals to amend Article 63(2) occurred in the run-up to the 1992 United Nations Conference on the Environment and Development (UNCED), which provided a fresh impetus and forum in which the issue might be raised. Meetings were held in St John's, Newfoundland, in 1990,[272] and in Santiago, Chile[273] and then in New York in 1991.[274] At the third meeting of the Preparatory Committee of UNCED, held 12 August–4 September 1991, a number of States submitted a proposal for the 'Conservation and management of living resources of the high seas'.[275] In the event, Chapter 17 of Agenda 21—the 'Earth's Action Plan' produced at Rio—identifies seven programme areas for protection of the oceans and their living resources, one of which is 'sustainable use and conservation of marine living resources of the high seas'.[276] Agenda 21 states that approximately 5% of total world landings of fish are derived from high seas fisheries. Straddling stocks are one issue identified as requiring specific action. Thus there is a call for the

[271] The principal Rio documents are reproduced in *International Legal Materials*, 31 (1992), at p. 814; see also Robinson (ed.), *Agenda 21 and the UNCED Proceedings* (1992–3), 6 vols.

[272] See further Orrego Vicuña, loc. cit. above (n. 185), at p. 86; and Lucchini, loc. cit. above (n. 5), at p. 866.

[273] Attended by experts from Canada, Chile, and New Zealand: see UN Division for Ocean Affairs and the Law of the Sea, *The Law of the Sea: Practice of States at the Time of Entry into Force of the United Nations Convention on the Law of the Sea* (1994), Part Five, 'Latin American and Caribbean States', at p. 188.

[274] With participation from Argentina, Australia, Barbados, Brazil, Canada, Chile, New Zealand, and the Forum Fisheries Agency: ibid. See also Orrego Vicuña, loc. cit. above (n. 185), at p. 86.

[275] Communicated by the Permanent Mission of Chile to the United Nations to the Office for Ocean Affairs and the Law of the Sea in Note Verbale No. 132/91 dated 17 September 1991, and reproduced in: Office for Ocean Affairs and the Law of the Sea, *Law of the Sea Bulletin*, No. 19 (October 1991), at pp. 42–4. It was co-sponsored by Argentina, Barbados, Canada, Cape Verde, Chile, Fiji, Guinea, Guinea-Bissau, Iceland, Kiribati, New Zealand, Peru, Samoa, Senegal, Solomon Islands and Vanuatu.

[276] Programme area (C), paras. 17.44–17.68.

convening of an intergovernmental conference under UN auspices to consider the more effective implementation of the provisions of the 1982 LOSC on, *inter alia*, straddling stocks.[277] States are also exhorted to '[g]ive full effect to [the provisions of the 1982 LOSC] with regard to fisheries populations whose ranges lie both within and beyond exclusive economic zones (straddling stocks)'.[278]

However, language which would have explicitly recognized the special interest of the coastal State in conserving straddling stocks beyond their exclusive economic zone was deleted from the final text. Not only was the necessity to 'co-operate to ensure that high seas fishing does not have an adverse impact on the marine living resources under the national jurisdiction of coastal States' deleted from the text as one of the objectives of sustainable use and conservation of high seas marine living resources,[279] but so too were management-related activities in this connection. The resulting text thus contains no mention of the obligation of the States whose vessels fish for straddling stocks on the high seas to co-operate with the coastal State in whose EEZ the straddling stocks occur, with a view to agreeing on high seas measures consistent with EEZ measures and giving effect 'to the special interest and responsibility of the coastal State with respect to the portion of the straddling stocks beyond the exclusive economic zones'.[280] Yet it was this special interest of the coastal State, in whose exclusive economic zone the straddling stocks spend part of their life cycle, in these stocks outside of the EEZ on the high seas, which has formed the foundation for Canadian criticisms both of Spanish and other fishing effort outside of the Canadian 200-mile zone,[281] and of the inadequacy of existing mechanisms within international and regional organizations to address the problem.

(b) *FAO*

A development which commenced prior to the 1992 UNCED but extended beyond it was the negotiation of the FAO's Code of Conduct on

---

[277] Paragraph 17.49(*e*). The oceans chapter was the last to be completed at UNCED PrepCom 4 in New York in March 1992; the call for a straddling stocks conference was an '11th hour compromise' said to have been brokered by the United States exploiting its position as a State with both coastal and distant water fishing concerns: Reiser (ASIL observer to the negotiations), *ASIL Newsletter*, November 1993.

[278] Paragraph 17.49(*a*).

[279] By the main Committee at UNCED: Nicholas Robinson (ed.), *Agenda 21: Earth's Action Plan* (1993), at p. 327, citing United Nations Document A/CONF.151/L.3/Add 17, 12 June 1992. The remaining objectives of programme area C are contained in paragraph 17.46.

[280] Robinson, ibid., at p. 329, n. 8.

[281] Fishing Zones of Canada Order 1977, made pursuant to the Territorial Sea and Fishery Zones Act 1964-5.

Responsible Fisheries.[282] Its origins may be traced back to the 1984 FAO World Conference on Fisheries Management and Development and other international instruments. At the 19th Session of the FAO in 1991, the FAO Fisheries Committee recommended the preparation of a Code of Conduct on Responsible Fishing[283] addressing, *inter alia*, EEZ and high seas fisheries, global overcapacity, inadequate flag State control, inadequate provision of data to both flag and coastal States, and domestic trade restrictions on environmental grounds which are contrary to GATT. In addition to the Straddling Stock Agreement negotiations, the FAO Code was negotiated within the context of the 1982 LOSC; the 1992 Rio Declaration and the provisions of Agenda 21 of UNCED; the conclusions of the 1992 FAO Technical Consultation on High Seas Fishing; and the 1992 Declaration of Cancun[284] which calls for the preparation of a Code of Conduct on Responsible Fisheries.[285]

The Code is global in scope, with the objectives, *inter alia*, of ensuring the effective conservation, management and development of living aquatic resources with due respect for the ecosystem and biodiversity, whilst recognizing the contribution of fisheries to global food security.[286] Article 6, which contains general principles, emphasizes that: 'The right to fish carries with it the obligation to do so in a responsible manner so as to ensure effective conservation and management of the living aquatic resources'. States[287] are urged to promote prevention of overfishing and the reduction of excess fishing capacity. The ecosystem approach,[288]

---

[282] FAO Doc. CL 108/20; 'Code of Conduct for Responsible Fisheries', *Environmental Policy and Law*, 25 (1995), nos. 4/5, p. 80. For discussion of the FAO and its functions, see further Birnie and Boyle, op. cit. above (n. 111), at pp. 498–502. See also the FAO Agreement to Promote Compliance with International Conservation and Management Measures by Fishing Vessels on the High Seas, a response to Agenda 21's call upon States to deter reflagging of fishing vessels to avoid compliance with applicable conservation measures, reproduced in *Yearbook of International Environmental Law*, 4 (1993), at p. 763.

[283] The title of the Code was changed from 'Fishing' to 'Fisheries' in the October 1994 consultations: Freestone, loc. cit. above (n. 5), at n. 90.

[284] This Declaration resulted from the first international conference on Responsible Fisheries organized by Mexico in collaboration with FAO at Cancun, 6–8 May 1992, in the immediate run up to UNCED.

[285] See Gherari, 'L'accord du 4 août 1995 sur les stocks chevauchants et les stocks de poissons grands migrateurs', *Revue générale de droit international public*, 100 (1996), p. 367, at pp. 370–1; see also Joyner and DeCola, loc. cit. above (n. 188). Article 3 of the FAO Code addresses its relationship with other instruments. Article 3.1 provides that the Code is to be interpreted and applied in conformity with the relevant rules of international law as reflected in the Law of the Sea Convention, and without prejudice to the rights, jurisdiction and duties of States under international law as reflected in that Convention. Article 3.2 also refers to the need to interpret and apply the Code consistently with other obligations, including the SSA, and various soft law declarations such as the 1992 Rio Declaration and Agenda 21.

[286] See further Article 1 (nature and scope) and Article 2 (objectives).

[287] References to States includes the EC in matters within its competence: Article 1.4. Indeed, the Code is open to members and non-members of FAO and addressed to individuals active in the fishing industry whether at the harvesting or processing stage: Article 1.2.

[288] Article 6.2. provides that '[m]anagement measures should not only ensure the conservation of target species but also species belonging to the same ecosystem or associated with or dependent upon the target species'.

maintenance of biodiversity,[289] and the application of the precautionary approach[290] are all included within these general principles of the Code.

Unlike the Straddling Stocks Agreement considered below, the FAO Code is not legally binding. However, though voluntary, its provisions are based on existing international law and to this extent some of its provisions may have binding force.[291] It goes beyond the SSA in the range of issues addressed in the twelve articles of the Code, which cover not only fisheries management,[292] research[293] and vessel operations[294] but also aquaculture,[295] coastal area management[296] and post-harvest practices including responsible international trade and laws and regulations relating to fish trade.[297] Thus the Code extends to all fishery operations, not just those on the high seas, and to the full 'life cycle' of the fishery. Duties of the flag and port State are also elaborated, addressing the need for effective flag State control.[298] The necessary flexibility to take account of inevitable changes in fishing technology is ensured by Article 4, which empowers the FAO, through its competent bodies, to revise the Code taking into account developments in fisheries.[299]

Work on the FAO Code was sidelined to some extent by negotiation of the Straddling Stocks Agreement, the outcome of which influenced final negotiations of the FAO Code. Canada and Peru, in particular, argued that work on the Code should await the outcome of the conference negotiating the Straddling Stocks Agreement; others, including the EU, 'appeared to attempt to use the process of drafting the Code to

[289] See further Article 6.6.

[290] See Article 6.5; the precautionary approach is further elaborated in Article 7 regarding fisheries management, in particular Article 7.5.

[291] Pannatier, *Le pillage des ressources biologiques de la haute mer* (forthcoming), at p. 26. The parallel FAO Agreement to Promote Compliance with International Conservation and Management Measures by Fishing Vessels on the High Seas, 'the Flagging Agreement', forms an integral part of the Code by FAO Resolution 15/93: text reproduced in *International Legal Materials*, 33 (1994), p. 968.

[292] Article 7.

[293] Article 12, which requires States to recognize that responsible fisheries require the availability of a sound scientific basis to assist fisheries management.

[294] Article 8 addresses fisheries operations, including harbours and landing places for fishing vessels as well as the rights and duties of flag and port States.

[295] Article 9.

[296] Article 10, which addresses the integration of fisheries into coastal area management.

[297] Article 11. Unilever, the world's largest fish buyer, has announced a scheme for the labelling of sustainable fish products: 'Unilever and WWF lay path to "sustainable fish" logo', *ENDS Report*, 254 (1996), p. 28. It is to be modelled on a similar programme established by the Worldwide Fund for Nature for timber products, indicating where the fish are caught and by what method.

[298] Article 8, which also includes obligations in respect of environmental protection and of abandonment of offshore installations and artificial reefs.

[299] Article 4 (implementation, monitoring and updating). The special requirements of developing States in respect of financial and technical assistance, technology transfer, training and scientific co-operation, are recognized in Article 5.

strengthen their negotiating positions for the UN Conference'.[300] In the event, the Code of Conduct was finally agreed on 16 March 1995 and formally adopted by the FAO on 31 October 1995 at its 28th Conference.[301]

(c) The EC/Canadian Agreement on the Conservation and Management of Fish Stocks in the NAFO Regulatory Area

Following the release of the *Estai* on 15 March 1995,[302] the EC, on behalf of its member States,[303] and Canada began negotiations to resolve their disagreements on the conservation and management of fish stocks in the NAFO Regulatory Area. These negotiations culminated in the signing of an 'Agreed Minute on the Conservation and Management of Fish Stocks' ('Agreed Minute')[304] in Brussels on 20 April 1995. At its annual meeting in September 1995, NAFO endorsed and adopted the main elements of this agreement, ensuring that the management and enforcement measures included in the Agreed Minute applied not only to the EC and Canada, but also to the other 13 NAFO States parties. The Canadian Minister of Fisheries and Oceans described such measures as

[300] Anon., 'Code of Conduct for Responsible Fisheries', *Environmental Policy and Law*, 25 (1995), nos. 4/5, p. 180.

[301] By Resolutions 4/95 and 5/95 at the 28th session of the FAO, 31 October 1995. Pannatier notes that the full force and effect of the Code awaits approval by the FAO Fisheries Commission of use guidelines to be submitted to its regularly scheduled meeting in 1997: op. cit. above (n. 291), at p. 25.

[302] The vessel was released on payment of a 500,000 Canadian dollar bail bond: see *The Independent*, 16 March 1995, p. 12. As part of the subsequent agreement between Canada and the EC, the bond given for the release of the *Estai*, and the bail paid for the release of its captain, were returned to the *Estai*'s captain. The *Estai*'s catch was also returned. The Canadian Government indicated that its Attorney-General had considered 'the public interest' in so doing and in giving his approval to the stay of prosecution proceedings: see letter from the Canadian Ambassador to the European Union of 16 April 1995, *International Legal Materials*, 34 (1995), pp. 1274–5.

[303] An EC delegation represents all EC member States at NAFO meetings. A member of the European Commission acts as the delegation's spokesman. The EC's own fisheries policy has evolved since the 1950s: see Song 'The EC's Common Fisheries Policy in the 1990s', *Ocean Development and International Law*, 26 (1995), pp. 35–45. Its Common Fisheries Policy ('CFP') was established in 1983 and *inter alia* allows for the establishment of TACs, national quotas, and the implementation of conservation measures. It is clear that the CFP has failed to tackle both the problem of overcapacity in the EC fisheries industry and the ability of modern fishing vessels to overfish; see Gwiazda, 'The Common Fisheries Policy: Economic Aspects', *Marine Policy*, July 1993, p. 253. In introducing wide-ranging amendments to the CFP at the end of 1992, the EC itself recognized that 'a number of stocks both in Community and non-Community waters have continued to decline and it is consequently necessary to improve and extend existing conservation measures': EC Council Regulation 3760/92 of 20 December 1992, OJ, 1992, L389/1. The CFP's inability to manage fish stocks in Community waters efficiently is exemplified by the need for the recently reported rather drastic 50% reduction in the TAC for North Sea herring: see *The Independent*, 3 July 1996, p. 2.

[304] Reproduced in *International Legal Materials*, 34 (1995), pp. 1260–72, and *Law of the Sea Bulletin*, 28 (1995), pp. 34–42. See also Freestone, 'The 1995 Agreement Between Canada and the EU over Fishery Control and Enforcement in the NAFO Regulatory Area', *European Environmental Law Review*, 4(10) (1995), pp. 270–2. Notwithstanding the name of this agreement, the Agreed Minute in the main focuses on enforcement procedures.

'the toughest set of control and enforcement measures of any fisheries management organisation in the world'.[305] There are several important elements to note concerning the EC/Canadian agreement.

(i) *Pilot project for observers and satellite tracking*

A pilot project was established providing for the presence of a trained observer on all fishing vessels in the NAFO Regulatory Area.[306] In addition, 35% of such fishing vessels had to be equipped with satellite tracking systems which will provide continuous information as to vessels' precise location.[307] This information will be made available to NAFO. The parties agreed to monitor the effectiveness of this scheme and to submit reports to NAFO by September 1997 with a view to establishing a permanent scheme.

It is the responsibility of each party to deploy one independent and impartial observer on each of their vessels. The observer will monitor and report on the fishing activities of the vessel in question including the nature of catches, net sizes and the location of the vessel whilst fishing. If the observer is satisfied that an infringement of NAFO conservation and management measures has taken place, the matter is to be reported within 24 hours to the NAFO Executive Secretary, who in turn will inform a NAFO inspection vessel. Commenting on this system in September 1995, the Canadian Minister of Fisheries and Oceans indicated that the '100% observer coverage has been demonstrated to be effective to ensure compliance with conservation rules. Since it was implemented by Canada and the EU,[308] Canadian inspectors have found

[305] See 'Tobin welcomes tough fisheries enforcement measures', *Canadian NewsWire*, 15 September 1995.
[306] A previous NAFO observer scheme had operated from 1992 to 1995: see EC Regulation No. 3928/92 of 20 December 1992, OJ, 1992, L397/78. Under this scheme observers were to be placed on fishing vessels to ensure 'a minimum of 10% of a [State's] total estimated fishing days . . . are subject to observation' (Article 1(i)). Under the provisions of the Agreed Minute *no vessel* may fish in the Regulatory Area unless accompanied by an observer. It is also of interest to note that the EC has implemented this part of the Agreed Minute by empowering the *European Commission* to 'assign Community observers to all Community fishing vessels engaged in, or about to engage in fishing activities, in the NAFO Regulatory Area': EC Regulation No. 3069/95 of 21 December 1995, OJ, L329/5, Article 1. Under the previous 1992–5 observer scheme, the 1992 Regulation had allowed the relevant flag State member to appoint observers. The new EC provisions could be interpreted as allowing the selecting of observers from EC member States other than that of the fishing vessel's flag State. This arrangement may have the advantage of improving the observer's perceived impartiality. It is of interest in this regard to note that the observer scheme established in the Convention on the Conservation and Management of Pollack Resources in the Central Bering Sea, loc. cit. above (n. 5), provides for the deployment on each fishing vessel of 'one observer of a Party other than its flag State Party, upon request of such Party, under conditions established bilaterally sufficiently in advance by the Parties concerned. If such an observer is not available, the fishing vessel shall have on board one observer from its flag State Party': Article 5(a).
[307] The satellite surveillance is a novel element to fisheries observer schemes generally.
[308] The observer scheme was initiated within 15 days of 20 April 1995, the date the Agreed Minute was signed.

only one violation by EU vessels compared to 19 during the same period last year.'[309]

(ii) *Inspections*

In addition to the observer scheme, each party having ten or more vessels fishing in the NAFO Regulatory Area will provide an inspection vessel for NAFO purposes. These vessels will carry out inspections in a non-discriminatory manner but the 'number of inspections shall be based upon fleet size, taking also into account their compliance records'.[310]

In addition, if a NAFO inspector cites an infringement of a specified conservation measure the breach of which is regarded as particularly serious,[311] the flag State of the vessel cited must itself inspect the vessel within 48 hours. In the meantime, the NAFO inspector has the power to seal the vessel's hold and remain on board in order to secure the evidence relating to the infringement. In these circumstances, the flag State's inspector may require the vessel to proceed to a nearby port 'for a thorough inspection under the authority of the flag State and in the presence of a NAFO inspector from any other Contracting Party that wishes to participate'.[312]

The Agreed Minute also stipulates that there 'shall be a transparent and effective legal process to follow up apparent infringements *using all necessary evidence available from all sources, including evidence from other Contracting Parties as required for effective prosecution*'.[313] It is apparent that co-operation between the EC and Canada has taken place in this respect since the signing of the Agreed Minute; in May 1995 the *Mayi Cuatro*, a Spanish trawler, was approached by Canadian NAFO inspectors and was seen to discard one of its nets. The trawler was ordered to return home by Spanish fishing authorities. Canadian fisheries protection officers managed to retrieve the net from the sea-bed. The net, together with other evidence obtained by the Canadian authorities, was passed over to EC officials for use in the subsequent Spanish prosecution.[314]

Penalties for infringements of NAFO conservation and management measures will be 'such as to provide an effective deterrent'.[315] The Agreed Minute stipulates that penalties '*may* include refusal, suspension

[309] Tobin, quoted in *Canadian NewsWire*, loc. cit. above (n. 305).
[310] Agreed Minute, annex I, paragraph II.1.
[311] These measures include a refusal to co-operate with a NAFO inspector or observer, net size violations, interference with on-board satellite equipment, and the misreporting of fish catches.
[312] Agreed Minute, annex I, paragraph II.9.ii.
[313] Agreed Minute, annex I, paragraph II.10 (emphasis added).
[314] See *Canadian NewsWire*, 27 July 1995, which also quotes the Canadian Minister of Fisheries and Oceans as stipulating: 'This is a first. It is the first time the EU has taken material evidence provided by Canada for use in a European Member State's court in legal proceedings against a vessel accused of violating NAFO conservation measures.'
[315] Agreed Minute, annex I, paragraph II.10.

or withdrawal of the authorisation to fish'[316] in the NAFO Regulatory Area. It is important to note that no obligation is placed on the flag State to prosecute alleged infringers, and also that ultimately it is left to the discretion of the flag State to determine the severity of any penalty imposed pursuant to the successful conclusion of any such proceeding.[317] The Agreed Minute does not address the problem that too often flag States do not seem willing, nor have any obvious incentive, to commence legal proceedings against alleged infringers of NAFO measures.[318]

(iii) *Dockside inspections and reporting requirements*

Vessels that have been fishing in the NAFO Regulatory Area will be subject to a dockside inspection at each port of call. The results of these inspections will be checked against the log book kept by the vessel's captain to ensure that both the dockside inspector's and the captain's recordings of catch sizes and composition of catches are the same. The results of these dockside inspections will be made available to the NAFO Executive Secretary in the form of annual reports.

(iv) *Other matters*

As part of the negotiated settlement, Canada agreed to repeal those provisions which prescribed EC vessels under the Coastal Fisheries Protection Act. The parties also confirmed their agreement to the 27,000 tonnes 1995 TAC for Greenland halibut, but reached agreement on the share-out of the TAC; Canada agreed to take no more than 10,000 tonnes of halibut in 1995 whilst EC vessels would not take more than 5,013 tonnes from 16 April 1995. This agreed share-out therefore achieved virtual parity of halibut catch for 1995 bearing in mind the catch landed by EC vessels prior to 15 April 1995. The agreed Canadian quota for 1995 represented an annual catch three times larger than its 1994 catch. The EC's 1995 quota represented approximately one-fifth of the total tonnage of halibut caught by EC registered vessels in 1994.[319]

As far as 1996 quotas were concerned, agreement was reached that a recommendation would be made to NAFO that 'allocations will be in the ratio of 10:3 for the European Community and Canada (aside from allocations to other Contracting Parties)'.[320]

---

[316] Ibid., annex I, paragraph II.10 (emphasis added).

[317] It is reported that Canada had wished to provide NAFO inspectors with the power to impose immediate fines on the captain of an infringing vessel, but this proposal was not accepted by the EC: see *The Independent*, 5 April 1995, p. 10.

[318] See above, n. 48 and accompanying text.

[319] See Government of Canada, *News Release*, 15 April 1995, Doc.NR-HQ-95-36E.

[320] Agreed Minute, annex II, paragraph III. A slight departure from this agreed ratio was made when NAFO established the 1996 halibut quota for that part of the NAFO Regulatory Area in which both the EC and Canada fish (NAFO divisions 3LMNO) at its annual meeting in September 1995; 11,070 tonnes were allocated to the EC and 3,000 tonnes to Canada: letter to co-author dated 24 July 1996 from Ms L. Fischer, Office of the Minister, Fisheries and Oceans (Canada). Japan's allocation totalled 2,050 tonnes, 2,550 tonnes was allocated to Russia, and 1,330 tonnes to other States parties to the Northwest Atlantic Fisheries Convention.

(v) *Assessment*

The long-term success of the enforcement mechanisms adopted in the Agreed Minute, and subsequently endorsed by NAFO, remains to be seen. There is no doubt that within the NAFO Regulatory Area, co-operation between the EC and Canada has improved. In addition, the 1996 TAC and national quotas for Greenland halibut would now seem to allow for the long-term replenishment of this fish stock. However, only when States parties to NAFO are minded to bring legal proceedings against the owners and captains of infringing vessels on a more regular basis, and to impose effective penalties on proven wrongdoers, will the measures introduced in the Agreed Minute begin to form part of a meaningful deterrent to those tempted to overfish. It should also be borne in mind that such agreement as to conservation and enforcement policies could seriously be undermined by the continued use of the objection procedure by a State party under the Northwest Atlantic Fisheries Convention, particularly at a time in the future when a unilateral decision is taken by such a State party that fish stocks have recovered to such an extent that TACs and national quotas should be increased.

The Straddling Stocks Agreement builds on, *inter alia*, this solution to conflict between members of a regional fishery organization. Indeed, the provisions of NAFO, the Agreed Minute, and the negotiated settlement of the straddling stocks conflict in the Central Bering Sea,[321] were very much present in the minds of the negotiators of the 1995 Agreement.

(d) *The 1995 Straddling Stocks Agreement*[322]

Kwiatkowska presciently observed in 1989 that a consequence of the 'determined position' of Canada and other States with an interest in straddling stocks was that 'it would be difficult to exclude certain

---

[321] Loc. cit. above (n. 5).

[322] UN Doc. A.CONF.164/38, reproduced in *International Legal Materials*, 34 (1995), p. 1542, and in *Law of the Sea Bulletin*, 29 (1995), pp. 25–55; *Revue générale de droit international public*, 99 (1995), at p. 730. See also Lévy and Schram (eds.), *United Nations Conference on Straddling Fish Stocks and Highly Migratory Fish Stocks: Selected Documents* (1996). For comment, see generally Anderson, 'The Straddling Stocks Agreement of 1995—an Initial Assessment', *International and Comparative Law Quarterly*, 45 (1996), p. 463; Gherari, 'L'accord de 4 août 1995 sur les stocks chevauchants et les stocks de poissons grands migrateurs', *Revue générale de droit international public*, 100 (1996), p. 367; Balton, loc. cit. above (n. 250), p. 124; Mack, 'International Fisheries Management: How the U.N. Conference on Straddling and Highly Migratory Fish Stocks Changes the Law of Fishing on the High Seas', *California Western International Law Journal*, 26 (1996), p. 313; Hayashi, 'The Role of the United Nations in Managing the World's Fisheries', in Blake *et al.* (eds.), *The Peaceful Management of Transboundary Resources* (1995); and Barston, 'United Nations Conference on Straddling and Highly Migratory Fish Stocks', *Marine Policy*, 19 (2) (1995), p. 159 (comment following the fourth session).

developments to this end in future'.[323] Most notably these developments have included the 'Turbot Wars' between Canada and Spain, described above, and, in 1995, the conclusion of an Agreement for the Implementation of the Provisions of the United Nations Convention on the Law of the Sea relating to the Conservation of Straddling Fish Stocks and Highly Migratory Fish Stocks.[324]

The Agreement was adopted without vote on 4 August 1995, after six sessions of negotiations spanning two years, and opened for signature on 4 December 1995.[325] It will enter into force 30 days after the thirtieth ratification.[326] No reservations are permitted, thus signalling the negotiators' intention that the Agreement embodies fundamental rules to be of uniform application.[327] At the time of writing the Agreement had received 32 signatures, including signature by four of the eight States which had supported amendment of Article 63(2) LOSC in 1982.[328] Canada has signed the Agreement but Spain has not.[329] The Agreement also makes provision for participation by international organizations such as the EC.[330] While it is not necessary to be a party to the LOSC in order to become a party to the Straddling Stocks Agreement (SSA),[331] there is

---

[323] Kwiatkowska, op. cit. above (n. 41), at p. 80. Burke prophesied that 'further extensions of national jurisdiction are the price of failure to agree on new mechanisms for dealing with transnational problems': op. cit. above (n. 151), at p. 350; see also Freestone, loc. cit. above (n. 5); and Treves, loc. cit. above (n. 209), at p. 231 (Article 63(2) not sufficient to ensure rational conservation of straddling stocks).

[324] Hereinafter 'Straddling Stocks Agreement' ('SSA').

[325] See UN General Assembly Resolution 47/192 of 22 December 1992 convening the conference. The resolution left open the form the final text would take; however, at the fourth negotiating session, at the insistence of coastal States in particular, the conventional form was agreed: Gherari, loc. cit. above (n. 322) at p. 372. A total of 138 States and a number of international organizations participated in the conference, which adopted working methods similar to the Third United Nations Conference on the Law of the Sea: Gherari, ibid.; see also Anderson, loc. cit. above (n. 322), at pp. 466–7. Of particular note was the full participation of the EC in the negotiations, with the Commission put forward as negotiator. All 15 member States refrained from speaking (save for British statements in respect of dependent territories: see further 'United Kingdom Materials on International Law,' this *Year Book*, 64 (1993), at pp. 674–5); 'This was the first legal or fisheries conference in the UN where this had been the procedure, although it had long been followed in NAFO and NASCO [the North Atlantic Salmon Conservation Organisation]': Anderson, ibid.

[326] Article 41 SSA provides for the provisional application of the Agreement, pending its entry into force, through notification in writing to the depositary.

[327] Gherari, loc. cit. above (n. 322), at p. 372. Article 42 precludes reservations, while Article 43 permits declarations and statements on signature, ratification or accession. These provisions mirror Articles 309 and 310 LOSC.

[328] Australia, Canada, Iceland, and Senegal. Another strong proponent of coastal State interests, Argentina, has also signed the Agreement.

[329] The Agreement will remain open for signature until 4 December 1996: Article 37.

[330] Article 47, whether competence is mixed (para. 1) or exclusive (para. 2).

[331] Unlike the 1994 Agreement relating to the Implementation of Part XI of the United Nations Convention on the Law of the Sea, adopted by UN General Assembly Resolution A/48/263 of 28 July 1994, Doc. A/RES.48/263. As at 31 December 1995 there were 125 parties to this Agreement, which both Canada and Spain have signed but not ratified.

Various provisions of the SSA are tailored to meet the potential difficulties arising from non-participation in the LOSC. For example, the dispute settlement procedures of Part XV LOSC are applicable to non-parties to the LOSC by virtue of Article 30(1) SSA.

clearly a close link between them. The Agreement was negotiated within the framework of the LOSC.[332] As a matter of treaty interpretation, the Law of the Sea Convention will be interpreted in the light of the SSA since both the 1994 Agreement on the Implementation of Part XI and the SSA constitute 'subsequent agreement between the parties regarding the interpretation of the treaty or the application of its provisions' for the purposes of Article 31(3)(a) of the Vienna Convention on the Law of Treaties.[333] The dispute settlement procedures of the Law of the Sea Convention apply *mutatis mutandis* to any dispute between States parties to the Agreement.[334]

This is the first global agreement to regulate high seas fisheries, providing for sustainable management of straddling fish stocks and highly migratory fish stocks and for peaceful resolution of any dispute arising from their exploitation. The Agreement is closely linked with Agenda 21, a relationship explicitly acknowledged in the preamble of the former, which states that the Agreement seeks 'to address the particular problem identified in Agenda 21, Chapter 17, Programme Area C . . . [that] the management of high seas fisheries is inadequate in many areas and that some resources are over-utilized'. In addition, problems of: (i) unregulated fisheries; (ii) over-capitalization; (iii) excessive fleet size; (iv) vessel reflagging to escape controls; (v) insufficiently selective gear; (vi) unreliable databases; and (vii) lack of sufficient co-operation between States, are identified.[335] The explicit objective of the Straddling Stocks Agreement 'is to ensure the long-term conservation and sustainable use of straddling fish stocks and highly migratory fish stocks through effective implementation of the relevant provisions of the [LOSC]'.[336]

(i) *Conservation and management*

Part II (Articles 5–7) of the Agreement addresses 'conservation and management of straddling fish stocks and highly migratory fish stocks', setting forth principles which apply to conservation and management of

[332] As Gherari observes, 'la conférence n'avait pas entière liberté pour définir le régime de son choix puisque ses travaux et ses résultats devaient être conformes aux dispositions de la Convention du 10 décembre 1982': loc. cit. above (n. 322), at p. 371. According to Anderson, it was largely at EC insistence that the conference confined its attention to straddling and highly migratory fish stocks in the context of the LOSC: loc. cit. above (n. 322), at p. 466.

[333] Anderson argues that 'it would be appropriate in construing either instrument [i.e. the LOSC and the SSA] to have regard to the other': ibid., at p. 468. Article 4 SSA addresses the relationship between the Straddling Stocks Agreement and the Law of the Sea Convention and provides, *inter alia*, that 'This Agreement shall be interpreted and applied in the context of and in a manner consistent with the Convention'.

[334] Article 30 SSA; on dispute settlement, see further above, Part II.

[335] Preamble, fifth paragraph.

[336] Article 2, SSA.

such stocks both within and beyond areas of national jurisdiction.[337] Article 5 sets forth general principles which are, in essence, 'international minimum standards on how to run a good fishery',[338] combining existing good practice with new environmental concepts. There is some overlap with the FAO Code of Conduct for Responsible Fisheries, suggesting a degree of international consensus regarding the applicable conservation and management measures.[339] The establishment of internationally agreed minimum standards for the conservation and management of straddling and highly migratory fish stocks was one of the key elements identified by the Chairman to ensure an effective outcome to the negotiations.[340] Moreover the SSA reinforces new environmental concepts[341] through the recognition in Article 5 of the precautionary principle,[342] the ecosystem approach,[343] conservation of biological diver-

---

[337] Article 3(1) and (2) SSA extend the provisions of Article 5 to areas within coastal State jurisdiction; see also Article 7 of the FAO Code on Responsible Fisheries, esp. 7.1.3–7.1.5. Gherari observes that the generality of the principles contained in Article 5 SSA no doubt helped to gain the acceptance by coastal States of the application of these principles within the EEZ/EFZ: loc. cit. above (n. 322), at p. 374. While coastal States were reluctant to see the Convention intrude within the EEZ, the US (with coastal and distant water fishing interests), Japan and the EU, *inter alios*, favoured such extension: see ASIL Briefing on UN Conference on Straddling Fish Stocks and Highly Migratory Fish Stocks by D. Walton, a member of the US delegation to the Conference: *ASIL Newsletter*, September 1994.

[338] See further Anderson, loc. cit. above (n. 322). These could constitute 'generally recommended international minimum standards' for the purposes of Articles 61(3) and 119(1) LOSC.

[339] See further Gherari, loc. cit. above (n. 322), at p. 374.

[340] Barston, loc. cit. above (n. 322), at p. 163, n. 38.

[341] Anderson emphasizes recognition of the precautionary principle and of large marine ecosystems: loc. cit. above (n. 322), at pp. 466 and 469; Gherari, sustainability and precaution: loc. cit. above (n. 322), at pp. 373–4.

[342] The precautionary approach is identified as a general principle in Article 5(c), which is further elaborated in Article 6 SSA ('application of the precautionary approach') and in Annex II. These are based, *inter alia*, on an FAO paper on 'The Precautionary Approach to Fisheries Management' produced at the request of the Straddling Stocks Conference for consideration at its fourth session in New York in March 1994.

Article 6(2) SSA states:

'States shall be more cautious when information is uncertain, unreliable or inadequate. The absence of adequate scientific information shall not be used as a reason for postponing or failing to take conservation and management measures.'

Of particular significance is Annex II to the Agreement which sets forth 'Guidelines for the Application of the Precautionary Reference Points in Conservation and Management of Straddling Fish Stocks and Highly Migratory Fish Stocks'.

Principle 15 of the 1992 Declaration of the UN Conference on Environment and Development, Rio de Janeiro, 3–14 June 1992, describes the concept of precautionary action as follows:

'In order to protect the environment, the precautionary approach shall be widely applied by States according to their capabilities. Where there are threats of serious or irreversible damage, lack of full scientific certainty shall not be used as a reason for postponing cost-effective measures to prevent environmental degradation.'

For background on the evolution and development of the precautionary principle or approach, see Freestone, 'The Precautionary Principle', in Churchill and Freestone (eds.), *International Law and Global Climate Change* (1991), pp. 21–40; and, more generally, Freestone and Hey (eds.), *The Precautionary Principle and International Law: The Challenge of Implementation* (1996).

[343] Article 5(d) and (e) SSA provide that coastal and high seas fishing States shall:

'(d) assess the impacts of fishing, other human activities and environmental factors on target stocks

sity,[344] and the objective of sustainable development of straddling stocks.[345]

In keeping with growing concerns regarding fishing techniques and high levels of incidental catches, there is also the obligation to minimize catch of non-target species through measures including 'to the extent practicable, the development and use of selective, environmentally safe and cost-effective fishing gear and techniques'.[346] Finally, any list of good practice in respect of fisheries conservation and management/ sustainable use would contain obligations to collect and share data, and to implement and enforce conservation and management measures through effective monitoring, control and surveillance. These basic obligations are also found in Article 5 and then amplified in later provisions of the Agreement.[347]

The application of the precautionary approach in Article 6 is particularly welcome, though it does not go so far as to prevent fishing even where stocks are threatened.[348] Thus it may be contrasted with the 'traffic lights' approach of the 1972 Convention for the Conservation of Antarctic Seals;[349] the SSA has green and amber lights, but no red.

and species belonging to the same ecosystem or associated with or dependent upon the target stocks;
(e) adopt, where necessary, conservation and management measures for species belonging to the same ecosystem or associated with or dependent upon the target stocks, with a view to maintaining or restoring populations of such species above levels at which their reproduction may become seriously threatened.'
The explicit direction to consider the impact of measures taken not only upon target stocks but upon dependent and associated species, contained in Article 5(e), is an approach also found in Article 61 LOSC.
The first international agreement explicitly to adopt an ecosystem approach to the conservation of marine living resources is the 1980 Convention for the Conservation of Antarctic Marine Living Resources: see further Lyster, *International Wildlife Law* (1985), chapter 9. On ecosystem approaches see further Freestone, 'The Conservation of Marine Ecosystems under International Law', in Bowman and Redgwell (eds.), *International Law and the Conservation of Biological Diversity* (1996), pp. 99–107. Freestone argues that the preservation of marine biodiversity requires a holistic, ecosystem approach and 'the development of principles and procedures to overcome the arbitrary juridical zones established by the LOSC where this is necessary to achieve these objectives' (at p. 106). The specific example provided is the 'compatibility' provision of what was to become Article 7 of the SSA, requiring conservation and management of stocks within and outside the 200-mile limit to be compatible: ibid., p. 106, n. 88.
[344] Article 5(g). For criticism of the failure of the 1992 United Nations Convention on the Conservation of Biological Diversity properly to address marine biodiversity conservation, see Freestone, ibid., at pp. 91–92.
[345] See Article 5(a) ('sustainability of straddling fish stocks . . .') and (h) ('sustainable use of fishery resources').
[346] Article 5(f).
[347] See in particular annex I, which sets forth standard requirements for collection and sharing of data. The inadequate and conflicting provision of data has been one of the criticisms of RFOs such as NAFO.
[348] Not even with what might be termed the 'modified abstention principle' in Article 16(2) (the 'enclave provision' designed to address the problem of the Sea of Okhotsk peanut hole).
[349] See Redgwell, 'The Protection of the Antarctic Environment', in Bowman and Redgwell (eds.), op. cit. above (n. 342), at p. 116. The traffic light analogy is found in Heap, 'Has CCAMLR Worked? Management Policies and Ecological Needs', in Jorgensen-Dahl and Ostreng (eds.), *The Antarctic Treaty System in World Politics* (1991), at p. 46.

Essentially the Agreement provides for the establishment of 'stock-specific reference points' which, if approached should not be exceeded; if exceeded, then action to restore the stocks is to be taken pursuant to Article 6(3)(*b*) which requires States to determine the reference points *and* to determine the action to be taken *if* they are exceeded. Thus it is left to States, co-operating through RFOs where extant and competent, to determine the consequences of exceeding pre-determined precautionary reference points, and not regulated by the Agreement.

The Agreement is explicitly designed to amplify the duty to co-operate contained in the 1982 LOSC (the 'Convention'),[350] and further clarifies the 'interests' of the coastal State referred to in Article 116 LOSC.[351] Coastal and fishing States are to 'adopt measures to ensure long-term sustainability of straddling fish stocks and highly migratory fish stocks and promote the objective of their optimum utilization' (Article 5(*a*)). The basis for setting such measures is not new, but relies on the approach taken in Article 61 (EEZ) and 119 (high seas) LOSC.[352] The need for this harmonization is obvious; not only is the Agreement explicitly stated to be an amplification of the Convention, but it would clearly be contrary to its basic objectives to provide for different criteria for establishing measures for the conservation and management of stocks on either side of a boundary. Indeed, one victory for coastal States is the recognition in Article 7 of the need to ensure compatibility of conservation and management measures within and beyond areas of national jurisdiction. However, this is done without significantly disturbing the delicate balance between the regulated high seas freedom of fishing and the sovereign rights of the coastal State over living marine resources within the EEZ/EFZ established under the LOSC.[353]

Agreement on this compatibility issue was seen by the Chairman of the Conference as one of the keystones of the Agreement.[354] NAFO's history, in particular the harmonization of international and coastal State standards, is the reason for the inclusion in Article 7 of detailed provisions relating to the compatibility of conservation and management measures.[355] With respect to straddling stocks, the relevant coastal and fishing States are to co-operate in order to agree upon measures necessary

---

[350] In particular, Articles 63(2), 64 and 117 LOSC. On the importance of co-operation in the Agreement, see further Gherari, loc. cit. above (n. 322), at pp. 377–81.

[351] Anderson, loc. cit. above (n. 322), at p. 468; see discussion of this point above, Part II.

[352] Though, of course, it is now not the coastal State alone which adopts the relevant measures but co-operation between the coastal States and States fishing on the high seas.

[353] Article 7(1) SSA, which does not accord an absolute priority to coastal State rights.

[354] '[L]'une "des clefs de voûte de l'Accord"': A/CONF. 164/35, 20 September 1995, as cited in Gherari, loc. cit. above (n. 322), at p. 376; see also Barston, loc. cit. above (n. 322), at p. 163.

[355] See discussion of NAFO above, n. 27.

for the conservation of the stocks in the adjacent high seas area.[356] Such co-operation may be direct or through the co-operation procedures contained in the Agreement in Articles 8–16 (Part III), which address 'mechanisms for international co-operation concerning straddling fish stocks and highly migratory fish stocks'. The provisions on compatibility underscore the importance and necessity of co-operation.[357] Article 7(2) further provides that conservation and management measures adopted for adjacent high seas areas and within national jurisdiction 'shall be compatible in order to ensure conservation and management of straddling fish stocks and highly migratory fish stocks in their entirety', and imposes a duty to co-operate to such end.

Criteria for determining compatibility are set out in Article 7(2). Of particular note is the obligation to take into account measures adopted within national jurisdiction[358] 'and ensure that measures adopted in respect of such stocks for the high seas do not undermine the effectiveness of such measures'.[359] In respect of previously agreed high seas measures, and of those agreed by the relevant RFO, there is merely the obligation to take such measures into account—if they exist.[360] Further evidence of the priority accorded coastal State interest is found in the obligation to take into account the biological unity of the stocks (a clear application of the ecosystem approach), 'including the extent to which the stocks occur and are fished in areas under national jurisdiction'.[361] The final criteria relate to the dependence of coastal and fishing States upon the stocks concerned, and the obligation to ensure that any measures agreed do not result in harmful impact on the living marine resources as a whole.[362] It remains to be seen whether the 'correct balance between the two interests, coastal and fishing' has been achieved.[363] It is certainly feasible that the application of the criteria

[356] Article 7(1) SSA. There is no definition of 'adjacent' in the Agreement; but cf. Barston, loc. cit. above (n. 322) (Russian proposal to define key terms in the Agreement).

[357] Gherari, loc. cit. above (n. 322), at p. 377. Referring in particular to Part III, he observes that '[c]e volet de l'Accord répond à une nécessité cruciale puisque l'aménagement des ressources concernées n'est pas sérieusement envisageable sans l'action commune de l'ensemble des Etats intéréssés'.

[358] Coastal States are obliged to inform relevant fishing States directly or through a RFO of measures adopted in respect of straddling and highly migratory stocks: Article 7(7). High seas States have a similar obligation to other States in respect of measures adopted regulating their fishing vessels on the high seas: Article 7(8).

[359] Article 7(2)(a). A requirement that high seas measures be 'no less stringent' than national measures was dropped owing to opposition from, inter alios, Poland and Korea: see further Barston, loc. cit. above (n. 322), at p. 163.

[360] Article 7(2)(b) and (c).

[361] Article 7(2)(d).

[362] Article 7(2)(e) and (f).

[363] Anderson, loc. cit. above (n. 322), at p. 470, does not reveal what the balance is—even, or tilted in favour of coastal or fishing State? The reiteration of the balance struck in the LOSC and preserved in Article 7(1) suggests that the intention was to strike the middle ground between these competing interests.

could result in a more favourable outcome for coastal States,[364] though this is not a necessary outcome.

Article 8 of Part III further elaborates upon the duty to co-operate either directly or through the relevant RFO. In the latter case, where the RFO has the competence to establish management and conservation measures for relevant stocks, the duty to co-operate of States fishing those stocks includes joining the relevant RFO[365] or agreeing to apply its measures. If no regional organization or arrangement exists, interested States are obliged to co-operate in the creation of such organization or arrangement.[366] There is particular urgency attached to negotiations to this end where stocks are under threat of over-exploitation or where a new fishery is being developed for such stocks.[367] The functions of RFOs and regional arrangements are set forth in Article 10.[368]

Thus the key to access to fishery resources to which regional conservation and management measures apply is through co-operative arrangements; otherwise fishing States do not have access to high seas stocks conserved and managed through an RFO or other arrangement.[369] These provisions are clearly aimed at the problem of new entrants to the

---

[364] See, for example, Gherari, loc. cit. above (n. 322), at p. 377:
'. . . la compatibilité peut déboucher sur un résultat plutôt favorable aux Etats côtiers dans la mesure où ceux-ci disposent d'un droit souverain pour fixer les mesures nationales auxquelles, pour rappel, les mesures internationales ne peuvent donc nuire, à quoi s'ajoutent certain éléments tel que la répartition des stocks et leur niveau d'exploitation dans les eaux nationales ou même l'aspect économique qui, dans certains cas, pourrait avantager ces mêmes Etats.'
Gherari considers that '[l]'avantage conféré à l'état côtier paraît plus visible encore' in Article 16, which addresses the particular problem of a high seas area surrounded by the maritime zone of a single State. This 'enclave' provision was included at the particular insistence of the Russian Federation concerned with overfishing in the high seas 'peanut hole' in the Sea of Okhotsk. In addition to importing the compatibility provisions of Article 7, Article 16(1) further requires that '[m]easures taken in respect of the high seas shall take into account the rights, duties and interests of the coastal State under the [LOS] Convention . . .'.
[365] In this connection Article 8(3) further provides that: 'The terms for participation in such organization or arrangement shall not preclude such States from membership or participation; nor shall they be applied in a manner which discriminates against any State or group of States having a real interest in the fisheries concerned'. The participation clauses of NAFO and the Bering Sea Convention may require reassessment in the light of this provision.
[366] Article 8(5). This is an obligation which exists under the LOSC in respect of highly migratory species, but not in respect of straddling stocks. Article 64(1) LOSC provides in respect of highly migratory species that '[i]n regions for which no appropriate international organization exists, the coastal State and other States whose nationals harvest these species in the region shall co-operate to establish such an organization and participate in its work'.
[367] Article 8(2), which further provides that, '[p]ending agreement on such arrangements, States shall observe the provisions of this Agreement and shall act in good faith and with due regard to the rights, interests and duties of other States'. Beyond observing the provisions of this Agreement, these obligations are consistent with States' general obligations under the LOSC and at customary law.
[368] Article 13 SSA obliges States to co-operate to strengthen RFOs in order to improve their effectiveness in establishing *and* implementing conservation and management measures, though no specific strengthening measures are specified. Compliance with the other provisions of the Agreement would contribute to such strengthening.
[369] Article 8(4). Nor does the failure to join or reach agreement free non-members/non-participants from the duty to co-operate in the conservation and management of straddling fish

fishery[370] and of re-flagging in non-parties to an RFO, both problems having been experienced under NAFO, the RFO which generally speaking was the Conference's model for such organizations.[371] Article 8 balances the obligation to participate in conservation arrangements to obtain access to the fishery with the right to participate in such organizations or arrangements. The sum total of these significant provisions is to ensure that no party acting in accordance with its obligations under the Agreement may fish unilaterally and unrestrictedly straddling and highly migratory fish stocks without being a member of the relevant RFO, participating in the relevant regional arrangement, or agreeing to apply regional measures. This is bolstered by the obligation on States which are non-members and non-participants to ensure that their fishing vessels are not authorized to engage in fishing activities in respect of those stocks to which regional conservation measures apply.[372] A serious question remains whether these provisions are consistent with the freedom of fishing on the high seas, and the extent to which the Agreement's further elaboration of the duty to co-operate is reflected in customary international law on the point.[373] Such an assessment may become pertinent for distant water fishing nations unhappy with the balance of rights and interests in the Agreement and searching for alternatives to participation therein.

(ii) *Compliance and enforcement*

Part VI (Articles 19–23) of the Agreement, on compliance and enforcement, 'was the subject of much debate'.[374] At the outset of the fourth negotiation session, the Canadian Fisheries Minister Brian Tobin 'summed up the general consensus that "the best conservation measures, supported by all States, will fail without effective enforcement"'.[375] The provisions of the SSA make a significant contribution in this regard. Provisions are divided between compliance and enforcement by the flag State (Article 19); international (Article 20) and regional (Articles 21 and

---

stocks and highly migratory fish stocks: Article 17(1). Indeed, such States are obliged under the Agreement to refrain from authorizing their fishing vessels to engage in fishing operations in respect of stocks subject to management and conservation measures by a RFO or other regional arrangement: Article 17(2).

[370] Article 11 SSA addresses the nature and extent of participatory rights for new entrants, listing criteria designed to balance coastal and DWFN interests in the stocks. The criteria listed are reminiscent of the *Fisheries Jurisdiction* cases, loc. cit. above (n. 119), in particular 'the needs of coastal communities which are dependent mainly on fishing for the stocks' and 'the needs of coastal States whose economies are overwhelmingly dependent on the exploitation of living marine resources', but balanced with, *inter alia*, 'the respective interests, fishing patterns and fishing practices of new and existing members or participants': Article 11 (*d*), (*e*), and (*b*).

[371] Anderson, loc. cit. above (n. 322), at p. 470.

[372] Article 17(2) SSA. Further flag State duties are contained in Article 18.

[373] See further Gherari, loc. cit. above (n. 322), at p. 379.

[374] Anderson, loc. cit. above (n. 322), at p. 471; see also Gherari, ibid., at pp. 381 ff.

[375] Canadian Permanent Mission to the United Nations, Press Release No. 6, 15 August 1994, as quoted in Barston, loc. cit. above (n. 322), at p. 164.

22) co-operation in enforcement; and measures by the port State (Article 23). Enforcement measures may thus be taken by the flag, coastal or port State.

The general duties of the flag State are addressed in Article 18, which mirrors the provisions of the 1993 FAO Agreement to Promote Compliance with International Conservation and Management Measures by Fishing Vessels on the High Seas.[376] Article 19 focuses specifically on compliance and enforcement, imposing on flag States the obligation to ensure compliance by their fishing vessels with RFO conservation measures for straddling stocks. This obligation is not geographically determined.[377] This point is reinforced by paragraph 1(a), which requires the flag State to enforce violations of such measures irrespective of where the violation occurs. Immediate investigation of any alleged violations, and prompt report to the State or RFO alleging the violation, are further obligations. In addition, any action taken consequent to the finding of a violation must be taken expeditiously, with sanctions of adequate severity to secure compliance and discourage recidivism.[378] Indeed, the flag State is to ensure the cessation of high seas fishing activities by a fishing vessel which has committed a serious violation until flag State sanctions have been fully complied with. Such sanctions must 'deprive offenders of the benefits accruing from their illegal activities' but it is left to the discretion of the flag State to determine the nature of such sanctions, which under the SSA may include refusing, withdrawing or suspending the authorization of masters and other officers of fishing vessels from serving in that capacity on such vessels.[379] It is only the flag State which may take, or authorize, the prosecution of violations committed by vessels flying its flag. The SSA therefore does not go as far as the Canadian Coastal Fisheries Protection Act.

The coastal State may, with flag State authorization, board and inspect on the high seas a vessel which is suspected of having been engaged in unauthorized fishing *within* an area under the jurisdiction of a coastal State.[380] There must be reasonable grounds for such belief, and there is no obligation on the flag State to grant consent; it is obliged to co-operate with the coastal State 'in taking appropriate enforcement action' and speedily and fully to investigate any such alleged unauthorized fishing where so requested by a coastal State. In respect of fisheries violations on *the high seas*, Article 21 contains innovative provisions which permit coastal State enforcement action in respect of violations of RFO meas-

---

[376] Text reproduced in *International Legal Materials*, 33 (1994), p. 968.

[377] Save for the geographic scope of the applicable RFO measures, e.g., the NAFO Regulatory Area.

[378] Article 19(1)(b) and 19(2).

[379] Article 19(2).

[380] Article 20(6); this is expressly without prejudice to Article 111 LOSC regarding the right of hot pursuit.

ures on the high seas.[381] A State party to the Agreement and also a member of a RFO may enforce the conservation provisions of that RFO against the fishing vessels of another party to the Agreement even where that party is not a member of the relevant RFO. It will be recalled that membership, or agreement to abide by the conservation measures, of the RFO, are preconditions for access to the high seas portion of the stocks.[382] Article 21(1) permits duly authorized inspectors[383] of the inspecting State to board and inspect fishing vessels flying the flag of another State party to the Agreement, for the purpose of ensuring compliance with applicable RFO measures. Basic procedures for boarding and inspection are set out in Article 22, and include obligations for both inspecting State and flag State.[384] Since the ability of the coastal State to exercise inspection powers on the high seas in connection with suspected fisheries violations is limited to the enforcement of multilaterally-adopted conservation measures, there will be a strong incentive to pursue agreement for the regulation of stocks in regions or subregions not presently subject to such international regulation.[385]

Article 21 further provides for the consequences of an inspection revealing a violation, with a distinction drawn between serious and non-serious violations. In the latter case, if an inspecting State has clear

[381] The complicated provisions of Article 21 are a result of the need to accommodate regional schemes such as NAFO and the Bering Sea Agreement of 11 February 1994: Anderson, loc. cit. above (n. 322), at p. 471. See also Article 20(7) which provides that, pending 'appropriate action' by the flag State, members of a RFO may take action in accordance with international law, including recourse to the enforcement provisions of the RFO itself, 'to deter vessels which have engaged in activities that undermine the effectiveness of or otherwise violate the conservation and management measures established by that organization or arrangement from fishing on the high seas in the subregion or region'.

[382] If no such arrangement exists, States are to co-operate to conclude such arrangement: Article 8(5).

[383] Article 21(4) further provides that inspecting States are obliged to inform all States fishing in the relevant high seas region of the form of identification issued to their duly authorized inspectors. Furthermore, as is the case under the LOSC, no 'undercover inspection vessels' are permitted: all vessels employed for inspection purposes must be clearly marked and identifiable as engaged in government service.

[384] For example, the inspecting State is to ensure that duly authorized inspectors follow the basic procedures in Article 22(1), which include the obligation to 'avoid the use of force except when and to the degree necessary to ensure the safety of the inspectors and where the inspectors are obstructed in the execution of their duties. The degree of force used shall not exceed that reasonably required in the circumstances.' The flag State is to ensure, inter alia, that inspectors are not obstructed in execution of their duties: Article 22(3). Article 22(4) addresses the circumstance where a master refuses to accept boarding and inspection in circumstances not warranted by generally accepted international regulations relating to safety at sea. The flag State shall direct the master to do so; failure further to comply requires the flag State immediately to suspend the vessel's authorization and order its immediate return to port. Further action taken by the flag State is then to be notified to the inspecting State.

[385] Mfodwo et al. note that the desire jointly to manage shared and highly migratory stocks in the region led to the conclusion of the Gulf of Guinea Convention and an agreement establishing the Sub-Regional Commission on Fisheries in the Northwest African coastal area: loc. cit. above (n. 208), at p. 461.

grounds for believing a violation of regional conservation and management measures has been committed, it may secure evidence and notify the flag State, which has 3 days in which to respond. Article 19 imposes on the flag State the obligation further to investigate and, if the evidence warrants, to take enforcement action, or authorize the inspecting State further to investigate but with the flag State responsible for any enforcement action against its vessel. Less latitude is afforded the flag State under the provisions of Article 21 in the case of a 'serious violation'[386] *and* where the flag State has failed to respond or failed to take the necessary investigatory and enforcement action. There the inspecting State may retain its investigators on board to collect further evidence and may require the vessel to be escorted to the nearest port. This possibility for dockside inspection is also found in the Agreed Minute. The flag State may intervene and exercise its investigatory and enforcement powers at any stage.[387] There is nothing in the Agreement which sanctions unilateral coastal State enforcement of coastal State fisheries conservation measures beyond the limits of national jurisdiction.

None the less Article 21 constitutes a significant advance in international co-operation regarding the enforcement of conservation measures on the high seas.[388] A measure of the importance of this innovation is the safeguard built into Article 22 should a RFO fail to adopt boarding and inspection procedures within two years of the entry into force of the SSA. Such failure will not impede the effective functioning of the crucial inspection and enforcement procedures of the SSA because of the detailed boarding and inspection procedures stipulated in Article 22 which apply in the event of such default.

Finally, Part VI permits measures to be taken by the port State in connection with fishing vessels voluntarily in port, including the inspection of gear and record books, and the prohibition of landing and transshipments of catch 'where it has been established that the catch has been taken in a manner which undermines the effectiveness of subregional, regional or global conservation and management measures on the high seas'.[389]

(iii) *Assessment*

In assessing the Straddling Stocks Agreement it is important to bear in mind that it does not address the problem of straddling and highly migratory fish stocks *de novo* but, at the insistence of the EC amongst

---

[386] A non-exhaustive list of 'serious violations' is contained in Article 21(11), ranging from fishing in a closed area or above quota to using prohibited gear and inaccurate record-keeping. It is open to RFOs to specify further such 'serious violations': Article 21(11)(i).

[387] Article 21(12).

[388] Anderson, loc. cit. above (n. 322), at p. 471.

[389] Article 23(3). Anderson notes that such steps have in the past raised questions of compatibility with the GATT: loc. cit. above (n. 322), at p. 472.

others, examines the issue within the existing framework of the Law of the Sea Convention. It continues the delicate balancing act between the high seas freedom of fishing and the rights, duties and interest of the coastal State set forth in the LOSC. This is seen most clearly in the continued reliance upon flag State jurisdiction to impose sanctions for violations of conservation measures by vessels flying their flag, and in the absence of explicit recognition of a 'special interest' of the coastal State.[390] In respect of the former, the Straddling Stocks Agreement does not take the approach of, for example, Article 228 LOSC (which is concerned not with fisheries but with pollution matters). That Article permits coastal States to *prosecute*[391] where, *inter alia*, the flag State has persistently failed to enforce applicable international rules and standards. Furthermore, Article 228 recognizes the special interest of the coastal State in prosecuting vessels for infringements of applicable coastal State law and regulations, or international rules and standards, in the EEZ which cause major damage to the coastal State. There is no parallel to these provisions in the Straddling Stocks Agreement, which stops short of conferring on coastal States prosecutorial powers against foreign flagged vessels in cases of serious violations of conservation measures. This constraint is no doubt explained in part by the fact that the Agreement is concerned with enforcement in adjacent high seas areas of regionally agreed conservation standards while the provisions of Article 228 apply within the EEZ to the enforcement of coastal State laws and regulations, or international rules and standards, regarding the protection of the marine environment.[392]

In other respects, however, the Agreement makes significant improvements upon the LOSC. There is now explicit recognition of the need for compatibility between conservation measures within and beyond national jurisdiction where straddling stocks are concerned. But, true to the balance struck in the LOSC, there is no priority given to coastal State measures. The SSA also goes much further in prescribing precautionary action in connection with setting TACs for straddling and highly migratory fish stocks, which has been a source of conflict in RFOs such as NAFO. The inspection and enforcement provisions of the SSA also

---

[390] It could be argued that the failure explicitly to acknowledge the special interest of the coastal State, in the manner of Article 7 HSC, has been traded off for an amplification of the rights, duties and jurisdiction of the coastal State under the SSA as a whole.

[391] The language of Article 228 is in fact broader, referring to 'proceedings to impose penalties'.

[392] Nor, and rightly so, does the same moral turpitude attach to over-fishing that attaches, say, to acts of terrorism and hijacking, for example, where 'prosecute or extradite' obligations have been established by treaty: see, for example, Article 7 of the 1970 Hague Convention for the Suppression of Unlawful Seizure of Aircraft, reproduced in *International Legal Materials*, 10 (1971), p. 133.

make a significant contribution to the effectiveness of fisheries conservation measures agreed through RFOs or other arrangements in consequence of the recognition of coastal State enforcement powers in the
area beyond national jurisdiction where giving effect to regionally agreed
conservation measures. A novel and innovative feature of the Agreement
is the ability of a coastal State party to a RFO to enforce within the
relevant regulatory area agreed conservation measures against non-
participants to the RFO. This meets head-on the problem of re-flagged
and other non-party vessels which seek to avoid compliance with
conservation measures established by the relevant RFO. Indeed, the
incentive to remain outside the RFO will be much diminished with the
coming into force of this Agreement, which encourages States to enter
into such arrangements where they do not presently exist, and to permit
new entrants where they do. The success of these measures will of course
depend upon widespread participation by high seas fishing States in the
Agreement where these additional inspection powers are grounded. In
respect of new participants to RFOs, the duty to co-operate is buttressed
by the inchoate right of participation contained in Article 8 of the
Agreement, but this right is only exercisable under the SSA by States
having a 'real interest in the fisheries concerned'. Whether a State
motivated by conservation concerns but not with imminent plans for
commercial exploitation of stocks in the region would be entitled to
participate in a regional RFO in consequence of this provision in the SSA
is not clear and will depend upon the interpretation of 'real interest'.

These novel provisions of the SSA are dependent for their effective
implementation upon co-operation between States, in particular through
RFOs; there is reference throughout the SSA to 'appropriate subregional
or regional fisheries management organizations or arrangements'. Thus,
while the SSA constitutes an amplification of the LOSC, it in turn will
require further amplification and implementation by States at the
regional level. Such implementation must take the conservation standards of the Agreement as a baseline, though implementation may take
the form of upward derogation from the provisions of, *inter alia*, Article
5 which sets international *minimum* standards for fisheries management.[393] The result is a three-tiered structure of LOSC, SSA and RFO,
with mutual reinforcement and dependence. Co-operation between
coastal and high seas fishing States is indispensable for the effective
operation of their provisions. Although the SSA does provide in certain
limited instances for automatic supplement of RFO measures (e.g.,
Article 22 on boarding and inspection), the success of the SSA will

---

[393] This does not imply that the measures contained in Articles 5 ff. set a minimal *level* for management and conservation.

ultimately be judged in the tier below. It is in this light that the Agreed Minute between Canada and the EC, and the provisions of NAFO and other RFOs, should be viewed.[394]

Notwithstanding NAFO's status as a role model for the negotiation of the SSA, one of the more serious weaknesses of NAFO (and many other fisheries organizations) is the objection procedure. The SSA does nothing to address the problem of a State party to NAFO objecting to a TAC, setting its own TAC and, in pursuance of that TAC, engaging in fishing activity which is not explicitly prohibited under NAFO. Indeed, the SSA could give rise to the anomalous situation where fishing above quota by a State party to the SSA but not to the RFO constitutes a serious violation of the conservation measures of the RFO, with the consequences attendant upon such violation, whilst a State party to the RFO which objects to a TAC in accordance with the procedures of the RFO may fish above the TAC without committing a serious violation. While such a scenario would fall outside the novel enforcement powers of the coastal State contained in the SSA in so far as enforcement of the RFO measures are concerned,[395] it might none the less still be viewed as contrary to the international minimum standards for fisheries conservation and management set forth in Articles 5 ff. of the SSA, and of Articles 61 and 119 LOSC. The enhanced enforcement powers of the coastal State under the SSA would be of no avail since their exercise is explicitly linked with RFO measures, leaving the inspecting non-flag State in the unsatisfactory position of relying on general principles of the LOSC and

---

[394] Provisions regarding satellite surveying, one mechanism for the effective inspection and enforcement of straddling stock conservation measures, are an example of a measure included in the Agreed Minute which does not find its counterpart in the SSA. However, it would be undesirable for the SSA to prescribe detailed technical standards which are best left to regional and other arrangements further to specify in accordance with the needs and capabilities of the parties. In this latter context, it should be noted that Part VII of the SSA addresses the requirements of developing States, including not only the obligation of States to co-operate in capacity-building measures in areas such as monitoring, surveillance, and compliance and enforcement (Article 25), but also an obligation to co-operate to establish special funds to assist in developing State implementation of the Agreement (Article 26).

[395] This assumes that such action by the objecting NAFO party does not constitute a serious violation within the meaning of Article 21(11)(c) which refers, *inter alia*, to fishing without, or after the attainment of, a quota established by the relevant RFO. If a State party to the RFO has employed lawfully the objection procedures of the RFO, then the quotas from which it has opted out could not be said to have been 'established' in respect of the objecting State. Savini, for example, has pointed out the tendency to label as 'guilty' parties which have lawfully exercised the objection procedure under, *inter alia*, NAFO and asks: 'Is it acceptable to take retaliatory measures against a country which has just exercised its legal right, a right which is specifically envisaged in the Convention?': Savini, 'Commentary', in Soons (ed.), op. cit. above (n. 5), at p. 382. Putting to one side his point on retaliation, analysis of which is beyond the scope of this article, our argument here is that use of the objection procedure does not absolve the objecting State from compliance with other applicable rules, including the objectives of conservation and management which must be applied in setting unilaterally a TAC.

of customary international law, which in respect of high seas fisheries matters acknowledge the exclusivity of flag State jurisdiction.[396]

Finally, while the SSA utilizes the innovative dispute settlement framework of the LOSC, a double standard exists. The failure properly to conserve high seas fish stocks is subject to compulsory dispute settlement under the LOSC, while coastal State measures in respect of the EEZ may be excluded, and there is no obligation of compulsory dispute settlement at customary international law.

IV. CONCLUSION

There is no doubt that the virtual lacuna which existed previously in respect of the regulation of straddling stocks has been filled with the amplification of the LOSC by the SSA. While it is too early to predict the likely date of the entry into force of the SSA, provisional application directly by States and through RFOs will ensure the wider dissemination of these 'international minimum standards on how to run a good fishery'. The future law of high seas fisheries will be governed by three levels of largely mutually compatible and reinforcing treaty obligations, ranging from the general provisions of the LOSC through the SSA to the RFOs. In practice these will not operate as three separate and conflicting sources of treaty law, since the principles contained at each level may be viewed as simply steps in the concretization of general norms of conservation, management and enforcement. Pending the entry into force of the SSA and subsequently, it will be the practice of RFOs and the steps which coastal States take within their jurisdiction, which will have the greatest effect on straddling stocks.

Many of these treaty obligations are also reflected in customary international law. The high seas freedom to fish is now a heavily

---

[396] Note, however, the innovative enforcement provisions contained in Article VI of the now discontinued Interim Convention on the Conservation of North Pacific Fur Seals, concluded 9 February 1957 (*UN Treaty Series*, vol. 314, p. 105), which permits the seizure of a vessel of another State party where these is reasonable cause to believe that prohibited pelagic sealing is taking place on the high seas of the North Pacific Region (Article VI(2)). However, it is only the flag State which has jurisdiction to try the case and to impose any penalties in connection with breach of the Convention: Article VI(3). The Convention was amended six times between 1963 and 1988 but is now discontinued: Birnie and Boyle, op. cit. above (n. 111), at p. 496, n. 17. See also the enforcement provisions of the Central Bering Sea Convention, loc. cit. above (n. 5), in particular Article XI(7)(c) which permits only the flag State to prosecute violations.

For a treaty example permitting intervention against vessels on the high seas by non-flag States in the pollution context, see the 1969 Convention Relating to Intervention on the High Seas in Cases of Oil Pollution Casualties (in force 6 May 1975), extended to other forms of pollution by a 1973 Protocol (in force 30 March 1983): text reproduced in Birnie and Boyle, *Basic Documents on International Law and the Environment* (1995), at p. 204. Intervention is restricted under Article I of the 1969 Convention to 'such measures on the high seas as may be necessary to prevent, mitigate or eliminate grave and imminent danger to their coastline and related interests from pollution or threat of pollution of the sea by oil . . .'. For analysis see Birnie and Boyle, op. cit. above (n. 111), at pp. 285–8. It should be noted that this does not *per se* permit the arrest of vessels.

regulated freedom curtailed by the obligation to conserve high seas fisheries, to co-operate with other States in their conservation and management, and even, *arguendo*, to use the precautionary approach in setting TACs unilaterally or through regional fora. An inchoate right of participation may be discerned, limited by treaty to States having a 'real interest in the fisheries concerned' but raising the intriguing prospect of wider participation in fisheries agreements by conservation-minded States. Whilst it might seem far-fetched to imagine regional fisheries organizations polarizing in the same manner as, for example, the International Whaling Commission, there is no doubt that increasing pressure on global fish stocks has consequences for the food security of both present and future generations.

Neither the treaties, nor the customary law principles, provide an easy answer to the problem of conserving and managing straddling stocks, a problem which necessarily finds its solution in co-operation between States.[397] In subjecting both EEZ and high seas conservation measures to the application of the principles of Article 5 SSA (reflected too in Article 61 (EEZ) and 119 (high seas) LOSC) and requiring consistency between them, the SSA ensures that long-term conservation and sustainable use of straddling fish stocks may be achieved through the qualification both of the high seas freedom of fishing *and* of the exercise of coastal States' sovereign rights within the EEZ.

Deficiencies in the present framework persist, however. The three tiers may falter on their foundation, the RFOs, in the ability of States parties to object to RFO measures including TACs. It is submitted that in such an instance the State or entity acting unilaterally to set its own TAC will still be subject to the general obligation to conserve stocks and to utilize the precautionary approach in setting the appropriate level of fishing effort. This is combined with the obligation to use the best scientific evidence available. Together, these form an obligation in respect of fisheries management schemes analogous to the emerging procedural obligation to conduct environmental impact assessment of projects likely to have a significant impact on the environment.

The continued hegemony of the flag State in respect of prosecution of violations of fisheries conservation measures on the high seas is a potentially grave defect in the edifice of LOSC/SSA/RFO. The SSA did not adopt the approach of the LOSC in respect of major pollution incidents in the EEZ and a recalcitrant flag State. The explanation for this restraint no doubt lies in the delicate balance between coastal and DWFN which the SSA seeks to maintain in its regulation of high seas fisheries, unlike the position in the EEZ where the coastal State enjoys

---

[397] For land-based co-operation in respect of migratory species, see the 1979 Convention on the Conservation of Migratory Species of Wild Animals (the Bonn Convention), reproduced in *International Legal Materials*, 19 (1980), at p. 15; for assessment, see Birnie and Boyle, op. cit. above (n. 111), at pp. 470–5.

sovereign rights and not even the residual character of this zone is now generally regarded as that of high seas. Yet placing the final obligation to impose sanctions[398] upon the flag State imposes this burden on the party least likely to benefit from zealous implementation of the obligation. This underscores the point made in a recent FAO document regarding the need to place high seas fisheries on a different economic footing from that of common property resource, providing greater economic incentive both to adopt conservation measures and effectively to enforce them.[399]

A persistent question is to whom the duty to conserve high seas living resources is owed. In this respect, international fisheries law may not substantially have progressed from the last century when the United States argued unsuccessfully that it was taking steps to conserve the Bering Fur seals for the benefit of humanity.[400] In the campaign for recognition of coastal States' 'special interest' in straddling stocks, there is the implicit assumption that high seas exploitation is necessarily over-exploitation whilst coastal States' resource exploitation is sustainable. Certainly the Canadian experience would suggest otherwise, notwithstanding the conservationist ethic behind more recent legislation. Giving priority to coastal State interests, and permitting the high seas extension of coastal State legislative and even enforcement jurisdiction, will not necessarily result in the long-term conservation and sustainable use of straddling fish stocks. It is submitted that widespread participation in the SSA, coupled with precautionary TACs implemented and enforced at the regional and sub-regional level, will achieve this objective.

---

[398] This is implied by Article 19(a) and (d) SSA, which provides that the flag State shall:

'(a) enforce [RFO conservation and management measures] irrespective of where violations occur;

. . .

(d) if satisfied that sufficient evidence is available in respect of an alleged violation, refer the case to its authorities with a view to instituting proceedings without delay in accordance with its laws and, where appropriate, detain the vessel concerned.'

Note, however, that while the flag State has an obligation to investigate, the obligation to take enforcement action is tempered with the exercise of its discretion in connection with the sufficiency of the evidence. Nor is there an explicit obligation to impose sanctions. Article 19(2) provides that '[s]anctions applicable in respect of violations shall be adequate in severity . . .', with the determination of applicability once again left to the flag State.

[399] FAO Fisheries Circular No. 853, *Marine Fisheries and the Law of the Sea: A Decade of Change* (1992), at p. 52.

[400] In the *Bering Fur Seals* arbitration, the United States argued unsuccessfully that it had a right of protection and of property in fur seals living on US islands in the Bering Sea when found outside the limits of the territorial sea: loc. cit. above (n. 106); see also Birnie and Boyle, op. cit. above (n. 111), at p. 493 ('The United States regarded itself as the trustee of the herd for the benefit of mankind'). For the text of the award of the tribunal see also Sands, Tarasofsky and Weiss (eds.), *Documents in Environmental Law* (1994), at p. 881.

Although in many ways the international regulation of fisheries presents a very different picture in the late 1990s from that of 100 years ago, it is salutary to recall the outcome of this 1893 arbitration. There is little in the SSA to suggest that notions of coastal, much less global, trusteeship or stewardship over straddling stocks are any more well developed today.

PROCEDURAL OBLIGATIONS IN INTERNATIONAL ENVIRONMENTAL AGREEMENTS*

By PHOEBE N. OKOWA‡

INTRODUCTION

One of the most significant developments since the UN Conference on the Human Environment (Stockholm)[1] is the proliferation of treaty instruments requiring States not so much to prevent environmental harm as to observe a number of discrete procedures before permitting the conduct of activities which may cause such harm.[2] The procedures may be described as instrumental, in so far as they are designed to ensure that the substantive decisions reached take into account anticipated environmental harm and the interests of those States likely to be affected. In general these obligations do not presuppose that anything has gone wrong; they are designed to come into play at the preliminary stages before any harm has occurred and usually before the potentially polluting or harm-generating activity has become operational. Thus States are increasingly required in a wide range of treaty instruments to conduct environmental impact assessments, notify potentially affected States of proposed activities which may entail environmental damage, exchange

---

* © Dr Phoebe N. Okowa, 1997.

‡ LLB (Nairobi), BCL, D Phil. (Oxon.); Lecturer in Law, University of Bristol.

[1] Report of the UN Conference on the Human Environment, UN Doc. A/CONF.48/14, at pp. 1–65 and Corr.1 (1972), *International Legal Materials*, 11 (1972), p. 1416.

[2] Although these duties have been most evident since 1972, the policy underlying the post-Stockholm developments may in fact be detected in a number of earlier treaties. This is especially the case in relation to treaties regulating the conduct of international watercourses. See, for instance, General Convention of 14 December 1931 between Romania and Yugoslavia concerning the Hydraulic System, *League of Nations Treaty Series*, vol. 135, p. 31; Agreement of 10 April 1922 for the Settlement of Questions Relating to Watercourses and Dykes on the German-Danish Frontier, *League of Nations Treaty Series*, vol. 10, p. 201; Treaty of 24 February 1950 between Hungary and the USSR concerning the Regime of the Soviet-Hungarian State Frontier, United Nations, *Legislative Texts and Treaty Provisions concerning the Utilization of International Rivers for other Purposes than Navigation* (hereinafter *Legislative Texts*), p. 823, No. 226; Convention of 23 September 1966 between Belgium and France on Radiological Protection with Regard to Ardennes Nuclear Power Station, *UN Treaty Series*, vol. 588, p. 227; Agreement of 8 July 1948 between Poland and the USSR concerning the Regime of the Polish–Soviet State Frontier, *UN Treaty Series*, vol. 37, p. 25; Treaty of 11 January 1909 between Great Britain and the United States of America relating to Boundary Waters and Questions concerning the Boundary between Canada and the United States, *Legislative Texts*, p. 260, No. 79; Convention of 11 May 1929 between Norway and Sweden on Certain Questions relating to the Law on Watercourses, *League of Nations Treaty Series*, vol. 120, p. 263; Treaty of 24 February 1950 between Hungary and the USSR concerning the Regime of the Soviet-Hungarian Frontier, *Legislative Texts*, p. 823, No. 226.

information on the effects of such activities, and where necessary enter into consultations. Because these obligations are designed to reconcile the interests of States proposing the conduct of activities and those likely to be affected, one recurrent theme in all these obligations is an attempt to ensure that, while some protection is given to putative victims, the sovereignty of the source State is also not unduly impeded in the process.

Despite the proliferation of procedural obligations in treaty and other non-binding instruments, very little explicit attention has been paid to the legal implications of these obligations. A systematic treatment of this subject is omitted in most of the major works.[3] In particular, the precise method of complying with the obligations in treaty instruments, as well as the legal consequences of non-compliance, remain unclear. Furthermore, it remains uncertain precisely which interests are regarded as falling within the ambit of procedural protection. The problem is particularly acute when proposed activities may cause harm to a multiplicity of States, For instance, the construction of a nuclear reactor, as the Chernobyl accident graphically demonstrates, could affect the territories of most States however far removed from the scene of an accident.[4] Yet it remains unclear which States are entitled to notification or consultation when nuclear installations are proposed or when accidents occur. Similarly, the contours of procedural protection in relation to activities with wide-ranging effects, such as transboundary air pollution, depletion of species or harm to the global commons, have never been clearly articulated.

The purposes of this article are to examine the nature and legal content of the procedural duties found in environmental treaties. The legal consequences of these obligations for the addressees, as well as the interpretation to be accorded to the specific duties and standards involved, will be considered. Finally, an attempt will be made to evaluate the impact of treaty obligations on the development of rules with a similar content in the sphere of customary law. An overall assessment of the strengths and weaknesses of these duties, as well as their legal significance outside the treaty regimes, will also be undertaken.

Although the content and stringency of procedural obligations may vary from one area of environmental regulation to another, it is suggested that in many cases the variations do not create significant distinctions of principle. The approach taken in this article is therefore in the form of a general survey rather than a detailed examination of the specific content

---

[3] But see Kirgis, *Prior Consultation in International Law* (Charlotsville, 1982); Sands, *Principles of International Environmental Law* (Manchester, 1994), chapter 16; Boyle, 'The Principle of Co-operation: The Environment', in Lowe and Wabrick (eds.), *The United Nations and the Principles of International Law* (London, 1994), p. 120.

[4] On the far-reaching effects of the Chernobyl accident, see NEA/OECD, *The Radiological Impact of the Chernobyl Accident in OECD Countries* (Paris, 1988); UKAEA, *The Chernobyl Accident and its Consequences* (London, 1987).

of procedural rules relating to the different sectors of the environment. No attempt will be made to consider the substantive content of these obligations in particular contexts. Rather, reference will be made to specific examples in order to illustrate the general propositions advanced, as well as any appreciable distinctions in the application of these duties in the different sectors of the environment.

I. THE RATIONALE OF PROCEDURAL OBLIGATIONS

Several underlying policy objectives may be detected in the diverse contexts in which States are required to observe procedural duties. First and foremost, it is clear that these obligations serve as a vehicle for the resolution of conflicts between States proposing the conduct of activities and those likely to be affected.[5] The conduct of environmental impact assessments, notification and consultation fosters the participation of interested parties in the decision-making process. This enables the parties affected to put forward their concerns, assess the impact of the proposed activities on the environment and take remedial measures accordingly.[6] Although it would seem that the putative victim States are not given a licence to dictate to the source State the manner and form of conducting activities on its territory, it is also the case that once their views are put forward a source State cannot ignore them without attracting legal consequences. The nature and form of these consequences will be discussed in some detail subsequently.

Secondly, it may be argued that the obligations are designed to ensure that the States contemplating the conduct of activities are appropriately advised as to the environmental effects of their actions at the domestic level as well as on the international scene. The requirement that States should conduct environmental impact assessments, enter into consultations and exchange information on a regular basis facilitates the collection and collation of relevant data on the effects of the proposed activities

---

[5] The role of consultation in the peaceful settlement of disputes is implicitly recognized in Articles 3(7) and 5 of the 1991 ECE Convention on Environmental Impact Assessment, *International Legal Materials*, 30 (1991), p. 802; Article 4(2) of the 1992 Convention on the Transboundary Effects of Industrial Accidents, *International Legal Materials*, 31 (1992), p. 1333; Kirgis, op. cit. above (n. 3), p. 375; Utton, 'International Environmental Law and Consultation Mechanism', *Columbia Journal of Transnational Law*, 12 (1973), p. 56 at p. 66; Sands, op. cit. above (n. 3), p. 606.

[6] This aspect of procedural duties is implicit in the following instruments: Chapter 40 of *Agenda 21, Report of the UN Conference on Environment and Development (UNCED)*, A/CONF.151/26/Rev.I, vol. 2, p. 9; Rio Declaration on Environment and Development, *International Legal Materials*, 31 (1992), p. 874; see also Preamble to the 1991 ECE Convention on Environmental Impact Assessment, loc. cit. above (n. 5).

on the environment. In this sense it may be argued that procedural obligations serve an instrumental function, since the observance of these standards is likely to assist the State of origin in reaching a substantively correct decision.[7] It is implicit in the environmental treaties that a commitment to procedural duties will help in shaping governmental policy, thus acting as a constraint against arbitrary decision-making, especially where the interests of other States are likely to be affected.

Thirdly, it may be argued that procedural obligations encompass a broad notion of fairness, a form of procedural due process which dictates that those individuals or States likely to be affected by proposed activities should be given a chance to participate in the decision-making process and have their interests or concerns taken into account.[8] In this sense the duties of environmental impact assessment, notification and consultation dictate a predetermined method of conducting the decision-making process without suggesting any particular outcome.

Finally it may be argued that procedural obligations epitomize new trends in international law in general and especially in relation to the protection of the environment, which are designed to ensure that governments involve those who are likely to be affected by proposed activities in the decision-making processes. This may require that citizens of the State of origin, as well as nationals of other States, be given a chance to present their views to those responsible for ultimate decision-making.[9]

---

[7] See Ludwik A. Teclaff, *Water Law in Historical Perspective* (New York, 1985), p. 240.

[8] This underlying objective is implicit in Articles 2(6) and 3(8) of the 1991 Environmental Impact Assessment Convention, which provides that the public in the territory of the affected State should be informed of, and be provided with possibilities for making comments or objections on, the proposed activity: loc. cit. above (n. 5). Under Article 6(1) the State of origin is obliged to take into account the comments received in deciding whether or not to proceed with the project. See also Article 9 of the Convention on the Transboundary Effects of Industrial Accidents, loc. cit. above (n. 5); Article III of the Convention relating to Intervention on the High Seas in Cases of Oil Pollution Damage, 1969, *UK Treaty Series*, No. 77 (1971) (Cmnd. 6056); the *Lake Lanoux* arbitration (1957), 24 ILR at p. 126; Birnie and Boyle, *International Law and the Environment* (Oxford, 1992), p. 103.

[9] See, for instance, Article 15 of the Report of the ILC Working Group on International Liability for the Injurious Consequences of Acts not Prohibited by International Law, Forty-Eighth Session, 1996, Doc. A/CN.4/L.5333, p. 62; see also Principle 10 of the Rio Declaration on Environment and Development, *Report of the UN Conference on Environment and Development*, op. cit. above (n. 6); Article 16 of the Convention on the Protection and Use of Transboundary Watercourses and International Lakes, *International Legal Materials*, 31 (1992), p. 1312; Article 3, paragraph 8, of the Convention on Environmental Impact Assessment in a Transboundary Context, loc. cit. above (n. 5); Article 17 of the Convention on the Protection of the Marine Environment of the Baltic Sea, UNEP, *Selected Multilateral Treaties in the Field of the Environment, Reference Series 3* (Nairobi, 1983), p. 405; Article 6 of the United Nations Framework Convention on Climate Change, *International Legal Materials*, 31 (1992), p. 849; 1974 Nordic Environment Protection Convention, *UN Treaty Series*, vol. 1092, p. 279; see also Sands, 'International Law in the Field of Sustainable Development', this *Year Book*, 65 (1994), pp. 357–8.

II. THE NATURE AND FORM OF PROCEDURAL OBLIGATIONS IN
ENVIRONMENTAL TREATIES

(i) *Environmental Impact Assessments*

In general it may be said that environmental impact assessment is a preliminary method of investigation aimed at determining not just the viability of a proposed project but also, and more significantly, the effect of the proposed activity on the domestic environment[10] as well as on the territory of other States, Environmental impact assessments are designed to ensure that decision-makers pay explicit attention to environmental factors at an early stage so that environmentally sound decisions can be made. These preliminary assessments have also been devised to enable States to develop appropriate anticipatory policies, thus assisting them to prevent, mitigate and monitor significant adverse impact in general and more specifically in a transboundary context.[11]

A large number of legal instruments expressly provide for the duty to conduct environmental impact assessments.[12] It is nevertheless arguable that even in those instances where no specific provision is made, environmental impact assessment may be taken to be implicit in other procedural duties, in particular the duty to notify other States of proposed activities that may entail transboundary harm.[13] In many of the environmental treaties under discussion, States are only under a duty to notify other States of planned activities if they entail a risk of causing

[10] The requirement in some treaty regimes that States should conduct environmental impact assessment at the domestic level, even when no direct transboundary effects are anticipated, illustrates the increasing acceptance that the management by a State of its own environment is a matter of international concern. See, for instance, Article 14 of the Convention on Biological Diversity, *International Legal Materials*, 31 (1992), p. 822; Article 4(*f*) of the Climate Change Convention, loc. cit. above (n. 9); Article 7 of the 1979 Convention on Long-range Transboundary Air Pollution, *United Kingdom Treaty Series*, No. 57 (1983) (Cmnd. 9034); Article 14 of the IAEA Convention on Nuclear Safety, *International Legal Materials*, 33 (1994), p. 1518.

[11] See Preamble to the 1991 ECE Convention on Environmental Impact Assessment in a Transboundary Context, loc. cit. above (n. 5); Birnie and Boyle, op. cit. above (n. 8), p. 96; see also ILC, Report of the Working Group on International Liability for the Injurious Consequences of Acts not Prohibited by International Law, loc. cit. above (n. 9), p. 50.

[12] See Principle 17 of the Rio Declaration on Environment and Development, loc. cit. above (n. 6); 1991 Agreement between the United States and Canada on Air Quality, *International Legal Materials*, 30 (1991), p. 676; Article 2 of the 1991 ECE Convention on Environmental Impact Assessment in a Transboundary Context, loc. cit. above (n. 5); Article 6 of the 1974 Nordic Environmental Protection Convention, loc. cit. above (n. 9); Article 206 of the 1982 United Nations Convention on the Law of the Sea, *International Legal Materials*, 21 (1982), p. 1261; the 1986 Convention for the Protection of the Natural Resources and Environment of the South Pacific Region (Noumea), *International Legal Materials*, 26 (1987), p. 38; UNEP Guidelines of 1987 on 'Goals and Principles of Environmental Impact Assessment', UNEP Resolution GC14/25; Article 8 of the Protocol to the Antarctic Treaty on Environmental Protection, *International Legal Materials*, 30 (1991), p. 1461; Article 12 of the 1983 Convention for the Protection and Development of the Marine Environment of the Wider Caribbean Region, *UK Treaty Series*, No. 38 (1988) (Cm 399).

[13] See Articles 5 and 8(*b*) of the 1979 ECE Convention on Transboundary Air Pollution, loc. cit. above (n. 10).

transboundary harm. However, the determination of harm for purposes of notification presupposes the existence of mechanisms for detecting the likely impact of proposed activities on the environment.[14] Moreover, meaningful consultations can only take place if the precise nature and effects of the proposed activity have been investigated. It is suggested that, unless a State has conducted a preliminary assessment, it will in most instances not be in a position to discharge this obligation.

Secondly, it may be argued that such assessments may be a relevant factor in determining whether a State has acted with the requisite degree of diligence in discharging its customary law or treaty-based duty to prevent environmental harm.[15] A State that fails to assess the impact of proposed activities on the territories of other States can hardly claim that it has taken all practicable measures with a view to preventing environmental damage. An argument to this effect was made by New Zealand in the 1995 proceedings involving France.[16] New Zealand maintained that it was not open to France to argue that it had taken all appropriate measures to prevent, reduce and control pollution in the environment area, when in the circumstances it had failed to conduct environmental impact assessment.[17] Like other procedural obligations discussed in the following paragraphs, environmental impact assessment serves an auxiliary role as a standard against which the diligence exercised by a State is to be measured. If damage occurs, it is suggested that the failure by a State to conduct environmental impact assessment may give rise to a presumption that 'due diligence' has not been observed.

In its dispute with the Slovak Republic concerning the construction and operation of the Gabcikovo-Nagymaros barrage system, Hungary laid emphasis on the likely environmental damage that the project could give rise to, and the fact that the nature of these risks had not been evaluated through appropriate environmental impact assessment procedures as required by international law.[18] Implicit in the argument is the suggestion that even where such assessments are not explicitly

---

[14] See Birnie and Boyle, op. cit. above (n. 8), p. 105.

[15] See Francioni in Lang, Neuhold and Zemanek (eds.), *Environmental Protection and the Environment* (London, 1991), p. 203; Handl, *Proceedings of the American Society of International Law*, 1980, pp. 223–5; Bilder, 'The Settlement of International Environmental Disputes', University of Wisconsin Sea Grant College Program *Technical Report 231*.

[16] *Request for an Examination of the Situation in accordance with paragraph 63 of the Court's Judgment of 20 December 1974 in the Nuclear Tests (New Zealand v. France) Case, aide-mémoire* of 21 August 1995, p. 17; see also the dissenting opinion of Judge *ad hoc* Sir Geoffrey Palmer, *ICJ Reports*, 1995, p. 381 at p. 411.

[17] Verbatim Record, CR95/20, Public Sitting of 12 September 1995.

[18] These arguments were advanced by Hungary in its Declaration made when terminating the bilateral treaty between her and Czechoslovakia regulating the project; see *International Legal Materials*, 32 (1993), p. 1260, esp. pp. 1268, 1273, 1274, 1275, 1276 and 1287. The parties subsequently agreed to submit the dispute to the International Court of Justice: see Hungary–Slovak Republic, Special Agreement for Submission to the International Court of Justice of the Differences between them concerning the Gabcikovo-Nagymaros Project, *International Legal Materials*, 32 (1993), p. 1293.

provided for, the discharge of the other duties imposed on States, in particular, the prevention of environmental damage, would usually necessitate some preliminary assessments.

(ii) *Is there a Consistent Body of Principles Governing the Conduct of Environmental Impact Assessment?*

The most straightforward answer would be to say that this will in each case depend on the terms of the treaty in question. This largely follows from the argument advanced elsewhere in this work that, with the exception of notification in emergency situations, none of the procedural obligations, including the duty to conduct environmental impact assessment, have passed into the corpus of customary international law. But even this fudges the issue. With the exception of the 1991 ECE Convention on Environmental Impact Assessment,[19] none of the existing treaties explicitly provide for the minimum content of a proper environmental impact assessment. It is therefore still necessary to determine the substantive content of environmental impact assessments even under treaty regimes. However, a caveat must nevertheless be entered. Even if a set of principles were agreed upon, their application is bound to be context-dependent, given the varied nature of activities that may require environmental impact assessment. On this reasoning, the kind of assessments that should precede the conduct of nuclear tests need not be identical with those required in relation to industrial activities.

With the exception of the arguments advanced by New Zealand in the *Nuclear Tests* cases,[20] it has not been possible to unearth any relevant State practice on the conduct of environmental impact assessment. Yet the issue is of central importance. As Bowett has suggested, unless the essential elements of environmental impact assessment were identified, 'there was a risk that a State might appear to have fulfilled its obligations by carrying out a study of some kind, whereas in reality, it had totally failed to have the potential risk properly assessed'.[21] It then becomes impossible to hold such a State accountable in the absence of standards against which its conduct may be judged.[22] An improper assessment may in fact undermine the entire structure of procedural obligations, for a State could simply avoid the notification and consultation duties, as well

---

[19] Loc. cit. above (n. 5).

[20] Loc. cit. above (n. 16); see also Declaration by the South Pacific Ministers adopted at their meeting at Brisbane, Australia, 16–17 August 1995, reproduced as Annex 8 in the *Request for an Examination of the Situation*, loc. cit. above (n. 16).

[21] See Summary Records of the Meetings of the Forty-Fifth Session, *Yearbook of the International Law Commission*, 1993, vol. 1, p. 34, para. 6.

[22] Professor Utton has suggested that the environmental impacts of proposed activities should be systematically considered in a third-party forum prior to the initiation of the activity: loc. cit. above (n. 5), p. 56 at p. 68.

as any form of external scrutiny, by concluding that the activity in question does not entail any form of adverse impact.

The International Law Commission's Working Group on International Liability for Injurious Consequences of Acts not Prohibited by International Law addressed its attention to the issue of content of environmental impact assessment, but decided that, given the varied nature of the contexts in which such assessments are required, the specifics should be governed by the domestic laws of the governments concerned.[23] However, this approach ignores the fact it may still be important to check the performance of domestic systems against external standards if a degree of consistency is to be maintained.

A broad range of standards and largely non-controversial principles may nevertheless be detected in existing treaty instruments. The 1991 ECE Convention on environmental impact assessment, for instance, specifies in some detail the minimum components of a good environmental impact assessment.[24] Given the unique nature of the 1991 ECE convention, it will be given extended treatment subsequently. The United Nations Environment Programme (UNEP) has also promulgated a set of fairly detailed rules and principles for the conduct of environmental impact assessment.[25] Although the UNEP principles are essentially non-binding, they have normative potential and are likely to influence the standards adopted in State practice.

(iii) *Five Principles Underlying Treaty Instruments on Environmental Impact Assessment*

The principle that the assessment must be carried out when the proposed activity is still at the planning stage and has not been put into effect seems to enjoy a substantial degree of support in treaty practice as

[23] International Law Commission, Report of the Working Group on International Liability for the Injurious Consequences of Acts not Prohibited by International Law, loc. cit. above (n. 9), p. 52.

[24] Loc. cit. above (n. 5).

[25] Principle 4 of the UNEP Guidelines on 'Goals and Principles of Environmental Impact Assessment', loc. cit. above (n. 12), lists the following as the essential components of a proper environmental impact assessment procedure:

'(a) a description of the proposed activity;

(b) a description of the potentially affected environment, including specific information necessary for identifying and assessing the environmental effects of the proposed activity;

(c) a description of practical alternatives, as appropriate;

(d) an assessment of the likely or potential environmental impacts of the proposed activity and alternatives, including the direct, indirect, cumulative, short-term and long-term effects;

(e) an identification and description of measures available to mitigate adverse environmental impacts of the proposed activities and alternatives and an assessment of those measures;

(f) an indication of gaps in knowledge and uncertainties which may be encountered in compiling the required information;

(g) an indication of whether the environment of any other state or areas beyond national jurisdiction is likely to be affected by the proposed activity or alternatives;

(h) a brief, non-technical summary of the information provided under the above headings.'

well as in the literature.[26] The rationale is not difficult to find; it would be pointless to continue with the procedure once the project in question has been completed.[27] Even if the exercise reveals that severe environmental consequences may result, it would be too costly to abandon the project. Most of the treaties that provide for environmental impact assessment reflect this principle and rightly provide that environmental impact assessment should precede the conduct of the activity in question.[28] For instance, Article 14 of the Convention on Biological Diversity provides:

1. Each Contracting party, as far as possible and as appropriate, shall:
(a) Introduce appropriate procedures requiring environmental impact assessment of its proposed projects that are likely to have significant adverse effects and where appropriate, allow for public participation in such procedures;
(b) Introduce appropriate arrangements to ensure that the environmental consequences of its programmes and policies that are likely to have significant adverse impacts on biological diversity are duly taken into account.[29]

In a few instances the nature of the activity may require periodic evaluation through further impact assessments.[30] As a corollary of the first principle, it is also generally provided in treaty instruments that the State proposing to conduct an activity that may entail transboundary harm should communicate the results of the environmental impact assessments to the potentially affected States or, where a multiplicity of States are involved, to an international organization.[31]

The second broad principle that finds support in treaty practice is that the activity in question must carry with it the risk of serious or

[26] Article 206 of the 1982 Convention on the Law of the Sea, loc. cit. above (n. 12); Article 6 of the 1974 Nordic Environmental Protection Convention, loc. cit. above (n. 9); Article 14(1) of the 1985 Association of South East Asian Nations Agreement on the Conservation of Nature and Natural Resources (ASEAN Agreement), *Environmental Policy and Law*, 15 (1985), p. 64; Articles 1 and 4 of the 1985 EC Environmental Assessment Directive, Council Directive 85/337/EEC, *Official Journal of the EC*, 1985, L175, p. 40; see also the *Report of the Expert Group on Environmental Protection and Sustainable Development: Legal Principles and Recommendations* (1986), pp. 58–60.

[27] See the argument of New Zealand in the *Nuclear Tests* case (*New Zealand* v. *France*), loc. cit. above (n. 16), p. 40, paragraph 82.

[28] See also Articles 4, 5, 26 and 53 of the 1988 Convention on the Regulation of Antarctic Mineral Resource Activities, *International Legal Materials*, 27 (1988), p. 868; Article 2(2) of the 1991 Protocol to the Antarctic Treaty on Environmental Protection, loc. cit. above (n. 12); Article 12 of the 1983 Convention for the Protection and Development of the Marine Environment of the Wider Caribbean Region, loc. cit. above (n. 12); Article 16 of the 1986 Convention for the Protection of the Natural Resources and Environment of the South Pacific Region, loc. cit. above (n. 12); Article 7 of the 1983 US-Mexico Agreement to Co-operate in the Solution of Environmental Problems in the Border Area, *International Legal Materials* 22 (1983), p. 1025; Articles 14, 19 and 20 of the ASEAN Agreement on Conservation of Nature and Natural Resources, loc. cit. above (n. 26).

[29] See also Article 206 of the 1982 Law of the Sea Convention, loc. cit. above (n. 12).

[30] The possibility of conducting a post-project analysis is clearly contemplated by Article 7 of the 1991 ECE Convention on Environmental Impact Assessment, loc. cit. above (n. 5).

[31] See Article 16 of the Noumea Convention for the Protection of the Natural Resources and Environment of the South Pacific Region, loc. cit. above (n. 12); Article XI of the 1978 Kuwait Regional Convention for Co-operation on the Protection of the Marine Environment from Pollution, *UN Treaty Series*, vol. 1140, p. 133.

substantial environmental harm. Thus, in general, a State is only under a duty to conduct environmental impact assessment if the proposed project falls within the range of activities deemed likely by it to have adverse impact.[32] The restriction can in part be explained. It is probably influenced by a desire not to overburden the source State. Rigidly applied to all activities, these procedures could very easily lead to indecision and stagnation. Environmental impact assessment procedures are costly and can be time-consuming. By restricting the application of environmental impact assessment to those instances where significant harm is anticipated, an attempt is made to balance the interests of the putative victim and the increased costs to the source State in carrying out such assessments.

With the exception of a few conventions,[33] it is widely provided that the State proposing the activity is the sole determinant of the likelihood or seriousness of adverse impact. This is unsatisfactory, for a State could simply evade conducting environmental impact assessment by stating that the proposed activity does not entail any significant risk for the environment. Furthermore, the determination of the source State is in many cases final, thus closing any possibility of external scrutiny. In almost all the treaty instruments, there is no obligation on the State of origin to supply any reasons supporting its decision.

However, in the *Nuclear Tests* cases (*New Zealand* v. *France*), New Zealand argued that a State likely to be affected must be given a chance to verify for itself the results of environmental impact assessment carried out by the State of origin, and an opportunity to propose additional or different investigations.[34] An argument to the same effect was advanced by the South Pacific Environment Ministers in their Brisbane Declaration.[35] While in general it is accepted that claims to sovereignty are not absolute and that encroachments may in fact take place under a title of international law, the interpretation placed by New Zealand on the content of environmental impact assessment requirement on the face of it appears too onerous. This is especially so when examined against the background of a marked reluctance on the part of States to accept

[32] Article 2 of the 1991 ECE Convention on Environmental Impact Assessment, loc. cit. above (n. 5); Principle 10 of the Rio Declaration on Environment and Development, loc. cit. above (n. 12); Principle 1 of the UNEP Goals and Principles of Environmental Impact Assessment, loc. cit. above (n. 12); see also commentary to Article 10 of the draft articles proposed by the International Law Commission's Working Group on Liability, loc. cit. above (n. 9); see also New Zealand arguments in *Request for an Examination of the Situation*, loc. cit. above (n. 16), p. 44.

[33] Appendix IV of the 1991 ECE Convention on Environmental Impact Assessment envisages joint reference to an inquiry commission, in those instances where the source and affected State are unable to agree on the environmental effects of proposed activities, above (n. 5); see also Article 3(5) of the Protocol to the Antarctic Treaty on Environmental Protection, above (n. 12).

[34] See *Request for an Examination of the Situation in accordance with paragraph 63 of the Court's Judgment of 20 December 1974 in the Nuclear Tests (New Zealand v. France) Case*, Verbatim Record, CR 95/20, p. 25.

[35] Loc. cit. above (n. 16), Annex 8, especially para 9.

mechanisms that unduly compromise their freedom of action. On the other hand, if obligations for the conduct of environmental impact assessments are seen as context-dependent, then onerous standards may be justified in relation to the conduct of nuclear tests. This may be especially the case where the State of origin has been far from candid in its relations with potentially affected States. It is, however, difficult to accept that the New Zealand interpretation of the essential elements of a good environmental impact enjoy general support, or that they can be of general application. None of the treaties under consideration permit third States to propose additional or different assessments if they are dissatisfied with those put forward by the State of origin.

The third general principle that may be suggested is that the nature of the activity as well as its likely consequences must be clearly articulated and communicated to those likely to be affected. Again the rationale is one of procedural fairness—that those likely to be affected by a decision should be fully apprised of its implications and given an opportunity to respond. Secondly, since most of the treaties considered require the parties to enter into consultations, such consultations cannot be meaningfully conducted until the results of the assessment have been communicated.

Fourthly, it is suggested that pending full consultations with those likely to be affected, a State proposing the conduct of an activity that entails transboundary harm should be debarred from proceeding with it. Any other conclusion would render nugatory the very aims of environmental impact assessment procedures.

The fifth and final principle that may be implied is that the State receiving notification of the intention to conduct an environmental impact assessment must respond within a reasonable time. The rationale underlying this suggestion is given extended treatment when the legal consequences of notification are considered. Here it suffices to note that in the absence of a temporal limitation, delay on the part of the notified State could effectively stultify the activities of the State of origin. The requirements of good faith therefore dictate that the notified State should respond promptly.

(iv) *Environmental Impact Assessment under the 1991 Espoo Convention*[36]

This Convention deserves extended treatment since it is the first multilateral treaty to consider the procedural obligations of States in some detail. It is also more specific in the delineation of the rights and duties of States, and provides for a systematic mechanism of supervision.

---

[36] 1991 ECE Convention on Environmental Impact Assessment in a Transboundary Context, loc. cit. above (n. 5).

The provisions of the convention are of a general character and apply to all activities the conduct of which may entail transboundary harm. The Convention requires States to conduct environmental impact assessments before permitting the construction and operation of a range of fixtures which include oil refineries, power stations, nuclear installations, smelters and waste disposal installations.[37]

Article 2 requires the States parties to establish an environmental impact assessment procedure. Appendix II, which forms an integral part of the Convention, sets out in detail the minimum content of environmental impact documentation which must be communicated to a potentially affected State. Again, the Agreement is unique in its attempt to standardize the nature and form of environmental impact assessment. As a minimum the documentation must include: a description of the proposed activity, reasonable alternatives if any, potential environmental impact and mitigative strategies, uncertainties as to likely impact, and monitoring/management programmes, as well as plans for post-project analysis. The State of origin is under a further duty to allow public participation for nationals of the affected State on the same terms as those accorded to its own nationals.[38]

The Convention further requires both the State of origin and the affected State to enter into consultations on the basis of the information supplied. The consultations must, in particular, take into account the outcome of the environmental impact assessment.[39] Moreover, the affected State may on its own motion require that an activity in the State of origin be subjected to environmental impact assessment even if it is not in the category of activities requiring automatic notification under Appendix I, if it has reason to believe that the activity as planned entails a significant risk of transboundary pollution.[40] This provision is significant in so far as it places responsibility on the potentially affected State to be vigilant in the protection of its interests. As a matter of principle, it is arguable that a State that stays silent after becoming aware that a proposed activity is likely to prejudice its rights may be precluded at a subsequent date from asserting the impermissibility of the activity, or that the regime of prevention enacted is not adequate.[41] The non-

---

[37] For an extensive list of activities which must be subjected to environmental impact assessment, see Appendix I, loc. cit. above (n. 5).

[38] Loc. cit. above (n. 5), Article 2(6).

[39] Loc. cit. above (n. 5), Article 6.

[40] Disagreements as to the likely environmental impact of proposed activities are to be referred to a Commission of Inquiry in accordance with the provisions of Appendix IV unless the parties agree on another method of settling the dispute.

[41] In the *Anglo-Norwegian Fisheries* case, the International Court implicitly acknowledged that a State that had been put on notice that conduct prejudicial to its own rights was taking place may be taken to have acquiesced if it fails to respond or protest: *ICJ Reports*, 1951, p. 116; see also counter-memorial of the Government of Denmark, *Great Belt* case (*Finland v. Denmark*), Pleadings, vol. I (1992), p. 255; Reisman, *Nullity and Revision* (New Haven, 1971), p. 385; see also Mendelson, in *Le droit international au service de la paix, de la justice et du développement: Mélanges Michel Virally*

protesting State may be taken to have waived its rights and acquiesced in the new state of affairs.

It is also interesting to note that the draft articles proposed by the Working Group of the International Law Commission in connection with its work on international liability for injurious consequences of acts not prohibited by international law also require a degree of vigilance on the part of the putative victim. In a curious provision, a potentially affected State may be required to conduct its own environmental impact assessment, if it has serious reason to believe that an activity proposed by the State of origin entails transboundary harm. The assessment of the risk is designed to enable it to have a legitimate basis for insisting on consultations with the State of origin,[42] in those circumstances when the State of origin has failed to notify it of proposed activities. If the assessment reveals that the activity proposed entails a serious risk of environmental harm, then the State of origin is required to pay an equitable share of the costs of the assessment. It is difficult to understand why the State of origin should in fact not be required to pay the entire amount, since in principle the obligation to conduct environmental impact assessment rests with source States as a necessary consequence of exercising their sovereign rights.

The effect of a provision of this nature is likely to be to encourage the State of origin to externalize costs of environmental impact assessments, knowing that should it turn out that the activity entails a risk of transboundary harm, it will only be required to pay an equitable share of the costs of such assessments. The provision is also likely to deter States with well-founded concerns about activities proposed by other States, since they may end up being saddled with the entire cost of the assessment, should it in fact turn out that the activity in question does not entail any environmental harm.

(v) *The 1991 Air Quality Agreement*[43]

Specific consideration of the environmental impact assessment requirement is also to be found in the 1991 Air Quality Agreement between the United States and Canada. Article V(i) of the Agreement requires each party to 'assess proposed actions, activities, and projects within the area under its jurisdiction that, if carried out would be likely to cause significant transboundary air pollution'. The party likely to be affected by the activity must be informed of the environmental impact assessment being undertaken. The State of origin is further under a duty

---

(Paris, 1991), p. 376 at p. 380; J. Bruhacs, *The Law of Non-Navigational Uses of International Watercourses* (Dordrecht, 1993), p. 178.

[42] Loc. cit. above (n. 9), Article 18.

[43] Loc. cit. above (n. 12).

to enter into consultations with States likely to be affected, but only if the latter so request. The comprehensive nature of these provisions was no doubt influenced by the fact that both the United States and Canada had for many years provided for environmental impact assessment in their domestic legislation.[44]

Perhaps the greatest shortcoming of the 1991 Air Quality Agreement is the lack of external control over environmental impact assessment. This could have the undesirable consequence that a State may carry out an assessment in a manner that minimizes the extra-territorial effects of the activity proposed. Since the notification and consultation duties are in fact dependent on a finding of adverse impact, a State may avoid scrutiny by simply presenting a favourable outcome of the assessment carried out. In the 1991 ECE Convention, this undesirable outcome is somewhat mitigated by the provisions of Article 3(7). The article provides that a State that has reason to believe that a proposed activity will cause significant transboundary harm may insist on an environ-mental impact assessment. If the parties concerned disagree as to the likely impact of a proposed activity, they may have the matter referred to an inquiry commission in accordance with the provisions of Appendix IV.

Neither the 1991 Air Quality Agreement nor the ECE Convention on Environmental Impact Assessment requires a State to refrain from the conduct of an activity should the consultations or conciliation prove unsuccessful. Indeed there is hardly any evidence in the practice of States which supports the cessation of a proposed project if a potentially affected State objects or when the resulting consultations are futile. The issue has been extensively discussed by the International Law Commis-sion without reaching any definitive result. Significantly, the 1996 Report of the Working Group on International Liability for Injurious Consequences of Acts not Prohibited by International Law has also refrained from endorsing any right of veto exercisable at the behest of a potentially affected State when the consultations prove futile.[45]

In a comprehensive survey of relevant State practice, the Secretariat of the United Nations was unable to uncover any instance where an activity was enjoined on account of the environmental risks it entailed, even though such requests had at times been made.[46] Pragmatic solutions have

---

[44] Canada, Environmental Assessment Act 1980 (Ontario); US, National Environmental Policy Act 1969, 42 USC ss. 4321–47.

[45] Loc. cit. above (n. 9).

[46] See Survey of State practice relevant to international liability for injurious consequences arising out of acts not prohibited by international law, *Yearbook of the International Law Commission*, 1985, vol. 2, part 1, especially at p. 71, para. 324 and para. 333. Although finding that no transboundary harm had actually occurred, the tribunal in the *Lake Lanoux* arbitration denied the existence of a veto exercisable at the behest of a potentially affected State: 24 ILR 101 at 130; Barboza, 'International Liability for the Injurious Consequences of Acts not Prohibited by International Law and Protection of the Environment', *Recueil des cours*, 247 (1994-III), p. 295 at p. 332.

from time to time been reached by States, but these it will be suggested, are not based on any consistent set of legal principles. The question whether potentially affected States should be entitled to enjoin activities proposed by other States under certain circumstances is of central importance to the entire topic under discussion, and will be given extended treatment after an examination of the content of the other relevant procedural obligations.

III. NOTIFICATION

(i) *The Varied Nature of the Duty to Notify*

There are a number of different contexts in which States are placed under a duty to notify other States of activities on their territories which are potentially harmful to the environment. The form and stringency of the obligation varies with the nature of the activity triggering it. Many treaties and international instruments require source States to notify potentially affected States of any projects on their territories which carry a risk of serious environmental harm.[47] Usually the obligation is directly provided for, but even when it is not, it must be taken as implicit in any requirement to conduct environmental impact assessment, since such assessments are carried out with a view to protecting the interests of third States.

The aim of the notification is to initiate a framework for consultations so that the State of origin can take into account the interests of those likely to be affected. The obligation may also be identified in relation to emergency situations such as industrial or nuclear accidents.[48] In the context of accidents, notification is intended to prepare the potential victim State and to give it a chance to adopt evacuation and other mitigative strategies. Although this is never clearly articulated, it would seem that factors such as the nature and seriousness of environmental

---

[47] See for instance Article 14(*d*) of the Convention on Biological Diversity, loc. cit. above (n. 10); Article 6 of the Convention on the Transboundary Movement of Hazardous Wastes and their Disposal, *International Legal Materials*, 28 (1989), p. 657; Article 14 of the Convention on the Protection and Use of Transboundary Watercourses and Lakes, loc. cit. above (n. 9); OECD Principles, Council Recommendation C(74) 224 (1974), Annex, Part F, in *OECD and the Environment* (Paris, 1986); ILA Montreal Rules on Transfrontier Pollution, Article 5, *Report of the 60th Conference* (Montreal, 1982); Principle 19 of the Rio Declaration on the Human Environment, loc. cit. above (n. 6); ILC Draft Articles on the Law of Non-Navigational Uses of International Watercourses, UN Doc.A/CN.4/L492 and Add. 1 (1994), Article 12; Articles 3 and 10 of the Convention on the Transboundary Effects of Industrial Accidents, loc. cit. above (n. 5); Article 3 of the Convention on Environmental Impact Assessment in a Transboundary Context, loc. cit. above (n. 5).

[48] Articles 2 and 3 of the Convention on Early Notification of a Nuclear Accident, *International Legal Materials*, 25 (1986), p. 1377; Article 10 of the Convention on the Transboundary Effects of Industrial Accidents, loc. cit. above (n. 5); Article 6 of the Convention on the Control of Transboundary Movements of Hazardous Wastes and their Disposal, loc. cit. above (n. 47).

harm that is likely to occur, geographical proximity of a State to the project proposed or accident that has occurred, as well as the importance of the interests likely to be affected, are all factors which may determine the stringency of the notification requirements.[49] The obligation is more rigorously and strenuously applied in relation to activities located in border areas. The seriousness of the resulting harm may also justify wide-ranging and fairly onerous notification requirements. Thus notification duties are rigidly applied in relation to nuclear installations located in border areas.[50]

Two problems nevertheless arise in relation to the scope of notification duties. In the first place the formula to be employed in determining a potentially affected State remains fraught with difficulty. This is especially the case where the activity in question by its very nature may affect the interests of a multiplicity of States. None of the treaties that provide for notification advert to this problem, but the issue has received some attention in the International Law Commission in its discussion of international liability for injurious consequences of acts not prohibited by international law, without any definitive result.

During the debate on the topic in 1986, Professor Ushakov pointed out that the repercussions of an accident of Chernobyl magnitude could have real consequences from one end of the earth to the other. This then raised the question whether the whole of mankind was to be notified, and if so, to which items the notification should relate.[51] The Special Rapporteur, as well as many members of the Commission who spoke on the topic, were of the view that where a plurality of States was likely to be affected by a proposed activity, then notification and consultations should take place within the framework of an international organization.[52] Although it is conceivable that international organizations such as UNEP and the IAEA may have a limited competence in this context, it is not immediately apparent that their institutional structures are designed to facilitate routine notifications and the attendant duty of consultation. It must be remembered that even where a multiplicity of States is involved, the actual implementation of notification and consultation duties is designed to take place in a bilateral context. The problem is a real one and the

[49] But see Appendix III of the 1991 ECE Convention, which contains similar criteria: loc. cit. above (n. 5).

[50] For a comprehensive survey of notification requirements in nuclear treaties, see Boyle, 'Nuclear Energy and International Law: An Environmental Perspective', this *Year Book*, 60 (1989), p. 257, especially at pp. 280 ff.

[51] See Summary Records of the Meetings of the Thirty-Eighth Session, *Yearbook of the International Law Commission*, 1986, vol. 1, p. 200.

[52] See Summary Records of the Meetings of the Forty-Second-Session, *Yearbook of the International Law Commission*, 1990, vol. 1, contributions by Calero Rodriguez, pp. 235–6; Ogiso, p. 262; see also Summary Records of the Meetings of the Forty-First Session, *Yearbook of the International Law Commission*, 1989 vol. 1, contributions by McCaffrey, p. 91; Shi, p. 94; Graefrath, pp. 105 and 106; Bennouna, p. 110.

utilization of offices of international organizations hardly seems a practical response, since there are very few such organizations.

The second problem relates to the general difficulty of identifying the types of activities and form of injuries which the State of origin has to notify to the potentially injured State. It appears from State and treaty practice that identification of relevant activities does not lend itself to a single formula. Sometimes it is the nature of the resources being used that is taken as the point of departure, such as shared rivers, the high seas, or the airspace. In other cases it is the potential scale or probability of harm to which the activity gives rise that may determine the nature and extent of notification. Given the changing character of technology and knowledge about the effects of activities, the International Law Commission has rightly refrained from drawing a definitive list of activities that should be subjected to the notification requirement.[53] The Commission observed that whether or not an activity requires notification should be determined on an *ad hoc* basis, having regard to all the surrounding circumstances.

(ii) *The Content of the Notification Requirement*

Despite the general absence of precision as to the normative content of notification in treaty instruments, it is suggested that a number of substantive principles must be implied if the obligation is not to be deprived of practical significance. In treaty regimes and in the works of codification bodies, it is frequently provided that the notification duty requires the State of origin to inform the State which might be affected of any activity on its territory (either planned or actual) which entails a risk of transboundary harm. It is also required to provide the potentially affected State with all the necessary information relating to the nature of the activity, the risks involved, as well as the injury it may cause.[54] This is to enable the potentially affected State to make its own evaluation of the situation. The notification is also intended to provide the parties with an opportunity for finding an amicable solution to the problems raised,

---

[53] See Barboza, Eighth Report on international liability for injurious consequences arising out of acts not prohibited by international law, *Yearbook of the International Law Commission*, 1992, vol. 2, part 1, p. 59 at p. 70; Report of the Commission to the General Assembly on the Work of its Forty-Fifth Session, *Yearbook of the International Law Commission*, 1993, vol. 2, part 2; Report of the Working Group on Liability for Injurious Consequences of Acts not Prohibited by International Law, Article 1 and commentary, loc. cit. above (n. 9).

[54] Barboza, Second Report on international liability for injurious consequences of acts not prohibited by international law, *Yearbook of the International Law Commission*, 1986, vol. 2, part 1, p. 152; ILC Draft Articles on the Non-Navigational Uses of International Watercourses, loc. cit. above (n. 47), Articles 11 and 12; Article 5 of the 1979 ECE Convention on Long-Range Transboundary Air Pollution, loc. cit. above (n. 10); Article 5 of the 1991 ECE Convention on Environmental Impact Assessment, loc. cit. above (n. 5); see also Articles 11 and 12 of the 1974 Nordic Convention, loc. cit. above (n. 9).

taking into account the interests of both the State of origin and the affected State.

For instance, in almost all treaties concerning transboundary air pollution, States are increasingly required to give notice to potential victim States before carrying out activities which may entail an appreciable risk of pollution. The 1979 ECE Convention, the 1991 US Canada Air Quality Agreement and a number of bilateral treaties on nuclear installations increasingly require States to give notice to potential victim States before carrying out activities that entail a significant risk of transboundary harm. It is suggested that the aim here, as in other procedural contexts, is to provide a mechanism for avoiding costly and unnecessary disputes, by promoting the exchange of views between interested States before the initiation of a project that may have significant transboundary consequences. The notified State then has the opportunity to assess the situation, and to have its views taken into account by the State of origin. This also gives the State of origin an opportunity to make the necessary adjustments with a view to avoiding appreciable transboundary harm.[55]

The main treaties that regulate the environment incorporate, in one form or another, the duty to give prior notice of planned activities that entail a significant risk of transboundary harm.[56] Article 8(b) of the 1979 ECE Convention on transboundary air pollution, for example, places the States parties under an obligation to provide information on major changes in national policies and in general industrial development, and their potential impact on transboundary air pollution.[57] The notification is to be made either to the Executive Body or to the States parties.

Similar notification requirements are to be found in the 1991 Air Quality Agreement, which places both Canada and the United States under a duty to notify each other before embarking on projects that may entail transboundary air pollution. Similarly, Article 5 of the 1974 Nordic Convention requires source States to notify any other States that may be affected by proposed activities, and to give such States an opportunity to comment on the project as proposed.

Extensive notification provisions are also set out in the 1991 ECE Convention on Environmental Impact Assessment. Article 3(1) of the Agreement provides:

> For a proposed activity listed in Appendix I that is likely to cause a significant adverse transboundary impact, the party of origin shall, for the purposes of ensuring adequate and effective consultations under Article 5, notify any party

---

[55] See *Lake Lanoux* arbitration, 24 ILR 101 at 140; Jiménez de Aréchaga, 'International Law in the Past Third of a Century', *Recueil des cours*, 159 (1978–I), p. 194 at p. 195.

[56] Loc. cit. above (n. 12).

[57] Loc. cit. above (n. 10).

which it considers may be an affected party as early as possible and no later than when informing its own public about that proposed activity.[58]

The rest of the paragraphs in Article 3 list in some detail the information which must accompany the notification. These include the nature of the proposed activity, as well as any available information on its possible transboundary impact. It must also indicate a reasonable time within which a response to the notification is required. This is a major improvement on the instruments previously considered, for it attempts to give a substantive content to the notification duty. The 1979 ECE Convention on Transboundary Air Pollution and the 1991 Canada/United States Air Quality Agreement are both silent on the information which should be contained in the notification and the obligations of the notified State.

With the exception of the 1991 ECE Convention on environmental impact assessment, none of the existing environmental treaties specify the legal consequences that are attached to the notification duty. The 1991 ECE Convention spells out in some detail the obligations of the notified State. Under Article 3(3), the affected party shall respond to the notification within the time specified by the State of origin in the communication, and indicate whether or not it wishes to participate in the environmental impact assessment proposed by the source State. The source State may also require the affected State to supply reasonably obtainable information relating to the likely environmental impact on the territory of the affected State. However, even in those treaties where no specific provision is made for a time within which a response to the notification should be communicated, it may be presumed, from the requirement that international obligations are to be performed in good faith, that a State should respond within a reasonable time.[59]

(iii) *Notification in Nuclear Treaties*

The duty to notify other States before embarking on an activity that may entail significant transboundary consequences assumes an added

---

[58] Loc. cit. above (n. 5).

[59] The Special Rapporteur of the ILC on the topic of international liability for injurious consequences arising out of acts not prohibited by international law suggested that a response to notification should be made within six months: see Barboza, Sixth Report, Draft Article 19, *Yearbook of the International Law Commission*, 1990, vol. 1, p. 226. However, the temporal element has been omitted in recent works, no doubt influenced by the non-binding character of the procedural obligations as proposed. A six-month limitation period has also been suggested by the ILC in its Draft Articles on the Non-Navigational Uses of International Watercourses: see Article 13, loc. cit. above (n. 47). On good faith see the *Nuclear Tests* cases, *ICJ Reports*, 1974, p. 268, para. 46, and p. 473, para. 49; see also the *Great Belt* case, counter-memorial of the Government of Denmark, *Pleadings*, vol. 1 (1992), p. 248, supporting the general argument that a response to notification should be made within a reasonable time.

importance in relation to the siting and construction of nuclear installations. This is largely due to the very serious risks inherent in the operation of nuclear reactors: understandably most States are apprehensive about them. A large number of bilateral treaties regulating the location and construction of nuclear installations contain elaborate provisions on notification and supply of information. Most of these regulate the construction of such installations in border or frontier areas. It is generally accepted that owing to their proximity to human settlements, serious accidents at border installations may have significant radiological impact on neighbouring States.

As a result, a long line of European treaties place installation States under a duty to notify other States that are likely to be affected of their intention to construct or licence the construction of a nuclear plant in a border area.[60] Most of these treaties must be considered against the background of a long-standing European tradition of subjecting issues affecting common borders to a special neighbourhood regime or *voisinage* even in the absence of a treaty. This principle of good neighbourship has been extensively examined in the literature. Although its exact implications cannot be stated with any precision, there is some agreement that it requires a State to take into account the detrimental effects of a proposed activity on neighbouring territories.[61]

The agreement between Denmark and the Federal Republic of Germany on nuclear installations along the common border is a pertinent example of the treaty mechanisms in this context. The key provision in Article 1 provides that:

The contracting party of the constructing state shall inform the contracting party of the neighbouring state of nuclear installations along the border and make available to it suitable documents. This applies to decisions regarding the location of a plant, to authorizations for its construction and operation, fundamental changes in such authorizations and to its termination . . . [62]

The article applies to all installations located in an area of approximately 30 km on either side of the common border. Similar agreements have been entered into between Spain and Portugal,[63] the Netherlands and the Federal Republic of Germany,[64] and also between Switzerland and the

[60] For a comprehensive discussion of these treaties, see Boyle, loc. cit. above (n. 50).

[61] Berber, *Rivers in International Law* (London, 1959), pp. 211–23; J. Andrassy, 'Les relations internationales de voisinage', *Recueil des cours*, 79 (1951-II), pp. 77–180; Wildhaber, 'External Relations of the Swiss Cantons', *Canadian Yearbook of International Law*, 12 (1974), pp. 211–21; Lammers, *Pollution of International Watercourses* (Dordrecht, 1984), pp. 563–9.

[62] *International Legal Materials*, 17 (1978), p. 274.

[63] 1980 Agreement between Spain and Portugal on Co-operation in Matters Affecting the Safety of Nuclear Installations in the Vicinity of the Frontier, in Ruster and Simma, *International Protection of the Environment*, vol. 27 (1980), p. 420.

[64] Memorandum for the Agreement on Consultation of Nuclear Installations near Borders between the Federal Republic of Germany and the Kingdom of the Netherlands, in Ruster and Simma, *International Protection of the Environment*, vol. 27 (1980), p. 275.

Federal Republic of Germany.[65] The Nordic countries of Denmark, Finland, Norway and Sweden have also adopted a set of guidelines to govern nuclear safety conditions in respect of border installations.[66] The objectives of these guidelines as stated in the preamble are to enable the authorities in a construction State to have all relevant information and viewpoints pertaining to the location, construction and operation of a nuclear installation before permitting its construction. The fact that these principles are formally designated as guidelines certainly detracts from their legal quality as binding obligations. Nevertheless they must be viewed against the background of a legally binding Nordic Environmental Protection Convention, the substantive provisions of which provide for notification before permitting the construction of installations or the carrying out of any activity that may entail transboundary consequences.[67]

Even though it is undeniable that the location of a nuclear installation within the vicinity of a common border is certainly a greater threat than one located in the heartland, the nuclear accident at the Chernobyl plant demonstrates that there may well be a case for extending the notification duty to all States in a region. In particular instances it may be necessary to notify the entire community of States. The far-reaching effects of the accident indicate that in ideal circumstances notification should not be restricted to States abutting on a common border.[68] However, with the exception of emergency situations, States do not as yet appear willing to extend the notification requirement to all States in a region, and the issue has not been addressed as a matter of principle either in treaty regimes or State practice. It was noted that the International Law Commission has considered the issue in general terms without arriving at any concrete result.[69]

Almost all the treaty regimes analysed in the previous paragraphs emphasize that a construction State is under a duty *promptly* to notify potential victim States of any activities proposed that may have significant transboundary consequences. In principle no specific time would seem to be implied, but since the overall purpose of the notification is to enable the potential victim State to put forward its views before the commencement of the activity, such notification should be given at any time before the construction is authorized. As a matter of policy it is

[65] Switzerland–Federal Republic of Germany Agreement on Mutual Information on Construction and Operation of Nuclear Installations in the Border Area, (1983) II *Bundesgesetzblatt*, p. 743.

[66] Guidelines for Nordic Co-operation concerning Nuclear Installations in the Border Areas between Denmark, Finland, Norway in respect of Nuclear Safety Conditions, *Nuclear Law Bulletin*, 19 (1977), p. 38.

[67] Article 5 of the 1974 Nordic Convention on Environmental Protection, loc. cit. above (n. 9).

[68] On the effects of the accident, see *The Radiological Impact of the Chernobyl Accident in OECD Countries*, op. cit. above (n. 4); United Kingdom Atomic Energy Agency, *The Chernobyl Accident and its Consequences*, op. cit. above (n. 4).

[69] Loc. cit. above (n. 52).

suggested that potential disputes should be addressed speedily, and this would invariably require prompt notification. Although the treaties are silent on this, it would seem that the requirement of good faith in the conduct of international relations dictates that pending the reply of the notified State, the source State is debarred from implementing its plan.

(iv) *Notification in Emergency Situations*

It is generally agreed that notification duties assume an added significance in emergency situations, especially where these entail appreciable transboundary consequences. It has already been noted that, in general, notification requirements invariably enable States at risk to prevent damage by adopting precautionary measures, such as the evacuation of persons at risk, and necessary restrictions on movement and consumption of foodstuffs.

In the literature, and in treaty regimes, there is general support for a duty to notify potential victim States of any sudden occurrences or emergency situations where these pose a significant risk of transboundary harm.[70] Of the treaty regimes providing for a duty to warn in emergency situations, the 1986 Convention on Early Notification of a Nuclear Accident is perhaps the most comprehensive and far-reaching.[71] This treaty, adopted in the aftermath of the Chernobyl disaster, entered into force in October 1986. It places source States under a duty to notify other States which may be physically affected by nuclear accidents occurring under their jurisdiction or control. Under Article 6, the source State is under a further duty promptly to respond to any request for further information or consultations sought by an affected State party. The accident must have actual or potential risk of transboundary radioactive contamination.[72]

The rationale behind prompt notification under the convention is to enable States at risk to minimize the radiological consequences of the accident, and to take necessary protective measures for the benefit of the environment and their citizens. The Convention is of course not exhaustive and many gaps remain in its application. For instance, the determination of 'radiological safety significance', for purposes of notification, is

---

[70] Schneider, *World Public Order of the Environment* (London, 1979), p. 159; Birnie and Boyle, op. cit. above (n. 8), p. 108; Sands, op. cit. above (n. 3), p. 608; Schachter, *International Law in Theory and in Practice* (Dordrecht, 1991), p. 373; 1982 Law of the Sea Convention, Arts. 198, 211(7), loc. cit. above (n. 12); Article 13 of the Basel Convention on the Transboundary Movement of Hazardous Wastes and their Disposal, loc. cit. above (n. 47).

[71] Loc. cit. above (n. 48); see also Adede, *The IAEA Notification and Assistance Conventions in Case of a Nuclear Accident* (Dordrecht, 1987).

[72] Articles 1 and 2, loc. cit. above (n. 48); Adede, op, cit. above (n. 71).

left to the discretion of the source State. This is a major shortcoming, since a source State could simply evade its duties by reaching the conclusion that the accident is not 'radiologically significant'.

Several bilateral treaties have been negotiated by other States as a direct consequence of the Convention.[73] The bilateral European treaties regulating the construction of nuclear installations within the vicinity of common borders, discussed in the previous section, also provide for the timely supply of information in cases of emergency. The 1974 Nordic Convention on Environmental Protection, the 1979 ECE Convention on Transboundary Air Pollution and its Protocols, and the 1991 Air Quality Agreement, as well many other treaties referred to previously, contain no specific provisions on notification duties in emergency situations. The obligations of the parties to these conventions are therefore determined by the content of customary law, considered subsequently.

(v) *Possible Consequences of Failure to Respond to Notification*

Two legal consequences of the duty to notify merit consideration. Although the treaty regimes are silent on the question of time frame within which a reply to notification should be received, it is arguable that the notified State is placed under a duty to respond to the notification within a reasonable time.[74] The restriction on time within which a response must be communicated is to ensure that notification does not impose an unnecessarily onerous obligation on the State of origin, for in the absence of a time limit a notified State could effectively paralyse the activities of the source State.[75] Secondly, it is suggested that failure to respond may give rise to a presumption of acquiescence in the proposed activity and preclude any subsequent assertion that the activity as proposed, planned or executed failed to take into account the interests of

---

[73] For the list of bilateral treaties negotiated since 1986 see Boyle, loc. cit. above (n. 50); see also 1987 Agreement between Belgium and the Netherlands on Co-operation, *Nuclear Law Bulletin*, 41 (1988), p. 42; Norway–Sweden Agreement on Exchange of Information and Early Notification relating to Nuclear Facilities, *Environmental Policy and Law*, 17 (1987), p. 41; Finland–USSR Agreement on Early Notification of a Nuclear Accident, *Nuclear Law Bulletin*, 39 (1987), p. 54; Brazil–Argentina Agreement on Early Notification and Mutual Assistance, *Nuclear Law Bulletin*, 39 (1987), p. 36; Denmark has also entered into similar agreements with Sweden and Poland, *Nuclear Law Bulletin*, 39 (1987), p. 35, and *Nuclear Law Bulletin*, 41 (1988), p. 49 respectively.

[74] See *Lake Lanoux* arbitration, 24 ILR 101 at 128; Barboza, Sixth Report on liability for injurious consequences of acts not prohibited by international law, *Yearbook of the International Law Commission*, 1990, vol. 2, part 1, Draft Article 19, p. 94. The temporal element has however been omitted in the subsequent reports of the Special Rapporteur and in the Report of the Working Group.

[75] *Lake Lanoux* arbitration, 24 ILR 101 at 128; see also *Railway Traffic between Lithuania and Poland*, PCIJ, Series A/B, No. 42, pp. 108 ff.

the affected State.[76] In his Sixth Report on Liability for Acts not Prohibited by International Law, the Special Rapporteur of the ILC, Mr Barboza, had proposed that any State that does not reply to a notification within six months should be presumed to have found the proposed measures satisfactory.[77]

Reisman also notes that silence in the face of a putative threat to established rights may give rise to a presumption of estoppel. He notes that a party:

. . . is expected to be vigilant in the protection of his rights. If he is not and thereby creates an impression of waiving his rights, and if others rely on this impression, . . . the law will not tolerate the belated exercise of the right.[78]

Although not specifically concerned with notification in the context of environmental obligations, the arguments of the parties in the *Great Belt* case had some bearing on the issues under consideration. In that case, it will be recalled, Finland challenged the right of Denmark to construct a bridge across the Danish straits on the ground that the bridge as planned would interfere with the Finnish rights of unimpeded passage through the straits in question.[79] A large part of the parties' respective arguments was devoted to the consequences that attach to the notification duty. In its counter-memorial, Denmark argued that Finland had failed to respond to a Danish notice, in which Denmark outlined its intention to construct a bridge across the Great Belt. The notice had been circulated by the Danish Government to all States that had an interest in the Great Belt. Denmark maintained that as a result of that notification, Finland was precluded from asserting, twelve years later, that the bridge would interfere with its entrenched rights under international law. In an important passage Denmark observed that:

In the interest of promoting stability in international relations based on general

---

[76] The decisions of the International Court in the following cases may be cited in support of the proposition: *Temple of Preah Vihear* case, *ICJ Reports*, 1962, pp. 22–3; *Gulf of Maine* case, *ICJ Reports*, 1984, p. 308; case concerning the *Frontier Dispute (Burkina Faso v. Mali)*, *ICJ Reports*, 1986, p. 554 at p. 575; and in the *Elettronica Sicula (ELSI)* case, the International Court observed that estoppel could in certain circumstances arise from silence when something ought to have been said: *ICJ Reports*, 1989, p. 6 at p. 44; Barboza, Sixth Report, *Yearbook of the International Law Commission*, 1990, vol. 2, part 1, Draft Article 19. Many writers subscribe to the view that unilateral acts of Governments including *notification* may give rise to distinct legal consequences. See Brownlie, *Principles of Public International Law* (4th edn., Oxford, 1990), p. 637; E. Suy, *Les actes juridiques unilatéraux en droit international public* (Paris, 1962), p. 22; Pellet, *Droit international public* (Paris, 1987), pp. 328–35; J. Bruhacs, op. cit. above (n. 41), p. 173.

[77] *Yearbook of the International Law Commission*, 1990, vol. 1, part 1, Draft Article 19; see also Article 13 of the ILC Draft Articles on the Non-Navigational Uses of International Watercourses, loc. cit. above (n. 47).

[78] Reisman, op. cit. above (n. 41), pp. 384–5; see also Schwarzenberger, 'The Fundamental Principles of International Law', *Recueil des cours*, 87 (1955–I), p. 195 at pp. 256–7; MacGibbon, 'Estoppel in International Law', *International and Comparative Law Quarterly*, 7 (1958), p. 468 at p. 501; Mendelson, loc. cit. above (n. 41), p. 376 at p. 380.

[79] *ICJ Reports*, 1991, p. 3.

concepts of good faith and equity, international law must require *protest* or some form of action on the part of states in order to preserve their legal positions, in cases where they believe that their legal rights may be infringed by acts performed or contemplated by another state . . . [80]

Denmark argued that since no objection had been presented to the successive Danish Governments in charge of the project until the Finnish reaction in 1990, more than twelve years after the initial notification, it had been entitled to rely on the silence of Finland in proceeding with the project.

It is significant that the memorial of Finland accepted the legitimacy of the argument in principle, but observed that on the facts no presumption of estoppel or acquiescence could be made. Finland argued that since the construction of the bridge had been postponed many times by Denmark, and was in fact the subject of domestic opposition, Finland was under the impression that an immediate response was not called for.[81] The Court did not pronounce on these issues as the case was discontinued and settled out of court.[82] Nevertheless, in its previous judgments the International Court has accepted that failure to respond to a state of affairs that has legal consequences for the party notified may give rise to a presumption of acquiescence or estoppel.[83]

(vi) *Some Conclusions on Notification*

The very limited nature of State practice in this area makes it difficult to state the essential components of a notification requirement with any degree of precision. The following principles, it is suggested, enjoy a substantial degree of support in the existing legal experience.

(*a*) In the first place the potentially affected State must be promptly notified before the activity takes place.

---

[80] *Great Belt* case, counter-memorial of the Government of Denmark, *Pleadings* (1992), p. 255 (original emphasis).

[81] *Great Belt* case, memorial of the Government of Finland, *Pleadings* (1991), pp. 170–80.

[82] Case concerning *Passage Through the Great Belt (Finland v. Denmark)*, order of 10 September 1992, *ICJ Reports*, 1992, p. 348; for note on the settlement, see *International Legal Materials*, 32 (1993), pp. 101–3; Koskenniemi, 'L'affaire du passage par le Grand Belt', *Annuaire français de droit international*, 38 (1992), p. 905.

[83] See, for instance, the *Temple of Preah Vihear* case, *ICJ Reports*, 1962, pp. 22–3. In the *Gulf of Maine* case a similar argument based on preclusion or estoppel was made by Canada. Canada had argued that since the United States was aware that Canada had issued sea-bed exploration permits over disputed areas of the Georges Bank and had failed to protest or react, the United States was precluded from challenging the validity of the Canadian claims. The judgment of the Chamber of the International Court, although accepting the argument in principle, concluded that no case for estoppel had been made on the facts: *ICJ Reports*, 1984, pp. 305–8; see also case concerning the *Frontier Dispute (Burkina Faso v. Mali)*, *ICJ Reports*, 1986, p. 554 at p. 575. In the *Elettronica Sicula (ELSI)* case, the International Court observed that estoppel could arise from a State's failure to respond when in light of the circumstances such a response was expected: *ICJ Reports*, 1989, p. 6 at p. 44; Sinclair, 'Estoppel and Acquiescence', in Lowe and Fitzmaurice (eds.), *Fifty Years of the International Court of Justice* (Cambridge, 1996), p. 104.

(*b*) The notification must be accompanied by information of a kind that would enable the potentially affected State to appreciate the effects of the proposed activity. The nature and form of information may vary with the nature of the activity as well as the risk it entails.

(*c*) The precise scope of the notification requirement in relation to activities that may affect a multiplicity of States remains uncertain.

IV. Duties Pertaining to the Exchange of Information

Apart from notification of discrete incidents that may entail a risk of transboundary harm, the treaties on environmental protection also require States parties to undertake the monitoring of sources and effects of pollutants on an on-going basis. The parties are further required to exchange the information so collected either bilaterally or through a supervisory organ charged with the implementation of these agreements. This information is particularly relevant to the understanding of the nature, extent and harmful effects of changes in the environment.[84] It enables the participating States to evaluate the effectiveness of measures taken in light of changing scientific evidence.[85]

Almost all the treaty instruments on environmental protection provide for the exchange of information on a regular basis.[86] A pertinent example is to be found in Articles 3, 4, 8 and 9 of the 1979 ECE Convention on Transboundary Air Pollution. Article 8 of this treaty is particularly relevant. It provides that the States parties are under a duty to exchange information bilaterally and within the framework of the Executive Body for the Convention on the following matters:

(*a*) data on emissions at periods of time to be agreed upon, of agreed air pollutants, starting with sulphur dioxide, coming from grid-units of agreed size; or on the fluxes of agreed air pollutants, starting with sulphur dioxide across national borders, at distances and at periods of time to be agreed upon;

(*b*) major changes in national policies and in general industrial development,

---

[84] ILA, First Preliminary Report of the Committee on Legal Aspects of Long-Distance Air Pollution, *Report of the 61st Conference* (1984), p. 402.

[85] Ibid., Draft Article 6, pp. 401–2; Schneider, op. cit. above (n. 70), p. 149.

[86] Convention on Biological Diversity, Article 17, loc. cit. above (n. 10); Convention on the Transboundary Effects of Industrial Accidents, Article 15, loc. cit. above (n. 5); Article 5 of the Vienna Convention on the Protection of the Ozone Layer, *UK Treaty Series*, No. 1 (1990) (Cm 910), in force 22 September 1988; Article 9(1) of the Montreal Protocol on Substances that Deplete the Ozone Layer, *UK Treaty Series*, No. 19 (1990) (Cm 977); Article 4(1)H of the Convention on Climate Change, loc. cit. above (n. 9); Principle 20 of the Stockholm Declaration, loc. cit. above (n. 1), and Principle 9 of the Rio Declaration, loc. cit. above (n. 6); Articles 61, 143, 200 and 244 of the 1982 Convention on the Law of the Sea, loc. cit. above (n. 12); Article 6(2) of the Protocol to the Antarctic Treaty on Environmental Protection, loc. cit. above (n. 12); Article 13 of the Convention on the Control of Transboundary Movement of Hazardous Wastes and their Disposal, loc. cit. above (n. 41).

and their potential impact, which would be likely to cause significant changes in long-range transboundary pollution;

(c) control technologies for reducing air pollution relevant to long-range transboundary air pollution; . . .

Similarly, Articles VI and VII of the 1991 US/Canada Air Quality Agreement contain the parties' basic duties with regard to monitoring and exchange of information. Under Article VI, the parties are obliged to carry out scientific and technical research 'in order to improve their understanding of transboundary air pollution concerns and to increase their capability to control such pollution'. Article VII requires the parties to exchange, on a regular basis and through the Air Quality Committee, information on emission monitoring, technologies, measures and mechanisms for controlling emissions, atmospheric processes and effects of air pollutants.

Arrangements along the same lines are also to be found in the agreements between Mexico and the United States in respect of their common border. In the 1980s, Mexico and the United States reached agreements of co-operation with regard to the protection and improvement of the environment in their common border.[87] Pursuant to those arrangements, a further agreement was reached on transboundary air pollution caused by copper smelters.[88] Article II of this agreement contains provisions on monitoring of emissions, record-keeping and reporting systems, with a view to providing each of the parties with adequate information necessary for pollution control.

The determination of breach of obligations of this character is bound to be problematic in so far as their performance cannot be tested objectively. There are no uniform principles or rules regulating the collection or dissemination of information. A State may decide to supply minimal information, or install inadequate monitoring equipment, but in the absence of institutional or third party mechanisms or criteria for determining the level of compliance it would be very difficult to make out a case of breach. However, there is a possibility of subjecting these duties to external scrutiny where supervisory organs have power to review on an on-going basis the performance of the parties. This is especially the case when information requirements are accompanied by a duty to submit periodic reports to an institution charged with monitoring compliance. Furthermore, should damage occur, failure to supply such information may be taken as evidence that the State on whom the duty is incumbent has not exercised due diligence over activities under its jurisdiction and control.

---

[87] *International Legal Materials*, 20 (1981), p. 696.
[88] *International Legal Materials*, 22 (1983), p. 1025.

V. THE DUTY TO ENTER INTO CONSULTATIONS

(i) *The Nature of the Duty*[89]

The duty to carry out environmental impact assessments, as well as the duties of notification and exchange of information, only make sense if in the end an objection by a notified State is taken into account. In other words, the ultimate goal of such notification and supply of relevant information is to require the State of origin to accommodate the interests of the notified State, and if need be to adopt mitigative strategies for its benefit.[90] The aim in each case is to ensure that the activity is carried out in a manner least harmful to the environment. Through consultations, both the notifying and the notified States have an opportunity to discuss the impact of the proposed activities, and where possible to try and counteract their potential or actual adverse effects.[91]

Although it is envisaged that such consultations will normally take place after the State of origin has notified a putative victim of its proposed activities, some treaties and legal instruments in fact provide that even where no particular notification has been received by the potentially affected State, the latter State may seize the initiative and insist on such consultations as soon as it becomes aware of proposed activities.[92] These instruments impose a parallel obligation on the State of origin to accede to such a request.[93] Presumably in the absence of such a right the putative victim State has no means of compelling the State of origin to enter into consultations, since as is argued[94] subsequently there is very little evidence to support the existence of an autonomous obligation to enter into consultations under customary law. In the draft articles proposed by the Working Group of the International Law Commission, a potentially affected State can only insist on consultations if it has *serious* reason to believe that the activity proposed will interfere

[89] Utton, loc. cit. above (n. 5), p. 56; Kirgis, op. cit. above (n. 3). For an interesting analysis on the nature of consultations in the context of space treaties, see Jerzy Sztucki, 'International Consultations and Space Treaties', *Proceedings of the Seventeenth Colloquium on the Law of Outerspace* (1974), p. 147.

[90] See Survey of State practice relevant to international liability for injurious consequences arising out of acts not prohibited by international law, prepared by the UN Secretariat, loc. cit. above (n. 46), p. 22; 1986 Report of the Working Group on Liability for Injurious Consequences of Acts not Prohibited by International Law, loc. cit. above (n. 9), pp. 69–70.

[91] ILA, op. cit. above (n. 84), p. 407; see also ILC Draft Articles on the Non-Navigational Uses of International Watercourses, Article 17, loc. cit. above (n. 47).

[92] Article 3(7) of the 1991 ECE Convention on Environmental Impact Assessment, loc. cit. above (n. 5); Article 4(2) of the Convention on the Transboundary Effects of Industrial Accidents, loc. cit. above (n. 5).

[93] Article 18 of the Draft Articles on the Law of the Non-Navigational Uses of International Watercourses, loc. cit. above (n. 41); Article 3(7) of the 1991 ECE Convention on Environmental Impact Assessment, loc. cit. above (n. 5); ILC, Report of the Working Group on International Liability for Injurious Consequences of Acts not Prohibited by International Law, Draft Article 18, loc. cit. above (n. 9), pp. 71–2.

[94] Report of the Working Group, loc. cit. above (n. 9), p. 71.

with its established rights under international law.[95] However, the requirement that a State insisting on consultations should back its request with documents containing its own assessment does seem unjustifiably onerous and is likely to have the undesirable effect of deterring many genuinely concerned States.

(ii) *The Content of Prior Consultation in Treaty Instruments*

In addition to environmental impact assessment and the notification duties considered previously, a large number of treaty instruments in the environmental context also require the States parties to enter into consultations.[96] Although it is not possible to discuss the substantive provisions in all these treaties, a consideration of the more prominent ones gives a broad overview of the content of consultation requirements. A good example is Article 5 of the 1979 ECE Convention on Long-Range Transboundary Air Pollution which provides for intergovernmental consultations on request between States that are actually affected, or exposed to a significant risk of pollution, and those from whose territories such pollution originates. The provisions of this article are complemented by the more general provisions on exchange of information to be found in Article 8. This article, as noted previously, provides for routine exchange of information bilaterally, and within the framework of the Executive Body for the management of the Convention on such matters as major changes in national policies and in general industrial development, and their potential impact on transboundary air pollution. Implicit in this provision is the requirement of routine consultation in those instances where major changes in industrial policy are likely to cause long-range transboundary pollution on the territory of other States.

Article 5 of the Air Quality Agreement between Canada and the United States also requires the parties to consult with respect to activities that are the subject-matter of notification if the notified State so requests. Consultations are also required with regard to 'any continuing actions, activities, or projects that may be causing significant transboundary air pollution', as well as changes to laws, regulations or policies that, if carried out, would be likely to affect transboundary air pollution. Paragraph 4 of Article 5 states that such consultations shall have as their object the adoption of mitigative strategies for the benefit of the affected party. Finally, under Article XI, the parties further undertake to consult on any matter within the scope of the treaty. Any matter not settled by

---

[95] Loc. cit. above (n. 9), p. 72.

[96] See, for instance, the 1974 Nordic Environmental Protection Convention, Article 11, loc. cit. above (n. 9); 1991 ECE Convention on Environmental Impact Assessment, loc. cit. above (n. 5), Article 5; 1992 Industrial Accidents Convention, Article 4, loc. cit. above (n. 5); 1968 African Convention on the Conservation of Nature and Natural Resources, *UN Treaty Series*, vol. 1001, p. 4; ASEAN Agreement, Articles 19(2)(*d*) and (*e*) and 20(3)(*b*) and (*c*), loc. cit. above (n. 26).

the parties after consultation is to be referred to third-party dispute settlement procedures in accordance with the provisions of the Agreement.[97] The provision on dispute settlement is a marked improvement on previous treaties, since it contemplates a failure to resolve differences through the consultation process and provides a mechanism for their resolution.

The 1974 Nordic Convention also contains fairly specific provisions on consultation. Article 11 of the Convention provides:

> Where the permissibility of environmentally harmful activities which entail or may entail considerable nuisance in another contracting State is being examined by the Government or by the appropriate minister or ministry of the State in which the activities are being carried out, consultations shall take place between the States concerned if the Government of the former State so requests.[98]

Article 12 of the Convention provides that the parties engaging in consultations in accordance with Article 11 may insist on the appointment of a commission to investigate the matter. The Chairman of the Commission under these circumstances is to be appointed jointly by the parties and is to be a national of a third State. The three other members of the Commission are to be appointed from each of the States concerned, and no decision is to be taken on the project that is the subject-matter of consultations until the Commission has delivered its opinion. Like the Air Quality Agreement, this Convention also anticipates that the parties may be unable to reach agreement through consultations, thus necessitating the intervention of a third party. However, the provision falls short of expressly requiring the parties permanently to forego the proposed activities should an environmentally acceptable regime prove impossible.

(iii) *Consultation and Nuclear Treaties*

It was noted previously that the regulation of nuclear installations, especially in border areas, is largely governed by special treaty regimes. In addition to notification and supply of information, these treaties also provide for intergovernmental discussions on siting, maintenance, and safety aspects at the request of any State exposed to the risk of transboundary harm.[99]

The 1980 Agreement between Portugal and Spain, on co-operation in

---

[97] See Article XIII: this provides that any dispute not settled by the parties through consultation shall first be subject to negotiation, and if still not resolved the parties may either refer the dispute to the International Joint Commission under Article IX or X of the Boundary Waters Treaty, or any other dispute settlement procedure of their choice.

[98] Nordic Convention on the Protection of the Environment, loc. cit. above (n. 9).

[99] For a general consideration of these treaties, see Boyle, loc. cit above (n. 50).

matters affecting the safety of nuclear installations,[100] limits such consultation to matters of radiological safety but excludes from the scope of consultations matters relating to the actual siting and licensing of nuclear installations. This is a major shortcoming of the provisions of this treaty. The location of a nuclear installation in the vicinity of a common border or in the neighbourhood of population settlements may have very serious implications for safety, and ought to be taken into account in any regulatory arrangement. The omission nevertheless reveals the deep anxiety and sensitivity felt by most governments in relation to issues pertaining to the regulation and control of nuclear energy.

Germany has also entered into agreements regulating the construction of nuclear installations with most of her neighbours. These agreements, unlike the bilateral agreement between Spain and Portugal, provide for consultation with regard to all aspects of nuclear regulation including siting and licensing of installations within the vicinity of the border. Article 6 of the agreement between Denmark and the Federal Republic of Germany provides:

> Consultations regarding safety conditions relating to a decision on the location, construction or operation of a nuclear installation along the border, . . . shall take place between the contracting parties of the constructing and neighbouring States, if one of them makes an appropriate request.

A similar agreement has been signed between the Federal Republic of Germany on the one hand and the Netherlands,[101] Switzerland[102] and France on the other. The Netherlands has also entered into similar arrangements with Belgium.[103] European Community law also requires Member States to enter into consultations before certain nuclear installations are constructed. Article 34 of the EURATOM Treaty obliges Member States to consult the Commission when they propose to conduct particularly dangerous nuclear experiments in their territories, and to obtain its consent if these are liable to affect other Member States. This in effect means that the Member State proposing the project may not proceed in the absence of the Commission's consent, and to that extent the provision is more stringent than the consultation requirements in the other treaty regimes discussed. Articles 41 and 43 go on to provide that Member States must consult with the Commission before constructing nuclear power stations or industries engaged in the nuclear fuel cycle.[104]

---

[100] Ruster and Simma, *International Protection of the Environment*, vol. 27 (1980), p. 420.

[101] Ruster and Simma, op. cit. above (n. 100), p. 275.

[102] See Switzerland–FRG Agreement on Mutual Information on Construction and Operation of Nuclear Installations in Border Areas, (1983) II *Bundesgesetzblatt*, p. 734.

[103] Agreement between Belgium and the Netherlands on Co-operation in Nuclear Safety, *Nuclear Law Bulletin*, 41 (1988), p. 42. Agreements have also been entered into between Belgium and France with regard to the installations of the Ardennes Nuclear Power Station, above (n. 2).

[104] See the EURATOM Treaty, 1957, *UN Treaty Series*, vol. 298, p. 162.

(iv) *Legal Consequences of the Consultation Process*

Few would dissent from the suggestion that the duty to enter into consultations is not a mere formality, but is in fact a procedural rule embodying a substantive value.[105] However, the nature of those values as well as the attendant legal consequences cannot always be stated with any degree of certainty. Although States have from time to time taken specific measures for the protection of the interests of potentially affected States, these, it will be suggested, have been in the form of pragmatic solutions, and were not necessarily grounded on any consistent set of legal principles. In other cases following on consultations, States have undertaken to guarantee compensation should damage occur. Nevertheless these too, it will be suggested, have been in the nature of *ex gratia* payments and therefore inconclusive for purposes of determining rules of general application.

(v) *What does Prior Consultation Entail?*

The majority opinion seems to favour the proposition that the duty to enter into consultations does not mean that the consent of an objecting State must be obtained before the initiation or continuation of an activity which poses a substantial risk of transboundary harm.[106] Rather, prior consultation requires that the views of the objecting State should be earnestly taken into account. The source State is required to endeavour to reconcile its own interests with those of the objecting State, and to seek to accommodate the interests of that State.[107]

The distinction between the requirements of prior consultation and prior consent was considered in the award of the international arbitral tribunal in the *Lake Lanoux* case.[108] Although the case was concerned with diversion of a shared water resource, the substance of the award is broad enough to encompass most cases of environmental interference. Spain had argued that both the traditional law of the Pyrenees as well as the specific provisions of the Treaty of Bayonne and the Additional Act dictated that no substantial change could be effected to the waters of

---

[105] *Lake Lanoux* arbitration, 24 ILR 101; ILC Report of the Working Group, loc. cit. above (n. 9), p. 67.

[106] Kirgis, op. cit. above (n. 3), p. 361; Utton, loc. cit. above (n. 5), p. 56 at p. 64; Birnie and Boyle, op. cit. above (n. 8), p. 106 at p. 107; Bruhacs, op. cit. above (n. 41), pp. 178–9. However, there is no reason in principle why prior consent should not be a condition for the legality of an activity if States desire: see, for instance, Article 6 of the Convention on the Control of Transboundary Movement of Hazardous Wastes, loc. cit. above (n. 47); Article 1 of the 1963 Nuclear Test Ban Treaty, *UN Treaty Series*, vol. 480, p. 43.

[107] Draft Article 8, ILA Committee on Legal Aspects of Transfrontier Pollution, op. cit. above (n. 84), p. 407; *Lake Lanoux* arbitration (1957), 24 ILR 101; see also Article 17 of the Draft Articles proposed by the ILC Working Group on International Liability for Injurious Consequences of Acts not Prohibited by International Law, loc. cit. above (n. 9), pp. 69–70.

[108] Loc. cit. above (n. 8).

Lake Lanoux without the prior consent or agreement of other riparian States.[109]

Rejecting the existence of any such requirement under treaty or customary law, the tribunal observed that such a restriction, if true, would amount to an intolerable interference with the sovereignty of France. The tribunal rejected the Spanish contention of a right to veto the proposed French project.[110] Referring more specifically to the requirements of consultation, the tribunal noted that France was under a duty to take into consideration all Spanish interests which were liable to be affected by the works proposed. It further observed that France was required to inform Spain of its intentions, hold consultations and pay reasonable regard to Spanish interests. It specifically emphasized that the discussions must be taken to have a substantive content and must not be limited to purely formal requirements such as taking note of complaints.[111]

The tribunal provided a catalogue of what it deemed unacceptable behaviour during the consultation process. This included breaking off discussions without justification, abnormal delays, disregard of the agreed procedures, systematic refusal to take into consideration adverse proposals or interests, and more generally violation of rules of good faith.[112] Although the tribunal noted that such behaviour may attract sanctions, it did not specify what form those sanctions might take. It may be argued that to the extent that procedural obligations are justiciable legal duties, a failure to conform with the basic tenets of the consultation process may attract the responsibility of the State in breach. The list provided by the tribunal is a useful guide as to what those tenets are, but these vary with the factual context of the consultations.

On the basis of the tribunal's pronouncements in the *Lake Lanoux* case and the jurisprudence of the International Court, two conclusions may be drawn. In the first place, where two States fail to arrive at a workable arrangement, the source State is perfectly entitled to carry on with the proposed project even in the face of opposition from potential victim States.[113] Moreover the potential victim State cannot insist that the

---

[109] Spanish memorial, at pp. 61–78, cited in 24 ILR at 112.

[110] Loc. cit. above (n. 8), pp. 129–30.

[111] Loc. cit. above (n. 8), p. 139.

[112] Loc. cit. above (n. 8). See also *North Sea Continental Shelf* cases (*Federal Republic of Germany* v. *Denmark* and *Federal Republic of Germany* v. *Netherlands*), judgment of 20 February 1969, *ICJ Reports*, 1969, especially paras. 85 and 86; see also the advisory opinion of the Permanent Court in *Railway Traffic between Lithuania and Poland, PCIJ*, Series A/B, No. 42, p. 116. In both cases the International Court and its predecessor emphasized the requirement to enter into negotiations in good faith and with a view to arriving at an agreement. Negotiation was not to be seen as a formal process which the parties undertook without any real intention of modifying their positions. It is suggested that although the Court was considering the essential components of negotiation duties, the requirements would equally apply to the consultation process.

[113] Bilder, 'The Settlement of International Environmental Disputes', loc. cit. above (n. 15), p. 2; Birnie and Boyle, op. cit. above (n. 8), p. 106.

activity should be carried out in any particular way or that any set of precautions be developed to safeguard its interests.[114] However, although State practice does not support the right of veto to be exercised at the behest of the potentially affected State, there is considerable evidence to suggest that in practice many States only carry out the proposed project after making specific undertakings to meet the concerns of the potentially affected State. It is necessary to consider the nature and form of these undertakings, as well their legal significance for the issues under consideration.

(vi) *The Nature of Settlements in State Practice*

There is some evidence in the practice of States to indicate that notwithstanding the absence of a general right to veto projects which entail environmental damage, States have been known to postpone, restructure, or even adopt specific measures to meet the concerns of the potentially affected State.[115] For example a dispute arose between Mexico and the United States concerning the operations of two United States companies (Payton Packing and Casuco) whose activities were causing environmental damage on the Mexican side of the border. Following an exchange of notes between the two governments, the United States companies undertook to modify the technical operations as well as the schedule of the plants' activities to ensure that inconvenience to Mexico was halted.[116] However, it is significant that the consultations that followed the exchange of notes made no reference to any legal principles.

The *Trail Smelter* arbitration was also preceded by fairly extensive study of the effects of sulphur fumes on farms located on the United States side of the border. In addition to awarding compensation, Canada was required to ensure that the Trail smelter plant did not exceed

---

[114] *Lake Lanoux* arbitration, 24 ILR 140–1; but see the proposals by Barboza, the ILC's Special Rapporteur on the topic of Liability for Acts not Prohibited by International Law. He envisages that in extreme situations, where a proposed activity entails a risk of serious transboundary harm, the activity should not be allowed to continue without the consent of the States threatened: Sixth Report, *Yearbook of the International Law Commission*, 1990, vol. 2, part 1, p. 94. It is nevertheless significant that this proposal was made *de lege ferenda*, and has been omitted in subsequent reports of the Rapporteur and of the Commission's working group. For a similar proposal see Jenks, 'The Scope and Nature of Ultra-Hazardous Liability in International Law', *Recueil des cours*, 117 (1966–I), p. 104 at pp. 173–4; Jiménez de Aréchaga, 'International Law in the Past Third of a Century', *Recueil des cours*, 159 (1978–I), p. 198.

[115] For a comprehensive survey of State practice, see Survey of State practice relevant to international liability for injurious consequences arising out of acts not prohibited by international law, prepared by the UN Secretariat, *Yearbook of the International Law Commission*, 1985, vol. 1, part 1, especially at pp. 71–4.

[116] See Whiteman, *Digest of International Law*, vol. 6 (Washington, 1968), pp. 258–9; see also the French decision to abandon the construction of some chemical factories following on German protestations, cited in ILA, 'Legal Aspects of the Conservation of the Environment', *Report of the 6oth Conference* (Montreal, 1982), p. 157 at p. 165.

emission limits during stated periods.[117] The legal context here was different since the modification was specifically mandated by a judicial tribunal. However, since Canada had in the past taken measures to meet United States concerns, it is equally conceivable that a similar outcome would have been reached through bilateral consultations. There is further evidence that, following the protests which accompanied the United States conduct of atmospheric nuclear tests at Bikini and Eniwetok atolls, the United States established danger zones for the protection specifically of Japanese interests.[118] In a border incident between France and Switzerland in 1892, the French Government decided to halt the military target practice exercises near the Swiss border until steps had been taken to avoid accidental transboundary injuries.[119]

In other instances where no feasible alternatives are envisaged, States of origin have either paid compensation or given guarantees to do so should harm result. The settlement between Finland and Denmark in relation to the dispute over the legality of the Danish proposal to construct a bridge over the main navigable channel of the Great Belt, to which reference has already been made, provides an interesting example of monetary compensation for potential inconvenience or interference with entrenched rights. Although not concerned with environmental damage, it nevertheless provides contemporary evidence of the arrangements that States may be prepared to make, before proceeding with activities that may cause harm to the interests of others.

It will be recalled that in its memorial submitted to the International Court of Justice, Finland had argued that the construction of a fixed link over the Great Belt as planned by Denmark would be incompatible with its right of innocent passage as guaranteed by international law.[120] After fairly protracted consultations between the two countries, Denmark paid Finland the sum of 90 million Danish Kroner which took into account the adjustments that the Finnish offshore industry would make to existing oil rig designs to enable passage through an alternative route or through the Great Belt in its modified condition.[121] The payment took an *ex gratia* form and involved no formal consideration of the legal principles at stake. It is nevertheless significant that Finland did not call for the abandonment of the Danish project, but

[117] *United Nations Reports of International Arbitral Awards*, vol. 3, p. 1907 at p. 1946; see also the examples cited by the UN Secretariat in its Survey of State practice relevant to international liability for injurious consequences arising out of acts not prohibited by international law, loc. cit. above (n. 115), at p. 73, paras. 328–35.

[118] Whiteman, *Digest of International Law*, vol. 4 (Washington, 1965), pp. 585 and 571.

[119] Guggenheim, 'La pratique suisse 1956', *Annuaire suisse de droit international*, 14 (1957), p. 168.

[120] Memorial of the Government of the Republic of Finland, *Pleadings* (1991), p. 183.

[121] *International Legal Materials*, 32 (1993), pp. 101–3.

rather its modification in a manner that would cost the least interference to Finnish rights.

The arbitration in the *Gut Dam* dispute was based on an agreement between Canada and the United States, under which the United States permitted the construction of a dam by Canada across the international boundary on the international section of the St Lawrence River. The permission was granted on the express understanding that Canada would compensate the United States for any damage attributable to the dam.[122] The subsequent settlement of claims was however made without prejudice to the legal position of either party. Similarly, in the *Trail Smelter* case, the smelter company was permitted to continue its activities, but the tribunal established a permanent regime which called, under certain conditions, for compensation for injury to the United States interests arising from fume emission even if the smelting activities conformed fully to the permanent regime as defined in the decision.

In a significant dispute between Canada and the United States regarding a plan for oil prospecting in the Beaufort Sea, near the Alaskan border, the Canadian Government undertook to guarantee payment for any damage that might be caused in the United States by the activities of the private corporation which was to undertake prospecting. Although the private corporation was to furnish a bond covering compensation for potential victims in the United States, the Canadian Government accepted liability on a subsidiary basis for payment of the cost of transfrontier damage should the bond prove inadequate.[123]

But what do these precedents represent? Are they of any relevance in the formulation of general rules that should govern the consultation process. In any case are general rules desirable in this context or should each consultation produce its *ad hoc* own result? On the one hand the precedents discussed appear to be no more than pragmatic bargains between a State of origin and the potentially affected State. It is plausible to argue that they have no legal value and are no more than extra-legal settlements determined by the exigencies of the situation.

Yet there is evidence to suggest that States rarely settle claims unless they are well founded in law.[124] It may therefore be argued that these incidents, although not laying down any hard rules, in fact represent what States perceive as the acceptable forms of solutions when faced with the threat of harm from activities proposed by other States. On this reasoning, a State proposing activities that in fact threaten the territory of other States is under a duty to take precautions for the benefit of the

---

[122] See Report of the United States Settlement of Gut Dam Claims, *International Legal Materials* 7 (1969), pp. 128–38.

[123] *International Canada*, vol. 7 (Toronto, 1976), pp. 84–5.

[124] The United States practice for instance limits the power of the executive to settle claims to those that are meritorious: 10 USC section 2734 (1964); 28 USC sections 2672, 2674 (1964); Kiss and Shelton, *International Environmental Law* (New York, 1991), p. 361.

potentially affected State, or to offer actual or guarantee some form of compensation. Failure to take steps of this nature may be taken as breach of the obligation to consult in good faith, thus calling into question the responsibility of the State of origin.

(vii) *The Approach of the International Law Commission*

The content as well as the legal consequences of procedural obligations of environmental impact assessment, notification, exchange of information and consultation has been central to the work of the International Law Commission, especially in its consideration of the topic of international liability for the injurious consequences of acts not prohibited by international law.[125] In a provision that largely mirrors earlier proposals by the Commission's Special Rapporteurs, Article 17 of the draft articles proposed by the Working Group on the 'liability topic' provides:

(1) The States concerned shall enter into consultations, at the request of any of them and without delay, with a view to achieving acceptable solutions regarding measures to be adopted in order to prevent or minimize the risk of causing significant transboundary harm, and cooperate in the implementation of these measures;
(2) States shall seek solutions based on an equitable balance of interests in light of article 19;
(3) If the consultations referred to in Paragraph 1 fail to produce an agreed solution the State of origin shall nevertheless take into account the interests of States likely to be affected and may proceed with the activity at its own risk, without prejudice to the right of any State withholding its agreement to pursue such rights as it may have under these articles or otherwise.

The set of factors in Article 19 which is designed to enable States to arrive at acceptable solutions includes:

(*a*) the degree of risk of significant transboundary harm and the availability of means of preventing or minimizing such risk or of repairing the harm;
(*b*) the importance of the activity, taking into account its overall advantages of a *social, economic,* and *technical* character, for the State of origin in relation to the potential harm for the States likely to be affected [emphasis supplied];
(*c*) the risk of significant harm to the environment and availability of means of preventing or minimizing such risk or restoring the environment;
(*d*) the *economic viability of the activity in relation to the costs of prevention demanded by the States likely to be affected* and to the possibility of carrying out the activity elsewhere or by other means or replacing it with an alternative activity [emphasis supplied];

[125] Barboza, Eighth Report on liability for injurious consequences of acts not prohibited by international law, *Yearbook of the International Law Commission*, 1992, vol. 2, part 1, Article IV; Ninth Report, *Yearbook of the International Law Commission*, 1993, vol. 2, part 1, Article 18; Article 17 of the ILC Draft Articles on the Non-Navigational Uses of Interantional Watercourses, loc. cit. above (n. 47).

(e) the degree to which States likely to be affected are prepared to contribute to the costs of prevention;

(f) the standards of protection which the States likely to be affected apply to the same or comparable activities and the standards applied in comparable regional or international practice.

These factors are not perceived as being exclusive and the parties remain free to take into account any other factors which they see as relevant to the realization of an equitable balance of interests.[126]

Although not expressly stated, it is apparent that the central philosophy underlying the Commission's approach to consultation is that the process should result in decisions which are *economically efficient*. This may be arrived at by taking into account the overall benefit of the proposed activity to the State of origin as against the costs of preventing transboundary harm. On this reasoning an economically beneficial activity should be allowed to continue notwithstanding the harm it generates. Similarly, if the costs of preventing harm are minimal and can be taken by the State of origin without incurring excessive expense, then efficiency dictates that the harm should be prevented.

The commentary to the article lays emphasis on the importance of activities that are usually the subject-matter of consultations to the economic development of States, and categorically rejects the existence of a right vested in the potentially affected State to veto proposed projects. Yet it is difficult to accept that economic efficiency should be an overarching goal when what are at stake are conflicts in the exercise of sovereign rights. By insisting that the State of origin should go ahead with the activity if the two States are unable to reach a solution, the Commission pays too much importance to the developmental interests of the State of origin, and ignores the fact that to proceed with the activity may in fact cause serious or irreparable harm to the potentially injured State.

It would seem that in formulating the set of factors to be taken into account during the consultation process, the Commission was influenced by economic approaches to the formulation of legal rules. These approaches have been much discussed[127] and equally discredited in the context of domestic law.[128] The balancing of interests on the basis of the benefit of an activity to a State of origin *vis-à-vis* the costs of preventing

---

[126] Report of the Working Group, loc. cit. above (n. 9), p. 70.

[127] Coase, 'The Problem of Social Cost', *Journal of Law and Economics*, 3 (1960), p. 1; Posner, *Economic Analysis of Law* (4th edn., Boston, 1992).

[128] Polinsky, 'Economic Analysis as a Potentially Defective Product: A Buyer's Guide to Posner's Economic Analysis of Law', *Harvard Law Review*, 87 (1974), p. 1655; Randall, 'Coasian Externality Theory in a Policy Context', *Natural Resources Journal*, 14 (1974), p. 35; C. Gray, *Judicial Remedies in International Law* (Oxford, 1987), p. 237; Ogus and Richardson, 'Economics and the Environment: A Study of Private Nuisance', *Cambridge Law Journal*, 36 (1977), p. 284.

transboundary harm can only make sense when both a State of origin and the State likely to be affected are going to benefit from the same activity. In domestic law the justification for efficient allocation of resources lies in the fact that it is likely to maximize the utilization of scarce resources for the common good. But such identity of interests is difficult to find in the relations between sovereign States. Moreover, the Commission's approach overlooks the fact that economic efficiency is not the only goal of the law. Justice and fairness are equally important.[129] Justice may require that an important activity likely to cause serious environmental damage to the territory of other States should in fact be prohibited, even if it may seem economically inefficient. In any case, the difficulty of quantifying damage to the environment[130] in monetary terms, and the presence of public order interests, make it difficult to balance the needs of the State of origin and the interests of the potentially affected State so as to achieve an economically efficient result.

This is a complex problem for it raises most starkly the difficulty in balancing concurrent sovereign claims that are both well-founded in law. It is suggested that the better solution is to determine what rights are at greater risk and therefore deserving of better protection. This balance cannot be struck at the right place, if it is assumed that in the end the right of the State of origin to proceed with the proposed activity should always have priority. Faced with a stark choice between the right of a State to meet its energy requirements through the use of nuclear installations or defence capacity through nuclear tests, and the right of a potentially affected State to be free from radiation-related risks, it is suggested *de lege ferenda* that the interests of a potentially affected State to be free from radiation are more important and therefore deserving of greater protection. This may justify vesting a right of veto in the potentially affected State, or in a body empowered to settle conflicting claims. But each case will involve a difficult weighing up of interests. The ILC proposals lean too heavily in favour of the State of origin.

Another major shortcoming of the draft articles proposed by the Commission is that they are pitched to take place in a distinctly bilateral framework. Yet activities that affect the environment are rarely confined to the bilateral interests of the parties. In the Commission's proposals no account is taken of the interest of the wider community of States in a decent environment, or what Willem Riphagen has elsewhere referred to

---

[129] Gray, op. cit. above (n. 128), p. 237.

[130] The very complex nature of determining harm to the environment has in fact received extended treatment in the International Law Commission. See Barboza, Eleventh Report on international liability for injurious consequences arising out of acts not prohibited by international law, Forty-Seventh Session, Document A/CN.4/468, 26 April 1995.

as the protection of *extra-State* interests.[131] It may be argued with a certain degree of cogency that environmental obligations do not always create bilateral rights which may be bargained away in pursuance of national interests. This is not to trivialize the direct interests of the State of origin and the potentially affected State, but these obligations usually raise public order concerns going beyond the immediate interests of the parties. A potentially affected State may in fact be prepared to waive its rights to a clean environment in return for monetary compensation under circumstances when the public interest may require prohibition.[132]

(viii) *The Question of Prohibition Examined*

Although the case for prohibition may seem attractive in those instances where an activity threatens to cause serious transboundary damage, it has been observed that it has found limited support. In its comprehensive survey of State practice, the Secretariat of the United Nations was unable to unearth a single incident where an activity had been enjoined as a result of the protests of a potentially affected State.[133]

However, in the literature as well as in the practice of States, a minority opinion exists for the view that where the likely effects of a proposed activity are serious, and no mitigative strategies are envisaged, a State should refrain from proceeding with the proposed activity should

---

[131] Riphagen, Second Report on the content, forms and degrees of State responsibility, *Yearbook of the International Law Commission*, 1981, vol. 2, part 1, p. 79 at p. 86; 'State Responsibility: New Theories of Obligation in Interstate Relations', in Macdonald and Johnston (eds.), *The Structure and Process of International Law: Essays in Legal Philosophy, Doctrine and Theory* (The Hague, 1983), p. 581, especially at pp. 602–10. In the *Barcelona Traction* case, the International Court of Justice drew a distinction between obligations in the field of diplomatic protection and those owed to the entire community of States: *ICJ Reports*, 1970, p. 4 at p. 32. Although the list of obligations having an *erga omnes* character did not include environmental obligations, it is clear from the context that they were not intended to be closed. Thus, in the literature, the category of obligations *erga omnes* has been extended to norms concerning the protection of the environment, in particular those prohibiting serious pollution of the atmosphere: see Ago, Third Report on State responsibility, *Yearbook of the International Law Commission*, 1976, vol. 2, part 1, pp. 28–54; Article 19(3)(d) of the Draft Articles provisionally adopted by the ILC, Report of the Commission to the General Assembly on the Work of its Twenty-Ninth Session, *Yearbook of the International Law Commission*, 1977, vol. 2, part 2; Australian memorial, *Nuclear Tests* cases, *ICJ Pleadings*, 1978, vol. 1, pp. 332–3, and New Zealand memorial, vol. 2, p. 264 at p. 265; Schachter, op. cit. above (n. 70), p. 211; American Law Institute, *Third Restatement* (St Paul, 1987), sections 702(h), 703, and 902; Birnie and Boyle, op. cit. above (n. 8), pp. 154–7.

[132] In relation to the transboundary movement of hazardous wastes, there is evidence to suggest that some poor States have been prepared to accept hazardous wastes in return for monetary considerations despite obvious risks to human health and the environment: see Kummer, *International Management of Hazardous Wastes* (Oxford, 1995), p. 7.

[133] Loc. cit. above (n. 46), p. 73, para. 331.

the notified State object.[134] This view has also received qualified support from the Rapporteur of the International Law Commission on the topic of liability of States for the injurious consequences of acts not prohibited by international law.[135]

Others are not so enthusiastic at such a prospect, pointing to the risk of abuse inherent in what in effect amounts to a unilateral injunction.[136] In the *Nuclear Tests* cases, Judge Ignacio-Pinto denied the legitimacy of the Australian argument that international law recognized the right of a State to veto projects proposed by another on the ground that it exposed it to an unacceptable degree of harm. He noted that:

if the Court were to adopt the contention of the Australian request it would be near to enforcing a novel conception in international law whereby states would be forbidden to engage in any risk-producing activity within the area of their own territorial sovereignty; but that would amount to granting any state the right to intervene preventively in the national affairs of other states.[137]

Nevertheless it is suggested that there is considerable merit in the suggestion that activities which entail a considerable risk of irreversible transboundary harm should be enjoined unless those risks can be contained. If it is obvious that a proposed activity is about to cause considerable harm, then in principle there is every reason why the activity should be prohibited. However, a balance is required between

---

[134] In the *Nuclear Tests* case (*New Zealand* v. *France*), application of 21 August 1995, New Zealand argued that France could only proceed with the conduct of underground nuclear tests if the environmental impact assessment demonstrated that no harm would result from the tests, and that 'the mere carrying out of an assessment does not mean that party can proceed in any event. It can only do so if the project is then approved as being environmentally acceptable following the full consideration of any objections'—in other words, that international law enjoined States from carrying out activities which entailed significant harm to the environment. In the literature a number of writers have suggested that prohibition remains the ultimate sanction since prevention of harm will usually be more important than any subsequent award of damages: see Gray, op. cit. above (n. 128), pp. 237–8; Barboza, 'Liability for the Injurious Consequences of Acts not Prohibited by International Law and the Protection of the Environment', *Recueil des cours*, 247 (1994-III), p. 295 at p. 332.

[135] Barboza, Sixth Report, Draft Article 20, *Yearbook of the International Law Commission*, 1990, vol. 1, p. 226. Some members of the Commission also gave cautious support to the proposal: see Summary Records of the Meetings of the Forty-Second Session, *Yearbook of the International Law Commission*, 1990, vol. 1, contributions by Caleros Rodrigues, p. 236; McCaffrey, p. 252; Bennouna, p. 254; Koroma, p. 266; Ajibola, p. 272; Mahiou, p. 276.

[136] Orrégo Vicuna, 'State Responsibility, Liability, and Remedial Measures under International Law: New Criteria for Environmental Protection', in Brown Weiss (ed.), *Environmental Change and International Law* (Tokyo, 1992), at p. 124. Although a number of members of the ILC supported the proposal that an activity should be enjoined if it carried an inescapable risk of transboundary harm, many of them were reluctant to confer an uncontrolled veto power on the potentially affected State. See the contributions by Mr Njenga, p. 112; Mr Al-baharna, p. 121; Mr Bennouna, p. 112; *Yearbook of the International Law Commission*, 1989, vol. 1, p. 112. The existence of a right to veto proposed activities was overwhelmingly rejected by the international arbitral tribunal in the *Lake Lanoux* case, 24 ILR 101 at 128.

[137] *Nuclear Tests* case (*Australia* v. *France*), order of 22 June 1973, *ICJ Reports*, 1973, p. 132; see also Judge de Castro, who also denied the existence of any right to enjoin an activity on the ground that it exposed other States to an unacceptable risk of harm: *ICJ Reports*, 1974, pp. 368–90.

the necessity for the source State to carry out activities on its territory as an inherent exercise of sovereignty, and fairness to the putative victim State so that the latter's environmental concerns are not unduly compromised. This balance cannot be pitched at the right place if the notified State is to be the final arbiter of the seriousness of the risks involved. It is therefore suggested that where two States are unable to agree on the degree of risk involved, the decision to prohibit the activity should in principle be taken by an independent body.[138] This however presupposes the existence of independent institutions with jurisdiction to hear disputes of that nature, as well as the initiative to issue anticipatory remedies in the form of injunctions or orders for specific performance when the likely harm is serious.[139] It is clearly the case that at the present stage of its development, there are very few if any institutions that have been endowed with authority to settle disputes of that nature.

The ILC Working Group on Liability for Injurious Consequences of Acts not Prohibited by International Law[140] and those members of the Commission who spoke on the topic were unequivocally of the view that the potentially affected State should be denied the right to veto the project.[141] These members noted that the State of origin could not reasonably be expected to refrain from undertaking a lawful activity especially when that activity was deemed indispensable to the country's development and there was no other solution.[142] Many members reiterated that there was no obligation on a State to refrain from proceeding with a project in the absence of mutually acceptable solutions, and that the obligation imposed on the State of origin required it to do no more than adopt an activity with a lesser risk. The Working Group has observed that although the State of origin is permitted to go ahead with the activity, it is still obliged to take into account the interests of the States likely to be affected.

Under the scheme proposed by the ILC, the State of origin conducts the activity at its own risk. Should any damage occur, the State of origin is under a duty to pay compensation. The provision is intended to protect

---

[138] See Utton, loc. cit. above (n. 5), p. 56 at pp. 66 ff.

[139] On the reluctance of tribunals to issue such orders in the absence of express authorization by the parties in a *compromis*, see Gray, op. cit. above (n. 128), pp. 12 and 95.

[140] Loc. cit. above (n. 9), p. 70.

[141] See Summary Records of the Meetings of the Forty-Fourth Session, *Yearbook of the International Law Commission*, 1992, vol. 1, in particular contributions by Mr Crawford, p. 95, para. 22; Mr Güney, p. 98, para. 8; Mr Koroma, p. 104, para. 5; Mr Robinson, p. 109, para. 55; Mr Sreenivasa Rao, p. 111, para. 65; Mr Bennouna, p. 116, para. 25; Mr Mahiou, p. 116, para. 36; Mr Shi, p. 118, para. 42; Mr Idris, p. 119, para. 47; see also Summary Records of the Meetings of the Forty-Fifth Session, *Yearbook of the International Law Commission*, 1993, vol. 1, in particular contributions by Mr Pellet, p. 28, paras. 8 and 10; Mr Bennouna, p. 30, para. 27; Mr Güney, p. 33, para. 44; Mr Koroma, p. 37, para. 25; Mr Sreenivasa Rao, p. 41, para. 61; Report of the Working Group, p. 70.

[142] See Report of the Commission to the General Assembly on the Work of its Forty-Fifth Session, *Yearbook of the International Law Commission*, 1993, vol. 2, part 2, p. 26.

the interests of the potentially affected State by allowing it to pursue such remedies or rights that it may have under other rules of international law. Under these proposals, the outcome of the consultation process will be one of the many factors to be taken into account in determining the amount of compensation payable. It deserves to be emphasized that the ILC proposals are perceived as part of the progressive development of the law and were expressly stated to be without prejudice to issues of responsibility.

VI. THE PERENNIAL PROBLEM OF PROCEDURAL OBLIGATIONS IN THE REALM OF CUSTOMARY LAW

The discussion of procedural duties has so far been exclusively concerned with treaty regimes and other non-binding legal instruments. However, the question whether a distinct regime has evolved in the realm of customary law requires separate examination. Although in theory this is a distinct possibility,[143] and a number of writers have in fact reached the conclusion that this has taken place,[144] it is suggested that the issue must nevertheless be approached with caution. The evidence in most cases is in fact patchy, equivocal, and inconclusive. It is argued in the following paragraphs that, with the exception of notification in emergency situations, it is doubtful whether the other procedural duties have passed into the corpus of customary law.[145]

---

[143] See *The Wimbledon* case (1923), *PCIJ*, Series A, No. 1, p. 25; see also *Panevezys-Saldutiskis Railway* case, *PCIJ*, Series A/B, No. 76, pp. 51–2, *per* Judge Ehrlich; *Nottebohm* case, *ICJ Reports*, 1955, pp. 22–3; Baxter, 'Treaties as Custom', *Recueil des cours*, 129 (1970-I), pp. 75–91.

[144] Schneider, op. cit. above (n. 70), p. 162; Jiménez De Aréchaga, loc. cit. above (n. 114), p. 197; Smith, *State Responsibility and the Marine Environment* (Oxford, 1988); Boyle, loc. cit. above (n. 50), p. 281; Schwebel, Third Report on the law of non-navigational uses of international watercourses, *Yearbook of the International Law Commission*, 1982, vol. 2, part 1, pp. 114–15; Birnie and Boyle, op. cit. above (n. 8), p. 103; Kirgis, op. cit. above (n. 3), chapter 2; Quentin-Baxter, Second Report on international liability for injurious consequences arising out of acts not prohibited by international law, *Yearbook of the International Law Commission*, 1981, vol. 2, part 1, p. 119, para. 69; Handl, *Proceedings of the American Society of International Law*, 1980, p. 223 at p. 224; Kiss and Shelton, op. cit. above (n. 124), pp. 115 ff; Sands, op. cit. above (n. 3), pp. 604, 606, 607; Kummer, op. cit. above (n. 132), p. 25; for a cautious endorsement, see Teclaff, op. cit. above (n. 7), p. 473.

[145] In the ILC many members were of the view that the procedural duties of notification, consultation and exchange of information were part of the progressive development of the law rather than its codification: see discussions on the topic of international liability for acts not prohibited by international law, Summary Records of the Meetings of Forty-First Session, *Yearbook of the International Law Commission*, 1989, vol. 1, contributions by Mr Calero Rodrigues, p. 109; Mr Razafindralambo, p. 120; Mr Al Khasawneh, p. 126; Mr McCaffrey, p. 91; Mr Reuter, pp. 94–5; Mr Tomuschat, p. 98; Mr Rao, p. 104; Mr Bennouna, p. 110; Mr Barsegov, pp. 119–20; Mr Sepulveda Gutierrez, p. 103. Doubt as to the customary law status of international environmental obligations is also expressed in general form in Kindred (ed.), *International Law* (Toronto, 1993), p. 746.

(i) *Treaty Practice as Evidence of Customary Norms*

The evidence that procedural obligations are now a general requirement in the field of environmental protection is derived from a number
of multilateral and bilateral treaties, including those referred to in the
previous paragraphs. It has been noted that the 1982 Law of the Sea
Convention, the UNEP Regional Seas Conventions,[146] treaties on the
conservation of nature,[147] as well as those on the utilization of international watercourses,[148] in one form or another provide for the procedural duties under consideration. These treaties in the aggregate create
rules and patterns of conduct that influence the behaviour of parties and
non-parties alike.

The evidence cited by proponents of an emergent principle of customary law includes the provisions of the 1982 Law of the Sea Convention
relating to the protection of the marine environment. It will be recalled
that Articles 197, 198, 200 and 201 require States to co-operate through
regular exchange of information, and notification, with a view to protecting the marine environment. Similar provisions are to be found in the
Regional Seas Conventions negotiated under the auspices of UNEP.
Thus, several articles of the Barcelona Convention for the Protection of
the Mediterranean against Pollution make provision for a general duty to
co-operate, especially in respect of matters pertaining to pollution
monitoring and exchange of scientific and technological information
which may be relevant in combating pollution.[149]

Other provisions on notification, exchange of information and consultation include: Articles 3 and 12 of the 1974 Helsinki Convention,[150]

---

[146] See Articles 3 and 12 of the 1974 Convention on the Protection of the Marine Environment of
the Baltic Sea Area, loc. cit. above (n. 9); Articles IX, X and XI of the 1978 Kuwait Convention on
the Protection of the Marine Environment from Pollution, loc. cit. above (n. 31); Articles 4–13 and
16–17 of the Abidjan Convention for Co-operation in the Protection and Development of the Marine
and Coastal Environment of the West and Central African Region, *International Legal Materials*, 20
(1981), p. 746.

[147] 1992 Convention on Biological Diversity, Articles 14 and 17, loc. cit. above (n. 10); 1968
African Convention on the Conservation of Nature, loc. cit. above (n. 96); see also Convention for
the Protection of the Natural Resources of the South Pacific Region, loc. cit. above (n. 12).

[148] See Article 12 of the 1964 Agreement concerning the Niger Commission, *UN Treaty Series*,
vol. 587, p. 19; 1973 US–Mexico Agreement on the Permanent and Definitive Solution to the
Problem of the Salinity of the Colorado River, *International Legal Materials*, 12 (1973), p. 1105;
1990 Agreement concerning Co-operation on Management of Water Resources in the Danube Basin
(EEC–Austria), *Official Journal of the EC*, No. L/90/20; 1959 Nile Waters Agreement, Ruster and
Simma, *International Protection of the Environment*, vol. 11, p. 5582; 1976 Convention on the
Protection of the Rhine Against Chemical Pollution, *International Legal Materials*, 16 (1977), p. 242;
for an extensive survey see Kirgis, op. cit. above (n. 3), chapter 2; McCaffrey, Second Report on the
law on non-navigational uses of international watercourses, *Yearbook of the International Law
Commission*, 1986, vol. 2, part 1, p. 139.

[149] UNEP, *Selected Multilateral Treaties in the Field of the Environment, Reference Series 3*
(Nairobi, 1983), p. 448. See Articles 9, 10 and 11.

[150] Convention on the Protection of the Marine Environment of the Baltic Sea Area, loc. cit.
above (n. 9).

Articles IX, X and XI of the 1978 Kuwait Regional Convention,[151] and the Abidjan Convention for Co-operation in the Protection and Development of the Marine and Coastal Environment of the West and Central African Region.[152] However, apart from the treaties themselves there is no evidence of State practice either based on the treaties or influenced by them.[153]

Evidence in support of procedural safeguards is also to be found in a long line of European treaties and State practice on the utilization of international watercourses.[154] These treaties provide for the procedural requirements that have to be satisfied before a State can unilaterally undertake measures that actually or may substantially interfere with the rights of other States. In the context of international watercourses, it is generally accepted that a State proposing to undertake works that may seriously impair the established rights of other States is under a duty to notify those States, enter into consultations with them, and generally seek to accommodate their interests before proceeding with the proposed works.[155] These procedural duties are also generally complied with even where there is no treaty obligation to do so. This practice has been considerably relied on by writers in support of the proposition that customary law in the context of shared water resources imposes an obligation to supply information, notify other States, and if need be enter into consultations.[156] What remains unclear is whether compliance with procedural obligations in that context can be extrapolated in support of a similar customary law requirement in relation to environmental obligations as a whole. One of the ILC Rapporteurs on International Watercourses, Professor McCaffrey, expressed grave reservations about such an exercise.[157] Given the long history of co-operation in the context of shared water resources, it is suggested that State practice in that context, although relevant, is nevertheless of limited value in the search for customary norms, given their *lex specialis* character.

It has also been noted that the 1979 ECE Convention, the 1991 US/Canada Air Quality Agreement, the 1991 UN Convention on industrial accidents and the ECE Environmental Impact Assessment

[151] Loc. cit. above (n. 31).

[152] See Articles 4–13 and 16–17, *International Legal Materials*, 20 (1981), p. 746.

[153] See Survey of State practice relevant to international liability for injurious consequences arising out of acts not prohibited by international law, prepared by the UN Secretariat, especially pp. 22–58, loc. cit. above (n. 46).

[154] These treaties are extensively discussed by Kirgis, op. cit. above (n. 3), especially chapter 2; the list of these treaties is extensive but the more important ones include the 1976 Convention on the Protection of the Rhine against Chemical Pollution, loc. cit. above (n. 148); the 1921 Barcelona Convention on the Regime of Navigable Waterways of International Concern, *League of Nations Treaty Series*, vol. 7, p. 35; the 1948 Convention regarding the Regime of Navigation on the Danube, *UN Treaty Series* vol. 33, p. 196.

[155] Kirgis, op. cit. above (n. 3); *Lake Lanoux* arbitration, loc. cit. above (n. 8), p. 146.

[156] Bruhacs, op. cit. above (n. 41), pp. 176–7.

[157] Summary Records of the Meetings of the Forty-First Session, *Yearbook of the International Law Commission*, 1989, vol. 1, p. 91.

Convention in varying degrees provide for duties of prior assessment, notification, exchange of information and consultation. These treaties may have some relevance in the evolution of customary norms. There is considerable evidence in support of the proposition that standardized treaties usually impose a uniform set of obligations on the addressees, thus contributing appreciably to the emergence of a distinct regime in the sphere of customary law.[158] Three arguments may be constructed on the basis of the treaty practice. It is arguable that the treaties are evidence of an emerging rule of customary law quite apart from their binding character *qua* treaty.[159] An equally plausible argument is to suggest that the requirements of customary law must now be interpreted in light of the changing standards of behaviour as reflected in the treaty regimes even if these have not attained the status of generally binding norms.[160] Thirdly, it is equally arguable that the very existence of numerous bilateral treaties points to the absence of customary law rules regulating the same subject-matter. It may be argued that had customary law provided for procedural duties, there would have been no need for States to enter into specific arrangements regulating the same issues.[161] All three hypotheses have received varying degrees of support in the literature and in the works of bodies charged with the codification and progressive development of international law as well as in the practice of States. This diversity of conclusions reached by these bodies on the same evidence does not strengthen the case for the existence of procedural norms under customary law.

(ii) *The International Law Commission*

It has already been observed that the nature, content, as well as the possible consequences of procedural rules has been central to the work of the International Law Commission both in the context of liability for injurious consequences of acts not prohibited by international law and in

[158] Schachter, op. cit. above (n. 70), p. 76.

[159] That this process is a distinct possibility was recognized by the Court in the *North Sea Continental Shelf* cases, *ICJ Reports*, 1969, p. 3 at pp. 42–3; see also the judgment in the case of *Nicaragua* v. *United States (Merits)*, *ICJ Reports*, 1986, p. 14 at pp. 92–7.

[160] A similar argument was made by Judge Jessup in the *South West Africa* cases, *ICJ Reports*, 1966, p. 6 at pp. 441–2, when he noted that although international law did not as such prohibit the policy of *apartheid*, South Africa's obligation as Mandatory, which required it to promote to the utmost the material well-being of the inhabitants, had to be interpreted in light of 'non-discriminatory standards in the international community'. The *Restatement*, s. 601(1)(*a*), op. cit. above (n. 131), also requires States to observe generally accepted international standards in discharging their obligations to prevent transboundary harm. Arguably such standards would include procedural norms. The ILC Working Group, loc. cit. above (n. 9), has suggested that the requirements of due diligence are in part dependent on compliance with procedural obligations: see commentary, pp. 84–5.

[161] H. Lauterpacht, *The Development of International Law by the International Court* (London, 1958), pp. 377–80; Kopelmanas, 'Custom as a Means of the Creation of International Law', this *Year Book*, 18 (1937), p. 127 at pp. 136–7.

the context of its work on the law of the non-navigational uses of international watercourses. In both contexts the Commission has attached considerable importance to the role of procedural safeguards in the management of the environment and, in particular, in the prevention of transboundary pollution.

(a) *The watercourses regime*

In 1994, the Commission adopted a set of draft articles on the law of non-navigational uses of international watercourses.[162] These draft articles contain a number of procedural safeguards to be observed by States in their utilization of shared water resources. Article 9 of the draft articles provides for a general obligation to co-operate; Article 11 places watercourse States under a duty to exchange information and consult with each other on the possible effects of planned measures on the condition of the watercourse system. Under Article 12, watercourse States are under a duty to issue timely notification to other States before permitting the implementation of planned measures which may have an appreciable adverse effect upon watercourse systems. Article 17 goes on to provide that the notifying State and the State making the communication shall enter into consultations and negotiations with a view to arriving at an equitable solution of the situation.

These provisions were adopted in the context of what was perceived as a framework convention, embodying elements of codification and progressive development of the law.[163] Judge Schwebel, as second Special Rapporteur on Non-Navigational Uses of International Watercourses, extensively reviewed State practice, as well as the practice of international organizations and arbitral tribunals that are relevant to notification and consultation duties. He concluded that these procedural safeguards constituted the 'indispensable minima' expected of a State under general international law.[164]

In formulating his 'indispensable minima', the Special Rapporteur had relied on a much broader practice, including the 1974 recommendations of the OECD in the field of transfrontier pollution,[165] and the UNEP principles of conduct governing natural resources shared by two or more States,[166] as well as treaties governing the uses of international watercourses. Arguably, given the extensive State practice in the context of international watercourses, it may be argued with some degree of

---

[162] ILC Draft Articles on the Non-Navigational Uses of International Watercourses, loc. cit. above (n. 47).

[163] Report of the International Law Commission to the General Assembly on the Work of its Thirty-Fifth Session on the Law of the Non-Navigational Uses of International Watercourses, *Yearbook of the International Law Commission*, 1983, vol. 2, part 2, p. 68.

[164] See Schwebel, Third Report on the law of the non-navigational uses of international watercourses, *Yearbook of the International Law Commission*, 1982, vol. 2, part 1, p. 103.

[165] OECD Council Recommendations C(74) 224; C(76) 55: loc. cit. above (n. 47).

[166] *International Legal Materials*, 17 (1978), p. 1091.

confidence that procedural duties in that context have passed into the corpus of general international law. But it would be unsound to rely on that practice to support the existence of customary norms in other areas such as the protection of species or atmosphere, or the regulation of the transboundary movement of hazardous waste.[167] Given its *lex specialis* character, it is suggested that State practice on water pollution, although relevant, is not automatically transferable to other environmental contexts.[168]

(b) *The ILC and liability for injurious consequences of acts not prohibited by international law*

Reference has already been made to the Commission's work on liability of States for the injurious consequences of acts not prohibited by international law. The conceptual basis of this project, which the ILC undertook in 1978, has never been properly explained. Many within the Commission and outside it remain unconvinced as to the potential utility of the project.[169] In its current form the project is an attempt to codify the primary rules in the field of environmental protection.

The Commission's project proceeds largely on the basis of two principles. The first general principle is that States are not precluded from carrying out activities not prohibited by international law, notwithstanding the fact that the activity in question may carry a risk of transboundary harm. On the other hand, their freedom of action is not unlimited, and in particular any damage suffered as a result of the activities must be paid for, notwithstanding the characterization of the activity as lawful. The thrust of the ILC's argument is that where States carry out activities which are prone to cause and which do cause

---

[167] Speaking as a member of the Commission during the discussion on the 'Liability' topic, the Special Rapporteur on International Watercourses, Professor McCaffrey, warned against the extrapolation of customary law rules from the State practice in that context. He was of the view that most of the procedural duties in the context of the law of international watercourses had been influenced by the unique features of watercourse systems. He noted that while the relationships between watercourse States could always be seen as bilateral for purposes of procedural rules, the multifaceted character of State relations in the case of air pollution raised difficult questions as to which States should be notified. He therefore called for caution when relying on the practice in the context of the relations between watercourse States. See Summary Records of the Meetings of the Forty-First Session, *Yearbook of the International Law Commission*, 1989, vol. 1, p. 91.

[168] This was in fact the view of the many members of the Commission who spoke on the liability topic. See generally the Summary Records of the Forty-First Session, ibid., contributions by Mr McCaffrey, p. 91; Mr Shi, p. 94; Mr Pawlak, p. 102; Mr Graefrath, p. 107; Mr Bennouna, p. 110; Mr Njenga, p. 112.

[169] See, for instance, Brownlie, *State Responsibility* (Oxford, 1983), p. 50; Boyle, 'State Responsibility and International Liability for Injurious Consequences of Acts Not Prohibited by International Law: A Necessary Distinction?', *International and Comparative Law Quarterly*, 39 (1990), p. 1. See also Summary Records of the Meetings of the Forty-Fourth Session, *Yearbook of the International Law Commission*, 1992, vol. 1, part 1, contributions by Mr Tomuschat, p. 115; Mr Bowett, p. 101; see also Summary Records of the Meetings of the Forty-Fifth Session, *Yearbook of the International Law Commission*, 1993, vol. 1, especially contributions by Mr Barboza, p. 34, para. 4; Mr Vereshchetin, p. 32, para. 37.

significant transboundary harm, even if those activities or their effects are not unlawful, a question of compensation for harm arises. Provisions on compensation are flexibly drafted and do not impose categorical obligations. Compensation is to be negotiated by taking into account a number of equitable factors, including the extent to which the State of origin has complied with its procedural duties.[170] Moreover, it has already been noted that the injurious consequences topic is clearly stated to be without prejudice to issues of State responsibility under general international law.

In addition to the work of the Special Rapporteur, the Commission in 1992 established a working group under the Chairmanship of the Special Rapporteur.[171] It was charged specifically with the task of consolidating the work already done on the topic and to see if provisional solutions to some unresolved questions could be arrived at with a view to producing a single text for transmission to the General Assembly. The nature of the procedural duties proposed by this working group has already been referred to. Like those contained in the successive reports of the Special Rapporteur, the procedural obligations proposed are not intended to impose a set of justiciable duties whose breach would entail responsibility. However, if damage occurs, non-compliance with the procedural duties will be one of the many factors determining the nature and extent of compensation.[172]

It should be emphasized that the approach of the Commission on the liability topic is novel and at times controversial. However, what is important for the present inquiry is that the Commission's work was always perceived as part of the progressive development of the law rather than its codification. In his sixth Report, the second Special Rapporteur, Mr Barboza, observed that, although the procedural duties contained in the Commission's work were relatively well established in the practice of States, they had not become firm obligations whose breach would entail international responsibility.[173] As noted above, the latest report of the Working Group of the Commission is also based on the premiss that these obligations do not impose 'hard obligations', breach of which entail the responsibility of a State. Although a substantial amount of State and

---

[170] See Draft Articles 18 and 23, Report of the ILC on the Work of its Forty-Second Session, *General Assembly Official Records*, Forty-Fifth Session, Supplement No. 10 (A/45/10).

[171] See Report of the Commission to the General Assembly on the Work of its Forty-Fourth Session, *Yearbook of the International Law Commission*, 1992, vol. 2, part 2, p. 51.

[172] Report of the Working Group, loc. cit. above (n. 9), Article 22.

[173] Barboza, Sixth Report on liability for injurious consequences of acts not prohibited by international law, *Yearbook of the International Law Commission*, 1990, vol. 2, part 1, p. 92. This is in marked contrast to the robust conclusion by Quentin-Baxter, the Commission's previous rapporteur on the same topic, that: 'the duties to provide information, to afford consultation, and to consider in good faith, representation made by another interested party are too well established to need elaboration': see Second Report on international liability for injurious consequences arising out of acts not prohibited by international law, *Yearbook of the International Law Commission*, 1981, vol. 2, part 1, p. 119, para. 69.

treaty practice has been referred to by the ILC, it is however not possible to discern any commitment on the part of the Commission to the view that these obligations have passed into the corpus of general international law.

(iii) *The Resolutions of the Institute of International Law and the International Law Association*

The difficulty of extrapolating customary law from treaty practice is evident in the different conclusions reached by the Institute of International Law and the International Law Association (ILA). The ILA's Committee on the Legal Aspects of Transfrontier Pollution, basing itself largely on treaty practice as well as on the recommendations of UNEP[174] and the OECD,[175] has reached the conclusion that the procedural duties of information, notification and consultation are already part of general international law.[176] The conclusion is surprising, since the reports do not cite any evidence of *opinio juris* in support of the proposition that customary law requires States to observe the procedural duties.[177] Rather, the repeated reaffirmation of the same principles in environmental treaties and in resolutions of international organizations is taken as conclusive evidence for the existence of those duties under customary law. With respect, this is a fundamental departure from established canons governing the creation of customary law rules.[178]

A more cautious and perhaps better informed position is adopted by the Institute of International Law. The Institute has been considering environmental problems in the context of transboundary air pollution

---

[174] UNEP, Principles of Conduct in the Field of the Environment Concerning Resources Shared by Two or More States, loc. cit. above (n. 166). The principles did not however receive the unqualified support of member States in the General Assembly of the United Nations. See UN General Assembly Resolution 34/186 (1979) and UN General Assembly Resolution 3129 (XXVIII). Five voted against the latter, 77 for and 43 abstained: Birnie and Boyle, op. cit. above (n. 8), p. 115.

[175] See OECD Recommendation C(74) 224 (1974), para. 6, loc. cit. above (n. 47).

[176] The preamble to the Draft Articles in fact stated that the ILA was restating existing rules of international law applicable to transfrontier pollution: Committee on Legal Aspects of Transfrontier Pollution, *Report of the 61st Conference*, op. cit. above (n. 84), p. 378.

[177] Yet even within the ILA divergent views may be detected. Professor Dietrich Rauschning, as Rapporteur on Legal Aspects of the Conservation of the Environment, concluded that there was insufficient evidence to support the conclusion that notification and consultation duties were already part of general international law: ILA, Report of the 59th Conference (1980, Belgrade), p. 549.

[178] The very stringent requirements for the creation of customary norms are well established. See *North Sea Continental Shelf* cases, *ICJ Reports*, 1969, p. 3 at pp. 32–43. In the case of *Nicaragua v. United States (Merits)*, *ICJ Reports*, 1986, p. 14 at pp. 108–9, para. 207, the Court referred to its judgment in the *North Sea* cases and observed that:

'. . . for a new customary rule to be formed, not only must the acts concerned "amount to a settled practice", but they must be accompanied by the *opinio juris sive necessitatis*. Either the States taking such action or other States in a position to react to it, must have behaved so that their conduct is "evidence of a belief that this practice is rendered obligatory by the existence of a rule of law requiring it. The need for such a belief, i.e., the existence of a subjective element, is implicit in the very notion of *opinio juris sive necessitatis*." '

and pollution of international watercourses. The draft articles on trans-boundary air pollution adopted by the Institute in 1987 are stated in *de lege ferenda* terms and were perceived by the Institute as part of the progressive development of international law rather than its codification.[179] Article 7 of the draft articles adopted by the Institute nevertheless would require the States concerned to make available on a regular basis information relating to the nature, sources and effects of air pollution. In addition, provisions are made for notification and consultation in those instances where a proposed activity poses a significant risk of transboundary pollution. It is significant that the Institute's Rapporteur on air pollution, Mr Nascimento e Silva, was of the unequivocal view that at the present stage of international development, procedural duties were merely contractual undertakings having no parallel in general international law. Only the duty to issue a warning in the event of a sudden increase of pollution was regarded by the Rapporteur as part of customary law.[180]

The discussions in the Institute, both in the context of air pollution and of pollution of rivers and lakes, reveal substantial differences between members of the Institute as to the customary law character of the procedural obligations. Rousseau, Seidl-Hohenveldern, McDougal, Sette Camara and Verzijl were of the view that procedural obligations were already part of general international law. On the other hand, Jennings and Colliard observed that State practice did not as yet support the existence of such duties in customary law.[181]

The American Law Institute's (*Third Restatement*) formulation of the general duties of States with respect to the environment does not contain any separate provision for procedural obligations. However, the comment and reporters' notes accompanying the formulation of the basic duty of States to prevent transboundary pollution state that the discharge of that duty in itself requires the observance of notification and consultation duties. Although it does not expressly say so, it is implicit from the context that procedural obligations are seen as complementing the substantive duties of States, rather than as the source of distinct duties.[182] There is no evidence from the commentary or the reporters' notes to suggest that these procedural duties were regarded by the Institute as the source of independent obligations under customary law.

---

[179] The Rapporteur Ambassador Nascimento e Silva was of the view that in the absence of a contractual obligation contained in a treaty, general international law did not impose any procedural duties on States: *Annuaire de L'Institut de Droit International*, 62: I (1987), pp. 220–1; see also the contribution of Mr Manner, ibid., 62: II (1987), p. 191.

[180] Loc. cit. above (n. 179), p. 221.

[181] See 'La pollution des fleuves et des lacs et le droit international', *Annuaire de L'Institut de Droit International*, 58: I (1979), pp. 296–309.

[182] *Third Restatement*, op. cit. above (n. 131), p. 107 at p. 114.

(iv) *State Practice in the Context of Particular Disputes*

It is to be emphasized that, in any assessment of obligations under customary international law, the concrete application of the principles discussed is more significant than any abstract expression of approval in international instruments. It is therefore essential to consider the actual application of these principles in the context of environmental disputes, especially those necessitated by an apprehension of threatened environmental harm. Again, the exercise is undertaken with a degree of caution as it is very difficult to find direct evidence of inter-State disputes settled on the basis of general international law in this field.

In the relations amongst European States, notification as well as consultation have generally taken place whenever a proposed activity entails significant transboundary consequences for the environment of other States.[183] Moreover, failure to notify or consult with States that may be affected by a proposed activity has usually been the subject-matter of protest by aggrieved States. For instance, the Swiss plan to construct a nuclear power plant at Ruthi about two kilometres away from its border with Austria was the subject of vehement protest by the Austrian Government and the Austrian state of Vorarlberg. At the request of the Austrian Government consultations were entered into with all the parties concerned with a view to examining the possible harmful consequences of the installation.[184]

The project was in any case shelved owing to domestic opposition to all forms of nuclear energy in Switzerland. The Swiss Government's position as to the applicable rules of general international law therefore remains unclear. The consultations were moreover legally mandatory under the provisions of the Convention on the Protection of Lake Constance from Pollution.[185] This latter fact considerably diminishes the precedent value of this case. Nevertheless it is significant that in the opinion of the Austrian Government there was a general obligation to enter into consultations.

The relations between Belgium and the Netherlands have also been based on routine consultations and exchange of information whenever activities in one State pose a substantial risk of transboundary harm to the territory of another.[186] A decision by the Belgian Government to construct refinery and petro-chemical units near its frontier with the Netherlands was the subject-matter of an objection by the Netherlands Government. The Government insisted on consultations before the

[183] For a very comprehensive survey see Lammers, op. cit. above (n. 61), pp. 206 ff.

[184] See *Österreichische Zeitschrift für Aussenpolitik*, 12 (1972), p. 349; ibid., 14 (1974), p. 224, cited in Lammers, op. cit. above (n. 61), p. 212.

[185] See Art. 1, para. 3, of the Convention on the Protection of Lake Constance from Pollution, in OECD Doc. AEU/TFP/ENV/75, p. 11 at p. 16.

[186] For an extensive discussion of these consultations, see Lammers, op. cit. above (n. 61), pp. 213–17.

actual construction of the proposed plans. The Netherlands argued that the proposed project threatened the nearby Netherlands national park as well as other neighbouring countries. Consultations were held between the two governments, with the Netherlands maintaining that the consultations were rendered mandatory by regional standards of behaviour.

In the accompanying debates in the Belgian House of Representatives, the Belgian Government also indicated that the consultations were a normal and necessary procedure of good neighbourship and were in any case expected of it under the Benelux accords.[187] There is, however, no conclusive evidence that the Belgian Government regarded such consultations as mandatory under general international law. It appears that both parties in holding consultations were largely influenced by regional standards of behaviour.

Franco/German relations have also been conducted on the basis of the existence of certain procedural constraints on the conduct of activities with transboundary implications. A recent example arose from the French Government's proposal to build a chemical industrial complex at Ottmarsheim (France). The complex was likely to give rise to significant air pollution in the German state of Baden-Wurttemberg. The German Federal Government sought further information from France with regard to the likely consequences of the proposed activities. In the resulting consultations, France agreed to abandon the construction of some of the factories in the complex with a view to reducing the resulting transboundary pollution.[188] The legal basis of this consultation remains unclear. While it is true that State consultations, even when founded on legal rules, do not always reveal the principles upon which they were grounded, it should not be assumed that in the absence of a treaty basis such consultations were mandatory under general international law.

It is also significant that in another dispute between France and Germany involving the French Government's intention to construct a lead/sulphate factory in Alsace,[189] Germany's objections were grounded on the procedural rules contained in the 1974 OECD principles[190] and the Resolution of the Committee of Ministers of the Council of Europe Concerning Air Pollution in Frontier Areas.[191] In the ensuing consultations France was apparently willing to take German air quality standards into account. The project was however shelved for reasons that had

[187] For a discussion of the dispute see *International Environmental Reporter*, 5 (1982), p. 480. For the discussion in the Belgian Parliament see *AP Chambre*, 1972–1973, 2 May 1973, p. 1625, cited in Lammers, op. cit. above (n. 61), p. 214, and Belgian Parliament, *Questions et réponses, Bulletin*, 17 July 1973.

[188] Grawe, 'Probleme des Umweltschutzes in deutsch-französischen Grenzgebiet', *Zeitschrift für ausländisches öffentliches Recht und Völkerrecht*, 34 (1974), p. 314, cited in ILA, 'Legal Aspects of the Conservation of the Environment' (1982), *Report of the 60th Conference*, op. cit. above (n. 47), p. 157 at p. 165.

[189] ILA Report, loc. cit. above (n. 47), p. 172.

[190] Loc. cit. above (n. 47).

[191] Council of Europe Resolution (71)5, *European Yearbook*, 22 (1971), p. 263.

nothing to do with the German objections.[192] This again emphasizes the equivocal nature of the incident as evidence of a legal duty requiring consultation.

Other less publicized cases include the dispute between Austria and Czechoslovakia over the construction of electric power reactors at Dukovany, located approximately 35 kilometres from the Austrian border. Owing to this proximity, the Austrian Ministry of Foreign Affairs insisted on being consulted. This was accepted by the Czechoslovak Government. Joint talks were subsequently held on the safety aspects of the project by the two governments.[193]

No specific legal principles were relied on, nor is there any evidence to suggest that there was a treaty instrument governing the relations between the two parties. However, in the earlier incident relating to the Swiss plan to construct a nuclear power plant at Ruthi on the Swiss–Austrian border, the Austrian minister for foreign affairs maintained that such consultations were required by the principle of good neighbourship. There is nothing to suggest that the Austrian Government regarded consultations as legally mandatory under international law. This conclusion may be deduced from the fact that the Austrian minister gave express consideration to the normative content of the applicable principles under international law.[194]

In the 1995 dispute concerning Slovakia's proposal to build a nuclear reactor at Mochovca, 72 miles from its border with Austria, consultations were held between the two governments with regard to the safety aspects of the project. Yet the background to the dispute does not unequivocally support the view that such consultations were legally mandatory under general international law. Slovakia had applied for a loan to enable it to complete the project from the European Bank of Reconstruction and Development. The Bank's guidelines on lending required a State seeking assistance to enter into consultations with neighbouring States as well as the general public on safety matters.[195]

Equally equivocal is the practice between Canada and the United States. Although a great deal of consultation has taken place in the relations between the two States, most of this has been conducted pursuant to the provisions of treaty obligations, including Article IX of the Boundary Waters Treaty,[196] and the 1980 US/Canada Memorandum

---

[192] See Lammers, op. cit. above (n. 61), p. 223.

[193] *Österreichische Zeitschrift für Aussenpolitik*, 15 (1975), p. 1, cited in Handl, 'Conduct of Abnormally Dangerous Activities in Frontier Areas: The Case of Nuclear Power Plant Siting', *Ecology Law Quarterly*, 7 (1978), p. 28; other relevant examples are discussed by the ILA, *Report of the 60th Conference*, op. cit. above (n. 47), p. 173.

[194] Reply to Question No. 2201/j/1978 of 28 November 1978, Austrian *Nationalrat*, cited in Lammers, op. cit. above (n. 61), pp. 212–13.

[195] On the dispute, see *International Environment Reporter*, 18 (1995), no. 2, p. 57.

[196] Boundary Waters Treaty, loc. cit. above (n. 2); Schachter, op. cit. above (n. 70), p. 374.

of Intent.[197] Furthermore, specific provisions for consultation with respect to transboundary air pollution have been expressly provided for in Article 5 of the 1991 Air Quality Agreement.[198]

A number of consultations have taken place under the auspices of the International Joint Commission (IJC) established under Article IX of the Boundary Waters Treaty. Consultations took place between the United States and Canada following the United States concern over the possible transboundary impact of the Poplar River power generating station. The United States insisted that the project should not continue until the two governments had received reports from the IJC.[199] Nevertheless, it is suggested that these treaty-based consultations provide no evidence of the existence of similar rules under customary law[200] in the absence of other evidence.

In the 1995 dispute between New Zealand and France concerning the legality of French underground nuclear tests in the South Pacific, New Zealand in addition to contesting the legality of the French tests *per se*, also argued that France was under a customary law duty to carry out environmental impact assessments before proceeding with the conduct of nuclear tests. The duty was formulated in general terms, for New Zealand observed that the

obligation to carry out such assessments exists in relation to any activity which is likely to cause significant damage to the environment, particularly where such effects are likely to be transboundary in nature.[201]

New Zealand further maintained that France could only proceed with the conduct of the tests if the environmental impact assessment indicated that no atmospheric contamination of the marine environment would result.[202] None of the treaty obligations so far considered has imposed such a stringent requirement. Indeed the law in this area has consistently shied away from enjoining activities on the ground that they are likely to

[197] US–Canada Memorandum of Intent, *United States Treaties and Other International Agreements*, vol. 32, p. 2521.

[198] Loc. cit. above (n. 12).

[199] See Contemporary Practice of the United States, *American Journal of International Law*, 72 (1978), p. 653; 1983 US–Mexico Agreement on Transboundary Air Pollution caused by Copper Smelters, *International Legal Materials*, 22 (1983), p. 1025; Annexes I–IV of 1986, *International Legal Materials*, 26 (1987); Kirgis, op. cit. above (n. 3), p. 116.

[200] It has been argued that one of the paradoxes of relying on treaties as evidence of customary law is that while many provide evidence of the existence of customary rules, repeated reliance on treaty provisions may also be an indicator that customary law does not regulate the issue under consideration: see Baxter, loc. cit. above (n. 143), pp. 75–91. This is based on the assumption that, had customary law provided for the matter in question, there would have been no need to enter into specific treaty arrangements.

[201] *Nuclear Tests* case (*New Zealand* v. *France*), loc. cit. above (n. 16). In further arguments developed during the oral hearing, New Zealand argued that not only was France under a duty to carry out environmental impact assessment, but that she was also obliged to allow other States (a) to propose additional or different investigations and (b) to verify for themselves the results of such investigations: Verbatim Record, 12 September 1995, CR 95/20.

[202] Loc. cit. above (n. 201), p. 58.

generate adverse impact.[203] But the conclusion as a matter of principle is sound. There would be no point in erecting elaborate procedures for environmental impact assessment if the findings can be ignored with impunity.

Yet in reaching the conclusion that customary law imposed such an obligation on France, New Zealand relied primarily on multilateral and bilateral treaties, as well as the draft principles governing the conduct of activities between two or more States promulgated by UNEP.[204] However, there is no independent evidence supplied by New Zealand to indicate that these obligations are regarded as legally mandatory outside the treaty regimes.[205]

(v) *The Case for a Customary Law Duty to Warn in Emergency Situations*

Of the procedural obligations discussed in the preceding paragraphs, the duty to warn States at risk in emergency situations has received substantial support in the literature as well as in the practice of States.[206] It is suggested that the existence of this duty in customary law may be argued on a rational basis. Its existence in general international law has received the endorsement of the International Court in the *Corfu Channel* case and in the *Nicaragua* case. In the *Corfu Channel* case, the Court referred to the obligation of Albania to warn shipping in general of the dangers to which they were exposed in Albania's territorial waters. Although the statement was made in the context of the right of States to unimpeded transit through international straits, it is clear that the Court

---

[203] See Survey of State practice relevant to international liability for injurious consequences of acts not prohibited by international law, prepared by the UN Secretariat, loc. cit. above (n. 46).

[204] *Request for an Examination of the Situation*, application of 9 May 1995, pp. 44–50.

[205] France did not address the substantive issues raised by the New Zealand application, maintaining that the Court manifestly lacked jurisdiction to hear the merits of the claim: see *aide mémoire* of 6 September 1995 submitted by France to the International Court. In its judgment of 22 September 1995, the International Court ruled that the basis of its 1974 judgment in the *Nuclear Tests* case (*New Zealand* v. *France*) had not been affected as required by paragraph 63 of that judgment, and that it therefore lacked competence to re-open the dispute which had been declared moot in 1974, and that the new application was concerned with underground nuclear tests whilst the 1974 case was exclusively concerned with atmospheric nuclear tests. As a result the application was dismissed: *ICJ Reports*, 1995, p. 288 at p. 306. In his dissenting opinion Judge *ad hoc* Sir Geoffrey Palmer regarded the principle requiring environmental impact assessment as *emergent*, but the language is cautious: ibid. at p. 412.

[206] See, for instance, OECD Principles concerning Transfrontier Pollution, OECD Doc. C(74) 224 (21 November 1974), loc. cit. above (n. 47), p. 242 at p. 246; 1982 Law of the Sea Convention, Art. 199, loc. cit. above (n. 12); Schneider, op. cit. above (n. 70), p. 162; Birnie and Boyle, op. cit. above (n. 8), p. 364; Schachter, op. cit. above (n. 70), p. 373; McCaffrey, Fifth Report on the law of the non-navigational uses of international watercourses, *Yearbook of the International Law Commission*, 1989, vol. 2, part 1, p. 91 at p. 113; *Third Restatement*, op. cit. above (n. 131), Comment (e), p. 107.

perceived the principle as one of general application.[207] In the *Nicaragua* case, the Court referred to its judgment in the *Corfu Channel* case and reaffirmed the duty of States to warn others of the dangers to which they had become exposed.[208]

The reaction of States to the Soviet Union's failure to issue a warning in the aftermath of the Chernobyl nuclear accident in 1986 provides further evidence that, in the view of a number of States affected, the Soviet Union was under a duty to warn them of the dangers to which they had become exposed. Thus the Group of Seven, meeting in Tokyo soon after the disaster, stressed the obligation of the Soviet Union to issue a warning and to supply information relating to the accident that had taken place on its territory. Since there was no treaty imposing such a duty on the Soviet Union, it can only be inferred that the Group of Seven were of the view that such notification was required under the existing principles of customary law.[209]

The Group of Seven noted *inter alia* that:

Each country, furthermore, is responsible for prompt provision of detailed and complete information on nuclear emergencies and accidents, in particular those with transboundary consequences. Each of our countries accepts that responsibility, and we urge the Government of the Soviet Union, which did not do so in the case of the Chernobyl, to provide urgently such information . . . [210]

It should however be pointed out that the Soviet Union denied the existence of any duty of notification or supply of information that was binding on it.[211] It is suggested that this defies logic and, like most of the Soviet statements in the aftermath of the Chernobyl accident, it cannot be taken as a defensible legal position. Although it is true that none of the affected States brought claims against the Soviet Union, it is generally agreed that this was largely due to reasons of political expediency since many of these States did not want to set a precedent that could be used in future claims against them and were in any case keen to win over Soviet co-operation.[212] In any case, and as a direct result of the Chernobyl disaster, a multilateral treaty on notification in case of a nuclear accident was adopted and has been ratified by most States that

---

[207] *ICJ Reports*, 1949, p. 22; that this duty is binding *lex lata* was recognized by the Special Rapporteur of the Institute of International Law, Mr Nascimento e Silva, in his Report on Transboundary Air Pollution, Part I, loc. cit. above (n. 179), p. 221.

[208] *Nicaragua* v. *United States (Merits)*, *ICJ Reports*, 1986, p. 4 at p. 112, para. 215.

[209] Adede, op. cit. above (n. 71), p. xx.

[210] See Tokyo Economic Summit of the Group of Seven Major Industrial Nations, consisting of Canada, France, Italy, Japan, FRG, UK and USA, *International Legal Materials*, 25 (1986), p. 1005.

[211] See text of the statement by President Gorbachev, IAEA Doc. GOV/INF/497, p. 10.

[212] Brownlie, 'State Responsibility and International Pollution: A Practical Perspective', in Magraw (ed.), *International Law and Pollution* (Philadelphia, 1991), p. 122; Birnie and Boyle, op. cit. above (n. 8), p. 309; Sands, *Chernobyl: Law and Communication* (Cambridge, 1988), p. 27.

possess nuclear reactors.[213] Although the conclusion of a treaty may in fact indicate that the subject-matter under consideration is not regulated by general international law, it is suggested that there are cogent reasons for concluding that the 1986 Treaty on Early Notification of a Nuclear Accident confirms an established position at customary law. These include the decisions of the International Court referred to, the unanimous position taken in codification bodies, and the available State practice.

VII. The Relationship between Procedural Obligations and Other Norms of Environmental Protection

Although the argument has been made that the bulk of procedural obligations have not been incorporated into the corpus of general international law, it is suggested that these duties nevertheless permeate other substantive obligations imposed on States in the context of environmental protection. That is to say, that even outside the treaty regimes procedural duties exist as a 'distinct category' which, although not attaining customary law status, contain fundamental standards to be taken into account in various contexts. Non-compliance with these standards, it is argued, may attract legal consequences of various kinds even for non-parties to treaty regimes. What then are these consequences?

It is widely accepted that general international law places States under a duty to act diligently in preventing transboundary harm.[214] Indeed, there is little dissent from the view that as a general rule States are placed under a duty to ensure that activities on their territory do not cause significant transboundary harm. However, a major shortcoming of customary law in this context is its failure to specify what diligent conduct entails or what concrete measures are required of States in order to fulfil their customary duty.[215]

Procedural obligations will in these circumstances play a crucial role in the determination of the content of 'due diligence' obligation of States.

---

[213] Loc. cit. above (n. 48). A large number of bilateral treaties on notification in case of nuclear accidents have been adopted by most States that possess nuclear reactors. These have been cited previously: see generally n. 73, above.

[214] See *Trail Smelter* case, loc. cit. above (n. 117), p. 1907 at p. 1965; Birnie and Boyle, op. cit. above (n. 8), p. 89; see also Principle 21 of the Stockholm Declaration on the Human Environment which reiterates the responsibility of States to ensure that activities within their jurisdiction or under their control do not cause damage to the environment of other States or to areas beyond the limits of national jurisdiction; Article 2(1) of the 1991 ECE Convention on Environmental Impact Assessment, loc. cit. above (n. 5); Eagleton, *The Responsibility of States in International Law* (New York, 1928), p. 80; see also ICJ advisory opinion on *Legality of the Threat or Use of Nuclear Weapons*, 8 July 1996, p. 15, para. 29.

[215] Birnie and Boyle, op. cit. above (n. 8), at p. 93.

These safeguards will be one of the many factors to be taken into account in determining whether a State has acted with the requisite degree of diligence under general international law.[216] A State that fails to conduct environmental impact assessment, notify potentially affected States or hold consultations can hardly claim that it has acted with the requisite degree of diligence should environmental harm occur.[217] In this sense procedural obligations play an auxiliary role as the standard against which the diligent conduct of governments is to be measured and complement the substantive duties imposed on them.

In the *Nuclear Tests* case, New Zealand argued that although the obligation to conduct environmental impact assessment was an independent legal duty, it was also an indispensable element in the implementation of the duty to prevent environmental harm. She argued that it was inconceivable that a State would be able to discharge its duty to prevent environmental harm without there being a legal duty to ensure, in advance, that an activity does not involve any unacceptable risk to the environment.[218] More specifically, counsel for New Zealand argued that France could not seriously assert that it was preventing, reducing and controlling pollution resulting from its nuclear activities as required by treaty obligations imposed on it, in the absence of such an environmental impact assessment.[219] The logic of the argument is apparent; due diligence is manifested in reasonable efforts by a State to inform itself of the factual and legal aspects of a contemplated course of action and to take appropriate measures in timely fashion to address them.[220] The importance of procedural obligations in the realization of those ends cannot be doubted.

Secondly, in the field of environmental protection, the conduct of governments is increasingly governed by a number of principles of indeterminate legal status. Many of these, such as the duty of co-operation, the sustainable use of resources, good neighbourliness and the precautionary approach to environmental protection, although important, are essentially programmatic and aspirational. However, their translation into practical concepts will to a large extent depend on the extent to which States are prepared to observe procedural standards. How else would one ensure, for instance, that resources are being used on a sustainable basis, without conducting environmental impact assessment? Co-operation also largely hinges on the observance of notification and consultation requirements.

---

[216] See American Law Institute, *Third Restatement*, op. cit. above (n. 131), p. 107 at p. 114.

[217] Birnie and Boyle, op. cit. above (n. 8), at p. 97.

[218] *Nuclear Tests* case (*New Zealand* v. *France*), Verbatim Record, CR 95/20, loc. cit. above (n. 17), p. 27.

[219] Verbatim Record, loc. cit. above (n. 17), p. 33.

[220] See Report of the Working Group, loc. cit. above (n. 9).

Thirdly, it may be argued that procedural obligations offer a basis for the implementation of, as well as the supervision of compliance with, treaty requirements. Environmental monitoring, routine exchange of information, notification and consultation all help to ensure that the parties are accountable to each other and to institutions charged with monitoring compliance. Consultation and exchange of information also enhance governmental understanding of the effects of activities on the environment. The improved scientific knowledge enables the parties continually to re-consider their obligations, and if need be undertake more stringent commitments.[221] By requiring parties to be in constant touch with each other and with institutions charged with monitoring compliance, it is suggested that these duties systematize co-operation and therefore ensure an on-going review of the parties' commitments as well as the efficacy of their implementation.

The International Law Commission has suggested, *de lege ferenda*, that non-compliance with procedural duties should be one of the many factors to be taken into account in determining the level of compensation payable. It was noted that Commission's driving philosophy is one of non-justiciability of procedural duties. Nevertheless these duties are assigned great importance at the compensation stage.[222] While general reservations have been expressed in relation to the secondary role assigned to procedural duties in the Commission's work, there is little doubt that non-compliance with procedural obligations will affect the level of compensation even under a State responsibility regime.

VIII. SOME GENERAL CONCLUSIONS

This study has revealed the very inchoate nature of procedural obligations in international law. In many contexts the obligations are not defined with precision, and much uncertainty persists as to their essential components. As found in treaty regimes, there is little doubt that these obligations have legal force for the parties to them. To that extent the obligations they impose are strictly speaking justiciable, notwithstanding their general imprecision. The suggestion in the ILC's work that these duties should not attract the normal consequences of responsibility is unfortunate and should be resisted. It must be seen as a retrograde step in an area where legal rules are in an embryonic state and practice

---

[221] This particular function of procedural obligations is reflected, for instance, in Article 9 of the 1991 ECE Convention on Environmental Impact Assessment, loc. cit. above (n. 5); Article 200 of the 1982 Law of the Sea Convention, loc. cit. above (n. 12), p. 1261; Protocol Relating to the Convention for the Prevention of Pollution from Ships, *International Legal Materials*, 17 (1978), p. 246; Article 7 of the Framework Convention on Climate Change, loc. cit. above (n. 9); Article 4 of the ECE Convention on Long-Range Transboundary Air Pollution, loc. cit. above (n. 10); Convention on Biological Diversity, loc. cit. above (n. 10), Article 23.

[222] Report of the Working Group, loc. cit. above (n. 9), p. 83.

incomplete. As independent legal duties, procedural obligations are likely to influence the behaviour of even the most reluctant of States.

It is suggested *de lege ferenda* that notwithstanding the general hostility to the question of prohibition, it may in certain circumstances be the only effective remedy when potentially affected States are faced with serious or irreversible harm. Prohibition as a last resort is bound to persuade even the most reluctant government to adopt stringent standards for the protection of the interests of third States.

The different conclusions reached by the main codification bodies illustrate the complexities involved in ascertaining the normative quality of procedural obligations outside the treaty regimes. Almost all of them rely on the same evidence either for or against the determination of the customary law status of procedural duties. The evidence from the law of international watercourses, although of some relevance in ascertaining the normative implications of procedural duties, nevertheless should not be applied without qualification to other environmental contexts. Most of the notification in that context has taken place within the framework of permanent institutions charged with adjusting the respective obligations of the parties on an on-going basis.[223]

It is suggested that the evidence relied on by the ILA in support of the proposition that customary law requires States to conduct environmental impact assessments and observe the duties of notification, supply of information and consultation has not occurred in a manner that indicates that a legal obligation *qua* custom is involved. Although the obligations have been repeatedly affirmed in international instruments as well as in the resolutions of international organizations, there is no evidence that States generally notify or consult other States before embarking on activities that entail transboundary harm in the absence of treaty commitments. To use the terminology of Article 38(1)(*b*) of the ICJ Statute, it cannot be said that the practice represents a 'uniform practice accepted as law'.[224]

The existence of *opinio juris* is particularly significant in evaluating the various consultations that have taken place between European States under principles of good neighbourliness. Like those between Canada and the United States, these consultations have taken place either under treaty arrangements or pursuant to principles of comity expected between friendly neighbours. It is difficult to conclude from the evidence that the practice has occurred in a manner that indicates that a rule of law *qua* custom is involved.

---

[223] McCaffrey, Summary Records of the Meetings of the Forty-First Session, *Yearbook of the International Law Commission*, 1989, vol. 1, p. 91, para. 26; Bloomfield and FitzGerald, *Boundary Waters Problems of Canada and the United States* (Toronto, 1958), pp. 39–40; Schachter, op. cit. above (n. 70), p. 374.

[224] See also *North Sea Continental Shelf* cases, *ICJ Reports*, 1969, p. 44, para. 77; *Nicaragua v. United States*, *ICJ Reports*, 1986, p. 14.

It is submitted that although a substantial amount of notification and consultation has taken place between States, it can hardly be said that the practice has occurred in a manner that indicates that a customary rule was involved. In most of the instances discussed, it is clear that the exchange of information and the consultation were distinct obligations imposed on the parties by the terms of an applicable treaty.[225] In other instances, it is not easy to discern evidence that the parties' conduct was motivated by a belief that the rules of international law required consultations and exchange of information.

Procedural obligations nevertheless have a crucial role to play in the implementation of the substantive obligation of States, especially obligations requiring them to prevent transboundary harm. However, it is suggested that in the absence of a normative regime in the sphere of customary law, procedural rules are useful criteria for determining whether or not a State has complied with its substantive duty diligently to prevent transboundary harm. A State that has failed to undertake environmental impact assessment or enter into consultations with affected States may be precluded from asserting that the harm did not occur for want of diligence.[226] Moreover, it has been noted that where a State fails to respond to a notification, it too may be taken to have acquiesced in the conduct of the activity and may be estopped from asserting that the activities as carried out are not compatible with its interests.[227]

There is nevertheless a credible amount of evidence in support of the existence in customary law of a duty to warn States in emergency situations of the dangers to which they have become exposed. It is therefore suggested that this duty can be taken to be an existing or at least an emergent rule of general international law.

[225] See Survey of State practice relevant to international liability for injurious consequences arising out of acts not prohibited by international law, loc. cit. above (n. 46), paras. 97–107.

[226] Second Report on international liability for injurious consequences arising out of acts not prohibited by international law, *Yearbook of the International Law Commission*, 1986, vol. 2, part 1, p. 153, para. 39.

[227] This argument has been considered at some length in the preceding paragraphs and is supported by the decision of the International Court in the *Gulf of Maine* case, *ICJ Reports*, 1984, p. 308.

THE CRITERIA FOR THE EQUITABLE UTILIZATION OF INTERNATIONAL RIVERS*

By XIMENA FUENTES‡

I. INTRODUCTION

In 1994 the International Law Commission adopted the Draft Articles on the Law of the Non-Navigational Uses of International Watercourses[1] recommending that they form a basis for the elaboration of a convention by the General Assembly or by an international conference of plenipotentiaries. Article 5.1 of the Draft Articles provides that:

> Watercourse States shall in their respective territories utilize an international watercourse in an equitable and reasonable manner. In particular, an international watercourse shall be used and developed by watercourse States with a view to attaining optimal utilization thereof and benefits therefrom consistent with adequate protection of the watercourse.[2]

The rule has been included in the Draft Articles as a crystallized rule of international law. This is evident from the commentary attached to Article 5.1, in which the ILC refers to equitable utilization as a 'well-established rule'. Furthermore, it states that:

> A survey of all available evidence of the general practice of States, accepted as law, in respect to the non-navigational uses of international watercourses—including treaty provisions, positions taken by States in specific disputes, decisions of international courts and tribunals, statements of law prepared by intergovernmental and non-governmental bodies, the views of learned commentators and decisions of municipal courts in cognate cases—reveals that there is overwhelming support for the doctrine of equitable utilization as a general rule of law for the determination of the rights and obligations of States in this field.[3]

In determining what is an equitable and reasonable utilization account is to be taken of all relevant factors and circumstances in the particular case.

*© Ximena Fuentes, 1997.

‡ Bachelor of Social and Legal Sciences (University of Chile). This article is part of the author's research as a D Phil. student at the University of Oxford. The author wishes to thank her supervisor, Professor Ian Brownlie, for his guidance and criticism of previous drafts of this work.

[1] See *Report of the International Law Commission to the General Assembly on the Work of its Forty-Sixth Session* (hereinafter, 1994 *ILC Report*), Doc.A/49/10 (1994), pp. 195 ff.

[2] Ibid., p. 218.

[3] Ibid., p. 222.

Article 6.1 of the Draft Articles contains a non-exhaustive catalogue of prospective criteria, including:

(*a*) geographic, hydrographic, hydrological, climatic, ecological and other factors of a natural character;
(*b*) the social and economic needs of the watercourse States concerned;
(*c*) the population dependent on the watercourse in each watercourse State;
(*d*) the effects of the use or uses of the watercourse in one watercourse State on other watercourse States;
(*e*) existing and potential uses of the watercourse;
(*f*) conservation, protection, development and economy of use of the water resources of the watercourse and the costs of measures taken to that effect;
(*g*) the availability of alternatives, of corresponding value, to a particular planned or existing use.[4]

There have been other attempts by international bodies to identify the criteria that ought to be taken into account in the establishment of an equitable regime for the utilization of international watercourses. In this connection, the International Law Association adopted in 1966 the Helsinki Rules on the Uses of Waters of International Rivers, of which Article V contains a list of relevant factors very similar to the one presented by the ILC. This provision states that:

1. What is a reasonable and equitable share within the meaning of Article IV is to be determined in the light of all relevant factors in each particular case.
2. Relevant factors which are to be considered include, but are not limited to:
    (*a*) the geography of the basin, including in particular the extent of the drainage area in the territory of each basin State;
    (*b*) the hydrology of the basin, including in particular the contribution of water by each basin State;
    (*c*) the climate affecting the basin;
    (*d*) the past utilization of the waters of the basin, including in particular existing utilization;
    (*e*) the economic and social needs of each basin State;
    (*f*) the population dependent on the waters of the basin in each basin State;
    (*g*) the comparative costs of alternative means of satisfying the economic and social needs of each basin State;
    (*h*) the availability of other resources;
    (*i*) the avoidance of unnecessary waste in the utilization of waters of the basin;
    (*j*) the practicability of compensation to one or more of the co-basin States as a means of adjusting conflicts among users;
    (*k*) the degree to which the needs of a basin State may be satisfied, without causing substantial injury to a co-basin State;
3. The weight to be given to each factor is to be determined by its importance in comparison with that of other relevant factors. In determining what is a

---

reasonable and equitable share, all relevant factors are to be considered together and a conclusion reached on the basis of the whole.[5]

Notwithstanding these lists of prospective criteria and the commentaries attached to the Draft Articles and to the Helsinki Rules, the relevance or relative weight of the different factors in the process of the establishment of an equitable regime for the utilization of international water resources is a question that remains open. It is true that 'the weight to be accorded to individual factors, as well as their very relevance, will vary with the circumstances';[6] nevertheless, this should not be a reason for negating the advantages of a more detailed examination of the role that the prospective relevant factors may play in the process. It is not the purpose of this article to find a general 'formula' applicable to all the various situations, but to assess the potential relevance of the various criteria, thus contributing to the determination of the possible outcome of a dispute between States concerning the utilization of the waters of an international river.

The practice of municipal courts of federal States in resolving inter-State river disputes has been particularly relevant to this study. This is so because these tribunals have applied the rule of equitable utilization and particularly because they have referred to it as a rule of international law applicable to inter-State water disputes. Complex disputes regarding the utilization of inter-State rivers have arisen between Indian, American and Argentinian States. In the case of American and Argentinian disputes, they can be settled by the Supreme Court of the respective country. Regarding the Indian States, the Constitution of India provides that for the resolution of this kind of dispute the central government can appoint a special tribunal. This was what happened in the case of the Krishna river dispute concerning the Indian States of Mysore, Maharashtra and Andhra Pradesh, and of the Narmada river dispute concerning the States of Madhya Pradesh, Gujarat, Rajasthan and Maharashtra.

The experience of maritime delimitation may also shed some light on the examination of the criteria applicable to the equitable utilization of international watercourses. The rule applicable to the delimitation of the continental shelf and the exclusive economic zone calls for the consideration of all the relevant circumstances in order to achieve an equitable result.[7] The equitable nature of the rule applicable to maritime delimitation makes it pertinent for the purposes of this study to examine the possibility of analogies and comparisons between the role ascribed by international tribunals to certain criteria in maritime delimitation and the

---

[5] ILA, *Report of the Fifty-Second Conference* (Helsinki, 1966), pp. 484 ff.
[6] 1994 *ILC Report*, p. 235.
[7] See *ICJ Reports*, 1984, para. 112, pp. 299–300.

role to ascribe to those criteria in the process of the establishment of an equitable regime for the utilization of international water resources.

The range of the criteria that might be considered in a dispute concerning the utilization of an international watercourse is unlimited. Because their status as relevant criteria is most likely to be in issue in disputes concerning the utilization of international rivers, the criteria examined here are:

(a) the economic and social needs of the States;
(b) existing uses;
(c) local customs;
(d) the efficiency of the different uses; and
(e) the geography and hydrology of the river.

The environmental impact of the use of the river on other basin States cannot be excluded as a relevant factor in the process of the establishment of a regime for the equitable utilization of an international river. However, this article does not examine this criterion in depth, and only the basic problems associated with its inclusion in the process are pointed out in section VII.

The aim of this study is twofold: on the one hand it explores the potential relevance of some of the prospective criteria to be taken into consideration in the establishment of an equitable regime for the use of international rivers; on the other, it attempts to identify certain guidelines that States and international tribunals should follow when applying the rule of equitable utilization.

II. The Relevance of the Social and Economic Needs of the States

According to Article 6.1(b) of the ILC Draft Articles on the Law of the Non-Navigational Uses of International Watercourses, the process of the establishment of an equitable regime for the utilization of international waters requires the consideration of the social and economic needs of the watercourse States[8] concerned. The ILC commentary to Article 6 does not provide any further explanation of the application of this criterion, but it is clear that Article 6.1(b) should be understood in connection with provisions 6.1(c) and 6.1(g), the first one concerning the population dependent on the watercourse in each watercourse State and the second

[8] The expression 'watercourse States' is preferred to 'riparian States' because the right to participate in the equitable utilization of a river not only pertains to the States that have a frontage on the river but also applies to States that contribute surface or underground water to the flow of the river or in whose territory part of the drainage area of the river is located. The ILC has defined watercourse State as 'a State in whose territory part of an international watercourse is situated': see Article 2 of the Draft Articles on the Law of the Non-Navigational Uses of International Watercourses, 1994 *ILC Report*, p. 199.

concerning the availability of alternatives, of corresponding value, to a particular planned or existing use.

The Helsinki Rules also require the consideration of the economic and social needs of the basin States, of the population dependent on the waters of the basin, of the comparative costs of alternative means of satisfying the economic and social needs of each basin State and of the availability of other resources. However, the ILA has not elaborated any further on the application of these criteria.

This part looks at the social and economic needs of the States concerned and their significance to the establishment of an equitable regime for the utilization of international rivers. It is asserted that this is one of the most important factors involved in the process, its importance deriving from the nature of the rule of equitable utilization which is in fact a rule concerned to ensure the fair distribution of water resources. However, it is probably the most difficult criterion to work with because it is likely to be manipulated. Therefore, for the implementation of this criterion it is fundamental that the real and objective water-related needs of the States concerned can be identified. Once the water needs of the parties are identified, it is necessary to examine how these needs operate within the process. The needs of the States may serve as a direct basis for a proportional division of the waters of the river, but the possibility of establishing priorities among the various needs must also be considered.

Before proceeding with the examination of the factors contributing to the identification of the needs of the States, it is important to make it clear that the inclusion of socio-economic elements in the application of the rule of equitable utilization does not necessarily transform what is to be a judicial decision into a political one. In the field of maritime delimitation it has been argued that the consideration of socio-economic elements involves questions on global resource policies and world politics which should not be solved by international tribunals because these questions go 'well beyond equity as a norm of law into the realm of social organization'.[9] This sort of argument denies the distributive aspect involved in the delimitation process. The origin of the reluctance of international tribunals to take into account the socio-economic elements involved in a delimitation is to be found in the *North Sea Continental Shelf* cases, in which the ICJ stated that its task was related essentially to the delimitation and not the apportionment of the areas concerned. The Court further explained that:

Delimitation is a process which involves establishing the boundaries of an area already, in principle, appertaining to the coastal State and not the determination *de novo* of such an area. Delimitation in an equitable manner is one thing, but not the same thing as awarding a just and equitable share of a previously

---

[9] See dissenting opinion by Judge Oda, *ICJ Reports*, 1982, para. 157, p. 255.

undelimited area, even though in a number of cases the results may be comparable, or even identical.[10]

The distinction between apportionment and delimitation is rather artificial. For this reason, it has not been possible to exclude the distributive aspect completely from the delimitation process. In fact, despite their general reluctance to admit economic considerations into the process, the tribunals have included certain social and economic factors. In this connection, a Chamber of the ICJ explicitly took into account the socio-economic element involved in the *Gulf of Maine* case, including the economic dependence of the coastal communities upon the resources of the area as a criterion to evaluate the equitableness of the delimitation. The Chamber did not consider economic dependence as an equitable criterion to be used in the determination of the delimitation line, but it used it as an auxiliary criterion to verify that the chosen line did not entail catastrophic repercussions to the livelihood and economic well-being of the coastal population of the States concerned.[11] The acknowledgement of the relevance of the presence of natural resources in the area to be delimited also entails a socio-economic aspect in so far as those resources are significant precisely because they can satisfy certain economic or social needs of the parties concerned. In the *Tunisia/Libya* case, for example, the ICJ admitted that the presence of oil-wells could be an element to be taken into account in the process of weighing all relevant factors to achieve an equitable result.[12] In the *Malta/Libya* case the Court asserted that the natural resources of the continental shelf under delimitation, so far as known or readily ascertainable, could well constitute a relevant circumstance to take into account.[13] Finally, in the *Jan Mayen* case, the ICJ, while rejecting the inclusion of socio-economic factors in the delimitation, took into account the equitable access to the capelin fishery resources present in the area.[14]

It must be concluded that the real objection to the inclusion of socio-economic factors does not lie in a *per se* extra-legal nature of the socio-economic criteria, but on *how* these factors should operate in the process of delimitation so that the decision does not intrude into the political realm. The correct approach should be to distinguish pertinent from non-pertinent socio-economic considerations in the delimitation process. While the reluctance of the maritime delimitation case law to include the socio-economic criteria should not be translated to the field of the utilization of international watercourses, the distinction between pertinent and non-pertinent economic considerations should be used in the selection of the appropriate socio-economic criteria to be taken into

---

[10] *ICJ Reports*, 1969, para. 18, p. 22.
[11] *ICJ Reports*, 1984, para. 237, p. 342.
[12] *ICJ Reports*, 1982, para. 107, pp. 77–8.
[13] *ICJ Reports*, 1985, para. 52, p. 42.
[14] *ICJ Reports*, 1993, paras, 75, 76 and 80, pp. 71–2 and 76.

account in the establishment of a regime of equitable utilization of international rivers.

The notion of non-pertinent socio-economic criteria refers to the comparison between levels of economic development of the States concerned. In the *Tunisia/Libya* case the ICJ dismissed the argument put forward by Tunisia of the relevance of 'its relative poverty vis-à-vis Libya in terms of absence of natural resources like agriculture and minerals, compared with the relative abundance in Libya, especially of oil and gas wealth as well as agricultural resources'.[15] In the view of the Court these economic considerations could not be taken into consideration because of the unpredictability of natural fortune or calamity. In the words of the Court, 'A country might be poor today and become rich tomorrow as a result of an event such as the discovery of a valuable economic resource'.[16] In the *Guinea–Guinea-Bissau* arbitration the economic factors invoked by the parties were dismissed because of the uncertain nature of the economic circumstances of the parties. In this regard, the Court of Arbitration was of the opinion that 'it would be neither just nor equitable to base a delimitation on the evaluation of data which changes in relation to factors that are sometimes uncertain'.[17] In the *Malta/Libya* case, the Court rejected the inclusion of Malta's absence of energy resources and its requirements as an island developing State because 'neither the rules determining the validity of legal entitlement to the continental shelf, nor those concerning delimitation between neighbouring countries, leave room for any considerations of economic development of the States in question'.[18]

It is apparent, therefore, that a comparison between the level of economic development of the disputing States has been regarded as immaterial to the process of maritime delimitation. This approach can be explained by the fact that such a comparison simply does not provide any help in determining to whom the areas to be divided should be allocated. In this connection Judge Oda was right when pointing out that the determination of the advanced industry or economy of one State as compared to the level of economic development of another one does not provide any satisfactory answer to the question of which of the two States should be given wider areas of the continental shelf or exclusive economic zone.[19] A satisfactory answer may only be given after the political issue whether or not to compensate the poor for their poverty is decided. In so far as this is a political decision, it should not be included in the process of the equitable delimitation of maritime zones or, for the same reason, in the

---

[15] *ICJ Reports*, 1982, para. 106, p. 77.
[16] Ibid., para. 107, p. 77.
[17] *Guinea–Guinea-Bissau* case, 77 ILR 689, para. 122.
[18] *ICJ Reports*, 1985, para. 50, p. 41.
[19] *ICJ Reports*, 1982, dissenting opinion of Judge Oda, para. 157, p. 255.

process of application of the rule of the equitable utilization of international watercourses. Therefore, it should be concluded that, as regards the utilization of international watercourses, the inclusion of the social and economic needs of the States should not consist in a comparison of stages of economic and social development of the States concerned.

It is interesting to mention that in his Third Report on the Law of the Non-Navigational Uses of International Watercourses the Special Rapporteur, Mr Schwebel, presented a list of factors relevant to the determination of the reasonableness and equitableness of the utilization of a watercourse, including the 'stage of economic development' of the riparian States.[20] This criterion was also included in the First Report of Dr Evensen, who succeeded Mr Schwebel as Special Rapporteur on the topic of the non-navigational uses of international watercourses.[21] One of the members of the ILC was right to point out that the reference to the stage of economic development of the States concerned 'did not make it clear whether preference should be given to developing or to developed countries'.[22] The stage of economic development was not mentioned as a relevant criterion in any of the subsequent revised versions of the list of relevant factors, and it is not included in the final wording of Article 6 of the Draft Articles on the Law of the Non-Navigational Uses of International Watercourses adopted by the ILC in 1994. Therefore, the relative economic poverty of the States concerned should not be admitted to affect the result. In other words, the question about the needs of the parties is a question about degrees of dependence and not stages of economic development.

The following pages examine how the degree of economic and social dependence can be determined. Two stages have been identified in this process: the first stage consists in the determination of the real needs of the States and the second one pertains to the possibility of establishing priorities among the various needs.

A. *The Determination of the Real Needs of the Parties*

The process of the establishment of an equitable regime for the utilization of international waters takes into account the social and economic needs of the parties in so far as the satisfaction of these needs depends on the use of the disputed waters. Various factors contribute to the determination of the degree of social and economic dependence of the States involved in a dispute concerning the utilization of a particular international river. These factors are examined below and the practice of municipal courts of federal States is used in the analysis.

---

[20] *ILC Yearbook*, 1982, vol. 2, part 1, p. 90, doc. A/CN.4/348.
[21] *ILC Yearbook*, 1983, vol. 2, part 1, p. 171, doc. A/CN.4/367.
[22] See remarks by Flitan, ibid., vol. 1, p. 213.

(1) *The determination of the territorial extent of the needs*

This should be the first question to be addressed. It has on occasion been argued that only the needs of the basin area[23] should be considered. This was one of the arguments produced by the Indian States of Maharashtra and Mysore against the State of Andhra Pradesh in the dispute concerning the allocation of the waters of the Krishna river.[24] The view was not shared by the Krishna Water Disputes Tribunal (1973), which stated that:

The need for diversion of water to another watershed may be a relevant factor in equitable apportionment. . . . Thus, the relevant consideration is the interest of the State as a whole and all its inhabitants and not merely the interest of the basin areas of the State.[25]

In the dispute concerning the waters of another Indian watercourse, the Narmada river, the State of Madhya Pradesh and the State of Maharashtra put forward the argument that:[26]

. . . the question of equitable apportionment [should] be related exclusively to the area and people within the river basin and the extension of irrigation to

[23] The basin area is the tract of land drained of both surface runoff and groundwater discharge. See Newson, *Hydrology and the River Environment* (Oxford, 1994), p. 149.

[24] The Krishna river dispute concerned the Indian States of Mysore, Maharashtra and Andhra Pradesh, all of which claimed a particular share of the waters of the river. The Constitution of India provides that for the resolution of this kind of dispute the Central Government can appoint a special tribunal. This was the case with the Krishna river. On 10 April 1969, the Government of India established the Krishna Water Disputes Tribunal, which rendered its decision in 1973. The Tribunal applied the rule of equitable apportionment, which was understood as a rule requiring the consideration of 'many variable yet important factors, such as, the hydrological, climatic and physical characteristics of the river basin, the volume of available supply, diversions and return of flow, the statewise drainage area and contribution to the supply, the respective needs of the States, the population dependent on the water supply and the degree of their dependence; alternative means of satisfying the needs, the extent of lawfully established uses in each State, the relative value of different uses, and the avoidance of unnecessary waste of water'. It further observed that in the application of the rule, 'the decisions of courts and tribunals and opinion of jurists on international law may be consulted': Government of India, *The Report of the Krishna Water Disputes Tribunal* (New Delhi, 1973), vol. 1, pp. 94–5.

[25] All the out-of-basin areas irrigated by the Krishna river lay in the territory of Andhra Pradesh: ibid., vol. 2, pp. 126–9.

[26] The Narmada river was the object of disputes between the Indian States of Madhya Pradesh, Gujarat, Rajasthan and Maharashtra. This dispute was decided in 1978 by the Narmada Water Disputes Tribunal, which in applying the rule of equitable apportionment pointed out that: 'The doctrine of Equitable Apportionment is derived from the basic concepts of international law. According to this doctrine, each State in the drainage basin of an international river system is entitled to a just and reasonable share of the benefits. What is just and equitable depends upon all the relevant facts in each particular case.' The following relevant factors were included in the process: 'the volume of the stream, the water uses already being made by the States concerned, the respective areas of land yet to be watered, the physical and climatic characteristics of the States, the relative productivity of land in the States, the Statewise drainage area, the population dependent on the water supply and the degree of their dependence, alternative means of satisfying the needs, the amount of water which each State contributes to the Inter-State stream, extent of evaporation in each State, and the avoidance of unnecessary waste in the utilisation of the water by the concerned States': Government of India, *The Report of the Narmada Water Disputes Tribunal* (New Delhi, 1978), vol. 1, pp. 113 and 115.

adjoining, extra-basin areas [could not] be justified on grounds of their dependence on use of the water or the easy commandability of such areas by the lower riparian State.[27]

The Narmada Tribunal (1978) also rejected that argument, maintaining that: ' . . . the need of diversion of water to another watershed can be a relevant factor in any question of equitable apportionment'.[28]

In truth, there is no ground for arguing either that the water-related needs of areas lying outside the basin should be disregarded or that the diversion of water outside a basin is unlawful. In this connection, the ILC Draft Articles refer to the needs of the watercourse States without establishing any territorial limit for the consideration of those needs other than the territorial extent of the respective States.[29] In addition, the Helsinki Rules state that each basin State is entitled *within its territory* to the equitable and reasonable use of an international drainage basin.[30] The conclusion should be, therefore, that the water requirements of the State as a whole must be taken into consideration. A related but different question is that concerning the possibility of preferring the needs of the basin over the needs of areas located outside the drainage area. The issue of preferences is examined in section B.

(2) *The population dependent on the waters of the river*

This factor is included in Article 6.1(c) of the ILC Draft Articles. The commentary to this provision states that its intention has been 'to note the importance of account being taken of both the size of the population dependent on the watercourse and the degree or extent of their dependence'.[31] The Helsinki Rules also included the population dependent on the waters of the basin in the list of relevant factors contained in Article V.[32]

The Narmada Water Disputes Tribunal maintained that 'the population of the States dependent on water supply and the degree of their dependence' was a relevant factor to take into account in the equitable division of the waters of the Narmada river.[33] A similar statement was made by the Krishna Water Disputes Tribunal when enumerating the factors to take into consideration in the process of the equitable apportionment of the Krishna river.[34] This factor was also taken into account by the Argentine Supreme Court (1987) in the dispute between the Argentinian provinces of La Pampa and Mendoza concerning the waters

[27] Ibid., para. 9.6.6, p. 122.
[28] Ibid., para. 9.6.10, p. 123.
[29] See Article 6.1(b) of the Draft Articles.
[30] See Article IV of the Helsinki Rules.
[31] See 1994 *ILC Report*, pp. 231–3.
[32] See Article V.2(f) of the Helsinki Rules.
[33] *Report of the Narmada Water Disputes Tribunal*, vol. 1, paras. 9.5.1 and 9.6.1, pp. 119 and 121.
[34] *Report of the Krishna Water Disputes Tribunal*, vol. 1, p. 94.

of the Atuel river.[35] The Argentine Supreme Court observed that 100,000 inhabitants in Mendoza were almost completely dependent on agriculture and, hence, on the waters of the Atuel river, while only 3,024 inhabitants in the province of La Pampa could have benefited from those waters.[36] Undoubtedly this fact influenced the decision of the Supreme Court to allocate the whole of the waters of the Atuel to the province of Mendoza.[37]

(3) *The extent of irrigated and irrigable land*

In many cases the dispute will refer to the water requirements of irrigation projects. In those cases the extent of irrigated and irrigable land may well be relevant factors to take into account. Irrigated land refers to land already under irrigation and cultivation and, thus, it is an existing use, while irrigable land includes existing as well as prospective irrigation. It will depend on the circumstances of the case if the relevant factor is one or the other. The Narmada Water Disputes Tribunal took into account the extent of irrigable land, observing that this was one of the most important criteria to take into account.[38] The Argentine Supreme Court also took into consideration the extent of irrigable land when dividing the waters of the Atuel river between the provinces of La Pampa and Mendoza. It was decided that Mendoza was entitled to use the whole of the waters of the Atuel, and in arriving at this conclusion the Court heavily relied on the fact that 75,761 hectares of irrigated land were located in Mendoza whereas just 15,000 hectares of irrigable land were located in La Pampa.[39] The Krishna Tribunal favoured irrigated land over irrigable land. The extent of the irrigable area would clearly have tipped the balance in favour of the States of Mysore and Maharashtra. Accordingly, these States worked out their claims on the basis of their cultivable area.[40] However, the State of Andhra Pradesh, having less extent of cultivable and irrigable area, was already using a large portion of the waters of the river. The position of the Tribunal was to

---

[35] The Argentine Supreme Court applied the rule of equitable utilization and stated that for the settlement of the dispute it was necessary to take into consideration the rules of customary international law: República Argentina, *Fallos de la Corte Suprema de Justicia de la Nación*, 1987, tomo 310, vol. 3, p. 2577.

[36] Ibid., p. 2490.

[37] The fact that the Argentine Supreme Court decided to allocate 100% of the waters of the Atuel river to one of the litigant provinces prompts the question whether such a solution could be applied between sovereign States. It must be noted that such a decision would disregard sovereignty entirely, and for this reason it is doubtful that it could be consonant with the rule of equitable utilization. But still this decision is useful in the identification of the relevant factors, although the importance of the social and economic dependence criterion could have been exaggerated by the Argentine Supreme Court.

[38] *Report of the Narmada Water Disputes Tribunal*, vol. 1, paras. 9.5.1 and 9.6.1, pp. 119 and 121.

[39] *Fallos de la Corte Suprema de Justicia de la Nación*, 1987, tomo 310, vol. 3, pp. 2545 and 2577.

[40] *Report of the Krishna Water Disputes Tribunal*, vol. 2, pp. 172–4.

favour the extent of irrigated land over irrigable areas, pointing out that:

. . . the various factors which have been mentioned in the statements filed by the States of Maharashtra and Mysore go to show that these two States, in spite of their need for water, could not or did not utilise the waters of the river Krishna in the past to the extent they would have been held entitled to do so had an equitable distribution taken place at some earlier date. But we are dividing the waters of the river Krishna on the basis of the conditions and circumstances as prevailing at present and for reasons which we have already given, we have held that uses made by all three States upto [sic] 1693.4 T.M.C. should prevail over the contemplated uses. It is earnestly submitted by the learned Advocate General of Maharashtra and the Counsel for the State of Mysore that to allocate any more water to the State of Andhra Pradesh out of the remaining water would be to perpetuate the inequity further. It would mean that the State which is making the least contribution and which has benefited to the largest extent would still claim more water at the expense of the States who are in dire need of water for irrigation. This, it is contended, is making the rich richer while the other States entitled to a much larger share will not even get the crumbs. . . .

We realise the force of the arguments of the learned Counsel for Maharashtra and Mysore. From the point of irrigable area, population or contribution to the total flow, the State of Andhra Pradesh for historical reasons is enjoying the benefit of the river Krishna to an extent which may appear to be disproportionate. But it has entered into field [sic] much earlier than the other States, and it has been able to develop its economy by bringing large tracts of land under cultivation in its territory by the hard labour and valiant efforts of its people and at great cost.[41]

It will be seen in section III below that existing utilization of the river by the States concerned does not possess any inherent superiority over other factors and, depending on the circumstances of the case, existing uses may have to give way to prospective utilization. What the Krishna Water Disputes Tribunal shows is that existing uses can be of great assistance in the establishment of economic and social dependence.

(4) *The extent of the economy of the States that is dependent on the river*

The determination of the degree of dependence of the States on the waters of a particular river is not only a question of comparing demographic figures or hectares of irrigable land, but it is also important to determine the extent of the economy of the States concerned that is dependent on the waters of the river. It is true that neither the ILC Draft Articles nor the Helsinki Rules refer explicitly to this criterion, but the International Law Association included it in the 'Statement of Principles upon which to base Rules of Law governing the Use of International Rivers' adopted at its Dubrovnik Conference in 1956.[42]

[41] Ibid., vol. 2, pp. 174–5. T.M.C.=thousand million cubic feet of water.
[42] See Principle V(*b*) of the Statement of Principles, in ILA, *Report of the Forty-Seventh Conference* (Dubrovnik, 1956), p. 242.

On the basis of this criterion a State with less population and irrigable land than others could be allocated more water than its neighbours as a result of the high degree of dependence of its economy on the utilization of that river. That was precisely the situation that came before the Krishna Tribunal. The State of Andhra Pradesh presented less population and irrigable land than the States of Maharashtra and Mysore. According to Mysore, 31.1% of the population of the three States and 33.9% of the population directly dependent on the Krishna basin lived in Andhra Pradesh. As regards cultivable area, only 26.6% of the cultivable land lay in Andhra Pradesh's territory.[43] In spite of that, Andhra Pradesh was able to prove that its economy was highly dependent on the waters of the river and, therefore, it was allocated almost 39% of the disputed water resources.[44]

In the dispute between the Argentinian provinces of La Pampa and Mendoza the extent of the economic dependence of Mendoza was crucial for the final decision of the Argentine Supreme Court, which allocated the whole of the waters of the Atuel river to this province. The Court observed that the economic development of two important zones within the province of Mendoza was essentially based on irrigation by the waters of the Atuel river and that 100,000 inhabitants in those zones depended on agriculture for their livelihood,[45] while in La Pampa only 3,024 inhabitants could have depended on those waters.[46]

With regard to the Columbia River and the Canadian intention to divert water from the Kootenay River into the Columbia River and from the Columbia into the Fraser River, the United States Department of State, in a Memorandum of 1958, held that the riparian States were entitled to a just and reasonable share in the use and benefits of international waters and that in determining what was a reasonable and just apportionment account was to be taken of the rights arising out of the extent of the dependence of each riparian upon the waters in question.[47]

(5) The existence of alternative water resources

Article 6.1(g) of the ILC Draft Articles provides that account should be taken of 'the availability of alternatives, of corresponding value, to a particular planned or existing use', and Article V.2(h) of the Helsinki Rules provides for the consideration of 'the availability of other resources'. The existence of alternative water resources for the satisfaction of the water-related needs of the States concerned implies that

---

[43] According to Maharashtra, 31.20% of the total population lived in Andhra Pradesh and only 26.40% of the cultivable area lay in Andhra Pradesh's territory. See *Report of the Krishna Water Disputes Tribunal*, vol. 2, pp. 172–3.

[44] Ibid., vol. 2, pp. 174–5 and pp. 226–7.

[45] *Fallos de la Corte Suprema de Justicia de la Nación*, 1987, tomo 310, vol. 3, p. 2577.

[46] Ibid. p. 2540.

[47] Cited in Whiteman, *Digest of International Law*, vol. 3 (1964), p. 940.

regarding those needs there is no real dependence on the waters of a particular river and, therefore, priority should be given to the satisfaction of the water requirements which cannot be met by other water supplies.

The Narmada[48] and the Krishna Water Disputes Tribunals[49] took this factor into account. The Narmada Tribunal rejected the State of Gujarat's claim for water for the irrigation of a certain extent of land (the Mahi area) because this area was already irrigated or intended to be irrigated by the Mahi river.[50] With regard to the equitable utilization of the Krishna river, the States of Maharashtra and Mysore claimed that the State of Andhra Pradesh could satisfy its needs by diverting water from the Godavari river into the Krishna. The Krishna Water Disputes Tribunal examined this proposal, concluding that at that moment the diversion of the Godavari river into the Krishna river was just a remote possibility, on which basis it could not cut down Andhra Pradesh's share of the waters of the Krishna river.[51] It is interesting to note, nevertheless, that the Tribunal would have arrived at a different conclusion had the diversion of the Godavari river been impending.

The Krishna Tribunal also took this factor into account when deciding 'on pragmatic considerations' what needs of the States could be satisfied on an equitable basis.[52] The Tribunal held that all the existing uses of water up to September 1960 were to be maintained. With regard to prospective utilization and to the projects undertaken after September 1960, the Tribunal examined the water requirements of each of these projects, taking particularly into account the possibility of satisfying those requirements with the amount of rainfall in each of the zones intended to be irrigated with waters of the Krishna river. If in the opinion of the Tribunal the water requirements of a particular irrigation scheme could be met by the amount of rainfall in the respective areas, then that project could not count as evidence of the water-related needs of the States.[53]

Finally, it should be noted that the alternative water supplies should be of a 'corresponding value'. The ILC has pointed out that the expression 'corresponding value' is intended to convey the idea of generally comparable feasibility, practicability and cost-effectiveness.[54] The Helsinki Rules contain a similar provision requiring the consideration of 'the comparative costs of alternative means of satisfying the economic and social needs of each basin State'.[55]

---

[48] *Report of the Narmada Water Disputes Tribunal*, vol. 1, para. 9.5.1, p. 119.
[49] *Report of the Krishna Water Disputes Tribunal*, vol. 1, p. 94.
[50] *Report of the Naramda Water Disputes Tribunal*, vol. 1, para. 6.5.2, p. 75.
[51] *Report of the Krishna Water Disputes Tribunal*, vol. 1, pp. 66–9.
[52] Ibid., vol. 2, pp. 178–9.
[53] Ibid., vol. 2, pp. 192–200.
[54] 1994 *ILC Report*, p. 233.
[55] See Art. V.2(g) of the Helsinki Rules.

(6) *The existence of alternative means of satisfying the needs of the States, other than alternative sources of water supply*

As has been said, Article 6.1(*g*) of the Draft Articles mentions the availability of alternatives, of corresponding value, to a particular planned or existing use. The ILC commentary to this provision further states that:

the alternatives may thus take the form *not only of other sources of water supply*, but also of other means—not involving the use of water—of meeting the needs in question, such as alternative sources of energy or means of transport.[56]

Article V.2(*g*) of the Helsinki Rules requires the consideration of the 'comparative costs of alternative means of satisfying the economic and social needs of each basin State'. The satisfaction of these needs might be related to water, but, as happens with food and electric power requirements, there can be alternatives not involving use of water.

All the above-mentioned factors may help in the determination of the real social and economic water-related needs of the States. These needs may serve as a basis for a proportional division of the waters of international watercourses. However, a question of preferences between the various needs may arise. Accordingly, the possibility of establishing such preferences is explored in the next section.

B. *The Relative Value of the Various Needs of the States. The Question of Preferences*

This section is not intended to challenge the principle that there is no pre-established hierarchy between the various factors that may be considered in the establishment of an equitable regime for the utilization of international rivers. Article 10.1 of the ILC Draft Articles prescribes that: 'In the absence of agreement or custom to the contrary, no use of an international watercourse enjoys inherent priority over other uses'. In a similar fashion, Article VI of the Helsinki Rules provides that: 'A use or category of uses is not entitled to any inherent preference over any other use or category of uses'. Nevertheless, in the process of assessment of the relevance of the various prospective factors it may be necessary to prefer certain uses to others. The following pages will attempt to establish which conditions may lead to the establishment of such preferences.

Article 10.2 of the ILC Draft Articles provides that:

In the event of a conflict between uses of an international watercourse, it shall be resolved with reference to the principles and factors set out in articles 5 to 7, with *special regard being given to the requirements of vital human needs* [italics added].

---

[56] 1994 *ILC Report*, p. 233 (emphasis added).

In the commentary attached to this provision, the ILC explains that the requirements of vital human needs include the supply of drinking water and the provision of the water required for the production of food in order to prevent starvation.[57] The various categories of uses which could be given priority are examined below.

(1) *Domestic uses*

In this connection, Lipper observes that there seems to be a tendency among governments and courts to give preference to drinking and other domestic uses.[58] In fact, the US Supreme Court has repeatedly stated that 'drinking and other domestic uses are the highest uses of water'.[59]

The 1909 Treaty between the United States and Great Britain relating to Boundary Waters established the following order of precedence among the different uses of boundary rivers: (i) uses for domestic and sanitary purposes; (ii) uses for navigation; and (iii) uses for power and for irrigation purposes.[60] The 1944 Treaty between the United States and Mexico relating to the Utilization of the Waters of the Colorado and Tijuana Rivers and of the Rio Grande also established an order of priority among the different water uses which should guide the International Boundary and Water Commission in the settlement of water disputes. In that list, domestic and municipal uses are mentioned in the first place, followed by agriculture and stock-raising, which in turn have to be preferred to electric power production. The Rau Commission (1942), an Indian conciliatory commission appointed to propose a solution to a dispute between the Indian provinces of Sind and Punjab concerning the utilization of the Indus river, suggested the following order of precedence between the different projects: (i) use for domestic and sanitary purposes; (ii) use for navigation, and (iii) use for power and irrigation.[61] The Krishna Water Disputes Tribunal stated that: 'use of water for drinking, house-hold purposes and watering of cattle is regarded as the primary use to which all other uses are subordinate'.[62]

The above-mentioned instances of international and municipal practice all ranked domestic uses in the first place. It is apparent, therefore, that domestic uses, so far as they are vital for the population, will in general have to be preferred to other uses. It does not follow from this,

---

[57] Ibid., p. 257.

[58] Lipper, 'Equitable Utilization', in Garretson, Hayton and Olmstead (eds.), *The Law of International Drainage Basins* (New York, 1967), p. 61.

[59] *Connecticut* v. *Massachusetts*, 282 US 660, 673 (1931). See also *Nebraska* v. *Wyoming*, 325 US 589, 656 (1945); *New Jersey* v. *New York*, 283 US 336 (1931); and *Wisconsin* v. *Illinois*, 281 US 179, 200 (1930). As for a definition of domestic use, the 1995 Protocol on Shared Watercourse Systems in the Southern African Development Community (SADC) Region has pointed out that it 'means use of water for drinking, washing, cooking, bathing, sanitation and stock watering purposes'.

[60] See Art. VIII of the 1909 Boundary Waters Treaty, text in Bloomfield and Fitzgerald, *Boundary Waters Problems of Canada and the United States* (Toronto, 1958), p. 211.

[61] *Report of the Indus (Rau) Commission* (Simla, 1942), vol. 1, p. 11.

[62] *Report of the Krishna Water Disputes Tribunal*, vol. 2, p. 138.

of course, that domestic uses should be accorded an automatic priority in the process of weighing up the various relevant factors, as any ascription of an automatic priority would bypass the necessary stage of determining what the real needs of the States are. In this connection, the International Law Association supported its rejection of a pre-established priority of domestic uses with the following example:

State B, for example, uses the waters of an international drainage basin for domestic purposes. State A, the upper riparian, uses the water for important industrial purposes, which result in the rising of the temperature of the water so as to make it unsuitable for drinking. An investigation discloses that only a relative handful of State B's inhabitants use the water for domestic purposes; that another equally convenient source of adequate quantities is available a few miles away; and that State A is prepared to pay any costs involved in making the change over. Is State A to be barred from its use merely because the conflicting use of State B happens to be a domestic use? A rule of artificial preference would dictate such a result, although manifestly unjust.[63]

This example refers to a situation in which the domestic needs of the population of State B could not be regarded as evidencing real dependence. However, once the genuineness of the domestic dependence is established, it is clear that domestic needs should be given priority.

(2) Irrigation

As regards the possibility of preferring irrigation to other uses, such as the production of electric energy, the question refers also to the vital character of the irrigation needs of the States. The Krishna Water Disputes Tribunal dealt with the problem, concluding that irrigation in the Krishna basin should prevail over hydro-electric use requiring diversion of the Krishna river. The Tribunal was of the opinion that no use possessed an *a priori* superiority, but it maintained that the examination of the factual circumstances of the case could lead to preference being given to a particular use. The special circumstances of India determined that irrigation was to be accorded priority. In 1972 the Irrigation Commission of India observed that:

5.19 To meet various long term requirements in an orderly manner, there should be an order of priority for water-use. The priority accorded to any particular requirement vis-à-vis others should depend upon its economic contribution and its significance to the well-being of the people. Domestic requirements must be given the highest priority . . .
5.21 Multipurpose river valley projects offer the best use of surface water resources; but apart from situations where both power generation and irrigation may be possible, there may be other cases in which a choice has to be made between the use of water either for irrigation or power generation. . . . In such cases, where a choice is involved, the priority has to be determined not only by

[63] ILA, *Report of the Fifty-Second Conference* (Helsinki, 1966), p. 491.

economic considerations but by recognition of the fact that irrigation is possible only by the use of water, whereas power can be generated from alternative sources such as coal, gas, oil and atomic fuels.[64]

The Krishna Tribunal, sharing the view of the Indian Irrigation Commission, stated that:

For irrigation use there is no substitute for water, but power may be generated from coal, oil, nuclear energy and other sources. In general, whenever production of hydro-electric power interferes with irrigation and the two uses cannot be reconciled increasing priority may be given to irrigation. Rapid growth in population calls for increased food production which in turn calls for intensified irrigation.[65]

Accordingly, the Tribunal took into consideration that:

75.8 percent of the population in the Krishna basin lies in rural areas and 68 percent of the working force is engaged as cultivators or agriculture labourers. The agrarian population is entirely dependent on the Krishna waters for irrigation. Having regard to the economic and social needs of the population, their dependence on the Krishna waters for irrigation and the hydrology, climate and physical characteristics of the basin, irrigation use is of prime importance and of the greatest value to the basin community as a whole. In view of the overall scarcity of the Krishna waters, preference should be given to irrigation use over power production by westward diversion of water.[66]

In the dispute concerning the Narmada river, the Narmada Tribunal also gave priority to irrigation over the production of hydro-electric power. The Tribunal was asked, among other things, to determine the level of the Navagam Canal and the height of the Sardar Sarovar Dam to be built by the State of Gujarat. The States of Madhya Pradesh and Maharashtra argued in favour of a low supply level for the canal and a low height for the dam. The acceptance of this claim would have meant a restriction on the possibilities of establishing irrigation by flow in the territories of Gujarat and Rajasthan. The opinion of the Narmada Tribunal was that:

10.10.1 At the outset the most important question for consideration is the conflict between providing flow irrigation to a reasonable extent for areas in Gujarat and Rajasthan and the generation of power by curtailing the extent of such irrigation by flow.

As a matter of law there is no fixed or automatic preference of one use over another (Article VI, Helsinki Rules). But one use may be preferred to another use in the circumstances of a particular case because of its greater value and importance to the community as a whole. . . .

. . .

---

[64] Ministry of Irrigation and Power, *Report of the Irrigation Commission* (New Delhi, 1972), vol. 1, pp. 89–90.

[65] *Report of the Krishna Water Disputes Tribunal*, vol. 2, p. 139.

[66] Ibid., p. 147.

10.10.3 For irrigation use, there is obviously no substitute for water, but power may be generated from coal, oil, nuclear energy and other sources. In general, whenever production of hydro-electric power interferes with irrigation and the two uses cannot be reconciled, increasing priority may have to be given to irrigation. Rapid growth in population calls for increased food production which in turn calls for intensified irrigation.

10.10.4 In countries with a hot and arid climate, water is absolutely indispensable for cultivation of the soil, and the use of water for irrigation is regarded as an ordinary or primary use for satisfying a natural want. In the arid and semi-arid parts of the country, irrigation makes the difference between waste land and highly productive crop land. . . .

10.10.5 . . . Indian economy is predominantly agrarian, as 75 per cent of the country's population depends on agriculture for livelihood. Nearly 60 per cent of total household consumption and 85 per cent of the commodity consumption of households are composed of agricultural products or manufactures based principally on agricultural raw materials. . . . The use of water resources for irrigation to the fullest extent possible is an essential condition for diversifying agriculture and increasing crop yields. Thus, irrigation plays a key role in the planned development of the country. Without irrigation, large arid tracts of the country would be permanently waste, while many other tracts having low and uncertain rainfall would be cultivated only in favourable seasons. . . .

10.10.6 We are accordingly of opinion that irrigation use of waters of Narmada should prevail over its hydroelectric use in case of any conflict of the two uses in the circumstances of the present case.[67]

(3) *The needs of the drainage area*

Finally, the possibility of preferring the needs of the drainage area to the needs of zones located outside the basin should be examined. It is true that there is no legal limitation on the use of the waters of a river in areas outside the drainage area, but nevertheless it has been claimed that the needs of this area should be accorded priority. The establishment of such a preference would imply that the diversion of water for the satisfaction of the needs of areas located outside the basin would be limited to the surplus waters left after the satisfaction of the needs of the drainage area, the justification being that drainage areas are, in general, more dependent on the basin waters than out-of-basin zones. It was on the basis of dependence that the Krishna Water Disputes Tribunal concluded that: 'In equitable allocation, future uses requiring diversion of water outside the basin are relevant, but more weight may be given to uses requiring diversion of water inside the basin'.[68] In so far as this priority is based on an assumed greater degree of dependence of the drainage areas, it is not pertinent to speak of intra-basin water requirements as a special category of preferential needs. If any preference is given to the water requirements of the drainage area this should be done

[67] *Report of the Narmada Water Disputes Tribunal*, vol. 2, pp. 8–10.
[68] *Report of the Krishna Water Disputes Tribunal*, vol. 2, p. 128.

on the basis of the vital character of those needs. The possibility of attributing this character to different categories of uses has already been discussed in terms that it would be immaterial to distinguish between intra- and extra-basin water requirements.

III. THE RELEVANCE OF EXISTING USES

Disputes concerning the utilization of the waters of an international watercourse may often consist in a dispute between a State that uses the waters and a State that intends to do so, and where the water available is not enough to satisfy both present and future utilization. In such a situation, the difficulty concerns the relevance to ascribe to the pattern of existing uses in the process of the establishment of an equitable regime for the utilization of an international river.

The Committee on the Uses of Waters of International Rivers of the American Branch of the International Law Association pointed out that: 'As a rule the protection of uses, lawful when they came into existence, so long as they remain beneficial, has been treated as an absolute first charge upon the waters'.[69] This contention of the American Branch of the ILA has found considerable doctrinal support. In fact, numerous commentators attribute a great degree of relevance to the pattern of existing uses on the basis that alongside other relevant factors the criterion is viewed as superior. In the first part of this section, it will be argued that such an approach is an overestimation of the real importance of this criterion. After demonstrating that to accord priority to this factor is not compatible with the rule of equitable utilization, the second part will attempt to define the proper role of the existing patterns of water utilization in the process of the establishment of an equitable regime for the use of international rivers.

A. *Is it Compatible with the Rule of Equitable Utilization to Accord Priority to the Existing Patterns of Utilization over other Relevant Factors?*

If the ILC Draft Articles on the Law of the Non-Navigational Uses of International Watercourses are taken as the starting point for the determination of the relevance of the pattern of existing uses, the result is quite disappointing for the advocates of the pre-eminence of this criterion. The ILC refers to existing and potential uses as criteria to be

---

[69] 'Principles of Law Governing Use of International Rivers', *Inter-American Bar Association Conference Report*, 10 (1957), p. 12, quoted by Johnston, 'Effect of Existing Uses on the Equitable Apportionment of International Rivers. I: An American View', *University of British Columbia Law Review*, 1 (1960), p. 394.

taken into account, and it emphasizes in the commentary attached to Article 6 of the Draft Articles that 'neither is given priority', recognizing that 'one or both factors may be relevant in a given case'.[70] However, some writers claim that existing patterns of water utilization should be accorded priority over other criteria. Jiménez de Aréchaga counted among them when stating that:

> In general, treaties are based on the respect for the existing uses, which is logical, because affecting such uses in another state would cause a substantial injury giving rise to compensation. . . . In this matter therefore, the maxim that priority of expropriation gives a better right, governs: 'prior in tempore, potior in jure'. This does not mean, however, that the existence of certain uses would inevitably prevent proposed works when they represent an improvement and better use of the water. In such a case the solution would be to find the technical means to ensure recognition of the existing uses as did France in the Lake Lanoux case, and when this is not possible, to provide monetary compensation for uses discontinued by new works.[71]

In the present chapter the validity of this argument is questioned. Can the rule of equitable utilization of international watercourses be construed as giving the existing patterns of utilization superiority of right over other relevant factors involved in the process of water apportionment? Positive answers have been founded on very different grounds. In this regard, many commentators have relied upon the case law of the Supreme Court of the United States of America, which has dealt at large with the argument of the priority of existing utilization. Also, instances of international State practice are often mentioned as authority for the protection of prior utilization. Such a view has also been based on the principle of *sic utere tuo ut alienum non laedas*. Arguments in favour of an alleged obligation to compensate for the termination or modification of existing uses have also been presented as providing additional support for the privileged position of this criterion. Finally, there have been attempts to apply the notion of 'acquired rights' to existing uses as a way to assimilate the termination of existing utilization to the expropriation of property in international law. In the next pages it will be demonstrated that all these arguments should be rejected.

(1) *The practice of the Supreme Court of the United States in which the principle of priority of appropriation has been applied to inter-State water disputes cannot be exported to the international sphere*

Reference to the case law of the US Supreme Court regarding inter-State water disputes seeks to assert the existence of a rule of general application providing for the priority of existing patterns of utilization in

[70] 1994 *ILC Report*, p. 233.
[71] Jiménez de Aréchaga, 'International Legal Rules Governing Use of Waters from International Watercourses', *Inter-American Law Review*, 2 (1960), pp. 335–6.

the process of water apportionment. It will be demonstrated that this American case law cannot be invoked in support of the priority of existing uses as a principle of international law.

In the United States, the protection of already existing utilization of a watercourse took the form of a set of rules based on the doctrine of prior appropriation that were to be distinguished from the rules of riparianism. Riparianism implied that only the owners of the land abutting a watercourse were entitled to its use, and that in case of competing incompatible utilizations by different riparians a reasonable and equitable adjustment was to be made. The doctrine of prior appropriation implied the respect of prior uses in terms that prior utilization was superior in right to uses commencing later in time. The rules based on the doctrine of prior appropriation originated in the Western States, whose water laws were shaped by the arid climatic conditions and the geography of the zone, and by the pattern of economic expansion existing during the nineteenth century, based mainly on mining activities.[72] The aridity of the American West determined that the amount of water was inadequate to supply everybody's needs, the geographical conditions determined that artificial irrigation was necessary and the pattern of economic expansion, based mainly on the mining industry, implied that miners applied the same rule as that governing mining claims to water rights claims, that is to say, the rule of priority of appropriation.[73] The rigidity of the rule was ameliorated by later developments in the law, in terms that the condition of a use being beneficial was said to be the basis, measure and limit of prior appropriation.[74] But the requirement that a certain use be beneficial can in no way be said to be similar to the requirement of reasonableness and equitableness applied by riparianism.

The decisions of the US Supreme Court rendered in inter-State water disputes cannot be exported to international law. The superiority of right of existing utilization of the waters of an inter-State river was admitted by the US Supreme Court when the States involved applied that doctrine as a rule within their own jurisdiction, and this is explained by the particularities of the American legal system. As has been stated by Tarlock:

The Court initially rejected local law as the basis for an apportionment, then accepted it as the basis among states that followed the same law, and finally downgraded local law to a 'guiding principle'. Fair allocation rather than consistency with locally generated expectations became the touchstone of equitable apportionment. Local law remains, however, central to an equitable apportionment inquiry. Although the Court has never been very precise about the source of the law of equitable apportionment, its early decisions make it

---

[72] Tarlock, Corbridge and Getches, *Water Resource Management* (New York, 1993), p. 150.
[73] Ibid., p. 153.
[74] Ibid., p. 195.

clear that the grant of original jurisdiction requires a federal law that will not allow one state to use its law to gain an unfair advantage over another. The use of local law as a basis for allocation is thus not compelled by the constitution. But local law may serve as a source of principles to apply since a federal common law must of necessity examine the most relevant sources of substantive law.[75]

A more detailed examination of the relevant decisions of the US Supreme Court will prove that the influence of the respective States' water laws dramatically modified the rule of equitable apportionment.

In *Wyoming* v. *Colorado* (1922),[76] the State of Wyoming sued the State of Colorado in order to prevent a proposed diversion by the latter of part of the waters of the Laramie River, contending that its existing uses would be rendered impracticable by the proposed Colorado diversion in so far as no water would be left in the stream sufficient to satisfy its prior and superior appropriations. In rendering its decision, the Supreme Court accepted the Wyoming contention, taking into account particularly the fact that both States applied within their jurisdiction the rule of prior appropriation. In the words of Justice Van Devanter:

. . . here the controversy is between states in both of which the doctrine of appropriation has prevailed from the time of the first settlements, always has been applied in the same way, and has been recognised and sanctioned by the United States, the owner of the public lands. Here the complaining state is not seeking to impose a policy of her choosing on the other state, but to have the common policy which each enforces within her limits applied in determining their relative rights in the interstate stream.

In *Nebraska* v. *Wyoming* (1945),[77] priority of appropriation was again taken into account in the apportionment of the waters of the North Platte River. In this case the Court intended to apply the rule of equitable apportionment, as distinct from the riparian rule or the prior appropriation one. Nevertheless, priority of appropriation was ascribed the role of a guiding principle in the process of allocation. The pre-eminent position attributed to prior appropriations was due to the fact that the three States involved, namely Colorado, Wyoming and Nebraska, applied that system within their territories.[78] Therefore, the 'guiding principle' consisting in the protection of existing uses cannot be seen as an element inherent in the rule of equitable utilization. It must be said that the Court did not really apply the rule of equitable apportionment, but a version of the rule conditioned by the States' legal systems.

---

[75] Tarlock, 'The Law of Equitable Apportionment Revisited, Updated and Restated', *University of Colorado Law Review*, 56 (1985), p. 394.
[76] *Wyoming* v. *Colorado*, 259 US 419 (1922).
[77] *Nebraska* v. *Wyoming*, 325 US 589 (1945).
[78] The Court stated that 'Since Colorado, Wyoming and Nebraska are appropriation States, that principle would seem to be equally applicable here'.

The idea of priority of appropriation as the guiding principle received further application in *Colorado* v. *New Mexico* (1982).[79] In this case, Colorado sued New Mexico in order to obtain an equitable apportionment of the waters of the Vermejo River. New Mexico argued on the basis of the rule of prior appropriation, in force in the two States, while Colorado based its case on the rule of equitable apportionment. The Supreme Court, as in the previous case, applied the rule of equitable apportionment and rejected New Mexico's contention that the Special Master appointed in the case was required to focus exclusively on the rule of priority. Nevertheless, priority of appropriation found its way into the reasoning of the Court in the same manner as it did in *Nebraska* v. *Wyoming* (1945). In fact, the Supreme Court repeated the statement that: 'When, as in this case, both States recognize the doctrine of prior appropriation, priority becomes the "Guiding principle" in an allocation between competing States'. The fact that the superiority of prior appropriations was taken as the guiding principle resulted in a dramatic shift of the burden of proof which transformed the requirement of reasonableness and equitableness of the uses into a mere nominal condition. This is shown by the following paragraph of the decision:

Under some circumstances . . . the countervailing equities supporting a diversion for future use in one State may justify the detriment to existing users in another State. This may be the case, for example, where the State seeking a diversion demonstrates *by clear and convincing evidence* that the benefits of the diversion *substantially outweigh* the harm that might result [italics added].

It is evident that in a situation where the termination or modification of existing uses needs to *substantially outweigh* the maintenance of the *status quo*, it is not possible to speak of an assessment of the impact of the various criteria on an equal footing, as the rule of equitable apportionment requires. In this regard, it should be noted that Article VIII(1) of the Helsinki Rules uses different language, providing that an existing reasonable use may continue in operation unless the facts justifying its continuance are *outweighed* by other factors, whereas the US Supreme Court decided that the maintenance of the existing pattern of usage should be *substantially outweighed* by other factors.

The separate opinion of Justice O'Connor, with whom Justice Powell joined, helps to clarify the consequences that might follow from *Colorado* v. *New Mexico* (1982). The relevant paragraphs of this separate opinion state that:

This case therefore highlights the restraint with which the Court should proceed in apportioning interstate waters between a State seeking a *future* use and a State with an existing economy dependent upon the waters to be apportioned. The Court can only invite litigation within its original jurisdiction

[79] *Colorado* v. *New Mexico*, 459 US 176, 103 S Ct. 539, 74 L Ed. 2d 348.

if it permits one State to obtain a diversion for a new use upon that State's allegation that the second State is engaging in 'wasteful' practices or that it can make 'better' use of the waters, even if the second State's uses are entirely reasonable . . .

. . . the Court should be moved to exercise its original jurisdiction to alter the status quo between States only where there is *clear* and *convincing* evidence[80] . . . that one State's use is unreasonably wasteful. To allow Colorado a diversion upon a lesser showing comports neither with the equality of rights of the litigants before us, . . . nor with the sparing use that should be made of the Court's equitable powers, . . . Further, such action would seriously undermine the Court's affirmation, . . . that priority of appropriation is the 'guiding principle' in allocating waters between two prior appropriation States [original emphasis].

The American Supreme Court, in *Colorado v. New Mexico* (1982), was not satisfied by the factual findings of the Special Master, and therefore it required additional findings of fact relevant to determining a just and equitable apportionment of the waters of the Vermejo River between the litigant States. These additional findings of fact were examined in *Colorado v. New Mexico* (1984), in which it is particularly interesting to observe how the shift of the burden of proof entailed by the application of priority of appropriation as a guiding principle makes it very difficult for a State seeking to outweigh existing utilization to succeed. On the one hand, the State of Colorado was requested by the Supreme Court to show by clear and convincing evidence that reasonable conservation measures could compensate for some or all of the proposed diversion and that the injury, if any, to New Mexico would be outweighed by the benefits to Colorado from the diversion. As the Court stated in its decision:

Colorado failed to meet this burden since it did not actually point to specific measures that New Mexico could take to conserve water, did not show how more rigorous water administration would actually preserve existing supplies, did not identify any financially and physically feasible means by which a river conservancy district could further eliminate or reduce inefficiency, did not present any evidence that it had undertaken reasonable steps to minimize the amount of diversion that would be required, has not committed itself to any longterm use for which future benefits could be studied and predicted, and did not specify how long its proposed interim agricultural use might or might not last.

On the other hand, New Mexico was just required to show real or substantial injury, which was not difficult since 'any diversion by Colorado would necessarily reduce the amount of water available to New Mexico users'. New Mexico was not required to show that it was undertaking a reasonable use of the water, nor was it required to prove that there were no means to make water available for Colorado. This

[80] Clear and convincing evidence is a high standard of proof. Ordinary civil cases are judged by a 'preponderance of the evidence' standard.

attitude of the Supreme Court has been criticized, and it has been suggested that:

By establishing prerequisites focusing both on clear and convincing evidence and on real and substantial injury or harm, the Court appears to be expressing its displeasure with its role in resolving interstate water conflicts. Resolving such conflicts is time-consuming and demanding of the limited resources of the Court. It is clear that the Court would prefer these conflicts to be resolved by some other means and in some other forum. It is equally clear, however, that the original intent of the framers of the Constitution was for the Court to resolve conflicts arising between states. The Court appears to be using burden of proof requirements to escape this responsibility.[81]

The cases examined above all relate to States that applied the rule of priority of appropriation within their territories, and it has been demonstrated that it is this very fact that ultimately has determined that, in the application of the rule of equitable apportionment, the Supreme Court of the United States of America has attributed a predominant role to prior utilizations. The situation has been very different in cases involving States that apply the doctrine of riparianism in their territories, as is demonstrated by *Kansas* v. *Colorado* (1906). The State of Kansas applied riparianism to solve disputes between users of water and, consequently, the Court made no reference to prior appropriation as a 'guiding principle' to solve the dispute between this State and the State of Colorado. The equitable water division that the Court attempted to make in this case was based on economic and social dependence rather than on a blind application of the rule of priority of appropriation, as is demonstrated by the following paragraph:

Appropriation of the waters of the Arkansas by Colorado, for purposes of irrigation, has diminished the flow of water into the state of Kansas; . . . the result of that appropriation has been the reclamation of large areas in Colorado, transforming thousands of acres into fertile fields, and rendering possible their occupation and cultivation when otherwise they would have continued barren and unoccupied; . . . while the influence of such diminution has been of perceptible injury to portions of the Arkansas valley in Kansas, particularly those portions closest to the Colorado line, yet to the great body of the valley it has worked little, if any, detriment, and regarding the interests of both states, and the right of each to receive benefit through irrigation and in any other manner from the waters of this stream, we are not satisfied that Kansas has made out a case entitling it to a decree. At the same time it is obvious that if the depletion of the waters of the river by Colorado continues to increase there will come a time when Kansas may justly say that there is no longer an equitable division of benefits, and may rightfully call for relief against the action of Colorado . . .

[81] Sherk, 'Equitable Apportionment After *Vermejo*: The Demise of a Doctrine', *Natural Resources Journal*, 29 (1989), pp. 579–80.

In the next case between Kansas and Colorado (1943) the Court emphasized that its central task was to determine if a State was using or threatening to use more than its equitable share of the benefits of a stream flowing into another State. In accomplishing this task, it stated that all the factors which created equities in favour of one State or the other should be weighed. Thus, the existence of prior uses was not attributed any higher status in the listing of relevant factors. Reference was made to the conduct of the parties which, though related to existing uses, is a different criterion and presents particular characteristics. It appears that for the Court the important thing was to compare the benefits of existing uses with the benefits of proposed future utilization. In this context, the Court said that if an upper State was devoting the water to a beneficial use, the question to be decided, in the light of existing conditions in both States, was whether and to what extent its action injured the lower State and its citizens by depriving them of a like or an equally valuable beneficial use. It follows from this that for the Supreme Court, prior appropriations could be terminated or modified if there was not a balance between the States, the imbalance consisting in one State preventing the other from a utilization of the waters similar in benefits.

In conclusion, the examination of the case law of the US Supreme Court demonstrates that it is not possible to invoke it in support of the assertion that prior utilization should have a predominant position in the process of the establishment of an equitable regime for international waters utilization. Therefore, attempts to interpret the American practice as an instance in which superiority of prior appropriation is still consonant with the rule of equitable apportionment should be rejected.[82]

(2) *Other instances of international State practice do not support the argument of the priority of existing uses*

Apart from the case law of the US Supreme Court, the claim that a watercourse State should not interfere with the existing patterns of utilization in another State is based on numerous treaties. In this section it will be argued that most of these precedents cannot be invoked as supporting the existence of a principle of international law that existing uses must always be protected. In most of these instances of State practice, factors other than the mere historical element have been crucial, in terms that the protection of existing utilization is more likely to be the outcome of the operation of these other factors, rather than the result of

---

[82] The Indus (Rau) Commission, constituted for the solution of a water dispute between the Indian Provinces of Punjab and Sind, made such an attempt when, after examining the US Supreme Court practice, it asserted that: '[t]he doctrine of appropriation . . . is consistent with equitable apportionment, provided that the prior appropriator is not allowed to exceed reasonable requirements': *Report of the Indus (Rau) Commission*, vol. 1, p. 37.

the application of an alleged principle of priority of existing uses. The most common of these other factors are:

(a) The purpose of establishing a pacific and definitive frontier between the States concerned;

(b) Respect for local customs; and

(c) The conduct of the parties.

(a) *The purpose of establishing a pacific and definitive frontier between the States concerned.* The greater part of the State practice on which the advocates of the superiority of right of existing uses rely consists of boundary treaties providing for the continuation of water rights acquired before their entry into force.[83] For example, Article 17 of the 1928 Convention relating to the Settlement of Questions arising out of the Delimitation of the Frontier between the Kingdom of Hungary and the Czechoslovak Republic (Frontier Statute) provides that:

> The Contracting Parties shall acknowledge legally-acquired rights over watercourses and [water-power] plant belonging thereto and established on frontier watercourses or on watercourses intersected by the frontier—in so far as the frontier affects the rights and plant in question—as also rights over frontier watercourses in general, provided that such rights can be proved by the production of official authority or evidence of long-standing rights.[84]

Article 14 of the Treaty between the German Reich and the Czechoslovak Republic regulating the Frontier described in Article 83 of the Treaty of Peace of Versailles, signed at Berlin on 3 February 1927, states that:

> Existing rights in respect of frontier watercourses intersected by the frontier—as regards the latter, in so far as these rights are affected by the tracing of the frontier—as also rights in respect of frontier waters in general, shall continue

---

[83] e.g., Treaty between the Republic of Austria and the Czechoslovak Republic regarding the Settlement of Legal Questions connected with the Frontier, signed at Prague, 12 December 1928, *League of Nations Treaty Series*, vol. 108, p. 57; General Convention concerning the Hydraulic System concluded between the Kingdom of Roumania and the Kingdom of Yugoslavia, signed at Belgrade, 14 December 1931, ibid., vol. 135, p. 31; Convention between Roumania and Yugoslavia concerning the Navigation and the Hydrotechnical System of the Bega (Beget-Begheu) Canal and River, signed at Belgrade, 14 December 1931, ibid., vol. 135, p. 73; Agreement concerning the Frontier between Germany and Belgium, signed at Aix-La-Chapelle, 7 November 1929, ibid., vol. 121, p. 327; Convention relating to the Settlement of Questions arising out of the Delimitation of the Frontier between the Kingdom of Hungary and the Czechoslovak Republic, signed at Prague, 14 November 1928, ibid., vol. 110, p. 425; Treaty between the German Reich and the Czechoslovak Republic regulating the Frontier described in Article 83 of the Treaty of Peace of Versailles of 28 June 1919, signed at Berlin, 3 February 1927, ibid., vol. 109, p. 219; Protocol regarding the Usufruct on the German-Saar Frontier, signed at SaarBruck, 13 November 1926, ibid., vol. 77, p. 249; Treaty between Germany and Poland for the Settlement of Frontier Questions, signed at Poznan, 27 January 1926, ibid., vol. 64, p. 419; Agreement between Germany and Poland regarding the Administration of the Section of the Warta forming the Frontier and Traffic on that Section, signed at Poznan, 16 February 1927, ibid., vol. 71, p. 369.

[84] Ibid., vol. 110, p. 433.

to be legally recognised by both States. The same applies to the joint use of frontier watercourses.[85]

No doubt, the main concern of these agreements was the maintenance of a definitive and pacific frontier. In this regard, the respect for the so-called 'acquired rights' of the parties was functional, and in no case can this State practice be invoked as demonstrating the existence of a principle of international law that established patterns of usage should always be maintained.[86]

(b) *Respect for local customs.* Local custom can constitute a relevant criterion for the establishment of an equitable regime for water utilization. This argument is further examined in section IV of this article. Examples such as the 1926 Agreement of Good Neighbourly Relations concluded between the British and French Governments on behalf of the Territories of Palestine, on the one part, and on behalf of Syria and Great Lebanon, on the other part,[87] and the 1926 Exchange of Notes between the Belgian and British Governments regarding the Frontier of Tanganyika–Ruanda-Urundi,[88] which provide that certain patterns of water and land usage should be maintained despite the new frontiers, should be understood in the context of respect for local customs.[89] Article III of the above-mentioned 1926 Agreement between the British and French Governments provides that:

All the inhabitants, whether settled or semi-nomadic, of both territories who, at the date of the signature of this Agreement enjoy grazing, watering or cultivation rights, or own land on the one or the other side of the frontier shall continue to exercise their rights as in the past. . . . All rights derived from local laws or customs concerning the use of the waters, streams, canals and lakes for the purposes of irrigation or supply of water to the inhabitants shall remain as at present.

The pertinent part of the 1926 Exchange of Notes between the Belgian and British Governments regarding the Frontier of Tanganyika—Ruanda-Urundi provides that: ' . . . notwithstanding the new boundary in Lake Tanganyika . . . all customary rights of fishing and passage exercised by natives living on either side of it should be preserved'.

The prevention of boundary disputes may explain the maintenance of the traditional usage of water in boundary treaties, but it may also be

---

[85] Ibid., vol. 109, p. 245.

[86] For a similar view see Lipper, 'Equitable Utilization', in Garretson, Hayton and Olmstead (eds.), op. cit. above (n. 58), p. 51.

[87] *United Nations Legislative Texts and Treaty Provisions concerning the Utilization of International Rivers for Purposes Other than Navigation,* hereinafter referred to as *UN Legislative Texts and Treaty Provisions,* ST/LEG/SER.B/12, 1964, p. 288.

[88] Brownlie, *African Boundaries, A Legal and Diplomatic Encyclopaedia,* hereinafter referred to as *African Boundaries* (London, 1979), p. 746.

[89] For a more comprehensive list of international agreements acknowledging the preservation of local customs with regard to water utilization, see below, section IV on Local Custom, pp. 373 ff.

argued that from the point of view of the equitable utilization of a river there is an inherent equity in the maintenance of the local customs. This argument will be further elaborated in section IV, but at this point it should be said that the maintenance of local customs operates as an independent criterion of water apportionment and its implementation cannot be explained by reference to the superiority of existing utilization.

(c) *The conduct of the parties.* The best example of judicial protection of existing patterns of water utilization is the decision rendered by the Krishna Water Disputes Tribunal in 1973. This protection was due to the conduct of the parties rather than to a preferential treatment of existing utilization. As has previously been said, the dispute involved three Indian States interested in the apportionment of the waters of the Krishna River, namely, the State of Maharashtra, the State of Mysore and the State of Andhra Pradesh. The State of Andhra Pradesh claimed recognition and protection of its water utilization up to September 1960, in terms that the decision of the Tribunal should ensure water supply for all the projects undertaken by Andhra Pradesh until that date.

In the absence of legislation or of an agreement on water apportionment by the States, the Tribunal concluded that it had to apply the rule of equitable apportionment of the benefits of the river, awarding to each party a fair share after due consideration of the relevant factors, among which existing uses received a very close examination. The conclusion of the Krishna Tribunal was that the water requirements of all the projects in operation or under construction as at September 1960 should be preferred to contemplated uses and, therefore, should be protected.[90] But in reaching this conclusion the Tribunal did not base its case on the existence of a general principle or a rule of law compelling it to do so. Instead, the main justification of the Tribunal for granting protection to certain existing uses was that no objections were raised by the riparian States to the utilization of water from the Krishna River until September 1960. The pertinent part of the decision reads as follows:

> We find that all commitment [*sic*] made up to September 1960 were made without any protest from any coriparian State under the bona fide belief that the committed utilisations will be allowed to continue.
>
> We also find that all commitments made after September 1960 were set up over the protest of coriparian States.
>
> Prima facie except by special agreement or concession of the parties a project committed after September 1960 is not entitled to any priority over contemplated uses.[91]

The Tribunal was very much influenced by an article written by Laylin

---

[90] *Report of the Krishna Water Disputes Tribunal*, vol. 1, p. 100.
[91] Ibid.

and Clagett,[92] in which these authors stated, as summarized by the Tribunal, that:

> . . . in case of competition between new or proposed beneficial uses and old lawfully established beneficial uses they know of no instance in which a State under the principle of equitable apportionment has been required to relinquish without full replacement from other sources, a lawfully established beneficial use in order to enable a coriparian State to develop a new use or uses of the same kind. To be lawfully established a beneficial use 'must not have been established over the timely protest of a coriparian State which offered to resolve by peaceful means . . . the question'.[93]

It is evident, then, that it was the lack of protest from Maharashtra and Mysore that led the Tribunal to admit Andhra Pradesh's claim that part of its existing uses were to be maintained.

(3) *The obligation to use an international river in such a way as not to cause significant harm to the other watercourse States does not imply the obligation to refrain from interfering with existing patterns of water utilization*

Can the duty to refrain from causing a significant harm to the other riparian States be construed as implying the protection and superiority of right of the existing pattern of usage in those other riparian States? Jiménez de Aréchaga gave a positive answer when asserting that the respect for the existing uses is logical, because affecting those uses in another State would cause a substantial injury giving rise to compensation.[94]

In general international law, States must refrain from causing wrongful injury to other States, and with regard to international watercourses this rule has generally been recognized by State practice.[95] The wrongful character of the injury is determined by its seriousness (it has to be significant) and by its inequitableness. As McCaffrey pointed out in his Second Report on the Law of the Non-Navigational Uses of International Watercourses:

> . . . an equitable use by one State could cause 'appreciable' or 'significant' harm to another State using the same watercourse, yet not entail a legal 'injury' or be otherwise wrongful. . . . the focus should be on the duty not to cause

[92] Laylin and Clagett, 'The Allocation of Waters of International Streams', in Smith and Castle (eds.), *Economics and Public Policy* (1964), cited ibid.

[93] Ibid.

[94] Jiménez de Aréchaga, loc. cit. above (n. 71), p. 335.

[95] See Articles 5 and 6 of the 1965 Draft Convention on the Industrial and Agricultural Use of International Rivers and Lakes, prepared by the Inter-American Juridical Committee, *ILC Yearbook*, 1974, vol. 2, part 2, pp. 349–50; the Preamble of the Draft European Convention on the Protection of Fresh Water against Pollution, ibid., p. 344; Article 2(1) of the 1992 ECE Convention on the Protection and Use of Transboundary Watercourses and International Lakes, Helsinki, 17 March 1992, Birnie and Boyle, *Basic Documents, International Law and the Environment* (Oxford, 1995), p. 347.

legal injury (by making a non-equitable use) rather than on the duty not to cause factual harm. This is not to deny by any means that there is a general duty to refrain from causing harm, in the factual sense, to another State; the point is simply that, in the context of watercourses, suffering even significant harm may not infringe the rights of the harmed State if the harm is within the limits allowed by an equitable allocation.[96]

The International Law Association and the International Law Commission have dealt with the possible conflict between the no-harm and the equitable utilization rules and they have concluded that, generally speaking, the application of the rule of equitable utilization may prevail over the operation of a rule that prohibits substantial injury. In 1986 the ILA acknowledged that there was a lack of adequate norms defining the interrelation between equitable utilization and possible injuries. Accordingly, it adopted complementary rules intended to fill the lacuna. Article 1 of these complementary rules provides that:

A basin State shall refrain from and prevent acts or omissions within its territory that will cause substantial injury to any co-basin State, provided that the application of the principle of equitable utilization as set forth in Article IV of the Helsinki Rules does not justify an exception in a particular case. Such an exception shall be determined in accordance with Article V of the Helsinki Rules.[97]

The ILA's commentary attached to this provision explains that:

. . . in some cases, which are not uncommon in practice, the reasonable and equitable share in the beneficial uses of the waters of an international drainage basin is not technically obtainable without affecting the rights of one or more of the co-basin States. In cases of this kind, the injurious effects may appear as unavoidable consequences of the application of the principle of equitable utilization.[98]

The International Law Commission has also acknowledged that there can be cases in which the equitable and reasonable utilization of an international watercourse entails a significant harm to another riparian State. In such a situation, the Commission states that: 'Generally, in such instances, the principle of equitable utilization remains the guiding criterion in balancing the interests at stake.'[99]

In the light of these provisions, it should be concluded that, in general, the rule of equitable utilization prevails over the rule that prohibits the causing of substantial injury. In this context, if the existing uses of a State are injured by the utilization of the waters of the river by another State, the measure in which that injury should be forbidden or compensated will depend on the degree of interference of one State on the

---

[96] *ILC Yearbook*, 1986, vol. 2, part 1, p. 133.
[97] ILA, *Report of the Sixty-Second Conference* (Seoul, 1986), p. 278.
[98] Ibid., pp. 281–2.
[99] See the commentary attached to Article 7 of the Draft Articles in 1994 *ILC Report*, p. 236.

equitable share of the other. To assert that any interference with existing patterns of water usage should be prohibited or compensated is to deny the operation of the rule of equitable utilization in those cases in which all or part of the waters of an international river are already being used, except for the surplus water if any.

(4) There is no obligation to compensate for the termination or modification of existing patterns of water utilization in general international law

Compensation was accorded a reduced importance by the Helsinki Rules. The ILA pointed out that: 'An existing reasonable use is entitled to significant weight as a factor and, as indicated in Article V, consideration must be given to protecting it'. These words have mistakenly been interpreted as requiring the payment of compensation for the termination or modification of an existing use. This interpretation should be dismissed because the ILA did not consider that the payment of compensation was an essential requirement for the discontinuance or impairment of existing uses. In fact, the ILA concluded that: 'a modification or termination, to be consistent with equitable utilization, *may*, in a particular case, require compensation to the user'.[100] In the Helsinki Rules, then, compensation is ascribed a rather secondary role in the process of the establishment of an equitable regime for the utilization of international rivers. In this regard, Article V.2(*j*) makes no reference to an obligation to compensate for the discontinuance of existing uses, but it only refers to 'the practicability of compensation to one or more co-basin States as a means of adjusting conflicts among users'.

It should also be pointed out that to require the payment of compensation in all cases of termination or impairment of existing uses is not consonant with the equality that must prevail between States. To make the termination or modification of an existing pattern of utilization conditional upon compensation would imply that the right of the State that seeks to utilize the waters of a river already used by another State should be bought from the State claiming a vested right in those waters.[101]

Authors often rely on the wrong State practice in support of the view that compensation should be paid when existing uses are terminated or modified. In this connection, it must be noted that not every payment of a certain amount of money by one State to another when the two are attempting to establish an equitable regime for water utilization amounts to the payment of compensation. Compensation is the 'payment for injury to an interest caused by the utilization of an international river or

---

[100] ILA, *Report of the Fifty-Second Conference* (Helsinki, 1966), p. 494 (italics added).
[101] Bourne, 'The Right to Utilise the Waters of International Rivers', *Canadian Yearbook of International Law*, 3 (1965), p. 233. This view is shared by Bruhács in *The Law of Non-Navigational Uses of International Watercourses* (Dordrecht, Boston, London, 1993), p. 133.

lake',[102] and it should be distinguished from the costs of protective measures envisaged to prevent injury from occurring.[103] It is for this reason that the 1960 Indus Water Treaty between India and Pakistan cannot support the existence of an obligation to compensate for the injury to existing utilization. The amount of money paid by India to Pakistan under Article 5 of the Treaty[104] was its contribution to the works intended to increase the available water supply so that injury to Pakistan could be avoided. The same should be said of the recommendations given on the same problem by the Indus (Rau) Commission in 1942. The Indus (Rau) Commission concluded that the province of Punjab should pay a certain amount of money to Sind, contributing in this way to the replacement of the old and wasteful irrigation system based on inundation canals existing in Sind. Unfortunately the Rau Commission spoke of 'a contribution from the Punjab by way of compensation for damage,'[105] where in fact the contribution from Punjab could not be characterized as compensation because it was supposed to finance preventive measures.

The payment of compensation for the injury to land or to installations on the river does not constitute compensation for the termination or impairment of a pattern of water utilization either. It is possible to think of compensation calculated on the basis of the cost of the canals that are to be replaced or calculated on the basis of the cost of the land to be flooded by the construction of a dam, but none of these payments includes the 'cost' of the termination or impairment of water utilization proper.

(5) *It is not possible to speak of 'acquired rights' in relation to the utilization of international rivers.*

Finally, it can be observed that States arguing in favour of the protection of their existing uses have on occasion referred to existing utilization as if it were an 'acquired right' or 'vested right', perhaps attempting to assimilate the termination of those existing uses to the expropriation of property in international law. Despite the fact that the application of the principle of 'acquired rights' in the field of expropriation of property has been doubted in international law,[106] the essential objection to the application of the principle of 'acquired rights' in the field of the equitable utilization of international rivers lies in the fact that

---

[102] Bush, 'Compensation and the Utilization of International Rivers and Lakes: The Role of Compensation in the Event of Permanent Injury to Existing Uses of Water', in Zacklin and Caflisch (eds.), *The Legal Regime of International Rivers and Lakes* (The Hague, Boston, London, 1981), p. 309.

[103] Ibid., p. 310.

[104] *UN Legislative Texts and Treaty Provisions*, p. 306.

[105] *Report of the Indus (Rau) Commission*, vol. 1, para. 39, p. 28.

[106] See Brownlie, *Principles of Public International Law* (4th edn., Oxford, 1990), p. 533.

it is difficult to speak of property rights with regard to the waters of an international river. In this respect, the Narmada Water Disputes Tribunal held that:

As a matter of law, no State has a proprietary right in a particular volume of water of an inter-State river on the basis of its contribution to the available flow or drainage area. It is well-established that the waters of a natural stream or other natural body of water are not susceptible of absolute ownership as specific intangible property.[107]

That it is not possible to speak of 'acquired rights' in relation to the water used by States is further demonstrated by the non-definitive character of judicial settlements in river disputes. The application of the principle of *res judicata* in international freshwater disputes is not complete, as the solution provided by a tribunal remains always open to be reviewed if there is a change in the circumstances that were taken into consideration when settling the dispute. In this connection, the Krishna Water Disputes Tribunal stated that:

. . . in determining the equitable share of the States, all the factors which create equities in favour of one State or the other have to be weighed as at the date when the current controversy is mooted. But population, engineering, economic, irrigation and other conditions constantly change and with changing conditions new demands for water continually arise. A water allocation may become inequitable when the circumstances, conditions and water needs upon which it was based are substantially altered.

For all these reasons, a review and modification of the allocations may become necessary to keep pace with changing conditions.

In order to ensure flexibility in the allocation the US Supreme Court usually retains jurisdiction to modify its decree and reserves liberty to the parties to apply for modification of the decree as and when future circumstances may require. On petitions filed from time to time under the clause reserving liberty to the parties at the foot of the decree, the Court has amended or superseded the earlier decree, taking cognizance of population and economic growth, or for other reasons.[108]

In conclusion, it has been demonstrated that all the arguments militating in favour of the priority of existing uses in the process of the establishment of an equitable regime for the utilization of international watercourses should be rejected. Therefore, it is not possible to assert that existing uses are 'an absolute first charge upon the waters'.[109] However,

---

[107] *Report of the Narmada Water Disputes Tribunal*, vol. 1, para. 8.8.1, p. 114.
[108] *Report of the Krishna Water Disputes Tribunal*, vol. 2, p. 158.
[109] See above, n. 69.

it still remains necessary to determine the proper role that existing uses can play in the process.

B. *The Proper Role to Ascribe to Existing Uses in the Process*

In the examination of this problem the experience of maritime delimitation can provide some guidelines. The historical element consisting in the long fishing practices of the coastal population was introduced by Norway when claiming the validity of its straight baseline system in the *Fisheries* case. It is important to remark that Norway did not base its case on mere 'long usage', but on long usage accompanied by economic dependence and the notion of vital interests. As O'Connell has pointed out, in the *Fisheries* case long usage was evaluated according to geographical, ecological, economic and sociological factors.[110]

It is in the *Gulf of Maine* case that the relationship between usage of natural resources and economic dependence can be fully appreciated. The argument based on long usage was put forward by the United States, contending that:

the fishing banks exploited by the two States should not be divided, but should be attributed to that State whose fishermen have fished the area a much longer time, to a much larger extent, and by a much larger number.[111]

This purely historical argument was to be confronted with the Canadian claim which, although based on the established patterns of exploitation of the fisheries of the disputed area, introduced the additional element of economic and vital dependence.[112] In the end, the Chamber divided the Georges Bank between the parties, justifying its decision in part on the avoidance of 'catastrophic repercussions' for the livelihood and economic well-being of the coastal population.[113]

What these decisions make clear is that in a dispute over access and apportionment of natural resources, the historic argument based on the utilization of the resource by the parties ought to be accompanied by and evaluated on the basis of other criteria, such as economic dependence and the vital needs of the population. It is this idea that should be used as a criterion in the assessment of existing utilization as a relevant factor in water apportionment if the role attributed to this criterion is to be consonant with the rule of equitable utilization in which no factor has a pre-established priority over the others. What is important is that

---

[110] O'Connell, *The International Law of the Sea* (Oxford, 1982), vol. 1, p. 438.
[111] *ICJ Pleadings*, 1984, vol. 6, p. 381.
[112] Ibid., Canadian memorial, vol. 1, paras. 311, 313, and 326 (b), pp. 128, 129, and 133.
[113] *ICJ Reports*, 1984, paras. 237 and 238, pp. 342–3.

existing uses as a relevant factor should not operate independently of the considerations of the social and economic needs of the parties. In this context, existing utilization is one of the criteria that will help in determining the degree of the social and economic dependence of the States concerned. Of course, since existing utilization generally creates economic dependence, it is most likely that its inclusion as a relevant factor will tip the balance in favour of its continuance, but it cannot be asserted that existing utilization has priority over the various other criteria that should be taken into consideration.

IV. The Relevance of Local Customs

A certain pattern of use of the waters of a river may have been established by local inhabitants constituting a local custom with regard to river utilization. Acknowledging that any definition of the concept of local custom is likely to be vague, it can be said that it refers to the traditional activities undertaken by a group of inhabitants using a river and its waters, whether they consist in a mere local traditional practice or in a practice in accordance with customary law. This section is not concerned with local custom as evidence of other criteria, such as the economic and social needs of the States concerned, but the analysis is referred to local custom as a relevant factor in its own right.

Boundary Agreements concluded by the European Powers for the division of their areas of influence in Africa often made reference to tribal customary rights over water and land, as is shown by Article III of the Memorandum to the Exchange of Notes between the British and French Governments Defining the Boundary between the Gold Coast and French Soudan of 1904, which stated that:

The villages situated in proximity to the frontier shall retain the right to use the arable and pasture lands, springs, and watering places which they have heretofore used, even in cases in which such arable and pasture lands, springs and watering places are situated within the territory of the one Power and the village within the territory of the other.[114]

The Protocol accompanying the Final Report of the Commissioners Appointed to Delimit the Boundary between the British and French Mandated Territories of Togoland, of 21 October 1929, provided in general clause (k) that:

---

[114] Brownlie, *African Boundaries*, p. 285.

It is understood that wherever the boundary follows a stream or river all existing watering and fishing rights on either side thereof, and all rights of passage up and down and across the stream or river, shall be preserved.[115]

In the same vein, the Protocol accompanying the 1924 Notes Exchanged between the United Kingdom and France Agreeing to the Ratification of the Protocol Defining the Boundary between French Equatorial Africa and the Anglo-Egyptian Soudan provided in general clause (a) that: 'Where the frontier follows a wadi, cuts a lake or rahad or changes its direction at either of such, the watering rights existing therein will be preserved by the inhabitants on either side'.[116] The 1926 Exchange of Notes between the Belgian and British Governments regarding the Frontier of Tanganyika–Ruanda-Urundi asserted that ' . . . notwithstanding the new boundary in Lake Tanganyika . . ., all customary rights of fishing and passage exercised by natives living on either side of it should be preserved'.[117] And Article 9 of the 1934 Agreement between the Belgian Government and the British Government regarding Water Rights on the Boundary between Tanganyika and Ruanda-Urundi provided that:

Any of the inhabitants of Tanganyika Territory or of Ruanda-Urundi shall be permitted to navigate any river or stream forming the common boundary and take therefrom fish and aquatic plants and water for domestic purposes and for any purposes conforming with their customary rights.[118]

As regards Asia, there are some instances in which local custom was taken into account by boundary treaties. The 1942 Exchange of Notes between the Government of Afghanistan and His Majesty's Government in the United Kingdom and the Government of India in regard to the

[115] Ibid., p. 273. See also the Agreement between Great Britain and France relative to the Frontier between the British and French Possessions from the Gulf of Guinea to the Niger of 19 October 1906, providing in its Annex 1, Article III that: 'The villages situated in proximity to the frontier shall retain the right to use the arable and pasture lands, springs and watering places which they have heretofore used, even in cases in which such arable and pasture lands, springs and watering places are situated within the territory of the one Power, and the village within the territory of the other': ibid., p. 171; Article IV of the Memorandum annexed to the Exchange of Notes recording the Agreement arrived at respecting the Frontier between the Gold Coast and the Ivory Coast of 1905, stating that: 'The villages situated in proximity to the frontier shall retain the right to use the arable and pasture lands, springs, and watering places which they have heretofore used, even in cases in which such arable and pasture lands, springs and watering places are situated within the territory of the one Power and the village within the territory of the other': ibid., p. 246; the Convention between the United Kingdom and France Supplementary to the Declaration of 21 March 1899 and the Convention of 14 June 1898, respecting Boundaries West and East of the Niger, which stated that: 'It is understood that when the boundary is said to follow a Wadi the existing rights of the inhabitants on either side of it to water therefrom are not prejudiced': ibid., p. 627; and the Agreement of Good Neighbourly Relations concluded between the British and French Governments on behalf of the Territories of Palestine on the one part and on behalf of Syria and Great Lebanon on the other part of 2 February 1926: *UN Legislative Texts and Treaty Provisions*, p. 288.
[116] In Brownlie, *African Boundaries*, p. 636.
[117] Ibid., p. 746.
[118] *UN Legislative Texts and Treaty Provisions*, p. 98.

Boundary between Afghanistan and India in the Neighbourhood of Arnawai and Dokalim stated:

(a) That the people of Dokalim shall be allowed to take water required for irrigation of their lands in Dokalim from the Arnawai Khwar above the boundary fixed.

(b) That the people of Arnawai Khwar may be allowed to float wood required for local use down that portion of the Arnawai Khwar which forms the international boundary.[119]

In respect to the demarcation of the north-west frontier between Afghanistan and Russia (1887), the circumstance that the populations on either side of the frontier performed traditional activities necessary for their livelihood was taken into consideration and, thus, a village was allowed to retain exclusive enjoyment of its irrigation canals in accordance with the customs in force, even though these canals took their rise in foreign territory.[120]

In the context of these boundary agreements the maintenance of traditional water utilization may have been regarded as a convenient provision, contributing to the stability of the frontiers. In this connection, geographers point out that boundary watercourses are likely to become the source of disputes between the inhabitants using the watercourse and, thus, they suggest that a good boundary agreement should foresee the possibility of disruption of the traditional rights of the people living near the boundary. As a solution, they propose that boundary agreements should define water rights clearly and that, as far as possible, they should provide for the continuation of those traditional rights.[121] However, apart from its practical convenience, the maintenance of traditional water usage may have also been regarded as an essentially equitable provision regardless of the real capacity of the local inhabitants to challenge the stability of the frontier. On the basis of this inherent equity, it is possible to claim that local customs should be included as a relevant factor in the process of the establishment of an equitable regime for water utilization. In other words, local custom may constitute a basis for the allocation of water in its own right.

The *Fisheries* case, though related to the delimitation of the territorial sea, can provide, by analogy, some authority in support of the previous assertion. The International Court, in determining whether or not the Norwegian system of delimitation of the territorial sea was in conformity with international law, emphasized the close relationship existing

[119] Ibid., p. 274.
[120] See Protocol No. 4 for the Demarcation of the North-West Frontier of Afghanistan of 1887: Aitchison, *A Collection of Treaties, Engagements and Sanads Relating to India and Neighbouring Countries* (Calcutta, 1909), vol. 11, pp. 351–4.
[121] See Adami, *National Frontiers in Relation to International Law* (London, 1927), p. 31, and Boggs, *International Boundaries. A Study of Boundary Functions and Problems* (New York, 1940), p. 97.

between local custom and the criteria of need and historic title. In this context, the Norwegian traditional practices were invoked as evidence of the economic interests peculiar to the region and of the historic title claimed by Norway.[122] Notwithstanding this, the judgment can still be construed as having recognized the relevance of the survival of traditional rights as such in the determination of the legality of the Norwegian system of straight baselines. In this regard, the Court was of the view that the survival of these traditional rights as such was a legitimate consideration to take into account when delimiting the territorial sea:

... the historical data produced ... by the Norwegian government lend some weight to the idea of the survival of traditional rights reserved to the inhabitants of the Kingdom over fishing grounds included in the 1935 delimitation ... Such rights, founded on the vital needs of the population and attested by very ancient and peaceful usage, may legitimately be taken into account in drawing a line, which, moreover, appears to the Court to have been kept within the bounds of what is moderate and reasonable.[123]

In this passage, the International Court did not ascribe to the traditional rights simply the role of evidencing needs and historic title. On the contrary, traditional rights were considered relevant in their own right, while long usage and the vital needs of the population were presented as auxiliary elements to attest to their existence and to evaluate their reasonableness.

As for an illustration of a case in which local custom was explicitly taken into account in a maritime delimitation process, mention should be made of the Torres Strait Treaty between Australia and Papua New Guinea of 18 December 1978.[124] This Treaty concerning sovereignty and maritime boundaries in the area between the two countries, including the area known as the Torres Strait, took into account the need to protect the livelihood and lifestyle of the local inhabitants. For this purpose, a Protected Zone was established in the following terms:

The principal purpose of the Parties in establishing the Protected Zone, and in determining its northern, southern, eastern and western boundaries, is to acknowledge and protect the traditional way of life and livelihood of the traditional inhabitants including their traditional fishing and free movement.[125]

The continuance of the local customs was allowed even in the case in which the respective territory in which to exercise those customs was under the jurisdiction of the other party.[126] Moreover, traditional fishing

[122] *ICJ Reports*, 1951, p. 133.
[123] Ibid., p. 142.
[124] *International Legal Materials*, 18 (1979), p. 291.
[125] Article 10(3) of the Torres Strait Treaty.
[126] See Article 12 of the Torres Strait Treaty.

rights were given a certain priority over the application of conservation measures.[127]

Apart from the intrinsic equity of maintaining the traditional uses of water by the local communities, there is also ground to assert that States are under a legal obligation to maintain traditional uses of natural resources. The existence of such an obligation has been acknowledged by international human rights law in general, and particularly by the international law concerning the rights of aboriginals. In this connection, Article 7 of ILO Convention 107, concerning the Protection and Integration of Indigenous and Other Tribal and Semi-Tribal Populations in Independent Countries, provided that:

1. In defining the rights and duties of the population concerned regard shall be had to their customary laws.
2. These populations shall be allowed to retain their own customs and institutions where these are not incompatible with the national legal system or the objectives of integration programmes.[128]

Article 14.1 of ILO Convention 169, concerning Indigenous and Tribal Peoples in Independent Countries, states that:

. . . measures shall be taken in appropriate cases to safeguard the right of the peoples concerned to use lands not exclusively occupied by them, but to which they have traditionally had access for their subsistence and traditional activities. Particular attention shall be paid to the situation of nomadic peoples and shifting cultivators in this respect.[129]

Article 15.1 of the same Convention provides that:

The rights of the peoples concerned to the natural resources pertaining to their lands shall be especially safeguarded. These rights include the right of these peoples to participate in the use, management and conservation of these resources.

More generally, Article 1.2 of the International Covenant on Civil and Political Rights (1966) provides that all peoples may freely dispose of their natural wealth and resources and that in no case may a people be deprived of its own means of subsistence.[130]

The recognition of the existence of a legal obligation binding upon States to respect local traditional utilization of natural resources has a very important implication for the definitive weight to be ascribed to local custom in the process of establishing an equitable regime for water utilization. As has been pointed out by Vanderzwaag and Pharand, if

---

[127] See Article 20 of the Torres Strait Treaty.

[128] *UN Treaty Series*, vol. 328, pp. 247 ff. The integrationist approach contained in this Convention was later suppressed by Convention 169.

[129] *International Labour Conventions and Recommendations 1919–1991* (Geneva, 1992), vol. 2, p. 1440.

[130] Brownlie, *Basic Documents on Human Rights* (Oxford, 1992), pp. 125 ff.

international law places a positive obligation upon States to protect aboriginal customs,[131] it should also make sure that the States would be materially capable of fulfilling that obligation.[132] With regard to the utilization of international watercourses, a necessary condition for the continuance of the local traditional use of those waters, enabling the States to respect traditional activities on the rivers, would be that local custom should be given a proper role in the process of the establishment of an international regime for the equitable utilization of freshwater resources. It is suggested, therefore, that local custom not only can be invoked as evidence of the economic and social needs of the parties, but it also may constitute a direct basis for the allocation of water to a State.

V. THE RELEVANCE OF EFFICIENT UTILIZATION

Article 6.1(f) of the ILC Draft Articles on the Law of the Non-Navigational Uses of International Watercourses requires that in the process of the establishment of an equitable and reasonable regime for the utilization of international rivers, account should be taken of the conservation, the protection, the development and economy of use of the water resources of the watercourse and the costs of measures taken to that effect. This provision is concerned, hence, with the efficient management of watercourses. The International Law Association also included the element of efficiency in its list of relevant factors. Article V.2(i) of the Helsinki Rules mentions the avoidance of unnecessary waste in the utilization of an international watercourse as one of the factors to be taken into consideration. When comparing the two provisions it seems that the scope of the criterion of efficiency is more broadly conceived in the ILC Draft Articles than it is in the Helsinki Rules. The ILA referred only to the avoidance of unnecessary waste, while the ILC seems to require more positive actions for the achievement of efficiency in the management of international water resources. Accordingly, the Helsinki Rules cannot be construed as promoting a real competition in efficiency between States. With regard to the ILC Draft Articles, they might be construed as ascribing a more important role to the element of efficiency, but it will be seen that the scope of its influence is in any case limited.

The examination of the factor of efficiency requires the distinction between the process of apportionment of volumes of water, on the one hand, and the process of accommodation of the different water uses, on

---

[131] Vanderzwaag and Pharand, as many other writers do, speak of aboriginal customs but the argument should be understood as applicable to local custom in general, even if it cannot be referred to a particular group of indigenous people.

[132] Vanderzwaag and Pharand, 'Unuit and the Ice: Implications for Canadian Arctic Waters', *Canadian Yearbook of International Law*, 21 (1983), p. 73.

the other. It will be shown that the criterion of efficiency has no relevance with regard to the division of volumes of water between States and that the ascription of a relevant role to this factor may only be made in connection with the accommodation process.

A. *The Role of Efficiency in the Process of Allocation of International Water Resources*

Regarding the impact of the factor of efficiency in the allocation of the waters of an international river, the ILA's view was that:

A 'beneficial use' need not be *the* most productive use to which the water may be put, nor need it utilize the most efficient methods known in order to avoid waste and ensure maximum utilization. As to the former, to provide otherwise would dislocate numerous productive and, indeed, essential portions of national economies; the latter, while a patently imperfect solution, reflects the financial limitations of many States; in its application, the present rule is not designed to foster waste but to hold States to a duty of efficiency which is commensurate with their financial resources. Of course, the ability of a State to obtain international financing will be considered in this context. Thus, State A, an economically advanced and prosperous State which utilizes the inundation method of irrigation, might be required to develop a more efficient and less wasteful system forthwith, while State B, an underdeveloped State using the same method might be permitted additional time to obtain the means to make the required improvements.[133]

The ILA certainly had in mind the long-lasting dispute concerning the Indus river and its tributaries, which originated before the 1947 partition of British India. In 1938, the province of Punjab contemplated the construction of a storage reservoir on the Sutlej river, a tributary of the Indus river. This reservoir, located upstream, would have interfered with the old system of irrigation of the province of Sind, namely, a system based on inundation canals. Irrigation by means of inundation canals consists in 'shallow cuts [that] are made through the river banks into which the excess water flows when the level of the water in the river rises higher in the floods which occur during the rainy seasons'.[134] A Commission (the Rau Commission) was appointed to give a report on the basis of which the parties could solve their dispute. The Commission rendered its report in 1942, observing that, in the absence of agreement between the parties, the applicable rule was equitable apportionment.[135]

[133] See commentary to Article V of the Helsinki Rules, ILA, *Report of the Fifty-Second Conference*, p. 487.
[134] Srinivason, *Irrigation and Water Supply* (Madras, 1991), p. 176.
[135] *Report of the Indus (Rau) Commission*, vol. 1, para. 14, p. 10.

The Rau Commission observed that 'the most important factor calling for notice [was] the large quantity of water that [was] running waste to the sea',[136] and it found that 'undoubtedly inundation canals [were] a wasteful anachronism'.[137] But it also took notice that a considerable number of people were dependent for their livelihood on this anachronistic and wasteful system of irrigation. And, what was more important, the Commission found that the explanation for the existence of this wasteful system of irrigation was the economic poverty of Sind, the government of which could not afford to install a weir-controlled method of irrigation.[138] In view of the paramount importance of irrigation for the survival of the population of Sind, the Commission adopted a preventive approach, concluding that it was reasonable to ask the province of Punjab to contribute in part to the cost of the replacement of the inundation canals.

The Indus river and its tributaries remained a source of disputes after the 1947 partition of British India. The partition line between India and the newly formed State of Pakistan left the principal irrigation canals in the territory of India,[139] whose prospective uses of the waters of the Indus river constituted a threat to the existing uses of Pakistan. The dispute was finally settled in 1960 when both parties concluded the Indus Waters Treaty, thanks to the good offices of the International Bank for Reconstruction and Development (World Bank). The Indus Waters Treaty provides for the continuation of Pakistan's existing uses. This was a key element during the negotiations, and the parties were able to agree on this point because it was materially possible to increase the availability of water in the basin. In fact, Pakistan's water storage capacity was increased; otherwise, there would have been no water available to satisfy Pakistan's existing uses and the needs of the Indian population. In this context, the 1960 Indus Waters Treaty did not address the question of dividing a fixed available water supply. Instead, it provided for an increase in the quantity of usable water in order to allocate water that prior to 1960 was running waste to the sea. A more efficient use of water was made possible by the construction of dams and new irrigation canals in the basin,[140] particularly in the territory of Pakistan, the cost of which was met by India and Pakistan, with financial aid from several other

---

[136] Ibid., vol. 1, para. 38, p. 27.

[137] Ibid., vol. 1, para. 69, p. 52.

[138] Ibid.

[139] Caponera, 'International Water Resources Law in the Indus Basin', in Ali, Radosevich and Ali Khan (eds.), Water Resources Policy for Asia (The Netherlands, 1987), p. 511.

[140] According to the Plan set out by the Treaty, it was necessary to build eight new link canals of nearly 400 miles in length, a dam on the Jhelum River, a dam on the Indus River, three barrages on Qadirabag, on the Ravi River and on the Sutlej River and additional works to integrate the new system with the old one. See Baxter, 'The Indus Basin', in Garretson, Hayton and Olmstead (eds.), op. cit. above (n. 58), p. 468.

countries.[141] Pakistan also received money on loan from the United States and from the World Bank.

Undoubtedly, the efficient management of the water resources had a part to play in the process of the establishment of an equitable regime for the utilization of the Indus river system. A more efficient management made it possible to increase the water available for allocation between the parties. However, the element of efficiency was not taken into account as a relevant factor when determining the parties' share in the augmented waters of the Indus river system. The Rau Commission in 1942 and the parties in 1960 had to resort to more efficient management of the basin as a way to solve the dispute, but they did not take this element into account as a basis for the apportionment of the waters. The situation would have been very different had there been no possibility of increasing Sind or Pakistan's efficiency in the use of their rivers. Without the intervention of the World Bank, it is reasonable to think that efficiency would not have been achieved in the short term, and in that case it is difficult to imagine the outcome of the dispute consisting in the denial of water to the inefficient party on account of its inefficiency alone.

Neither the province of Sind nor Pakistan were wilfully wasting their water resources and for this reason the efficiency criterion could not play a part in the determination of their equitable share in the waters of the Indus river basin. It follows, then, that efficiency can only play a part in the process of allocating waters of a river when one of the parties is intentionally or negligently wasteful. It is only in such extreme case that the issue of efficiency can be related to entitlement, justifying a denial of water to the wasteful State. In this connection Lipper states that:

While the use must bestow a benefit upon the user, the benefit need not be commensurate with the optimum possible utilization of the waters, provided however, that no user may be wilfully wasteful or inefficient when it has the means to reduce inefficiency.[142]

In the same line of thought, the Narmada Tribunal maintained that:

8.6.1 The doctrine of Equitable Utilisation is also not concerned with the protection of abstract or hypothetical rights of riparian States. To be protected, the use must be of a beneficial nature. . . . This does not however mean that the use must be the most beneficial to which the water must be put or that the method of utilisation must be maximally efficient. But the rule does mean that the States will not be permitted to waste inter-State river waters. The rule certainly enjoins upon the riparian States the duty of efficiency in the use of such waters which is commensurate with their respective financial resources. There is hence little doubt that an inter-State Tribunal would not countenance waste due

---

[141] Australia, Canada, Germany, New Zealand, the United Kingdom and the United States contributed to form the Indus Basin Development Fund.

[142] Lipper, 'Equitable Utilization', in Garretson, Hayton and Olmstead (eds.), op. cit. above (n. 58), p. 47.

to wilfulness or indifference by a riparian State where the waters of the river are insufficient to meet the needs of all riparian States . . .

. . .

8.6.3 Where, however, inefficiency stems not from misfeasance but from limitations of technical and financial resources, the result must be different. It may be unreasonable . . . to require an underdeveloped State to meet the standards of efficiency for the utilisation of irrigation waters prevalent in parts of highly developed countries.[143]

Intentional wastefulness evidences the absence of real need for the water. For this reason it is better to understand the denial of water to a wasteful party as a result of this absence of need rather than as a sanction for the failure to achieve a minimum standard of efficiency. Accordingly, it should be concluded that efficiency as such has no role in the allocation of water resources between States, and this is further demonstrated by the practice of municipal courts of federal States.

The Krishna Water Disputes Tribunal pointed out that: 'Needless waste of water should be prevented and efficient utilisation encouraged'.[144] However, it is not enough for a judicial decision to state that efficient utilization of water should be encouraged to conclude that the element of efficiency has been relevant in the resulting allocation of waters between the contending parties. In fact, the Tribunal also recognized that 'an established use may have to be protected though the same amount of water may produce more in other sections of the river'.[145] The Krishna Tribunal mentioned efficiency as a desirable goal, but it did not really consider this element when apportioning the waters of the river between the respective States. Instead, it provided for the protection of existing uses in so far as they evidenced the economic dependence of the respective populations.

The fact that the element of efficiency has no role to play in the allocation of the waters of a river, except for the most unusual case of a party being wilfully wasteful, can be fully appreciated in the 1987 Argentinian water dispute between the provinces of La Pampa and Mendoza. The Argentinian provinces, like the Indian and the American States, have full jurisdiction over the water resources occurring in their territories. In a situation of inter-provincial water disputes they are free to solve it by agreement, and if they fail to agree on a solution they can resort to the jurisdiction of the Argentine Supreme Court. In the dispute between La Pampa and Mendoza, the province of La Pampa sued the province of Mendoza in order to obtain an equitable share of the waters of the Atuel river, founding its claims entirely on the criterion of efficiency. La Pampa argued that Mendoza was inefficiently using the

---

[143] *Report of the Narmada Water Disputes Tribunal*, vol. 1, p. 112.
[144] *Report of the Krishna Water Disputes Tribunal*, vol. 1, p. 94.
[145] Ibid.

whole of the waters of the Atuel, leaving no water in the stream for the use of La Pampa.

Accordingly, the Argentine Supreme Court examined the efficiency of Mendoza's water utilization and the capability of this province to improve its irrigation system. It is important to note that the Supreme Court analysis was focused on the possible finding of a gross inefficiency ('*grave ineficiencia*') and a big waste ('*gran derroche*') on the part of Mendoza.[146] The general efficiency of Mendoza's irrigation system was estimated at 0.30. That is to say, 70% of the Atuel's waters diverted for irrigation were lost before reaching the crops.[147] At first sight, a 0.30 level of efficiency seems to be a very poor achievement, but according to the Argentine Supreme Court it was not. The Court maintained that this level of efficiency was the general level to be found in Argentina, as well as in other countries.[148] Notwithstanding that the experts appointed by the Court to report on the technical issues of the case described Mendoza's irrigation system as precarious, very old, in bad working condition and lacking in maintenance, the degree of efficiency of the respondent province was still considered a normal one by the Supreme Court. The Court was absolutely persuaded that Mendoza was not intentionally inefficient. Therefore, it was reasonable for it to conclude that there was no abusive use by Mendoza and, consequently, the main argument of La Pampa was to be rejected.

The Supreme Court reinforced its rejection of La Pampa's claim by asserting that even a dramatic improvement in efficiency would make no difference to the situation. In this connection, the Court found that the additional water resulting from improving the level of efficiency to 0.50 would first have to supply the land under cultivation in Mendoza, which was short of adequate irrigation. In the opinion of the Supreme Court, the only possibility of obtaining a surplus of water for use by La Pampa was the construction of major engineering works for the purpose of avoiding the huge natural losses of water occurring in Mendoza.[149] Altogether, the cost of the improvement in efficiency and of the engineering works was estimated at US$676,000,000, a sum that in the view of the Court:

exceeds at length any financial and economic viability in view of the relatively poor results in production and benefits that could be obtained, considering only the Northwest of the province of La Pampa [author's translation].[150]

---

[146] *Fallos de la Corte Suprema de Justicia de la Nación*, 1987, tomo 310, vol. 3, para. 98, p. 2550.
[147] Ibid., para. 99, p. 2551.
[148] Ibid., para. 100, p. 2551.
[149] Ibid., p. 2558.
[150] 'Supera ampliamente toda factibilidad económica financiera ante los relativamente magros resultados de producción y beneficios que podrían obtenerse considerando solamente el noroeste de la Provincia de La Pampa': ibid., para. 113, p. 2559.

For this reason the Argentine Supreme Court did not find many difficulties in rejecting the applicant's claim.[151] In the words of the Argentine Supreme Court:

... the existence of highly inefficient uses has been ruled out. There are no doubts as well that La Pampa was far from demonstrating that its intended uses are more important than the existing ones. And it is evident that the works intended for the irrigation of an area of about 15,000 hes. in La Pampa are inconvenient because its onerous cost is disproportionate to the benefits that could be obtained [author's translation].[152]

La Pampa v. *Mendoza* demonstrates how difficult it is to prove that a State is wilfully or negligently inefficient in the management of its water resources. However, the identification of intentional waste is not impossible, but it usually goes together with the absence of real need for the waters in question. The Narmada river dispute provides an example of a situation in which one of the parties was denied a portion of water because the Tribunal considered that in the utilization of that portion the State was contemplating a wasteful usage. This case evidences the close relationship between intentional wastefulness and the absence of real need for the water.

As has already been said, the Narmada Water Disputes Tribunal was established, among other things, to apportion a certain volume of water of the Narmada river between the States of Gujarat and Madhya Pradesh. The two States founded their respective claims on various factors, the principal being their irrigation needs. In this regard, Gujarat claimed that it needed water to irrigate a total of 71.38 lakh acres,[153] of which 11 lakh acres were located in the areas known as the Little and the Great Rann of Kutch, the Banni and the Mahi Command area. The amount of water needed to irrigate these 11 lakh acres was estimated at 6.36 MAF.[154] In the end, this claim of Gujarat was rejected on two different grounds. In relation to the Mahi Command area, this land was already receiving adequate irrigation from the Mahi river. As regards the Great and Little Rann of Kutch and Banni areas, the Tribunal did not see a reasonable justification for the irrigation of these lands, which were described as 'admittedly barren and sparsely populated'. The soil condition was characterized by a very high salinity and a very low permeability, and the area was subject to high evaporation and low rainfall.[155] In short, the diversion of water of the Narmada river to

---

[151] Ibid., para. 117, p. 2560.

[152] '... ha quedado descartada la existencia de usos altamente ineficaces. No hay dudas tampoco, de que La Pampa estuvo lejos de demostrar que los usos pretendidos superen en importancia a los actuales. Y resulta evidente que las obras destinadas a regar una superficie de alrededor de 15.000 has. de La Pampa son inconvenientes, pues su onerosidad resulta desproporcionada con los beneficios que se prodrían obtener': ibid., p. 2577.

[153] 1 lakh acre=100,000 acres.

[154] MAF=million acres feet.

[155] *Report of the Narmada Water Disputes Tribunal*, vol. 1, para. 9.9.6, p. 126.

irrigate these barren soils would have been a waste of water. As the Tribunal asserted, 'Even if it is assured that the area could be reclaimed and develop with the quantity of water indicated by Gujarat, the project would be highly uneconomic'.[156] The rejection of Gujarat's claim to irrigate barren lands demonstrates that when a State wilfully wastes or intends to waste its water resources, then the authenticity of its need for the water should be doubted.

The rejection of Gujarat's claim also prompts the question of the impact on the Tribunal's reasoning of the fact that this claim was based on a prospective use rather than on an already existing irrigation scheme. Perhaps the outcome would have been different had Gujarat already used water of the Narmada river for irrigating the poor and infertile soils of the Rann of Kutch and Banni areas. Accordingly, there would be some ground for the view that it is easier to claim intentional inefficiency against a party that intends to utilize a river than against a party already using it.

Finally, it is interesting to note that, when mentioning the factors that it took into account in the apportionment of 27.25 MAF of water of the Narmada river between the States of Gujarat and Madhya Pradesh, the Narmada Tribunal did not include the element of the efficiency in the use of the waters as a relevant criterion in its own right. The relevant factors, as mentioned by the Tribunal, were: (a) the cultivable area of the States; (b) the population dependent on the waters of the basin in each State; (c) the drought areas in each State; and (d) the economic needs including the irrigation requirements of each State.[157] It is reasonable to think, therefore, that efficiency had a part to play in the allocation of the Narmada waters, only because of its connection with these factors, all of which serve to establish the social and economic needs of the parties.

The conclusion that can be drawn with regard to the impact of the factor of efficiency on the allocation of waters between States is that, in general, the factor has no role to play in the process of water allocation. Only intentional inefficiency can have an impact upon the resulting allocation of the waters of an international river because it evidences the absence of real need for water. The denial of water in such a case is not a question of imposing a sanction on the inefficient party.

B. The Role of Efficiency in the Accommodation of Different Uses

It has been shown that, in general, the criterion of efficiency has no impact in the determination of volumes of water to be allocated between

---

[156] Ibid.
[157] Ibid., vol. 1, para. 9.6.1, p. 121.

the parties to a dispute. By contrast, this section attempts to show that efficiency can have a very important role in the accommodation of the different water uses contemplated by the parties, provided that this reconciliation does not involve a question of allocation of water.

The Narmada Water Disputes Tribunal, in addition to the problem of allocating 27.25 MAF of water between the States of Gujarat and Madhya Pradesh, was also faced with the task of accommodating the various water uses of these two States plus the States of Maharashtra and Rajasthan. The State of Gujarat complained that the contemplated water projects of the States of Madhya Pradesh and Maharashtra would prejudicially affect its own utilization of the Narmada river. The State of Madhya Pradesh had entered into an agreement with the State of Maharashtra jointly to construct the Jalsindhi Dam on the Narmada river and Gujarat objected to this proposal on the basis that the dam would restrict the height of the dam it itself proposed to build across the river, causing a permanent detriment to the irrigation and power benefits in its territory and in the State of Rajasthan. During the proceedings, the parties involved in the dispute agreed that Gujarat was entitled to build a dam and an irrigation canal, leaving for the decision of the Tribunal the question about the height of the dam and the level of the irrigation canal.

The rule applied by the Tribunal to these questions was the same that it applied when apportioning waters of the Narmada between Gujarat and Madhya Pradesh, that is to say, the rule of equitable utilization. However, the criterion of efficiency was to receive a different treatment now that the Tribunal was faced with the task of accommodating the interests of Gujarat, Rajasthan, Madhya Pradesh and Maharashtra, in relation to the height of the Sardar Sarovar Dam and the level of the Navagam Canal to be built by Gujarat on the Narmada river. The canal was intended to irrigate land in Gujarat and Rajasthan. The adequate level claimed by Gujarat was a full supply level (FSL) of a minimum of 320 feet. Madhya Pradesh and Maharashtra objected to this proposal, arguing that the canal should not exceed a FSL of 190 feet, as any level higher than 190 feet would require the construction of a higher dam involving submergence of their territory and loss of power potential. Rajasthan and Gujarat claimed that a canal of a maximum of 190 feet would deny the benefits of flow irrigation in the areas concerned, relegating considerable areas of irrigable land to lift irrigation.[158] The Court was of the view that if lift irrigation was necessary, then the question of cost was to be taken into consideration.[159] In this connection, the Tribunal found that under the circumstances lift irrigation was undoubtedly an inefficient method of irrigation.

[158] Ibid., vol. 2, p. 7.
[159] Ibid., vol. 2, para. 10.9.1, p. 8.

Among the factors that the Tribunal took into account in rejecting a maximum level of 190 feet for the Navagam Canal was the priority of irrigation over power generation projects. This was explained by the special circumstances of the case and, more generally, by the situation of India, a country in great need of food supply for its growing population.[160] Besides this priority issue, the Tribunal also took into account the level of efficiency in irrigation that could be achieved by the different proposals. A canal with a full supply level of no more than 190 feet, as proposed by Madhya Pradesh and Maharashtra, would have irrigated a total of 42.97 lakh acres, of which 10.70 were to be irrigated by lift. As against these figures, a canal with a full supply level of more than 300 feet could irrigate 54.02 lakh acres, of which only 4.62 were to be irrigated by lift.[161] The Tribunal also observed that:

the power required for lifting water to a particular height for providing lift irrigation is substantially more than that which can be generated by the same quantity of water with that height. . . . In other words, 40 per cent more power is required to lift water to a given height than can be generated by the same quantity of water dropped through the same height.[162]

With regard to the height of the dam to be built by Gujarat, the Tribunal also assessed the efficiency to be achieved by the different proposals, taking into account the following factors: (i) the submergence of areas, (ii) the storage capacity; (iii) the facility for regulating supplies for the Navagam Canal; (iv) the irrigation benefits; and (v) the power benefits.[163] Gujarat claimed that the adequate height of the dam was a full reservoir level (FRL) of more than 455 feet. Madhya Pradesh and Maharashtra claimed that it could not exceed a FRL of 210 feet. The Tribunal favoured Gujarat's claim, and in reaching this conclusion the criterion of efficiency proved to be decisive. In fact, when fixing the height of the dam at a FRL of 455 feet the Tribunal attempted to achieve the best efficiency in water utilization. In this connection, it pointed out that:

The water resources of the Narmada have to be utilised in a manner that would ensure the least wastage of water to the sea. Also irrigation should be done by flow to the maximum extent feasible, as lift irrigation is expensive and imposes a perpetual burden on the irrigators.[164]

The avoidance of waste of water was mentioned by the Tribunal when rejecting Madhya Pradesh and Maharashtra's proposal of constructing

---

[160] In this regard, the Tribunal said that: 'For irrigation use, there is obviously no substitute for water, but power may be generated from coal, oil, nuclear energy and other sources. In general, whenever production of hydroelectric power interferes with irrigation and the two uses cannot be reconciled, increasing priority may have to be given to irrigation. Rapid growth in population calls for intensified irrigation': ibid., vol. 2, para. 10.10.3, p. 9.

[161] Ibid., vol. 2, para. 10.10.10, p. 11.

[162] Ibid., vol. 2, para. 10.10.7, p. 10.

[163] Ibid., vol. 2, p. 52.

[164] Ibid., vol. 2, para. 13.5.2, p. 55.

the Jalsindhi Dam on their territory and a dam in Gujarat of no more than a FRL of 210 feet. In the opinion of the Narmada Tribunal, this proposal gave 'Madhya Pradesh and Maharashtra the benefit of power generation but by sacrificing the irrigation interest of Gujarat and wasting to the sea appreciable water resources of the river'.[165]

With regard to the storage capacity of the dam, the Tribunal found that it was necessary to provide carryover capacity in order to allow the storage of flood flows occurring in the respective catchment area, floods that otherwise would run down to the sea without being put to use. To allow the flood to go waste to the sea was considered an unacceptable waste.

Concerning the submergence of land, a dam of no more than a FRL of 210 feet height, as proposed by Madhya Pradesh and Maharashtra, would submerge 7,550 acres consisting mainly of uncultivable land, whereas a higher dam like the one proposed by Gujarat would submerge 91,500 acres of land of which 30,000 were cultivable. The Tribunal found that the submergence of land by a dam of a FRL of 455 feet was not excessive in relation to its capacity when compared with a number of other projects.

Particularly important were the irrigation benefits that could be achieved by a high dam of the type proposed by Gujarat. A Sardar Sarovar Dam of a FRL of 210 feet would be able to supply a canal of just a FSL of 190 feet. This meant that irrigation could only serve an area of 42.97 lakh acres, and that in Rajasthan irrigation was to be served entirely by lift. By contrast, a dam of a FRL of 455 feet would irrigate a zone of 56.92 lakh acres almost entirely by flow.

Finally, in relation to the power generation benefits, a Sardar Sarovar dam of FRL of 455 feet proved to be more productive than the Jalsindhi Dam and a low Sardar Sarovar Dam together. As the construction of a high Sardar Sarovar Dam would make unfeasible the construction of the Jalsindhi Dam, the Tribunal decided that the power needs of Madhya Pradesh and Maharashtra should be satisfied by the high Sardar Sarovar Dam to be built in Gujarat.

In conclusion, it is evident that efficiency played a major part in the accommodation of the various interests of the parties involved in the dispute concerning the height of the Sardar Sarovar Dam and the level of the Navagam Canal. This higher degree of relevance, as compared to the general irrelevance of efficiency in the division of volumes of water from the Narmada river, requires some further explanation that the judicial settlements examined above are unable to provide on their own. The following section, therefore, attempts to find an explanation by examining other instances of international law in which efficiency in the

---

[165] Ibid.

management of a certain natural resource has been invoked as a basis for entitlement.

C. The Experience of Maritime Delimitation Cases with regard to the Efficiency Element and its Assistance in Explaining the role of Efficiency in the Process of the Establishment of an Equitable Regime for the Utilization of International Rivers

The delimitation of maritime zones and the establishment of a regime for the equitable utilization of international rivers are two areas of international law that have much in common. In this connection, the establishment of a regime for the equitable utilization of international watercourses involves a sort of delimitation in so far as the allocation of certain volumes of water may be at issue. Moreover, in the two areas the aim of the applicable rule is to achieve an equitable result. For this reason, the experience of maritime delimitation cases with regard to the element of efficiency may shed some light on the application of this factor to the case of the utilization of international watercourses.

In the *Gulf of Maine* case concerning the delimitation of the continental shelf and the fisheries jurisdiction areas between the United States of America and Canada, the United States put forward the argument that the delimitation should take into account the principle that the delimitation should facilitate the conservation and the management of the natural resources of the area.[166] Accordingly, the United States argued that the delimitation should give exclusive jurisdiction over the Georges Bank to a single State, as this would facilitate the conservation and the management of the fisheries of that area.[167] In the view of the United States, a single State management avoided the division of the responsibility for conserving and managing a natural resource between the parties and, allegedly, a delimitation providing for this single management would have protected 'the resources from the uncertain fate of conservation by agreement',[168] thus avoiding the uncoordinated exploitation which eventually results in the waste or destruction of the resources.[169] The reasoning of the United States was intended to justify its claim to the allocation of the whole of the Georges Bank. In support of this argument, the United States referred to the Court's decision in the *North Sea Continental Shelf* cases, which mentions the unity of any deposits as one of the factors to be taken into consideration in the delimitation of areas of continental shelf as between adjacent States.[170]

---

[166] *ICJ Pleadings*, 1984, *Gulf of Maine* case, US memorial, p. 63.
[167] Ibid., p. 74.
[168] Ibid.
[169] Ibid., para. 247, p. 95.
[170] *ICJ Reports*, 1969, para. 97, p. 51.

Canada rejected the monopolistic claim of the United States on the basis that it was inconsistent with the law applicable to the delimitation of fisheries jurisdiction zones, which was to be effected so as to obtain an equitable result. The Canadian counter-memorial argued that:

Since the solution proposed by the United States would be inequitable in this case, the question whether 'single-State management' is more efficient or expedient than co-operative management must be irrelevant.[171]

In Canada's view, the element of efficiency in the conservation and management of the resources of the area, in the particular form it assumed in the United States memorial, could not be invoked as a principle applicable to the delimitation in so far as it contradicted the rule of equitable delimitation. Canada contended that:

It is beyond question that the proper conservation and management of the resources of the sea and the avoidance of international disputes are valid objectives and important rules of behaviour. But their distortion into false principles of delimitation that rule out equitable division of the resources of the relevant area is almost perverse. The United States has misapplied two perfectly reasonable concepts to justify the most unreasonable results. For its theory of 'single-State management' would deny to Canada—and to other coastal States similarly placed—the sovereign rights and jurisdiction flowing from the distance principle enshrined in the 1982 Convention on the Law of the Sea and in customary international law.[172]

With regard to the *North Sea Continental Shelf* cases, Canada maintained that when the Court referred to the unity of any deposits as one of the factors to be taken into account in a delimitation of the continental shelf, the Court was not suggesting that the whole of a deposit should go to one of the parties in an undivided condition.[173] Canada was right in this interpretation of the decision rendered in the *North Sea Continental Shelf* cases. It must be recalled that the Court's task in the *North Sea Continental Shelf* cases was to indicate to the parties the principles applicable to the delimitation, but not to effect the delimitation itself. In this context, the Court's references to the deposits that often lie on both sides of the dividing line, to the possibility of exploiting those deposits from either side of the line, to the risk of wasteful or prejudicial exploitation of the transboundary deposits and to the appropriateness of joint exploitation by the parties, have to be understood as the description of a factual situation which the Court thought was convenient for the parties to take into account in their future negotiations.[174]

In the end, the Chamber dismissed the argument of the single State management presented by the United States. It is to be noted that the

[171] *ICJ Pleadings*, 1984, Canadian counter-memorial, para. 230, p. 84.
[172] Ibid., para. 497, p. 186.
[173] Ibid., para. 503 p. 189.
[174] Ibid.

Chamber did not find real difficulties in dismissing efficiency as a principle of delimitation. In fact it devoted only one paragraph to this argument, stating that:

... the Chamber considers that there is no need to overestimate any difficulties that may arise from the division of Georges Bank, with the resources of its waters and subsoil, resulting from the delimitation line which it has drawn in accordance with law and with the equitable criteria whose application is called for by the law itself. It is unable to discern any inevitable source of insurmountable disputes in the fact that its decision has not endorsed the single management of this Bank's fisheries, and the assignment to one country of the task of conserving them, which the United States would have preferred to see instituted. ... Canada and the United States have to their credit too long a tradition of friendly and fruitful co-operation in maritime matters, as in so many other domains, for there to be any need to fear an interruption of that co-operation, which clearly now becomes all the more necessary, not only in the field of fisheries but also in that of hydrocarbon resources. By once more joining in a common endeavour, the Parties will surely be able to surmount any difficulties and take the right steps to ensure the positive development of their activities in the important domains concerned.[175]

Clearly this paragraph is mainly concerned with rejecting the argument that the delimitation should avoid disputes between the parties, rather than the argument that the delimitation should also assure the best management of the resources of the area. It seems that for the Chamber the latter argument was subsumed into the former. It may be concluded, therefore, that the Chamber was of the view that the achievement of efficiency was more an issue for the parties to solve than for the Chamber to adjudicate.

What is the relevance of the *Gulf of Maine* case in relation to the prospective role of efficiency in the establishment of an equitable regime for the utilization of international watercourses? The decision of the Chamber in the *Gulf of Maine* case not only demonstrates that the element of efficiency cannot be used as the basis of a monopolistic claim but, and more importantly, it also shows that efficiency cannot be invoked as a criterion for entitlement to natural resources. In this connection, it is interesting to note that Canada put forward the argument that a claim based on the element of efficiency struck at the very legal basis of title of the coastal State.[176]

The rule of equitable delimitation of certain maritime areas has developed into various criteria applicable to the delimitation process, which have been divided into different categories: equitable principles, relevant factors and auxiliary criteria to test the equitableness of the result. These equitable criteria can be classified in two groups, one related to the concept of sovereignty and the other related to the relative

[175] *ICJ Reports*, 1984, para. 240, p. 344.
[176] *ICJ Pleadings*, 1984, Canadian counter-memorial, para. 29, p. 11.

economic needs of the parties. In the process of maritime delimitation, international tribunals have applied criteria which are directly related to legal title over the respective areas, but they have also admitted the inclusion of the economic element, though this factor has had a lesser impact upon the delimitation process than the others. The economic element has adopted the form of the economic dependence of the local communities, which was a factor used to test the equitableness of the result in the *Gulf of Maine* case,[177] and the form of equitable access to the natural resources of the area, which was a factor applied by the ICJ in the *Jan Mayen* case.[178] Within this legal framework, the criterion of efficiency in the management of the resources of the respective maritime zones does not fit as a criterion for the delimitation of the continental shelf or of the exclusive economic zone, because it can be related neither to title nor to the needs of the parties. For this reason the element of efficiency was not taken into account in the *Gulf of Maine* case, not even as a factor to test the equitableness of the result as was the case with the economic dependence of the local communities concerned. In short, efficiency has no relation whatsoever to the institution of the continental shelf or the exclusive economic zone. The jurisdiction of the State over offshore areas is an extension of the State's coastal sovereignty for the purpose of exercising jurisdiction and control over those areas, including the right to exploit the natural resources located therein. It is evident, then, that efficiency does not play any part in the existence of the coastal State's right over offshore areas and, accordingly, its prospects of becoming a relevant criterion for the equitable delimitation of those areas are very poor.

The allocation of waters of an international river has to be effected by applying the rule of equitable apportionment, which also implies the consideration of two main groups of factors: those related to sovereignty and those related to the social and economic needs of the States concerned. The outcome of the application of these factors to the allocation of international waters might differ from the results obtained in the process of maritime delimitation in so far as, in the process of dividing the waters of a river, sovereignty is ranked lower than the criterion of need. But, with regard to the element of efficiency, it must again be stated that it simply does not fit into the allocation process. International watercourses separate or traverse the territory of the various watercourse States, and it is on this basis that the States are entitled to the equitable use of the waters for the satisfaction of their needs. Of course, efficiency in the utilization of rivers should be a goal envisaged by States in the management of their water resources, but this

---

[177] *ICJ Reports*, 1984, para. 237, p. 342.
[178] *ICJ Reports*, 1993, paras. 72, 73 and 76, pp. 70 and 72.

factor cannot be invoked as a criterion affecting the entitlement of the parties to a share in the waters of a river.

D. *Conclusion*

It must be concluded that the element of efficiency cannot operate as a factor in the apportionment of waters from an international river between the various riparian States. The fact that inter-State tribunals have not admitted the factor of efficiency to operate in the process of allocation of volumes of water from the respective rivers is consonant with the requirements of the rule of equitable utilization. If efficiency were to play a more important role in the process of allocation, the key elements that determine entitlement to the equitable utilization of rivers, that is to say, the element of State sovereignty and need, would be blatantly contradicted.[179] When the task does not consist in dividing the waters of a river, but in accommodating different water uses, the element of efficiency can play a role as a relevant factor to take into consideration in the process. This is so because the accommodation of the different water uses does not involve a question of entitlement to participate in the utilization of a river.

It is interesting to note that the most efficient method of river utilization, that is to say, integral management of international water resources, is not prescribed by the rule of equitable utilization. In other words, States are not obliged to join with their neighbours for the purpose of exploiting the waters of an international river. Certainly, 'parallel independent development of a river by each riparian is likely to prove economically wasteful',[180] but it seems that the rule of equitable apportionment admits this inefficient utilization of rivers because it ranks the element of sovereignty as a relevant factor and reduces the element of efficiency to a desirable outcome. It is true that Article 5.1 of the ILC Draft Articles provides that:

... an international watercourse shall be used and developed by watercourse States with a view to attaining optimal utilization thereof and benefits therefrom consistent with adequate protection of the watercourse.

But this provision cannot be construed as forcing States to join with the other co-riparians in the exploitation of the waters of a river. In fact, it can only imply the establishment of a duty to co-operate. The reference to optimal utilization in the Draft Articles is no more than a cautious call for a sound management of water resources by the States concerned. The

---

[179] This does not mean that every solution in order to be consonant with the rule of equitable utilization must embody these two elements. In theory, at least, it is perfectly possible to imagine a case in which needs override the influence of sovereignty.

[180] Lipper, 'Equitable Utilization', in Garretson, Hayton and Olmstead (eds.), op. cit. above (n. 58), p. 38.

ILC itself makes clear that the scope of this reference to optimal utilization is very limited, stating that:

The expression 'with a view to' indicates that the attainment of optimal utilization and benefits is the objective to be sought by watercourse States in utilizing an international watercourse. Attaining optimal utilization and benefits does not mean achieving the 'maximum' use, the most technologically efficient use, or the most monetarily valuable uses much less short-term gain at the cost of long-term loss. Nor does it imply that the State capable of making the most efficient use of a watercourse—whether economically, in terms of avoiding waste, or in any other sense—should have a superior claim to the use thereof. Rather, it implies attaining maximum possible benefits for all watercourse States and achieving the greatest possible satisfaction of all their needs, while minimizing the detriment to, or unmet need of, each.[181]

VI. The Relevance of Geography and Hydrology

Article 6 of the ILC Draft Articles on the Law of the Non-Navigational Uses of International Watercourses includes, as relevant criteria for the determination of what is an equitable and reasonable utilization of an international watercourse, the geographical, hydrographic and hydrological factors. The ILC commentary to this provision details that:

'Geographic' factors include the extent of the international watercourse in the territory of each watercourse State; 'hydrographic' factors relate generally to the measurement, description and mapping of the waters of the watercourses; and 'hydrological' factors relate, *inter alia*, to the properties of the water, including water flow, and to its distribution, including the contribution of water to the watercourse by each watercourse State.[182]

The Helsinki Rules also refer to geography and hydrology as relevant factors to be taken into account in the process of the establishment of an equitable regime for water utilization.[183] For the International Law Association, geography relates in particular to the extent of the drainage area in the territory of each basin State, and hydrology includes the contribution of water by each basin State.

In this context, it is obvious that the geographical and hydrological factors have a certain role to play in the process, and this section attempts to determine the degree of their potential relevance. This study is not concerned with the technical function that these factors may perform in the process. The technical function, as opposed to the legal one, relates generally to the collection of hydrological and geographical data contributing to a more accurate knowledge of the physical properties of the

[181] 1994 *ILC Report*, pp. 218–19.
[182] Ibid., p. 232.
[183] See Articles V.2(*a*) and V.2(*b*) of the Helsinki Rules.

watercourse, and usually it is unrelated to the creation of entitlement to the waters of an international river. In this respect, the geography and the hydrology of a river may influence the viability of harnessing its waters as well as the suitability of the technology to be applied for that purpose. What is important for the purposes of this study is that these factors might have an impact upon the formulation of the arguments that States may produce in support of their respective claims to the utilization of the waters of an international river, and this is what is called their legal function.

Two extreme positions can be taken as to the proper role of the geography and the hydrology of a watercourse in the process. The first of these extreme positions argues that geography and hydrology are not relevant factors in their own right. In this connection, Lipper claims that the unique relevant factor to take into account in the establishment of an equitable regime for water utilization is need.[184] Therefore, geography and hydrology should prove their relation to need in order to be included in the balancing process. The opposing view assumes that the geographical and the hydrological elements of an international watercourse are the most important criteria in the process of allocation as they are factors creating legal rights, while the inclusion of other factors is made to adjust the situation already established by them.[185]

It is not possible to agree with either of these extreme views. The first assumes that need is the unique applicable equitable criterion and ignores that there are other criteria relevant for solving claims over transboundary natural resources. The second view wrongly assumes that the rule of equitable utilization is a rule to be applied as a 'corrective' of an apportionment already effected by nature. Therefore, the relevance of the geographical and the hydrological factors has to be determined somewhere in between these two extreme viewpoints.

It is convenient to point out that in the past, geography and hydrology have had a predominant place in certain doctrines related to the formulation of the rules for the utilization and allocation of international rivers and their waters, such as the absolute territorial sovereignty and the territorial integrity doctrines. The former maintains that riparian States have the right to dispose freely of the waters flowing through their respective territories and the latter argues in favour of the right of lower riparians to demand the continuation of the natural flow of the waters

---

[184] In this regard Lipper claims that: 'equality of right is the equal right of each coriparian state to a division of the waters on the basis of its economic and social needs, consistent with the corresponding rights of its coriparian states, and excluding from consideration factors unrelated to such needs': see 'Equitable Utilization', in Garretson, Hayton and Olmstead (eds.), op. cit. above (n. 58), p. 63.

[185] Chauhan, *Settlement of International Water Law Disputes in International Drainage Basins* (Berlin, 1981), pp. 217–25.

coming from upstream.[186] It is common for these doctrines to coincide with the respective claims of upstream and downstream States: upstream States usually present a claim based on absolute territorial sovereignty and downstream States often produce the opposing absolute territorial integrity argument.[187] The rule of equitable utilization represents the abandonment of both these two extreme applications of the concept of territorial sovereignty, but from this it does not follow that territorial sovereignty has no further role to play in water utilization disputes. The question relates to the form that territorial sovereignty must assume in order to find its way into the rule of equitable utilization.

That territorial sovereignty is an element with a potential to influence the establishment of an equitable regime for water utilization is demonstrated by the fact that treaties concerning the utilization of international rivers, which generally adhere to the rule of equitable utilization, often include a reference to the sovereign rights of the parties which, in their view, ought to be respected. In this connection, Article 2 of the 1963 Act regarding Navigation and Economic Co-operation between the States of the Niger Basin provides that:

The utilisation of the River Niger, its tributaries and sub-tributaries, is open to each riparian State in respect of the portion of the River Niger basin lying in its territory and without prejudice to its sovereign rights in accordance with the principles defined in the present Act and in the manner that may be set forth in subsequent special agreements.[188]

Article 3 of the Statute relating to the Development of the Chad Basin states that:

The Chad Basin is open to the use of all Member States parties to the present Convention, without prejudice to the sovereign rights of each, as stipulated in the present Statute, revision thereof, or subsequent regulations thereunder or by special agreement.[189]

In Article 4 of the Treaty for Amazonian Co-operation of 3 July 1978, the parties declared that:

. . . the exclusive use and utilization of natural resources within their respective territories is a right inherent in the sovereignty of each state and that the exercise

---

[186] For an account of these doctrines see, Lipper, 'Equitable Utilization', in Garretson, Hayton and Olmstead (eds.), op. cit. above (n. 58), p. 18, and Lammers, *Pollution of International Watercourses* (The Hague, 1984), pp. 557 and 562.

[187] See Dellapenna, 'Treaties as Instruments for Managing Internationally-Shared Water Resources: Restricted Sovereignty vs. Community of Property', *Case Western Journal of International Law*, 26 (1984), p. 35; Naff and Matson, *Water in the Middle East. Conflict or Cooperation?* (Boulder and London, 1984), pp. 164–5.

[188] Hohmann (ed.), *Basic Documents of International Environmental Law* (London, Dordrecht, Boston, 1992), vol. 1, p. 1263.

[189] Sohn, *Basic Documents of African Regional Organizations* (New York, 1972), p. 1048.

of this right shall not be subject to any restrictions other than those arising from International Law.[190]

In Article 4 of the Agreement on Co-operation for the Sustainable Development of the Mekong River Basin of 5 April 1995, the parties agreed 'To co-operate on the basis of sovereign equality and territorial integrity in the utilization and protection of the water resources of the Mekong River Basin'.[191]

Article 2.1 of the 1995 Protocol on Shared Watercourse Systems in the Southern African Development Community (SADC) Region provides that:

The utilisation of shared watercourse systems within the SADC region shall be open to each riparian or basin State, in respect of the watercourse systems within its territory and without prejudice to its sovereign rights, in accordance with the principles contained in this Protocol . . .

Other international instruments also refer to the respect for the sovereign rights of the States concerned, such as the Recommendations of the United Nations Water Conference, held in Mar del Plata in March 1977. Recommendation 90 states that:

It is necessary for States to co-operate in the case of shared water resources in recognition of the growing economic, environmental and physical interdependencies across international frontiers. Such co-operation, in accordance with the Charter of the United Nations and principles of international law, must be exercised on the basis of equality, sovereignty and territorial integrity of all States . . . [192]

Some significance should also be attached to the fact that the characterization of international watercourses as shared natural resources was rejected by the ILC. After long discussions,[193] the ILC rejected the use of the expression 'shared natural resource' because it was not the purpose 'of drafting general rules to iron out the natural inequalities in resources between States, or to depreciate the importance of the principle of national sovereignty over natural resources'.[194]

Therefore, it may be concluded that territorial sovereignty over watercourses has a potential relevance in the establishment of an equitable regime for water utilization. The particular form that this relevance may adopt is still uncertain. However, it is possible from the outset to exclude dogmatic views such as those expressed by Chad:

[190] *International Legal Materials*, 17 (1978), p. 1045.
[191] *International Legal Materials*, 34 (1995), p. 869.
[192] *Report of the United Nations Water Conference* (Mar del Plata, 14–25 March 1977), E/CONF.70/29.
[193] See *ILC Yearbook*, 1980, vol. 1, and 1983, vol. 1.
[194] *ILC Yearbook*, 1979, vol. 2, part 2, para. 130, p. 165.

... watercourses are gifts of nature, and the latter did not take equity into account when distributing them among States. Consequently, it would not be very logical for a State having a large part of a watercourse to have to agree to equitable utilization with other States which only have a small part of the same watercourse.[195]

A claim for the apportionment of the waters of an international river which is based on territorial sovereignty might be related to some of the geographical and hydrological aspects of the watercourse, namely, the length of the river frontage of the riparian States, the extent of the drainage area of the watercourse in the territory of the basin States and the contribution to the flow of the watercourse by the basin States. The role of these geographical and hydrological aspects is examined below.

A. *The Length of the Frontage of the Riparian States on the River*

The ILC has included 'the extent of the international watercourse in the territory of each watercourse State' among the geographical factors mentioned in Article 6.1 of the Draft Articles on the Law of the Non-Navigational Uses of International Watercourses.[196] In the case of surface waters, the extent of the watercourse located in the territory of the States concerned is in great measure determined by river frontage. In this context, it is possible for the relationship between the lengths of river frontage to be invoked as a relevant criterion in the establishment of an equitable regime for the utilization of an international river. However, the practice of States shows that this criterion has seldom been invoked as a basis for the allocation of the waters of an international river. This is illustrated by the situation of the Nile and the Colorado rivers, which present an evident disparity of river frontage lengths that has been ignored by the respective States.

The Colorado river measures 1,300 miles.[197] It flows through the territory of the United States and for 20 miles it constitutes the boundary between this country and Mexico, then it flows through Mexican territory for 100 miles until it reaches the sea.[198] The allocation of the waters of this river was a matter of extended negotiations between the riparian States. These negotiations came to an end with the signature of the 1944 Treaty relating to the Utilization of the Waters of the Colorado and Tijuana Rivers, and of the Rio Grande (Rio Bravo).[199] In the course

---

[195] This was Chad's observation to the ILC Draft Articles on the Law of the Non-Navigational Uses of International Watercourses, A/CN.4/447/Add. 1, p. 8.

[196] See the ILC's commentary attached to Art. 6.1(a) of the Draft Articles, 1994 *ILC Report*, p. 232.

[197] Meyers, 'The Colorado Basin', in Garretson, Hayton and Olmstead (eds.), op. cit. above (n. 58), p. 486.

[198] Ibid., p. 546.

[199] *UN Legislative Texts and Treaty Provisions*, pp. 236 ff.

of the negotiations it was obvious that Mexico, which was seeking the delivery of more than 2,000,000 acres feet of the Colorado's waters into Mexican territory, would not give emphasis to the fact that less than 10 per cent of the river flowed through its territory. But particularly interesting is the fact that the United States, in whose territory most part of the river flows, did not argue on this basis. In this case, the United States preferred to use the criterion of existing uses for the allocation of the waters of the Colorado. This is clear from the Memorandum sent by the Under Secretary of State to the Mexican Ambassador, of 27 December 1939, which reads as follows:

> . . . it is believed that it would be advisable that an agreement be entered into between the two Governments confirming the present uses of the Lower Colorado River waters on Mexican lands and similar uses of Lower Rio Grande waters on American lands in the state of Texas.[200]

In the result, Article 10 of the 1944 Treaty provided for the allocation of 1,500,000 acres feet to Mexico. The United States acceded to this delivery because of its interest in obtaining a greater share of the waters of the Rio Grande. The length of the sections of the Colorado river flowing in the respective territories, as a criterion for allocation, was never at issue.

The other river in relation to which the disparity between the lengths of the river frontage of the riparian States is evident is the Nile. It is one of the largest rivers in the world and its basin is shared by nine different States.[201] Up to the present, the only States that have been directly involved in disputes concerning the waters of the Nile are Egypt and the Sudan.[202] For this reason the analysis will refer only to these two countries.

The Nile flows 6,695 kilometres from its source in Burundi to its discharge into the Mediterranean Sea in the Nile delta.[203] As regards the portion of the Nile flowing through Sudanese and Egyptian territory, 70 per cent of this section is located in the Sudan. Notwithstanding this fact, the agreements concluded by both States for the allocation of water of the Nile river show that the Sudan has never been allocated that percentage of the water of the Nile.

Egypt has always attempted to preserve its 'acquired rights' to the Nile, and in this task it has been successful. In the 1929 Exchange of Notes between the United Kingdom and the Egyptian Government in regard to the Use of the Waters of the River Nile for Irrigation

---

[200] *Foreign Relations of the United States*, 5 (1940), p. 1029.
[201] These States are: Burundi, Rwanda, Tanzania, Kenya, Zaire, Uganda, Ethiopia, the Sudan and Egypt. See Lowi, *Water and Power* (Cambridge, 1993), p. 67, and Waterbury, *Hydropolitics of the Nile Valley* (Syracuse, 1979), p. 14.
[202] Lowi, op. cit. above (n. 201), p. 69.
[203] Naff and Matson, *Water in the Middle East* (Boulder and London, 1984), p. 125.

Purposes,[204] those 'acquired rights', consisting in existing uses, were recognized and protected.[205] At that time it was evident that the Sudan needed to develop further its irrigation scheme, while Egypt was already wholly dependent on the Nile river. In January 1925, a Commission had been constituted 'for the purpose of examining and proposing the basis on which irrigation [in the Sudan could be] carried out with full consideration of the interests of Egypt and without detriment to her natural and historic rights'.[206] Accordingly, the Commission 'decided to approach its task with the object of devising a practical working arrangement which would respect the needs of established irrigation, while permitting such programme of extension as might be feasible'.[207] The basic proposal of the Commission consisted in the division of the year into two seasons, reserving to Egypt the natural flow of the whole river during the low season.[208] The consequence of the Commission's Report was that Egypt's 'acquired rights' were maintained and fixed at 48 billion cubic meters (bcm), the Sudan's share was fixed at 4 bcm, and the flow of the river was reserved for the benefit of Egypt from 19 January to 15 July of each year. The ratio of allocation was 1:12 favouring Egypt,[209] despite the fact that the Sudan's river frontage was much longer than that of Egypt.

After Sudanese independence, the terms of a new allocation agreement were discussed. On 8 November 1959, Egypt and the Sudan signed the Agreement for the Full Utilization of the Nile Waters.[210] By means of this treaty, Egypt obtained a total share of 55.5 bcm and the Sudan obtained 18.5 bcm. The ratio of allocation was 1:3 favouring Egypt.[211] This new proportion was achieved without detriment to the 'acquired rights' fixed in the 1929 Exchange of Notes and, again, the length of the river frontage of the negotiating States was not mentioned as a criterion for the allocation of water. During the negotiation of the 1959 Agreement, the Sudan claimed that the allocation of the waters of the Nile was to be made on the basis of the relative populations of the two States and on the basis of the cultivable areas in both countries.[212] It is to be noted that the Sudanese arguments did not contemplate the possibility of a comparison between the length of the river frontages.

The experience of the Colorado and the Nile rivers has to be regarded with caution. It must be borne in mind that none of these cases referred

---

[204] Text in *UN Legislative Texts and Treaty Provisions*, pp. 100 ff.

[205] See paras. 2 and 4(6) of the 1929 Exchange of Notes, ibid.

[206] See text of the Exchange of Notes creating the Commission in *League of Nations Treaty Series*, vol. 93, p. 92.

[207] See paragraph 21 of the Report of the Commission, ibid., p. 58.

[208] See paragraph 29 of the Report of the Commission, ibid.

[209] Lowi, op. cit. above (n. 201), p. 71.

[210] *UN Treaty Series*, vol. 453, pp. 64 ff.

[211] Lowi, op. cit. above (n. 201), p. 71.

[212] Ministry of Irrigation of the Sudan, *The Nile Waters Question* (Khartoum, 1955), p. 43.

to the establishment of an equitable regime for the utilization of those rivers. Accordingly, the fact that the States which were in the privileged position of claiming a greater share in the waters of the respective rivers did not resort to this argument cannot imply that the length of the river frontage of the riparian States on the river should be dismissed as a criterion for the equitable apportionment of a watercourse. Nevertheless, the examples of the Colorado and the Nile show that a claim based on this criterion was not considered persuasive enough to convince Mexico or Egypt to accept smaller volumes of waters from the rivers in question. For this reason, even if there is still a certain logic in using river frontage length as a potential criterion for the determination of what is an equitable utilization of an international river, it is likely that the degree of its potential relevance will be rather low. The extent of that potential is examined below.

The first thing that must be borne in mind is that the rule of equitable utilization entails two important principles: the principle that the basin States do not have proprietary rights over the waters of international rivers and the principle of equality between the basin States. The result of the combination of these two principles is that basin States have an equal right to benefit from the waters of an international river traversing their territories regardless of the length of their frontage on the river. Equality of right does not mean that the water will be divided into equal portions, but it means that the ratio between the frontages of the riparian States on the river should not be used as a direct basis for the allocation of water. In other words, equitable utilization is not a rule to ameliorate a division already effected by nature. In this context, the length of the frontage of the riparians on the river may only be used to adjust an allocation effected on the basis of other factors.

In order to determine the particular form in which the length of the river frontage of the riparian States on the river may be admitted in the process of the determination of what is an equitable utilization of an international watercourse, it will be useful to consider a set of four hypothetical situations in which a river flows through the territory of States A, B and C:

(i) The frontages of the three riparian States on the river are similar in length. On the basis of various criteria, namely, the social and economic needs of the States, their existing uses and the local customs, the percentage of water that each State is entitled to use is fixed as follows: 10 per cent for State A, 30 per cent for State B and 60 per cent for State C. There is enough water in the river to supply these requirements totally. Should the fact that the frontage lengths are similar justify an adjustment to the allocation?

(ii) The frontages of the three riparians differ in length: 10 per cent of the river runs through the territory of State A, 30 per cent flows through the territory of State B and 60 per cent of the river is located in the territory of State C. On the basis of the above-mentioned criteria, the waters of the river are divided equally between the three States There is enough water in the river to supply these water requirements totally. Should the fact that the frontage lengths differ justify an adjustment to the allocation?

In these two situations an adjustment to the allocation on the basis of frontage length would be inequitable. In the first example, if the share of States A or B is increased in view of the lengths of their frontages on the river, it can be the case that these States do not have the capacity to use the augmented share and, even if they could, it would be for superfluous purposes that did not count as evidencing real need for the water. The same applies to the second example if the share of State C were to be increased on the basis of the length of the State's frontage on the river.

(*iii*) The frontages of the three riparians are similar in length. On the basis of the socio-economic needs of the States, their existing uses and local customs, the waters of the river are allocated to the riparians as follows: 10 per cent of the waters for State A, 30 per cent for State B and 60 per cent for State C. The problem is that the waters of the river are not sufficient to satisfy all the water requirements of the three States. Suppose that for the total satisfaction of their water requirements State A required 20 per cent, State B required 60 per cent and State C required 120 per cent of the available waters of the river. Should the fact that the lengths of the river frontage of the States are similar justify a modification of the figures of allocation in order to reflect that similarity in lengths? Would it be consonant with the rule of equitable utilization to give to State A 20 per cent of the waters of the river and to reduce the share of State C to 50 per cent?

(*iv*) The frontages of the three riparians differ in length: 10 per cent of the river runs through the territory of State A, 30 per cent flows through the territory of State B and 60 per cent of the river is located in the territory of State C. On the basis of socio-economic criteria, the waters of the river should be divided equally between the three States. But the problem is, again, that there is not enough water in the river to satisfy the water requirements of the three States as each State requires 50 per cent of the waters of the river and not just 33.3 per cent. Should the fact that the lengths of the river frontages differ justify a modification of the figures of allocation in terms that the apportionment would reflect the difference? Would it be consonant with the rule of equitable utilization to give to State A less than 33.3 per cent of the waters in order to increase the share of State B on whose territory most of the river is located?

In the last two situations it is not possible to say that the adjustment automatically transforms the allocation into an inequitable one. In fact, if the share of any of the States is increased up to the extent of its respective needs, the whole of the waters of the river will anyway be used for productive purposes and no genuine water requirement would be sacrificed for the satisfaction of superfluous needs. Therefore, in situations (iii) and (iv) the lengths of the frontage of the riparian States on the river can be given some weight in the process of the establishment of an equitable regime for the utilization of international freshwater resources.

In conclusion, river frontage may be included in the process of the establishment of an equitable regime for the utilization of international waters, but only as a factor to adjust the apportionment effected on the basis of other criteria and provided that its inclusion does not imply the apportionment of volumes of water to a State that does not really need them. As will be shown below, this approach should also be applied to the other geographical and hydrological criteria, namely drainage area and contribution of water to the flow of the river.

B. *The Extent of the Drainage Area Lying in the Territory of the Basin States*

Drainage area is often confused with the concept of catchment area, despite the fact that the two concepts denote different things. The catchment area refers to the area that supplies surface runoff to a river or a stream. Runoff occurs when precipitation (rainfall) or snowmelt moves across the land surface. The part of it which does not remain on the surface for evaporation and which does not infiltrate through the ground surface eventually reaches rivers and lakes.[213] Therefore the concept of catchment area refers to the area supplying runoff to a watercourse, 'whereas a drainage basin for a given stream is the tract of land drained of both surface runoff and groundwater discharge'.[214] Despite the conceptual difference between the two terms, in the literature on international watercourses, as has been pointed out, the two concepts are often confused. Most of the time writers refer to catchment area when they really intend to refer to the drainage area.[215] For the purposes of this study, the pertinent concept is that of drainage area and the reference to writers or documents which speak of catchment area is made on the understanding that they really intended to refer to the drainage area of the watercourse. Fortunately, the definition contained in the Helsinki Rules complies with what hydrologists understand by drainage area:

... a geographical area extending over two or more States determined by the watershed limits of the system of waters, including surface and underground waters, flowing into a common terminus.[216]

---

[213] Newson, op. cit. above (n. 23), p. 149; Ward, *Principles of Hydrology* (Great Britain, 1975 [1967]), pp. 5–6.

[214] Newson, op. cit. above (n. 23), p. 149.

[215] One of the few instances in which the two concepts have been distinguished is the decision of the Narmada Water Disputes Tribunal.

[216] See Article II of the Helsinki Rules.

Article V of the Helsinki Rules included the extent of the drainage area located in the territory of each basin State as a relevant factor to be taken into account when deciding whether or not an international watercourse is being used in an equitable and reasonable manner. The ILC Draft Articles have not been that explicit, but they mention as relevant factors the extent of the watercourse in the territory of each watercourse State and the distribution of water therein, defining the term watercourse as a 'system of surface waters and groundwaters constituting by virtue of their physical relationship a unitary whole and normally flowing into a common terminus'.[217]

It has been claimed that drainage area may determine the territorial area where water should preferentially be used. This issue has been discussed in relation to the factor of the social and economic needs of the States. In that section it was asserted that diversion of water to areas lying outside the basin is not *per se* unlawful and that there are no grounds to prefer the water needs of the basin to the needs of extra-basin areas. It must be recalled that the ILC Draft Articles refer to the needs of the watercourse States, without establishing any territorial limit for the consideration of those needs, other than the territorial extent of the respective States.[218] In addition, the Helsinki Rules state that each basin State is entitled *within its territory* to the equitable and reasonable use of an international drainage basin.[219] The unlawfulness of extra-basin diversions and the claim that only the needs of the basin should be considered as the basis for the determination of the real needs of the parties concerned were rejected by the Krishna and the Narmada Water Disputes Tribunals.[220] Finally, the argument that the social and economic needs of the drainage area should be preferred to the needs of areas lying outside the basin should also be dismissed, in so far as this preferential treatment can only be justified by reason of the greater water dependence of the basin areas. If dependence is the decisive element, then whether the intra-basin areas are more dependent on the river than the areas lying outside the basin is a question of fact which has to be answered in accordance with the circumstances of the case.[221]

Apart from the issue of preferential use, it is suggested that the extent of the drainage area lying in the territory of the States concerned can still be included as a relevant factor in the process of the establishment of an equitable regime for water utilization. The argument could have been produced by the Sudan against Egypt in the dispute concerning the apportionment of the waters of the Nile river. If allocation had been

---

[217] See Article 2 of the ILC Draft Articles on the Non-Navigational Uses of International Watercourses.

[218] See Article 6(*b*) of the Draft Articles.

[219] See Article IV of the Helsinki Rules.

[220] See *Report of the Krishna Water Disputes Tribunal*, vol. 2, p. 126, and *Report of the Narmada Water Disputes Tribunal*, vol. 1, para. 9.6.9 and para. 9.6.10, p. 123, and para. 9.9.4, p. 126.

[221] See above, pp. 355 ff.

made proportional to the drainage area located in each of the respective States, the Sudan would have obtained 'the lions' share, while Egypt would have hardly survived with its part'.[222] Despite this fact, the Sudan did not argue on this basis during the negotiations leading to the 1959 Agreement for the Full Utilization of the Nile Waters.

The argument was produced in the dispute concerning the allocation of 27.25 million acres feet (MAF) between the Indian States of Madhya Pradesh and Gujarat. In that dispute, Madhya Pradesh included the extent of the drainage area in its territory as one of the bases for the apportionment. According to the Narmada Tribunal, 97.59 per cent of the drainage area was located in the territory of Madhya Pradesh, while only 0.53 per cent lay in the territory of Gujarat. However, the Tribunal was of the opinion that the most important factors for consideration were the social and economic needs of the parties, and on this basis concluded that the apportionment of water between Madhya Pradesh and Gujarat should be in a ratio of 11.694:19.410. The exact application of this ratio would have left Gujarat with 37.59 per cent and Madhya Pradesh with 62.41 per cent of the waters to be shared.[223] Drainage area was not taken into account in this calculation. However, the Tribunal was unable to dismiss this criterion totally, observing that:

It is also necessary to take into account the circumstance that the drainage area of Gujarat is 180 square miles (0.53%) and of Madhya Pradesh 33,150 square miles (97.59%) and that the contribution of Gujarat at 75% dependability flow is 2.68 MAF and that of Madhya Pradesh 26.20 MAF. We have already rejected the argument of Madhya Pradesh that the drainage area and contribution of water by each State should be given equal weight along with the other factors mentioned in the Helsinki Rules. But in our opinion, some weight should be given to the factors of drainage area and contribution of water by each basin State in the circumstances of this particular case.[224]

The result was that 33 per cent of the waters to be divided between the two States were allocated to Gujarat and 67 per cent to Madhya Pradesh. This decision shows that drainage area was not used in the establishment of the prima facie equitable apportionment, and it was only used to adjust the allocation arrived at by the application of other criteria.

C. *The Contribution of Water to the Flow of the River by the Basin States*

This element is mentioned as a relevant factor by the Helsinki Rules and by the ILC Draft Articles. The settlement of an international water

---

[222] Jovanovic, 'Ethiopian Interests in the Division of the Nile River Waters', *Water International*, 10 (1985), p. 82.

[223] *Report of the Narmada Water Disputes Tribunal*, vol. 1, p. 127.

[224] Ibid., pp. 127–8.

dispute on the sole basis of this criterion would amount to the application of the absolute territorial sovereignty doctrine. In this context, claims based on the contribution element usually constitute the initial position adopted by upstream States. The argument has been produced by Turkey in relation to the waters of the Euphrates river and by Ethiopia in relation to the waters of the river Nile. As regards the Euphrates, Turkey contributes 30 billion cubic metres per year (bcm/y) out of the 32 bcm/y of the natural flow of the river.[225] In other words, Turkey contributes 94 per cent of the flow of the river,[226] and for this reason it is not surprising that this State argues that: 'Water is an upstream resource and downstream users cannot tell [Turkey] how to use [its] resource'.[227]

Ethiopia contributes 60 per cent of the flow of the main stream of the Nile river.[228] Until now, Ethiopia has not been able to use these waters, but since 1956 it has been asserting its right to the Nile on the basis of contribution. In 1957 the Ethiopian Government stated that:

The Imperial Ethiopian Government has ascertained the fact that certain discussions have been taking place concerning the division of the waters of the Nile. Ethiopia alone supplies 84% of those waters, as well as the immense volume of alluvium fertilizing the lower reaches of the Nile. In view of this fact and the overwhelming importance which such waters and soils represent with reference to the total water and other resources of Ethiopia, the Imperial Ethiopian Government finds it important once again to make clear the position and rights of Ethiopia in this matter and would, in this connexion, invite attention to the official communiqué published on this subject by the Ministry of Foreign Affairs on the 6th February, 1956.

Just as is the case of all other natural resources on its territory, Ethiopia has the right and obligation to exploit the water resources of the Empire and, indeed, has the responsibility of providing the fullest and most scientific measures for the development and utilisation of the same, for the benefit of present and future generations of its citizens, in pace with and in anticipation of the growth in population and its expanding needs. The Imperial Ethiopian Government must, therefore, reassert and reserve now and for the future, the right to take all such measures in respect of its water resources and in particular, as regards that portion of the same which is of the greatest important to its welfare, namely, those waters providing so nearly the entirety of the volume of the Nile, whatever may be the measure of utilisation of such waters sought by recipient states situated along the course of that river.

[225] Hillel, *Rivers of Eden* (Oxford and New York, 1994), p. 95.

[226] Kirmani and Rangeley, 'International Inland Waters', World Bank Technical Paper No. 239 (1994), p. 8.

[227] Turkey's Official Statement (words of Suleiman Demirel), quoted by Hillel, op. cit. above (n. 225), n. 5, at p. 305.

[228] Jovanovic, loc. cit above (n. 222), p. 82; Bulloch and Darwish, *Water Wars* (London, 1993), p. 99.

. . . Under these circumstances, Ethiopia, alone the source of nearly the entirety of the waters involved, must, once again, make it clear that the quantities of waters available to others must always depend on the ever-increasing extent to which Ethiopia, the original owner, is and will be required to utilise the same for the needs of her expanding population and economy.[229]

The idea that the factor consisting of the contribution of water to the watercourse creates a proprietary right over the waters of an international river should be totally rejected. But its potential as a relevant factor on a basis different to that of proprietary rights should not be denied.

It is true that in many international river disputes the criterion has been overlooked. In the case of the Nile river, all riparian States, except for Egypt, make some contribution to the flow of the river; however, Egypt has managed to obtain three-quarters of the flow.[230] In the case of the Colorado river, despite the fact that the United States contributes the total flow of the river, Mexico has obtained 1,500,000 acres feet of its waters. During the negotiations of the agreement the United States entirely omitted the argument based on contribution. As was pointed out with regard to the length of river frontage, these examples can only suggest that the relevance of this factor might be low in hierarchy, but they cannot be used for denying that contribution of water to the flow of the river may have some relevance in the process of the establishment of an equitable regime for the utilization of international rivers.

The contribution of water by the watercourse States influenced the division of the waters of the Narmada river between the Indian States of Madhya Pradesh and Gujarat. The factor of contribution was ranked lower than the factor of the social and economic needs of the States, but it was still relevant for the final apportionment. As has already been said, on the basis of the water needs of the States concerned, the Narmada Tribunal concluded that, in principle, 37.59 per cent of the water should be allocated to Gujarat and 62.41 per cent to Madhya Pradesh. In view of the fact that Madhya Pradesh contributed 99.5 per cent of the flow of the river, the Tribunal decided to give some weight to this factor, modifying its provisional apportionment and allocating 33 per cent of the waters to Gujarat and 67 per cent to Madhya Pradesh. The Narmada Tribunal did not resort to the criterion of the contribution of water for the calculation of the prima facie equitable allocation of the waters of the Narmada river. This factor was only used to adjust the allocation arrived at by the application of other criteria.

---

[229] *Aide mémoire* of the Ethiopian Government circulated to diplomatic missions at Cairo, dated 23 September 1957, quoted by Whiteman, *Digest of International Law*, vol. 3, pp. 1011–12.
[230] Lowi, op. cit. above (n. 201), p. 71.

D. *The Role Ascribed by the Narmada Water Disputes Tribunal to the Factors Consisting of the Drainage Area and Contribution of Water*

The Narmada Tribunal took into account the extent of the drainage area lying in the territories of the parties and their contribution of water to the flow of the river. The result of the consideration of these factors was that the preliminary apportionment of the waters of the Narmada river was modified or adjusted in terms that Madhya Pradesh, instead of obtaining 62.41 per cent of the waters, obtained 67 per cent. The prima facie equitable apportionment was done on the basis of the needs of the parties, and a mathematical approach was adopted in the application of this criterion. In fact, the provisional division of the waters of the Narmada river was proportional to the ratio between the water requirements of the two States. But the Tribunal refused to apply the arithmetical perspective to the criteria of drainage area and contribution of water. Accordingly, these factors were only ascribed a role in the adjustment of the provisional allocation figures established by the Tribunal.

In the light of this jurisprudence, it is possible to assert that the rejection of the mathematical perspective in relation to a particular factor, which at least in principle has the potential of serving as a basis for a proportional division of the disputed object, shows that the role ascribed to that criterion is low in the hierarchy of relevant factors. This is consistent with the rule of equitable utilization, because to admit these factors to function as a direct basis for the allocation of waters would not be in keeping with the principle of equality between the basin States.

The role accorded to these factors by the Narmada Tribunal was consistent with the rule of equitable utilization on an additional basis: the adjustment to the provisional allocation of waters was made in a situation where there was not enough water (27.25 MAF) to satisfy the water requirements of the parties totally (31.104 MAF), and the adjustment did not exceed the requirements of Madhya Pradesh, which were estimated at 19.41 MAF, that is to say, 71.23 per cent of the water available for division.

VII. THE ENVIRONMENTAL IMPACT OF THE USE OF THE RIVER ON OTHER BASIN STATES

The utilization of an international watercourse by a watercourse State may cause significant environmental harm to the other basin States. For example, the use of a river for irrigation purposes may cause the pollution of the river, and the construction of a dam may increase water temperature, and affect the migration of fish and the equilibrium of the ecosystem of the watercourse. These detrimental environmental effects should be taken into account in the establishment of an equitable regime for water utilization. The operation of this criterion prompts the fundamental question whether or not any significant harm to the environment consequential upon the use of an international watercourse should be deemed inequitable. It has previously been pointed out that the operation of the rule of equitable utilization may tolerate that certain uses cause significant harm to the interests of other co-basin States. In this connection, the impairment or termination of existing uses was considered as one possible effect of the application of the rule of equitable use. However, it has been claimed that significant harm to the environment is a special category of injury that automatically transforms that harmful utilization into an inequitable use of the watercourse.[231] The opposing view considers that the detrimental environmental effects have to be approached from the overall perspective of what constitutes an equitable utilization. This was the opinion of the International Law Association, according to which:

> The optimum goal of international drainage basin development is to accommodate the multiple and diverse uses of the co-basin States. The concept of equitable utilization of the waters of an international drainage basin has the purpose of promoting such an accommodation. Thus, uses of the waters by a basin State that cause pollution resulting in injury in a co-basin State must be considered from the overall perspective of what constitutes an equitable utilization.
>
> Any use of water by a basin State, whether upper or lower, that denies an equitable sharing of uses by a co-basin State conflicts with the community of interests of all basin States in obtaining maximum benefit from the common resource. Certainly a diversion of water that denies a co-basin State an equitable share is in violation of international law. A use that causes pollution to the extent of depriving a co-basin State of an equitable share stands on the same basis. By parallel reasoning, a State that engages in a use or uses causing pollution is not required to take measures with respect to such pollution that would deprive it of equitable utilization.[232]

The International Law Commission has not adopted a clear position on this issue, which has been approached from the perspective of the existence of a conflict between the equitable utilization and the no-harm rules. Therefore, the discussion has focused on which of the two rules should prevail.[233] In the 1991 Draft Articles on the Law of the Non-Navigational Uses of International Watercourses the no-harm rule was accorded priority. In this context, pollution and significant environmental harm in general were viewed as *per se* contrary to the equitable

---

[231] Nollkaemper, *The Legal Regime for Transboundary Water Pollution: Between Discretion and Constraint* (Dordrecht, 1993), pp. 68–9.

[232] ILA, *Report of the Fifty-Second Conference* (Helsinki, 1966), p. 499. See also Art. X of the Helsinki Rules.

[233] McCaffrey, 'The International Law Commission adopts Draft Articles on International Watercourses', *American Journal of International Law*, 89 (1995), p. 399.

utilization of an international watercourse.[234] In 1993 the Special Rapporteur, Mr Rosenstock, proposed a redraft of Article 7, concerning the obligation of watercourse States not to cause significant harm to other watercourse States. The intended result of the revision was a regime in which equitable and reasonable utilization was the decisive criterion in determining which harmful uses of a watercourse were to be allowed. In any case, Rosenstock's new version of Article 7 would have given a special treatment to pollution, which was conceived as a defeasible presumption of inequity.[235] In 1994, the Commission adopted the view that, in general, the harmful consequences of a certain water utilization have to be weighed up according to the rule of equitable use. In this context, 'the fact that an activity involves significant harm, would not of itself necessarily constitute a basis for barring it'.[236] The commentary attached to Article 7 explains that:

In certain circumstances 'equitable and reasonable utilization' of an international watercourse may still involve significant harm to another watercourse State. Generally in such instances, the principle of equitable and reasonable utilization remains the guiding criterion in balancing the interests at stake.[237]

Pollution is not mentioned in the 1994 definitive version of Article 7. On this basis it could be concluded that pollution has not been considered as an extraordinary harmful situation in which the rule of equitable utilization should be subordinated to the no-harm principle. However, the ILC acknowledges the existence of a general obligation to protect and preserve the ecosystems of international watercourses (Article 20) and the obligation to prevent, reduce and control pollution of an international watercourse that may cause significant harm to other watercourse States or their environment (Article 21.2). Unfortunately, there is no further explanation of the interrelation between these obligations and the rule of equitable utilization. The commentary attached to Article 21.2 simply states that: 'This paragraph is a specific application of the general principles contained in articles 5 and 7'.[238] The fundamental question whether the scope of the rule of equitable utiliza-

---

[234] *ILC Yearbook*, 1982, vol. 2, part 1, pp. 91–101 and p. 144; *ILC Yearbook*, 1983, vol. 2, part 1, pp. 181–4.

[235] The proposed Article 7 provided that: 'Watercourse States shall exercise due diligence to utilize an international watercourse in such a way as not to cause significant harm to other watercourse States, absent their agreement, except as may be allowable under an equitable and reasonable use of the watercourse. A use which causes significant harm in the form of pollution shall be presumed to be an inequitable and unreasonable use unless there is: (*a*) a clear showing of special circumstances indicating a compelling need for ad hoc adjustment; and (*b*) the absence of any imminent threat to human health and safety'. See, Rosenstock, First Report on the Law of the Non-Navigational Uses of International Watercourses (1993), doc. A/CN.4/451, p. 10.

[236] 1994 *ILC Report*, p. 236.

[237] Ibid.

[238] Ibid., p. 291.

tion is limited by the operation of these environmental obligations remains unanswered.

Some commentators have interpreted Articles 7, 20 and 21 of the Draft Articles as establishing due diligence as the decisive criterion. According to this interpretation, significant harm resulting from a failure to exercise due diligence violates the rule of equitable utilization, and 'where significant harm is caused despite the exercise of due diligence it will be prima facie inequitable'.[239] The problem with this interpretation is that the standard of due diligence can only assist in determining the form in which certain activities should be conducted, but it is of no assistance in deciding which uses of a certain river should be permitted. The failure to exercise due diligence may be inequitable, but there is no basis to conclude that significant harm caused despite the exercise of due diligence is prima facie inequitable. In the second case, the inequity of certain harmful activities cannot be established by reference to standards of responsibility.

The purpose of this section has been to point out that the environmental impact of the utilization of an international river on the co-basin States is a relevant factor that should be taken into consideration in the establishment of an equitable regime of water utilization and to describe the problems that the operation of this criterion may present. A more detailed examination of those problems exceeds the scope of this article, which has focused on the examination of the criteria directly and indirectly related to the social and economic needs of the basin States and to their territorial sovereignty.

VIII. CONCLUSION

The rule of equitable utilization of international watercourses cannot be interpreted as authorizing international tribunals to decide a dispute *ex aequo et bono*. The rule has a normative content and its application requires weighing up all the prospective relevant factors which create equities in favour of the States concerned. While States are free to agree on any solution which they consider equitable, international tribunals, if asked to settle a dispute concerning the utilization of an international river, should follow certain guidelines in the selection of the criteria to take into consideration in the process of the establishment of an equitable regime for water utilization. These guidelines emanate from the fundamental principle of equality of States and from the principle that States do not have proprietary rights over the waters of a river. Within this framework, the present study has attempted to assess the potential

---

[239] Brunnée and Toope, 'Environmental Security and Freshwater Resources: A Case for International Ecosystem Law', *Yearbook of International Environmental Law*, 5 (1994), p. 64.

relevance of various prospective criteria, and for this purpose it has examined the experience of the equitable delimitation of maritime zones and the experience of inter-State river disputes settled by municipal courts of federal States. In the light of this jurisprudence, it should be concluded that the most relevant factors to be taken into account are those related to the water requirements of the States concerned. The criteria related to territorial sovereignty over the portions of the river system lying in the territory of the States concerned might also be included in the process, but their relevance should be low.

Not all the prospective criteria to be included in the process of the establishment of an equitable regime for the utilization of international watercourses have been examined here. However, the assessment of the relevance of some of these criteria might illustrate the kind of process that international tribunals may be asked to undertake in future disputes concerning international freshwater resources.

THE LEGAL FRAMEWORK GOVERNING UNITED NATIONS SUBSIDIARY ORGANS*

By DANESH SAROOSHI‡

I. INTRODUCTION

The six principal organs of the United Nations (UN) possess the authority to establish and utilize subsidiary organs in the attainment of their Charter objectives.[1] There is, however, an important distinction to be made between the legal considerations relating to the establishment and termination of a subsidiary organ and the lawfulness of the activities of a subsidiary organ. The establishment and termination of UN subsidiary organs is governed by a legal framework consisting of the relevant provisions of the UN Charter and those parts of the general law of international institutions that relate to this activity, while the lawfulness of the acts of subsidiary organs will depend on the subsidiary complying with the legal mandate conferred on it by the principal. The former deals with the competence of principal organs to establish and

* © Danesh Sarooshi, 1997.

‡ B Comm., LL B (NSW), LL M (London); Doctoral Candidate (LSE); Lecturer in Public International Law, University College London. The author would like to express his gratitude to his supervisor Judge (formerly Professor) Rosalyn Higgins of the International Court of Justice for her continual support and encouragement and for her valuable advice on an earlier version of this article. He would also like to express his great appreciation to Professors Ian Brownlie, James Crawford and Maurice Mendelson, Mr David Hutchinson and Mr Amazu Asouzu for their very helpful comments on an earlier version of this article. Any opinions expressed are, unless the contrary is stated, solely those of the author.

[1] Article 7(1) of the Charter establishes the following principal organs of the United Nations: the General Assembly; the Security Council; the Economic and Social Council; the Trusteeship Council; the International Court of Justice; and the Secretariat. For the scope of the authority of principal organs to establish subsidiary organs, see section III, below. The literature on UN subsidiary organs has not been extensive. The main works include: Torres Bernardez, 'Subsidiary Organs', in Dupuy (ed.), *Manuel sur les organisations internationales* (1988), p. 109; Ramcharan, 'Lacunae in the Law of International Organizations: The Relations between Subsidiary and Parent Organs with Particular Reference to the Commission and Sub-Commission on Human Rights', in Nowak *et al.* (eds.), *Festschrift Ermacora* (1988), pp. 37–49; Reuter, 'Les Organes Subsidiaires des Organisations Internationales', in Chaumont (ed.), *Hommage d'une génération de juristes au Président Basdevant* (1958), pp. 415–30; Klepacki, *The Organs of International Organizations* (1973), pp. 17 ff; Schermers and Blokker, *International Institutional Law* (1995); Dutheil de la Rochère, 'Etude de la composition de certains organes subsidiaires récemment créés par l'Assemblée générale des Nations Unies dans le domaine économique', *Annuaire français de droit international*, 13 (1967), p. 307; and commentaries to Articles 7, 22, 29, and 68 of the Charter in the following works: Goodrich and Hambro, *The Charter of the United Nations* (1949); Bentwich and Martin, *A Commentary on the Charter of the United Nations* (1950); Cot and Pellet (eds.), *La Charte des Nations Unies* (1991); and Simma (ed.), *The Charter of the United Nations: A Commentary* (1994).

terminate subsidiary organs, while the latter is concerned with the subsidiary remaining within the bounds of its delegated mandate. This article is concerned primarily with the identification of those elements of the general legal framework that govern the processes of establishment and termination of UN subsidiary organs. This framework applies to all UN principal and subsidiary organs: it is all-encompassing in scope. This is attested by the fact that once subsidiary organs are lawfully established by a principal organ, they become subsidiary organs of the United Nations as a whole and not just subsidiary organs of the particular principal organ.[2] Accordingly, the practice of all UN principal organs in establishing and terminating subsidiary organs needs to be considered in order to construct this unified legal framework.

The operation of this framework is illustrated by reference to, *inter alia*, certain cases where the Security Council has established subsidiary organs as part of its efforts to maintain or restore international peace. For example, the establishment of the UN War Crimes Tribunals for the former Yugoslavia and Rwanda and the UN Iraq-Kuwait Boundary Demarcation Commission are considered in some detail. Moreover, these cases illustrate, *inter alia*, the degree of flexibility that subsidiary organs add to the work of the principal organs. The establishment of subsidiary organs has allowed the Security Council to ensure the performance of certain tasks which, though essential to the maintenance of international peace and security, it arguably could not itself perform.

II. UN SUBSIDIARY ORGANS: ISSUES OF DEFINITION

Issues of form are not of major importance when considering what constitutes a UN subsidiary organ.[3] Thus although they have usually

---

[2] In the discussion on the current Article 7(2) of the Charter at the San Francisco Conference, this argument was made by the representative of the Netherlands in the Coordination Committee: 30 May 1945, meeting 8, UN Doc. WD 60; CO/29, *Documents of the United Nations Conference on International Organization*, vol. 17, p. 37. As a result, UN subsidiary organs enjoy, for example, privileges and immunities under the Convention on the Privileges and Immunities of the United Nations and the capacity to conclude treaties and to contract with private entities. The UN Legal Counsel has found the Convention on the Privileges and Immunities of the United Nations applicable to UN subsidiary organs in the case of, among others, the United Nations Joint Staff Pension Fund: see further *UN Juridical Yearbook*, 1978, p. 186.

[3] Moreover, issues of form should not constitute a legal bar to the effective functioning of subsidiary organs. In a memorandum to the Secretary of ECOSOC, the UN Legal Counsel pointed to the fact that there are several examples in the practice of the General Assembly and ECOSOC where subsidiary organs have met and proceeded to discharge their mandate even though for one reason or another it was not possible to appoint the full complement of members provided for in the resolution authorizing the establishment of the body concerned. The UN Legal Counsel continued: 'The conclusion that may be drawn from these precedents is that the fact it is not possible to secure the appointment of all the members envisaged in a resolution establishing an organ has not been considered a bar to convening the organs in question and to permitting them to proceed with their work' (Memorandum to the Secretary of ECOSOC, *UN Juridical Yearbook*, 1984, p. 168). In this

been composed of representatives of States,[4] in certain cases members have been appointed in their personal capacity.[5] It is not, moreover, a requirement that the membership of a subsidiary organ should reflect or draw upon the membership of the particular principal organ or even of the Organization.[6] The only requirement regarding membership is that if States are proposed to be members of the subsidiary organ, they must either be members of the United Nations or States that are assessed for contributions by the General Assembly on the basis of their participation in the activities of the subsidiary organ.[7]

The Charter nowhere defines the term 'subsidiary organ'.[8] There have, however, been several attempts made at a definition. For instance,

opinion, the UN Legal Counsel applied the principle of effectiveness, as formulated for example in Article 28(1) of the Charter in respect of the Security Council, to the context of the operation of UN subsidiary organs. The relevant section of Article 28(1) provides: 'The Security Council shall be so organized as to be able to function continuously'. Thus, the Legal Counsel stated: '[t]he fact that a particular group entitled to be represented on a subsidiary organ of the United Nations does not desire to participate in the work of that organ should not have the effect of preventing the organ concerned from being effectively, albeit incompletely, constituted and from carrying out the functions entrusted to it. In our view this in effect constitutes a waiver by the group concerned of its right to be represented on the organ in question' (Memorandum to the Secretary of ECOSOC, ibid., p. 169).

[4] In cases where a subsidiary organ is composed of States, their membership may include all member States—as in the case of the Committee on arrangements for a conference for the purpose of reviewing the Charter (General Assembly Resolution 992 (X))—or a number of specified member States, in which case commissions or committees are often designated as special or ad hoc commissions or committees. There is, however, an important distinction between a subsidiary organ and a committee which is part of the principal organ: see further below, n. 14 and corresponding text.

[5] This occurred in the case, for example, of the UN Representative for India and Pakistan (Repertory of Practice of UN Organs (1955), vol. 2, p. 121). Moreover, the Council has recommended to the Secretary-General that he appoint a UN Mediator in respect of Cyprus (Repertoire of the Practice of the Security Council, 1964–1965, p. 71); a Personal Representative in respect of the Dominican Republic (Repertoire of the Practice of the Security Council, 1964–1965, p. 72), the Middle East (Repertoire of the Practice of the Security Council, 1966–1968, p. 76), and Liberia (Security Council Resolution 788 of 19 November 1992); and that he send a Special Envoy to Abkhazia, Georgia (Security Council Resolution 849 of 9 July 1993). As the UN Legal Counsel has noted: '[o]ther subsidiary organs consist of several individuals, or of a single individual, appointed in their individual expert capacity. In some instances, as in the case of the Technical Assistance Board (Economic and Social Council Resolution 222 A (IX)), a subsidiary organ is composed of the executive heads, or their representatives, of the United Nations and the specialized agencies. The Administrative Committee on Co-ordination established by Economic and Social Council resolution 13 (III), which is a subsidiary organ of the Council, also consists of the executive heads of the United Nations and of the specialized agencies' (UN Juridical Yearbook, 1963, p. 169).

[6] Certain non-member States have been included as members of a UN subsidiary organ when deemed appropriate: see, for example, the Executive Board of UNICEF (General Assembly Resolution 417 (V)) or the Governing Council of the Special Fund (General Assembly Resolution 1240 (XIII)): see further UN Juridical Yearbook, 1963, p. 169.

[7] Accordingly, the UN Legal Counsel stated, in respect of membership of the UN Environmental Programme: 'In the absence of guidance from the General Assembly there would not appear to be a sufficient basis for the Governing Council to include as members of the proposed subsidiary organ States that meet neither of these criteria' (UN Juridical Yearbook, 1983, p. 170).

[8] The Repertory of Practice points out that the term 'subsidiary organ' has not been defined by any organ of the United Nations, and that, in the practice of the Organization, 'such expressions as "commissions", "committees", "subsidiary organs", and "subsidiary bodies" have been used interchangeably' (Repertory of Practice of United Nations Organs, vol. 1, p. 224). For examples of

subsidiary organs were defined in a United Nations document as follows:

A subsidiary organ is one which is established by or under the authority of a principal organ of the United Nations, in accordance with Article 7, paragraph 2, of the Charter, by resolution of the appropriate body. Such an organ is an integral part of the Organization . . . Most subsidiary organs have in common their establishment by parent bodies which presumably may change their terms of reference and composition, issue policy directives to them, receive their reports and accept or reject their recommendations. Generally speaking, a subsidiary organ may be abolished or modified by action of the parent body.[9]

Similarly, the *Repertory of Practice of United Nations Organs* lists the following, almost identical, common features of a UN subsidiary organ:

(a) A subsidiary organ is created by, or under the authority of, a principal organ of the United Nations;
(b) The membership, structure and terms of reference of a subsidiary organ are determined, and may be modified by, or under the authority of, a principal organ;
(c) A subsidiary organ may be terminated by, or under the authority of, a principal organ.[10]

Both definitions contain two of the preconditions for the lawful establishment of a UN subsidiary organ: that it be established by a UN principal organ, and that it be under the authority and control of a UN principal organ.[11] There is, however, the additional precondition that the establishment of the subsidiary organ does not violate the delimitation of Charter powers between the principal organs.[12] The satisfaction of these preconditions of establishment is necessary before an entity can be considered as a lawfully established UN subsidiary organ. These preconditions derive from the definition of a UN subsidiary organ, and, moreover, the law of international institutions.[13] However, in defining a subsidiary organ there is an additional element which is required: that the subsidiary organ necessarily possesses a certain degree of independence from its principal organ. This is necessary since otherwise the entity in question would simply be a part of the principal organ. This degree of independence can, as a definitional element of a subsidiary organ, be used to distinguish an entity which is part of a principal organ from a UN

such practice, see further Gordon, *The United Nations at the Crossroads of Reform* (1994), pp. 72 ff. Cf. below, n. 14 and corresponding text.

[9] 'Summary of internal Secretariat studies of constitutional questions relating to agencies within the framework of the United Nations'. This document was subsequently proposed to the 9th Session of the General Assembly. See further *General Assembly Official Records*, 9th Session, Annexes, Agenda Item 67, at p. 13, A/C.1/758, paras. 1 and 2.

[10] *Repertory of Practice of United Nations Organs*, vol. 1, p. 228.

[11] For detailed consideration of these preconditions, see section IV(1) and (2), below.

[12] For detailed consideration of this precondition, see section IV(3), below.

[13] See section IV, below.

subsidiary organ.[14] This occurred during the debates of the 6th Committee of the General Assembly where there was discussion as to whether committees of the General Assembly should be regarded as subsidiary organs or as integral components of the Assembly itself.[15] In the ensuing debates it was accepted that a Main Committee is not usually a subsidiary organ, but a part of the General Assembly itself, since the two are identical in membership.[16] It was, nevertheless, generally agreed that if a committee continued to operate during the interval between two General Assembly sessions it would probably be a subsidiary organ, with the result that the Assembly would have to consider its work.[17] The test that emerged to determine whether an entity is a subsidiary organ is that it will depend on whether the entity is exercising powers and functions in a manner which is distinct from the internal workings of the principal organ. An additional element is whether the subsidiary organ is performing functions which the principal organ does not itself possess.[18]

[14] Accordingly, Torres Bernardez states: ' "subsidiary organs" should be distinguished from bodies (e.g., committees, commissions, working parties, etc.) which may be set up within a given "principal organ" as integral parts thereof. These bodies are not distinct entities or distinct "organs", albeit "subsidiary", but elements of the internal organization of the "principal organ" concerned' (loc. cit. above (n. 1), p. 130).

[15] General Assembly Official Records, 2nd Session, 6th Committee, 57th meeting, p. 143.

[16] Ibid., at pp. 142–4. However, the fact that the membership of an entity is identical to that of the principal organ which established it does not in itself mean that the entity is a committee of the principal organ. Many subsidiary organs established by the Security Council are recognized as such even though they mirror the membership of the Council, for example, the sanctions committees established by the Security Council to monitor and ensure implementation of economic sanctions imposed by the Council against the following non-State and State entities: Southern Rhodesia, the sanctions committee was initially established by Resolution 253 (1968) in the form of a committee of limited membership of 7, but later, on 1 October 1970, the membership was expanded to include all Security Council members (Repertoire of the Practice of the Security Council, 1966–1968, p. 78, and Repertoire of the Practice of the Security Council, 1969–1971, p. 63); Iraq (Security Council Resolution 661 (1990)); the former Yugoslavia (Security Council Resolution 724); Libya (Security Council Resolution 748); Somalia (Security Council Resolution 751); Haiti (Security Council Resolution 841); and Angola (Security Council Resolution 864).

[17] See, for example, the statement by the representative of the USSR: General Assembly Official Records, 2nd Session, 6th Committee, 57th meeting, p. 143. Even if this is the case, it does not follow that if a committee meets during the period when a principal organ is in session, it cannot be considered as a subsidiary organ. As Torres Bernardez argues: 'Categorizations made in the "internal law", or in administrative internal arrangements, of some international organizations between "standing" and "special" or ad hoc bodies, between "sessional" and "intersessional" bodies, etc., are not always of help as criteria to determine if a given body is an integral part of a "principal organ" or a "subsidiary organ", because both such criteria are susceptible of application to both these kinds of bodies without distinction' (loc. cit. above (n. 1), p. 131). What if the case were such that a committee of a principal organ were assigned the performance of functions which the principal organ did not itself possess? The mere fact that such a committee met during the same period as the principal organ cannot in itself preclude such a committee being considered to be a subsidiary organ of the principal organ. Moreover, the case of committees of the General Assembly is arguably unique, since the Assembly is the only principal organ that has in a decision—paragraph 34 of Decision 34/401—stipulated that its subsidiary organs are not to meet during sessions of the Assembly unless explicitly authorized to do so.

[18] See further on this issue n. 54 and corresponding text, below.

This requirement of independence means that the establishment of sessional committees, sub-committees, and working groups of UN principal organs does not represent the establishment of subsidiary organs.[19] Similarly, the appointment of UN staff by the Secretary-General under Article 101(1) of the Charter does not represent the establishment of subsidiary organs under Article 7(2),[20] since UN staff are in legal terms considered an integral part of the UN Secretariat,[21] a UN principal organ under Article 7(1). However, in the case of the International Court of Justice, the exercise of its power under Article 26 of its Statute, to establish 'Chambers', to deal with particular categories of cases (a 'Special Chamber') or on an *ad hoc* basis,[22] does represent the establishment by the Court of subsidiary organs, since these entities fulfil the preconditions of establishment of subsidiary organs, and, moreover, there is a degree of independence of these Chambers from the Court.[23] These Chambers are not as such part of the Court, they are a separate organ established by the Court to exercise the functions of the Court.[24] This independence does not mean, however, that a Chamber is not an integral part of the work of the Court in terms of both the peaceful settlement of disputes between States and the development of inter-

---

[19] Thus the constitutional basis of such entities is not the general authority to establish organs, but those articles in the Charter which authorize the principal organs to adopt their own rules of procedure. See also Simma, op. cit. above (n. 1), p. 197.

[20] Cf. Kelsen, *The Law of the United Nations* (1951), p. 139.

[21] Article 97 of the Charter provides, in part, the following: 'The Secretariat shall comprise a Secretary-General and such staff as the Organization may require'. See also Simma, op. cit. above (n. 1), pp. 1088–9; and Alexandrowicz, 'The Secretary-General of the United Nations', *International and Comparative Law Quarterly*, 11 (1962), p. 1109, at p. 1112.

[22] There is an additional Chamber of the Court, the Chamber of Summary Procedure, which is established by Article 29 of the Court's Statute. This Chamber cannot be considered as a UN subsidiary organ, since it is established not by a principal organ but by the constituent instrument of the international organization, in this case the Court's Statute which is part of the Charter. See further, on the precondition of establishment that a subsidiary organ be established by a principal organ, Section IV(1), below.

[23] The relevant sections of Article 26 of the Court's Statute state: '1. The Court may from time to time form one or more chambers, composed of three or more judges as the Court may determine, for dealing with particular categories of cases . . . 2. The Court may at any time form a chamber for dealing with a particular case. The number of judges to constitute such a chamber shall be determined by the Court with the approval of the parties. 3. Cases shall be heard and determined by the chambers provided for in this article if the parties so request.' See further on this provision Rosenne, *The World Court: What It Is and How It Works* (1995), pp. 75–6; and the judgment of the International Court of Justice in the *Land, Island and Maritime Frontier Dispute (El Salvador/Honduras)*, *Application to Intervene*, *ICJ Reports*, 1990, p. 3. For the authority and control which the Court exercises over its Chamber, see Section IV(2), below.

[24] See also Rosenne, who goes even further when he states: 'It follows from the Statute and the Rules of the Court that, once a chamber is constituted under article 27(2) of the Statute, the Court itself has nothing more to do with the chamber or with the case . . . the chambers envisaged in article 26 do not act in the name of the Court, but as independent organisms, no doubt established by the Court under powers conferred by the Statute, but, as regarding an ad hoc chamber, established and acting exclusively at the request of the parties' ('Article 27 of the Statute of the International Court of Justice', *Virginia Journal of International Law*, 32 (1991), p. 213 at pp. 228, 230).

national law.[25] The fact that the Chamber is composed of judges who are members of the principal organ, the Court, is not a barrier to the consideration of the Chamber as a subsidiary organ. It has already been explained that such matters of form are not of prime importance in determining what constitutes a subsidiary organ.[26] Accordingly, Goodrich and Hambro also consider that the establishment by the Court of Chambers constitutes the establishment of a subsidiary organ by the International Court.[27] However, *ad hoc* and Special Chambers of the Court are to be considered as a *sui generis* type of subsidiary organ. They differ from a normal subsidiary organ since there is a special condition that must be fulfilled for their establishment: the International Court must obtain the consent of States that are to be parties to the case for a Chamber to be established.[28] The International Court could suggest to States that a Chamber may be the best forum to determine a dispute, but under Article 26 of the Court's Statute, the Court could never require States to have their case heard by a Chamber. Once, however, the parties to a case request the establishment of a Chamber to hear the case, Article 26 makes it clear that it is within the sole discretion of the Court to decide to establish an *ad hoc* Chamber and, arguably, to determine its composition.[29] The characterization of these *ad hoc* and Special Chambers of the

---

[25] It is in this sense that Judge Jennings has observed: 'A Chamber constituted under Article 26.2 of the Statute of the Court, like all Chambers of the Court, is in no wise to be regarded as a body which is independent of the Court as a whole' ('Chambers of the International Court of Justice and Courts of Arbitration', in *Humanité et droit international: Mélanges René-Jean Dupuy* (1991), p. 197 at p. 199). The Chambers facility provides the International Court and prospective parties with the flexibility that may be necessary in a particular case to settle a dispute under the authority, and using the procedures, of the Court, and thus should be increasingly used. See also Jennings, ibid., at p. 200; de Aréchaga, 'The Amendments to the Rules of Procedure of the International Court of Justice', *American Journal of International Law*, 67 (1973), p. 1; Robinson, Colson and Rashkow, 'Some Perspectives on Adjudicating Before the World Court: The Gulf of Maine Case', ibid., 79 (1985), p. 578 at p. 582; Leigh and Ramsay, 'Confidence in the Court: It Need Not be a Hollow Chamber', in Fisler-Damrosch (ed.), *The International Court of Justice at a Crossroads* (1987), p. 106; Jessup, 'To Form a More Perfect United Nations', *Recueil des cours*, 129 (1970–I), p. 21; and Hyde, 'A Special Chamber of the International Court of Justice—An Alternative to Ad Hoc Arbitration', *American Journal of International Law*, 62 (1968), p. 439.

[26] See further n. 3 and corresponding text, above.

[27] Goodrich and Hambro, *Charter of the United Nations: Commentary and Documents* (1946), p. 91.

[28] The lawful establishment of a Chamber is dependent on the request for and consent of both parties to a case: see further Article 17 of the Court's revised Rules of Procedure, below, n. 29. Moreover, see further Oda, 'Further Thoughts on the Chambers Procedure of the International Court of Justice', *American Journal of International Law*, 82 (1988), p. 556 at p. 559; de Aréchaga, loc. cit. above (n. 25), pp. 2–3; Ostrihansky, 'Chambers of the International Court of Justice', *International and Comparative Law Quarterly*, 37 (1988), p. 30 at p. 49; Mosler, 'The ad hoc Chambers of the International Court of Justice', in *International Law at a Time of Perplexity* (1989), p. 449 at p. 457; and Rosenne, loc. cit. above (n. 24), p. 215.

[29] For the content of Article 26 of the Court's Statute, see above, n. 23. The cogency of this contention is illustrated by the *Gulf of Maine* case, where the Court expressly notes that it '*Decides to accede to the request of the Governments of Canada and the United States of America to form a special Chamber of five judges to deal with the case*' (*Gulf of Maine, Constitution of Chamber* case, *ICJ Reports*, 1982, p. 3 at p. 8). See also *Frontier Dispute (Burkina Faso/Mali), Constitution of*

Court as subsidiary organs is of considerable importance in determining the precise nature of their relationship with the Court.[30]

Chamber case, *ICJ Reports*, 1985, p. 6; *Elettronica Sicula (ELSI) (US/Italy), Constitution of Chamber* case, *ICJ Reports*, 1987, p. 3; and *Land, Island and Maritime Frontier Dispute (El Salvador/Honduras), Constitution of Chamber* case, *ICJ Reports*, 1987, p. 10. There has, however, been concern expressed that Article 17 of the revised Rules of the Court affects this sole prerogative of the Court to decide to establish an *ad hoc* Chamber and to determine its composition. Article 17 provides: '1. A request for the formation of a Chamber to deal with a particular case . . . may be filed at any time until the closure of the written proceedings. Upon receipt of a request made by one party, the President shall ascertain whether the other party assents. 2. When the parties have agreed, the President shall ascertain their views regarding the composition of the Chamber, and shall report to the Court accordingly. . . . 3. When the Court has determined, with the approval of the parties, the number of its Members who are to constitute the Chamber, it shall proceed to their election, in accordance with the provisions of Article 18 . . . '. The view has been expressed that this provision gives parties to a case the power to 'approve' of the composition of the Chamber and is thus contrary to the Court's Statute which gives the Court the sole competence to establish Chambers and to determine their composition. (See, for example, Judge Shahabuddeen in his dissenting opinion in the *Land, Island and Maritime Frontier Dispute* case, *Application to Intervene*, *ICJ Reports*, 1990, p. 18 at p. 23; McWhinney, 'Special Chambers within the International Court of Justice: the Preliminary, Procedural Aspect of the Gulf of Maine case', *Syracuse Journal of International Law and Commerce*, 12 (1985), p. 1 at pp. 8–10; and Brauer, 'International Conflict Resolution: The ICJ Chambers and the Gulf of Maine Dispute', *Virginia Journal of International Law*, 23 (1983), p. 463.) However, the Court in the *Gulf of Maine*, the *Frontier Dispute*, the *ELSI* and the *Land, Island and Maritime Frontier Dispute* Chamber cases expressly treats consultation with the parties 'as to the composition of the proposed chamber' as being in accordance with Article 26(2) of the Statute (*Gulf of Maine, Constitution of Chamber* case, *ICJ Reports*, 1982, p. 3; *Frontier Dispute (Burkina Faso/ Mali), Constitution of Chamber* case, *ICJ Reports*, 1985, p. 6; *Elettronica Sicula (ELSI) (US/Italy), Constitution of Chamber* case, *ICJ Reports*, 1987, p. 3; and *Land, Island and Maritime Frontier Dispute (El Salvador/Honduras), Constitution of Chamber* case, *ICJ Reports*, 1987, p. 10). Moreover, the General Assembly in Resolution 3232 (XXIX) (1974) on a 'Review of the Role of the International Court of Justice' expressly endorsed the provisions of Article 17 when it declared: '*Considering* that the International Court of Justice has recently amended the Rules of Court with a view to facilitating recourse to it for the judicial settlement of disputes, *inter alia*, by simplifying the procedure, reducing the likelihood of undue delays and costs and allowing for greater influence of parties on the composition of *ad hoc* chambers, *Draws the attention* of States to the possibility of making use of chambers as provided in Articles 26 and 29 of the Statute of the International Court of Justice and in the Rules of Court, including those which would deal with particular categories of cases'. See further Schwebel, 'Chambers of the International Court of Justice Formed for Particular Cases', in *International Law at a Time of Perplexity* (1989), p. 739 at pp. 754–61; and Oda, loc. cit. above (n. 28). Moreover, several Judges of the Court and other commentators correctly place more emphasis on the fact that the ultimate decision on the composition of the Chamber is still that of the Court, and thus do not find the provisions of Article 17 of the revised Rules problematic. (Judge Lachs puts this persuasive point well when he observed: 'It is one thing for the Court to agree with the views of the parties as an element of judicial policy, another for it to act under an obligation to comply with the wishes of the parties as a matter of law. While the revision of the Rules was aimed at breathing life into the institutions of the chambers, those concerned were equally aware that it would be improper to suggest that the Court would be bound by the view of the parties' ('Some Comments on Ad Hoc Chambers of the International Court of Justice', in *Humanité et droit international: Mélanges René-Jean Dupuy* (1991), p. 203 at pp. 206–7). See further Lachs, 'Arbitration and International Adjudication', in Soons (ed.), *International Arbitration: Past and Prospects* (1990), p. 45; Schwebel, ibid., pp. 746, 752; Valencia-Ospina, 'The Use of Chambers of the International Court of Justice', in Lowe and Fitzmaurice (eds.), *Fifty Years of the International Court of Justice: Essays in Honour of Sir Robert Jennings* (1995), p. 503 at pp. 514–16; Hambro, 'Will the Revised Rules of Court Lead to Greater Willingness on the Part of Prospective Clients?', in Gross (ed.), *The Future of the International Court of Justice* (1976), p. 369, and also 'Quelques observations sur la revision du Règlement de la Cour Internationale de Justice', in *Mélanges offerts à Charles Rousseau* (1974), pp. 128–34; and de Aréchaga, loc. cit. above (n. 25), pp. 2–3.)

[30] See further n. 187 and corresponding text, below.

In conclusion, the four definitional elements of a subsidiary organ are important in determining whether a particular subsidiary organ has been lawfully established. However, these preconditions stipulate only the way in which a lawful exercise of the authority of establishment by a principal organ takes place. If a principal organ were to exceed the scope of authority which it possesses to establish a subsidiary organ, or were it not to satisfy the preconditions of establishment, then it has acted unlawfully. But this does not in itself mean that the law will treat its acts as utterly non-existent and not attach legal consequences to them.[31]

Before proceeding, it must be emphasized that the effect of an invocation by States of the elements of the legal framework governing UN subsidiary organs, which of course includes the preconditions of establishment, before the particular principal organ will often depend on the other, often political, considerations that a UN principal organ, with the exception of the International Court, will take into account when making decisions. However, this does not detract from the restraints which the legal framework governing the establishment and termination of subsidiary organs places on principal organs when engaged in this activity. The principal organs possess a discretion in this regard, but the exercise of this discretion does not take place outside the legal framework. In terms of the institutional mechanism that can ensure that the principal organs comply with the requirements of this framework, the most authoritative is a review of their decisions by the International Court.[32] The use of this mechanism is not, however, unproblematic. The review of the legality of decisions of principal organs by the Court can only proceed once the Court has established some basis for its jurisdiction in accordance with Article 36 of its Statute.[33]

It is convenient, before examining the preconditions of establishment, to determine the scope of the authority of principal organs to establish subsidiary organs.

---

[31] See *Expenses* case, *ICJ Reports*, 1962, p. 151 at p. 168. See further on this issue Osieke, 'Ultra Vires Acts in International Organizations', this *Year Book*, 48 (1976–7), p. 259, and also 'The Legal Validity of Ultra Vires Decisions of International Organizations', *American Journal of International Law*, 77 (1983), p. 239; Morgenstern, 'Legality in International Organizations', this *Year Book*, 48 (1976–7), p. 24; Jennings, 'Nullity and Effectiveness in International Law', in *Cambridge Essays in International Law* (1965), p. 64; E. Lauterpacht, 'The Legal Effect of Illegal Acts of International Organizations', ibid., p. 88; and Cahier, 'La nullité en droit international', *Revue générale de droit international public*, 76 (1972), p. 645.

[32] See further below, n. 289.

[33] See, for example, the *Expenses* case, *ICJ Reports*, 1962, p. 151; and the *Namibia* case, *ICJ Reports*, 1971, p. 6.

III. The Authority of UN Principal Organs to Establish Subsidiary Organs

The UN Charter gives UN principal organs the authority to establish subsidiary organs.[34] Article 7(2) seems to give all UN principal organs a general authority to establish subsidiary organs, while Articles 22, 29 and 68 provide this authority in specific terms for the General Assembly, the Security Council and the ECOSOC, respectively.[35] What is unclear, however, is the nature of the relationship between the two types of authority, the legal consequences of the distinction that exists, and the content of any limitations that restrict their exercise.

The general authority to establish subsidiary organs in Article 7(2) provides in a non-restrictive way for the establishment of '[s]uch subsidiary organs as may be found necessary'. The existence of a substantive authority to establish such organs under this provision was confirmed during the debate in the 74th meeting of the First Committee of the General Assembly on the establishment of an interim committee. The representative of Belgium, for example, stated that the General Assembly 'certainly had the right to create subsidiary bodies, and would have it even if Article 22 of the Charter did not exist'.[36] Moreover, the Netherlands argued before the International Court in the *Effect of Awards of Compensation made by the UN Administrative Tribunal* case (the '*Administrative Tribunal* case')[37] that the General Assembly had the authority to establish the Administrative Tribunal as its subsidiary organ

---

[34] In so doing the Charter entered new territory as compared to the League of Nations Covenant, and opened up possibilities for the institutional development of the United Nations system. The League of Nations Covenant did not expressly provide for the establishment of subsidiary organs, although in practice a large number of subsidiary organs were established by the League: see further commentary to Article 7 in Cot and Pellet, op. cit. above (n. 1), p. 207.

[35] Article 7(2) of the Charter provides: 'Such subsidiary organs as may be found necessary may be established in accordance with the present Charter'. Articles 22 and 29 share the following common formulation: '[The relevant principal organ] may establish such subsidiary organs as it deems necessary for the performance of its functions'. Article 68 provides: 'The Economic and Social Council shall set up commissions in economic and social fields and for the promotion of human rights, and such other commissions as may be required for the performance of its functions'.

[36] *General Assembly Official Records*, 2nd Session, First Committee, 74th meeting, p. 143. It seems that the Belgian delegate considered Article 7 as the source of this general competence of the Assembly to establish subsidiary organs, although it is arguable that he may have been referring to a general authority of organs of an international organization to establish subsidiary organs. For example, Schermers and Blokker argue that under the law of international institutions there may be created subsidiary organs to which powers may be delegated even where the constituent instrument in question contains no such provision for this process (op. cit. above (n. 1), para. 224). Moreover, Gold states that in the practice of the IMF '[t]he Board of Governors has no express power to appoint committees, but has appointed them on numerous occasions since the earliest days of the Fund' (*Voting and Decisions in the IMF* (1972), p. 203). See also Seyersted, 'Objective International Personality of Intergovernmental Organizations', *Nordisk Tidsskrift for International Ret*, 34 (1964), p. 1 at p. 111.

[37] *Administrative Tribunal* case, *ICJ Reports*, 1954, p. 47.

by virtue of Article 7(2) of the Charter.[38] To summarize, Article 7(2) is *per se* a source of authority to establish subsidiary organs.[39]

However, nowhere in the Charter does it specify which principal organs possess this general authority. The question thus arises: do all principal organs possess this general authority or is it only some of them? To determine this it is necessary to examine the relationship between the general and the specific authority to establish subsidiary organs. If the phrase 'in accordance with the Charter' in Article 7(2) is read restrictively, then it is arguable that only the General Assembly and Security Council may establish 'subsidiary organs', since Articles 22 and 29, which give this authority specifically to the General Assembly and the Security Council, are the only other Charter articles which expressly refer to 'subsidiary organs' as such.[40] The contention is that the general authority to establish 'subsidiary organs' in Article 7(2) relates only to those principal organs which have been given the specific authority to establish 'subsidiary organs' elsewhere in the Charter.[41] According to such an interpretation, even Article 68 does not empower ECOSOC to establish subsidiary organs since there is no mention made in this Article of the term 'subsidiary organ'.[42] However, this restrictive interpretation of Article 7 is not appropriate for three reasons. First, reading Article 7 as a whole, the general authority in Article 7(2) can be said to relate to all six principal organs named in Article 7(1) and not just the General Assembly and Security Council, which possess the specific authority of establishment. This follows from the principle of treaty interpretation that a treaty provision is to be read in the context of the treaty as a whole.[43] Second, if the authority to establish subsidiary organs under Articles 22 and 29 represents the totality of the general authority of

---

[38] *Administrative Tribunal* case, *ICJ Pleadings*, 1954, p. 379.

[39] Accordingly, Commission I of the San Francisco Conference stated in respect of Article 7(2) that it provided 'the constitutional authority for the creation of subsidiary agencies' (*United Nations Conference on International Organization*, vol. 6, p. 207).

[40] This argument is pointed out by Kelsen, op. cit. above (n. 20), p. 138.

[41] It is arguable that the International Court of Justice impliedly accepted this position in the *Expenses* case when it stated: 'The general purposes of Article 17 are the vesting of control over the finances of the Organization, and the levying of apportioned amounts of the expenses of the Organization in order to enable it to carry out the functions of the Organization as a whole acting through its principal organs and such subsidiary organs as may be established under the authority of Article 22 or Article 29' (*ICJ Reports*, 1962, p. 151 at p. 162).

[42] For the text of Article 68, see n. 35, above.

[43] The importance of reading a treaty as a whole is well accepted as a rule of treaty interpretation: see Article 31(1) of the 1969 Vienna Convention on the Law of Treaties and the following case law of international tribunals: *Competence of the ILO to Regulate Agricultural Labour*, PCIJ, Series B, No. 2 (1922); *Interpretation of Peace Treaties with Bulgaria, Hungary and Romania (Second Phase)*, *ICJ Reports*, 1950, p. 221; *Expenses* case, *ICJ Reports*, 1962, p. 151; and the case concerning the *Interpretation of the Air Transport Services Agreement between the United States of America and France, Signed at Paris on 27 March 1946*, *Reports of International Arbitral Awards*, vol. 16, p. 75. In the first *Admissions* case, the International Court used Article 4(2) in order to arrive at an interpretation regarding Article 4(1) of the Charter (*Conditions of Admission of a State to Membership in the United Nations*, *ICJ Reports*, 1948, p. 57 at p. 64).

establishment in Article 7(2), then there was clearly no need for the inclusion of the latter article in the Charter. However, the need for the inclusion of all three articles in the Charter was expressly endorsed at the San Francisco Conference.[44] Third, the interpretation of the Charter, as the constituent instrument of an international organization, requires more emphasis to be placed on the teleological or objects and purposes approach to treaty interpretation rather than upon the literal approach.[45] *In casu*, the object and purpose of Article 7(2) is to give UN principal organs the authority to establish subsidiary organs to assist them in the exercise of both their express and implied powers under the Charter. As the International Court in the *Application for Review* case observed:

The object of both those Articles (7(2) and 22) is to enable the United Nations to accomplish its purposes and to function effectively. Accordingly to place a restrictive interpretation on the power of the General Assembly to establish subsidiary organs would run contrary to the clear intention of the Charter.[46]

Using this object and purpose, it is contended that the term 'subsidiary organ' in Article 7(2) should be given a broad meaning to include any kind of UN organ that has been lawfully established by any of the six principal organs and that possesses the requisite degree of independence from its principal organ.[47] Accepting this interpretation of Article 7(2) leads to the position that the authority to establish subsidiary organs is not restricted to Articles 22 and 29.[48] This approach is, moreover, reflected in the practice of the United Nations.[49] Thus it may be said that

[44] The Advisory Committee of Jurists of the San Francisco Conference considered Articles 22 and 32 (now 29) in connection with the current Article 7 and agreed that all three provisions should remain in the Charter. The only changes which the Jurists recommended were those which brought the language of the three Articles into conformity: UN Doc. WD 253; CO/35(3) vol. 18, p. 134.

[45] See *Polish Postal Service in Danzig, PCIJ*, Series B, No. 11 (1925), at pp. 33–40; *Expenses* case, *ICJ Reports*, 1962, p. 151 at p. 157; and the *Applicability of Article VI, Section 22, of the Convention on the Privileges and Immunities of the United Nations*, advisory opinion, *ICJ Reports*, 1989, p. 177 at para. 53. See further Rosenne, *Developments in the Law of Treaties 1945–1986* (1989), pp. 237–42.

[46] *Application for Review of Judgment No. 158 of the United Nations Administrative Tribunal* case, *ICJ Reports*, 1973, p. 166 at p. 172.

[47] See also Kelsen, op. cit. above (n. 20), p. 138, and Simma, op. cit. above (n. 1), p. 202. For the preconditions of establishment that are necessary for the lawful establishment of a UN subsidiary organ, see Section IV, below. For the requisite degree of independence of a subsidiary organ from its principal organ, see n. 14 and corresponding text, above.

[48] This position may lead to the question whether the specific authority of establishment under Articles 22 and 29 is thus redundant. However, the position of the Advisory Committee of Jurists of the San Francisco Conference was that all three articles should be included in the Charter: above, n. 44. The only explanation for this position may be the importance that was attached to the General Assembly and the Security Council possessing the authority to establish subsidiary organs.

[49] For example, in the case of ECOSOC, Article 68 of the Charter—which authorizes ECOSOC to 'set up Commissions in economic and social fields and for the promotion of human rights, and such other commissions as may be required for the performance of its functions'—is considered in practice as authority for ECOSOC to establish Article 7(2)-type 'subsidiary organs'. Note the following four examples of cases in which the UN Legal Counsel has either expressly or implicitly

all UN principal organs possess the general authority under Article 7(2) of the Charter to establish 'subsidiary organs'.[50] Moreover, in the case of the General Assembly and the Security Council it is clear that they have a specific authority to establish subsidiary organs under Articles 22 and 29, respectively.

There is, however, an important distinction between the general and specific authority to establish subsidiary organs.[51] Under the specific authority of establishment, the relevant principal organ can only establish subsidiary organs to perform, in the terms of Articles 22 and 29, 'its [the principal organ's] functions'. However, in the case of the general authority of establishment under Article 7(2) there is no such functional limitation: subsidiary organs may be established under Article 7(2) to perform functions which the principal organ cannot itself perform. This was clearly established by the International Court in the *Administrative Tribunal* and the *Application for Review* cases.[52] Thus the general authority in Article 7(2) is broader than the specific authority in Articles

affirmed the right of ECOSOC to establish 'subsidiary organs': first, in a letter to the Legal Counsel of the FAO, the UN Legal Counsel expressly refers to the general authority under Article 7(2) to establish subsidiary organs and then goes on to refer to the more specific authority of the General Assembly under Article 22, the Security Council under Article 29, and the Economic and Social Council under Article 68, to create 'subsidiary organs' (*UN Juridical Yearbook*, 1963, p. 169); second, the UN Legal Counsel, in a memorandum to the Secretary of ECOSOC when advising on whether the Committee on Crime Prevention and Control was a subsidiary organ of ECOSOC, stated that 'it is clear . . . [the] Committee possesses the characteristics of a subsidiary organ of the Council, since it was the Council which determined its size, appointed its members and instructed it to report to certain subsidiary organs of the Council' (ibid., 1971, p. 206); third, in a memorandum to the Secretary of the ECOSOC, concerning the modalities to be followed by ECOSOC in connection with the request by the General Assembly that the Council consider granting membership in one of its subsidiary bodies to Namibia, the UN Legal Counsel refers to the Executive Committee of the Programme of the United Nations High Commissioner for Refugees as a 'subsidiary organ' of ECOSOC (ibid., 1982, p. 185); and, finally, in a memorandum to the Assistant Secretary-General at the Centre for Human Rights concerning the participation of National Liberation Movements in sessions of the Sub-Commission on Prevention of Discrimination and Protection of Minorities, the UN Legal Counsel implicitly affirmed the right of ECOSOC to establish its own 'subsidiary organs' under its rules of procedure, the source of constitutional power of which is presumably Article 7(2) or Article 66 of the Charter (ibid., 1983, p. 189).

[50] It is thus arguable, for example, that the International Court could, if it obtains the consent of the parties to a case, establish a Chamber to decide a case under its general authority of establishment, even in the absence of a specific authority to do so.

[51] This distinction is of considerable practical importance. As will be seen below, where a principal organ establishes a subsidiary organ to exercise powers and functions which it cannot itself exercise, there are limitations as to the degree of authority and control which the principal can exercise over its subsidiary. See Section IV(2), below.

[52] *Administrative Tribunal* case, *ICJ Reports*, 1954, p. 47. See further on this case, n. 57 and corresponding text, below. In the *Application for Review* case, the Court found that the General Assembly had the competence to operate in the area of staff administration, and therefore that it could establish a body with judicial functions which it could not itself exercise under the Charter: *ICJ Reports*, 1973, p. 166. Moreover, as Ciobanu had earlier noted, 'in setting up subsidiary organs, the principal organs do not necessarily confer on them the character of their own jurisdiction. Consequently, in any effort to ascertain the jurisdiction of subsidiary organs the only reliable sources are their constituent instruments' (*Preliminary Objections to the Jurisdiction of the United Nations Political Organs* (1975), p. 30). Cf., however, the following dissenting opinions of judges of the

22 and 29, which is only for the purpose of carrying out the 'functions' of the General Assembly and Security Council, respectively. There is, however, a limitation on this general authority of establishment: the principal organ must possess either an express or implied power under the Charter to be able to establish such a subsidiary organ. This follows from the position that the authority of principal organs to establish subsidiary organs is not in itself enough for the lawful establishment of a subsidiary organ. The principal organ must itself possess either the express or implied power which it seeks to delegate to its subsidiary.[53] However, as just noted, this does not preclude a principal organ from possessing an implied power to establish a subsidiary organ to exercise

International Court of Justice: Judge Morozov who argues that a subsidiary organ can only be created by a principal organ which has a specific power to establish subsidiary organs for the performance of the functions of the principal organ concerned, and that where this is not the case the principal organ cannot use the general power of establishment under Article 7 of the Charter (*Application for Review* case, *ICJ Reports, 1973*, p. 166 at p. 298). *In casu*, the judge found the fact that the General Assembly had created the Committee on Applications for Review of Administrative Tribunal Judgments to exercise functions which the Assembly itself did not possess meant that 'the Committee created in 1955 cannot be considered as an organ of the United Nations within the meaning of Articles 7 and 22 of the Charter' (ibid.); Judge Alvarez, who states that the 'only purpose of the subsidiary organ is to assist the principal organs to discharge their duties' (*ICJ Reports, 1954*, p. 70); Judge Hackworth, who argues that as the only power of the General Assembly to create a subsidiary organ is in Article 22 of the Charter, the Assembly must therefore be subject to the constraints of that article (ibid., pp. 78–9); Judge Onyeama who states that a characteristic feature of a subsidiary organ is that it has been established to carry out certain functions in aid of the principal organ establishing it—functions embraced within the overall functions, and closely corresponding to the legitimate activities of the principal organ. It was on this basis that the judge concluded that the General Assembly could not legally establish a subsidiary body to perform functions which were not within the range of the Assembly's functions (*ICJ Reports, 1973*, p. 226). Cf. also Kelsen, who argues: 'If an organ is competent to establish a "subsidiary" organ, it may establish it for the performance of some or of all of its functions; but only for the performance of "its" functions, that is to say, the functions assigned to it by the Charter' (op. cit. above (n. 20), p. 137). Cf., finally, the opinion of the Committee on International Criminal Jurisdiction, established to make recommendations regarding the establishment of an international criminal court, which in its report to the General Assembly observed: 'Under the Charter, the court could only be established as a subsidiary organ. The principal organ would presumably be the General Assembly, but a subsidiary organ could not have a competence falling outside the competence of its principal, and it was questionable whether the General Assembly was competent to administer justice' (*General Assembly Official Records*, 7th Session, Supplement No. 11 (A/2136), p. 3). Thus it was argued that since under Article 22 the General Assembly was only entitled to create subsidiary organs to assist it in the performance of its functions, and that since the functions of the Assembly did not include the exercise of criminal jurisdiction over individuals, it could not delegate such functions to a subsidiary organ (ibid.).

[53] As Bowett states: 'The establishment of a subsidiary organ simply cannot be divorced from the functions *entrusted* to the organ . . . . In other words a resolution which contemplates a subsidiary organ with a given function has to find its constitutional basis first and foremost in the articles justifying the functions—and not in an article giving a general power to establish subsidiary organs' (*United Nations Forces* (1964), p. 178). Thus Bowett points out that in the *Expenses* case the Court did not rely on Article 22 as the source of the constitutional power of establishment of UNEF, but turned to the more substantive powers of the General Assembly, in particular Article 14 (ibid., p. 178, n. 46). See also Ciobanu, 'The Power of the Security Council to Organize Peace-Keeping Operations', in Cassese (ed.), *United Nations Peace-Keeping: Legal Essays* (1978), p. 19 at p. 23.

functions which it does not itself possess.[54] In such a case the power to establish such a subsidiary organ may even be implied from the general competence of the principal organ to operate in the particular area.[55] The principal may not itself possess the competence to perform certain functions, but the establishment and exercise of these functions by a subsidiary organ may nonetheless be necessary for the effective exercise by the principal organ of its powers and functions in an area in which it has the competence to operate.[56] This is what occurred in the *Administrative Tribunal* case where the International Court found that the General Assembly had the competence to establish a judicial body, the Administrative Tribunal.

The majority of the Court in the *Administrative Tribunal* case found that the General Assembly did not under the Charter possess the judicial function which the Tribunal was exercising, and thus '[b]y establishing the Administrative Tribunal, the General Assembly was not delegating the performance of its own functions: it was exercising a power which it had under the Charter to regulate staff relations'.[57] It was the opinion of the Court that the General Assembly possessed the implied power to establish such a subsidiary organ, and that this power could be implied from its competence to operate in the area concerned, the regulation of staff relations.[58] The Court then found it necessary to undertake 'the

---

[54] See n. 52 and corresponding text, above.

[55] The word competence is being used here to describe what an organ of an international organization is specifically empowered to do. In this way the competence of an organ refers to the range of activities which an organ is entitled to undertake, and the conditions attached thereto, in the pursuit of its Charter designated functions and purposes. See also Bekker, *The Legal Position of Intergovernmental Organizations: A Functional Necessity Analysis of Their Legal Status and Immunities* (1994), p. 75.

[56] The implication of powers by an international organization from its constituent treaty is a well-accepted doctrine under international law. The International Court in relation to the UN stated in the *Reparation for Injuries* case: 'Under international law, the Organization must be deemed to have those powers which, though not expressly provided in the Charter, are conferred upon it by necessary implication as being essential to the performance of its duties. . . . the rights and duties of an entity such as the Organization must depend upon its purposes and functions as specified or implicit in its constituent documents and developed in practice' (*ICJ Reports*, 1949, p. 174 at pp. 180, 182).

[57] *ICJ Reports*, 1954, p. 61. Cf. Judge Hackworth, who in his dissenting opinion argues that the doctrine of implied powers is designed to implement, within reasonable limits, and not to supplant or vary, express powers. Thus, in his opinion, the Assembly could only establish a Tribunal needed for the implementation of its functions, as required by Article 22. He states that: 'It is not, therefore permissible, in the face of this express power, to invoke the doctrine of implied powers to establish a tribunal of a supposedly different kind, nor is there warrant for concluding that such a thing has resulted' (ibid., pp. 80–1).

[58] The Court implied from Article 101(1) of the Charter the power of the General Assembly to 'establish a tribunal to do justice between the Organization and the staff members' (ibid.). See also the *Expenses* case, where the International Court of Justice—having recognized the power of the General Assembly to act in the area of maintaining and restoring international peace—recognized the power of the Assembly to establish subsidiary organs under Article 22 through which it could

further enquiry as to the agency by which it may be exercised'.[59] The Court decided that the source of authority of the General Assembly to establish such a subsidiary organ was the general authority under Article 7(2) of the Charter. Accordingly, the Court found that 'the power to establish a tribunal to do justice between the Organization and the staff members may be exercised by the General Assembly'.[60]

This use of the general authority to establish subsidiary organs to perform functions which the principal cannot itself exercise is of considerable importance when determining the legality of the recent establishment by the Council of several subsidiary organs: in particular, the UN War Crimes Tribunals for the former Yugoslavia and Rwanda.[61]

The Security Council in Resolution 808 determined that the establishment of the War Crimes Tribunal for the former Yugoslavia would contribute both to putting an end to the commission of war crimes and to the restoration of peace in the former Yugoslavia.[62] Resolution 808 requested the Secretary-General to make a report to the Council on how best to establish such a tribunal. In his subsequent report, the Secretary-General states that such a tribunal should be established under Chapter VII of the Charter as a subsidiary organ of the Council. Subsequently, the Security Council, in Resolution 827, acting expressly under Chapter VII, established the War Crimes Tribunal for the former Yugoslavia. In the *Tadic* case the validity of the establishment of the Tribunal was challenged by the defence.[63] The issues which arose from this challenge were not dealt with by the Trial Chamber in any detail.[64] However, the Appeal Chamber of the Tribunal in the *Tadic* case found that it could decide the issue of the lawfulness of the establishment of the Tribunal as

---

exercise its functions. The Court observed: 'Such implementation is a normal feature of the functioning of the United Nations. Such committees, commissions, or other bodies or individuals, constitute, in some cases, subsidiary organs established under the authority of Article 22 of the Charter' (*Expenses* case, *ICJ Reports*, 1962, p. 165). See further as to the Court's affirmation of an implication of power in the *Administrative Tribunal* case, Amerasinghe, *The Law of the International Civil Service* (1994), pp. 27, 34–7; Gomula, 'The International Court of Justice and Administrative Tribunals of International Organizations', *Michigan Journal of International Law*, 13 (1991), p. 83 at p. 93; and Campbell, 'The Limits of the Powers of International Organisations', *International and Comparative Law Quarterly*, 32 (1983), p. 523 at p. 524.

[59] *ICJ Reports*, 1954, p. 57.

[60] Ibid., p. 58.

[61] Moreover, the lawful establishment of the Iraq-Kuwait Boundary Demarcation Commission by the Security Council is affirmed below: see n. 268 and corresponding text.

[62] The case of the Yugoslav War Crimes Tribunal only is examined here. However, the analysis that follows applies *mutatis mutandis* to the case of the Rwandan War Crimes Tribunal.

[63] See defence motions in the *Tadic* case, Case No. IT–94–I–T, 23 June 1995, paras. 3–4.

[64] The Trial Chamber dismissed the defendants' arguments on this point on the basis that the objections did not go 'so much to its jurisdiction, as to the unreviewable lawfulness of the actions of the Security Council' (*Tadic* case, decision on the defence motion on the jurisdiction of the Tribunal, Case No. IT–94–I–T, 10 August 1995, para. 40).

part of its competence to determine its own jurisdiction.[65] The Appeal Chamber expressly found that 'the establishment of the International Tribunal falls squarely within the powers of the Security Council under Article 41'.[66] The Appeal Chamber is not, however, suggesting that Article 41 provides a basis for the exercise by the Council of the judicial functions which have been entrusted to the Tribunal. It is clear that the purely judicial function which the Tribunal is to perform—the determination of criminal liability of individuals[67]—is a function which the Council does not itself possess under the Charter. As the Appeal Chamber held:

> The establishment of the International Tribunal by the Security Council does not signify, however, that the Security Council has delegated to it some of its own functions or the exercise of some of its own powers. Nor does it mean, in reverse, that the Security Council was usurping for itself part of a judicial function which does not belong to it but to other organs of the United Nations according to the Charter. The Security Council has resorted to the establishment of a judicial organ in the form of an international criminal tribunal as an instrument for the exercise of its own principal function of the maintenance of peace and security, *i.e.*, as a measure contributing to the restoration and maintenance of peace in the former Yugoslavia.[68]

What the Appeal Chamber of the Tribunal is indicating is that the Council possesses an implied power to establish the War Crimes Tribunal to exercise judicial functions from its express powers in Article 41, since it is a measure necessary for the effective exercise of its powers

[65] The Appeal Chamber stated that prominent among the attributes of the judicial function, which the Tribunal was exercising, is the power known as '*compétence de la compétence*': the incidental or inherent jurisdiction of any judicial tribunal to determine its own jurisdiction: 'jurisdiction to determine its own jurisdiction' (*Prosecutor* v. *Dusko Tadic*, IT–94–1–AR72, 2 October 1995, *International Legal Materials*, 35 (1996), p. 32, para. 18). See also the *Nottebohm* case, *ICJ Reports*, 1953, p. 7 at p. 119. On this issue of '*compétence de la compétence*' as a general principle of law, see further Cheng, *General Principles of Law as applied by International Courts and Tribunals* (1987), pp. 275–301. For an examination of the other issues dealt with in the *Tadic* case, see further Greenwood, 'International Humanitarian Law and the *Tadic* case', *European Journal of International Law*, 7 (1996), p. 265; and Fenrick, 'Some International Law Problems Related to Prosecutions before the International Criminal Tribunal for the Former Yugoslavia', *Duke Journal of Comparative and International Law*, 6 (1995), p. 103.

[66] *Tadic* case, loc. cit. above (n. 65), para. 36. Moreover, in a report of a committee of French jurists set up by the French Government to examine the establishment of the War Crimes Tribunal, it was argued that the establishment of the Tribunal was based on a power implied from Chapter VII of the Charter—specifically Article 41—since the establishment of the War Crimes Tribunal would be likely to help restore international peace and security (S/25266, pp. 12–13). See also Szasz, 'The Proposed War Crimes Tribunal for Ex-Yugoslavia', *New York University Journal of International Law and Politics*, 25 (1993), p. 405 at p. 412; Shraga and Zacklin, 'International Criminal Tribunal for the Former Yugoslavia', *European Journal of International Law*, 3 (1994), p. 360; and O'Brien, 'The International Tribunal for Violations of International Humanitarian Law in the Former Yugoslavia', *American Journal of International Law*, 87 (1993), p. 638 at p. 643.

[67] The Security Council in Resolution 808 decided 'that an international tribunal shall be established for the prosecution of persons responsible for serious violations of international humanitarian law committed in the territory of the former Yugoslavia since 1991'.

[68] *International Legal Materials*, 35 (1996), p. 32, para. 38.

to act to maintain or restore international peace. Additionally, or in the alternate, it seems clear that the Council possesses an implied power to establish the Tribunal from its competence to act to maintain or restore international peace under Article 24(1) and, more generally, Chapter VII of the Charter.[69] Accordingly, the Secretary-General in his report to the Council on the establishment of the Tribunal stated: 'the International Tribunal should be established by a decision of the Security Council on the basis of Chapter VII . . . Such a decision would constitute a measure to maintain or restore international peace and security, following the requisite determination of the existence of a threat to the peace, breach of the peace or act of aggression.'[70] The report notes that the Security Council had already made the determination that the situation of widespread violations of international humanitarian law occurring in the former Yugoslavia constituted a threat to international peace and security.[71] The Secretary-General thus contends that the establishment of the Tribunal would be justifiable both 'in terms of the object and

[69] Thus the Japanese representative to the Security Council stated in the Council meeting at which Resolution 827 was adopted: 'the establishment of this Tribunal to judge and punish war crimes is an instrument for the promotion of international peace and security' (S/PV.3217, pp. 29–30). See also the following statements by States' representatives in the Council debates preceding the adoption of Resolution 827: the New Zealand representative stated: 'As is noted in the resolution [S/RES/808] and in the Secretary-General's report, the establishment of the Tribunal and the prosecution of persons suspected of crimes against international humanitarian law is closely related to the wider efforts to restore peace and security to the former Yugoslavia' (S/PV.3217, p. 22); the Spanish representative stated that the Council: 'is only attempting to create an *ad hoc* mechanism that, by applying existing laws, will assign responsibility for acts committed in an ongoing conflict that has already been seen to threaten and undermine peace; a mechanism that contributes, by means of recourse to justice and punishment of the guilty, to restoring the peace and ensuring its maintenance, so as to deter the repetition of similar acts in the future' (S/PV.3175, p. 22); and also the French and US delegates stated that in establishing the Tribunal the source of the power of establishment was the fact that the Security Council was acting within the framework of its powers under Chapter VII to maintain or restore international peace and security: France (S/PV.3175, p. 9), and USA (S/PV.3175, p. 13). Similarly, in the case of the Rwandan Tribunal, the Secretary-General states: 'Having determined on two previous occasions that the situation in Rwanda constituted a threat to peace and security in the region, the Council, in its resolution 955 (1994), determined that the situation in Rwanda continued to constitute a threat to international peace and security and, accordingly, decided to establish the International Tribunal for Rwanda under Chapter VII of the Charter of the United Nations' (S/1995/134, para. 6). Moreover, the Secretary-General gave more reasons than was done in the case of the Yugoslav Tribunal why the establishment of the Rwandan Tribunal should be under Chapter VII of the Charter. He states: '[this] was necessary to ensure not only the cooperation of Rwanda throughout the life-span of the Tribunal, but the cooperation of all States in whose territory persons alleged to have committed serious violations of international humanitarian law and acts of genocide in Rwanda might be situated. A Tribunal based on a Chapter VII resolution was also necessary to ensure a speedy and expeditious method of establishing the Tribunal' (ibid.).

[70] S/25704 of 3 May 1993, p. 7.

[71] Ibid. Moreover, the Hungarian representative to the Council observed: 'On the basis of the information that has reached us from several sources, as well as from the Commission of Experts established by the Security Council, the Council, in resolution 808 (1993), noted that the violations of international humanitarian law, because of their gravity and their generalized character, constituted a threat to international peace and security, which, in our view, fully justifies the competence of the Security Council in this sphere' (S/PV.3217, p. 20).

purpose of the decision [to restore and maintain international peace] . . . and of past Security Council practice'.[72]

Once it is clear that the Council possessed the implied power to establish the Tribunal, then there is no legal objection to the Council using its authority under Article 7(2) to establish the Tribunal as a UN subsidiary organ.[73] The Council could not have been acting under Article 29, since, as noted above, the Council in establishing the War Crimes Tribunal is not delegating to the Tribunal the performance of its own functions.[74]

To conclude, the general rule regarding the lawful exercise of the general authority of principal organs to establish a subsidiary organ under Article 7(2) of the Charter is that the possession of an express power or function to be delegated to a subsidiary organ is not necessary.[75] What will however preclude the lawful establishment of a subsidiary organ is if the principal organ does not possess the express or implied power under the Charter to establish a subsidiary organ to perform certain functions in the area. In the case of an implied power, this may depend on whether the subsidiary organ has been established in an area in which the principal organ has a competence to exercise its powers and functions.

---

[72] S/25704, p. 7. In respect of such practice, the Secretary-General observed: 'the Security Council has on various occasions adopted decisions under Chapter VII aimed at restoring and maintaining international peace and security, which have involved the establishment of subsidiary organs for a variety of purposes. Reference may be made in this regard to Security Council resolution 687 (1991) and subsequent resolutions relating to the situation between Iraq and Kuwait' (S/25704, p. 8). With regard to the Iraq-Kuwait Boundary Demarcation Commission, see further nn. 268–71, below.

[73] However, the powers of the Security Council to act to establish an international criminal court without reference to a particular situation which constitutes a threat to or breach of international peace is highly doubtful. As a report of a committee of French jurists set up by the French Minister of State and Minister of Foreign Affairs states: 'If it was a matter of establishing a jurisdiction with universal competence, however, the Committee would be very reluctant to consider the United Nations as being competent to establish an international criminal court with binding force. There are no provisions in the Charter that could be invoked as giving the Security Council or the General Assembly such powers' (S/25266, p. 11). See also the statement by Mr Arangio-Ruiz in the International Law Commission, 2300th meeting, *Yearbook of the International Law Commission*, 1993, vol. 1, pp. 16–17, 26. Cf. Pellet, *Yearbook of the International Law Commission*, 1993, vol. 1, p. 17.

[74] Compare, however, the opinion of the UN Secretary-General who in his report to the Security Council on the establishment of the Tribunal states: 'In this particular case, the Security Council would be establishing, as an enforcement measure under Chapter VII, a subsidiary organ within the terms of Article 29 of the Charter, but one of a judicial nature' (S/25704, p. 8). The Secretary-General took the same approach in the case of the Rwanda Tribunal: see further: S/1995/134, para. 8. However, what the Secretary-General probably means when he says 'a subsidiary organ within the terms of Article 29 . . . but one of a judicial nature' is that the Tribunal is an Article 29-type 'subsidiary organ' of the Council—being established under Article 7(2)—, and not necessarily that the Tribunal is being established under Article 29, since if the latter were the case the Tribunal would be restricted to performing only those functions which the Council itself can perform. This reflects the difference between the general and specific authority to establish subsidiary organs: see further n. 51 and corresponding text, above.

[75] See n. 52 and corresponding text, above.

IV. PRECONDITIONS FOR THE LAWFUL ESTABLISHMENT OF UN SUBSIDIARY ORGANS

1. *Establishment must be by a Principal Organ*

The precondition that a subsidiary organ be established by a principal organ is a requirement under the general law of international institutions.[76] Application of this precondition to the UN context enables a distinction to be made between subsidiary organs and other types of organs: in particular, auxiliary organs and organs established by intergovernmental agreement.

A distinction between UN subsidiary organs and other kinds of UN auxiliary organs was arguably envisaged at the San Francisco Conference: perusal of the *travaux préparatoires* of Article 7(2) reveals that the term initially used in the French text was '*organe auxiliaire*' which was later replaced in the final text of the Charter by that of '*organe subsidiaire*'.[77] This distinction is illustrated by the case of the Military Staff Committee. Article 47(1) of the Charter provides for the establishment of a 'Military Staff Committee to advise and assist the Security Council on all questions relating to the Security Council's military requirements for the maintenance of international peace and security, the employment and command of forces placed at its disposal, the regulation of armaments, and possible disarmament'. Clearly the Military Staff Committee is to assist the Security Council in the exercise of its Chapter VII powers. However, Article 47(2) of the Charter directly establishes the Military Staff Committee when it states that the Committee 'shall consist of the Chiefs of Staff of the permanent members of the Security Council or their representatives'.[78] Thus the Committee, having been established by the Charter and not by a principal organ, does not meet the precondition that establishment be by a principal organ.[79] Accordingly, the Military Staff Committee cannot be considered as a 'subsidiary organ' within the meaning of Article 7(2).[80] This conclusion has been affirmed by the UN Legal Counsel, who stated before the Court in the *Administrative Tribunal* case that there are a few organs which cannot be

---

[76] See, for instance, Torres Bernardez, loc. cit. above (n. 1); and Schermers and Blokker, op. cit. above (n. 1).

[77] See also the commentary to Article 7 of the Charter in Cot and Pellet, op. cit. above (n. 1), p. 207.

[78] There are also other provisions of the Charter which authorize non-principal organs to set up auxiliary organs not designated as 'subsidiary organs'. For example, Article 47(4) provides: 'The Military Staff Committee, with the authorization of the Security Council and after consultation with appropriate regional agencies, may establish regional subcommittees'.

[79] Cf. Torres Bernardez, who argues that the term subsidiary organ can cover organs which are established by the constituent instrument of an international organization (loc. cit. above (n. 1), p. 115).

[80] See also Kelsen, op. cit. above (n. 20), p. 138. Cf. Goodrich and Hambro, who argue that the Military Staff Committee is a subsidiary organ of the Security Council: op. cit. above (n. 1), p. 231.

characterized as either principal or subsidiary under Article 7 of the Charter, and he included in this category the Military Staff Committee, which, he noted, is directly established by Article 47 of the Charter.[81] The practical consequence of this position is that the Security Council, as a UN principal organ, cannot exercise authority and control over such an auxiliary organ.[82] The control of such an auxiliary organ, where established by the Charter, is regulated by the relevant provisions of the Charter. Thus the Security Council could not, for example, terminate the life of the Military Staff Committee or *require* it to perform tasks which have not been specified in the Charter.[83]

The precondition of establishment by a principal organ enables a distinction also to be made between UN subsidiary organs and other entities established by intergovernmental agreement: for example, UN specialized agencies which are all established either by intergovernmental agreement or on a legal basis separate from that of the United Nations.[84] As Cot and Pellet's commentary on the Charter states:

---

[81] *Administrative Tribunal* case, *ICJ Pleadings*, 1954, p. 295.

[82] On the authority and control which a principal organ possesses over its subsidiary organ, see further, Section IV(2), below.

[83] This may not necessarily, however, preclude an auxiliary organ like the Military Staff Committee from voluntarily accepting to undertake additional tasks which the Security Council has requested it to perform. In such a case, it would seem that the Military Staff Committee would be established and acting as a subsidiary organ of the Council for the performance of these additional functions. As such, the Military Staff Committee would be subject to the authority and control of the Council when it is acting pursuant to the discharge of these functions.

[84] There are, however, a group of organs which, though their establishment is provided for in a treaty, are so closely linked with the United Nations that they are considered organs of the Organization. The UN Legal Counsel has termed these 'treaty organs' of the United Nations: *UN Juridical Yearbook*, 1969, pp. 207–10, and ibid., 1976, p. 200. These organs are not, however, to be considered 'UN subsidiary organs'. The UN Legal Counsel notes that these include the following: the former Permanent Central Opium Board, established by an Agreement of 1925 (*League of Nations Treaty Series*, vol. 51, p. 337) but made a United Nations organ by General Assembly Resolution 54(I) of 19 November 1946 and the protocol of amendment annexed thereto; the former Drug Supervisory Body, established by a Convention of 1931 (*League of Nations Treaty Series*, vol. 139, p. 301) but made a United Nations organ by General Assembly Resolution 54(I) of 19 November 1946 and the protocol of amendment annexed thereto; the International Bureau for Declarations of Death, established by the Convention on the Declaration of Death for Missing Persons (*United Nations Treaty Series*, vol. 119, p. 99), adopted by a United Nations conference on 6 April 1950; the Appeals Committee established under the Protocol for Limiting and Regulating the Cultivation of the Poppy Plant, the Production of International and Wholesale Trade in, and Use of Opium (*United Nations Treaty Series*, vol. 456, p. 56), adopted by a United Nations Conference on 23 June 1953; the International Narcotics Control Board, established under the Single Convention on Narcotic Drugs (*United Nations Treaty Series*, vol. 520, p. 151), adopted by a United Nations Conference on 30 March 1961; and the Committee on the Elimination of Racial Discrimination (*UN Juridical Yearbook*, 1969, pp. 207–8). The UN Legal Counsel states: 'Except for the mode of their creation, these organs are in the same position as recognized subsidiary organs of the United Nations' (ibid.). In a separate opinion the Legal Counsel states 'It makes no difference that the treaty in this case [establishing the International Committee on the Elimination of Racial Discrimination] was itself adopted as a decision of the General Assembly; the Assembly did not directly create the Committee, as it does in establishing subsidiary organs, but the Committee came into being only when a sufficient number of States had bound themselves by the Convention to bring it into force in accordance with its terms' (ibid., p. 200). The Legal Counsel went on to state that the

Un organe subsidiaire *est créé par une manifestation de volonté de l'organe principal* . . . il n'est pas créé par accord entre Etats. . . . Un acte de l'organisation est soumis aux limites de compétence de l'Organisation alors qu'un accord entre Etats membres ne le serait pas: créé par un accord entre Etats, l'organe subsidiaire ne serait plus le subordonné mais l'égal de l'organe principal; il ne jouerait plus le rôle de l'organe d'exécution complémentaire par rapport aux besoins de l'organe principal.[85]

However, the case of subsidiary organs jointly established by a UN principal organ together with another international organization is somewhat different. In an opinion in 1963, the UN Legal Counsel states the general proposition that '[t]he setting up of committees jointly with other international organizations would be considered as permissible in

Committee on the Elimination of Racial Discrimination is not a subsidiary organ of the General Assembly, and that 'it falls into a special category of "treaty organs of the United Nations", which are organs whose establishment is provided for in a treaty, for the purpose of carrying out its provisions, but are so closely linked with the United Nations that they are considered organs of the Organization' (*UN Juridical Yearbook*, 1976, p. 200).

[85] Cot and Pellet, op. cit. above (n. 1), p. 212 (original emphasis). This has not however prevented the Security Council from calling upon UN specialized agencies to undertake, or, as the case may be, to refrain from taking certain action. (For example, Security Council Resolution 662 of 9 August 1990 '*Calls upon* all States, international organizations and specialized agencies not to recognize that annexation, and to refrain from any action or dealing that might be interpreted as an indirect recognition of the annexation'. In its response to the crisis in the former Yugoslavia, the Security Council in Resolution 757, when imposing sanctions on Serbia and Montenegro, '*Calls upon* all States . . . and all international organizations, to act strictly in accordance with the provisions of the present resolution, notwithstanding the existence of any rights or obligations conferred or imposed by any international agreement or any contract entered into . . . prior to the date of the present resolution'.) Moreover, in some cases the Council has gone further to require specialized agencies to implement certain measures. When expanding the scope of economic sanctions already imposed against Iraq in response to its invasion of Kuwait, the Security Council expressly referred to Article 48 in the preamble of Resolution 670 and then went on to affirm 'that the United Nations Organization, the specialized agencies and other international organizations in the United Nations system are required to take such measures as may be necessary to give effect to the terms of resolution 661 (1990) and this resolution'. However, in the absence of a relationship agreement, the specialized agencies are under no legal obligation under the Charter to carry out such a directive by the Security Council. The obligation which exists in such a case rests with UN member States and not the specialized agencies. It is precisely because UN specialized agencies are not bound by Security Council decisions that the IMF Board of Governors has been able to consult directly with States that are the subject of UN sanctions, namely Serbia and Montenegro, and Haiti. Cf. the legal opinion of the Secretariat of the United Nations Industrial Development Organization (UNIDO), which states: 'As far as UNIDO is concerned, it is in accordance with its Constitution a subject of international law. As such—and as an international organization of the United Nations system—it has to comply with decisions of the Security Council that are binding on all states, including UNIDO's Member States, even if the resolution does not specifically address international organizations.' Thus, in the context of Security Council Resolution 661 which imposed an arms embargo against Iraq, the legal opinion went on to state: 'It follows that UNIDO may not undertake any activity in furtherance of the activities banned by the Security Council or request others to commit such activities' (Memorandum by the Secretariat of UNIDO dated 29 August 1990, *UN Juridical Yearbook*, 1990, at pp. 311–12). Article 48(2) of the Charter requires UN member States to carry out the Security Council's decisions through the specialized agencies of which they are members: see further Cot and Pellet, op. cit. above (n. 1), p. 215. It is due to the fact that the Council is unable to exercise authority and control over specialized agencies, since they are not UN subsidiary organs, that all the agreements concluded between the UN and the specialized agencies contain a clause on the issue of United Nations resolutions and, in particular, a provision on assistance to the Security Council.

appropriate circumstances by application of the provisions of the United Nations Charter relating to the establishment of subsidiary organs of the Organization'.[86] The reason that such an entity is classified prima facie as a UN subsidiary organ is that it has resulted from an expression of the will of a UN principal organ. However, such a classification depends of course on the other preconditions of establishment also being fulfilled. This provides a good example of the way in which all the preconditions of establishment must be satisfied for a particular entity to be considered a lawfully established UN subsidiary organ. Thus these preconditions are of some importance when, for example, identifying the legal requirements which must be met when considering whether the Security Council can jointly establish a subsidiary organ with a regional organization in order to exercise command and control over a force consisting of troops from both the regional organization and other UN member States.[87]

In those cases where there are two principal organs of the UN involved in the establishment of a subsidiary organ, it may not be immediately apparent to which the subsidiary belongs. In many cases the principal organ may have chosen to delegate its power of establishment to one of the other principal organs to exercise.[88] The principal organ which appoints the members of the subsidiary organ may not necessarily be the principal organ to whom the subsidiary belongs.[89] The test to ascertain which is the establishing principal organ will depend on which principal organ possesses the authority under the Charter to establish the subsidiary organ in question.[90] In the case where both principal organs possess the authority under the Charter to establish the subsidiary organ in question, then it may be a case of both principal organs being able to

---

[86] *UN Juridical Yearbook*, 1963, p. 168. Accordingly, the UN Legal Counsel went on to note that 'the joint United Nations FAO Inter-Governmental Committee for the World Food Programme, which consists of 20 nations members of FAO and the United Nations, was established on behalf of the United Nations by General Assembly Resolution 1714 (XVI)' (ibid., p. 169).

[87] For an example of a subsidiary organ exercising powers of command and control over a force carrying out military enforcement action, see nn. 115–16 and corresponding text, below.

[88] See, for example, n. 94 and corresponding text, below.

[89] In an opinion given on the status under the UN Charter of the Group of Governmental Experts on International Cooperation to Avert New Flows of Refugees, the UN Legal Counsel observed: 'This characterization of the Group as a subsidiary organ of the Assembly is not affected by the fact that the members of the Group are appointed by the Secretary-General ... Nor does the characterization of the body as an "Expert Group" affect this conclusion. Members of subsidiary organs of the General Assembly have been appointed in a large variety of ways, other than directly by the Assembly, and subsidiary organs not infrequently report through other bodies to the Assembly' (*UN Juridical Yearbook*, 1983, p. 177). Examples of this great variety of appointing methods, reporting procedures, and titles for subsidiary organs of the General Assembly can be found in UN Document A/AC.202/1 of 28 March 1980.

[90] See also the case of the United Nations Mediator for Palestine: *Repertoire of the Practice of the Security Council, 1946–1951* (1972), pp. 223–4.

exercise authority and control over the subsidiary,[91] or there may have been a case of subsequent adoption by one principal organ of the subsidiary as its own to the exclusion of the other.[92] The determination of which principal organ is the 'establishing organ' is an important inquiry. This will determine which principal organ can exercise authority and control over the subsidiary. The issue of which UN principal organ can exercise authority and control over a subsidiary organ has arisen in the case of UN peace-keeping forces.

It is clear that UN peace-keeping forces are UN subsidiary organs.[93] In every case where the Council has established a UN peace-keeping force, it has, to date, been the consistent practice of the Council to delegate to the Secretary-General its Chapter VII power to constitute that force.[94] The Secretary-General does not himself possess the

[91] For example, General Assembly Resolution 31/93 of 14 December 1976 and ECOSOC Resolution 2008 (LX) of 14 November 1976 jointly established the Committee on Programme and Co-ordination (which was originally established as a subsidiary organ of ECOSOC only) 'as the main subsidiary organ of the Economic and Social Council and the General Assembly' for planning, programming, and coordination of UN activities with financial implications. (See also Simma, op. cit. above (n. 1), p. 204.) See further, for other examples where principal organs of international organizations have shared a subsidiary organ, Torres Bernardez, loc. cit. above (n. 1), p. 134, nn. 95 and 96.

[92] An example of this is provided by the United Nations Trust Fund for Population Activities (as the UNFPA was originally known). The UNFPA was initially established in 1969 by the UN Secretary-General (UN Juridical Yearbook, 1979, p. 171). However, the General Assembly in Resolution 3019 (XXVII) of 18 December 1972 decided to place the UNFPA under the authority of the Assembly and decided further 'without prejudice to the overall responsibilities and policy functions of the Economic and Social Council, that the Governing Council of the United Nations Development Programme, subject to conditions to be established by the Economic and Social Council, shall be the governing body of the United Nations Fund for Population Activities'. It was on this basis that the UN Legal Counsel observed: 'As a consequence of the adoption of General Assembly resolution 3019 (XXVII) the Fund ceases to be a trust fund of the Secretary-General and became a Fund under the authority of the General Assembly with an intergovernmental governing body, having its own financial regulations and rules. It thus . . . became a subsidiary organ of the Assembly similar to other Funds having intergovernmental supervisory bodies such as UNICEF, the Capital Development Fund and the United Nations Special Fund. In this respect, it should be noted that Article 22 of the Charter authorizes the Assembly to create "subsidiary organs" which are to be distinguished from principal organs specified in the Charter or completely autonomous bodies which have to be established by separate intergovernmental agreement' (ibid., p. 172).

[93] See the Expenses case, ICJ Reports, 1962, p. 151 at p. 165. See also, for example, the following: 'Article 29', Repertory of Practice of UN Organs, Supplement No. 3, p. 82 at p. 83; Higgins, United Nations Peacekeeping, vol. 1 (1969), p. 271; Bowett, op. cit. above (n. 53), p. 67; Simma, op. cit. above (n. 1), pp. 590–1; and Draper, 'The Legal Limitations upon the Employment of Weapons by the United Nations Force in the Congo', International and Comparative Law Quarterly, 12 (1963), p. 387 at p. 392.

[94] Two examples suffice to provide insight into this process. First, in the case of the establishment of ONUC the Security Council delegated to the Secretary-General in paragraph 2 of Resolution 143 the following broad power: '[The Security Council] Decides to authorize the Secretary-General to take the necessary steps, in consultation with the Government of the Republic of the Congo, to provide the Government with such military assistance, as may be necessary, until, through the efforts of the Congolese Government with the technical assistance of the United Nations, the national security forces may be able, in the opinion of the Government, to meet fully their tasks'. Second, France, the Netherlands and the UK agreed on 7 June 1995 to create a 'rapid reaction force (RRF)' to be placed at the disposal of UNPROFOR in Bosnia. It is clear that the RRF is a part of

authority under the Charter to establish UN peace-keeping forces:[95] it is only the Security Council and General Assembly that possess such a power. Accordingly, the establishment of UN peace-keeping forces by the Secretary-General represents the exercise of a delegated power.[96] It is clear that UN peace-keeping forces are UN subsidiary organs that are established under the authority of either the Security Council or, as the case may be, the General Assembly.[97] The legal basis for, and mandate of, a UN peace-keeping force are rooted in a resolution of either the Council or the Assembly. It follows that the Secretary-General does not possess the competence unilaterally to terminate a UN peace-keeping force—a subsidiary organ under the overall authority and control of another UN principal organ—unless this power has been expressly delegated to him by the relevant principal organ.[98] Moreover, the Secretary-General cannot infer the power to terminate a peace-keeping force from the terms of the resolution which delegated to him the

UN peace-keeping operations in the former Yugoslavia, that it is under the UN chain of command and is to operate under existing UN rules of engagement (S/1995/470, Annex). The Security Council delegated to the Secretary-General the power to establish this force in Resolution 998 (1995) of 16 June 1995 in the following terms: '[The Security Council] . . . 9. *Welcomes* the letter of the Secretary-General of 9 June 1995 on the reinforcement of UNPROFOR and the establishment of a rapid reaction capacity to enable UNPF/UNPROFOR to carry out its mandate; 10. *Decides* accordingly to authorize an increase in UNPF/UNPROFOR personnel, acting under the present mandate and on the terms set out in the above-mentioned letter, by up to 12,500 additional troops, the modalities of financing to be determined later; 11. *Authorizes* the Secretary-General to carry forward the implementation of paragraphs 9 and 10 above, maintaining close contact with the Government of the Republic of Bosnia and Herzegovina and others concerned'. See further, for the practice of the Council in this area, White, *Keeping the Peace: The United Nations and the Maintenance of International Peace and Security* (1993), pp. 215–56; and the commentary to Article 40 in Cot and Pellet, op. cit. above (n. 1), p. 667.

[95] As Higgins has observed: 'There is a general consensus that the Secretary-General cannot establish a force even with the consent of all the parties directly involved . . . . The Secretary-General's powers under Articles 97–99 of the Charter, even where taken with the consent of the host state and all parties concerned, apparently are not a sufficient basis for a United Nations peace-keeping mission' ('A General Assessment of United Nations Peace-Keeping', in Cassese (ed.), *United Nations Peace-keeping* (1978), p. 1 at p. 7).

[96] See also Alexandrowicz, 'The Secretary-General of the United Nations', *International and Comparative Law Quarterly*, 11 (1962), p. 1109 at pp. 1122–3.

[97] See, for example, the statement by the UN Secretary-General in the 'Summary Study of the experience of UNEF' that '[t]he Force was recognized as a subsidiary organ of the General Assembly, established under the authority of Article 22 of the Charter of the United Nations (regulation 6)' (A/3943, 'Summary Study of the Experience of UNEF', 9 October 1958, as contained in Higgins, loc. cit. above (n. 93), p. 287).

[98] Moreover, the Secretary-General does not possess the competence to change unilaterally the mandate of a peace-keeping force. In response to pressure during a phase of the operation in the Congo for the Secretary-General to use ONUC to carry out disarmament of certain rebellious groups in the Congo, he stated: 'this [the disarmament] cannot be done by me or the United Nations Force short of new instructions from the Security Council' (S/4629, p. 4).

authority to establish the force.[99] This is confirmed in a message by the Secretary-General to the President of the Republic of Congo:

Such a determination can be made only by the Security Council itself or on the basis of its explicit delegation of authority. It is of no special importance that only the Security Council can decide on the discontinuance of the [peace-keeping] operation, and that, therefore, conditions which, by their effect on the operation, would deprive it of its necessary basis, would require direct consideration by the Security Council, which obviously could not be counted upon to approve of such conditions unless it were to find that the threat to peace and security had ceased.[100]

This approach follows from the position that the legal basis for the peace-keeping force is to fulfil the mandate specified by the Council or Assembly and that some form of decision by the relevant principal organ is thus required to terminate the force.[101] Accordingly, the unilateral decision by the Secretary-General to order the withdrawal of UNEF from Egyptian territory was *ultra vires*.[102]

It is convenient to reiterate the general point, that a UN subsidiary organ must be established by some form of expression of the will of a UN principal organ.[103]

---

[99] The issue may be raised whether the Secretary-General has no emergency powers to withdraw a peace-keeping force in a situation where the position of such a force may be imperilled. However, this approach is not appropriate since, as already explained in the text, there is no legal basis for the Secretary-General to exercise such a power either under the Charter or, unless the contrary is expressly stated, the resolution that establishes a peace-keeping force.

[100] Message dated 8 March 1961, *Security Council Official Records*, 16th year, Supplement for January–March, vol. 2, S/4629, p. 35.

[101] On the question of the requirements for the effective termination of a subsidiary organ by a principal organ, see further n. 162 and corresponding text, below.

[102] The Secretary-General ordered the withdrawal of UNEF from Egypt without obtaining the authorization of the General Assembly, the political organ which had established the Force. In the report of the Secretary-General on the matter, it was contended that the Secretary-General had undertaken all reasonable consultation with the Advisory Committee on UNEF and the troop-contributing States that could in the circumstances have been expected. The report points to the failure of the Advisory Committee to convene the General Assembly and the practical difficulties in so doing as a large part of the justification for the unilateral decision which was taken (Higgins, loc. cit. above (n. 93), pp. 271–3). However, these considerations are of a pragmatic nature and do not address the relevant issue: whether the Secretary-General has the competence to terminate a UN peace-keeping mission. See also, Higgins, ibid., p. 271; and Garvey, 'United Nations Peacekeeping and Host State Consent', *American Journal of International Law*, 64 (1970), p. 241. Cf., however, Di Blase, 'The Role of the Host State's Consent With Regard to Non-Coercive Actions by the United Nations', in Cassese (ed.), *United Nations Peace-keeping* (1978), pp. 70–3; and Elaraby, 'United Nations Peacekeeping by Consent: A Case Study of the Withdrawal of the United Nations Emergency Force', *New York University Journal of International Law and Politics*, 1 (1968), p. 149.

[103] However, even in those cases where an entity has not been initially established by a principal organ it is possible for a principal organ to subsequently adopt the entity as its subsidiary organ. An example of such adoption is illustrated by the opinion of the UN Legal Counsel in a memorandum on the status of the Ad Hoc Committee of the International Conference on Kampuchea. The Ad Hoc Committee was established not by the General Assembly but by a conference convened by the General Assembly. The UN Legal Counsel nevertheless found that the General Assembly had

There are no strict requirements of form which a principal organ must follow in order to establish a subsidiary organ. As already noted, the *raison d'être* of the precondition is that a principal organ express its intention that it wishes to establish a subsidiary organ.[104] As the commentary to Article 7 in Cot and Pellet's commentary on the Charter states: 'Un organe subsidiaire *est creé par une manifestation de volonté de l'organe principal*, quelle que soit la dénomination précise de la mesure prise—résolution, recommandation, décision . . . '.[105] The form by which a principal organ can establish a subsidiary organ will thus depend on the principal organ in question.

In the case of the International Court of Justice, the form will be by a decision of the Court.[106] In the cases of the Security Council, General Assembly, Trusteeship Council and ECOSOC, the most obvious form is by a resolution.[107] This resolution may be phrased in terms of a decision or even a non-binding recommendation. In the case of a recommendation, the International Court found in the *Expenses* case that the General Assembly has the power, under Article 14 of the Charter, to recommend to States that they organize peace-keeping operations—which it found were subsidiary organs—with the consent of the States concerned.[108] In fact, the non-binding nature of this form of establishment of the subsidiary organ was of considerable importance to the International Court in finding that the peace-keeping forces in question had been lawfully established.[109]

An interesting instance of this use of a recommendation to establish a subsidiary organ arose in the case of the UN's response to the invasion by North Korean forces of the Republic of Korea on 25 June 1950. After having determined in an earlier resolution that the 'armed attack'

---

adopted the Ad Hoc Committee as its own subsidiary organ by approving the conference report. The Legal Counsel observed: 'In these circumstances the Committee must be considered as being an organ of the Conference which established it and also an organ of the General Assembly which was the convening authority of the Conference and which approved and gave effect to the Conference's decision to establish the Committee' (*UN Juridical Yearbook*, 1984, p. 160). Moreover, both Higgins and Bowett have noted that the United Nations Treaty Supervision Organization (UNTSO), while initially organized and developed by the UN Mediator for Palestine, was later adopted by the UN Security Council as its subsidiary organ: see further Higgins, loc. cit. above (n. 93), p. 60; and Bowett, op. cit. above (n. 53), p. 63.

[104] Above, n. 85 and corresponding text.
[105] Cot and Pellet, op. cit. above (n. 1), p. 212 (original emphasis).
[106] For the voting requirements for such a decision by the Court, see further n. 120, below.
[107] However, it is arguably not restricted to this form. In the case, for example, of the Security Council, Woods has stated the following ways by which the Council expresses its intention: 'The Security Council acts in various ways: there are resolutions, statements made on its behalf by the President of the Council, letters from the President (normally addressed to the Secretary-General) and other decisions (generally recorded in official documents)' ('Security Council Working Methods and Procedure: Recent Developments', *International and Comparative Law Quarterly*, 45 (1996), p. 150 at p. 151). It is not clear, however, whether, for example, a statement by the Security Council would be sufficient to establish a subsidiary organ.
[108] *Expenses* case, *ICJ Reports*, 1962, pp. 163–5.
[109] See further n. 220 and corresponding text, below.

constituted a 'breach of the peace',[110] the Security Council, in Resolution 83, recommended that the members of the United Nations 'furnish such assistance . . . as may be necessary to repel the armed attack'.[111] Subsequently, the Council, in Resolution 84, recommended that 'all Members providing military forces and other assistance pursuant to the aforesaid Security Council resolutions make such forces and other assistance available to a unified command under the United States',[112] and requested the United States to designate the commander of such forces.[113] This unified command, or UN Command as it later became known,[114] was established by the Security Council as its subsidiary organ, since it acted on behalf of and as 'agent' for the Security Council,[115] had the requisite degree of independence from the Council, and was under the overall authority and control of the Council.[116] The

---

[110] Security Council Resolution 82 of 25 June 1950.

[111] Security Council Resolution 83 of 27 June 1950.

[112] Security Council Resolution 84 of 7 July 1950. The recommendation by the Council that the member States contributing forces place them under the unified command of the United States did not involve any legal obligation on the member States to do so. The fact that this occurred was the effect of a voluntary agreement by these members. See also Kelsen, op. cit. above (n. 20), p. 940.

[113] On 8 July 1950, President Truman announced that he had designated General MacArthur as 'the commanding general of the military forces which the members of the United Nations place under the unified command of the United States pursuant to the United Nations' assistance to the Republic of Korea in repelling the unprovoked armed attack against it' ('Military Situation in the Far East', Hearings Before the Senate Committee on Armed Services and the Committee on Foreign Relations, 82nd Congress, 1st Session, part 5, p. 3373).

[114] Higgins points out that 'the contributing governments used the term "United Nations Command" when communicating with it; the agreements between them and the United States employed the same term; and UN resolutions referred either to UN Forces or to the UN Command' (*United Nations Peacekeeping*, vol. 2 (1970), p. 197).

[115] Thus, for example, the UK Prime Minister in the House of Commons on 28 June 1950, the day after the adoption of Resolution 83, stated: 'The House will wish to know what action His Majesty's Government is taking in pursuance of the resolution of the Security Council passed yesterday calling on all Members of the United Nations to furnish assistance to the Republic of Korea. We have decided to support the United States action in Korea by immediately placing our Naval forces in Japanese waters at the disposal of the United States authorities to operate *on behalf of the Security Council* in support of South Korea. Orders to this effect have already been sent to the Naval Commander-in-Chief on the spot' (as cited in S/PV.476, *Security Council Official Records*, 5th year, 476th meeting (1950), p. 11 (emphasis added)). The view that the US was the 'agent' of the UN was made clear by the testimony of the first UN Force Commander, General MacArthur, when he testified before the United States Senate that: 'The Agreement that was . . . made between the United Nations and the United States Government was that the . . . Government should be the agent for the United Nations in the campaign in Korea. The orders that came to me were from the American Government, but they had under that basis the validity of both the United States Government and the United Nations . . . My instructions from the Joint Chiefs of Staff acting as the agency for the United Nations, ha[d] modified the military conditions under which I operate[d]' ('Military Situation in the Far East', Hearings before the Senate Committee on Armed Services and Foreign Relations, 82nd Congress, 1st Session, part 3, p. 1937).

[116] It is overall authority and control by the relevant principal organ which is important in terms of characterizing an entity as a subsidiary organ, and not necessarily that the principal be able to exercise operational control over its subsidiary organ. Accordingly, the seeming lack of operational command and control by the Council over the UN Command is of no significance to the issue of its

United States Government carried out a number of activities on behalf of the UN Command acting as 'the executive agent of the United Nations Forces in Korea'. For example, the US Government acting as the 'executive agent' concluded formal agreements with some of the nations who contributed troops to the action in Korea.[117] The execution of these treaties was mostly in the hands of the UN Command and the United States Government. This did not, however, prevent the UN from invoking the provisions of the treaties concluded by the UN Command when the situation called for intervention of the Organization.[118] Such action is in conformity with the legal position that the UN Command (and in some cases the US Government acting on its behalf), acting as a subsidiary organ of the Council, entered into agreements on behalf of the Council which the UN could thus rely on, the undertakings being entered into by its subsidiary organ. To reiterate the main point of this example, the UN's principal organs can use the form of a recommendation to establish a subsidiary organ.

In the majority of cases of establishment of a subsidiary organ, the expression of the will of a principal organ will require that the particular voting requirements of the relevant principal organ be satisfied. It is clear from the express provisions of the Charter that in the cases of the General Assembly, ECOSOC and the Trusteeship Council, the consent of the majority of States present and voting is sufficient to establish a subsidiary organ.[119] Similarly, in the case of the International Court of Justice, Article 55 of the Statute stipulates: 'All questions shall be decided by a majority of the judges present'.[120]

---

characterization as a subsidiary organ. In respect of this lack of operational command and control in the case of Korea, see further Higgins, op. cit. above (n. 114), pp. 195–7. Importantly, the establishment of the Unified Command also fulfilled the remaining precondition of establishment that there be no violation of the delimitation of powers between the principal organs. See further on this precondition of establishment Section IV(3), below.

[117] See, for example, the Agreement between the US and the Netherlands concerning participation of Netherlands Forces, 18 May 1952, *UN Treaty Series*, vol. 177, p. 234, contained in Higgins, op. cit. above (n. 114), pp. 204–5. Moreover, other international agreements entered into in connection with the UN action in Korea were concluded not by the Secretary-General acting for the UN, but by the United States Government (expressly stated to be 'the executive agent of the UN Forces in Korea') or the UN Command. For example, an agreement with the UN Korean Reconstruction Agency for the Relief and Rehabilitation of Korea (UNKRA), a UN organ, was concluded by the United States acting in its capacity as UN Command pursuant to UN resolutions. (Summary contained in *US Department of State Bulletin*, 25 (1951), p. 232.)

[118] See further Seyersted, *United Nations Forces* (1966), p. 104.

[119] See the following corresponding provisions of the Charter for the General Assembly, the Economic and Social Council and the Trusteeship Council, respectively: Articles 18, 67 and 89. See further the commentaries on these articles in Cot and Pellet, op. cit. above (n. 1); Simma op. cit. above (n. 1); and Goodrich and Hambro, op. cit. above (n. 1).

[120] The following are the provisions of the 1978 Rules of Procedure of the Court that apply Article 55(1) to the establishment of Chambers, the election of the Registrar, and the appointment of assessors:

Article 18(1) of the 1978 revised Rules of Procedure of the Court applies Article 55(1) to the establishment of Chambers by the Court: 'Elections to all Chambers shall take place by secret ballot.

The case of the Security Council is, however, more complicated, owing to the issue of the veto power which permanent members possess when voting on questions of a non-procedural nature. Article 27(2) of the Charter requires an affirmative vote of nine members on procedural matters for a resolution of the Security Council to be lawfully adopted, while Article 27(3) requires 'an affirmative vote of nine members *including the concurring votes of the permanent members*' on non-procedural matters.[121] Thus if the establishment of a subsidiary organ of the Security Council is considered to be a non-procedural decision, then it is subject to the power of veto by the permanent members of the Council.

This question was first discussed at the 70th meeting of the Security Council, on 20 September 1946. At this meeting, a draft resolution proposing to establish a commission of investigation in connection with the Ukrainian complaint against Greece was not adopted owing to the negative vote of a permanent member.[122] Accordingly, Goodrich and Hambro consider that the establishment of a subsidiary organ in this case was regarded as a non-procedural issue, subject to the veto.[123] However, the approach of the members of the Security Council was somewhat different when considering the establishment of a sub-committee to deal with the Corfu Channel question. At the 114th meeting, the UK representative considered that, as the establishment of a subsidiary organ was a procedural matter, he was not required to abstain from voting by

The Members of the Court obtaining the largest number of votes constituting a majority of the Members of the Court composing it at the time of the election shall be declared elected. If necessary to fill vacancies, more than one ballot shall take place, such ballot being limited to the number of vacancies that remain to be filled.'

The election of the Registrar is covered by Article 22 of the 1978 Rules of Procedure of the Court, the relevant provisions of which are as follows: '1. The Court shall elect its Registrar by secret ballot from amongst candidates proposed by Members of the Court. . . . 4. The candidate obtaining the votes of the majority of the Members of the Court composing it at the time of the election shall be declared elected.'

Article 9(3) of the 1978 Rules of Procedure provides that 'assessors shall be appointed by secret ballot and by a majority of the votes of the judges composing the Court for the case'.

See further in respect of all of these provisions Rosenne, 'The 1972 Revision of the Rules of the International Court of Justice', *Israel Law Review*, 8 (1973), p. 197 at p. 210, and id., *Procedure in the International Court of Justice, A Commentary on the 1978 Rules of the International Court of Justice* (1983), pp. 45–6.

[121] Despite extensive practice under these provisions, their meaning remains uncertain and controversial. See further commentary to Article 27 in Cot and Pellet, op. cit. above (n. 1), p. 495, and in Simma, op. cit. above (n. 1), p. 430; Blum, *Eroding the United Nations Charter* (1993), chapter 9; Kelsen, op. cit. above (n. 20), pp. 245–58; McDougal and Gardner, 'The Veto and the Charter: An Interpretation for Survival', *Yale Law Journal*, 60 (1951), p. 209; Bailey, *Voting in the Security Council* (1969), pp. 26–41, and *Procedure of the Security Council* (1988), pp. 200–23; Caron, 'The Legitimacy of the Collective Authority of the Security Council', *American Journal of International Law*, 87 (1993), p. 552, at pp. 566–88; and Gross, 'Voting in the Security Council: Abstention in the Post-1965 Amendment Phase and its Impact on Article 25 of the Charter', ibid., 62 (1968), p. 315.

[122] *Repertoire of the Practice of the Security Council, 1946–1951*, p. 158.

[123] Goodrich and Hambro, op. cit. above (n. 1), p. 222.

Article 27(3). The President of the Council, the representative of Belgium, ruled that:

Article 27 . . . does not debar members of the Security Council who are parties to a dispute from voting, except with regard to decisions to be taken by the Council 'under Chapter VI'. But Chapter VI does not mention decisions of the kind which we have now to take. We have to establish a purely advisory subcommittee, whose only task will be to assist the Council in the submission of facts; this body will take no decisions; it will confine itself to formulating conclusions intended to help the Council in taking a decision. The sole function of the future sub-committee will be to facilitate the Council's work by classifying information submitted to the Council; there is no question in this case of undertaking an investigation.[124]

The nature of the powers to be exercised by the subsidiary organ thus assumes importance for the purpose of determining whether the creation of the subsidiary is a procedural matter. The US representative, after agreeing with the statement of the President, took, however, a somewhat broader approach to the powers which could be delegated to the subsidiary when he observed:

It is unthinkable that the Security Council should not be able to establish a sub-committee, as the Council's own servant, to examine matters referred to it by the Council and to make recommendations and clarifications for the furtherance of the Council's own work. The Council's decision would be taken on the report of the sub-committee, which would have no power other than that of making recommendations . . . .[125]

A similar approach was taken by the US representative when considering a draft resolution which would appoint a sub-committee to receive or hear evidence, statements, and testimony on the Czechoslovak question in 1948. At the 288th meeting on 29 April 1948, the US representative stated that the decision to establish the sub-committee was

clearly a procedural decision. It is a decision under Article 29 of the Charter, not under Chapter VI. The Charter contains a clear indication that this type of matter is procedural. Article 29 is one of the five articles in the portion of Chapter V of the Charter entitled 'Procedure'. Consequently, under the language of the Charter, a Security Council decision pursuant to Article 29 must be considered as procedural . . . .[126]

---

[124] *Repertoire of the Practice of the Security Council, 1946–1951*, p. 204.
[125] Ibid.
[126] Ibid. Moreover, the representative of Canada considered that the draft resolution represented a 'convenient way of carrying on the further enquiries of the Security Council and, as such, was clearly a procedural matter under Article 29' (ibid.).

However, at the 288th meeting the representative of the USSR disagreed with these arguments, pointing out that the activities of the sub-committee required it to deal with substantive, non-procedural, issues.[127] As a result, the Chilean draft resolution to establish the sub-committee was not adopted owing to the veto of the former Soviet Union, the effect of which other States seemed to accept.[128] At the 303rd meeting on 24 May 1948, the Council voted on the preliminary question of whether the draft resolution was non-procedural.[129] The President gave the word 'investigation' found in the San Francisco Declaration[130] its 'widest meaning' when he interpreted the vote as a 'decision to consider the vote on the resolution as one of substance'.[131] This interpretation was challenged and put to the vote. The ruling was upheld, and the draft resolution was not adopted.[132] In the Security Council debates on the proposed establishment of a sub-committee to investigate and report on the situation in Laos, the representatives of Japan and Argentina stated that the establishment of the sub-committee under the terms of Article 29 was a matter of procedure. At the 847th meeting of the Council on 7 September 1959, the Panamanian representative stated that in his delegation's opinion the setting up of the sub-committee, which could not draw conclusions or submit recommendations but would confine itself to submitting the facts to the Council, did not imply any judgement whatsoever of the situation described, and was thus clearly a procedural matter which could be established by a procedural decision.[133] The US representative argued that the Four-Power Statement[134] itself recognizes

---

[127] Accordingly, Goodrich and Hambro have stated: 'The Soviet Union has consistently taken the position that a resolution to establish a sub-committee or commission to take evidence or investigate and report is a substantive matter, that the decision is a political decision' (op. cit. above (n. 1), p. 231).

[128] *Repertoire of the Practice of the Security Council, 1946–1951*, p. 205.

[129] *Security Council Official Records*, 3rd year, No. 73, 303rd meeting (1948), p. 19.

[130] Paragraph 4 of the San Francisco declaration states: 'decisions and actions by the Security Council may well have major political consequences and may even initiate a chain of events which might, in the end, require the Council under its responsibilities to invoke measures of enforcement under Section B, Chapter VIII. This chain of events begins when the Council decides to make an *investigation* . . . It is to such decisions and actions that unanimity of the permanent members applies . . . ' (Statements by the Delegations of the four sponsoring governments, 7 June 1945: *Documents of the United Nations Conference on International Organization*, Doc. 852, III/1/37(1)). On the chain-of-events theory, see further Kelsen, op. cit. above (n. 20), pp. 255–7; commentaries to Article 27 in Cot and Pellet, op. cit. above (n. 1), and in Simma, op. cit. above (n. 1); and Bailey, op. cit. above (n. 121).

[131] Loc. cit. above (n. 129), p. 21.

[132] Ibid. p. 26.

[133] *Repertoire of the Practice of the Security Council: Supplement 1959–1963*, p. 119. Moreover, the representative of France, arguing in favour of the procedural nature of the draft resolution, observed that the decision would affect only members of the Council ('a sub-committee of itself') by providing them with appropriate means for further deliberations and would not prejudge any future Security Council decisions (ibid.).

[134] See *Documents of the United Nations Conference on International Organization* (San Francisco, 1945), vol. 11, p. 711.

the establishment of a subsidiary organ as a procedural decision.[135] However, at the 848th meeting the representative of the former USSR stated that the proposal was 'a question of substance and a question of great importance, on which no decision should be taken without full consideration of all its possible political consequences'.[136] Moreover, he argued that as the proposed sub-committee was 'essentially a sub-committee for investigation', then the chain-of-events theory established by the San Francisco Declaration meant that the decision was one which was subject to the veto.[137] After the vote was taken to determine the question whether the vote on the draft resolution should be considered a procedural one, the President of the Council stated that it was 'the interpretation of the Chair, shared by the overwhelming majority of the members, that the draft resolution falls clearly under Article 29 of the Charter . . . '.[138] Moreover, since Article 29 appeared in the Charter under the heading of 'Procedure', the establishment of the sub-committee was deemed to be a procedural matter.[139] Thus the draft resolution was adopted notwithstanding the negative vote of the USSR.[140] The UK representative stated that '[t]here were no doubts that it was in accord with the letter and the spirit of the Charter that a decision of the Council to establish such a body to assist the Council in its work should be treated as a matter of procedure'.[141] Moreover, the UK representative correctly attached a degree of importance to the fact that paragraph 2 of the San Francisco Declaration, which dealt with the decisions that could be taken by a procedural vote, included the establishment by the Council of 'such bodies or agencies as it may deem necessary for the performance of its functions'.[142]

The rule which the above practice establishes is that there is a general presumption that a decision by the Security Council to create a subsidiary organ will be classified as a procedural matter and thus not be subject

[135] The US representative observed: 'Part I, paragraph 2 of the Statement provides: "For example, under the Yalta formula a procedural vote will govern the decisions made under the entire Section D of Chapter VI."—This section of the Dumbarton Oaks proposal is equivalent to Articles 28 to 32 inclusive of the Charter and of course includes Article 29—"This means that the Council will, by a vote of any seven of its members, . . . establish such bodies or agencies as it may deem necessary for the performance of its functions" ' (*Repertoire of the Practice of the Security Council: Supplement 1959–1963*, p. 119).

[136] Ibid.
[137] Ibid.
[138] Ibid.
[139] Ibid.
[140] *Security Council Official Records*, 14th year, 848th meeting, paras. 131–2. The draft resolution was adopted as SC/RES/132 (1959). The legality of the decision establishing the sub-committee was contested by the former USSR at the 848th meeting, but to no avail (ibid., paras. 133–9).
[141] *Repertoire of the Practice of the Security Council 1959–1963*, p. 119. The Representative of Japan similarly stated that the establishment of a sub-committee by the Security Council under the terms of Article 29 was a matter of procedure (ibid.).
[142] Ibid.

to the veto.[143] However, this presumption can be rebutted where it is proposed that a subsidiary organ be established to exercise powers which are non-procedural in nature. In this case the decision of the Council is non-procedural and will thus be subject to the veto. Accordingly, if the Security Council were to establish a subsidiary organ to which it purports to delegate certain of its Chapter VII decision-making powers then the establishment of the subsidiary is arguably subject to the veto of any of the five permanent members. This is an important check on the powers of the Council. Were it otherwise, it might be possible for the Security Council to decide to establish a subsidiary organ to exercise its Chapter VII powers without this decision being made subject to the veto.

There is an important distinction to be made between the decision by a principal organ to establish subsidiary organs as just discussed and the role of the individual member State in this process. In the case of UN peace-keeping, for example, it is clear that there is a distinction which must be made between the consent of the principal organ establishing the peace-keeping force and the consent of both the States which contribute troops to the force and the State where the force is to be deployed. It is a fundamental requirement of UN peace-keeping that the deployment of a peace-keeping force is conditional on the consent of both the States contributing troops to such a force and the host State where the force is to be deployed.[144] The fact however that a State has voted within the principal organ concerned in favour of the establishment of a peace-keeping force does not estop that State from later refusing either to allow the deployment of the peace-keeping force on its own territory or to contribute troops to the force. The participation by a State in the

---

[143] Thus Klepacki argues that resolutions setting up subsidiary organs are considered as procedural resolutions 'in the majority of organizations, especially those of a universal character, and require a normal majority of votes' (Klepacki, op. cit. above (n. 1), p. 17). Similarly, Bowett argues that the decision to establish a subsidiary organ through which to act is really secondary, and could, as a separate decision, be regarded as procedural under Article 29 (op. cit. above (n. 53), p. 67). However, he goes on to state that if the vote is taken as a single step rather than by distinguishing between the two stages of deciding to act and establishing an organ through which to act, the vote ought to be a non-procedural vote (ibid.).

[144] As the UN Secretary-General, in paragraph 9 of his second and final report on the plan for an emergency international force of 6 November 1956, observed: 'While the General Assembly is enabled to *establish* the Force with the consent of the parties which contribute units to the Force, it could not request the Force to be *stationed* or *operate* on the territory of a given country without the consent of the Government of that country' (A/3302, contained in Higgins, op. cit. above (n. 93), p. 263 (original emphasis)). Moreover, the International Court of Justice has observed in respect of peace-keeping forces: 'the way in which such subsidiary organs are utilized depends on the consent of the State or States concerned' (*Expenses* case, *ICJ Reports*, 1962, p. 165). On the necessity and role of consent in such operations, see further Garvey, 'United Nations Peacekeeping and Host State Consent', *American Journal of International Law*, 64 (1970), p. 241, and Di Blase, loc. cit. above (n. 102), p. 55.

establishment of a subsidiary organ cannot affect the rights which a State may otherwise enjoy under the Charter.[145]

In conclusion, for an entity to be considered a UN subsidiary organ it must be either established or subsequently adopted as such by some form of expression of will by a UN principal organ. In those cases where there are more than two principal organs involved in the establishment of the subsidiary, the principal which exercises authority and control over the subsidiary can in general be determined by ascertaining under whose authority the subsidiary organ was established.

2. A Principal Organ must Exercise Authority and Control over its Subsidiary Organ

The *Repertory of Practice of United Nations Organs* notes that an essential characteristic of a subsidiary organ is that it be under the authority and control of a principal organ.[146] Thus, for example, the UN Legal Counsel has observed:

The Council for Namibia was established as a subsidiary organ of the General Assembly by resolution 2248 (S-V) of 19 May 1967. As a subsidiary organ, it is responsible to, and under the authority of, the General Assembly in the same way as any other subsidiary organ.[147]

This characteristic flows from the subordinate nature of a subsidiary organ in relation to its principal.[148] The notion of ultimate control of the activities of a subsidiary organ is clear: it rests with the principal organ

---

[145] Moreover, the rights which States or other entities possess with regard to a principal organ of the UN they also possess in respect of its subsidiary organs. This was illustrated in a UN legal opinion on the legal status of the International Trade Centre (ITC) and the applicability to the Centre of General Assembly resolutions regarding the participation of the PLO in UN meetings. In particular the question was whether the PLO could participate as an observer in a session of the Joint Advisory Group (JAG) on the ITC. The UN Legal Counsel noted that the General Assembly in Resolution 3237 (XXIX) of 22 November 1974 had invited the PLO to participate as an observer in the sessions and the work of all international conferences convened under the auspices of the General Assembly. The UN Legal Counsel then found that since, *inter alia*, the ITC had been recognized by the General Assembly as a subsidiary organ of the United Nations (*UN Juridical Yearbook*, 1990, p. 272), the PLO was accordingly able to participate as an observer in JAG meetings (ibid.).

[146] Above, n. 10.

[147] Memorandum to the Representative of the Director General of the International Atomic Energy Agency to the United Nations: *UN Juridical Yearbook*, 1982, p. 164. Similarly, the Legal Counsel has observed in respect of the Committee of Contributions, 'The Committee, as a subsidiary organ of the General Assembly . . . is bound to carry out its tasks in accordance with any directives addressed to it by the Assembly' (ibid., p. 182).

[148] As Judge Hackworth observed in his dissenting opinion (on another point) in the *Administrative Tribunal* case: 'The term "subsidiary organ" has a special and well recognised meaning. It means an auxiliary or inferior organ; an organ to furnish aid and assistance in a subordinate or secondary capacity. This is the common acceptation of the term' (*ICJ Reports*, 1954, p. 79). However, several writers have pointed out that this subordinate nature of a subsidiary organ does not mean that there is a hierarchy of functions between principal and subsidiary organs, in the sense that the latter deal only with minor tasks: see Torres Bernardez, loc. cit. above (n. 1), p. 104; and Bentwich and Martin, op. cit. above (n. 1), p. 28.

unless the instrument establishing the subsidiary organ stipulates otherwise.[149] There are two main consequences of the precondition that a subsidiary organ be under the authority and control of a principal organ.

First, it enables a clear distinction to be made between UN subsidiary organs and other entities. Accordingly, a private corporation which is incorporated within a State cannot lawfully be established as a UN subsidiary organ, since the organ would be subject to the laws of the State in question and would thus not be under the sole authority and control of a UN principal organ. This issue arose when UNICEF asked whether it could become a shareholder in a printing company incorporated in a member State. In reply, the UN Legal Counsel observed:

The participation of UNICEF as a shareholder in a private company would submit the Organization to the regulations and rules of the national law governing corporate entities, and would thus be incompatible with the character and status of the United Nations, of which UNICEF is a subsidiary organ. As a United Nations organ, UNICEF enjoys, under Article 104 of the United Nations Charter and the Convention on the Privileges and Immunities of the United Nations, certain privileges and immunities, including immunity from legal process. Yet, as a shareholder in a private corporation, UNICEF would be subject to any legislative controls imposing fiduciary duties and liabilities for the acts of the corporation.[150]

The second consequence is that the principal organ possesses the competence to determine the membership, structure, mandate and

[149] This was illustrated by the opinion of the UN Legal Counsel in his memorandum to the Secretary of ECOSOC where he stated in respect of the *Ad Hoc* Committee of ECOSOC that if 'any question arises as to the composition of the *Ad Hoc* Committee, this could be settled in the first instance in the *Ad Hoc* Committee and ultimately by the parent body, the Economic and Social Council' (Memorandum to the Secretary of ECOSOC, *UN Juridical Yearbook*, 1984, p. 168). Similarly, in a memorandum to the Under-Secretary-General for Political and General Assembly Affairs, the UN Legal Counsel states: 'Where the terms of reference are not clear and a question arises as to the competence of a subsidiary organ to take action on a particular matter it would, in the first instance, be settled by that organ in accordance with its rules of procedure. Should the manner in which it is settled be questioned again in the parent organ it would then be for the parent organ to decide the issue, and its decision would be final' (ibid., p. 135). However, if the subsidiary organ wishes to take action contrary to a decision of its principal organ there is no legal impediment to the subsidiary obtaining the permission of its parent organ: permission being either express or implied. Accordingly, in a cable to the Chief of the Governing Council Secretariat of the United Nations Environmental Programme on the question whether a subsidiary organ can provide that one of its own subsidiaries use fewer languages than itself, the UN Legal Counsel stated: 'If a choice of languages is desired that would contravene a General Assembly or Economic and Social Council decision, then the permission of the Assembly or Council must be secured. This can be granted by an explicit resolution or decision, or implicitly through the approval of a financial implications statement anticipating the use of fewer languages than those normally authorized' (*UN Juridical Yearbook*, 1983, p. 169).

[150] Ibid., 1990, p. 256. See also the opinion given by the UN Legal Counsel on whether the United Nations Development Programme could become a founding member of a corporate body under the national law of a member State: ibid., p. 259. An additional consideration here is that such an entity would not be subject to the budgetary control of the General Assembly which is required by the Charter: see further nn. 272–5, below.

duration of existence of its subsidiary organ.[151] The scope of the competence to terminate a subsidiary organ is the least clear and most controversial of these competencies.

There are many instances of an express termination of the life of a subsidiary organ by formal decision of the Security Council.[152] What is not so clear is whether there can be implied termination. The Security Council considered the procedure for the termination of a subsidiary organ when deciding what the effect of the liquidation of the Commission set up to investigate the Greek frontier incident would be on its sub-subsidiary organ, the 'Subsidiary Group'.[153] In this case the Greek Frontier Commission—the subsidiary organ of the Council—had set up its own subsidiary organ: the 'Subsidiary Group'. It follows from the fact that the Frontier Commission was the subsidiary organ of the Council that the latter could exercise authority and control over the 'Subsidiary Group'. At the 188th meeting of the Council, the UK representative argued that both subsidiary organs in this case 'can be terminated only by an affirmative decision of the Council'.[154] Moreover, the representative of the United States stated: 'I entirely support the President's ruling that the Group and the Commission should remain in existence until the Council takes affirmative action'.[155] The issue was resolved by the US representative, who introduced at the 202nd meeting a draft resolution to remove the question from the list of matters of which the Security Council was seised. There could be no doubt, he stated, that in taking such a decision the Council would be destroying both subsidiary organs in question.[156] At the same meeting the US draft resolution was adopted.[157] The Greek question was accordingly removed from the list of matters and the Commission of Investigation was deemed to be terminated.[158] Thus implied termination was effected in the Greek case by removing the question from the list of matters of which the Security Council was seised. What was considered important for effective termination was not the form of determination, but that the principal organ clearly evinced its intention that the subsidiary organ was to be terminated. The position is well summarized by Cot and Pellet's commentary on the Charter: '[l]es conditions de suppression d'un organe subsidiaire

---

[151] As the International Court in the *Administrative Tribunal* case observed: 'There can be no doubt that the Administrative Tribunal is subordinate in the sense that the General Assembly can abolish the Tribunal by repealing the Statute, that it can amend the Statute and provide for review of the future decisions of the Tribunal and that it can amend the Staff Regulations and make new ones' (*ICJ Reports*, 1954, p. 61). See also Simma, op. cit. above (n. 1), p. 197.

[152] For example, the termination of the United Nations Commission for India and Pakistan on 17 May 1950: see further *Repertory of Practice of United Nations Organs* (1955), vol. 2, p. 21.

[153] *Repertoire of the Practice of the Security Council, 1946–1951*, pp. 207–8.

[154] Ibid., p. 208.

[155] Ibid.

[156] Ibid.

[157] Ibid.

[158] Ibid.

sont symétriques des conditions de création: la suppression résulte d'une manifestation de volonté de l'organe principal créateur'.[159] Accordingly, there cannot be implied termination of a subsidiary organ simply because the task which the subsidiary was established to carry out has been completed. This approach has been confirmed by the UN Legal Counsel. In reply to the question whether the life of the UN Council for Namibia was to be considered as automatically terminated after the achievement by Namibia of its independence, the Council's very reason for existence,[160] the Counsel stated:

While the constitutive resolution (2248 (S-V) of 19 May 1967) and subsequent resolutions of the General Assembly imply in substantive terms that the mandate of the Council is fulfilled and that, therefore, the Council ceases to exist upon Namibian independence, no automatic dissolution of the Council is foreseen in these resolutions. The independence of Namibia ... will not, therefore, automatically trigger the dissolution of the Council, which will continue to exist from a purely legal point of view as a duly constituted subsidiary organ of the General Assembly until such time as the Assembly itself decides otherwise. ... As far as the question of status is concerned, therefore, one may conclude that the legal status of the Council for Namibia as a subsidiary organ of the General Assembly remains unchanged until such time as the General Assembly decides otherwise.[161]

The general rule in this area is that the fulfilment by a subsidiary organ of the task for which it was created does not automatically terminate its life.[162] The expression in some form by a principal organ that it intends the life of the subsidiary organ to be terminated is required for effective

---

[159] Cot and Pellet, op. cit. above (n. 1), p. 216.

[160] The UN Council for Namibia was a subsidiary organ which was created by General Assembly Resolution 2248 (S-V) of 19 May 1967 and which was endowed with broad administrative, executive, and legislative powers to help achieve the independence of Namibia. The fact that it is a subsidiary organ of the Council is affirmed by the UN Legal Counsel in a memorandum to the Officer-in-Charge of the Office of the UN Commissioner for Namibia: see further *UN Juridical Yearbook*, 1990, p. 271.

[161] *UN Juridical Yearbook*, 1990, p. 271. The General Assembly decided to terminate the life of the Council by Resolution 44/243 of 11 September 1990, which states: '*Taking note* of the declaration of the United Nations Council for Namibia adopted at its special plenary meetings ... by which the Council decided to recommend to the General Assembly its own dissolution as a result of Namibia's attainment of freedom and independence, ... [the General Assembly] (2) *Decides* that the United Nations Council for Namibia, having fulfilled the important mandate entrusted to it by General Assembly Resolution 2248 (S-V) relating to the Territory, is hereby dissolved' (General Assembly Resolution 44/243 of 11 September 1990, *General Assembly Official Records*, 44th Session, Supplement No. 49A (A/44/49/Add.1) (1991), pp. 2–3).

[162] This does not however mean that a subsidiary organ will be able to continue carrying out functions in respect of a task which the principal organ has decided has already been completed. As the UN Legal Counsel observed in respect of the effect of Namibia attaining its independence upon the UN Council for Namibia: 'This is not to say, of course, that all of the activities of the Council will survive the independence of Namibia. Some activities of the Council will automatically lose their *raison d'être* or will by their very nature be assumed by the new Government of Namibia' (*UN Juridical Yearbook*, 1990, p. 271).

termination to occur.[163] For example, a principal organ may expressly provide in the resolution establishing a subsidiary that its life is to be terminated upon, for example, the expiration of a certain time period.[164]

This general rule is of considerable importance to the work of the UN War Crimes Tribunal for the former Yugoslavia. In the case of the War Crimes Tribunal, the Secretary-General, in his Report to the Security Council on the establishment of the Tribunal, states:

As an enforcement measure under Chapter VII, however, the life span of the international tribunal would be linked to the restoration and maintenance of international peace and security in the territory of the former Yugoslavia, and Security Council decisions related thereto.[165]

It would not be accurate to suggest that the Secretary-General means by this statement that when the determination that international peace has been restored in the former Yugoslavia is made by the Security Council, the mandate of the Tribunal would be automatically terminated.[166] There is the additional requirement which must be satisfied for effective termination to occur: *in casu*, there would need to be a clear expression of intention by the Council that the Tribunal is to be terminated.[167] This does not, however, impinge on the Council's prerogative to decide to abolish the Tribunal or to exclude from the jurisdiction of the Tribunal a whole range of cases (thereby granting in effect immunity to persons falling within a specified category).

The case of termination by the International Court of the life of an *ad hoc* Chamber is of particular interest. It is clear that an important

[163] Accordingly, the Security Council in Resolution 689 notes in respect of the UN Iraq-Kuwait Observation Mission that 'the decision to set up the observation unit was taken in paragraph 5 of Resolution 687 (1991) and can only be terminated by a decision of the Council. The Council shall therefore review the question of termination or continuation every six months' (S/RES/689 (1991)).

[164] See, for example, the establishment by the Security Council in Resolution 186 (1964) of the United Nations peace-keeping force in Cyprus (UNFICYP) for an initial time-period of three months. Thus the existence of UNFICYP has, to date, depended on the Council continually renewing its mandate. See further on this issue of a time-limit in UN peace-keeping forces Di Blase, loc. cit. above (n. 102), pp. 75–6.

[165] S/25704, p. 8.

[166] Cf. the defence motion in the *Tadic* case, which states: 'the legal ground for the Tribunal would probably fall away precisely at that moment it would be likely to be able to do most, namely when peace has returned' (Case No. IT–94–I–T, 23 June 1995, para. 3.5.5).

[167] A possible reason for this may be that the Council wants to use the threat of prosecution as a bargaining chip to force the leaders in the former Yugoslavia to conclude a binding peace: see further Szasz, loc. cit. above (n. 66); and D'Amato, 'Peace vs. Accountability in Bosnia', *American Journal of International Law*, 88 (1994), p. 500. In response to D'Amato's articles, cf. the letters to the editor of the *American Journal of International Law* by Jordan Paust, Benjamin Ferencz and Payam Akhavan: 88 (1994), p. 715, ibid., p. 717, and 89 (1995), p. 92, respectively. The competence of the Council to terminate the life of the Tribunal, its subsidiary organ, is a cogent argument against an International Criminal Court being established, if the Council has the competence, as a UN subsidiary organ. See further on the various arguments surrounding the establishment of this Court, *Yearbook of the International Law Commission*, 1993, vol. 1, and 1994, vol. 1.

element of the authority and control which the International Court can exercise over an *ad hoc* Chamber is the power to decide to dissolve the Chamber at any time.[168] However, the Court has itself decided to impose a restriction on the exercise of this power. This has been expressly provided for in Article 16(3) of the revised Rules of the Court, which states: 'The Court may decide upon the dissolution of a Chamber, *but without prejudice to the duty of the Chamber concerned to finish any cases pending before it*'.[169] There is no restriction that prohibits the Court, as the entity possessing the competence to exercise authority and control over its subsidiary organ, from itself imposing such a limitation on the exercise of its authority and control.

This is an example of a wider issue which arises in the context of the authority and control that a principal organ exercises over its subsidiary: to what extent can limitations be placed upon the exercise of this authority and control?

The International Court in the *Administrative Tribunal* case expressly rejected the argument that a principal organ establishing a subordinate or subsidiary organ is inherently incapable of giving this organ the competence to make decisions that bind its creator.[170] The Court found that this question cannot be determined on the basis of the nature of the relationship between the General Assembly and the Tribunal, that is 'by considering whether the Tribunal is to be regarded as a subsidiary, a subordinate, or a secondary organ, or on the basis of the fact that it was established by the General Assembly'.[171] The answer depends on the intention of the General Assembly in establishing the Tribunal.[172] Thus the relevant question is: did the principal organ intend the subsidiary to have the power to make such binding decisions? Such an intention can be inferred from a variety of indicia. In the *Administrative Tribunal* case the Court looked primarily at the nature of the functions conferred upon the Administrative Tribunal by its Statute.[173] The fact that the Tribunal was established as a judicial body to exercise judicial functions which the General Assembly did not itself possess[174] was of primary importance to the Court in reaching the decision that the Administrative Tribunal was established 'not as an advisory organ or a mere subordinate committee of the General Assembly, but as an independent and truly judicial body

---

[168] See further Ostrihansky, loc. cit. above (n. 28), p. 41.

[169] As contained in Rosenne, *Procedure in the International Court: A Commentary on the 1978 Rules of the International Court of Justice* (1983), p. 38 (emphasis added). Rosenne contends that the phrase 'case pending before the chamber' includes any phase of proceedings after the filing of the document instituting them (loc. cit. above (n. 120), pp. 210–11).

[170] *ICJ Reports*, 1954, p. 61.

[171] Ibid.

[172] Ibid.

[173] Ibid.

[174] The International Court found that the General Assembly 'was not delegating the performance of its own functions', since the 'Charter does not confer judicial functions on the General Assembly' (ibid.).

pronouncing final judgments without appeal within the limited field of its functions'.[175] In reaching this decision, the Court noted that the terms 'tribunal', 'judgment', and competence to 'pass judgment upon applications', which appeared in the Tribunal's Statute, are generally used with respect to judicial bodies.[176] The degree of independence required in order to decide whether the decisions of a subsidiary can bind the principal may also be indicated by such factors as the method of appointment of the members of the subsidiary organ, whether these members serve in an individual capacity, and the degree to which the subsidiary organ is given the power to make decisions and act on its own.[177] The Court thus found that the decisions of the Tribunal did in fact bind the Assembly.[178] Accordingly, the Court established the principle that a UN principal organ which establishes a subsidiary to exercise powers and functions that it cannot itself exercise cannot change individual decisions of its subsidiary which are an exercise of those unique powers and functions. This is important, since if it were otherwise, then the principal organ would in effect be performing the very functions which it does not itself possess under the Charter. This is of importance to the work of the UN War Crimes Tribunal for the former Yugoslavia.[179]

As explained above, the Security Council does not have the authority under the Charter to perform the judicial functions entrusted to the Tribunal.[180] The Tribunal is established to determine individual criminal responsibility for violations of international humanitarian law in the former Yugoslavia.[181] The fact that the War Crimes Tribunal is exercising a judicial function which the Council does not itself possess is of considerable importance in ascribing to the Tribunal a degree of independence which prohibits interference by the Council in the conduct of individual cases. As the International Tribunal itself observed at the appeal stage of the *Tadic* case:

---

[175] Ibid., p. 53.

[176] Ibid., p. 52.

[177] See also, in the context of UN Administrative Tribunals, Gomula, loc. cit. above (n. 58), p. 83.

[178] As the Court in the *Administrative Tribunal* case stated: 'The Statute has provided for no kind of review. As this final judgment has binding force on the United Nations Organization as the juridical person responsible for the proper observance of the contract of service, that Organization becomes legally bound to carry out the judgment and to pay the compensation awarded to the staff member. It follows that the General Assembly, as an organ of the United Nations, must likewise be bound by the judgment' (*ICJ Reports*, 1954, p. 53).

[179] The following analysis in the text, although limited to the Tribunal for the former Yugoslavia, applies *mutatis mutandis* to the Rwandan Tribunal.

[180] Above, nn. 67–8 and corresponding text.

[181] In the context of the War Crimes Tribunal for the former Yugoslavia, the New Zealand representative to the Council states: 'We must remember, however, that the Tribunal is a court. Its task is to apply independently and impartially the rules of customary international law and, we believe, conventional law applicable in the territory of the former Yugoslavia' (S/PV.3217, p. 23).

To assume that the jurisdiction of the International Tribunal is absolutely limited to what the Security Council 'intended' to entrust it with, is to envisage the International Tribunal exclusively as a 'subsidiary organ' of the Security Council . . . a 'creation' totally fashioned to the smallest detail by its 'creator' and remaining totally in its power and at its mercy. But the Security Council decided to establish a subsidiary organ (the only means available to it for setting up such a body), it also clearly intended to establish a special kind of 'subsidiary organ': a tribunal.[182]

The Statute of the War Crimes Tribunal, like the Statute of the Administrative Tribunal, refers to the terms 'tribunal' and 'judgment'. Also in the case of the Tribunal, its Statute refers to it as a 'Court' and provides for no external review over its decisions. The Spanish representative to the Council stated in the debates preceding the adoption of Resolution 827 that the Tribunal exercises a large degree of independence in the exercise of its functions. He argues that this independence derives from the following:

the qualifications required of its members and from the procedure for their selection, which includes the participation of the Security Council and the General Assembly. It derives above all from the autonomy of its machinery, which is not subject to any external review. . . . We should recall that this independence is not at all incompatible with its formal character as a subsidiary organ of the Council, as is borne out by the jurisprudence of the International Court of Justice with respect to the United Nations Administrative Tribunal and its relations with the General Assembly.[183]

Accordingly, it is clear that the War Crimes Tribunal was established as an independent judicial body pronouncing final judgments without external review of its decisions within the limited field of its functions.[184] This degree of independence prevents the Council from reviewing individual decisions of the Tribunal.[185] If this were not the case then the Council would in effect be exercising judicial functions in specific cases. To prevent this from occurring, the Secretary-General stated in his report dealing with the establishment of the War Crimes Tribunal 'that it [the Tribunal] should perform its functions independently of political considerations and not be subject to the authority or control of the

---

[182] *Tadic* case, loc. cit. above (n. 65), para. 15. Accordingly, the Appeal Chamber of the War Crimes Tribunal in the *Tadic* case stated that prominent among these attributes of judicial function is the power known as *'compétence de la compétence'*: see further n. 65, above.

[183] S/PV.3217, pp. 39–40.

[184] Article 25 of the Statute of the Tribunal does, however, provide for the possibility of appellate proceedings *within* the International Tribunal. In fact, in the Appeals Chamber decision in the *Tadic* case the Tribunal found: 'This provision stands in conformity with the International Covenant on Civil and Political Rights which insists upon a right of appeal' (loc. cit. above (n. 65), para. 4).

[185] As Alvarez has stated: 'As the Tribunal's decisions issued to date suggest, in at least some of these instances the body is "subsidiary" in name only and can render final judgments that even the Council is not authorized to disturb—and that in turn can disturb the Council by suggesting limits on its powers' (Alvarez, 'Judging the Security Council', *American Journal of International Law*, 90 (1996), p. 1 at p. 11).

Council with regard to the performance of its judicial functions'.[186] This position was adopted by the Council when it adopted the Secretary-General's report in Resolution 827.

However, the competence of a subsidiary organ to take decisions that bind the principal organ that established it does not necessarily depend on the subsidiary performing functions which the principal cannot itself perform. One may recall the statement by the Court in the *Administrative Tribunal* case that this will depend on the intention of the principal organ in establishing its subsidiary. Accordingly, in the case of *ad hoc* Chambers of the International Court of Justice, both the principal organ, the Court, and subsidiary organ, the Chamber, can perform the same functions, but it is clear from Article 27 of the Court's Statute that the decisions of the Chamber bind the Court. Article 27 provides that a decision of a Chamber 'shall be considered as rendered by the Court'.[187] Accordingly, the Court, when establishing a Chamber, must be deemed to be acting with this intention in mind. As Judge Elias has stated: 'It must follow [from Article 27] that the Court and all its Members are bound by the judgment of a Chamber'.[188] Put differently, the Court's Statute provides for the automatic delegation of the power of binding decision in a particular case from the Court to the Chamber once it has been lawfully established. As Judge Schwebel has observed in commenting on Article 27, 'there can be no question of appeals from a chamber to the full Court'.[189] Thus, the authority and control which the Court exercises over its Chambers does not allow it to intervene in a particular case to substitute its judgment for that of the Chamber once the Chamber has been lawfully established. This restriction on the authority and control of the Court to intervene in a case being heard by a Chamber extends to issues both of procedure and of substance.[190]

This issue came into sharp focus before the International Court in respect of Nicaragua's request for permission to intervene in the *Land,*

---

[186] S/25705 and Add. 1. Similarly, in the case of the Rwandan War Crimes Tribunal the Secretary-General has stated: 'The International Tribunal for Rwanda is a subsidiary organ of the Security Council . . . . As such, it is dependent in administrative and financial matters on various United Nations organs; as a judicial body, however, it is independent of any one particular State or group of States, including its parent body, the Security Council' (S/1995/134, para. 8).

[187] See further on Article 27 Rosenne, loc. cit. above (n. 24), and Schwebel, loc. cit. above (n. 29), p. 741.

[188] Judge Elias in the *Land, Island and Maritime Frontier* case, *ICJ Reports*, 1990, p. 9. Cf. Rosenne who states that 'article 27 can only refer to the finality of the judgment and, thus, to the obligations contained in article 94 of the Charter, the undertaking to comply with the decisions of the Court, and the recourse to the Security Council in the event of non-compliance by the judgment debtor with a judgment of a Chamber' (Rosenne, loc. cit. above (n. 24), at pp. 218–24).

[189] Schwebel, loc. cit. above (n. 29), p. 741.

[190] Cf. Judge Shahabuddeen in the *Land, Island and Maritime Frontier* case who stated: 'The full Court, having set up a chamber, cannot interfere in its actual work; but I think it retains a continuing responsibility to ensure that the composition of the chamber is such as to enable it to function with a sufficient degree of procedural rectitude in order to qualify it as a convincing manifestation of the Court as a court of justice' (*ICJ Reports*, 1990, p. 57).

Island and Maritime Frontier Dispute case.[191] As a preliminary issue in the case, the Court had to decide whether Nicaragua's request for permission to intervene in the case should be decided by the Chamber or the full Court. Nicaragua contended that its request was a 'matter exclusively within the procedural mandate of the full Court'.[192] The Court, however, found that it was for the Chamber to decide the request for permission to intervene, since 'every intervention is incidental to the proceedings in a case',[193] and 'it is for the tribunal seised of a principal issue to deal also with any issue subsidiary thereto . . . a chamber formed to deal with a particular case therefore deals not only with the merits of the case, but also with incidental proceedings arising in that case'.[194] More specifically, the Court found that the question of whether an application for permission to intervene in a case under Article 62 of the Statute should be granted requires a judicial decision as to whether the State seeking to intervene 'has an interest of a legal nature which may be affected by the decision in the case'.[195] The Court found that this decision 'can therefore only be determined by the body which will be called upon to give the decision on the merits of the case'.[196] The Court thus dismissed the following contention:

Nicaragua in the alternative would request that, for those reasons of elemental fairness explained above . . . the Court should, in any case, exclude from the mandate of the Chamber any powers of determination of the juridical situation of maritime areas both within the Gulf of Fonseca and also in the Pacific Ocean and, in effect, limit the Chamber's mandate to those aspects of the land boundary which are in dispute between El Salvador and Honduras.[197]

The Court found that since it decided to leave the issue to be decided by the Chamber, then this contention, dependent on the Court deciding the application for permission to intervene, did not need to be addressed.[198] However, the reason for the Court not limiting the mandate of the Chamber in such a way, it must be emphasized, is that the Chamber had already been established and that the Court could not interfere in the conduct of the case by the Chamber once it had been lawfully established and seised of the case. This does not, however, prevent the Court from deciding, when forming the Chamber, to limit the mandate of the

[191] See further in respect of this case Shaw, 'Case concerning the Land, Island and Maritime Frontier Dispute (El Salvador/Honduras: Nicaragua Intervening), Judgment of 11 September 1992', in 'International Court of Justice: Recent Cases', *International and Comparative Law Quarterly*, 42 (1993), p. 929; and Rosenne, *Intervention in the International Court of Justice* (1993), p. 179.

[192] As quoted in Rosenne, ibid., p. 179.

[193] *Land, Island and Maritime Frontier* case, *ICJ Reports*, 1990, p. 4, quoting the *Haya de la Torre* case, *ICJ Reports*, 1951, at p. 76.

[194] *ICJ Reports*, 1990, p. 4.

[195] Ibid., p. 5.

[196] Ibid.

[197] As quoted in the judgment of the Court, ibid.

[198] Ibid., p. 6.

Chamber so as to exclude consideration of certain issues. This would represent a valid exercise by the Court of the authority and control which it possesses over the Chamber, its subsidiary organ. The limiting of the mandate of a Chamber would, however, require the consent of the parties to the case, since the formation of a Chamber of the Court and its hearing of a case is dependent on the consent of the parties to the case.[199] However, to restrict the mandate of the Chamber in the way that, for example, Nicaragua requested in the *Land, Island, and Maritime Frontier* case would probably require a decision by the Court at this early stage that the State seeking to make a request for permission to intervene does in fact have a legal interest in the claim. However, one may recall the statement by the Court in the *Land, Island, and Maritime Frontier* case, '[the decision that] an application for permission to intervene in a particular case under Article 62 of the Statute should be granted requires a judicial decision whether the State seeking to intervene 'has an interest of a legal nature which may be affected by the decision' in the case, and can therefore only be determined by the body which will be called upon to give the decision on the merits of the case'.[200] In other words, an attempt by the Court to restrict the competence of the Chamber before its formal establishment may be to prejudge the validity of the claim of the State seeking to intervene in the case. None the less, the Court does possess such a competence by virtue of the general authority and control which it can exercise over a Chamber as its subsidiary organ.[201] Accordingly, if a State wishes to have its application for permission to intervene in a case heard by the full Court, it will depend on its timing in making its request for intervention. The State seeking to intervene must do so at the time that the parties request the Court to establish the Chamber. It is at this stage the Court can decide such an issue, and, accordingly, decide to limit the competence of the Chamber, subject to the consent of the parties concerned.

In conclusion, the authority and control which a principal organ possesses over its subsidiary organ enables the principal to review and change the decisions of its subsidiary organ and terminate the life of the

---

[199] See further n. 28, above.

[200] *ICJ Reports*, 1990, p. 4.

[201] This authority and control which the Court can exercise over its Chamber at the time of its formation is evidenced in express terms by, for example, Article 31(4) of the Court's Statute, which ensures that the right of a State to appoint an *ad hoc* judge to the Court where there is no judge of its nationality on the Court is applied to Chambers of the Court. Article 31(4) provides that 'In such cases, the President shall request one or, if necessary, two of the members of the Court forming the chamber to give place to the members of the Court of the nationality of the parties concerned, and, failing such or if they are unable to be present, to the Judges specially chosen by the parties'. Accordingly, this provision saw the President of the Court in the *Gulf of Maine* case request one of the judges elected to the *ad hoc* Chamber to give up his place to the judge *ad hoc* chosen by Canada (*Gulf of Maine* case, *ICJ Reports*, 1984, p. 246 at p. 252). (The US did not have to appoint an *ad hoc* judge, since it already had a judge of its nationality on the Court.)

subsidiary with immediate effect. The all-important degree of independence of the subsidiary organ, which determines whether a decision of the subsidiary can bind the principal organ, is ascertained by reference to the intention of the principal organ when establishing its subsidiary.

3. *The Establishment of a Subsidiary Organ must not Violate the Delimitation of Powers between Principal Organs Specified by the Charter*

The UN Charter gives certain powers to certain principal organs and certain other powers to certain other principal organs. There is in many cases a good deal of overlap of powers and functions of the principal organs. However, even in these cases there are limits to when a principal organ can exercise certain powers. Under the law of the United Nations, it is not possible for UN principal organs to impinge on each other's Charter-mandated delimitation of powers.[202] Applying this principle to our enquiry, it follows that UN principal organs cannot establish a subsidiary organ whose activities would violate the delimitation of Charter powers between principal organs.[203] This section ascertains the contours of the delimitation of Charter powers between principal organs and examines how this operates as a limitation on the authority of principal organs to establish subsidiary organs in the following three areas: international peace and security; the exercise of judicial functions in contentious cases between States; and United Nations finances.

(a) *International peace and security*

Article 24(1) of the Charter confers on the Council the 'primary responsibility for the maintenance of international peace and security'. However, it is well established that this does not prevent the General Assembly from exercising a secondary responsibility for maintaining international peace and security.[204] The question which has arisen in practice is whether the General Assembly has the authority to establish subsidiary organs to perform functions in respect of the maintenance of international peace and security. This issue has been highly controversial. It was the issue of the delimitation of Charter powers that in

---

[202] See also the following: Koskenniemi, 'The Police in the Temple. Order, Justice and the UN: A Dialectical View', *European Journal of International Law*, 6 (1995), p. 325 at pp. 337–8; Fitzmaurice, *The Law and Procedure of the International Court of Justice* (1986), p. 103; Bindschedler, 'La délimitation des compétences des Nations Unies', *Recueil des cours*, 108 (1963–I), p. 312; and the statement by Mr Phleger (USA), *United Nations Administrative Tribunal* case, *ICJ Pleadings*, 1954, p. 322.

[203] Simma's *Commentary*, although less equivocal, states: 'The exercise by one such [principal] organ of its powers [to establish subsidiary organs] should not lead to a disturbance of the balance established between principal organs by the Charter' (Simma, op. cit. above (n. 1), p. 386).

[204] See the *Expenses* case, *ICJ Reports*, 1962, p. 163; Cot and Pellet, commentary to Article 24, op. cit. above (n. 1), p. 447; and Kelsen, op. cit. above (n. 20), p. 283.

part provided the basis for a claim in the *Expenses* case that the General Assembly did not possess the competence to establish the first UN peace-keeping force in the Middle East (UNEF I).[205] However, the first instance where this issue arose was during discussion in the First Committee of the General Assembly on the proposed establishment of an Interim Committee by the General Assembly to deal with matters relating to international peace and security.

The Interim Committee of the General Assembly was intended to function in between the sessions of the main Assembly, its purpose being to ensure continuity in the control the Assembly could exercise over major political problems. The Committee was to have the power to discuss important disputes or situations submitted to the Assembly, to conduct investigations, and to advise, if necessary, that there should be a convening of a special session of the Assembly.[206] A major objection to the establishment of the Interim Committee was the contention that the functions proposed for the Committee were those which belonged to the Security Council and not the General Assembly. It was the representative of the Soviet Union who argued that when definite measures for the solution of a problem relating to international peace and security were to be taken, Article 11(2) of the Charter required the General Assembly to submit the matter to the Security Council.[207] Moreover, he argued, the empowering of the Interim Committee to conduct investigations and to appoint commissions of inquiry was a function of the Security Council, and not the General Assembly.[208] The Soviet Representative contended that the 'true purpose' was to create a new organ 'to weaken, circumvent, and act as a substitute for the Security Council, on which the Charter placed primary responsibility for maintaining peace and security'.[209] The opposing, better, view expressed was that the Assembly, as well as the Security Council, could take certain measures in relation to the maintenance of international peace and security and that the Assembly accordingly possessed the competence to establish the Committee.[210] The arguments in favour of the establishment of the Committee prevailed and the Interim Committee was established by resolution of the General Assembly.[211] For present purposes it is significant that in the debates, the UK representative argued that the Committee would be

---

[205] See n. 214 and corresponding text, below.
[206] UN Doc.A/C.1/SR74 and Doc.A/PV.82, p. 60. See also Bowett, *The Law of International Institutions* (4th edn., 1982), p. 49.
[207] *Repertory of Practice of United Nations Organs* (1955), vol. 1, p. 675.
[208] Ibid.
[209] UN Doc.A/C.1/SR 74. See also Doc. A/PV.110.
[210] Ibid.
[211] *General Assembly Official Records*, 2nd Session, Doc.A/519, p. 15.

subservient to the Security Council, which had the primary responsibility for the maintenance of international peace and security.[212] This allayed fears that the Committee, as a subsidiary organ, would be used to supplant the delimitation of powers between the Security Council and the General Assembly as established by the Charter.[213] However, until the *Expenses* case the exact contours of the delimitation of powers between the Council and the Assembly in the area of international peace and security remained unclear.

In the *Expenses* case, the delimitation of Charter powers between the Security Council and the General Assembly in the area of international peace and security was one of the bases upon which the constitutionality of UNEF I, which had been established by the General Assembly, was questioned. The argument made was that matters pertaining to the maintenance of international peace and security were, according to the Charter, to be dealt with solely by the Security Council, and that therefore only the Security Council could establish a UN peace-keeping force. The Court rejected this argument on the basis that the primary responsibility conferred on the Council by Article 24 for matters pertaining to international peace and security is ' "primary", not exclusive'.[214] The Court went on to state that '[t]he Charter makes it abundantly clear that the General Assembly is also to be concerned with international peace and security'.[215] However, the Court did find that there was a delimitation of Charter powers between the two organs that would prohibit the General Assembly from exercising certain powers. The Court found that ' . . . it is the Security Council which is given a power to impose an explicit obligation of compliance if for example it issues an order or command to an aggressor under Chapter VII. *It is only the Security Council which can require enforcement by coercive action against an aggressor.*'[216] Thus the Court found that the delimitation of Charter powers here means that the General Assembly could not impose a requirement on States to carry out military enforcement action. Put differently, if a force were established by the General Assembly to carry

[212] The UK representative stated that the Committee would have no power of direct recommendation—as the Council has—nor would it be able to send a commission of inquiry to a country without the consent of the Council (ibid., p. 159).

[213] This point was made in somewhat more general terms by the French representative: see further, ibid., p. 162. Moreover, the Interim Committee was required to take account of the limitations imposed upon it by Articles 11(2) and 12(1) of the Charter. This illustrates the principle that a subsidiary organ is constrained, at a minimum, by the same limitations under the Charter as its principal organ. In fact, as Goodrich and Hambro point out, Article 12(1) became a greater limitation upon the Interim Committee than upon the General Assembly. They observed: '[under Article 12] The General Assembly, while it may not make any recommendations concerning the question of which the Council is seized, may discuss that question. However, the Interim Committee could not even discuss any question of which the Council was seized' (Goodrich and Hambro, op. cit. above (n. 1), p. 197).

[214] *Expenses* case, *ICJ Reports*, 1962, p. 163.

[215] Ibid., p. 163.

[216] Ibid. (emphasis added).

out military enforcement action that purported to require States to contribute troops to the force, then its establishment would be *ultra vires*. The International Court went on to decide, however, that this particular delimitation of Charter powers did not apply to the case in question, since contributions to the force were on a voluntary basis. Moreover, the Court rejected the argument with regard to the delimitation of Charter powers in this case by giving a narrow interpretation to the word 'action' in Article 11(2).[217] The Court found that 'action' refers to coercive enforcement action.[218] As UN peace-keeping does not in theory involve the use of coercive enforcement measures against a State,[219] the Court rejected the argument that the application of Article 11(2) of the Charter prevented the General Assembly from lawfully establishing the peace-keeping force. The delimitation of Charter powers did not prevent the General Assembly from exercising its power under Article 14 of the Charter to recommend—such recommendations of course being non-binding—to member States that they establish a peace-keeping force.[220]

Consideration of the above two cases reveals that, in determining the effect of the delimitation of Charter powers on the authority of principal organs to establish subsidiary organs, the Charter provisions are to be given a broad interpretation in the area of international peace and security. The possibility of the overlapping of functions of the Security Council and the General Assembly is not in itself a barrier to their possessing concurrent jurisdiction[221] and thus both possessing the authority to establish subsidiary organs to perform functions in the relevant area. However, the delimitation of Charter powers in this area is such that it does preclude the General Assembly from establishing a UN

[217] Article 11(2) provides that certain 'action' is within the sole province of the Security Council, to the exclusion of the General Assembly. The relevant section of Article 11(2) of the Charter provides as follows: 'Any such question on which action is necessary shall be referred to the Security Council by the General Assembly either before or after discussion'.

[218] *ICJ Reports*, 1962, pp. 163–5.

[219] The Court stated: 'UNEF and ONUC were not enforcement actions within the compass of Chapter VII of the Charter' (*ICJ Reports*, 1962, p. 166). See also the opinion by the UN Legal Counsel regarding the implementation of Article 43 of the Charter: *UN Juridical Yearbook*, 1982, pp. 183–4.

[220] *ICJ Reports*, 1962, pp. 163–5.

[221] Moreover, subsequent to the Court's decision in the *Expenses* case, the delimitation of powers between the Security Council and the General Assembly provided for in Article 12 in respect of the maintenance of international peace and security has, through practice, become even less clear. Article 12(1) of the Charter states: 'While the Security Council is exercising in respect of any dispute or situation the functions assigned to it in the present Charter, the General Assembly shall not make any recommendation with regard to that dispute or situation unless the Security Council so requests'. However, the General Assembly, when dealing with the situation in the former Yugoslavia, passed Resolution 47/121 of 18 December 1992, which urges the Security Council to exempt the Republic of Bosnia and Herzegovina from the arms embargo imposed on the former Yugoslavia under Security Council Resolution 713. This resolution was passed at the same time that the Council was considering the question of the former Yugoslavia: an apparent violation of Article 12 of the Charter. See further on Article 12 Blum, 'Who Killed Article 12 of the United Nations Charter?', chapter V, *Eroding the United Nations Charter* (1993), pp. 103–32.

force, a subsidiary organ, that would require a contribution of troops from UN member States to carry out military enforcement action.

(b) *The exercise of judicial functions in contentious cases between States*

Article 92 of the Charter establishes the International Court of Justice as the principal judicial organ of the United Nations. As such, the Court has the primary responsibility for the exercise of judicial functions within the UN system. This primary responsibility does not mean, however, that the Court has an exclusive competence to exercise judicial functions within the UN system. As Rosenne has observed, 'The fact that the Court is the only judicial organ established by the Charter and is the principal judicial organ of the United Nations does not mean that it is the only judicial organ that may be established, either by the United Nations as an organization or by its individual members'.[222] The status of the Court as the 'principal judicial organ of the United Nations' does not prohibit other UN principal organs from establishing subsidiary organs to exercise judicial functions when this is necessary for the effective exercise of their powers.[223] What is, however, of more concern is when, for example, the Security Council purports to act like a judicial tribunal and make judicial decisions.[224] Among the UN principal organs, it is the Court alone that has the competence to exercise judicial functions. This contention does not rest on any false distinction between a 'legal dispute' or a 'political dispute';[225] on the fact that a complementarity of functions between the Court and the Security Council only allows the simultane-

---

[222] Rosenne, *The World Court: What It Is and How It Works* (1995), p. 33. See also Article 95 of the Charter that provides: 'Nothing in the present Charter shall prevent Members of the United Nations from entrusting the solution of their differences to other tribunals by virtue of agreements already in existence or which may be concluded in the future.'

[223] See further, for an example, nn. 258–61 and corresponding text, below.

[224] The Security Council, for example, has often assumed the power to make quasi-judicial determinations as part of its efforts to maintain or restore international peace. See further on this issue the following: Higgins, 'The Place of International Law in the Settlement of Disputes by the Security Council', *American Journal of International Law*, 64 (1970), p. 1; id., *Problems and Process: International Law and How We Use It* (1994), pp. 181–4; E. Lauterpacht, *Aspects of the Administration of International Justice* (1991), p. 39; Schachter, 'The Quasi-Judicial Role of the Security Council and the General Assembly', *American Journal of International Law*, 58 (1964), p. 960; Gowlland-Debbas, 'Security Council Enforcement Action and Issues of State Responsibility', *International and Comparative Law Quarterly*, 43 (1994), p. 55 at pp. 63–90; Harper, 'Does the United Nations Security Council Have the Competence to Act as Court and Legislature?', *New York University Journal of International Law and Politics*, 27 (1994), p. 103; Kirgis, 'The Security Council's First Fifty Years', *American Journal of International Law*, 89 (1995), p. 506; and Kelsen, op. cit. above (n. 20), pp. 359–450.

[225] See also Higgins, 'Policy Considerations and the International Judicial Process', *International and Comparative Law Quarterly*, 17 (1968), p. 58 at pp. 63–75; Acevedo, 'Disputes under consideration by the UN Security Council or Regional Bodies', in Fisler-Damrosch (ed.), *The International Court of Justice at a Crossroads* (1987), p. 242 at pp. 244–8; Gordon, 'Legal Disputes under Article 36(2) of the Statute', ibid., p. 183; and Harper, loc. cit. above (n. 224).

ous exercise of functions that are different, not the same;[226] nor on there being a clear separation of powers between the Security Council, as the *de facto* executive organ of the United Nations, and the International Court, as the UN's principal judicial organ.[227] The contention rests on the distinction between the legal and political *processes of determination*

---

[226] It is clear that the Court and the Council can exercise their powers of appreciation in complementarity. Accordingly, the Court has heard cases at the same time as they are being dealt with by the Council under Chapter VII. (See, for example, the *Expenses* case, *ICJ Reports*, 1962, p. 151; *Hostages* case, *ICJ Reports*, 1980, pp. 21–2; *Nicaragua* case, *ICJ Reports*, 1984, p. 434; and the *Lockerbie* case, *ICJ Reports*, 1992, pp. 20–1, 132–3.) However, this complementarity of functions does not mean that the Council and the Court can exercise *identical* functions in respect of the same issue. As Skubiszewski states: 'There is no obstacle to the simultaneous submission of a dispute to the Security Council and the Court provided the delimitation of functions is respected' ('The International Court of Justice and the Security Council', in Lowe and Fitzmaurice (eds.), *Fifty Years of the International Court* (1996), p. 606). Moreover, as the Court in the *Nicaragua* case observed: 'The Council has functions of a political nature assigned to it, whereas the Court exercises purely judicial functions. Both organs can therefore perform their separate but complementary functions with respect to the same events' (*ICJ Reports*, 1984, p. 435, para. 96). The Court brings its judicial powers to bear on a dispute while the Security Council uses its political powers. As Judge Bedjaoui has stated: 'The respective missions of the Security Council and the Court are thus on two distinct planes, have different objects and require specific methods of settlement consistent with their own respective powers. Such a situation, involving two distinct procedures before two principal organs of the United Nations having parallel competencies, is, I might add, not an unusual one . . . ' (*Lockerbie* case, *ICJ Reports* 1992, p. 144). Moreover, Judge Ni, when commenting in the *Lockerbie* case on this delimitation, yet complementarity, of functions between the Court and the Council, stated: 'Here the mention of *complementary* functions should not be overlooked. Although both organs deal with the same matter, there are different points of emphasis. In the instant case, the Security Council, as a political organ, is more concerned with the elimination of international terrorism and the maintenance of international peace and security, while the International Court of Justice, as the principal judicial organ of the United Nations, is more concerned with legal procedures such as questions of extradition and proceedings in connection with prosecution of offenders and assessment of compensation, etc. But these functions may be correlated with each other. What would be required between the two is co-ordination and co-operation, not competition or mutual exclusion' (ibid., p. 134 (original emphasis)). As the Court in the *Hostages* case found, 'it does not seem to have occurred to any member of the Council that there was or could be anything irregular in the simultaneous exercise of their respective functions by the Court and the Security Council' (*ICJ Reports*, 1980, pp. 22–3), the reason for this being: 'Whereas Article 12 of the Charter expressly forbids the General Assembly to make any recommendation with regard to a dispute or situation while the Security Council is exercising its functions in respect of that dispute or situation, no such restriction is placed on the functioning of the Court by any provision of either the Charter or the Statute of the Court. The reasons are clear. *It is for the Court, the principal judicial organ of the United Nations, to resolve any legal questions that may be in issue between parties to a dispute* . . . . This is indeed recognised by Article 36 of the Charter' (ibid. (emphasis added)). See also Gowlland-Debbas, 'The Relationship between the International Court of Justice and the Security Council in the Light of the *Lockerbie* Case', *American Journal of International Law*, 88 (1994), p. 643 at pp. 655–8.

[227] Whether such a separation of powers, albeit desirable, exists under the Charter is a controversial issue. There are arguments made that it does not as yet exist under the Charter: see further the *Nicaragua* case, *ICJ Reports*, 1984, p. 433, para. 92; and Judge Weeramantry in the *Lockerbie* case, *ICJ Reports*, 1992 p. 114 at p. 165. Cf., however, Brownlie, 'The Decisions of Political Organs of the United Nations and the Rule of Law', in Macdonald (ed.), *Essays in Honour of Wang Tieya* (1993), pp. 91 ff.

used to resolve a dispute.[228] The point is that the International Court and the Security Council (as a political organ) have been invested by the Charter with certain institutional characteristics that determine how, or more precisely in what way, they can exercise their powers when dealing with a dispute. They cannot seek to go beyond these institutional restraints and perform a function which is antithetical to the processes of decision-making with which they have been invested by the Charter. The UN political organs clearly have not been established to carry out the functions of a judicial tribunal.[229] This flows from their institutional characteristics as political organs.[230] The International Court has accepted this approach in respect of UN political organs when it found in the *Administrative Tribunal* case that the General Assembly could not act as a judicial organ and exercise judicial functions:

> The Court is of the opinion that the General Assembly itself, in view of its composition and functions, could hardly act as a judicial organ—considering the arguments of the parties, appraising the evidence produced by them, establishing the facts and declaring the law applicable to them . . . .[231]

Moreover, in the context of the Security Council, the following statement by the Appeal Chamber in the *Tadic* case may be recalled:

> Nor does it mean . . . that the Security Council [by establishing the Tribunal]

---

[228] As Higgins has observed in respect of the real issue when discussing the traditional view of a distinction existing between a 'political dispute' and a 'legal dispute': ' . . . *the terms "political dispute" and "legal dispute" refer to the decision-making process which is to be employed in respect of them, and not to the nature of the dispute itself.* A dispute is a "legal" dispute if it is to be resolved by authoritative legal decision, no matter what the component elements of that dispute. In other words, there is little reality in any definition of a political, or legal question; what is relevant is the distinction between a *political method* and a *legal method* of solving disputes' (Higgins, loc. cit. above (n. 225), p. 74 (original emphasis)). See also Jennings, 'Gerald Gray Fitzmaurice', this *Year Book*, 55 (1984), p. 18.

[229] As the representative of Brazil stated during discussion of the Corfu incident in the Security Council: 'The Security Council is not and cannot be a tribunal . . . Ours is not a judicial function, nor do we meet here as international judges' (*Security Council Official Records*, 2nd year, No. 32, S/PV.125, p. 686). It is contended that in this light the following statement by Judge Fitzmaurice in the *Namibia* case should be interpreted: ' . . . where the matter turns, and turns exclusively, on considerations of a legal character, a political organ, even if it is competent to take any resulting action, is not itself competent to make the necessary legal determinations on which the justifications for such action must rest. This can only be done by a legal organ competent to make such determinations' (*ICJ Reports*, 1971, p. 6 at p. 299). See also Kelsen, op. cit. above (n. 20), pp. 476–7.

[230] As Higgins has stated: 'Whether it would be wise or prudent for the Security Council to move . . . into the heart of what we normally see as judicial activity—that is to say, functions that tribunals are by their training and experience and familiarity with the relevant norms very well placed to carry out, must be doubtful' (Higgins, op. cit. above (n. 224), p. 184). Moreover, as Bowett has observed in respect of the right to a hearing before the Council: 'The Charter provisions in Articles 31, 32 and 44 do not, *expressis verbis*, confer on a Member State the right to be heard before sanctions are imposed upon it: and the maxim *audi alteram partem* is invoked in connection with judicial or quasi-judicial hearings, rather than hearings in a political organ' ('The Impact of Security Council Decisions on Dispute Settlement Procedures', *European Journal of International Law*, 5 (1994), p. 89 at p. 96). See further Harper, loc.cit. above (n. 224), pp. 132–42.

[231] *ICJ Reports*, 1954, p. 56.

was usurping for itself part of a judicial function which does not belong to it but to other organs of the United Nations according to the Charter.[232]

Accordingly, the delimitation of Charter powers in the area of the exercise of judicial functions derives from the position that the UN's political organs do not possess the institutional competence to exercise a judicial function.[233] This represents a specific example of the point made by Brownlie when discussing the limits on the powers of the Security Council. He states: 'The conclusion must be that the Security Council is subject to the test of legality in terms of its designated institutional competence'.[234] The application of the delimitation of Charter powers in this area thus means that the exercise of the judicial function should be left by the Council and the Assembly for the Court.[235] Just as the Court will never pronounce on a political matter using political processes to arrive at a decision,[236] the institutional characteristics of the Council, as a political organ, proscribe it from acting as a judicial tribunal and exercising primarily judicial functions. It is the exercise of the judicial function by the Council which is objectionable and not the exercise of its political powers of appreciation. This applies even in the case of the

---

[232] *International Legal Materials*, 35 (1996), p. 32, para. 38.

[233] As Judge Weeramantry stated in the *Lockerbie* case: 'As a judicial organ, it will be the Court's duty from time to time to examine and determine from a strictly legal point of view matters which may at the same time be the subject of determination from an executive or political point of view by another political organ of the United Nations. The Court by virtue of its nature and constitution applies to the matter before it the concepts, the criteria and the methodology of the judicial process which other organs of the United Nations are naturally not obliged to do. The concepts it uses are juridical concepts, its criteria are standards of legality, its method is that of legal proof. Its test of validity and the bases of its decisions are naturally not the same as they would be before a political or executive organ of the United Nations. . . . What pertains to the judicial function is the proper sphere of competence of the Court' (*ICJ Reports*, 1992, pp. 165–6). It may be for this reason that some authors contend that Article 36(3) of the Charter should be interpreted to mean that when resolving disputes the Security Council should as a general rule always leave legal disputes to be referred by the parties to the International Court of Justice in accordance with the provisions of the Statute of the Court. Thus, Bowett, for example, states that 'the clear implication [of Article 36(3)] is that legal disputes are not the business of the Council' (loc. cit. above (n. 230), p. 90). Cf. Simma, op. cit. above (n. 1), p. 545. Article 36(3) of the Charter provides in part: ' . . . the Security Council should also take into consideration that legal disputes should as a general rule be referred by the parties to the International Court of Justice in accordance with the provisions of the Statute of the Court'.

[234] Brownlie, loc. cit. above (n. 227), at p. 96. Moreover, the International Court in the *First Admissions* case states: 'The political character of an organ cannot release it from the observance of the treaty provisions established by the Charter when they constitute limitations on its powers or criteria for its judgment. To ascertain whether an organ has freedom of choice for its decisions, reference must be made to the terms of its constitution' (*ICJ Reports*, 1948, p. 57 at p. 64).

[235] As Graefrath has stated: 'The Security Council remains a political organ that takes political decisions. Even if the Council decides legal disputes and exercises "quasi-judicial functions" it neither applies judicial methods nor reaches judicial results, and its conclusions never attain the quality of a judicial decision. Its decision therefore cannot replace rulings of the Court or make them superfluous. The Security Council should leave to the Court what belongs to the Court' (Graefrath, 'Leave to the Court What Belongs to the Court: The Libyan Case', *European Journal of International Law*, 4 (1993), p. 184 at p. 204). See also Harper, loc. cit. above (n. 224), p. 109.

[236] See, for example, the *Rights of Minorities in Upper Silesia (Minority Schools)* case, PCIJ, Series A, No. 15, at p. 23.

exercise by the Council of its Chapter VII powers.[237] This is an application of the general point made by Brownlie, who states:

Even if the political organs have a wide margin of appreciation in determining that they have competence by virtue of Chapter VI or Chapter VII, and further, in making dispositions to maintain or restore international peace and security, it does not follow that the selection of the modalities of implementation is unconstrained by legality.[238]

However, there is, as briefly noted above, an important exception to the general rule that prohibits the exercise of judicial functions by the UN's political organs: where a political organ establishes a subsidiary organ to exercise judicial functions.[239] This process of establishment of subsidiary organs to exercise judicial functions does not violate the delimitation of powers between the principal organs, since the political organs are not themselves exercising judicial functions which they cannot themselves perform, but have entrusted this function to a subsidiary organ which can operate as a truly judicial organ. Thus the delimitation of Charter powers in these cases does not prevent the establishment of a subsidiary organ by a political (principal) organ to exercise judicial functions, but rather requires it. Specifically, the mandate and mode of operation of such subsidiary organs can be specified by the political organ so as to ensure such basic institutional requirements of a judicial organ as explained above by the Court in the *Administrative Tribunal* case.[240] In this way the use of subsidiary organs affords the Security Council and the General Assembly a large degree of flexibility in being able to achieve their Charter objectives in a lawful manner.

The issue of a judicial determination by the Security Council arose after the Gulf War in the context of where the boundary lay between Iraq and Kuwait. The Security Council, in Resolution 687, states:

[A]cting under Chapter VII of the Charter, . . . Demands that Iraq and Kuwait respect the inviolability of the international boundary and the allocation of islands set out in the 'Agreed Minutes Between the State of Kuwait and the Republic of Iraq Regarding the Restoration of Friendly Relations, Recognition and Related Matters', signed by them in the exercise of their sovereignty at Baghdad on 4 October 1963 and registered with the United Nations and published by the United Nations . . . Decides to guarantee the inviolability of the above-mentioned international boundary and to take as appropriate all necessary measures to that end in accordance with the Charter of the United Nations.[241]

---

[237] Moreover, the argument may be made that since Article 36 falls within Chapter VI of the Charter it cannot affect the exercise by the Council of its powers under Chapter VII. However, the interpretation of a Charter provision is to be determined by reference to the context of the Charter as a whole. See further n. 43, above.

[238] Brownlie, loc.cit. above (n. 227), p. 102.

[239] Above, n. 223 and corresponding text.

[240] Above, n. 231 and corresponding text. See also Bowett, loc. cit. above (n. 230), p. 89.

[241] Resolution 687, para. 2.

One view of this Council resolution is that the boundary between Iraq and Kuwait had already been delimited by the 1963 Agreed Minutes between the State of Kuwait and the Republic of Iraq[242] and thus the Council was not itself engaged in fixing or determining 'the international boundary contested by Iraq'.[243] This interpretation suggests that the Council was only giving its support to a treaty concluded between the two parties establishing the boundary, and that their compliance with this arrangement was determined by the Council to be an essential element for keeping the peace and for respecting the territorial integrity of Kuwait.[244] This was the position adopted by the majority of the members of the Security Council.[245] The important consideration which such an argument ignores, however, is that the boundary, at the time that the Council resolution was adopted, was contested by Iraq: the validity of the 1963 Agreement was being called into question on a series of legal grounds.[246] The fact that these arguments lacked cogency does not detract from the issue.[247] It was essentially left to individual members of the Council to decide the validity of Iraq's claims as to the legal force of the 1963 Agreement. For example, the representative of China held: 'In our view, the Agreed Minutes, long ago registered with the United Nations, constitutes an effective and legal document'.[248] The decision of the Council in Resolution 687 was a legal pronouncement that the 1963 Agreement was the instrument governing the delimitation of the Iraq-

[242] Post, 'Adjudication as a Mode of Acquisition of Territory?', in Lowe and Fitzmaurice (eds.), *Fifty Years of the International Court of Justice* (1996), p. 237 at p. 249.

[243] Sur, 'Security Council Resolution 687 of 3 April 1991 in the Gulf Affair: Problems of Restoring and Safeguarding Peace', *UNITAR Research Paper*, No. 12 (1992), p. 19; and Murphy, 'Force and Arms', in Schachter and Joyner (eds.), *United Nations Legal Order*, vol. 1 (1995), p. 272.

[244] Sur, loc. cit. above (n. 243).

[245] See, for example, the following statement by the representative of the United Kingdom: 'The resolution is not attempting to settle the boundary between these two countries; that was done by the 1963 Agreement between them, which was registered with the United Nations. But the failure to demarcate that boundary and the determination of Iraq to raise territorial claims that are incompatible with the 1963 Agreement are at the roots of this dispute, and they must be addressed. My Government is well aware of the great sensitivity to many Members of the Organization of the question of defining boundaries. We have no desire and no intention of overturning the principle that it is for the parties in question to negotiate and reach agreement, as was done in this case in 1932 and 1963. But, naturally, the Security Council has a duty to respond when disputes over boundaries arise and come to threaten international peace and security' (S/PV.2981, p. 113). See also, for example, the statement by the Indian representative: S/PV.2981, p. 78.

[246] As Brownlie has observed: 'It is probable that the alignment as such was disputed (and there is also a question of title to certain islands) and that, therefore, the adoption of a particular alignment by the Security Council involved rather more than a "demarcation" ' (Brownlie, loc. cit. above (n. 227), p. 97).

[247] For an analysis of the competing legal arguments in this case, see further Mendelson and Hulton, 'La revendication par l'Iraq de la souveraineté sur le Koweit', *Annuaire français de droit international*, 36 (1990), p. 195.

[248] S/PV.2981, p. 96 (emphasis added).

Kuwait boundary.[249] It is precisely this judicial determination by the Council which is of concern to Higgins, who states the following:

The Resolution [687] also determined that the international boundary should be delimited on the basis of what had been agreed between them in [1963]. It is one thing for the Security Council to insist that one state cannot use force to settle its frontier with another. It is another thing for it to purport to determine, in a sentence or two, where the frontier should run. Although I believe that legal analysis would show that the [1963] agreement was still in effect between the states concerned, the Security Council's determination of these matters simply ignores the recent Iraqi claims that for various reasons the [1963] treaty no longer applied. Had the matter of where the boundary lay fallen for determination by a legal tribunal, it would have been expected that an opportunity would have been given for these arguments to be deployed, and legal reasons for rejecting them (if that was the tribunal's conclusion) would have been given.[250]

As Brownlie has stated: 'It is one thing to effect a restoration of Kuwaiti sovereignty on the basis of the status quo prior to Iraq's invasion; it is quite another to impose a boundary in the absence either of bilateral negotiation and agreement or an arbitration or reference to the International Court'.[251] A cogent legal objection to the Council exercising a judicial power of determination in this case is that, as noted above, the Council cannot act as a judicial tribunal and exercise judicial functions in respect of competing claims between States,[252] since it lacks such necessary institutional judicial safeguards as, for example, due process for the parties.[253]

---

[249] See also Harper, loc. cit. above (n. 224), p. 116.

[250] Higgins, op. cit. above (n. 224), pp. 184–5.

[251] Brownlie, loc. cit. above (n. 227), p. 97.

[252] The main legal objection to the determination of the Iraq-Kuwait Boundary may be that the Council was exercising a permanent legislative power under Chapter VII. However, in casu, see further n. 256, below, as to a possible source of the Council's power to determine international boundaries in such a way.

[253] See also Bowett, loc. cit. above (n. 230), p. 89. Thus it was that the representative of Ecuador to the Council stated: 'In taking a position on the territorial boundary between Iraq and Kuwait and in requesting the Secretary-General to make arrangements with both countries to demarcate the boundary, acting within the scope of Chapter VII of the Charter, the Council has made the interpretation that this case is one of the exceptions envisaged in Article 36, which says that the Security Council: " . . . should also take into consideration that legal disputes should as a general rule be referred by the parties to the International Court of Justice in accordance with the provisions of the Statute of the Court." Ecuador does not share this interpretation of the Charter' (S/PV.2981, pp. 107–8). Cf. the position of Dr Gray, who, writing in this Year Book, states in respect of the Ecuadorian argument: 'In so far as this is an argument based on the separation of powers between the Security Council and the Court it is not convincing, given the consistent practice of the Security Council and jurisprudence of the Court on the relation between them. The Court has repeatedly said that there is no strict separation of powers and that the Security Council and the Court are complementary in their functions. Nor is it an attractive argument coming from States that have not accepted the Optional Clause or submitted any of their disputes to the International Court' (Gray, 'After the Ceasefire: Iraq, the Security Council and the Use of Force', this Year Book, 65 (1994), p. 136 at p. 147). With regard to this issue of complementarity of functions, see further n. 226, above.

However, the delimitation of powers does not automatically render the Council's decision in Resolution 687 *ultra vires*. The delimitation of powers in this area relies on the fact that the Council does not possess the institutional competence to act like a judicial tribunal. Accordingly, the subsequent reaction of both Iraq and Kuwait is of vital importance when determining the legal effect of the resolution. This was accepted by the resolution in paragraph 33 which '*[d]eclares* that, upon official notification by Iraq to the Secretary-General and to the Security Council of its acceptance of the provisions above, a formal cease-fire is effective between Iraq and Kuwait and the member States cooperating with Kuwait in accordance with resolution 678 (1990)'. Accordingly, the Council in Resolution 687 purports to make demands of Iraq, but it was then left to Iraq whether to accept the terms of these demands as part of the cease-fire agreement. Iraq's subsequent acceptance of the terms of the resolution[254] is thus of some significance in attributing to the terms of the resolution a legal obligation of a binding nature.[255] As the consent of Iraq was given to the purported decision of the Council in Resolution 687, then Iraq accepted, or at least acquiesced in, the position that the boundary between itself and Kuwait is that which is delimited in the 1963 Agreement and that it no longer contends that the Agreement is unlawful. The voluntary proffering of the consent of Iraq in this case thus means that there was no longer a legal dispute in respect of the delimitation of its boundary with Kuwait. Accordingly, the Council was not exercising a judicial function, since there was no dispute between the States.[256] This does not of course mean that at the time of the adoption

---

[254] Letters of 6 April 1991 addressed to the Security Council and to the Secretary-General, S/22456.

[255] Accordingly, the Secretary-General found that the acceptance expressed by Iraq constituted the necessary element of consent by the two parties for the terms of the resolution to have legal effect (letter of 30 April 1991, from the Secretary-General to the Minister of Foreign Affairs of Iraq, S/2258, pp. 8–9).

[256] As an alternative legal basis, the expression of consent by Iraq to the terms of Resolution 687 may be considered as a delegation of a power of disposition of title to the Council. As Brownlie has noted: ' . . . the fact is that states may agree to delegate a power of disposition to a political organ of the United Nations, at least where the previous sovereign has relinquished title and there is no transfer of sovereignty and no disposition of a title inhering in the Organization. The latter acts primarily as a referee' (Brownlie, *Principles of Public International Law* (4th edn., 1990), p. 173). Brownlie had earlier identified two bases for this exercise of 'power of disposition': 'If a political organ like the Security Council does not decide the issue judicially and in accordance with the law, it is simply exercising a power of disposition which may be derived from the Charter (this is a difficult question) or from a treaty specially conferring such power' (ibid., p. 137). Importantly, Crawford contends that the Council does, in any case, possess such a power of disposition under the Charter: ' . . . transfers of territory may take place either by consent of parties affected before a formal peace settlement (and the Security Council would be competent, if such transfer was regarded as necessary to "maintain or restore international peace and security", to require and enforce it) . . . . The point is that such action would seem to be fully authorized by the terms of Chapter VII; and that the exercise of dispositive authority by the Council cannot therefore be said

of the Council resolution the dispute did not exist. The point is, however, as Mendelson and Hulton have contended in this *Year Book*, that the effect of Iraq's consent is that 'even if procured by duress, the express consent of Iraq to the demarcation was sufficient to cure [retroactively] any possible defect in the Council's authority'.[257] The acceptance by Iraq of the determination by the Council of where the boundary lay was the defining act which conferred legal effect on the terms of Security Council Resolution 687.

The Council could have avoided this somewhat tortuous legal (and political) route with respect to Resolution 687 by establishing a judicial tribunal to decide in final terms the delimitation of the boundary between Iraq and Kuwait.[258] In this case, the Council could be said to possess an implied power to establish such a tribunal from the object and purpose of Chapter VII of the Charter, since it was a measure that was necessary for the restoration and maintenance of international peace and security,[259] the object and purpose of Chapter VII being that the Security Council should be able to take such action, within the confines of the Charter, as it deems necessary to maintain or restore international peace and security.[260] Once the Council can be said to possess the implied power to establish the Commission, it is clear that it can use its authority under

to be contrary to the "structure" of the Charter. Whether it would be contrary to the "purposes and principles of the United Nations" would of course depend on the specific case' (Crawford, *The Creation of States in International Law* (1979), p. 329). In a case where the League of Nations Council was delegated such a power of disposition of title, see further Boggs, *International Boundaries* (1940), pp. 148–9. In the context of the Iraq-Kuwait boundary, see further Mendelson and Hulton, 'The Iraq-Kuwait Boundary', this *Year Book*, 64 (1993), p. 135 at p. 146; and Gray, loc.cit. above (n. 253), pp. 147–8. Cf., in general, Judge Fitzmaurice in the *Namibia* case, who stated the following: 'Even where the Security Council is acting genuinely for the preservation or restoration of peace and security, it has no competence as part of that process to effect definitive and permanent changes in territorial rights, whether of sovereignty or administration . . .' (*ICJ Reports*, 1971, p. 6 at p. 216). Cf. also Bowett, who states: ' . . . the Council could not order a State to transfer any part of its own territory to another, for no such power exists in the Charter' (loc. cit. above (n. 230), p. 96).

[257] Mendelson and Hulton, loc. cit. above (n. 256), p. 179. See also Article 75 of the 1969 Vienna Convention on the Law of Treaties.

[258] Assuming the establishment of such a tribunal was by decision of the Council, then by virtue of Article 25 of the Charter the tribunal would have a compulsory jurisdiction and its decision would be final and binding upon member States. See further in respect of Article 25 of the Charter Cot and Pellet, op. cit. above (n. 1); Simma, op. cit. above (n. 1); Higgins, 'The Place of International Law in the Settlement of Disputes by the Security Council', *American Journal of International Law*, 64 (1970), p. 1, and 'The Advisory Opinion on Namibia: Which UN Resolutions are Binding under Article 25 of the Charter?', *International and Comparative Law Quarterly*, 21 (1972), p. 270; Kelsen, op. cit. above (n. 20), pp. 95–8, 293–5, 444–50; Bailey, op. cit. above (n. 121); and Suy, 'Some Legal Questions Concerning the Security Council', in *Festschrift Schlochauer* (1981), p. 676.

[259] There would, however, seem to be insuperable difficulties if the Council were to seek to establish a tribunal for determining a boundary in the absence of the consent of at least one of the parties, a major reason for this being that the tribunal, although possibly possessing legal competence, would lack legitimacy: see further, on the issue of the legitimacy of Security Council action, n. 267, below.

[260] The ability of the Council to imply powers from this object and purpose has previously been validated by the International Court of Justice in the *Expenses* case: see, for example, the oft-quoted

Article 7(2) of the Charter to establish such a subsidiary organ. The point has already been made in this *Year Book* by Mendelson and Hulton that the determination of where the boundary lay between Iraq and Kuwait was necessary for the restoration and continued maintenance of international peace and security.[261] The contention here, however, is that this should have been carried out by a subsidiary organ, a judicial tribunal, which was under the authority and control of the Council.[262] The argument would run that the Security Council, as the main guarantor of international order,[263] has in such cases a responsibility to ensure that justice is seen to be done between the parties by referring the matter to the International Court or establishing a judicial tribunal which can decide the matter by judicial process. The point is that the choice of institutional response is of crucial importance also in determining the long-term effectiveness of the Council's actions.[264] A tribunal would have provided the appropriate judicial safeguards to ensure that the arguments of both States were fully heard and given due weight in a subsequent decision.[265] This would contribute significantly to the perception by the parties that justice was in fact done between them,[266] and,

statement by the Court when upholding the implied power of the Council to establish UN peace-keeping forces: 'It cannot be said that the Charter has left the Council impotent in the face of an emergency situation when agreements under Article 43 have not been concluded' (*Expenses* case, *ICJ Reports*, 1962, p. 151 at p. 167). This is an expression of the more general point made earlier by Grayson Kirk who in 1946 had observed: 'The general principle . . . which runs consistently throughout the Charter, was that the Council should have the greatest possible flexibility in handling a situation which menaces the peace of the world' (Kirk, 'The Enforcement of Security', *Yale Law Journal*, 55 (1946), p. 1081 at p. 1088).

[261] Mendelson and Hulton, loc. cit. above (n. 256), p. 146.

[262] See also Harper, loc. cit. above (n. 224), p. 143.

[263] See further, for this notion that the Security Council is established to deal with issues relating to international order, Koskenniemi, loc. cit. above (n. 202).

[264] This is of particular importance in the context of a boundary delimitation. As Whittemore Boggs has stated: 'The acceptance of a decision relating to so vital a matter as a national boundary may depend upon confidence in the impartiality and integrity of character of an arbitrator or of commission members even more than upon the competence in all of the relevant fields of technical knowledge' (Boggs, op. cit. above (n. 256), p. 197).

[265] The importance of this depoliticized process has been recognized by Alvarez who states in respect of the War Crimes Tribunal: 'While the Council did not establish the Yugoslav Tribunal to buttress its own legitimacy, this and other subsidiary bodies were created as mechanisms for more impartial and apolitical judgments than are possible within the Council. Through these delegations of authority the Council has created potential alternatives to its own politicized processes' (Alvarez, loc. cit. above (n. 185), p. 11). Moreover, the tribunal should possess such a degree of independence from the Security Council that the Council could not, as explained above, interfere in the exercise of these judicial functions. Importantly, the Court stressed in the *Administrative Tribunal* case that a particular award of the Tribunal could be subject to review only if there was an express provision to that effect in the Tribunal's Statute. The Court stated: 'In order that the judgments pronounced by such a judicial tribunal could be subjected to review by any body other than the tribunal itself, it would be necessary, in the opinion of the Court, that the statute of that tribunal or some other legal instrument governing it should contain an express provision to that effect' (*ICJ Reports*, 1954, p. 56).

[266] Accordingly, one may recall the pertinent observation by Mendelson and Hulton in the context of the Council's determination of the Iraq-Kuwait boundary: 'the failure to pay more attention to the legal niceties has unnecessarily given Iraq ammunition with which

it is thus submitted, a significant contribution would be made to the legitimacy of any subsequent enforcement action by the Council that may be necessary to enforce the decision of the tribunal.[267]

These considerations are of considerable importance in finding the establishment by the Security Council of the Iraq-Kuwait Boundary Demarcation Commission as having been lawful.[268] Whether the acitivity of the Commission was justified, to the extent that it engaged in delimitation of some areas of the Iraq-Kuwait boundary,[269] will depend on the mandate conferred on the Commission by the Council.[270] The fact, however, that the Council in Resolution 833 expressly adopted the final decision of the Commission is sufficient indication that it authorized the exercise of such a power of judicial determination by the Commission.[271]

In conclusion, the institutional inadequacy of the UN's political organs to exercise judicial functions requires a dispute involving the

to attack the work of the Commission. It was of course evident from the outset that the Baghdad Government would challenge the validity of the process and the substance of the decisions reached, even if the legal difficulties had been more carefully grappled with. Nonetheless, it is feared that its task has been made the easier by an apparent failure to make sufficiently strenuous efforts, in what was after all a very novel and controversial proceeding, to ensure that justice was not only done, but manifestly seen to be done' (loc. cit. above (n. 256), p. 195).

[267] On the issue of the legitimacy of Security Council action in general, see further Caron, 'The Legitimacy of the Collective Authority of the Security Council', *American Journal of International Law*, 87 (1993), p. 552; and Murphy, 'The Security Council, Legitimacy, and the Concept of Collective Security After the Cold War', *Columbia Journal of Transnational Law*, 32 (1994), p. 201.

[268] Security Council Resolution 687 directed the Secretary-General 'to develop and present to the Security Council for decision . . . the composition of the Commission'. The composition of the Commission was determined by the Secretary-General and it was subsequently established as a subsidiary organ of the Council (S/22559 of 2 May 1991, p. 2.).

[269] As Mendelson and Hulton have noted in this *Year Book*: 'The Commission was not merely marking out on the ground a boundary which had already been defined with some precision in a treaty. So far as concerned the boundary in the Khowr Abd Allah, there was no treaty definition at all; and, as for the land boundary, the treaty definition was so vague as to require considerable elaboration (to use a neutral term). Secondly, the effect of the Commission's decision was to locate the land boundary in the northern sector further north than had previously been treated as the correct position in practice' (loc.cit. above (n. 256), p. 192). See also Mendelson and Hulton, 'Les décisions de la Commission Nations Unies sur la démarcation de la frontière entre l'Iraq et le Koweit', *Annuaire français de droit international*, 39 (1993), p. 178; Post, loc. cit. above (n. 242), p. 261; and Klabbers, 'No More Shifting Lines? The Report of the Iraq-Kuwait Boundary Demarcation Commission', *International and Comparative Law Quarterly*, 43 (1994), p. 904 at p. 911.

[270] Mendelson and Hulton argue that delimitation of part of the boundary in the Khowr Abd Allah was envisaged by the Council: loc. cit. above (n. 256), p. 179.

[271] This judicial determination led Post to contend that the final (and binding) decision of the IKBDC 'has produced a constitutive effect' and that as a result 'part of the IKBDC decisions can then be said to provide support for the point of view that, within international law, indeed, such a way of acquiring territory is perfectly possible' (Post, loc. cit. above (n. 242), p. 262). Post goes on to argue: 'By sanctioning in this resolution [833] the decisions of the IKBDC just mentioned, the Security Council has produced the same constitutive effect' (ibid., p. 263). Moreover, although Iraq initially protested, it eventually accepted the final decision of the Commission in a letter to the President of the Security Council dated 12 November 1994 (UN Doc. S/1994/1288).

exercise of a judicial function to be resolved by a judicial organ: either the 'principal judicial organ' of the United Nations—the International Court of Justice—or by a subsidiary organ established by, for example, the Security Council as a judicial tribunal to hear the case.

(c) *United Nations finances*

The International Court of Justice in the *Expenses* case found that Article 17 of the Charter vested in the General Assembly the 'control over the finances of the Organization, and the levying of apportioned amounts of the expenses of the Organization in order to enable it [the Assembly] to carry out the functions of the Organization as a whole acting through its principal organs and such subsidiary organs as may be established under the authority of Article 22 or Article 29'.[272] Moreover, the Court found that Article 17 gave the General Assembly an exclusive right to consider and approve the UN budget.[273] Accordingly, a UN principal organ cannot purport to establish a subsidiary organ which has control over its finances such that it can determine its own budget, since the subsidiary would thus be capable of usurping the power of the General Assembly under Article 17 to decide the budget of the Organization.[274] The delimitation of powers under the Charter with respect to the authority to determine and apportion the UN budget means that an essential precondition for an entity to be lawfully established as a UN subsidiary organ is that the General Assembly exercise complete control over its budget. An entity which exercises exclusive control over its finances cannot be considered as a UN subsidiary organ.[275]

The controversial issue which arises from the consequences of this delimitation of powers is whether the General Assembly can use its exclusive control over the UN budget to limit the competence of the other principal organs to establish subsidiary organs. Klepacki argues

[272] *ICJ Reports*, 1962, p. 162.

[273] The Court observed: 'Article 17 is the only article in the Charter which refers to budgetary authority or to the power to apportion expenses, or otherwise to raise revenue, except for Articles 33 and 35, paragraph 3, of the Statute of the Court which have no bearing on the point here under discussion' (ibid.). The one possible exception to this position is where the General Assembly establishes a subsidiary organ to carry out judicial functions which may lead to costs being incurred by the UN where the General Assembly has intended that the decision of the subsidiary organ is to be final and binds even itself. Thus in the *Administrative Tribunal* case the Court dismissed the argument that it was not possible to establish a subsidiary organ which could in effect impose legal limitations on the General Assembly's express Charter powers to determine the UN budget. The Court concluded on this point: 'The Court therefore considers that the assignment of the budgetary function to the General Assembly cannot be regarded as conferring upon it the right to refuse to give effect to the obligation arising out of an award of the Administrative Tribunal' (*ICJ Reports*, 1954, p. 59). See further, on the general issue of decisions by subsidiary organs which bind their principal organ, n. 170 and corresponding text, above.

[274] The importance of this budgetary control is emphasized when one considers that the General Assembly fully funds and, more importantly, fully controls the budget of United Nations treaty bodies: for example, the UN Human Rights Committee. See further, in respect of these UN treaty bodies, n. 84, above.

[275] This view has been confirmed by the UN Legal Counsel when determining the status of the

this in general terms when he contends that if the activity of a subsidiary organ involves costs to be borne by the whole organization, then the consent of the 'top organ is, as a rule, required. In this manner the top organ to some extent controls the setting up of these subsidiary organs.'[276] Klepacki later states that the 'top organ' is the most important of the principal organs. It is, however, unclear whether this 'top organ' is the principal organ responsible for setting the budget of the international organization. In the context of the UN it seems that this may be the case: the UN Legal Counsel has stated:

the pre-eminence of the General Assembly as the most significant of the principal organs flows from its power of the purse (Article 17) and its power to discuss 'any matters . . . relating to the powers and functions of any organ' (Article 10).[277]

If this is indeed the case, then in the context of the United Nations the consent—albeit not formally expressed—of the General Assembly would be needed every time a principal organ wanted to establish a subsidiary organ. It should be emphasized that there is of course no formal procedure whereby the Council must approach the Assembly for the approval of the establishment of individual subsidiary organs. However, the point is that the Assembly can, by virtue of the delimitation of Charter powers in this area, exercise a degree of control over the activities of, for example, the Security Council.[278] So that while in theory the Security Council may have unchallengeable authority to establish a particular subsidiary organ, if, however, the General Assembly does not apportion any funds for its operation out of the UN budget, then in practice it will be able to survive in name only. An example of how this

Special Commission established by General Assembly Resolution 38/161 of 19 December 1983 entitled 'Process of Preparation of the Environmental Perspective to the Year 2000 and Beyond'. He observed: 'After careful consideration and largely because the Commission, once established, is to have complete control over its finances, we have come to the conclusion that the Commission, which has adopted the name "World Commission on Environment and Development", should not be considered as having the status of a United Nations organ or as being a part of the United Nations' (*UN Juridical Yearbook*, 1984, p. 163). Cf. Morgenstern, who argues that often an important reason for the establishment of subsidiary bodies is to separate their finances, largely based on voluntary contributions, from those of the parent (principal) organization (*Legal Problems of International Organizations* (1986), pp. 23–4).

[276] Klepacki, op. cit. above (n. 1), p. 17.

[277] *UN Juridical Yearbook*, 1982, p. 190. The fact that the General Assembly is the only plenary organ of the UN may also be of some importance in arguing that it is Klepacki's 'top organ'. Moreover, Simma's *Commentary* states: 'It may be maintained that the General Assembly enjoys a primary position among the principal organs because Article 15 [of the Charter] provides that it shall receive and consider reports from the other principal organs' (Simma, op. cit. above (n. 1), p. 196). However, the commentary goes on to note: 'but this right of information does not include the right of the General Assembly to issue directives to the other principal organs where there is no such authority under other articles of the Charter' (ibid.).

[278] This is however qualitatively different from saying that the Assembly has the competence to question the way in which the Security Council has exercised its powers. Serge Sur, for example, argues that under the Charter the General Assembly does not have the competence to question the

could occur nearly arose in the case of the establishment of the War Crimes Tribunal for the former Yugoslavia. The Security Council in Resolutions 808 and 827 established the Tribunal as a measure to assist in the restoration of international peace and security in the former Yugoslavia.[279] However, in Article 32 of the Statute of the Tribunal the Security Council stated that the expenses of the Tribunal 'shall be borne by the regular budget of the United Nations in accordance with Article 17 of the Charter of the United Nations'.[280] A note by the UN Secretariat to the General Assembly concerning this issue provides:

In the view of the Secretary-General . . . there was no legal bar to the Security Council reaching its own conclusions as to the appropriate financing of the International Tribunal and including a provision on the matter in the Statute which it adopted. Nevertheless, such conclusions are without prejudice to the authority of the General Assembly under the Charter to consider and approve the budget of the Organization and to apportion the expenses of the Organization among its Members.[281]

However, in the view of the General Assembly this clearly impinged on its sole prerogative to make determinations regarding the UN budget. The General Assembly voiced its discontent when it '[e]xpress[ed] concern that advice given to the Security Council by the Secretariat on the nature of the financing of the International Tribunal did not respect the role of the General Assembly as set out in Article 17 of the Charter'.[282] As a result the General Assembly did not initially pledge full financing of the Tribunal.[283] Although the General Assembly subsequently agreed to continue to finance the activities of the Tribunal, the

---

way in which the Security Council exercises its competence, especially under Chapter VII (loc. cit. above (n. 243), p. 7). See also, Fitzmaurice, loc. cit. above (n. 256). Cf., however, the statement by the Venezuelan representative at the San Francisco Conference in the context of matters pertaining to international peace and security who claimed for the General Assembly the right to control the Security Council in order to prevent it from transgressing established legal principles (*Documents of the United Nations Conference on International Organization*, vol. 4, p. 253 (General Doc. 2, G/7(d)(1), of 5 May 1945, p. 12), and ibid., vol. 11, p. 768 (Commission III, Security Council Doc. 360, III/1/16, 15 May 1945, p. 4)). Cf. also Koskenniemi, who argues that the General Assembly should use whatever powers it has at its disposal to impose restraint on the Council in order to achieve international justice in certain cases (loc. cit. above (n. 202)); and Alvarez, loc. cit. above (n. 185), p. 10.

[279] Above, n. 62 and corresponding text.

[280] The Secretary-General in his report on the establishment of the Tribunal stated that this provision is without prejudice to the role of the General Assembly in the administrative and budgetary aspects of the question of establishing the Tribunal (S/25704, para. 21).

[281] A/47/1002, para. 12. Note, moreover, the earlier practice of the Security Council when, while establishing subsidiary organs, it indicated the method of financing of the subsidiary: see further 'Article 29', *Repertory of Practice of United Nations Organs*, Supplement No. 3, (1972), p. 81 at p. 84, para. 12.

[282] A/47/1014, para. 3.

[283] The Assembly only '[e]ndorse[d] the recommendation of the Advisory Committee on Administrative and Budgetary Questions to authorize the Secretary-General to enter into commitments in an amount not exceeding 500,000 United States dollars to provide for the immediate and urgent requirements of the Tribunal for its initial activities' (A/47/104, para. 5).

emphasis placed by it on retaining its sole prerogative over UN finances is significant. The Assembly's sole competence in respect of UN finances may in the future be used to restrict the effective establishment of subsidiary organs by the Council.

However, in the case of the exercise of Chapter VII powers by the Council, this possibility seems remote owing to the emphasis the Charter places on the maintenance of international peace and security and the Council's primary role therein. This was of considerable importance to the International Court in the *Expenses* case when it found that the Security Council could establish a peace-keeping force, that 'it must be within the power of the Security Council to police a situation even though it does not resort to an enforcement action against a State',[284] and, moreover, that the costs of such an operation would constitute 'expenses of the Organization within the meaning of Article 17, paragraph 2'.[285] Moreover, it may be argued that if the Security Council decides to establish a subsidiary organ which it deems necessary for the maintenance or restoration of international peace, then UN member States are under an obligation under Article 25 of the Charter to carry out this decision. Thus the argument would run that when voting in the Assembly, States should vote in favour of the provision of funds to enable the effective establishment of such a subsidiary organ. In formal terms, however, there would be no obligation on the General Assembly, but only on the member States of which it is composed. Such an idea is not new to the law of the United Nations. When the Security Council makes a decision under Chapter VII of the Charter, this does not *per se* bind other international organizations.[286] However, UN member States are placed under an obligation by Articles 25 and 48(2) of the Charter to vote or act in these international organizations in a manner which will enable the implementation of the Council's decision.[287] It is, nonetheless, contended that the obligation under Article 25 does not apply to States when voting in the General Assembly on the question of the budget of the Organization. The obligation on States under Article 25 is that they 'carry out the decisions of the Security Council *in accordance with the present Charter*'.[288] In the case of the establishment of a UN subsidiary organ, it has already been explained that the Charter requires that the General Assembly apportion funds from the UN budget for its effective establishment. Moreover, the provisions of the Charter dealing with the right of States to vote in the General Assembly place no restriction on the exercise of a State's individual discretion, as part of its sovereign

[284] *ICJ Reports*, 1962, p. 151, at pp. 165–7.
[285] Ibid.
[286] See also Simma, op. cit. above (n. 1), p. 653.
[287] For examples of this practice, see n. 85, above. See further Cot and Pellet, op. cit. above (n. 1), p. 751; and Simma, op. cit. above (n. 1), p. 653.
[288] Emphasis added.

prerogative, to vote as it deems fit. Accordingly, to require States to vote in the General Assembly in a particular way would not be in accordance with the Charter. Thus States are free to vote in the General Assembly as they deem fit when deciding whether to apportion funds for a UN subsidiary organ.

V. Concluding Remarks

The flexibility that UN subsidiary organs provide for the principal organs is of considerable importance to their being able to act effectively and within the law. In particular, the use by UN principal organs of their general authority to establish subsidiary organs to exercise functions which they do not themselves possess may be recalled. As such, UN principal organs should increasingly resort to subsidiary organs to assist them in their work.

The increasing establishment and usage of subsidiary organs in a variety of diverse areas is an indication of the greater degree of *de facto* international governance being undertaken by the United Nations and its Specialized Agencies. As such, the legal framework governing the establishment of subsidiary organs by these organizations will prove to be of considerable importance to States and others whose rights and duties will increasingly be decided upon by these organs. Moreover, the law pertaining to subsidiary organs may well have wider significance. In particular, what is of interest is how this legal framework may be used by the International Court of Justice if it decides to review the legality of the establishment by, for example, the Security Council of a subsidiary organ. It remains unclear whether the Court does possess such a power of review.[289] If, however, the Court finds that it does and that it has some basis for asserting its jurisdiction in a particular case, then, in the context

---

[289] On the issue of the review by the International Court of the legality of decisions by the Security Council, see further Brownlie, loc. cit. above (n. 227); Bowett, loc. cit. above (n. 230), p. 89; Bedjaoui, *The New World Order and the Security Council: Testing the Legality of Its Acts* (1994); Gowlland-Debbas, 'The Relationship between the International Court of Justice and the Security Council in the Light of the Lockerbie Case', *American Journal of International Law*, 88 (1994), p. 643; Alvarez, loc.cit. above (n. 185); McWhinney, 'The International Court as Emerging Constitutional Court and the Co-ordinate UN Institutions (Especially the Security Council): Implications of the Aerial Incident at Lockerbie', *Canadian Yearbook of International Law*, 30 (1992), p. 261; Franck, 'The "Powers of Appreciation": Who is the Ultimate Guardian of UN Legality?', *American Journal of International Law*, 86 (1992), p. 519; Reisman, 'The Constitutional Crisis in the United Nations', ibid., 87 (1993), p. 83; Herdegen, 'The 'Constitutionalization of the UN Security System', *Vanderbilt Journal of Transnational Law*, 27 (1994), p. 135; and Watson, 'Constitutionalism, Judicial Review, and the World Court', *Harvard International Law Journal*, 34 (1993), p. 1.

of the establishment of subsidiary organs, the legal framework governing this process may well provide an important corpus of law by reference to which the Court can review the legality of Security Council action.[290]

---

[290] For other grounds which may constitute a basis for review by the Court, see further Brownlie, loc. cit. above (n. 227); and Bowett, loc. cit. above (n. 230).

NOTE

THE EXTERNAL REPRESENTATION OF THE DOMINIONS, 1919–1948: ITS ROLE IN THE UNRAVELLING OF THE BRITISH EMPIRE*

By LORNA LLOYD *and* ALAN JAMES‡

Throughout the inter-war period there was considerable uncertainty about the exact international status of the self-governing British dominions. Not least was this so because Britain wished to discourage any moves which threatened the unity of her empire. Reflecting both these circumstances, the arrangements made by the dominions for their representation abroad tended either not to follow normal diplomatic lines or to do so only after having surmounted some difficulties. However, the important principle was established that they were entitled to set up the usual sort of diplomatic missions in foreign (i.e. non-British-Commonwealth) States. This and associated developments in the dominions' external representation were pointers to their inexorable assumption of full independence, and may also have encouraged their own and others' recognition of the fundamental alteration in their status which was under way. Thus by 1939 a series of seemingly esoteric events in the field of diplomatic protocol had contributed notably to the unravelling of the British empire. It only remained for the Second World War to ratify, as it were, this important development.

INTRODUCTION

Somewhat in keeping with Britain's lack of a written constitution, the developments which brought her 'old' dominions to independence took place in a conceptual fog. Throughout the inter-war period there was confusion in many quarters about the precise status of these 'self-governing' entities—Canada, Australia, New Zealand, South Africa and, after 1922, the Irish Free State.[1] Even those dominions which were pushing hard for change were not disposed to

* ©Lorna Lloyd and Alan James, 1997.

‡ Department of International Relations, Keele University. The authors would like to acknowledge their gratitude to Professor Norman Hillmer for his valuable comments on an earlier draft.

[1] Newfoundland and India are excluded from this article. Newfoundland was a dominion in 1919, but did not participate in international relations. Its financial difficulties led to the re-assumption of direct British control in 1933 (and it became a Canadian Province in 1949). India, although enjoying a measure of international personality from 1919 onwards, was not a dominion until its independence in 1947.

press for fundamental issues to be fully clarified. For her part, Britain had no wish to examine too closely the status of the dominions, let alone to advance it. This lack of clarity reflects what some might regard as a characteristic British way of doing things. The wider world looked on in some bemusement and, not infrequently, with suspicion. Eventually, however, it became clear that what had been going on was not some devious British scheme but the unravelling of a most important section of the modern world's greatest empire.

One area in which this conceptual uncertainty manifested itself concerned the 'diplomatic unity' of the empire and, concomitantly, the external representation of the dominions. Until the First World War the British empire was unquestionably a single (and a cohesive) unit. This was not an insuperable bar to the establishment by the dominions of external offices. Just as a commercial concern may despatch and maintain an agent abroad, so also could the dominions seek to do likewise. As long as the limited extent of their agents' competence was unambiguously established, Britain did not object. No threat was presented to the unity of the empire, or to Britain's controlling role over it. Before 1914 the dominions' agents definitely did not enjoy diplomatic status, but once the underlying political reality was such as to raise the issue of whether they should, in some manner, be seen as diplomats, concern began to be expressed in Whitehall.

The competence to send and receive diplomatic missions is limited to territorial entities which have sovereign status. Despite the apparent implication of the oft-used phrase 'the right of legation', a sovereign State possesses neither the legal right to establish a diplomatic mission in another State, nor the duty to receive such a mission. The setting up of diplomatic missions, like the condition of being in diplomatic relations on which it is premised, is contingent upon the agreement of both the sending and the receiving States. But no question will be raised regarding their formal capacity to make these moves. The possession of sovereign statehood entitles an entity to engage in diplomatic activity.

The smooth operation of this system is dependent upon clarity regarding the nature of sovereignty and upon its individual manifestations. Although much comment on the matter suggests the contrary, there is no uncertainty at all— among States—as to what it is which makes them, in international terms, sovereign. Constitutional independence is the essential requirement.[2] And as this condition is in almost all twentieth-century circumstances very easily operationalized and identified, there is hardly ever confusion about whether a particular entity is or is not sovereign. In consequence, fundamental diplomatic arrangements run smoothly.

The emergence on to the diplomatic stage of the self-governing British dominions, however, provides an exception to this statement. Even after the 1931 Statute of Westminster (which decreed that Britain's parliament was no longer entitled to legislate for the dominions except in those areas where they chose to remain subordinate), questions remained about their exact international status. Two of them—Australia and New Zealand—expressly requested that the Statute should not be applied to them until they enacted legislation to that effect, which they did not do until 1942 and 1947 respectively. As to the others, the

---

[2] See Alan James, *Sovereign Statehood: The Basis of International Society* (London: Allen and Unwin, 1986), pp. 22–31.

imperial *inter se* doctrine, which declared that intra-Commonwealth relations were of a different nature from relations with foreign States, meant that—within as well as outside the empire—there was still obscurity about the position of the dominions. The most striking manifestation of this situation was the lack of clarity which existed throughout the inter-war years as to whether the King— the head of State of all the dominions[3]—could in his several capacities be at the same time both at war and at peace. In this context it is not surprising that there was also initial uncertainty about whether the dominions had the capacity to make diplomatic appointments, and whether their existing external agents enjoyed diplomatic status.

This situation was fostered and accentuated by two powerful political factors. On the one hand, most of the dominions were unclear about the precise international status which they sought. Furthermore, they did not agree about the speed at which they should travel to whatever destination might lie at the end of the constitutional road along which they were straggling. Thus they never presented Britain with anything remotely resembling a united front about the status of their external representatives.

On the other hand, Britain was prepared to make concessions to the dominions but she was reluctant to approve arrangements which could be seen as diluting the dominions' position within the empire. With the wisdom of a seasoned political campaigner, Britain was not outrightly obstructionist. But she discouraged decisive steps, being uneasy about the implications for her inter- national reputation and role of a heightened standing for dominion representa- tives. Of course, to the extent that Britain's policy-makers recognized the mother country's decline, their attitude was also a reflection of the truism that States on the way down in international politics rarely seek to give the process an added head of steam.

None the less, there *were* significant developments during the inter-war period with regard to the diplomatic status of the dominions' external representatives. As these developments were fragmented, and had on the whole to do with what was generally perceived to be the rather esoteric realm of protocol, they did not achieve the notice which they deserved. They were important for three connected reasons. Firstly, the grant of clear diplomatic status to the head of a dominion's external mission was hardly compatible with that dominion being part of an empire. Secondly, the grant of a status which was only doubtfully diplomatic nevertheless suggested that some loosening of the imperial bond was under way. And, thirdly, the provision of places on the international stage for representatives of either kind afforded them an ongoing opportunity to express views which were distinguishable from those of Britain, thus putting into question the tightness of the relationship between Britain and the relevant dominions. There was also the real possibility that the attractiveness of such freedom of expression would encourage its increased use.

---

[3] There were, however, Irish reservations on this point after the coming into force in 1937 of a new Irish Constitution. It was this Constitution which led to the Irish Free State becoming 'Eire'.

I. Dominion Representation at the Paris Peace Conference

Representatives of the dominions, or of colonial territories which were to unite into or become dominions, had attended international conferences and participated in international organizations since the middle of the nineteenth century. But these activities did not relate to high politics, and in no way implied that the empire was not a single diplomatic entity. Moreover, such representatives were usually members of, or attached to, the British delegation. On those occasions where the dominions were represented in their own right, there was no thought in any quarter that this was because they had somehow become independent, or that a form of diplomatic status had thereby been conferred on their spokesmen.

However, the notable contribution which the dominions made to the war effort in 1914–18 meant that it was hardly possible to deny them a part in the subsequent peace settlement. In January 1915 Britain expressly promised to consult the dominions about the terms of peace, and did so again in 1917 when establishing the Imperial War Cabinet (which gave the dominions a voice in the conduct of the war). In 1917, moreover, the Imperial Conference had proclaimed the right of the 'autonomous nations of the Imperial Commonwealth' to have 'an adequate voice in foreign policy'.[4] The time had passed for Britain to be the sole representative at the peace conference of the entire empire. Thus, when her Prime Minister, Lloyd George, urged dominion leaders to proceed swiftly to London to participate in deliberations 'to determine the line to be taken at the [peace] conferences by the British[sic] Delegates',[5] Sir Robert Borden of Canada swiftly rejoined that 'new conditions must be met by new precedents': the Canadian press, people and Cabinet all required that Canada should be separately represented.[6]

Britain was unenthusiastic about this, and the idea emerged that dominion representatives might be included in the British delegation. Australia and Canada objected vociferously, and were supported by the other dominions. The upshot was that the Imperial War Cabinet agreed that the dominions should have the same number of representatives as Belgium—one of (in the unashamedly hierarchical terminology of the time) the 'Lesser Allies'. In addition, it endorsed the Canadian Prime Minister's proposal for a 'British Empire panel' that could provide alternate members of the British delegation. If the dominions appear to have been trying to have their cake and eat it, it was a reflection of what they were 'primarily interested in at Paris'—'their own status in the Empire and the world. They were in a position to do something about

---

[4] Resolution IX, *Extracts from Proceedings and Papers laid before the Imperial War Conference, 1917–18* (Cmd. 8566), p. 61.

[5] Telegram from Lloyd George to dominion Prime Ministers, 27 October 1918; quoted in 'Introduction' to R.A. Mackay (ed.), *Documents on Canadian External Relations*, vol. 2, *The Paris Peace Conference of 1919* (Ottawa: The Queen's Printer for Department of External Affairs, 1969), p. vi.

[6] Telegram from Borden to Lloyd George, secret, private, personal, 29 October 1918; quoted in ibid., p. viii, n. 1.

their status, and they pursued this object with determination and considerable success.'[7]

First, however, Lloyd George had to overcome the distinct unease of the American President that the proposed scheme would give additional votes to what the latter saw as the British group. Wilson gave way when told that the conference was not going to operate on that sort of basis. The question then turned to the number of representatives which the dominions should have. It was agreed that Canada, Australia and South Africa should each have two (as would the different-again case of India), and New Zealand one. However, the dominions were not separately represented on any of the general commissions of the conference. Instead, they were part of the British delegation, which was now termed that of the 'British Empire' rather than that of 'Great Britain'. (It was, in effect, a continuation of the wartime Imperial War Cabinet.)

This arrangement meant that the dominions were not separately listed as parties to the various peace treaties of 1919. It was just the 'British Empire' which was so described. But in the lists of plenipotentiaries their delegations were included in the Treaty of Versailles in the following way. 'His Majesty the King of the United Kingdom of Great Britain and Ireland and of the British Dominions beyond the Seas, Emperor of India' is listed as represented by named individuals. Then the words 'And for the Dominion of Canada' introduce the names of the Canadian representatives (as representatives of the most senior dominion), and so on. At the end of the Treaty, signatures appear in the same order as in the list of plenipotentiaries, so that each dominion (except Newfoundland) could be said to have signed in her own right.[8]

But what that right was, exactly, remained obscure. Not everyone would go as far as the analyst who later declared that the dominions had secured the 'right to participate as sovereign States'.[9] Another, also looking back, spoke of the empire delegation as 'a group of separate and almost sovereign states, with the United Kingdom *primus inter pares*'.[10] Assertive dominion nationalists might have thought that way, but contemporary British observers hardly saw the United Kingdom in such a light. In truth, and in keeping with current developments in imperial relations, the British empire delegation was 'an anomaly in terms of international diplomacy'.[11] It was a 'freak', in the sense that 'the British Commonwealth appeared both as several nations and as a united Empire'—and spoke in that dual way, too.[12] *The Times*, after commenting along these lines, added, a trifle smugly, that it was 'No wonder that the technical intricacies of

[7] C. P. Stacey, *Canada and the Age of Conflict*, vol. 1, *1867–1921* (Toronto, Buffalo, London: University of Toronto Press, 1984 [first published 1979]), p. 251.

[8] H. A. Smith, *Great Britain and the Law of Nations. A Selection of Documents Illustrating the Views of the Government in the United Kingdom upon Matters of International Law* (London: P.S. King & Son, 1932), p. 51.

[9] F. S. Marston, *The Peace Conference of 1919. Organization and Procedure* (London, New York, Toronto: Oxford University Press for Royal Institute of International Affairs, 1944), p. 62.

[10] R. C. Snelling, 'Peacemaking, 1919: Australia, New Zealand and the British Empire Delegation at Versailles', *The Journal of Imperial and Commonwealth History*, vol. 4, no. 1 (October 1975), p. 15.

[11] Ibid.

[12] C. A. W. Manning, *The Policies of the British Dominions in the League of Nations* (London: Oxford University Press, 1932), pp. 13–14.

[the dominions'] position puzzle foreign observers'.[13] There is something of a similar air in the comment of the British Cabinet Secretary that 'We [sic] have really given the Dominions a most magnificent show'.[14]

Technically, this last observer might have been correct in claiming that the dominions' performance was premised on British liberality. But in political as in diplomatic terms the dominions had undoubtedly taken a huge stride forward. The structure of the empire's delegation was 'a striking confirmation of the progress already achieved in the remodelling of imperial relations since the outbreak of war'.[15] It was unlikely that its full diplomatic implications could long be denied. Indeed, things would never be the same again.

II. Dominion Representation at the League of Nations

The most immediate, and most obvious, consequence of the dominions' representation at the Peace Conference in relation to their diplomatic standing was that they (Newfoundland again excepted) became founder—and full—members of the League of Nations. Britain had not envisaged this. However, when Australia and Canada protested that their exclusion would be unacceptable, no problems were raised about dominion membership, nor over that of India. The League's Covenant was Part I of both the Treaty of Versailles (the German Peace Treaty) and the Treaty of Saint-Germain (the Austrian). Accordingly, the provisions for membership in the League mirrored the arrangements which had been made for the dominions' signature of the treaties, which in turn reflected the nature of their representation in the peace negotiations. The League's original members, an annex to the Covenant declared, included the signatories (on the victorious side only) of the treaty of peace. They were then listed alphabetically (commencing, in the English version, with the 'United States of America'—an expression of that country's 'happy philological discovery' at the Hague Conference of 1907 that for purposes of diplomatic protocol its official name began with the letter 'A'![16]). Among them was not 'Great Britain', but the 'British Empire'; and indented under this name came the dominions in order of seniority, the oldest, Canada, coming first.[17]

There was, therefore, some ambiguity about the exact international status of these members, the difference between them and the other members being 'symbolically indicated by a quarter of an inch of difference in type alignment'.[18] The existence of such a difference was perhaps also hinted at in an Annex to the League of Nations Covenant, which distinguished between the Covenant's

[13] Editorial, 30 January 1919.
[14] Hankey to Esher, 10 February 1919, Hankey papers, Cambridge, Churchill College Archives Centre 4/11.
[15] Snelling, loc. cit. above (n. 10).
[16] Lord Gore-Booth (ed.), Satow's Guide to Diplomatic Practice (London and New York: Longman, 5th edition, 1979), p. 25. It is unclear whether Satow is here quoting J. B. Scott (Le Francais, langue diplomatique).
[17] The Covenant of the League of Nations with a Commentary thereon, Cmd. 151, HMSO, Misc. No. 3 (1919), p. 13.
[18] David Hunter Miller (President Wilson's Legal Adviser at the Peace Conference); quoted in F. H. Soward, Canada and the League of Nations (Ottawa: League of Nations Society in Canada, 1931), p. 12.

'Signatories' and certain non-signatory 'States' which were invited to accede to it. Furthermore, Article 1 of the Covenant referred to the possible addition to the League's membership of 'Any fully self-governing State, Dominion, or Colony'. Thus any dominion claim that its membership was indicative of its sovereignty, and hence of its competence to engage in normal diplomatic relations, would carry something less than complete conviction. And it may be confidently assumed that when the British Government spoke of the Covenant as a 'solemn agreement between sovereign States',[19] it was thinking only of those members whose names had not suffered the quarter-of-an-inch indentation.

It may be added that when the Irish Free State became a member of the League in 1923, it did so (at least from the League's point of view) as a dominion. That was the status Britain gave it in 1922. And the report of the relevant League committee on the Free State's application for membership noted that it was 'a Dominion forming part of the British Empire upon the same conditions as the other Dominions which are already members of the League'.[20]

But unquestionably, whatever their wider constitutional status, the dominions were no less members of the League than any other member. They might have been 'lately developed entities', but it remained the position that they shared 'with their elders the dignity and responsibilities of League membership'.[21] And, it may be added, the opportunities. For the League was a godsend to those dominions who wanted to emphasize and extend their diplomatic personality. The majority did.

From the start this was something which concerned Britain. The Colonial Secretary, Viscount Milner (the renowned imperialist), publicly expressed the view that 'Anything like dissension between different British [sic] States in the Councils of the League would be so overwhelmingly condemned by public opinion in all of them that it should be an easy task for statesmanship to avoid it'.[22] But in private he was not so sanguine. In a circular telegram to Governors-General in 1920, he warned:

To us it seems essential that arrangements should be devised without delay which will ensure that on doubtful or controversial issues, we should present a united front, and that any differences of point of view . . . should be previously discussed and harmonised between ourselves. There is otherwise a real danger . . . [of an outcome which] would seriously weaken in international affairs the position and influence of the British Empire, and could hardly fail to have an unfortunate reaction on its internal relations.[23]

Accordingly, Britain suggested that, with a view to the harmonisation of policy, all imperial communications with Geneva should go through an office attached to the (British) Cabinet's Secretariat. (In fact, the League Secretariat had initially thought in terms of dealing with the dominions through London.)

---

[19] Cmd. 151 (above, n. 17), p. 13.

[20] Quoted in Manning, op. cit. above (n. 12), p. 8.

[21] Ibid, p. 9.

[22] Quoted in H. Duncan Hall, *The British Commonwealth of Nations. A Study of its Past and Future Development* (London: Methuen, no date: ?1921), p. 344. Also Manning, op. cit. above (n. 12), p. 129.

[23] Colonial Secretary to Governor-General, paraphrase telegram, secret, 22 January 1920, in Lovell C. Clark (ed.), *Documents on Canadian External Relations*, vol. 3, *1919–1925* (Ottawa: Department of External Affairs, 1970) (hereinafter *DCER*, vol. 3), p. 392.

bound, sooner or later, to cause trouble',[24] the dominions would have none of it. They correctly saw that it would smother their emerging identities, and insisted on communicating individually with Geneva. They were, in 1920, agreeable to Britain transmitting to the League's Secretary-General the names of their representatives to the Assembly. (Britain did this in separate letters, since a single letter listing British and dominion delegates might 'accentuate the six-fold representation of the British Empire'.)[25] But as the Foreign Office Legal Adviser had anticipated, only India and New Zealand were agreeable to Britain, rather than the dominion Governors-General, issuing the letters of credence which each delegate had to carry to Geneva. And as to their presentation, it was 'generally agreed' at a meeting prior to the first League Assembly that this 'should be left to the representatives of the Dominions and India to arrange as they thought best'.[26]

In these possibly arcane ways, League membership enabled those dominions who wished to do so to underline their individual diplomatic personalities. Another such device was the appointment of permanent missions to the League—which, in time, were established by most members. The Irish Free State made the running, establishing an office in Geneva in the summer of 1921, even before the negotiation of the Irish 'Treaty' (which, in the face of fierce British protests, was registered by the Irish with the League). Then, in 1924, Canada appointed a Permanent Advisory Officer to Geneva to represent its interests at the League (and at the International Labour Organization). The position of Commonwealth representatives was not a normal diplomatic one, in that they were not accredited to a head of State and—unlike some other representatives—were not given diplomatic rank by their own governments. In consequence, they did not automatically receive the usual privileges and immunities which were enjoyed by diplomats. But the Swiss Government had very early accepted that it was dealing with at least a quasi-diplomatic situation, and in 1922 granted diplomatic status to the permanent delegates. And, as the first such Canadian said, 'I soon found my diplomatic functions were legion'.[27] It was he who, during the 1926 crisis over membership of the League Council, originated the idea of allowing States to be re-elected so that those who could regularly count on sufficient votes would become 'semi-permanent' members of the Council. He became 'acting dean of the Genevan diplomatic corps [sic]'.[28] He often represented his country at important League meetings. In fact, he was representing his State in much the same way as an ambassador would—but in a novel, multilateral, environment. In 1938 the title of the post was changed to that of Permanent Delegate of Canada to the League of Nations, thus bringing it into line with similar representatives of other States. By this time South Africa had also made such an appointment.

---

[24] Sir James Allen at British Empire Delegation (hereinafter BED), 39th Conference, secret, 8 November 1920, London, Public Record Office (hereinafter PRO), W 2692/22/98 FO 371/7033.

[25] Minute by Hurst (Foreign Office Legal Adviser), 4 November 1920, PRO, W 1662/160/98 FO 371/5479.

[26] BED, 39th Conference, 8 November 1920.

[27] Walter Alexander Riddell, *World Security by Conference* (Toronto, Halifax, Vancouver: The Ryerson Press, 1947), p. 28.

[28] H. Gordon Skilling, *Canadian Representation Abroad: From Agency to Embassy* (Toronto: The Ryerson Press, 1945), p. 168.

The establishment of permanent missions to the League by some Commonwealth countries, and the treatment accorded them by Switzerland, helped to establish the idea that the dominions were entitled to engage in the usual sort of diplomatic activity. It was, however, in the formal meetings of the League that they were best able to draw attention to their diplomatic individuality. They were seated apart from Britain, on an alphabetical basis. They kept in very close touch with Britain, but by no means always publicly agreed with her, or with each other. (Reference was made in 1932 to a facetious comment asserting that it was only on the question of whether to establish an Institute of Intellectual Co-operation that 'Great Britain and the Dominions voted solidly: they all voted against it'.)[29] In 1929 intra-Commonwealth differences over the signature of the Optional Clause of the Statute of the Permanent Court of International Justice resulted in the Irish Free State storming out of Commonwealth discussions.[30] Sometimes it was a dominion, rather than (as was usual) Britain, which called a meeting to discuss a specific item on the Assembly's agenda. Irish representatives even went so far as to address the Assembly in French, to emphasize their separateness from Britain.[31] And after Canada was elected to the Council in 1927, it became accepted that a dominion would occupy a non-permanent seat. (Dominion eligibility for Council membership had been explicitly stated in 1919.) Indeed, when the Irish Free State ran (successfully) for Council membership in 1930, she did not do so as a member of the dominion group.

It was not always easy for Britain to take on board the fact that the imperial ground rules were changing in these sorts of ways. In London in November 1924, in his first speech as Foreign Secretary, Austen Chamberlain said that

The first thoughts of any Englishman on appointment to the Office of Foreign Secretary must be that he speaks in the name not of Great Britain only, but of the British Dominions beyond the seas . . . Our interests are one. Our intercourse must be intimate and constant, and we must speak with one voice in the councils of the world.[32]

He proceeded to do just that at Geneva, saying in the Council that he spoke the minds not of one but of six governments. Canada pointed out that he could not make such a claim without specific authorization.[33] In 1925 a British delegate appeared, in one of the League's commissions, to be speaking for the whole Empire. The dominion delegations met with Britain's to clear the matter up.[34]

---

[29] Manning, op. cit. above (n. 12), p. 69.

[30] See Lorna Lloyd, ' "Equality means freedom to differ": Canada, Britain and the World Court in the 1920s', *Diplomacy and Statecraft*, vol. 7, no. 2 (July 1996), and idem, *Peace through Law. Britain and the World Court in the 1920s* (Royal Historical Society, *Studies in History*, forthcoming).

[31] Max Beloff, *Imperial Sunset*, vol. 2, *Dream of Commonwealth 1921–1942* (London: Macmillan, 1989), p. 78, n. 10. When the Irish Free State took up League membership, President Cosgrave 'made his opening speech in Gaelic, to the dismay of some members of his delegation who had no idea what he was talking about'!: Vernon Bartlett, *This is My Life* (London: Evergreen Books, 1941), pp. 129–30.

[32] Sir Charles Petrie, *The Life and Letters of Sir Austen Chamberlain* (London: Cassell, 1940), vol. 2, p. 251.

[33] Telegram from Mackenzie King to Chamberlain, 8 March 1925; quoted in C. P. Stacey, *Canada and the Age of Conflict*, vol. 2, *1921–1948. The Mackenzie King Era* (Toronto, Buffalo, London: University of Toronto Press, 1981), p. 63.

[34] See Minutes of the First Committee, *League of Nations Official Journal*, Special Supplement No. 34 (1925), pp. 22 and 23–4; Lorna Lloyd, 'Le Sénateur Dandurand, pionnier du règlement pacifique des différends', *Études Internationales*, vol. 23, no. 3 (September 1992), p. 606.

The same sort of statement by Chamberlain in 1926 led to strong dominion protests.[35] In 1929 the failure of Britain's (Labour) Prime Minister to appreciate that he represented only *one* of His Majesty's governments at Geneva, and his paternal attitude towards the others, elicited much resentment.[36]

This last event upset even Australia. However, generally she was content to lead a quiet life in Geneva, and to stick closely to Britain's line. Indeed, her cultural identification with and sense of strategic dependence on Britain 'could occasionally surface in quite extraordinary expressions of colonial self-efface-ment'.[37] New Zealand went further in this direction, having no desire at all to cut an independent figure. William Massey, who as Prime Minister had attended the Peace Conference, took this approach to the point of believing that the dominions should not have been admitted to the League. He would have been content with the right to transmit views to Britain on the various questions that arose.

The other dominions, however, consciously used their membership in the League to advance their international status. They might have started out in a category which was distinct from—and in a sense inferior to—that of the other members. But no one could deny them their right to exercise all the prerogatives of membership. By so doing, they greatly strengthened their claim to be seen as belonging in the same category as the rest. Lesser States, in some respects maybe, but States nonetheless. The Genevan efforts in this direction of Canada, South Africa, and the Irish Free State thus gave a very powerful stimulus to the diplomatic unravelling of the empire. The League might be an unusual edifice in the realm of international diplomacy. But it was not so removed from the rest of diplomatic life as to prevent any conclusions which might be drawn from the dominions' behaviour there from being applied in a broader setting. And, as it happened, diplomatic developments of essentially the same kind had throughout the period been afoot beyond the League.

III. Dominion Representation in London

Following the establishment of the federation (and Dominion) of Canada in 1867, its government had come to see the desirability of having its own representative in London. The Colonial Office agreed, but was unable to contemplate the position having anything in the nature of a diplomatic charac-ter. The outcome was the appointment of a Canadian 'High Commissioner' in 1880. Similar appointments were made by New Zealand in 1905 (two years before the colony achieved dominion status), Australia in 1910, and South Africa in 1911.

In retrospect, the appointment of High Commissioners can be seen as the first

[35] Dandurand to Skelton, 26 June 1926, in Alex I. Inglis (ed.), *Documents on Canadian External Relations*, vol. 4, *1926-30* (Ottawa: Department of External Affairs, 1971) (hereinafter *DCER*, vol. 4), p. 611.

[36] 'Optional Clause. Report of Inter-Commonwealth Discussions received by Canada from Saorstat [Irish] Delegation', 12 September 1929, National Archives of Canada, Ottawa (hereinafter NAC), RG 25, vol. 3424, file 1–1929/10.

[37] W. J. Hudson, *Australia and the League of Nations* (Sydney: Sydney University Press, 1981), p. 112.

step towards the diplomatic unravelling of the empire. Although formally not diplomatic agents, the High Commissioners came, naturally enough, to assume something like a normal representative role. Thus their governments occasionally used High Commissioners to communicate with the Colonial Office, and sometimes High Commissioners took independent initiatives. This was little to the liking of Britain's Governors-General in the dominions, who felt that one of their traditional roles as the official medium of communication between London and the colonies was being undermined.

In the inter-war period these developments were extended and reinforced. Already in 1918 the feisty and abrasive Australian Prime Minister, Hughes, had demanded that dominion Prime Ministers should by-pass not just their Governors-General but also the 'crusted, procrastinating, bureaucratic inefficiency and ineptitude of the Colonial Office',[38] and deal directly with British ministers, including the Prime Minister. Governors-General protested, some vehemently, but to all practical purposes one dominion Prime Minister—Borden—was already corresponding with Lloyd George, and Britain felt obliged to recognize that Hughes had a point. It was therefore allowed that dominion Prime Ministers had the right of direct communication in special circumstances as determined by the dominion Prime Ministers. An important formal step forward had been taken. And when in 1931 dominion ministers gained the right of direct access to the sovereign, and so the right to tender their advice, they gained the same rights as UK ministers.

Meanwhile, those High Commissioners who enjoyed the confidence of their Prime Ministers had increasingly been used by both Britain and the dominions as the channel of communication in important matters. Usually High Commissioners dealt with the Colonial Office (prior to the creation of the Dominions Office in 1925), but they were also entitled to approach most other departments of State. This draws attention to a distinction between ambassadors and High Commissioners, in that the representatives of foreign States could only have dealings with the Foreign Office. This office was the one department to which, initially, High Commissioners had no right of access. However, by the end of 1924 the British Foreign Secretary (and by implication his officials) had agreed to see High Commissioners when they wanted information or consultation. This reflected the fact that essentially a High Commissioner was doing exactly the same kind of representational job, and performing it in exactly the same kind of way, as an ambassador.

Formally speaking, however, High Commissioners and their staffs were not diplomats. The High Commissioners did not present letters of credence. Nor were they grouped with the diplomatic corps for purposes of precedence. And neither they nor the members of their missions received the privileges and immunities which were automatically accorded to those who held that status. Thus, they did not have immunity from demands that they appear in British courts. From the very institution of the office of High Commissioner, these discriminatory aspects had rankled. The first Canadian appointee had complained that 'the only proper definition of his rank, and the only way to ensure

---

[38] Quoted in P. G. Edwards, *Prime Ministers and Diplomats. The Making of Australian Foreign Policy 1901–1949* (Melbourne, Oxford, Wellington, New York: Oxford University Press in association with the Australian Institute of International Affairs, 1983), p. 41. Borden supported him.

proper respect' was to be listed as a diplomat, for 'these "arrogant insulars" turn up their noses' at mere colonials.[39] The thorny question of precedence on formal occasions was raised at the 1923 Imperial Conference, as a result of which it was agreed that High Commissioners should immediately follow Secretaries of State. But this not only carried an implied message about their relationship to the Colonial Secretary (or, as from the establishment of a Dominions Office, the Dominions Secretary); it also placed the High Commissioners well below ambassadors, ministers, and envoys. So far as fiscal privileges were concerned, dominion dissatisfaction resulted in British legislation in 1923 and 1928 which exempted High Commissioners and their staffs from payment of customs duties, British income tax and certain other taxes which were not levied on foreign diplomats. However, in terms of status a significant gulf still existed between High Commissioners and heads of 'normal' diplomatic missions.

In 1927 the Canadian Prime Minister had told his House of Commons that 'the British Government hope to give increasingly to the High Commissioners of the several dominions [sic] that recognition which, in the eyes of the world, will cause them to appear in the light of ambassadors'.[40] This was a case of the wish, rather than the reality, being father to the thought. Britain had no desire at all to see the status of the High Commissioners move in that direction. As late as 1937 very short shrift was given in Whitehall to the news that South Africa proposed to raise the matter at the forthcoming Imperial Conference. She wanted High Commissioners to be used in the same manner as ambassadors (so that all their dealings would be with the Foreign Office) and for them to be assimilated into the diplomatic corps. The Dominions Office regarded South Africa's idea as stupid, an inter-departmental committee drawing attention to what it saw as the clinching objection: that the proposal failed to distinguish between Commonwealth and foreign relations. For its part, the Foreign Office was far from keen to be additionally burdened in this way. In the event, South Africa was dissuaded from bringing the matter up formally.

In any event, by 1939 the High Commissioners had become an established part of London's representational scene. It remained the situation, however, that the grant of diplomatic status was firmly withheld. Accordingly, their position in London was still widely seen as inferior to that of the vast majority of their *de facto* colleagues. On the other hand, there could be no doubting that they enjoyed a quasi-diplomatic presence. Furthermore, by this time the dominions had made substantial (if somewhat unclear) advances on both the constitutional and the political fronts. Full diplomatic status for their representatives was unlikely to be very long in coming.

IV. CONSEQUENTIAL ARRANGEMENTS, AND INTER-DOMINION REPRESENTATION

The use of High Commissioners in London as a channel of communication between dominion governments and the British Government raised a question

---

[39] O. D. Skelton, *The Life and Times of Sir Alexander Tilloch Galt* (Toronto: 1920); quoted in Skilling, op. cit. above (n. 28), p. 97.

[40] Quoted in Skilling, op. cit. above (n. 28), p. 116.

about the role in the dominions of the Governors-General. Thus, by the early 1920s it was becoming clear that the task of representing the King in his dominions was increasingly incompatible with the job of speaking for the British Government of the day. The former role required the Governor-General to be an impartial constitutional guardian. But when, on occasion, he had to take such decisions as whether to grant a Prime Minister's request for the dissolution of parliament, he could be catapulted into a controversy that led—owing to his latter role—to perceptions of partiality. The sensitivity of Canada, South Africa and the Irish Free State about their growing prerogatives only underlined the importance of hiving off the Governor-General's role as spokesman for the British Government, and leaving him solely with the job, in effect, of representative of the King.

As early as the second decade of the century, the Canadian Prime Minister, Borden, had thought the Governor-General's status was already analogous to that of the King. Despite the dissent of Newfoundland and New Zealand, the 1926 Imperial Conference agreed that this was how the role of Governor-General should now be conceived. Before long, Newfoundland entered a kind of constitutional limbo, while New Zealand chose to continue with the old system. As her High Commissioner in London put it in 1935: 'You may say that we are an old-fashioned lot . . . but I say it is only another instance of New Zealand's warmth, loyalty and devotion to Great Britain, to her King and custom and tradition'.[41] Elsewhere, however, Governors-General became simply the personal representatives of the monarch—and New Zealand followed suit in 1939.

But if the Governor-General was not to act on behalf of the British Government, who was? In principle the answer was not hard to find—a specially appointed representative, on the analogy of the dominion High Commissioners in London. But the fleshing out of this answer led to a tussle between the Dominions Office and the Foreign Office (each of whom wanted any appointee to come under its wing), and there was also a need to consult the dominions and their Governors-General. Eventually, in 1928 a representative of the British Government went to Canada, and was given the title of High Commissioner. This set both the representational and the usual terminological pattern, and in ensuing years British High Commissioners were appointed to other dominions. By 1939, when one went to New Zealand and a 'Representative' was despatched to Ireland, Britain was represented in all the dominions.[42]

Contrary to what the Foreign Office had wanted, none of Britain's early High Commissioners had diplomatic experience, and only two of them came from the Dominions Office. But none the less, what had been begun was a kind of Dominions Office overseas service, and in functional terms it was broadly

[41] Sir James Parr, bidding farewell to the newly-appointed Governor-General of New Zealand in early 1935: *United Empire*, April 1938 (*sic*), p. 198; quoted in Angus Ross, 'Reluctant Dominion or Dutiful Daughter? New Zealand and the Commonwealth in the Inter-War Years', *Journal of Commonwealth Political Studies*, vol. 10, no. 1 (1972), p. 34.

[42] Despatch of a British representative to Dublin was delayed owing to Ireland's refusal to accept a High Commissioner and Britain's refusal to designate him as Ambassador or Minister. In October 1939 it was agreed that Ireland would call him the 'British Representative' and Britain would call him the 'UK Representative': Joe Garner, *The Commonwealth Office 1925–1968* (London: Heinemann, 1978), pp. 236, 176.

diplomatic. However, as had been the case with appointments to Britain, High Commissioners were sent not from or to a head of State (which would have been a case of the King appointing someone to himself) but from one Prime Minister to another. On this ground neither side saw them as diplomats. Consequentially, they were not members of the local diplomatic corps, and did not receive all the customary diplomatic immunities and privileges.

But none the less, by the end of the inter-war period a largely complete and quasi-diplomatic representational system between Britain and the dominions was in place. Inter-dominion representation, however, lagged notably behind. This reflected the fact that hard interests, such as would justify the expense of permanent missions, were none too prominent as between individual pairs of dominions. But then the growing prospect of war resulted in closer attention being given to the matter, and its outbreak was a sharp spur, a number of High Commissions being established either immediately or within a few years. One case, which predated the war, also resulted in a different terminology. Canada had agreed that South Africa's representative could be called 'Accredited Representative', South Africa's object being to insinuate that her relations with Canada were diplomatic. (Ireland, too, tried at the last minute to secure a more diplomatic-sounding title for her appointee to Canada, but the Canadians said it was too late.) However, Canada insisted that the status, privileges and immunities of South Africa's agent were just those of a High Commissioner. This did not stop the agent in question (Meyer) describing himself 'as the first diplomatic representative of one Dominion in another',[43] and demanding accordingly that the British High Commissioner was his junior and should therefore call on him first. But in 1943, after asserting that Meyer's rank was no higher than a Trade Commissioner, South Africa quickly backtracked and accepted he had the status of a High Commissioner. In 1945, following Canadian representations about Meyer's 'ambiguous and meaningless title',[44] his successor was designated High Commissioner.

In relation to foreign, as opposed to Commonwealth, countries, the dominions had been much more representationally active in the inter-war period. In this area, however, they ran into substantial problems with Britain. As the mother country saw it, it was one thing to facilitate intra-Commonwealth contact through the appointment of distinctively Commonwealth representatives; quite another to go along with arrangements which, being of a normal diplomatic kind, might make it look as if the British empire was less than a single international unit.

V. DOMINION REPRESENTATION IN FOREIGN STATES

Given the part which the dominions had played during the First World War, and the extent to which they have been brought within the counsels of the empire, it was to be expected that they might soon think about separate foreign

---

[43] Holmes to Harding, 15 July 1939; quoted in Brian Douglas Tennyson, *Canadian Relations with South Africa. A Diplomatic History* (Washington DC: University Press of America, 1982), p. 90.

[44] Holmes memorandum for Wrong, 15 November 1944; quoted in Tennyson, op. cit. above (n. 43), p. 105.

representation. In a memorandum drawn up by their Prime Ministers at the 1919 Peace Conference, the conviction was expressed that their 'right . . . to send diplomatic envoys to foreign states should be recognized'. Yet in the same document they also said that this process must 'take into account the necessity for preserving the unity of the British Commonwealth'.[45]

Already, in 1917, the Colonial Secretary had agreed in principle that a Canadian could be attached to the British Embassy in Washington. However, Borden swiftly deemed this insufficient and proposed to appoint a 'high commissioner' with independent powers. The British Ambassador's warnings about the expense of a separate establishment were sufficiently daunting for Borden to decide instead to establish a War Mission, which continued after the war in anticipation of independent diplomatic representation. In the autumn of 1919 Borden told Britain that he had decided to appoint a minister to Washington. There was Colonial Office concern at this 'separatist move'.[46] However, the Colonial Secretary, Milner, suggested Canada might have a branch in the Washington embassy and an equal say in, and an equal right to provide, ambassadors. Since, as Curzon (the Foreign Secretary) put it, this went 'rather unnecessarily far',[47] Britain proposed that a Canadian minister should be second-in-command at the British embassy in Washington.

This did not mean, Britain emphasized, that the empire's unity would be lost; nor that relations between the United States and Canada would be on a par with those which existed between other foreign States. Certainly, despite assertions to the contrary, it is difficult to see Britain's agreement as establishing a general rule that the dominions had the right to establish diplomatic missions, for there was no question here of a separate Canadian legation. For her part, Canada naturally tried to maximize the benefit which could be obtained from the position which had been offered. She wanted her representative to enjoy a higher place in the order of precedence than would be normal for an ambassador's deputy. This caused exasperation in the Foreign Office. Eyre Crowe (an outstanding official) asked: 'Why should all the rules of the world be thrown overboard at the desire' of the Canadian Government? The Permanent Under-Secretary, Hardinge, grumbled that the Canadians seemed to be 'trying to see how much they can make us swallow'.[48] In the event, failure to find the right man for the job and a change in Canada's government resulted in the whole thing falling through. Still, it was a significant straw in the wind.

From the British angle, this episode showed Whitehall's strong reluctance, in the early post-war years, to contemplate dominion appointments which could be construed as diplomatic. Such a development was, to those in London, almost literally inconceivable. Some change was, of course, recognized. Thus, in the

[45] 'Dominions' Right of Legation', confidential, 25 February 1919. It is not known whether this memorandum was presented to Lloyd George or discussed in the full British Empire Delegation: *DCER*, vol. 3, p. 1.

[46] Philip Wigley, *Canada and the Transition to Commonwealth, British-Canadian Relations 1917–1926* (Cambridge, London, New York, Melbourne: Cambridge University Press, 1977), p. 108.

[47] Curzon's secretary to Reading, 17 October 1919; quoted in Robert Bothwell, 'Canadian Representation at Washington: a Study in Colonial Responsibility', *The Canadian Historical Review*, vol. 53, no. 2 (June 1972), p. 144.

[48] Minute by Crowe, 5 April 1920 and undated minute by Hardinge, FO 371/4566, 4567; quoted in Wigley, op. cit. above (n. 46), p. 110.

House of Commons in 1921, Lloyd George pointed out that the dominions had been given 'equal rights with Great Britain in the control of the foreign policy of the Empire'. But, he added, the machinery for foreign policy making was that 'of the British Government . . . [and] must remain here'. He claimed this had been 'accepted by all the Dominions as inevitable'. To the dominions, however, that did not seem much like the 'joint control' of which the Prime Minister spoke—and they can hardly have been greatly mollified by his picture of 'joint responsibility': 'when the burden of Empire has become so vast it is well that we should have the shoulders of these young giants under the burden to help us [sic] along'.[49] As the Permanent Under-Secretary of the Canadian Department of External Affairs put it a few years later, 'Diplomatic unity of the Empire means, for the Dominions, a minimum of control and a maximum of responsibility'.[50]

Two developments sharply accentuated the restiveness of some dominions with this system. In the first place there was considerable dissatisfaction with certain aspects of British-determined policy. The Near East (Chanak) crisis of 1922 highlighted in a particularly vivid way the sort of problem which could arise. At its start, for example, most of the dominions were far from happy at Britain's blithe assumption that they would immediately respond to her call to provide armed backing for her position. Then, the exclusion of the dominions from the peace conference at Lausanne led to bitter protests from Australia. And the signature (by Britain) of a peace treaty in the name of the whole empire elicited furious objections from Canada. It took two months of Anglo-Canadian negotiations before Britain felt able to proceed with the treaty's ratification—and then only on the understanding that Canada would interpret for herself what bearing the treaty had on her legal obligations. Meanwhile, the Irish Free State pointedly distanced herself from the whole episode.

From Britain's point of view there were good reasons for at least some of her behaviour. Crowe (by now Permanent Under-Secretary) believed that admitting the dominions to the Lausanne conference 'would serve no purpose and could only produce friction with the allies, as well as retard the negotiations'.[51] But the wider question which underlay this approach was whether Britain could justifiably act as the sole representative of the empire. The same issue arose in 1924 when Britain's new Labour government recognized the Soviet Union without first consulting the dominions. It was, however, a question which Britain was in no hurry to ask.

Secondly, there were growing worries in the dominions about what, under the existing system, Britain was omitting to do for them. Bluntly put, some of them felt that the protection and advancement of their individual interests in particular countries were not best conducted by Britain's embassies. The problem, as Canada saw it in relation to the United States, was described as follows. Sir Joseph Pope, the Under-Secretary of the Department of External Affairs,

had been obliged to go to the British Embassy at Washington to discuss Canadian affairs.

[49] Quoted in Skilling, op. cit. above (n. 28), p. xiv.

[50] 'The Locarno Treaties: Proposed Imperial Conference', typewritten copy of undated notes by Skelton, January 1926, NAC, RG 25, vol. 3419, 1–1926/22.

[51] Minute, 6 November 1923, FO 371/7909; quoted in Wigley, op. cit. above (n. 46), p. 83.

He could not entrust most of his mandates to the Ambassador himself. The Ambassador appointed one of his attachés from London to represent Canada, and Sir Joseph had to give him a few lessons in geography and explain to him the details of the record. While the attaché was a brilliant young man and did his best, he knew little of Canada, never having set foot in this country. After corresponding with him for a time, and before the mandate was carried out, Sir Joseph would find that that young attaché had been transferred to another embassy, and the correspondence would cease. Then Sir Joseph would have to journey again to Washington and begin over again to post another young attaché on Canadian affairs, giving him a few lessons in geography, handing him a brief and sending him along with it.[52]

If, however, a member of the Commonwealth had her own independent representative in a foreign State, the danger (as Britain saw it) was that the 'diplomatic unity of the empire' might be lost. This phrase was reiterated time and again by Britain as indicative of the essential bottom line. Its exact content was never precisely spelled out. Nevertheless, undoubtedly it embraced keeping in sharp diplomatic step on important political matters, establishing and breaking diplomatic relations in unison (the breach of such relations then being a more significant act than it was to become after 1945), and, above all, making war and peace as one. To ensure that there was no breaking of ranks on such issues, the Permanent Under-Secretary at the Foreign Office said (in 1926) that it was 'vital' that on matters affecting the empire as a whole, 'we [sic] should conduct *all* political negotiations'.[53]

The clear ambiguity of this statement was a sufficient indication that Britain was no longer in unquestioned command. Already, in 1923, a Canadian-American treaty (albeit 'only' on fish) had been signed by a Canadian and an American alone. At the Imperial Conference of that year, Britain had had to accept that foreign policy was 'necessarily subject to the action of the Governments and Parliaments of the various portions of the Empire'.[54] And in 1924 the first dominion legation to a foreign State was established: that of the Irish Free State to the United States.

Its head (a professor) had been in the United States as Ireland's representative without diplomatic status since 1922. His elevation to diplomatic rank (as Minister) had to wait upon the co-operation of Britain, for two reasons. The first was that the Americans would not receive him as such without the approval of Britain and her formal notification of his appointment. The second was that the King had to sign his letter of credence. Of course, in technical terms that was in his capacity as head of the Irish State, but in the early 1920s it was most unlikely that the King's co-operation would have been easily forthcoming without the assent of his British ministers. And these ministers were unhappy about the whole matter, so there were protracted negotiations with the Irish. Eventually Britain acquiesced. Given the 1920 offer to Canada, the Foreign Office felt it could not refuse the Free State high-level representation. But it was not

[52] Quoted in Alan James, 'Diplomatic Relations and Contacts', this *Year Book*, 62 (1991) p. 367.
[53] Minute, 10 November 1926; quoted in Norman Hillmer, 'The Foreign Office, the Dominions and the Diplomatic Unity of the Empire, 1925–1929', in David Dilks (ed.), *Retreat from Power: Studies in Britain's Foreign Policy of the Twentieth Century*, vol. 1, *1906–1939* (London: Macmillan, 1991), p. 64.
[54] Quoted in C. P. Stacey, *Canada and the Age of Conflict*, vol. 2, *1921–1948, The Mackenzie King Era* (Toronto, Buffalo, London: University of Toronto Press, 1981), p. 69.

prepared to have a representative of the Free State within the British embassy, entailing British 'responsibility for action over which they would, in fact, have no control'.[55] A full-blown Irish legation was the result.

To emphasize his independence of Britain, the Irish Minister presented his letter of credence to the American President without the sponsoring presence of the British Ambassador. It was argued that the arrangement did not conclusively prove the dominions had a right to establish diplomatic missions. But there was no real comfort to be had in this direction. For the oldest dominion, Canada, was actively seeking an independent appointment to Washington.

This had become in external matters the Canadian Government's 'first priority',[56] and a Canadian legation to the United States was established in 1927. However, as 'the price of British co-operation and goodwill', Canada agreed that 'matters which are of Imperial concern or which affect other Dominions . . . in common with Canada will continue to be handled as heretofore by [the British] Embassy'.[57] Furthermore, the British Ambassador accompanied the Canadian Minister when he presented his letters of credence to the President in order to 'make clear to the public that Great Britain approved . . . and that the two missions were on friendly terms'.[58] The American President took the opportunity to improve his geography, asking 'whether Toronto was near the Lake [sic]'![59]

But, friendship or no, the essential thing about this development was the existence of two separate missions. And soon there was another independent mission, Canada's hitherto non-diplomatic office in Paris being raised in 1928 to the status of a legation. In this connection Britain repeated the formula which had been used in respect of the appointment to Washington about her continued handling of imperial matters. This reservation reflected the fact that while Britain no longer actively opposed the establishment of legations, there were some Foreign Office fears—shared by the leader of the Canadian Opposition— that it would be 'impossible' to have different members of the Commonwealth conducting their own foreign policies. 'Impossible' meant 'disaster and ultimate disruption', which in turn meant that 'the British Empire would lose weight and prestige in the councils of the Great Powers'.[60] Britain would go 'to almost any length in the matter of the autonomous rights of the Dominions', the Canadian Prime Minister was told. But 'the conception of unity within the Empire' had to be maintained.[61]

However, at the 1926 Imperial Conference a powerful committee of all the

[55] Foreign Office to Colonial Office, 20 March 1924, CO 886/10/90; quoted in Wigley, op. cit. above (n. 46), p. 225.

[56] John Hilliker, *Canada's Department of External Affairs*, vol. 1, *The Early Years, 1909–1946* (Montreal and Kingston, London, Buffalo: McGill-Queen's University Press, 1990), p. 111.

[57] British Chargé d'Affaires in Washington to US Secretary of State, 19 November 1925, *DCER*, vol. 4, p. 15.

[58] Vincent Massey, *What's Past is Prologue* (London: Macmillan, 1963), p. 122.

[59] Massey, diary entry, 18 February 1927; quoted in ibid. and Hilliker, op. cit. above (n. 56), p. 115.

[60] Memorandum by Percy Koppell (head of the Dominions Information Department of the Foreign Office), 16 January 1926; quoted in Hillmer, loc. cit. above (n. 53), p. 65.

[61] Mackenzie King diary, 17 October 1926, recording conversation with Harding (Assistant Under-Secretary of the Dominions Office) (Toronto: University of Toronto Press, 1973), transcript 57.

dominion Prime Ministers under Lord Balfour's chairmanship had been charged with 'tidying up the confusion which had been apparent in the British Commonwealth's foreign relationships during the previous four years'. It declared that 'equality of status' was 'the root-principle' governing inter-imperial relations.[62] When, therefore, the Canadian legation was opened in Paris, Canada protested that Britain's arrogation to herself of imperial matters was inconsistent with the Balfour formula. South Africa and Ireland—who were planning to open legations—also objected.

Intensive intergovernmental discussions were therefore set in train about the precise compatibility of such diplomatic appointments by the dominions with the idea of the empire's diplomatic unity. The Canadian Prime Minister, Mackenzie King, also found himself having to defend his country's establishment of legations to the King, who told him 'frankly . . . I don't like them'. The King added that 'it looked as if separate legations might make for separation'. The Prime Minister's sincere reply—that he 'thought the opposite would be the case'[63]—was a remarkable testimony to the contemporary pervasiveness of the imperial ideology.

Until this issue was resolved Britain was intent on delaying the opening of further diplomatic missions by the dominions. Eventually, in mid-1929, it was agreed that while the British Ambassador 'would be the channel for making common imperial views known to the authorities in the host country',[64] the existence of such a common view was neither to be assumed nor insisted upon. Thus the empire's diplomatic unity now consisted of no more than an obligation to consult on matters of common concern. It was also agreed that each dominion would be responsible for its own diplomatic appointments, so that in signing letters of credence the King would unequivocally be acting only on the advice of his ministers in the dominion concerned.

The way was now open for Canada to make the third of its desired appointments: a Minister to Japan. The wife of the British Ambassador in Tokyo was not pleased. After discovering that the official who had been sent ahead of the Minister to open the legation 'could speak a more or less intelligible form of English', she 'bombarded' him with 'inquiries as to why Canada should be opening diplomatic offices abroad, especially in Japan. "Quite unnecessary, you know; we don't mind looking after things for you, and, of course, we have had a long experience. So silly of you".'[65] However, legations were costly and domestically controversial, provoking cries of 'separatism'. So it was not until 1939 that Canada made a further appointment, establishing legations in Belgium and the Netherlands under a Minister accredited to both countries.

The Irish Free State and South Africa were only slightly more active. Mention has already been made of the Irish legation to the United States. Since 1925 that country had also had a colourful representative in Brussels, a Count, who persistently laid claim to membership of the diplomatic corps. A British

---

[62] W. K. Hancock, *Survey of British Commonwealth Affairs*, vol. 1, *Problems of Nationality 1918–1936* (London, New York, Toronto: Oxford University Press for Royal Institute of International Affairs), pp. 262, 263.

[63] Mackenzie King diary (above, n. 61), 11 October 1928, transcript 63.

[64] Hilliker, op. cit. above (n. 56), p. 113.

[65] H. L. Keenleyside, *Memoirs of Hugh L. Keenleyside*, vol. 1, *Hammer the Golden Day* (Toronto: McLelland & Stewart, 1981), p. 269.

embassy official loftily expressed the view that the Irish Government ('who are quite ignorant of these matters') had been persuaded by the Count to designate him as 'Representative of the Irish Free State' on the sort of basis 'in which they would at home call the "odd man" the butler if it made him happier'.[66] Following the 1929 agreement, some unquestionably more regular appointments were made: to the Holy See, Paris (to which Brussels was now attached), Berlin and Madrid. The penultimate one of these gave rise to a problem when, early in the Second World War, Ireland wished to make a new appointment to Berlin. The British Foreign Secretary thought Ireland would appreciate the 'difficulties arising over the formal procedure such as asking the King to sign credentials addressed to Herr Hitler'. The matter was not pressed, and the Irish mission in Berlin was left in the hands of a chargé d'affaires.[67]

South Africa's initial diplomatic plans ran into a substantial difficulty when, in 1928, she made it known that she planned to raise the status of her Trade Commissioner to Canada and the US to that of chargé d'affaires. But her scheme in this way to blur the distinction between the Commonwealth and foreign States failed. The Foreign and Dominions Offices disapproved. But, more importantly, Canada would not hear of it. Besides setting a possibly dangerous precedent and threatening the legal distinctiveness of the empire (about which, it might be thought, Canada had not herself been the most scrupulous), it affronted Canadian dignity and it rather hinted at the possibility of North American integration. In due course a separate appointment was made to Washington. By 1936 South Africa had also sent a diplomatic representative to Rome, and made joint appointments to the Hague and Brussels, Berlin and Stockholm, and Paris and Lisbon.

The remaining two dominions showed no inclination to proceed down the diplomatic path. Australia was conscious of the financial cost, and of the implications for her defence, if the idea gained ground that she stood on her own in the world. In 1925 the leader of the Australian Labour Opposition thought that his country should not participate in international relations. The country's Prime Minister, Bruce (who was later a distinguished international figure), was happy to tolerate special representational cases, such as those of Canada in Washington or the Irish Free State at the Holy See. Otherwise, the opening of legations was a 'mistake', and bound to lead to a 'hopeless mess'.[68] Even in the 1930s, when China, Japan, and the United States were pressing Australia for diplomatic exchanges, she was disinclined to accede. There was some talk of appointing an Australian 'Commissioner' to Washington, but it fell through when it was pointed out that such an 'unorthodox' position[69] would result in its holder, owing to his lack of diplomatic status, 'being at the end of the line where

---

[66] Memorandum by Wingfield, 4 January 1926, DO 35/12; quoted in Robert F. Holland, *The Commonwealth in the British Official Mind: A Study in Anglo-Dominion Relations 1925–1937*, Ph.D thesis, Oxford, St Antony's College (1977), p. 90.

[67] Garner, op. cit. above (n. 42), p. 247, n. By then the King's only role in respect of Eire was (under Article 3 of Eire's 1936 External Relations Act) to sign letters of credence and approve international agreements.

[68] Bruce to R. G. Casey, 20 March 1929; quoted in Edwards, op. cit. above (n. 38), p. 77, and W. J. Hudson and M. P. Sharp, *Australian Independence: Colony to Reluctant Kingdom* (Melbourne: Melbourne University Press, 1988), p. 102.

[69] Edwards, op. cit. above (n. 38), p. 116.

he would necessarily always remain'.[70] Instead, and as an experiment, it was decided to send an official to join the British embassy in Washington in 1937. This device was not a success (partly because Australia was not yet equipped to service even minuscule overseas representation) and lasted only for a year—during which period Australia's future Foreign Minister, Evatt, said how much 'it galled him to find Canada, Ireland and South Africa well set-up and playing a role here, and then to find Australia's representative in a cubby-hole at the end of a long corridor in the British Embassy'.[71] But in 1939, although worrying that it might give the impression of imperial disunity, Australia decided that the time had come to open legations in Washington and Tokyo. It was a while before she implemented this decision, and then only in relation to the United States.

New Zealand was even less enthusiastic than Australia for the diplomatic life. Following the 1923 Imperial Conference her Prime Minister, Massey, 'wanted to put an end to the wicked nonsense that was being talked about the Dominions having become sovereign states'.[72] Shortly afterwards Massey was said to regard the idea of separate representation as 'the first step towards the disruption of the Empire'. He thought it 'essential that all territories of the Crown should be united in their relations to Foreign Powers', and believed that this necessitated just 'a single representative of the Crown in every foreign capital'.[73] Some years later a member of the British Foreign Office who had been seconded to the Prime Minister's Department in New Zealand thought that most of his hosts 'are neither desirous nor particularly capable of taking an intelligent interest in foreign affairs'.[74] Certainly there was no desire to get involved internationally. Until 1942 New Zealand's sole overseas representative was her High Commissioner in London. A separate Department of External Affairs was not created until 1943 and the leader of the 1949 National Government entered office intending to close the Department. From a British angle, such fealty resulted in 'the famous phrase attributed to a British statesman, jaded by the course of negotiations with other countries: "Thank God for New Zealand" '.[75]

Nevertheless, although two dominions were less than keen on developing their diplomatic identities, the crucial point was the establishment of the principle that the dominions might be separately represented in foreign capitals. Inasmuch as such permanent bilateral contact between sovereign States made up the core of the diplomatic system, the full diplomatic status of the dominions could no longer be denied. Concomitantly, the diplomatic unity of the empire had, in essence, been undone. The Second World War was to make that abundantly clear—and so to provide the impetus for the grant to High Commissioners of the same status as that enjoyed by their diplomatic colleagues.

[70] Cordell Hull (Secretary of State) to President Roosevelt, 21 September 1935; quoted in Edwards, op. cit. above (n. 38), p. 116.
[71] Moffat diary, 24 October 1938; quoted in Edwards, op. cit. above (n. 38), p. 118.
[72] R. M. Budon, *The New Dominions. A Social and Political History of New Zealand* (London: Allen & Unwin, 1965), p. 184.
[73] Jellicoe (Governor-General) to Colonial Secretary, 3 May 1924; quoted in Ross, loc. cit. above (n. 41), pp. 32–3.
[74] Philip Nichols, 'New Zealand Impressions', 16 April 1930, PRO U 80/32/750 FO 426/2.
[75] F. L. W. Wood, 'The Anzac Dilemma', *International Affairs*, vol. 29, no. 2 (April 1953), p. 185.

VI. The Impact of the Second World War

The outbreak of war in 1939 provided the categoric answer to the issue which had troubled constitutional theorists since the Balfour formula of 1926, and especially since the Statute of Westminster of 1931: whether the sovereign could, through different policies being pursued by the dominions, be at the same time both at war and at peace. The answer came through the dominions' making their individual declarations of war, at different times. Eire (which the rest of the Commonwealth formally regarded as a dominion) made the point even more emphatically by remaining neutral. The experience of war only underlined the dominions' international stature, and the war also saw the establishment by Australia and even New Zealand of diplomatic missions in Washington. By 1945, therefore, there could be no doubt that the dominions enjoyed the same status as other States. This removed any ground for distinguishing their diplomatic activities from those of other, non-Commonwealth, States.

By 1948 dominion restiveness at the maintenance of the distinction could no longer be maintained, and the matter was therefore discussed at the Prime Ministers' meeting. (By then India, Pakistan and Ceylon had been added to the ranks of the dominions.) Britain remained averse to assimilating High Commissioners with the diplomatic corps and thought such a step was unnecessary. However, the overwhelming view was that High Commissioners should rank with ambassadors, taking precedence among them (as was the case with ambassadors) according to their formal date of arrival. This was therefore agreed and, in consequence, High Commissioners were no longer ranked according to their countries' seniority as Commonwealth members. (A movement to change the name of High Commissioners to ambassadors was, however, unsuccessful and, in time, the former title came to be preferred.)

It was left to each individual member to arrange for the detailed implementation of the new scheme in its own jurisdiction. In December 1948 Britain and all the dominions other than Pakistan announced the necessary changes in respect of precedence. In so doing, Britain proposed to respond to any objections by saying that her announcement 'ha[d] simply given formal recognition to what has long been the rightful place of High Commissioners as representatives of ambassadorial status exchanged between the countries of the Commonwealth'.[76] (This was a somewhat less than historically accurate representation of Britain's view of the matter; but it was a splendid illustration of the British faculty of making the best of a bad job.) As far as privileges and immunities in Britain were concerned, the necessary legislation came into force in 1952. The imprimatur of the society of States on the assimilation of High Commissioners with ambassadors was granted (indirectly) by Article 14(1) of the 1961 Vienna Convention on Diplomatic Relations—which is recognized as the universally applicable law on diplomacy.

There were still a few distinctions between High Commissioners and ambassadors. Britain treated High Commissioners and ambassadors 'as separate

---

[76] Memorandum by Escott Reid (Canadian Acting Under-Secretary of External Affairs) on 'Precedence and Titles of High Commissioners', for Lester Pearson (Acting Secretary for External Affairs), 29 November 1948, in Hector Mackenzie (ed.), *Documents on Canadian External Relations*, vol. 14, *1948* (Ottawa: Department of Foreign Affairs and International Trade, 1994), p. 1475.

groups on a footing of equality', adopting a system of 'interleaving' at functions where both groups were represented.[77] Britain also considered it 'inappropriate that a subject of The King (which all High Commissioners then were) should be the Doyen of diplomatic representatives in his capital [sic], since he was technically not accredited to The Sovereign'. But 'this inhibition, which never existed at all in other Commonwealth capitals, lapsed in 1972'.[78] And as the sovereign cannot accredit someone to herself, High Commissioners from countries recognizing the Queen as Head of State carry letters of commission from their Prime Minister to the Prime Minister of the receiving State. But they are not denied their twenty minutes or so with the sovereign on arrival, being received in a private, informal, audience. It was also the case in London until the merging (in 1968) of the Foreign Office and the Commonwealth Relations Office (the 1947 successor to the Dominions Office) that High Commissioners principally conducted their business through the latter.

However, these were the merest technicalities. In the initial membership roster of the United Nations there was no question of listing Canada and the rest as a British empire group; they appeared in their individual alphabetic places, no distinctions being drawn between them and the other member States. Intra-Commonwealth diplomatic relations were, by the end of 1948, to all intents and purposes on the same footing as all others. Likewise, independent Commonwealth countries—who shrugged off the term 'dominion' as demeaning—were represented in foreign States on normal diplomatic lines. These fundamental changes in the external representation of the former dominions indicated that the British empire, which a mere generation before had been so imposing, had to this extent lost its cohesion. It might have been in the process of re-birth as an inter-governmental body. But as a diplomatic unit it had unravelled.

---

[77] Note by Attlee on 'Status of High Commissioners', 13 October 1948, secret, PRO, P.M.M. (48) 9, CAB 133/88. This had not found favour with dominion representatives, who thought it unnecessary and 'not consistent with the equality of status with Ambassadors which it was now proposed to secure for High Commissioners' (Report of the Committee of High Commissioners and officials on status of High Commissioners, 19 October 1948, secret, PRO, P.M.M. (48) 14, CAB 133/88).

[78] Gore-Booth, op. cit. above (n. 16), p. 388.

REVIEWS OF BOOKS

Cuadernos de Cátedra. Edited By VICTORIA ABELLÁN. Barcelona: Bosch, 1994–6. Volume 1: *El Arreglo Pacífico de Controversias en la Organización de Naciones Unidas*. By A. BADIA MARTÍ. 126 pp. Volume 5: *Las Reservas a Los Tratados Internacionales*. By J. BONET PÉREZ. 207 pp. Volume 6: *La Cuestion de Timor Oriental*. Edited by VICTORIA ABELLÁN HONRUBIA. 270 pp. No price stated.

Cuadernos de Cátedra is a series of monographs published in Spanish under the editorship of Dr Victoria Abellán, Professor of Public International Law at the University of Barcelona. The series provides a forum for the publication of research carried out in the area of public international law and international relations by members of the Department of International Law and Economics, as well as work carried out in collaboration with the Department through seminars and conferences. As such, the content of each monograph is as varied as one would expect from any legal journal. In addition to the three volumes reviewed here, the series also contains three others which translate as: *Generality and Particularity in the Law on the Use of International Waterways* by A. Pigrau Solé; *Codification and Progressive Development of the Law relating to International Organizations* by X. Pons Ràfols; and *Territorial Sea Limits* by J. Saura Estapà.

The series begins with an analysis of peaceful dispute resolution both as a principle contained within the UN Charter and in its practical application by the organs of the United Nations, with particular reference to the Security Council. The study covers: (1) the principle of peaceful dispute resolution: the behavioural duty of States; (2) the United Nations' peaceful resolution function; (3) the competence of the organs of the United Nations; and (4) actual tendencies based on UN practice. The author argues that the classification of a certain set of facts as a 'dispute' is subject to much discretion, and as such is determined by the political arena. To bring the practice of dispute resolution more into line with the principle of peaceful dispute settlement, certain control mechanisms are suggested, such as the judicial weight of an opinion from the International Court of Justice, as well as an endorsement by the General Assembly.

The second title reviewed covers reservations to international treaties. This monograph considers the regulation of international treaty reservations through both its codification and international practice. The study criticizes the codification of the legal institution of entering reservations in the Vienna Convention of 1969 (supplemented by the Conventions of 1978 and 1986) as ambiguous and imprecise; and welcomes the decision taken in 1993 by the International Law Commission to include in its long-term programme 'the law and practice of treaty reservations'. Having discussed the codification of reservations, the concept of a reservation in international law, the formulation of reservations, and their legal effects, the author highlights some particularly significant problems with regard to their codification. These include: the absence of a real definition of a reservation which creates great difficulty in distinguishing between a reservation and an interpretative declaration; the doubts as to whether reservations can be made to bilateral treaties or how extensive or crucial reservations to multilateral treaties can be; and the precise legal effects that are created between two States where one has entered a reservation to an agreed treaty provision. This paper poses some interesting analytical questions and highlights problems encountered in the international law of reservations, but leaves suggestions for its reform for another day.

Unlike the previous titles, the third report reviewed from this series is the product of a symposium held in November 1995 by the Universities of Barcelona and Oporto, on the international legal aspects of the East Timor question. The symposium took place following Portugal's proceedings in the International Court of Justice against Australia's recognition of East Timor as part of Indonesia, and was held nearly four years to the day from the Santa Cruz massacre when many young Timorians were killed demonstrating for freedom and self-determination. The report begins by painting an historical and political picture of East Timor before examining the issues of international law: the right to self-determination; the situation with regard to human rights; the judgment in the *East Timor (Portugal* v. *Australia)* case; and the possibility of a peaceful resolution to the East Timor situation. The symposium proceedings conclude with papers by a student from East Timor, convinced that the East Timor question will only be resolved by way of dialogue and negotiation between Jakarta and the resistance movement even though previous efforts at negotiation have failed, and a Professor from the University of Barcelona, examining the part to be played by the United Nations and urging that the situation be resolved through the people of East Timor being allowed to exercise their right to free (self) determination. The papers contained in this final report are well-written in a style which the non-native speaker will find easier to read than the other volumes and provide an interesting overview of the situation in East Timor.

KISCH BEEVERS

The United Nations Mission in El Salvador: A Humanitarian Law Perspective. By TATHIANA FLORES ACUÑA. The Hague: Kluwer Law International, 1995. xvi + 253 pp. £56.

Although this work starts from a wide base in Chapter 1 which contains a general legal exposition on the role of the Security Council and the Secretary-General, Chapters 2 and 3, which look at the mandate and powers of ONUSAL and its role in the area of international humanitarian law, are quite narrowly focused. The author makes the following claim in the Introduction:

The ONUSAL Mission is the first UN mission to have consisted of the three phases an ideal mission should have. In its Peace-making phase, during the development of the hostilities, the Mission created the right atmosphere for a cease-fire. As a Peace-keeping mission, it performed tasks to assure the demobilization of the parties and the seizure of the weapons. As the first post-conflict peace-building mission, the ONUSAL collaborated in reforming governmental institutions, monitoring 1994 elections and supervising land reform. Without any precedents in history, the ONUSAL was the first UN mission to accomplish its tasks of verification and observation of the respect for human rights and international humanitarian law during a non-international armed conflict. (p. xv)

The uniqueness of ONUSAL is indisputable, though the same could be said, and has been said, of many other UN forces. In many ways, ONUSAL is a variation of so-called 'second generation' peace-keeping, which combines consensual peace-keeping with peaceful settlement, as opposed to traditional or 'first generation' peace-keeping in which a force is consented to with the limited purpose of supervising provisional measures (cease-fires and withdrawals) agreed to by the parties, and 'third generation' forces which cross the threshold from consensual, non-aggressive, peace-keeping, to become quasi-enforcement actions (as in Somalia). Under the so-called 'second generation' peace-keeping model, the various ways in which peaceful settlement of the conflict may be agreed to (although the goal is invariably the holding of free elections) results in forces with different specific mandates. In the case of ONUSAL, concerned with a particularly dirty civil war, there was a need to incorporate a human rights component into the model.

Although there are some fleeting references to Somalia and Rwanda in Chapter 1, these are insufficient to put ONUSAL into context, with the result that the claim that ONUSAL was a significant development in peace-keeping remains largely unsubstantiated. The experiences in Cambodia of UNTAC, which was operating at about the same time, could have been usefully referred to given that it too had a concern for human rights. In addition, it is also difficult to evaluate ONUSAL's work when the other aspects of its mandate, including the supervision of elections, are not referred to.

Nevertheless, the focus of the book is on ONUSAL's role in the protection of humanitarian law. Despite the fact that ONUSAL's own interpretation of its mandate put more emphasis on human rights law (pp. 80–1), the author makes a strong case for overlap between the norms of human rights law and humanitarian law (pp. 33–6), arguing that ONUSAL's mandate was as much concerned with the latter as the former. Indeed, the author's description of ONUSAL's work in protecting and promoting norms of humanitarian law (pp. 55–71) illustrates that despite doctrinal confusion and serious flaws in its work (see, for example, the ambivalent relationship with the ICRC: pp. 72–3), ONUSAL made an important contribution to the development of supervisory mechanisms in the field of humanitarian law. The point the author makes well is that there are hard lessons to be learnt from ONUSAL's experiences (pp. 82–4), but that if these lessons are taken on board by the UN, the marriage of peace-keeping and the protection of humanitarian law and human rights may well be a fruitful one in the future.

One final point to note is that the actual text is 103 pages in length (including a useful bibliography). The rest of the book consists of an appendix containing the first three reports of ONUSAL. A much more detailed set of documents on the UN's Mission in El Salvador can be found in *The United Nations Blue Book Series*, volume 4, *The United Nations and El Salvador, 1990–1995* (New York: United Nations Department of Public Information, 1995).

N.D. WHITE

Self-Determination of Peoples. By ANTONIO CASSESE. Cambridge: Cambridge University Press, 1995. xviii + 375 pp. £60.

This work is a welcome addition to the current debate on self-determination. By an author who needs no introduction, it is divided into five parts and twelve chapters. In Chapter 1 the author sets out the parameters of his work, stating it to be doctrinal, or *lex lata*, eschewing legal theory (pp. 2, 7). But he also aims to go beyond the law, adopting a contextual approach in which history, politics and jurisprudence play a role (pp. 2–3). He additionally introduces us to the significance of the principle of self-determination. It is both radical and progressive, subversive and threatening, a challenge to established authority. Internally, it has empowered the people, while externally it has operated so as to increase membership of the international community by bringing new States to independence. Therein, however, lies the paradox, because without limits the principle of self-determination has the capacity to dismantle the very fabric of international society (pp. 1–2, 5–6).

Following an account of the historical dimension (Chapter 2), Cassese proceeds to consider the development of self-determination as an international legal standard (Part II), including, in addition to internal self-determination, the principle of non-interference and the right to permanent sovereignty over natural resources (Chapter 3). The evolution of the customary rules of self-determination is also reviewed (Chapters 4 and 5). An analysis of State practice and the pronouncements of bodies such as the UN General Assembly and the International Court of Justice leads to the conclusion that self-determination, expressed as the 'need to pay regard to the freely expressed will of peoples', is a general principle of customary international law. Only the most conservative would argue with this assessment. Indeed, Cassese finds that it is a principle *erga omnes* (an observation reinforced by the International Court of Justice in the *East Timor* case, which unfortunately came too late to be included in this study), and, controversially, that it is a norm of *jus cogens*. The author relies principally on the *opinio juris* of States to support his bold assertion (pp. 133–40). This general principle is nevertheless composed of a number of specific rules on the external self-determination of colonial peoples and peoples under foreign military occupation, and on internal self-determination for racial groups. The author also makes the important point that national minorities do not generally have a right to secession. Such a right would exist only *in extremis*, where a racial group inhabiting an authoritarian State is persecuted or denied its democratic rights (pp. 122–4).

The enforcement of the right to self-determination is a crucial issue (Chapter 6). One particularly controversial question is whether national liberation movements have a right to use force and to assistance. Cassese concludes that they have a licence, but not a right, to use force (which applies equally to oppressed racial groups fighting for internal self-determination) and are entitled to receive assistance falling short of accepting military units. Third States are under a minimum obligation to refrain from frustrating the goal of self-determination. (On this point the *dicta* in the *East Timor* case, to the effect that for Australia and Indonesia East Timor remains a non-self-governing territory and its people have the right to self-determination, are again instructive.)

How has the right of self-determination operated in practice (Part III)? What impact has it had on traditional international law (Chapter 8)? The author finds that the law on personality, territorial sovereignty, State responsibility, the use of force and the principle of non-interference, and the humanitarian law of armed conflict, have all been affected. Even so, the impact 'has not been so decisive as to change the structure of international law. It has, however, had an enormous influence on the content of some fundamental international norms and . . . on the outlook of States towards the present world community' (p. 165). However, the political impact could be said to be much more significant.

Some complex and topical disputes are then re-examined. In Chapter 9 Cassese considers the cases of Gibraltar, the Western Sahara, Eritrea, East Timor, Palestine and Quebec, and in each instance provides an incisive and thought-provoking treatment. The dissolutions of the USSR and Yugoslavia merit separate attention in a particularly illuminating analysis (Chapter 10). Here, after discussing the different situations, the author draws the following conclusions which may have wider repercussions. First, self-determination 'operated at the level of political rhetoric, as a set of political principles legitimizing the secession of national States from central, oppressive State structures'. Secondly, it 'provided the legal tools for establishing the demands of the seceding people to achieve independent statehood': referenda were held to ascertain the wishes of the people. Thirdly, third States, in particular the member States of the European Community, established general criteria for the recognition of new States, notably, a commitment to democratic values, the rule of law and human and minority rights, and respect for the wishes of the people as expressed through referenda (p. 273).

What other significant trends appear to be emerging (Part IV)? Both the Helsinki Declaration 1975 and the Algiers Declaration were important political and moral developments in that there was wider recognition of internal self-determination (Chapter 11). Crucially, the participants at the Helsinki Conference were careful not to provide even a modicum of support for separatism (pp. 287–9).

Cassese brings all these strands together in a final chapter (Chapter 12). In addition, he proposes a blueprint for action. First, he urges the setting aside of short-term interests and their replacement by long-term policies consonant with international law and international peace and security. This will require a radical change in the present outlook of much of the international community which could be overcome, however, through political will and through pressure exerted by international organizations and third States (pp. 344–5). Secondly, a more liberal approach should be taken towards the rights of peoples under human rights treaties (pp. 345–6). The author also calls for the internal dimension of self-determination to be emphasized. In particular, it is important to disassociate self-determination from independence. In this context, self-determination recognizes group rights and provides alternative constitutional frameworks, through autonomous status or federalism, which meets the legitimate aspirations of these groups, such as has occurred in Spain. Once this is achieved it would then be possible to grant self-determination to ethnic and national minorities without disrupting the territorial integrity of States.

This is an excellent book. Its scholarship is of the highest standard. It is a thoroughly interesting and thought-provoking study. It combines an analysis of the evolution of the principle of self-determination and its various ramifications with its practical application to a number of case studies and suggestions for its future development. It is required reading.

GINO J. NALDI

Issues in Global Governance. Papers written for the COMMISSION ON GLOBAL GOVERNANCE. The Hague: Kluwer Law International, 1995. 496 pp. £75.

On 3 February 1995, Ambassador Peter Osvald, the Permanent Representative of Sweden to the United Nations, presented the United Nations Secretary-General with a summary of *Our Global Neighbourhood*—the report of the Commission on Global Governance which began its work in September 1992.[1] Created as part of the Stockholm Initiative on Global Security and Governance of April 1991, and co-chaired by Ingvar Carlsson and Shridath Ramphal, the Commission was charged with the responsibility of addressing the challenges affecting global governance as a whole—clearly a formidable task, but one which the Commission's twenty-eight members responded to with a mixture of optimism and pragmatism.

Issues in Global Governance is an assembly of eighteen of the papers produced for the Commission at various stages of its work, and it is frankly admitted in the Co-Chairmen's Foreword (at p. xii) that '[t]he extent to which the ideas expressed in these papers is reflected in the Commission's [final] report will be found to vary greatly, but that extent is not, by any means, a reliable measure of their importance or of their relevance to the discussion of several areas of public policy'. While this may be an interesting matter for examination, this review will confine itself to the broad contents of this volume. That the Commission has decided to release these working papers for general consumption is itself a move to be welcomed, not least because it provides the reader with a useful idea of the range of issues which confronted the Commission, and, of course, some understanding of the way (and possibly the reasons for the way) in which the Commission prioritized the items on its agenda.

The volume is divided into six sections—global values, global security, global development, global institutional reform, the global rule of law and global governance. To introduce us to the general work of the Commission, the first section outlines the 'global values' envisaged in an international system where interdependence and global concerns dominate the politics of nations. Professor James N. Rosenau's very useful 'Changing Capacities of Citizens, 1945–95' sets the climate of the study: citizens of today differ significantly from those of yesteryear in terms of their attributes and their desires

---

[1] UN Docs. A/50/79 and S/1995/106 (6 February 1995). This summary is reproduced as an Annex in this volume, at pp. 449–64.

and expectations and in terms of the political, economic, social, technological and cultural environment in which they find themselves. The reality of the new generation of citizen is brought home to us so that (at p. 51) 'the challenges posed by the dynamics of world-wide change may receive a fair hearing among major segments of the world's citizens'.

The importance of defining the 'global values' of the international system becomes clearer when one reads the paper prepared by Professor Lincoln P. Bloomfield. In his essay on 'Enforcing Rules in the International Community: Governing the Ungovernable?', we are reminded of the inherent virtue of identifying the common ideals of any community which is legally organized and functions according to accepted principles of behaviour. He writes, at p. 221, that 'People generally accept their community's rules because of a sense of commonality, be it ethnic, linguistic, religious, or philosophical, and because of a governance system if that protects their physical environment from threats' (elsewhere, at p. 279, Professor Rosenau offers 'the long-term absence [in Russia] of shared national values [which] underlies a continuing deterioration that may well culminate in sheer disarray and lack of any authoritative institutions capable of fashioning a modicum of social order' as a veritable lesson for the international system). Given this relationship between the values which a community endorses and the effectiveness of its laws, it is to be regretted that the first section does not deal with the envisaged global values in a more coherent or detailed way (as is done in *Our Global Neighbourhood*). Apart from the changing aspirations of the citizens of the world, corruption is depicted as a necessary evil in the overall scheme of things and the equality of nations and peoples is espoused as a meritorious principle, but the reader is left to piece together a picture of those values (e.g. democracy, the rule of law, representative law-making and organizational efficiency). These collected papers would have had greater resonance if they had developed from a more definitive elaboration of these global values—values which inform and permeate the whole work of the Commission.

International lawyers will be reassured by the essay of Professor Rahmatullah Khan on 'The Thickening Web of International Law', which provides a balanced appreciation of the conceptual foundations of the international legal system (if international law is going to work, it first needs to be understood). Law, it is rightly asserted, has an indispensable role in the management of the challenges of the future: e.g. international crime and the protection of the environment (on which there is a most lucid piece by Peter M. Haas). We are also alerted to the stark realities of the limitations of international institutions—a theme which recurs in many of the papers in this volume—and the 'regional-functional route' is advocated (at p. 262) as a complementary apparatus in enhancing the effectiveness of the institution of law in the regime of global governance. This alternative introduces its own series of difficulties, none of which are really given rigorous consideration, something which is vital if a serious case is to be made for a devolution of powers and responsibilities from the global to the regional level.

By way of final comment, it may be said that the organizational unit of the international system—the State—could perhaps have been given more analytical prominence in this set of essays, since it is the State that remains at the centre of the system we have and it is the State (as well as international organizations) which will remain the vehicle of change on any question of global governance. Professor Rosenau's essay on 'Changing States in a Changing World' (one of three superb contributions to this volume) fills this breach to an extent, but a more thoroughgoing treatment of the role of States and the trappings of statehood in the age of global governance (the resurgence of new States in today's world underscores the importance of this issue) would not have gone amiss. These eighteen papers help to define some, but by no means all, of the issues which now require attention and also offer possible ideas and solutions on how governance on a number of issues can be reformed and improved.

DINO KRITSIOTIS

Allocation of Law Enforcement Authority in the International System (Proceedings of an International Symposium of the Kiel Institute of International Law, March, 23 to 25, 1994). Edited by J. DELBRÜCK. Berlin: Duncker & Humblot, 1995. 196 pp. DM 78.

The publication of the 1994 symposium of the Kiel Institute of International Law follows on from the 1989 conference on regionalism and universalism, and the 1992 symposium on international law enforcement, both of which were also published in this series. As a set, they make an excellent introduction to the problems of institutional law enforcement. Their weakness is that, in the nature of conference proceedings, there is no real development from interesting ideas and thoughts to detailed exposition and criticism.

In many ways the proceedings of the symposium encapsulate the diverse, often conflicting, approaches to world order that have prevented international legal and political theory from achieving any sort of consensus on the development and direction of international organizations. The reader is left with the feeling that writers in the field are struggling to make sense of the explosion in institutional activity that has occurred with the end of the Cold War. However, this is not only a problem for academics but also for people working for international organizations, as illustrated by the first paper entitled 'Centralized and Decentralized Law Enforcement: The Security Council and the General Assembly Acting under Chapters VII and VIII' by Paul Szasz, which contains a pragmatic run-through of the powers of the UN. While adopting a realist viewpoint that the UN reflects the power structures prevalent within the world order, the author does highlight legal difficulties created by the ever-expanding competence of the Security Council, without, however, providing any overarching principles. Nevertheless, the problems he points to—the development of the concept of a 'threat to the peace', the legal basis of military measures under Chapter VII, the relationship between self-defence and enforcement action, and the legality of the Uniting for Peace Resolution—are well-worn issues on which there is considerable disagreement, as the discussions and remaining papers in this symposium show.

The paper by Fred Morrison entitled 'The Role of Regional Organizations in the Enforcement of International Law' widens the questions raised to include the relationship of regional organizations to the United Nations under Chapter VIII of the UN Charter. Again the analysis is useful though mainly descriptive. Furthermore the controversial, but increasingly relevant, doctrine of 'inherent powers', championed by Professor Seyersted in the mid 1960s, is touched upon and dismissed in a summary fashion (p. 46). The increasing autonomy of regional organizations in the area of enforcement, and the extremely flexible interpretation of the UN Charter by the Security Council, can only be explained by the recognition that international organizations have evolved from being simple arenas for debate to becoming powerful autonomous actors on the international plane, with a handful possessing supranational characteristics. To accommodate this evolution it is necessary to recognize that the constituent documents of international organizations are 'living instruments' in which the purposes and functions of the organization take precedence over the literal meaning of particular provisions, providing always that the action undertaken in pursuit of the organizations' goals does not entail something which is prohibited by the constituent document (see the excellent comment by Schreuer, pp. 82–3). Morrison's argument that a 'group of states cannot collectively convey a power or authority which none of them originally had' (p. 47) seems to miss this point, and ignores the widening gap between institutional enforcement action and a State's right to self-defence.

Furthermore, to recognize the doctrine of 'inherent powers' is not to give organizations unlimited powers, for, as Seyersted pointed out, it is to subject them to two clear legal limitations (on top of any practical limitations there may be): that the action in question

achieves the purposes of the organization, and secondly that it does not breach any of the
express provisions of the Charter. An international judicial doctrine of *ultra vires* could
develop along these lines (for discussion of the review powers of the World Court see, for
example, pp. 77, 83 and 85).

The positivist/realist legal analysis of Szasz and Morrison tends to leave many
questions unanswered, and certainly does not provide any clear guidance as to how to
improve the system or how it will develop in the future. As Klaus Dicke suggests in his
interesting comment, this is perhaps the role of the political scientist, although his point
that the legalistic approach may actually work against such hypothesizing because it tends
to reinforce the *status quo* and freeze the situation (p. 58) is well made. Indeed, Dicke's
comment and proposals for reform provide food for thought in understanding and
reforming the current system, issues which a legal analysis tends to avoid. However, most
of the discussion which follows, with the odd exception (see for example p. 72), focuses
on the narrower legal issues. Of the remaining papers and discussion, the paper by
Torsten Stein entitled 'Decentralized International Law Enforcement: The Changing
Role of the State as Law Enforcement Agent' is the most thought-provoking because it
attempts to resolve many of the legal problems raised by other papers within a broader
conceptual framework.

On the whole this is a very enjoyable book, encapsulating as it does many of the legal
issues concerning law enforcement by international organizations. Inevitably it only
scratches the surface of the problem and almost entirely focuses on collective security to
the exclusion of interesting institutional developments in the areas of human rights and
the environment. In addition, the imbalance between legal and political perspectives is to
be regretted. One way forward from this debate is for a greater integration between legal
and political approaches to the subject.

N.D. WHITE

*International Institute of Humanitarian Law: San Remo Manual on
International Law Applicable to Armed Conflicts at Sea.* Edited by LOUISE
DOSWALD-BECK. Cambridge: Cambridge University Press, 1995. ix +
257 pp. £14.95 (paper); £40 (hardback).

The Iran-Iraq war during the 1980s demonstrated that questions of the legal regulation
of the use of force at sea remain important. Was it permissible to attack foreign flag oil
tankers bound to or from an enemy State that used oil exports to fund its war effort?
Could combatant warships subject all foreign merchant ships in the region to visit and
search, even if there was no specific ground for suspecting a particular vessel of carrying
contraband? What, indeed, is contraband? Could British warships use force to protect
foreign flag vessels owned or chartered by British companies? Could foreign merchant
ships be not merely protected, but escorted in convoy, by warships? May neutral coastal
States suspend the rights of passage of ships of the combatant States, while allowing other
ships to pass? Many such questions arose and have been extensively discussed in the legal
literature.

Behind these questions lie two doctrinal debates. First, have the traditional Laws of
War, as set out in instruments such as the 1907 Hague Conventions, survived the advent
of the UN Charter? Or do the principles of necessity and proportionality implicit in
Article 51 of the Charter now constitute the sole legal source of the *jus in bello* as well as
the *jus ad bellum*? Secondly, how far does the law applicable to armed conflict permit
derogations from the normal peacetime rules of the law of the sea? There is in addition
a fundamental practical question: do the rules make sense in the context of modern
weaponry and ways of using force? States have given a variety of answers to these and
similar questions, reflecting the very different doctrinal positions that they hold. As in
most areas of life, it is probably more important that the answers be clear than that they

be right. And it is certainly much more important that States conform to an agreed set of rules than that they share a common position on why they so conform. The peculiar strength of the *San Remo Manual* is that it manages to give clear answers which meet the practical concerns, but without always resolving the underlying doctrinal debates.

The *Manual* is chiefly the work of a small group of experts: Messrs Amer (Egypt), Doyle (USA), Fenrick (Canada), Greenwood (UK), Heintschel von Heinegg (Germany), Robertson (USA) and Van Hegelsom (Netherlands), and Ms Doswald-Beck (Switzer-land), who also edited the *Manual* and co-ordinated its drafting. But the text is a result of lengthy, detailed debates over drafts and discussion papers by a much larger group. International lawyers and naval officers from 30 or so States, from all parts of the globe, have participated in the San Remo project at some stage since it began in 1987 (and this reviewer must declare an interest as a participant in the initial preliminary meeting). This breadth of expertise lends the *Manual* authority; but more importantly, it gives it practicality. The rules have been designed to meet the exigencies of war at sea, by a group which has direct experience of naval operations.

The *Manual* consists of 183 crisply stated paragraphs, divided into six parts: (I) general provisions; (II) regions of operations; (III) basic rules and target discrimination; (IV) methods and means of warfare at sea; (V) methods short of attack—interception, visit, search, diversion and capture; (VI) protected persons, medical transports, and medical aircraft. There follows a detailed paragraph-by-paragraph explanation of the rules, which describes the thinking behind the rules and the main lines of debate on points that proved controversial. Some of the premises, such as the assumptions concerning the extent to which the 1982 Law of the Sea Convention represents customary international law, might be questioned by some readers. So may some of the rules, such as that forbidding non-humanitarian assistance to the aggressor and permitting assistance to the victim in cases where there is a Security Council resolution identifying a State as responsible for an act of aggression or breach of the peace. And some will find holes to pick in the drafting: for example, in the rule (paragraph 52) which appears to elide the distinction between the character of individual ships and that of classes of ships, when stipulating what are legitimate targets.

Ultimately, such criticisms matter little. The *Manual* is essentially a practitioner's text. Its value is to be measured not by its doctrinal purity or logical consistency, nor by the precision and elegance of its drafting, but by its practical utility. In the search for a consensus over a workable set of rules it is inevitable that there will be compromises and finessing of doctrinal differences. There has not been a serious international codification of the law of naval warfare since the 1913 *Oxford Manual*, and one was desperately needed as a focus for the development of doctrine and, indeed, of State practice. The robust pragmatism of the *San Remo Manual* promises to fulfil that need, and to lay down for a generation the framework within which the legality of naval operations will be evaluated.

VAUGHAN LOWE

Declining Jurisdiction in Private International Law. Edited by JAMES J. FAWCETT. Oxford: Clarendon Press, 1995. lxi + 447 pp. £60.

This book forms the first in a series of *Oxford Monographs in Private International Law* under the general editorship of P.B. Carter. It consists of up-to-date reports presented to the XIVth Congress of the International Academy of Comparative Law held at Athens in 1994 and revised after the conference, together with a synopsis and survey provided by the editor. The reports, based on a questionnaire reproduced in the Appendix, follow a model of international jurisdiction, *forum non conveniens* and *lis alibi pendens*, choice of jurisdiction and arbitration arrangements. The reports, which come largely from first world countries, constitute the book's chapters. Quebec has a report separate from the common law districts of Canada, but other federal States, including the USA and

Switzerland, are treated in one chapter, as are Scotland and England. One or two reports have been published elsewhere but usually neither in English nor in journals easily accessible to Anglo-American lawyers. The length of the reports is generally in proportion to the amount of international litigation. As may be expected, reports from Sweden and Japan are shorter than those from Great Britain and the USA, and the Argentinian report is brief with little explication, whereas the one from Belgium (by Fallon) is detailed. The national reports are largely restricted to civil and commercial matters as understood in western Europe. A similar volume concerned with family matters would be useful.

Books in the series are intended for both scholars and practitioners. The conflict of laws is certainly one area where there is substantial cross-fertilisation. The work of Lawrence Collins in the UK published as *Essays in International Litigation and the Conflict of Laws* exemplifies this tendency. Because the present book is one for reference, practitioners will find much useful information. Over time, of course, this information will lose its value as laws change, and so it is as a scholarly work that the book must be judged. There is no work of similar coverage, a fact which in itself makes this book important. Fawcett's contentions that '[t]he great virtue of the *forum non conveniens* approach is its flexibility' (p. 39), whereas its 'great vice' is the grant of a negative declaration that the court first seised is an inappropriate forum, repay study. The competing paradigm, first to the court, is simple but its disadvantages are aptly summarized at pp. 34–5 in the context of the Brussels and Lugano Conventions. The contrary approach is neatly put by Trocker in his Italian report (p. 301, footnotes omitted).

It is doubtful, however, whether . . . other problems related to the phenomenon of concurrent jurisdiction and parallel proceedings, in particular the problems of improper fora and of excessive forum-shopping, can adequately be resolved by the means of a *forum non conveniens* doctrine. What seems to be needed are carefully structured rules of jurisdiction reflecting the idea of international due process and carefully designed conflict-of-laws rules attuned to the exigencies of inter-state and international justice.

The book well demonstrates the dichotomy between civil law and common law models of jurisdiction. The former in general adopts a rigid rule: if a court has jurisdiction it must take it, and the lack of a doctrine of *forum non conveniens* is explained by the precise rules on jurisdiction. The Brussels Convention on Jurisdiction and the Enforcement of Judgments in Civil and Commercial Matters 1968, which was drafted before the United Kingdom acceded to the EC, exemplifies this model. The latter, also in general, has wide jurisdictional rules (such as service outside the jurisdiction without leave in New Zealand) which is tempered by principles permitting the forum to decline jurisdiction by staying proceedings. In England a writ may be served on a person who is within the jurisdiction simply to see the races. He or she may have no assets in the country, need not be domiciled or habitually resident in England, or a British national, and so on. Such exorbitant jurisdiction is rendered acceptable to common lawyers by the discretion to be exercised judicially to forgo hearing the action. The contrast between the two models may be strong. Article 21 of the Brussels Convention adopts a simple rule that the court first seised is to hear the issue and the court second seised is not. In the event of a dispute, a party is well advised to select the forum and act expeditiously. The effect is an unseemly rush to the courts, a process which Beaumont (p. 232) calls 'arbitrary', and 'unacceptable' where there is not a context of a 'tight-knit framework' of narrow grounds of jurisdiction and a virtually mechanical system of recognition. Besides the encouragement of forum-shopping given by Article 21, there is the problem of defining when a court is definitively seised: as Briggs has pointed out, practitioners should not, as they do in England, send a letter before action because to do so may prompt the other party to commence proceedings elsewhere, thereby depriving the English courts of jurisdiction contrary to the interests of one of the parties.

The distinction between the civil law and common law countries is not always clear-cut and the general report makes pellucid the variations among law districts. US long-arm statutes are matched by Article 14 of the French *Code Civil*. The distinction, furthermore, in the United Kingdom may be on the point of breaking down. It is a paradox that at about the same time as the English courts accepted the doctrine of *forum non conveniens* they were faced with applying the Brussels Convention. Judgments on and the mode of thinking behind the hard and fast rules of the Convention will over time influence the purely domestic law, and perhaps the doctrine will receive its quietus at not too distant a date. There remains, however, debate at present whether the doctrine is still applicable in England when there is a forum outside the EC: see *Re Harrods (Buenos Aires) Ltd.* and *The Nile Rhapsody*. Unfortunately for those wanting a settled answer, the former case was referred to the European Court of Justice (Case 314/93, *Ladenimor SA v. Intercomfinanz SA*) but the dispute was settled; the latter action was not referred because of the cost and delay of a reference. Continental opinion is strongly opposed to the incorporation of the doctrine into the Convention (cf. Droz, quoted at p. 139: il faut 'tuer dans l'oeuf cette source de chicane'). It is interesting to note that one civil law country not affected by the Convention, Quebec, is moving the other way, from rules to flexibility.

In the book there is an investigation of the problem of parallel proceedings and potentially inconsistent judgments, and restraining foreign actions by injunction (the so-called antisuit injunction now countered by anti-antisuit injunction). Some countries do not permit antisuit injunctions, but refusal to recognize foreign judgments may have the same effect (though Article 28 of the Brussels and Lugano Conventions generally speaking prohibits investigation of the original court's jurisdiction). The reader is referred to pp. 14–15 for a good summary comparing the British and US doctrines of *forum non conveniens* and to pp. 20 and 420 for a rapid listing of the advantages of litigating personal injury claims in the USA. There is a good, succinct introduction (by Epstein) to cross-vesting (p. 32) followed by a discussion of why the States and Territories of Australia are moving towards becoming one law district, and there is an interesting perspective (by Del Duca and Zaphiriou) on the development of *forum non conveniens* in US Federal Courts (pp. 403–5). Powers similar to this doctrine such as *fraude à la loi* and the abusive exercise of rights are considered. There are some suggestions for reform, such as the use of an autonomous interpretation of pendency within Article 21 of the Brussels Convention. There are insights into other countries' laws: for instance, California at one time adopted the attitude that the UK was not a suitable place for the trial of a product liability action (*in casu* oral contraceptives manufactured in California and taken in the UK) because the UK did not have a regime of strict liability for defective products.

The work is very well produced. Translations from the French are smooth. The present writer would have separately indexed Scottish and English cases and would not have put cases on the Brussels Convention under the heading of the European Court of Justice. As a source of information the book has no rival.

MICHAEL JEFFERSON

Le Droit et les Minorités. Analyses et Textes. By ALAIN FENET, GENEVIÈVE KOUBI, ISABELLE SCHULTE-TENCKHOFF and TATIANA ANSBACH. Bruxelles: Établissements Émile Bruylant, 1995. 462 pp. Belgian francs 2880.

Despite or perhaps because of the reserved attitude of the French State towards minority rights, there exists a considerable literature in French on minority rights, much of it from authors with French citizenship. The Bruylant publishing house has been responsible for some mainstream writings in this area, including works of recent vintage. The authors of this volume explore related but distinct subject-matters. Schulte-

Tenckhoff and Ansbach deal generally with minorities in international law, and their section incorporates reflections on the rights of indigenous peoples, currently under development at the United Nations. Their writing has something of the quality of the textbook (not a bad thing)—and could be used as such in view of its generality and tight organization.

Fenet's contribution deals with minorities and Europe, and he is also responsible for organizing the useful collection of texts on minority rights, including bilateral arrangements (not all in French), and documents on gypsies and indigenous peoples. The gypsy issue is also addressed in his review of law and policy, which is well argued, critical, perceptive and wide-ranging. Fenet incorporates reflections on regionalism and the EU into his analyses, as well as the to-be-expected review of the work of the OSCE and the Council of Europe. He is acutely aware of the limitations of the European Convention on Human Rights as an instrument for the protection of minorities.

Koubi offers the most abstract of the discussions: on minority rights in France, and the theory of minority rights. The former section tackles difficult issues for the French State in its approach to international treaties which attempt to guarantee and promote minority rights. She says a great deal about 'the right to be different', and appraises the ambivalence of the French position, its perplexing features and potential for change. The final theory section is written in terms of arguments concerning definition, individual and collective rights, and cultural and juridical pluralism. Her style and approach challenge the foreigner with a very particular deployment of concept, vocabulary and argumentation, but the dogged reader may be rewarded by grasping some mysteries of the French legal and political psyche.

The book reads well and is not blighted with heavy footnotes. Understanding better the French approach to minority rights, including its modes of analysis and argument, is more than intruding into the travails and agonies of one nation. Regrettably, the French State, guardian of the Revolution and bringer of liberty, is presently stuck with an almost uniquely backward-looking attitude to the development of international standards on minority rights. The book provides evidence that there is a debate within France of a high intellectual quality, the resonances of which could eventually percolate through to levels of government, perhaps promoting some necessary reconceptualizations.

PATRICK THORNBERRY

The Handbook of Humanitarian Law in Armed Conflicts. Edited by DIETER FLECK. Oxford: Oxford University Press, 1995. xvi + 589 pp. £90.

This work is much more than a 'handbook'. It provides a very detailed and scholarly account of the main topics within the field of humanitarian law applicable in armed conflicts. It is, however, unusual in taking its key statements from the Joint Service Regulations of the German armed forces (promulgated in 1992) and commenting upon them. The result is a work which has some similarities to the British *Manual of Military Law Part III* (soon to be replaced by a tri-Service manual). It has brought the official German view of humanitarian law to a wider audience, a matter of some importance when the *opinio juris* is being considered to determine the development of customary international law. In *The Prosecutor* v. *Tadic* (1995) the President of the Appeals Chamber of the International Criminal Tribunal for the Former Yugoslavia relied upon the German Military Manual to show the German view that 'grave breaches of international humanitarian law include some violations of common Article 3 [to the Geneva Conventions of 1949]' (at paras. 83 and 131 of the judgment of President Cassese).

The book contains chapters on the historical development and legal basis, the scope of application of humanitarian law, combatants and non-combatants, the methods and means of combat, the protection of the civilian population, the wounded and sick, prisoners of war, religious personnel, cultural property, armed conflicts at sea, neutrality and the enforcement of international humanitarian law. All the chapters are written by academics of standing within their fields.

The editor states (at p. x) that the 'publication of the [Joint Service Regulations] follows intensive co-operation between practitioners and scholars . . . [which] has benefited not only the wording of the Joint Service Regulations but also the commentary'. It is therefore, perhaps, surprising to find some commentators pointing out the inaccuracy of some of the Joint Service Regulations (which are printed in bold type). Thus, Ipsen in his excellent chapter on combatants and non-combatants is at pains to correct the view in para. 315 of the Joint Service Regulations (hereafter, the Regulations) that non-combatant members of the armed forces 'have the right to defend themselves or others against attacks contrary to international law'. He states, correctly, that 'the non-combatants' right of self-defence is not restricted to those attacks which involve prohibited methods and means of warfare'. The difficulty caused in the Regulations is that German law draws a distinction in the personnel of its armed forces between combatant and non-combatant members, which, apart from medical personnel and chaplains, is not recognized under international law. He also warns the reader about the ambiguity in para. 321 of the Regulations, which seems to suggest that only members of the armed forces can be brought within the definition of spies in Article 29 of the Hague Regulations 1907. Fischer draws attention to a further ambiguity in para. 701 of the Regulations.

As one might expect of a book of this nature, statements of government policy are contained within the Regulations. There are, for instance, seven Regulations concerning nuclear weapons. Regulation 430 concludes that 'The new rules introduced by Additional Protocol I . . . do not influence, regulate, or prohibit the use of nuclear weapons'. This may be compared with the declarations of both the UK and the USA upon signature of Additional Protocol I, where the language is not quite so unequivocal. A further example might include Regulation 211 which states that 'German soldiers like their allies are required to comply with the rules of international humanitarian law in the conduct of military operations in all armed conflicts however such conflicts are characterized'. No attempt is made to consider the practical consequences of such a statement, although Greenwood, in a very balanced chapter, properly draws attention to it, at p. 49. The decision of the Appeals Chamber in *The Prosecutor* v. *Tadic* (1995) that the grave breach provisions of the 1949 Geneva Conventions apply only during an international armed conflict illustrates the difficulties of transferring humanitarian law applicable in an international armed conflict into one which is of a non-international character. It has already been pointed out that the Regulations include a breach of common Article 3 to the 1949 Geneva Conventions as a grave breach, although they are not so styled in the Conventions themselves. Given Regulation 211, it is difficult to see why this is necessary or why breaches of Additional Protocol II are deemed to be grave breaches (see Regulation 1209) under German law.

With some eleven contributors there is a danger that the complete work might display a variation in the depth of analysis and style with each contribution. This has been largely avoided through careful editing. In most of the chapters the commentaries are first-rate with useful footnotes, although in the chapter on religious personnel there is little by way of commentary where one is clearly required (see Regulation 816). In places the cross-referencing might have been improved. This is but a minor quibble. Dr Fleck is to be congratulated on producing a well researched and scholarly work which will find a place in the established literature of international humanitarian law.

PETER ROWE

Law, Power, and the Sovereign State. The Evolution and Application of the Concept of Sovereignty. By MICHAEL ROSS FOWLER and JULIE MARIE BUNCK. University Park: Penn State Press, 1995. xiv + 200 pp. £25.50 (cloth); £12.50 (paper).

This book, written by two American scholars, focuses on the use and relevance of the concept of sovereignty. As such, its very appearance is heartily to be welcomed, for (as it seems to this reviewer) the idea of sovereignty receives far too little attention, particularly in Britain. Furthermore, the book's content calls for no less than two resounding cheers.

After an introduction in which they ask why sovereignty is ambiguous, the authors deal in each of their chapters with other central questions: why is sovereignty important? what constitutes a sovereign State? how is sovereignty applied in theory, and in practice? why is sovereignty useful? and will sovereignty prosper or decline? They believe that the concept is 'on the whole a useful and largely positive feature of modern international life' (p. 152), and that there is no sign of its demise. This conclusion is reached on the basis of a thorough examination of a very wide range of statements and opinions about sovereignty. The authors do not hide their own views, but are scrupulously fair in their marshalling of competing contentions. Moreover, they write throughout in admirably clear and uncluttered prose. Theirs is an excellent guide to contemporary thinking about sovereignty.

Why, then, might there be some hesitation about giving full voice to the final cheer? In the first place, rather more might have been made of the significance of sovereignty in identifying those entities to which full international personality is ascribed. Attention is certainly paid to this matter. But the spotlight is not very brightly turned on what is surely the fundamental role of sovereignty in delineating the territorial constituents of the international society. Without some such process, it is difficult to see how international relations (in actuality and as a field of study) and international law could, as we know them, exist.

Secondly, a little unease is aroused by a central aspect of the book's exposition: the concept of sovereignty as a 'chunk'. This is how the authors characterize the absolute concept of sovereignty—'like a chunk of stone. Every state has one of these stones, and . . . all are exactly alike' (p. 64). More specifically, this concept refers to the 'unalterable and irreducible quantity of rights and immunities which automatically accrue to any state' (a writer quoted on p. 65). This approach is contrasted with the concept of sovereignty as a 'basket', that is, a variable quantity of rights and duties. The authors are themselves advocates of the basket, and make a number of telling criticisms of those who think in terms of a chunk. But arguably, a belief in the value of an absolute concept of sovereignty (as for the purpose indicated in the previous paragraph) does not necessarily find expression in the idea of a chunk of international legal rights. Instead, it can refer to no more (and no less) than the distinctive status enjoyed by entities possessing a constitution which is unconnected with any other.

This draws attention to a more basic point. At all times the authors depict their quest as an effort to elucidate 'the' concept of sovereignty. But, as their book attests on every page, while the focus is on a single *term*, that term gives rise to a number of different *concepts*. It may be thought that the authors would have done well to meet this head on. Comment could still have been made on the cogency and helpfulness of the individual concepts which all happen to sail under a common name. But there would then have been no need to try to reach an overall conclusion about 'sovereignty'. That is both an elusive task, and one which does not diminish the confusion which habitually attaches to the term.

It remains, however, that Drs Fowler and Bunck have splendidly prepared the ground for those wishing to follow the debate on and clarify their thoughts about sovereignty—an exercise which underlines the connectedness between international law and international relations. An awareness of these links, and of their importance, is not uncommon in the United States, as indicated by the fact that although the authors of this book are political scientists, they include a two-page table of cases. (Nothing comparable is ever seen here.) It is to be hoped that their work will encourage a similar level of awareness in Britain.

ALAN JAMES

The International Covenant on Civil and Political Rights and United Kingdom Law. Edited by DAVID HARRIS and SARAH JOSEPH. Oxford: Oxford University Press, 1995. xviii + 699 pp. £60.

Raising the profile of the International Covenant on Civil and Political Rights (ICCPR) amongst both the academic and the practising legal community in the United Kingdom is central to the aim of this book. To this end it provides a survey of both its present and its potential relevance to the law in the United Kingdom. The Covenant certainly needs to be more closely studied by British lawyers, both academics and practitioners. Its local rival, the European Convention on Human Rights and Fundamental Freedoms 1950 (ECHR), is now well established as an important implement in the protection of the rights and freedoms of people in Britain, but a similar status for the wider United Nations Covenant has never been fully recognized. Focusing on the ECHR is understandable because the individual can take a case to the European Court of Human Rights and obtain a judgment on a particular rights issue which the UK is then obliged by treaty to recognize and uphold. This direct access has heightened its profile as more and more cases are taken against the UK and other contracting States so that all parties to the legal and political process can easily comprehend its utility. Despite the possibility of a similar individual petition in the case of the Covenant through the First Optional Protocol (OP1), no such simple access is offered because the UK has not accepted this OP1. Without acceptance of the individual petition, as Rosalyn Higgins points out, the potential and importance of the Covenant in guaranteeing rights has never been realized. Neglect of the possibilities of using the Covenant also arises from the widespread ignorance of its existence and extent. This book performs a valuable service in addressing and redressing this latter problem.

The editors have drawn together an eminent group of contributors and have carefully directed them in their task so that although each chapter is different they link together and carry similar thematic lines of enquiry. In the foreword Rosalyn Higgins, then a member of the United Nations Human Rights Committee, introduces some of the reasons behind the limited interest and knowledge surrounding the Covenant, and criticizes its system from a number of aspects. She rightly points to the lack of its use by the media, parliament, NGOs and the legal community within the UK and suggests that before its full impact can be felt these shortcomings need to be dealt with. In pursuit of this object the introduction provides a general consideration of the guarantees offered by the Covenant, the nature of its implementation and its direct relevance for the UK. This last aspect is further considered in Chapter 2. The chapters which follow then discuss, for various facets of the legal structure, the substantive provisions of the Covenant, along with their relevance to the law in the UK, and assess whether UK law complies with its international requirements. The authors also reflect on the relationship between the ECHR and the ICCPR in the relevant subject areas. Each chapter is thoroughly researched and comprehensive in its factual material, covering current and often controversial legal problems (see especially the chapters by Nigel Rodney on terrorism and Stephen Bailey on fair trial etc.) which arise in the UK and on which the ICCPR has some bearing. The approach is relevant to both the academic and the practitioner: of particular importance may be the introduction of the Covenant to the judiciary, who through judgments can do most to aid its implementation in spirit and the parliamentarian who can influence law-making. If each of these groups is strategically placed to facilitate implementation, it has to be acknowledged that, for the latter group, the scale and density of the legal text is daunting.

The calculation of the editors and sponsors (the Airey Neave Foundation) has clearly been that before any popularizing approach can be effective, the awareness and understanding of the legal profession (academic and professional) needs to be aroused. As already indicated, this function has been fulfilled most effectively. What is perhaps less on offer is a more analytical and critical approach. It has to be accepted however that this would both have added to an already substantial text and, more significantly, might have detracted from its main aim: introduction to and consideration of the Covenant in the UK environment.

On its own terms therefore the book performs admirably. When so much is offered it may seem churlish to point to absences, but the book would have gained in both accessibility and impact if two omissions had been repaired. The reader would have been helped if the text of the Covenant itself had been reproduced as a whole and in one place: various relevant Articles are reprinted within individual chapters, but not everyone has easily to hand the complete text. More damaging for the 'missionary' purpose of the volume is the lack of an explicit concluding chapter. Again, some of this function is briefly provided within the introduction (pp. 46–55), but a more expansive discussion would have enhanced the book's effectiveness for its central objectives: increasing the knowledge, and raising the profile, of the Covenant. These comments, however, should not obscure the point that this is an informative and scholarly work which should have a salutary impact on the legal community.

KATHERINE S. WILLIAMS

Art. 6 ERMK und kantonale Verwaltungsrechtspflege. By RUTH HERZOG. Bern: Verlag Stämpfli & Cie.AG, 1995. lv + 427 pp. DM 121.

Administrative law is an extensive and, it seems, ever expanding area of law which affects many areas of our daily lives. It is therefore important to ensure that proper attention is paid to the protection of individuals' rights within areas affected by it. This book, based on a thesis, addresses the question of the execution and supervision of administrative law in the context of Article 6 of the European Convention on Human Rights. The book's main concern is to assess how well the administrative law system within the Swiss cantons (in so far as administrative law disputes fall within Article 6) satisfies the guarantees to a fair trial set out in that article.

The book is divided into three unequal sections. The first contains a description of the development of Article 6, in particular the meaning of 'civil rights and obligations' and 'any criminal charge'; the second, a description of Swiss administrative law, identifying the areas within administrative law as either being civil or criminal, or falling outside the scope of Article 6; and the third assesses the consequences for the Swiss cantons of ensuring that their administrative law systems comply with the requirements of Article 6.

The first section on the development of Article 6 is broken down into several subsections looking at the text of the ECHR, case law, and finally analysis. Although following a well-marked path, the treatment is thorough and there are plenty of examples highlighting the possible difficulties of Article 6 for those with an interest in administrative law. Interestingly, the section on the substance of the guarantees provided by Article 6 is not included here, but at the end of the section on Swiss administrative law. Although there is a certain logic to its inclusion here, the organization of part one might be thought to lead more naturally to the insertion of the material on the substance of the right to a fair trial at the end of that section.

The second section, which is based mainly on the administrative law in Bern, is by far the longest in the book, and therein lies the difficulty for a non-Swiss lawyer: the description of the different types of administrative law is extensive. Further, in each case, whether disputes will be considered as 'civil' or criminal matters, or even whether Article 6 applies is considered. This is, no doubt, of much interest and relevance to Swiss lawyers, but from the external perspective there is perhaps too much detail, and too many examples. However, notwithstanding this section's length (or perhaps because of it), the book underscores the importance of administrative law and how arbitrary the distinction is between those who will be able to rely on Article 6 and those who cannot. The final section, again, probably has more relevance to the Swiss lawyer than to the majority of international human rights lawyers, dealing as it does with the particular problems for the cantons of complying with the requirements of Article 6. It may be, however, that these problems will be recognized in other federal systems and may also be of relevance to those who are interested in the difficulties of ensuring the implementation of the Convention in domestic legal systems.

Overall this book is thorough and well researched. Further, the information within it has been, on the whole, logically structured and organized. For someone with an interest in this particular question, it must have great relevance. How great an audience it will find outside this is a different question, as such a large part of the book relates specifically to the Swiss situation, although the problems encountered in applying Article 6 in the administrative context, which the book highlights, are present in many, if not all, member States.

LORNA WOODS

Whither Jerusalem? Proposals and Positions Concerning the Future of Jerusalem. By MOSHE HIRSCH, DEBORAH HOUSEN-COURIEL and RUTH LAPIDOTH. The Hague: Martinus Nijhoff, 1995. xi + 182 pp. £59.

There can be little doubt that the future status of Jerusalem has been one of the main stumbling-blocks to a settlement of the Palestinian-Israeli or Arab-Israeli conflicts. For a mixture of religious, historical and political reasons, Jerusalem has achieved an importance out of all proportion to its economic or strategic significance. United under Israeli control since 1967, the Israeli Knesset, or parliament, passed a law in 1980 proclaiming that 'Jerusalem, whole and united, is the capital of Israel'. For its part, the Executive Committee of the PLO reaffirmed its commitment, in February 1985, to '[e]nding the Zionist occupation of the occupied Arab territories, including Jerusalem', while, in December 1973, an Arab League Summit Conference had called for '[l]ibera-tion of the Arab city of Jerusalem, and rejection of any situation which may be harmful to complete Arab sovereignty over the Holy City'.[1]

The present book, written and compiled by international law scholars at the Hebrew University of Jerusalem, offers a useful overview and analysis of the bewildering variety of proposals and positions which have been adopted concerning the future of Jerusalem, beginning in 1916 with the Sykes-Picot Agreement. The proposals and positions take up the greater part of the book and are set out in Chapter Two. In the preceding chapter, Dr Moshe Hirsch considers the legal status of Jerusalem. While generally fair-minded and balanced in his approach, certain historical events, perhaps inevitably, are portrayed from an Israeli perspective. For example, Dr Hirsch refers to the establishment of the State of Israel as 'triggering an invasion by Arab states' (p. 3). That is a legitimate viewpoint; however it is by no means the only one. The Arab States portrayed their action as, *inter alia*, intervention at the behest of the Arab population of Palestine, following the termination of the League of Nations Mandate, and as a form of humanitarian

---

[1] See, respectively, Y. Lukacs (ed.), *The Israeli-Palestinian Conflict* (Cambridge University Press, 1992), pp. 369, 463.

intervention.[2] While one need not necessarily accept such arguments at face-value, neither should the notion of an Arab 'invasion' be treated as unproblematic. Similarly, in discussing the circumstances in which Israel occupied the Old City and east Jerusalem in 1967, Dr Hirsch perhaps places excessive emphasis on the belligerence of Jordanian forces at the time and on Israel's apparently 'defensive' posture (p. 6). The truth, as so often in the Middle East, is more complex. Thus, Israel's occupation of the Old City *followed* the adoption of a ceasefire resolution by the UN Security Council, on 6 June, which the Jordanian Government had formally (and apparently sincerely) accepted.[3]

Nevertheless, Dr Hirsch is to be commended for setting out the range of official and scholarly opinion on the legal status of Jerusalem under international law. As he acknowledges, many of the positions taken on this topic 'derive from their espousers' ideological-political approach to the Arab-Israeli conflict' rather than from a dispassionate analysis of international law.

Chapter Two, which accounts for well over half the book, offers an overview of successive proposals and positions adopted concerning the future of Jerusalem. The documentary source, date and background to each of the proposals or positions is given. However, the proposals and positions themselves are merely summarized. I must confess to a preference for primary texts, wherever possible. Summaries, though useful, may nevertheless distort or modify the meaning of the original proposals in some way, particularly where there is an element of ambiguity (deliberate or otherwise) in the primary text. Summaries are also much less interesting to read. However, these criticisms concern form rather than substance. Regarding matters of substance, I am puzzled at the omission of any reference to the Husein-McMahon correspondence of 1915–16, in which Great Britain pledged her support for Arab independence in an area that apparently included Jerusalem. In these letters, Sir Henry McMahon, the British High Commissioner in Egypt, affirmed that 'Great Britain will guarantee the Holy Places against all external aggression and will recognize their inviolability'.[4] Surely this 'proposal', however out-dated, merits inclusion quite as much as the contemporaneous (and inconsistent) Sykes-Picot Agreement.

Chapter Three, although rather short, is useful in drawing together the key elements of the various proposals and positions surveyed earlier. These are considered in terms of (a) national aspirations, (b) the holy places and (c) municipal administration. While (b) and (c) are relatively straight-forward, the notion of 'national aspirations', as used by the authors, is wide-ranging, encompassing: 'sovereignty over the city . . . arrangements concerning citizenship and the political rights of the inhabitants, the city's demilitarization and neutrality, as well as various forms of international supervision over the institutions that are to be entrusted with the city's administration' (p. 138).

Chapter Four, written by Professor Ruth Lapidoth, presents a 'Lexicon of Terms'. In fact, this is far more than a lexicon in the conventional sense, offering historically-informed and wide-ranging essays on a range of topics and concepts relevant to the proposals surveyed concerning the future of Jerusalem. These include 'autonomy', 'condominium', 'internationalization' and 'sovereignty'. Some of these entries, such as the one on sovereignty, are masterly overviews of a complex and multi-faceted, subject, extending to no more than a page and a half. The book concludes with a short bibliography.

As a contribution to the continuing quest to devise a widely acceptable solution to the status of Jerusalem, this book is to be commended. While it must be used in conjunction with a collection of the most important primary texts, it undoubtedly has value. The 1993

[2] See, generally, I. Pogany. *The Security Council and the Arab-Israeli Conflict* (Gower, 1984), pp. 37–41.

[3] Ibid., p. 92.

[4] See, e.g., T. G. Fraser (ed.), *The Middle East 1914–1979* (Edward Arnold, 1980), p. 12, at p. 13.

Israel-PLO Declaration of Principles on Interim Self-Government Arrangements calls for 'permanent status negotiations' to deal with particularly thorny issues such as Jerusalem, to commence not later than the beginning of the third year of the interim period. This book can certainly be used or consulted with profit by participants in such talks and by other interested parties. However, goodwill and an overriding commitment to peace remain imperative and, unfortunately, elusive.

ISTVAN POGANY

International Organizations and Civil Wars. By HILAIRE McCOUBREY and NIGEL D. WHITE. Aldershot: Dartmouth, 1995, xiii + 294 pp. £40.

This well-researched and clearly-written book is both a little less and a little more than might be deduced from the evidence of its title. Less, in the sense that (as is suggested by the identity of the authors) its focus is largely on legal matters; and more in the sense that it extends beyond the activities of organizations to examine the legal principles which relate to non-international armed conflicts.

The book commences with an examination of the international legal framework which is applicable to civil wars, and of the powers of the various international organizations which have become involved in such wars. It then proceeds to a detailed scrutiny of these matters. On the relevant law, individual chapters are devoted to the status of the parties, constraints upon the conduct of hostilities, humanitarian assistance, the question of refugees and the associated matter of 'ethnic cleansing', and the issue of criminal liability. The role of organizations is explored through chapters on observation and fact finding, election monitoring, peace-keeping forces, and the use of coercion.

As the authors recognize, attempts by or on behalf of the international society to exert a purchase on the conduct of civil wars tend to run up against the extreme sensitivity of the State on whose territory the war is being conducted. None the less, many issues which bear on civil wars have come on to the international agenda, especially of late. The unsurprising result, so far as international law is concerned, is that it is beset with uncertainty and difficulty. In this respect the authors cite, *inter alia*, the issue of the recognition, and hence what will be seen as the legitimation, of dissident groups. They also point (connectedly) to the poorly developed condition of that part of the law (the 'Hague' division) which concerns the conduct of (internal) hostilities. At the same time, however, they demonstrate that the law has unquestionably begun to extend to civil conflicts, sometimes with relative certainty—as in the case of refugees.

Regarding the work of international organizations in civil wars, the legal bases of such activities are explored, and attention is drawn to the difficulties of applying the *jus in bello* to military forces mounted by international organizations on a multi-national basis. On peace-keeping (now often called 'traditional' peace-keeping), the authors identify the key principles as consent, impartiality, and the use of force only in self-defence. They point to the problems which frequently attend the effort to act on this basis in an intra-State context, and give a number of illustrations drawn both from the UN's experience and from that of other organizations. But they are also very clear—and convincing—in their belief that, as a practical matter, it is a mistake to try to combine peace-keeping and enforcement within a single operation.

On enforcement, the authors distinguish between economic and military measures, arguing that the effectiveness of the former depends on immediate, mandatory, and comprehensive action. With regard to armed coercion, they suggest that it is not a misuse of power for the UN Security Council to authorize an *ad hoc* coalition to act on its behalf—provided that the objectives of the operation are clearly established by the Council at the outset, so enabling the UN to be in effective overall control. As the armed action in Korea in the early 1950s was not so controlled, strong doubt is expressed as to whether the Council's delegation of authority to the United States was constitutional. With regard to the sanctioning of military action by other organizations, such as NATO in Bosnia-Herzegovina and the Economic Community of West African States in Liberia, the authors note that the UN appears not to worry whether the body concerned is empowered by its own constituent treaty so to act.

The authors do not attempt to draw any general conclusions from this mixed story. It would be possible to sum it up along the lines of the glass which was perceived either as half empty or as half full. The tenor of this very useful work suggests that its two authors would place themselves in the latter camp.

ALAN JAMES

Judge Shigeru Oda and the Progressive Development of International Law. By EDWARD MCWHINNEY. Dordrecht: Martinus Nijhoff, 1993. 667 pp. £123.50. *Judge Manfred Lachs and Judicial Law-Making.* By EDWARD MCWHINNEY. Dordrecht: Martinus Nijhoff, 1995. 424 pp. £101.

These volumes inaugurate a new series, entitled *The Judges*, bringing together the individual opinions of leading members of the International Court of Justice and reviewing the contribution of the judges concerned to international law and adjudication. Each volume has the same format: first a biographical essay of about 100 pages analysing the subject's judicial work and setting it in the wider context of his professional career, then a much longer section reproducing the opinions themselves and certain related material. There is also a bibliography of the judge's principal publications and, in the case of the Lachs volume, a section containing a number of public letters and statements. In the volumes under review, the biographical essays are by Professor Edward McWhinney, who knew Judge Lachs well, and who is also general editor of the series.

The decision to begin the series with volumes devoted to Judges Oda and Lachs may seem a little surprising. The former, though elected to the Court in 1975, was re-elected in both 1984 and 1993 and, as his declaration in the Cameroon/Nigeria *Land and Maritime Boundary* case (1996) has recently demonstrated, continues to articulate a distinctive point of view. An assessment of Judge Oda published in 1993 must therefore be in the nature of an interim report. Judge Lachs, though sadly no longer with us, was a member of the Court from 1966 to 1993, but unlike Judge Oda, wrote relatively few individual opinions for the judicial biographer to scrutinize. How, in the light of these different constraints, has Professor McWhinney handled his task?

As regards the Oda volume, the constraint is perhaps more apparent than real. Although the latest opinion considered is Judge Oda's dissent in the *Land, Island and Maritime Frontier* case (1992), the subject's writings, both judicial and extra-judicial, were already so extensive as to provide ample material for commentary. Indeed, while recognizing the value of Judge Oda's contributions, particularly on law of the sea issues, McWhinney is critical of the length of some of his opinions, a view which others may share. The emphasis, however, quite rightly, is on content rather than form, and a fascinating account is provided of the personal and cultural taproots of Judge Oda's thought. Judge Lachs, too, produced a good deal of extra-judicial writing, made full use of by the editor, who supplements the three main individual opinions and larger number of short declarations by including, in the documents section, passages from judgments of the Court which Lachs is thought to have written. The latter, of course, cannot be formally attributed, but as the editor explains, Lachs's forte as a judge was as a conciliator and a 'team player'. Accordingly, this broader treatment of his judicial work is well justified. In courts, as in other institutions, those who work behind the scenes may be equally, if not more important than those whose activity is more prominent. It is therefore right that the contributions of the former should be properly acknowledged.

A commendable feature of both books is that the work of each judge is related not simply to his personal philosophy and background, but also to the work of the Court as a whole, considered from both the substantive and the institutional aspect. Thus in each volume there is discussion of, among other matters, the evolution of the chambers procedure, following its inception in the *Gulf of Maine* case, the Court's formulation and application of the principles of continental shelf delimitation, which prompted dissents from both Lachs (in the *North Sea* cases), and Oda (in the *Libya/Tunisia* and *Libya/ Malta* cases), and the various UN Administrative Tribunal cases, which were also controversial. It is not possible to discuss the many interesting points raised in the editor's essays here, but two in particular call for brief comment. A recurrent theme is what the editor sees as the significant difference between the 'new' progressive Court of the Lachs/Oda era and the 'old' positivist Court, whose apogee (or nadir) was the decision in the 1966 *South West Africa* cases. This is a contrast Professor McWhinney has drawn before, but, as the reviewer has argued elsewhere, when closely inspected it does not seem very convincing (see *International and Comparative Law Quarterly*, 35 (1986), p. 737). Likewise, not everyone will be persuaded that the dismissal of the *Nuclear Tests* cases in 1974 was the master-stroke of judicial pragmatism that the editor applauds (see pp. 85–6 of the essay on Judge Lachs, but also the more cautious assessment on p. 80).

A point concerning the documents contained in these volumes should also be noted. Including the full texts of a judge's individual pronouncements is unquestionably useful, but when these are voluminous is an indulgence which makes for a large and very expensive book. Further volumes are planned and will, it is understood, include edited versions of lengthier opinions, instead of the full text. This should bring them within the reach of law libraries, which may be put off by the price of the volumes under review, but which will certainly wish to add this series to their collections.

J. G. Merrills

Principles of International Environmental Law. Volume I: *Frameworks, Standards and Implementation.* By Philippe Sands. Manchester University Press, 1995. 773 pp. £90 (hardback); £29.99 (paper).

Philippe Sands's intention in writing this book is 'to provide a comprehensive overview of those rules of public international law which have as their object the protection of the environment' (p. xv). Bearing in mind the remarkable growth in the number of rules and principles in this area over the last twenty-five years, the author's task is a considerable one.

The book is divided into three parts. Part I is entitled 'The Legal Institutional Framework' and includes chapters covering the historical development of international environmental law, the main actors involved in that development (including both IGOs and NGOs), and the sources of law. In addition, a chapter addresses the question of enforcement of international rules and the various procedures that may be available to settle disputes. The author rightly stipulates that rules in this area 'have developed as a result of a complex interplay between governments, non-governmental actors and international organisations', and that improvements in our scientific knowledge of the sensitivity of the environment to human activities have played a 'significant catalytic role' in such development (p. 26).

The second part of the book includes an analysis of those rules and principles that have general applicability to the protection of the environment (such as the obligation to co-operate, Principle 21 of the 1972 Stockholm Declaration, the concept of sustainable development, and the preventive and precautionary principles). In addition, separate chapters discuss the law and principles which have developed with specific application to the protection of the atmosphere, the oceans, international watercourses, and both the Arctic region and Antarctic continent. Discussion also addresses the law as it relates to waste management, activities and substances of a particularly hazardous nature, and to the conservation of biological diversity; it is a sobering thought that it 'has been estimated that continued loss at the current rate would destroy up to fifteen per cent of the earth's species over the next twenty five years' (p. 369).

It is refreshing to note that the author includes a chapter on European Community environmental law and throughout the book makes reference to developments at Community level. A substantial body of law has developed at the EC level and the importance of the need to protect the environment is reflected in the EC Treaty which, post-Maastricht, stipulates that one of the tasks of the Community shall be 'to promote . . . throughout the Community . . . sustainable and non-inflationary growth respecting the environment' (Article 2). Whilst it is clear that question marks remain over the EC's ability to provide protection for the Community's environment, international lawyers would do well to reflect on efforts made within this regional economic organization and, in particular, on the ability of the Community both to influence international debate and to develop a body of environmental rules and principles which bind fifteen Western European States. The apparent ineffectiveness of enforcement procedures within the EC both at national and at Community level could usefully have been more thoroughly addressed, as well as the circumstances governing the applicability of the EC doctrine of 'direct effect' (a footnote on p. 586 would seem incorrectly to refer the reader to an earlier discussion on this issue).

Part III usefully addresses various techniques utilized to implement rules and principles. The procedural technique of environmental impact assessment is clearly and concisely discussed. Developments to improve the accuracy, exchange and availability of environmental information are assessed, the author indicating that the 'original reporting, consultation and notification obligations which are well established in international law have been supplemented by a second generation of rules . . . [which] aim to increase the public availability of information by creating rights of access and encouraging greater dissemination to consumers at various levels' (p. 626).

The issue of liability for environmental damage is addressed, including the difficulties in defining the content of the rules governing State liability for such damage. A chapter on trade and competition includes an overview of those GATT panel decisions with implications for environmental measures, and of the EC's approach in situations where national environmental laws conflict with the principle of free movement of goods.

The final chapter concentrates on the availability of financial resources to developing countries both to induce them to sign up to international rules that seek to protect the environment, and subsequently to facilitate their implementation of such obligations.

The law is stated as of 1 January 1993 although the author has been able to include reference to some subsequent developments. Inevitably important developments (such as the adoption of the 1995 Straddling Fish Stocks Agreement and the 1994 Nuclear Safety Convention) escape comprehensive assessment. However, this underlines the rapidly evolving nature of the subject rather than any failing on the author's part.

At times the text could be criticized for lacking detail; for instance, treatment of the 1979 Convention on Long Range Transboundary Air Pollution and its protocols could have been improved by a more detailed evaluation of the merits of a 'critical load' rather than a 'flat rate' approach to emission reductions, an indication that neither the United Kingdom nor the United States ratified the 1985 Sulphur Protocol, and by greater emphasis being placed on the important role of the Executive Body and the 'framework' nature of the convention. However, it should be noted that each chapter is accompanied by a very useful select bibliography to enable the reader to read further on matters of particular interest.

Overall, this book is to be highly commended as it has succeeded in providing the reader with an overview of those rules and techniques applicable to environmental protection at the international level. It is sure to prove an important source of reference to those wishing to appreciate and study the large body of law now applicable in this area.

The book is accompanied by two further volumes which provide the text of various relevant international and EC documents.

P. G. G. Davies

Justice in International Law. By Stephen M. Schwebel. Cambridge: Cambridge University Press, 1994. viii + 630 pp. £80.

This handsome volume brings together 36 of more than 100 of the writings of Judge Schwebel, as published in the years from 1952 to 1994 and now selected by him for reprinting. Several of the pieces were co-authored (Essays 10, 27); others were written as part of collective work for bodies such as the ILA (Essay 23 (1957)) or in an official capacity as an assistant legal adviser within the State Department (e.g. Essay 20, which argues persuasively for the automatic and mandatory application of Article 19 of the Charter to member States in arrears with their financial contributions; he is, consistently, critical of the subsequent change in the US position on this issue: Essay 22 (1994)).

The collection is organized under five main themes, which very much reflect Judge Schwebel's work and preoccupations during these years: the International Court (on which he has served since 1981), international arbitration, the United Nations, international contracts and expropriation, and a fifth miscellaneous category covering use of force, compliance with international law and the role of the government legal adviser. Schwebel's various roles and offices are thus firmly reflected here, and since he has rarely been cast as an unengaged commentator, many of the pieces have either the air of occasional work, or of restrained reflections on incidents in which his role of participant was more important than that of observer.

The sense of restraint is conveyed, for example, by repeated statements of the need 'to confine my remarks to the substance of what I have earlier expressed in Court opinions' (p. 140; see also pp. 134–5)—a statement which betrays the fact that those were separate, or more often dissenting, opinions. The *Nicaragua* case, in particular, casts a long shadow: see especially Essays 7 and 8. But this is not to suggest that the pieces lack interest or balance. While critical of the Court's handling of the *Nicaragua* case—and of some aspects of the handling of that case who could not be critical?—he notes that one of the major divisive issues there was one of fact, and that the United States did not assist its case by its failure to appear at the Merits phase (p. 134; see also pp. 142, 144). But his discussion of the issues is itself not assisted by a failure to distinguish between collective measures taken on the territory of the requesting State and those taken on the territory of a third State said to be assisting insurgents. It was the latter situation that the Court was addressing in *Nicaragua*.

The sense of occasion is conveyed, for example, in a series of pieces which comment on themes specific to the time of writing, whether in an address (e.g. Essays 1, 8), a comment on a paper delivered that day (e.g. Essays 14, 28) or otherwise. Thus some of the pieces, including some of the more recent, seem rather dated—or, which may be a polite way of saying the same thing, precisely located in time past. For example, Essay 6 (1989) extols the use of *ad hoc* chambers, but who now thinks they will have a major role in the next phase of the Court's history? Similarly Essay 19 (1973) argues against the admission of mini-States to the United Nations—a bridge long ago crossed, and in my view, rightly, in the direction of universality of membership. On the other hand, some of the individual pieces are classics on their subject; this is particularly true of the pieces in Part II on arbitration, where Schwebel speaks with great authority and assurance, and of his still valuable early work on the international character of the UN Secretariat (Essays 15, 16, 17).

The overall impression one gains is of a doughty proponent of legal positions associated over time with the United States—but also, and increasingly, of a temperate and realistic proponent of internationalism. The tone is caught, for example, by his remark that the

International Court is—whatever one may think of *Nicaragua*—'a body of high achieve-ment and unused potential' (p. 4), or by the observation, in the same essay, that 'There is no use in pretending that we have the sort of international law we need simply because we need it' (p. 13). And it is caught in his remark on government legal advising, that 'The Legal Adviser acts not only as the conscience of the Foreign Ministry; he is its advocate, if not apologist as well. Indeed, it might be said that he is customarily its advocate and occasionally its conscience' (Essay 36 (1967) at p. 610). That remark is redolent of the balances which underlie a career, but for Schwebel, given the distinguished contributions he made to the International Law Commission and is making to the International Court, it was only part of a career.

In a collection of previously published work, to say that any part of this volume comes as a surprise would be little more than a confession of not keeping up with the literature. But for all that, this is a most useful compilation of pieces, as well as a distinguished reflection of a distinguished—and fortunately unfinished—career.

JAMES CRAWFORD

Enforcing EC Law. By JOSEPHINE STEINER. London: Blackstone Press Limited, 1995. xxxii + 194 pp. £18.95.

The title of this work is a little misleading in that 'enforcing EC law' might raise the expectation that the book would look at the range of methods by which obligations arising under Community law are enforced against institutions, member States and private parties. However, Steiner's work is more narrowly focused and deals only with the enforcement of Community *rights* by individuals. As a consequence, topics which one would expect in a general work on enforcement are omitted, such as a thorough discussion of Article 169 of the EC Treaty and the problems faced in enforcing Community obligations against individuals and other private legal persons. Turning to what the book does cover, Steiner introduces the Community legal system and its main institutions before moving on to outline the doctrines of direct effect and indirect effect and the principle of State liability for breaches of Community law laid down in the landmark case of *Francovich*. The second section of the book, which is the main part, examines the enforcement of Community rights by the national courts of the member States, while the third section considers the scope for claims by individuals for redress against the Community institutions. The final section considers briefly various non-judicial methods of obtaining redress, a useful perspective often ignored by lawyers when considering remedies.

The book's main strength lies in the second section, where Steiner takes the reader through the general principles of Community law covering the circumstances in which national courts must provide a remedy for a breach of an individual's Community rights, and then examines the public and private law remedies available in England and Wales in the light of these Community requirements. The reader is invited to view what may be the familiar territory of remedies, such as judicial review, injunctions, declarations and damages, with 'European eyes' and to consider the extent to which those national remedies satisfy the Community requirement that there be an effective remedy for any breach of a Community right. Where an existing remedy does not wholly satisfy this criterion, Steiner is prepared to suggest how the existing remedy might be remodelled or adapted. This survey of national remedies leads the author to conclude that the demands of Community law relating to remedies have been, and can be, met without major alteration of the traditional domestic remedies, with the significant exception of the area of State liability for breaches, the *Francovich* principle. Noting the areas of uncertainty which remain in relation to *Francovich*, she emphasizes the value of introducing uniform Community rules for the application of this principle. This raises the very interesting issue of the way in which much of Community law in this area has developed on a case by case basis and the advantages and limitations of such an approach for uniform enforcement of the law. As may be seen from the bibliography, there is a good deal of periodical literature on the area of national remedies but much of it tends to concentrate on particular aspects of the issue. Steiner's work is helpful in bringing together various remedies and providing an overall perspective.

The third section of the book considers the opportunities for individual action against the Community institutions and appears to have been included for the sake of completeness and a desire to provide a comprehensive account of the methods of redress of individual grievances. It provides an outline of the relevant routes to litigating against an act of one of the institutions (although the division of jurisdiction between the Court of Justice and the Court of First Instance is not addressed), but adds little to what has already been written on this area by many authors including Steiner herself, and the level of discussion here sits a little uncomfortably in the shadow of the earlier section. This unevenness in depth may cause one to wonder for whom the book is designed. Those unfamiliar with Community law might require more on the general machinery of the system, whereas those looking for a more specialist account of remedies might very well dispense with the outline of institutions and other matters dealt with in the first chapter. Notwithstanding this, however, since most litigation involving individuals and Community law takes place in the national courts, this book should prove useful to practising lawyers in England and Wales who need to be familiar not only with the substance of Community law but also with the procedures for obtaining effective redress for breaches. More generally, it supplies a helpful starting-point for students and academic lawyers seeking an introduction to the interface between Community and English law on remedies.

ANN SHERLOCK

The United Nations at Age Fifty: A Legal Perspective. Edited by CHRISTIAN TOMUSCHAT. The Hague: Kluwer Law International, 1995. xvii + 327 pp. £84.

This is a collection of essays from seventeen distinguished scholars marking the fiftieth anniversary of the United Nations. As Christian Tomuschat says in his Foreword, much has been written concerning the UN's influence as a political force over the past fifty years—and rightly so—but there is also room for an analysis of its influence as a manager of the international community through the legal process and championship of the rule of law. The professed claim of this collection is to contribute to that analysis by garnering the views of scholars from across the international spectrum, to imitate imperfectly the diversity of the UN itself. Although not formally representing their governments or the UN, there are pieces from nationals of each of the five permanent members of the Security Council, from individuals intimately connected with the working of the organization and its legal offices, and from nationals representing the geographical groups that make up the General Assembly. This is one of the great attractions of this book, for represented here in a single volume are the different approaches to the UN's legal functions that operate every day on the floor of the committees and organs of the organization. In this vein, and although primarily about the UN as a 'juridical entrenched form of international cooperation' (Foreword, p. xi), it is entirely appropriate that the contributors have not cast aside political considerations. All of the contributions are shot through with a realism that makes them all the more compelling. It is right that Qizhi He (China) laments the UN's 'unlawful' exclusion of China until 1971 and emphasizes that it must refrain from interfering in the internal affairs of States, that Mohamed Bennouna

(Morocco and Arab World Institute) asserts that the Security Council is not subject to any review of the legality of its actions, whereas Thomas Franck (USA) argues that it must be and Pemmaraju Rao (India and Member of the ILC) thinks it could be, if set within proper bounds. In so far as the seventeen contributors differ in their analysis of the many legal functions of the UN, this reflects the political nature of the tasks entrusted to the organization and emphasizes the nature of the community in which these legal powers are to be exercised.

The essays are divided into two Parts: Part I on Issues of International Peace and Security; and Part II on Other Main Fields of Activity of the United Nations. It is in Part I that the single weakness of this collection is to be found. As Tomuschat rightly says, the purposes of a study like the present one should be to use the lessons of the past as beacons for the future. With this in mind, there is perhaps too much repetition in these essays of the history and background of the UN's legal powers. Most readers of this work will not need reminding more than once—if at all—of how the UN grew out of the failure of the League of Nations as an effective guardian of international peace and security, or of how Chapters VI and VII of the UN Charter recast the UN's powers in this regard. It is difficult to find a different angle on such matters and none such exists here. For this reader, a brief introduction would have been enough, but then I was not faced—as was Tomuschat—with such a powerful array of scholars each with a point to make and a scene to set.

It is always invidious to pick out individual contributions from a work of this calibre, for (as here) omission does not always imply criticism. However, I must commend Thomas Franck's piece on 'The United Nations as Guarantor of International Peace and Security: Past Present and Future', Winrich Kuhne on 'The United Nations, Fragmenting States and the Need for Enlarged Peacekeeping', Allain Pellet's 'The Road to Hell is Paved with Good Intentions' and Rao's piece giving an Indian perspective on the UN and international peace and security. Undoubtedly, this selection reveals my bias for those brave enough to grope for the future. Franck is thoughtful and imaginative as always, echoing themes now found in his *Fairness in International Law and Institutions*, and whether or not one agrees with his argument (and many will not), he has given us his own vision of the future of international peace management. Likewise with Kuhne and Pellet, both of whose contributions are light on history and heavy on analysis. Rao's essay is perhaps the most extensively researched and suffers from none of the superficiality that (understandably) touches some of the other pieces—the footnotes alone make a good starting-point for anyone taking to his topic for the first time. His analysis is penetrating and his view of the relative role of the Security Council and ICJ has, in this reviewer's opinion, the stamp of authority and common sense.

Part II has six essays on a wider range of topics. As one would expect, Tomuschat on 'International Law' is well written, informative and readable. It makes clear again just how important the UN is in the structure of the international legal system. It fits well with Wolfrum's canter through the developments which led to widespread ratification of the UN Convention on the Law of the Sea 1982. I particularly liked Andronico Adede's piece on 'International Protection of the Environment', which is detailed enough to carry the expert further, but broad enough to engage those who so far have touched this area of international law only fleetingly.

There is no doubt that this book is a very timely and scholarly tribute to the juridical persona of the United Nations. The existence of a sub-theme in Part I makes this a valuable set of essays for those concerned with the future of international peace-keeping and peace enforcement, while the diverse nature of Part II will hold something of interest for other readers. Bound in UN blue, it is a worthy addition to the *Legal Aspects of International Organization* series.

MARTIN DIXON

The Svalbard Treaty; From Terra Nullius to Norwegian Sovereignty. By
GEIR ULFSTEIN. Oslo: Scandinavian University Press, 1995. 572 pp.
including index and appendices.

Article 1 of the Svalbard Treaty, 1920, applies to the several islands situated within
given co-ordinates in the north Barents Sea, but principally to Spitzbergen, the largest
island (p. 22). A surprisingly large number—some 42 States—are now parties (pp. 65,
162), including several non-European States (p. 163). It seems fair to say that most
international lawyers are relatively ignorant of this Treaty regime, though the same
author (with Robin Churchill) has already analysed the question of the application of the
Treaty to the various maritime zones around Svalbard in a previous book, *Marine
Management in Disputed Waters: The Case of the Barents Sea*, 1992, Chapter 2 (reviewed
in this *Year Book*, 63 (1992), p. 467). In Chapter 7 of the present work, similar
conclusions are reached on such maritime matters; and it is thus concluded that the treaty
regime does apply to the territorial sea (pp. 415, 417), and also (after much discussion) by
'an extensive interpretation or an analogy' to the continental shelf and 200–mile zone
(p. 441).

After World War I, an international legal regime was thought necessary (p. 38) for this
remote region of Europe, most particularly to control mining (p. 193). A specially-
formed Spitzbergen Commission never considered granting Norway a (conventional)
mandate over Svalbard under the League of Nations (p. 49) (though the Treaty regime
is seen to bear some similarities thereto (p. 50)). One of the three main Treaty elements
was the granting of sovereignty there to Norway (p. 49). The author cites the other two
main features as being (i) preservation of the *terra nullius* status through non-discrimination and by allowing accession by all States (p. 158); and (ii) ensuring peaceful utilization.
Under Article 8(1) of the Treaty, Norway undertook to provide 'mining regulations'
there. The latter article is fleshed out in the annexed Mining Code, which the author finds
not only to be an integral part of Norwegian law (p. 137) but also an 'internationally
binding instrument' (see pp. 136–49). The important legal effect of this finding is that
Norway may not unilaterally amend the Code (p. 341) (the view of the former USSR
(pp. 147–8)) though it may adapt it through 'interpretation' (pp. 148–9, 314).

Whereas in the early 1920s several nations were involved in mining on Spitzbergen,
such mining is now the preserve of just Norway and Russia (p. 65). Indeed the (then)
USSR even suggested in 1944 that most of Svalbard should become a Soviet/Norwegian
condominium (p. 66), an idea which had been floated even pre-World War I. It is thus
not surprising that such diplomatic protests that have arisen in more recent times have
almost exclusively come from the USSR/Russia as the main protagonist of treaty rights
on Norwegian actions such as imposition of regulations (p. 272); establishing a telemetric
(ESRO) station there (p. 67); establishment of a 200–mile zone around Svalbard (p. 446);
and other matters mentioned below. Accordingly, the author sees *lack* of Russian protest
(as, e.g., in the case of Norwegian rejection of the application by the Russian Trust,
Artikugol, to commence commercial aviation) as 'acquiescence and relevant subsequent
State practice in the interpretation of the Treaty' (p. 199) on the basis that interpretation
by 'the two principal actors on Svalbard' should 'carry considerable weight' (p. 200). But
at another point (p. 78), we are warned (rather inconsistently) that the 'bilateral practice'
of Norway and Russia should not be all-pervasive from an interpretative point of view
(e.g., over placing Svalbard under NATO command in 1950 (p. 368)). At times (e.g., in
Chapter 5 on 'Demilitarisation'), one feels that perhaps the author has downplayed too
much the many and consistent Russian protests in reaching his interpretative conclusions
(as, e.g., p. 378). Ironically, when the treaty was signed in 1919, the USSR was not a
party (the original parties being the USA, UK, France, Japan, Italy, Norway, Sweden,
Denmark and the Netherlands (p. 157)); and it only ratified in 1935. Following the break-
up of the Soviet Union, the problem of State succession arises in this regard (pp. 159–60);

not surprisingly it is concluded that Russia is still a party to the treaty, whereas the other former Republics are not (p. 161).

Although coal mining has been the main basis for Norwegian and Russian settlements in Svalbard, this bilaterality of interest may be diminishing. For the potential of oil discoveries (p. 67) may attract other active participants (p. 79). Recent oil exploration in the region—as well as coal mining—present increasing conservation concerns for the environment generally (p. 187). (Article 2(2) of the Treaty only refers to 'preservation' of the 'fauna and flora' (p. 187).) For example, since 1973 mining rights may not be acquired on designated nature reserves (p. 324). It must not be forgotten that the earlier history of Svalbard did indeed evidence conflicts between different nationalities in respect of hunting for the region's rich natural resources (p. 34) at which time the archipelago was considered to be a *terra nullius*.

The fact that Article 1 of the Treaty grants 'full and absolute sovereignty to Norway'— subject to 'the stipulations' of same (p. 124) leads the author to concluded that such 'sole sovereignty' should prevail unless otherwise provided in the treaty (p. 125). Not surprisingly, the USSR had some initial reservations to such Norwegian sovereignty and only accepted this by a later verbal note of 1924 (p. 56). In 1925 under the Norwegian Svalbard Act, the archipelago was officially placed under this sovereignty (p. 64). This Norwegian sovereignty (considered in detail in Chapter 2) is concluded to be 'subject only to obligations established in international law' (p. 81), most particularly so as to serve 'the interests of the international community rather than Norwegian national interests' (p. 83) as an 'objective regime' in the same mould as, e.g., arrangements for international waterways (p. 166). Though *third States* had no rights under the Treaty as such (p. 172), Norway's non-discrimination obligation may work in their favour (p. 225). For instance, it is surprising to learn that seemingly unlike anywhere else in the world (apart from Antarctica), visitors to the (main) Longyearbyen airport need no passport (p. 177). (However he also concludes that Norway may restrict access to Svalbard provided the measures are non-discriminatory (p. 269).)

Such sovereignty was reinforced in 1975 in various ways to the sound of Russian protests (p. 69), though since the ending of the Cold War there has been more Russian inclination to accept such Norwegian moves (p. 69), even in the Russian settlements (p. 71). Prior to this date the Norwegian exercise of jurisdiction in Svalbard had been 'rather passive' (p. 82), though one forms the impression of its getting increasingly active—e.g., in the maritime area against non-Russian ships (pp. 448–9).

A constant theme of the author is that it is strictly incorrect to say that Svalbard was 'internationalised', as Norway only has treaty restrictions on certain specified 'sovereign rights' (p. 128). For example, Norway cannot enter into treaties violating the rights of States parties (p. 130). This would, e.g., preclude a unilateral transfer to an international organization (p. 131). The implications of Norwegian sovereignty in Svalbard *vis-à-vis* potential Norwegian EU membership are considered (pp. 299–308, 455–9), as is its present membership of the European Economic Area (EEA) (a special protocol *excluding Svalbard* seemingly being (respectively) a potential or actual feature of both (p. 299)). The implications of Norwegian membership of the UN are considered later (p. 385).

The supposed original benefit of granting sovereignty in Svalbard to Norway—then seen as a neutral country—was not just that it resolved the problem of previous competing jurisdiction (p. 50), but also (more obviously) that it assisted *peaceful* utilization. However, Norway appears to get little benefit itself out of its sovereign rights: any revenue from Svalbard has by Treaty to be retained there (under Article 8(2) taxes cannot be used anywhere outside Svalbard); and the level of taxes is so low anyway as to cause Norway to subsidize the administration of the archipelago (pp. 285, 296) (having been at the same level since 1925! (p. 297)). Even the raising of the annual fee for mining beyond the originally set level in the Mining Code—in part justified by inflation!—led to initial Russian protest (p. 325).

The insertion of the non-discrimination principle was largely aimed at preserving previous rights (p. 50), even for all States ratifying the Treaty at a later date (p. 51). The *terra nullius* status *ante quo* is constantly reiterated in the book, and in this connection the author sees it as appropriate to apply an interpretative principle of 'effectiveness' to ensure such rights (p. 129). The requirement of 'equal treatment' (or non-discrimination) is exhaustively analysed in Chapter 3 (including its various attributes) based here on *nationality* alone (p. 231), as it affects such 'disparate activities as hunting and fishing, mining, commercial activities, real property and telecommunication' (p. 175). The gist of this obligation comes in Article 7(1) of the Treaty under which Norway undertakes to 'grant to all nationalities of the High Contracting Parties treatment based on complete equality . . . ' (p. 212). In the past this has not caused significant legal or practical problems with the other most involved State, the USSR (Russia), but increased activity in Svalbard by more nations could change this (p. 175) as well as the fact that Russia is considering new ways of maintaining its population on Svalbard through economic activities (p. 283). (One instance of alleged discrimination against a Russian company is cited at p. 239; but elements of 'most-favoured-nations' are also detectable—for example, Russians were the only nationals exempted from licensing of weapons for polar bear hunting in 1970 (p. 243)!)

The third feature of the 1925 Treaty—'peaceful utilization'—is dealt with in Chapter 5. Here Article 9 is of main importance as it prohibits the establishment of naval bases and fortifications and use of Svalbard for 'war-like purposes' (an article that has been much invoked by the USSR (p. 344) (with its largest naval base at Kola strategically near the area) in connection with Norwegian NATO membership; the ESRO station (above) (p. 355); an airport on Svalbard; and visits by Norwegian ships and aircraft (p. 344)). Does this imply that Svalbard is neutralized or that all military activities are forbidden there? The author thinks not entirely (p. 352)—most obviously if Norwegian self-defence of Svalbard is involved (p. 360). Only during World War II does there appear to have been a breach of the Treaty's non-military requirements—by Germany (p. 359). In response to the many Russian protests on this score, Norway has stated that Article 9 of the Treaty does not forbid *all* military activities there (p. 375).

In essence the book takes the form of a detailed (and almost ritualistic) legal analysis of the main provisions of the 1920 Treaty—the wording of which is 'not always well drafted' (p. 73)—and the annexed Mining Code. Much of this exposition makes for heavy reading, particularly in the case of the Mining Code (Chapter 4). Accordingly, much time is taken up with the legal rules applicable to treaty interpretation. The writer concludes (p. 87) that, although the starting-point should be the facts and law at the Treaty's inception in 1920, this should be tempered by a presumption that the parties intended a 'viable regime', taking into account developments in international law and changing social needs, a factor requiring a 'dynamic interpretation', e.g., in respect of modern more extensive nature conservation measures (p. 278), which would now include 'touristic purposes' (p. 279). Amongst the problems here he opines that in cases of ambiguity, an interpretative principle should be applied which (p. 90) 'places the least restriction on Norwegian sovereignty'. (On this restrictive interpretation principle alone some 31 pages are spent analysing academic viewpoints and international case law!)

One recurrent interpretative problem is that the treaty regime is now very dated having been in existence some 75 years. Thus the author makes frequent reference to modern problems not expressly covered by the Treaty. For example: Does Article 4 (which makes, incidentally, the only reference in the whole Treaty to 'aircraft' (pp. 218, 228–9)), include modern telecommunications apart from 'wireless telegraph stations' (p. 217)? How is the requirement to mark a discovery point under section 9(1) of the Mineral Code (which involves, *inter alia*, making 'marks in solid rock' to visibly locate the claim) to be satisfied *at sea* (p. 319)? (Here Norway has in practice accepted a mark on the nearest land! (p. 320) though it is 'hard to imagine how the principle of the first finder's right is to be applied to the continental shelf' (p. 445)!) Does Article 9 (prohibiting Norwegian fortifications or naval bases) also apply to military aircraft? (At p. 351 he concludes surely yes.) And there is no provision of 'explicit rights' relating to scientific research and meteorology (p. 390) (though Norway has in fact allowed open access in such matters (p. 391)). Because of such changing circumstances and needs, he ultimately (at p. 486) considers whether the Treaty (and Mining Code) needs to be amended or terminated. He recommends neither—merely 'adaptation' through interpretation (p. 487) because this 'has the benefit of preserving the basic legal regime' (p. 488).

Throughout the book there are only occasional analogies made to other comparable 'internationalized' regimes—e.g., most obviously Antarctica, or neutralized areas (e.g., Panama canal, Aaland Islands (p. 364)). This may be because the author ultimately concludes (p. 488) that it is 'hard to imagine that such an arrangement would be acceptable for any other territory'. The author disapproves of the term 'internationalization' to apply to Svalbard (p. 482). He also points out (at p. 388) that other 'demilitarization' regimes are 'more extensive in their substantive scope' because they are 'regarded or managed as global commons', whereas Svalbard is under Norwegian sovereignty. For this reason he sees closer analogies with the regime relating to the Aaland Islands and the Greek islands off Turkey (p. 478). Interestingly, the word 'neutralization' is not used in the Svalbard Treaty, but subsequent State practice indicates this status (p. 367). The Arctic, unlike Antarctica, has not been designated a natural reserve (p. 280). Furthermore Antarctica is, unlike Svalbard, protected by a 50-year moratorium on mineral activities (p. 282). He does briefly discuss the comparative aspect of non-discrimination in regard to other treaty regimes (pp. 472–5). The 1920 Treaty is found to be 'unique in the sense that it provides for the acquisition of non-discriminatory rights through accession on a land territory under national sovereignty' (p. 475)—a right 'only known in the case of global commons and international waterways' (p. 480).

Further analogous references to more general international law might have been used, e.g., to the deep sea-bed regime in discussing whether Norway can reject a mining licence or attach conditions (p. 322); or to the provision on 'nationals' who have 'habitually fished in the zone' in Article 62(3) of the 1982 LOSC, in discussing the share-out of fish stocks around Svalbard (pp. 451–2).

In conclusion, this is a useful study on an area not well known to non-Norwegian lawyers. It is well produced and misprints are commendably few. A niggling complaint is that many of the footnotes are in Norwegian, as also, perversely, is the wording of the many Soviet (Russian) protest notes—the worst example of this is in connection with the placement of Svalbard under NATO (at pp. 368, 369), where no fewer than three such notes are placed in the text in Norwegian, only to be translated into English in the footnotes! What relevance does the Svalbard experiment have for solving other international disputes? At most the author sees present-day application of such a regime in the case of 'other disputed territories' (p. 489) being limited to the *disputing States* alone (p. 489). One gets, then, the impression that the Treaty—a bold pioneering venture at its inception—may have little relevance for today.

CLIVE R. SYMMONS

Aspects of the Protection of Individual and Social Rights. Edited by S. VASSILOUNI. Athens: Hestia Publishers, 1995. 354 pp.

This book on the protection of 'individual and social' rights contains a collection of essays with a diversity of styles, languages, and subject-matters. The book is divided into three sections, the first dealing with the international protection of human rights, the second with the protection of economic and social rights at the European level, and the third with the national protection of economic and social rights. Each section contains four or five essays. Of the fifteen essays, two are in English, four in French, five in German, and four in Greek. An initial unsatisfactory aspect of the book is the lack of summaries in alternative languages. Whilst there is nothing objectionable about a book containing essays in a variety of languages, unless the reader is conversant with all four languages, the overall impact of the book will be severely limited. Indeed, the second section of the book contains three potentially interesting articles on the protection of social rights in Europe, the 'social demands and institutional availabilities' of European integration, and the Community Charter on Social Rights and European industrial law, all of which were in Greek and inaccessible to this reviewer.

Whilst the book as a whole appears to focus predominantly upon the issues relating to the protection of socio-economic rights, the title, referring as it does to 'individual' and 'social' rights, suggests a slightly wider focus. Indeed, the first section of the book is more wide-ranging, and somewhat less coherent than the second and third sections. The essays of Tardu (the protection of human rights after the Vienna Conference), Graham (the implementation of the International Convenant on Civil and Political Rights) and Nowak (the interrelationship between the Covenant on Civil and Political Rights and the European Convention on Human Rights) are all interesting, and in the latter case particularly, informative. They provide, in essence, a snapshot of some of the current concerns of the international human rights community. That they do not cohere well with the other contributions in the book, all of which address more specifically the issue of socio-economic rights, is perhaps excusable.

One curious aspect of the book, which is reflected both in its title and in one or two individual contributions, is the tendency to distinguish between 'social' rights and 'individual' rights. As ordinarily construed, in international human rights treaties at least, 'social rights' are no less 'individual' than are 'political' or 'civil' rights, for example. The distinction to which the editor was apparently referring is generally premised upon one of two arguments. First, that social rights, defined as rights attributed to individuals in virtue of their position in society (e.g. trade union rights, rights to social security), may be distinguished from other individual rights that are enjoyed by all irrespective of their social status (e.g. the right to freedom from torture). Secondly, that whereas individual rights may be directly justified by an appeal to individual dignity or autonomy, social rights are essentially instrumental, and have significance only in so far as they contribute to more basic individual values. Neither of these arguments is beyond criticism, or at least debate. The first distinction may well be correct as a descriptive categorization, but does not in itself lead to any immediate conclusions as to status, or necessitate any particular differences in performance. The second is a more fundamental distinction, but is one that is entirely dependent upon the justificatory discourse pursued. While an appeal to autonomy may well serve to privilege a small range of what are termed civil rights, it has to be recognized that alternative constructions, which might be founded upon a notion of basic needs for example, could underscore the fundamental importance of certain socio-economic rights. What is clear from the book is that, although socio-economic rights have formed a central part of human rights standard setting, there is still considerable confusion as to their nomenclature, justification and operational characteristics.

Most of the essays on socio-economic rights within the first two sections of the book focus upon the activities of various organs and organizations. Nicolas Valticos writes about the work of the ILO, Arghyrios Fatouros about the activities of the OSCE, OECD and UNCTAD, Fritz Fabricius about the European Social Charter, and Jochen Frowein about the European Court of Human Rights. Each chapter provides a brief, but useful, overview. Professor Simma, writing as one of the independent experts of the UN Committee on Economic, Social and Cultural Rights, addresses a slightly wider theme. He begins by noting that the promotion of socio-economic rights has been set back by the collapse of the Soviet bloc in Central and Eastern Europe and by the predominance of competitive, laissez-faire economic policies in the West. He argues, however, with specific reference to the UN Convenant on Economic, Social and Cultural Rights, that contrary to many assumptions, the recognition and promotion of such rights does not require the maintenance of a centralized economic and political system. Rather, the Covenant embodies what the ILC would refer to as 'obligations of result' (as opposed to 'obligations of conduct') which allow States considerable discretion as to the means of implementation employed. Whilst this is undoubtedly the best means of rationalizing the openly welfarist implications of the Covenant in light of the forces of privatization and liberal economic policy, it would be wrong to assume that the UN Covenant makes no stipulations as to the legitimate functions and responsibilities of the State. As a matter of practical organization, the State may wish to divest itself of control over the day to day operation of essential social and educational services, but it still remains ultimately responsible under the terms of the Covenant for their operation. There is a cautious acceptance of the practicalities of privatisation, but a rejection of the normative concept of the 'minimal State'. The fact that the type of obligation undertaken by the State has been transformed from an obligation to 'provide' to an obligation to 'guarantee the provision' is perhaps irrelevant, but nevertheless indicative of the change in emphasis.

Even if socio-economic rights pose interesting questions in the field of international law, as is often the case it is the experience at the national level which is of critical importance. The final section of the book provides several useful and interesting accounts of the protection of economic and social rights in Germany (Fritz Fabricius), Italy (Tiziano Treu), the Benelux countries (Danny Pieters), and Hungary (Andras Baka). One point is very clear, namely, that the level and type of protection afforded to socio-economic rights varies substantially from one State to another. In some States, little or no recognition is given to socio-economic rights as such. In others, a limited range of socio-economic rights (or perhaps social freedoms) have been given Constitutional recognition. Even then, however, whether or not the judiciary will take cognisance of the Constitutional provisions will frequently depend upon the particular constitutional tradition or prevailing political climate. One cannot help feeling that more often than not it is actually the idea of social rights, rather than the reality, that is the greatest obstacle to their effective recognition and implementation.

MATTHEW CRAVEN

International Economic Organizations in the International Legal Process. By SERGEI A. VOITOVICH. Dordrecht: Martinus Nijhoff, 1995. xviii + 199 pp. £62.

In his preface, Mr Voitovich undersells his book:

> The subject-matter of the present inquiry necessarily deals with a lot of procedural and technical issues, as well as a number of quotations from various documents. Thus the author must apologize for those parts of his presentation which will inevitably be somewhat dry.

It cannot be denied that Mr Voitovich's survey of the practice of international economic organizations is extensive, but it is equally the case that—on the whole—he presents his material lucidly and clearly. The central thesis of this work is that international economic law has been characterized by a shift from bilateralism to multilateralism. Unlike other fields in which a trend to multilateral regulation is apparent, in economic law this has taken place within an institutional context. As the cut-off point for this study was 1 June 1993, it does not examine developments associated with the World Trade Organization. This is a serious substantive omission given the subject-matter of this work, but it is not fatal given the nature of Voitovich's analysis.

The aim of this monograph is to examine how organizations participate in the creation and implementation of international economic law. Voitovich deliberately excluded any consideration of transnational corporations as actors in the international economic system because they do not operate at the inter-State level. Although direct economic relations occur at the non-inter-State level, his focus is on the inter-State co-ordination of economic policies. Although the relationships involved here are more political than economic *per se*, these constitute the predominant part of international economic law.

In essence, this monograph is one which examines international institutional law rather than economic law *per se*. The method adopted is one of an extensive comparative analysis of how international economic organizations deal with specific issues. Frequently this analysis is then employed to generate an elaborate classification either of organizations themselves or of methods of dealing with specific issues. Voitovich sees this as being important in itself, arguing that the classification and comparative analysis can inform the drafting of new constitutive instruments of economic organizations and indicate how existing mechanisms can best be amended.

The monograph is neatly structured. The first part locates organizations within international economic law, as well as considering organizations' legal personality and classification. To an extent, this includes an exposition of general principles of institutional law. Voitovich then proceeds in the second part to examine the modes by which international economic organizations participate in law-making, concentrating on the conclusion of treaties and other methods of standard-setting. The third part considers organizations' methods of implementing the law, covering matters such as interpretation, the supervisory role of organizations, methods of dispute settlement and the imposition of sanctions. This is a fairly schematic approach, but it works. The arrangement of the material has been very clearly thought through—a necessity given the extensive range of practice which forms the comparative analysis of institutions which lies at the heart of the book, and it has been very well executed.

It should not be thought that this work is simply a collation, comparison and classification of organizational practice. It is also a critical evaluation of that practice which offers some sharp insights, for instance, in the discussion of the utility of sanctions as a tool of enforcement. Moreover, the general review of non-conventional normative acts of international economic organizations is excellent. This encompasses a perceptive and evaluative consideration of the role of soft law as a regulatory tool, as well as an examination of the normative worth of organizational recommendations and decisions.

Since the end of the Cold War, the work of Eastern European publicists has become more accessible. Western publishers should, however, realize that they owe an obligation to their authors. An irritating feature of this book is that it has been badly proof-read, and on one or two occasions the English fractures completely—for instance, Voitovich states that international economic law 'has a developed structure of links with other hormone and normative institutes of public international law'. There also appears to be a slight internal contradiction in the discussion of the doctrine of implied powers (compare pages 145, 151 and 168). These problems could have easily been avoided by proper copy-editing. These minor problems aside, this is an intelligent and useful addition to the literature whose significance transcends the field of international economic law. It is also a contribution to the understanding of international institutional law.

IAIN SCOBBIE

Incentives and Foreign Direct Investment. Report by the UNITED NATIONS CONFERENCE ON TRADE AND DEVELOPMENT, Current Studies, Series A, No. 30. New York and Geneva: UNCTAD, 1996. 99 pp. $30.

The impact that multinational corporations' investment decisions can have on the domestic economies of the States in which they locate cannot be underestimated. The possibility of increased wealth, employment and the ability to exploit valuable technological innovations ensures that countries are keen to encourage the location of such companies within their territory. This is particularly notable in developing countries, which may offer significant financial and fiscal incentives which they may not be able to afford in order to influence that location decision.

This report is the latest in a long series of studies undertaken by the Division of Transnational Corporations of UNCTAD and attempts to assess the importance that the offer of incentives plays in the multinationals' decision to locate. It is divided into six main sections, each dealing with important aspects of the offering of incentives to attract

FDI, from the theoretical basis to the adverse affects that competition for FDI may have on the competing countries. Most importantly, the report's findings show that incentives only play a part in the decision where other region-specific factors are equal, and that consolidated efforts between countries may have a more beneficial effect overall than if countries within a region all compete for the same location decision. The report includes several attempts at regulation including those by the OECD, the Uruguay Round attempts, and finally the CARICOM initiative, all of which have had varying degrees of success. It concludes that it is only with a combination of controls that success can be guaranteed, particularly in the national arena using a method of review, or alternatively, at a multilateral level by the establishment of an Eminent Persons Group.

The review is of particular interest to those whose fields of research cover international company law, international trade law and the law as it relates to developing countries. It is widely researched and includes a number of specific case examples, as well as numerous statistical tables, which are of a varying degree of clarity. It is an essential addition to the ever expanding library of reports and material on this economically significant area of law.

FIONA SMITH

DECISIONS OF BRITISH COURTS DURING 1996 INVOLVING QUESTIONS OF PUBLIC OR PRIVATE INTERNATIONAL LAW

A. PUBLIC INTERNATIONAL LAW*

State immunity—State Immunity Act 1978, sections 1(1), 5—torture committed outside the United Kingdom—jus cogens rules

Case No. 1. *Al-Adsani* v. *Government of Kuwait and others*, [1996] Times LR 192, CA, leave to appeal denied. Section 1(1) of the State Immunity Act 1978 provides immunity to foreign States before courts in the United Kingdom, except in certain instances as specified in the Act.[1] One such instance is set out in section 5, which reads:

A State is not immune as respects proceedings in respect of—
(*a*) death or personal injury; or
(*b*) damage to or loss of tangible property,
caused by an act or omission in the United Kingdom.

The Court of Appeal held that the combined effect of sections 1(1) and 5 is that a foreign State is immune from the jurisdiction of courts in the United Kingdom in respect of death or personal injury, or damage to or loss of tangible property, caused by an act or omission *outside* the United Kingdom. This is the case even if such a death or personal injury is inflicted through torture.

Suleiman Al-Adsani was a national of both the United Kingdom and Kuwait. He was a pilot in the Kuwaiti airforce. When Iraq invaded Kuwait in 1990 he went underground as a member of the resistance movement. During this time he came into possession of certain videotapes belonging to the second defendant, Sheikh Jaber Al-Sabah/Al-Saud Al-Sabah. These tapes were said to show embarrassing matter of a sexual character. The content of these tapes became common knowledge, which caused great offence to the second defendant. After the Iraqi army was expelled from Kuwait, the second defendant, together with the third and fourth defendants, Sheikh Talal Al-Sabah and Saad Al-Saad, allegedly kidnapped Al-Adsani and took him to the State security prison, where he was repeatedly beaten by security guards. They then took him to a private house where he was again tortured and severely burned. He fled to London where he allegedly suffered psychological harm as a result of anonymous and threatening telephone calls. These telephone calls, which he attributed to agents of the State of Kuwait, warned him not to publicize his case or commence a legal action. The Kuwaiti ambassador in London allegedly made similar threats. Despite these threats, Al-Adsani commenced an action in the English courts

* © Dr Michael Byers, 1997.
[1] Section 1(1) reads: 'A State is immune from the jurisdiction of the courts of the United Kingdom except as provided in the following provisions of this Part of this Act'.

against the State of Kuwait and the three other defendants for their alleged actions in Kuwait and in England.

This decision of the Court of Appeal dealt solely with the issue of jurisdiction over the State of Kuwait. It was clear from section 5 of the Act that Kuwait could not have benefited from immunity, had it caused harm to Al-Adsani in England. However, neither the Court of Appeal nor the judge at first instance was satisfied that the telephone calls were attributable to agents of Kuwait, or that the Kuwaiti ambassador had caused Al-Adsani harm.[2]

For the purpose of resolving the jurisdictional issue, it was assumed that Kuwait was vicariously liable for the acts of the security guards, if indeed such acts had been committed by them. This was the correct approach, because State immunity concerns jurisdiction and not the substance of a case. It was also accepted that the acts in question, if proved, were of sufficient gravity to constitute torture. However, the language of sections 1(1) and 5, together with the fact that the acts had been committed outside the United Kingdom, indicated that Kuwait could benefit from immunity. Although sections 134 and 135 of the Criminal Justice Act 1988 had implemented the 1984 Convention against Torture and Other Cruel, Inhuman or Degrading Treatment or Punishment[3] in English law, they dealt with substantive criminal law only and did not conflict with the immunity from civil jurisdiction conferred by the State Immunity Act.

Al-Adsani argued that since the State Immunity Act dealt with inter-State relations and had been passed to give effect to changes in customary international law, it should be read as being subject to international law. The prohibition against torture was one of a relatively small number of rules of international law having a *jus cogens* or peremptory character, which rendered all other rules in conflict with that prohibition void.[4] This, he argued, meant that the territorial restriction, which was implicit in section 5 as a result of section 1(1), did not preclude an English court from asserting jurisdiction over a foreign State for torture committed abroad.

The Court of Appeal rejected this argument, thus affirming the judgment at first instance. It held that section 1(1) was unambiguous in conferring immunity on foreign States, unless it could be shown that a case came within one of the exceptions set out in the Act. In this particular case section 5 clearly did not apply.

The Court did accept that the prohibition against torture was a rule of customary international law. For example, Stuart-Smith LJ said:

---

[2] The judgment of Mantell J of 3 May 1995 remains unreported. An earlier judgment of the Court of Appeal granting leave to serve proceedings out of the jurisdiction is found at 100 ILR 465.

[3] United Nations General Assembly Resolution 39/46 of 10 December 1984, Misc. 12 (1985) (Cmnd. 9593).

[4] On *jus cogens* rules, see Articles 53 and 64 of the 1969 Vienna Convention on the Law of Treaties, *United Nations Treaty Series*, vol. 1155, p. 331; Hannikainen, *Peremptory Norms (Jus Cogens) in International Law* (1988); Kadelbach, *Zwingendes Völkerrecht* (1992). On the *jus cogens* character of the prohibition against torture, see Higgins, 'Derogations under Human Rights Treaties', this *Year Book*, 48 (1976-7), pp. 281, 282; Rodley, *The Treatment of Prisoners in International Law* (1987), p. 70; Hannikainen, op. cit., pp. 499-513; Kadelbach, op. cit., pp. 291-4.

In international law, torture is a violation of a fundamental human right, it is a crime and a tort for which the victim should be compensated.[5]

However, Stuart-Smith LJ also held that:

[The State Immunity Act] is a comprehensive code and is not subject to overriding considerations. At common law, a sovereign state could not be sued at all against its will in the courts of this country. The 1978 Act, by the exceptions therein set out, marks substantial inroads into this principle. It is inconceivable, it seems to me, that the draughtsman, who must have been well aware of the various international agreements about torture, intended section 1 to be subject to an overriding qualification.[6]

In coming to this conclusion Stuart-Smith LJ relied heavily on several cases from the United States which were authority for the proposition that section 1605(a)(5) of the 1976 Foreign Sovereign Immunities Act (the equivalent of section 5 of the State Immunity Act) does not allow a denial of immunity in respect of non-commercial torts committed outside the United States.[7]

The approach taken by Ward LJ was more compelling. Faced with a statutory provision which was 'as plain as plain can be', he referred to several judicial pronouncements of the doctrine of parliamentary supremacy as it applies in such situations.[8] He concluded, rightly, that in the case of an unambiguous statutory provision, it is irrelevant for the purposes of English law whether that provision is inconsistent with customary international law.

Although the decision of the Court of Appeal was correct, several points may be made in connection with it. First, on the same facts immunity might not have been available at common law.[9] It has been established that customary international law is part of English law and that English courts are not bound by the

---

[5] Approved transcript at 6–7. In support of this conclusion Stuart-Smith LJ referred to Articles 1, 2 and 3 of the Declaration on the Protection of All Persons from being subject to Torture and Other Cruel, Inhuman or Degrading Treatment or Punishment, United Nations General Assembly Resolution 3452 (XXX) of 9 December 1975; Article 3 of the European Convention for the Protection of Human Rights and Fundamental Freedoms, *United Nations Treaty Series*, vol. 213, p. 221, *UK Treaty Series*, No. 71 (1953) (Cmnd. 8969); Articles 1, 2 and 3 of the Convention against Torture and Other Cruel, Inhuman or Degrading Treatment or Punishment, United Nations General Assembly Resolution 39/46 of 10 December 1984, Misc. 12 (1985) (Cmnd. 9593); and sections 134 and 135 of the Criminal Justice Act 1988.

[6] Approved transcript at 8–9. Stuart-Smith LJ thus ignored the substantial inroads which may have been made into the doctrine of absolute State immunity, before the enactment of the Act, as a result of the Court of Appeal's decision in *Trendtex Trading Corp.* v. *Central Bank of Nigeria*, [1977] 2 WLR 356, [1977] 1 All ER 881, this *Year Book*, 48 (1976–7), pp. 353–62. On the restrictive doctrine of State immunity in the common law subsequent to 1978, see, e.g., *Planmount Ltd.* v. *Republic of Zaïre*, [1981] 1 All ER 1110, [1980] 2 Lloyd's Rep. 393, this *Year Book*, 51 (1980), pp. 325–7; *I Congreso del Partido*, [1983] 1 AC 244, [1981] 3 WLR 328, [1981] 2 All ER 1064, this *Year Book*, 52 (1981), pp. 314–19.

[7] The 'FSIA' is found at 28 USC §§ 1330, 1602–11 (1976). The first case was *Argentine Republic* v. *Amerada Hess Shipping Corporation*, 488 US 428 (1989), which did not involve a violation of the prohibition against torture, but which was nevertheless followed in *Siderman de Blake* v. *Republic of Argentina*, 965 F 2d 699 (9th Cir. 1992), which did.

[8] *Theophile* v. *Solicitor-General*, [1950] AC 186 at 195 (*per* Lord Porter); *Alcom Ltd.* v. *Republic of Colombia*, [1984] 1 AC 580 at 600B (*per* Lord Diplock); *Lesa* v. *Attorney-General of New Zealand*, [1983] 2 AC 20 at 33 (*per* Lord Diplock).

[9] This may have implications in respect of a few matters specifically excluded from the Act, particularly proceedings in relation to visiting armed forces. See section 16 of the Act; *Littrell* v. *United States of America (No. 2)*, [1995] 1 WLR 82, [1994] 4 All ER 203, this *Year Book*, 65 (1994), pp. 491–6.

doctrine of *stare decisis* when applying rules of customary international law.[10] It is also widely accepted that *jus cogens* rules are rules of customary international law which have effects additional to those identified in the 1969 Vienna Convention on the Law of Treaties.[11] English courts, when dealing with questions in respect of which the legislator has not spoken, should therefore take into account the development of the concept of *jus cogens* and the fact that certain rules of customary international law now possess a *jus cogens* character. In cases involving torture outside the United Kingdom, the *jus cogens* character of the prohibition against torture may have rendered void any rule of customary international law which might otherwise have required English courts, when applying the common law of State immunity, to grant immunity to foreign States.[12]

A recent decision of the New Zealand Court of Appeal supports this

---

[10] See *Trendtex Trading Corp* v. *Central Bank of Nigeria*, [1977] 2 WLR 356 at 365–6, 388, [1977] 1 All ER 881 at 890, 910–11 (*per* Lord Denning MR and Shaw LJ), this *Year Book*, 48 (1976–7), pp. 353–62.

[11] On the customary international law character of *jus cogens* rules, see Brownlie, *Principles of Public International Law* (4th edn., 1990), p. 513; Kadelbach, op. cit. above (n. 4), p. 186; Byers, 'Conceptualising the Relationship between *Jus Cogens* and *Erga Omnes* Rules', *Nordic Journal of International Law*, 66 (1997) (forthcoming).

The Vienna Convention is found at *United Nations Treaty Series*, vol. 1155, p. 331. According to Articles 53 and 64, *jus cogens* rules render pre-existing or emerging treaties in conflict with them void. The additional effects of *jus cogens* rules include: (1) precluding persistent objection (see Rozakis, *The Concept of Jus Cogens in the Law of Treaties* (1976), p. 78; Brownlie, op. cit. above (n. 11), p. 514; Case 9647 (*United States*) (Inter-American Commission of Human Rights), in Buergenthal and Norris (eds.), *Human Rights: The Inter-American System* (Booklet 21.3, 1988), pp. 61, 78–9); (2) making it more difficult for the principles of effectiveness and extinctive prescription to operate when territory has been occupied in a manner which violates one or more such rules (see Jennings, 'Nullity and Effectiveness in International Law', in *Cambridge Essays in International Law* (1965), pp. 64, 70–8; Crawford, *The Creation of States in International Law* (1979), pp. 81–4 and 420; Brownlie, op. cit. above (n. 11), p. 80); (3) causing the loss of certain privileges, such as the rule that belligerent States are not responsible for damage caused to subjects of neutral States by military operations (see Schwarzenberger, *International Law* (3rd edn., 1957), vol. 1, p. 646, Brownlie, op. cit. above (n. 11), p. 514; Article 33(2)(a) of the ILC Draft Articles on State Responsibility (Part One), in Report of the ILC on the work of its 32nd session, *Yearbook of the International Law Commission*, 1980, vol. 2, part 2, p. 26).

[12] The argument advanced by Zimmermann, 'Sovereign Immunity and Violations of International *Jus Cogens*—Some Critical Remarks', *Michigan Journal of International Law*, 16 (1995), pp. 433, 438, to the effect that the prohibition against torture and the rules of State immunity 'do not interact with each other' and that a *jus cogens* rule can only render void another rule dealing with 'the very same question', may be regarded with scepticism. The *erga omnes* character of this and most, if not all, other *jus cogens* rules would seem to enable States, not only to deny immunity in response to serious human rights violations abroad, so as to allow private parties to pursue legal actions against other States, but also to take more proactive measures, such as the making of inter-State claims. Although the International Court of Justice in the *East Timor* case, *ICJ Reports*, 1995, p. 102, para. 29, made a distinction between the *erga omnes* character of a rule and the jurisdicitional requirements of appearance before the Court, the development of the doctrine of restrictive State immunity in international law has demonstrated that immunity from the jurisdiction of national courts is not subject to the same consensual requirements as jurisdiction before the International Court. On the *erga omnes* character of certain rules, see *Barcelona Traction* case *(Second Phase)*, *ICJ Reports*, 1970, p. 32, paras. 33–5; Schachter, *International Law in Theory and Practice* (1991), pp. 208–13; Frowein, 'Reaction by Not Directly Affected States to Breaches of Public International Law', *Recueil des cours*, 248 (1994–IV), pp. 345, 405–22; Byers, loc. cit. above (n. 11).

suggestion.[13] In *Controller and Auditor-General* v. *Sir Ronald Davison* four separate judgments (the fifth judge concurred) relied on or expressed support for a 'public policy' exception in the common law of State immunity, in this case in respect of the involvement of a foreign State in the evasion of taxes payable in New Zealand.[14]

Second, the State Immunity Act should probably be amended so as to modify the territorial restriction which is implicit in section 5 as a result of section 1(1).[15] In this context, the following passage from Stuart-Smith LJ's judgment may be questioned:

A moment's reflection is enough to show that the practical consequences of the Plaintiff's submission would be dire. The Courts in the United Kingdom are open to all who seek their help, whether they are British citizens or not. A vast number of people come to this country each year seeking refuge and asylum, and many of these allege that they have been tortured in the country whence they came. Some of these claims are no doubt justified, others are more doubtful. Those who are presently charged with the responsibility for deciding whether applicants are genuine refugees have a difficult enough task, but at least they know much of the background and surrounding circumstances against which the claim is made. The Court would be in no such position. The foreign state would be unlikely to submit to the jurisdiction of the United Kingdom Court, and in its absence the Court would have no means of testing the claim or making a just determination.[16]

There is no reason to believe that a modification of the territorial restriction in section 5 would result in any significant increase in the amount of litigation before the courts. As is the case in any civil action, the burden of proof in an action against a foreign State rests on the plaintiff. The normal rules concerning service apply, including (in England and Wales) those rules under Order 11 of the Rules of the Supreme Court controlling service out of the jurisdiction. The doctrine of *forum non conveniens* will continue to be used to preclude actions when a better forum is available.[17]

The argument that the courts would not have sufficient knowledge of the background and surrounding circumstances of non-commercial torts committed by foreign States abroad may also be questioned. The danger that foreign States will choose not to appear in order to defend themselves against such actions would be minimized by the possibility of default judgments combined with

---

[13] Unlike the United Kingdom and the United States, New Zealand does not have a State immunity statute.

[14] [1996] 2 NZLR 278 at 290 (*per* Cooke P), 304–7 (*per* Richardson J, McKay J concurring), 309 (*per* Henry J), 310 (*per* Thomas J). Cooke P said (at 290): 'One can speculate that the law may gradually but steadily develop, perhaps first excepting from sovereign immunity atrocities or the use of weapons of mass destruction, perhaps ultimately going on to except acts of war not authorised by the United Nations'.

[15] The United States has recently modified the territorial restriction in section 1605(a)(5) of the FSIA. The Antiterrorism and Effective Death Penalty Act of 1996, Public Law 104–32, lifts that restriction in respect of civil actions taken by United States nationals against any State which has been designated by the Executive as a 'State sponsor of terrorism'. The limitation to United States nationals suggests a connection to the concept of diplomatic protection rather than to the law of human rights, while the limitation to designated States reflects the political motives behind this modification.

[16] Approved transcript at 11–12.

[17] On *forum non conveniens*, see, e.g., *Spiliada Maritime Corporation* v. *Cansulex*, [1987] AC 460, [1986] 3 WLR 972, this *Year Book*, 57 (1986), pp. 429–34.

execution against property owned by those States within the United Kingdom. Moreover, the courts seem satisfied with their current degree of knowledge in cases arising out of the commercial activities of foreign States abroad. Why should non-commercial torts pose any greater difficulty?[18]

In fact, it is incongruous that, although foreign States are immune from jurisdiction in respect of non-commercial torts committed outside the United Kingdom, they are not similarly immune in respect of their commercial activities.[19] It may be possible to explain this difference on the basis that different national legal systems have different conceptions of public policy and therefore of what constitutes a tort, whereas contracts by their very nature identify a breach. However, there is no disagreement among legal systems in respect of the most serious of non-commercial torts, namely those violations of human rights that are prohibited by *jus cogens* rules. For this reason, an amendment to section 5 which removed the territorial restriction only in respect of the most serious of human rights violations would not offend foreign conceptions of public policy. It would also reflect developments within international law, and especially the development of *jus cogens* rules, which are the 'public policy' rules of the international legal system.[20]

State immunity—employment contracts—submission to the jurisdiction—evidence relevant to immunity arising on appeal—member of the mission—commercial purposes—State Immunity Act 1978, sections 2(2), 4(3), 16(1)(a)

Case No. 2. Ahmed v. *Government of Saudi Arabia,* [1996] 2 All ER 248, 104 ILR 673, CA; *Case No. 3. Arab Republic of Egypt* v. *Gamal Eldin and another,* [1996] 2 All ER 237, 104 ILR 673, Employment Appeals Tribunal. Ahmed was a British national employed as a secretary in the Saudi Arabian embassy in London, initially without a written contract of employment. She was given a copy of a solicitors' letter of advice addressed to the military attaché, which stated that any staff member who was dismissed would have rights under English law. She later signed a contract of employment with the government of Saudi Arabia. The contract provided for termination at the discretion of the

[18] The passage from Stuart-Smith LJ's judgment may also be read to suggest that the granting of asylum and the recovery of civil damages are related in some way additional to the fact that the same evidence may be relevant to both claims. However, the two claims are in fact distinct. Refugee law concerns each State's obligation not to force individuals to return to another State, when those individuals have a well-founded fear of being persecuted there. Tort law concerns the compensation of individuals for past wrongs by those who have committed those wrongs. There is no reason why an individual should be denied a civil remedy just because the United Kingdom has had to consider whether the United Kingdom risks violating a separate obligation in respect of how it treats him, i.e. by returning him to a persecuting State.

[19] See section 3, State Immunity Act 1978.

[20] Although torture has been criminalized in the United Kingdom by sections 134 and 135 of the Criminal Justice Act 1988, this development contributes little to the argument that section 5 of the State Immunity Act should be modified, although it does reflect the existence of a general prohibition against torture. Despite the fact that an individual who commits torture does so in performance or purported performance of official duties or at the instigation of a public official, it is the actions of individuals which have been criminalized and not those of States. There is nothing in the State Immunity Act which suggests that an individual who commits torture abroad is immune from the jurisdiction of courts in the United Kingdom.

government, without reasons having to be given therefor. She was dismissed one year later without reasons being given, and brought a claim for unfair dismissal before an industrial tribunal.

The Court of Appeal held that on the plain meaning of section 16(1)(a) of the State Immunity Act 1978 a foreign State enjoyed immunity in respect of proceedings concerning the employment of a staff member in the administrative and technical service of the embassy because such a person was 'a member of the mission' within the meaning of Article 1 of the 1961 Vienna Convention on Diplomatic Relations.[21] It did not matter that Ahmed's appointment had not been notified to the Foreign and Commonwealth Office, as it was a 'separate and irrelevant question whether she herself [was] entitled . . . to enjoy privileges and immunities'.[22] The scope of Article 1 was not limited to those who were actually or notionally sent to the United Kingdom by the foreign State, nor was it linked to nationality.[23]

The solicitors' letter was not a 'written agreement' for the purposes of submission to the jurisdiction in accordance with sub-sections 2(1) and 2(2) of the State Immunity Act because it was not a complete agreement in writing between the parties, nor was there anything on the face of the letter which showed that it was intended by Saudi Arabia to be an offer open for acceptance by Ahmed upon her entering into a contract of employment.[24] Furthermore, the letter did not purport to be an agreement to submit to the jurisdiction; it merely contained the solicitors' opinion for the benefit of the military attaché. In any event, for the letter to have constituted a submission to the jurisdiction, it would have had to be shown either that the head of the mission had so submitted, or that the person who entered into the alleged contract by the letter did so 'on behalf of and with the authority of' Saudi Arabia, as required by section 2(7) of the State Immunity Act.[25]

In *Arab Republic of Egypt* v. *Gamal Eldin and another* two Egyptian nationals resident in London were employed under contracts of employment made in the United Kingdom as drivers at the medical office of the Egyptian embassy. The medical office was concerned with the procurement, in the United Kingdom for

---

[21] *United Nations Treaty Series*, vol. 500, p. 95, *International and Comparative Law Quarterly*, 10 (1961), p. 600. The Vienna Convention is relevant because section 16(1) of the State Immunity Act reads, *inter alia*: 'This part of this Act does not affect any immunity or privilege conferred by the Diplomatic Privileges Act 1964 . . . and—(a) section 4 above [the exception to immunity in respect of employment contracts] does not apply to proceedings concerning the employment of the members of a mission within the meaning of the Convention scheduled to the said Act of 1964 . . . '.

[22] [1996] 2 All ER 248 at 251. For support of this conclusion Gibson LJ referred to *R* v. *Secretary of State for the Home Department, ex parte Bagga*, [1990] 3 WLR 1013, [1991] 1 All ER 777, [1991] 1 QB 485, this *Year Book*, 61 (1990), pp. 391–4.

[23] For support of the latter conclusion Gibson LJ referred to *Sengupta* v. *Republic of India*, [1993] ICR 221 at 225 (*per* Browne-Wilkinson J).

[24] Sub-section 2(1) reads: 'A State is not immune as respects proceedings in respect of which it has submitted to the jurisdiction of the courts of the United Kingdom'.
Sub-section 2(2) reads: 'A State may submit after the dispute giving rise to the proceedings has arisen or by a prior written agreement; but a provision in any agreement that it is to be governed by the law of the United Kingdom is not to be regarded as a submission'.

[25] Section 2(7) reads: 'The head of a State's diplomatic mission in the United Kingdom, or the person for the time being performing his functions, shall be deemed to have authority to submit on behalf of the State in respect of any proceedings; and any person who has entered into a contract on behalf of and with the authority of a State shall be deemed to have authority to submit on its behalf in respect of proceedings arising out of the contract'.

Egyptian nationals, of certain medical services which were not otherwise obtainable within the Egyptian health service. The office was physically separate from the embassy and had little day-to-day contact with it.

The two drivers were dismissed from their employment and brought claims for unfair dismissal before an industrial tribunal. Although no notice of appearance was served on behalf of the embassy, the chief medical officer wrote two letters to the tribunal, asserting that the drivers were Egyptian nationals subject only to Egyptian law. The tribunal found that it had jurisdiction. On appeal Egypt provided affidavit evidence on the issue of State immunity.

The Employment Appeal Tribunal held that, if an industrial tribunal failed to give effect to an immunity enjoyed by a foreign State as a result of not having had all the relevant evidence before it, it was the duty of the Appeal Tribunal to correct the error.[26] It held that the chief medical officer was not authorized to submit to the jurisdiction on behalf of Egypt because he was not the head of the mission and had not entered into the contracts of employment,[27] that the sending of the letters to the tribunal did not constitute the entering of a notice of appearance, and that neither the sending of the letters nor their contents constituted a submission to the jurisdiction within the meaning of section 2(1) of the State Immunity Act.[28] The Appeal Tribunal also held that the drivers, as employees in the administrative and technical service of the mission, were members of the mission because the medical office had been certified by the Foreign and Commonwealth Office to be part of the Egyptian embassy for the purposes of the Diplomatic and Consular Premises Act 1987. Therefore, Egypt benefited from immunity in respect of their employment as a result of section 16 of the State Immunity Act.[29] Even if the drivers had not been part of the embassy staff, the purposes and activities of the medical office were not 'commercial purposes' falling within section 4(3) of the State Immunity Act, but were instead within the sphere of governmental or sovereign activity.[30] In coming to the latter conclusion the Appeal Tribunal relied on the decision of the

---

[26] The Appeal Tribunal referred to section 1(2) of the State Immunity Act, which reads: 'A court shall give effect to the immunity conferred by this section even though the State does not appear in the proceedings in question'. It also referred to its own decision in *United Arab Emirates* v. *Abdelghafar*, [1995] ICR 65, this *Year Book*, 66 (1995), p. 501, fn. 48.

[27] The Appeal Tribunal referred to section 2(7) of the State Immunity Act. See above, n. 25.

[28] See above, n. 24.

[29] See above, n. 21. Mummery J said: 'Drivers form part of the administrative and technical staff. As is clear from the decision in *Sengupta* v. *Republic of India* [1983] ICR 221 at 229 the immunity extends to members of staff of the mission carrying out work of the mission "in however humble a role" ': [1996] 2 All ER 237 at 246.

[30] Sub-sections 4(1), 4(2)(a) and 4(3) were all relevant here:

'(1) A State is not immune as respects proceedings relating to a contract of employment between the State and an individual where the contract was made in the United Kingdom or the work is to be wholly or partly performed there.

(2) Subject to subsections (3) and (4) below, this section does not apply if —

    (a) at the time when the proceedings are brought the individual is a national of the State concerned; . . .

    . . .

(3) Where the work is for an office, agency or establishment maintained by the State in the United Kingdom for commercial purposes, subsection 2(a) . . . above do[es] not exclude the application of this section unless the individual was, at the time when the contract was made, habitually resident in that State.'

Court of Appeal in *Littrell* v. *United States of America (No. 2)*,[31] and looked 'at all the circumstances in relation to the activities and their context'.[32]

Patent dispute—foreign banknotes—non-justiciability—act of State—State immunity

Case No. 4. *A Ltd.* v. *B Bank*, [1996] Times LR 518, CA, leave to appeal granted. The appellant was the registered proprietor of a United Kingdom patent relating to a type of security paper suitable for use in the manufacture of banknotes. The respondent was a commercial bank in England. The intervener was the central bank of a foreign State ('State X'). The central bank had security paper manufactured for it in Italy, on which banknotes were printed and issued as the currency of State X. The commercial bank disposed of some of these banknotes in England. The appellant alleged that this disposal infringed its patent, contrary to section 60(1)(*a*) of the Patents Act 1977.[33]

The central bank argued that the issuance of the banknotes as currency was at the centre of the dispute. Although the central bank could alter the paper on which its banknotes were printed in the future, it would be impossible to separate currency already circulating abroad from currency circulating at home.

Leggatt LJ held that the banknotes were not currency in this instance but were instead commodities. He held that there was nothing to show that the central bank had put the banknotes into circulation in the United Kingdom, and if it had, that would not have been a sovereign act as no State had the right to insist on the circulation of its banknotes in a foreign State.

The central bank relied on the House of Lords decision in *Buttes Gas & Oil Co. Ltd.* v. *Hammer (No. 3)* to argue that the court should decline jurisdiction when required to adjudicate upon the transactions of a foreign State.[34] If the court held that the commercial bank had infringed the patent, then it would necessarily be holding that anyone else, such as the central bank, who did the same thing would also be infringing the patent.

Leggatt LJ distinguished *Buttes Gas & Oil Co. Ltd.* v. *Hammer (No. 3)* as a case in which the issues of sovereignty were raised by the defendant's plea of justification and by his counterclaim. This case revolved around a comparison of the paper on which the banknotes were printed and the patent specification. The case against the commercial bank in no way depended upon showing that the central bank was a party to any infringement, and the relief claimed by the appellant would not interfere with the circulation within State X of its currency.

---

[31] [1995] 1 WLR 82, [1994] 4 All ER 203, this *Year Book*, 65 (1994), pp. 491–6.

[32] [1996] 2 All ER 237 at 247.

[33] According to section 60(1)(*a*) the patent would be infringed by a person if in the United Kingdom and without the consent of the patent proprietor 'he makes, disposes of, offers to dispose of, uses or imports the product or keeps it whether for disposal or otherwise'. Since the rights conferred by the patent were territorial, the appellant made no allegations of infringement against State X or the central bank.

[34] [1982] AC 888, [1981] 3 All ER 616, [1981] 3 NLR 787, this *Year Book*, 53 (1982), pp. 259–68.

Moreover, adjudication of the claim entailed no adjudication upon the transactions of a foreign State nor any enquiries into acts done in the exercise of a foreign State's sovereignty within its own territory. The relevant acts were the keeping and disposal within the United Kingdom of banknotes to which the patent was alleged to relate. They were not sovereign or public acts, but commercial banking transactions which were devoid of any governmental or political purpose. They also occurred within the territorial jurisdiction of the English courts, where, if State X did these acts, it would itself enjoy no immunity from suit.[35]

In his judgment, Morritt LJ insisted on a distinction between the principles of State immunity and non-justiciability, although he noted that State immunity which had been removed by the State Immunity Act 1978 should not be reintroduced under the guise of non-justiciability.[36] He also explained that act of State issues only arise when the outcome of a case turns upon the validity of an official act by a foreign sovereign within its own territory. In this case the connection between the appellants and the central bank arose from the latter's choice of paper and not its decision to issue currency. The choice of paper was not by its nature an act of State.

Employees of international organizations—non-justiciability—immunity of officials of international organizations

Case No. 5. Arab Monetary Fund v. Hashim and others, [1996] 1 Lloyd's LR 589, CA. This case is related to but nevertheless distinct from the litigation which resulted in the 1991 House of Lords decision in *Arab Monetary Fund v. Hashim and others (No. 3)*.[37] That case arose out of Hashim's alleged embezzlement of money, whereas this case arose out of his alleged acceptance of a bribe.

The Arab Monetary Fund (AMF) was formed by agreement between 20 Arab States and Palestine in 1977. It had its headquarters in Abu Dhabi. Hashim was its first President. Bernard Sunley & Sons (BSS) was a construction company which formed a Middle East subsidiary (BSME) in Abu Dhabi in 1977. A contract for the construction of the AMF headquarters was entered into between the AMF and BSME. AMF alleged that a payment made by BSS to a Swiss bank account was a bribe paid to Hashim in connection with that contract. It claimed the amount of that payment, or damages, from BSS, BSME and Hashim on the basis of quasi-contract, restitution, unjust enrichment, and contract. BSS and BSME denied liability and argued that the payment was not authorized by them and was therefore *ultra vires*. Hashim also denied liability and contended that the claims against him were non-justiciable and that he was

---

[35] Section 7(b) of the State Immunity Act 1978 reads: 'A State is not immune as respect proceedings relating to— . . . (b) an alleged infringement by the State in the United Kingdom of any patent, trade-mark, design, plant breeders' rights or copyright'.

[36] In support of this proposition Morritt LJ referred to Kerr LJ's judgment in *Maclaine Watson & Co. Ltd. v. International Tin Council*, [1988] 3 All ER 257 at 375–6, [1988] 3 WLR 1169 at 1188, CA, this *Year Book*, 60 (1989), pp. 461–73.

[37] [1991] 2 AC 114, [1991] 2 WLR 729, [1991] 1 All ER 871, this *Year Book*, 62 (1991), pp. 433–7.

entitled to the immunity allowed to officials of international organizations under international law.

Evans J in the Queen's Bench Division held that the payment was not *ultra vires* the two companies.[38] This holding was not in dispute on appeal. He also held that the payment was a bribe or secret commission, but accepted an argument that the claims were statute-barred.

The Court of Appeal agreed that the payment was a bribe. It held that the relationship between Hashim and the AMF involved private contractual rights and obligations on both sides, and that these rights and obligations were governed by the law of Abu Dhabi. Therefore the Court did not lack subject-matter jurisdiction, since the claims in no way concerned either the inter-State relationships which had been created by the AMF treaty, or any other matters of public international law. As Saville LJ explained:

As to justiciability, the argument was, in essence, that Dr Hashim's appointment was made pursuant to the public international law rights and obligations created by the AMF treaty, which has not been incorporated into English law, so that English law could not apply at all to the relationship between the AMF and Dr Hashim. As Mr Justice Evans pointed out, the fallacy in this argument is that it assumes that what must have been some form of engagement between the AMF and Dr Hashim is not governed by some municipal law. There is simply no basis for this assumption and to my mind it is clear that the relationship between Dr Hashim and the AMF created private contractual rights and obligations on both sides. Given that this is so, it is equally clear that these rights and obligations are governed by the law of Abu Dhabi, since the AMF is an Abu Dhabi legal entity which engaged Dr Hashim there. It further follows that the existence of such private rights and obligations militates conclusively against the further suggestion that the Court lacked 'subject matter jurisdiction' of the kind described by Lord Wilberforce in *Buttes Gas & Oil Co. Ltd.* v. *Hammer*, [1982] AC 888 at p. 937.[39] The claims are in no way concerned with the relationship between states created by the AMF treaty or any other matters of public international law.[40]

The plea of immunity was similarly unsustainable. Saville LJ continued:

As to the plea of immunity, it is accepted that this could at best only apply to official acts. To my mind the proposition that Dr Hashim was engaged in official acts for the AMF when secretly agreeing and accepting a bribe for his own benefit (and not that of the AMF) has only to be stated to be rejected. Furthermore, and even if I am wrong about this, it seems to me that the immunity is one which exists for the benefit of the organization concerned and can be waived by that organization; which the AMF clearly have done in the present case.[41]

With regard to the claims in quasi-contract, for restitution, and of unjust enrichment, the applicable law was that of Abu Dhabi. Regardless of whether the AMF was correct in arguing that it had a right under the law of Abu Dhabi to claim damages in tort from the companies and Hashim, that right had been lost in the English courts by reason of the applicable statute of limitations, which was article 298(1) of the Civil Code of the United Arab Emirates. The same conclusion applied to the claim for unjust enrichment. However, according to

---

[38] [1993] 1 Lloyd's Rep. 543.
[39] This *Year Book*, 53 (1982), pp. 259–68.
[40] [1996] 1 Lloyd's Rep. 589 at 596.
[41] Ibid.

Islamic Shari'a law the limitation period in respect of the claim in contract was fifteen years. The claim in contract was therefore allowed.

Extradition—right to a fair trial—transfer of sovereignty—Extradition Act 1989, section 12(1)—non-justiciability—whether ministerial discretion non-justiciable in respect of an extradition decision taken on political grounds

Case No. 6. R v. *The Secretary of State for the Home Department, ex parte Launder,* [1996] Times LR 603, QBD. In this case the Divisional Court considered section 12(1) of the Extradition Act 1989, which reads:

> Where a person is committed under Section 9 above and is not discharged by order of the High Court . . . , the Secretary of State may by warrant order him to be returned unless his return is prohibited . . . by this Act, or the Secretary of State decides under this section to make no such order in his case.

It held that under this section the Secretary of State has both a wide discretion to extradite and a personal responsibility to ensure that it would not be unjust or oppressive to extradite the individual concerned.

The Governor of Hong Kong sought the extradition of Launder to face charges of corruption. Launder was alleged to have received bribes amounting to some £4.5 million over a period of six months. He challenged the decision to return him to Hong Kong on the basis that he would not be given a fair trial there.

Section 12(2) of the Extradition Act places what are known as 'mandatory requirements' on the Secretary of State's general discretion under section 12(1). It reads:

> Without prejudice to his general discretion as to the making of an order for the return of a person to a foreign state, Commonwealth country or colony—
> (a) the Secretary of State shall not make an order in the case of any person if it appears to the Secretary of State in relation to the offence, or each of the offences, in respect of which his return is sought, that
>   (i) by reason of its trivial nature; or
>   (ii) by reason of the passage of time since he is alleged to have committed it or to have become unlawfully at large, as the case may be; or
>   (iii) because the accusation made against him is not made in good faith in the interests of justice,
>   it would, having regard to all the circumstances, be unjust or oppressive to return him; and
> (b) the Secretary of State may decide to make no order for the return of a person accused or convicted of an offence not punishable with death in Great Britain if that person could be or has been sentenced to death for that offence in the country by which the request for his return is made.

The question in this case was whether the Secretary of State had erred in law in making an order for the return of Launder to Hong Kong. It was already clear that the factual decision was not irrational or '*Wednesbury* unreasonable'.[42] Under section 11 of the Extradition Act the Divisional Court had similar duties

---

[42] On '*Wednesbury* principles' of reasonableness, see *Associated Provincial Picture Houses Ltd.* v. *Wednesbury Corporation,* [1948] 1 KB 223.

to those of the Secretary of State, and had, in an earlier decision on an application for a writ of habeas corpus, reached the same conclusion as him in respect of Launder.[43] Therefore, this ground for judicial review of the Secretary of State's decision did not apply.

On the first issue, namely that of unreasonable delay, it was clear that the Secretary of State and the Divisional Court in its earlier decision had both adopted the same analysis. They had divided into four parts the time which had elapsed since the period (June 1982—the end of 1983) in which the bribes were allegedly received. The Secretary of State had found that there was no unreasonable delay on the part of the authorities and that much of the delay had resulted from the concealment by Launder of his crime. In this instance, the Court was satisfied that this did not constitute a reviewable error.

The Court was also satisfied that the Secretary of State had acted with procedural fairness, addressing himself to the right issues and acting within the confines of his discretion, and that he had considered Launder's personal circumstances.

The Court then turned to what it referred to as 'the China point', the crux of the application for judicial review. It considered that it was realistic to proceed on the basis that any trial of Launder for these offences would take place after the transfer of sovereignty over Hong Kong to the People's Republic of China (PRC) at midnight on 30 June 1997. The same would obviously be true of the serving of any sentence imposed, were Launder to be convicted. While it was accepted that the current legal, penal and judicial system in Hong Kong properly protected Launder's right to a fair trial and provided for appropriate humane punishment, there was a real risk that those safeguards would not survive the 'hand-over'.

The Secretary of State pointed to the existence of a treaty, the Joint Declaration, entered into with the PRC in 1984, which aimed to preserve the present way of life in Hong Kong for a period of fifty years from hand-over. The Secretary of State argued that as the PRC had not repudiated the treaty, one had to proceed on the basis that it would respect its treaty obligations.

Launder argued that this approach relied too much on the letter of the treaty and did not have regard to the realities of the situation. Evidence was submitted that the PRC had a very poor human rights record, that it retained the death penalty for corruption offences involving sums in excess of £850, and that Amnesty International had monitored 97 death sentences and executions in the PRC within the six-month period from July to December 1994. Furthermore, in 1995 the *Far Eastern Economic Review* reported the execution of a man who had been extradited from Thailand to the PRC upon the latter's assurance that he would face a maximum fifteen-year term of imprisonment. There was also a concern whether the specialty provisions required by section 6(4) of the Extradition Act 1989 would be in place and survive the transfer of powers in the absence of agreement to this effect from the PRC. The Court held that, subject to questions of justiciability, this evidence should be taken into account in assessing the risks of: (i) an unfair trial; (ii) inhumane or inappropriate

[43] Decision of 14 December 1994 (Glidewell LJ and Curtis J), unreported. Leave to appeal to the House of Lords was denied on 9 March 1995.

punishment following such a trial; and (iii) the specialty protections not remaining in place after hand-over.

The Secretary of State contended that review was being sought of a decision based on a political judgment by the Executive as to the good faith of a foreign sovereign State and whether it would adhere to its treaty obligations, and that this was non-justiciable. The Secretary of State relied for support on, *inter alia*, the House of Lords judgment in *Buttes Gas & Oil Co. Ltd.* v. *Hammer (No. 3)*,[44] the decision of Colman J in *Westland Helicopters Ltd.* v. *Arab Organization for Industrialization*,[45] and the unreported 1992 Divisional Court judgment in *R* v. *Secretary of State for the Home Office, ex parte Osman.*

Founding himself on the authority of the European Court of Human Rights decision in the *Soering* case in respect of Article 13 of the European Convention for the Protection of Human Rights and Fundamental Freedoms (the right to an effective remedy),[46] Launder argued that he must be entitled to attempt to satisfy the Court that no reasonable Secretary of State could conclude that there was not a serious risk that the protections as to due process, fair punishment and specialty would not be available in Hong Kong after hand-over. If he could not do so because the issue was non-justiciable, then he would effectively be deprived of that part of his section 12(1) protection.

The Court considered the following statement of the European Court of Human Rights in the *Soering* case to be uncontroversial:

According to the United Kingdom Government, a court would have jurisdiction to quash a challenged decision to send a fugitive to a country where it was established that there was a serious risk of inhuman or degrading treatment, on the ground that in all the circumstances of the case the decision was one that no reasonable Secretary of State could take. Although the Convention is not considered to be part of the United Kingdom law . . . the Court is satisfied that the English courts can review the 'reasonableness' of an extradition decision in the light of the kind of factors relied on by Mr Soering before the Convention institutions in the context of Article 3.[47]

In respect of the issue of non-justiciability, the Court noted that the unreported judgment in *R* v. *Secretary of State for the Home Office, ex parte Osman* was not authority for the proposition relied upon by the Secretary of State. Although a decision to extradite might be highly politically charged, that judgment conspicuously did not say that the decision was unreviewable, only that it should be scrutinized with care. Although the Court considered the two reasons for judicial abstention put forward by Lord Wilberforce in *Buttes Gas & Oil Co. Ltd.* v. *Hammer (No. 3)*, namely the possibility of embarrassment in the foreign relations of the United Kingdom and the possible absence of judicial or manageable standards by which the Court may judge the issues, it

---

[44] [1982] AC 888, [1981] 3 All ER 616, [1981] 3 NLR 787, this *Year Book*, 53 (1982), pp. 259–68.

[45] [1995] QB 282, [1995] 2 WLR 126, [1995] 2 All ER 387, [1994] 2 Lloyd's Rep. 608, this *Year Book*, 66 (1995), pp. 491–6.

[46] Judgment of 7 July 1989, Series A, No. 161, this *Year Book*, 60 (1989), pp. 552–6.

[47] Series A, No. 161, at pp. 47–8, para. 121. The Court referred to *R* v. *The Secretary of State for the Home Department, ex parte Bugdaycay*, [1987] 1 AC 514, [1987] 1 All ER 940, this *Year Book*, 58 (1987), pp. 429–33 as additional authority that the decision of the Secretary of State was subject to review. See also discussion of *R* v. *Ministry of Defence, ex parte Smith and other appeals*, below, p. 552.

held that these reasons did not apply in an extradition case. As both the judgment and the United Kingdom's submissions in the *Soering* case indicated, the section 12 discretion is normally justiciable. No exception could be justified in respect of politically sensitive cases, as the protection of judicial review was most needed in those situations where the interests of the State and the interests of the fugitive were in direct conflict, when there was a possibility that the Secretary of State might regard himself bound by Government policy to extradite a person without regard to the consequent risks to his life and liberty.

The Court then examined the Secretary of State's responsibilities and concluded that his decision called for the most anxious scrutiny, because of its critical importance to Launder. Moreover, it held that the decision involved a heavy personal responsibility for the Secretary of State, which could not be outweighed by his collective responsibility as a member of Cabinet. The Secretary of State, in proceeding on the basis that he was bound by a Cabinet decision, i.e. the Joint Declaration, had erred fundamentally in the exercise of his section 12 discretion. This deprived Launder of his main safeguard, namely a Minister who would exercise personal judgment as to the real risks of breach of the treaty safeguards.[48]

Although this case is interesting in a number of respects, it is perhaps most important for its departure from the traditional policy of the English courts in extradition cases, namely of non-enquiry into the standards of justice in the requesting State.[49] Despite the fact that in this case the Court was operating in the limited context of a review of whether the possible exercise of ministerial discretion was properly considered, the character of its enquiry was no different from that which might be applied generally. In both instances the courts would have to consider whether it would be unjust or oppressive to extradite the individual concerned, given the factual situation in the requesting State. As a departure from the traditional policy, this case will either create an important precedent, or be overruled on appeal.[50]

[48] Two other aspects of the case may be mentioned. First, with regard to an argument founded on Article 48 of the 1957 EC Treaty (*United Nations Treaty Series*, vol. 294, p. 17), the Court held that extradition came within the public policy exception. The Court relied on *Re the Habeas Corpus Application of Narinder Singh Virdee*, [1980] 1 CMLR 709; *Re Carthage Healy's Habeas Corpus Application*, [1984] 3 CMLR 575. Second, with regard to the European Convention for the Protection of Human Rights and Fundamental Freedoms (*United Nations Treaty Series*, vol. 213, p. 221, *UK Treaty Series*, No. 71 (1953) (Cmnd. 8969)), the Court held that, unless or until the Convention was incorporated into English law, breaches of it could not be relied on in English courts. The Court relied on *R v. Secretary of State for the Home Department, ex parte Brind*, [1991] 1 All ER 720, [1991] 1 AC 696, [1991] 2 WLR 588, this *Year Book*, 62 (1991), pp. 437–40; *R v. Secretary of State for the Home Department, ex parte Chinoy* (unreported CO/156/91, 10 April 1991, Bingham LJ). See discussion of *R v. Ministry of Defence, ex parte Smith and other appeals*, below, p. 552.
[49] In the context of Hong Kong, the Divisional Court has twice held that extraditions would not be refused on the grounds that specialty undertakings given by the Government of Hong Kong would not be binding on the PRC. See *R v. Governor of Brixton Prison, ex parte Osman (No. 3)*, [1992] 1 WLR 36, [1992] 1 All ER 122, this *Year Book*, 63 (1992), pp. 515–16; *R v. Governor of Pentonville Prison, ex parte Lee*, [1993] 1 WLR 1294, [1993] 3 All ER 504, this *Year Book*, 64 (1993), p. 452, fn. 42.
[50] For a similar case in the United States, see *Lui Kin-Hong, a.k.a. Jerry Lui v. United States*, USDC Mass., 7 January 1997, 1997 US Dis. *LEXIS* 801.

Unimplemented treaty—relevance in national law—judicial review—European Convention for the Protection of Human Rights and Fundamental Freedoms

Case No. 7. R v. *Ministry of Defence, ex parte Smith and other appeals,* [1996] 1 All ER 257, [1996] 2 WLR 305, [1996] QB 517, [1995] Times LR 567, CA, leave to appeal denied. This judgment affirmed a decision of the Divisional Court reviewed in the previous volume of this *Year Book* and may assist in clarifying the role of the European Convention for the Protection of Human Rights and Fundamental Freedoms ('the European Convention') in administrative law cases.[51]

The four applicants had challenged the legality of their discharge from the armed forces on the basis that the blanket policy prohibiting the service of homosexual men and women in the armed forces was irrational. The Court of Appeal held that it could only interfere with the exercise of an administrative decision where it was satisfied that the decision was unreasonable, i.e. where the decision was beyond the range of responses open to a reasonable decision-maker. Nevertheless, the human rights context was clearly important, and the more substantial the interference with human rights, the more the Court could require by way of justification.[52] Sir Thomas Bingham MR said:

It is important to note that, in considering whether English law satisfies the requirement in article 13 of the European Convention that there should be a national remedy to enforce the substance of the Convention rights and freedoms, the European Court of Human Rights has held that it does, attaching very considerable weight to the power of the English courts to review administrative decisions by way of judicial review.[53]

However, the Court confirmed that the United Kingdom's obligation to secure compliance with the European Convention is unenforceable by the national courts. In response to an argument based on Article 8 of the European Convention,[54] Sir Thomas Bingham MR said:

It is, inevitably, common ground that the United Kingdom's obligation, binding in international law, to respect and secure compliance with this article is not one that is enforceable by domestic courts. The relevance of the Convention in the present context is as background to the complaint of irrationality. The fact that a decision-maker failed to take account of Convention obligations when exercising an administrative decision is not of itself a ground for impugning that exercise of discretion.[55]

---

[51] [1995] 4 All ER 427, this *Year Book*, 66 (1995), pp. 509–12 (the decision of the Court of Appeal is discussed briefly at p. 512, fn. 116). The European Convention is found at *United Nations Treaty Series,* vol. 213, p. 221, *UK Treaty Series,* No. 71 (1953) (Cmnd. 8969).

[52] In coming to this conclusion the Court relied on *Bugdaycay* v. *Secretary of State for the Home Department,* [1987] 1 All ER 940, [1987] AC 514, this *Year Book,* 58 (1987), pp. 429–33; *Brind* v. *Secretary of State for the Home Department,* [1991] 1 All ER 720, [1991] 1 AC 696, [1991] 2 WLR 588, this *Year Book,* 62 (1991), pp. 437–40.

[53] [1996] 1 All ER 257 at 264, [1996] 2 WLR 333 at 337, referring to *Vilvarajah* v. *UK,* (1992) 14 EHRR 248 at 291, 292. See also discussion of the *Soering* case, above, p. 550.

[54] Article 8 concerns the right to respect for private and family life.

[55] [1996] 1 All ER 257 at 266–7, [1996] 2 WLR 333 at 340. Although Sir Thomas Bingham MR expressed scepticism in respect of the Ministry of Defence's position on Article 8, he concluded that these were not 'questions to which answers may properly or usefully be proffered by this court which has seen none of the evidence which would be relied on if it were this court, and not the European Court of Human Rights, with whom the responsibility for deciding this issue lay': [1996] 1 All ER 257 at 267, [1996] 2 WLR 333 at 340.

Henry LJ was of the same view. He questioned the utility of English courts considering how matters before them might be dealt with by the European Court of Human Rights. He affirmed that the European Convention was relevant only as 'background to the complaint of irrationality', and that the present constitutional role of English courts in respect of the European Convention was to exercise 'a secondary or reviewing judgment'.[56] He explained that '[t]his court does not entertain hypothetical questions', and that there were four reasons why that principle was particularly important in this case:

First, Parliament has not given our judges primary jurisdiction over the human rights issues contained in the Convention. Without such jurisdiction, the court should not speculate. Second, the evidence and submissions before us were directed to our secondary or review jurisdiction, and not to the primary jurisdiction. We should not opine on a case not argued before us. Third, if the Convention were to be made (or possibly be held to be) part of our domestic law, then in the exercise of the primary jurisdiction the court in, for it, a relatively novel constitutional position, might well ask for more material than the adversarial system normally provides, such as a 'Brandeis brief'. The court could well appear to be taking too narrow a view if it hypothetically answered a different question on limited evidence. Lastly, the dangers of speculation and the absence of what Simon Brown LJ refers to as the 'tide of history' from the published tide tables both point to judicial silence on any eventual primary judicial judgment on article 8 in this case.[57]

This judgment not only confirms the limited role of the European Convention in English administrative law, it also makes it highly unlikely that the European Convention will be accorded greater influence in the future through the introduction of the doctrine of proportionality.[58] The standard applied was clearly one of irrationality rather than proportionality. In this respect this judgment represents a restrictive interpretation of the House of Lords decision in *Brind* v. *Secretary of State for the Home Department*,[59] and does nothing to redress the current imbalance between human rights and ministerial discretion which exists in this country in the absence of legislation implementing the European Convention.

[56] [1996] 1 All ER 257 at 272, [1996] 2 WLR 333 at 345.

[57] [1996] 1 All ER 257 at 272, [1996] 2 WLR 333 at 345. In his judgment on the case in the Divisional Court, Simon Brown LJ had said: 'The tide of history is against the ministry. Prejudices are breaking down; old barriers are being removed. It seems to me improbable, whatever this court may say, that the existing policy can survive for much longer': [1996] 2 WLR 305 at 319. Thorpe J, the third member of the Court of Appeal, agreed with Sir Thomas Bingham MR and Henry LJ. See also discussion of *R* v. *The Secretary of State for the Home Department, ex parte Launder*, above, pp. 548–51 and 551, n. 48. In respect of another set of arguments based on the 1957 EC Treaty (*United Nations Treaty Series*, vol. 294, p. 17), and Council Directive (EEC) 76/207 ('Council Directive on the implementation of the principle of equal treatment for men and women as regards access to employment, vocational training and promotion, and working conditions'), the Court held that neither document covered discrimination on the grounds of sexual orientation.

[58] On the possible application of the doctrine of proportionality in English law, see Jowell and Lester, 'Beyond *Wednesbury*: Substantive Principles of Administrative Law', *Public Law*, 1987, p. 368, esp. pp. 375–6; Laws, 'Is the High Court the Guardian of Fundamental Constitutional Rights?' *Public Law*, 1993, p. 59, esp. pp. 69–74. Cf. Wade, *Administrative Law* (7th edn., 1994), p. 403.

[59] [1991] 1 All ER 720, [1991] 1 AC 696, [1991] 2 WLR 588, and especially this *Year Book*, 62 (1991), pp. 437–40. See also the discussion of the Divisional Court decision in this case, as well as of *R* v. *Secretary of State for the Home Department, ex parte McQuillan*, [1995] 4 All ER 400, QBD, in this *Year Book*, 66 (1995), pp. 509–12.

Refugees—'serious non-political crime'—Geneva Convention relating to the Status of Refugees 1951, Article 1F(b)—relationship of the 'serious non-political crime' exception in refugee law to the 'political offence' exception in extradition law

Case No. 8. T v. *Secretary of State for the Home Department*, [1996] AC 742, [1996] 2 All ER 865, [1996] 2 WLR 766, [1996] Times LR 323, [1996] Imm AR 443, HL. T was an Algerian national who applied for asylum in the United Kingdom after having been arrested as an illegal entrant. The request for asylum was rejected by the Secretary of State, who ordered T's removal to Algeria. Subsequent appeals were rejected by a special adjudicator, the Immigration Appeals Tribunal and the Court of Appeal.

The special adjudicator accepted that T was a member of the Islamic Salvation Front (FIS). The FIS is an Algerian political organization which seeks to establish a fundamentalist Islamic State. In pursuing this goal the FIS has engaged in considerable violence. In December 1991 it secured a majority in a first round of national elections. However, a second round of elections was cancelled by those in power. Algeria has since been ruled by the military, and in March 1992 the FIS was declared an illegal organization.

The special adjudicator accepted that T had a well-founded fear of persecution if returned to Algeria and that he therefore fell within the definition of a refugee under Article 1A of the 1951 Geneva Convention relating to the Status of Refugees (the 'Geneva Convention').[60] This point was also conceded by the Secretary of State. However, the special adjudicator, the Immigration Appeals Tribunal and the Court of Appeal (in a decision reviewed in the previous volume of this *Year Book*[61]) were of the view that T was excluded from the application of the Geneva Convention on the basis of Article 1F(b), which reads:

> The provisions of this Convention shall not apply to any person with respect to whom there are serious reasons for considering that: . . . (b) He has committed a serious non-political crime outside the country of refuge prior to his admission to that country as a refugee; . . .

There were serious reasons for considering that T was involved in an FIS bomb attack on an airport in Algeria, in which ten people were killed, as well as in a raid on an army barracks, in which one person was killed. Glidewell LJ, giving the judgment of the Court of Appeal, said:

> [I]t cannot properly be said that these particular offences qualify as political. In our judgment the airport bombing in particular was an atrocious act, grossly out of proportion to any genuine political objective. There was simply no sufficiently close or direct causal link between it and T's alleged political purpose. It offends common sense to suppose that the FIS's cause of supplanting the government could be directly advanced by such an offence.[62]

---

[60] *United Nations Treaty Series*, vol. 189, p. 137, Cmnd. 9171, as modified by the 1967 Protocol relating to the Status of Refugees, Cmnd. 3906. The question of the application of the Convention in national law arose for determination on account of section 8(1) of the Asylum and Immigration Appeals Act 1993, which provides that: 'A person who is refused leave to enter the United Kingdom under the . . . [Immigration Act 1971] may appeal against the refusal to a special adjudicator on the ground that his removal in consequence of the refusal would be contrary to the United Kingdom's obligations under the [Geneva] Convention'.

[61] This *Year Book*, 66 (1995), pp. 501–5.

[62] [1995] 2 All ER 1042 at 1056, [1995] 1 WLR 545 at 559–60.

This case therefore concerns the 'serious non-political crime' exception to the application of the Geneva Convention. Although this exception is closely related to the 'political offence' exception to the obligation to extradite pursuant to extradition treaties, the issues are nevertheless distinct. Lord Mustill, in his judgment on this case in the House of Lords, explained one of the differences between the two issues:

A substantial point of difference between extradition and asylum is that where the former is in issue the political nature of the offence is an exception to a general duty to return the fugitive, whereas in relation to asylum there is a general duty *not* to perform a refoulement unless the crime is non-political.[63]

Nevertheless, Lord Mustill, Lord Slynn and Lord Lloyd (Lords Keith and Browne-Wilkinson concurring) all relied heavily on the case law concerning the political offence exception to extradition in rendering their judgments on this issue of refugee law. Lord Lloyd said:

There is no English authority on the meaning of 'non-political crime' in the 1951 Convention. But it was common ground that the words must bear the same meaning as they do in extradition law. Indeed, it appears from the travaux préparatoires that the framers of the Convention had extradition law in mind when drafting the Convention, and intended to make use of the same concept, although the application of the concept would, of course, be for a different purpose.[64]

In dealing with the issue, Lord Lloyd adopted what has been described as a 'traditional approach'.[65] He began by reviewing earlier cases in the English courts. In *Re Castioni* murder 'in furtherance' of an armed uprising had been held to constitute a political offence,[66] as had violent measures taken to avoid being prosecuted for political opinions within a totalitarian State in *Ex parte Kolczynski*.[67] In *Re Meunier* the acts of an anarchist 'directed primarily against the general body of citizens' had not been considered political offences,[68] whereas in *Schtraks* v. *Government of Israel* Viscount Radcliffe had said:

In my opinion the idea that lies behind the phrase 'offence of a political character' is that a fugitive is at odds with the state that applies for his extradition on some issue connected with the political control or government of the country.[69]

In *Tzu-Tsai Cheng* v. *Governor of Pentonville Prison* an offence which had been committed in the United States but which was directed against another State was held not to be a political offence for the purposes of extradition to the United States.[70]

---

[63] [1996] 2 All ER 865 at 886, [1996] 2 WLR 766 at 787, emphasis in original.
[64] [1996] 2 All ER 865 at 891, [1996] 2 WLR 766 at 792.
[65] Hopkins, 'What is a Political Offence?', *Cambridge Law Journal*, 55 (1996), pp. 417, 419.
[66] [1891] 1 QB 149, [1886–90] All ER 640.
[67] [1955] 1 QB 540.
[68] [1894] 2 QB 415.
[69] [1962] 3 All ER 529 at 540, [1964] AC 556 at 591.
[70] [1973] 2 All ER 204, [1973] AC 931. *Ex parte Cheng* was referred to by Henry LJ in another case in the year under review, namely *R* v. *Governor of Belmarsh Prison, ex parte Dunlayici*, [1996] Times LR 476, QB. This case concerned a request by Germany for the extradition of a Kurd who had organized a series of attacks on Turkish property in Germany. Applying Lord Mustill's analysis in *T* v. *Secretary of State* (see below), Henry LJ held that, since the dominant motive behind the attacks was directed against the Turkish Government and not the requesting German Government, the attacks were not political offences within section 6(1)(a) of the 1989 Extradition Act.

Lord Lloyd then considered several cases from other jurisdictions. In the United States, the Court of Appeals (Seventh Circuit) had said in *Eain* v. *Wilkes*:

The [political offence] exception does not make a random bombing intended to result in the cold-blooded murder of civilians incidental to a purpose of toppling a government, absent a direct link between the perpetrator, a political organization's political goals, and the specific act.[71]

In *McMullen* v. *Immigration and Naturalization Service* the Court of Appeals (Ninth Circuit) had distinguished between terrorist acts directed at military or official agencies of the State, and random acts of violence against ordinary citizens which are intended only to promote social chaos. Only the former would be considered political offences.[72]

In Canada, the case of *Re Gil and Minister of Employment and Immigration* concerned a bomb attack in Iran which had been designed to injure the commercial interests of supporters of the Khomeini regime, but which had also killed many innocent bystanders.[73] Hugessen J of the Federal Court of Appeal said:

[A]lthough there is no doubt as to the extremely repressive nature of the regime in Iran, the appellant's claim fails for other reasons: notably the lack of nexus between the crimes and any realistic political objective, and the fact that the means employed are unacceptable as a form of political protest against any regime, no matter how repressive, totalitarian or dictatorial.[74]

Lord Lloyd also referred to the UNHCR Handbook[75] and the 1977 European Convention on the Suppression of Terrorism.[76] Both documents identify elements to be considered when determining whether an offence is political in character.

He then provided the following definition, or what he referred to as a 'description of an idea', of 'political crime':

A crime is a political crime for the purposes of art 1F(b) of the 1951 convention if, and only if: (1) it is committed for a political purpose, that is to say, with the object of overthrowing or subverting or changing the government of a state or inducing it to change its policy; and (2) there is a sufficiently close and direct link between the crime and the alleged political purpose. In determining whether such a link exists, the court will bear in mind the means used to achieve the political end, and will have particular regard to whether the crime was aimed at a military or governmental target, on the one hand, or a civilian target on the other, and in either event whether it was likely to involve the indiscriminate killing or injuring of members of the public.[77]

Applying this definition to the facts of the case, Lord Lloyd said:

[I]t is clear that the FIS is a political organization which was thwarted in an attempt to

---

[71] 641 F 2d 504, 521 (1981).
[72] 788 F 2d 591 (1986).
[73] (1994) 119 DLR (4th) 497.
[74] Ibid. at 517–18.
[75] Office of the United Nations High Commissioner for Refugees, *Handbook on Procedures and Criteria for Determining Refugee Status* (re-edited 1992).
[76] *UK Treaty Series*, No. 93 (1978) (Cmnd. 7390), *European Treaty Series*, No. 90.
[77] [1996] 2 All ER 865 at 899, [1996] 2 WLR 766 at 801.

become the government of Algeria by democratic means. T's motive in becoming involved in the bombing of the airport is not in doubt. He was attempting to overthrow the government by what he regarded as the only remaining available means. He therefore satisfies the first, or subjective, condition.[78]

Lord Lloyd went on to hold that T did not satisfy the second condition:

Although the airport itself could be regarded as a governmental target, the crime as carried out was almost bound to involve the killing of members of the public. The means used were indiscriminate, and therefore the link between the crime and the political object which T was seeking to achieve was too remote.[79]

Lord Mustill considered this approach to be flawed because it left open the question of how tests of remoteness, causation or proportionality are to be applied. He said:

[T]o say that the political aim must cause the crime, or that the crime must not be too remote from the aim, does no more than assert that the crime must be really political in nature to fall within the exception. But to prescribe causation or remoteness as tests which must as a matter of law be applied . . . only multiplies the problems.[80]

He added:

To strike a balance the official or adjudicator in the receiving state would have to evaluate, amongst other facts: (i) the unacceptableness of the state of affairs which the crime is designed to improve; (ii) the extent to which the crime would, or at least might, bring about an improvement; (iii) the conformity or otherwise of the crime with local conceptions of the way in which, if need be, political change can be brought about; (iv) the practicability of achieving the same result by other and less drastic means.[81]

Lord Mustill adopted a different approach, which he described as 'writing "terrorism" into the modern concept of the political crime'.[82] He explained that the situation within which the political offence exception had developed was different from that which exists today:

Those who were intended to benefit from the political exception had taken up arms, having no other means, to relieve from oppression those who could not fend for themselves. The human rights of the individual who sought refuge in fear of persecution therefore coincided with those of the oppressed, and the evil of violence could be tolerated without threat to the world order in the greater interest of making the world a better place. Whether this was sound thinking no longer matters, for the scene has changed. Those who use violence and fear to struggle against oppression may themselves be oppressors, causing as much suffering to the defenceless as those whom they seek to displace. When they flee to a foreign country the impulse to protect them from persecution remains, but it is muted. The community as a whole has a moral right to protection, which should not be compromised by offering too ready a refuge to those who, having embroiled the population in violence, find themselves on the losing side. . . . To my mind, the whole trend of the more modern decisions and writings is towards an acceptance that certain acts of violence, even if political in a narrow sense, are beyond the

---

[78] [1996] 2 All ER 865 at 899, [1996] 2 WLR 766 at 801.
[79] [1996] 2 All ER 865 at 899, [1996] 2 WLR 766 at 801.
[80] [1996] 2 All ER 865 at 882, [1996] 2 WLR 766 at 783.
[81] [1996] 2 All ER 865 at 883, [1996] 2 WLR 766 at 785.
[82] [1996] 2 All ER 865 at 885, [1996] 2 WLR 766 at 786.

pale, and that they should not be condoned by offering sanctuary to those who commit them.[83]

Lord Mustill's approach involves what he described as 'the recognition that some characteristic of the crime can disconnect it from its political origins'.[84] He explained that this approach 'concentrates on the method of the offence, rather than its physical manifestation'.[85] It was therefore important that:

The terrorist does not strike at his opponents; those whom he kills are not the tyrants whom he opposes, but people to whom he is indifferent. They are the raw materials of a strategy, not the objectives of it. The terrorist is not even concerned to inspire terror in the victims, for to him they are cyphers. They exist only as a means to inspire terror at large, to destroy opposition by moral enfeeblement, or to create a vacuum into which the like-minded can stride. It seems to me in a real sense that a political crime, the killing of A by B to achieve an end, involves a direct relationship between the ideas of the criminal and the victim, which is absent in the depersonalised and abstract violence which kills twenty, or three, or none. I find it hard to believe that the human rights of the fugitive could ever have been intended to outweigh this cold indifference to the human rights of the uninvolved.[86]

Lord Mustill suggested that the term terrorism is divorced from criteria such as remoteness, causation, atrociousness and proportionality, for 'once it is made clear that terrorism is not simply a label for violent conduct of which the speaker deeply disapproves, the term is capable of definition and objective application'.[87] He concluded by adopting the definition of terrorism set out in the 1937 Convention for the Prevention and Punishment of Terrorism (a convention which he recognized had never come into force), namely:

'[A]cts' of terrorism mean criminal acts directed against a State and intended or calculated to create a state of terror in the minds of particular persons, or a group of persons or the general public.[88]

This case is likely to have a significant impact, not only on the serious non-political crime exception to the application of the Geneva Convention, but also on the political offence exception in extradition law. Lord Lloyd's judgment, in particular, may replace the tests concerning the political offence exception which were set out in *Schtraks* v. *Government of Israel*[89] and *Tzu-Tsai Cheng* v. *Governor of Pentonville Prison*.[90] Whether this is a good thing is another question, especially given that this was not an extradition case and that the judges themselves recognized important differences between the serious non-political crime and political offence exceptions. On the other hand, this may not be a serious concern in terms of extradition law, for the simple reason that the judges treated this case as if it were an extradition case. The problem lies in the

---

[83] [1996] 2 All ER 865 at 870, [1996] 2 WLR 766 at 771.
[84] [1996] 2 All ER 865 at 885, [1996] 2 WLR 766 at 786–7.
[85] [1996] 2 All ER 865 at 885, [1996] 2 WLR 766 at 787.
[86] [1996] 2 All ER 865 at 885–6, [1996] 2 WLR 766 at 787.
[87] [1996] 2 All ER 865 at 886, [1996] 2 WLR 766 at 787.
[88] Hudson, *International Legislation* (1935–7), vol. 7, p. 862 (no. 499).
[89] [1962] 3 All ER 529 at 535 (*per* Lord Reid), 540 (*per* Viscount Radcliffe), 552–3 (*per* Lord Hodson), [1964] AC 556 at 583, 591, 612.
[90] [1973] 2 All ER 204 at 207 (*per* Lord Hodson), 209 (*per* Lord Diplock), [1973] AC 931 at 942, 945.

fact that in so doing, they overlooked that this was a refugee case, and thus largely ignored the 'general duty *not* to perform a refoulement unless the crime is non-political', to which Lord Mustill did refer.[91] Thus they failed to fulfil their primary responsibility in this case, as it exists in all *asylum* cases, namely towards the individual facing return.

Despite the consistent rejection of T''s arguments at all levels of the judiciary, and the apparent consistency of this judgment of the House of Lords with the case law in the United Kingdom and elsewhere, the decision may nevertheless be regarded with scepticism. It is possible that T was not simply facing persecution on his return to Algeria, but, as a known opponent of the military government, would probably face particularly severe treatment.

The uncertainty as to whether Article 1F(*b*) deprived T of the benefit of the protection of the Geneva Convention could have been resolved by looking to international law more generally. Other treaties and, arguably, customary international law contain an absolute prohibition on the return of an individual to torture. In particular, Article 3 of the 1984 Convention against Torture and Other Cruel, Inhuman or Degrading Treatment or Punishment ('the Torture Convention'), which the United Kingdom ratified in 1988, reads:

1. No State Party shall expel, return (*'refouler'*) or extradite a person to another State where there are substantial grounds for believing that he would be in danger of being subjected to torture.

2. For the purpose of determining whether there are such grounds, the competent authorities shall take into account all relevant considerations including, where applicable, the existence in the State concerned of a consistent pattern of gross, flagrant or mass violations of human rights.[92]

There is no serious non-political crime exception in the Torture Convention. Moreover, for the purposes of this case Article 3(2) might be redundant: even the Secretary of State agreed that T faced persecution if returned to Algeria. Alternatively, the human rights situation in Algeria should have been considered in order to determine whether that persecution would be serious enough to constitute torture, with any uncertainty being resolved in favour of T, as a result of the Court's general duty *not* to perform a refoulement.

Subsequent to the rejection of T''s arguments by the House of Lords, the absolute prohibition on return to torture was confirmed by the European Court of Human Rights in the case of *Chahal* v. *The United Kingdom*.[93] Chahal was a

[91] [1996] 2 All ER 865 at 886, [1996] 2 WLR 766 at 787, emphasis in original. See full quotation, above, p. 555.

[92] United Nations General Assembly Resolution 39/46 of 10 December 1984, Misc. 12 (1985) (Cmnd. 9593). On Article 3 of the Torture Convention, see the decisions of the United Nations Committee against Torture in *Mutombo* v. *Switzerland*, 27 April 1994, Communication No. 13/1993, UN Doc. CAT/C/12/D/13/1993, *International Journal of Refugee Law*, 7 (1995), p. 322; *Kahn* v. *Canada*, 15 November 1994, Communication No. 15/1994, UN Doc. CAT/C/13/D/15/1994; *Alan* v. *Switzerland*, 8 May 1996, Communication No. 21/1995, UN Doc. CAT/C/16/D/21/1996, *International Journal of Refugee Law*, 8 (1995), p. 440. The first two decisions are discussed in Goodwin-Gill, *The Refugee in International Law* (2nd edn., 1996), pp. 153–5.

[93] 15 November 1996, judgment 70/1995/576/662. The absolute character of this prohibition was again upheld by the ECHR in *Ahmed* v. *Austria*, 17 December 1996, judgment 71/1995/577/663. The decision of the Court of Appeal in *R* v. *Secretary of State for the Home Department, ex parte Chahal*, [1995] 1 WLR 526, [1995] 1 All ER 658, was reviewed in this *Year Book*, 66 (1995), pp. 501–3.

Sikh activist who faced return to India on the basis of Article 33(2) of the Geneva Convention, which normally allows States of asylum to refuse a claim

by a refugee whom there are reasonable grounds for regarding as a danger to the security of the country in which he is, or who, having been convicted by a final judgment of a particularly serious crime, constitutes a danger to the community of that country.

The Court found that his return would violate Article 3 of the European Convention for the Protection of Human Rights and Fundamental Freedoms ('the European Convention'), which reads:

No one shall be subjected to torture or to inhuman or degrading treatment or punishment.[94]

The Court said:

Article 3 enshrines one of the most fundamental values of democratic society. The Court is well aware of the immense difficulties faced by States in modern times in protecting their communities from terrorist violence. However, even in these circumstances, the Convention prohibits in absolute terms torture or inhuman or degrading treatment or punishment, irrespective of the victim's conduct. . . . The prohibition provided by Article 3 against ill-treatment is equally absolute in expulsion cases. . . . In these circumstances, the activities of the individual in question, however undesirable or dangerous, cannot be a material consideration.[95]

Article 3 of the Torture Convention has not been incorporated into the national law of the United Kingdom.[96] It is nevertheless of importance in a case, such as this one, where a provision of a United Kingdom statute dealing with the return of refugee claimants is less than clear. Although it was uncertain whether there were substantial grounds for believing that T was in danger of being subjected to torture, in interpreting Article 1F(*b*) of the Geneva Convention (as implemented by section 8(1) of the Asylum and Immigration Appeals Act 1993), the House of Lords should have followed the basic tenet expressed by Lord Diplock in *Garland* v. *British Rail*:

[I]t is a principle of construction of United Kingdom statutes . . . that the words of a statute passed after the Treaty has been signed and dealing with the subject matter of the

[94] *United Nations Treaty Series*, vol. 213, p. 221; *UK Treaty Series*, No. 71 (1953), Cmnd. 8969.

[95] 15 November 1996, judgment 70/1995/576/662, paras. 79 and 80. Goodwin-Gill, *The Refugee in International Law* (2nd edn., 1996), pp. 106–7, came close to saying the same thing:

'Article 1F excludes "persons", rather than "refugees" from the benefits of the [Geneva] Convention, suggesting that the issue of a well-founded fear of persecution is irrelevant and need not be examined at all if there are "serious reasons for considering" that an individual comes within its terms. In practice, the claim to be a refugee can rarely be ignored, for a balance must also be struck between the nature of the offence presumed to have been committed and the degree of persecution feared. A person with a well-founded fear of very severe persecution, such as would endanger life or freedom, should only be excluded for the most serious reasons. If the persecution feared is less, then the nature of the crime or crimes in question must be assessed to see whether criminal character in fact outweighs the applicant's character as a *bona fide* refugee.'

Goodwin-Gill also suggested that the 'inclusion of the principle *aut dedere aut judicare* in instruments aimed at suppressing certain crimes with an international dimension is further acknowledgement that even the serious criminal may deserve protection against persecution or prejudice, while not escaping trial or punishment': ibid., p. 149, footnote omitted.

[96] Sections 134 and 135 of the Criminal Justice Act 1988 only criminalized torture. They did not set out a requirement of non-refoulement in respect of probable torture victims.

international obligation of the United Kingdom, are to be construed, if they are reasonably capable of bearing such a meaning, as intended to carry out the obligation, and not to be inconsistent with it.[97]

This case also raises an important issue concerning democracy. Although the FIS may be considered a terrorist organization, it may also have some claim to legitimacy. The elections held on 26 December 1991 were the first multiparty elections in Algeria in thirty years.[98] They were also generally considered to be free from serious irregularities. The FIS won 189 of the 231 parliamentary seats distributed in the first round of those elections. Moreover, FIS attacks in Algeria are not necessarily random acts of violence. Although frequently abhorrent, they are often directed either at the military government or at those segments of the population which support the government in some way. In the light of these facts, Lord Lloyd's attempt to balance various factors seems somewhat mis-informed, while Lord Mustill's designation of the bombing of the airport as a terrorist act is perhaps open to question.

It is possible that another, largely unspoken, factor may have been weighing on the judges' minds. The FIS had made it clear during the elections that, if victorious, it intended to abolish future elections. The elections were suspended, in part, because it was clear that the FIS was about to achieve the two-thirds parliamentary majority needed to amend the Algerian constitution so as to achieve this goal. In short, the FIS can be seen as a democratically elected anti-democratic party, and as such very difficult to fit into the traditional political conceptions which gave rise to the serious non-political crime and political offence exceptions. It may be possible that members of anti-democratic groups are regarded as undeserving of the protection of international law when they engage in violent activities—even if they have the support of the majority of their State's population in so doing. Such an approach might find support in recent writings about democracy and international law.[99] However, to make such a judgment is to seek to protect existing liberal democratic States and not to adjudicate the seriousness and political character of a particular crime. It is an exercise of judgment allowed by Article 33(2) of the Geneva Convention, to the effect that the refugee is 'a danger to the security of the country in which he is'. Yet this was not asserted to be the case with T.

---

[97] [1983] 2 AC 751 at 771A, [1982] 2 All ER 402 at 415, [1982] 2 WLR 918 at 934–5, this *Year Book*, 53 (1982), pp. 291–3. See also *R v. Secretary of State for the Home Department, ex parte Brind*, [1991] 1 All ER 720 at 722–3 and 733–4, [1991] 2 WLR 588 at 591–2 and 603–4 (*per* Lord Bridge and Lord Ackner), this *Year Book*, 62 (1991), pp. 437–40; *Mortensen v. Peters*, (1906) 8 F(JC) 93 at 103–4 (*per* Lord Kyllachy). As Lord Bridge and Lord Ackner made clear in their judgments in *R v. Secretary of State for the Home Department, ex parte Brind*, [1991] 1 All ER 720 at 722–3 and 734, [1991] 2 WLR 588 at 591–2 and 604, the statutory provision in question need not have been enacted for the purpose of giving effect to the treaty to which reference is made.

[98] On the factual background, see generally Fox and Nolte, 'Intolerant Democracies', *Harvard International Law Journal*, 36 (1995), pp. 1, 6–7. Fox and Nolte argued that international law allows States to impose limits on democratic participation in order to protect democracy against organizations like the FIS.

[99] See, e.g., Franck, 'The Emerging Right to Democratic Governance', *American Journal of International Law*, 86 (1992), p. 46; Crawford, 'Democracy and International Law', this *Year Book*, 64 (1993), p. 113; Fox and Nolte, loc. cit. above (n. 98); Marks, 'The European Convention on Human Rights and its "Democractic Society" ', this *Year Book*, 66 (1995), p. 209.

Ironically, an alternative avenue was open to the Secretary of State. As Lord Mustill pointed out in his judgment,[100] the United Kingdom has assumed jurisdiction over precisely the kind of criminal act committed by T, irrespective of the offender's nationality and of the place where the act was done. It has done so by enacting the Aviation and Maritime Security Act 1990, section 1(1) of which makes it an offence triable in the United Kingdom

for any person by means of any device, substance or weapon intentionally to commit at an aerodrome serving international civil aviation any act of violence [defined in such a manner as to include murder, manslaughter, offences against the person and the use of explosive devices] which—(a) causes or is likely to cause death or serious personal injury, and (b) endangers or is likely to endanger the safe operation of the aerodrome or the safety of persons at the aerodrome.

Refugees—Geneva Convention relating to the Status of Refugees, Article 33—'safe third country'—evidence made available to special adjudicators in reviewing the Secretary of State's designation of a third State as 'safe'—risk of refoulement by the third State

Case No. 9. Abdi and another v. Secretary of State for the Home Department and another, [1996] 1 WLR 298, [1996] 1 All ER 641, [1996] Imm. AR 288, [1996] Times LR 88; *Case No. 10. Mohammed A.S. Al-Mass'ari v. Secretary of State for the Home Department,* Appeal No. HX 75955/94, 5 March 1996, unreported. By Article 33 of the 1951 Geneva Convention relating to the Status of Refugees ('the Geneva Convention') the contracting States, including the United Kingdom, undertook not to 'expel or return *("refouler")* a refugee in any manner whatsoever to the frontiers of territories where his life or freedom would be threatened on account of his race, religion, nationality, membership of a particular social group or political opinion'.[101]

These two cases concern the introduction, in 1993, of the concept of the 'safe third country' into the regulations which govern how the United Kingdom goes about fulfilling its obligations under Article 33, and more specifically, the role of special adjudicators in reviewing the Secretary of State's designation of a third State as 'safe'. According to paragraph 345 of the Immigration Rules:

If the Secretary of State is satisfied that there is a safe country to which an asylum applicant can be sent his application will normally be refused without substantive consideration of his claim to refugee status. A safe country is one in which the life or freedom of the asylum applicant would not be threatened (within the meaning of Article 33 of the Convention) and the government of which would not send the applicant elsewhere in a manner contrary to the principles of the Convention and Protocol. The

---

[100] [1996] 2 All ER 865 at 877, [1996] 2 WLR 766 at 778.

[101] *United Nations Treaty Series,* vol. 189, p. 137, Cmnd. 9171, as modified by the 1967 Protocol relating to the Status of Refugees, Cmnd. 3906. The question of the application of the Geneva Convention in national law arose for determination on account of section 8(1) of the Asylum and Immigration Appeals Act 1993, which provides that: 'A person who is refused leave to enter the United Kingdom under the . . . [Immigration Act 1971] may appeal against the refusal to a special adjudicator on the ground that his removal in consequence of the refusal would be contrary to the United Kingdom's obligations under the [Geneva] Convention'.

Secretary of State shall not remove an asylum applicant without substantive consideration of his claim unless:

(a) the asylum applicant has not arrived in the United Kingdom directly from the
country in which he claims to fear persecution and has had an opportunity, at the
border or within the territory of a third country, to make contact with that country's
authorities in order to seek their protection; or

(b) there is other clear evidence of his admissibility to a third country.

Provided that he is satisfied that a case meets these criteria, the Secretary of State is under
no obligation to consult the authorities of the third country before the removal of an
asylum applicant.[102]

In *Abdi and another* v. *Secretary of State for the Home Department and another*
the applicants were Somali nationals who had claimed asylum in the United
Kingdom. On their way from Somalia to the United Kingdom they had passed
through Spain. The Secretary of State refused their request for asylum without
giving them a substantive hearing. He did so on the basis that they were
returnable to Spain as there was no reason to believe that Spain, which had
ratified the Geneva Convention, would not comply with its obligations towards
them. He accordingly issued certificates that the applicants' claims (that their
removal from the United Kingdom would be contrary to the United Kingdom's
obligations under the Geneva Convention) were without foundation. On appeal
the special adjudicators held that both applicants had had time to apply for
asylum in Spain and had not done so, and that, in the absence of material
suggesting that Spain was not a 'safe third country', they were entitled to rely on
the Secretary of State's certificate to that effect.

In the House of Lords, Lord Lloyd, for the majority, held that the lack of any
requirement in the Immigration Rules for the Secretary of State to provide an
explanatory statement of facts did not imply that he was obliged to disclose the
material facts by other means. Moveover, Lord Lloyd held that this case did not
concern the substantive right to asylum, but rather the procedural question
whether the substantive hearing should take place in the United Kingdom, or in
another State. He emphasized the need for short time limits:

The longer the delay between the arrival of the appellant in the United Kingdom and his
return to a safe third country, the less likely it is that that country will be willing to
undertake the substantive hearing, in which case, if there is no other country to which the
appellant can be sent, he would inevitably be returned again to the United Kingdom. So
if the procedure . . . is to be effective at all . . . , it must be fast.[103]

This, Lord Lloyd explained, did not mean that justice was being sacrificed in
the interest of speed. Under the Immigration Rules special adjudicators could
always apply for an extension of the time limits, both for giving notice of the
appeal and for determining it.[104] Special adjudicators had also built up their own
expertise in respect of what constituted a 'safe third country', and could always
exercise their powers to ask for the particulars of the Secretary of State's case.
Therefore, Lord Lloyd was 'not persuaded that justice required that the Home
Secretary should give discovery in asylum appeals, even if it were possible

---

[102] (1993–94) HC 395.
[103] [1996] 1 WLR 298 at 314, [1996] 1 All ER 641 at 657.
[104] See rules 5(7) and 31 of the Asylum Appeals (Procedure) Rules 1993 (SI, 1993, No. 1661).

(which it is not) to reconcile such an obligation with the express provisions of the 1993 appeals procedure rules'.[105] Indeed,

if the courts were to supplement the rules by imposing some such obligation on the Secretary of State, there would be a risk of frustrating the evident legislative purpose that 'without foundation' appeals should be considered with all due speed.[106]

Lord Slynn disagreed. He said:

It is for the Secretary of State to show that the decision was the right one for the special adjudicators to adopt for themselves. That is the nature of their inquiry.[107]

He continued:

It is clear that Parliament has not provided expressly for such material to be laid before the adjudicator. That, however, is not conclusive if the nature of the function imposed on him by Parliament and 'fair play in action' require that such material should be made available.[108]

Lord Slynn emphasized the procedural fairness which should permeate the appeal process, rather than a strict interpretation of the rules and time limits:

In my view, the justified wish to give a quick refusal to hopeless applications for asylum cannot override the importance of giving due consideration to those applications for asylum which are or may be genuine and well founded. The time limits are not therefore conclusive. . . . In my view, even more, the nature of the special adjudicator's task in reviewing the Secretary of State's certificate makes it necessary that the material available to the Secretary of State should be available to the special adjudicator.[109]

He pointed out that, although the adjudicator may be provided with a bundle of documents relating to the appeal, this 'bundle' does not include material relating to the asylum-seeker's contention that the third State is not 'safe'. The documents are limited to those which support the Secretary of State's decision. In Lord Slynn's opinion, this did not enable the special adjudicators fully to perform their task and was 'calculated to produce unfairness'[110].

Lord Slynn's approach is preferable to that adopted by the majority. As Goodwin-Gill has explained, albeit in the slightly different context of the 'safe country of origin':

The problem with the general assessments implied by the safe country of origin device is

---

[105] [1996] 1 WLR 298 at 315, [1996] 1 All ER 641 at 657.

[106] [1996] 1 WLR 298 at 315, [1996] 1 All ER 641 at 657. On the subsidiary issue of whether the certificates constituted evidence in support of the Secretary of State's case, Lord Lloyd considered that, in view of the Home Secretary's knowledge and experience, they did. Thus they constituted sufficient evidence on which the adjudicators were entitled to uphold the certificates. Lords Mustill and Slynn both dissented on this point, and found that the certificates did not go beyond bare certification.

[107] [1996] 1 WLR 298 at 305, [1996] 1 All ER 641 at 648. In support of this conclusion, Lord Slynn referred to Lord Bridge's statement in *Bugdaycay* v. *Secretary of State for the Home Department*, [1987] 1 All ER 940 at 952, [1987] AC 514 at 531, this *Year Book*, 58(1987), pp. 429–33: 'The most fundamental of all human rights is the individual's right to life and when an administrative decision under challenge is said to be one which may put the applicant's life at risk, the basis of the decision must surely call for the most anxious scrutiny'.

[108] [1996] 1 WLR 298 at 305, [1996] 1 All ER 641 at 648, referring to *Wiseman* v. *Borneman*, [1969] 3 All ER 275 at 278, [1971] AC 297 at 309 (*per* Lord Morris).

[109] [1996] 1 WLR 298 at 306, [1996] 1 All ER 641 at 649.

[110] [1996] 1 WLR 298 at 307, [1996] 1 All ER 641 at 650.

precisely that they are general, and consequently operate at a quite different level from the realm of the particular which is central to the refugee definition laid down in the 1951 Convention. Their role can only be evidential, and while good information is the surest basis for good refugee decisions, there will always be a danger of *refoulement* wherever the general is preferred to the particular circumstances of the individual case.'''

The case of *Mohammed A. S. Al-Mass'ari* v. *Secretary of State for the Home Department* concerned a national of Saudi Arabia who, together with some others, had founded the Committee for the Defence of Legitimate Rights (CDLR). He was imprisoned in Saudi Arabia for his activities, as were other members of his family. He fled to Yemen, and there obtained a passport under false pretences so that he could travel to the United Kingdom. He applied for asylum in the United Kingdom shortly after his arrival. However, the Secretary of State served a notice on him, informing him that he was an illegal immigrant. His application for asylum was not considered substantively and directions were issued for his removal to Yemen. He appealed against these directions. The Deputy Chief Adjudicator concluded that 'Yemen is not safe if it cannot protect him and it cannot be said that, by attempting to return Dr Al-Mass'ari to the Yemen, no issue as to the UK's obligations under Article 33 will arise'.'''2

The Secretary of State then announced that he had decided to refuse the application for asylum without substantive consideration of the claim, and to remove Al-Mass'ari to Dominica, which had ratified the Geneva Convention. He claimed that removal to Dominica would not raise any issue of the United Kingdom's obligations under the Geneva Convention.

The decision to remove Al Mass'ari to Dominica was reviewed by the Chief Adjudicator, Judge Pearl. The parties agreed that the burden of proof was on the Secretary of State to establish that Al-Mass'ari's removal would not violate the United Kingdom's obligations under the Geneva Convention, and that Judge Pearl had to consider the merits of the case in deciding this issue. They agreed that the principal question was whether Dominica was a 'safe third country' within the meaning of paragraph 345 (*b*) of the Immigration Rules, which would have entitled the Secretary of State to certify that the claim that removal to Dominica would violate the United Kingdom's obligations was without founda- tion.'''3 They also agreed, following *In re Musisi*, that Judge Pearl was required to subject the decision to remove Al-Mass'ari to the most anxious scrutiny.'''4

Judge Pearl considered Al-Mass'ari's activities both in Saudi Arabia and in the United Kingdom, where he had sent faxes on behalf of the CDLR aimed at 'removing injustice, supporting the oppressed and defending the rights that were given to man by the Shari'a (the Islamic law)'.'''5 He also considered evidence that the Saudi Arabian Government had in the past taken violent action against its opponents, both within Saudi Arabia and elsewhere. He concluded that there 'is "some" suggestion, which is in no way fanciful, that the Saudi Government has been involved in extra-territorial violence in the past'.'''6

''' Goodwin-Gill, *The Refugee in International Law* (2nd edn., 1996), p. 348.
'''2 Appeal No. HX/75955/94, 7 March 1995, Approved Transcript at 15.
'''3 HC 395. See quotation above, p. 562.
'''4 [1987] AC 514 at 531, [1987] 1 All ER 940 at 952, this *Year Book*, 58 (1987), pp. 433–8.
'''5 Declaration of the CDLR, 3 May 1993, quoted in the Approved Transcipt at 6.
'''6 Approved Transcript at 12.

Moreover, there was evidence that threats had been made to Al-Mass'ari in the United Kingdom. Judge Pearl noted:

It would seem the Government has kept under review the possibility that the appellant might be at physical risk in the UK. He has been provided with police advice on security matters, although it has not been judged necessary to offer him special protection.[117]

With regard to Dominica, although the evidence suggested that there was local opposition to Al-Mass'ari's arrival, more important was the evidence in respect of the legal safeguards available there. Dominica had no defence force and all security matters were dealt with by a small police force. The history of Dominica also illustrated a considerable degree of political vulnerability. Indeed, the evidence suggested that the local people considered the decision to receive the appellant to be based entirely on political considerations. Judge Pearl said:

[I] have arrived at the conclusion that Dominica's vulnerability is such that pressure placed on it to remove the appellant and expel him again to Saudi Arabia itself or another third country, other than the UK, may not be capable of being resisted.[118]

Assurances in respect of Al-Mass'ari's safety in Dominica had been made to the United Kingdom rather than to Al-Mass'ari himself. The Geneva Convention was not part of Dominican law, so that, were Dominica to attempt to expel him, any challenge to that decision would have to rely on untested principles of Dominican administrative law. Judge Pearl continued:

I reject the suggestion that even if Dominica were to expel the appellant there would be no real risk of breach of the Convention because all they would do would be to return him to the UK. There is no evidence of this, and it would fly in the face of evidence I have heard that the UK does not want him, and Saudi Arabia does not want him in the UK. In my view there is a real risk of refoulement.

It is my finding, therefore, giving the matter the most anxious scrutiny in an area of factual information which is surrounded by uncertainty, that the Secretary of State has not established that Dominica is a safe third country within the meaning of the Immigration Rules such that he is entitled to refuse the appellant's asylum claim without substantive consideration. Accordingly, he was not entitled to certify the claim as without foundation.[119]

Judge Pearl referred the case to the Secretary of State for reconsideration under paragraph 5(6) schedule 2 of the 1993 Asylum and Immigration Appeals Act, with a strong recommendation that he consider the substantive claim to asylum as expeditiously as possible and in any event within one month of the date of judgment.

The actions of the Secretary of State and the decision of Judge Pearl in this case are both controversial. Nevertheless, Judge Pearl's understanding of the United Kingdom's obligations under the Geneva Convention when removing an asylum seeker to a third State is compelling. Article 33(1) prohibits expulsion or

[117] Approved Transcript at 13–14.

[118] Approved Transcript at 16.

[119] Approved Transcript at 17. A second issue concerned whether the removal without substantive consideration was in breach of Article 3 of the Geneva Convention, which reads: 'The contracting States shall apply the provisions of this Convention to refugees without discrimination as to race, religion or country of origin'. Judge Pearl found that there was no breach of Article 3.

return in 'any manner whatsoever', which clearly includes sending an asylum-seeker to a third State when there is a risk that he will be returned to his State of origin despite a well-founded fear of persecution.[120] In the light of this and of the fact that the parties agreed that Judge Pearl was required to subject the decision to remove Al-Mass'ari to the most anxious scrutiny, his conclusions are at least credible ones.

Refugees—1951 Geneva Convention relating to the Status of Refugees, Article 1A(2)—whether fraudulent claim an automatic barrier to a grant of asylum

Case No. 11. M v. *Secretary of State for the Home Department,* [1996] 1 WLR 507, [1996] 1 All ER 870, [1996] Imm. AR 136, [1995] Times LR 575, CA, leave to appeal denied. M was a national of Zaïre who was found to have made a fraudulent asylum claim in the United Kingdom. The case found its way to the Court of Appeal on the issue of whether it is possible for a person whose claim for asylum has been found to be fraudulent, nevertheless to benefit from the terms of the 1951 Geneva Convention relating to the Status of Refugees ('the Geneva Convention').[121] The Court held that it is possible. Millett LJ wrote:

A person who puts forward a fraudulent and baseless claim for asylum may be guilty of an attempt to pervert the course of justice and, in theory at least, at risk not only of having his claim dismissed but of finding himself the subject of criminal proceedings. But he is not thereby deprived of the protection of the convention.[122]

Millett LJ noted that, although there are express exceptions to the obligation of non-refoulement in the Geneva Convention, these exceptions 'do not include the case where the applicant for asylum has made a previous claim which has been found to be fraudulent and baseless'.[123] However, such an applicant faced serious difficulties in advancing a second claim:

He will have to explain why he voluntarily exposed himself to the risk of persecution where none previously existed by making a false claim which was liable to be exposed. . . . Even if he does satisfy the Secretary of State that he has a genuine fear of persecution for having made a fraudulent application which failed, it will not be easy for him to satisfy the Secretary of State that this is fear of persecution for a convention reason. Failed asylum seekers are not a social or political group. Nor are liars. Such

---

[120] See Crawford and Hyndman, 'Three Heresies in the Application of the Refugee Convention', *International Journal of Refugee Law*, 1 (1989), pp. 155 at 171: 'It is . . . clear that more than one State may share joint responsibility for decisions which result in the *refoulement* of a refugee . . . It follows that a State may not rely on the obligation of another State party to the Convention, even where there are good grounds for saying that the latter State is indeed under a particular obligation with respect to the refugee, if that reliance is likely to result in a violation of Article 33.'

[121] *United Nations Treaty Series*, vol. 189, p. 137, Cmnd. 9171, as modified by the 1967 Protocol relating to the Status of Refugees, Cmnd. 3906. The question of the application of the Geneva Convention in national law arose for determination on account of section 8(1) of the Asylum and Immigration Appeals Act 1993, which provides that: 'A person who is refused leave to enter the United Kingdom under the . . . [Immigration Act 1971] may appeal against the refusal to a special adjudicator on the ground that his removal in consequence of the refusal would be contrary to the United Kingdom's obligations under the [Geneva] Convention'.

[122] [1996] 1 WLR 507 at 513, [1996] 1 All ER 870 at 876.

[123] [1996] 1 WLR 507 at 513, [1996] 1 All ER 870 at 876.

persons do not necessarily hold any particular political opinion. . . . If they are persecuted on their return this is not persecution for a convention reason . . . If, on the other
hand, the applicant claims to have a well-founded fear of persecution because of the
nature of the evidence he gave to support his false claim, he will have to satisfy the
Secretary of State that there is a real risk that the evidence will come to the attention of
the authorities, and that he is likely to be ill-treated in consequence because of the risk
that his claims to have been engaged in political activities which were disbelieved by the
tribunal in this country will nevertheless be believed by the authorities in his own.[124]

*Refugees—1951 Geneva Convention relating to the Status of Refugees, Article
1A(2)—'particular social group'*

Case No. 12. *Secretary of State for the Home Department* v. *Sergei Vasilyevich
Savchenkov*, [1996] Imm. AR 28, CA; Case No. 13. *R* v. *Immigration Appeal
Tribunal and another, ex parte Shah*, The Times, 12 November 1996, QB.
Savchenkov was a Russian national who had been one of a number of security
guards at a hotel in St Petersburg. He had been asked to act as an informer for
the mafia. When he refused, he was harassed, physically assaulted and threatened with death. The Immigration Appeal Tribunal had concluded that he was
a member of a 'particular social group' within the scope of Article 1A(2) of the
1951 Geneva Convention relating to the Status of Refugees ('the Geneva
Convention').[125]

The Court of Appeal reversed that decision. It held that the concept of a
'particular social group' must have been intended to apply to social groups
which existed independently of persecution, and that in such cases the risk of
persecution must therefore arise by reason of an individual's membership within
such an independently existing group.[126]

In *R* v. *Immigration Appeal Tribunal and another, ex parte Shah* the refugee
claimant was a national of Pakistan. She was a battered wife who had fled to the
United Kingdom. On her arrival, she had discovered that she was pregnant. She
had since given birth and, if returned to Pakistan, would have nowhere to go
apart from her husband's home. The special adjudicator found that, if she were
obliged to return, she had a credible fear of being accused of having conceived
the child adulterously, thus exposing her to death by stoning according to

---

[124] [1996] 1 WLR 507 at 514, [1996] 1 All ER 870 at 877.
[125] *United Nations Treaty Series*, vol. 189, p. 137, Cmnd. 9171, as modified by the 1967 Protocol
relating to the Status of Refugees, Cmnd. 3906.
  Article 1A(2) defines a refugee as any person who, 'owing to well-founded fear of being persecuted
for reasons of race, religion, nationality, membership of a particular social group or political opinion,
is outside the country of his nationality and is unable or, owing to such fear, is unwilling to avail
himself of the protection of that country; or who, not having a nationality and being outside the
country of his former habitual residence as a result of such events, is unable or, owing to such fear,
is unwilling to return to it'.
  The question of the application of the Geneva Convention in national law arose for determination
on account of section 8(1) of the Asylum and Immigration Appeals Act 1993, which provides that:
'A person who is refused leave to enter the United Kingdom under the . . . [Immigration Act 1971]
may appeal against the refusal to a special adjudicator on the ground that his removal in consequence
of the refusal would be contrary to the United Kingdom's obligations under the [Geneva]
Convention'.
[126] In coming to this conclusion the Court relied on the Canadian case of *Canada (Attorney-
General)* v. *Ward*, [1993] 2 SCR 689, and the Australian case of *Morato* v. *Minister for Immigration,
Local Government and Ethnic Affairs*, [1992] 106 ALR 367.

Shari'a law. Sedley J held that these facts were capable of bringing her within the scope of Article 1A(2) of the Geneva Convention as a member of a particular social group.

Sedley J's decision is consistent with some developments in other jurisdictions.[127] Women accused of adultery and facing death in accordance with the legal system applicable in their State of origin are clearly members of an independently existing social group having a well-founded fear of persecution.[128] However, the facts in this case might easily have been more difficult. What if Shah had not been pregnant? Would the mere fact that she was a battered wife have been sufficient to bring her within the scope of Article 1A(2), or would the lack of direct State involvement have been fatal to her claim?[129]

Discretion of the court to stay proceedings on grounds of abuse of process—whether luring to United Kingdom by trickery and deception constitutes an abuse of process— criminal jurisdiction over offences committed outside the United Kingdom

Case No. 14. R v. Latif, R v. Shahzad, [1996] 1 All ER 353, [1996] 1 WLR 104, HL. The appellants had been charged and convicted under section 170(2)

---

[127] See, e.g., *Cheung* v. *Minister of Employment and Immigration*, [1993] 2 FC 314 at 322, where Linden JA of the Canadian Federal Court of Appeal held that 'women in China who have [more than] one child and are faced with forced sterilization satisfy enough of the . . . criteria to be considered a particular social group'. The United States has recently recognized forced sterilization as a basis for the granting of asylum, albeit within the scope of persecution for 'political opinion'. On 30 September 1996 Congress adopted the Illegal Immigration Reform and Immigrant Responsibility Act of 1996 which amended the definition of a refugee under section 101(a)(42) of the Immigration and Nationality Act (to be codified at 8 USC §1101(a)(42)) to include 'a person who has been forced to abort a pregnancy or to undergo involuntary sterilization, or who has been persecuted for failure or refusal to undergo such a procedure or for other resistance to a coercive population control program . . . [or] who has a well founded fear that he or she will be forced to undergo such a procedure or subject to persecution for such a failure, refusal, or resistance . . .'.

[128] See discussion of *Secretary of State for the Home Department* v. *Sergei Vasilyevich Savchenkov*, above, p. 568. In Canada, the following test for 'particular social group' was set forth by Mahoney JA of the Trial Division of the Federal Court in *Minister of Employment and Immigration* v. *Mayers*, [1993] 1 FC 154 at 165: '(1) a natural or non-natural group of persons with (2) similar shared background, habits, social status, political outlook, education, values, aspirations, history, economic activity or interests, often interests contrary to those of the prevailing government, and (3) sharing basic, innate, unalterable characteristics, consciousness, and solidarity or (4) sharing a temporary but voluntary status, with the purpose of their association being so fundamental to their human dignity that they should not be required to alter it'. This test was relied upon by the Canadian Federal Court of Appeal in *Cheung* v. *Minister of Employment and Immigration*, [1993] 2 FC 314 at 321–2, and by the Supreme Court of Canada in *Ward* v. *Attorney-General of Canada*, [1993] 2 SCR 689 at 739. For the situation in Australian law, see *Morato* v. *Minister for Immigration, Local Government and Ethnic Affairs*, [1992] 106 ALR 367 at 375–7.

[129] The Trial Division of the Canadian Federal Court has twice held that domestic violence may be a sufficient basis for the granting of asylum. See *Navarez* v. *Minister of Employment and Immigration*, [1995] 2 FC 55; *Diluna* v. *Minister of Employment and Immigration*, [1995] 29 Imm.LR (2d) 156. Goodwin-Gill, *The Refugee in International Law* (2nd edn., 1996), p. 362, wrote: 'From the perspective of the 1951 Convention, the problem with much of the violence against women is precisely that it is perceived, either as "domestic" or as individual and non-attributable to the State or other political structure'. However, he went on to suggest that '[w]hat might at first glance appear "domestic" may enter the public arena and therefore the traditional refugee domain when it passes into the ambit of State-sanctioned or State-tolerated oppression', and that particular social groups of women may be 'identifiable by reference to the fact of their liability, exposure, or vulnerability to violence in an environment that denies them protection': ibid., pp. 363 and 365.

of the Customs and Excise Management Act 1979 ('the Customs and Excise Act') with the offence of being knowingly concerned in the fraudulent evasion of the prohibition on importation of a controlled drug. They appealed on the grounds, *inter alia*, that an informer and customs officer had, by subterfuge, incited one of them—Shahzad—to commit the offence, and had then lured him into the jurisdiction, and that this constituted an abuse of process.

The facts were as follows: Honi, a shopkeeper in Pakistan, was an informer employed by the United States Drugs Enforcement Agency. Shahzad approached Honi and proposed an export of 20 kilograms of heroin to the United Kingdom. They agreed that Shahzad would deliver the drug in Pakistan to Honi, who would then arrange for an airline pilot to carry it to the United Kingdom. Honi would take delivery of the drug there and then Shahzad, or somebody acting on his behalf, would collect it and arrange for its distribution.

Honi, on receiving the drug, delivered it to a Drugs Enforcement Agency officer. A customs and excise officer from the United Kingdom then travelled to Pakistan to collect the drug and bring it back to the United Kingdom. Honi also travelled to the United Kingdom where he set about persuading Shahzad to come to take delivery of the drug. Shahzad came, as did Latif, and together with Honi they discussed arrangements for delivery of the drug. A customs officer arrived with bags made to look like the packages of heroin, and both Shahzad and Latif were arrested.

Shahzad argued that the customs officer had not only encouraged him to commit the offence, but had actually committed the offence himself. The Court held that it was Shahzad who had taken the initiative. The most that could be said was that Honi had given him the opportunity to commit, or to attempt to commit, the crime of importing heroin into the United Kingdom, if he were so minded. It also held that the customs officer was himself guilty of offences under sections 50(3) and 170(2) of the Customs and Excise Act.

In determining whether the illegal actions of the customs officer constituted an abuse of process, the Court held that it had to balance the requirement of not being seen to condone the criminal conduct or malpractice of law enforcement agencies with the necessity of protecting the public from serious crime. Since a fair trial was still possible in the circumstances, the judge had a discretion as to whether there was an abuse of process which amounted to an affront to the public conscience.

Lord Steyn, giving the opinion of the House of Lords and referring to its judgment in *Bennett* v. *Horseferry Road Magistrates' Court*,[130] said:

In this case the issue is whether, despite the fact that a fair trial was possible, the judge ought to have stayed the criminal proceedings on broader considerations of the integrity of the criminal justice system. The law is settled. Weighing countervailing considerations of policy and justice, it is for the judge in the exercise of his discretion to decide whether there has been an abuse of process, which amounts to an affront to the public conscience and requires the criminal proceedings to be stayed. . . . *Bennett* was a case where a stay was appropriate because a defendant had been forcibly abducted and brought to this country to face trial in disregard of extradition laws. The speeches in *Bennett* conclusively

---

[130] [1993] 3 All ER 138, *sub nom. R* v. *Horseferry Road Magistrates' Court, ex parte Bennett*, [1994] 1 AC 42, this *Year Book*, 64 (1993), pp. 447–52.

establish that proceedings may be stayed in the exercise of the judge's discretion not only where a fair trial is impossible, but also where it would be contrary to the public interest in the integrity of the criminal justice system that a trial should take place. An infinite variety of cases could arise. General guidance as to how the discretion should be exercised in particular circumstances will not be useful. But it is possible to say that in a case such as the present the judge must weigh in the balance the public interest in ensuring that those that are charged with grave crimes should be tried and the competing public interest in not conveying the impression that the court will adopt the approach that the end justifies any means.[131]

The Court felt that the judge had reached the right decision after balancing the competing interests, and that the conduct of the customs officer was not so shameful as to constitute an affront to the public conscience requiring the proceedings to be stayed.

Shahzad also submitted that the court did not have jurisdiction to try the offence, since the attempts at evasion were made in Pakistan. The Court, following its decision in *Director of Public Prosecutions* v. *Stonehouse*,[132] rejected this argument. It stated:

The English courts have jurisdiction over such criminal attempts even though the overt acts take place abroad. The rationale is that the effect of the criminal attempt is directed at this country.[133]

The Court approved the reasoning of Lord Griffiths in *Somchai Liangsiriprasert* v. *US Government*[134] to the extent that '[a]s a matter of policy jurisdiction over criminal attempts ought to rest with the country where it was intended that the full offence should take place'.[135] In any event, one of the attempts at evasion was committed in the United Kingdom.

This case is interesting in two respects. First, it clarifies how English courts may exercise their discretion to stay criminal or extradition proceedings on the grounds of abuse of process, when the individual concerned has been brought to the United Kingdom improperly or illegally. Read together with the House of Lords' decisions in *Bennett* v. *Horseferry Road Magistrates' Court*[136] and *In re Schmidt*,[137] it suggests that at least three factors will be considered by the courts in such cases. The first of these is the seriousness of the crime. The abuse of process argument was allowed to prevail in a case concerning fraud (*Bennett*), but not in cases concerning drug trafficking (*Schmidt* and *Latif/Shahzad*). The second factor is whether the individual was brought to the United Kingdom against his will (*Bennett*), or was tricked into coming on his own (*Schmidt* and *Latif/Shahzad*), with the latter approach to acquiring custody being preferred over the former. The third factor is whether the impropriety or illegality on the part of the law enforcement agency in question concerned the procedures

---

[131] [1996] 1 All ER 353 at 361, [1996] 1 WLR 104 at 112–13.

[132] [1977] 2 All ER 909, [1978] AC 55, [1977] 3 WLR 143, this *Year Book*, 49 (1978), pp. 279–81.

[133] [1996] 1 All ER 353 at 365, [1996] 1 WLR 104 at 116.

[134] [1990] 2 All ER 866 at 877–8, [1991] 1 AC 225 at 250.

[135] [1996] 1 All ER 353 at 365, [1996] 1 WLR 104 at 116.

[136] [1993] 3 All ER 138, *sub nom. R* v. *Horseferry Road Magistrates' Court, ex parte Bennett*, [1994] 1 AC 42, this *Year Book*, 64 (1993), pp. 447–52.

[137] [1995] 1 AC 339, [1994] 3 WLR 228, [1994] 2 All ER 65, this *Year Book*, 65 (1994), pp. 500–2.

normally available to bring the individual to the United Kingdom, i.e. the Extradition Act 1989, in which case the abuse of process argument may be accorded greater weight (*Bennett*), or whether the impropriety or illegality concerned an unrelated aspect of the law of the United Kingdom (*Latif/ Shahzad*), or elsewhere (*Schmidt*). This last factor indicates that the doctrine of abuse of process, as it is currently applied by the House of Lords, seeks to protect the integrity of national law and is not directed at violations of international law, as such. In the light of these three factors, it nevertheless remains open to question whether proceedings would have been stayed on the grounds of abuse of process if an individual who had engaged in serious human rights violations abroad were brought to the United Kingdom against his will, in a manner which circumvented the Extradition Act 1989.[138]

It is also noteworthy that this case appears to affirm the protective principle of criminal jurisdiction, in that the Court was prepared to assert jurisdiction over the offence, even though it took place outside the United Kingdom, on the basis of the harmful effects that it would have had here.[139] The judges apparently did not consider the possibility of asserting jurisdiction on the basis of the universality principle, although such an approach might also have been justified, given the seriousness with which many States now regard the international drug trade.[140]

Diplomatic protection—export credit guarantees—discretion of Crown to retain moneys recovered

Case No. 15. Lonrho Exports Ltd. v. *Export Credits Guarantee Department*, [1996] 4 All ER 673, QB. Lonrho Exports Ltd. (LEL) exported goods to Zambia. In 1975 it entered into export credit guarantees with the Export Credits Guarantee Department (ECGD), which is a department of the Secretary of State. On the basis of the guarantees the ECGD was entitled to recover outstanding debts from foreign debtors, and under common Article 24 of the guarantees, it was required to pay LEL a part of the debt recovered in proportion to LEL's uninsured loss.

Following a multilateral agreement for the rescheduling of its long, medium

---

[138] For abduction cases, see, e.g., *Attorney-General* v. *Eichmann* (Israel, District Court 1961, Supreme Court 1962), 36 ILR 5 at 57–76 and 304–8; *United States* v. *Alvarez-Machain* (United States, Supreme Court), 112 S Ct. 2188 (1992); *S* v. *Ebrahim* (South Africa, Supreme Court), [1991] 2 SA 553.

[139] See *Rocha* v. *US*, 288 F 2d 545 (9th Cir. 1961), 32 ILR 112 (concerning a conspiracy to defraud the United States); Sahovic and Bishop, 'The Authority of the State; Its Range with respect to Persons and Places', in Sörensen (ed.), *Manual of Public International Law* (1968), pp. 311, 362–5; Akehurst, 'Jurisdiction in International Law', this *Year Book*, 46 (1972–3), pp. 145, 157–9; Bowett, 'Jurisdiction: Changing Patterns of Authority over Activities and Resources', this *Year Book*, 53 (1982), pp. 1, 10–11.

[140] See, e.g., Akehurst, 'Jurisdiction in International Law', this *Year Book*, 46 (1972–3), pp. 145, 160–6. Cf. Bowett, 'Jurisdiction: Changing Patterns of Authority over Activities and Resources', this *Year Book*, 53 (1982), pp. 1, 11–14, who concluded that universal jurisdiction only exists in respect of piracy, and Gilmore, 'Hot Pursuit: the Case of *R* v. *Mills and Others*', *International and Comparative Law Quaterly*, 44 (1995), p. 949, discussing an English case in which jurisdiction over drug smugglers on the high seas was based on the doctrine of 'hot pursuit' rather than on the principle of universal jurisdiction.

and short term debts, Zambia entered into a bilateral agreement with the United Kingdom for the payment of its outstanding debts, including those which the ECGD sought to recover. The agreement, which was negotiated by the ECGD as representative of the Crown, applied to all of LEL's debts.

In 1984 the Bank of Zambia made a payment to the ECGD pursuant to the bilateral agreement, but failed to confirm the list of debts outstanding. The ECGD paid the money into the Consolidated Fund, which is a general fund, as required by section 14 of the Export Guarantees and Overseas Investment Act 1978. It was not until 1991 that it paid three instalments of the dividend to LEL. LEL then brought an action claiming interest on its proportion of the 1984 payment, on the basis that the ECGD had held the moneys on trust for it during the period between 1984 and 1991, and, alternatively, that the guarantees contained a contractually implied term that the moneys would be paid upon receipt. The ECGD argued, *inter alia*, that as the payment was made in intended performance of an international treaty, the ECGD held the moneys as a beneficial owner free from any obligation to LEL and the other policyholders until it voluntarily decided to treat a substantial part of the 1984 payment as a recovery under Article 24 of the guarantees.

Lightman J held that it was up to the Executive to decide whether, before the end of 1990, there had been an agreement as to the debt lists and for payment to the creditors out of the 1984 payment. The ECGD's decision that there was no such agreement was therefore conclusive. Nevertheless, at the request of counsel and in anticipation of a possible appeal, Lightman J analysed the facts for himself and found that there was indeed no agreement as to the debts prior to December 1990. He based this conclusion, in part, on a series of principles of English law, which he identified as follows:

(1) The conclusion of a treaty by the United Kingdom is a sovereign act carried out by the Crown in the exercise of the royal prerogative (see *Rustomjee v. R* (1876) 2 QBD 69).

(2) Treaties do not form part of English domestic law unless given effect by statute. Unless given such effect by statute, they can neither create new, nor take away existing, rights recognised by English law (see *Maclaine Watson & Co. Ltd. v. Dept of Trade and Industry, Maclaine Watson & Co. Ltd. v. International Tin Council* [1989] 3 All ER 523 at 529–530, 544–545, [1990] 2 AC 418 at 480–482, 500 per Lord Templeman and Lord Oliver[141]).

(3) When the Crown espouses claims (e.g. of nationals who are creditors of foreign states or nationals) and affords diplomatic protection (e.g. by the negotiation of a treaty providing for payment to the Crown for distribution to its nationals), under international law the Crown is maintaining its own right in its own name to such protection of its nationals (see *Re Barcelona Traction Light and Power Co. Ltd.* 1970 ICJ Rep 3 at 78–79).

(4) (Subject to (5) below) in concluding and performing the obligations under such a treaty, the Crown does not act as agent or trustee for the nationals; and irrespective of the terms of the treaty and (as it seems to me) the characterisation of the payments by the treaty, payments made to the United Kingdom pursuant to such treaties are received by the Crown in a sovereign capacity and form the absolute property of the State (see *Civilian War Claimants Association Ltd. v. R* [1932] AC 14, [1931] All ER Rep 432 and consider the decision to the like effect of the Swiss Federal Court in *Gschwind v. Swiss Confederation* (1932) 6 Annual Digest 242 at 244–245 and the statement to like effect in

[141] This *Year Book*, 60 (1989), pp. 461–73.

the third American Law Institute's *Restatement of Foreign Relations Law* vol. II p. 348).

(5) There is nothing to prevent the Crown acting as agent or trustee if it chooses to do so (see *Nissan* v. *A-G* [1969] 1 All ER 629 at 650–651, [1970] AC 179 at 223 per Lord Pearce[142]). It may be that the Crown can, when it concludes or performs a treaty, act as a trustee or agent for one or more nationals or corporations (see *Civilian War Claimants Association Ltd.* v. *R* [1932] AC 14 at 26–27, [1931] All ER Rep 432 at 436 per Lord Atkin and *Buck* v. *A-G* [1964] 2 All ER 663 at 669, [1965] Ch 745 at 759 per Wilberforce J,[143] but see *Rustomjee* v. *R* (1876) 2 QBD 69 at 74 per Lord Coleridge CJ). But, if this is so, there is a strong presumption against the Crown fettering in this way its ability to conduct foreign relations in the interests of the United Kingdom as a whole and the Crown must expressly declare its intention to act in this capacity before it will be held to have done so (see *German Property Administrator* v. *Knoop* [1933] Ch 439 at 455–456 per Maugham J, citing Lord Atkin in the *Civilian War Claimants* case). For this purpose it is quite insufficient that the Crown has espoused the individual's cause, obtained from him his co-operation (including details of his claims to take up with the foreign government) and indeed has obtained acceptance of such claims by the foreign government. The fact that under municipal law the Crown would be held (if negotiating a private agreement rather than a treaty) to be negotiating as agent or trustee is not sufficient if it is negotiating a treaty, where the Crown must represent the national interest and take account of the widest range of considerations (see the cases cited above). There can be (as it seems to me) no reason why the Crown cannot commit itself to hold any sum received under a treaty as agent or trustee if the necessary intention is sufficiently clearly established, though this would be quite exceptional.

(6) The entitlement of the Crown to retain the payments made to it is not, as a matter of English law, affected by the terms of the treaty or whatever the treaty may provide regarding their distribution. Nor can the terms of the treaty affect or qualify the sovereign character of the Crown's receipt of such payments or imbue such receipt with the character eg of a recovery. The Crown has under English law no legal or equitable, but at best a mere moral, obligation to fulfil those terms. If the Crown fails to do so, the only remedies lie in Parliament or (at the instance of the foreign government) in international law proceedings (see *Philipp Bros* v. *Republic of Sierra Leone* [1995] 1 Lloyd's Rep. 289).

(7) The Crown in distributing any payments received pursuant to a treaty may determine the character to be borne by the payments it makes and earmark such payments (e.g. as mere bounty or a payment in respect of the insured or uninsured element of a loss) and such determination and earmarking binds third parties (e.g. insurers) (see *Burnand* v. *Rodocanachi Sons & Co.* (1882) 7 App Cas 333).

(8) Subject to (9), the interpretation of treaties not by statute incorporated into municipal law and the decision whether or not they have been complied with are matters exclusively for the Crown in its conduct of foreign relations. The court must speak with the same voice as the Executive and accordingly seek and follow the interpretation adopted by the Crown, and not venture its own interpretation (let alone its own interpretation if at variance with that of the Crown). Nor may it seek to determine whether the parties have implemented its provisions in good faith as required by international law (see *British Airways Board* v. *Laker Airways Ltd.* [1983] 3 All ER 375 at 402–403, [1984] QB 142 at 192–193 per Donaldson MR;[144] [1984] 3 All ER 39 at 49, [1985] AC 58 at 85–86 per Lord Diplock,[145] *Littrell* v. *USA (No. 2)* [1994] 4 All ER 203

---

[142] This *Year Book*, 43 (1968–9), pp. 217–26.
[143] This *Year Book*, 41 (1965–6), pp. 435–8.
[144] This *Year Book*, 55 (1984), pp. 331–6.
[145] Ibid.

at 210–211, 216, [1995] 1 WLR 82 at 89, 94[146] and *Westland Helicopters Ltd.* v. *Arab Organisation for Industrialisation* [1995] 2 All ER 387 at 399, [1995] QB 282 at 294[147]). For an example of the possible difficulties created where the court does construe a treaty, see Oppenheim *International Law*, (9th edn, 1992) vol. 1 para 612, footnote 2.

(9) As exceptions (actual or apparent) to (8), (a) there are circumstances when the court may be called on to interpret a treaty (eg if its terms are incorporated into a domestic contract); and (b) reference may be made to the conclusion of a treaty and its terms for evidential purposes as part of the factual background against which a particular issue is to be determined (see *Maclaine Watson & Co. Ltd.* v. *Dept of Trade and Industry, Maclaine Watson & Co. Ltd.* v. *International Tin Council* [1989] 3 All ER 523 at 545, [1990] 2 AC 418 at 500–501 per Lord Oliver[148] and *Littrell* v. *USA (No. 2)* [1994] 4 All ER 203 at 215, [1995] 1 WLR 82 at 93 per Hoffmann LJ[149]).

(10) The courts will not adjudicate upon the transactions of or between sovereign states, and in all matters relating to foreign relations, judges should be circumspect and rarely should judges intervene where diplomats fear to tread (see *Maclaine Watson & Co. Ltd.* [1989] 3 All ER 523 at 544, [1990] 2 AC 418 at 499 per Lord Oliver[150] and *R* v. *Secretary of State for Foreign and Commonwealth Affairs, ex p Pirbhai* (1985) Times, 17 October).

Lightman J, applying these principles to the facts of the case, held that the Crown did not negotiate as trustee or agent for the policyholders, and that it owed no duties to them. As part of a framework to deal with Zambia's economic crisis, the bilateral agreement concerned the relations between two States. The conduct of the Crown in respect of the agreement was not open to evaluation by the Court, and the agreement could not and did not confer any rights on the policyholders.

However, Lightman J also held that, depending on the language of Article 24, the Crown could have bound itself by the guarantees to deal with the sums received from Zambia as there provided. In addressing the construction of Article 24, Lightman J first considered whether, as a matter of law, LEL had a proprietary interest in recoveries made by the ECGD. He held that where an insurer enforces a cause of action belonging beneficially to the insured for their joint benefit, the principles which apply lie in the law of mortgages. Thus, a chargee who receives payment in excess of his rights holds the surplus recoveries on trust for the mortgagor. Similarly, if LEL could establish that the 1984 payment included recoveries in respect of its debts, the ECGD might have held the 1984 payment on trust for it. The identity and qualities of the insurer would be irrelevant, the issue being whether the 1984 payment constituted a recovery within the meaning of article 24 of the guarantees.

Lightman J held that the 1984 payment 'was an inter-state payment made by the government of Zambia in satisfaction of a claim, not by the policyholders, but by the United Kingdom'.[151] Moreover, and although he considered it impermissible to analyse the character of the 1984 payment by reference to the terms of the bilateral agreement, such an analysis revealed that the Crown was intended to be free to deal with the payment in a manner which would be

---

[146] This *Year Book*, 65 (1994), pp. 491–6.
[147] This *Year Book*, 66 (1995), pp. 491–6.
[148] This *Year Book*, 60 (1989), pp. 461–73.
[149] This *Year Book*, 65 (1994), pp. 491–6.
[150] This *Year Book*, 60 (1989), pp. 461–73.
[151] [1996] 4 All ER 673 at 693.

inconsistent with a finding that the payment was a recovery under Article 24. At the date of the 1984 payment, determinations remained to be made as to the debts owed to creditors, and the priority and proportions of their payment. The payment was therefore a sovereign receipt available for distribution at the discretion of the Crown and not a recovery under any of the ECGD policies, unless or until distributed as such. Accordingly, LEL never had a proprietary interest in the 1984 payment, and the ECGD was at no time trustee or subject to fiduciary duties in respect of the moneys. Having thus found that the ECGD was absolutely entitled to the 1984 payment from the date of its receipt, Lightman J also dismissed the contractual claim.

MICHAEL BYERS

1 *Exclusive jurisdiction and the Brussels Convention: Jarrett* v. *Barclays Bank plc;*[1] *In re Hayward, deceased*[2]

Article 16 of the Brussels Convention[3] gives exclusive jurisdiction, regardless of the domicile of the defendant, to certain courts. Article 16(1)(*a*)[4] does so 'in proceedings which have as their object rights *in rem* in, or tenancies of, immovable property . . .'. It has been established[5] that proceedings have such rights as their object when the action is founded on the existence in the plaintiff of a vested right *in rem*. This excludes from Article 16(1) an action brought to acquire a right *in rem* presently vested in someone else, and also an action to enforce an existing right *in personam*, such as equitable title to immovable property. Moreover, it is not sufficient that a right *in rem* is a part of the action which the plaintiff brings; it is required that it be the principal component of the action.[6] The result is, and is meant to be, that Article 16(1) is construed restrictively.

An easy illustration of a case which fell outside its provisions was provided by the Court of Appeal in *Jarrett* v. *Barclays Bank plc.* The Jarretts had been unwise enough to buy into a time-share scheme in holiday accommodation in the Algarve, Portugal. Payment to the Portuguese vendor was made by use of a credit card, the credit card company being reimbursed by the customer at the due time. Predictably enough, the purchase was alleged to have been procured by lies; and the plaintiffs sought to enforce the liability owed to them by reason of the misrepresentations. Rather than suing the Portuguese owners in Portugal, the plaintiffs relied on their right under the Consumer Credit Act 1974 to sue the defendant creditor.[7] Section 75 of the Act makes the creditor jointly and severally liable with the supplier for breach and misrepresentation. But the defendant contended that the claim against it fell within Article 16(1), and had, on that account, to be brought in Portugal. The Court of Appeal rejected the contention, which was as unattractive as it was misconceived, and allowed the action to proceed in England.

Two points arose. First, did the time-share scheme create a tenancy for the purposes of Article 16(1)? This required the Court first to decide which system of law was to be looked to for the answer. It rejected the view that the *lex situs* applied for the purpose. It preferred the view that the term 'tenancy' had an autonomous meaning, which was not dictated by the contents of national law. The Schlosser Report had indicated[8] that the *lex situs* was to be used for this

* © Adrian Briggs, 1997.
[1] [1997] 2 All ER 484, CA (Morritt, Ward, Potter LJJ).
[2] [1997] Ch. 45, Ch. D (Rattee J).
[3] Civil Jurisdiction and Judgments Act 1982, Sch. 1 (as amended).
[4] Article 16(1) of the Brussels Convention was amended by the addition of sub-paragraph (*b*), dealing with certain short holiday lettings. But this provision requires both landlord and tenant to be natural persons; here the landlord was not. No further reference needs to be made to Article 16(1)(*b*).
[5] *Webb* v. *Webb*, [1994] ECR I–1717, ECJ.
[6] Cf. *Hacker* v. *Euro-Relais GmbH*, [1992] ECR I–1111, ECJ, where it was not.
[7] That is, the party who provided credit to finance the purchase.
[8] *Official Journal*, 1979, C59/71, at paragraph 168.

task, but Morritt LJ considered that this proposition had been rejected by the Court of Justice,[9] in the interests of uniformity of interpretation. Although the Court of Justice had not provided a general definition of 'tenancy', the Court of Appeal considered that a right to exclusive occupation for a specified period, and in return for a sum of money, amounted to a tenancy.[10] The virtue of the test adopted is that it avoids the need to draw the kind of qualitative distinction which might have led to the exclusion of time-shares, and other short-term residential arrangements, from Article 16(1); and in the light of the jurisprudence of the Court of Justice it is probably correct.

But this did not mean that the proceedings against the creditor had the tenancy as their object. For although section 75 provided that the debtor had a 'like claim' against the creditor to that which he had against the supplier, it was plainly unreal to interpret this as meaning a claim which was in all material respects identical to that which lay against the supplier. In terms of remedy at least, that cannot have been true. Moreover, the claim against the creditor was to enforce a personal liability for misrepresentation. Although this had a factual connection to the tenancy of Portuguese land, it was not an action to enforce the rights arising under that tenancy; it did not depend upon the plaintiff being a tenant; and it did not involve application of the law of landlord and tenant. In short, none of the indicia of a claim which falls within Article 16(1) were present; and the action was rightly allowed to proceed in England.

More difficult was the application of Article 16 as it arose in *re Hayward*. An owner of a half share of land in Minorca, Spain, had died some years after being made bankrupt. After his death, his widow procured the transfer to her of his half share in the land in question, and caused herself to be registered as sole proprietor in the local land register. The trustee in bankruptcy then applied for an order against the widow for a declaration that the half share formed part of the bankrupt estate, and for an order that the widow procure the rectification of the Minorcan land register. The widow claimed that the proceedings had as their object a right *in rem* in Spanish land, so that the Spanish courts had exclusive jurisdiction under Article 16(1); and that the proceedings had as their object the validity of an entry in a public register, so that the Spanish courts had exclusive jurisdiction under Article 16(3). Rattee J agreed, on both grounds.

If one applies the test of whether the claim was brought by a party claiming to have an existing right *in rem* in the property, it was arguable that this was the case. The trustee in bankruptcy maintained his claim on the ground that the property of the bankrupt had already vested in him by operation of law, and that he was the lawful holder of a right *in rem*. The judge considered that the claim advanced by the trustees was one claiming a right to legal ownership, which was, as he put it, the clearest of rights *in rem*. This can be supported, though, only on the basis that the trustee claimed that he already owned that right for, as *Webb* v. *Webb*[11] appears to have decided, a claim that a plaintiff was entitled to be constituted holder of a right *in rem* did not bring the case within Article 16(1). Did the trustee make such a claim? Or did he claim that he was entitled to

---

[9] In *Reichert* v. *Dresdner Bank*, [1990] ECR I-27, ECJ; *Hacker* v. *Euro-Relais* (n. 6, above).

[10] A definition strikingly (but doubtless coincidentally) similar to that found in English law: cf. *Street* v. *Mountford*, [1985] AC 809, HL.

[11] [1994] ECR I-1717, ECJ; action by beneficiary of resulting trust for transfer of legal title to land was not within Article 16(1).

receive something, but something which was not yet his? Without sight of the pleadings it is difficult to say for sure, but with the Minorcan property register recording the fact that the present legal owner was the widow, it is difficult to imagine that the trustee was claiming that he already owned the legal estate (or its Spanish equivalent). If that is correct, his claim to acquire it would not fall within Article 16(1), for the same reason as applied to the claim of the father in *Webb*: a claim that one is entitled to be instituted legal owner of immovable property does not mean that the proceedings have as their object a right *in rem* in that property.

But if the case arguably fell outside Article 16(1), did it follow that it fell within Article 16(3), as having as its object the validity of the entry in the Minorcan land register? The judge thought that it did; and his conclusion is probably right. The point and purpose of the proceedings was to obtain an order that the land register should be rectified to divest the widow of half her recorded holding. Although the order would not be directed at the land registrar, it seems natural to accept that the validity of the existing entry on the register was the central issue in the dispute. To reason that, as the order sought was *in personam* against the widow, the proceedings did not have the validity of the register as their object is possible,[12] but unacceptable. If the point of the proceedings is to obtain an order that a land register should be rectified, all manner of questions of Spanish land registration law—how, when, with what evidence, with what consequences for third parties, with or without compensation, and so on—may arise. The prospect that these could be dealt with in the Chancery Division was simply unreal; and despite the nature of the relief sought, the claim was properly covered by Article 16(3).

All this presupposes, though, that the Convention applied to the claim at all. After all, the claim was brought by a trustee in bankruptcy, who claimed his interest by reason of (and only by reason of) the law of bankruptcy. As Article 1 excludes bankruptcy[13] from the Convention altogether, how did the judge reach the conclusion that Article 16 applied at all? It is, in truth, very difficult to say. The Court of Justice had explained that 'bankruptcy' encompassed an action by a liquidator against directors of an insolvent company, as the right to recover a contribution from them was based solely on the provisions of the law of bankruptcy.[14] The *locus standi*, and the actual claim, of the trustee arose solely from the law of bankruptcy. But, said the judge, the claim was more in the nature of an ordinary action to recover debts or other property: bankruptcy had nothing to do with the claim made. If the deceased had been alive and solvent, an action by him to recover property would have nothing to do with bankruptcy; if he were alive but bankrupt, the nature of the action would have been identical, save for its being brought by a trustee in bankruptcy. The specific *jus actionis* asserted would be essentially the same in each case; the difference would lie only in the fact that it was being brought by a different plaintiff.

[12] Such reasoning is found in the common law to explain why an action which appeared to concern title foreign land, and over which the court would accordingly lack jurisdiction, was not precluded by the rule.

[13] The Convention also excludes itself from succession; and it was also argued that this was a case upon succession. The argument was dismissed by the judge, as no issue of succession law appeared to be remotely relevant. He was probably right about this, and the issue is not examined further.

[14] *Gourdain* v. *Nadler*, [1979] ECR 733, ECJ.

It is not obvious that the judge was correct in his interpretation. After all, if the transferee has no title to the land, or has a defeasible title to the land, this arises from the impact of the bankruptcy. It all depends on whether Article 1, and the exclusions from the scope of the Convention, are intended to be given a narrow meaning. It is evident that within the field of application of the Convention, it is permissible to promote or restrict certain of the jurisdictional rules in order to advance the internal purposes of the Convention. But it is less clear that a similar approach may properly be taken to the definition of the outer edges of the Convention, for there is no basis for supposing that the contracting parties intended this to have a wide or a narrow scope. The judge appears to have given a distinctly narrow interpretation to the exclusion made in respect of bankruptcy: a claim which existed only by reason of the law of bankruptcy was nevertheless not held to have bankruptcy as its subject-matter. It is clear from the judgment that the judge had the benefit of full submissions on the point. It follows that a commentator can simply voice doubt as to whether the interpretation of 'bankruptcy' accepted by the judge was really to be preferred over that which he rejected.

2 *Special jurisdiction under the Brussels Convention: Kleinwort Benson Ltd. v. City of Glasgow DC*[15]

This protracted[16] litigation, it will be recalled, concerns whether an action to recover money paid over pursuant to an interest rate swap agreement, which was void in law as being *ultra vires* the local authority, fell within the special jurisdiction provisions of the Brussels Convention. Hirst J had held that it did not:[17] that such a claim was neither a matter relating to a contract within the meaning of Article 5(1), nor a matter relating to tort, delict or quasi-delict within Article 5(3). As a result the claim had to be brought in Scotland, where the defendant was domiciled. A trip to the Court of Justice proved abortive:[18] the Court held that as the particular dispute was to be disposed of by provisions of internal United Kingdom law, it had no jurisdiction to accede to a request for a ruling on the corresponding (and in all material senses, identical) provisions of the Brussels Convention. On the resumed hearing in the Court of Appeal it was held, by a majority, that the claim fell within Article 5(1). Leave to appeal to the House of Lords was granted by the Court of Appeal.

A preliminary point concerned the relationship between the rules of the Convention, and the rules of internal United Kingdom law as set out in section 16 and Schedule 4 to the 1982 Act. As a matter of European law, the

---

[15] [1996] QB 678, CA (Leggatt, Roch, Millett LJJ).

[16] Leggatt LJ observed that the transactions were entered into 13 years ago; that there had been four hearings (and leave was granted for a fifth) to establish whether the lending bank was entitled to sue in England. The merits of the dispute may still be years from their resolution.

[17] [1993] QB 429 (noted in this *Year Book*, 64 (1993), p. 467).

[18] The decision to refer is at [1994] QB 404, CA; the ruling of the Court of Justice at [1995] ECR I-615, ECJ.

Convention often ascribes jurisdiction to the courts of the United Kingdom:[19] the United Kingdom is the contracting party. Thereafter it is no concern of European law how the legal order of the United Kingdom chooses to allocate jurisdiction to one or another court. There was no obligation, as far as European law was concerned, to resolve this by reference, direct or indirect, to the rules which had given jurisdiction to the United Kingdom in the first place; but Parliament had enacted, in section 16 and Schedule 4, jurisdictional rules which were closely copied from the text of the Convention. Though Parliament had also provided that there was a power to make departures from the corresponding text of the Convention,[20] no such manifestation of intent had been made in relation to Articles 5(1) and 5(3) of Schedule 4. It was therefore for the Court of Appeal to decide what was the relationship between the meaning of these provisions in the Convention and in Schedule 4. It was held by the majority, Leggatt LJ dissenting, that the interpretation was intended to be the same. In other words, the true construction of Article 5 of the Convention according to European law dictated the meaning of Article 5 of Schedule 4.[21] The view of the majority has much to commend it. Although there was a difference in wording between the statutory duties of an English court to follow the jurisprudence of the Court of Justice ('judicial notice shall be taken . . . ' in relation to the application of the Convention,[22] whereas 'regard shall be had' to it in relation to the application of Schedule 4[23]), this was held to be a distinction without a difference. For Leggatt LJ, it was significant that the Court of Justice had refused to give a ruling, precisely because the English court would not be obliged to follow it in relation to the internal legislation of the United Kingdom. But, with respect, all this establishes is that in the eye of European law, there is no such duty upon the national court. It does not follow that Parliament could not have imposed a duty *sua sponte*.[24] According to the majority, it had done. The harmonious development of the law on civil jurisdiction is aided by this conclusion; the Convention is problematic enough without a separate set of slightly (and unpredictably) different interpretations in relation to analogous provisions in Schedule 4.

Leggatt LJ's views on the interpretation of Article 5 of Schedule 4 may be thought to be affected by his conclusion that he was not obliged to discern and then to apply the meaning which these provisions had in European law. He appears to have taken to heart the argument, arguably misleading, that because as a matter of English law, restitutionary claims are not (in substantive law) contractual in nature, they are therefore not (for jurisdictional purposes) within the rule for matters relating to a contract. But the majority considered that the

---

[19] This was true in the present case: the defendant was domiciled in the United Kingdom. If the Convention applied at all, Article 2 of it gave jurisdiction to the courts of the United Kingdom (though the Convention may not have applied at all, on the ground that in a dispute wholly internal to the United Kingdom, no question of *international* jurisdiction arose).

[20] Section 47(3).

[21] Presumably as the interpretation of Article 5 as a matter of European law changes with elucidation by the Court of Justice, the content of internal United Kingdom law, as set out in Schedule 4, will change as well.

[22] Section 3(2).

[23] Section 16(3).

[24] Though this unilateral act could not operate to widen the jurisdiction of the Court of Justice.

claim was to be seen, for jurisdictional purposes, as a matter relating to a contract, and was therefore within Article 5(1). It is thought that this is correct, both in theory and on pragmatic grounds. As far as theory is concerned, the unwinding of a contract, which both parties supposed was valid but which turned out to be void, is still a matter which relates to that 'void contract'. Now there is a sense in which a 'void contract' is a nonsense, for if it is void it is not a contract; if it is void, the remedial claim cannot relate to it, for there is nothing to relate to. But such playing with words is disreputable. If one accepts that a contract, for the purposes of Article 5(1), has a meaning which is wider than that encountered in national law,[25] and if one accepts that a contract for these purposes requires an obligation freely entered into with regard to another,[26] then the relationship which the parties entered into is contractual in that sense and for that purpose. That it may have led only to obligations imposed by law is nothing to the point, for many terms in contracts arise that way. The obligation to repay arose as a direct consequence of the agreement the parties freely entered into and freely performed; that the agreement did not give rise to the legal consequences which they expected does not alter the fact. Theory aside, a contrary decision would have been potentially disastrous in many ways. It would have meant that a court could have special jurisdiction to determine whether a contract was valid, but no jurisdiction to impose remedies if it concluded that it was not. It would mean that a consumer could bring a claim to enforce a contract in accordance with the consumer contract provisions of the Convention,[27] but would have no such right if he claimed to recover his money in the event of the contract's being void. If the court which ruled on the validity of a contract had no jurisdiction to deal with the purely remedial consequences of its ruling, it would be wholly discreditable to the law.

The majority explained, as must be obvious, that not every restitutionary claim will fall within Article 5(1). The spread of the collection of restitutionary claims—'category' is hardly the word for it—is uncertain, and under unending critical examination. Within England, no two restitutionists will come up with the same answer; it is fair to suppose that when foreign lawyers enter the debate, the disagreement will be greater, not less. There would be no basis for making a sweeping classification of all such claims, for the purposes of the Convention or for any purpose. Instead, such claims as relate to a contract will fall within Article 5(1). It does not mean that they are to be classified and dealt with as contractual for the purposes of substantive law, or for choice of law purposes. But if they relate to a contract, they follow the jurisdictional scheme for such claims.

This in turn requires it to be decided which is the obligation in question, which identifies the court which has special jurisdiction. Little attention was devoted to this point in the judgments, possibly because of the fact, as had been recorded by Hirst J at first instance, that it was common ground that the place for performance of the obligation in question was England. As all payments under the supposed contract were to have been made to bank accounts in

---

[25] *Martin Peters Bauunternehmung GmbH* v. *Zuid Nederlandse Aannemers Vereniging*, [1983] ECR 987, ECJ.

[26] *Handte & Cie. GmbH* v. *Traitements mécano-chimiques des surfaces*, [1992] ECR I-3967, ECJ.

[27] Section 4 of Title II.

London, and all repayments to Kleinwort Benson Ltd. were due in London, this was not a serious issue in the case. But that is not to say that there are no problems which will emerge in other cases. The choice lies between the performance obligation under the supposed contract, and the remedial obligation which arises once the contract is recognized as having been a nullity. Millett LJ indicated that the former represented the correct choice. The solution has practical virtue in a case where the action is brought also for damages for breach; and this may be sufficient to justify it. Certainly it avoids the problem of asking where an obligation to make repayment after a contract has been avoided was required to be performed. The strain of pragmatism which characterises the majority judgments supports this approach.

It was not necessary for the majority to consider the alternative view, that if this was not a matter relating to a contract, it was a matter relating to tort within Article 5(3). Initial surprise at the simplistic oddness of this proposition recedes in the light of the jurisprudence of the Court of Justice which gave rise to it;[28] but Leggatt LJ was wholly unpersuaded that it was correct as a matter of European law, quite apart from Schedule 4. It is possible to take issue with his interpretation of the ruling and reasoning in *Kalfelis*; certainly there is support for the view that actions based on allegations of unjust enrichment, other than those which fall under Article 5(1), must fall under Article 5(3). It remains to be seen whether the path to Leggatt LJ's preference may be found in the proposition that an action complaining of unjust enrichment does not seek to establish *liability*, properly so called: the defendant is not liable because and to the extent that he has done wrong, but is required to disgorge that which it is unjust for him to retain, with wrong having nothing to do with it. Perhaps the House of Lords will feel that after so much time and money has been invested in it, it is appropriate to examine this aspect of the decision before it goes off to be tried on the merits.

3 *Special jurisdiction under the Brussels Convention: Boss Group Ltd. v. Boss France SA;*[29] *Agnew v. Lansförsäkringsbolagens AB*[30]

Article 5(1) of the Brussels Convention gives special jurisdiction[31] in matters relating to a contract to the courts of the place for performance of the obligation in question. The questions for the Court of Appeal were whether this provision was available to a plaintiff who sought a declaration of non-liability on the ground that a contract alleged against him by his opponent was non-existent; and if so, what exactly was the obligation in question whose location identified the court with special jurisdiction. It held that such a claim did fall within Article 5(1), and that the obligation in question was that which the defendant alleged the plaintiff was required, by the disputed contract, to perform.

[28] *Kalfelis v. Bankhaus Schröder Münchmeyer Hengst & Co.*, [1988] ECR 5565, ECJ; and see also paragraph 102 of the Opinion of the Advocate General in *Shearson Lehmann Hutton Inc. v. Treuhand für Vermögensverwaltung und Beteiligungen mbH*, [1993] ECR I-139, ECJ.

[29] [1997] 1 WLR 351, CA (Russell, Saville, Otton LJJ).

[30] [1996] 4 All ER 978, QBD (Mance J).

[31] That is, jurisdiction over a defendant domiciled in another contracting State.

The starting point was to decide whether the definition 'matters relating to a contract' could in principle cover a claim for a declaration of non-liability. There was no relevant guidance from the Court of Justice, nor from national courts. One solution might have been to accept that when both parties admitted the existence of a contract, but disagreed whether it had been broken, a claim for a declaration of non-liability, such as a declaration that there had been no breach, would be a matter relating to a contract; but where the claim was for a declaration that there was no contract, the opposite would be the case. But this would have encouraged careful pleaders to plead in the alternative; and the distinction would rapidly disappear. Moreover, a declaration that a contract had been rescinded *ab initio*, or avoided for material non-disclosure, or had been void for mistake, or illegality, would have created difficulties of its own. Pragmatism really required an answer to be of general application: all such claims, or no such claim, would have to be acknowledged as relating to a contract.

It had been established by the Court of Justice that it is not open to a court to gloss the jurisdictional provisions of the Convention by reference to discretionary considerations of *forum conveniens*,[32] either to confer jurisdiction where the Convention denies it, or to deny it where the Convention confers it. It had been obscurely established by English courts that there was a general suspicion of actions for declarations of non-liability.[33] The grounds of this suspicion included the apprehension that the procedure could be used for forum shopping, or to create a *res judicata* through a clash of judgments, or to force into court before he was ready a party who had not yet formulated his claim or decided whether to sue, or to put other improper pressure on an opponent. The impact of the jurisprudence of the Court of Justice means that the traditional objections to declarations of non-liability had to be disentangled, so that weight was no longer placed on the defendant's allegation that the plaintiff was forum shopping. Once that was done, as the Court recognized, the only question really left to be asked was whether there was a live and genuine issue between the parties, or whether (by contrast) the plaintiff had contrived an issue from nothing. As in the present case the defendant had taken action in the French courts to seek to enforce the contract it alleged to exist, it did not lie in its mouth to say that there was no genuine dispute between the parties. The result is that the court may use its discretion[34] not to grant a declaration if there are good reasons to do so; and where jurisdiction is founded on rules of the common law[35] rather than the Convention, it may still make a ruling on jurisdiction[36] which makes an adverse judgment upon forum shopping. But the complaint of forum

---

[32] *Custom Made Commercial Ltd.* v. *Stawa Metallbau GmbH*, [1994] ECR I–2913, ECJ.

[33] *Re Clay*, [1919] 1 Ch. 66, CA; *Camilla Cotton Oil Co.* v. *Granadex SA*, [1976] 2 Lloyd's Rep. 10, HL; *First National Bank of Boston* v. *Union Bank of Switzerland*, [1990] 1 Lloyd's Rep. 32, CA. It is obscure, because the precise reasons had never been disentangled. And there were a number of cases where such declarations had been foreseen with no difficulty whatsoever: cf. *Gulf Bank KSC* v. *Mitsubishi Heavy Industries Ltd.*, [1994] 1 Lloyd's Rep. 323, QBD.

[34] RSC, Order 15, rule 16.

[35] On the footing that jurisdiction under Article 4 is not incompatible with the application of national rules on *forum conveniens* which are an integral part of those jurisdictional rules.

[36] For example, by setting aside the order granting leave to serve the writ out of the jurisdiction.

shopping is not admissible where the plaintiff has invoked the jurisdictional rules of the Brussels Convention. This seems eminently right.

But to accommodate the claim within Article 5(1) it was necessary also to identify and give a location to the obligation in question. Authority had interpreted this to mean the obligation which founded the basis of the plaintiff's claim. As the plaintiff denied there was a contract, so the argument ran, it equally denied all obligations, and could not point to an obligation as that upon which it founded its claim. But the prima facie error in the reasoning was plain: once it had been decided that a claim for a negative declaration fell within Article 5(1), the obligation in question naturally became that which the defendant alleged, and the plaintiff denied, that the plaintiff was obliged to perform. The contrary conclusion was not unarguable: it might have been reasoned that in a case where the plaintiff relied upon no obligation, the matter could not have related to a contract. Even so, there were reasons of judicial policy which favoured the construction favoured by the Court. It is not uncommon for a plaintiff to claim damages for breach but, if he fails to establish that there was a contract, to seek the return of his payment. It would have been unwelcome for the first, but not the second, head of claim to be capable of being brought within Article 5(1);[37] yet this result would have followed from the conclusion that a claim for a declaration that there was no contract did not fall within Article 5(1). Moreover, if the courts for the place of performance of the obligation are well placed to adjudicate upon a claim brought to enforce the contract, they appear to be just as well placed to determine other issues of contractual validity and construction. Finally, if one took the view that the question of who was plaintiff and who defendant was no more than an accident of who sued first and for what, it was unacceptable that the interpretation of Article 5(1) should be affected by this accident of litigation.[38] It is hard to disagree, except on the doctrinaire ground that as Article 5(1) confers special jurisdiction, it is to be construed restrictively. Restrictive construction is one thing; destructive construction is quite another.

The judgments of the Court of Appeal in *Kleinwort Benson Ltd*. and in *Boss Group Ltd*. mean that, so far as the English courts are concerned, claims which arise in connection with a contract will be seen to fall within Article 5(1). They also lead to the conclusion that the 'obligation in question', which is indicative of the existence of jurisdiction, need not be a contractual obligation narrowly so called. An awkward, earlier, decision, but one which had read this limitation into Article 5(1), was that of Rix J in *Trade Indemnity plc* v. *Försäkringsaktiebolaget Njord*.[39] In an action to obtain a declaration that a reinsurance contract was entitled to be avoided for material non-disclosure, it had been held that the obligation in question, from which Article 5(1) identifies the court with special jurisdiction, had to be a *contractual* obligation. It had further been deduced that the duty to make a fair presentation, which arose prior to the contract, and which gave rise to no claim for damages or other performance if broken, was not a contractual obligation in the material sense. Although it was difficult to establish at the time that Rix J had been led into error at the date of his judgment, it

---

[37] It would have been even more objectionable if it had carried across into the provisions on consumer contracts in section 4 of Title II of the Convention.

[38] A conclusion supported by the judgment in *The Tatry*, [1994] ECR I–5439, ECJ.

[39] [1995] 1 All ER 796.

became evident that his judgment could not stand with the two subsequent decisions of the Court of Appeal. Indeed, *Kleinwort Benson* made it perfectly clear that the obligation relied on, and which indicated the existence of Article 5(1) jurisdiction, need not be seen as contractual as a matter of domestic law.[40] And if Article 5(1) encompassed claims for repayment after a supposed contract had been held to be void, and claims for a declaration that there was no contract between the parties, it plainly embraced a claim that a contract was entitled to be avoided for non-disclosure. In *Agnew* v. *Lansförsäkringsbolagens AB*, Mance J duly so held, not following *Trade Indemnity* on the point. In the light of the later authorities he was plainly bound to do so.

Two final points, which arise from the decision in *Boss Group*, should be noted. The case underlines one aspect of the construction of Article 21. The first side to get to court was Boss France SA, which obtained various forms of interlocutory relief from the French courts. But it appeared from the evidence that the claims with which the French courts were seised were separate and distinct from any claim on the merits of the dispute. Such a claim would need, as a matter of French law, to be brought separately, and in a different court. Perhaps the fact that Boss France SA took its eye off this particular ball and did not institute substantive proceedings allowed Boss Group Ltd. to seise the English courts as it did; that it did so would mean that Article 21 and the English proceedings prevented Boss France from commencing substantive proceedings for breach of the alleged contract in France. Overall, if the decision represents the manner in which the Convention prevents forum shopping, it appears to be making a rather imperfect job of it. Finally, the provisional character of the French proceedings also had an impact on the potential application of the rules on recognition of judgments. Though the Convention required the English courts to recognize the French interlocutory judgments, the findings made by the French court (as to the existence, validity and construction of the alleged contract) were not sufficient to give rise to an issue estoppel as a matter of English procedural law, as they represented provisional conclusions only, and not the final decision of the French courts on the points in question.[41]

4 Special jurisdiction and the Brussels Convention: Shevill v. Presse Alliance SA[42]

The only private international law case to be decided by the House of Lords in 1996 was the most inconsequential, and it is noted here only for completeness. After the preliminary ruling of the Court of Justice,[43] the case of *Shevill* v. *Presse Alliance SA* returned for a brief and unexpected hearing. It will be recalled that Shevill complained that an article in *France Soir*, which was published by a French defendant, had libelled her; that she had sued[44] alleging that dissemina-

---

[40] See Roch LJ at 667, Millett LJ at 671.
[41] For the rejection of a heretical view that a non-finding by a court may be treated as a finding for these purposes, see *Berkeley Administration Inc.* v. *McClelland*, [1996] ILPr. 772, CA.
[42] [1996] AC 959, 980, HL (Lord Keith of Kinkel, Lord Ackner, Lord Jauncey of Tullichettle, Lord Lowry, Lord Browne-Wilkinson).
[43] [1995] ECR I–415, ECJ.
[44] After amendment of her pleading.

tion of the newspaper in England had libelled her; and that the ruling of the Court was to the effect that she was entitled by reason of Article 5(3) of the Convention to do so.[45] The Court of Justice also ruled that the question whether harm of any sort needed to be proved, or was entitled to be presumed, was a matter for national law, and was not something for the Court of Justice to specify. For reasons which appear only to reflect the bitterness of the particular litigation, the defendant obtained a further hearing, contending that there were still loose ends to be tied up. The defendant contended that as Article 5(3) gave jurisdiction to the place of the harmful event, there had to be proof of qualifying harm. The argument was, on the face of it, flatly inconsistent with what the Court of Justice had said; and the House of Lords so held. If English law presumes harm, that is sufficient. It is hard to see what the defendant can have been thinking of.

5 *Forum non conveniens and unavailable courts: Mohammed v. Bank of Kuwait and the Middle East KSC;*[46] *Connelly v. Rio Tinto Zinc Corporation plc;*[47] *Connelly v. Rio Tinto Zinc Corporation plc (No. 2)*[48]

Where the defendant contends that the natural forum for the trial of a claim against him is in a foreign country, but this court is one in which the plaintiff alleges that he is, in practice, unable to sue, should a stay of proceedings be granted? The test laid down by the House of Lords in *Spiliada*[49] is two-limbed. It first requires that the defendant identify a foreign court, to whose jurisdiction he is amenable, in which justice can more conveniently be done. If he does this, the burden shifts to the plaintiff, who has to show, second, that it would be unjust to require him to bring his claim in that foreign court.[50] Where the particular factual objection is the difficulty which the plaintiff will have in bringing a claim at all in the foreign court, does the objection fit within the first or the second of the two limbs of the *Spiliada* test? If it belongs to the first limb, it may leave the defendant unable to demonstrate that there is another forum in which justice can be done; and the stay will not be granted. But if it belongs to the second—this would mean that, under the first limb, all the defendant need do is to show that there is a court to whose personal jurisdiction he is in principle amenable—the plaintiff will have the burden of proving why this factor makes it unjust for a stay to be granted. In *Mohammed v. Bank of Kuwait and the Middle East*, the Court of Appeal held that this particular factor belonged to the first, and not the second, limb of *Spiliada*. The defendant was therefore unable to

---

[45] On the footing that this was where the harm had occurred.
[46] [1996] 1 WLR 1483, CA (Evans, Saville, Morritt LJJ).
[47] [1996] QB 361, CA (Neill, Waite, Swinton Thomas LJJ).
[48] 2 May 1996, CA (Sir Thomas Bingham MR, Evans, Ward LJJ).
[49] *Spiliada Maritime Corporation v. Cansulex Ltd.*, [1987] AC 460, HL.
[50] These cases did not raise, and this comment does not discuss, the operation of these principles in a case in which the plaintiff has a good cause of action under the law which will be applied by an English court, and may win, but does not have a good cause of action (and will lose) under the law which will be applied by the other court. Principle and even-handedness suggest that this fact ought to be irrelevant; but these cases furnish a cautionary reminder that such things should not be taken for granted.

show that there was a foreign court in which justice could more conveniently be done; and it had accordingly failed to make out a case for a stay.

Mohammed was an Iraqi national who had been employed by the defendant bank in Kuwait. He had returned to Iraq when war broke out; he was prevented, by Iraqi and by Kuwaiti law, from returning to Kuwait thereafter. He had a claim for money due to him on the termination of his contract, and he commenced proceedings in London[51] to recover it. The bank contended that Kuwait was the natural forum for the claim; it was certainly a forum to the jurisdiction of which it was amenable. It therefore applied for a stay, and contended that by pointing to Kuwait, it had satisfied the first limb of the *Spiliada* test. But the plaintiff contended that the defendant had to go further, and show that Kuwait was available as a forum to the plaintiff, not just in the sense that the defendant could, in principle, be sued there, but that the *plaintiff* could fairly be expected to sue the defendant there. The court agreed, holding that the other forum was not available unless it could be said that it was 'available in practice to this plaintiff to have his dispute resolved',[52] and that the question whether the plaintiff would obtain substantial justice, or 'the fair resolution of the dispute',[53] in that other forum was an aspect of the first limb of the test. As it was found that the plaintiff could not lawfully enter Kuwait, could not participate in the compulsory conciliation which was required before the case could come to trial, and would have to instruct lawyers from outside Kuwait, give instructions and follow the trial by fax and telephone, Kuwait was not in practice an available forum. It followed that the defendant had not discharged the burden imposed on him by the first limb of *Spiliada*, and that a stay would not be granted.

As a result, the court was able to treat questions of whether the Kuwaiti court would have treated the plaintiff fairly, which questions would arise, it said, at the second stage, as irrelevant. In a sense, they were; but Evans LJ went on to say that he did not 'find any justification for holding that Kuwaiti judges would not have acted fairly if an Iraqi citizen appeared as plaintiff before them, whenever that might have occurred'.[54]

The fact that the difference appears to involve nothing more than the burden of proof should not be under-estimated. In delicate areas like this one, where the courts will be especially careful not to make disparaging or politically incorrect assessments of a foreign court or its procedure, the question of who has the burden of proof under each *Spiliada* limb may well be crucial. The party who has to persuade a judge to go on the record and find that the other court is unfair or untrustworthy may struggle to succeed. It is clear from the passage cited above that if the burden of proving that Kuwaiti procedure was unfair had lain on Mohammed, he would probably have failed; but as this was not for him to prove, he did not fail. But it is not obvious that it makes sense to separate the broad availability of a court from the fairness of the procedure which that court will adopt, for there may be no sharp line to be seen: the nature of the procedure may be unfair; or it may be *so* unfair that the court is not in practice available to the plaintiff at all. It may have been better to do as *Spiliada* almost certainly

[51] The bank was present in London, and could be served as of right.
[52] At 1490.
[53] At 1491.
[54] At 1496.

intended, and accept that all questions relating to whether it is fair to expect the plaintiff to go and make his case to the foreign court fit properly within the second limb of the *Spiliada* test.

The argument in favour of giving a narrow and value-free interpretation to the point about availability can be underlined by reference to the decision in *Connelly* v. *RTZ Corp. plc*: it is strongly arguable that *Mohammed* is inconsistent with *Connelly*. The plaintiff had sustained an industrial injury while working for the defendant (or one of its subsidiaries) at a uranium mine in Namibia. He commenced proceedings in England, but the defendant sought a stay in favour of the courts of Namibia. It was plain that in terms of the location of the tort, the witnesses, and the applicable law, Namibia was far and away the most appropriate forum. It was equally plain that if the case was stayed, the courts of Namibia were not available to the plaintiff. He had a good claim to legal aid for litigation in England, but no means whatever to support litigation in Namibia. Yet the court stayed the English proceedings. In doing so, it must have accepted that the fact that it was wholly impossible for the plaintiff to sue in Namibia did not prevent Namibia being an available natural forum. It is true that the court reached its conclusion, in part at least, because the Legal Aid Act 1988, section 31, directed it to disregard the rights conferred by the Act when exercising its discretion.[55] This meant that the court was precluded from reasoning that the availability of legal aid constituted a reason why it would be unjust to send the plaintiff to the Namibian courts: a second-stage factor. But the unavailability of legal aid in Namibia, and the fact that Connelly could not instruct Namibian lawyers from outside Namibia or at all, had no bearing at all upon whether Namibia was 'an alternative forum available to the plaintiff for . . . the fair resolution of the dispute'.[56] Unless it was sufficient that the courts of Namibia were available to the plaintiff in the same way as was once said of the Ritz Hotel, they were not open to him. He could, as a matter of practical fact, no more gain admission to the Namibian courts than could Mohammed to the Kuwaiti courts. Yet the possible impact of *Connelly* was not considered in *Mohammed*. The result is that a jurisprudence of 'availability' is at risk of being developed within the first limb of *Spiliada*. This will lead to argument about whether the particular factor relied on relates to curial availability or curial fairness (and hence to the burden of proof). It is very unsatisfactory indeed; and the view preferred here is that, whilst the decision in *Mohammed* is understandable on the facts, the court was wrong to see the case as falling under the first limb of *Spiliada*. According to the most straightforward reading of *Spiliada*, it was wrongly decided.

For the sake of completeness, let us return to *Connelly*. After the stay, the case took an unexpected turn. Relying upon the power recently conferred by the Courts and Legal Services Act 1990, Connelly withdrew his application for legal aid, and entered into a conditional fee arrangement with his English solicitor. He contended that this meant that the stay should be lifted. A stay had been granted because, in part at least, the court was prevented by statute from taking any account of the fact that legal aid was available in England. But now that the

---

[55] There was no authority which held that this statutory requirement applied when considering a stay on *forum non conveniens* grounds; but the wording of the statute was absolute on its face.

[56] Cf. *Mohammed* at 1491.

funding of the English litigation was secured by private funds, not public money, a material fact had changed. The Court of Appeal, in *Connelly (No. 2)*, and not without expressions of disquiet, re-examined the new facts, and lifted the stay. Again, it did not do so on the ground that Namibia was not an available forum, but because it would be unjust, in *Spiliada* terms, to deprive the plaintiff of the right to a trial of his claim (a second-stage argument). That Sir Thomas Bingham MR also mused that there might be a violation of Article 6(1) of the European Convention for the Protection of Human Rights and Fundamental Freedoms, if a citizen of a contracting State was deprived of his right to a trial, may lay the ground for a whole new line of argument by the plaintiff desperate to deploy any argument to forestall a stay of proceedings.

One final point should be noted from the judgment in *Mohammed*. The facts of the case had altered between the issue and service of the writ and the hearing in the Court of Appeal. There was disagreement as to which was the date upon which the court was required to assess the facts and arguments relevant to the application for a stay. The court, surely correctly, decided that the date of the hearing must in principle be correct: were it otherwise, and were the court required to determine whether a stay should have been granted as at an earlier date, there would be a fresh application, even at the date of the appeal, when the change of facts might be thought to warrant it. To encourage or require such formality would be absurd. By contrast, when an application is made under RSC, Order 12, rule 8, to have the court set aside service of the writ, the material date is the date upon which leave to serve out was granted (or if leave was not required, the date of issue of the writ). The application in such a case is to have the order granting leave, and all subsequent acts, cancelled; the question is whether the order should have been made in the first place. The cases are quite different, because the nature of the relief sought, and the grounds for granting it, are quite different.

6 *Jurisdiction agreements and third parties: The Mahkutai*[57]

The question of whether a third party is entitled to rely on, or is bound by, a jurisdiction clause contained in a contract to which he is not party is, ultimately, simply a question of contract. Assume a contract between A and B which provides for the exclusive jurisdiction of the courts of State X. Any action falling within the four corners of the clause will, in principle,[58] be subject to it. But what if C sues B, or A sues C? Is the contractual clause, in either case, binding upon the litigants, or is it irrelevant to a dispute when the litigants are not the two parties to the agreement?

In *The Mahkutai*, a time charterer issued a bill of lading which contained a clause giving exclusive jurisdiction to the courts of Indonesia, and stipulating Indonesian law as the governing law. The performance of the carriage was sub-contracted to the shipowner. The cargo was damaged, and the cargo owners issued a writ against the *Mahkutai* in Hong Kong. The sub-contractor ship-

---

[57] [1996] AC 650, PC (Lord Goff of Chieveley, Lord Jauncey of Tullichettle, Lord Nicholls of Birkenhead, Lord Hoffmann, and Sir Michael Hardie Boys), on appeal from the courts of Hong Kong.

[58] On the assumption that the clause is valid and enforceable as a matter of general law.

owners sought a stay of the proceedings in favour of the courts of Indonesia, purporting to rely on the choice of jurisdiction clause in the bill of lading to which they were not party. The cargo owners denied that the shipowners were entitled to rely on the jurisdiction clause against them, as they were strangers to the contract containing it. The shipowners sought to invoke the clause via the mechanism of the 'Himalaya' clause in the bill of lading, or alternatively through the principles of bailment. Both arguments failed. The Privy Council held that the shipowners were not entitled to invoke the jurisdiction clause, and refused to order a stay of the proceedings.

The detail of the reasoning is part of the domestic law of contract, and is beyond the scope of a comment such as this. But both arguments advanced by the shipowner sought to show that, in accordance with English principles, the benefit of holding the cargo owners to the jurisdiction clause, which benefit (if such it was) was originally granted by the cargo owners to the time charterer, could be claimed by the sub-contracting shipowner. It was never going to be easy. First, the mechanism of a 'Himalaya' clause operates to make a grant from the owner to the contracting carrier's sub-contractor of the benefit of 'exceptions, limitations, provisions, conditions and liberties . . . benefiting the carrier'. That form of words, said the Board, did not extend to encompass a choice of court agreement. The question is one of contractual construction; it is hard to quibble with the answer given. Second, with regard to the reasoning derived from bailment, it is agreed that if A bails goods to B on condition that B may sub-bail them to C on any terms B chooses, A will be bound by the sub-bailment to C, even including a jurisdiction clause if there was one in the sub-bailment from B to C: A is taken to have agreed to it. This had been recently illustrated in *The Pioneer Container*.[59] But the reasoning did not work in reverse. If there was a sub-bailment from B to C, which contained nothing by way of jurisdiction clauses, but there was such a clause in the contract between A and B, there was nothing in *The Pioneer Container* to support the argument that A had agreed, on bailing the goods, to bind himself to C in relation to the contents of the jurisdiction clause. Both arguments accordingly failed.

Two points should be noted. First, the difficulties arose in part at least from the doctrine of privity of contract. This piece of the common law of contracts has been sniped at for decades, and the Law Commission has proposed[60] substantial reform (which means abolition) of the doctrine. But they chose to exclude jurisdiction clauses from their proposed legislation;[61] and unless second thoughts are had, problems of the sort encountered in *The Mahkutai* will continue to test the wits of common lawyers.

Second, the bill of lading contract was expressly governed by Indonesian law. Yet nothing was said about the possible effect of Indonesian law, save that 'no question arises in the present case with regard to the choice of law provision'.[62] Presumably that means that there was no evidence that Indonesian law was materially different from the law of Hong Kong. But suppose it had been:

---

[59] [1994] 2 AC 324, PC.

[60] *Privity of Contract: Contracts for the Benefit of Third Parties*, Law Commission Report No. 242 (Cm 3329, July 1996).

[61] Clause 6(2)(*e*) of the draft bill. Presumably the reason is that jursidiction clauses are not ordinarily (nor otherwise) thought of as contracts for the benefit of third parties.

[62] At 666.

suppose Indonesian law had supported the argument that on its true construction, the shipowners were entitled to enforce the jurisdiction clause against the cargo owners. Would Indonesian law have been applied, to reach the conclusion that a stay would be granted, even though the law of Hong Kong would not have seen the shipowner as implicated by the jurisdiction clause? In principle the answer seems to be affirmative, even though there is room for doubt. Even without the benefit of the interference of the Law Commission, there is still some thinking through to be done upon the way jurisdiction clauses operate in certain common commercial contexts.

7 *Lis alibi pendens, forum non conveniens and the Brussels Convention: Sarrio SA v. Kuwait Investment Authority*[63]

It is generally accepted that when a court is exercising jurisdiction which is given to it by the Brussels Convention, it has no power to accede to a plea that the court of another contracting State is the *forum conveniens* for the dispute.[64] The reasons are principally those of European law: the scheme of the Convention does not permit such discretionary stays of jurisdiction; such a mechanism is generally unknown in the contracting States, and it would arguably[65] distort the operation of the Convention if the courts of one contracting State had such a power; plaintiffs should not have to spend money in commencing proceedings in accordance with the Convention, only to find that they have wasted time and money when a United Kingdom court decides that it is a *forum non conveniens*.[66] But there is a principle of English law as well: a court which stays its proceedings remains seised of the dispute, and may at any time lift the stay and resume hearing the case.[67] That being so, there will not be a court in another contracting State which has jurisdiction, for Article 21 of the Convention would require any such court to regard itself as second seised, and hence without jurisdiction. The first limb of the *Spiliada* test would not therefore be satisfied by the defendant; and there would be no stay.

It is less clear how much, if any, of this reasoning applies when the English court is exercising jurisdiction by reason of Article 4 of the Convention. If a defendant is not domiciled in a contracting State, it is at least arguable that Article 4 authorizes the court to apply the full panoply of its national law rules on jurisdiction. If these include power to stay proceedings on grounds of *forum non conveniens*, then it may stay. If the natural forum is another contracting State, then this is the court in favour of which a stay may be granted, for Article 4 constitutes a jurisdictional doorway leading out of the Convention, back into

---

[63] [1997] 1 Lloyd's Rep. 113, CA (Evans, Peter Gibson, Brooke LJJ).

[64] If authority is needed, it can be found in *Re Harrods (Buenos Aires) Ltd.*, [1992] Ch. 72, CA. There, the court stayed proceedings based on Article 2 in favour of the courts of a non-contracting State (*in casu*, Argentina); it explained that it was entitled to do so outside the field of the Convention even though it would have been prohibited from doing so in an intra-contracting State case.

[65] It is not clear that this a bad thing, nor that it was meant to be prevented by the Convention: the Convention does not seek to harmonize rules of procedure properly so called: *Kongress Agentur Hagen GmbH v. Zeehaghe BV*, [1990] ECR I–1845, ECJ. But it may not be proper to describe a *Spiliada* stay as procedural in this sense.

[66] See the Schlosser Report (*Official Journal*, 1979, C59/71) at paragraph 78.

[67] *Rofa Sport Management AG v. DHL International (UK) Ltd.*, [1989] 1 WLR 902, CA.

the outside world. On the other hand, a court may not exercise Article 4 jurisdiction if another contracting State was seised first,[68] and a judgment based on Article 4 jurisdiction is still a judgment which qualifies for recognition under the Convention. The proposition, that a case founded on Article 4 jurisdiction is in some sense 'outside' the Convention, may be too simplistic to be really reliable.

In *Sarrio v. KIA*, the defendant was domiciled in Kuwait. Exactly what sort of body it was, whether it had a claim to sovereign immunity,[69] how and where it could be served, were all equally obscure. But service was made in London; and so far as the English courts were concerned, jurisdiction was based on Article 4 of the Convention and hence on rules of national law. It was argued by the defendant that, for various reasons, the natural forum for the dispute was Spain. An issue of principle half arose before the Court of Appeal: if it was indeed true that Spain was the natural forum, was it lawful to order a stay of proceedings? The court concluded that Spain was not the natural forum, not least because the delays which such a finding would entail were unacceptable. But had Spain been shown to be the natural forum, the court would have been prepared to order a stay of proceedings. What a Spanish court would then have done remains unknown.

The reasoning adopted by the court supported the conclusion which it reached. It involves making a distinction between 'pure' Convention jurisdiction, and that based on Article 4. So far as it goes, this cannot be faulted. The hostility in the Schlosser report to the principle of *forum non conveniens* was sidelined, on the footing that it was directed to the possibility that a court with 'pure' Convention jurisdiction might seek to stay its proceedings in favour of another contracting State court. This is probably an accurate statement of what Professor Schlosser had in mind. It then deduces that as the power to stay proceedings is part of the national law whose operation is authorized by Article 4, the power may be exercised without any relevant limitation being imposed by the Convention. This is much more difficult, for a variety of compelling reasons.

First, Article 4 does not just authorize courts, but plaintiffs as well: 'as against such a defendant, any person domiciled in a contracting State may, whatever his nationality, avail himself in that State of the rules of jurisdiction there in force, and in particular those specified in the second paragraph of Article 3[70] . . . '. From the point of view of the plaintiff, he may have read this empowering text, and have concluded that, in England, he had the right to invoke that jurisdictional rule of English law which permits a defendant to be proceeded against once he has been served within the jurisdiction with the writ. It is an odd-looking right if such a plaintiff may lose it again by the application of the principle of *forum non conveniens*. And his waste of time and money will be no less than it would have been had he tried to rely on a rule of 'pure' Convention jurisdiction.

Secondly, if the argument by the defendant succeeded, the court would stay its proceedings; and it would remain seised of them. This is settled doctrine at

---

[68] *Overseas Union Insurance Ltd. v. New Hampshire Insurance Co.*, [1991] ECR I-3317, ECJ.

[69] On the suggested footing that it was an aspect of the Treasury of the Emir of Kuwait.

[70] That is, asserting jurisdiction by service within the jurisdiction, a rule which Article 3 spells out in order to prohibit its use against a defendant domiciled in a contracting State.

the level of the Court of Appeal, but it is also transparently factually true. A stay is not a dismissal of the proceedings; it may be lifted on the application of either party, and there is no question of the proceedings having to be started all over again.[71] If that is so, how could a Spanish court be persuaded that it had jurisdiction to hear the case, if the English court was first seised, and remained seised, of it? Evans LJ saw the problem. He proposed that the solution was to consider that the jurisdiction of the English court was, in such a case, not 'established'. But this is an illusion. Article 21[72] provides that until such time as the jurisdiction of the court seised first is 'established', the court seised second shall stay its proceedings. The obligation on the court seised second to dismiss its proceedings does not crystallize until the jurisdiction of the court first seised is established. But the court seised second is not authorized to hear the case unless there is not a court seised by virtue of an earlier act of seisin. It is an inescapable fact that the English court remains seised; and until English law, or the remedy, is amended, this appears to provide a fatal objection to the ordering of a stay. Moreover, can it really be true that if the Spanish court were persuaded to hear the case, it would then be impossible for the stay to be lifted, even for blatant breach of an undertaking given to the court, on the ground that the Spanish court was now seised first? It all goes to show how the reasoning proposed by the court leads into more and more difficulty as the procedural options are teased out.

Thirdly, the court was impelled towards its conclusion by the concession, made entirely correctly by counsel for plaintiff, that it would be different if proceedings had been commenced by service out of the jurisdiction under RSC, Order 11. In such a case, the defendant is entitled to allege (among other things) that the English court is not the *forum conveniens*; and, if the argument is sustained, the service of the writ will be set aside, and/or the court will declare that it has no jurisdiction. The result will be that the English court is not, or is no longer, seised; and there will be no bar to proceedings being commenced in another contracting State. The court found it difficult to accept that arguments on *forum conveniens* could be relevant if service had been made under Order 11, but not if it had been made within the jurisdiction, as of right. But even if it appears odd, this is correct. A defendant served out of the jurisdiction applies by means of RSC, Order 12, rule 8, for an order which leads to the dismissal, or denial, or relinquishing of jurisdiction. A defendant who seeks a stay does not, and probably may not, apply by RSC, Order 12, rule 8,[73] and does not ask the court to find that it has no jurisdiction. Any oddness may derive from the proven state of English procedural law;[74] but while English law remains in that condition, the conclusion favoured by the Court of Appeal cannot be correct.

The reasons why Spain could not be shown by the defendant to be the natural

---

[71] With a defendant which had behaved in as slippery a fashion as KIA evidently had, there would have been very good reason for the remedy being a stay, and not something more final. And, after all, if the stay is granted on undertakings given by the defendant, how could these be enforced if the case were dismissed rather than stayed?

[72] As amended.

[73] Though *Mohammed* v. *Bank of Kuwait and the Middle East KSC*, noted above, appears to accept, at 1492, that such an application may be made under RSC, Order 12, rule 8.

[74] For recent confirmation that this sharp difference is well founded in law, see *Mohammed* v. *Bank of Kuwait and the Middle East KSC*, at 1492–3.

forum are unimportant. But it was argued by the defendant that as the plaintiff had also commenced proceedings in Spain, which were still pending at first instance, and as these had (at least) some connection with those in England, Article 22 of the Convention permitted the English court, as the court seised second, to stay or dismiss its proceedings. (This submission also supports the proposition that jurisdiction under Article 4 is still, for some purposes at least, a jurisdiction located within, and not beyond, the framework of the Convention.) Whether this was so depended upon the two sets of proceedings being shown to be 'related' in the sense of Article 22. It had been held by the Court of Justice[75] that 'related proceedings' did not require proceedings to be so closely inter-linked that there was a risk that the judgment in one would be mutually irreconcilable with the judgment in the other. It was sufficient that 'the reasoning adopted by the court hearing the earlier proceedings may concern issues likely to be relevant to its own decision'.[76] What was arguably left unclear in this formulation was whether it was to be interpreted expansively (so that if there was a risk that the court might make findings ancillary to, or observations not required for, its judgment, this definition was satisfied) or restrictively (so that only matters which were strictly required to be decided in order for the court to give judgment were to be taken into account in deciding whether the proceedings were related). The Court opted for the restrictive interpretation, and concluded that the proceedings were not related in the material sense.

Its answer is to be applauded. The effect of Article 22 is to deprive a plaintiff of an immediate hearing by reference to proceedings in another court. It is one thing to do so when the first court may be required, and can be expected, to rule on matters in issue in the second court; it is another thing altogether if a plaintiff may lose his day in court because the court seised first may deal, gratuitously or in passing, with facts or matters which bear on proceedings in the court seised second. As the two proceedings in *Sarrio* were not related, there was no need for the court to consider whether, if they had been, it should have dismissed the proceedings for these to be consolidated with the Spanish proceedings, or have stayed, to await judgment in the Spanish proceedings. The test of the Convention gives no indication which remedy is to be preferred, or when one or the other is to be selected. But sooner or later the question will arise. Is there any obvious solution to it?

Not obvious, perhaps. But a key to it may be found in the decision of the Court of Justice in *The Tatry*, and in *Sarrio* itself. In *The Tatry*, there were multiple cargo claims brought by various owners of cargo carried on the one ship; in Holland there was a claim for a declaration of non-liability. But as between the courts of England and Holland, the lists of plaintiffs and defendants were not identical. Against that background, it would have made no sense to stay the English proceedings, but every sense to dismiss for consolidation with the Dutch ones. Had the Dutch court given judgment first, its findings would not have been *res judicata* in the English proceedings, which involved different parties; there was nothing to be gained, so far as concerned the English trial, by awaiting the outcome of the Dutch proceedings. But it would have made every sense to have the proceedings heard all in one omnibus trial. There was one

---

[75] *The Tatry* (also reported as *The Maciej Rataj*), [1994] ECR I–5439, ECJ.
[76] At paragraph 28 of the judgment.

cause of action, one ship, one form of contract, one allegation of default against the carrier, and a single species of damage to the cargo. It would have made every sense for the proceedings to be heard together in one set, so that all parties were bound by the single finding of a single court on a single point of fact and law. But it is different if the parties to the two actions are the same, but the claims are different in substance. If the second action is dismissed to be tried together with the first, the result will be that the first court has to investigate all the facts and matters arising within two actions. If anything, this may even delay the trial in the first court.[77] But if the court seised second stays its proceedings, it may save time and costs. The result of the first trial will be binding on the parties to the second set of proceedings, and questions decided by the first court may have the status of *res judicata* for the second court. The result may even be that there is no need to proceed with the second trial, because the first court has, by its findings, made the outcome obvious. In such a case, a stay would have assisted the administration of justice; but dismissal-for-consolidation would not have. It is thought that this makes rough sense of the undifferentiated powers conferred on the court seised second; and it means that in *Sarrio* the choice offered by Article 22 was to stay or not; not to dismiss-for-consolidation.

8 Foreign judgments and res judicata: Desert Sun Loan Corp. v. Hill[78]

The doctrine of *res judicata* in relation to foreign judgments is a developing one. A novel, and far from straightforward, example of it arose in *Desert Sun Loan Corp.* v. *Hill*. Hill had been a partner in an American property venture. A creditor of the partnership, the Desert Sun Loan Corporation, brought proceedings against the partnership and against Hill personally, in the courts of Arizona. It obtained judgment against all the defendants. It then sought to enforce the judgment by action against Hill in England. Defending the application for summary judgment, Hill contended that he had not submitted to the jurisdiction of the Arizona court, and that as a result its judgment could not be recognized and enforced against him. Up to that point the case is uncomplicated.

But in the proceedings in Arizona, a lawyer had appeared, purporting to do so on behalf of Hill. Hill claimed to know nothing of this. When he discovered that judgment had been sought and given against him personally, he instructed another lawyer to apply to have the judgment against him vacated, on the ground that he had not authorized the first lawyer to appear on his behalf. The application was unsuccessful. But the judgment creditor fastened upon it to argue that Hill was estopped from contesting the finding of the Arizona court— which court he, Hill, had asked to make the finding—that he had in fact instructed the lawyer to appear on his behalf in the original proceedings. The question for the Court of Appeal was therefore whether Hill could be and was estopped from arguing that he had not voluntarily appeared in the original proceedings by reason of the conclusion of the court in the later proceedings that he had. The judgments of the Court of Appeal are not easy to reconcile. It appears that all agreed that an estoppel was, in principle, possible; but that it was

---

[77] In *Sarrio*, this was exactly what was feared.
[78] [1996] 2 All ER 847, CA (Evans, Roch and Stuart-Smith LJJ).

not made out, for Order 14 purposes, on the facts. The Court disagreed on whether the fact that Hill had invoked the jurisdiction of the Arizona court as he had led to the conclusion that he had submitted to its jurisdiction on this issue. Evans and Stuart-Smith LJJ held that it did; Roch LJ disagreed. It is submitted that the majority were wrong and Roch LJ right.

The theoretical problems for the judgment creditor in making good the plea of estoppel were two. First, was the nature of the later Arizona proceedings such as could give rise to a finding upon which an estoppel could be founded? And second, was the nature of the participation of Hill in those proceedings such as to bind him to the finding of the Arizona court? If these were overcome, there was a third, factual, question as well: had the Arizona court actually made the finding upon which the judgment creditor wished to rely?

There is no difficulty with founding an estoppel upon a final judgment on the merits of a dispute between the parties. That a judgment on a procedural matter could be final for these purposes had been established in *The Sennar (No. 2)*;[79] all that was required was that the ruling be the adjudicating court's last word, and not just a provisional conclusion, on the subject. Evans and Stuart-Smith LJJ accepted that the Arizona court's decision on a procedural question, as long as it was not in the nature of a provisional conclusion, was sufficient. In this they were probably correct. Even so, it is wise to remember as Evans LJ did, the cautious words of Lord Wilberforce in *Carl Zeiss Stiftung* v. *Rayner & Keeler Ltd. (No. 2)*,[80] to the effect that issue estoppel must not be derived mechanically from a foreign judgment. As the basic principle is that it is unfair to require a party to prove a second time that which he has succeeded in proving once, there will be cases where it is still unreasonable to confine a party to making his challenge in a foreign court, and then to being shut out from raising the same issue in England. Moreover, the perception that there is more interlocutory litigation than there used to be, especially upon jurisdictional issues, may mean that these preliminary skirmishes in foreign courts have a greater force and effect outside the immediate context in which they arise.

But before any such ruling binds a litigant, it must be established that the judgment in which the ruling was contained was, as a matter of English private international law, entitled to be recognized as against him. This will require the party to be subject, as a matter of English private international law, to the international jurisdiction of the adjudicating court. As Hill was at no material time present or resident within the jurisdiction of the Arizona court, it had to be shown that he had submitted to the jurisdiction of the court. On his evidence, Hill had not submitted in respect of the first Arizona proceedings. But did the position change when he instructed a lawyer to seek to have the judgment set aside?

At first sight this is an odd question to ask in respect of a plaintiff or applicant. Though a defendant may argue that he did not appear or submit in proceedings brought against him, a plaintiff has, *ex hypothesi*, chosen the court and hence submitted to its jurisdiction. For Evans and Stuart-Smith LJJ this appears to have been sufficient: Hill had elected to submit the issue to the adjudication of the Arizona court, and nothing else needed to be, nor was, said on the point. But

[79] [1985] 1 WLR 490, HL.
[80] [1967] 1 AC 853.

the contrary view of Roch LJ is to be preferred. He pointed out that a statutory definition of non-submission is contained in the Civil Jurisdiction and Judgments Act 1982, section 33, and that according to this a person 'is not to be regarded as having submitted to the jurisdiction of the court by reason only of the fact that he appeared[81] . . . (a) to contest the jurisdiction of the court'. As section 33 deals generally with the recognition of judgments based on submission to a foreign court, it applied to any case in which a foreign judgment was to be recognized against a party to that decision. Only Roch LJ examined the application of section 33; and he deduced from it that Hill had not thrown away his shield and submitted to the Arizona court when he applied to it for a finding that it had had no jurisdiction over him and for the first judgment to be vacated.[82] Once section 33 cut away the basis for an argument that Hill had (or was estopped from denying that he had) submitted to the Arizona court, there was no basis for an estoppel to work against him. It is submitted that this approach is unassailable, and that the majority fell into error in making no mention of section 33.[83] Nor should it have been relevant that Hill made his jurisdictional challenge after a trial and judgment on the merits of which he knew nothing. It is impossible to believe that he is protected by section 33 if he makes an application at the appropriate stage in the original trial but (in a case where he learns nothing of it until the trial is over, but makes it as soon thereafter as he can) not if he makes the same argument by application after the trial. And it is impossible to contend that making an application which falls within section 33 leads to an estoppel arising out of the result of the application, for that would deprive the statute of all effect. Yet that, in effect, is the result produced by the majority. It cannot be correct.

That should have sufficed to deprive the argument about estoppel of its very foundation. The further fact that it was not possible to determine from the Arizona judgment exactly what issue or issues the court had decided added to the case for Hill. The Arizona court had concluded on the second hearing that it had had jurisdiction at the first. This did not necessarily mean that the lawyer who had appeared the first time was found to have been authorized: there may have been other bases upon which the Arizona court was prepared to find that it had had jurisdiction. All three members of the court agreed that there was, on the facts, no estoppel which could be teased out of the Arizona judgment. But in doing so, Roch LJ again put his finger on an issue of real difficulty. For an estoppel to work, it was necessary to find that Hill had, as a matter of English law, submitted to the jurisdiction of the Arizona court. If the Arizona court had expressly found that he had submitted, would it have decided the same issue as the English court had to? Or would the fact that it had found submission according to the law of Arizona suffice to make the issue a different one, and to

---

[81] It is not specified that he must appear as defendant, respondent, or anything else.

[82] This conclusion supposes that the application made by Hill was properly characterized as one in which he contested the jurisdiction of the court. It could have been argued, against the analysis adopted by Roch LJ, that the application actually made by Hill was not one to contest the jurisdiction of the Arizona court within the meaning of section 33(1)(a), but was a challenge to the entering of judgment otherwise than on jurisdictional grounds. But this is probably not supportable, and it does not appear to be the basis of the judgments of the majority.

[83] It may be argued that as the majority found that the Arizona court had not made a finding on the point in issue, it was unnecessary for them to deal with this point. Such an argument does not really correspond to the structure of the majority judgments.

prevent estoppel? This is not well explored in the authorities, but it may be that the fact that (as Evans LJ observed) courts apply their own law of procedural issues has led to the perception that estoppel does not arise from judgments on procedural questions. If so, it is time for it to be reconsidered.

Finally, the majority indicated that in an appropriate case the doctrine of abuse of process could be used to overcome technical gaps in the construction of an estoppel. This malign doctrine has recently acquired new vitality in the area of estoppel and foreign judgments;[84] it appears to bring out a strain of judicial impatience with a judgment debtor who has the temerity to point out that it is open to him to challenge the conclusive effect of a foreign judgment. It is to be regretted that the careful and tidy lines of the law on recognition of foreign judgments may be overridden by the juggernaut of abuse of process. How soon will it be before it is said to be an abuse of process to plead fraud in opposition to the enforcement of a foreign judgment when this plea has not been taken, or no fresh proceedings brought, in the foreign court itself? How soon will it be before it is said to be an abuse of process not to bring a claim which could have been brought in a foreign court which has very wide provision for joinder of causes of action? To the extent that the judgments of the majority lend any support to the operation of this doctrine in its subversion of the law on recognition of judgments, it is to be regretted on this ground as well.

9 *Foreign judgments and res judicata: Republic of India* v. *India Steamship Co. Ltd. (The Indian Grace) (No. 2)*[85]

For the second time the *Indian Grace* made its way to the Court of Appeal on an application to strike out the action.[86] Mention is made of it only to complete the story. It will be recalled that this was the case where a claim in respect of short delivery of a consignment of munitions was successfully brought before the courts of Cochin, India, but that this success was used by the defendants, owners of the *Indian Grace*, to prevent the plaintiffs bringing a claim in England for damage to the remainder of the cargo. The first time around it had been decided by the House of Lords that the seemingly absolute bar to the second action, created by the Civil Jurisdiction and Judgments Act 1982, section 34, was to be seen as a defence, and not as the statutory removal of jurisdiction to hear any such action; that this defence was susceptible to loss by waiver or estoppel; and that the case should be remitted to the Admiralty judge for him to evaluate the case further. Clarke J duly held[87] that the defendants were precluded from reliance on section 34, and that they were not debarred by the principle in *Henderson* v. *Henderson* from bringing the claim. As to the argument on the difference between the configuration of the proceedings, which were

[84] The origins (though not as to foreign judgments) lie in *Henderson* v. *Henderson*, (1843) 3 Hare 100. See, for example, *House of Spring Gardens Ltd.* v. *Waite*, [1991] 1 QB 391, CA; *Owens Bank Ltd.* v. *Etoile Commerciale SA*, [1995] 1 WLR 44, PC; and *The Indian Grace (No. 2)* [1996] 2 Lloyd's Rep. 12, CA (noted below).

[85] [1996] 2 Lloyd's Rep. 12, CA (Staughton, Simon Brown and Auld LJJ).

[86] The first action is reported at [1993] AC 410, HL (noted in this *Year Book*, 64 (1993), p. 470).

[87] [1994] 2 Lloyd's Rep. 331.

in personam against the owners in India but commenced *in rem* in England, Clarke J held that this also carried the case outside the scope of section 34. The Court of Appeal reversed Clarke J on all points, and held that the plaintiffs were prevented from bringing the action in respect of the whole cargo in England. Along with finding that a judgment from the courts at Cochin for a trifling sum prevented a claim for a sum 360 times that sought and recovered in Cochin, the court was harshly critical of the conduct of the plaintiffs, attributing their defeat to 'incompetence' in the bringing of the first claim in India to begin with. One may wonder whether all will immediately agree that the failure of an Indian plaintiff, suing an Indian defendant in India, to see so far down the road should be characterized quite so unkindly.

As the House of Lords had already decided that estoppel or waiver could lead in principle to the loss of the section 34 defence, the analysis of the facts and of the law on estoppel undertaken by the Court of Appeal is of local interest only. More significant is the difficulty which was caused by the Indian proceedings having been *in personam* against the owners of the *Indian Grace*, but the later English proceedings having been commenced *in rem* against the ship. In the English proceedings the owners acknowledged service, and the proceedings then continued *in personam* and *in rem*. But section 34 required, so the plaintiffs contended, the action brought in England to be between the same parties (or their privies), and in respect of the same cause of action, as were the foreign proceedings. As the action in England was brought *in rem*, whatever may have happened to it afterwards, section 34 did not apply to it. The court disagreed, whilst seeing that there were difficulties arising from the operation of section 34 in an Admiralty context. On the one hand, it accepted that for some purposes at least an Admiralty action *in rem* should be seen *ab initio* as having as defendants those interested in the ship. It did so by reasoning from the interpretation of the Brussels Convention[88] back to a purely domestic statute—an unexpected pattern of reasoning, it must be said. On the other, it did not consider that Parliament necessarily intended to affect the doctrine of Admiralty law that an action *in rem* could be brought by a plaintiff with an unsatisfied judgment *in personam*, and an action *in personam* could be brought by a plaintiff who had only partially obtained satisfaction by an action *in rem*. Yet if section 34 applied, abolition would be the result if the first action were brought in a foreign (but not in an English) court. In the end it accepted that section 34 applied on the facts of the case, taking what it called a purposive construction of the section. The purpose was therefore seen as being to prevent second actions by partially successful plaintiffs, and the procedural character of the different actions was not particularly relevant. That this involved, and will probably generate,[89] some rough interpretation of the statute and of the legal character of an Admiralty action *in rem*, was not allowed to stand in the way of the reasoning.

But the court was not finished. Had the shipowners lost on the interpretation of section 34, so that this did not debar the plaintiffs from proceeding, it would still have been an abuse of process for the plaintiffs to sue in England in respect

---

[88] In *The Deichland*, [1990] 1 QB 361, CA; *The Tatry* (also known as *The Maciej Rataj*), [1994] ECR I–5439, ECJ.

[89] For example, is an action by a minority shareholder against the majority shareholder in one court an obstacle to an unfair prejudice petition against the company pursuant to Companies Act 1985, s. 459?

of the whole of the damaged cargo after bringing the piffling action in respect of 51 jettisoned shells in Cochin. This comes as no surprise, for the courts have recently adopted this doctrine as the fallback solution to overcome a party of whose previous performance there is judicial disapproval. *The Indian Grace* is one of the rarer cases where it has been used in the context of a foreign judgment to defeat a plaintiff. Though the court admitted that in principle exceptions may be made for special circumstances, it found no cause for any in the present case. Having chosen to sue in Cochin, the plaintiffs were obliged, so far as English law was concerned, to bring all their claim in Cochin. Presumably it would have been different if there had been a real obstacle to bringing the whole cargo claim in Cochin. Even so, the careful limits which Parliament may have been thought to have foreseen and created by section 34 would still have been overridden by this bullying doctrine. There is a real danger, it is submitted, that the enthusiasm shown for this principle, almost wholly discretionary in content, means that courts are losing sight of the law by which commercial men advise themselves. It may also be wondered whether the House of Lords, when remitting the case to the Admiralty judge, had appreciated the fact that the *Henderson* v. *Henderson* principle would provide such a short cut to the eventual result.

10 *Injunctions to restrain foreign proceedings: Airbus Industrie GIE* v. *Patel*[90]

It has been re-established in recent years that an English court may grant an injunction to restrain a party over whom it has jurisdiction *in personam* when the prosecution by that party of proceedings in a foreign court is vexatious or oppressive. There are doubtless other grounds upon which equity may be persuaded to intervene, but in the context of such an 'anti-suit' injunction, this is by far the most commonly encountered formulation. In the leading recent authority,[91] it had been said in addition that for equity to intervene on this ground, it was generally presupposed that England should be the natural forum for the litigation of the differences between the parties. The question whether this presupposition was well founded was examined by the Court of Appeal in *Airbus* v. *Patel*; and a negative answer was given. As a result, it appears that the grant of an injunction may not be prevented on the ground that England is not, or that some other court is, the natural forum for the resolution of the dispute between the parties.

Bereaved and other victims of an aviation catastrophe in India had commenced proceedings in the courts at Bangalore. The principal defendants were the Indian airline and the airport authorities, and also the French aircraft manufacturer, Airbus GIE. But a commission of enquiry carried out in India had effectively exonerated Airbus; and the claim against the other defendants was prosecuted with little vigour. Some time later, the plaintiffs commenced proceedings in Texas against Airbus.[92] Airbus sought dismissal of the claim from the Texas courts, but were not immediately successful. They also applied

[90] [1997] ILPr. 230, CA (Hobhouse, Aldous, Nourse LJJ).
[91] *SNI Aérospatiale* v. *Lee Kui Jak*, [1987] AC 871 (PC).
[92] It is not recorded whether the initiative came from the plaintiffs or from the Texas lawyers themselves. Airbus had no real choice but to defend proceedings in an American court.

to the courts at Bangalore for an anti-suit injunction. This was granted, but as the plaintiffs were not resident in India they were not in practice compelled to obey it.[93] But they were resident in England. Airbus therefore applied to the English courts for an injunction to restrain the plaintiff-respondents from proceeding further in Texas. Colman J held that he had power to make such an order, but declined, in his discretion to do so. The Court of Appeal reversed him on the exercise of discretion, and made the order sought.

At first sight the decision is attractive and highly sensible. If—as the Court found—it was vexatious or oppressive for the plaintiffs to sue Airbus in Texas, this conclusion does not obviously depend upon finding the proper place for the litigation to be England. If equity is justified in acting whenever those subject to its personal jurisdiction are behaving oppressively, why should it be further required that England constitute the natural forum? In *Airbus v. Patel* itself, not only was England not the natural forum, it was not even an *available* forum for a claim against Airbus.[94] Nor was that all. Not only were the plaintiffs suing in a forum which was grotesquely inappropriate, but they were doing so in defiance of an order from the Indian court to refrain from doing so. It appeared that only the English court was in a position to make an order which would be practically effective against the plaintiff-respondents; and the Court of Appeal saw no sufficient ground for not doing so. As well it might.

But at second sight, matters are less straightforward. For if *Airbus v. Patel* is correct, there appears to be no obvious restriction upon the disciplinary role of equity over all those within its jurisdiction: it would be acting as governess to the world. Though Hobhouse LJ insisted that the case was an exceptional one, it is rather difficult to see how any such exception is to be defined. For if the respondent is within the jurisdiction, and is behaving oppressively, what more is left, or required, to make out an exception? One possibility might be where the court which is the appropriate one to grant an injunction is unable to make an order which will be effective, and the applicant, having exhausted his remedies there, is then free to apply to the English courts. But if this is a pre-condition, it may mean that it will be several years before the applicant is free to seek the injunction in England; and delay may be fatal to its being granted. So this is unlikely to be required, in all cases at least.

The problem may in fact be broader than this. When an injunction is sought on the basis of an infringement of a legal right[95] not to be sued overseas, such as may be based on a choice of court or arbitration agreement, a choice of law rule stands between the jurisdiction of the court and the ordering of any remedy. Only if the proper law of the agreement confirms that there is such a legal right

[93] The judgment of the Bangalore court, as a non-money judgment, could not in any event be enforced by action in England.

[94] Since it was domiciled in France, and no other provision of the Brussels Convention gave a jurisdictional basis for a claim against Airbus in England, any claim against it would have had (submission apart, and as a matter of English law) to have been brought in France.

[95] In *British Airways Board* v. *Laker Airways plc*, [1985] AC 58, Lord Diplock appeared to confine injunctions to those granted in aid of legal rights and those in aid of equitable rights. In *South Carolina Insurance Co.* v. *Assurantie Maatschappij 'de Zeven Provincien' NV*, [1987] AC 24, it was suggested that the anti-suit injunction may, in some cases at least, constitute an exception to this analysis. But the reasoning was not developed further, and it is not clear that it would be desirable if it were: the injunction needs to be based on a proper understanding of theory if it is to operate in a satisfactory way.

does the question of remedy arise. But where an injunction is sought, as here, on the ground of oppressive or vexatious conduct, the cases have not so far recognized that a choice of law has to be undertaken. In *Airbus* v. *Patel* there was no connection whatever with England or English law (save for the amenability of the respondents to the jurisdiction of the court); it is difficult to see the justification for the application of English law or equity. It is this, it is thought, which leads to the incoherence of the observation in *Airbus* v. *Patel* that the case was an exceptional one. The conflict of laws has, since time out of mind, prevented the inappropriate application of English law by means of choice of law rules. If equity is nevertheless free to operate without this restriction, it is still claiming to work as it did in the Middle Ages. The control mechanism, which Hobhouse LJ did not identify, may be that an injunction should not be granted unless the law which governs the particular allegation of wrongdoing agrees that the applicant has a right not to be sued. In the present case, that may well have been Indian law: India was, on any view, the natural forum for the litigation, and as a matter of Indian law the proceedings in Texas were wrongfully brought.[96] Perhaps this should have been the factor which explained why the approach of the court was not one which opens the floodgates.

If this is not accepted, why else might it have been appropriate to grant an injunction? The Indian injunction obviously could not be enforced[97] as such in England, with this result: the court which should[98] have dismissed the proceedings on forum grounds (Texas) would not do so; and the court in which the claim should have been (and had in fact been) brought could not make an order which was internationally effective. Given the ineffective rules on foreign judgments, for the English court to wish to act in aid of the Indian court was understandable. But this could not be the legal basis for the order made. The law on judicial co-operation is almost wholly confined to statute, and often requires a formal request from the foreign court itself. Nothing like that was present in Airbus. All that is left, therefore, was the finding that the behaviour of the respondents was oppressive or vexatious. Indeed, the list spelled out with clarity by Hobhouse LJ makes plain his view that it came very high indeed on the scale of unconscionability. The meretricious advantages of Texas law and procedure for a plaintiff, who wishes to coerce a commercial defendant who dare not let an American court enter judgment in default, are all too well known. In response to the contention that it was unjust to deprive the plaintiff of these (to him) advantages, Hobhouse LJ was satisfyingly robust. In his view, an oppressive advantage was no advantage at all, though his criticism of Texas choice of law rules (which would have called for the application of Texas law to a foreign tort) only 90 days after English choice of law rules in tort had been changed to remove

---

[96] Ordinarily this will be a matter for pleading and proof of Indian law. But the decision of the court at Bangalore would, in the present case, have made this considerably easier.

[97] This is not to say that the conclusions of an Indian court could not have established that certain issues were *res judicata* when the same points arose for decision in an English court. This would involve recognition, rather than enforcement, of the judgment. This would require that the Patels be subject (in English eyes) to the jurisdiction of the Indian court; and as they had commenced proceedings in that court, it was not difficult to conclude that they had submitted to its jurisdiction.

[98] In English eyes.

centuries of application of the *lex fori* should perhaps have been done with tongue in cheek.

The result is that the scope of the court's power to grant an anti-suit injunction has been considerably widened, and without a proper theoretical underpinning, Hobhouse LJ's statement that the case was an exceptional one may be no more than a hope. The right result was reached, but there is more work to be done in finding a durable justification for it.

11 *Choice of law and restitutionary claims: Arab Monetary Fund v. Hashim;*[99] *Macmillan Inc. v. Bishopsgate Investment Trust plc (No. 3)*[100]

A much-debated question of choice of law concerns the correct approach to restitutionary claims.[101] As choice of law in contract and tort is now governed mostly by statute,[102] this remains the one area of the law of obligations where the common law rules of choice of law hold sway. Sadly, the common law rules are largely undeveloped; and in the two cases in which the Court of Appeal had an opportunity to say something on the topic, the approach adopted made little detailed contribution to the debate. The starting point in the textbooks has long been *Dicey & Morris's* Rule 201,[103] which proposes that 'the obligation to restore the benefit of an enrichment obtained at another person's expense is governed by the proper law of the obligation'. This is then particularized: in connection with a contract, this is the law applicable to the contract; otherwise[104] it is the law of the country where the enrichment occurs. But the case law from which this is deduced is remarkably sparse.

In *AMF* v. *Hashim*, a claim was made by an employer to recover the sum paid by a third party as a bribe to an employee. The contract of employment was governed by the law of Abu Dhabi; any tort committed was in substance committed in Abu Dhabi; the bribe was received in Abu Dhabi. So far as concerned any quasi-contractual action to recover the sum paid, Saville LJ expressly accepted the general statement of the governing law set out in Rule 201. In his opinion, this required the nature of the complaint to be examined in detail, in order that it could be decided which law applied to the claim. On the footing that the essence of the claim was abuse by briber and bribe-taker of the relationship of each with the employer, and that these were governed by the law of Abu Dhabi, the proper law of the alleged obligation to pay over the bribe was the law of Abu Dhabi. It is evident from this approach that one looks at the juridical nature of the particular claim, and at the facts giving rise to it; one then asks which is the law with which that claim has its closest connection. It is probably not realistic to expect greater precision than that; the approach of

[99] [1996] 1 Lloyd's Rep. 589, CA (Nourse, Saville, Hutchison LJJ).

[100] [1996] 1 WLR 387, CA (Staughton, Auld, Aldous LJJ).

[101] As to whether this is a category which is disciplined enough to have a choice of law rule, there is room for doubt; see also the comment upon *Kleinwort Benson Ltd.* v. *City of Glasgow DC*, above.

[102] Contracts (Applicable Law) Act 1990 (applicable to contracts made on or after 2 April 1991); Private International Law (Miscellaneous Provisions) Act 1995 (applicable to torts committed on or after 1 May 1996).

[103] Dicey & Morris, *The Conflict of Laws* (12th edn., 1993).

[104] Omitting reference to unjust enrichment in connection with immovable property, where the *lex situs* will govern.

Saville LJ has the virtue of being adaptable to accommodate almost any claim which can be described as restitutionary. If the claim lies close to a contract, it will almost inevitably produce the result that the law which governs the contract will be the law governing the obligation to make restitution, and it obviates the need for a separate sub-rule to deal with such cases. It also explains, wholly satisfactorily, why the law governing the contract, or the supposed contract, will govern the restitutionary obligation. This will not come about because the claim is a contractual claim, but because the relationship to which the obligation relates was itself governed by a law which overshadows the restitutionary claim.[105]

The Court was also required to consider whether the claim was limited or prescribed by the law of Abu Dhabi, and, if it was, whether the Foreign Limitation Periods Act 1984, section 2, allowed the period fixed by Abu Dhabi law to be set aside on the ground that its operation offended public policy by causing undue hardship to a party to the proceedings. Saville LJ explained that this test was satisfied when the operation of the period gave rise to 'greater hardship than the circumstances warrant', and if the consequences were out of proportion to the plaintiff's fault, that fact sufficed to show undue hardship. He further explained that if section 2 led to the disapplication of the foreign limitation period, the English period would apply by default, as part of the procedural law of the forum.[106] It follows that the statute has not wholly abolished the rule of the common law that statutes of limitation are procedural, but has simply suppressed it with a statutory scheme; if for some reason the statutory scheme is inapplicable, the common law rule is revived to fill the gap.

The approval of the *Dicey & Morris* Rule in *AMF* v. *Hashim* stands in contrast to the studied refusal to endorse it in the earlier decision in *Macmillan* v. *Bishopsgate*. In some ways this was wholly justifiable, for the Court of Appeal did not appear to believe that it was required to identify the law which governed a restitutionary claim. There had been a transfer of shares which were not his, engineered by Robert Maxwell to guarantee loans made to private family companies. The plaintiff, the beneficial owner of the shares, knew nothing of this dealing; and the transferees claimed not to know that the shares were beneficially owned by the plaintiff. In an action for a declaration that the transferees took their interest in the shares subject to the equitable title of the plaintiff, the plaintiff argued that its claim was a restitutionary one, governed by the law identified by Rule 201. The Court of Appeal disagreed, but for reasons and to an extent which lack clarity. Even so, the decision lends no real support to the analysis in Rule 201.

Staughton LJ was prepared to 'accept without deciding' that Rule 201 identified the law which would govern a restitutionary claim. But he denied that the issue for decision was as to the law which governed a restitutionary claim. As far as he was concerned, the issue for decision was distinct and narrower; it was which law governed the issue of whether the purchasers took for value in good

---

[105] The theory at this point troubled Lord Penrose, in the Outer House of the Court of Session, in *Baring Brothers & Co. Ltd.* v. *Cunninghame DC* (24 May, 1996), who appears to have preferred the view that the law which governed the (supposed) contract will often govern, not because the claim is contractual, but because this is the law with the closest connection to the claim for recovery.

[106] Cf. *The Komninos S*, [1991] 1 Lloyd's Rep. 371, CA.

faith so as to obtain title. This, he decided, was to be decided by the law of place of incorporation, which was the *lex situs* of the shares. Auld LJ considered that the highest it could be put was that there was a tendency in the cases, none of which bound the court, to endorse Rule 201. But he saw the issue as one of priority of ownership of shares, and as such as governed by the *lex situs* of the shares. Aldous LJ simply denied that Rule 201 applied to the case before the court, and applied the law of the place of incorporation. The case is therefore authority for the view that questions of title to, and of priority as between titles to, shares are governed by the law of the place of incorporation, as the *lex situs* of the shares. That conclusion appears to be in line with traditional understanding.

But the reason why the court characterized the issue as one of priority of title to shares is less clear. It appears to have been accepted that any and all claims which the plaintiff could have advanced were liable to be defeated if, according to the law which governed the particular issue, the defendants had better title to the shares than did the plaintiff. Now this may have been so; and it may have been conceded in argument that it was so. But it is a rather unexpected piece of methodology. If the claim brought by the plaintiffs was properly seen as being a proprietary claim to the shares, the approach of the Court would have been entirely expected. But was it? What if the correct analysis was that they brought a claim for restitution, for the observance of an obligation owed to them; and the factor of bona fide purchase was simply a potential defence to that claim? Because if that were so, there are two reasons for not simply applying the English choice of law rule applicable to such a plea. First, the law which governed the claim itself may make no allowance for such a defence. It may simply take the view that there is no obligation to make restitution, and leave it at that. Were that to be so, it is not clear what purpose would have been served by isolating the particular issue with which the Court dealt, and choosing the law for it. Second, if there is a claim governed by one law, but a defence exists which would otherwise be governed by a separate choice of law rule, there is a classic incidental question. Orthodoxy has it that the incidental question is answered, not according to what English law regards as the law chosen for it, but by the law which is identified for it by the law which governs the main question. If that analysis were applied to *Macmillan*, one would need to enquire what law governed the claim made, so that the choice of law provisions of *that* system of law could deal with the defence which might be raised. As a result of the way the judgments are presented in *Macmillan*, we know a lot more than we did about the English choice of law rules for questions of priority of title to shares. But we do not know quite so well why, in the context in which the issue arose and had to be analysed, this was the right question to be asking.

ADRIAN BRIGGS

DECISIONS ON THE EUROPEAN CONVENTION ON HUMAN RIGHTS DURING 1996*

Following the scheme which has been employed in recent volumes of this *Year Book*, this survey is divided into four parts. Part One contains full notes on the more important cases decided in the period under review. Part Two contains summaries of other cases which were decided on the merits. Part Three lists those cases in which the only issue was that of just satisfaction under Article 50. And Part Four lists those which were removed from the list following a friendly settlement, or where there was no decision on the merits for some other reason. Within each part the decisions are in chronological order.

PART ONE: SELECTED DECISIONS

Freedom of expression (Article 10)—freedom of association (Article 11)—dismissal of a teacher on account of her political activities—the margin of appreciation

Case No. 1. Vogt case.[1] In this case, which concerned Germany, the Court held by 10 votes to 9 that the dismissal of a teacher on account of her political activities on behalf of the German Communist Party constituted a violation of Articles 10 and 11 of the Convention. It further held, unanimously, that it was not necessary to examine the case under Article 14 of the Convention, taken in conjunction with Article 10, and by 17 votes to 2 decided that the issue of compensation under Article 50 should be reserved.

In 1972 the applicant, Mrs Vogt, joined the German Communist Party (DKP). In 1979 she was appointed to a permanent teaching post in a secondary school in Lower Saxony. Under German law this gave her the status of a civil servant with tenure for life. She taught German and French and her professional qualifications and performance were fully satisfactory. However, under federal and Länder legislation civil servants owed a duty of political loyalty, and when Mrs Vogt increased her activity on behalf of the DKP, disciplinary proceedings were begun against her. These culminated in her dismissal in October 1987. Appeals against this decision were unsuccessful, but in 1991, following the repeal of the relevant local legislation, Mrs Vogt was reinstated.

In her application to the Commission in February 1991 Mrs Vogt complained that her dismissal had violated her rights to freedom of expression and freedom of association, as guaranteed by, respectively, Articles 10 and 11 of the Convention. In its report in November 1993 the Commission expressed the

* © Professor J. G. Merrills, 1997. Thanks are due to the Registrar of the Court for his co-operation in making material available to me for the preparation of these notes. Cases decided in the latter part of 1996, which appeared too late for inclusion in the present survey, will be covered in the next issue of the *Year Book*.

[1] European Court of Human Rights (ECHR), judgment of 26 September 1995, Series A, No. 323, decided by a Grand Chamber.

opinion that both provisions had been violated. The Commission and the Government then referred the case to the Court.

The main issue in this case concerned Article 10, which provides:

1. Everyone has the right to freedom of expression. This right shall include freedom to hold opinions and to receive and impart information and ideas without interference by public authority and regardless of frontiers. This Article shall not prevent States from requiring the licensing of broadcasting, television or cinema enterprises.

2. The exercise of these freedoms, since it carries with it duties and responsibilities, may be subject to such formalities, conditions, restrictions or penalties as are prescribed by law and are necessary in a democratic society, in the interests of national security, territorial integrity or public safety, for the prevention of disorder or crime, for the protection of health or morals, for the protection of the reputation or rights of others, for preventing the disclosure of information received in confidence, or for maintaining the authority and impartiality of the judiciary.

The Court began by considering the applicability of this provision. In the *Glasenapp* and *Kosiek* cases,[2] where the same federal legislation had been challenged, the Court held Article 10 to be inapplicable. However, it distinguished those cases here on the ground that they had involved access to the civil service, which the Convention does not protect, whereas the present case involved dismissal.[3] As the Court had emphasized in the earlier cases, the Convention's guarantees exist to protect civil servants no less than other citizens. It followed that Mrs Vogt was entitled to rely on Article 10.

The next question was whether the interference with her right to freedom of expression could be justified under Article 10(2). The Court found that the measure complained of was 'prescribed by law' and also that it pursued legitimate aims, namely protecting national security, preventing disorder and protecting the rights of others. On this second point the Court noted the relevance of Germany's political history and specifically the adoption of the principle that it should be a 'democracy capable of defending itself' (*wehrhafte Demokratie*). The key issue, as in most cases involving limitations to the Convention's guarantees, was therefore whether the treatment of Mrs Vogt was 'necessary in a democratic society' for the achievement of the above aim and, specifically, whether it should be considered disproportionate.

After reiterating the principles laid down in its earlier case law, including the central importance of freedom of expression, the Court reviewed the facts of the case. It noted that the reference to 'duties and responsibilities' in Article 10(2) has a special significance for members of the civil service and that this justifies leaving the national authorities a certain margin of appreciation. On the other hand, even in the light of Germany's history, the duty of loyalty laid down in Germany was exceptionally strict. Dismissing a teacher was a severe sanction; there was no suggestion that Mrs Vogt's political views had influenced her teaching; the DKP was a lawful organization and there was no evidence that the applicant had ever made unconstitutional statements. In the light of these

---

[2] ECHR, judgments of 28 August 1986, Series A, Nos. 104 and 105, and this *Year Book*, 57 (1986), p. 466.

[3] Judgment, para. 44. See, however, the dissenting opinion of Judge Jambrek, para. 7, and the supplementary dissenting opinion of Judge Gotchev.

factors the Court concluded that Mrs Vogt's dismissal had been disproportionate. It therefore concluded that there had been a violation of Article 10.
The other claim concerned Article 11, which provides:

1. Everyone has the right to freedom of peaceful assembly and to freedom of association
with others, including the right to form and to join trade unions for the protection of his
interests.
2. No restriction shall be placed on the exercise of these rights other than such as are
prescribed by law and are necessary in a democratic society in the interests of national
security or public safety, for the prevention of disorder or crime, for the protection of
health or morals of for the protection of the rights and freedoms of others. This Article
shall not prevent the imposition of lawful restrictions on the exercise of these rights by
members of the armed forces, of the police or of the administration of the State.

The issues here were very similar to those considered under Article 10. Again
the protected right had been interfered with and so the question was one of
justification. It will be noted that Article 11(2) closely resembles Article 10(2),
although the last sentence is different. The Court, however, considered that the
reference to the 'administration of the State' should be interpreted narrowly
with account taken of the nature of the individual's work. Moreover, even if
teachers were to be regarded as included, Mrs Vogt's dismissal must be regarded
as disproportionate to the legitimate aim pursed. The Court therefore concluded
that there had also been a violation of Article 11.

The decision of the Grand Chamber was arrived at by the narrowest majority
and the nine judges who dissented[4] explained that they had done so because they
regarded Mrs Vogt's dismissal as within the respondent's margin of appreciation. There is, as they pointed out, an obvious contradiction involved in
professing loyalty to the constitutional order, while actively supporting a
political party financed from abroad and devoted to installing a communist
government. However, there is perhaps also a certain contradiction between
allowing a party such as the DKP to exist and at the same time seeking to
penalize anyone who supports it and happens to be a State employee. Sacking a
person on grounds of security or for incompetence is one thing, dismissing
someone for extramural political activity is another, which according to the
majority cannot be reconciled with the Convention.

*Right to life (Article 2)—shooting of IRA members by the SAS—when killing can
be justified under Article 2(2)(a)—just satisfaction (Article 50)*

Case No. 2. McCann and others case.[5] In this case, which concerned the
United Kingdom, the Court held by 10 votes to 9 that there had been a violation
of Article 2 of the Convention. As just satisfaction under Article 50 the
Government was ordered to pay the applicants £38,700, less the sums paid by
the Council of Europe as legal aid, in respect of their costs and expenses.

[4] See the joint dissenting opinion of Judges Bernhardt, Gölcüklü, Matscher, Loizou, Mifsud
Bonnici, Gotchev, Jungwiert and Kuris, and the dissenting opinion of Judge Jambrek. It is
interesting to note that the Grand Chamber for this case included four judges from former
communist States (Judges Gotchev, Jungwiert, Kuris and Jambrek) and that all four voted against
the judgment.
[5] ECHR, judgment of 27 September 1995, Series A, No. 324, decided by a Grand Chamber.

The applicants in this case were the parents of S, M and F, three members of the Provisional IRA, who in March 1988 were shot dead in Gibraltar by members of the SAS, which is part of the British Army. The killings took place because intelligence information had indicated that a car bomb was to be detonated in Gibraltar by a remote control device. When S left a car in Gibraltar it was decided to arrest all three before they crossed the border into Spain, but when arrests were attempted S, M and F made movements which led the soldiers to believe that they were about to detonate the bomb, and so they were shot and killed. S, M and F were not in fact carrying any remote control devices, or weapons, and the car contained no explosives. They were, however, members of an IRA active service unit and had left a car containing explosives in Spain with the intention of using it in Gibraltar. At an inquest into the killings in Gibraltar in September 1988 the jury returned verdicts of lawful killing. An attempt to bring an action against the Ministry of Defence arising out of the above events in the High Court in Northern Ireland was unsuccessful.

In their application to the Commission in August 1991 the applicants relied on Article 2 of the Convention which protects the right to life. In its report in March 1994 the Commission by a majority expressed the opinion that this provision had not been violated. The Commission then referred the case to the Court.

Article 2 of the Convention provides:

1. Everyone's right to life shall be protected by law. No one shall be deprived of his life intentionally save in the execution of a sentence of a court following his conviction of a crime for which this penalty is provided by law.
2. Deprivation of life shall not be regarded as inflicted in contravention of this Article when it results from the use of force which is no more than absolutely necessary:
   (a) in defence of any person from unlawful violence;
   (b) in order to effect a lawful arrest or to prevent the escape of a person lawfully detained;
   (c) in action lawfully taken for the purpose of quelling a riot or insurrection.

This is the first case in which the Court has been required to apply Article 2[6] and so it began the judgment with a number of general observations. Stating that Article 2 is one of the most fundamental provisions of the Convention, the Court indicated that the exceptions in paragraph 2 cover both intentional and unintentional killing and in the former case require the most careful scrutiny, taking into account not only the actions of the agents of the State, but also the surrounding circumstances, including such matters as the planning and control of the actions in question.

Addressing first the obligation of the State to protect life in Article 2(1), the Court ruled that Article 2 of the Gibraltar Constitution, which covers the right to life and lays down the relevant national standard, was compatible with the Convention. It also held that effective protection of the right to life calls for proper procedures for reviewing the lawfulness of any use of lethal force, but

---

[6] However, issues closely related to Article 2 were discussed by the Court in the *Soering* case, Series A, No. 161, and this *Year Book*, 60 (1989), p. 552, and the *Open Door and Dublin Well Woman* case, Series A, No. 246, and this *Year Book*, 64 (1993), p. 491.

decided that the inquest, which had been very thorough, had fulfilled this requirement.[7]

The Court then considered the application of Article 2 to the particular events. Noting that the facts themselves were uncontested, the Court rejected the applicants' argument that the killings were premeditated executions, then turned to what it regarded as the crucial issue in the case, viz. the conduct and planning of the operation. The Court recognized that the situation was difficult. The authorities had to protect the people of Gibraltar, while using minimum resort to lethal force. The ruthlessness of the IRA was known, but the authorities had time to plan their reaction, although their information was also limited. How, then, should the operation be assessed?

The Court exonerated the soldiers who had carried out the shootings on the ground that they honestly believed that it was necessary to shoot the suspects in order to prevent them detonating a bomb, which was what they had been led to believe. However, it was more critical of the planning of the operation. It questioned why the suspects had not been arrested when they entered Gibraltar, and noted that a number of erroneous assumptions concerning the details of the bombers' plan had been made. In the Court's view there had been insufficient allowance for other possibilities and this omission was especially significant in the light of the soldiers' training which was to shoot to kill, as a consequence of which their 'reflex action' lacked 'the degree of caution in the use of firearms to be expected from law enforcement personnel in a democratic society'.[8] In view of these factors the Court rejected the argument that the killing of the three terrorists constituted a use of force which was no more than absolutely necessary in defence of persons from unlawful violence within the meaning of Article 2(2)(a). It therefore concluded that there had been a breach of Article 2.

The only remaining issue was just satisfaction under Article 50, which provides:

> If the Court finds that a decision or a measure taken by a legal authority or any other authority of a High Contracting Party is completely or partially in conflict with the obligations arising from the . . . Convention, and if the internal law of the said Party allows only partial reparation to be made for the consequences of this decision or measure, the decision of the Court shall, if necessary, afford just satisfaction to the injured party.

The applicants sought a sum as financial compensation, but as S, M and F had been intending to plant a bomb in Gibraltar, the Court, not surprisingly, rejected this part of their claim. Its award under Article 50 was therefore limited to the applicants' costs and expenses.

This was the first of eleven cases involving the United Kingdom decided in the period under review[9] and in political terms was certainly the most controversial. Reaction to the decision in Government circles was a mixture of outrage and bafflement, but dispassionate analysis indicates that neither response can really be justified. Far from encouraging terrorism, as some have suggested, the judgment accepted almost all of the arguments put forward by the

---

[7] Evidence in support of the applicants' submissions on this point was given by Amnesty International and a number of other human rights organizations.

[8] Judgment, para. 212. But see also the joint dissenting opinion, paras. 21 to 24.

[9] See Cases Nos. 5, 6, 9, 12, 13, 15, 19, 20, 37 and 51.

Government and placed the finding of a violation on the narrowest possible ground. That nine members of the Grand Chamber could take a different view[10] demonstrates not that the reasoning of the majority was necessarily flawed, but rather that when issues are finely balanced, judges are always likely to disagree about the significance of different factors and the latitude available to the authorities.[11]

Right to the peaceful enjoyment of possessions (Article 1 of Protocol No. 1)—retrospective legislation removing a cause of action—just satisfaction (Article 50)

Case No. 3. Pressos Compania Naviera SA and others case.[12] In this case, which concerned Belgium, the Court held by 8 votes to 1 that retrospective legislation dealing with liability for shipping accidents had resulted in a violation of Article 1 of Protocol No. 1 to the Convention. As just satisfaction the Court awarded the applicants 8,000,000 Belgian francs in respect of their costs and expenses.

The twenty-six applicants in this case were shipowners, mutual insurance associations of shipowners and the trustee in bankruptcy of a shipping company. All had brought actions for damages against the Belgian State and a private pilot services operator following shipping accidents in the Scheldt estuary, and at the time of the present case most of these actions were still pending. In 1983 the Court of Cassation, in a decision which changed the legal position, held that the owner or the charterer of a ship which suffered an accident while a pilot was on board could sue the organizer of the pilot service for compensation. In 1988, however, this decision was reversed by an Act which was given thirty years' retroactive effect. Attempts to challenge the Act in the Belgian courts were unsuccessful.

In their application to the Commission in January 1991 the applicants complained *inter alia* of violations of Article 1 of Protocol No. 1 and Article 6(1). In its report in July 1994 the Commission expressed the opinion that the first of these provisions had been violated, but that there had been no violation of Article 6(1), except in respect of two of the applicants. The Commission and the Government then referred the case to the Court.

After noting that one of the applicants had elected not to pursue its claim, and dismissing a preliminary objection from the Government relating to the exhaustion of domestic remedies (Article 26), the Court turned to the main issue in the case which concerned Article 1 of Protocol No. 1. This provides:

Every natural or legal person is entitled to the peaceful enjoyment of his possessions. No one shall be deprived of his possessions except in the public interest and subject to the conditions provided for by law and by the general principles of international law.

The preceding provisions shall not, however, in any way impair the right of a State to

[10] See the joint dissenting opinion of Judges Ryssdal, Bernhardt, Thór Vilhjálmsson, Gölcüklü, Palm, Pekkanen, Sir John Freeland, Baka and Jambrek.
[11] Such divisions of opinion have been particularly prominent in cases involving action against terrorism. See, for example, the *Murray* case, Series A, No. 300A, and this *Year Book*, 66 (1995), p. 522.
[12] ECHR, judgment of 20 November 1995, Series A, No. 332, decided by a Chamber.

enforce such laws as it deems necessary to control the use of property in accordance with the general interest or to secure the payment of taxes or other contributions or penalties.

The applicants' complaint was that the 1988 Act violated this provision in two respects. By limiting liability for negligence it imposed an excessive burden on the applicants; and because it was retrospective it deprived them of their claims for compensation. On the second point the Government denied that any 'possession' of the applicants had been affected and maintained that Article 1 was inapplicable. The Court, however, followed the Commission's view and its previous case law[13] and rejected the submission. Since the Court was satisfied that there had been an 'interference' with the applicants' right, the case turned on whether the interference could be justified.

In determining what is 'in the public interest' the Court has always granted the national authorities a significant margin of appreciation.[14] Satisfied that this requirement was fulfilled, the Court found that the key issue in the present case was that of proportionality. The Government argued that the 1988 Act was needed because the 1983 judgment of the Court of Cassation had enormous financial implications, had created considerable uncertainty and made Belgian law different from that of its neighbours. The Court rejected the uncertainty point and held that the other considerations could have warranted prospective legislation, but did not justify retrospectively depriving the applicants of their claims for compensation. Finding that the interference was therefore disproportionate, the Court concluded that there had been a violation of Article 1 of Protocol No. 1.

Noting that the applicants' complaints under Article 6(1), which concerned the right to a fair trial, overlapped with those they had raised under Article 1, the Court decided that it was unnecessary to rule on these complaints.[15] As regards just satisfaction, the Court awarded the applicants a substantial sum in respect of their costs and expenses, but found that it was necessary for the Belgian courts to establish liability and damage in respect of the applicants' accident claims. It therefore held that the question of compensation for damage was not ready for decision.

Judge Thór Vilhjálmsson dissented on the ground that when all the circumstances were taken into account the interference with the applicants' rights had not been shown to be disproportionate. As he pointed out, the Convention does not prohibit retrospective legislation in the civil sphere; consequently cases like this are always likely to generate disagreement. It is otherwise, of course, in the criminal law where the *SW* and *CR* cases (Cases Nos. 5 and 6) and *G* v. *France* (Case No. 23) show the questions which can arise under Article 7. In the period under review the Court decided a good many other cases involving Article 1 of Protocol No. 1: see the *Velosa Barreto* case (Case No. 4); the *Phocas* case (Case No. 16); the *Gustaffson* case (Case No. 18); the *Spadea and Scalabrino* case (Case

---

[13] See the *Pine Valley Developments and others* case, Series A, No. 222, and this *Year Book*, 63 (1992), p. 551.

[14] See, for example, the *James and others* case, Series A, No. 98, and this *Year Book*, 57 (1986), p. 450.

[15] In a separate opinion Judge De Meyer indicated that he considered that Article 6(1) had been violated.

No. 24); the *Scollo* case (Case No. 25); the *British American Tobacco Company* case (Case No. 35); and the *Agrotexim* case (Case No. 52).

Right to respect for private and family life (Article 8)—right to the peaceful enjoyment of possessions (Article 1 of Protocol No. 1)—restriction on a landlord's right to terminate his tenant's lease

Case No. 4. *Velosa Barreto* case.[16] The Court held by 8 votes to 1 that the Portuguese courts had not infringed the applicant's rights under either Article 8 of the Convention, or Article 1 of Protocol No. 1, when they prevented him from recovering possession of a house which he had let, and now wished to live in.

The applicant, who married in 1979 and had a child in 1980, lived with his family at the home of his wife's parents. One of his wife's brothers and two of her aunts also lived there at various times. The house had four bedrooms, a kitchen, a living-cum-dining room and a basement. In 1982 he inherited his parents' house which for nearly twenty years had been let to a man who lived there with his wife. In 1983 the applicant began proceedings to evict the tenant, claiming that he wished to live in the house with his family. In 1989, however, a local court gave judgment against him on the ground that he had not proved he really needed the house. On appeal, this ruling was upheld on the ground that the house where the applicant currently lived was large enough for all the people who resided there.

In his application to the Commission in March 1991 Mr Velosa Barreto relied exclusively on Article 8 of the Convention, which guarantees respect for private and family life. However, in its decision on admissibility the Commission expressed the view that the case would also be considered under Article 1 of Protocol No. 1, which provides for the right to the peaceful enjoyment of possessions. In its report in June 1994 the Commission, by a majority, expressed the opinion that there had been a violation of Article 8, but not of Article 1 of the Protocol. The Commission and the Government then referred the case to the Court.

Article 8 of the Convention provides:

1. Everyone has the right to respect for his private and family life, his home and his correspondence.
2. There shall be no interference by a public authority with the exercise of this right except such as is in accordance with the law and is necessary in a democratic society in the interests of national security, public safety or the economic well-being of the country, for the prevention of disorder or crime, for the protection of health or morals, or for the protection of the rights and freedoms of others.

In its extensive case law the Court has established that the object of this provision is to protect the individual against arbitrary interference by the public authorities, but that it can also give rise to positive obligations, particularly the obligation to ensure respect for private and family life, even in the sphere of

---

[16] ECHR, judgment of 21 November 1995, Series A, No. 334, decided by a Chamber.

interpersonal relations.[17] In such cases a fair balance must be struck between the general interest and the interest of the individuals concerned.[18] In the present case the decisions complained of had prevented the applicant from living in the house as he intended. However, in the Court's view, 'effective protection of respect for private and family life cannot require the existence in national law of legal protection enabling each family to have a home for themselves alone. *It does not go so far as to place the State under an obligation to give a landlord the right to recover possession of a rented house on request and in any circumstance.*'[19]

Finding that the legislation in question pursed a legitimate aim, namely the protection of tenants, the Court observed that the only point in issue was whether, when deciding on the applicant's need, the Portuguese courts had infringed his right to respect for his private and family life. It decided that they had not, because both courts had considered the various questions of fact and law and carefully examined the arguments. In particular, they had taken into account an improvement in the applicant's situation when his wife's brother and two of her aunts had moved away. Since the courts had not acted arbitrarily, and had sought to strike the necessary fair balance, the Court decided that there had been no violation of Article 8.

The other issue concerned Article 1 of Protocol No. 1, which was quoted in Case No. 3. The Court held that this provision was applicable, since the restriction on the applicant's right to terminate the lease amounted to control of the use of his property. However, it pointed out that the application of this provision involved the same requirement of a 'fair balance' that the Court had already considered in relation to Article 8. It therefore concluded that there had been no violation of Article 1.

Judge Gotchev dissented on both issues, holding that the right to establish an independent family home is a basic element of both Article 8 and Article 1 of Protocol No. 1. This is a persuasive view, but the present decision should be compared with those in the *Spadea and Scalabrino* case (Case No. 24) and the *Scollo* case (Case No. 25) where this aspect of Article 1 was again considered. Article 8 was examined in two other cases in the period under review: the *Gül* case (Case No. 10), and the *Boughanemi* case (Case No. 47).

Protection against retroactive law (Article 7(1))—application to convictions for marital rape

Cases Nos. 5 and 6. SW v. *United Kingdom. CR* v. *United Kingdom.*[20] In these cases, which concerned developments in the law relating to marital rape in the United Kingdom, the Court held unanimously that there had been no violation of Article 7 of the Convention.

[17] See, for example, *X and Y* v. *Netherlands*, Series A, No. 91, and this *Year Book*, 56 (1985), p. 344. See also Merrills, *The Development of International Law by the European Court of Human Rights* (2nd edn., 1993), pp. 104–5.

[18] See, for example, the *Gaskin* case, Series A, No. 160, and this *Year Book*, 60 (1989), p. 549. See also Robertson and Merrills, *Human Rights in Europe* (3rd edn., 1993), pp. 135–6.

[19] Judgment, para. 24 (emphasis added).

[20] ECHR, judgments of 22 November 1995, Series A, Nos. 335B and 335C, decided by the same Chamber.

The facts of these cases were very similar. In each case after a long period of marital difficulties the applicant sexually assaulted his wife. In SW's case this occurred when she threatened to leave him and in CR's case after they had been living apart. SW was charged with rape, threatening to kill and assault; CR with attempted rape and assault. Both applicants were convicted on all charges and given custodial sentences. When CR was tried in July 1990, he argued that the common law did not recognize the offence of marital rape. However, the trial judge rejected this defence on the ground that CR's conduct fell within exceptions to this immunity established in the case law. On appeal the Court of Appeal confirmed the conviction on the wider ground that the immunity in question no longer existed, and this decision was subsequently confirmed by the House of Lords.[21] SW was tried in April 1991 after the decision of the Court of Appeal in the CR case and the trial judge, holding himself bound by that decision, ruled that it was not open to SW to rely on the immunity. In both cases the courts decided that the definition of rape in section 1(1) of the Sexual Offences (Amendment) Act 1976 was no obstacle to deciding that the marital immunity to rape no longer existed.[22]

In applications to the Commission in March 1992 both applicants relied on Article 7(1) of the Convention, which prohibits the retrospective creation of offences. In its reports in June 1994 the Commission, by majorities of 11 to 6 and 14 to 3, expressed the opinion that this provision had not been violated. The Commission then referred both cases to the Court.

Article 7(1) of the Convention provides:

No one shall be held guilty of any criminal offence on account of any act or omission which did not constitute a criminal offence under national or international law at the time when it was committed. Nor shall a heavier penalty be imposed than the one that was applicable at the time the criminal offence was committed.

Recent case law on this provision has been concerned with the scope of the second sentence and, in particular, with the meaning of the word 'penalty'.[23] The present cases raised a different, and more fundamental question about the first sentence and, as there has been little discussion of this in the Court's jurisprudence to date, it prefaced its treatment of the particular facts with a review of general principles.

Pointing out that the importance of Article 7 is underlined by the fact that no derogation from it is permitted under Article 15, the Court stated that it must be construed and applied 'in such a way as to provide effective safeguards against arbitrary prosecution, conviction and punishment'.[24] Thus, as explained in the *Kokkinakis* case,[25] it followed that only the law could define a crime and

---

[21] See *R* v. *R*, [1991] 1 All ER 747 (Owen J); [1991] 2 All ER 257 (CA); and [1991] 4 All ER 481 (HL).

[22] This provided that the offence of rape was committed where a man had 'unlawful sexual intercourse with a woman who at the time of the intercourse does not consent to it . . . '. In November 1994 the Criminal Justice and Public Order Act 1994 replaced this with a new provision which omitted the word 'unlawful'.

[23] See the *Welch* case, Series A, No. 307A, and the *Jamil* case, Series A, No. 320; this *Year Book*, 66 (1995), pp. 530 and 555.

[24] *SW* judgment, para. 34.

[25] ECHR, judgment of 25 May 1993, Series A, No. 260A, and this *Year Book*, 64 (1993), p. 519.

prescribe a penalty; that the criminal law should not be extensively construed to an accused's detriment; and that offences should be clearly defined. On the other hand, an element of judicial interpretation, elucidation and adaptation was inevitable in any legal system. Article 7 did not outlaw this process, so long as any development was 'consistent with the essence of the offence and could reasonably be foreseen'.[26]

Turning to the facts, the Court recalled that it is for the national authorities to interpret and apply national law, and saw no reason to disagree with the Court of Appeal's interpretation of the Sexual Offences (Amendment) Act 1976, which continued a line of case law dismantling the marital immunity for rape.[27] In view of the evolution of the law, total removal of the immunity had become a reasonably foreseeable development. Furthermore, the essentially debasing character of rape was so manifest that the decisions of the Court of Appeal and House of Lords could not be said to conflict with the object and purpose of Article 7, nor with the fundamental objectives of the Convention, namely respect for human dignity and freedom. The Court therefore concluded that neither applicant's conviction had violated Article 7(1).

The reasoning by which the Court supported its conclusion is generally convincing and few will disagree with its decision. The situation which prompted these applications is, however, most unsatisfactory. Given the seriousness of the offence in question, it cannot be right for the availability or otherwise of an important defence to depend on guesses about future decisions of the courts. While the law can never be completely certain, it does not seem unreasonable to regard issues of principle concerning the scope of rape and other serious offences as matters which should be settled in advance by Parliament.

In the period under review Article 7 was also considered in *G* v. *France* (Case No. 23) below.

Inhuman and degrading treatment (Article 3)—allegations of police violence—the burden of proof—just satisfaction (Article 50)

Case No. 7. Ribitsch case.[28] The Court held by 6 votes to 3 that there had been a violation of Article 3 of the Convention as a result of the applicant's treatment by the police while he was in custody in Austria. As just satisfaction the Government was ordered to pay the applicant 100,000 Austrian schillings as compensation for non-pecuniary damage, together with 200,000 schillings, less the sum paid by the Council of Europe as legal aid, in respect of his costs and expenses.

In May 1988 the Austrian police searched the flat where the applicant and his wife lived as part of a criminal investigation into two deaths from heroin overdoses. Ten days later after a further search the applicant and his wife were arrested and taken into police custody on suspicion of drug trafficking. When they were released, nearly 48 hours later, the applicant complained of ill-treatment to several people and on visiting the local hospital was found to have

---

[26] *SW* judgment, para. 36.
[27] For an outline of this evolution see the *SW* judgment, paras. 22–27.
[28] ECHR, judgment of 4 December 1995, Series A, No. 336, decided by a Chamber.

bruising on his right arm. Following broadcast reports of the incident, criminal proceedings were begun against three police officers, one of whom was convicted of assault occasioning bodily harm.

The officer concerned then appealed and, after a forensic report had been prepared indicating that the injury might have been caused by falling against a car door (as the defence had claimed), the appeal was allowed, partly for lack of physical evidence and partly because the appeal court regarded the applicant, who was unemployed and had a previous criminal conviction, as an untrustworthy witness. In further proceedings in the Constitutional Court the applicant's complaint regarding ill-treatment was rejected, although the court held that the applicant's arrest and detention, as well as the searches of his home, had all been unlawful.

In his application to the Commission in August 1991 Mr Ribitsch relied on several provisions of the Convention, including Article 3 (prohibition of inhuman and degrading treatment). In its report in July 1994 the Commission by a majority expressed the opinion that Article 3 had been violated. The Commission then referred the case to the Court.

Article 3 of the Convention provides:

> No one shall be subjected to torture or to inhuman or degrading treatment or punishment.

Cases involving this provision normally raise two issues: whether the alleged ill-treatment can be proved; and if it can, whether it is sufficiently serious to amount to 'inhuman or degrading treatment'. In the present case the Government did not deny that the applicant's injuries, if inflicted deliberately, were prohibited by Article 3, and the Court, in an important statement of principle, held that 'in respect of a person deprived of his liberty, any recourse to physical force which has not been made strictly necessary by his own conduct diminishes human dignity and is in principle an infringement of the right set forth in Article 3 of the Convention'.[29] Thus the crucial issue was that of proof.

In its decision in the *Tomasi* case[30] the Court decided that where an applicant suffers injuries whilst in police custody the onus is on the authorities to provide an explanation. However, if the matter has been fully investigated by the domestic courts, the Court will not usually undertake its own investigation.[31] The three members of the Court who dissented in the present case considered that this was the position here.[32] The Court, however, disagreed. Pointing out that the trial court and the appeal court had reached different conclusions, and that the latter had taken into account considerations relating to the applicant's circumstances and character unrelated to the incident complained of, it noted that the acquittal of the officer concerned was not in itself sufficient to discharge the authorities' obligation to provide a plausible explanation of the applicant's injuries. In view of the incomplete nature of the forensic evidence,[33]

---

[29] Judgment, para. 38.

[30] ECHR, judgment of 27 August 1992, Series A, No. 241A, and this *Year Book*, 63 (1992), p. 592.

[31] See the *Klaas* case, Series A, No. 269, and this *Year Book*, 65 (1994), p. 509.

[32] See the joint dissenting opinion of Judges Ryssdal, Matscher and Jambrek.

[33] In addition to the bruising on his arm the applicant alleged that he had suffered various other injuries which, if established, could not have been caused by falling against a car door.

it considered that they had failed to do this. It therefore concluded that there had been a violation of Article 3.

The only remaining issue was just satisfaction under Article 50. The applicant claimed a substantial sum as compensation for pecuniary loss and was supported by the Commission, which argued that 'a relatively high sum should be awarded in order to encourage people in the same position as Mr Ribitsch to bring court proceedings'.[34] The Court awarded Mr Ribitsch a significant sum, albeit less than he was claiming, together with his costs and expenses, but again on a reduced basis.

Right of access to the courts (Article 6(1))—the need for clarity in domestic law— just satisfaction (Article 50)

Case No. 8. Bellet case.[35] The Court held by 8 votes to 1 that the applicant had not had a practical, effective right of access to the French courts, with the result that there had been a violation of Article 6(1) of the Convention. As just satisfaction the respondent was ordered to pay the applicant 1,000,000 French francs as compensation for loss of opportunities and non-pecuniary damage, and 50,000 francs in respect of his costs and expenses.

The applicant in this case was a haemophiliac who became infected with HIV as a result of being exposed to contaminated blood or blood products. In 1991 he brought an action for damages against the National Blood Transfusion Foundation and in 1992 submitted a claim to the recently established Compensation Fund for Haemophiliacs and Transfusion Patients. Although the Compensation Fund made Mr Bellet an offer, which he accepted, he continued his legal action and in September 1992 was awarded damages totalling 1,500,000 francs. In 1993, however, the Paris Court of Appeal quashed this judgment on the ground that as the applicant had been fully compensated through the Compensation Fund, his action was inadmissible. In 1994 an attempt to challenge this ruling in the Court of Cassation was unsuccessful and in November 1995 Mr Bellet died.

In his application to the Commission in March 1994 Mr Bellet complained that he had been denied his right of access to a court, contrary to Article 6(1) of the Convention. In its report in January 1995 the Commission expressed the opinion that this provision had been violated. The Commission and the Government then referred the case to the Court.

The relevant part of Article 6(1) of the Convention lays down that:

In the determination of his civil rights and obligations . . . everyone is entitled to a . . . hearing by [a] . . . tribunal . . .

In the *Golder* case[36] in 1975 the Court decided that this provision confers a right of access to the courts and has subsequently indicated that while this right is not absolute, any limitation must ensure that the 'very essence' of the right is not impaired. In the present case Mr Bellet had accepted the offer from the

---

[34] Judgment, para. 45.
[35] ECHR, judgment of 4 December 1995, Series A, No. 333B, decided by a Chamber.
[36] ECHR, judgment of 21 February 1975, Series A, No. 18, and this *Year Book*, 47 (1973-4), p. 391.

Compensation Fund, while under the impression that his action for damages would be unaffected. The Court of Appeal, however, had ruled his claim inadmissible. Did this mean he had been denied his right of access to the courts?

The Court decided that it did, essentially on the ground that the legislation creating the Compensation Fund, when read in the light of the relevant parliamentary proceedings, appeared to suggest that claims for compensation could still be pursued through the courts. The Court of Appeal had decided otherwise, and while the European Court was not empowered to interpret French law, it stated that it must assess the adequacy of the system in the light of Article 6(1), and in particular decide whether the system was sufficiently clear, or sufficiently attended by safeguards, to avoid the possibility of misunderstanding. The Court recognized that the creation of a special compensation scheme for those infected with AIDS displayed 'a remarkable spirit of solidarity',[37] but following its own previous case law,[38] ruled that 'For the right of access to be effective, an individual must have a clear, practical opportunity to challenge an act that is an interference with his rights'.[39] Because that had not been provided, it decided that there had been a violation of Article 6(1).[40]

The sum awarded as just satisfaction represented the difference between the sum Mr Bellet received from the Compensation Fund and the sum he would have received from the Court of Appeal if it had held itself competent to address the merits.

Right to a fair trial (Article 6(1))—the presumption of innocence (Article 6(2))—the privilege against self-incrimination—the right to legal assistance (Article 6(3)(c))—just satisfaction (Article 50)

Case No. 9. Murray case.[41] The Court held by 14 votes to 5 that there had been no violation of Articles 6(1) and 6(2) of the Convention arising out of the drawing of adverse inferences from the applicant's silence during police interrogation and at his trial in Northern Ireland. It also held by 12 votes to 7 that there had been a violation of Article 6(1), taken in conjunction with Article 6(3)(c), as regards the applicant's lack of access to a lawyer during the first 48 hours of his police detention. As just satisfaction the applicant was awarded £15,000 in respect of his costs and expenses, less the sums granted by the Council of Europe by way of legal aid.

In January 1990 the applicant was arrested in a house in which an IRA informer had been held captive. Pursuant to the Northern Ireland (Emergency Provisions) Act 1987, the police decided to delay his access to a solicitor for 48

---

[37] Judgment, para. 33.

[38] See the *de Geoffre de la Pradelle* case, Series A, No. 253B, and this *Year Book*, 64 (1993), p. 505.

[39] Judgment, para. 36.

[40] Judge Pettiti delivered a dissenting opinion containing a detailed discussion of the relevant provisions of French law, and Judges Walsh, Pekkanen and Jambrek gave shorter concurring opinions.

[41] ECHR, judgment of 8 February 1996, decided by a Grand Chamber. Series A of the Court's publications was discontinued on 1 January 1996. Cases decided after that date will therefore be reported in a new publication entitled *Reports of Judgments and Decisions*.

hours on the ground that such access would interfere with police operations against terrorism. The applicant was cautioned under the Criminal Evidence (Northern Ireland) Order 1988 that adverse inferences might be drawn if he failed to answer questions at the pre-trial stage. The applicant was interviewed twelve times over two days, but remained silent. He saw a solicitor before the final two interviews, but the solicitor was not allowed to attend them. In May 1991 the applicant was tried before the Lord Chief Justice of Northern Ireland, sitting without a jury, convicted, and sentenced to eight years' imprisonment for aiding and abetting a false imprisonment. The judge, exercising his discretion under the 1988 Order, drew adverse inferences from the applicant's failure to explain his presence at the house and from his silence at the trial. An appeal against this conviction was dismissed.

In his application to the Commission in August 1991 Mr Murray complained *inter alia* of violations of Article 6(1), taken together with Articles 6(2) and 6(3)(c). In its report in June 1994 the Commission rejected the first claim, but accepted the second. The Commission and the Government then referred the case to the Court.

The relevant parts of Article 6 of the Convention provide:

1. In the determination of . . . any criminal charge against him, everyone is entitled to a fair and public hearing within a reasonable time by an independent and impartial tribunal established by law . . .
2. Everyone charged with a criminal offence shall be presumed innocent until proved guilty according to law.
3. Everyone charged with a criminal offence has the following minimum rights:
. . .
(c) to defend himself in person or through legal assistance of his own choosing or, if he has not sufficient means to pay for legal assistance, to be given it free when the interests of justice so require.

The Court began by considering the scope of the right to silence and its earlier ruling in the *Funke* case.[42] It pointed out that:

Although not specifically mentioned in Article 6 of the Convention, there can be no doubt that the right to remain silent under police questioning and the privilege against self-incrimination are generally recognised international standards which lie at the heart of the notion of a fair procedure under Article 6 . . . By providing the accused with protection against improper compulsion by the authorities these immunities contribute to avoiding miscarriages of justice and to securing the aims of Article 6.[43]

However, in an important ruling, the Court held that these immunities are not absolute. Rather, whether the drawing of adverse inferences from an accused's silence infringes Article 6 is a matter to be determined in the light of all the circumstances of the case, having particular regard to the situations where inferences may be drawn, the weight attached to them by the national courts, and the degree of compulsion inherent in the situation.

Turning to the particular facts, the Court pointed out that the applicant was able to remain silent and under the 1988 Order was a non-compellable witness. Moreover, domestic case law established that silence alone could not be regarded

[42] ECHR, judgment of 25 February 1993, Series A, No. 256A, and this *Year Book*, 64 (1993), p. 510.
[43] Judgment, para. 45.

as an admission of guilt, and the case was tried before an experienced judge. In addition, the drawing of inferences under the Order was subject to an important series of safeguards designed to respect the rights of the defence and limit the extent to which reliance could be placed on inferences. Thus it had been established that the question in each case is whether the evidence adduced by the prosecution is sufficiently strong to require an answer. Here there was a good deal of evidence against the accused, including evidence from the victim. Having regard to the weight of the evidence, drawing inferences from his refusal to provide an explanation was a matter of common sense and could not be regarded as unfair or unreasonable. Accordingly, it could not be said that drawing such inferences had shifted the burden of proof and infringed the presumption of innocence. The Court therefore decided that there had been no infringement of Articles 6(1) and 6(2).

The other issue in the case concerned the refusal to provide the applicant with access to a lawyer. The Court observed that Article 6(3) is relevant to pre-trial procedures where these may seriously prejudice the fairness of the trial.[44] In the Court's view, the scheme set out in the 1988 Order, and in particular the possibility of adverse inferences being drawn from silence, made it essential for an accused to have access to a lawyer during the initial stages of police interrogation. It therefore decided that there had been a violation of Article 6(1), taken in conjunction with Article 6(3)(c). However, finding that this ruling was in itself sufficient just satisfaction, it confined its award under Article 50 to a sum representing a proportion of the applicant's costs and expenses and declined to award him damages.

Five members of the Grand Chamber voted against the Court's decision on the scope of the right to silence[45] and seven against the ruling on Article 6(3)(c).[46] For the former, whose views were supported by comments from Amnesty International and a number of other human rights organizations,[47] the right to silence must be treated as absolute and the drawing of adverse inferences from silence always infringes the presumption of innocence. For the latter, on the other hand, the Court was wrong to rule that the scheme of the Order made access to a solicitor essential, and instead of basing itself on this general ground, should have considered whether, on the particular facts, withholding access had resulted in injustice. In effect, the Court's decision was a compromise between these positions, investing the right to silence with a relative character, but stipulating access to a lawyer as a necessary safeguard.

In the period under review Article 6(2) was also in issue in the *Leutscher* case (Case No. 46) and Article 6(3)(c) in the *Benham* case (Case No. 19).

---

[44] See the *Imbrioscia* case, Series A, No. 275, and this *Year Book*, 65 (1994), p. 516.

[45] See the partly dissenting opinion of Judge Walsh, joined by Judges Makarczyk and Löhmus, and the partly dissenting opinion of Judge Pettiti, joined by Judge Valticos.

[46] See the joint partly dissenting opinion of Judges Ryssdal, Matscher, Palm, Foighel, Sir John Freeland, Wildhaber and Jungwiert.

[47] These comments included references to the 1966 United Nations Covenant on Civil and Political Rights (Article 14(3)(g)); to the Rules of Procedure and Evidence of the International Criminal Tribunal for the Former Yugoslavia (Rule 42(A)); and to the Draft Statute for an International Criminal Court (Article 26(6)(a)(i)).

Right to respect for family life (Article 8)—application to immigration—the meaning of 'family life'—the scope of positive obligations—the margin of appreciation

Case No. 10. Gül case.[48] The Court held by 7 votes to 2 that the refusal of the Swiss authorities to allow the applicant's son to join him in Switzerland had not involved a breach of Article 8 of the Convention.

Until 1983 the applicant lived in Turkey with his wife and his two sons, T, born in 1971 and E, born in 1983. In 1983 he moved to Switzerland and applied for political asylum. In 1987 he was joined by his wife, who suffered from epilepsy, and in 1989 the applicant, his wife and a daughter, born in 1988, were granted a residence permit on humanitarian grounds. The applicant then requested permission for T and E to join him in Switzerland but this was refused, mainly on the grounds that his flat was unsuitable and his means insufficient to provide for his family. In 1991 an appeal against this decision was dismissed, the cantonal government taking the view that as the holder of a residence permit, the applicant had no right to be joined by the other members of his family. As regards E, the authorities concluded that the applicant had insufficient means to support him in Switzerland and that his wife was incapable of looking after him.[49] A further appeal was dismissed in 1993.

In his application to the Commission in December 1993 Mr Gül complained *inter alia* of a violation of Article 8 as regards E. In its report in April 1995 the Commission by a majority expressed the opinion that this provision had been violated. The Commission and the Government then referred the case to the Court.

It will be recalled from the *Velosa Barreto* case (Case No. 4) that Article 8 protects the right to respect for family life. In the present case there were two questions: whether this provision was applicable, which depended on whether in relation to E 'family life' had been established; and, if so, whether the Swiss authorities had interfered with the applicant's right. As regards the first question, the Court's case law establishes that a bond amounting to family life is created on the birth of a child to a married couple and that only exceptional events can break this link.[50] Here the applicant had left Turkey when E was only three months old, but had repeatedly sought to bring him to Switzerland as well as making a number of visits to Turkey. The Court was therefore satisfied that the bond of 'family life' had not been broken.

The second question was more difficult. As regards both the positive and the negative obligations of the State under Article 8, the Court has indicated that a balance must be struck between the interests of the individual and those of the community[51] and that the State enjoys a certain margin of appreciation. The latter is particularly significant in immigration cases because 'as a matter of well established international law and subject to its treaty obligations, a State has the

---

[48] ECHR, judgment of 19 February 1996, decided by a Chamber.

[49] On account of her epilepsy, Mrs Gül had never been able to look after her daughter, who since birth had been cared for in a home in Switzerland.

[50] See, for example, the *Hokkanen* case, Series A, No. 299 A, and this *Year Book*, 66 (1995), p. 547.

[51] See, for example, the *Velosa Barreto* case (Case No. 4, above).

right to control the entry of non-nationals into its territory'.[52] Furthermore, the Court has also laid down that where immigration is concerned, Article 8 does not impose an obligation to respect a married couple's choice of their country of matrimonial residence, nor does it always require family reunion.[53]

Reviewing the facts, the Court pointed out that Mr Gül had brought about the separation from E by leaving Turkey and his recent visits to that country suggested that his reasons for applying for political asylum were no longer valid. The applicant currently received various social security benefits in Switzerland, but most of these would continue to be payable if he returned to Turkey. As regards Mrs Gül, it had not been shown that she could not receive medical treatment if she returned to Turkey and she had recently visited the country with her husband. In addition, the applicant and his wife did not have a permanent right of abode in Switzerland and could, if they wished, establish their family life in Turkey, where E had always lived. In these circumstances the Court, whilst acknowledging that the Güls' family situation was 'very difficult from the human point of view',[54] found that Switzerland had not interfered with the applicant's family life. It therefore decided that there had been no violation of Article 8.

Judge Martens, with whom Judge Russo agreed, dissented, maintaining that the Commission had been correct to identify the issue as whether the Government's actions could be justified under Article 8(2), and that when full account was taken of the circumstances, they could not. Immigration has presented the Court with some particularly delicate questions and it is perhaps not surprising that the majority preferred a cautious approach. Cases in which there is a challenge to the expulsion of an alien raise issues under Article 8 parallel to those considered here, and the present decision should be compared with that in *Boughanemi* (Case No. 47), where the Court was again divided.

Right to a fair hearing (Article 6(1))—role of the procureur du Roi *in civil proceedings in Belgium—precedent—just satisfaction (Article 50)*

Case No. 11. Vermeulen case.[55] The Court held by 15 votes to 4 that proceedings in the Court of Cassation in Belgium had infringed the applicant's right to adversarial proceedings, contrary to Article 6(1) of the Convention. As just satisfaction, the respondent was ordered to pay the applicant 250,000 Belgian francs in respect of his costs and expenses.

In 1987 the applicant was adjudged bankrupt and his business consultancy declared insolvent. After an unsuccessful appeal against this decision, the case was referred to the Court of Cassation, which rejected the applicant's arguments. At the end of the hearing a submission had been presented by the *avocat général*, who had also taken part in the Court's deliberations.

In his application to the Commission in November 1991 Mr Vermeulen claimed *inter alia* that the participation in the proceedings of the *avocat général*,

---

[52] Judgment, para. 38.

[53] See the *Abdulaziz, Cabales and Balkandali* case, Series A, No. 94, and this *Year Book*, 56 (1985), p. 352.

[54] Judgment, para. 42.

[55] ECHR, judgment of 20 February 1996, decided by a Grand Chamber.

a member of the *procureur général's* department, had violated his right to adversarial proceedings, as guaranteed by Article 6(1). In its report in October 1994 the Commission, by a majority, expressed the opinion that this provision had been violated. The Commission and the Government then referred the case to the Court.

In the *Borgers* case[56] in 1991 the Court held that a violation of Article 6(1) had occurred when the Belgian *avocat général* made submissions to which a defendant in criminal proceedings was unable to reply, and was subsequently present during the court's deliberations. The only question in the present case was whether a similar prohibition operates in civil cases. The Belgian Government maintained that it did not, arguing that the function of the *procureur général's* department was to advise the court independently and that in civil proceedings the *avocat général* could not possibly be perceived as a litigant's ally or opponent. The Court, however, disagreed. Although recognizing that the *procureur général's* department acted with complete objectivity, the Court found that its role was identical in civil and criminal cases and pointed out that its advice would clearly affect the applicant's position. Accordingly, the Court considered that the same principle must apply in both civil and criminal cases and therefore concluded that Article 6(1) had been violated.

As just satisfaction the applicant claimed a considerable sum in respect of alleged pecuniary and non-pecuniary damage, but the Court agreed with the Government and the Commission that no case for compensation had been made out. It therefore awarded Mr Vermeulen only his costs and expenses.

The importance of this case is indicated by its reference to a Grand Chamber, and the controversial nature of the point in issue by the fact that four judges dissented.[57] In their view it was not illogical to treat civil and criminal proceedings differently, especially when the Belgian system was based on a tradition which the institution of the Advocate-General at the Court of Justice of the European Communities and the role of the Commission at Strasbourg show to be by no means dead. There is force in this argument, but in another decision on the same day, *Lobo Machado* (Case No. 42), a differently composed Grand Chamber unanimously followed the present decision. Accordingly, the point must now be regarded as settled.

Right to take proceedings to challenge the lawfulness of detention (Article 5(4))—application to detention of juveniles during Her Majesty's pleasure—just satisfaction (Article 50)

Cases Nos. 12 and 13. Singh case. *Hussain* case.[58] In these cases, which concerned the United Kingdom, the Court held unanimously that there had been a violation of Article 5(4) of the Convention because the applicants, who had both been sentenced to be detained during Her Majesty's pleasure, were

---

[56] ECHR, judgment of 30 October 1991, Series A, No. 214B, and this *Year Book*, 63 (1992), p. 538. For the significance of this decision see Merrills, *The Development of International Law by the European Court of Human Rights* (2nd edn., 1993), pp. 189–90.

[57] See the joint dissenting opinion of Judges Gölcüklü, Matscher and Pettiti and the dissenting opinion of *ad hoc* Judge Van Campernolle.

[58] ECHR, decisions of 21 February 1996, decided by the same Chamber.

unable to have the lawfulness of their continued detention or redetention reviewed by a court. As just satisfaction the applicants were awarded £13,000 and £19,000 respectively as compensation for their legal costs and expenses, subject in each case to the amounts received by way of legal aid.

The applicants, when aged 15 and 16 respectively, were separately convicted of murder and on account of their youth sentenced to be detained during Her Majesty's pleasure. Mr Singh was released on licence in 1990 after he had been detained for seventeen years, but his licence was then revoked for alleged misbehaviour and he was redetained on the recommendation of the Parole Board. Mr Hussain's case was considered by the Parole Board on four occasions during his detention, but initially he was not allowed to see the reports which the Board considered. He was eventually transferred to an open prison.

In their applications in March 1993 and January 1994 the applicants relied on Article 5(4) of the Convention, which guarantees the right to take proceedings to challenge the lawfulness of detention. In its reports in October 1994 the Commission expressed the unanimous opinion that this provision had been violated. The Commission and the Government then referred the cases to the Court.

Article 5(4) of the Convention provides:

> Everyone who is deprived of his liberty by arrest or detention shall be entitled to take proceedings by which the lawfulness of his detention shall be decided speedily by a court and his release ordered if the detention is not lawful.

There has been a good deal of case law on this provision, much of it involving the United Kingdom. This has established, on the one hand, that an adult who is given a mandatory life sentence cannot rely on Article 5(4) because the element of judicial control required by this provision is incorporated in the original conviction,[59] and, on the other, that one who receives a discretionary life sentence can rely on Article 5(4) because once the initial tariff has expired, detention can only be justified by a finding of continued dangerousness, which should be open to challenge at reasonable intervals.[60] In the present cases the government argued that the situation was like that in the mandatory life sentence cases, and the applicants that the parallel was with the discretionary life sentence cases. Not surprisingly, the Court agreed with the Commission that the Government's argument must be rejected. After the initial tariff period, the applicants' detention could only be justified by the need to protect the public, and this necessarily required an assessment of the applicants' character and mental state which were susceptible to change over time. Accordingly, the applicants were entitled to take proceedings to have these issues decided by a court at reasonable intervals and Article 5(4) applied. Finding that neither the Parole Board's limited powers to recommend release, nor its procedures, satisfied the requirements of Article 5(4), the Court held unanimously that the Convention had been violated and awarded the applicants their costs and expenses.[61]

---

[59] See the *Wynne* case, Series A, No. 294A, and this *Year Book*, 65 (1994), p. 545.

[60] See the case of *Thynne, Wilson and Gunnell*, Series A, No. 190A, and this *Year Book*, 62 (1991), p. 479. The 'tariff' is a period of detention set by the Home Secretary for the purposes of retribution and deterrence.

[61] Claims for compensation for damage were rejected, however.

This was an entirely predictable decision. If the Government expected to win, it was poorly advised; if it did not, instead of wasting the Court's time with casuistry, it should have changed the law.

In the period under review there was only one other case involving Article 5(4), the *Iribarne Pérez* case (Case No. 34).

Right to a fair hearing (Article 6(1))—right to examine witnesses (Article 6(3)(d))—anonymous witnesses—role of the domestic courts

Case No. 14. Doorson case.[62] In this case, which concerned a criminal trial in the Netherlands, the Court held by 7 votes to 2 that various restrictions on the rights of the defence had involved no violation of Article 6(1) of the Convention, taken together with Article 6(3)(d).

In 1988 the applicant was convicted of various drug offences and in 1989 the Amsterdam Court of Appeal, after quashing the trial court's judgment, made a fresh assessment of the evidence and again found the applicant guilty. In reaching its decision the Court of Appeal took into account the evidence of four witnesses: A and B, who had been heard anonymously; C, who had implicated the applicant, but withdrawn his statement in court; and D who had also implicated the applicant in a statement to the police, but had then disappeared. The Court of Appeal also refused to hear evidence from an expert, E, called by the defence, while admitting evidence from F, a prosecution witness, on the same subject.

In his application to the Commission in June 1992 Mr Doorson relied on a number of provisions of the Convention, including Article 6(1) and Article 6(3)(d). In its report in October 1994 the Commission expressed the opinion by a narrow majority that these provisions had not been violated. The Commission then referred the case to the Court.

Article 6(1) of the Convention, which was quoted in Case No. 9, guarantees the right to a fair trial and Article 6(3) provides:

3. Everyone charged with a criminal offence has the following minimum rights:

. . .

(d) to examine or have examined witnesses against him and to obtain the attendance and examination of witnesses on his behalf under the same conditions as witnesses against him.

Since the requirements of Article 6(3) are particular aspects of the right to a fair trial guaranteed by Article 6(1), the Court normally considers the two provisions together and it adopted that approach here. It is also well established that the admissibility of evidence is primarily a matter for national law, as is its assessment. Thus the Court's task in cases of this type is not to substitute its own evaluation for that of the national courts, but to ascertain whether the proceedings as a whole, including of course the way the evidence was taken, have been fair.

The first and most difficult question concerned the evidence of the anonymous witnesses, A and B. The use of such evidence has been considered in earlier

---

[62] ECHR, judgment of 26 March 1996, decided by a Chamber.

cases and the Court has indicated that whilst anonymity is in principle undesirable, it may nevertheless be acceptable when it is necessary in the interests of witnesses or victims, and appropriate safeguards are provided.[63] Here the Court was satisfied that anonymity had been guaranteed in order to persuade A and B to give evidence without fear of reprisals. Furthermore, the investigating judge had been aware of the witnesses' identities and the applicant's counsel had been able to question them. A and B had identified the applicant from a photograph and had described him accurately. Finally, the applicant's conviction had not been based wholly or largely on their evidence and the Court of Appeal had used it cautiously. The Court therefore decided that the Convention had been complied with.

The second question concerned the evidence of C, who had retracted his statement, and D, who had disappeared. As regards C, the Court rejected the view that evidence given in court must always be relied on in preference to earlier statements; and as regards D, the Court was satisfied that efforts had been made to secure his attendance and held that in the circumstances it was open to the Court of Appeal to rely on his statement, especially as it was corroborated by other evidence.

The third and final issue concerned the evidence of the expert, E, and the prosecution witness, F. As regards E, the Court considered that as his evidence had already been covered by another expert, the Court of Appeal was entitled to disallow it, while F's evidence had been properly admitted. The Court therefore concluded that none of the alleged shortcomings considered individually suggested that the trial had been unfair, nor was this so when they were considered together, especially as the various items were corroborative of each other. The Court therefore decided that there had been no violation of Article 6(1), taken together with Article 6(3)(d).[64]

There were two other cases involving Article 6(3)(d) in the period under review: the *Pullar* case (Case No. 20); and the *Baegen* case (Case No. 53).

Freedom of expression (Article 10)—protection of journalistic sources—the margin of appreciation—just satisfaction (Article 50)

Case No. 15. Goodwin case.[65] The Court held by 11 votes to 7 that measures to compel a journalist in the United Kingdom to disclose his sources of information had involved a violation of Article 10 of the Convention. As just satisfaction under Article 50 the Government was ordered to pay the applicant £37,595.50, less the sum paid by the Council of Europe as legal aid, in respect of his costs and expenses.

In 1989 the applicant, a trainee journalist employed on a periodical called *The Engineer*, was given unsolicited information concerning the affairs of an engineering firm, the T company, which he was told was in financial difficulties. The

---

[63] See the *Kostovski* case, Series A, No. 166, and this *Year Book*, 60 (1989), p. 564.

[64] Judges Ryssdal and De Meyer voted against the decision and in a short dissenting opinion explained that they saw the right to examine witnesses as vital and considered that in the present case it had been denied as regards the witnesses A, B and D.

[65] ECHR, judgment of 27 March 1996, decided by a Grand Chamber. Judge Pekkanen was originally a member of the Grand Chamber but subsequently withdrew.

applicant sought the comments of the T company on the information and subsequently prepared a draft article on the subject. However, the T company obtained an *ex parte* interim injunction to prevent publication of the applicant's article, followed by an order from the High Court requiring the applicant to disclose his notes on the ground that it was necessary 'in the interests of justice', within the meaning of section 10 of the Contempt of Court Act 1981, for the identity of the source to be disclosed, the purpose being to enable the T company to recover the draft of its corporate plan on which it believed the applicant's information was based, to obtain an injunction preventing further publication, or to seek damages. Appeals against this order, first to the Court of Appeal, and then to the House of Lords, were unsuccessful. The applicant, however, refused to disclose his notes and in 1990 the High Court fined him £5,000 for contempt.

In his application to the Commission in September 1990 Mr Goodwin claimed that the disclosure order violated his right to freedom of expression, as guaranteed by Article 10. In its report in March 1994 the Commission, by a majority, expressed the opinion that this provision had been violated. The Commission then referred the case to the Court.

Article 10, which was quoted in Case No. 1, has generated a considerable case law, but this is the first case in which the Court has had to consider the particular issue of journalistic confidentiality. It was undisputed that the measures complained of interfered with the applicant's freedom of expression[66] and the Court was satisfied that the interference was 'prescribed by law' and pursued a legitimate aim, namely the protection of the T company's rights. Everything therefore depended on whether the disclosure order could be regarded as 'necessary in a democratic society', as Article 10(2) requires.

Before examining the facts, the Court outlined the relevant general principles. It pointed out that protecting journalistic sources is one of the basic conditions of press freedom and noted that this is recognized in national and international practice.[67] In the light of these considerations the Court held that ordering a journalist to disclose his or her sources could only be justified by 'an overriding requirement in the public interest'.[68] Turning to the particular circumstances, the Court stated that the disclosure order had to be seen against the background of the earlier interim injunction, which had been notified to the press and, as Lord Donaldson had acknowledged in the Court of Appeal, which had already prevented dissemination of the confidential information.

Since reinforcing the injunction was not, in the Court's view, enough to justify the order for disclosure, another justification was required. The House of Lords had accepted that the risk of dissemination other than through the press, unmasking a disloyal employee and obtaining compensation provided such

[66] But see on this point the separate dissenting opinion of Judge Walsh.

[67] As regards national practice, the President of the Court had, during the proceedings, granted leave to *Article 19* and *Interights*, two London-based non-governmental organizations, to submit observations. As regards international practice, the Court cited as examples the Resolution on Journalistic Freedoms and Human Rights, adopted at the 4th European Ministerial Conference on Mass Media Policy (Prague, 1994), and the Resolution on the Confidentiality of Journalists' Sources by the European Parliament, 18 January 1994, *Official Journal of the European Communities*, No. C 44/34.

[68] Judgment, para. 39.

justification, but the Court disagreed. Deciding that there was not a reasonable relationship of proportionality between the legitimate aim and the disclosure order, it held that, notwithstanding the respondent's margin of appreciation, the disputed measures could not be regarded as 'necessary in a democratic society'. The Court therefore concluded that there had been a violation of Article 10 and awarded the applicant a sum in respect of his costs and expenses.[69]

The Court, like the Commission, found this a difficult case, and in a strong dissenting opinion seven members of the Grand Chamber explained why they considered that the respondent had been treated too harshly.[70] In essence their argument was that the national courts had reached their decisions after carefully weighing all the relevant factors and that, as their conclusion was not unreasonable, the matter should be regarded as within the national margin of appreciation. This is reminiscent of the argument put forward almost twenty years ago by the dissenting judges in the first *Sunday Times* case.[71] The present decision does not mean that journalists can never be compelled to disclose their sources, but, like the earlier case in a different context, attests the weight of the presumption favouring freedom of expression.

Right to the peaceful enjoyment of possessions (Article 1 of Protocol No. 1)—trial within a reasonable time (Article 6 (1))

Case No. 16. Phocas case.[72] In this case, which concerned France, the Court decided by 7 votes to 2 that there had been no violation of Article 1 of Protocol No. 1 to the Convention, and by various majorities that there had been no violations of Article 6(1).

Although the facts of this case were complex, the situation which gave rise to the proceedings at Strasbourg was relatively simple. The applicant owned a building at the intersection of two roads which he anticipated might be expropriated following the approval of a road widening scheme in 1960. When the expropriation did not take place, the applicant, having moved his business from the building, applied for planning permission to convert it into flats. The application was made in 1965 and after a series of events which need not be described, proceedings were terminated in 1982 with a judgment awarding him financial compensation for the property. In separate proceedings in 1986 additional compensation was awarded, but an appeal and proceedings seeking further compensation were unsuccessful, the final judgment being given in 1995.

In his application to the Commission in November 1990 Mr Phocas relied on Article 1 of Protocol No. 1 to the Convention and Article 6(1) (trial within a reasonable time). In its report in July 1994 the Commission expressed the unanimous opinion that there had been a violation of Article 1 and that it was

---

[69] It should be noted, however, that the Court rejected the applicant's claim for compensation for alleged non-pecuniary damage and that the sum awarded in respect of costs and expenses was significantly less than the sum claimed.

[70] See the joint dissenting opinion of Judges Ryssdal, Bernhardt, Thór Vilhjálmsson, Matscher, Walsh, Sir John Freeland and Baka.

[71] ECHR, judgment of 26 April 1979, Series A, No. 30, and this *Year Book*, 50 (1979), p. 257.

[72] ECHR, judgment of 23 April 1996, decided by a Chamber.

unnecessary to consider the claim under Article 6(1). The Commission then referred the case to the Court.

The applicant's main claim concerned Article 1 of Protocol No. 1,[73] where the first question was whether there had been an interference with the applicant's right of property. The Government argued that the Court could not take into account events before 3 May 1974 when France had ratified Protocol No. 1. The Court, however, decided that from 1965 to 1982 the crossroads scheme had been an obstacle to the applicant's development of his land for which he had not been compensated. It therefore concluded that this constituted a continuous interference which allowed it to take into account events from the very beginning.

The next question was whether the interference could be justified. The relevant principles have been extensively discussed in the case law and the Court's task was to apply those principles to the facts. Finding that the applicant's complaint was a general one relating to the peaceful enjoyment of his property, the Court indicated that its task was to determine whether a fair balance had been struck between the demands of the community interest and the individual's rights. In finding that it had, the Court treated as decisive the fact that in cases of possible planning blight the law offered owners the option of having their land purchased by the local authority. This was the procedure Mr Phocas had eventually used, but since he could have used it earlier, the Court held that there had been no violation of Article 1.

The other issue concerned the length of the proceedings, which the applicant claimed amounted to a violation of Article 6(1). The Court held that it could only take into account proceedings between May 1974, when France ratified the Convention, and November 1990, when Mr Phocas applied to the Commission. There were three sets of proceedings within this period, but having regard to the complexity of the case and the applicant's conduct, the Court decided that there had been no violations of Article 6(1). On the first set of proceedings, which had lasted two years and two months, the Court was unanimous; on the second set (four years and three months) the vote was 7 to 2; and on the third set (eight years and five months) the vote was 5 to 4.

Right to a fair hearing by an impartial tribunal (Article 6(1))—racist remark by juror—just satisfaction (Article 50)

Case No. 17. Remli case.[74] The Court held by 5 votes to 4 that there had been a violation of Article 6(1) of the Convention when a French court, which was trying the applicant, refused to take formal note of a racist remark, allegedly made by one of the jurors outside the courtroom. As just satisfaction the respondent was ordered to pay the applicant 60,000 French francs in respect of his costs and expenses.

---

[73] For the text of Article 1 of Protocol No. 1 see Case No. 3.
[74] ECHR, judgment of 23 April 1996, decided by a Chamber.

In 1985 the applicant, who was Algerian, killed a warder while attempting to escape from a prison in France. In the course of his trial for murder, which took place in 1989, the applicant's lawyers asked the court to take formal note of a racist remark made by one of the jurors shortly before the trial began. The remark had been overheard by a woman, Mrs M, who was unconnected with the trial and who had made a signed statement. The court refused to take formal note of the remark, but agreed that Mrs M's statement should be appended to the record. The applicant was convicted and an appeal against the decision was unsuccessful.

In his application to the Commission in May 1990 Mr Remli relied *inter alia* on Article 6(1) of the Convention. In its report in November 1994 the Commission expressed the opinion that this provision had been violated. The Commission then referred the case to the Court.

The substantive issue in this case concerned Article 6(1) of the Convention, which, it will be recalled from case No. 9, guarantees a 'fair . . . hearing . . . by an independent and impartial tribunal'. Before dealing with this issue, however, the Court had to consider preliminary objections from the Government concerning the exhaustion of domestic remedies and the six-month rule (Article 26).[75] Both were rejected, the Court ruling that all relevant remedies had been exhausted and that the application was not out of time.

On the merits of the case, the Court observed that the principles laid down in its case law concerning the impartiality and independence of tribunals apply to jurors as well as to judges. It noted that the applicant had asked the trial court to take formal note of Mrs M's statement, but it had refused to do so, or to take evidence to verify what had been reported. As a result, the applicant had been unable either to challenge the juror concerned or to rely on Mrs M's statement in his appeal. In the Court's view Article 6(1) placed an obligation on a national court to check whether it was 'an impartial tribunal' if, as here, a plausible challenge was made. Because the trial court had not done so, the Court decided that there had been a violation of Article 6(1).[76]

The remaining issue was just satisfaction under Article 50. The Court did not consider that compensation for non-pecuniary damage was appropriate, and rejected the applicant's request for a retrial or reduction of sentence on the familiar ground that these remedies were not within its powers. It did, however, award the applicant a sum in respect of his costs and expenses.

In the period under review the question of impartiality was also considered in the *Pullar* case (Case No. 20); the *Diennet* case (Case No. 22); the *Procola* case (Case No. 26); the *British American Tobacco Company* case (Case No. 35); the *Bulut* case (Case No. 44); and the *Thomann* case (Case No. 49).

---

[75] Article 26 provides:
'The Commission may only deal with the matter after all domestic remedies have been exhausted, according to the generally recognized rules of international law, and within a period of six months from the date on which the final decision was taken.'

[76] Four members of the Chamber voted against the decision and delivered dissenting opinions. Judges Pettiti and Mifsud Bonnici considered that the defence could have asked for the case to be transferred to another court, and Judges Thór Vilhjálmsson and Lopes Rocha that the complaint was too trivial to be entertained.

Freedom of association (Article 11)—employer's refusal to enter a collective agreement—right to the peaceful enjoyment of possessions (Article 1 of Protocol No. 1)—right of access to the courts (Article 6(1))—the right to a remedy (Article 13)

Case No. 18. Gustaffson case.[77] In this case, which concerned the refusal of a Swedish restaurant owner to participate in a collective bargaining arrangement, the Court held by 11 votes to 8 that Article 11 of the Convention was applicable to the facts complained of, but by 12 votes to 7 that it had not been violated. It also held by 13 votes to 6 that Article 1 of Protocol No. 1 was inapplicable; by 14 votes to 5 that Article 6(1) was inapplicable; and by 18 votes to 1 that Article 13 was inapplicable.

The applicant owned a restaurant and youth hostel on the island of Gotland and hired employees on a seasonal basis. There are two associations of restaurant employers in Sweden, but the applicant did not belong to either. As a result, he was not bound by any collective agreement between them and the Restaurant Workers Union (HRF). The applicant could have signed a substitute agreement with the HRF which would have brought a collective agreement into effect for his establishment, but did not do so. The HRF therefore picketed the restaurant and declared a boycott of it; consequently, following sympathy measures by other unions, supplies to the restaurant were stopped. The applicant then asked the Government to prohibit the picketing and order the unions concerned, or the State, to pay damages. The Government, however, rejected the request on the ground that it concerned a legal dispute between private parties which could only be decided by a court. An application for judicial review of this decision was unsuccessful.

In his application to the Commission in July 1989 Mr Gustaffson relied on several articles of the Convention, including Articles 11 and 13. In its report in January 1995 the Commission expressed the opinion that these provisions had been violated, but also considered that there had been no violation of Article 6(1) and that it was not necessary to examine the complaint under Article 1 of Protocol No. 1, taken together with Article 17.[78] The Commission then referred the case to the Court.

The main issue in this case concerned Article 11 of the Convention, which protects freedom of association and was quoted in Case No. 1. The Court began by deciding that this provision was applicable because the applicant was under pressure, and to meet the union's demand that he be bound by a collective agreement he could have either joined an employers' association, or signed a substitute agreement. To a degree the enjoyment of his freedom of association was thereby affected. The situation therefore fell within Article 11.

The next question was whether Article 11 had been complied with. It is clear from the Court's case law that, on the one hand, the national authorities may be obliged to intervene in relationships between private individuals to protect the individual's right not to belong to an association,[79] and, on the other, the

[77] ECHR, judgment of 25 April 1996, decided by a Grand Chamber.
[78] Article 17 is intended to prevent abuse of the Convention's rights and freedoms.
[79] See, for example, the *Young, James and Webster* case, Series A, No. 44, and this *Year Book*, 52 (1981), p. 340.

Convention recognizes the legitimacy of trade union action,[80] which can include the negotiation of collective agreements. In view of the sensitivity of these issues and the wide divergency of national practice, the Court added that this is an area in which States enjoy a wide margin of appreciation.

Applying the above principles to the facts, the Court noted that signing a substitute agreement would not have affected the applicant's freedom of association and was a genuine alternative to joining an employers' association. It appeared that the applicant's objection to this course was his disagreement with the collective bargaining system in Sweden. However, Article 11 did not guarantee a right not to enter into a collective agreement. Moreover, the legitimacy of collective bargaining was recognized by a number of international instruments, the actions of the HRF pursued legitimate interests, given the importance of collective agreements in Sweden, and the applicant had not substantiated his contention that the terms of employment he offered were more favourable than those required by a collective agreement. In the light of the foregoing and having regard to the margin of appreciation, the Court did not find that Sweden had failed to secure the applicant's rights under Article 11. It therefore decided that this provision had not been violated.

The applicant's other claims can be dealt with more briefly. His claim under Article 1 of Protocol No. 1 was rejected on the ground that the interruption of the applicant's supplies did not result from government action, and was concerned exclusively with private contractual relationships. Likewise, the Court rejected the claim under Article 6(1) because the applicant's complaint was essentially that the union action had been lawful, whereas the Convention does not guarantee any particular content for 'civil rights and obligations' in the Contracting States. Finally, the claim under Article 13 was rejected because it is established in the Court's case law that this provision does not go so far as to guarantee a remedy allowing a Contracting State's laws, as such, to be challenged before a national authority,[81] and the applicant's complaint was again directed against the lawfulness of the union action.

This was an unusually divisive case and every ruling was the object of some disagreement.[82] The most contentious issues concerned Article 11 where both the decision on applicability[83] and the decision on violation[84] provoked significant dissents. However, the Court has rarely been inclined to treat the scope of the Convention narrowly, yet, on the other hand, when applying Article 11 in the context of industrial relations has always emphasized the margin of

---

[80] See, for example, the *National Union of Belgian Police* case, Series A, No. 19, and this *Year Book*, 48 (1976–7), p. 373.

[81] See, for example, the *Leander* case, Series A, No. 116, and this *Year Book*, 58 (1987), p. 476.

[82] In addition to the views referred to in notes 83 and 84, Judges Martens, Matscher, Walsh and Morenilla indicated in their dissenting opinions that they had voted against the ruling on Article 1 of Protocol No. 1, and Judge Morenilla that he had also voted against the rulings on Article 6(1) and Article 13.

[83] See the partly dissenting opinion of Judges Ryssdal, Spielman, Palm, Foighel, Pekkanen, Loizou, Makarczyk and Repik.

[84] See the dissenting opinion of Judge Martens, joined by Judge Matscher, containing a detailed and cogent argument; and the dissenting opinions of Judges Walsh, Morenilla, Mifsud Bonnici and Jambrek.

appreciation. On both points therefore the judgment in the present case follows the Court's previous jurisprudence.

Right to liberty (Article 5(1))—imprisonment of a poll tax defaulter—the meaning of 'lawful' in Article 5(1)(b)—the right to legal assistance (Article 6(3)(c))—the meaning of 'criminal charge' in Article 6(1)—just satisfaction

Case No. 19. Benham case.[85] In this case, which concerned the imprisonment of a 'poll tax' defaulter in the United Kingdom, the Court held by 17 votes to 4 that there had been no violation of Article 5(1) of the Convention, with the result that Article 5(5) did not apply. However, it also held unanimously that the fact that the applicant had not been entitled to legal aid to enable him to be represented at the hearing constituted a violation of Article 6(1) and 6(3)(c), taken together. As just satisfaction the respondent was ordered to pay the applicant £10,000 in respect of his costs and expenses, less the sum already paid as legal aid by the Council of Europe.

In April 1990 the applicant became liable to pay the community charge (poll tax), the sum due being £325. He did not pay and as a result appeared before Poole Magistrates' Court in March 1991 for an inquiry to be made into his means and the reasons for his failure to pay. The magistrates concluded that Mr Benham had no assets, but that his failure to pay was due to his culpable neglect since he was capable of earning money, and committed him to prison for thirty days. The applicant was not represented at the hearing. On appeal to the Divisional Court in October 1991, the order for detention was quashed on the ground that there had been insufficient evidence to support the magistrates' finding of culpable neglect, and that alternatives to prison should also have been considered. Although Mr Benham had spent eleven days in prison, no possibility of obtaining compensation for his detention was available.

In his application to the Commission in September 1991 Mr Benham relied on Articles 5(1), 5(5) and 6(3)(c) of the Convention. In its report in November 1994 the Commission expressed the opinion that all three provisions had been violated. The Commission and the Government then referred the case to the Court.

The relevant part of Article 5(1) provides:

Everyone has the right to liberty and security of person. No one shall be deprived of his liberty save in the following cases and in accordance with a procedure prescribed by law;

. . .

(b) the lawful arrest or detention of a person for non-compliance with the lawful order of a court or in order to secure the fulfilment of any obligation prescribed by law.

The main issue to be determined in the present case was whether the disputed detention was 'lawful' and whether it complied with 'a procedure prescribed by law'. Here, as in other parts of the Convention, the references to lawfulness refer primarily to national law, although it is for the Strasbourg institutions to exercise a general supervision. In English law a distinction is made between

---

[85] ECHR, judgment of 10 June 1996, decided by a Grand Chamber.

errors made by a magistrates' court which are so grave as to deprive the court of jurisdiction, and other less serious mistakes. In the former case, orders made by the court are null and void *ab initio*, which renders any detention unlawful. In the latter case, however, the order is valid until overturned, and so any intervening detention is lawful.

In Mr Benham's case the Divisional Court had found that there was insufficient evidence to support the magistrates' ruling, but there was no explicit finding as to whether they had exceeded their jurisdiction. In these circumstances the Court considered that it had not been established that the initial order for detention was unlawful. Since the Court also found that the magistrates had not acted in bad faith, or failed to perform their duty, it decided that the detention was not arbitrary, and so concluded that there had been no violation of Article 5(1).[86]

Article 5(5), which the applicant also relied on, guarantees an enforceable right to compensation for those who have been arrested or detained in contravention of Article 5. However, since the Court had decided that there was no violation of Article 5(1) in this case, it concluded that Article 5(5) was not applicable.

The only other substantive issue concerned Article 6(3)(*c*), which the Court considered in conjunction with Article 6(1). It will be recalled from Case No. 9 that Article 6(3)(*c*) guarantees the right to free legal assistance to those charged with a criminal offence, who lack the necessary means, and when 'the interests of justice so require'. It is well established that the words 'criminal charge' in Article 6 have an autonomous meaning independent of the classification of the proceedings under domestic law.[87] In view of the nature of the committal proceedings for non-payment of the community charge and the relative severity of the maximum sanction (three months' imprisonment), the Court had no difficulty in deciding that Article 6 was applicable.

This left the question of whether the interests of justice required Mr Benham to be provided with free legal representation at the magistrates' hearing. The Court concluded that they did on the ground that the applicant's liberty was at stake and the application of the relevant law was not straightforward, as was demonstrated by the success of the applicant's appeal. Although two types of legal aid provision had been available to Mr Benham,[88] neither provided for representation at the hearing as of right. The Court therefore concluded that there had been a violation of Article 6(1) and Article 6(3)(*c*) taken together.

On the issue of just satisfaction the Court declined to award compensation for the applicant's detention on the ground that it could not speculate as to whether the absence of legal representation had affected the magistrates' decision. It did,

---

[86] Four members of the Grand Chamber held that Article 5(1) had been violated because Mr Benham's detention had not been lawful, and thus considered that Article 5(5) was applicable. See the partly dissenting opinions of Judges Bernhardt, Thór Vilhjálmsson, de Meyer and Foighel. Judges De Meyer and Foighel also considered that compensation should have been awarded.

[87] See, for example, the *Öztürk* case, Series A, No. 73, and this *Year Book*, 55 (1984), p. 370. See also Robertson and Merrills, *Human Rights in Europe* (3rd edn., 1993), pp. 92–3.

[88] Under the Green Form scheme Mr Benham was entitled to advice and assistance from a solicitor prior to the hearing, but not to legal representation in court. Under the Assistance by way of Representation (ABWOR) scheme, the magistrates could at their discretion have appointed a solicitor to represent him.

however, award Mr Benham a sum in respect of his costs and expenses, although on a reduced basis in view of the failure of his claims under Article 5.

Right to a fair hearing by an impartial tribunal (Article 6(1))—impartiality of a juror—right to examine witnesses (Article 6(3)(d))

Case No. 20. *Pullar* case.[89] The Court held by 5 votes to 4 that there had been no violation of Article 6(1) of the Convention arising out of the composition of a jury which had tried the applicant's case in Scotland. The Court also held unanimously that there had been no violation of Article 6(1) and Article 6(3)(d) taken together with regard to witness evidence produced to the court which heard the applicant's appeal.

In 1992 the applicant was tried and convicted of having corruptly solicited money from M, a partner in a firm of architects, and C, a partner in a firm of quantity surveyors, while an elected member of Tayside Regional Council. M and C were the two principal prosecution witnesses and one of the jurors selected for the case, F, was a junior employee in M's firm, although he had been given a notice of redundancy which was to take effect in the following month. F and M informed the sheriff clerk about this connection while the jury was being selected, but he did not inform the sheriff. When the applicant discovered the connection between F and M, he appealed to the High Court of Justiciary, claiming that F's presence on the jury amounted to a miscarriage of justice.

Before the appeal hearing the prosecution took a written statement from M which was made available to the applicant and the High Court judges. The applicant did not object to its contents. In its judgment the High Court accepted that if the sheriff had been aware of F's position he would probably have been excused from the jury, but decided that there was no evidence that he had not been impartial and that the conviction should not be quashed. Certain procedural recommendations were also made in order to avoid this type of situation recurring.

In his application to the Commission in May 1993 Mr Pullar relied on Articles 6(1) and 6(3)(d) of the Convention. In its report in January 1995 the Commission unanimously expressed the opinion that Article 6(1) had been violated, but decided that it was not necessary to examine the case under Article 6(3)(d). The Commission then referred the case to the Court.

As noted earlier in Case No. 17, Article 6(1) provides that legal tribunals must be impartial. According to the Court's case law, impartiality has two aspects, requiring that the tribunal be both free of actual bias (subjective impartiality), and free from the suspicion of bias (objective impartiality).[90] In the present case there was no evidence of actual bias and the Court rejected the applicant's submission that because a jury was involved, the presumption of impartiality should be set aside. The case thus turned on the issue of objective impartiality.[91] Rejecting the argument that a personal connection necessarily creates prejudice, the Court pointed out that F was a junior employee under notice of redundancy

[89] ECHR, judgment of 10 June 1996, decided by a Chamber.
[90] See, for example, the *Piersack* case, Series A, No. 53, and this *Year Book*, 53 (1982), p. 321.
[91] The applicant's submission was that because it is impermissible to inquire into the workings of a jury, the presumption is inappropriate where the impartiality of jurors is concerned.

and had had no connection with the transactions in issue. In addition, he was only one of fifteen jurors, who had all taken an oath of impartiality and had been carefully directed. In these circumstances the Court decided that there had been no violation of Article 6(1).[92]

In relation to M's witness statement, the applicant complained that he had had no opportunity to test it by cross-examination. The Court, however, pointed out that the applicant's counsel had neither objected to the statement being put before the appeal judges, nor reserved his position as to its accuracy. Furthermore, he had not sought to call M to give evidence to the High Court as he could have done. Not surprisingly, therefore, the Court held that there had been no violation of Article 6(1) in conjunction with Article 6(3)(d).

Right to liberty (Article 5(1))—detention of persons claiming refugee status (Article 5(1)(f))—the meaning of 'victim' in Article 25—the meaning of 'deprived of his liberty' and 'in accordance with a procedure prescribed by law' in Article 5(1)—just satisfaction (Article 50)

Case No. 21. Amuur case.[93] In this case, which concerned detention in the transit zone of a French airport, the Court held unanimously that Article 5(1) of the Convention was applicable and had been violated. As just satisfaction, the Court ordered the respondent to pay the applicants 57,000 French francs, less the sum paid by the Council of Europe as legal aid, in respect of their costs and expenses.

In March 1992 the three applicants, who were all nationals of Somalia, arrived at Orly Airport on a flight from Damascus and claimed political asylum. They were detained at a hotel near the airport for twenty days and then, having been refused entry by the Ministry of the Interior, were returned to Syria. Two days later a French court held that their detention was unlawful and ordered their release.

In their application to the Commission, which was made while the applicants were in France, they relied *inter alia* on Article 5(1) of the Convention.[94] In its report in January 1995 the Commission by a majority expressed the opinion that there had been no violation of this provision. The Commission then referred the case to the Court.

The relevant part of Article 5(1) of the Convention provides:

Everyone has the right to liberty and security of person. No one shall be deprived of

---

[92] Four members of the Chamber voted against the decision on Article 6(1). Judges Ryssdal and Makarczyk in a partly dissenting opinion, which was joined by Judges Spielman and Lopes Rocha, held that the authorities had failed in their obligation to ensure that a jury was selected which was unquestionably impartial. It is interesting to note that in the *Remli* case (Case No. 17), which raised a similar point, Judge Lopes Rocha reached the opposite conclusion.

[93] ECHR, judgment of 25 June 1996, decided by a Chamber.

[94] Two days before the applicants were removed from France the President of the Commission, acting under Article 36 of the Commission's Rules of Procedure, had requested the Government to delay their return to Somalia. Recommendations under Article 36 are, however, not legally binding; see the *Cruz Varas* case, Series A, No. 201, and this *Year Book*, 62 (1991), p. 500. See also Merrills, *The Development of International Law by the European Court of Human Rights* (2nd edn., 1993), pp. 82–4.

his liberty save in the following cases and in accordance with a procedure prescribed by law;

. . .

(f) the lawful arrest or detention of a person to prevent his effecting an unauthorized entry into the country or of a person against whom action is being taken with a view to deportation or extradition.

After rejecting a preliminary objection from the Government based on Article 25,[95] the Court began by considering whether Article 5 was applicable to the facts. The Commission had concluded that it was not, mainly on the ground that the applicants could have ended their detention at any time by returning to Syria. The Court, however, rejected this argument and, pointing out that the right to leave any country, including one's own, is guaranteed by Protocol No. 4 to the Convention, held that the fact than an asylum seeker can voluntarily abandon the country of intended asylum does not in itself prevent detention there from constituting a deprivation of liberty. It recognized the right of States to restrict the liberty of would-be immigrants, but pointed out that such confinement is acceptable only when it is compatible with the State's international obligations, including the European Convention on Human Rights and the 1951 Geneva Convention relating to the Status of Refugees. Here the applicants had been held for twenty days without access to the courts, or to legal and social assistance. In these circumstances the Court was satisfied that the detention was equivalent to a deprivation of liberty and therefore came within Article 5.

The next question was whether Article 5(1) had been complied with, which turned on whether the applicants' detention was 'in accordance with a procedure prescribed by law'. The Court recalled that this requires not only that detention must be lawful under domestic law, but also that the law in question satisfies the 'qualitative' requirement of the Convention and is compatible with the rule of law. Here the applicants had been subject to French law throughout and the relevant provisions of domestic law had failed to provide them with adequate protection against arbitrary interferences by the authorities with the rights safeguarded by the Convention. Thus the legal rules in force at the time, as applied in the present case, did not sufficiently guarantee the applicants' right to liberty. Accordingly, there had been a violation of Article 5(1).

As just satisfaction the Court awarded the applicants their costs and expenses, but decided that no compensation for damage was required in the particular circumstances.

This is the first case in which the Court has considered the position of those seeking asylum under Article 5(1)(f), but its approach was generally similar to that adopted in the *Bozano* case[96] where it examined the analogous issue of deportation. Its recognition that in cases of this kind the existence of a

---

[95] Article 25 requires an individual applicant to show that he or she is the 'victim' of a violation of the Convention. The Court rejected the Government's argument that the applicants lacked this status on account of the belated decision from the domestic court upholding their rights.

[96] ECHR, judgment of 18 December 1986, Series A, No. 111, and this *Year Book*, 58 (1987), p. 460.

'deprivation of liberty' is not simply a matter of physical conditions,[97] but also involves the length of detention, the availability of assistance and the possibility of judicial review, is, however, an important development.

PART TWO: OTHER CASES DECIDED ON THE MERITS

Right to a public hearing by an impartial tribunal (Article 6(1))—application to proceedings for professional misconduct—just satisfaction (Article 50)

Case No. 22. Diennet case.[98] In this case, which concerned France, the Court held unanimously that because proceedings against a doctor had not been heard in public, there had been a violation of Article 6(1) of the Convention. However, it also decided by 8 votes to 1 that the composition of the tribunal in question had not infringed the applicant's right to an impartial tribunal, guaranteed by the same provision. As just satisfaction for the violation of Article 6(1) the Court awarded the applicant 20,000 French francs in respect of his costs and expenses.

The applicant, a doctor, was found guilty of professional misconduct by a Regional Council of the *Ordre des médecins* and on appeal by the disciplinary section of the National Council of the Ordre. This decision was then quashed by the courts, which remitted the case to the National Council for a rehearing. When the case was heard again, three of the seven members constituting the section had taken part in the earlier decision. The applicant complained that the disciplinary proceedings had not been held in public and that the rehearing was not held before an impartial tribunal. In the absence of any reason for confidentiality the Court held that Article 6(1) had been violated on the first point, but decided that, as no reason for doubting the tribunal's impartiality had been shown, the second claim must be rejected.[99] On both points the Court agreed with the Commission.

Protection against retroactive law (Article 7(1))

Case No. 23. G v. France.[100] The Court held unanimously that there had been no violation of Article 7(1) of the Convention.

The applicant, a driving test examiner, was charged with indecent assault and corruption, convicted and sentenced to three years' imprisonment. In his application to the Commission he argued that in relation to the assault charge he had been convicted of an offence which, when it was committed, did not

---

[97] Thus the Court was unmoved by the Government's argument that the conditions in the hotel in which the applicants were detained had been described as satisfactory in the report of the European Committee for the Prevention of Torture and Inhuman or Degrading Treatment or Punishment.

[98] ECHR, judgment of 26 September 1995, Series A, No. 325A, decided by a Chamber.

[99] Judge Morenilla voted against the judgment on this point and explained his vote in a dissenting opinion. In the *Bulut* case (Case No. 44), which raised a similar point, Judge Morenilla discussed this issue further.

[100] ECHR, judgment of 27 September 1995, Series A, No. 325B, decided by a Chamber.

constitute a recognized offence. The Commission rejected the complaint and the Court agreed. It pointed out that the offences with which G was charged fell within the scope of former articles of the Criminal Code and that the new legislation which had been applied, although not in force at the time of the offence, downgraded the offence and provided for a more lenient sanction. Its application, though retrospective, had therefore operated in the applicant's favour. Accordingly, the Court concluded that there had been no violation of Article 7(1).[101]

Right to the peaceful enjoyment of possessions (Article 1 of Protocol No. 1)—non-discrimination (Article 14)—the margin of appreciation

Case No. 24. Spadea and Scalabrino case.[102] In this case, which concerned measures to deal with a housing shortage in Italy, the Court held unanimously that there had been no violation either of Article 1 of Protocol No. 1 to the Convention, or of Article 14 read in conjunction with Article 1 of Protocol No. 1.

In April 1982 the applicants bought two adjoining flats in Milan with the intention of making their home in them. In the meantime they let the flats to two elderly ladies. In October 1982 they gave notice to the tenants to quit the premises in December 1983 when the leases expired, but were unable to regain possession of the flats until August 1988 and February 1989, on account of successive legislative decrees protecting the tenants. The applicants' first claim was that these measures violated their right to the peaceful enjoyment of their possessions, contrary to Article 1 of Protocol No. 1. However, the Court rejected this argument on the ground that in implementing social and economic policies the authorities enjoy a wide margin of appreciation, particularly in the field of housing. The suspension of evictions between 1984 and 1988 was motivated by the need to deal with a large number of expiring leases and to avoid social unrest. It thus had a legitimate aim, and in view of the content of the legislation could also be considered proportionate.

The applicants also complained that since owners of residential and non-residential property had been treated differently, there had been a violation of Article 14, read in conjunction with Article 1 of Protocol No. 1. Article 14 provides:

> The enjoyment of the rights and freedoms set forth in this Convention shall be secured without discrimination on any ground such as sex, race, colour, language, religion, political or other opinion, national or social origin, association with a national minority, property, birth or other status.

However, the Court, like the Commission, also rejected this argument. Given the aim of the legislation, the distinction was objective and reasonable, while a further argument that there was a difference in treatment between landlords and tenants raised the issue of proportionality which the Court had already considered when examining Article 1 of the Protocol alone.

[101] For the text of Article 7(1), see Cases Nos. 5 and 6 above.
[102] ECHR, judgment of 28 September 1995, Series A, No. 315B, decided by a Chamber.

Right to the peaceful enjoyment of possessions (Article 1 of Protocol No. 1)—trial within a reasonable time (Article 6(1))—just satisfaction (Article 50)

Case No. 25. Scollo case.[103] In this case, which concerned Italy, the Court held unanimously that there had been violations of both Article 1 of Protocol No. 1 to the Convention and Article 6(1). As just satisfaction the Government was ordered to pay the applicant 13,634,280 lire in respect of pecuniary damage, 30 million lire in respect of non-pecuniary damage and 14,280,000 lire in respect of his costs and expenses.

The situation in this case was similar to that in *Spadea and Scalabrino* (Case No. 24). Again the applicant was a flat owner who found it impossible to evict a tenant on account of successive decrees protecting the tenant. The applicant, who wanted to live in the flat himself, eventually regained possession only in 1995, some twelve years after beginning proceedings. As in the previous case, the applicant relied on Article 1 of Protocol No. 1, but as the proceedings had taken so long, also invoked Article 6(1), which guarantees the right to a hearing within a reasonable time.

The Court agreed with the Commission that Article 1 of Protocol No. 1 had been violated because the authorities had failed to apply the relevant legislation properly. Here therefore, unlike *Spadea and Scalabrino*, the Court considered that the disputed measures had been disproportionate. It also decided that there had been a violation of Article 6(1), because the time taken to deal with the case had been excessive.

Right to a hearing by an impartial tribunal (Article 6(1))—the meaning of 'civil rights and obligations'—just satisfaction (Article 50)

Case No. 26. Procola case.[104] The Court held unanimously that the handling of an issue by the Judicial Committee of the *Conseil d'Etat* in Luxembourg had involved a violation of Article 6(1) of the Convention because that organ was not impartial. As just satisfaction the applicant was awarded 350,000 Luxembourg francs in respect of its costs and expenses.

The applicant in this case was a dairy which successfully challenged decisions relating to the milk quota system applicable under EEC Regulations Nos. 856/84 and 857/84 of 31 March 1984. The relevant Minister of State then drew up a new regulation on the matter which was submitted to the *Conseil d'Etat*, acting in its advisory capacity, and approved subject to certain amendments. When the new regulation came into force the Minister made orders under it which the applicant challenged. However, the Judicial Committee of the *Conseil d'Etat* rejected the case, four of its five members having previously given advice on the new regulation.

The applicant claimed that Article 6(1) had been violated because the Judicial Committee lacked independence and impartiality. Having decided that this provision was applicable because the case involved a dispute concerning 'civil

---

[103] ECHR, judgment of 28 September 1995, Series A, No. 315C. This case was decided by the same Chamber as the *Spadea and Scalabrino* case (Case No. 24).
[104] ECHR, judgment of 28 September 1995, Series A, No. 326, decided by a Chamber.

rights and obligations',[105] the Court held that it was unnecessary to consider the Committee's independence, but that its combination of advisory and judicial functions was capable of casting doubt on its structural impartiality.

Right to a fair and public hearing before an impartial tribunal (Article 6(1))—the need for a dispute over a 'right'

Case No. 27. *Masson and Van Zon* case.[106] In this case, which concerned the Netherlands, the Court held by 8 votes to 1 that Article 6(1) of the Convention did not apply to the procedure for obtaining compensation for pre-trial detention following acquittal. It therefore held unanimously that it had not been violated.

The applicants in this case were both convicted of various offences, but subsequently had their appeals allowed. As they had been detained on remand, they claimed compensation under the Code of Criminal Procedure for damage they had allegedly suffered and reimbursement of their legal costs. However, the Court of Appeal, sitting *in camera*, refused their claims for compensation and the President of the Court, also sitting *in camera*, awarded them only a small part of their costs. At Strasbourg the applicants claimed that contrary to Article 6(1) they had been denied their right to a fair and public hearing before an impartial tribunal. However, the Court held that this provision was inapplicable because under the law of the Netherlands the courts have a power to award compensation for pre-trial detention and legal expenses, but no duty to do so.[107] Accordingly, whether or not the impugned proceedings involved a 'dispute', they did not involve a 'right' as Article 6(1) requires.[108]

Right of access to the courts (Article 6(1))—immunity from being prosecuted twice for the same offence (Article 4 of Protocol No. 7)—validity of a reservation (Article 64(2))—just satisfaction (Article 50)

Cases Nos. 28 to 33. *Schmautzer* case. *Umlauft* case. *Gradinger* case. *Pramstaller* case. *Palaoro* case. *Pfarrmeier* case.[109] In these cases, all of which concerned Austria, the Court held unanimously that there had been a violation of Article 6(1) of the Convention on account of a lack of access to the courts. In the *Gradinger* case it also held that there had been a violation of Article 4 of Protocol

---

[105] The Commission had reached a different conclusion on this point.

[106] ECHR, judgment of 28 September 1995, Series A, No. 327A, decided by a Chamber.

[107] Although the Convention is part of the law of the Netherlands, it does not guarantee either the reimbursement of expenses incurred in the course of criminal proceedings ending in an acquittal, or compensation for lawful restrictions on liberty. Consequently, as the Court explained, whether such rights exist in any particular case depends on the position in domestic law. Six months after this decision the Court employed the same reasoning in the *Leutscher* case (Case No. 46).

[108] One Judge held that Article 6(1) was applicable, but considered that it had not been violated.

[109] ECHR, judgments of 23 October 1995, Series A, Nos. 328A–C and 329A–C, decided by the same Chamber.

No. 7,[110] which prohibits being tried twice for the same offence. As just satisfaction under Article 50 all the applicants were awarded sums in respect of their costs and expenses.

The applicants in these cases had all been convicted of minor offences and sentenced to fines, enforceable by imprisonment. Because Austrian law classified the offences in question as 'administrative offences', the sentences in question had been imposed by administrative authorities with only a limited power of review by the courts. In these circumstances the Court agreed with the Commission that there had been a violation of Article 6(1).[111] In Mr Gradinger's case the administrative proceedings, which related to a drink-driving charge, followed criminal proceedings based on the same facts. Deciding that an Austrian reservation to Article 4 of Protocol No. 7 was invalid,[112] the Court held that this provision had also been violated.[113]

Right to take proceedings to challenge the lawfulness of detention (Article 5(4))—application to detention in France following trial in Andorra

Case No. 34. Iribarne Pérez case.[114] The Court held unanimously that the inability of a person convicted of an offence in Andorra to take proceedings in the French courts to challenge the lawfulness of his detention in France did not constitute a violation of Article 5(4) of the Convention.

In November 1985 the *Tribunal de Corts* in Andorra sentenced the applicant to twelve years' imprisonment for drug trafficking and unlawful possession of a firearm. The applicant chose to serve his sentence in France[115] and then sought to challenge the lawfulness of his detention there, but was unable to do so.[116] The applicant claimed that this violated Article 5(4) of the Convention, which was quoted earlier.

The Court, however, agreed with the Commission that the complaint must be rejected. As already noted, the Court's case law establishes that the review

[110] Article 4 of Protocol No. 7 provides:
'1. No one shall be liable to be tried or punished again in criminal proceedings under the jurisdiction of the same State for an offence for which he has already been finally acquitted or convicted in accordance with the law and penal procedure of that State.
2. The provisions of the preceding paragraph shall not prevent the re-opening of the case in accordance with the law and penal procedure of the State concerned, if there is evidence of new or newly discovered facts, or if there has been a fundamental defect in the previous proceedings, which could affect the outcome of the case.
3. No derogation from this article shall be made under Article 15 of the Convention.'
[111] In a separate opinion Judge Martens indicated that he disagreed with some of the Court's reasoning.
[112] This was because the reservation in question did not contain 'a brief statement of the law concerned' as Article 64(2) of the Convention requires.
[113] Protocol No. 7 came into force in 1988 but this is the first case in which the Court has applied Article 4.
[114] ECHR, judgment of 24 October 1995, Series A, No. 325C, decided by a Chamber.
[115] As there are no facilities for long term prisoners in Andorra, the law there allows a person who has been sentenced to more than three months' imprisonment to choose between serving the sentence in France and in Spain.
[116] Among the reasons for this were that Andorra is not regarded as a subject of international law, with the result that its courts are not treated as foreign courts for the purposes of the Code of Criminal Procedure.

required by Article 5(4) is normally incorporated in the decision of the trial court which imposes a sentence of imprisonment. Subsequent review may be required in cases of detention of persons of unsound mind, or where a court has imposed an indeterminate sentence.[117] Here, however, no such special circumstances were present. The *Tribunal de Corts* was a 'competent court' for the purposes of Article 5(1)(a) and the necessary review was incorporated in its judgment. Moreover, the rights of the defence had been respected and so there had been no denial of justice. The Court therefore decided that there had been no violation of the Convention.[118]

Right to a fair and public hearing before an impartial tribunal (Article 6(1))—possibility of access to the civil courts—right to the peaceful enjoyment of possessions (Article 1 of Protocol No. 1)

Case No. 35. British American Tobacco Company Ltd. case.[119] In this case, which concerned appellate proceedings relating to patent claims in the Netherlands, the Court decided unanimously that there had been no violation of Article 6(1) of the Convention and that no separate issue arose under Article 1 of Protocol No. 1.

The applicant was involved in a claim over a patent in the Netherlands which was eventually rejected by the Appeal Division of the Patent Office. At Strasbourg it argued that Article 6(1) of the Convention had been violated because the Appeal Division was not an impartial tribunal and had not held a fair and public hearing. The Commission accepted the argument, but the Court rejected it. The basis for its decision was that whether or not the Appeals Division satisfied the requirements of Article 6(1),[120] the law of the Netherlands provided the applicants with the possibility of challenging a decision before the civil courts on procedural grounds and, if such a challenge was successful, obtaining a ruling from the courts on the merits. In reaching this conclusion the Court relied on its previous decision in the *Oerlemans* case[121] and rejected the applicant's argument that in the earlier case it had misunderstood the law of the Netherlands.

The applicant also relied on Article 1 of Protocol No. 1. However, the Court, like the Commission, held that it was unnecessary to consider this provision, the complaint under this head, namely denial of a judicial remedy, being in substance identical to that already considered and rejected under Article 6(1).

[117] As in the *Hussain* and *Singh* cases, Cases Nos. 12 and 13 above.
[118] For a review of other issues raised by trials in Andorra see the *Drozd and Janousek* case, Series A, No. 240, and this *Year Book*, 63 (1992), p. 589.
[119] ECHR, judgment of 20 November 1995, Series A, No. 331, decided by a Chamber.
[120] The Court left this point undecided, but observed that 'in a domain as technical as that of the granting of patents there may be good reasons for opting for an adjudicatory body other than a court of the classic kind integrated within the standard judicial machinery of the country . . . ': judgment, para. 77.
[121] ECHR, judgment of 27 November 1991, Series A, No. 219, and this *Year Book*, 63 (1992), p. 548. The Court also distinguished the position from that in the *Van de Hurk* case, Series A, No. 288, and this *Year Book*, 65 (1994), p. 529. In the latter the civil courts had held that the administrative tribunal in question provided sufficient safeguards.

Trial within a reasonable time (Article 6(1))—application of Article 6(1) to judicial investigation procedures

Case No. 36. Acquaviva case.[122] The Court held by 8 votes to 1 that Article 6(1) of the Convention was applicable to judicial investigation proceedings in France which had been instituted following a civil party complaint, but decided unanimously that the length of the proceedings in question had not exceeded a reasonable time.

This case was brought by the father and brother of a militant Corsican nationalist who was killed while on the run by a farmer, R, who claimed to be acting in self-defence. Criminal proceedings were begun against R and in December 1987 the applicants sought to join them as a civil party. Following investigations, the proceedings were finally concluded in April 1992. The applicants claimed that the length of the proceedings violated their right to a hearing within a reasonable time, as guaranteed by Article 6(1). The Court accepted that the proceedings in question concerned the applicants' 'civil rights and obligations', since under the procedure employed, establishing criminal liability was a prerequisite of obtaining compensation.[123] It decided, however, that the length of the proceedings was largely accounted for by the unstable political situation in Corsica at the relevant time and held that in these circumstances there had been no violation of Article 6(1).[124]

Right to a fair hearing before an independent tribunal (Article 6(1))—application to planning proceedings in the United Kingdom

Case No. 37. Bryan case.[125] In this case, which concerned the United Kingdom, the Court held unanimously that proceedings to challenge a planning enforcement notice had not involved a violation of Article 6(1) of the Convention.

In December 1989 the applicant received an enforcement notice from his local authority requiring him to demolish two brick buildings on his property because they had been erected without planning permission. He appealed against the decision, first to the Planning Inspector on grounds of fact and law, and then to the High Court on points of law, but in both cases was unsuccessful. He then took his case to Strasbourg, where he argued that the domestic proceedings had not complied with Article 6(1) of the Convention. The Commission, however, rejected the claim and the Court agreed.

Although the Court was satisfied that the proceedings before the Planning Inspector were fair, it held that the power of the Secretary of State for the Environment to revoke the Inspector's power to decide an appeal at any time was sufficient to deprive the Inspector of the appearance of independence required by Article 6(1).[126] Everything therefore turned on the powers of review

[122] ECHR, judgment of 21 November 1995, Series A, No. 333A, decided by a Chamber.
[123] Judge Baka dissented on this point.
[124] The Commission had reached the opposite conclusion.
[125] ECHR, judgment of 22 November 1995, Series A, No. 335A, decided by a Chamber.
[126] See, for example, the *Langborger* case, Series A, No. 155, and this *Year Book*, 60 (1989), p. 537.

exercisable by the High Court. An appeal to the latter was limited to points of law, but the High Court had jurisdiction to entertain all the grounds of appeal pleaded and could have quashed the Inspector's decision if it had been made by reference to irrelevant factors, or had failed to take account of relevant factors, or if the evidence relied on was incapable of supporting the Inspector's conclusions, or the decision was perverse or irrational. Holding that such an approach was reasonable in specialized areas of law, especially where there had already been a quasi-judicial procedure, the Court concluded that the scope of the High Court's power of review was enough to satisfy the requirements of Article 6(1).[127]

Trial within a reasonable time (Article 6(1))—just satisfaction (Article 50)

Cases Nos. 38 and 39. Ciricosta and Viola case. Terranova case.[128] Both cases concerned Italy, In the first, the Court decided unanimously that civil proceedings relating to the use of land for building had not exceeded a reasonable time; in the second, it decided unanimously that the length of proceedings in the Court of Audit had violated Article 6(1) and awarded damages and costs as just satisfaction. In the *Ciricosta and Viola* case the proceedings had begun in 1980 and were still unfinished. However, the Court considered that the delays were largely the applicants' responsibility. In the *Terranova* case, on the other hand, the proceedings had been concluded after more than eight years, but there were no extenuating circumstances.

Trial within a reasonable time (Article 6(1))—cases requiring 'exceptional diligence'—just satisfaction (Article 50)

Case No. 40. A and others v. *Denmark.*[129] The Court held by 6 votes to 3 that eight of the ten applicants in this case had suffered a violation of their rights under Article 6(1) of the Convention because civil proceedings in which they were involved had exceeded a reasonable time. With regard to the remaining two, it decided unanimously that there had been no violation. The successful applicants were awarded various sums as compensation for non-pecuniary damage, together with reimbursement of their legal costs and expenses.

The applicants in this case were all haemophiliacs, or the widows or parents of haemophiliacs now deceased. The applicants or their deceased relatives were all infected with HIV as a result of using contaminated blood products. Proceedings to obtain compensation were begun by the Danish Association of Haemophiliacs acting on behalf of the applicants. For various reasons the proceedings were prolonged, the relevant periods for the purpose of Article 6(1) ranging from four years to more than six years. In previous cases involving litigation over HIV infection the Court has indicated that, in view of the

---

[127] This is not the first time this type of issue has arisen. See, for example, the *Zumtobel* case, Series A, No. 268A, and this *Year Book*, 65 (1994), p. 536.

[128] ECHR, judgments of 4 December 1995, Series A, Nos. 337A and 337B, decided by the same Chamber.

[129] ECHR, judgment of 8 February 1996, decided by a Chamber.

claimants' reduced life expectancy, 'exceptional diligence' is called for on the part of the authorities.[130] Following this approach in the present case, it found that with only two exceptions the claims under Article 6(1) must be upheld.[131]

Right to a fair hearing (Article 6(1))—just satisfaction (Article 50)

Case No. 41. Botten case.[132] The Court held by 7 votes to 2 that proceedings in the Supreme Court of Norway had violated Article 6(1) of the Convention. However, it also decided unanimously that no award was necessary under Article 50.

In 1987 the applicant, an officer in the Norwegian Air Force, was Commander of the Telecommunications Station on Jan Mayen Island in the Arctic Ocean. In the course of an attempt to bring an injured fisherman ashore, using a rubber dinghy, the fisherman and one of the applicant's colleagues were drowned, leaving the applicant as the only survivor. Proceedings were then instituted in which the applicant was charged with negligence. At the trial he was acquitted, but on appeal the Supreme Court convicted him, giving a new judgment after a hearing at which the applicant's counsel was present, although the applicant himself was not.

The applicant maintained that the proceedings before the Supreme Court had violated Article 6(1) and the Court, by a majority, agreed. The key question was whether in giving a new judgment the Supreme Court had violated the applicant's right to a fair hearing by not summoning and hearing him in person. The Court answered the question in the affirmative because (*a*) the issue of guilt called for an assessment of complex facts and (*b*) the sentence required an assessment of the applicant's personality and character. In the light of these findings the Court considered that a fair trial required a direct assessment of the evidence given by the applicant in person. It therefore agreed with the Commission that there had been a violation of Article 6(1).[133]

Right to a fair hearing (Article 6(1))—just satisfaction (Article 50)

Case No. 42. Lobo Machado case.[134] In this case, which concerned proceedings before the Supreme Court of Portugal, the Court decided unanimously that there had been a violation of Article 6(1) of the Convention. As just satisfaction the Government was ordered to pay the applicant 1,500,000 escudos in respect of his costs and expenses.

[130] See *X* v. *France*, Series A, No. 236, and this *Year Book*, 63 (1992), p. 576; the *Vallée* case, Series A, No. 289A, and this *Year Book*, 65 (1994), p. 543; and the *Karakaya* case, Series A, No. 289B, and ibid., p. 546.
[131] Judges Ryssdal, Matscher and Foighel dissented on the ground that the applicants' actions were mainly responsible for delays in the proceedings.
[132] ECHR, judgment of 19 February 1996, decided by a Chamber.
[133] Judges Ryssdal and Gölcüklü dissented on the ground that the Supreme Court had decided the case on the basis of legal considerations exclusively and that if the applicant had been concerned about the sentence he could have sought leave to address the Supreme Court.
[134] ECHR, judgment of 20 February 1996, decided by a Grand Chamber.

In 1986 the applicant, who was retired, brought proceedings in an industrial tribunal on a point relating to his pension rights. The tribunal rejected his claim and its judgment was upheld by the Lisbon Court of Appeal. The applicant then appealed to the Supreme Court. After pleadings had been exchanged, the file was sent to the Attorney-General's department, which recommended in writing that the appeal should be dismissed. The Supreme Court then met in private to consider the case with a representative of the Attorney-General's department present and decided that the applicant's appeal should be dismissed.

The applicant claimed that the proceedings in the Supreme Court had violated Article 6(1) of the Convention and the Commission and Court agreed. Although it considered that the involvement of the Attorney-General could be justified on grounds of public interest, the Court considered that withholding his report from the applicant had infringed his right to adversarial proceedings, contrary to Article 6(1), and that this violation had then been compounded by the presence of the Deputy Attorney-General at the Supreme Court's private sitting.[135] In view of these rulings the Court held that it was unnecessary to consider the applicant's allegation that the Supreme Court had also failed to act as an independent and impartial tribunal.

As indicated earlier, the issue in this case was essentially identical to that considered on the same day by a different Grand Chamber in the *Vermeulen* case (Case No. 11), and the result was the same. It is interesting to note that the Belgian Government, which was the respondent in *Vermeulen*, was permitted to submit written observations in the present case.[136]

Right to a fair hearing by an impartial tribunal (Article 6(1))—the meaning of 'criminal charge' in Article 6(1)—the right to a remedy (Article 13)

Case No. 43. Putz case.[137] The Court held by 7 votes to 2 that Articles 6 and 13 of the Convention did not apply to pecuniary penalties imposed on the applicant for disrupting court proceedings in Austria and that, as a result, there had been no violation of those provisions.

In the course of criminal proceedings brought against the applicant for, *inter alia*, bankruptcy, several fines were imposed on him for 'disrupting court proceedings', the offending behaviour consisting of insulting and unfounded accusations directed against various judges. At Strasbourg the applicant complained of violations of Articles 6(1) and 13 of the Convention. The Commission upheld the first complaint and held that it was unnecessary to consider the second. The Court, however, rejected both complaints. As regards Article 6(1) in its 'criminal' aspect, the Court pointed out that there were three criteria laid down in its case law to determine the applicability of this provision, viz. the classification of the offence in national law; the nature of the offence; and the

---

[135] In a concurring opinion Judge Lopes Rocha indicated that his support for the decision was based only on the second of these points. On the first point see also the Court's decision in the *Bulut* case (Case No. 44), which was given on the same day.

[136] See judgment, paras. 6 and 27.

[137] ECHR, judgment of 22 February 1996, decided by a Chamber.

nature and severity of the penalty.[138] Although these are alternatives, it considered that none was satisfied in the present case.[139] As for Article 13, because Article 6 was inapplicable, there was no alleged violation of Convention rights calling for a national remedy. That provision too was therefore inapplicable.

Right to a fair and public hearing by an impartial tribunal (Article 6(1))—just satisfaction (Article 50)

Case No. 44. Bulut case.[140] In this case, which concerned Austria, the Court held by 8 votes to 1 that the Attorney-General's submission to the Supreme Court of a statement which was not communicated to the defence constituted a violation of Article 6(1) of the Convention. However, allegations that this provision had been violated in other respects were rejected by 8 votes to 1. As just satisfaction for the violation which had been identified, the Government was ordered to pay the applicant 75,000 Austrian schillings, less the sum already paid as legal aid, in respect of his costs and expenses.

In 1990 the applicant was convicted of attempting to bribe civil servants and sentenced to a fine which was suspended. One of the trial judges, Judge S, had already taken part in the preliminary proceedings as investigating judge, and although the applicant was aware of this, he did not object. When the case went to the Supreme Court the applicant argued that Judge S was disqualified from trying him. In a note which was not passed to the defence, the Attorney-General's office proposed that the applicant's appeal should be dismissed after a private deliberation. This was done and after remission of the case to the Court of Appeal the applicant's sentence was increased.

In his application to the Commission Mr Bulut claimed that the above events had given rise to a number of violations of Article 6(1). The Commission and the Court accepted that the action of the Attorney-General had violated the principle of equality of arms,[141] but rejected the argument that Judge S should not have taken part in the trial[142] and that the Supreme Court should have held a hearing.[143] Since Judge S had played only a minor role in the preliminary proceedings and there was no evidence of bias, his participation in the trial was unobjectionable. As regards the procedure adopted by the Supreme Court, since the grounds of appeal had raised no question of fact bearing on the assessment of the applicant's guilt or innocence, but had only challenged the trial court's assessment of the evidence, no hearing had been necessary.

---

[138] See, for example, the *Ravnsborg* case, Series A, No. 283B, and this *Year Book*, 65 (1994), p. 542.

[139] Judges De Meyer and Jungwiert dissented on this point and also considered that there had been a violation of Article 13. The former's dissenting opinion contains a well argued critique of the Court's case law on this type of issue.

[140] ECHR, judgment of 22 February 1996, decided by a Chamber.

[141] Judge Matscher dissented on this point.

[142] Judge Morenilla dissented on this point, repeating the argument he had put forward in the *Diennet* case (Case No. 22).

[143] Judge De Meyer dissented on this point and, like Judge Morenilla, also reviewed the Court's treatment of the issue of impartiality in its previous case law.

Trial within a reasonable time (Article 6(1))—just satisfaction (Article 50)

Case No. 45. Mitap and Müftüoğlu case.[144] The Court held unanimously that there had been a violation of Article 6(1) of the Convention on account of the length of criminal proceedings brought against the applicants in Turkey. As just satisfaction under Article 50 the Court awarded them 80,000 French francs in respect of non-pecuniary damage, and 60,000 francs, less the sum received as a legal aid, as reimbursement of their costs and expenses.

The applicants, who were suspected of being members of a left-wing revolutionary organization, were arrested in 1981, held in detention and eventually tried and convicted in proceedings which concluded in December 1995.

Complaints that the excessive length of their pre-trial detention contravened Article 5(3) and that the court which had tried them did not satisfy the requirements of Article 6(1) were, the Court found, outside its jurisdiction, because Turkey's declaration under Article 46 of the Convention covered only facts or events occurring since 22 January 1990, when the declaration was deposited. However, their complaint concerning the length of the proceedings could be considered for the period between the date of the declaration and the termination of the proceedings in 1995. Applying the principles to be found in its case law, and taking into account the state of the proceedings in January 1990, the Court decided that there had been a violation of Article 6(1) and made an award of compensation.

Right to a fair hearing (Article 6(1))—the need for a dispute over a 'right'—the presumption of innocence (Article 6(2))

Case No. 46. Leutscher case.[145] In this case, which concerned the Netherlands, the Court held unanimously that Article 6(1) of the Convention did not apply to the procedure under the law of the Netherlands allowing a person who had been acquitted to seek reimbursement of counsel's fees, and that the relevant decision of the domestic court had not violated Article 6(2).

The applicant was tried in the Netherlands on a charge of tax evasion and initially convicted, but on appeal the proceedings were discontinued on the ground that the criminal charge had not been determined within a reasonable time, as required by Article 6(1) of the Convention, which is part of the law of the Netherlands. The applicant then sought reimbursement of his legal costs and expenses, but was awarded only a fraction of his claim on the ground that since the original conviction was correct, there was nothing to justify reimbursement.

In his application to Strasbourg Mr Leutscher claimed that the reimbursement proceedings had been unfair, contrary to Article 6(1), and that the reason given for rejecting his claim had violated the presumption of innocence, contrary to Article 6(2).[146] The Court held that the first of these claims must fail in view

[144] ECHR, judgment of 25 March 1996, decided by a Chamber.
[145] ECHR, judgment of 26 March 1996, decided by a Chamber.
[146] For the text of Article 6(2), see Case No. 9 above.

of its recent decision in the case of *Masson and Van Zon* (Case No. 27), where the situation was identical. As regards the presumption of innocence, the Court recognized that this could be engaged by proceedings relating to the reimbursement of expenses, but held that it had not been violated in the present case. Reimbursement had been denied in the exercise of a wide discretion, the national court was fully entitled to have regard to the circumstances, and in the Court's view had not made a finding as to the applicant's guilt.[147] The claim under Article 6(2) must therefore also fail.

Right to respect for private and family life (Article 8(1))—application to deportation decision

Case No. 47. Boughanemi case.[148] The Court held by 7 votes to 2 that the applicant's deportation from France did not constitute a violation of the Convention.

The applicant in this case was born in Tunisia in 1960, but in 1968 arrived in France and settled there with his family. He also claimed to have cohabited briefly with a woman of French nationality, Miss S, who bore him a child in 1993. In 1988 he was deported from France after had had been convicted of various offences and sentenced to four years' imprisonment for *inter alia* living on the earnings of prostitution. He returned illegally, but in 1994 was deported again. In his application to Strasbourg Mr Boughanemi relied on Article 8 of the Convention, which was quoted in Case No. 4, and which protects the right to respect for private and family life.

The Commission upheld his complaint, but the Court rejected it. Although not entirely convinced by the evidence of family ties between the applicant and Miss S, the Court decided that the applicant's recognition of his paternity, and his own family links with France, were enough to bring the case within Article 8. It pointed out, however, that the applicant had not severed his links with Tunisia[149] and had been convicted of serious offences. In these circumstances the Court was not prepared to hold that his deportation was disproportionate to the legitimate aims pursued, namely the prevention of disorder and the prevention of crime. It therefore concluded that there had been no violation of Article 8.

---

[147] The Court referred in its judgment to the *Lutz* case, Series A, No. 123, and this *Year Book*, 58 (1987), p. 490. Surprisingly, however, it did not cite the *Sekanina* case, Series A, No. 266A, and this *Year Book*, 64 (1993), p. 538, although the latter is a more recent decision in which Article 6 (2) was found to have been violated. On the scope of the Court's jurisprudence concerning the presumption of innocence, see Robertson and Merrills, *Human Rights in Europe* (3rd edn., 1993), pp. 105–8.

[148] ECHR, judgment of 24 April 1996, decided by a Chamber.

[149] In the Court's view this factor distinguished the present case from previous cases in which deportation had been found to violate Article 8. See, for example, the *Beldjoudi* case, Series A, No. 234A, and this *Year Book*, 63 (1992), p. 572; and the *Nasri* case, Series A, No. 324, and this *Year Book*, 65 (1995), p. 556.

Trial within a reasonable time (Article 6(1))—just satisfaction (Article 50)

Case No. 48. Ausiello case.[150] In this case, which concerned Italy, the Court decided unanimously that there had been a violation of Article 6(1) of the Convention on account of the length of proceedings brought by the applicant in the Court of Audit. It also decided that no award of just satisfaction was necessary.

The proceedings in question had lasted for more than six years, including a period of more than two years when they had lain dormant for which the Government had no explanation. The Court therefore had no difficulty in agreeing with the Commission's conclusion that there had been a violation of Article 6(1).

Right to a fair hearing by an impartial tribunal (Article 6(1))—successive trials before the same judges

Case No. 49. Thomann case.[151] In this case, which concerned Switzerland, the Court decided unanimously that there had been no violation of Article 6(1) of the Convention.

In May 1989 the applicant was tried and convicted *in absentia* on various charges of fraud. He then successfully requested a retrial, but was informed that the retrial was to be conducted by the three judges who had sat in the original trial. The applicant's objection to this arrangement was considered by a different court, but was rejected. The retrial was then held and the applicant was again found guilty. In his application Mr Thomann claimed that his retrial had not been conducted by an impartial tribunal as Article 6(1) requires. The Court, however, agreed with the Commission that the complaint must be rejected. Pointing out that there was no reason to question the judges' subjective impartiality, the Court considered that the requirement of objective impartiality was also satisfied. At the retrial the judges were in no way bound by their original decision and undertook a completely fresh review of the case. Moreover, it would be wrong to give defendants who had been tried *in absentia* an advantage over those who appeared for trial, by allowing the former to obtain a second hearing of their case by different judges, a concession which would also slow down the work of the courts. The Court therefore concluded that there had been no violation of Article 6(1).

PART THREE: DECISIONS ON THE ISSUE OF JUST SATISFACTION

Case No. 50. Papamichalopoulos v. *Greece.* ECHR, judgment of 31 October 1995, Series A, No. 330B, decided by a Chamber. The Court decided unanimously that the respondent must return to the applicants within six months a substantial area of land which it had unlawfully taken over, including the

---

[150] ECHR, judgment of 21 May 1996, decided by a Chamber.
[151] ECHR, judgment of 10 June 1996, decided by a Chamber.

buildings on the land. Failing such restitution, it was to pay the applicants a large sum in respect of pecuniary damage.[152] It was also to pay them compensation for non-pecuniary damage and a further sum in respect of costs and expenses. Finally, it was to pay experts who had valued the land at the Court's request a sum representing the costs and fees involved in writing their report. It will be noted that in this case the Court took the unusual step of ordering restitution. Other notable features were that the Government sought unsuccessfully to challenge the validity of the experts' report and was required to pay for it, although these costs had not been incurred in the normal way. For the Court's decision on the merits, finding a violation of Article 1 of Protocol No. 1, see ECHR, judgment of 24 June 1993, Series A, No. 260B, and this *Year Book*, 64 (1993), p. 532.

Case No. 51. Welch v. *United Kingdom*, ECHR, judgment of 26 February 1996, decided by a Chamber. Compensation for alleged pecuniary and non-pecuniary damage was denied on the ground that no case for such compensation had been demonstrated. Compensation for costs and expenses incurred in the Article 50 proceedings was also denied on the ground that the claims for damages had been rejected. For the Court's decision on the merits, finding a violation of Article 7 of the Convention, see ECHR, judgment of 9 February 1995, Series A, No. 307A, and this *Year Book*, 66 (1995), p. 530.

PART FOUR: CASES IN WHICH THERE WAS NO DECISION ON THE MERITS

Case No. 52. Agrotexim v. *Greece*, ECHR, judgment of 24 October 1995, Series A, No. 330A, decided by a Chamber. Application based on Articles 6 and 13 of the Convention and Article 1 of Protocol No. 1 rejected by 8 votes to 1 on the ground that the applicants lacked the status of 'victim' within the meaning of Article 25 of the Convention. The applicants' main complaint was that shares which they held in the FB company had fallen in value as a consequence of measures taken against the latter's property. The Court, however, ruled that the applicants lacked standing, citing in support the decision of the International Court of Justice in the *Barcelona Traction* case.[153] Judge Walsh dissented.

Case No. 53. Baegen v. *Belgium*, ECHR, judgment of 27 October 1995, Series A, No. 327B, decided by a Chamber. Application based on Articles 6(1) and 6(3)(*d*) of the Convention struck out, following failure by the applicant to pursue the case (Rule 51(2) of Rules of Court B).[154]

[152] It is interesting to note that when calculating the sum due, the Court said that it had found the decisions of international courts and tribunals in expropriation cases to be 'a precious source of inspiration': judgment, para. 36.

[153] *Barcelona Traction, Light and Power Company Ltd.*, judgment of 5 February 1970, *ICJ Reports*, 1970, p. 3.

[154] Rule 51(2) of Rules of Court B provides:
'When the Chamber is informed of a friendly settlement, arrangement or other fact of a kind to provide a solution of the matter, it may, after consulting, if necessary, the parties and the Delegates of the Commission, strike the case out of the list.

The same shall apply where the circumstances warrant the conclusion that a party who filed an application by virtue of Article 48 § 1 (e) of the Convention does not intend to pursue the application or if, for any other reason, further examination of the case is not justified.'

Case No. 54. Fouquet v. *France*, ECHR, judgment of 31 January 1996, decided by a Chamber. Application based on Article 6(1) of the Convention struck out, following a friendly settlement, providing for the payment of compensation (Rule 49(2) of Rules of Court A).[155]

J. G. MERRILLS

[155] This provision is identical to Rule 51(2) of Rules of Court B quoted above.

DECISIONS OF THE COURT OF JUSTICE OF THE EUROPEAN COMMUNITIES DURING 1996*

I *External relations—accession by the Community to the ECHR Convention— Opinion under Article 228(6) of the EC Treaty—embargo against the Federal Republic of Yugoslavia (Serbia and Montenegro)—impounding of an aircraft— customs procedure applicable to products originating in the Faroe Islands—concept of originating products—post-clearance recovery of customs duties—free movement of goods—Common Customs Tariff—common commercial policy—goods from non-Member countries—retroactivity of judgment*

I.1 *Opinion 2/94, Accession by the Community to the European Convention for the Protection of Human Rights and Fundamental Freedoms*, 28 March 1996.¹ The Court of Justice was asked by the Council of the European Union to give an Opinion pursuant to Article 228(6) of the EC Treaty² as to whether accession by the Community to the European Convention for the Protection of Human Rights and Fundamental Freedoms of 4 November 1950 (ECHR Convention) would be compatible with the EC Treaty.

A number of Member States argued that the request for an Opinion was premature. No draft agreement on Community accession had been created which the Court of Justice could examine. Further, the Council have not even adopted a decision in principle to open accession negotiations.

On the question whether the request was admissible, the Court of Justice pointed out that the purpose of the procedure under Article 228(6) was to pre-empt complications which would result from legal disputes concerning the compatibility with the EC Treaty of international agreements binding upon the Community.³

The Court of Justice considered that the possible accession of the Community raised two questions, (*a*) the competence of the Community to conclude the agreement in question and (*b*) the compatibility of the agreement with the EC Treaty and, in particular, its compatibility with those provisions relating to the jurisdiction of the Court of Justice.

As to the question of competence, the Court repeated its earlier ruling in *Opinion 1/78*,⁴ that it is in the interests of all concerned to have any issue of competence clarified from the outset of negotiations and even before the main points of the agreement are negotiated. The sole condition required is that the purpose of the agreement is known before negotiations are commenced.

---

* © Sara Masters, 1997.
¹ [1996] ECR I-1759.
² Article 228 (6) provides:
   'The Council, the Commission or a Member State may obtain the opinion of the Court of Justice as to whether an agreement envisaged is compatible with the provisions of this Treaty. Where the opinion of the Court of Justice is adverse, the agreement may enter into force only accordance with Article N of the Treaty on European Union.'
³ See also *Opinion 3/94* of 13 December 1995, [1995] ECR I-4577.
⁴ [1979] ECR 2871.

Applying this principle to the present request for an Opinion, the Court concluded that the purpose of an agreement providing for Community accession to the ECHR was clear. No formal Council decision to open negotiations was necessary. Further, to ensure the effectiveness of the procedure set out in Article 228(6) of the EC Treaty, the question of competence could be referred to the Court of Justice not only when negotiations had already begun, but also prior to their commencement. Accordingly, the Court of Justice concluded that the request for an Opinion was admissible in so far as it concerned the Community's competence to accede to the ECHR Convention.

Turning to the question whether accession to the ECHR Convention was compatible with the EC Treaty, and in particular with Articles 164 and 219 thereof relating to the jurisdiction of the Court of Justice,[5] the Court concluded that it was not in a position to give an Opinion. The Court did not have sufficient information on how the Community would submit to the mechanisms of judicial control established under the ECHR Convention.

On the substance of the question of the Community's competence to accede, the Court of Justice concluded that the Community had no competence to accede to the ECHR Convention unless and until the EC Treaty was amended. First, the Court pointed out that no Treaty provisions conferred any general power upon the Community institutions to enact rules on human rights or to enter into international agreements in this field. The Court thus went on to examine whether Article 235 of the EC Treaty[6] could form the legal basis for accession, noting that Article 235 could not be used as a basis for widening the scope of Community powers beyond the framework created by the EC Treaty as a whole.

The Court of Justice emphasized the importance of respect for human rights enshrined both in the preamble to the Single European Act and in various provisions of the Treaty on European Union,[7] and reaffirmed that fundamental rights form an integral part of the fundamental principles of Community law. The Court of Justice noted, in particular, that the ECHR had a special significance.[8] Accordingly, the Court concluded that respect for human rights was a condition for the lawfulness of all Community acts.

Accession by the Community to the ECHR would, however, entail a substantial change in the present system for protecting human rights under Community law. The Community would be entering into a distinct institutional

---

[5] Articles 164 and 219 of the EC Treaty provide:
Article 164
The Court of Justice shall ensure that in the interpretation and application of this Treaty the law is observed.
. . .
Article 219
Member States undertake not to submit a dispute concerning the interpretation or application of this Treaty to any method of settlement other than those provided for therein.'

[6] Article 235 provides
'If action by the Community should prove necessary to attain, in the course of the operation of the common market, one of the objectives of the Community and this Treaty has not provided the necessary powers, the Council shall, acting unanimously on a proposal from the Commission and after consulting the European Parliament, take the appropriate measures.'

[7] See the preamble to Article F.(2), the fifth indent of Article J.1(2), and Article K.2(1) of the Treaty on European Union.

[8] See, in particular Case C–260/89, *ERT*, [1991] ECR I–2925.

system. Further, all provisions of the ECHR would have to be integrated into the Community legal order. Such changes would be of constitutional significance and would therefore go beyond the scope of the use of Article 235 of the EC Treaty as a legal basis. Accession to the ECHR would require amendment to the EC Treaty.

I.2 *Case C–84/95, Bosphorus Hava Yollari Turizm ve Ticaret AS v. Minister for Transport, Energy and Communication and others*, 30 July 1996. By Council Regulations (EEC) No. 990/93 concerning trade between the European Economic Community and the Federal Republic of Yugoslavia (Serbia and Montenegro),[9] the Community implemented certain aspects of the sanctions taken by the United Nations Security Council against the Federal Republic of Yugoslavia arising out of the conflict in the Balkans.[10]

Bosphorous Hava Yollari Turizm ve Ticaret AS ('Bosphorous Airways'), a Turkish company, took in April 1992 a 'dry lease'[11] over two aircraft owned by the Yugoslavian national airline, JAT, for a period of four years. Pursuant to the 'dry lease', Bosphorus Airways provided the cabin and flight crew and had complete control of the management of the aircraft for the period of the lease. JAT, however, remained beneficial owner. Whilst one of the aircraft was preparing for take off at Dublin Airport, the Minister for Transport, Energy and Communications in Ireland ordered that it be impounded under Article 8 of Council Regulation 990/93 on the grounds that it was an aircraft in which a majority or controlling interest was held by a person or undertaking operating from the Federal Republic of Yugoslavia.

Proceedings were commenced by Bosphorus Airways before the Irish courts, and a question was referred to the Court of Justice on the question whether Article 8 of Council Regulation (EEC) No. 990/93[12] applied to the impounded aircraft.

Bosphorus Airways first submitted that Article 8 did not apply to aircraft whose day to day control had been entrusted under a lease to an undertaking which was not based in or operating from the Federal Republic of Yugoslavia. In support, it argued that the purpose of the Regulation was to penalize the Federal Republic of Yugoslavia and its nationals but was not to extend the sanctions unnecessarily to wholly innocent undertakings pursuing their activities from a neighbouring State with which the Community has friendly relations.

This argument was rejected by the Court of Justice. It held that the scope of Article 8 of Regulation 990/93 must be determined according to the text and aims of the Security Council resolutions to which it was designed to give effect and, in particular, paragraph 24 of Resolution 820(1993) which stated that:

---

[9] OJ, 1993, L102/14.

[10] See, in particular, United Nations Security Council Resolution 713 (1991) adopted on 25 September 1991, United Nations Security Council Resolution 787 (1992) adopted on 16 November 1992, and United Nations Security Council Resolution 820 (1993), adopted on 17 April 1993.

[11] An aircraft 'dry lease' is a lease under which an aircraft but no cabin and flight crew are provided.

[12] The first paragraph of Article 8 provides, *inter alia*:

'All vehicles, freight vehicles, rolling stock and aircraft in which a majority or controlling interest is held by a person or undertaking in or operating from the Federal Republic of Yugoslavia (Serbia and Montenegro) shall be impounded by the competent authorities of the Member States.'

all States shall impound all vessels, freight vehicles, rolling stock and aircraft in their territories in which a majority of controlling interest is held by a person or undertaking in or operating from the Federal Republic of Yugoslavia.

There was nothing in the resolution to indicate that it was necessary for the person or undertaking with ownership of the aircraft to have day to day control of it. Moreover, the word 'interest' contained in paragraph 24 of Resolution 820 (1993) could not, on any view, exclude ownership as a determining criterion for impounding. Further, the impounding of an aircraft leased to a non-Yugoslav undertaking was consistent with the aims of the sanction, namely to put pressure on the Republic.

By contrast, the use of day to day control as a criterion for the application of Article 8 of the Regulation would jeopardize the effectiveness of the strengthening of the sanctions. It would permit Yugoslav nationals to transfer the day to day operation and control of means of transport to evade application of the sanctions.

As a second line of attack, Bosphorous Airways argued that the impounding of a Yugoslav owned aircraft subject to a 'dry lease' infringed Bosphorus Airways' fundamental rights, in particular, its right to peaceful enjoyment of its property and freedom to pursue a commercial activity, as the impounding of the aircraft would destroy its air charter business. Bosphorus Airways also argued that the action was disproportionate.[13] Rental payable to JAT under the lease was being held in a blocked account. Thus, the impounding of the aircraft was unnecessary.

This argument was also rejected by the Court of Justice. The Court considered that any measure imposing sanctions affecting property rights and the freedom to pursue commercial activity would affect wholly innocent third parties. On the facts, however, the importance of the aims pursed by the sanctions were such as to justify damages, even of a substantial nature, to some operators. The Court thus concluded that, compared with the fundamental general interest for the international community of putting an end to the war and to the massive violations of human rights and humanitarian rights and humanitarian international law in the Republic of Bosnia-Herzegovina, the impounding of the aircraft leased to Bosphorus Airways could not be regarded as disproportionate.

I.3 *Joined Cases C–153/94 and C–204/94, The Queen v. Commissioners of Customs and Excise, ex parte Faroe Seafood Co. Ltd. and others*, 14 May 1996.[14] Faroe Seafood, an English company, imported into the United Kingdom from the Faroe Islands under cover of EUR1 certificates[15] shrimps and prawns which came, *inter alia*, from Foroya Fiskasola, a co-operative governed by Faroese law.

---

[13] The doctrine of proportionality has been developed by the Court of Justice in a number of cases. In summary, it provides that a provision of Community law satisfies the principle of proportionality if the means used are suitable for achieving the aims of the measure in question, provided that the means used do not go beyond what is necessary to achieve those aims. For a good recent example of the application of the doctrine, see Case C–426/93, *Germany* v. *Council*, [1995] ECR I–3723, paragraph 42 of the judgment.

[14] [1996] ECR I–2465.

[15] EUR1 movement certificates are used to indicate the originating status of certain goods for customs tariff purposes.

Arthur Smith acted as shipping, stevedoring and forward agent in relation to a number of the consignments imported.

Under Community law, crustaceans and molluscs originating in the Faroe Islands could be imported free of customs duties into the United Kingdom upon production of a EUR1 certificate completed by the Faroese competent authorities proving that the prawns and shrimps fulfilled certain criteria.[16]

In 1991, a mission of enquiry conducted by the Commission visited the Faroe Islands. It concluded that a number of EUR1 certificates had been wrongly issued and should be cancelled. The Faroese authorities disputed the Commission's conclusions and maintained that the certificates were valid. In reliance upon the Commission's Report, the United Kingdom customs authorities proceeded to demand uncollected customs duties on imports from the Faroe Islands between May 1989 and September 1991. Faroe Seafoods received a demand for almost £500,000, whilst the sum of more than £1,000,000 was claimed from Arthur Smith.

Proceedings were commenced before the English High Court and a number of questions referred to the Court of Justice concerning the rules for determining the origin of goods and post-clearance recovery of import duties not initially demanded. A substantial number of questions were referred to the Court of Justice.

The Court of Justice's judgment is lengthy and complex. It does, however, raise a number of interesting issues as to the division of powers between the State of exportation and State of importation on the question of the validity of EUR1 certificates designating the originating status of goods, and also as to the party bearing the burden of proof of the originating status of the goods.

After setting out in detail the legislative provisions applicable for applying the preferential system for certain goods of Faroese origin, the Court concluded that whilst the issue of EUR1 certificates by the competent Faroese authorities indicated that the goods were of Faroese origin, it nevertheless remained open to the Commission to check by sending a mission of enquiry. Confirming its previous judgment in Case C–12/92, *Huygen and others*,[17] the Court held that where a subsequent verification does not confirm that the goods are of the origin stated, it must be concluded that the goods are of unknown origin and that the EUR1 certificate was wrongly granted. In such circumstances, a Member State must in principle carry out post-clearance recovery of the duty that should have been paid.

---

[16] See Article 2(2) of Regulation No. 2051/74 on the customs procedure applicable to certain products originating in and coming from the Faroe Islands (OJ, 1974, L212/33). For further legislative background to these proceedings, see Commission Regulation (EEC) No. 3184/74 concerning the definition of the concept of 'originating products' and methods applicable to certain products originating in and coming from the Faroe Islands (OJ, 1974, L344/1), Council Regulation (EEC) No. 1697/79 on the post-clearance recovery of import duties or export duties which have not been required of the person liable for payment on goods entered for a customs procedure involving the obligation to pay such duties (OJ, 1979, L197/1), and Commission Regulation (EEC) No. 2164/91 of 23 July 1991 laying down provisions for the implementation of Article 5(2) of Council Regulation (EEC) No. 1697/79 (OJ, 1991 L201/16).

[17] [1993] ECR I–6381, at paragraphs 17 and 18 of the judgment.

The Court then went on to consider whether such a duty still existed in circumstances where the Member State of exportation disputed the Commission's findings. In a number of judgments,[18] the Court of Justice had interpreted similar provisions and concluded that determination of the origin of goods was based upon a division of powers between the customs authorities parties to the relevant agreements. The mechanism established for determining the origin of goods could only function if the customs authorities of the importing State accepted the determinations legally made by the exporting State.

On the facts of the present case, however, the Court distinguished its decision in *Les Rapides Savoyards*. It concluded that the customs authorities of the importing State were not bound by the fact that the Faroese authorities continued to insist that the certificates had been validly issued.

The Court reasoned that the need for the customs authorities of the importing Member States to recognize assessments made by the customs authorities of the exporting State did not arise in the same way where the preferential system was established not by an international agreement binding the Community to a non-member country on the basis of reciprocal obligations, but by a unilateral Community measure, namely the legislative provisions granting preferential treatment to certain goods originating from the Faroe Islands. Furthermore, unlike the legislative background to the Court of Justice's judgment in *Les Rapides Savoyards*, there did not exist in this case a procedure for the settlement of disputes concerning origin. Finally, the rules applicable in the present case differed from those entered into subsequently under the free-trade agreement concluded between the Community and the Government of Denmark and the Home Government of the Faroe Islands.[19] The annexes to that free trade agreement contained a protocol concerning the definition of the concept 'originating product' and methods of administrative cooperation. In particular, Article 25(3) of that agreement laid down the principle that disputes were to be settled by a joint customs committee.

On the question of the party bearing the burden and means of proof of the originating status of the goods,[20] the Court of Justice noted that rules as to the burden and means of proof of the originating status of the goods were governed by national law only in so far as they are not covered by Community law. The Court repeated that under the Community rules applicable in this case, where a subsequent verification of the origin of the goods did not confirm that the rules on origin were complied with, the EUR1 certificates and preferential tariff were wrongly granted. In such circumstances, the Court of Justice concluded that the

[18] Case 218/83, *Les Rapides Savoyards and others* v. *Directeur des Douanes et Droits Indirects*, [1984] ECR 3105, where the Court of Justice considered the free trade agreement concluded between the (then) EEC and the Swiss Confederation on 22 July 1972 (OJ, English Special Edition 1972 (31 December), p. 190); Case C–12/92, *Huygen and others*, [1993] ECR I–6381, where the Court of Justice considered the free trade agreement between the (then) EEC and the Republic of Austria on 22 July 1972 (OJ, English Special Edition (31 December 1972), p. 3); Case C–432/92, *Anastasiou and others*, [1994] ECR I- 3087, where the Court of Justice considered the agreement of 19 December 1972 establishing an association between the (then) EEC and the Republic of Cyprus (OJ, 1973, L133/1). Each of these agreements contains a protocol concerning the concept of 'originating products' and methods of administrative co-operation.

[19] Approved on behalf of the Community by a Council Decision of 2 December 1991 (OJ, 1991, L371/1).

[20] For the purposes of applying Council Regulations Nos. 2051/74 and 3184/74.

burden lay on the exporter to show proof, by furnishing all appropriate supporting documents, that the shrimps and prawns of Faroese origin had been separated from the shrimps of other origins. In the absence of such proof, the shrimps and prawns could no longer be regarded as being Faroese, with the result that the EUR1 certificates and the preferential tariff must therefore be regarded as having been wrongly granted.

I.4 *Case C–126/94, Société Cadi Surgelés and others* v. *Ministre des Finances and others,* 7 November 1996. This reference from the Tribunal d'Instance (District Court), Paris XII, allowed the Court of Justice to return once more to the subject of certain charges, the *octroi de mer* (dock dues) and the *droit additionel* (additional duty), levied by the French authorities upon certain goods upon their entry into the French overseas departments. The nature and effect of these charges had already been considered in detail by the Court of Justice in Case C–163/90, *Administration des Douanes et Droits Indirects* v. *Legros and others,*[21] and Joined Cases C–363/93 and C–407/93 to C–411/93, *Lancray* v. *Direction Générale des Douanes.*[22]

In the light of the Court's previous judgments in *Legros* and *Lancray*, the sole question that arose in the present case was whether a Member State was permitted to levy charges such as the *octroi de mer* and the *droit additionel* on imports of goods from non-Member States which are not linked to the Community by special agreement.

The Court of Justice noted that the Community Customs Union created by Article 9(1) of the EC Treaty involved not only the prohibition of customs duties based on imports and exports, but also the adoption of a common customs tariff in trade between Member States and third countries. The fact that no mention was made in the section on the setting-up of the common customs tariff of 'charges having an equivalent effect' was not material. Accordingly, Member States had not been competent, since 1 July 1968,[23] to introduce unilaterally new charges on goods imported from non-Member countries or to raise the level of those charges in existence at the time.[24]

The Court of Justice, however, considered that the position was different in the case of charges which already existed when the Common Customs Tariff came into force. Member States could retain such charges in effect. However, as a derogation from the rules contained in the common commercial policy, the option for a Member State to retain existing charges should be narrowly construed. It was for the national court to determine whether the charge in

[21] [1992] ECR I–4625, where the Court of Justice ruled that a charge proportional to the customs value of the goods, levied by a Member State on goods from another Member State by reason of their entry into the territory of the former Member State, constitutes a charge having an effect equivalent to a customs duty, even if the charge is also imposed on goods entering that region from another part of the same State.

[22] [1994] ECR I–3957, where the Court of Justice ruled that a charge such as the *octroi de mer*, which is levied on all goods entering a region within the Member State in question, constitutes a measure having an equivalent effect to a customs duty not only when it is levied on goods entering that region from other Member States, but also when it is levied on goods entering that region from another part of the same State.

[23] The date upon which the Common Customs Tariff came into effect.

[24] In its conclusions, the Court of Justice re-affirmed its decision in Joined Cases 37 and 38/73, *Diamantarbeiders* v. *Indiamex*, [1973] ECR 1609.

question, having regard to all of its essential characteristics, could be regarded as an existing charge. Further, any increase, however small, in the level of the charge introduced since 1 July 1968 was incompatible with Community law.[25] Accordingly, the Court of Justice concluded that a tax such as the *droit additionnel*, whether categorized as a mere increase or as a new charge, was incompatible with Community law.

In the event that the Court of Justice found that the charges at issue were incompatible with Community law, the French Government requested that the effect of the judgment be limited in time, i.e. that the judgment be prospective only. In *Legros*, the French Government had successfully persuaded the Court of Justice to limit the retroactivity of its judgment. There the Court had held that, owing to overriding considerations of legal certainty, provisions of the EC Treaty could not be relied upon in support of claims for the reimbursement of charges such as dock dues paid before the date of the Court of Justice's judgment (16 July 1992), except by claimants who had initiated legal proceedings or made a claim before that date.

In the present case, the Court of Justice followed its ruling in *Legros* but rejected any further restriction on the retroactivity of its judgment after 16 July 1992. The Court held that, following its judgments in *Diamantarbeiders* and *Legros*, the French Government could not have reasonably believed that the levy of the *droit additionel* or the *octroi de mer* (in so far as it could not be characterized as an existing charge) on the import of goods from third countries, not linked to the Community by a special agreement, was compatible with Community law.

II. *Liability of a Member State in damages for breach of Community law—free movement—goods—services—breaches attributable to the national legislature— conditions for Member State liability—Telecoms Directive 90/531/EEC—liability for incorrect implementation of Directive 90/314/EEC on package travel, package holidays and package tours—non-transposition—liability of a Member State in damages*

II.1 In the course of 1996, the Court of Justice had four opportunities to discuss the principle, set out its judgment in Joined Cases C–6 & 9/90, *Francovich* v. *Italy*[26] ('*Francovich*'), of the liability of a Member State to compensate an individual for loss suffered by reason of that Member State's breach of Community law.

II.2 *Joined Cases C–46 and 48/93, Brasserie du Pêcheur SA v. Germany; R v. Secretary of State for Transport, ex parte Factortame Ltd. and others.*[27] In this long-awaited judgment from the Court of Justice, the Court considered in detail the effect of its judgment in *Francovich*.

---

[25] See Joined Cases 37 and 38/73, *Diamantarbeiders* v. *Indiamex*, [1973] ECR 1609.
[26] [1991] ECR I–5357.
[27] [1996] ECR I–1029.

Brasserie du Pêcheur, a French company claimed damages[28] in the sum of 1,800,000 DM against the German Government for loss suffered. In late 1981, it was forced to discontinue the export of French beer to Germany owing to the fact that the beer did not comply with German law laying down purity requirements.[29] By its judgment in Case 178/84, *Commission v. Germany*,[30] the Court had ruled that the prohibition on marketing beers imported from other Member States which did not comply with German purity laws was incompatible with Article 30 of the EC Treaty.

In 1988, Factortame and a number of other companies brought an action in the English High Court to challenge the compatibility of Part II of the Merchant Shipping Act 1988[31] with Community law and, in particular, Article 52 of the Treaty. By its judgment in Case C-221/89, *Factortame II*,[32] the Court of Justice ruled that conditions laid down under the registration system as to nationality, residence and domicile were contrary to Community law, but a requirement for registration that a vessel be managed and its operations directed and controlled from within the United Kingdom was not.

At the same time, the Commission brought infringement proceedings under Article 169 of the EC Treaty against the United Kingdom. Following an application for interim measures, the President of the Court of Justice ordered suspension of the nationality conditions contained in the Merchant Shipping Act 1988.[33] Finally, by a judgment dated 4 October 1991,[34] the Court of Justice confirmed that the registration conditions were contrary to Community law.

In the meantime, the Divisional Court in the United Kingdom made[35] an order designed to give effect to the Court of Justice's judgment[36] in *Factortame II* and at the same time directed the plaintiffs to give detailed particulars of their claims for damages.

The first issue addressed by the Court of Justice in its judgment in *Brasserie du Pêcheur* was whether the principle of Member State liability for breaches of Community law confirmed by the Court in *Francovich* had any application

---

[28] Pursuant to section 839 of the *Bürgerliches Gesetzbuch* ('BGB') and Article 34 of the *Grundgesetz* ('GG').

   Section 839 of the BGB provides, *inter alia*:
   'If an official wilfully or negligently commits a breach of official duty incumbent upon him as against a third party, he shall compensate the third party for any damage arising therefrom.'
   Article 34 of the GG provides:
   'If a person infringes, in the exercise of a public office entrusted to him, the obligations incumbent upon him as against a third party, liability therefor shall attach in principle to the State or to the body in whose service he is engaged.'

[29] Namely sections 9 and 10 of the *Biersteuergesetz* of 14 March 1952 (Act on Beer Duty), in the version dated 14 December 1976.

[30] [1987] ECR 1227.

[31] The Merchant Shipping Act 1988 entered into force on 1 December 1988, subject to a transitional period expiring on 31 March 1989. Under the Act, a new register for British fishing boats was introduced and registration upon that register, including the registration of vessels already previously registered in the United Kingdom, was made subject to certain conditions relating to the nationality, residence and domicile of the owners. Fishing boats ineligible for registration were deprived of the right to fish in British waters.

[32] [1991] ECR I-3905.

[33] Case C-246/89R, *EC Commission v. United Kingdom*, [1989] ECR 3125.

[34] Case C-246/89, *EC Commission v. United Kingdom*, [1991] ECR I-4585.

[35] On 2 October 1991.

[36] Of 25 July 1991, [1991] ECR I-3905.

where the national legislature was responsible for the infringement of Community law in question. A number of Member States[37] had argued that Member States could only be liable to individuals if the provisions in question were not directly effective and that the judgment in *Francovich* was intended merely to fill a lacuna in the system of safeguarding individual rights. The Court of Justice rejected such an approach to actions for damages. It repeated its previous case law[38] and confirmed that the principle of direct effect is only a minimum guarantee and is not sufficient in itself to secure, in every case, the rights of individuals to have the benefit of the rights conferred on them by Community law. In the event of the breach of a directly effective Treaty provision:

the right to reparation is the necessary corollary of the direct effect of the Community provision whose breach caused the damage sustained.[39]

The German Government then argued that a general right to compensation could not be created by judicial decision but must be created by legislation. This, too was rejected by the Court of Justice which, confirming its judgment in *Francovich*, held that the principle of State responsibility, was inherent in the system of the Treaty. The Court relied upon Article 215(2) of the EC Treaty[40] and concluded that:

29. The principle of the non-contractual liability of the Community expressly laid down in Article 215 of the Treaty is simply an expression of the general principle familiar to the legal systems of the Member States that an unlawful act or omission gives rise to an obligation to make good the damage caused. That provision also reflects the obligation on public authorities to make good damage caused in the performance of their duties.
30. In any event, in many national legal systems the essentials of the legal rules governing State liability have been developed by the courts.

Finally, the Court of Justice concluded that the principles set out in *Francovich* were applicable whatever the organ of the State responsible for the breach. The obligation to compensate could not depend on domestic rules as to the division of powers between constitutional authorities.

Next the Court of Justice considered the conditions, as a matter of Community law, under which a Member State might incur liability. Drawing extensively on its case law upon the non-contractual liability of the Community under Article 215(2) of the EC Treaty, the Court of Justice considered that, in developing the system of rules applicable to the liability of Community institutions for legislative acts, the Court had had regard to the wide discretion available to the institutions in implementing Community policy. Accordingly, in circumstances where a Member State acted in a field where it had a wide discretion in implementing Community policies, the conditions under which it might incur liability must, in principle, be the same as those under which

---

[37] Namely Germany, Ireland and the Netherlands.
[38] See, in particular, Case 168/85, *Commission v. Italy*, [1986] ECR 2945, Case C–120/88, *Commission v. Italy*, [1991] ECR I–621, and Case C–119/89, *Commission v. Spain*, [1991] ECR I–641.
[39] At paragraph 22 of the judgment.
[40] Which provides:
'In the case of non-contractual liability, the Community shall, in accordance with the general principles common to the laws of the Member States, make good any damage caused by its institutions or by its servants in the performance of their duties.'

Community institutions incur liability under Article 215(2). On the facts, the Court of Justice concluded that both the United Kingdom and Germany had acted in fields in which they had a wide discretion.

The Court then listed the three conditions set out in its judgment in *Francovich*[41] which must be fulfilled before Member State liability in damages may be incurred, namely (*a*) the rule infringed must be intended to confer rights on individuals, (*b*) the breach must be sufficiently serious and (*c*) there must be a direct causal link between the breach and the damage sustained by the injured parties, and applied them to the facts before it.

On the first issue, the Court concluded that both Articles 52 and 30 of the EC Treaty conferred a right on individuals which must be protected by the national courts.[42]

Turning to the question of breach, the Court confirmed that the decisive test was the same as that set out under Article 215 of the EC Treaty, namely whether the Member State or the institution concerned had manifestly and gravely disregarded the limits on its discretion. Relevant factors included:

56. . . . the clarity and precision of the rules breached, the measure of discretion left by the rule to the national or Community authorities, whether the infringement and the damage caused was intentional or involuntary, whether any error of law was excusable, the fact that the position taken by a Community institution may have contributed towards the omission, and the adoption or retention of national measures or practices contrary to Community law.

The Court indicated, however, that a breach of Community law was sufficiently serious if it persisted despite a judgment finding an infringement or a preliminary ruling of the Court of Justice, or in situations where it was clear from case law that there had been a breach.

Applying these principles to ascertain whether the conduct of the United Kingdom in adopting Part II of the Merchant Shipping Act 1988 was sufficiently serious, the Court considered that the relevant factors included legal disputes on certain aspects of the common fisheries policy, the attitude of the Commission which was made known to the United Kingdom in good time, and the assessments made by the national courts in the proceedings for interim measures. In addition, the Court considered that if the allegation that the United Kingdom failed to adopt immediately the measure needed to comply with the order of the President of the Court of Justice for interim measures[43] was correct, this should be regarded by the national court as a manifest breach of Community law.

Finally, the Court considered that proof of the direct causal link between the breach of Community law and the loss alleged was a matter for the national courts.

The Court noted, however, that, although the three conditions set out were a necessary minimum to found liability as a matter of Community law, Member States were free to impose stricter conditions if they so wished.

[41] At paragraphs 38–41 of its judgment.
[42] See Case 74/76, *Ianelli & Volpi* v. *Meroni*, [1977] ECR 557 (Article 30), and Case 2/74, *Reyners*, [1974] ECR 631 (Article 52).
[43] [1989] ECR 3125.

Having dealt with the substance, the Court turned to consider the application of domestic rules to govern a Member State's liability to pay damages. The Court considered that, in principle, a Member State must compensate in accordance with national rules on liability. However, the Court added its oft used caveat on the application of domestic procedural rules,[44] namely that conditions for compensation under national law must not be less favourable than those relating to similar domestic claims and must not in practice make it excessively difficult to obtain compensation.

On the facts before it, the Court gave two helpful indications. First, the condition imposed under German law, which made liability in damages dependent on the legislature's action or omission being referable to an individual situation, would make it excessively difficult to obtain compensation. An identical conclusion was reached in respect of any condition that might be imposed by English law requiring proof of misfeasance in public office.

The German court had also asked whether the national court was entitled to make liability in damages dependent upon proof of fault (either intentional or negligent). The Court responded that any supplementary requirement of fault going beyond that of a sufficiently serious breach of Community law was not acceptable.

Both courts had referred questions on the extent of damages payable in the case of breach and, in particular, whether national rules which restricted the recovery of certain heads of damages were acceptable. The Court responded that the level of compensation payable must be commensurate with the loss or damage sustained to ensure effective protection of Community rights. The Court indicated, however, that it was acceptable for the national court to enquire whether the injured party had taken reasonable steps to limit the extent of loss and damage suffered by him[45] and, in particular, whether all legal remedies available had been exhausted. The Court rejected an argument put forward by the German Government that loss of profit could not be recovered in a claim for damages, holding that a total exclusion of loss of profit would make adequate compensation practically impossible. Finally, on the question whether exemplary damages could be awarded, the Court concluded that such an award could not be ruled out if such damages would be awarded under a similar claim founded upon domestic law.

Further, the German court had asked whether compensation must be paid to cover any periods arising prior to a judgment finding that the Member State had breached Community law. The Court considered that the necessity of a prior judgment finding a breach would preclude an action for damages unless the Commission had taken infringement proceedings under Article 169 of the EC Treaty against the Member State in question. The right of an individual to be compensated could not depend on the Commission's assessment of the expediency of commencing infringement proceedings.[46] The Court thus concluded

---

[44] See, for example, Case 199/82, *Amministrazione delle Finanze dello Stato* v. *San Giorgio*, [1983] ECR 3595.

[45] For an application of the principle of mitigation in an action for damages against a Community institution, see Joined Cases C–104/89 and C–37/90, *Mulder and others* v. *EC Council and EC Commission*, [1992] ECR I–3061.

[46] See, in particular, Joined Cases 314–316/81 and 83/82, *Waterkeyn and others*, [1982] ECR 4337.

that the right to compensation could not be limited to periods arising after a judgment by the Court of Justice finding a breach.

Finally, the German Government requested that the effect of its present judgment be prospective only, limited to loss or damage sustained after the judgment had been given. Such an approach was not accepted by the Court of Justice, which pointed out that, had the claims for damages been brought under national and not Community law, they would not have been so limited. Accordingly, the conditions under which claims based upon Community law were brought should not be less favourable than those attaching to similar domestic claims.

II.3 *Case C–392/93, The Queen v. HM Treasury, ex parte British Telecommunications plc*, judgment of 26 March 1996.[47] In this case, the Court of Justice was faced with a different but connected issue, the liability of a Member State to compensate an individual for loss suffered by incorrect implementation of a directive into national law.

British Telecommunications plc ('BT') brought proceedings against the United Kingdom Government in the English High Court challenging the validity of those provisions of the Utilities Supply and Works Contracts Regulations 1992 which purported to implement Article 8(1) of Council Directive 90/531/EEC on the procurement procedures of entities operating in the water, energy, transport and telecommunications sectors[48] ('the Directive'). BT also claimed damages for loss suffered by reason of having to comply with the 1992 Regulations.

In implementing the Directive, the United Kingdom had excluded all telecommunications operators in the UK except for BT and Kingston Communications (Hull) plc. These two companies were subject to the Directive in respect of voice-telephony services, basic data-transmission services, the provision of private leased circuits and maritime services. Before the English court, BT argued that the United Kingdom had incorrectly implemented the Directive. It should have simply transposed the relevant criteria set out in Article 8(1) into domestic law, rather than purporting to apply them to each contractual entity.

The first question referred essentially sought an answer from the Court of Justice to BT's submissions before the English High Court. In response, the Court of Justice supported BTs arguments and held that it was for the contractual entities alone to determine whether or not they fell within the scope of Article 8(1). The Court considered that if the Member States were competent to exclude certain entities from the scope of the Directive, economic operators would be denied recourse to the legal remedies set out in Council Directive

---

[47] [1996] ECR I–1631.
[48] OJ, 1990, L297/1. Article 8(1) provides:
'This directive shall not apply to contracts which contracting entities . . . award for purchases intended exclusively to enable them to provide one or more telecommunications services where other entities are free to offer the same services in the same geographical area and under substantially the same conditions.'

92/13/EEC[49] if a Member State infringed Community rules on public procurement. Further, it was important to ensure equality of treatment between contracting entities and their suppliers by making them subject to the same rules.

The Court of Justice next considered whether the criteria set out in Article 8(1) were to be applied purely as a matter of law, or also as encompassing matters of fact. The Court of Justice ruled that both issues of law and fact were important and concluded that:

33. Consequently, the criterion laid down by Article 8(1) is to be interpreted as meaning that other contracting entities must not only be authorized to operate in the market for the services in question, . . . , but must also be in a position actually to provide the services in question under the same conditions as the contracting entity.

34. In those circumstances, a decision to exclude certain services from the scope of the directive must be taken on an individual basis, having regard in particular to all their characteristics, the existence of alternative services, price factors, the dominance or otherwise of the contracting party's position on the market and the existence of any legal constraints.

On the question of damages for incorrect implementation, the Court of Justice reaffirmed the application of the principles laid down in Joined Cases C-46 and 48/93, *Brasserie du Pêcheur SA* v. *Germany; R* v. *Secretary of State for Transport, ex parte Factortame Ltd. and others*[50] to situations where a Member State had incorrectly implemented a directive. The Court considered, however, that in circumstances where a Member State enjoyed a wide discretion to enact legislation, a restrictive approach to liability was necessary. Only this would ensure that the exercise of legislative functions was not hindered by the prospect of actions for damages whenever a Member State was required, for the general interest, to adopt measure which could adversely affect individual interests.

The Court noted that, in principle, it was for the national court to determine whether the conditions for Member State liability were fulfilled, but considered that it had sufficient information before it to decide whether the breach of Community law committed by the United Kingdom legislature was sufficiently serious. On the facts, the Court ruled that Article 8(1) was imprecisely worded and was reasonably capable of bearing the meaning given to it by the United Kingdom in good faith. Accordingly, the Court concluded that BT had no right to be awarded damages.

II.4 *Case C-5/94, The Queen* v. *Ministry of Agriculture, Fisheries and Food, ex parte Hedley Lomas (Ireland) Ltd.*, 23 May 1996.[51] Between April 1990 and 1 January 1993, the Ministry of Agriculture, Fisheries and Food ('the Ministry') refused to grant licences for the export of live animals to Spain for slaughter on the grounds that their treatment in Spanish slaughterhouses was contrary to Council Directive 74/577/EEC on stunning of animals before slaughter[52] ('the Directive'). In October 1992, Hedley Lomas Ltd. applied for an export licence

---

[49] Of 25 February 1992, co-ordinating the laws, regulations and administrative provisions relating to the application of Community rules on the procurement procedures of entities operating in the water, energy, transport and telecommunications sectors (OJ, 1992, L76/14.)

[50] [1996] ECR I-1029.

[51] [1996] ECR I-2553.

[52] OJ, 1974, L316/10.

to export live sheep. Its application was refused despite information obtained by Hedley Lomas that the slaughterhouse had been approved since 1986 and was complying with Community directives on animal welfare.

Hedley Lomas brought proceedings in the English High Court seeking a declaration that the Ministry's refusal to grant an export licence was contrary to Article 34 of the EC Treaty, and also seeking damages. The Ministry accepted that its refusal to grant an export licence was a quantitive restriction on exports, but argued that its conduct was justified under Article 36 of the Treaty.

The first issue raised by the questions referred to the Court of Justice was whether a Member State may rely on Article 36 of the EC Treaty 'extra-territorially' to justify a restriction on exports to another Member State when it believed that the second Member State was failing to comply with obligations laid down in a harmonizing directive. Further, the directive contained no procedure to monitor compliance with those obligations nor any penalties in the event of their breach.

In its decision, the Court of Justice began by repeating the Community law legislative doctrine of 'the occupied field', namely that a Member State may no longer have recourse to Article 36 of the EC Treaty where the harmonization necessary to safeguard the specific objectives laid down in Article 36 had been achieved by Community legislation. The fact that the Directive did not lay down a Community monitoring procedure did not change that conclusion. In such circumstances, the Member States were obliged[53] to take all measures necessary to guarantee that Community law was applied effectively. Accordingly, the Member States must trust each other to carry out inspections in their respective territories to ensure that Community obligations are complied with.[54] The Court of Justice concluded, however, that a Member State may not adopt unilateral measures of 'self help' designed to obviate any breach by another Member State of rules of Community law.[55]

The Court of Justice then considered the question of damages for breach of Article 34 of the EC Treaty. The Court repeated the three conditions which must be met before damages may be awarded for a breach of Community law described in detail in its judgment in *Brasserie du Pêcheur* and applied them to the facts before it.

As to the first condition, breach of a provision of Community law intended to confer rights on individuals, the Court confirmed that Article 34 not only imposed a prohibition on Member States, but also created individual rights which Member States must protect.[56]

As to the second condition, namely that the breach must be sufficiently serious, the Court of Justice considered that, in circumstances where the Member State was not called upon to make legislative choices and had very little, if any, discretion, the mere infringement of Community law might make the breach sufficiently serious.

---

[53] In accordance with Article 5 and Article 189 of the EC Treaty.

[54] See Case 46/76, *Bauhuis* v. *Netherlands*, [1977] ECR 5, paragraph 22 of the judgment.

[55] Applying the principles laid down in Joined Cases 90/63 and 91/63, *Commission* v. *Luxembourg and Belgium*, [1964] ECR 625, and also in Case 232/78, *Commission* v. *France*, [1979] ECR 2729, paragraph 9 of the judgment.

[56] See Case 83/78, *Pigs Marketing Board* v. *Redmond*, [1978] ECR 2347, paragraphs 66 and 67 of the judgment.

Finally, on the question of causation, the Court repeated that it is the function of the national court to determine the casual link between the breach of a State's Community law obligations and the damage sustained by the injured parties.

II.5 *Joined Cases C–178/94, C–179/94, C–188/94 and C–190/94, Erich Dillenkofer and others* v. *Federal Republic of Germany*, 8 October 1996. A number of actions were brought in the Landgericht of Bonn claiming damages against the Federal Republic of Germany for loss suffered by its failure to transpose Council Directive 90/314/EEC on package travel, package holidays and package tours[57] ('the Directive') within the prescribed period. Questions were referred to the Court of Justice on the conditions necessary for a Member State to be held liable in damages.

The first issue raised was whether the failure of a Member State to implement a directive within the prescribed period gave a right *per se* to be compensated for loss suffered or whether other conditions nevertheless had to be fulfilled. Maintaining the distinction made in its earlier case law[58] between those areas in which Member States of Community institutions enjoy a measure of discretion in implementing the legislative measure in question or applying Community law, and those areas in which a Member State was not called upon to make legislative choices or had very little discretion, the Court of Justice considered that a breach of the obligation contained in Article 189(3) of the EC Treaty to implement a directive within the time limit was a manifest and grave disregard of the limits of a Member State's discretion. It was thus a sufficiently serious breach to form the basis of an award for damages.

The Court of Justice went on to consider whether the result prescribed by Article 7 of the Directive[59] entailed the grant of rights to individuals and whether the content of those rights could be sufficiently identified in the provision itself.[60] Rejecting arguments put forward by the United Kingdom and German Governments that the primary purpose of the Directive was to ensure freedom to provide services and freedom of competition, the Court held that the purpose of the Directive was to protect consumers against the financial risks arising from the insolvency of package travel operators. This clearly entailed the grant of individual rights to consumers. Further, the content of the rights, namely that purchasers of package travel would be given refunds and repatriated if the organizer became insolvent, could be determined with sufficient precision.

The German courts asked two other interesting questions on the interpretation of Article 7 of the Directive. The first was whether organizers fulfilled

---

[57] OJ, 1990, L158/59.

[58] See Joined Cases C–46 and 48/93, *Brasserie du Pêcheur SA* v. *Germany, R* v. *Secretary of State for Transport, ex parte Factortame Ltd. and others*, [1996] ECR I–1029; [1996] 1 CMLR 889; Case C–392/93, *The Queen* v. *HM Treasury, ex parte British Telecom plc*, [1996] ECR I–1631; Case 5/94, *R* v. *Ministry of Agriculture, Fisheries and Food, ex parte Hedley Lomas*, [1996] ECR I–2553.

[59] Article 7(1) provides:

'The organiser and/or retailer party to the contract shall provide sufficient evidence of security for the refund of money paid over and for the repatriation of the consumer in the event of insolvency.'

[60] For an explanation of the importance of these factors as a pre-condition for Member States' liability in damages, see Joined Cases C–6/90 and C–9/90, *Francovich* v. *Italy*, [1991] ECR I–5357.

the requirement to provide 'security for the refund of money paid over' if they supplied the consumer with documents guaranteeing a direct right against the actual provider of the services (the airline or hotelier). The Court of Justice responded in the negative, stating that the protection guaranteed by Article 7 would be impaired if consumers were made to enforce credit vouchers against third parties who themselves were not required to enforce them and could also become insolvent.

Second, the Court of Justice was asked if the Directive required Member States to adopt specific measures to protect package travellers from their own negligence. Noting that this requirement was neither expressly nor implicitly contained in the Directive, the Court concluded that the national court was free to enquire whether the injured party had taken reasonable care to avoid or mitigate the loss suffered.

III *Law governing the institutions—principles concerning observance of rights of the defence in criminal proceedings—no jurisdiction in areas outside the scope of Community law*

III.1 *Case C-144/95, Ministère Public v. Jean-Louis Maurin and Metro SA*, 13 June 1996. A question was referred by the Tribunal de Police, Toulouse, France about provisions of French procedural law concerning the interpretation of the principles of the rights of the defence and the adversarial nature of proceedings. The questions referred arose in the context of the criminal prosecution of Mr Maurin who was charged with selling food products after the expiry of their sell-by date in breach of certain provisions of French criminal law.

The relevant Community law at the time that Mr Maurin was charged was contained in Council Directive 79/112/EEC on the approximation of the laws of the Member States relating to the labelling, presentation and advertising of foodstuffs for sale to the ultimate consumer[61] ('the Directive'). The Directive provided that the date by which the product in question must be used should be indicated on the product labelling. It also provided that Member States must prohibit trade in products which did not comply with its provisions. The Directive did not, however, regulate the sale of products complying with its labelling requirements but which were sold after the use-by date had expired.

The Court of Justice held that the offences with which Mr Maurin was charged were outside the scope of Community law. For that reason, the Court of Justice concluded that it did not have jurisdiction to answer whether the domestic procedural rules applicable were compatible with the principles concerning rights of the defence and the adversarial nature of proceedings.

IV *Equal treatment—domestic procedural law—discrimination on grounds of nationality—security for costs—services—establishment—discrimination—judicial procedure*

IV.1 *Case C-43/95, Data Delecta Aktiebolag and Ronny Forsberg v. MSL Dynamics Ltd.*, judgment of 26 September 1996. In this reference from the

[61] OJ, 1979, L33/1 as amended by Council Directive 89/395/EEC (OJ, 1989, L186/17).

Swedish Supreme Court, the Court of Justice extended the scope of its decision in Case C–398/92, *Mund and Fester* v. *Hatrex International Transport.*[62]

In *Mund and Fester*, the Court of Justice ruled that a provision of German law that distinguished, in the conditions for granting an order for seizure of assets, between judgments to be enforced in Germany and judgments to be enforced in other Member States, was incompatible with the principles of discrimination now contained in Article 6 of the EC Treaty, read in conjunction with Article 220 EC Treaty. In *Data Delecta Aktiebolag and Ronny Forsberg* v. *MSL Dynamics Ltd.*, the Court of Justice extended this principle to domestic rules ordering security for costs. This decision thus confirms the decision in *Fitzgerald* v. *Williams*,[63] where the English Court of Appeal held that the English rules on security for costs[64] were indirectly discriminatory and that accordingly the English court should never exercise its discretion in favour of ordering security for costs against a foreign Community national.

MSL Dynamics, an English company, brought an action in Sweden. It was forced to pay security for the costs of the proceedings in circumstances where a Swedish company would not be so required. MSL Dynamics argued that the difference in treatment was unlawful discrimination contrary to Article 6 of the EC Treaty.

The Court of Justice endorsed that view. The question that the Court faced was whether rules for security for costs fell 'within the scope of application of the Treaty', a pre-condition for the application of Article 6. Unlike the situation in *Mund and Fester*, this was not a procedural rule linked to the enforcement of a judgment and thus within the scope of Article 220 of the EC Treaty.

The Court of Justice considered that a national procedural rule on security for costs, although not intended to regulate commercial activity, had the effect of placing traders established in another Member State at a disadvantage as regards access to the courts. The corollary of the freedom of movement of goods and services in the Community guaranteed by Community law must be the right to bring actions to resolve disputes arising out of economic activities in the courts of a Member State on the same terms as nationals of that Member State. Accordingly, the Court concluded that the rule did fall within the scope of the Treaty.

The Court of Justice took the opportunity to reaffirm its ruling in Case C–326, *Phil Collins* v. *Imrat Handelsgesellschaft mbH*[65] that, by reason of their effect on intra-Community trade in goods and services, Article 6 of the EC Treaty may be applicable to national provisions on its own without there being any need to link the application of the principle of non-discrimination contained in Article 6 to

---

[62] [1994] ECR I–467, noted in this *Year Book*, 65 (1994), p. 561.

[63] [1996] QB 657.

[64] Contained in Rules of the Supreme Court, Order 23, rule 1 (*a*), which provides:
  'Where, on the application of a defendant to an action or other proceedings in the High Court, it appears to the Court—
  (a) that the plaintiff is ordinarily resident out of the jurisdiction . . .
    . . .
  then if, having regard to all the circumstances of the case, the Court thinks it just to do so, it may order the plaintiff to give such security for the defendant's costs of the action or other proceedings as it thinks just.'

[65] Reported in English in [1993] 3 CMLR 773.

more specific Treaty provisions such as Articles 30, 36, 59 and 66 of the EC Treaty.

Accordingly, the Court of Justice concluded that the difference in treatment between nationals and those established in other Member States permitted under the Swedish security for costs rule was contrary to Community law.

IV.2 *Case C–177/94, Gianfranco Perfili* v. *Lloyd's of London*, judgment of 1 February 1966.[66] Mr Perfili, a jeweller in Rome, took out an insurance policy with Lloyd's of London ('Lloyd's'). Two years later he made a claim under his policy for theft. Mr Perfili was charged in Italy on charges of falsely reporting an unlawful act and attempted fraud, both serious criminal charges. Lloyd's general representative in Italy conferred on a lawyer a special power of attorney pursuant to Italian rules of procedure, so that he could intervene in the criminal proceedings to seek damages against Mr Perfili on behalf of Lloyd's.

As a matter of Italian procedural law,[67] a person seeking to intervene in criminal proceedings to claim damages through the intermediary of a representative must give the representative a special power of attorney. The general power of attorney conferred by Lloyd's on its Italian representative did not confer on him a special power of attorney to take part in the criminal proceedings brought against Mr Perfili. Under English law, however, a general power of attorney given to a representative may implicitly signify an intention to grant such a power.

The Italian court considered that Lloyd's was restricted by the existence of a special set of rules which did not exist under its national legal system and concluded that there was unequal treatment between Italian and British nationals. Accordingly proceedings were stayed and two questions referred to the Court of Justice.

By its first question, the Italian court asked whether the provision of Italian procedural law at issue was compatible with Articles 2, 3 and 6 of the EC Treaty. The Court of Justice first confirmed that, on the facts, the relevant article of the EC Treaty was Article 6. Then, in contrast to its more recent approach in Case C–43/95, *Data Delecta Aktiebolag and Ronny Forsberg* v. *MSL Dynamics Ltd*,[68] the Court ruled that the general principle of discrimination contained in Article 6 of the EC Treaty was not 'free standing' but could only apply in conjunction with the special provisions of the Treaty.

On the facts, the Court of Justice considered that EC Treaty provisions on the freedom of establishment and the freedom to provide services were applicable, holding that:[69]

National legislation governing the procedure for bringing suit as a civil party in criminal proceedings affects the ability of an insurance company established in another Member State to defend its interests under civil law in the host State and must be examined in the light of the Treaty's provisions concerning freedom of establishment or freedom to provide services in the host State.

---

[66] [1996] ECR I–161.
[67] Set out in Article 78 of the Italian Code of Procedure.
[68] Noted above at paragraph 4.1.
[69] At paragraph 16 of the judgment.

The Court noted, however, that Articles 6, 52 and 59 of the EC Treaty were not concerned with differences in treatment arising from disparities in national law, so long as they affected all persons subject to them equally and without distinction on the grounds of nationality.[70]

On the facts referred, the Court of Justice considered it was unable to determine how and in what circumstances the national legislation could constitute an unjustifiable restriction on the freedom of establishment or the freedom to provide services. Accordingly, the Court concluded that the requirements of Italian procedural law were not incompatible with Articles 52 and 59 of the EC Treaty.

The Italian Court also asked whether the provision of Italian law was compatible with Article 6 of the European Convention for the Protection of Human Rights and Fundamental Freedoms.[71] The Court of Justice, repeating its ruling in Case C–159/90, *Society for the Protection of Unborn Children, Ireland* v. *Grogan*,[72] confirmed that the Court had no jurisdiction to examine the compatibility of national legislation falling outside the scope of Community law with the European Convention.

V *Free movement—persons—national of a Member State established in non-Member State employed by embassy of another Member State—discrimination in conditions of employment*

V.1 *Case C–214/94, Ingrid Boukhalfa* v. *Federal Republic of Germany*, 30 April 1996.[73] Mrs Boukhalfa was a Belgian national employed on the local staff of the German Embassy in Algiers. She was permanently resident in Algeria. Her contract of employment had been concluded in Algeria and was subject to Algerian law. The German law governing Diplomatic Service employment[74] distinguished between local staff with German nationality and those of other nationalities. Mrs Boukhalfa asked to receive the same treatment as local German staff but was refused.

The question whether such a difference in treatment was compatible with Article 48(2) of the EC Treaty and Articles 7(1) and (4) of Council Regulation No. 1612/68[75] was referred to the Court of Justice by the Bundesarbeitsgericht (Federal Labour Court). The Court held that the refusal to grant equal treatment to a worker in the same position as Mrs Boukhalfa was discriminatory and incompatible with EC law.

The decision was based upon the Court's previous rulings that Community law may apply to professional activities pursued outside the Community if there is a sufficiently close link between the employment relationship and the law of a

---

[70] See Case 1/78, *Kenny* v. *Insurance Officer*, [1978] ECR 1489, Joined Cases C–251/90 and C–252/90, *Wood and Cowie*, [1992] ECR I–2873, and Joined Cases 185/78 and 204/78, *Van Dam en Zonen and others*, [1979] ECR 2345.

[71] Concluded on 4 November 1950.

[72] [1991] ECR I–4685.

[73] [1996] ECR I–2253.

[74] *Gestez über den Auswärtigen Dienst* (German Law on the Diplomatic Service, *Bundesgesetzblatt*, I, p. 1842).

[75] On freedom of movement for workers within the Community (OJ, English Special Edition 1968 (II), p. 475).

Member State and thus the relevant rules of Community law.[76] In the present case, the Court of Justice identified three factors that led to the conclusion that Community law applied. First, Mrs Boukhalfa's contract of employment was entered into under provisions of German law. The fact that her conditions of employment were determined under Algerian law was a result of the application of that German law. Second, her contract of employment contained a jurisdiction clause giving jurisdiction over any dispute arising under the contract to the German courts. Third, Mrs Boukhalfa's pension rights were administered through the German social security system and she was subject, to a limited extent, to German income tax.

VI *Brussels Convention—documents to be produced by a party applying for enforcement of a judgment—recognition of a decision—definition of a defendant in default of appearance*

VI.1 *Case C–275/94, Roger van der Linden v. Berufsgenossenschaft der Feinmechanik und Elektronik*, 14 March 1966.[77] This reference from the Hof van Cassatie van België raised an issue as to the interpretation of Article 47(1)[78] of the Brussels Convention of 27 September 1968 on Jurisdiction and the Enforcement of Judgments in Civil and Commercial Matters[79] ('the Brussels Convention').

A German insurance company, Berufsgenossenschaft der Feinmechanik und Elektronik, had applied for the enforcement in Belgium of two default judgments obtained against Mr van der Linden. Upon appeal against the decision authorizing enforcement, Mr van der Linden argued that the application for enforcement made by the insurance company had not fulfilled the documentary requirements of Article 47(1) of the Brussels Convention. No document had been attached to the application lodged to show that the default judgments had been served upon the defendant and were enforceable. Belgian law provided that proof of service of the judgment of which enforcement was sought could be produced after the application for enforcement had been lodged.

The Court of Justice held that domestic procedural rules regarding the form of the application for enforcement may provide for the documentary requirements contained in Article 47(1) of the Brussels Convention to be regularized after the application has been lodged by production of proof of service of the judgment, providing that the objectives pursued by, in particular, Article 33(3)[80] and Article 47(1) of the Convention are respected. The purpose of serving the judgment upon a defendant is to notify him that it has been given and to enable him to satisfy the judgment voluntarily before an application for enforcement is

---

[76] See Case 237/83, *Prodest v. Caisse Primaire d'Assurance Maladie de Paris*, [1984] ECR 3153; Case 9/88, *Lopes da Veiga v. Staatssecretaris van Justitie*, [1989] ECR 2989; Case C–60/93, *Aldewereld v. Staatssecretaris van Financiën*, [1994] ECR I–2991.

[77] [1996] ECR I–1393.

[78] Article 47 (1) provides:
  'A party applying for enforcement shall also produce:
  (1) documents which establish that, according to the law of the State of origin, the judgment is enforceable and has been served.'

[79] As amended most recently by the Convention of 26 May 1989 (San Sebastian Convention).

[80] Article 33(3) provides:
  'The documents referred to in Articles 46 and 47 shall be attached to the application.'

made. The Court of Justice ruled that domestic procedural rules which permit the court hearing the application for enforcement to take into consideration proof that the judgment has been served were not incompatible with the purpose provided that the party against whom enforcement was sought was given a reasonable time to satisfy the judgment voluntarily and provided that the party seeking enforcement bears all the costs unnecessarily incurred.

VI.2 *Case C–78/95, Bernardus Henrikman and Maria Feyen* v. *Magenta Druck & Verlag GmbH*, 10 October 1996. A national court considering the recognition and enforcement of a judgment obtained in another Member State may refuse to recognize the judgment only on very limited grounds.[81] These include the fact that the judgment was obtained in default of appearance by the defendant.[82] This reference from the Hoge Raad der Nederlanden (Supreme Court of the Netherlands) raised the question whether Article 27(2) could be relied upon by a defendant who was not duly served with or notified of the documents instituting the proceedings and who was not validly represented. As a matter of Dutch law, the judgment had not been obtained in default, as someone purporting to represent the defendant had appeared before the Court hearing the action.

Before the Court of Justice, the German Government argued that the aim of Article 27(2), namely the right of a defendant to defend himself, was satisfied if a lawyer not authorized to act nevertheless appeared on behalf of the defendant. In such circumstances, the Court hearing the case was obliged to rely on what that lawyer said unless and until he was shown to have no authority.

Somewhat unsurprisingly, that argument was rejected by the Court of Justice. The Court held that where proceedings are begun against a defendant without his knowledge, but nevertheless a lawyer purports to appear on his behalf, the defendant is powerless to defend himself. Accordingly, such a defendant is entitled to rely on Article 27(2) of the Brussels Convention even if the proceedings in which the judgment was given became, as a matter of form, *inter partes* proceedings. The Court of Justice concluded that it was a matter for the court from whom recognition was sought to see whether such exceptional circumstances exist.

VII *Social policy—Council Directive 93/104/EC concerning certain aspects of the organization of working time—action for annulment*

VII.1 *Case C–89/94, United Kingdom of Great Britain and Northern Ireland* v. *Council of the European Union*, 12 November 1996. The United Kingdom made an application under Article 173 of the EC Treaty to annul Council Directive

---

[81] See Articles 27, 28 and 34 of the Brussels Convention.
[82] See Article 27 of the Brussels Convention which provides:
'A judgment shall not be recognised–
. . .
2. Where it was given in default of appearance, if the defendant was not duly served with the document which instituted proceedings or with an equivalent document in sufficient time to enable him to arrange for his defence.'

93/104/EC concerning certain aspects of the organization of working time[83] ('the Directive'). In the alternative, the United Kingdom argued that certain provisions of the Directive should be annulled.[84]

The United Kingdom first argued that the legal base chosen for the Directive was defective. The Directive was adopted on the basis of Article 118a of the EC Treaty, which permits measures to be adopted by qualified majority voting.[85] The United Kingdom contended that the Directive should have been adopted pursuant to Article 100 of the EC Treaty, one of the legal bases for harmonizing legislation, or alternatively, Article 235 of the EC Treaty.[86] Further, as Article 118a must be regarded as an exception to Article 100 of the EC Treaty, it must be strictly interpreted.

On the question of the scope of Article 118a of the EC Treaty, the Court reaffirmed that Article 118a granted the Community legislative competence in the field of social policy.[87] The existence of other Treaty provisions could not restrict the scope of Article 118a. It constituted a more specific legal base than Articles 100 and 100a of the Treaty. Further, there was nothing in Article 118a to indicate that the concepts of 'working environment', 'safety' and 'health' used there should be interpreted restrictively:

and not as embracing all factors, physical or otherwise, capable of affecting the health and safety of the worker in his working environment, including in particular, certain aspects of the organization of working time.[88]

On the contrary, the wording of Article 118a militated towards a broad interpretation of the powers which Article 118a conferred upon the Council for the protection of the health and safety of workers.

Accordingly, the Court concluded that:[89]

where the principal aim of the measure in question is the protection of the health and safety of workers, Article 118a must be used, albeit such a measure may have ancillary effects on the establishment and functioning of the internal market.

The Court of Justice then went on to consider the United Kingdom's submission that the legal basis for the Directive was defective. The Court noted

---

[83] OJ, 1993, L307/18.

[84] Namely Article 4, the first two sentences of Article 5, Article 6(2) and Article 7.

[85] Article 118a of the Treaty provides, *inter alia*:

'1. Member States shall pay particular attention to encouraging improvements, especially in the working environment, as regards the health and safety of workers, and shall set as their objective the harmonization of conditions in this area, while maintaining the improvements made.

2. In order to help achieve the objective laid down in the first paragraph, the Council, acting in accordance with the procedure referred to in Article 189c and after consulting the Economic and Social Committee, shall adopt by means of directives, minimum requirements for gradual implementation, having regard to the conditions and technical rules obtaining in each of the Member States.

Such directives shall avoid imposing administrative, financial and legal constraints in a way which would hold back the creation and development of small and medium-sized undertakings.

3. The provisions adopted pursuant to this Article shall not prevent any Member State from maintaining or introducing more stringent measures for the protection of working conditions compatible with this Treaty.'

[86] Both of these provisions require unanimity within the Council

[87] See *Opinion 2/91* of 19 March 1993, [1993] ECR I–1061, paragraph 17.

[88] At paragraph 15 of the judgment.

[89] At paragraph 22 of the judgment.

that the sixth recital in its preamble stated that the Directive constitutes a practical contribution towards creating the social dimension of the internal market. However, the fact that the Directive fell within the scope of Community social policy did not mean that the Directive could not be based on Article 118a so long as it contributed to encouraging improvements in the health and safety of workers. Indeed, the Court of Justice accepted the Advocate General's Opinion[90] that the organization of working time was not necessarily conceived as an instrument of employment policy. The Court of Justice considered that the aim of the Directive was to view the organization of working time as a means of improving the health and safety of workers and concluded:

while . . . it cannot be excluded that the directive may affect employment, that is clearly not its essential objective.[91]

Next, the United Kingdom argued that the connection between the health and safety of the worker and the measures laid down in the Directive was too tenuous to use Article 118a as its legal base. In response, the Court of Justice drew a distinction between the second sentence of Article 5[92] of the Directive, laying down the weekly rest period, and its other provisions. The second sentence of Article 5 provided that, in principle, the minimum weekly rest period should include Sunday. The Court of Justice, whilst accepting that the decision whether to include Sunday was ultimately a matter for the Member States, having regard to their own cultural, ethnic and religious considerations, ruled that, nevertheless, the Council had failed to explain why Sunday was more intimately connected with the health and safety of workers than any other day of the week. Accordingly, the second sentence of Article 5 of the Directive would be annulled.

So far as the other measures were concerned which laid down minimum rest periods, length of work, shift work and the pattern of the working day, the Court of Justice concluded that they related to the 'working environment' and were consistent with protecting the health and safety of workers. Accordingly, the Court of Justice concluded that Article 118a and not Article 100a or Article 235 was the correct legal basis for the Directive.

The United Kingdom's third submission was that Article 118a of the EC Treaty permitted the Council to adopt only 'minimum requirements'. The measures contained in the Directive were excessive and breached the principle of proportionality. Applying the classic doctrine of proportionality,[93] the Court of Justice concluded that the measures were not disproportionate. The provisions on the organization of working time contained in the Directive, save for the second sentence of Article 5, contributed directly to the improvement of health and safety protection for workers and could not therefore be regarded as

---

[90] See points 85 to 90 of his opinion.
[91] At paragraph 30 of the judgment
[92] Article 5 provides:
  '*Weekly rest period*
  Member States shall take the measure necessary to ensure that, per each seven-day period, every worker is entitled to a minimum uninterrupted rest period of 24 hours plus the 11 hours' daily rest referred to in Article 3.'
[93] For an explanation of this doctrine, see n. 13, above.

unsuited to the objective pursued. Further, the Council did not commit any manifest error in concluding that the measures were necessary.

Finally, the United Kingdom raised the argument that, in breach of Article 190 of the EC Treaty,[94] the Directive was not adequately reasoned because it failed to demonstrate the causal connection relied on by the Council between health and safety and the majority of the measures concerning working time. Alternatively, the reasoning was defective. The Court's response was succinct, stating:

> . . . the preamble clearly shows that the measures introduced are intended to harmonize the protection of the health and safety of workers.[95]

The Court of Justice thus concluded that the Directive was adequately reasoned.

Accordingly, save for directing that the second sentence of Article 5 of the Directive be annulled, the United Kingdom's application was dismissed and costs were awarded against it.

SARA MASTERS

---

[94] Which provides that regulations, directives and decisions shall state the reasons on which they are based and shall refer to any proposals or opinions which were required to be obtained under the EC Treaty.

[95] At paragraph 75 of the judgment.

UNITED KINGDOM MATERIALS ON INTERNATIONAL LAW 1996*

Edited by GEOFFREY MARSTON[1]

[*Editorial note*: Attention is drawn to the editorial note in UKMIL 1983, p. 361. Delay in the appearance of the bound volumes has made it impossible to make any corrections which might be necessary to the column references in volumes 281–287 of the House of Commons Debates and to volume 576 of the House of Lords Debates.]

INDEX[2]

* Editorial arrangement and comments © Geoffrey Marston, 1997. Copyright in the materials cited is in the original copyright holders.

[1] LL M, Ph.D (Lond.): Lecturer in Law, University of Cambridge: Fellow of Sidney Sussex College. The assistance of Mr A. Aust, CMG, Legal Counsellor, Foreign and Commonwealth Office, the Treaty and News Departments, Foreign and Commonwealth Office, and the staff of the Official Publications Department, University Library, Cambridge, is gratefully acknowledged.

[2] Based on the *Model Plan for the Classification of Documents concerning State Practice in the field of Public International Law* adopted by the Committee of Ministers of the Council of Europe in Resolution (68) 17 of 28 June 1968. For a more detailed index of subject-matter, readers are referred to the general index to this volume.

Abbreviations

HC Debs	*Hansard*, House of Commons Debates (6th series)
HL Debs	*Hansard*, House of Lords Debates (5th series)
Cmnd	Command Paper (5th series)
Cm	Command Paper (6th series)
UKMIL	*United Kingdom Materials on International Law*
TS	*United Kingdom Treaty Series*
EC	European Community
EU	European Union
FCO	Foreign and Commonwealth Office
WA	Written Answers

Part One: I. *International law in general—nature, basis, purpose*

(See Part Twelve: II. H. 1. (item of 24 September 1996), below)

Part One: II. A. *International law in general—relationship between international law and internal law—in general*

In the course of a debate in the House of Lords on 3 July 1996 on the subject of the United Kingdom's existing constitutional settlement, and of the implications of proposals for change, the Lord Chancellor, Lord Mackay of Clashfern, stated:

While the functions of government are not compartmentalised, the basic principles and divisions are clear. The primary function of law making rests with Parliament, the supreme law-making body. The Government, the Executive branch, must act within the law and the courts must apply and give effect to it. The role of the courts in developing the common law should not be underestimated; but that role is developing principle, not creating wholly new law. Statute is the supreme source of law, and in any conflict between the common law and the clearly expressed will of the legislature in an Act of Parliament, the Act must prevail. But even here the function of the courts is by no means purely mechanical: they must construe and apply these Acts and, in doing so, they may rely on historical common law principles of interpretation and application.

What they cannot do, and show no sign of attempting to do, is refuse to give effect to an Act of Parliament or to question its validity. It is sometimes said that your Lordships' House has already, in the *Factortame* case, struck down an Act of Parliament by reference to a higher order which dilutes or reduces the sovereignty of Parliament; namely, the law and institutions of the European Community or the European Union. I think that that is an incorrect analysis of the *Factortame* decision.

It is important to be clear that Community law, including decisions of the European Court of Justice, has authority here by virtue of an Act of Parliament—namely, the European Communities Act 1972, with subsequent amendments to it. The *Factortame* decision rests on the basis that the Merchant Shipping Act had to be read in the context of the European Communities Act, which expressly provided that all other statues should be construed and have effect subject to the provisions giving Community law primacy in our legal system. That was enough, in the absence of a clear provision in the 1988 Act overriding the 1972 Act, to reverse the rule that, in a conflict between two Acts of Parliament, the later takes precedence. Accordingly the English court correctly proceeded on the basis that Parliament did not intend to override Community law in passing the Merchant Shipping Act. It is open to Parliament expressly to override the 1972 Act and, if it did so, the courts would be bound to give effect to this, even though that might be a breach of obligations under the Community treaties. But that would be a problem for the Government and Parliament to deal with, rather than the courts.

Similar considerations apply to our membership of other international organisations, such as the United Nations. Resolutions of the Security Council bind us in international law but, where they need to have legal force in this country, they can be implemented under the United Nations Act 1946 by an Order in Council.

It may also be argued that Parliament's sovereignty is limited by various other legal conventions and treaties. Again, as a matter of legal theory, I believe that that is not correct. Conventions operate by agreement of the parties. The process of entering into them is not irreversible: however, it is open to a party to withdraw under conditions that may be specified. If the power of Parliament in that respect is subject to any limits, those limits are due to political considerations—and considerations of international comity—rather than purely legal considerations.

(HL Debs., vol. 573, cols. 1450–1: 3 July 1996)

Part One: II. B. *International law in general—relationship between international law and internal law—international law in national courts*

(See also Part One: II. A., above)

The following paragraph is taken from a paper issued by Her Majesty's Government on 18 December 1996 on the subject of public interest immunity in court proceedings in the United kingdom:

International relations

5.14 The Government has similarly refined and clarified the basis on which it proposes to assert claims in this area. As elsewhere, it has taken as a starting point the Code of Practice on Access to Government Information. It has also had in mind section 3 of the Official Secrets Act 1989, which is concerned with 'damaging disclosure' in this field.

5.15 Under the Government's approach, a document would attract PII if its disclosure would harm the United Kingdom's interests or those of its dependent territories. A document could be the subject of a PII claim because it revealed the Government's policies towards other states or because it exposed a negotiating position. Another could be the subject of a PII claim because, by disclosing information given in confidence by another state, it would jeopardise future communications or relations with that state. These are merely examples. The common theme is however that real damage is anticipated to British interests in the area of international relations.

(Text provided by the FCO; see also HL Debs, vol. 576, cols. 1507–17: 18 December 1996, and HC Debs., vol. 287, cols. 949–58: 18 December 1996)

The FCO sent the following letter, dated 4 December 1996, to a firm of solicitors in London:

You seek information regarding Iraq in connection with, I presume, legal proceedings either current or contemplated. It might be helpful if I explain the practice of the FCO with regard to such requests.

When not party to legal proceedings, the FCO adopts a strictly neutral position. In such cases the FCO will normally provide information only on matters which are peculiarly within the knowledge of the Secretary of State eg whether HMG recognises an entity as a State. Furthermore, such information is usually provided only on the application of both or all parties, and normally in the form of a certificate, statutory or non-statutory as the case may be. It has been also found from experience that it is better not to issue a certificate unless it has been established that an issue which can properly be certified *needs* to be resolved for the proper disposition of the legal proceedings. It is therefore usually better and more convenient for a question to be formulated by the Court once it has been able to form a view, with the assistance of both or all parties, whether a certificate is required in order to enable the Court to dispose of the issue and, if so, on what question.

I trust that the above fully explains the position. You may care to arrange for this letter to be circulated within your firm.

(Text provided by the FCO)

Part One: II. D. 1. *International law in general—relationship between international law and internal law—implementation of international law in internal law—treaties*

In the course of its fourth periodic report, dated 14 October 1994, made to the UN Human Rights Committee under Article 40 of the International Covenant on Civil and Political Rights, the UK Government wrote:

In the debates on human rights issues that have occurred in Parliament and elsewhere in recent years, the Government has maintained the long-established principle that the rights and freedoms recognized in international instruments and in the constitutions of those countries that have enacted a comprehensive Bill of Rights are inherent in the United Kingdom's legal system and are protected by it and by Parliament unless they are removed or restricted by statute. The Government does not consider that it is properly the role of the legislature to confer rights and freedoms which are naturally possessed by all members of society. It also believes that Parliament should retain the supreme responsibility for enacting or changing the law, including that affecting individual rights and freedoms, while it is properly the role of the judiciary to interpret specific legislation.

The incorporation of an international human rights instrument into domestic law is not necessary to ensure that the United Kingdom's obligations under such instruments are reflected in the deliberations of government and of the courts. The United Kingdom's human rights obligations are routinely considered by Ministers and their officials in the formulation and application of Government policy, while judgements of the House of Lords have made clear that such obligations are part of the legal context in which the judges consider themselves to operate:

'There is a *prima facie* presumption that Parliament does not intend to act in breach of international law, including therein specific treaty obligations; and if one of the meanings which can reasonably be ascribed to the legislation is consonant with the treaty obligations and another or others are not, the meaning which is consonant is to be preferred.' (*Salomon* v. *the Commissioners of Customs and Excise* [1967] 2 QB 116.)

The application of this principle (extended to the common law) in relation to the European Convention on Human Rights may be seen in *Derbyshire County Council* v. *Times Newspapers Limited* [1992] 3 WLR 28. (The decision was upheld on different grounds in the House of Lords, where their Lordships found no ambiguity in the common law, [1993] AC 534.)

(CCPR/C/95/Add. 3, pp. 4–5)

During a debate on the above report in the UN Human Rights Committee on 20 July 1995 the UK delegate, Mr Halliday, stated:

The draft Human Rights Bill had been introduced as a Private Members' Bill measure into Parliament in late 1994, and had been debated during the first half of 1995 in the House of Lords. Designed to incorporate the European Convention on Human Rights into British domestic legislation, the Bill had sparked considerable debate in Parliament, including among members of the senior judiciary. The Bill had not been supported by the Government, nor had it made progress in the House of Commons. The series of parliamentary debates to which it had given rise in the House of Lords had, however, shown the high level of interest accorded by British institutions to developing measures to protect human rights in the country, and had led the Government to review its relevant policies.

It had long been held in the United Kingdom that freedoms—which included those guaranteed by the Covenant and by the European Convention on Human Rights—were naturally possessed by all members of society and need not be conferred. The United Kingdom enjoyed regular elections with full adult suffrage, parliamentary sovereignty, ministerial accountability, a free press and supervision by the courts of executive action by way of judicial review proceedings. That practice permitted executive action to be tested against broad principles of rationality, fairness, justice and legality, not themselves conferred by the Covenant or the Convention. In the view of the Government, the incorporation of those instruments was not a measure of the health of human rights in British society.

10. The British courts, demonstrating that they were indeed aware of that country's human rights obligations, increasingly referred to both the Covenant and the Convention in the course of their deliberations. The significance of that phenomenon could not be overestimated. The Government nevertheless continued to hold firmly to the position that those human rights obligations should not be incorporated into British law. The record indicated that in cases where they could duly invoke the terms of human rights instruments without trespassing on the legislative prerogative of Parliament, the courts had been scrupulous in so doing. Therefore, the fact that neither the Covenant nor the Convention were incorporated into domestic law did not preclude their use by the courts.

(CCPR/C/SR.1432, pp. 3–4)

The Chairman of the Committee then posed a number of questions, the first of which ran as follows:

(a) has any consideration been given to incorporating the Covenant into domestic law and adopting a bill of rights pursuant to the undertaking of the delegation during the consideration of the third periodic report to review governmental policy in that regard in the light of the Committee's comments (see A/46/40, para. 357)?

In reply, the UK representative, Mr Halliday, stated:

. . . the Government had reviewed the arguments for and against the incorporation of the European Convention on Human Rights into British law in the context of the parliamentary debates surrounding the draft Human Rights Bill. The Government's position remained unchanged since the time of its last appearance before the Committee. In its view, incorporation of either the Covenant or a bill of rights into domestic law was neither necessary nor desirable. It was unnecessary to incorporate the Covenant because current constitutional arrangements already established individual rights and freedoms under the law. It was unnecessary to incorporate a bill of rights because such rights were already inherent in the United Kingdom's legal systems and were protected by them and by Parliament until the point where that body determined that the needs of society were such that they should be restricted in some way. Incorporation of either was considered undesirable because it would alter the long-established balance among Parliament, the executive and the courts, in which Parliament was primarily responsible for matters affecting the rights and duties of individuals. In the view of the British Government such a fundamental change to the United Kingdom's constitutional arrangements should be made only if and when a clear need arose and a national consensus emerged. Members of the Committee would surely recall that the United Kingdom had in 1966 accepted the right of individual petition under the European Convention on Human Rights as well as the jurisdiction of the European Court of Human Rights, and on those occasions when that body had determined that breaches of the Convention had occurred, steps had at once been taken to remedy the matter. Having reviewed the record of those countries that had incorporated the European Convention on Human Rights into their legal arrangements, the Government found no evidence to support the notion that such a step would provide greater safeguards for individuals. The provisions of the Covenant were admittedly broader in some respects than those of the Convention. However, in the context of a legal system that itself safeguarded rights and freedoms, the Government had deemed that the jurisdiction of the European Court of Human Rights provided sufficient additional safeguards.

(Ibid., pp. 6–7; see also UKMIL 1995, pp. 592–602 passim)

The Parliamentary Under-Secretary of State, Department of Transport, Viscount Goschen, stated in the House of Lords:

I beg to move that the International Tribunal for the Law of the Sea (Immunities and Privileges) Order 1995 be approved. In moving that Motion it may be for the convenience of the House if I also speak to the International Sea-Bed Authority (Immunities and Privileges) Order 1995 and to the Merchant Shipping (Prevention of Pollution) (Law of the Sea Convention) Order 1995.

These three orders will enable the Government to implement the provisions of the 1982 United Nations Convention on the Law of the Sea, with a view to the United Kingdom's forthcoming accession to the Convention.

The convention was the product of the third United Nations Conference on the Law of the Sea, which was held over ten years between 1973 and 1982. The aim of the convention was to establish a comprehensive legal regime for the oceans. In this it is largely successful and is beneficial to United Kingdom interests. It confirms important rights, such as the freedom of navigation and overflight. It provides for a package of maritime limits: notably a maximum of 12 miles for the territorial sea and 200 miles for the exclusive economic zone, within which coastal states have jurisdiction for the conservation of natural resources and the protection and preservation of the marine environment. These maximum limits are generally accepted and have caused some states to withdraw more extravagant and unjustified claims. The convention also contains extensive provisions on the peaceful settlement of maritime disputes.

(HL Debs., vol. 568, cols. 1178–9: 25 January 1996)

In the course of a debate in the House of Lords on 3 July 1996 on the subject of the United Kingdom's existing constitutional settlement, and of the implications of proposals for change, the Lord Chancellor, Lord Mackay of Clashfern, stated:

I have already referred to the process of evolution by which the constitutional principles of this country have been built up. The result is a network of arrangements ensuring good government and fairness to individuals. Essential to it is the interplay between historical common law principles and the application of statutes. I take the view that common law principles have embedded in them certain settled concepts, which provide broad and flexible protection of individuals' rights. One of the principles of interpretation to which I have referred is that the courts will have regard to these basic tenets when interpreting statutes, resolving ambiguities so as to minimise the effect on essential and particularly important elements of the common law. I personally consider this approach more satisfactory and better for the individual than one based on written and therefore less flexible principles. That is one reason why the Government do not favour the elaboration of a Bill of Rights or the incorporation of the European Convention on Human Rights into domestic law.

Your Lordships have debated the question of a Bill of Rights, whether in the form of the European Convention or in some other form, on several occasions. I will today merely state what I believe to be a few of the salient points. The question of whether the European Convention is incorporated or not is, in my view, of little relevance to the real standard of legal protection afforded by the state to individuals in this country. Nor is there any evidence, in my view, that it would reduce the number of cases going from this country to the human rights court in Strasbourg. Our record at Strasbourg has been questioned; but if account is taken of relative population sizes and length of time the right of individual petition and jurisdiction of the court has been accepted here, we are about in the middle of the field.

Legal traditions, legislative and judicial approaches lead in practice to the same or a higher level of protection of human rights provided in a number of other ways. Unwritten principles, for example, of rationality and legality can be greatly superior to the list of rights set out in the convention. There is also a presumption applied by the courts in cases of ambiguity that Parliament does not intend to legislate inconsistently with the United Kingdom's international obligations.

Enacting a Bill of Rights in terms similar to the convention, or incorporating the convention itself would give courts wide discretion over matters which in my view are properly the preserve of Parliament. It is for Parliament to legislate so that our legal arrangements comply with convention principles, taking account, for example, of the margin of appreciation allowed to member states under Strasbourg case law. The extent to which that margin of appreciation is used is clearly, in my judgment, a matter for political balance but would have to be decided by our courts on the basis of a generally worded provision if the convention were incorporated in our law in terms such as I have mentioned. This contrasts strongly with our own legislative drafting tradition and would leave much scope for judicial interpretation and of course litigation. I think it would also have the effect of creating the impression that the Strasbourg court was in the nature of a court of appeal from the House of Lords.

Moreover, the scope for judicial interpretation would inevitably draw judges into making decisions which are essentially political rather than legal in nature. For example, the courts might be asked to decide sensitive matters such as the conditions under which abortions should be allowed. That has been put forward as a constitutional question in some other jurisdictions which will occur quite readily to your Lordships. In my view our tradition is clearly that such matters should be decided by Parliament. Against such a background a strong demand would emerge for judges to be chosen for their social or political views rather than their legal qualities and impartiality. It would be a short step to the kind of senatorial hearings on the appointment of judges which we see in the United States. In my view that would be a fundamental change in the nature of our judiciary, and an unwelcome one.

(HL Debs., vol. 573, cols. 1451–2: 3 July 1996)

[*Editorial note*: The following extract from the speech in the same debate by the Lord Chief Justice, Lord Bingham of Cornhill, although not given by a member of Her Majesty's Government, is reproduced here for its general interest:

There is just one issue upon which, with your Lordships' leave, I wish to touch; that is, the constitutional relationship between the British courts, the European Court of Human Rights in Strasbourg and the current status of the European convention in our courts. I raise that topic not to argue any case, but to record where, as I understand, we now are on the principle that it is desirable to know where one is before deciding where, if anywhere, one wishes to go.

The starting point is, of course, that we are a state that ratified the convention; we are bound in international law to honour the obligations which we have undertaken. When any breach of the convention has been established on the part of any public authority, we are bound to amend our law and procedures to make good the breach and prevent a recurrence. That is an obligation which has, I believe, been scrupulously observed by successive governments of both political colours.

But the convention is not part of our domestic law. The courts have no powers to enforce convention rights directly. If domestic legislation plainly conflicts with the enforcement of the convention, then the courts apply the domestic legislation. That is a principle which your Lordships' House, sitting judicially, has unambiguously laid down and it is a rule which the courts have loyally observed, despite ingenious and persistent invitations by counsel to depart from it.

In some countries treaties, once ratified, have the force of law. That is not so here and it is that fact which gives continuing vitality to the debate on incorporation. It might be thought to follow from that that the convention is a matter for Parliament and the Government, with which the courts have nothing whatever to do. But that, I suggest, would not be entirely right and I hope that your Lordships will permit me to touch briefly on six respects in which I suggest the convention can, and in practice does, have an influence in our domestic proceedings.

First, as the noble and learned Lord the Lord Chancellor observed, where a United Kingdom statute is capable of two interpretations, one consistent with the convention and one inconsistent, then the courts will presume that Parliament intended to legislate in conformity with the convention and not in conflict with it. In other words, the courts will presume that Parliament did not intend to legislate in violation of international law. That may be thought by your Lordships to be a modest presumption.

Secondly, if the common law is uncertain, unclear or imcomplete, the courts have to make a choice; they cannot abdicate their power of decision. In declaring what the law is, they will rule, wherever possible, in a manner which conforms with the convention and does not conflict with it. Any other course would be futile since a rule laid down in defiance of the convention would be likely to prove short-lived.

There is, of course, one field—freedom of expression—in which respected Members of this House have declared that they see no inconsistency between the common law and the convention. That is reassuring; it is also wholly unsurprising since we have a long record as a pioneer in the field of freedom of expression. But it means that the courts are encouraged to look to the convention and the jurisprudence of the European Court of Human Rights when resolving problems on the common law.

Thirdly, when the courts are called upon to construe a domestic statute enacted to fulfil a convention obligation, the courts will ordinarily assume that the statute was intended to be effective to that end. That is mere common sense, but common sense is the stock-in-trade of much judicial decision-making.

Fourthly, where the courts have a discretion to exercise—that is, they can act in one way or another—one or more of which violates the convention and another of which does not, they seek to act in a way which does not violate the convention. That again is usually common sense and requires no elaboration. However, it is not an invariable rule and your Lordships' House, sitting judicially, gave an important judgment only yesterday in which the convention right to privacy was held to be obliged to give way to the greater interests of justice.

Fifthly, when, as sometimes happens, the courts are called upon to decide what, in a given situation, public policy demands, it has been held to be legitimate that we shall have regard to our international obligations enshrined in the convention as a source of guidance on what British public policy requires.

Sixthly and lastly, matters covered by the law of the European Community— that is, the law administered by the European Court of Justice in Luxembourg and not Strasbourg—on occasion give effect to matters covered by convention law. The Court of Justice takes the view that on matters subject to Community law, the law common to the member states is part of the law which applies. All member states are parties to the convention and it so happens from time to time that laws derived from the convention are incorporated as part of the law of the Community. That of course is a law which the courts in this country must apply since we are bound by Act of Parliament to do so, and that is a means by which, indirectly, convention rights find their way into domestic law.

(Ibid., cols. 1465–7)]

Later in the same debate, the Minister of State, FCO, Baroness Blatch, stated:

It is too easy at times to take the safeguards and the protection that we enjoy for granted. We must not fall into the trap of doing so. We should be proud of those fundamental parts of our heritage and not seek to change them where there is neither a clear need nor an advantage in doing so. Some noble Lords have argued that, instead of a Bill of Rights, or as a first step towards one, the United Kingdom should incorporate the European Convention on Human Rights, or the International Covenant on Civil and Political Rights, into our domestic law. For the reasons I have already explained, the Government do not believe that seeking to codify individual rights and freedoms in our law, whether in the form of an incorporated treaty or a free-standing bill of rights, is either necessary or desirable.

Those who suggest that the United Kingdom's record on breaches of the ECHR is the worst in Europe are simply misinformed. The UK's record of compliance with the European Convention on Human Rights compares well with the record of any other country. Listening to the noble and learned Lord, Lord Bingham, I had to ask myself: what is the practical benefit of incorporation? On the contrary, incorporation would have required the Appellate Committee of the House of Lords to decide on yesterday's case in another way.

Perhaps I may give your Lordships some examples of the records of other countries as regards breaches of the ECHR: 27 allegations of violation respectively against the Portuguese and Greek Governments were declared admissible by the Commission; 28 against the Austrian Government; 39 against the Government of the Netherlands; 57 against the Turkish Government; 148 against the French Government; and 453 against the Italian Government. Over the same period, only 24 allegations against the United Kingdom were declared admissible. Those figures hardly support the claim that incorporation reduces the number of cases going forward to Strasbourg. I agree with the powerful speech of my noble friend Lord Kingsland when he argued that incorporation is not necessary and, if it were suggested, it would only be futile.

(Ibid., cols. 1567–8)

In the course of oral questions in the House of Commons on the subject of the European Court of Human Rights, the Secretary of State for the Home Department, Mr Michael Howard, stated:

I believe that the best way forward is to reform the court in the way in which we are seeking to do, rather than incorporate the convention into our domestic law, which would require our courts to make political judgments about a wide range of matters that are at present determined by our elected and democratically accountable Parliament. Such judgments are the proper function of Parliament, not the courts.

(HC Debs., vol. 286, col. 1193: 5 December 1996)

Part One II. D. 3. *International law in general—relationship between international law and internal law—implementation of international law in internal law—other sources*

The FCO presented a memorandum, dated 27 March 1996, to the HC Joint Committee on Statutory Instruments on the subject of the United Nations (International Tribunal) (Former Yugoslavia) Order 1996 (Statutory Instruments 1996, No. 716). The memorandum started as follows:

1. This Order enables the United Kingdom to comply with international obligations which have been imposed by the United Nations Security Council. Resolution 827 (1993) established the International Tribunal for the Prosecution of Persons Responsible for Serious Violations of International Humanitarian Law Committed in the Territory of the Former Yugoslavia since 1991 and adopted the Statute of the Tribunal (which is scheduled to the Order).
2. The Statute imposes obligations on Member States of the United Nations to co-operate with the International Tribunal in the investigation and prosecution of accused persons and to comply with any request for assistance or an order issued by a Trial Chamber. This may involve, among other things, the identification and location of persons, the arrest, detention and delivery up to the International Tribunal of accused persons or of witnesses who fail to comply with a subpoena, the taking of testimony and the production of evidence and the service of documents. The Order contains provisions enabling the United Kingdom to comply with its international obligations, subject to necessary safeguards.

(Text provided by the FCO)

Part Two: I. *Sources of international law—treaties*

A legal committee within the Council of the European Union circulated a questionnaire on the subject of the conclusion of international agreements. The following questions were amongst those asked:

1. What criteria, if any, are used by your authorities to distinguish treaties from instruments without legally binding force in public international law?
2. Are there any special procedures to be followed before the signing or approval of the latter instruments?
3. Are there any mandatory legal rules preventing delegation of signing or approval of such instruments?

The FCO replied on 9 May 1996 as follows:

1. INSTRUMENTS WITHOUT LEGALLY BINDING FORCE

1. What distinguishes a treaty from an instrument without legally binding force is an intention by the parties to enter into binding relations in international law. In UK practice, such an intention is evidenced by the use of particular language indicating an intention to create a binding legal relationship. The terms of an informal, non-binding, document will be drafted as mere expressions of intent. The UK's practice was recently described in more detail in PESC/LON COREU 772 of 6 September 1994.
2. There are no special procedures to be followed before the signing or approval of non-binding instruments.
3. There are no legal rules defining the persons who may be authorised to sign or approve international instruments, whether binding or non-binding. In practice, however, all such instruments are usually concluded by official Government representatives.

(Text provided by the FCO)

In a press release dated 20 December 1996, the Secretary of State for Foreign and Commonwealth Affairs, Mr Malcolm Rifkind, stated in part:

British policy in Hong Kong is governed by the Sino-British Joint Declaration on the question of Hong Kong of 1984 (the JD). The JD is a binding treaty between Britain and China, registered at the United Nations

(Text provided by the FCO)

Part Two: II. *Sources of international law—custom*

In the course of a debate on the implementation of provisions designed to facilitate the accession by the UK to the 1982 Law of the Sea Convention, the Parliamentary Under-Secretary of State, Department of Transport, Viscount Goschen, stated:

The noble Lord raised the issue of whether some of the provisions contained in the convention are not already part of the legal system, agreements or arrangements. The noble Lord is right. Many of the provisions are now customary in international law, but the law is obviously much more certain when agreed internationally by the convention. It confirms a number of those points.

(HL Debs., vol. 568, cols. 1185–6: 25 January 1996)

Part Two: VIII. *Sources of international law—restatement by formal processes of codification and progressive development*

The following statement on behalf of the European Union was made on 27 February 1996 by Professor Mauro Politi to the Special Committee on the Charter of the UN and on the Strengthening of the Role of the Organization:

I have the honour to speak on behalf of the European Union.

This statement of the European Union is devoted to the topic of the Status of the Repertory of Practice of United Nations Organs and of the Repertoire of Practice of the Security Council. We are grateful to the Legal Counsel, Mr. Hans Corell, for his introduction to the Note issued by the Secretariat on this question. This note provides useful background information and indicates, both with respect to the U.N. Organs' Repertory and the Security Council's Repertoire, the difficulties encountered by the Secretariat in their preparation and update, and the possible courses of action for the future.

The European Union regards the publication of the Repertory of Practice of U.N. Organs and of the Repertoire of Practice of the Security Council as a matter of the utmost importance. We see these repertories as essential instruments for recording United Nations practice, and providing a summary of it to be used not only by Governments of Member States and offices of the Secretariat, but also by institutions outside the U.N., universities and individual scholars. The idea behind the decisions, taken shortly after the birth of the United Nations, that the preparation of these repertories would contribute to the knowledge and understanding of the Charter, remains extremely valid. There is a need to make available to all potential users the repertories as sources of reference for assessing the evolution of U.N. practice and, more generally, of international law.

The mandate given to the Charter Committee to consider the status of the Repertory of Practice and of the Security Council's Repertoire reflects the concern, which we fully share, over the present difficulties and delays in updating these publications. The last Supplement to the Repertory of Practice, issued in 1986, covers the period 1970–1978. The last Supplement to the Security Council's Repertoire, issued in 1992, covers the period 1982–1984. We are aware of the problems of human and budgetary resources encountered by the Secretariat in this respect and outlined in the Note of 21 February. At the same time, we are convinced that, in a spirit of cooperation and mutual understanding, every effort should be made to overcome those problems and progressively reduce the existing backlog.

We take note of the various suggestions made by the Secretariat for possible courses of action in this matter. We are ready to discuss in more detail the different ways and means, outlined by the Secretariat, that could allow prompt resumption and effective work on the publication of the repertories. While the difficulties concerning the Security Council's Repertoire appear, to a certain extent, less complex, the questions raised in connection with updating the U.N. Repertory deserve particularly careful consideration. All options which are consistent with the idea that the publication of the repertories must continue should be considered.

In conclusion, the European Union would like to stress once again the great interest that it takes in this subject. It is an interest based on the profound conviction that collecting and handing down U.N. practice is an essential duty of the Organization, and an activity of primary importance for the knowledge and progress of international law.

(Text provided by the FCO)

Speaking on 12 November 1996 in the Sixth Committee of the UN General Assembly discussing the report of the work of the International Law Commission, the UK representative, Sir Franklin Berman, stated:

I conclude this section of my statement with just one comment, which goes to the Commission's intriguing analysis of the relationship between codification and progressive development. The Commission take the view that the distinction between the two 'is difficult if not impossible to draw in practice, especially when one descends to the detail . . . necessary . . . to give more precise effect to a principle.' It is hard to cavil at that. There remains, however, a difference in kind, reflected in turn in the elusive but tantalising words of article 15 of the Commission's Statute. It would be worth an attempt to explore more deeply what it was that the General Assembly seemed to have in mind in 1947. However that may be, the distinction exists and the blurring of the dividing line which has characterised most of the Commission's work over the years may also have led to the blurring of another factor which to my mind remains very important . . .

'Codification' is a process designed to pin down the unique 'right solution' which represents what the law is at the given moment. 'Progressive development', on the other hand, necessarily entails an element of choice as to how the law *should* develop; various solutions are possible, none uniquely right, even if one seems (to the Commission) better than others. It is quite possible that over the years the Commission, in eliding the distinction, has been guilty of disguising this element of choice. Policy choices have been presented in the language of codification, as if they were uniquely right solutions, or at least uniquely preferable solutions. It would seem far better for the Commission to acknowledge the element of choice, indeed to go out of its way to identify the choices and explain the criteria. To provide guidance in this way would not only make the entire process of choice and recommendation more transparent, it would also be of positive benefit to Governments in their responses if the Commission guided them on their way, possibly by pointing out the consequences foreseen from making one choice rather than another. This would not prevent, or even inhibit, the Commission from stating what its own preference would be. But it would be a service to States. And I have a strong feeling that it would facilitate the dialogue with this Committee which the Commission rightly seeks to improve.

(Text provided by the FCO; See also A/C.6/51/SR. 38, p. 7)

Part Two: IX. *Sources of international law—comity*

(See Part One: II.A., above)

Part Three: I. A. 1. *Subjects of international law—States—international status—sovereignty and independence*

Speaking in the UN Security Council on 12 July 1996, the UK Permanent Representative, Sir John Weston, referred to conditions in Georgia and the mandate of the UN Observer Mission in Georgia (UNOMIG). He went on:

We believe that UNOMIG continues to have a valuable role in sustaining the conditions necessary to allow a lasting settlement to emerge. But—and we always say this on these occasions—it is up to the parties, and in particular the Abkhaz leadership, to demonstrate that they are prepared to work earnestly and constructively towards a settlement. The British Government continues to believe that any such settlement, if it is to be viable, must fully respect Georgia's sovereignty and territorial integrity within its internationally recognized borders.

(S/PV. 3680, pp. 8–9)

In a speech to the UN General Assembly on 24 September 1996, the Foreign Minister of the Republic of Ireland, on behalf of the EU, stated:

The European Union observes once again that the current status quo in Cyprus is not acceptable. It reaffirms its strong support for the efforts of the Secretary-General of the United Nations aimed at a negotiated and lasting solution to the Cyprus question which will respect the sovereignty, independence, territorial integrity and unity of the country in accordance with the relevant United Nations resolutions.

(A/51/PV. 6, p. 11)

The following Presidency statement on behalf of the EU was issued on 28 October 1996:

The European Union reaffirms its strong commitment to the sovereignty, independence, territorial integrity and national unity of Afghanistan, and urges all States to refrain from interfering in the internal affairs of Afghanistan.

(*Bulletin of the European Union*, 1996–10, p. 64)

Part Three: I. A. 2. *Subjects of international law—States—international status—non-intervention and non-use of force*

The following Presidency statement of behalf of the EU was made on 13 February 1996, the seventh anniversary of the *fatwa* against Salman Rushdie:

On the seventh anniversary of the publication of the fatwa condemning the British author Salman Rushdie to death and calling for his assassination, the European Union recalls and repeats the solemn affirmation it made on 13 February 1995 according to which the fatwa, decided in defiance of the Universal Declaration of Human Rights and the principle of the sovereignty of States, in particular regarding the protection by the latter of their nationals, remains null and void.

The European Union will continue to take advantage of its critical dialogue with Iran to defend fundamental rights and freedom of expression. Recalling the conclusions of the European Council in Madrid on 15 and 16 December 1995, the European Union renews its demand that Iran abide by international law and calls upon the Iranian authorities to join the EU's efforts to obtain a satisfactory solution in respect of Salman Rushdie.

(*Bulletin of the European Union*, 1996–1/2, p. 78)

Part Three: I. A. 3. *Subjects of international law—States—international status—domestic jurisdiction*

(See also Part Four: VII. (item of 18 December 1996), below)

In July 1996, the FCO published a document entitled *Human Rights in Foreign Policy* which contained the following paragraphs:

NATIONAL SOVEREIGNTY: ARE WE INTERVENING IN INTERNAL AFFAIRS?

17. The duty not to intervene in matters within the domestic jurisdiction of other states is a recognised principle of international law, reflected in Article 2(7) of the United Nations Charter. However, Articles 55 and 56 of the Charter set out the obligation of all Members of the United Nations to promote universal respect for, and observance of, human rights. This obligation, reinforced over the years by the creation of a framework for international promotion and discussion of human rights and by the elaboration of international human rights law, means that human rights violations are no longer insulated from external criticism on the grounds that the matter is exclusively a domestic one. This was expressly recognised at the World Conference on Human Rights (Vienna, 1993), which declared that:

'*The promotion and protection of all human rights is a legitimate concern of the international community*'.

18. In practice the argument that to raise concerns at violations of human rights constitutes interference in the internal affairs of a state is heard less and less frequently. Governments are becoming used to the fact that human rights issues

are discussed in international bodies and in relations between countries, and will continue to be discussed. In 1995 alone we participated with our EU partners in 157 EU statements, declarations and public or confidential démarches to 51 governments of countries where human rights had been violated. We also made numerous bilateral representations. Even those countries which object to human rights criticism often implicitly accept its legitimacy by themselves criticising others. As a corollary, we must be prepared to discuss human rights issues in the United Kingdom when these are raised with us.

19. It follows from the above that, if asked whether we will take up a human rights violation with another State on behalf of one or more of its own nationals, it is wrong to take the line that this is an internal affair in which we have no standing. Where British nationals are involved, we do of course also have an additional consular standing to raise a human rights issue.

. . .

Bilateral Action

23. We take a wide range of bilateral action. For example:
— confidential representations (Prime Ministerial, Ministerial and at all official levels) about a general problem (such as torture, disappearances or detention without charge) or about individual cases;
— public statements;
— curtailment of aid (eg to Malawi in 1991—restored in 1993) or restrictions on aid (eg to Nigeria in 1993 and 1995, to the Gambia in 1994);
— enquiries about individual cases of concern to the British public or Parliament;
— attending trials (eg in Iran in 1994);
— sending observers to elections (eg South Africa, Nepal and Ukraine in 1994 and Belarus and Russia in 1995);
— looking for opportunities to support local human rights work (eg Post using Heads of Mission Small Projects Scheme to finance human rights training courses for public security force in Honduras from 1992 to 1994; Post using AUS Programme Budget to support human rights seminar in Cameroon in 1995; British Council initiating and funding an African regional workshop on freedom of expression in Zambia in 1995);
— arranging sponsored visits for people whose work relates to human rights;
— maintaining contacts with the supporting local human rights organisations.

(FCO *Foreign Policy Document* No. 268)

Part Three: I. B. 1. *Subjects of international law—States—recognition—recognition of States*

(See also part One: II. B. (item of 4 December 1996), above)

The following statement was issued by the FCO on 9 April 1996:

STATEMENT ON UK RECOGNITION OF THE FEDERAL REPUBLIC OF YUGOSLAVIA

The Foreign Secretary Malcolm Rifkind will be writing to President Lilic to inform him that the United Kingdom recognises the Federal Republic of Yugoslavia as an independent sovereign state.

We shall be upgrading the level of our diplomatic representation at Belgrade to that of Ambassador.

This is a welcome development which reflects the changed circumstances in the region following signature of the Bosnia Peace Agreement, and underlines our and the EU's balanced approach to the states of former Yugoslavia, all of which we now recognise.

Both we and our EU partners have made it clear that the development of good relations with the FRY and the evolution of its position within the international community will depend on a constructive approach by the FRY to a range of key issues. These include:

— fulfilment of its Bosnia Peace Agreement commitments including co-operation with the International Criminal Tribunal;
— full co-operation in implementing the Basic Agreement on Eastern Slavonia;
— full respect for human rights, minority rights and the right to return of all refugees and displaced persons and the granting of a large degree of autonomy for Kosovo within the FRY;
— mutual recognition among all the former Yugoslav republics, and agreement by them on succession issues.

(Text provided by the FCO; see also HC Debs., vol. 277, WA, col. 89: 7 May 1996)

The following Presidency statement on behalf of the EU was made on 9 April 1996:

On behalf of the European Union, the Presidency expresses appreciation for the agreement signed yesterday by the Federal Republic of Yugoslavia (FRY) and the former Yugoslav Republic of Macedonia (FYROM) authorities to the effect of settling their bilateral relations and exchanging diplomatic representatives at ambassadorial level. This development, which was considered important by the European Union, represents a substantial contribution to peace and stability in the region of former Yugoslavia and opens the way to recognition by the Member States, in accordance with their respective procedures, of the Federal Republic of Yugoslavia as one of the successor States to the Socialist Federal Republic of Yugoslavia. The European Union will welcome further steps by the Federal Republic of Yugoslavia leading the country to the full normalization of its relations with the international community.

The European Union considers that hereafter the development of good relations with the Federal Republic of Yugoslavia and of its position within the international community will depend on a constructive approach by the FRY to the following:

☐ mutual recognition among all the states of the former Yugoslavia, including between the Republic of Croatia and the Federal Republic of Yugoslavia. The

EU urges the Federal Republic of Yugoslavia and the Republic of Croatia to overcome all remaining obstacles to the mutual recognition and full normalization of relations without delay;

□ progress in the fulfilment of the commitments made in the Paris Peace Agreement, including cooperation with the International Tribunal;

□ agreement among all the states of the former Yugoslavia on succession issues;

□ full cooperation in implementing the basic agreement on Eastern Slavonia, and

□ full respect for human rights, minority rights and the right to return of all refugees and displaced persons and the granting of a large degree of autonomy for Kosovo within the FRY.

The European Union places a particular emphasis on human rights and rights of national and ethnic groups. It recalls the Federal Republic of Yugoslavia's commitments made in the Paris Peace Agreement and its agreement at the London Peace Implementation Conference to the continuation of the Working Group on ethnic and national minorities and communities with its present terms of reference. This Group's mandate is to recommend initiatives for resolving ethnic questions in the former Yugoslavia on the basis of agreed principles concerning human rights and rights of national and ethnic groups. The European Union understands that the commitments in the Paris Peace Agreement and the acceptance of the continuation of this Group by the Federal Republic of Yugoslavia entails acceptance of these principles. This understanding is communicated to the Federal Republic of Yugoslavia and progress in implementing these principles will be carefully monitored.

(*Bulletin of the European Union*, 1996–4, p. 58.)

On 10 April 1996, the following message was sent to President Lilic of the Federal Republic of Yugoslavia by the Secretary of State for Foreign and Commonwealth Affairs, Mr Malcolm Rifkind:

I am writing to place on record that the British Government formally recognises the Federal Republic of Yugoslavia as an independent sovereign state.

In doing so may I also say that we expect the Federal Republic of Yugoslavia to adopt a constructive approach on all the points set out in the statement of 9 April of the European Union.

We have decided to upgrade the level of our diplomatic representation in Belgrade to that of Ambassador. I can confirm that, as appropriate, we regard treaties and agreements in force to which the United Kingdom and the Socialist Federal Republic of Yugoslavia were parties as remaining in force between the United Kingdom and the Federal Republic of Yugoslavia.

I take this opportunity to send the best wishes of the British people to the people of the Federal Republic of Yugoslavia.

(Text provided by the FCO)

On 11 April 1996, the FCO sent a telegram to all missions for use publicly in statements. Part of the telegram read as follows:

Is UK rewarding Milosevic/Serbs/ethnic cleansing?
– No. We recognise states, not governments. Recognition is not a reward. Our recognition of the FRY, along with our European partners, reflects the changed circumstances in the region in the light of the Bosnia Peace Agreement, and the EU's balanced policy to the states of the region.

. . .

Why wait so long to recognise the FRY?
– In many respects non-recognition of the FRY was a legal anomaly. For instance, the UK has witnessed a treaty—the Bosnia Peace Agreement—which the FRY signed; and we have maintained an Embassy in Belgrade (at Chargé d'Affaires level). Recognition was withheld for political reasons, which in the light of the changed circumstances post-Dayton are now overtaken.
Link with mutual recognition between the FRY and Macedonia?
– EU Foreign Ministers decided on 29 January that the EU declaration should be published only after FRY/Macedonia mutual recognition. The FRY and Macedonia recognised each other on 8 April, and the EU declaration was published on 9 April.
Practical consequences of recognition?
– Limited. The ban on social contacts with FRY diplomats is now lifted. Defence attachés can now have normal contact with FRY DAs. Sanctions on the FRY remain suspended, and the UN/EU arms embargo on all states of former Yugoslavia remains in force.

. . .

Terminology?
– The UK is recognising the Federal Republic of Yugoslavia (FRY). It comprises Serbia and Montenegro. We used to call the FRY 'FRY (Serbia and Montenegro)'. Kosovo, Vojvodina and Sandjak are part of Serbia. The FRY is not (not) the same as former Yugoslavia. Former Yugoslavia comprises Serbia and Montenegro (now the FRY), Bosnia (officially 'Bosnia and Herzegovina'), Croatia, Slovenia, and Macedonia. Bosnia, Croatia etc are not (not) part of the FRY. FRY is not (not) an acronym for former Yugoslavia. The Bosnian Serbs in the Republika Srpska live in Bosnia, not the FRY: the Republika Srpska is one of the two Entities comprising Bosnia (the other being the Bosniac-Croat Federation).

(Text provided by the FCO)

In an action brought in the Chancery Division of the High Court of Justice by the Bank of Credit and Commerce International (Overseas) Ltd. (in liquidation) against Price Waterhouse and others, it was sought to join a number of third parties, including (i) Abu Dhabi, (ii) the Emirate of Abu Dhabi, (iii) the Government of Abu Dhabi, (iv) His Highness, the Ruler of Abu Dhabi, (v) the Abu Dhabi Investment Authority, (vi) His Excellency, Mohammed Habroush al Suweidi, (vii) His Excellency, Jauan Salem al Dhaheri, and (viii) His Excellency, Ghanem Faris al Mizrui. These claimed immunity pursuant to the terms of the State Immunity Act 1978, the Diplomatic Privileges Act 1964, and the common law. At an interlocutory hearing before the Vice-Chancellor, Sir Richard Scott, on 5 June 1996, an Order was made pursuant to which the FCO was to be requested in a letter signed jointly by the defendants' and third parties' solicitors (Messrs Herbert Smith and Macfarlanes respectively) and initialled by the Vice-Chancellor to provide a certificate in relation to specified questions.

The joint letter, initialled by the Vice-Chancellor, was dated 13 June 1996 and asked the following questions:

(In the following questions, reference to 'the Emirate' are references to Abu Dhabi or the Emirate of Abu Dhabi. Please state in each case in which it is felt able to provide an answer whether the recognition referred to is (or, as appropriate, was) accorded to 'Abu Dhabi' or 'the Emirate of Abu Dhabi'.)

1. Pursuant to the prerogative powers of the Crown, does Her Majesty's Government recognise Sheikh Zayed bin Sultan al Nahyan as a personal ruler exercising sovereign authority over the territory of the Emirate?
2. Prior to the creation of the United Arab Emirates:
   (a) did Her Majesty's Government recognise the ruler and/or the Emirate as exercising sovereign authority over its territory, if not,
   (b) what other recognition, if any, did Her Majesty's Government accord to the ruler and/or the Emirate?
3. The Provisional Constitution of the United Arab Emirates having been adopted, does Her Majesty's Government now recognise the Emirate as enjoying sovereign authority over its territory within the terms of the Provisional Constitution of the United Arab Emirates?
4. Pursuant to section 21 of the State Immunity Act 1978, does Her Majesty's Government recognise:
   (a) the Emirate as a state for the purposes of part I of the Act; and
   (b) His Highness Sheikh Zayed bin Sultan al Nahyan as a Head of State as Ruler of the Emirate for those purposes; or
   (c) His Highness Sheikh Zayed bin Sultan al Nahyan as Head of State as the President of the United Arab Emirates for those purposes?
5. Pursuant to section 21 of the State Immunity Act 1978, does Her Majesty's Government recognise the Emirate as a constituent territory of the United Arab Emirates as a federal state for the purposes of part I of the Act?
6. If Her Majesty's Government recognises the Emirate as a constituent territory of the United Arab Emirates as a federal state for the purposes of part I of the State Immunity Act 1978, does Her Majesty's Government recognise the Emirate as having any other attributes of sovereignty?

The following reply, dated 17 July 1996, was addressed to the respective solicitors by Mr G. J. Dorey, Acting Head of the Middle East Department, FCO:

BCCI (OVERSEAS) LIMITED AND OTHERS V. PRICE WATERHOUSE AND OTHERS V. ABU DHABI AND OTHERS

I refer to your joint letter of 13 June 1996 and to the judgment of the Vice-Chancellor given on 5 June 1996 in the above matter. I enclose a certificate by the Secretary of State for Foreign and Commonwealth Affairs given under section 21 of the State Immunity Act 1978, which should be taken as the response to Questions 4(a) and (c) and 5 in the joint letter.

As to Questions 3 and 6, it is not the practice of Her Majesty's Government to accord recognition to the constituent entities of federal States, nor is there power under section 21 to certify as to their status except as specified in that section. Whether Her Majesty's Government would enter into official dealings with any such constituent entity is a matter to be decided in the light of all the relevant circumstances of the particular case, including the attitude of the authorities of the federal State.

As to Question 2, I am instructed to state that, prior to the establishment of the United Arab Emirates on 2 December 1971, Her Majesty's Government recognised the State of Abu Dhabi as an independent sovereign State in special treaty relations with the United Kingdom. By virtue of the special treaty relations, Her Majesty's Government were generally responsible for the conduct of the international relations of Abu Dhabi and for its defence. Her Majesty's Government recognised His Highness Sheikh Zayed bin Sultan Al Nahyan as the sovereign Ruler of the State of Abu Dhabi.

As to Questions 1 and 4(b), it is my understanding that His Highness Sheikh Zayed bin Sultan Al Nahyan is the Ruler of Abu Dhabi, but I am instructed to state that that fact is not one peculiarly within the knowledge of the Secretary of State or Her Majesty's Government.

I am instructed finally to add that the names 'Abu Dhabi' 'Emirate of Abu Dhabi' and 'Abu Dhabi (United Arab Emirates)' are all in use by Her Majesty's Government, but that no special significance should be attached to the use of any one or other of them.

Attached to the above letter was the following certificate, dated 16 July 1996 and signed by the Secretary of State for Foreign and Commonwealth Affairs, Mr Malcolm Rifkind:

CERTIFICATE

in the matter of

BCCI (OVERSEAS) LIMITED AND OTHERS V. PRICE WATERHOUSE AND OTHERS V. ABU DHABI AND OTHERS

I, the Rt. Hon. Malcolm Rifkind QC MP, Her Majesty's Principal Secretary of State for Foreign and Commonwealth Affairs, refer to the request for a certificate made pursuant to the Order of the Court of 5 June 1996 in the above proceedings and issue the following certificate:

Pursuant to section 21 of the State Immunity Act 1978 (the 'Act'), I hereby certify that

— the United Arab Emirates is a State for the purposes of Part I of the Act;
— Abu Dhabi is a constituent territory of the United Arab Emirates, a federal State, for the purposes of Part I of the Act;

— His Highness Sheikh Zayed bin Sultan Al Nahyan is to be regarded for the purposes of Part I of the Act as head of State of the United Arab Emirates.

(Texts provided by the FCO)

Part Three: I. B. 2. *Subjects of international law—States—recognition—recognition of governments*

In the course of replying to oral questions on the subject of Cyprus, the Secretary of State for Foreign and Commonwealth Affairs, Mr Malcolm Rifkind, stated:

The Government of the Republic of Cyprus are recognised as the Government of a country that covers the whole island . . .

(HC Debs., vol. 273, col. 325: 6 March 1966)

Part Three: I. B. 4. *Subjects of international law—States—recognition—retroactive effects of recognition*

On 11 April 1996, the FCO sent a telegram to all missions setting out material for use in briefing in respect of the recognition of the Federal Republic of Yugoslavia. The telegram contained the following item:

Is recognition retroactive?
For legal purposes, in accordance with usual practice, recognition, once granted, dates back to the actual commencement of the activities of the recognised authority.

(Text provided by the FCO)

Part Three: I. B. 5. *Subjects of international law—States—recognition—non-recognition*

(See also Part Three: I. B. 1. (item of 11 April 1996), above)

On 2 October 1989, the following certificate was issued by the FCO for the purposes of litigation involving the case mentioned below:

Under the authority of Her Majesty's Principal Secretary of State for Foreign and Commonwealth Affairs conferred on me in accordance with Section 21 of the State Immunity Act 1978, I, David Colin Baskcomb Beaumont, Head of Protocol Department at the Foreign and Commonwealth Office, hereby certify that the so-called Turkish Republic of Northern Cyprus is not a State for the purposes of Part 1 of the State Immunity Act 1978.

In the course of a case in the Queen's Bench Division of the High Court, *In re an Application for Judicial Review: The Queen* v. *The Commissioners for the Inland Revenue, ex parte Resat Caglar*, the following affidavit was sworn on 5 May 1995:

I, HAYDON BOYD WARREN-GASH of King Charles Street, London, member of HM Diplomatic Service, make oath and say as follows:

1. I am Head of the Southern European Department of the Foreign and Commonwealth Office and am authorised to swear this Affidavit under the authority of Her Majesty's Principal Secretary of State for Foreign and Commonwealth Affairs. I have held my present position since 9 June 1994 and I make this Affidavit as a result of information I have obtained in the course of my duties in the Foreign and Commonwealth Office. This affidavit is intended to supplement the information provided by Mr John Buck in his affidavit sworn on 25th April, 1994. [See UKMIL 1994, pp. 590–1]

2. As the second paragraph of the aforesaid affidavit of Mr John Buck makes clear, Her Majesty's Government recognises only one State in the island of Cyprus, namely the Republic of Cyprus established in 1960 under the Treaties of Guarantee and Establishment which are attached as exhibits 1 and 2 to the affidavit of Mr Buck. Article 1 of the Treaty of Establishment and Section 2(1) of the Cyprus Act 1960 provide that the territory of the Republic of Cyprus comprises the entirety of the island of Cyprus with the exception of the two United Kingdom Sovereign Base Areas.

3. Her Majesty's Government maintains full and friendly relations in all fields with the Government which is currently led by President Glafcos Clerides as the Government of the Republic of Cyprus. It maintains diplomatic relations and has normal government to government dealings with that Government including the conclusion of international agreements.

4. Her Majesty's Government does not maintain diplomatic relations or have normal government to government dealings with any other entity on the island of Cyprus.

In proceedings before the Special Commissioners of Inland Revenue, in the *Appeals of Resat Caglar and others*, the following further affidavit was sworn on 10 January 1996:

I, HAYDON BOYD WARREN-GASH of King Charles Street, London, Member of HM Diplomatic Service, make oath and say as follows:

1. I am head of the Southern European Department of the Foreign and Commonwealth Office and am authorised to swear this Affidavit under the authority of Her Majesty's Principal Secretary of State for Foreign and Commonwealth Affairs. I have held my present position since 9 June 1994 and I make this Affidavit as a result of information I have obtained in the course of my duties in the Foreign and Commonwealth Office.

2. Her Majesty's Government has not accorded any form of recognition to the so-called 'Turkish Republic of Northern Cyprus (TRNC)'. I refer to the certificate sent by the Foreign and Commonwealth Office to the taxpayers' solicitors on 2 October 1989, a copy of which is attached as exhibit HBWG 1 to this Affidavit, which stated that the so-called TRNC was not a State for the purposes of section 1 of the State Immunity Act 1978. I am authorised to state that the terms of that certificate continue to represent the position of Her Majesty's Government.

3. Her Majesty's Government recognises only one State in the island of Cyprus, namely the Republic of Cyprus established in 1960 under the Treaties of

Guarantee and Establishment to which the United Kingdom, Greece, Turkey and the Republic of Cyprus are parties, and which are attached as exhibits HBWG 2 and HBWG 3 to this Affidavit. Article 1 of the Treaty of Establishment and section 2(1) of the Cyprus Act 1960 provide that the territory of the Republic of Cyprus comprises the entirety of the island of Cyprus with the exception of the two United Kingdom Sovereign Base Areas. In Article 11 of the Treaty of Guarantee, Greece, Turkey and the United Kingdom undertook inter alia to recognise and guarantee the independence, territorial integrity and security of the Republic of Cyprus.

4. Following a Greek-inspired coup against the legitimate Government of the Republic of Cyprus in 1974, the Turkish army intervened on the grounds that intervention was necessary to protect the Turkish Cypriot community. Violence was halted when the United Nations Force in Cyprus (UNFICYP), with the agreement of the parties, established cease-fire lines between the northern and southern parts of the island. These lines do not constitute an international boundary, but demarcate a buffer zone between the positions of the Greek Cypriot military forces on the one hand and the Turkish Army and Turkish Cypriot forces on the other.

5. On 13 February 1975 the Turkish Cypriot community in northern Cyprus declared the so-called 'Turkish Federated State of Cyprus (TFSC)' in the area north of the buffer zone. The legality of this declaration was not accepted by Her Majesty's Government. The 'TFSC' did not purport to be a state in the international sense, and, to the best of my knowledge, was not recognised as such by any other State.

6. On 15 November 1983 the Turkish Cypriot community in northern Cyprus purported to declare independence and established the so-called 'TRNC'. The declaration of independence of the 'TRNC' was declared legally invalid by the Security Council in Resolution 541 of 18 November 1983, which is attached as exhibit HBWG 4 of this Affidavit. In addition, this resolution called upon all States to recognise the sovereignty, independence, territorial integrity and non-alignment of the Republic of Cyprus and not to recognise any Cypriot State other than the Republic of Cyprus.

7. With the exception of Turkey, no other State has recognised the 'TRNC'. On 11 May 1984 the United Nations Security Council adopted Resolution 550, which is attached as exhibit HBWG 5 to this Affidavit. Resolution 550 declared illegal and invalid the purported exchange of Ambassadors between Turkey and the Turkish Cypriot leadership and repeated the call to all States not to recognise the 'TRNC'. It further called on them not to facilitate or assist the 'TRNC' in any way.

8. Her Majesty's Government maintains full and friendly relations in all fields with the Government, which is currently headed by President Glafcos Clerides, as the Government of the Republic of Cyprus. It maintains diplomatic relations and has normal government-to-government dealings with the Government. Those dealings include the conclusion of international agreements. A list of the international agreements concluded between the United Kingdom and the Republic of Cyprus since 1974 is attached as exhibit HBWG 6 to this Affidavit. Ministers from the Republic of Cyprus make official visits to the UK and are regularly seen by UK Ministers when they do so. Those from the so-called TRNC who make visits to the UK do so on a private basis and are not seen by

UK Ministers. The Government headed by President Clerides represents the Republic of Cyprus in the United Nations, of which the Republic has been a member since 1960, and has diplomatic relations with the governments of most other members of the United Nations, including all the members of the European Union.

9. Her Majesty's Government does not maintain any diplomatic relations or have any normal government-to-government dealings with any other entity on the island of Cyprus. Her Majesty's Government does, however, have regard to the interests of the Turkish Cypriot community. For this reason it has maintained contacts with the leaders of the Turkish Cypriot community since the establishment of the Republic of Cyprus in 1960. In addition, there are functional contacts between police forces and other UK agencies and law enforcement officials in the 'TRNC' for the purposes of addressing law enforcement issues.

10. It is in that context that Her Majesty's Government allows the office in London, which is the subject of the present proceedings, to operate in the interests of the Turkish Cypriot community. Her Majesty's Government does not treat that office as representing a foreign state, nor does the Foreign and Commonwealth Office accord the 'TRNC' office in London the facilities which it normally extends to diplomatic missions. The Foreign and Commonwealth Office deals with the staff only on the basis that they are representatives of the Turkish Cypriot community and accords them no formal status. An office representing the Turkish Cypriot community within the Republic of Cyprus was established in London well before the Turkish Cypriot community declared the so-called Turkish Federated State of Cyprus on 13 February 1975.

11. The office is not a diplomatic mission and its staff are not diplomatic agents. On 2 October 1989 the Foreign and Commonwealth Office issued certificates under section 4 of the Diplomatic Privileges Act 1964, an example of which is attached as exhibit HBWG 7 to this Affidavit. Those certificates state that the taxpayers in the present proceedings had not been notified to the FCO as members of a diplomatic mission. I am authorised to state that the terms of those certificates continue to represent the position of Her Majesty's Government, The 'TRNC' maintains a number of similar offices in other States but these are not, to the best of my knowledge and belief, accorded the status of diplomatic missions in those States nor are their staff accredited as diplomats under the terms of the Vienna Convention on Diplomatic Relations 1961.

12. The Republic of Cyprus is a member of the Commonwealth and, in accordance with Article 6 and Annex D of the Treaty of Establishment, all persons of Cypriot origin, both Greek and Turkish, are citizens of the Republic of Cyprus and consequently are Commonwealth citizens. Turkish Cypriots are admitted to this country on the basis that they are members of the Turkish Cypriot community and thus citizens of the Republic of Cyprus. Her Majesty's Government regard passports issued by the so-called 'TRNC' as no more than evidence of identity and not as constituting recognition of separate 'TRNC' nationality. No official United Kingdom stamps are placed in 'TRNC' passports.

(Texts provided by the FCO (exhibits not reproduced))

In the course of a debate in the House of Commons on the subject of Taiwan, the Minister of State, FCO, Mr Jeremy Hanley, stated:

Let me make the Government's position clear. We acknowledge the Chinese Government's position that Taiwan is a province of China. The Taiwanese should be singularly ill-advised were they to proceed to a declaration of independence or some similar initiative. Our understanding is that the Taiwanese authorities seek negotiations about reunification, not independence.

(HC Debs., vol. 273, col. 943: 13 March 1996)

In reply to the question whether the Prime Minister will make it his policy to support the application by Taiwan to join the United Nations and to seek support from Commonwealth and EU partners for it, the Prime Minister wrote:

No. Membership of the United Nations is open only to states. Her Majesty's Government does not recognise Taiwan as a state.

(HC Debs., vol. 274, WA, col. *408*: 25 March 1996)

In reply to a question, the Minister of State, FCO, wrote:

Those entities which some claim to be states, but which are not recognised as such by the UK are:

Palestine
Taiwan
The Saharan Arab Democratic Republic
The Turkish Republic of Northern Cyprus.

(HC Debs., vol. 277, WA, col. *364*: 13 May 1996)

The following letter, dated 16 May 1996, was sent by the FCO to the Attorney-General's Chambers, Hong Kong, for use in litigation in the High Court of Hong Kong:

HIGH COURT ACTION NO. 5805 OF 1991: QUESTIONS BY THE COURT ABOUT THE STATUS OF TAIWAN

1. You asked in your letter of 8 May for answers to two questions posed by Mr Justice Leonard on 23 April 1996 in the above action. I set out below the questions and our response, which we would be happy for you to pass to the judge.

Question 1

What government, state or authority, if any, does HM Government recognise as the de facto or de jure government in Taiwan?
Her Majesty's Government does not recognise Taiwan as a state, and does not have any official dealings with the authorities there. In March 1972, the United Kingdom signed a Joint Communiqué with the People's Republic of China

(PRC) on the exchange of Ambassadors, in which the British Government acknowledged the position of the Government of the PRC that Taiwan was a province of the PRC and recognised the PRC Government as the sole legal government of China. This remains the Government's position. There has been no official UK representation in Taiwan since 1972, when, in consequence of the upgrading of relations with the PRC, the consulate at Tamsui was withdrawn.

Question 2

What dealings generally does HM Government have with any regime situate in Taiwan and purporting to exercise authority in Taiwan and, in particular, what dealings does HM Government have with any regime on a government to government basis?

The British Government has no official dealings with the authorities in Taiwan on a Government to Government basis. Those contacts with the authorities in Taiwan that do take place, primarily of an economic and commercial nature, do so on an unofficial basis, through the medium of the unofficial British Trade and Cultural Office (BTCO) in Taipei. The authorities in Taiwan maintain unofficial offices in London, through which similar unofficial contacts also take place.

(Text provided by the FCO)

In reply to an oral question on the subject of East Timor, the Minister of State, FCO, Mr Jeremy Hanley, stated in part:

The hon. Gentleman will be aware that the United Kingdom does not recognize Indonesian sovereignty over East Timor.

(HC Debs., vol. 279, col. 303: 12 June 1996)

In reply to a question, the Minister of State, FCO, wrote:

We do not recognise the self-proclaimed Tibetan Government in exile. We do, however, consider that Tibetans should have a greater say in the running of their own affairs in Tibet, and we have consistently urged the Chinese authorities and Tibetan Buddhist leaders to enter into a constructive dialogue, without preconditions.

(HC Debs., vol. 279, WA, col. *320*: 17 June 1996)

In an interview on London Greek Radio on 11 December 1996, the Secretary of State for Foreign and Commonwealth Affairs, Mr Malcolm Rifkind, stated:

But I would like to emphasise that we in no way intend to recognise the so-called Turkish Republic of Northern Cyprus. We do not recognise it. We acknowledge that north Cyprus is an occupied territory and in my meeting with Mr Denktash I will be meeting him in his capacity as leader of the Turkish-Cypriot community.

In an interview on the same day on the CNN network, Mr Rifkind was asked the following question:

You are making an unprecedented visit to the northern part of the island, the Turkish-occupied part of the island. Is that not in fact going to be viewed as a de facto recognition?

Mr Rifkind replied:

Most certainly not. We do not recognise any question of a separate Turkish Cypriot republic.

In an interview on BBC TV on the same day, Mr Rifkind stated:

There is no change in our position that we do not recognise the so-called Republic of Northern Cyprus; that has not changed, no country recognises that.

(Texts provided by the FCO)

In the course of a debate on the subject of human rights in China and Tibet, the Government spokesman, Lord Inglewood, stated:

Successive British Governments have regarded Tibet as autonomous while recognising the special position of China there. That continues to be the Government's view. Tibet has never been internationally recognised as independent. But we believe that the Tibetans should have a greater say in running their own affairs in Tibet, and have urged the Chinese authorities to respect the distinct cultural, religious and ethnic identity of the Tibetans.

(HL Debs., vol. 576, col. 1590: 18 December 1996)

Part Three: I. C. 1. *Subjects of international law—States—types of States—unitary States, federal States and confederations*

(See Part Three: I.B.1. (FCO Letter dated 17 July 1996), above)

Part Three: I. C. 4. *Subjects of international law—States—types of States—dependent States and territories*

(See also Part Eleven: II.A.1. (item of 17 July 1996), below)

The following letter, dated 10 June 1996, was sent by the Secretary of State for Foreign and Commonwealth Affairs, Mr Malcolm Rifkind, to the Governor of Hong Kong, Mr Christopher Patten:

I have the honour to refer to the draft Agreement for the purpose of providing the framework for air services between Hong Kong and the Republic of India, the text of which was negotiated during the period from May to December 1989.

The United Kingdom remains responsible for the external relations of Hong

Kong until 30 June 1997. However, the United Kingdom Government hereby entrusts to you authority:

(*a*) to conclude the said Agreement;
(*b*) in accordance with prior specific authorisations in that behalf from the United Kingdom Government, to agree and confirm amendments to the said Agreement;
(*c*) to carry into effect and to exercise the other powers conferred upon a Contracting Party by the said Agreement.

Further, with the prior agreement of the United Kingdom Government, you may terminate the said Agreement in accordance with its terms.

If action is required to be taken relating to the international conventions referred to in the said Agreement it shall be taken either by the United Kingdom Government or, as appropriate, by the Hong Kong Government acting under the authority of the United Kingdom Government.

Following the coming into force of the said Agreement, the United Kingdom Government will register it on behalf of the Hong Kong Government.

(Special Supplement No. 5 to the *Hong Kong Government Gazette*, vol. 138 (1996), p. E446; see also ibid., p. E395 (letter of 8 July 1996 in respect of draft air services agreement between the Hong Kong and Italian Governments))

Part Three: I. D. 2. *Subjects of international law—States—formation, continuity and succession of States—identity, continuity and succession*

On 11 April 1996, the FCO sent a telegram to all missions setting out briefing material in respect of the recognition of the Federal Republic of Yugoslavia. The telegram contained the following item:

Is FRY continuation of old Yugoslavia?
– The FRY is one of the successor states of the Socialist Federal Republic of Yugoslavia (SFRY). This has no consequences for the continuing debate on the division of assets and debts amongst the successor states.

(Text provided by the FCO)

Part Three: I. E. *Subjects of international law—States—self-determination*

(See also Part Eight: II. A (item of 27 September 1996), below)

In the course of a debate in the House of Lords on the subject of Chechnya, the Minister of State, FCO, Baroness Chalker, stated:

Any cessation from membership of the Russian Federation has to be mutually agreed, and it has been a longstanding part not only of British policy but certainly of other OSCE countries too that the right to self-determination does not equate automatically with the right to [secession].

(HL Debs., vol. 568, col. 586: 16 January 1996)

In the course of a debate on the subject of Chechnya, the Government spokesman in the House of Lords, Lord Chesham, stated:

The right to self-determination does not equate automatically with a right to secession. Chechnya is internationally recognised as part of the Russian Federation. A negotiated settlement needs to find an effective way to enable the Chechen people to express their identity within the framework of the consitution of the Russian Federation.

(HL Debs., vol. 569, col. 971: 20 February 1996)

In the course of a debate on the subject of Spanish attitudes towards Gibraltar, the Minister of State, FCO, stated:

We shall not let the people of Gibraltar pass under the sovereignty of another state against their freely and democratically expressed wishes.
. . .
My Lords, Gibraltar is British. As long as the people of Gibraltar want her to remain British, that is what they will voice in their elections.

(HL Debs., vol. 572, cols. 385–6: 14 May 1996)

In the course of a press interview in Madrid on 6 June 1996, the Secretary of State for Foreign and Commonwealth Affairs, Mr Malcolm Rifkind, stated:

Our interest in Gibraltar is that in the modern world, and in a modern democratic world, it is the wishes of the people of Gibraltar who must be given priority, and it is for them to decide, in our view, that consistent with the legal situation, and the Treaty of Utrecht, it is important for the people of Gibraltar's wishes to be taken into account.

(Text provided by the FCO)

In reply to a question, the Minister of State, FCO, wrote in part:

We continue to believe that a referendum of [sic] self-determination represents the best solution to the conflict in the Western Sahara.

The following question was asked of Her Majesty's Government:

Whether they consider themselves in any way still bound, by the terms of the 1917 Balfour Declaration, by which their predecessors sought 'the establishment in Palestine of a national home for the Jewish people . . . it being clearly understood that nothing shall be done to prejudice the civil and religious rights of existing non-Jewish communities in Palestine . . .'?

In reply, the Minister of State, FCO, wrote:

We support Israel's right to exist. We also support the principle of self-determination for the Palestinian people, and the right of all religions to have freedom of access to the Holy Places. We support UN Security Council Resolutions 242 and 338.

(HL Debs., vol. 574, WA 104–5: 23 July 1996)

At a press conference in New York on 24 September 1996, the Secretary of State for Foreign and Commonwealth Affairs, Mr Malcolm Rifkind, was asked to explain differences of policy towards Hong Kong and the Falkland Islands. He replied:

The legal position with regard to Hong Kong is that British sovereignty over Hong Kong is based on a treaty between the United Kingdom and China under which a large part of what is now Hong Kong was transferred to the United Kingdom 100 years ago in a 99 year lease, and once that lease expired, which it will do in June of next year, we have no legal basis to continue the administration of a large part of Hong Kong, and therefore that is the reason for the policy in respect of Hong Kong.

So far as the Falkland Islands is concerned, we believe, and it should be a view shared by the United Nations, that the fundamental principle is self-determination. Here is a territory which is a dependent territory. The people of the Falkland Islands have shown overwhelmingly their desire to remain citizens of the United Kingdom. That is a view that should be respected. The United Nations is built on the principle of the right of people to live according to their own free will, free choice. There is no legal argument to the contrary and therefore that is the basis of our position. It is quite clear and it has not changed.

(Text provided by the FCO)

Part Three: II. A. 1 (a). *Subjects of international law—international organizations—in general—legal status—personality*

On 30 May 1996, the Government of the UK and the International Oil Pollution Compensation Fund concluded a Headquarters Agreement. Among its provisions is the following:

ARTICLE 3

Legal personality

The 1992 Fund shall have legal personality. It shall in particular have the capacity to contract, to acquire and dispose of movable and immovable property and to be a party in legal proceedings.

(TS No. 78 (1996); Cm 3354)

The Bosnia and Herzegovina (High Representative) Order 1996 (Statutory Instruments 1996, No. 268), which entered into force on 18 March 1996, has the following explanatory note attached to it:

This Order, made under the United Nations Act 1946, confers the legal capacities of a body corporate upon the High Representative for Bosnia and Herzegovina established pursuant to the General Framework Agreement for Peace in Bosnia and Herzegovina (Cm 3154), as required by Security Council resolution 1031 (1995) of 15th December 1995.

The European Police Office (Legal Capacities) Order 1996 (Statutory Instruments 1996, No. 3157), which was made on 19 December 1996, was accompanied by the following explanatory note:

This Order confers the legal capacities of a body corporate on the European Police Office ('Europol'). This legal capacity is conferred in accordance with Article 26 of the Convention based on Article K.3 of the Treaty on European Union, on the Establishment of a European Police Office (Europol Convention) (Cm 3050). The Order will enable Her Majesty's Government to give effect to Article 26 of that Convention, and will come into force on the date on which the Convention enters into force in respect of the United Kingdom.

Part Three: II. A. 1. (c). *Subjects of international law—international organizations—in general—legal status—privileges and immunities*

In moving the consideration by the House of Commons First Standing Committee on Delegated Legislation of the draft Merchant Shipping (Prevention of Pollution) (Law of the Sea Convention) Order 1995, the International Sea-Bed Authority (Immunities and Privileges) Order 1995, and the International Tribunal for the Law of the Sea (Immunities and Privileges) Order 1995, the Minister of State, FCO, Sir Nicholas Bonsor, stated:

The two draft orders deal with privileges and immunities. The International Seabed Authority and the international tribunal for the law of the sea are established by the convention. Privileges and immunities need to be conferred on the authority and members of the tribunal in order for Her Majesty's Government to fulfil their obligations under part XI, subsection (G) and annex VI of the convention. The former provides for privileges and immunities for the authority, its staff and for representatives of states parties attending meetings of the authority. The annex provides for diplomatic privileges and immunities for members of the tribunal in the exercise of their functions.

So far as the authority is concerned, the privileges are to be similar to those provided for in the 1947 convention on the privileges and immunities of the specialised agencies of the United Nations.

. . .

I can tell my hon. Friend that someone with dual nationality would not get privileges and immunities. With regard to the Maastricht Treaty, the privileges and immunities under the International Organisations Act 1968 are the same as those with a more general application and in no way affect whatever was in the Maastricht Treaty . . .

So far as the members of the tribunal are concerned, the privileges are similar to those conferred upon the members of the International Court of Justice. However, as the authority is located in Jamaica and the tribunal in Hamburg, many of the privileges and immunities set out in the draft Order in Council are unlikely to have much practical effect in the United Kingdom. In practice, there are likely to be claims only for refunds of VAT on goods and services purchased in the United Kingdom for the official purposes of the organisation. For the most part, we will only need to accord the relevant privileges and immunities to the Authority's officials, representatives of member states of the authority and members of the tribunal if they attend any official meetings or conferences, which may be held in the United Kingdom. I would like to emphasise that the privileges and immunities provided for in the orders are, of course, granted in accordance with the limitations imposed by the International Organisations Act 1968, as amended, under the provisions of which the orders are made.

The Joint Committee on Statutory Instruments considered the draft instruments and had no comments.

(HC Debs., 1995–96, First Standing Committee on Delegated Legislation, 23 January 1996, col. 6)

In moving the approval by the House of Lords of the draft International Tribunal for the Law of the Sea (Immunities and Privileges) Order and the draft International Sea-Bed Authority (Immunities and Privileges) Order, the Parliamentary Under-Secretary of State, Department of Transport, Viscount Goschen, stated:

[These] two draft orders confer privileges and immunities on two new international institutions established by the Law of the Sea Convention: the International Sea-Bed Authority and the International Tribunal for the Law of the Sea. Privileges and immunities need to be conferred in order for the Government to meet their international obligations under the convention.

In relation to the International Sea-Bed Authority, the privileges and immunities are to be similar to those provided for in the 1947 Convention on the Privileges and Immunities of the Specialised Agencies of the United Nations. As regards the International Tribunal for the Law of the Sea, they are similar to those conferred on the International Court of Justice.

The authority is located in Jamaica and the tribunal in Hamburg. In practice, therefore, there are only likely to be claims for refunds of VAT on goods and services purchased in the UK for the official purposes of the organisations. The privileges and immunities conferred by the orders are, of course, granted in accordance with the limitations imposed by the International Organisations Act 1968, as amended, under which the orders are made. I commend the orders to the House.

(HL Debs., vol. 568, col. 1180: 25 January 1996)

The International Tribunal for the Law of the Sea (Immunities and Privileges) Order 1996 (Statutory Instruments 1996, No. 272), made on 14 February 1996, has the following explanatory note attached to it:

This Order confers privileges and immunities on the members of the International Tribunal for the Law of the Sea. These privileges and immunities are conferred in accordance with Annex VI of the United Nations Convention on the Law of the Sea (Cmnd. 8941). The Order will enable Her Majesty's Government to give effect to that Convention and will come into force on the date on which the Convention enters into force in respect of the United Kingdom.

The International Sea-Bed Authority (Immunities and Privileges) Order 1996 (Statutory Instruments 1996, No. 270), made on 14 February 1996, has the following explanatory note attached to it:

This Order confers privileges and immunities on the International Sea-Bed Authority, its officials, representatives of its members and experts performing missions for it, and on the Enterprise, an organ of the Authority. These privileges and immunities are conferred in accordance with the United Nations Convention on the Law of the Sea (Cmnd. 8941). The Order will enable Her Majesty's Government to give effect to that Convention, and will come into force, with the exception of Article 13, on the date on which the Convention enters into force in respect of the United Kingdom. Article 13 will come into force when the Enterprise operates independently of the Secretariat of the Authority.

In moving the approval by the House of Lords of the draft International Oil Pollution Compensation Fund 1992 (Immunities and Privileges) Order, the Government spokesman, Lord Chesham, stated:

A protocol amending the 1971 Fund Convention was agreed in 1992 and this will establish a new International Oil Pollution Compensation Fund. This will be a separate legal entity to be known as the 1992 fund. However, for practical purposes it will have the same director and staff and will work in much the same way as the existing fund. The intention is that the 68 member states to the existing fund will gradually denounce the 1971 Fund Convention and ratify the 1992 protocols, until eventually the existing fund is dissolved. Under the transitional provisions of the protocols, the United Kingdom will be a member of both funds simultaneously for a period of up to two years, before being required to denounce the 1971 Fund Convention.

The existing fund has its headquarters in the International Maritime Organisation's building in London, where it operates under the provisions of the IOPCF (Immunities and Privileges) Order which this House approved in July of that year. The 1992 fund will be based there too when the protocols come into force.

The draft order is necessary to give effect in UK law to the draft headquarters agreement negotiated in respect of the 1992 fund. I should like to indicate to the House that the privileges and immunities accorded are the same as those approved by your Lordships in July 1979 for the existing fund. I should also emphasise that we consider that they are no more than is necessary for the effective operation of the 1992 fund in the United Kingdom. They are granted in accordance with the limitations imposed by the International Organisations Act 1968, as amended, under whose provisions the order is made.

The scale of privileges and immunities is broadly similar to that accorded to most of the other international organisations having their headquarters here, except that the fund's immunity from suit is more limited in certain significant respects. For example, actions may be taken against the fund in the courts of this country in relation to the compensation provisions of the convention.

The order needs to be formally made at the meeting of the Privy Council on 15th May 1996, so that the headquarters agreement which will enter into force on signature, and the order, can come into force on 30th May. It is for that reason that the order is before your Lordships today.

The Joint Committee on Statutory Instruments considered the draft instrument and had no comments.

(HL Debs., vol. 571, cols. 1741–2: 1 May 1996)

The International Oil Pollution Compensation Fund 1992 (Immunities and Privileges) Order 1996 (Statutory Instruments 1996, No. 1295), made on 15 May 1996, has the following explanatory note attached to it:

This Order confers privileges and immunities on the International Oil Pollution Compensation Fund 1992, on representatives of its members and on its officers and experts. These privileges and immunities are conferred in accordance with an Agreement which has been negotiated between the Government of the United Kingdom and the International Oil Pollution Compensation Fund 1992 (Cm 3241). The Order will enable Her Majesty's Government to give effect to the Agreement, which will enter into force on signature. The Order will come into force on the date on which the Agreement enters into force.

On 30 May 1996, the Government of the UK and the International Oil Pollution Compensation Fund concluded a Headquarters Agreement. Among the provisions are the following:

ARTICLE 5

Immunity

(1) Within the scope of its official activities the 1992 Fund shall have immunity from jurisdiction and execution except:
  (a) to the extent that the 1992 Fund waives such immunity from jurisdiction or immunity from execution in a particular case;
  (b) in respect of actions brought against the 1992 Fund in accordance with the provisions of the Convention;
  (c) in respect of any contract for the supply of goods or services, and any loan or other transaction for the provision of finance and any guarantee or indemnity in respect of any such transaction or of any other financial obligation;
  (d) in respect of a civil action by a third party for damage arising from an accident caused by a motor vehicle belonging to, or operated on behalf of, the 1992 Fund or in respect of a motor traffic offence involving such a vehicle;
  (e) in respect of a civil action relating to death or personal injury caused by an act or omission in the United Kingdom;
  (f) in the event of the attachment, pursuant to the final order of a court of law, of the salaries, wages or other emoluments owed by the 1992 Fund to a staff member of the 1992 Fund;
  (g) in respect of the enforcement of an arbitration award made under Article 23 of this Agreement; and

(h) in respect of a counter-claim directly connected with proceedings initiated by the 1992 Fund;

(2) The 1992 Fund's property and assets wherever situated shall be immune from any form of administrative or provisional judicial constraint, such as requisition, confiscation, expropriation or attachment, except in so far as may be temporarily necessary in connection with the prevention of, and investigation into, accidents involving motor vehicles belonging to, or operated on behalf of, the 1992 Fund.

ARTICLE 6

Archives

The archives of the 1992 Fund shall be inviolable. The term archives includes all records, correspondence, documents, manuscripts, photographs, films, recordings, discs and tapes belonging to or held by the 1992 Fund.

(TS No. 78 (1996); Cm 3354)

Part Three: II. A. 3. *Subjects of international law—international organizations—in general—legal effect of acts of international organizations*

(See Part Eight: II.A. (item of 6 September 1996), below)

Part Three: II. B. 1. *Subjects of international law—international organizations—particular types of organizations—universal organizations*

The following question was asked of Her Majesty's Government:

Whether, in the light of threats from (a) Israel (*The Times*, 19th April 1996, 'Israel sees Iran as next in line for punishment') and (b) the United States (Secretary of Defence Perry and others, *International Herald Tribune*, 20th April 1996, 'America to Gadhafi: stop poison gas plant or face an attack'), they will state that Britain will not take part in any attack on any country, including Iran and Libya, except with UN approval?

In reply, the Minister of State, FCO, wrote:

The UK conducts its foreign and defence policy fully in accordance with the Charter of the United Nations.

(HL Debs., vol. 571, *WA 145*: 1 May 1996)

In the course of a debate on the subject of the 50th anniversary of the United Nations, the Minister of State, FCO, Mr Jeremy Hanley, stated:

The UN has done excellent, unsung humanitarian work through the United Nations High Commissioner for Refugees. It has been a motor for democracy, sustainable development and the rule of law. Its record on human rights has been outstanding in setting universal standards and in progressively canalising pressure from democracies and non-governmental organisations to address the problems of human rights violations where and when they occur.

Britain, for its part, remains wholeheartedly committed to the purposes and principles of the UN charter. We have been at the heart of the UN for the past 50 years. Britain helped to draft the UN charter, which has stood the test of time and remains a testament to the vision of the founding fathers. Britain hosted the first meetings of the UN General Assembly and the Security Council in London in 1946.

British forces have a long record of service with the UN, from Cyprus 30 years ago . . . to Kuwait, Rwanda, Angola and Bosnia more recently. Britain can be proud of its contribution. From 1993 to 1995, we were one of the major UN troop contributors, and the UK has made strenuous efforts to find a long-term solution to many of those problems.

As a permanent member of the Security Council, Britain is at the centre of decision making. Our permanent seat on the council gives us an important point of leverage in international affairs, and we bring a wealth of experience to the council.

We have contributed strongly in ideas and constructive proposals to the continuing process of United Nations reform, to which my hon. Friend referred. I agree with him that the United Nations' financial crisis is its greatest challenge. Its perennial cash flow problems result principally from the continued failure of some member states to fulfil their international treaty obligation to pay their assessed contributions to the UN promptly and in full.

(HC Debs., vol. 277, cols. 617–18: 10 May 1996)

Part Four: I. *The individual (including the corporation) in international law—nationality*

In reply to an oral question asking whether there are plans to amend nationality legislation to allow the transmission of citizenship to the grandchildren of British citizens, the Parliamentary Under-Secretary of State, Home Office, Mr Timothy Kirkhope, stated in part:

> None. We remain of the view that, as a general rule, British citizenship should not be transmitted beyond the first generation born abroad.
>
> . . . The position—as it was deemed right by the House in the 1970s, and supported by the Labour party in its Green Paper—is that citizenship should be a mixture of rights and duties, that there should be some commitment on the part of those who seek to acquire it and that there must be some concern and interest with the country of their choice.

(HC Debs., vol. 273, col. 1091: 14 March 1996)

In reply to a question on the subject of the status of persons of South Asian origin lawfully present in Hong Kong on 1 July 1997, the Minister of State, FCO, wrote:

Those members of Hong Kong's ethnic minorities who have British Dependent Territories citizenship and no other form of nationality will continue to hold British nationality after the transition—either in the form of British Nationality (Overseas) or British Overseas citizenship. They will also, under the terms of the 1984 Sino-British Joint Declaration, retain the right of abode in Hong Kong.

(HL Debs., vol. 575, *WA* 59: 6 November 1996)

In the course of the Second Reading in the House of Commons of the British Nationality (Hong Kong) Bill, introduced by a private member, the Minister of State, FCO, Baroness Blatch, stated:

The British Nationality Act 1981 provides for different forms of British nationality to be acquired according to the circumstances of the particular case. Each form of British nationality is perfectly acceptable and valid. It is absolutely legitimate for someone to have, say, British dependent territories citizenship and no other nationality, and right of abode only in the relevant territory. There are many thousands of people in the world who have one of these other forms of British nationality and who have right of abode only in a particular territory. The ethnic minorities are not unique in having a form of British nationality which is not British citizenship and in not having a right of abode in the United Kingdom. This global situation has to be taken into account.

(HL Debs., vol. 576, col. 1230: 12 December 1996)

Part Four: II. *The individual (including the corporation) in international law—diplomatic and consular protection*

On 4 December 1996, the FCO issued the following statement:

In view of interest in Hong Kong on the question of consular protection for British nationals in Hong Kong after 30 June 1997, the British Government wishes to reaffirm its position as follows.

The British Government draws no distinction whatsoever between British citizenship acquired under the British Nationality Selection Scheme or acquired in any other way. There is only one form of British citizenship. All British citizen passports are identical.

The British Government, and the future British Consulate-General, will offer consular protection to British nationals in Hong Kong in exactly the same way as in any other part of the world.

Every British national in Hong Kong will be entitled to consular protection from the future British Consulate-General, irrespective of how that British nationality was obtained, except in cases of dual nationality.

In such cases, we accept that international law limits the ability of the UK to provide full consular protection to dual nationals in the country or territory of their other nationality. But it is a matter for the UK to decide what representations it makes in any individual case; and we do not accept that the way in which a British citizen obtained his or her passport would of itself be evidence of dual nationality.

In cases of disputed dual nationality, our practice in Hong Kong will be exactly the same as anywhere else in the world. If an individual claimed to be a solely British national, we would take that at face value and act on his or her behalf, unless and until we were presented with acceptable evidence of dual nationality. Even if we were persuaded that he or she were a dual national, that would not in itself stop us from making representations on his or her behalf. The British Government takes particularly seriously its responsibilities towards all British nationals in Hong Kong, irrespective of how their British nationality was obtained and of whether they hold Chinese nationality. We would not regard any claim by the local authorities that a British passport had been obtained under the British Nationality Selection Scheme as of itself relevant or acceptable evidence of dual nationality.

It is for the British Government and the British Government alone to determine whether or not an individual holds British nationality. The British Government rejects any suggestion that this can ever be a matter for any other government.

(Text provided by the FCO)

Part Four: V. *The individual (including the corporation) in international law—statelessness, refugees*

In the course of the Second Reading debate in the House of Commons on the British Nationality (Hong Kong) Bill, introduced by a private member, the Minister of State, FCO, Baroness Blatch, stated:

It has been argued very strongly today that because of their unique position those members of the ethnic minorities with whom the Bill is concerned should be given British citizenship as a form of insurance against what might happen to them after June next year. Parliament concluded, when the British Nationality (Hong Kong) Bill was debated in 1990, that no special citizenship arrangements were needed or appropriate.

One of the arguments for special citizenship measures has been that the ethnic minorities concerned will become stateless on 1st July 1997. The Government do not accept that argument. Specific provision was made in Article 6 of the Hong Kong (British Nationality) Order 1986 to deal with the possibility of statelessness. Under the terms of the order people who have only British nationality—in the form of Hong Kong British dependent territories citizenship or British nationality (overseas)—before 1997 will keep British nationality, primarily as British nationals (overseas) but, alternatively, as British overseas citizens if they fail to register as British nationals (overseas) and would otherwise be stateless. The children of these people will automatically become British overseas citizens if they would otherwise be stateless. The anti-statelessness provisions even extend to their grandchildren who will have an entitlement to acquire British overseas citizenship by registration if they would otherwise be stateless.

It is thus clear from Article 6 of the 1986 order that the ethnic minorities will not be stateless. I cannot stress that enough. Another issue is the often-repeated claim that the ethnic minorities will have no right of abode after 1997. The solely British ethnic minorities have a right of abode only in Hong Kong at the moment. They will continue to have a right of abode there because the Joint Declaration and Article 24(6) of the Basic Law guarantee it for people who do not have a right of abode elsewhere. That has been reaffirmed in recent discussions with the Chinese Government.

Most of the Hong Kong population will be in the same position as the ethnic minorities in that they will have the same rights of abode after the change of sovereignty as before, with the vast majority not having the right of abode in the United Kingdom. The Government's view is that the change of sovereignty will not impact upon the ethnic minorities in any way which justifies their being given special treatment in the form of a right of abode in the United Kingdom.

(HL Debs., vol. 576, cols. 1228–9: 12 December 1996)

Part Four: VI. *The individual (including the corporation) in international law—immigration and emigration, extradition, expulsion and asylum*

In the course of a debate on the subject of Dr Muhammad al Mas'ari, a Saudi Arabian national for whom the UK authorities had issued a deportation order to Dominica, the Minister of State, Home Office, Baroness Blatch, stated:

... the important point is that a safe place is found for Dr. al-Mas'ari. However, it has to be accepted that Dr. Al-Mas'ari is an illegal immigrant. He has used the hospitality of this country to wage a campaign to bring down the Saudi Government. The decision to remove him to a safe third country was taken strictly within our obligations under national and international law.

... our understanding is that we have acted entirely within the law and under our obligations to international law.

(HL Debs., vol. 568, cols. 259–60: 11 January 1996)

The following letter, dated 23 January 1996, was sent by Ms Ann Widdecombe, Minister of State, Home Office, to Mr George Galloway MP:

Thank you for your letter of 3 January about the proposed removal of Dr Al-Mass'ari, a Saudi Arabian national.

This decision was made in accordance with United Kingdom and international law on asylum. The Immigration Rules provide that an asylum application may be refused without substantive consideration if there is clear evidence of admissibility to a safe country. The Home Secretary was satisfied, following receipt of a letter from the Prime Minister of Dominica, that not only would Dr Al-Mass'ari be admitted there but he would be granted refugee status should he wish to apply. The Home Secretary believes that Dominica is a safe country within the meaning of the 1951 United Nations Convention relating to the Status of Refugees. If he had thought otherwise the decision to remove him there would not have been taken. Dominica has an excellent human rights record with freedom of speech and worship being enshrined in the Constitution.

It is the government's view that Dr Al-Mass'ari's wish for international protection under the 1951 Convention does not entitle him to pick and choose which country will protect him. It is relevant in this context that he also had no ties with this country before entering illegally and he has publicly acknowledged that he did this to take advantage of our communication network in order to campaign against the Saudi government.

We have made no secret of the fact that the action taken in Dr Al-Mass'ari's case took account of the United Kingdom's economic and strategic interest in the stability of Saudi Arabia. On being satisfied that Dr Al-Mass'ari was not at risk of persecution in Dominica or return from there to a country in which he feared persecution, it was entirely proper to give very wide consideration to the United Kingdom's overall interests.

(Text provided by the FCO)

In reply to a question, the Parliamentary Under-Secretary of State, Home Office, wrote:

All applications for asylum in the United Kingdom are considered in the light of all available information and in accordance with the criteria set out in the 1951 United Nations convention relating to the status of refugees.

Those seeking asylum in this country are expected to act within the law. If an asylum seeker undertakes activities in the United Kingdom which are inconsistent with his previous beliefs and behaviour and calculated to create or substantially enhance his claim to refugee status, this may damage the credibility of his claim

(HC Debs., vol. 271, WA, col. *314*: 8 February 1996)

In the course of the third reading debate in the House of Commons on the Asylum and Immigration Bill, the Secretary of State for the Home Department, Mr Michael Howard, stated:

The Government are determined to maintain the United Kingdom's honourable tradition in providing a safe haven for those fleeing persecution. We shall continue to meet in full our international obligations, including those under the 1951 United Nations convention on refugees.

(HC Debs., vol. 272, col. 542: 22 February 1996)

In the course of the second reading debate in the House of Lords on the Asylum and Immigration Bill, the Minister of State, Home Office, Baroness Blatch, stated:

It has consistently been our view that effective immigration control is a necessary condition for achieving that aim, and that this entails a readiness to deal with abuses and to operate a fair and objective system. We are determined to honour our obligations under the 1951 United Nations Convention on Refugees and the 1984 Convention on Torture and Cruel or Inhuman Treatment. We do not, and will not, remove people to countries where they have a well-founded fear of persecution or where there are substantial grounds for believing that they would be tortured. Those are the principles underlying this Bill. I must also stress that nothing in the Bill will change the immigration status of anyone who currently has the right to come to this country to live.

(HL Debs., vol. 570, col. 959: 14 March 1996)

In reply to the question whether the threat to a woman or girl of being subjected to genital mutilation is accepted as sufficient grounds for asylum, the Minister of State, Home Office, wrote:

To qualify for refugee status, applicants need to show that they have a well founded fear of persecution based on one of the reasons contained in the 1951 UN Convention Relating to the Status of Refugees. Those who do not meet the requirements of the 1951 convention may nevertheless be granted exceptional leave to remain if there are compelling humanitarian reasons for doing so. Cases are considered in the light of their individual circumstances.

(HL Debs., vol. 572, *WA 3*: 7 May 1996)

In reply to a question, the Minister of State, FCO, wrote:

Entry clearance officers at British posts overseas are guided by the following advice on asylum matters: 'In accordance with the 1951 Geneva convention and the 1967 New York protocol on the status of refugees the United Kingdom is under no obligation to accept a request for asylum overseas. Entry clearance officers have discretion, however, to accept outside the immigration rules an application for entry clearance for the United Kingdom where a foreign national demonstrates his circumstances meet the definition of the 1951 convention, he has particularly close ties with the United Kingdom and this is the most appropriate country of long-term refuge. Any such application is to be referred to the Home Office for decision.'

HC Debs., vol. 282, WA, col. *40*: 22 July 1996)

The following question was asked of Her Majesty's Government:

Whether they accept that in matters involving the UN Convention, the word 'refugee' applies to asylum seekers from the moment they make their claim and if not, how they reconcile the view with Article 31.1 of the Convention?

In reply, the Minister of State, Home Office, wrote:

In the Government's opinion the Convention does not entitle asylum seekers to be treated as refugees until their refugee status has been recognised. The Government's view is entirely consistent with Article 31.1.

(HL Debs., vol. 574, *WA 169*: 25 July 1996)

The following question was asked of Her Majesty's Government:

...which clause of the Geneva Convention allows the return of asylum applicants to safe third countries?

In reply, the Minister of State, Home Office, wrote:

Article 33.1 provides that no contracting state shall expel or return a refugee to the frontiers of territories where his life or freedom would be threatened on account of his race, religion, nationality, membership of a particular social group or political opinions. Removing asylum applicants to safe third countries is entirely compatible with that requirement.

(Ibid., *WA 170*)

The following question was asked of Her Majesty's Government:

Whether the Secretary of State for Social Security's claim on 15th July (H.C. Deb., col. 854) that 'we are taking away benefit only from illegal immigrants' is compatible with Article 31.1 of the UN Convention on Refugees, and if so, how?

In reply, the Minister of State, Home Office, wrote:

My right honourable friend said: 'We are taking away benefit only from illegal immigrants, from people who change their story after they have arrived in Britain claiming to be something other than asylum seekers, and from people found not to be genuine refugees'. The Government are satisfied that their policy is entirely compatible with the UN Convention.

(Ibid.)

Speaking on 3 October 1996 in the Sixth Committee of the UN General Assembly considering measures to eliminate international terrorism, the UK representative, Ms Elizabeth Wilmshurst, stated:

The United Kingdom has a long and proud tradition of affording asylum to persons fleeing from persecution. The 1951 Refugee Convention created essential safeguards for those fleeing persecution and the United Kingdom complies fully with its obligations under the Convention.

(Text provided by FCO; see also A/C.6/51/SR. 10, p. 5)

Part Four: VII. *The individual (including the corporation) in international law—protection of human rights and fundamental freedoms*

(See also Part One: II. D. 1. and Part Three: I. A. 2., above)

The following letter for the Government of the UK, dated 12 January 1996, was registered at the Secretariat-General of the Council of Europe on 19 January 1996:

Your Excellency,

I have the honour to refer to Mr Boothby's letter dated 14 January 1966 which declared the recognition by the Government of the United Kingdom of Great Britain and Northern Ireland, in respect of the United Kingdom only, of the jurisdiction of the European Court of Human Rights, and to Mr Marshall's letter dated 11 January 1991 which prolonged, until 13 January 1996, the period of such recognition.

On instruction from Her Majesty's Principal Secretary of State for Foreign and Commonwealth Affairs, I now have the honour to inform you that the Government of the United Kingdom hereby renew for the United Kingdom of Great Britain and Northern Ireland the declaration made in Mr Boothby's letter of 14 January 1966 referred to above, further prolonging the said period for a further five years, to end on 13 January 2001. Except in relation to the date of expiry of this period, the terms of the said declaration shall remain unaffected.

(signed) R. C. BEETHAM

(TS No. 69 (1996); Cm 3364, p. 14)

In reply to an oral question, the Minister of State, Baroness Chalker, stated:

... the decision to renew the United Kingdom's acceptance of the compulsory jurisdiction of the court for five years, as well as the right of individual petition, was announced on 13th December and has been communicated to the Council of Europe. Parliament has been kept fully informed.

(HL Debs., vol. 569, col. 717: 15 February 1996)

In the course of a debate on the subject of Chechnya, the Government spokesman in the House of Lords, Lord Chesham, stated:

... as a member of the Council of Europe, Russia will be required to comply with the full range of Council of Europe principles. Those include early signature of the European Convention on Human Rights.

(HL Debs., vol. 569, col. 972: 20 February 1996)

In a paper dated 4 March 1996 presented by the UK Government to the Council of Europe Bureau of the Steering Committee for Human Rights, the following passage appeared:

Note on the position of the British Government

1. The British Government has always been a strong supporter of the European Convention on Human Rights. The principles it enshrines have guided the countries of Western Europe for the last 50 years and now provide common standards for the new, wider Europe. The Convention is as important as it has ever been, and the machinery set up under it faces the challenge of adapting to an enlarged Council of Europe. The United Kingdom was among the first to ratify Protocol 11 to the Convention. We wish to play our part in trying to establish good working procedures before its new arrangements come into effect.

2. The British Government has been concerned about some recent judgments of the Court, and would like to see certain changes to promote fairness and to ensure that the Strasbourg institutions take all factors into account. We have a number of specific suggestions for discussion, and are keen to know the views of others. We hope that significant improvements can be achieved, both for the present Commission and Court and the new Protocol 11 Court.

(Text provided by the FCO)

In reply to a question, the Minister of State, FCO, wrote:

Officials have repeatedly pressed the Burmese authorities to allow humanitarian and human rights organisations to operate freely in Burma. We were closely involved in the drafting of the recent UN Commission on Human Rights resolution on Burma, which invited the ruling military regime in Burma to 'respect its obligations under the Geneva Convention of 12 August 1949 and to avail itself of such services as may be offered by impartial humanitarian bodies'.

(HL Debs., vol. 572, *WA 168*: 12 June 1996)

In reply to a question, the Minister of State, Department of Trade and Industry, wrote:

The UK Government are firmly opposed to abuses of fundamental human rights such as forced labour and the exploitation of child labour, wherever this occurs. But we believe that these would be tackled within the appropriate UN framework, which is the International Labour Organisation, and not by the World Trade Organisation.

(HC Debs., vol. 282, WA, col. *35*: 22 July 1996)

In July 1996, the FCO published a document entitled *Human Rights in Foreign Policy*. It contained the following paragraph:

2. Promoting respect for human rights is one of the UK's central foreign policy objectives; the Government regards respect for human rights as a fundamental value in its own right. This policy is also based on the UK's national and international interests: events have repeatedly demonstrated that respect for human rights is one of the crucial elements for a just and secure international order, leading to long-term stability and prosperity. Under the United Nations Charter, promoting and protecting human rights is also a legal obligation on the UK, as on all other United Nations members.

(FCO Foreign Policy Document No. 268)

Later in the document, the following paragraphs appeared:

WHAT ARE HUMAN RIGHTS?

5. The *United Nations Charter* (1945) represented a breakthrough for human rights. Under Articles 55 and 56, all members of the United Nations pledge themselves to promote 'universal respect for, and observance of, human rights and fundamental freedoms for all without distinction as to race, sex, language or religion'. This pledge reflects one of the purposes of the United Nations: 'To achieve international cooperation . . . in promoting and encouraging respect for human rights and for fundamental freedoms for all without distinction as to race, sex, language or religion' (Article 1 Paragraph 3).

6. However there was then no internationally agreed definition of what constituted these human rights and fundamental freedoms. That definition came in 1948 in the *Universal Declaration of Human Rights*. Although not a legally binding treaty, the Declaration establishes an internationally recognised set of standards. No country voted against it, although a handful abstained. The Declaration makes clear that human rights transcend national, religious, cultural and ideological frontiers.

7. These rights are often divided into two categories: civil and political rights and economic, social and cultural rights. Civil and political rights have often been regarded as the means of protecting the individual from the arbitrary exercise of power by the state. Economic, social and cultural rights are concerned with the material, social and cultural welfare of persons, and also require an active response by the state to provide the conditions for their achievement. Some civil rights are normally regarded as absolute in that they cannot be restricted or derogated from in any circumstances. Others may be subject to restrictions on grounds of, for example, public order or health, or during a proclaimed public emergency.

8. Using the Universal Declaration as the starting point, the international community has since drawn up a wide-ranging legal framework for the protection of human rights. Standard-setting work continues to this day, although the focus has increasingly shifted to implementation of existing standards. The *International Covenant on Civil and Political Rights* and the *International Covenant on Economic, Social and Cultural Rights* (both 1966) put most of the rights in the Universal Declaration into legally binding treaty form. They came into force in 1976. By December 1995 there were 132 States Parties to the Civil and Political Covenant, and 133 to the Economic, Social and Cultural Covenant, drawn from all regions of the world.

9. The United Kingdom ratified both Covenants in 1976. The duties and obligations of governments have been further elaborated in a number of other United Nations human rights instruments, which relate to particular aspects of the protection of human rights.

10. In addition to international human rights treaties open to all States, there are regional arrangements for the protection of human rights:

— *the European Convention on Human Rights (Council of Europe)*;

— *the European Social Charter (Council of Europe)*;

— *the American Convention on Human Rights (Organisation of American States)*;

— *the African Charter on Human and Peoples' Rights (Organisation of African Unity)*;

— *the Organisation for Security and Cooperation in Europe.*

ARE HUMAN RIGHTS UNIVERSAL?

11. Some assert that human rights are essentially Western values, and that promoting them is tantamount to cultural imperialism. We deal below with the issue of human rights and Islamic/Asian values. British policy takes as a basic premise the fact that human rights are universal. The Charter of the United Nations in its preamble states that the peoples of the United Nations

'reaffirm faith in fundamental human rights, in the dignity and worth of the human person, in the equal rights of men and women and of nations large and small'.

This, combined with the Article 55/56 commitment to universality referred to in para 5 above, and the subsequent Universal Declaration, are clearly based on the assumption that they applied to all countries, not just those in the West. They were drafted and agreed by representatives of countries from all regions. States with many different religious and cultural traditions have felt able to take on legal obligations by ratifying human rights treaties. And those countries which have joined the United Nations since the original definitions of human rights were drafted all agreed to accept and carry out the obligations of the Charter, including those on human rights.

12. At the World Conference on Human Rights in Vienna in 1993, the international community affirmed that 'the universal nature of human rights and fundamental freedoms was beyond doubt'. It also stated that:

> 'While the significance of national and regional particularities and various historical, cultural and religious backgrounds must be borne in mind, it is the duty of States, regardless of their political, economic and cultural systems, to promote and protect all human rights and fundamental freedoms'.

13. There is no perfect and universally applicable way of *implementing* human rights. But that the *standards* are universal should no longer be open to question. We should be prepared to argue for these standards in all countries. Where appropriate, we should urge countries which have not yet done so to ratify the International Covenants and other human rights instruments. Particular sensitivity will be required in exchanges with Islamic Governments, where special attention is called for in explaining the UK's *locus standi*.

(Ibid.)

In reply to a question, the Minister of State, FCO, wrote:

Where legislation is contemplated, Government departments should ensure that it is compatible with the international human rights obligations of the United Kingdom, and the European Convention on Human Rights in particular. Every proposal for legislation should be accompanied by a statement that this has been done. Legal advice should be obtained in the first instance from departmental lawyers, who consult as necessary the Foreign and Commonwealth Office legal advisers.

(HL Debs., vol. 574, *WA 177*: 15 October 1996)

In the course of a debate in the UN Security Council on 16 October 1996, the UK Permanent Representative, Sir John Weston, stated:

We have made clear our strong objections to violations of fundamental human rights. In particular, we are gravely concerned about measures implemented to restrict girls' rights to education and women's rights to employment. We have major concerns in this regard about the prospects for many households where women in that country are the only providers. They face destitution as a result of these measures. We call on all the factions to respect international human rights norms and to act in accordance with those international instruments which Afghanistan has signed and ratified, for example the International Covenant on Economic, Social and Cultural Rights, and the Covenant on Civil and Political Rights.

(S/PV. 3705, p. 16)

A Presidency statement on behalf of the EU issued on 28 October 1996 contained the following paragraph:

The European Union strongly urges the leaders of the various factions in Afghanistan to respect and act in accordance with the principles laid down in the Universal Declaration of Human Rights and the United Nations Charter, as well as all the other conventions on human rights to which Afghanistan is a signatory.

(*Bulletin of the European Union*, 1996–10, p. 64)

In reply to the question why Her Majesty's Government have not ratified Protocol No. 4 to the European Convention on Human Rights, the Minister of State, FCO, wrote:

The UK has signed but not ratified Protocol 4 to the European Convention on Human Rights. Her Majesty's Government believes that Article 3(2) of the Protocol could conflict with UK immigration and nationality legislation by giving British Dependent Territories Citizens, British Overseas Citizens, British Subjects and British Nationals (Overseas) a right of entry to the UK that they no longer possess.

The UK therefore has no plans to ratify Protocol 4 to the ECHR.

(HL Debs., vol. 575, *WA 92*: 12 November 1996)

In reply to the question why Her Majesty's Government have not ratified Protocol No. 6 to the European Convention on Human Rights, the same Minister wrote:

The Government have not ratified Protocol 6 to the European Convention on Human Rights because they believe that the reintroduction of capital punishment for murder and its abolition for the offence for which it is still available is a matter for Parliament to decide.

(Ibid., *WA 93*)

In reply to a question about the treatment of Mr Khadar Mubarak by the Israeli authorities, the Minister of State, FCO, wrote:

My right honourable and learned friend the Foreign Secretary raised human rights issues when he met the Israeli Defence Minister on 20th November. We are concerned at the Israeli High Court's decision to permit Israeli authorities to go beyond internationally accepted interrogation practices in the case of Khadar Mubarak. We urge Israel to take account of the recommendations of the UN Committee Against Torture.

(HL Debs., vol. 576, *WA 43*: 3 December 1996)

In the course of a debate on the subject of human rights in China and Tibet, the Government spokesman, Lord Inglewood, stated:

I should like to start with some general comments. Obviously we are deeply concerned about reports of human rights violations wherever they may occur.

We believe that human rights are universal and apply to everyone equally. They are not just western standards; they apply to all countries and regions. All governments have a moral and legal obligation to their citizens to protect these rights. That concept is enshrined in the United Nations Charter under Articles 55 and 56. At the Vienna World Conference on Human Rights, China accepted the universality of human rights and the legitimacy of international debate.

The subject of human rights is no longer viewed as it was by some in the past as a form of interference in a country's domestic affairs. The United Kingdom has rightly taken a leading role in the promotion of international standards in this area. We believe that the best way to do so is through a process of constructive engagement at every level. We pursue that approach bilaterally with countries whose human rights performance concern us, and also in international fora, such as the United Nations, where we work closely with European Union partners and other like-minded governments.

. . .

In our exchanges with the Chinese authorities, both bilaterally and with our EU partners, we have urged the Chinese Government to take real steps to improve the human rights situation in China, including Tibet. As I mentioned, we have encouraged China to accede to the International Covenant on Economic, Social and Cultural Rights. China is already a party to a number of international human rights instruments such as the Convention against Torture and Other Cruel, Inhuman or Degrading Treatment or Punishment (ratified by them in 1988) and the Convention on the Rights of the Child. We have encouraged China to open further its system to the outside world. In November/December 1994 the UN Special Rapporteur on Religious Intolerance visited China at the invitation of the Ministry of Foreign Affairs International Organisations Department. The UN Special Rapporteurs on Torture and on Extrajudicial, Summary or Arbitrary Execution have also reported on China, although it is a matter of real regret that they have not been invited to visit the country. We continue to encourage China to take measures to improve human rights related legislation in accordance with international standards and to adopt measures to ensure the right to freedom of expression and association.

. . .

The noble Baroness, Lady Blackstone, the right reverend Prelate the Bishop of Bristol and my noble friend Lord Ashbourne also raised the question of religious freedom. Freedom of worship is a basic human right and reports of the harassment and detention of individuals on the basis of their religious belief in China, including Tibet, is a cause of great worry. We continue to urge the Chinese authorities to look on religious freedom as fulfilling a basic human need, and not as a threat. As I have already mentioned, the United Nations Special Rapporteur on Religious Intolerance visited China in 1994, and in his report he raised a number of concerns, including restrictions on Christians and Buddhists to practise their religion openly. We look to the Chinese authorities to address the concerns expressed in the special rapporteur's report.

(HL Debs., vol. 576, cols. 1585–90 *passim*: 18 December 1996)

Part Five: II. *Organs of the State—Ministers*

In reply to a question asking for examples of categories of powers exercised by Ministers exclusively under the royal prerogative, the Lord Privy Seal, Viscount Cranborne, wrote:

Examples of prerogative powers exercised by Ministers on behalf of the Sovereign are the issue of passports and some treaty-making functions.

(HL Debs., vol. 569, *WA 46*: 13 February 1996)

Part Five: IV. *Organs of the State—diplomatic agents and missions*

(See also Part Thirteen: II. A. (item of 20 May 1996), below)

In reply to a question, the Minister of State, FCO, wrote:

Twenty-eight alleged serious offences by persons entitled to diplomatic immunity were drawn to the attention of the Foreign and Commonwealth Office in 1995. 'Serious offences' are defined in accordance with the Report to the Foreign Affairs Committee, *The Abuse of Diplomatic Immunities and Privileges (1985)*, as offences which fall into the category which in certain circumstances attract a maximum penalty of 6 months' imprisonment or more: the majority involved drinking and driving and shoplifting.

Five diplomats or members of their families were withdrawn at our request from post in Britain as a result of alleged offences, compared with six the previous year.

(HL Debs., vol. 571, *WA 125*: 29 April 1996)

Part Five: VII. *Organs of the State—armed forces*

In reply to questions about the legal basis under which the United States army, with other United States forces, is stationed at Menwith Hill, the Minister of State for the Armed Forces wrote:

The basis on which the US army, along with other United States forces, is stationed in the UK is contained in the NATO status of forces agreement of 1951.

(HC Debs., vol. 274, WA, col. *286*: 21 March 1996)

Part Five: VIII. A. *Organs of the State—immunity of organs of the State— diplomatic and consular immunity*

The FCO issued the following Circular No. 117/96 dated 14 March 1996 to all Missions and staff:

DIPLOMATIC & CONSULAR IMMUNITY OVERSEAS

Summary

1. The purpose of the international legal rules on Diplomatic/Consular immunity is to ensure the efficient performance of the functions of diplomatic and consular Missions, and not to benefit individuals. International law requires those enjoying immunity to respect the laws and regulations of the receiving State. *HMG takes this requirement very seriously indeed, and expects the highest standards of conduct from foreign diplomats and consuls in London and from British diplomats and consuls and their families overseas.*
2. There has been an increase in the number of cases that have arisen as a result of guidance not being followed properly. This circular should be brought to the attention of all staff.

Diplomatic Immunity

3. Staff who are granted the status of *diplomatic agent* ('diplomatic status') by the receiving State are entitled to immunity from the criminal and (with certain limited exceptions) from the civil jurisdiction of the receiving State. *Administrative and Technical* (A&T) staff members of Embassies are entitled to immunity from the criminal jurisdiction of the receiving State, and from its civil jurisdiction in respect of acts carried out in the course of their official functions. *Members of the families* of diplomatic and A&T staff enjoy analogous immunity from the receiving State's jurisdiction to that enjoyed by the officer, although this may be affected by spouse employment (see Annex A to this circular).

Consular Immunity

4. Staff who have consular status have more limited immunity. As a general rule (there are exceptions) they are immune from local jurisdiction only in respect of acts carried out in the exercise of their consular functions.
5. Diplomatic or Consular immunity belongs to the diplomat or consul's State, not to the individual. So it can only be waived by the sending State at the request of the receiving State. In practice this means that *all* requests for waiver of immunity of a UK diplomat or consul must be made through the local MFA [Ministry of Foreign Affairs] and not directly by the local judiciary or police. *Under no circumstances should a court summons or other legal request be acknowledged without prior consultation with Personnel Policy Unit (PPU).*
6. Immunity is a privilege not a perk. It carries with it certain obligations. HMG's staff overseas must ensure that they do not abuse this privilege, and must maintain the UK's reputation for the high standards of behaviour of its staff overseas. The main objective must be to preserve the efficient working of Missions overseas and to protect staff from hostile action on the part of local authorities. This can only be done if staff respect local laws and regulations, and do not abuse their immunity by seeking to avoid penalties properly applicable to them, or to evade their legal duties.

HMG's General Policy on Waiver of Immunity

7. HMG's general policy is that *immunity should not be unreasonably maintained.* In practice all staff are expected to answer to any criminal or civil charge brought

against them. In some countries this may present practical or political problems, and so decisions about the waiving or claiming of immunity may only be taken after consultation with PPU. In making any decision the following factors will have to be considered:

— whether local laws are alien to British ideas of justice;
— whether there are doubts about the impartiality or efficiency of local judicial procedures;
— whether the alleged offence appears to have been contrived by the receiving State for political or other reasons;
— whether there are valid security reasons (eg if the officer was privy to sensitive information which may be put in jeopardy through imprisonment or intensive police questioning);
— whether the functioning of the Mission would be seriously impeded.

8. The most common cases where waivers are sought are traffic accidents, drink-drive offences, LE staff redundancies and Industrial Tribunals, and requests to appear as witnesses. Detailed guidance is given in the annexes B, C, and D to this Circular, but the general principles which should be applied in all cases are:
i) Any request for an officer to appear in court proceedings or give evidence should be made through the MFA and addressed to the Mission, not the individual;
ii) The Mission should immediately consult their local Legal Adviser and then inform PPU. *No decision on whether to claim or waive immunity should be taken before this point;*
iii) The Mission should try and obtain as much information as possible about the charges or claims being made. It is useful to know
— whether the alleged offence/summons relates to a criminal or civil charge,
— what the officer's status is, i.e diplomatic, A&T or consular and whether they are employed by an OGD,
— whether there is any scope for an out of court settlement, and if so, how much would have to be paid,
— whether the charge is in substance levelled at HMG as the individual's employer in respect of acts carried out in the course of the individual's duties, or at the individual concerned in his/her own right,
— how long the judicial process would take if HMG were to defend the allegation(s),
— a brief description of the judicial process that would follow in the case in question.
9. One factor in determining an approach in individual cases will be the way in which the Host Government handles matters of this kind in respect of its own staff in London. In some cases it may be desirable to withdraw an officer if that is also the Host Government's preferred way of handling the matter, before the case develops to a point where a formal request for a waiver of immunity is made.
10. Even if for these or other reasons it is decided not to waive immunity, internal disciplinary proceedings may still be instituted if the officer's conduct constitutes a breach of Diplomatic Service Regulations.

Local Guidance

11. Many Posts issue local guidance to staff about the recommended procedures to be followed in the event of being involved in a traffic accident or offence. PPU can provide on request, copies of the guidance issued to foreign missions in London by Protocol Department. Any local guidance issued by Posts should reflect the same standards that are applied to foreign missions in London. PPU are happy to advise.

. . .

Annex A

SPOUSE EMPLOYMENT

1. Under the Vienna Convention on Diplomatic Relations (VCDR), diplomats and A&T staff do *not* enjoy immunity from civil jurisdiction in respect of an action relating to any professional or commercial activity exercised in the receiving State outside of their official function.
2. The same rule applies to spouses wishing to seek employment outside of the Mission. Because of the embarrassment which might arise if a spouse contravened local laws in the course of their activities, it is of paramount importance that Heads of Mission and Management Officers, when advising spouses and officers about outside employment, draw attention to the implications of any contravention of local law. The spouse should be made aware that any wilful breach of local laws, might, depending on the circumstances, jeopardise the position of the officer through whom that immunity is enjoyed.
3. HMG has reached agreements about employment of diplomatic spouses with an increasing number of countries. Under these, members of a family enjoying immunity from the civil and administrative jurisdiction of the receiving State, under the VCDR or any other international instrument, will not be entitled to such immunity in respect of their employment. This means that working family members are also liable to pay income tax and national insurance contributions on their earnings.

. . .

Annex B

TRAFFIC OFFENCES

1. Posts are responsible for issuing local guidance to staff on dealing with cases where they are involved in traffic accidents. The main principles are as follows.

Traffic/Parking violations

2. HMG's staff overseas are expected to respect and comply with local laws. Normally we would expect *all* officers to pay any fines for minor offences. However, Heads of Mission have authority to insist that formal requests for payment, or alleged charges be sent to the Mission via the MFA. A&T staff

should continue to pay fines on the spot, unless liability is contested by the officer.

3. If liability is contested the officer should point out that as a member of the Mission he/she is '*entitled* to immunity from jurisdiction under the Vienna Convention, and that any further action should be addressed to the mission through the MFA'. No indication of whether immunity will be claimed or waived should be indicated until PPU have been consulted.

Drinking and Driving

4. If an officer is stopped on suspicion of drink driving they should decline to take a breath test using the form of words in para 3 and then inform their Line Manager. However, it should be pointed out that in serious cases, particularly where there is violence or injury to a third party, an officer may have to be withdrawn from post. For a second offence, the officer would be automatically withdrawn from post. *It should also be remembered that drink driving offences whether committed in the UK or overseas are disciplinary offences under [Diplomatic Service Regulations].*

Process of Waiving/Claiming Immunity

5. In respect of any traffic offence, a waiver of immunity sought by the host Government must be communicated to the Mission through the MFA. After consulting a local legal adviser, Post should refer the matter to PPU. Post should provide the following information;

— whether there is a risk of a custodial sentence,
— whether the charge is regarded in local law as a civil or criminal offence,
— whether by waiving immunity to allow the officer to answer the charge, we would prejudice our right to claim immunity from execution of the judgement,
— an outline of the judicial process in the case.

6. All serious traffic infringements should be reported to the FCO (PMD and PPU). A record of minor offences where fines have been paid should be kept in Post.

Annex C

REQUESTS FOR STAFF TO APPEAR OR GIVE STATEMENTS AS WITNESSES

1. HMG would normally expect all staff to assist local police and judicial authorities if called upon to do so. If staff are asked to give a statement or to appear in court as a witness, they should say that the request should be transmitted to the Mission through the MFA. PPU should then be consulted. Local legal advisers should also be consulted in such cases.

2. Consideration would have to be given to whether the demands made on the officer's time by the court would impede the efficiency of the Mission, and whether, in all the circumstances, it was appropriate that the officer should give evidence.

Annex D

INDUSTRIAL TRIBUNAL/UNFAIR DISMISSAL OF [LOCALLY ENGAGED] STAFF

1. . . . To summarise, we would expect all employment issues relating to LE staff to be handled, as far as is practicable, in line with local employment law. Normally we would wish to challenge any allegation of unfair dismissal.

2. Any summons connected with such allegations should be presented to the Mission through the MFA. After consulting the local legal adviser, PPU should be consulted before any decision on whether to claim/waive immunity is taken.

(Text provided by the FCO)

In reply to a question on the subject of the fatal shooting in 1984 of Woman Police Constable Fletcher outside the Libyan People's Bureau in London, the Secretary of State for the Home Department wrote:

The investigation of crime is a matter for the police. As my right hon. Friend the Minister of State made clear to the House on 8 May, the police were unable to obtain enough evidence to sustain a prosecution without the full co-operation of those concerned in the Libyan's People's Bureau. Such co-operation was not forthcoming. None the less, the police were of the view that it was likely that the murder was committed by one of two people who were in the bureau. Both of them possessed diplomatic immunity and could not be prosecuted under English law even if the necessary evidence had been available.

(HC Debs., vol. 278, WA, col. *19*: 20 May 1996)

In the course of a statement made on 26 November 1996 to the Sixth Committee of the UN General Assembly considering the report of the Committee on Relations with the Host Country, the Representative of Ireland, on behalf of the European Union, stated:

Last year, in the context of the application of traffic laws, the European Union drew attention to the importance which it attaches to Articles IV and V of the Headquarters Agreement of 1947 and Articles 29 and 31 of the Vienna Convention of 1961 concerning inviolability and immunity from criminal, civil and administrative jurisdiction in the receiving State. The European Union regrets having to say that it is somewhat disappointed with the rate of progress achieved in this area. For example, the Union notes that the Committee has been informed of instances where legally parked diplomatic cars had received parking tickets, sometimes even when parked in lots especially reserved for them, and that such lots are sometimes occupied by non-diplomatic vehicles. In addition, some allocated parking lots are inadequate in practice as they have to be shared amongst several Permanent Missions. While recognising the obligations arising from Article 41 of the Vienna Convention for all persons enjoying diplomatic privileges and immunities to respect the laws and regulations of the Host Country, the European Union rejects the suggestion that diplomats should accept the jurisdiction of the national courts to claim that a traffic ticket has been improperly served. It would appreciate therefore receiving an assurance from the authorities of the Host Country that it will take the necessary measures, including appropriate instruction of traffic police, to resolve these problems in regard to parking.

(Text provided by the FCO)

Part Six: I. A. *Treaties—conclusion and entry into force—conclusion, signature, ratification and accession*

(See also Part Five: II., above and Part Eleven: II. A. 1. (item of 24 January 1996), below)

Lord Lester of Herne Hill introduced in the House of Lords a private member's bill, the Treaties (Parliamentary Approval) Bill, whereby treaties concluded by the UK which are subject to ratification should be approved by Parliament before they are ratified. Giving the government's view on the Bill, the Minister of State, FCO, Baroness Chalker, stated during the second reading debate on the Bill:

The Bill provides that no treaty shall be ratified by Her Majesty's Government without its first having been approved by Parliament. The Government share the noble Lord, Lord Lester's concern that the international obligations of the United Kingdom should be the subject of a proper scrutiny by Parliament. The real question—which I am not sure that we have yet answered in the drafting of the Bill—is what is the best way for this to be carried out. We may need more thought and clarification on that.

The present arrangement for parliamentary consideration of treaties is flexible. It provides for proper opportunity for debate and, as the noble Lord, Lord Bridges, said, the system works rather well. It has worked remarkably well considering its age—but then, in this House, I am a great respecter that good things last a long while.

The Bill worries me because it would introduce fixed procedures which could impinge upon Parliament's timetable and yet do little to further the democratic scrutiny of international agreements concluded by the Government. Successive British Governments have long recognised the importance of ensuring that their international obligations and responsibilities are well understood, publicised, and that Parliament is kept fully informed. That is why this Government, like all governments before them since 1924, comply with the Ponsonby rule, as we have discussed tonight. Under that rule it is settled practice that treaties requiring ratification, acceptance, approval or accession are laid before Parliament for 21 sitting days before the Government deposit their instrument of ratification, acceptance or approval. It provides opportunities for comment and debate if Parliament so desires.

In addition, to the extent that any treaty would alter the law or require legislation for its implementation, it is settled practice to ensure that the necessary legislation has been passed before the treaty is entered into. This is exactly what my noble and learned friend Lord Howe meant when he spoke for the flexibility of the Ponsonby rule.

There are special cases in which, by convention, treaties are not entered into without parliamentary sanction. Noble Lords will remember that Parliament expressly provided in the European Assembly Elections Act 1978 that no treaty which provides for an increase in the powers of the European Parliament may be ratified by the United Kingdom unless it has been approved by an Act of Parliament. That is certainly something of which the noble Lord, Lord Bruce of Donington, definitely approves.

In addition to that special case, there are five situations where treaties are not concluded without parliamentary approval, usually in the form of statute. Those are where they require an amendment to UK law; where they affect private rights; where they create a charge on public funds; where they attribute new powers to the Crown; or where they cede British territory.

There are then other cases where Parliament sanctions in advance, by general legislation, the conclusion of bilateral treaties in particular fields within the minutes laid down. Examples here are extradition treaties, double taxation treaties, and reciprocal social security benefit treaties. Here it is often provided that the terms of the treaty take immediate effect on being scheduled to an Order in Council

I shall turn now to some of the points raised in the debate. The noble Lord, Lord Wallace of Saltaire, was worried that parliamentary sovereignty is infringed by the Crown's prerogative to ratify treaties. I do not believe that is so, because parliamentary sovereignty requires that while the Government may make treaties without parliamentary approval, it must seek approval by means of prior legislation where existing law is affected. That is why the European Communities Act was required to give effect to the Treaty of Rome. That is why on other occasions in recent years we have had some long and interesting debates in the House which I well remember.

Whenever we are talking about bringing more information to Parliament, the reason given for it, as given by the noble Lord, Lord Lester of Herne Hill, and by others today, is that there is a democratic deficit. I am not sure whether there is a democratic deficit here, because the power to make treaties is not vested in the Crown only, it is exercised by the Secretary of State for Foreign and Commonwealth Affairs. He must consult those of his colleagues whose departments are responsible for implementing the provisions of a particular treaty. The authority of the Government rests upon a democratic mandate, and effective government requires the support of the majority of the Members of the other place.

While Parliament may not invariably have a formal role in the ratification of the treaties, unless it decides to debate them, it has every opportunity to scrutinise their provisions. Through Parliament, governments will always be democratically accountable for their actions. They include the making of international treaties.

I have been involved in a number of signings over the past 10 years. I cannot remember a case where, when there was something to be questioned, it has not been questioned. Others may differ in their view on that matter. Others may say that the Bill is a safeguard. But I believe that this is something about which the Foreign and Commonwealth Office is a good deal more diligent, as the noble

Lord, Lord Bridges, intimated, than the House may have assumed from having listened to the debate.

. . .

I remember well the concern about the European Convention on Human Rights, because the noble Lord, Lord Lester, has queried matters of that nature with me previously. It is important to note that when the European Convention on Human Rights was to be ratified, long before I came into Parliament, the convention was laid under the Ponsonby rule on 23rd January 1951. Members' attention was drawn to it on 5th February 1951 in a Written Answer from the then Minister of State for Foreign Affairs, Mr. Kenneth Younger. There were no objections raised, despite the fact that that Written Answer actually invited them, and therefore the convention was duly ratified. That seems to me a very sensible way under the existing system to proceed, to notify by Written Answer that if objections are not made within the 21 days after the convention has been laid, then it will be duly ratified. That obviously does not answer the noble Lord, Lord Lester, or the noble Lord, Lord Wallace of Saltaire.

One of the things I believe we can do is to look at these cases in a positive light: that is to say, to look at these cases and see on each occasion how it has been dealt with. The noble Lords, Lord Bridges and Lord Lester, both asked me about Protocol 11 of the European Convention on Human Rights. Once again, the protocol was laid before Parliament in the normal way. The Ponsonby rule was completely complied with and an opportunity was given for debate, though none was in fact held on that occasion.

When we come to the inevitably interesting question of the ratification of European Community treaties, which was raised by the noble Lord, Lord Lester of Herne Hill . . . one has to realise that all European Community matters require the government to introduce legislation. I have already given the example of the European Communities Act 1972. Any proposal for one of the communities themselves to enter into a treaty is already submitted under cover of an explanatory memorandum to the Scrutiny Committees of both Houses, so in a sense part of what the noble Lord, Lord Lester, is asking for is actually carried out in that case.

The noble Lord, Lord Wallace, asked me about third pillar agreements, as did a number of other noble Lords. The Government have already undertaken to provide Parliament with texts of draft third pillar conventions while they are still under negotiation. I think this is very important. Normal ratification as at present would proceed after signature, but the very fact that there is to be prior notice while negotiation is going on is certainly a step forward. I noted what the noble Lord, Lord Wallace of Saltaire, said about the liberties of citizens. May I just say to him that common positions, joint actions or joint positions adopted under the second and third pillars, while they may impose legally binding obligations, are not normally subject to ratification. That is why they do not occur under the Ponsonby rule. Also I must point out that under this Bill they would not be subject to that process either.

The noble Baroness, Lady Blackstone, asked how many treaties might come before us if this Bill were to be given Royal Assent. That is a matter which, as we answered in a Parliamentary Question, varies from year to year, some 72 treaties having been ratified between 1st January 1991 and 31st December 1995:

in other words, the number is running at between 10 and 15 a session. I should also like to point out that 280 treaties have entered into force for the United Kingdom in the same period, either on signature or by a notification contained in an exchange of diplomatic notes. Of course, neither of these two circumstances would be covered by this Bill.

I believe, too, that although there may be only 10 or 15 treaties a Session requiring resolutions from both Houses, there would be a significant additional amount of parliamentary time required under the noble Lord's Bill without necessarily demonstrably contributing to the better scrutiny of the treaty-making process. It seems to me that that scrutiny should come rather earlier in the process than when one is at the final treaty stage. Undoubtedly there are problems with a number of the elements of the Bill which, if it is given a Second Reading, I am sure your Lordships will want to go into at a later stage.

I turn now to the comments made by the noble Lord, Lord Bridges, about the article in the *Financial Times* of last Saturday by Mr. A Hermann, and especially the comment made by the noble Lord about secrecy. After my 10 years in the Foreign Office, I am absolutely convinced that the ratification process is not secret. A distinguished noble Lord who is a former member of the Diplomatic Service will know full well the amount of quizzing about treaties which takes place.

One of the difficulties involved is the point raised by the noble Baroness, Lady Williams of Crosby; namely, that there are complex treaties. Indeed, there are treaties which, except to experienced lawyers such as the noble Lord, Lord Lester of Herne Hill, and my noble and learned friend Lord Howe of Aberavon, are not clear. But there is no question, as the writer of the article in the *Financial Times* said, that it is a secret matter. The Foreign Office has no interest in keeping secret things which can be shared. I believe that that is the right way to proceed.

A number of questions were asked about practice in other countries. Certainly the essentials of our practice on treaty making and the balance of responsibilities between the Executive and the legislature is actually common to most countries. In the majority of OECD countries, parliamentary approval is required for certain types of treaty. But in most other countries, unlike the UK, the treaties take effect directly in national law upon ratification.

In the United States, treaties are subject to presidential ratification and require approval by two-thirds of the Senate. But the American constitution also provides that, 'all treaties made under the authority of the United States shall be the supreme law of the land and that the judges in every state shall be bound by them, notwithstanding anything to the contrary in the constitution or laws of any state'. That is obviously not the case in the United Kingdom; treaties cannot and do not take effect in our law without implementing legislation.

There are countries, such as Denmark, where treaties are not self-enacted. Prior parliamentary approval is required for the ratification of treaties requiring implementation in national law in that country. The purpose of that is to prevent its government from undertaking international obligations which its parliament might refuse to implement.

However, it is the consistent practice of HMG not to ratify any treaty requiring implementation in UK law until such legislation has actually been passed. As regards the question put to me by the noble Baroness, Lady

Blackstone, of how it affects other European countries, perhaps I may write to her on the matter because I do not have details of the situation in each country to hand at present. Those situations vary and it would take me a considerable amount of time to explain them.

We have heard a good deal tonight about the Australian constitution. Although there is much talk in Australia at present about a change in the matter, I am sure that neither there nor, indeed, in New Zealand or Canada are the treaties subject to parliamentary approval. We answered the noble Lord, Lord Lester, on that point in a Written Answer a short while ago.

I am happy to put in writing the detail about the Australian Federal Parliament, but it is a situation which has been very much akin to our own. The difficulty is that the Australian Parliament did not actually use the practice which it was afforded by its written constitution. The Parliament had 12 sitting days prior to ratification, but those concerned allowed their system to fall into disuse. They then overtook the practice that they had previously kept to by tabling treaties in bulk every six months, with the result that many treaties were tabled after ratification. That is why there has been a great debate in Australia. Your Lordships would be right and, indeed, would have every reason to complain had we followed such a practice of tabling treaties in bulk. We have not done that. If our Australian friends had used something like the Ponsonby rule on treaties effectively one by one they would not be in the situation in which they now find themselves.

We are very different from the Australian Government in this. We are committed to a policy of open government. The full texts of all treaties are published. We give guidance on the treaty practice and procedures. That has been laid in both Houses, and it is available to the public on request from the Foreign and Commonwealth Office.

There has been some comment tonight about lack of information to answer the questions of the noble Lord, Lord Lester. This is a recent matter in terms of the great interest that the noble Lord, Lord Lester, has brought to the subject. We have been computerising treaty records. Some 12,000 items, dating back to 1835, are now being entered on to computer. No doubt, bit by bit, we shall be able to do an analysis of them which might answer the questions that the noble Lord, Lord Lester of Herne Hill, keeps asking me. I do not know whether I can do that quickly, but it may come.

Several times I have spoken about openness and have mentioned the explanatory memorandum. It is the practice of the Foreign Office to be as open as possible to the public and, of course, Parliament. There has been a massive increase in openness in the last 10 years since I first went to the Foreign Office. I hasten to add that that has nothing to do with me, although I am very much in favour of it. Ministerial speeches and correspondence are a growing feature of government business. In 1994 the Foreign Office exchanged 11,000 letters with Members of Parliament. That is a much higher figure than ever before. We make available verbatim copies of all ministerial speeches. I have already mentioned the treaty series, which is published by the Foreign Office.

However, that may not be enough. That was the point that the noble Baroness, Lady Williams of Crosby, made. The suggestion concerning explanatory memoranda is one that is worthy of further consideration whether or not this Bill becomes law. We should try to see that suggestion in the positive light in which I know it has been proposed. I shall want to examine it further with my colleagues before giving a definitive answer, but it seems a sensible way to proceed.

Certainly, I can assure your Lordships that if an MP or one of the Select Committees ever writes asking for an explanation, not only of a treaty but of anything else, they receive one. Frequently it is in memorandum form. I can assure the noble Lord, Lord Bruce of Donington, that I will not sign any explanatory memorandum without having not only read it but also learnt to understand it. Sometimes that takes a little more work than may at first sight be apparent.

As the noble Lord, Lord Bridges, says, it is more than 70 years since Arthur Ponsonby put the case forcefully against a measure such as that which the noble Lord, Lord Lester of Herne Hill, wishes to introduce. I believe that the noble Lord, Lord Bridges, used the same quotation that I had picked out from that speech. Arthur Ponsonby said: 'Resolutions expressing Parliamentary approval of every Treaty before ratification would be a very cumbersome form of procedure and would burden the House with a lot of unnecessary business'. Today, I would not use the word 'unnecessary'. It is probably quite time consuming, but your Lordships might deem it necessary.

It is clear that the Ponsonby rule, as it has been applied consistently over many years, has the great merit of allowing flexibility. My noble and learned friend Lord Howe said that the Bill of the noble Lord, Lord Lester, might impose inescapable burdens. That is a matter that your Lordships need to examine very carefully at a later stage in the Bill. We want not only the flexibility but the efficiency of the Ponsonby rule, while preserving the sovereignty and prerogatives of Parliament. Parliament has ample opportunity, whenever neces-sary, to examine and discuss new international responsibilities. But admin-istrative and procedural costs must be minimised as well as making sure that the information is always available. We want parliamentary control which is effective. We want scrutiny maintained. It is not, as many noble Lords seemed to imply tonight, that the Foreign and Commonwealth Office or any other government department would feel greatly hampered by the Bill. What we must not do is to burden Parliament in such a way that Parliament cannot cope with the Bill. That is why I do not have an open-handed welcome for the Bill but a little scepticism (if I may so put it) about whether this is the best way for Parliament to go.

The Government will not seek to impede the progress of the Bill of the noble Lord, Lord Lester of Herne Hill, in this House. What we shall ask your Lordships to do is to give it strict scrutiny. It is in those terms that I welcome the debate that we have had tonight.

(HL Debs., vol. 569, cols 1556–62: 28 February 1996)

A working party within the Council of the European Union circulated to Member States a questionnaire on the subject of the conclusion of international agreements. The following questions were amongst those asked:

II. INSTRUMENTS WITH LEGALLY BINDING FORCE APPROVABLE UNDER A
SIMPLIFIED PROCEDURE

4. Does your national law distinguish between treaties requiring and treaties
not requiring parliamentary approval? What are the determinants in such a
distinction?

5. What is the procedure to be followed for treaties not requiring parliamentary approval?

6. In the case of treaties requiring parliamentary approval, is there any
simplified procedure for having some of them concluded? What are its
features?

7. Is any such simplified procedure explicitly confined to certain kinds of
treaties?

8. If there is no express provision for any such procedure, does a de facto one
exist in practice? Under what circumstances, on what conditions and in
what form?

9. If not, are there any legal impediments to simplification of procedures?

10. Are there any categories of treaties which are excluded (or would in any
event be excluded) from the application of a simplified procedure?

11. Should a simplified procedure not be possible, are there any written rules or
any practices allowing an urgent or fast-track procedure to be followed for
certain treaties?

The FCO replied on 9 May 1996 as follows:

II. INSTRUMENTS WITH LEGALLY BINDING FORCE APPROVABLE UNDER A
SIMPLIFIED PROCEDURE

4. In the United Kingdom, the power to conclude treaties is vested in the
Executive and, subject to the one exceptional case mentioned below, Parliamentary approval is not in law required before the Government exercises that
power. However:

(a) If the treaty requires legislation to enable it to be given effect in the UK,
it is UK practice not to express its consent to be bound by a treaty,
whether by signature, ratification or accession, before such legislation has
been adopted; and

(b) if the treaty is signed subject to ratification, it is UK Government practice
to lay a copy of the treaty before Parliament for a minimum of 21 days
before depositing its instrument of ratification. This gives an opportunity
for Parliamentary scrutiny and debate, but does not amount to a legal
requirement for Parliamentary approval of the treaty.

The only exception laid down by legislation to the general rule is that treaties
providing for an increase in the powers of the European Parliament must be
approved by an Act of Parliament before they can be ratified by the UK
(section 6, European Parliamentary Elections Act 1978).

5. See answer to question 4.

6. In the one case where prior Parliamentary approval is required (see answer 4
above) no simplified procedure for obtaining that approval is possible: under
the terms of the 1978 Act an Act of Parliament is necessary.

7. Not applicable.

8. No.

9. No, apart from in the exceptional case referred to in answers 4 and 6 above, when an Act of Parliament is required.

10.Not applicable.

11.See answer to question 6.

(Text provided by the FCO)

In reply to a question, the Minister of State, FCO, wrote:

We accept that explanatory memoranda can usefully supplement the established Ponsonby procedures by bringing to the attention of Parliament the main features of the treaties with which they are laid. In future therefore every international agreement laid under the Ponsonby Rule will be accompanied by an explanatory memorandum. This new procedure will apply to all international agreements signed after 1st January 1997 which are laid under the Ponsonby Rule, namely those agreements which are concluded subject to ratification, accession, acceptance or approval, and which are laid for a period of 21 sitting days after signature and before ratification or its equivalent.

Arrangements will be made to lay copies of the note for departments entitled Guidelines on Explanatory Memoranda for Treaties in the Libraries of both Houses.

We should like to thank the noble Lord, Lord Lester, whose initiative led directly to the introduction of the new arrangements.

(HL Debs., vol. 576, *WA 101*: 16 December 1996)

Part Six: I. B. *Treaties—conclusion and entry into force—reservations and declarations to multilateral treaties*

Article IX of the Genocide Convention, 1948 (TS No. 58 (1970)) reads as follows:

ARTICLE IX

Disputes between the Contracting Parties relating to the interpretation, application or fulfilment of the present Convention, including those relating to the responsibility of a State for genocide or for any of the other acts enumerated in article III, shall be submitted to the International Court of Justice at the request of any of the parties to the dispute.

In acceding to the above Convention, Malaysia made the following reservation:

That with reference to Article IX of the Convention, before any dispute to which Malaysia is a party may be submitted to the jurisdiction of the International Court of Justice under this article, the specific consent of Malaysia is required in each case.

(TS No. 21 (1995); Cm 3048, p. 19)

In acceding to the above Convention, Singapore made the following reservation:

That with reference to Article IX of the Convention, before any dispute to which the Republic of Singapore is a party may be submitted to the jurisdiction of the International Court of Justice under this Article, the specific consent of the Republic of Singapore is required in each case.

(TS No. 114 (1995); Cm 3309, p. 7)

On 20 March 1996, the UK Government filed the following objection with the UN Secretary-General as depositary:

The Government of the United Kingdom of Great Britain and Northern Ireland have consistently stated that they are unable to accept reservations to Article IX. In their view, these are not the kind of reservations which intending parties to the Convention have the right to make.

Accordingly, the Government of the United Kingdom do not accept the reservations entered by the Governments of Singapore and Malaysia to Article IX of the Convention.

(TS No. 96 (1996); Cm 3528, pp. 16–17)

Speaking on 12 November 1996 in the Sixth Committee of the UN General Assembly discussing the report of the work of the International Law Commission, the UK representative, Sir Franklin Berman, stated:

The work on *Reservations to Treaties* is equally full of promise for a genuinely useful outcome. My delegation understands the reasons why less time was available for detailed discussion this session, but we commend the energetic approach of the Special Rapporteur which we have tried to fuel with information about British treaty practice as requested in his detailed questionnaire. We have of course taken note (as we are sure other Governments will also do) of Professor Pellet's thoughtful analysis of whether the law embodies, or indeed requires, what he refers to as a 'normative diversification' under which different reservations regimes would, as a matter of general law, apply to different types of treaty. Like him, we had noted that the International Court of Justice, when it laid the foundation for the Vienna Convention regime in its Advisory Opinion on the *Genocide Convention*, was already dealing with a human rights treaty *par excellence* and drew on that specific fact in its Opinion. The Commission should be encouraged to press ahead with its thoroughly worthwhile efforts to bring similar clarity to other aspects of this confused area of international law and State practice. The Special Rapporteur has judiciously reserved his view for the moment on whether a guide to practice would be needful. We for our part should be very surprised if it were not.

(Text provided by the FCO; see also A/C.6/51/SR.38, p. 6)

In the course of a statement made on 9 December 1996 in the UN General Assembly, the representative of Ireland, on behalf of the European Union, observed:

Article 309 of the [Law of the Sea] Convention prohibits reservations and exceptions other than the very few expressly permitted in other Articles. Although Article 310 indicates that declarations or statements are permissible, the European Union wishes to reiterate the prohibition on States making declarations or statements which purport to exclude or modify the legal effects of the provisions of the Convention in their application to those States. Many declarations and statements have been made by States and the European Union is concerned that many of these are not in conformity with the Convention. It therefore urges all States that have made statements or declarations to review them in the light of the provisions of Articles 309 and 310, and to withdraw those that are not in conformity with those provisions. While of course any declaration or statement which purports to exclude or modify the legal effect of the provisions of the Convention is devoid of effect, its maintenance on the record is misleading. It may cast doubt on the commitment of the State concerned to the Convention and can only have a weakening effect on the Convention. We note that a number of States have made clear on the record the unacceptability of such statements and declarations.

(Text provided by the FCO)

Part Six: II. A. *Treaties—observance, application and interpretation—observance*

In reply to a question on the subject of Her Majesty's Government's policy towards the security of human rights in Hong Kong after 1 July 1997, the Minister of State, FCO, wrote:

The Sino-British joint declaration on the question of Hong Kong, which is a binding treaty between Britain and China, provides for continuing human rights protection in Hong Kong after the handover. Specifically, in the last paragraph of chapter XIII of annex I to the joint declaration, China pledges to ensure that the provisions of the international covenants on civil and political rights and on economic, social and cultural rights, as applied to Hong Kong, remain in force after 30 June 1997.

(HC Debs., vol. 278, WA, col. 516: 6 June 1996)

Part Six: II. C. *Treaties —observance, application and interpretation—interpretation*

(See Part Nine: IX. (second item of 8 May 1996) and Part Ten: III. (item of 17 April 1996), below)

Part Six: II. E. *Treaties—observance, application and interpretation—treaty succession*

By an Exchange of Notes dated 29 August 1996 and 16 September 1996 respectively it was agreed that the bilateral agreements and arrangements which were valid on 31 December 1992 between the Czech and Slovak Federal Republic and the United Kingdom of Great Britain and

Northern Ireland which are listed below will be regarded as remaining in force between the Czech Republic and the United Kingdom of Great Britain and Northern Ireland, without prejudice to the possibility that any provision in any other bilateral agreement might remain in force between the two countries in accordance with international law–

	Date	Treaty Series and Command Nos.
Exchange of Notes between Great Britain and Czechoslovakia relative to the importation from Great Britain into Czechoslovakia of Opium and similar Drugs	Prague 24 Mar., 1921 and 4 Aug., 1921	
Convention between the United Kingdom of Great Britain and Northern Ireland and the Czechoslovak Republic relative to Legal Proceedings in Civil and Commercial Matters	London 11 Nov., 1924	6/1926 Cmd. 2637
Convention between His Majesty in respect of the United Kingdom and the President of the Czech Republic Supplementary to the Convention of November 11, 1924 to facilitate the Conduct of Legal Proceedings	Prague 15 Feb., 1935	30/1935 Cmd. 4980
Exchange of Notes between His Majesty's Government in the United Kingdom and the Government of Czechoslovakia in regard to Passports for Seamen	London 13 Feb., 1935 and 4 Mar., 1935	11/1935 Cmd. 4865
Agreement between the Government of the United Kingdom of Great Britain and Northern Ireland and the Government of the Czechoslovak Republic for the Mutual Upkeep of War Graves	Prague 3 Mar., 1949	31/1949 Cmd. 7691
Agreement between the Government of the United Kingdom of Great Britain and Northern Ireland and the Government of the Czechoslovak Republic for Air Services between and beyond their respective Territories	Prague 15 Jan., 1960	26/1960 Cmnd. 1036

	Date	Treaty Series and Command Nos.
Agreement for Co-operation in the Field of Applied Science and Technology between the Government of the United Kingdom of Great Britain and Northern Ireland and the Government of the Czechoslovak Socialist Republic	Prague 26 Mar., 1968	57/1968 Cmnd. 3697
Agreement between the Government of the United Kingdom of Great Britain and Northern Ireland and the Government of the Czechoslovak Socialist Republic on International Road Transport	Prague 10 Nov., 1970	59/1971 Cmnd. 4747
Co-operation Agreement between the United Kingdom of Great Britain and Northern Ireland and the Czechoslovak Socialist Republic	Brno 8 Sept., 1972	70/1973 Cmnd. 5335
Consular Convention between the United Kingdom of Great Britain and Northern Ireland and the Czechoslovak Socialist Republic	Prague 3 Apr., 1975	107/1976 Cmnd. 6683
Agreement between the Government of the United Kingdom of Great Britain and Northern Ireland and the Government of the Czechoslovak Socialist Republic on Co-operation in the Field of Medicine and Public Health	Prague 23 Apr., 1976	74/1976 Cmd. 6561
Agreement between the Government of the United Kingdom of Great Britain and Northern Ireland and the Government of the Czechoslovak Socialist Republic on the Settlement of Certain Outstanding Claims and Financial Issues (with amending Exchange of Notes)	Prague 29 Jan., 1982	21/1982 Cmnd. 8557

	Date	Treaty Series and Command Nos.
Agreement between the Government of Great Britain and Northern Ireland and the Czechoslovak Federative Republic on Co-operation in the Fields of Education, Science and Culture	London 3 Apr., 1990	57/1990 Cm 1198
Agreement between the Government of Great Britain and Northern Ireland and the Czech and Slovak Federal Republic for the Promotion and Protection of Investments, with Protocol	Prague 10 July, 1990	42/1993 Cm 2277
Exchange of Notes between the Government of the United Kingdom of Great Britain and Northern Ireland and the Government of the Czech and Slovak Federal Republic amending the Agreement for the Promotion and Protection of Investments, signed in Prague on 10 July 1990	Prague 23 Aug., 1991	42/1993 Cm 2277
Memorandum of Understanding between the Government of the United Kingdom of Great Britain and Northern Ireland and the Government of the Czech and Slovak Federal Republic concerning Co-operation in Matters of Terrorism, Drug Trafficking, Organised Crime and General Policing and Enforcement Matters	Prague 23 July, 1990	
Exchange of Notes between the Government of the United Kingdom of Great Britain and Northern Ireland and the Government of the Czech and Slovak Federal Republic concerning the Abolition of Visas	Prague 18 Sept., 1990	6/1991 Cm 1396

	Date	Treaty Series and Command Nos.
Convention between the Government of the United Kingdom of Great Britain and Northern Ireland and the Government of the Czech and Slovak Federal Republic for the Avoidance of Double Taxation with respect to Taxes on Income and Capital Gains	London 5 Nov., 1990	54/1992 Cm 2016
Agreement between the Government of Great Britain and Northern Ireland and the Government of the Czech and Slovak Federal Republic on the Establishment and Activities of Cultural Centres	London 12 Dec., 1991	31/1992 Cm 1938

(TS No. 96 (1996); Cm 3528, pp. 8–9)

Part Six: IV. C. *Treaties—invalidity, termination and suspension of operation—termination, suspension of operation, denunciation and withdrawal*

By a written communication dated 26 July 1995, the Government of the UK gave notice to the Government of the Russian Federation of the decision to denounce the Exchange of Notes of 13 April 1964 concerning the mutual abolition of consular fees on visas.

(TS No. 70 (1996); Cm 3383, p. 47)

Part Eight: I. A. *State territory and territorial jurisdiction—parts of territory, delimitation—frontiers, boundaries*

(See also Part Eight: II. A. (item of 14 February 1996), below)

In the course of a debate in the House of Lords on the subject of Chechnya, the Minister of State, FCO, Baroness Chalker, stated:

The OSCE principle which works throughout the countries signed up to it is that frontiers are inviolable but they can be changed peacefully and by agreement. The examples of peacefully agreed frontier changes obviously include German unification, the establishment of separate Czech and Slovak republics and the dissolution of the Soviet Union. Chechnya is internationally recognised as part of the Russian Federation. That is why we say that we are looking for a solution within the framework of the Russian Federation.

(HL Debs., vol. 568, col. 586: 16 January 1996; see also ibid., vol. 569, col. 971: 20 February 1996)

Part Eight: II. A. *State territory and territorial jurisdiction—territorial jurisdiction—territorial sovereignty*

(See also Part Three: I. E. (item of 14 May 1996), above)

The following question was asked of Her Majesty's Government:

Whether, during the period of British rule over Eritrea, the Hanish Islands were treated as part of the territory, and whether they will place in the Library of the House of Lords copies of any maps showing the extent of the territory at the time which are held in the archives of the Foreign and Commonwealth Office?

The Minister of State, FCO, wrote in reply:

The status of the Hanish Islands has remained indeterminate since the 1923 Treaty of Lausanne, which provided that the future of the islands would be settled by the parties concerned. Maps of the region at that time are now with the Public Record Office.

(HL Debs., vol. 568, *WA 43*: 16 January 1996)

On 7 September 1994, the UK Government informed the UN Secretary-General that it was extending the application of the Convention on the Rights of the Child to, *inter alia*, the Falkland Islands, South Georgia and the South Sandwich Islands (TS No. 81 (1995); Cm 3063, p. 23). On 3 April 1995, the Government of Argentina communicated the following objection to the Secretary-General:

The Government of Argentina rejects the extension of the application of the 'Convention on the Rights of the Child' done in New York on 20 November 1989 to the Malvinas Islands, South Georgia and the South Sandwich Islands, effected by the United Kingdom of Great Britain and Northern Ireland on 7 September 1994, and reaffirms its sovereignty over those islands, which are an integral part of its national territory.

(TS No. 69 (1996); Cm 3364, pp. 19–20)

In response on 16 January 1996, the UK Government communicated the following declaration to the Secretary-General:

The Government of the United Kingdom has no doubt about the sovereignty of the United Kingdom over the Falkland Islands and over South Georgia and the South Sandwich Islands and its consequential right to extend the said Convention to these Territories. The United Kingdom Government rejects as unfounded the claims by the Government of Argentina and is unable to regard the Argentinian objection as having any legal effect.

(TS No. 70 (1996); Cm 3383, p. 19)

In the course of a debate in the House of Lords on the subject of human rights in Turkey, the Minister of State, Baroness Chalker, referred to the situation in south-east Turkey and continued:

That is one of the problems that Turkey has at home in the south-east: how it deals with the terrorism that is undoubtedly there. I know that for Turkey one crucial issue raised by the conflict is that of territorial integrity. We have no intention of questioning Turkey's territorial integrity. No one should be in any doubt about that.

(HL Debs., vol. 569, col. 693: 14 February 1996)

In the course of a press interview given in Moscow on 23 March 1996, the Secretary of State for Foreign and Commonwealth Relations, Mr Malcolm Rifkind, stated:

We recognise that Chechnya is an integral part of the Russian Federation, but it is important that within that framework a political solution is found to this particular problem.

(Text provided by the FCO)

On 13 March 1996, the Government of Argentina sent a message to the Executive Secretary of the Commission for the Conservation of Antarctic Marine Living Resources (CCAMLR) in Hobart, Australia in which the following passage appeared:

The intent of the United Kingdom to exercise unilateral jurisdiction over matters pertaining to fisheries in waters adjacent to the South Georgia and South Sandwich Islands which fall within Statistical Subareas 48.3 and 48.4 of the Convention for the Conservation of the Antarctic Marine Living Resources has come to the attention of the Republic of Argentina.

The Republic of Argentina has officially reiterated its rejection of these pretensions by the United Kingdom and has reasserted its sovereign rights over the aforementioned islands and their related maritime areas.

In a letter dated 8 May 1996, the Polar Regions Section, South Atlantic and Antarctic Department, FCO, referred to the above message and to another from the Government of Argentina dated 14 March 1996, and informed the Executive Secretary of CCAMLR:

The letters imply that the United Kingdom's actions are contrary to international law, including CCAMLR. The United Kingdom does not accept that.

Sovereignty over South Georgia and the South Sandwich Islands

The Argentine letter of 13 March 1996 appears to deny the United Kingdom's sovereignty over South Georgia and the South Sandwich Islands. Although it is not a matter within the scope of the Convention, it is desirable that the position of the United Kingdom be placed on record.

The United Kingdom has no doubt about its sovereignty over South Georgia and the South Sandwich Islands and its right to exercise maritime jurisdiction around the islands in accordance with the rules of international law.

(Texts provided by the FCO)

On the 25 July 1996, the Government of Argentina addressed a letter to the Executive Secretary of the Commission for the Conservation of Antarctic Marine Living Resouces (CCAMLR) which read in part as follows:

SOVEREIGNTY OVER SOUTH GEORGIA AND THE SOUTH SANDWICH ISLANDS

The Republic of Argentina reaffirms its sovereignty over South Georgia and the South Sandwich Islands and over their corresponding maritime areas, and repeats yet again that it rejects that alleged right of the United Kingdom to exercise unilateral jurisdiction in those areas.

The Republic of Argentina notes that these islands are subject to a sovereignty dispute between the Republic of Argentina and the United Kingdom. This dispute has been formally acknowledged by both countries and the UN General Assembly, which has adopted several resolutions urging the Parties to the dispute to seek a peaceful settlement and to refrain from adopting decisions which unilaterally modify the existing situation, as long as those territories remain under the procedures recommended by Resolutions 2065 (XX) and 3160 (XXVIII). Actions taken unilaterally by the United Kingdom are contrary to the letter and the spirit of these Resolutions.

Argentina also reiterates that the British claims to exercise unilateral jurisdiction over those areas are contrary to the Convention, they contravene International Law in general, and they enable any State Party to bring the dispute before the Commission and to resort to the provisions for the resolution of disputes established in Article XXV of the Convention.

Consequently, the Republic of Argentina firmly rejects the claims of the United Kingdom to be regarded as a coastal State in the South Atlantic because, as has been explained above, these territories, presently under British occupation, are subject to a widely recognised international dispute. Therefore, the provisions made for certain States in the Statement by the Chairman are not applicable to the United Kingdom.

In response, the Polar Regions Section, South Atlantic and Antarctic Department, FCO, replied on 6 September 1996 through the Executive Secretary as follows:

'The sovereignty dispute'

The Argentine letter says that a sovereignty dispute has been 'formally acknowledged' by both States. The position is that the United Kingdom acknowledges that Argentina first claimed sovereignty over SGSSI in 1927, over 150 years after Captain Cook took possession in the name of the King, and almost 20 years after the Royal Letters Patent of 1908 formally constituted SGSSI (among other territories) as Dependencies of the Falkland Islands. By the time of the Argentine claim the British presence on South Georgia included a resident magistrate, customs and police officers, a post office, wireless station and marine laboratory. Between 1947 and 1955, the British Government offered to submit the dispute over Argentine claims to SGSSI to the International

Court of Justice; but the matter could not be pursued because Argentina declined to accept the jurisdiction of the Court.

The Argentine letter also notes that the UN General Assembly adopted Resolutions 2065 (XX) and 3160 (XXVIII) regarding SGSSI, and asserts that actions by the United Kingdom are contrary to the letter and spirit of the Resolutions. I would point out that not only do the Resolutions have no legal effect, but that the United Kingdom abstained on both.

. . .

The assertion that the United Kingdom has failed to invoke its sovereign rights over SGSSI and its maritime areas is also misconceived. The declaration of the SGSSI Maritime Zone, the enactment of implementing legislation and the enforcement of that legislation are the clearest example of the exercise of the United Kingdom's sovereignty.

(Text provided by the FCO)

In exercising a right of reply in the UN General Assembly on 27 September 1996, the UK representative, Mr S. Gomersall, stated:

British sovereignty over Gibraltar was clearly established in the Treaty of Utrecht. This legal fact is uncontrovertible. Furthermore, Britain stands by its commitment to the people of Gibraltar in the preambles to the 1969 Constitution. Her Majesty's Government will not enter into any arrangement under which the people of Gibraltar would pass under the sovereignty of another State against their freely and democratically expressed wishes.

We do not consider that the notion of territorial integrity is at all relevant in this case.

(A/51/PV.13, p. 27)

In reply to the following question:

To ask the Secretary of State for Foreign and Commonwealth Affairs if he will make it a condition of Spain joining the integrated military structure of the North Atlantic Treaty Organisation that there will be no Spanish military influence or control over Gibraltar or its territorial waters,

the Minister of State, FCO, wrote:

There can be no question of Spanish command over the territory of Gibraltar, or of any arrangement which allowed Spain to use NATO to take forward its claim to sovereignty over Gibraltar.

(HC Debs., vol. 286, WA, col. 80: 25 November 1996)

Part Eight: II. D. *State territory and territorial jurisdiction—territorial jurisdiction—extra-territoriality*

The following Presidency statement was made on 11 October 1995 on behalf of the EU:

The European Union would like Cuba to have a peaceful transition to democracy and respect for human rights. It takes the view that maintaining the political dialogue and encouraging economic relations are the means most suited to promote evolution towards democracy and Cuba's return to the international community.

The European Union therefore views the House of Representatives' approval on 21 September of the Helms-Burton bill in a negative light and takes the opportunity to reiterate its opposition to the adoption of any measure with extra-territorial application which is in conflict with the rules of international organizations, including those of the WTO.

(*Bulletin of the European Union*, 1995–10, pp. 72–3)

In reply to a question, the Minister of State, FCO, wrote in part:

We do not support the US boycott of Cuba and have passed legislation which counteracts any extra-territorial provisions in the US legislation. We continue to lobby against extra-territorial elements in proposed US legislation to tighten the boycott.

(HL Debs., vol. 568, *WA 85*: 25 January 1996)

In reply to a question, the Secretary of State for the Home Department wrote in part:

With some exceptions, the jurisdiction of courts throughout the United Kingdom is territorially based. There are long-standing arguments of principle and of practicality which support this approach.

It is right, however, that we should, from time to time, examine whether those arguments remain valid in the light of changing circumstances. With the agreement of my right hon. Friend the Secretary of State for Scotland and my right hon. Friend the Secretary of State for Northern Ireland, I have established an inter-departmental review to look at the implications for both policy and procedure of any change to the current position on jurisdiction over offences committed by United Kingdom nationals overseas throughout the United Kingdom.

The review is under way and is expected to take four or five months to complete.

(HC Debs., vol. 270, WA, col. *874*: 1 February 1996)

In the course of oral questions, the Government spokeswoman in the House of Lords, Baroness Miller of Hendon, stated:

. . . the US embargo on Cuba is a bilateral matter between the states involved. We are, however, deeply concerned about the latest US legislation, which contains extra-territorial powers which seek to impose US law on UK companies. We shall be examining the legislation carefully to determine the appropriate response.

. . .

. . .we agree with my noble friend that this is a serious matter and may very well be contrary to the principles of free trade. We are studying the legislation carefully with our European partners to determine its compatibility with the United States' international obligations under GATT and other international agreements.

(HL Debs., vol. 570, cols. 842–3: 13 March 1996)

In reply to an oral question on the subject of the Helms-Burton Act in the United States, the Minister of State, FCO, Sir Nicholas Bonsor, stated:

The Helms-Burton Act has two particularly objectionable clauses: title III, which gives United States citizens the right to sue in the American courts British and other foreign companies that traffic, as they put it, with Cuba and in Cuba; and title IV, which claims the right to exclude from the United States anyone connected with any company that may be trafficking in that way, and that appears to include shareholders and their families. The Government view that as unacceptable legislation, with very high extra-territorial content.

Therefore, we are making bilateral complaints to the United States Government, the most recent of which was a diplomatic note that we sent today. . .. We are also joining with our European Union colleagues to see what steps can be taken collectively to persuade the United States to think better of this unfortunate move. The permanent representatives will be meeting later this week to discuss this and the Foreign Affairs Council will be meeting towards the end of the month. The British delegation to both meetings will make strong representations that we should exert pressure on the United States to change its mind.

(HC Debs., vol. 275, col. 378: 3 April 1996)

The diplomatic note of 3 April 1996 mentioned by the Minister of State—Note No. 46—read as follows:

Her Britannic Majesty's Embassy present their compliments to the Department of State and have the honour to refer to HR927, the Cuban Liberty and Democratic Solidarity (LIBERTAD) Act of 1996.

As the Administration is aware, the United Kingdom is deeply concerned about certain provisions of the Cuban Liberty and Democratic Solidarity (LIBERTAD) Act of 1996 ('the Act'), which the President signed on 12 March.

There can be no excuse for the Cuban airforce action which resulted in the death of those on board the two aircraft shot down on 24 February. The United Kingdom supported the tough Security Council presidential statement on 27 February, which strongly deplored the shooting down, and the statement issued by the EU on 26 February which strongly condemned it. The British Government also condemned the detention of members of the Concilio Cubano and called for their release. These developments highlight the need for fundamental reform, political and economic, in Cuba.

The Governments of the United States and the United Kingdom agree on this aim: the disagreement is about the means. The United Kingdom seeks to follow with Cuba the policies on engagement and dialogue which served so well with many other communist, now ex-communist, countries. To this end, the Government of the United Kingdom is committed to protecting legitimate trading interests and intends to continue to support British companies wishing to do business in Cuba, either through trade or investment, notwithstanding the passage of the Act.

The provisions of the Act which cause particular concern are those which would involve the exercise of extra-territorial jurisdiction and which attempt to deter foreign companies who wish to pursue trading relations with Cuba from doing so. If rigorously implemented, these provisions would cause significant commercial disruption, not least for companies in the US owned by British parents. Since the United Kingdom is the biggest direct investor in the United States, this causes the British Government great concern.

Title IV seeks to exclude from the United States certain foreign nationals and their families because of their involvement with Cuba. The British Government recognises the right of the United States to decide whom it shall admit through its borders. But the conditions for refusing admission set out in Title IV far exceed the normal conditions imposed on applicants for entry to the United States. The definition of 'trafficking' in Title IV is so wide as potentially to catch very large numbers of business people whose connection with operations in Cuba may be remote.

Title III also presents major difficulties. It would have extra-territorial effect if applied to acts committed by foreign nationals outside United States territory. It would also have extra-territorial effect if applied to foreign nationals or companies who are not within the United States, and to subsidiaries which do not carry on business within the jurisdiction. Exercise of extra-territorial jurisdiction in this way would be a major irritant in the trading relationship between the United States and its partners. The new uncertainties introduced by the Act would discourage foreign companies considering starting, or expanding, operations in the United States. The Act also provides United States companies with avenues for vexatious litigation directed at overseas competitors choosing to do legitimate business in Cuba. The width of the definition of 'traffics' gives rise to concern. Persons engaging in a commercial activity may, for example, be quite unaware that the activity is benefiting from confiscated property. The British Government is also considering whether Title III is contrary to international obligations undertaken by the United States in the World Trade Organisation. In the light of these considerations the British Government urges the President in due course to exercise the discretion to suspend the effective date of Title III granted to him in Section 306 of the Act.

The British Government is also concerned by Section 104(b) which provides in certain circumstances for the withholding of United States payments to international financial institutions. Such actions could be in breach of provisions of the relevant international agreements, and in any case are likely adversely to affect their proper functioning.

The British Government hopes that in practical implementation of the legislation, the United States Government will take note of these major concerns about the Act and will work to minimise its practical impact on the economic relationship between the United States and the United Kingdom.

(Text provided by the FCO)

In the course of a speech to a trade conference in London on 2 May

1996, the Parliamentary Under-Secretary of State, Department of Trade and Industry, Mr Ian Taylor, stated in part:

The question of US bilateral relations with Cuba should be a matter for the two countries to resolve between themselves. US has practised such a unilateral trade embargo for the last 30 years and more. Helms/Burton legislation is merely the latest example of this. It is disruptive of normal trade relations. It imposes costs on the US too—ask any American smoker about the impact of his country's policy upon the price and availability of the best quality Cuban cigars. Most importantly, it rarely, if ever, brings the political dividends sought. The more reflective US commentators readily admit this. The world has changed radically over the last 30 years. We believe that the way to bring Cuba into the the global community is through trade and investment, not isolation.

The US has the right to conduct its foreign policy in the light of its own convictions. But the UK is not obliged to follow its lead. When the methods used by the US to enforce its unilateral embargo on Cuba interfere with the legitimate trading interests of third parties, we must express our concern to the US. Particularly when they are seeking to impose US laws on foreigners on an extraterritorial basis.

US businessmen are not unknown in Havana. US business interests are often channelled through Mexico, or Canada, the other 2 members of NAFTA.

The US has shown a tendency to export its laws and its domestic and foreign policy objectives—those of you with long memories may recall the Siberian Pipeline affair. This has been a source of friction for some time.

It is a matter for profound regret that the Helms/Burton legislation follows some bad precedents in seeking to impose US law on transactions involving third parties. It would be thoroughly unwelcome on these grounds alone.

We have had differences with the US over Cuba in the past. The 1992 Cuban Democracy Act sought to oblige UK subsidiaries of US companies to comply with US embargo legislation. On that occasion, the Government issued an Order and Directions under the Protection of Trading Interests Act prohibiting UK companies from complying with this attempt to impose US law upon them.

Now I am sorry to say that we find ourselves faced with another US attempt to punish third parties for doing business with Cuba. The UK Government intends to speak up for the interests of UK businesses which might be affected.

The Cuban Liberty and Democratic Solidarity (LIBERTAD) Act of 1996, better known as the Helms/Burton Act, has now been in force for just under two months. It is a classic example of how a bad piece of law, passed in a particular political climate, can create friction between the closest of friends and disrupt normal trading relations.

It is no secret that the UK Government was deeply concerned by this legislation and had made a number of representations about it both to the US Administration and to the Congress.

We have lodged a strongly worded diplomatic note protesting at the provisions of the legislation. We have also been very active in pressing both our EU partners and other states whose interests are affected by the legislation (Canada and Mexico in particular) to take action both bilaterally and internationally. We shall continue to do so vigorously.

Important to underline this. The bilateral UK/US aspect of the response to Helms/Burton is just a part of the story. The US legislation potentially affects everybody who trades with Cuba, whatever their nationality.

The US has made a series of international commitments designed to promote the liberalisation of world trade under the WTO and the rules of the OECD. It has been active in pressing others to abide in full by these obligations and must do so itself. We and our EU partners shall, therefore, be making a point of raising the Helms/Burton legislation whenever we have the opportunity.

The EU has agreed to initiate consultations in the WTO in response to this legislation. We will be raising the issue at the forthcoming OECD Ministerial meeting on 22/23 May. We have already done so in the Committee on International Investment and Multinational Enterprises. We will continue to raise it in the context of the newly-created Transatlantic Dialogue between the EU and US, including at the forthcoming summit meeting in June.

Provisions of the legislation

Certain provisions which are of particular interest to a business audience. Our immediate aim must be to try and mitigate the worst effects of a broadly drafted piece of legislation.

(i) provision which seeks to exclude from the US 'persons who are allegedly trafficking outside the US in property expropriated from a US national in Cuba'.

This is remarkably widely drawn. It includes company officers, their families, controlling shareholders and the like. This provision is already in force though it has not yet been applied in practice.

Without accepting the validity of the underlying legislation we are pressing the United States authorities to implement the provisions in as transparent and flexible a way as possible. As it stands it could possibly be used to ban a five year old child from visiting Disneyland if one of its parents were linked to a company potentially affected by the legislation.

(ii) the provision which gives a right of action in US courts to US nationals, whose property has been expropriated in Cuba, against third country nationals allegedly trafficking in such property outside the US.

Again, this is drafted in very broad terms. One problem is that we will not know the precise meaning of terms such as 'trafficking' until cases get into the US courts.

This attempt to extend the effect of US law on an extraterritorial basis is fundamentally objectionable to the UK. It also poses serious issues of principle.

The US has laid great stress in defending the Helms/Burton legislation upon the right to compensation of its citizens and companies whose property was expropriated in Cuba. In fact, the UK negotiated a settlement of claims over expropriated property with the Cuban Government many years ago.

It is strange that the US should seek to compensate its own citizens by permitting them to pursue claims against the rights and assets of companies from other friendly states. Particularly, when this may mean seizing the company's US assets, supposedly to compensate for the expropriation of someone else's property in a third country a generation or more ago.

The first cases cannot be brought before 1 November. In the meantime, President Clinton can choose to suspend the legislation on a six monthly basis provided certain conditions are met. We shall continue to make every effort to encourage him to do so.

The US should not be left in any doubt that its actions against the UK and other trading partners are likely to have an adverse impact upon US interests both internationally and domestically. There will be a price to be paid.

I would note that British firms invested a record US $27 billion in the US in 1995. Measures like the Helms/Burton legislation can do nothing for the attractiveness of the United States as a destination for overseas investment. The views of UK investors should be taken into account by US authorities.

It is particularly important then that companies which are substantial employers and taxpayers in the US should make their concerns known to the US Administration too.

The Government is also reviewing a range of potential domestic counter-measures—in terms of action in direct response to UK companies, of individuals being affected by the Helms/Burton legislation and more generally. We are keeping all our options open.

Options include the use of the Protection of Trading Interests Act, as well as the possible use of entry permission procedures.

Much will depend upon how the United States legislation is implemented in practice. We will, of course, consider our response in the context of the many legal and business issues that are raised.

Effect on US/UK relations

Her Majesty's Government is not looking to pick a trade fight with the USA, which remains a major trading partner and a close ally. Close friends have a duty to speak bluntly to each other. The Helms/Burton legislation is undeniably a blight on the friendly relationship we have with our American partners. It has the potential to disrupt normal trading relationships in a way which my Ministerial colleagues and I would deeply regret. The objection is one of principle rather than over the US/Cuba issue alone.

This is not just a UK quarrel with the US. We shall, therefore, make the fullest possible use of the various multinational bodies which have an interest in the free and unhindered flow of international trade and investment to register our opposition to this legislation. We shall continue to work in the closest consultation with our EU partners and others whose interests are affected by this legislation.

I can however assure you that, whatever the precise methods used, we shall take all appropriate steps to protect the legitimate trading interests of the UK.

(Text provided by the FCO)

The following question was asked of Her Majesty's Government:

What measures they are taking to implement the recommendations of the Ministers of the Council of Europe concerning extra-territorial jurisdiction, adopted on 9th September 1991 (Document R (91)11, in particular part 11, 2 to 4)?

In reply, the Minister of State, FCO, wrote:

We are taking positive steps to assist those countries where child prostitution exists and to strengthen action against those in the UK who organise sex tours or who encourage others to travel abroad for the purposes of sexually exploiting children. In this context, the Government are supporting a Sexual Offences (Conspiracy and Incitement) Bill, the purpose of which is to make it an offence for persons in the UK to conspire with or incite others to commit sexual acts against children abroad which would be offences if committed in the UK.

An interdepartmental review is considering the general issues of extra territorial jurisdiction. But the UK police already provide assistance to local police forces directly and through participation in training sessions arranged by Interpol. The National Criminal Intelligence Service also provides assistance through Interpol to police in countries receiving sex tourists in order to help identify British sex tourists.

(HL Debs., vol. 571, *WA 58*: 16 April 1996)

In the course of the debate at the committee stage in the House of Lords of the Civil Aviation (Amendment) Bill, the Minister of State, Home Office, Baroness Blatch, stated:

The United Kingdom regularly opposes attempts by other countries to impose their laws on United Kingdom companies or nationals, when outside the territory of the state concerned. There have, for example, been attempts recently by some countries to impose their laws on the conduct of people in British aircraft flying to their countries, to the detriment of the airlines concerned. We resist these attempts by foreign states to impose their laws on our companies and therefore we cannot seek to impose our laws on others in similar circumstances.

(HL Debs., vol. 571, col. 1231: 24 April 1996)

In reply to a question on the subject of the United States legislation regarding Cuba, the Parliamentary Under-Secretary of State, Department of Trade and Industry, Mr Ian Taylor (Minister for Science and Technology), wrote:

I made a speech to a seminar hosted by the Caribbean trade advisory group on 2 May setting out Her Majesty's Government policy in respect of this legislation and how the interests of United Kingdom business could be protected if threatened by its provisions.

. . .

As I indicated in that speech, we are still seeking to clarify certain areas of deep concern about this potentially damaging piece of legislation. Our objection is to its attempts to interfere with the legitimate trade of UK companies outside US. In this connection, my officials will be meeting US State Department officials this week to establish details on how the latter intend to implement the provisions covering the exclusion of persons from the US. We will take the opportunity to reiterate the UK's concern that the Helms/Burton legislation could disrupt normal trading relationship with the USA. We shall consider carefully how to coordinate our response with our EU partners.

(HC Debs., vol. 277, WA, col. *297*: 10 May 1996)

During a press interview in Washington DC, on 29 May 1996, the Secretary of State for Foreign and Commonwealth Relations, Mr Malcolm Rifkind, stated:

. . . along with many other countries, including Canada, Mexico, Western European countries, we believe that the American claim for extra-territorial jurisdiction, a secondary boycott against countries that may be trading with Cuba, we think that is unfortunate and misplaced.

(Text provided by the FCO)

The following question was asked of Her Majesty's Government:

What effect, if any, they consider there will be on the principle of extra-territorial jurisdiction over offences committed by any persons in relation to internal armed conflicts, as a result of Article 14 of the Protocol on Prohibitions or Restrictions on the Use of Mines, Booby Traps and Other Devices, adopted at the 14th Plenary Meeting of the Conference of the States Parties to the Convention on prohibitions or restrictions on the use of certain conventional weapons which may be deemed to be excessively injurious or to have indiscriminate effects?

In reply, the Minister of State, FCO, wrote:

Article 14 of Amended Protocol II of the UN Weaponry Convention provides for States Parties to take appropriate measures to ensure the imposition of penal sanctions against persons, who, in relation to an armed conflict and contrary to the Protocol, wilfully kill or cause injury to civilians, and to bring such persons to justice. The Government accept that jurisdiction may be exercised in such cases pursuant to international agreements. We are however currently assessing the full implications of the Amended Protocol.

(HL Debs., vol. 573, *WA 2*: 17 June 1996)

In the course of a debate in the House of Lords on the subject of the Helms-Burton Act, the Minister of State, Department of Trade and Industry, Lord Fraser of Carmyllie, stated:

. . . certainly we hope that we have made clear to the United States authorities where we stand on the Helms-Burton legislation. As recently as last week, prior to the President's decision, my right honourable friend the President of the Board of Trade in a speech to the American Chamber of Commerce made it clear that the United Kingdom Government deplored the action that had been taken.

We need to separate the two issues; first, the reform in Cuba, which the United Kingdom firmly supports, and, secondly, unilateral actions against United Kingdom companies and others, which we deplore. We cannot accept that in applying a principle of extra-territoriality the United States has the right to attack the interests of UK individuals and companies in order to impose its approach to foreign policy issues on its partners.

(HL Debs., vol. 574, col. 998: 18 July 1996)

The Civil Aviation (Amendment) Act 1996 received the Royal Assent on 18 July 1996. Its long title reads: 'An Act to amend the Civil Aviation Act 1982 so as to provide for the prosecution of persons committing offences on foreign aircraft while in flight to the United Kingdom and for connected purposes'. In the course of the second reading debate on the Bill in the House of Lords, the Minister of State, Home Office, Baroness Blatch, had remarked:

The Bill will give us jurisdiction over any offence committed on board a foreign registered aircraft landing in the United Kingdom.

(HL Debs., vol. 570, col. 1803: 27 March 1996)

In reply to a question, the Minister of State, Home Office, wrote:

My right honourable friend the Home Secretary is today publishing the report of the review which he set up with the agreement of my right honourable friend and Secretary of State for Northern Ireland. . . . The review advised against any general extension of extra-territorial jurisdiction because of the implications which so substantial an extension of jurisdiction would have for the procedures and rules of evidence of the United Kingdom courts. It recommended, however, in favour of the adoption of a set of policy guidelines, against which proposals for taking extra-territorial jurisdiction over individual offences should be judged. These are:

where the offence is serious (this might be defined, in respect of existing offences, by reference to the length of sentence currently available);
where, by virtue of the nature of the offence, the witnesses and evidence necessary for the prosecution are likely to be available in the United Kingdom territory, even though the offence was committed outside the jurisdiction;
where there is international consensus that certain conduct is reprehensible and that concerted action is needed involving the taking of extra-territorial jurisdiction;
where the vulnerability of the victim makes it particularly important to be able to tackle instances of the offence;
where it appears to be in the interests of the standing and reputation of the United Kingdom in the international community;
where there is a danger that offences would otherwise not be justiciable.

Meeting any of the guidelines would not mean automatically that jurisdiction would be taken, but it would establish a *prima facie* case for considering the issue further.

The review advised that sexual offences committed against children abroad satisfied a number of these criteria, and that extra-territorial jurisdiction should be taken over these offences. The review also recommended in favour of the assumption of jurisdiction over acts of incitement and conspiracy committed in this country in respect of offences abroad. This will assist our efforts to control the activities of foreign extremists who use this country as a base to plan or encourage criminal acts abroad.

We have accepted all of these recommendations. Legislation to give effect to them will be brought forward at the earliest possible opportunity. In respect of those aspects relevant to the activities of foreign extremists, we shall also be taking account of the findings of Lord Lloyd's Inquiry into Counter-Terrorism Legislation.

(HL Debs., vol. 574, *WA 117–18*: 23 July 1996)

In reply to a question, the Minister of State, FCO, wrote:

My right hon. and learned Friend the Foreign Secretary has discussed the Helms-Burton Act with the United States ambassador and the US Secretary of State, Warren Christopher.

We consider that this legislation sets a dangerous and unwelcome precedent. It is against the spirit, if not the letter, of international trade law. While we agree with the US objective to promote democracy in Cuba, we disagree fundamentally on the means to achieve this. US sanctions against British companies are not the way forward. We have put firmly on record with the US Administration and Congress bilaterally, and also collectively with our EU partners, our views and our objections to the legislation. The EU has requested World Trade Organisation disputes panel to rule on the issue. Countermeasures are under consideration in Brussels. The Government are determined to do everything possible to protect our legitimate business interests and the law-based international trading system.

(HC Debs., vol. 284, WA, col. *35*: 28 October 1996)

In the course of a speech to the UN General Assembly on 12 November 1996 on the subject of US political relations with Cuba, the Permanent Representative of the UK to the UN in New York, Sir John Weston, made the following observations in the name of the EU:

Having made clear our views on the situation that exists in Cuba, the European Union wishes to reiterate its rejection of attempts to apply national legislation on an extra-territorial basis. We have always rejected attempts by the United States to coerce other countries into complying with the commercial measures it has adopted unilaterally against Cuba.

For this reason, we continue to oppose United States legislation which provides for the application of United States law to companies and individuals outside the jurisdiction of the United States, including provisions designed to discourage third country companies from trading with, or investing in, Cuba. We cannot accept that the United States may unilaterally determine or restrict the European Union's economic and commercial relations with any other State. Measures of this type violate the general principles of international law and the sovereignty of independent states.

The European Union has therefore initiated proceedings in the World Trade Organisation to have the Helms-Burton legislation declared contrary to the obligations assumed by the United States as a member of that organisation. The European Union has also agreed upon legislation to counter the extra-territorial effects of the United States measures.

(Text provided by the FCO)

In reply to a question, the Minister of State, Department of Trade and Industry, wrote:

The General Affairs Council on 28 October agreed the text of an EC regulation which is designed to protect against the effects of the extraterritorial application of legislation adopted by a third country. The regulation specifically identifies the US Cuban Liberty and Democratic Solidarity Act 1996 and other legislation relating to Cuba, and the Iran and Libya Sanctions Act 1996. It was adopted on 22 November 1996 and entered into force on 29 November 1996.

The regulation applies to all legal persons incorporated within the Community and to all natural persons resident in the Community whether or not they are EC nationals as well as certain other categories of persons, for example certain shipping companies.

Those covered by the regulation are obliged to inform the European Commission either directly or through their national authorities if their financial and economic interests are directly or indirectly affected by the operations of the foreign legislation in question and they are prohibited from complying with any requirements or prohibitions which may be imposed on them under the legislation. Procedures have been established whereby those affected may seek waivers allowing them to comply in circumstances where non-compliance with the foreign legislation would seriously damage their interests or those of the European Community.

The regulation also provides that judgments given by foreign courts under the specified foreign legislation will not be enforceable within the European Community and that those persons covered by the regulation can recover any damages, including legal costs, caused to them by the application of that legislation or by actions based thereon or resulting therefrom. This recovery may be obtained, anywhere in the European Community where there are assets, from the natural or legal person or any other entity causing the damages or from any person acting on its behalf or from an intermediary.

Member states are obliged to provide for sanctions for breaches of the notification and non-compliance obligations. We shall be proposing an appropriate order to Her Majesty in Council to accomplish this which will then be laid before Parliament.

A joint action commitment agreed in parallel to the regulation commits Member states to protect the interests of those natural and legal persons covered by the regulation to the extent that the regulation itself does not do so.

(HC Debs., vol. 286, WA, cols. 585–6: 3 December 1996)

In reply to the question 'is it the Government's view that the Helms-Burton Act is or is not lawful under international law', the Government spokeswoman in the House of Lords, Baroness Miller of Hendon, referred to the dispute settlement panel established by the World Trade Organization and continued:

... we very much hope that the panel will find that the US action is inconsistent with her obligations under international trade rules. The case is complex and that is the very best answer I can give at this time.

(HL Debs., vol 576, col. 581: 3 December 1996)

The Extraterritorial US Legislation (Sanctions against Cuba, Iran and Libya) (Protection of Trading Interests) Order 1996, which was made on 19 December 1996 and came into force on 28 January 1997, was accompanied by the following explanatory note:

This Order—
 (a) makes it an offence to breach Article 2 or 5 of Council Regulation (EC) No. 2271/96 of 22nd November 1996 protecting against the effects of the extraterritorial application of legislation adopted by a third country, and
 (b) disapplies sections 1(1) and (3), 2 and 6 of the Protection of Trading Interests Act 1980 to the extent that the Council Regulation applies.

The offence in (a) is punishable by an unlimited fine on indictment or a fine not exceeding the statutory maximum (currently £5,000) on summary conviction: these are the penalties imposed for breach of sections 1(1) and (3) and 2 of the 1980 Act, disapplied as in (b). The offence cannot be committed as a result of acts or omissions in another member state or the acts or omissions outside any member state of nationals of other member states, bodies incorporated in other member states, ship-owners with no relevant connection with the United Kingdom or individuals who were not resident in the United Kingdom at any relevant time.

Part Eight: III. B. *State territory and territorial jurisdiction—acquisition and transfer of territory—transfer*

Speaking on 24 September in the UN General Assembly, the Minister of State for Foreign and Commonwealth Relations, Mr Malcolm Rifkind, stated:

The peaceful transfer of sovereignty over a territory of six million free and prosperous people is an event unparalleled in modern times. A transfer on the basis of an international treaty—registered here at the United Nations—a Treaty between two members of the Security Council, which guarantees that for fifty years after 1997 there will be 'one country, two systems', and that the 'Hong Kong people will rule Hong Kong'.

(A/51/PV.6, p. 11)

Part Eight: IV. *State territory and territorial jurisdiction—regime under the Antarctic Treaty*

(See Part Nine: IX., below)

Part Nine: I. A. *Seas, waterways, ships—territorial sea—delimitation, baselines*

(See also Part One: II. D. 1. (item of 25 January 1996), above and Part Nine: X., below)

In a *démarche* dated 14 December 1994 addressed to the Islamic Republic of Iran, the German Embassy in Tehran, also on behalf of the EU, wrote in part:

The Embassy of the Federal Republic of Germany in Tehran presents its compliments to the Ministry of Foreign Affairs of the Islamic Republic of Iran and, on behalf of the European Union, has the honour to invite its attention to the following:

The European Union has examined the Act on the Marine Areas of the Islamic Republic of Iran in the Persian Gulf and in the Oman Sea adopted by the Islamic Republic of Iran on 2 May 1993. The Act refers, in the matter of baselines, to Decree No. 2/250–67 dated 31 Tir 1352 (22 July 1973) of the Council of Ministers.

The European Union notes that the Islamic Republic of Iran has employed the method of straight baselines along practically the entire coastline, even where it is not deeply indented and cut into and there is no fringe of islands along the coast in its immediate vicinity.

The European Union considers that although the United Nations Convention on the Law of the Sea, which entered into force on 16 November 1994, does not stipulate any maximum length for baseline segments, several of the segments where the straight baseline method has been employed by the Islamic Republic of Iran are excessively long.

The European Union would further recall that the islands may only be used in defining internal waters where they form part of a genuine system of straight baselines or where they constitute the line which delimits a bay.

. . .

The European Union considers that the aforementioned provisions of the Act of 2 May 1993 are not in conformity with the rules of international law, in particular articles 5, 7, . . . of the United Nations Convention on the Law of the Sea. Consequently, the States members of the Union reserve their position and their rights in respect of those provisions.

The acceding States, namely Austria, Finland and Sweden, endorse this démarche.

(*Law of the Sea Bulletin*, No. 31 (1996), pp. 60–1)

The Territorial Sea (Amendment) Order 1996 (Statutory Instruments 1996, No. 1628) was made on 26 June 1996 under powers conferred by the Territorial Sea Act 1987, and came into force on 1 August 1996. It revokes the Territorial Waters (Amendment) Order 1979 (UKMIL 1979, p. 366). An explanatory note attached to the Order reads as follows:

The Order amends the Schedule to the Territorial Waters Order in Council

1964 by redefining specified points between Cape Wrath and the Mull of Kintyre which are joined by geodesics to form baselines from which the breadth of the territorial sea adjacent thereto is measured. The amendments make minor changes to two points which have been shown to be necessary by the publication of a new larger scale chart of part of the area.

Part Nine: I. B. 1. *Seas, waterways, ships—territorial sea—legal status—right of innocent passage*

In a *démarche* dated 14 December 1994 addressed to the Islamic Republic of Iran, the German Embassy in Tehran, also on behalf of the EU, wrote:

The Embassy of the Federal Republic of Germany in Tehran presents its compliments to the Ministry of Foreign Affairs of the Islamic Republic of Iran and, on behalf of the European Union, has the honour to invite its attention to the following:

The European Union has examined the Act on the Marine Areas of the Islamic Republic of Iran in the Persian Gulf and in the Oman Sea adopted by the Islamic Republic of Iran on 2 May 1993. The Act refers, in the matter of baselines, to Decree No. 2/250–67 dated 31 Tir 1352 (22 July 1973) of the Council of Ministers.

. . .

It also notes that the Islamic Republic of Iran does not consider the passage of foreign vessels through its territorial sea to be innocent if they engage in any act aimed at collecting information prejudicial to the economic interests of the Islamic Republic of Iran (although article 19, paragraph 2(c), of the United Nations Convention on the Law of the Sea merely refers to the collecting of information to the prejudice of the defence or security of the coastal State) or any act of pollution of the marine environment contrary to the rules and regulations of the Islamic Republic of Iran (although article 19, paragraph 2 (h), of the United Nations Convention on the Law of the Sea merely refers to any act of wilful and serious pollution contrary to this Convention); that the Islamic Republic of Iran is subjecting the entry into its territorial sea of warships, submarines, nuclear-powered ships and vessels or any other floating objects or vessels carrying nuclear or other dangerous or noxious substances harmful to the environment to prior authorization, and that the Islamic Republic of Iran prohibits any activity in its exclusive economic zone and continental shelf that is inconsistent with its rights and interests.

The European Union considers that the aforementioned provisions of the Act of 2 May 1993 are not in conformity with the rules of international law, in particular articles . . . 19, 56, 58 and 78 of the United Nations Convention on the Law of the Sea. Consequently, the States members of the Union reserve their position and their rights in respect of those provisions.

The acceding States, namely Austria, Finland and Sweden, endorse this démarche.

(*Law of the Sea Bulletin*, No. 31 (1996), pp. 60–1)

Part Nine: VII. A. 1. *Seas, waterways, ships—the high seas—freedoms of the high seas—navigation*

The following paper, dated 23 October 1996, was submitted by the delegation of the UK to the Commission for the Conservation of Antarctic Marine Living Resources (CCAMLR):

PROPOSED VESSEL NOTIFICATION AND VESSEL MONITORING SYSTEMS: LEGAL BASIS

Delegation of the United Kingdom

At the 1995 meeting of the CCAMLR Commission certain reservations were expressed by some Parties about the legality of a CCAMLR Vessel Notification System (VNS) or Vessel Monitoring System (VMS). It was considered by those Parties that the approach proposed by the Secretariat (paragraph 2.41 of the SCOI Report) would be incompatible with general international law and with the UN Convention on the Law of the Sea of 1982 (UNCLOSC); in particular that requiring prior notification from vessels bound to or from the CCAMLR area (or navigating through it but not intending to fish or conduct fisheries research there) would be incompatible with the freedom of navigation on the high seas and in EEZs, as well as with the right of innocent passage through the territorial sea. The view was also expressed that CCAMLR was not a regional fisheries organisation, and that it was therefore not appropriate to follow approaches taken by such organisations. To do so would require an amendment to the Convention to transform CCAMLR into a regional fisheries organisation (CCAMLR-XIV, Annex 5, paragraph 2.43).
2.   This paper discussed the legal basis for the proposed systems, and the nature of CCAMLR.

VNS AND VMS SYSTEMS

3. Systems such as those proposed by the Secretariat have become well-established means of enhancing the ability of States to monitor the conduct of fishing vessels. They operate in various parts of the world, within territorial waters, EEZs and on the high seas.
4. Whereas a State may apply the systems to its flag vessels on the high seas, it may not do so for *foreign* flag vessels without the consent of the flag State. Consent can be given ad hoc, on a bilateral basis or in a multilateral agreement. Such an agreement could be reached regarding observation and inspection. Agreements relating to the conservation of marine living resources are encouraged by Article 118 of UNCLOSC. Such an agreement, as that reached in CCAMLR on observation and inspection, goes beyond merely conservation measures, such as TACs. It deals with the vitally important questions of compliance with the enforcement of conservation measures.
5. There is no legal barrier to a CCAMLR agreement on VNS and VMS being applied to CCAMLR members' flag vessels which are on the high seas bound to or from the CCAMLR area, or navigating through it without any intention of fishing or conducting fisheries research there. Requiring notification or monitor-

ing of them would not be in any way inconsistent with freedom of navigation, which is not an absolute right. Any State may agree that its flag vessels may be subject to requirements which limit the freedom. By agreeing to the establishment of a VNS or VMS system, a CCAMLR Member State would be accepting that, to the extent required for the effective operation of the systems, its flag vessels' movements would be reported or monitored. The fact that such a vessel may not be intending to fish or conduct fishery research in the CCAMLR area does not affect the position. That the vessel is bound to or from [or] navigating through, the CCAMLR area is reason enough to verify its position and intentions and to ensure that those intentions do not change during the passage of the vessel through the CCAMLR area.

NATURE OF CCAMLR

6. CCAMLR is without doubt a regional fisheries organisation. The fact that the title of the Convention refers to the 'conservation' of Antarctic marine living resources does not alter the substance of the Convention, for Article II of the Convention defines 'conservation' as including rational use i.e. harvesting. In a similar vein, Article 61 of UNCLOSC is entitled 'Conservation of the Living Resources' yet it is clear from its contents that this is no more than a general phrase to cover all aspects of fishing. For example, paragraph 1 requires a coastal State to 'determine the allowable catch of the living resources in its EEZ'. No two regional fishing organisations are alike, but one common factor is that they seek to control, generally by TACs, the harvesting of certain species.

(CCAMLR–XV/25—text provided by the FCO)

Part Nine: VII. F. *Seas, waterways, ships—the high seas—conservation of living resources*

The Joint Statement of the delegations of the UK and Mauritius Governments of 27 January 1994, which established a British–Mauritius Fisheries Commission, provided:

4. The definition of the maritime area in the waters of concern to the British Indian Ocean Territory (Chagos Archipelago), which the Commission will consider in relation to the conservation of fish stocks, will be agreed upon by both Governments.

On 17 March 1995, a Joint Communiqué was issued following the second meeting of the Commission. It read in part as follows:

8. Following on from discussions in the first meeting of the Joint Fisheries Commission and taking account of scientific advice, the Commission agreed to recommend to their governments, that the area of waters of concern to the Commission under paragraph 4 of the Joint Statement on the Conservation of Fisheries should be based on the area within the following points:

Latitude 0° 0′ (Equator), Longitude 53° 0′ East
Latitude 0° 0′ (Equator), Longitude 77° 0′ East

Latitude 25° 0' (South), Longitude 77° 0' East
Latitude 25° 0' (South), Longitude 53° 0' East

but excluding the Exclusive Economic Zones of the neighbouring countries. The area would therefore include the Fisheries Conservation and Management Zone of the BIOT (Chagos Archipelago), the Mauritian Exclusive Economic Zone and intervening international waters.

(Texts provided by the FCO)

Part Nine: VII. G. *Seas, waterways, ships—the high seas—pollution*

In moving the approval by the House of Lords of the draft Merchant Shipping (Prevention of Pollution) (Law of the Sea Convention) Order, the Parliamentary Under-Secretary of State, Department of Transport, Viscount Goschen, stated:

The Merchant Shipping (Prevention of Pollution) (Law of the Sea Convention) Order will help us to enforce the regulations on marine pollution from ships. Currently, we are only able to bring prosecutions for pollution offences which occur in our territorial waters. This is not a satisfactory state of affairs, as we are sometimes able to identify ships which pollute waters just outside the 12-mile limit. At present, our only recourse in such cases is to report the incident to the ship's flag state. Experience has demonstrated, however, that that is rarely an effective means of bringing sanctions against polluters.

This order will permit the Department of Transport to make regulations which will greatly increase our ability to prosecute polluters. As proposed by the inquiry of the noble and learned Lord, Lord Donaldson, we will take powers to the maximum extent consistent with international law. That will allow us to bring prosecutions for illegal discharges which occur up to 200 miles from the UK coastline. We will also introduce provisions to enhance our co-operation with neighbouring states by making it possible for UK courts to prosecute ships which have polluted other states' waters.

(HL Debs., vol. 568, col. 1179: 25 January 1996)

In reply to questions, the Parliamentary Under-Secretary of State, Department of Transport, wrote:

The 1969 international convention on civil liability for oil pollution damage and the 1971 international convention on the establishment of an international fund for compensation for oil pollution damage, implemented in the United Kingdom by the Merchant Shipping Act 1995, provide for compensation for pollution damage caused by spills from vessels carrying oil in bulk. The criteria for admissibility of these claims is described in the claims manual produced by the International Oil Pollution Compensation Fund. Copies of the claims manual have been placed in the Library of the House.

(HC Debs., vol. 274, WA, col. *103*: 19 March 1996)

Part Nine: VII. H. *Seas, waterways, ships—the high seas—jurisdiction*

In reply to the question what representations Her Majesty's Government had made 'to countries in South America and the Caribbean about the anti-drug work of the West Indies guardship, its access to territorial waters and its powers to board vessels registered in these countries', the Minister of State, FCO, wrote:

We have made no such representations regarding the West Indies guardship—WIGS. I have, however, made representations to the Venezuelan Government, following the refusal by the Venezuelan authorities to grant permission to the Royal Fleet Auxiliary Gold Rover, which operates in support of WIGS, for US law enforcement officers embarked on the RFA to board a Venezuelan flagged vessel suspected of drug trafficking. I made clear this Government's view that article 17 of the 1988 UN drugs convention, which the United Kingdom and Venezuela have ratified, provides the legal framework for maritime anti-narcotics co-operation.

(HC Debs., vol. 287, WA, col. *20*: 9 December 1996)

Part Nine: VIII. *Seas, waterways, ships—continental shelf*

(See also Part Nine: XIV., below)

On 27 June 1996, the Governments of the United Kingdom and France signed an Agreement on Maritime Delimitation concerning Montserrat and Guadeloupe (Cm 3359). In the preamble to the Agreement (which is not yet in force), the parties recognised 'the need to delimit in a precise and equitable manner the maritime areas between the United Kingdom (Montserrat) and the French Republic (Guadeloupe)'. The Agreement reads in material part as follows:

ARTICLE 1

The maritime delimitation between the United Kingdom (Montserrat) and the French Republic (Department of Guadeloupe) shall be based on the principle of equidistance. Delimitation shall be effected by using the baselines from which the territorial sea of each State is measured.

ARTICLE 2

1. The maritime delimitation referred to in Article 1 shall be formed by geodesic lines joining, in the order in which they are given, the following points identified by their geographical co-ordinates:

Point 1	15° 50' 31"N	62° 48' 50"W
Point 2	15° 56' 54"N	62° 38' 58"W
Point 3	16° 07' 41"N	62° 24' 19"W
Point 4	16° 25' 52"N	62° 03' 10"W
Point 5	16° 39' 28"N	61° 51' 04"W

2. The geographical co-ordinates given in this Article are expressed in the geodesic reference system WGS 84 (World Geodesic System 1984).

3. This line has been drawn by way of illustration on the map in the Annex to this Agreement [reproduced at p. 783].

ARTICLE 3

It has not been possible, for the time being, to complete the maritime delimitation beyond point 5. It is however agreed between the Parties that the delimitation between point 5 and the tripoint between the maritime areas under the jurisdiction respectively of the Parties and of Antigua and Barbuda shall be completed at the appropriate time by applying the same methods as those used to determine the limit between points 1 to 5.

On 27 June 1996, the Governments of the United Kingdom and France signed an Agreement on Maritime Delimitation concerning Anguilla, on the one hand, and Saint Martin and Saint Barthelemy, on the other (Cm 3360).

In the preamble to the Agreement (which is not yet in force), the parties recognised 'the need to delimit in a precise and equitable manner the maritime areas between the United Kingdom (Anguilla) and the French Republic (Saint Martin and Saint Barthelemy)'. The Agreement reads in material part as follows:

ARTICLE 1

The maritime delimitation between the United Kingdom (Anguilla) and the French Republic (Saint Martin and Saint Barthelemy) shall be based on the principle of equidistance. Delimitation shall be effected by using the baselines from which the territorial sea of each State is measured.

ARTICLE 2

1. The maritime delimitation referred to in Article 1 shall be formed by geodesic lines joining, in the order in which they are given, the following points identified by their geographical co-ordinates:

Point 1	17° 57' 35"N	63° 36' 57"W
Point 2	18° 02' 03"N	63° 28' 26"W
Point 3	18° 05' 53"N	63° 12' 34"W
Point 4	18° 10' 51"N	62° 56' 55"W
Point 5	18° 11' 25"N	62° 52' 35"W
Point 6	18° 09' 21"N	62° 44' 22"W
Point 7	18° 13' 19"N	62° 29' 46"W
Point 8	18° 18' 29"N	62° 13' 59"W

2. The geographical co-ordinates given in this Article are expressed in the geodesic reference system WGS 84 (World Geodesic System 1984).

3. This line has been drawn by way of illustration on the map in the Annex to this Agreement [reproduced at p. 784].

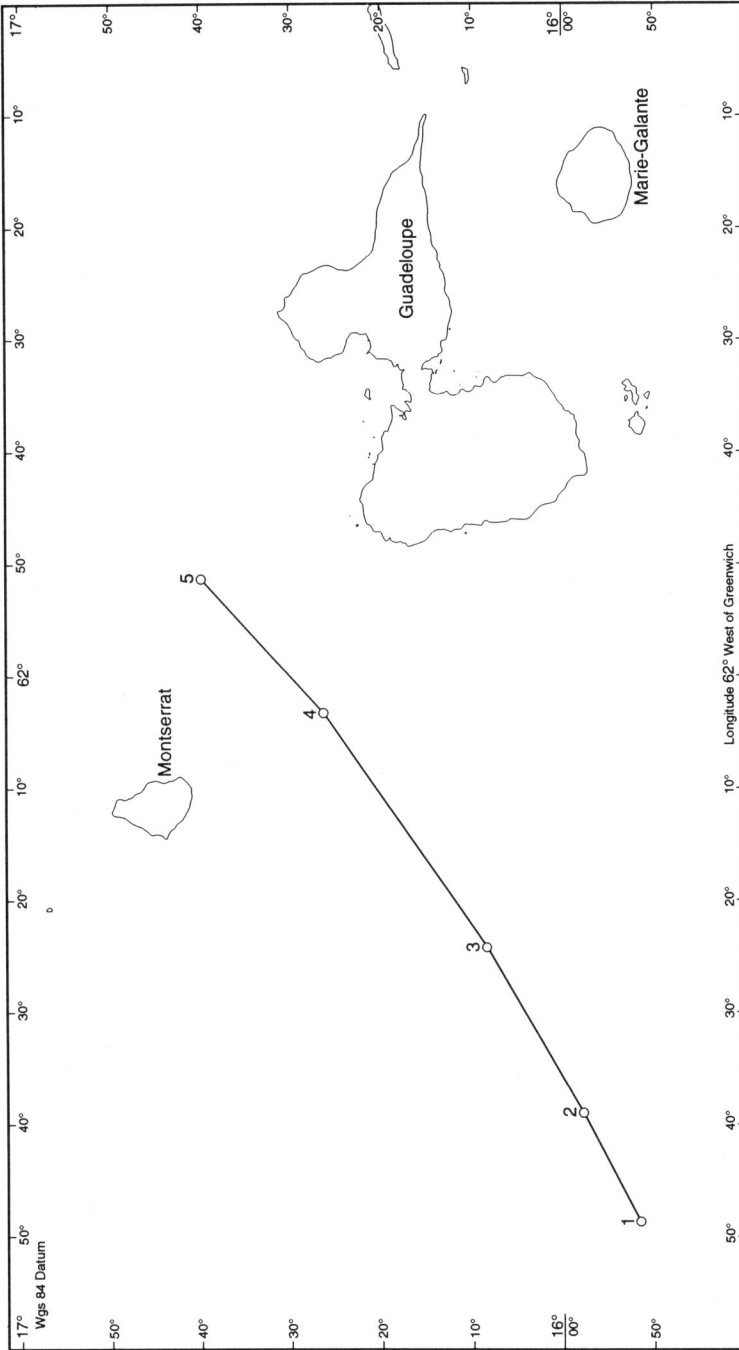

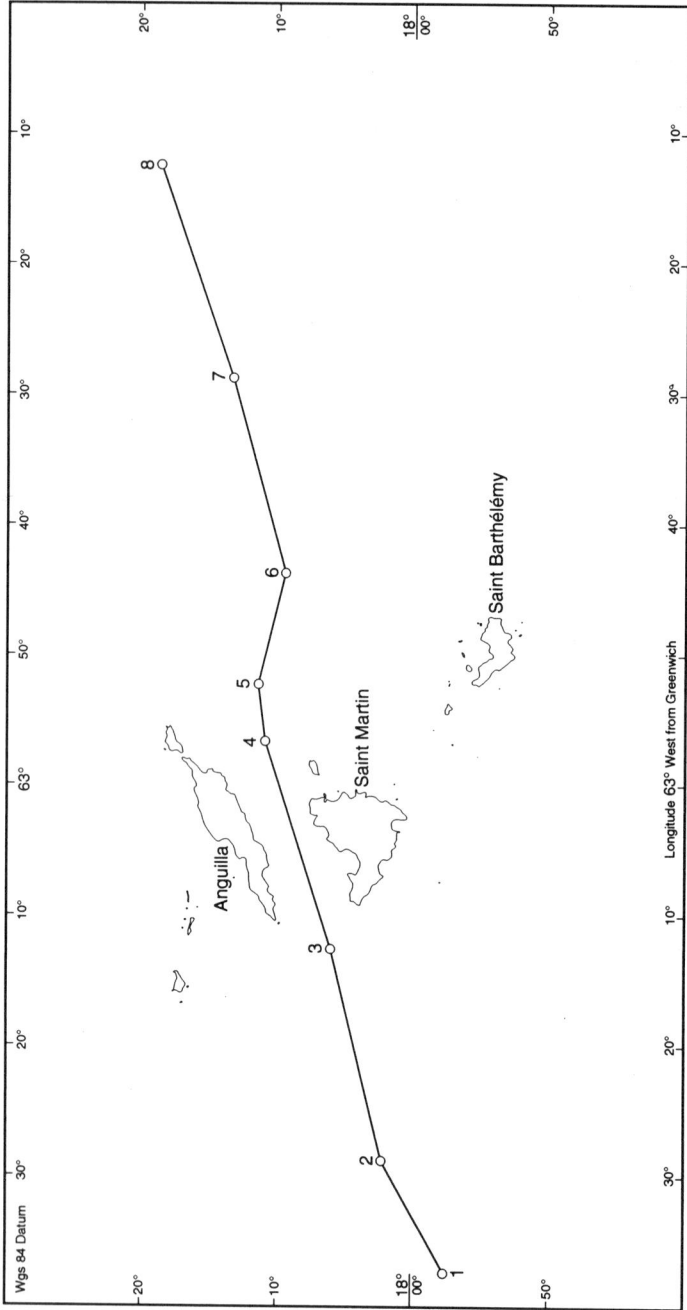

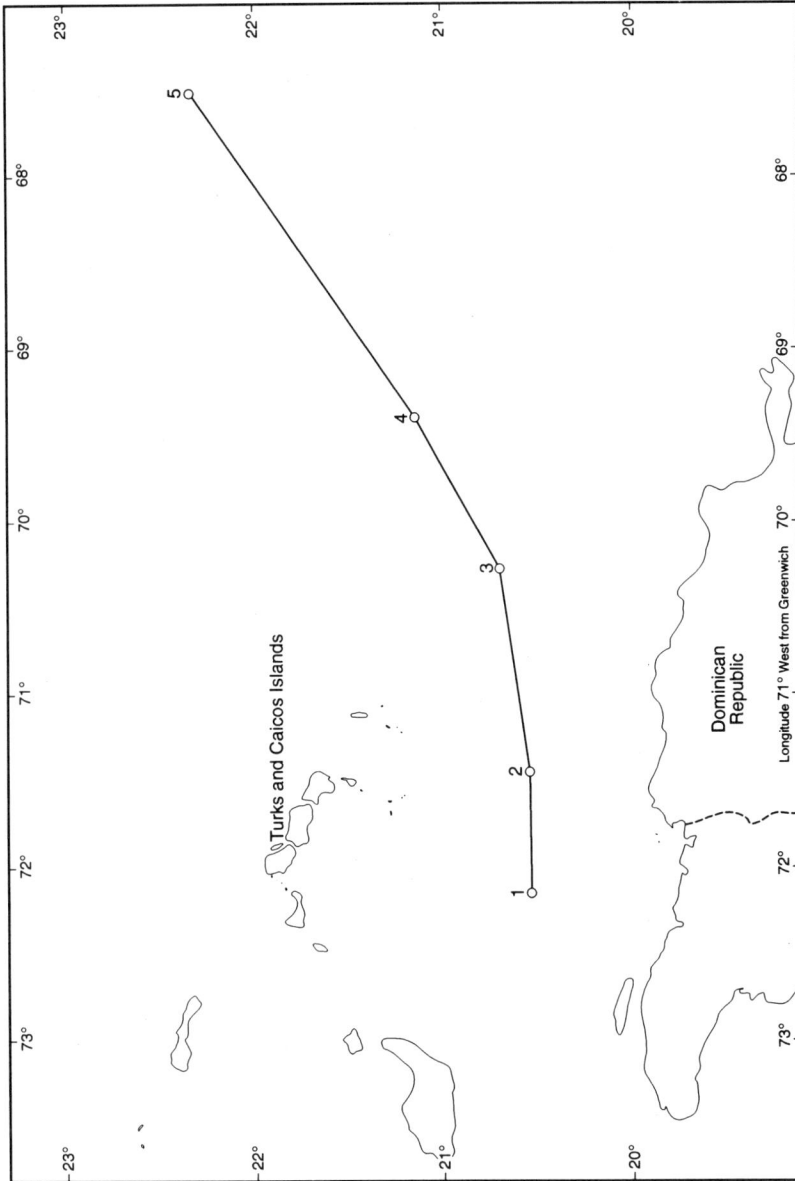

ARTICLE 3

It has not been possible, for the time being, to complete the maritime delimitation before point 1 and beyond point 8. It is, however, agreed between the Parties that the delimitation:

(a) from point 1 to the tripoint between the limits of the maritime areas under the jurisdiction respectively of the Parties and of the Kingdom of the Netherlands, and

(b) From point 8 to the tripoint between the limits of the maritime areas under the respective jurisdiction of the Parties and of Antigua and Barbuda,

shall be completed at the appropriate time by applying the same methods as those used to determine the limit between points 1 and 8.

On 2 August 1996, the Governments of the UK and the Dominican Republic signed an Agreement on Maritime Delimitation (Cm 3461). In the preamble to the Agreement (which is not yet in force), the parties expressed the wish 'to delimit the maritime areas between the Dominican Republic and the Turks and Caicos Islands in accordance with the principles of international law'. The Agreement reads in material part:

ARTICLE 1

(1) The maritime boundary between the Dominican Republic and the Turks and Caicos Islands shall be a geodesic line joining in the order specified the points listed in the Schedule to this Agreement [not reproduced].

(2) The boundary line defined in paragraph 1 is illustrated on the chart annexed to this Agreement [reproduced at p. 785].

Part Nine: VIIIa. *Seas, waterways, ships—inland seas and lakes*

The following question was asked of Her Majesty's Government:

Whether a legal regime for the Caspian Sea and for the exploitation of its resources has yet been agreed; whether in their view the status of that sea and its seabed is a matter to be resolved by the littoral states of the Caspian Sea themselves; whether they consider it appropriate that the Azerbaijan Government should dispose of oil from the seabed of the Caspian without consulting the governments of the other littoral states; and meanwhile under what legal regime the relevant British firms are preparing to engage in exploitation of the oil resources there?

In reply, the Government spokesman in the House of Lords wrote:

The legal status of the Caspian Sea and its seabed is not clearly defined in international law. There is, as yet, no generally agreed view of its status among the littoral states, to whom it falls to resolve that matter. Her Majesty's Government consider that, whatever the outcome of the debate on the Caspian

Sea's status, commitments under existing contracts on exploitation of the Caspian's resources should not be called into question.

(HL Debs., vol. 568, *WA 96*: 29 January 1996)

Part Nine: IX. *Seas, waterways, ships—exclusive fishery zone*

(See also Parts Nine: VII. A. 1 and Nine VII. F., above)

The following letter, dated 22 March 1996, was sent by Sir Nicholas Bonsor, Minister of State, FCO, to Sir Michael Shersby MP:

I promised to write to you with a fuller explanation of our policy towards fishing around South Georgia.

Fish stocks in sub-Antarctic waters were fished heavily in the 1960s and 1970s and there was serious concern about overfishing. A multilateral treaty, the Convention for the Conservation of Antarctic Marine Living Resources (CCAMLR), was concluded in 1980 primarily to deal with the problem of overfishing throughout the sub-Antarctic area. That area includes in FAO sub-area 48.3 the waters around South Georgia.

The Commission established by the Convention adopts each year conservation measures binding on its Member States. But the Commission has no enforcement powers, and it is left primarily to flag States to ensure that their vessels comply with the conservation measures. However, the Convention recognises that Parties to it with islands within its area of application may exercise coastal state jurisdiction in respect of their islands. Such jurisdiction may be exercised in respect of all vessels, including those of countries which are not Parties to the Convention e.g. Belize and Panama. The exercise of such jurisdiction with respect to important fishing grounds in the waters around such islands is therefore a particularly effective way of enforcing the CCAMLR conservation measures.

Accordingly, in 1993 a 200 nm Maritime Zone was proclaimed around South Georgia and the South Sandwich Islands (SGSSI), and a Fisheries (Conservation and Management) Ordinance enacted by the Commissioner of SGSSI. This provides for comprehensive regulation of fishing within the Zone. In particular, licences are required for fishing and granted only in a manner consistent with the conservation measures adopted by the CCAMLR Commission, and this is abundantly clear from the terms of the Ordinance. The licences are conditional on the observation of the appropriate CCAMLR Conservation Measures e.g. type of fishing gear allowed, season opening and closing dates and measures to avoid incidental killing of seabirds.

Fisheries Protection Vessels, and RN vessels, patrol the zone. Vessels found fishing illegally are arrested and their operators prosecuted. There have been four prosecutions since 1993.

The 1995 season for toothfish began on 1 March. In order to avoid the Total Allowable Catch (TAC)—set by the CCAMLR Commission for the whole area at 4000 tonnes—being exceeded, the Government of SGSSI limited the number of licences available to 10 licences, although there was greater demand. Experience has shown that to issue an unlimited number of licences would be counter-productive as the economic returns on catches would be low and that in turn only encourages illegal fishing after the TAC has been reached.

The SGSSI legislation has always applied to all vessels, including Argentine-registered vessels. Until last year when a small number of Argentine-vessels reported to CCAMLR (after the season had closed) fishing catches taken from inside the SGSSI Zone, no Argentine vessels had fished in the Zone. This year it became evident that several Argentine flag vessels were intending to fish in the Zone without applying for a licence. We believe that many of them were in fact not Argentine-owned but were Chileans reflagging in order to gain access to new grounds.

In short, we believe that Argentine-registered vessels were going to be used this season in a way which would not only have breached SGSSI law but, if nothing were done by SGSSI, would have seriously undermined the credibility of the Convention and threatened the conservation of fragile fish stocks. It was therefore right, both legally and politically, to insist that owners of *all* vessels apply for licences.

(Text provided by the FCO)

In reply to a question, the Minister of State, FCO, wrote:

Her Majesty's Government and the Government of South Georgia and the South Sandwich Islands are determined to protect the South Georgia fishery. The waters around South Georgia fall within the area of the convention for the conservation of Antarctic marine living resources. The CCAMLR Commission regulates fishing in the area by means of conservation measures. In order to enforce these measures more effectively, because of serious concern about fishing in the area in recent years in violation of the conservation measures, the Commissioner for South Georgia introduced legislation in 1993 establishing a maritime zone around South Georgia. This requires operators of fishing vessels to acquire licences in order to fish and provides for enforcement measures such as arrest of vessels and prosecution for unlicensed fishing. The legislation and the enforcement of it is in full conformity with international law and CCAMLR convention.

(HC Debs., vol. 274, WA, col. *386*: 22 March 1996)

In the course of a debate on the subject of Antarctica, the Minister of State, FCO, Sir Nicholas Bonsor, stated:

I refer next to South Georgia and the South Sandwich Islands and to the convention on the conservation of Antarctic marine living resources—which was not specifically raised by the hon. Member for Islington, North but is important in this context. I wrote to my hon. Friend for Uxbridge (Sir M. Shersby) on 22 March with a full explanation of our policy towards fishing around South Georgia. A copy of that letter has been placed in the Library. I am grateful for the additional opportunity to point out the steps that we have taken to ensure the conservation of fish stocks around South Georgia—something to which I attach particular importance, as I do to the conservation of all stocks in the Antarctic sea area. I know that sentiment is shared by the hon. Gentleman.

We are in no doubt about our sovereignty over South Georgia and the South Sandwich Islands, and hence our right to exercise coastal state jurisdiction around the islands. Fishing in sub-Antarctic waters, including the waters around South Georgia, is regulated by a multilateral treaty—the convention on the conservation of Antarctic marine living resources, or CCAMLR. The commission established by the convention adopts conservation measures binding on its member states, but the commission has no enforcement powers. It is left to flag states to ensure that their vessels comply with the conservation measures. The commission was established in 1980, but flag state enforcement of the conservation measures has been largely ineffective. Over-fishing continued throughout the 1980s and into the 1990s and was increasing.

Non-members of the convention are not bound by the conservation measures, but the convention recognises that parties to it with sovereign islands within its area of application may exercise coastal state jurisdiction in respect of those islands. Such jurisdiction may be exercised in respect of all vessels, including those of countries that are not parties to the convention.

In recognition of the continuing threat posed by over-fishing to the conservation of the fish stocks, a 200-nautical mile maritime zone was proclaimed in 1993 around South Georgia and the South Sandwich Islands. A fisheries ordinance was enacted, which provides for comprehensive regulation of fishing within the zone. Licences are required for fishing there. Licences are granted only in a manner consistent with the conservation measures adopted by the CCAMLR commission.

. . .

Argentina asserts that our licensing regime is a new development that impinges on the fishing activities of Argentine-flagged vessels. The licensing regime operated by the Government of the territory has been no different this season from that in force in the previous two seasons. Since the introduction of the fisheries ordinance, all vessels have been required to obtain a licence before fishing in the waters around South Georgia. Unlicensed vessels are subject to arrest and prosecution.

This year it was apparent that a number of vessels, including several Argentine-flagged vessels, intended to target this limited fishery, and that this number was far greater than the total allowable catch could withstand. The projection was for a fishing pressure of about 40 vessels, targeting a 4,000 tonne TAC. There would have been three results: first, a rapid exhaustion of the allowable catch; secondly, an uneconomic take for the majority, if not all, of the vessels involved; and, thirdly, there would have been the inevitable risk of large-scale illegal fishing as vessels attempted to ensure viable, economic returns on their fishing efforts.

The South Georgia licensing regime does not preclude vessels from fishing unhindered outside of South Georgia waters. But with due regard to the TAC, and other conservation measures, the commissioner for South Georgia limited the number of licences available to 10, although there was far greater demand. Licences were required by Chilean, Korean, Russian and US vessels. In addition, one Argentine vessel voluntarily applied for, and was granted, a licence. The vessel operator subsequently arranged to transfer the licence to another non-Argentine vessel as part of a commercial arrangement. The allegation that we put pressure on the vessel to apply for a licence was wholly unfounded.

The South Georgia fisheries regime is legal in terms of our international obligations under the convention on the conservation of Antarctic marine living resources. Moreover it is wholly consistent with the convention in terms of its conservation measures.

(HC Debs., vol. 275, cols. 489–92: 3 April 1996)

On 13 March 1996, the Government of Chile sent the following message to the Executive Secretary of the Commission for the Conservation of Antarctic Marine Living Resources (CCAMLR) in Hobart, Australia:

On March 6 this year, while the Chilean flag vessel *Antonio Lorenzo* was in Statistical Subarea 48.3 of the Commission for the Conservation of Antarctic Marine Living Resources (CCAMLR) in compliance with the provisions of CCAMLR Conservation Measure 93/XIV, it was detained by vessels from the United Kingdom.

The British Government has indicated to the Chilean Government that the reason for the arrest was that the vessel was not carrying a fishing licence issued by the Government of South Georgia and the South Sandwich Islands.

In this regard, we would like to begin by notifying the Secretariat that before the opening of the current fishing season the Government of Chile had made representations to the British Government that it is inadmissible, within the framework of CCAMLR, to apply measures limiting the number of vessels and to charge for fishing licences, as has been done on this occasion.

In view of the above, Chile was surprised at this arrest and in consequence was obliged to express its protest to the United Kingdom, explaining the need to release the vessel as soon as possible, thus allowing vessels flying the Chilean flag which comply with the regulatory measures of CCAMLR as is the case of the *Antonio Lorenzo*, to carry out normal fishing activities in this fishery.

In informing the Secretariat of this situation, Chile also wishes to advise that it is at present undertaking an analysis of the scope of CCAMLR in order to decide whether it is possible to use the latter's mechanisms to find a solution for this impasse, which is adversely affecting the fishing interests of Chile, thus avoiding the repetition of similar irregular incidents in the abovementioned area in the future.

In view of the above, the Government of Chile requests the Executive Secretary to inform the Chairman of CCAMLR and its Members of this situation.

On the same day, the Government of Argentina sent the following message to the Executive Secretary:

The intent of the United Kingdom to exercise unilateral jurisdiction over matters pertaining to fisheries in waters adjacent to the South Georgia and South Sandwich Islands which fall within Statistical Subareas 48.3 and 48.4 of the Convention for the Conservation of the Antarctic Marine Living Resources has come to the attention of the Republic of Argentina.

The Republic of Argentina has officially reiterated its rejection of these pretensions by the United Kingdom and has reasserted its sovereign rights over the aforementioned islands and their related maritime areas.

Also, the Republic of Argentina has informed the United Kingdom that its pretensions are contrary to the Convention for the Conservation of the Antarctic Marine Living Resources, contrary to International Law in general, particularly to the Law of the Sea, and might, in consequence, give rise to repercussions in terms of international responsibility.

The Government of the Republic of Argentina has also mentioned to the United Kingdom that, considering the current situation, it might be appropriate to resort to the mechanisms of peaceful resolution of dispute outlined in Article XXV of the Convention. Accordingly it has invited the United Kingdom to hold urgent consultations in order to initiate immediate negotiations aimed at resolving this disagreement.

This mechanism, naturally, does not exclude the timely intervention of the Commission for the Conservation of Antarctic Marine Living Resources, so that it can become cognisant of the history of the problem and exercise its authority in accordance with the Convention.

The opportunity for this intervention will arise at the XV Meeting of the Commission. However the Republic of Argentina reserves its right to make use of other mechanisms envisaged in the Convention, depending on the circumstances.

The Republic of Argentina requests the urgent distribution of this note to all Members of the Commission.

On 14 March 1996, the Government of Argentina sent the following further message to the Executive Secretary:

The unlawful arrest of the Chilean flag vessel *Antonio Lorenzo* in Statistical Subarea 48.3 by vessels from the United Kingdom of Great Britain and Northern Ireland while it was conducting fishing activities in accordance with the Convention for the Conservation of the Antarctic Marine Living Resources and its later transfer to the Malvinas/Falkland Islands have been damaging to both the Convention and the International Scheme of Scientific Observation established by this Convention.

The Republic of Argentina has become aware of the fact that the CCAMLR International Scientific Observer designated by the Republic of Argentina to undertake work on board the *Antonio Lorenzo* has been taken to the Malvinas/Falkland Islands where he remains deprived of his liberty in that he is forbidden to disembark and has had severe restrictions imposed on his means of communication.

The Republic of Argentina points out that these types of action breach the letter and spirit of the Convention for the Conservation of the Antarctic Marine Living Resources, and particularly the rules pertaining to the International Scheme of Scientific Observation.

Hindering the work of an International Scientific Observer designated in accordance with the Convention for the Conservation of Antarctic Marine Living Resources while carrying out duties in compliance with Conservation Measures in force which have been adopted by the Commission, constitutes an act of discrimination which, in view of its severity may seriously affect the proper operation of the Convention and the fulfilment of its objectives.

It is the opinion of the Republic of Argentina that all Members should be informed as soon as possible when events of this nature take place. Therefore it is requested that this note be circulated by the Secretariat without delay.

(Texts provided by the FCO)

In response, the Polar Regions Section, South Atlantic and Antarctic Department, FCO, sent to the Executive Secretary two letters, dated 8 May 1996, the first of which read in material part as follows:

SOUTH GEORGIA AND THE SOUTH SANDWICH ISLANDS: COMMUNICATION
FROM CHILE

I refer to your circular letter (COMM CIRC 96/16) of 15 March 1996, to which was attached a letter dated 13 March from the Government of Chile.

The letter refers to the arrest last month in the Maritime Zone of South Georgia and the South Sandwich Islands (SGSSI) of a Chilean-registered fishing vessel, the *Antonio Lorenzo*. The vessel was arrested for fishing without a licence, but has been released on the posting of a bond. The owners have been charged with offences under SGSSI fishing legislation. As indicated in the letter of 13 March, the Government of Chile has protested to the British Government about the arrest.

The Chilean letter refers to representations made to the British Government regarding the limitation by the Government of the SGSSI on the number of vessels licensed to fish in the SGSSI Maritime Zone as from 1 March this year, and about the charges made for licences. The requirement to acquire a licence and the limitation of effort has existed since the SGSSI fisheries regime was established in 1993. These measures are in conformity with the 1980 Chairman's Statement.

We do not accept therefore that it is incompatible with CCAMLR to apply such measures, and a detailed explanation of the background to the exercise of coastal State jurisdiction by the Government of SGSSI and its compatibility with CCAMLR is contained in my letter of today's date in reply to letters to you from the Government of Argentina.

The decision by the Government of SGSSI to limit the number of vessels licensed to fish for *Dissostichus eleginoides* in the SGSSI Maritime Zone was taken in conformity with the 1980 Chairman's Statement, and with due regard to the TAC set by the CCAMLR Commission for sub-area 48.3. This year it was apparent that the number of longliners intending to target this limited fishery was far greater than the TAC could withstand. The projection was for a fishing presence of around 40 vessels targeting a 4,000 tonne TAC. The result would have been three-fold: a rapid exhaustion of the allowable catch, an uneconomic take for the majority, if not all, vessels involved, and the inevitable risk of large scale illegal fishing as vessels attempted to ensure viable, economic returns on their fishing effort. In order to reduce fishing pressure, at least within that part of sub-area 48.3 which lies within the territory's zone, the Government of the territory limited the number of licences available to 10, although there was greater demand. This clearly did not preclude vessels from fishing unhindered in the remainder of sub-area 48.3 in conformity with CCAMLR conservation measures.

The second letter read as follows:

SOUTH GEORGIA AND THE SOUTH SANDWICH ISLANDS: COMMUNICATIONS FROM
ARGENTINA

I refer to your circular letter (COMM CIRC 96/16) of 15 March 1996 to which were attached two letters received from the Government of Argentina.

. . .

Management and Conservation

The CCAMLR Commission adopts each year conservation measures binding on its Members. But the Commission has no enforcement powers. Rather flag States have a duty to ensure that their vessels comply with the conservation measures; and Coastal States play an important part in ensuring compliance.

It became increasingly obvious by the early 1990s that a considerable amount of fishing in contravention of the conservation measures was being carried out, especially in sub-area 48.3. Some was being done by vessels of non-CCAMLR Members, but the majority was done by vessels registered in CCAMLR States. The effect was to undermine the objectives of the Convention. Attempts by the Commission to prevent this were not successful and the problem increased.

Legislation of South Georgia and the South Sandwich Islands

In order to deal more effectively with the problem of overfishing and its impact on stocks, a 200 nm Maritime Zone was proclaimed in 1993 around South Georgia and the South Sandwich Islands, and a Fisheries (Conservation and Management) Ordinance enacted by the Commissioner of the territory. This provides for comprehensive regulation of fishing within the Zone. In particular, licences are required for fishing and are granted in a manner consistent with the conservation measures adopted by the CCAMLR Commission. This is abundantly clear from the terms of the Ordinance which includes numerous references to the Convention, its principles and objectives. The licences are conditional on the observation of the appropriate conservation measures e.g. type of fishing gear allowed, season opening and closing dates and measures to avoid incidental killing of seabirds. Fisheries protection vessels patrol the Zone. Vessels found fishing illegally are subject to arrest and prosecution. There have been four prosecutions since 1993, including one of a vessel registered in a non-CCAMLR State.

By the enactment of this legislation, and its enforcement, the Government of the territory is better able to enforce the conservation measures adopted by the Commission in respect of any vessel, whether or not it is registered in a CCAMLR State.

In any discussion of conservation measures, one should draw a clear distinction between the adoption of measures by the CCAMLR Commission and their actual enforcement. Mere adoption of a measure is no guarantee that it is going to be respected by fishermen. That can only be ensured by putting in place provisions for enforcing the measures by practical and effective means. This is what has been done by the Government of the territory. But the legislation also makes it clear that the regulations on fishing do not apply to that area of the South Georgia and the South Sandwich Islands Zone which is south of latitude 60° south ie within the Antarctic Treaty Area; nor is there any restriction in the Zone on vessels engaged in bona fide scientific research activities which have been notified to the CCAMLR Secretariat.

Coastal State jurisdiction

The right to enact and enforce such legislation derives from the right of the United Kingdom to exercise coastal State jurisdiction in respect of the territory. The Convention recognises this right. Sub-paragraph 2(b) of Article IV by its terms recognises that Parties may exercise coastal state jurisdiction in respect of islands within the area of application of CCAMLR.

In respect of those islands there is provision for a modified regime. The Final Act of the Conference on the Conservation of Antarctic Marine Living Resources includes the text of a formal statement made by the Chairman of the Conference on 19 May 1980 (the so-called 'Chairman's Statement') regarding the application of CCAMLR to the waters adjacent to the French islands of Kerguelen and Crozet. The statement sets out four understandings, followed by a final paragraph which provides that the understandings

'also apply to waters adjacent to the islands within the area to which the Convention applies over which the existence of State sovereignty is recognised by all Contracting Parties'.

The Final Act records that no objection was made to the statement.

In interpreting the CCAMLR Convention one must have regard to

'any agreement relating to the treaty which was made between all the parties in connexion with the conclusion of the treaty'

(*Vienna Convention on the Law of Treaties 1969*, Article 31(2) (a)).

The Chairman's Statement falls squarely within this provision. (See also the statement by Australia on 3 November 1995 at the Fourteenth Meeting of the CCAMLR Commission.)

The phrase 'over which the existence of State sovereignty is recognised by all Contracting Parties' was most carefully formulated. Its purpose was to cover those islands which Parties agreed were subject to the sovereignty of some State even though another may claim it. The key phrase is 'the existence of'. It is the recognition of the *existence* of State sovereignty which is referred to, not the recognition of the sovereignty of a particular State.

Application of the understandings in the Chairman's Statement to South Georgia waters

Accordingly, the application of the four understandings in the Chairman's Statement to South Georgia waters has the following effects:

(1) National conservation measures in effect for South Georgia before the coming into force of CCAMLR remain in effect until modified by the territory acting within the framework of CCAMLR, or otherwise.

Such national measures do not have to be internationally recognised. (South Georgia had laws relating to marine living resources in its territorial sea prior to the entry into force of the CCAMLR.)

(2) The United Kingdom may exclude South Georgia waters from the area of application of a specific conservation measure under consideration by the CCAMLR Commission, and the territory may adopt national measures for those waters. (This has been done by other Parties in respect of their islands on a number of occasions.)

(3) When the United Kingdom participates in discussions within the CCAMLR Commission on conservation measures, it can nevertheless authorise national measures for South Georgia which are either more strict than those eventually adopted by the Commission, or which deal with other matters. (For example the territory has promulgated more extensive data collection requirements.) If consensus cannot be reached within the Commission, the territory is free to promulgate any national measures for South Georgia which it deems appropriate.

(4) Enforcement of measures, whether adopted under CCAMLR or national measures, in respect of South Georgia waters, is done by the territory. Observation and inspection measures in those waters are subject to the agreement of the territory. (The territory does not, however, exclude from its waters the System of Observation adopted under CCAMLR.)

The Antonio Lorenzo

The Argentine letter of 14 March refers to the arrest of the Antonio Lorenzo, a Chilean-registered fishing vessel. Please see my letter of today's date to you in answer to a letter from the Government of Chile on this matter.

The arrest of the vessel did not infringe in any way the rights of the CCAMLR Scientific Observer who was on board at the time. The presence of such an observer affords no immunity to the vessel in respect of infringements of CCAMLR conservation measures or national legislation enforcing them. In view of the immigration regulations, the observer in question was asked whether he wished to leave the Falkland Islands by air or remain on board the vessel until it sailed. The UK kept the Argentine Government in touch with developments. The observer chose to remain on the vessel. During that time he was free to communicate by any means available to him.

(Texts provided by the FCO)

On 31 October 1996, the UK delegation made the following observations at the 15th Meeting of the CCAMLR held at Hobart, Australia:

The right of the United Kingdom to exercise coastal state jurisdiction is rooted in Article IV (2) (b) of the Convention and paragraph 5 of the Chairman's Statement. Paragraph 5 includes the critical phrase

'over which the *existence* of state sovereignty is recognised by all Contracting Parties'.

This was most carefully formulated. Its sole purpose was to cover the islands which Parties accept are subject to the sovereignty of some state, even though there may be a dispute as to which. It is the recognition of the *existence* of state sovereignty which is referred to, not the recognition of the sovereignty of a particular state. There is no doubt that South Georgia and the South Sandwich Islands is sovereign territory, nor that the United Kingdom exercises sovereignty over it *de facto*, and we of course believe *de jure*.

Like Argentina, we have no wish to bring a discussion on sovereignty before this Commission, but the Commission will understand that the interpretation of the Chairman's Statement is intimately liked to the sovereignty question. The reason the issue of the exercise of coastal state jurisdiction cannot be resolved is because of Argentina's claim to sovereignty.

As we have indicated in our note of 6 September, the United Kingdom offered to take the sovereignty dispute to the International Court of Justice in the 1950s. A formal application was made to the Court. That Argentina rejected this offer was unfortunate. Had they not done so none of us would be in the position we find ourselves today.

A word commonly used yesterday during the debate on the Chilean Agenda Item 12 was 'harmonisation'. In seeking to integrate the national legislation of South Georgia with the multilateral Conservation Measures of CCAMLR, we have been acutely aware of the need for harmonisation. If Parties study the fisheries legislation of South Georgia, they will see that it is explicitly linked to CCAMLR. It contains references to the Convention, to its principles and objectives, and to its Conservation Measures. The Commissioner for South Georgia and the Director of Fisheries are required by the legislation to carry out their functions in accordance with the Conservation Measures.

In addition, and in explicit recognition of the Antarctic Treaty regime, the South Georgia legislation on fisheries is *not* applied south of 60 degrees of latitude—that is into the Antarctic Treaty area. Moreover, within our Maritime Zone there is no hindrance of those scientific research activities which have been notified to the Secretariat of this Commission under the provisions of Conservation Measure 64/XII.

But our regime, though intimately linked to CCAMLR, is not worthless. We all know that the management of fisheries worldwide cannot rely on the goodwill and altruism of fishermen. Sound management is only possible through *effective enforcement* of the measures this Commission adopts. The fisheries laws of South Georgia and the South Sandwich Islands are complementary to, and in no way conflict with, the Conservation Measures that we adopt in this Commission.

That we enforce those measures through the imposition of a licensing regime is nothing new. Since the turn of the century, South Georgia, as a territory of the United Kingdom, has managed harvesting of marine living resources (i.e. whaling and sealing) through leasing and licensing arrangements, both in South Georgia and in its territorial waters. Companies involved with this include those from at least three members of this Commission, in addition to ourselves.

The United Kingdom extended its maritime jurisdiction in 1993 in response to the actions by Argentina in 1991, when its baselines law purported to claim a 200 mile EEZ for South Georgia. Our actions are wholly consistent with UNCLOS and CCAMLR.

What prompted us to take further action in 1993, through the introduction of fisheries legislation, was the increasing level of illegal fishing of *Dissostichus* in our waters. A brief glance through the reports of the Commission will show that the United Kingdom has not been backward in bringing our concerns on this to the attention of the Commission. Those concerns included activities by both vessels of Member and non-Member states.

But unfortunately our concerns were not adequately addressed. Flag States have apparently been unable to deal with the matter with sufficient vigour. Accordingly, to ensure greater conservation of stocks, we felt compelled to take action as a coastal state. Furthermore it is only by use of coastal state jurisdiction that one can combat fishing by vessels of non-Members of the Commission.

We therefore share more than a degree of sympathy with South Africa and other coastal states, which are, or may be, facing a similar plundering of their marine living resources. The problems experienced by South Georgia have it seems simply moved to another part of the Southern Ocean. The issue of illegal fishing is a very real and worrying problem which this Commission (and in particular its flag State Members) needs to address if the credibility of CCAMLR is to be maintained.

Were we to end the effective means of enforcement of Conservation Measures that we have now established for South Georgia waters, we would return to the longlining free for all that was witnessed until recently.

Mr Chairman, I have tried to bring to the Commission's attention the fact that the South Georgia fisheries regime is not in any way at odds with CCAMLR. The United Kingdom remains totally supportive of the aims and objectives of the Convention and of the work of this Commission. But in the spirit of yesterday's debate on item 12, we are nevertheless prepared to explore with the Commission and with those Parties who fish in our waters whether further harmonisation can be achieved.

(Text provided by the FCO)

In reply to questions, the Parliamentary Under-Secretary of State, Home Office, wrote:

In those areas where French vessels are permitted to fish within 12 miles of the Bailiwick of Guernsey, no distinction is made between classes of vessel.

A temporary agreement with France covering these waters was recently terminated by the United Kingdom at the request of the Guernsey authorities, who did not think it operated in a way which was fair to the Bailiwick.

In reply to the question 'what rights French fishermen currently have to fish within the Sark box,' the same Minister wrote:

The position in international law is disputed, and the matter is currently the subject of discussion with France.

(HC Debs., vol. 287, WA, col. 656: 18 December 1996)

Part Nine: X. *Seas, waterways, ships—exclusive economic zone*

(See also Parts Nine: VII.F. and Nine: IX., above)

In reply to the question 'what is the status of Rockall, within the UN law of the sea convention 1982', the Minister of State, FCO, wrote:

Rockall is an island within the meaning of article 121(1) of the United Nations convention on the law of the sea and has a territorial sea of 12 miles. Measuring British fishing limits from Rockall is believed to be inconsistent with the provision in article 121(3) of UNCLOS that rocks which cannot sustain human habitation or economic life of their own shall have no exclusive economic zone.

(HC Debs., vol. 281, WA, col. *442*: 17 July 1996; see also HL Debs., vol. 573, *WA 120–1*: 5 July 1996)

Part Nine: XII. *Seas, waterways, ships—bed of the sea beyond national jurisdiction*

In moving the consideration in the House of Commons First Standing Committee on Delegated Legislation of the draft Merchant Shipping (Prevention of Pollution) (Law of the Sea Convention) Order 1995, the International Sea-Bed Authority (Immunities and Privileges) Order 1995, and the International Tribunal for the Law of the Sea (Immunities and Privileges) Order 1995, the Minister of State, FCO, Sir Nicholas Bonsor, stated:

The text of the law of the sea convention was laid before Parliament in 1983. But the United Kingdom did not sign it in 1983–84 because we objected to its part XI, which established a regime for mining of the deep sea bed beyond the limits of national jurisdiction which was unacceptable not only to the United Kingdom but to other industrialised countries.

It was only in 1994 that an agreement on the implementation of part XI, which addressed our concerns, was concluded at the UN. That agreement, which has also been laid before Parliament, effectively modifies part XI to our satisfaction and that of like-minded governments. As a result, we were able to announce to the House our intention to accede to the convention, and to sign the implementing agreement, in July 1994.

My right hon. and loyal Friend the Foreign Secretary explained the problems with part XI to the House in December 1984 and it might be useful to mention how those objections have been addressed in the implementation agreement.

The original part XI set up a highly burdensome regime for mining of the deep sea bed, both bureaucratically and fiscally. It would have hit companies and developed countries. Moreover, it would not have assisted developing countries. The regime was centered on the International Seabed Authority, a new international institution created by the convention and the 'enterprise' arm of the authority, which would compete on favourable terms with deep sea bed mining companies. Under the part XI implementation agreement, the following changes have been made.

The burdensome regulatory mechanism has been scaled down. The redistributive role of the International Seabed Authority has been removed. The possibility of unfair competition from the enterprise arm, an operator linked to the regulator, has also been removed. The regime for sea bed mining will be based on market principles, free trade and, importantly, respect for the environment. The authority will operate on the principle of cost-effectiveness. What might have been a major new international bureacracy has been cut down to size.

The United Kingdom played a major role in the negotiations that led to part XI agreement. The agreement reflects closely our 1984 objections. It is a good result for our diplomacy and a vindication of our decision not to sign in 1984. Eighty four nations are now party to the convention, including Germany, Italy and Australia. Most other major nations are making preparations to join them or have proposed to do so to their legislatures.

(HC Debs., 1995–96, First Standing Committee on Delegated Legislation, 23 January 1996, cols. 4–5)

Part Nine: XIV. *Seas, waterways, ships—international regime of the sea in general*

(See Part One: II. D. 1. (item of 25 January 1996), above)

In moving the consideration in the House of Commons First Standing Committee on Delegated Legislation of the draft Merchant Shipping (Prevention of Pollution) (Law of the Sea Convention) Order 1995, the International Sea-Bed Authority (Immunities and Privileges) Order 1995, and the International Tribunal for the Law of the Sea (Immunities and Privileges) Order 1995, the Minister of State, FCO, Sir Nicholas Bonsor, stated:

These three orders will enable the Government to implement provisions of the United Nations convention on the law of the sea, which was adopted in 1982 and entered into force in 1984.

The convention was the product of the third United Nations conference on the law of the sea which took place from 1973 to 1982. It is an ambitious and largely successful attempt to lay down a comprehensive international regime for the oceans. The law of the sea convention provides either the framework for further action or detailed rules on almost every aspect of international maritime affairs.

That is of itself a significant benefit if the substance is right. We believe that the substance is now right. It confirms important rights of navigation and overflight which are essential to our interests as a trading nation and for defence purposes. It provides for a package of maritime limits, notably a maximum of 12 miles for the territorial sea and 200 miles for the exclusive economic zone, including fisheries and pollution jurisdiction, which are generally accepted and have caused some nations to withdraw from previous extravagant and unjustified claims. And the convention contains important provisions for the protection of the marine environment which all hon. Members will welcome.

It may help if I give some examples of the advantages for the United Kingdom of accession to the United Nation's convention on the law of the sea.

As a trading nation the United Kingdom depends on the freedom of ships to ply the world, bringing us raw materials and exporting our products. That trend will increase as markets in the far east and Latin America open up to our traders. The City of London is an important centre for marine services. The law of the sea convention guarantees merchant ships the freedom to transit straits unhindered by bordering countries. In the case of oil from the Gulf, the convention would apply to the straits of Hormuz and the straits of Malacca. Without such freedom, international trade could be severely obstructed.

The convention is also important for defence purposes. It gives the warships of the Royal Navy, for example on passage to the Gulf through the straits of Hormuz, the same rights as merchant ships. It also allows submarines the right to pass through such straits submerged. Military planes have a parallel right of overflight of straits.

The convention has also halted the trend towards creeping jurisdiction, such as the unjustified extension of the territorial sea and has caused states to pull back from claimed territorial seas of 200 miles to 12 miles. Argentina, Brazil, Ghana, Guinea and Senegal have all pulled back from 200-mile territorial sea claims since the conclusion of the convention. Gabon, Madagascar, Mauritania and Tanzania have pulled back from lesser but excessive claims. That also helps ensure the freedom of navigation on the world's seas.

The convention contains a balanced framework for the control of pollution. That will be welcomed by Opposition Members. Consistent with its terms we are establishing listing [sic] a pollution jurisdiction of 200 miles to protect our coasts. The convention ensures that the similar jurisdiction of other states is not abused to impede world trade.

The convention establishes generally accepted rules that allow British scientists to carry out research off the coasts of other states. British flagged marine research vessels range far and wide, from Brazil to Oman, from Norway to South Africa. Part XIII of the convention ensures that they cannot be unreasonably refused permission to carry out research in the waters of those countries, or have unreasonable conditions imposed upon them.

The law of the sea convention provides for our jurisdiction over the potentially oil-bearing continental shelf beyond 200 miles. This is of great importance for the United Kingdom, especially in the west of Scotland. Its comprehensive provisions for the peaceful settlement of disputes, and in particular the new international tribunal for the law of the sea should help to ensure that fewer maritime disputes lead to shots being fired or nets cut.

(HC Debs., 1995–96, First Standing Committee on Delegated Legislation, 23 January 1996, cols. 3–4)

In reply to a question, the Minister of State, FCO, wrote:

It is the Government's intention that the United Kingdom will accede to the United Nations convention on the law of the sea in due course. In the light of a number of continuing uncertainties in the international situation with regard to fisheries issues, the Government have concluded that now is not an appropriate time to accede to the convention. The timing of accession remains under review and Parliament will be informed as soon as the Government have taken a decision.

(HC Debs., vol. 282, WA, cols. *185–6*: 23 July 1996)

Part Ten: II. A. 2. *Air space, outer space—air navigation—civil aviation—treaty regime*

In the course of the second reading debate in the House of Lords on the Civil Aviation (Amendment) Bill, the Minister of State, Home Office, Baroness Blatch, stated:

Article 13 of the Tokyo Convention allows the commander of an aircraft landing in the UK to deliver to the British police any person who has committed an act on board the aircraft which would be an offence according to the law of the state of registration

Article 13 imposes also an obligation on the UK to take delivery of that person; and a further obligation to take that person into custody, but only 'upon being satisfied that the circumstances so warrant'. Custody may last only 'for such time as is reasonably necessary to enable criminal or extradition proceedings to be instituted'. . . .

In our view UK law implements that article. A person may be taken into custody on being delivered to the British police by the commander of an aircraft if the circumstances warrant it. Custody will be justified either by a provisional warrant under the Extradition Act 1989 or by the bringing of criminal proceedings, if the offence is one over which we have jurisdiction.

We do not consider that that part of the convention means that the UK must take criminal jurisdiction over all offences committed by persons who may be delivered to the British police under Article 13. Had that been the intention, the convention would have said so in Chapter 2. Moreover, the convention cannot be read as envisaging custody without the prospect of subsequent proceedings, either criminal or extradition. That would be contrary to other, more fundamental, principles of international law.

However, the effect of the Bill is to go beyond the convention by extending UK jurisdiction to offences committed on incoming aircraft. That will make it more likely that a person delivered to British police under Article 13 will be held in custody for the purpose of prosecution.

Therefore, detention would be warranted if an offence was committed on a British registered aircraft or if a provisional warrant had been issued under the Extradition Act. As has already been said, the police would also detain someone who had committed an act of violence which endangered the safety of the aircraft or who has seized the aircraft, whatever the nationality of the offender or the state of registration of the aircraft. Those provisions flow from the Hague and Montreal Conventions rather than the Tokyo Convention . . .

(HL Debs., vol. 570, cols. 1802–3: 27 March 1996)

The following letter was sent to the Secretary-General of the UN during the meetings of the Sixth Committee of the UN General Assembly:

MEASURES TO ELIMINATE INTERNATIONAL TERRORISM

Letter dated 9 October 1996 from the Permanent Representative of the United Kingdom of Great Britain and Northern Ireland to the United Nations addressed to the Secretary-General

I have the honour to refer to the letter dated 14 September 1996 from the Deputy Prime Minister and Acting Minister for Foreign Affairs of Iraq addressed to you, in which he stated that the Iraqi authorities had requested a report on the interrogation by the United Kingdom police authorities of those arrested for the hijack of a Sudan Airways aircraft to the United Kingdom on 27 August 1996, and had sought their extradition to Iraq.

I have the honour to inform you that, on 5 September 1996, the United Kingdom authorities fulfilled their obligation under article 6, paragraph 4, of the 1970 Convention for the Suppression of Unlawful Seizure of Aircraft by informing the Iraqi interests section of the Embassy of the Hashemite Kingdom of Jordan in London of the fact that seven Iraqi nationals had been charged under section 1 (1) of the United Kingdom Aviation Security Act 1982, and by giving their names.

Article 7 of the aforementioned Convention provides that if a party does not extradite an alleged offender, it must submit the case to its competent authorities for the purpose of prosecution. The United Kingdom has followed the latter course.

I should be grateful if you would have the text of the present letter circulated as a document of the General Assembly, under agenda item 151.

(*Signed*) John WESTON
Permanent Representative

(A/C.6/51/3)

Part Ten: III. *Air space, outer space—outer space*

(See also Part Eleven: II. A. 1. (items of 26 February, 11 March and 26 July 1996), below)

In reply to the question whether Her Majesty's Government are content for space to be 'weaponised', the Minister of State, FCO, wrote:

Both the United Kingdom and the United States are parties to the 1967 Treaty on Principles Governing the Activities of States in the Exploration and Use of Outer Space, including the Moon and Other Celestial Bodies (the 'Outer Space Treaty'). Article IV of the Treaty contains an undertaking not to place in orbit around the earth, install on the moon or any other celestial body, or otherwise station in outer space nuclear or any other weapons of mass destruction. It also limits the use of the moon and other celestial bodies exclusively to peaceful purposes and expressly prohibits their use for establishing military bases; testing weapons of any kind; or conducting military manoeuvres.

(HL Debs., vol. 569, *WA 48*: 14 February 1996)

The following question was then asked:

Why, in answering a Question about the weaponisation of space (14 February 1996, *WA 48*), they quoted only Article IV of the 1967 Space Treaty, and not Article I, which states that 'the exploration and use of outer space . . . shall be carried out for the benefit and in the interests of all countries, irrespective of their degree of economic and scientific development, and shall be the province of all mankind', and whether they do not consider that current and proposed United States uses severally and unambiguously breach this article?

In reply, the Minister of State wrote:

The specific provisions relating to the military use of outer space, including the moon and other celestial bodies, are contained in Article IV of the Outer Space Treaty. We do not believe that the United States is in breach of its obligations under the treaty.

(Ibid., *WA 87*: 26 February 1996)

In reply to a question about the possible landing in the UK of a Chinese satellite, the Minister of State, Home Office, Baroness Blatch, stated in part:

. . . there is absolutely no doubt that if the satellite landed on UK soil, or, indeed, in UK waters we would have an obligation to return it to China and to do so as soon as possible.

(HL Debs., vol. 569, col. 1364: 27 February 1996)

The following question was asked of Her Majesty's Government:

Whether, in answering questions about the weaponisation of space (14th and 26th February 1996) they quoted only Article IV of the 1967 Space Treaty, and not Article I which states that 'the exploration and use of outer space . . . shall be carried out for the benefit and in the interests of all countries, irrespective of their degree of economic and scientific development, and shall be the province of all mankind', because they hold that Article IV is not to be interpreted in the light of Article I but rather as limiting the application of Article I, thereby allowing all military activity in space which is not cited in Article IV; and whether this interpretation is now and always has been accepted by the non-superpower signatories?

In reply, the Minister of State, FCO, wrote:

The terms of a treaty have to be interpreted in their context, which includes the whole of the text of the treaty. Article I is a general provision governing the exploration and use of outer space. Article IV is a more specific provision concerning (1) nuclear weapons and (2) the use of the moon and other celestial bodies exclusively for peaceful purposes. The position remains as set out in my earlier answers (Official Report), *cols. WA 48* and *WA 87*).

(HL Debs., vol. 571, *WA 72*: 17 April 1996)

The following question was asked of Her Majesty's Government:

Whether it is their belief that any military activity other than those specifically precluded by Article 4 of the space treaty is (a) permitted, and (b) is not governed by Article 1 of the Treaty?

In reply, the Minister of State, FCO, wrote:

The Outer Space Treaty as a whole applies to all activities in outer space. Whether particular activities in outer space are lawful depends on whether they are consistent with the Treaty (and, as reflected in Article III, with international law generally).

The following question was then asked:

Whether it has been generally understood by signatories of the space treaty that only those military activities specifically precluded by Article 4 of the space treaty are prohibited and that no other military activity in space is governed by Article 1 of the Treaty.

In reply, the same Minister of State wrote:

It is for each party to a treaty to express its own understanding of its provisions.

(HL Debs., vol. 571, *WA 156–7*: 2 May 1996)

On 6 February 1996, the Governments of the UK and the People's Republic of China concluded an Exchange of Notes concerning liability for damage during the launch stage of the Apstar-IA and Apstar-IIR satellites. The Notes included the following provisions:

The Ministry of Foreign Affairs of the People's Republic of China presents its compliments to the Embassy of the United Kingdom of Great Britain and Northern Ireland in China and has the honour to confirm on behalf of the Government of the People's Republic of China that, with respect to the liability for damage to other states or their nationals arising during the launch phase (from ignition of the launch vehicle to the separation of the satellite from the launch vehicle) of the Apstar-IA and Apstar-IIR respectively, the two parties, after friendly consultations, have reached the following agreement:

1. The Government of the People's Republic of China (hereinafter referred to as 'China') and the Government of the United Kingdom of Great Britain and Northern Ireland (hereinafter referred to as the 'United Kingdom') note that China Great Wall Industry Corporation will launch the Apstar-IA and Apstar-IIR for APT Satellite Company Limited in the first half of 1996 and in the first half of 1997 respectively, from the People's Republic of China.

2. China and United Kingdom also note that both of them are parties to the Convention on International Liability for Damage Caused by Space Objects of 1972 (hereinafter referred to as the 'Liability Convention') and the Treaty on Principles Governing the Activities of States in the Exploration and Use of Outer Space, including the Moon and Other Celestial Bodies of 1967 (hereinafter referred to as the 'Outer Space Treaty').

3. China and United Kingdom agree that, with regard to the compensation for damage to other states or their nationals arising during the launch phase (from ignition of the launch vehicle to the separation of the satellite from the launch

vehicle) of Apstar-IA and Apstar-IIR, China shall assume the liability, as between them, under the liability Convention and the Outer Space Treaty and other principles of international law, and, subject to Article 4 below, shall indemnify the United Kingdom for compensation claims for the above mentioned damage for which the United Kingdom may be liable.

4. China and United Kingdom agree:

(i) In the event that a claim for compensation for damage within the scope of Article 3 above is brought against the United Kingdom, the United Kingdom shall, as soon as possible after receiving notice of such claim, notify China thereof.

(ii) The United Kingdom shall not make any settlement with any such claimant without full consultation with China.

(iii) In the event that China objects to the terms of a proposed settlement between the United Kingdom and any such claimant, the United Kingdom shall submit the claim to a claims commission as provided for in the Liability Convention or to a claims commission whose procedures accord with the procedures in Article XIV to XX inclusive thereof. In this event, China shall compensate the United Kingdom for any settlement of such claim up to and not exceeding the amount recommended by the claims commission. Subject to Articles XV, XVI and XVII of the Liability Convention with respect to failure to select a commission member, selection of members by the United Kingdom shall require prior consultation with, and the approval of China.

(TS No. 52 (1996); Cm 3274)

The following question was asked of Her Majesty's Government:

What are the definitions of 'outer space' currently in use, whose definitions they are, whether the military satellites of the United States, Russia and other countries are now operating in 'outer space', and if not where, in international law, they are operating?

In reply, the Minister of State, FCO, wrote:

There is no internationally agreed definition of outer space. We do not consider it necessary to take a legal view on the question raised by the noble Lord in the absence of a specific challenge based on the relevant UN treaties.

(HL Debs., vol. 575, *WA 101*: 13 November 1996)

Part Eleven: II. A. 1. *Responsibility—responsible entities—States—elements of responsibility*

(See also Part Ten: III. (item of 27 February 1996), below)

In reply to the question

what approaches have been made to the Governments of the former Soviet Union, under the principles of the polluter pays, to seek compensation for the effects in the United Kingdom of the Chernobyl explosion, the Minister of State, FCO, wrote in part:

Just after the 1986 nuclear disaster at Chernobyl, on 10 July 1986, we notified the Soviet Union that we were reserving the right to file claims for damage which had occurred in the United Kingdom.

However, we came to the conclusion that it was unrealistic to expect the Soviet Union to honour such claims.

It was not possible to base a claim for compensation against the Soviet Union on relevant international conventions, in particular the 1963 Vienna convention on civil liability for nuclear damage, as it was not a party to these conventions. The Soviet Union now no longer exists. The Russian Federation and Ukraine are considering accession to the 1963 Vienna convention. However, any such accession would not have retrospective effect.

(HC Debs., vol. 270, WA, cols. *226–7*: 24 January 1996)

The following EU comment was made on 26 February 1996 about the shooting down of two civilian aircraft by the Cuban authorities between Cuba and Florida:

The European Union strongly condemns the shooting-down of two civilian aircraft on Saturday by the Cuban air force. It regrets the deaths of the four people on board the aircraft and calls for moderation and restraint from all involved in the handling of this incident.

The EU requests that an immediate investigation be carried out in order to ascertain the details and responsibilities in this case.

Irrespective of the circumstances of the incident, there can be no excuse for not respecting international law and human rights norms.

(*Bulletin of the European Union*, 1996–1/2, pp. 76–7)

The following question was asked of Her Majesty's Government in respect of the same incident:

Whether the relevant article in the International Civil Aviation Agreement of December 1944 and the Montreal Protocol of 10th May 1984 to which the United Nations Security Council Declaration refers is in effect; whether either the United States or Cuba have ratified it and are bound by it; and whether it is expected that the International Civil Aviation Organisation will examine the overall context of the events off Cuba, including earlier incursions and warnings and communications?

In reply, the Minister of State, FCO, wrote:

Article 3 bis of the International Convention on Civil Aviation of 7th December 1944 added by the Montreal Protocol of 10th May 1984 is not yet in force. Neither the United States nor Cuba has ratified it. However, the provisions of Article 3 bis, which state that weapons must not be used against civil aircraft in flight, reflect a general principle of international law.

In addition, Annex 2 to the Chicago Convention, which deals with the rules of the Air, has an attachment which sets down the specific actions to be followed by a state if it decides that it has to intercept a civil aircraft. Those actions do not include the use of weapons.

The International Civil Aviation Organisation (ICAO) Council adopted a resolution on 6th March directing the Secretary General of ICAO to initiate immediately an investigation of the incident in its entirety to determine all relevant facts and technical aspects in accordance with the United Nations Security Council Presidential Statement.

(HL Debs., vol. 570, *WA 44–5*: 11 March 1996)

In the course of a debate on the question whether Her Majesty's Government will make appropriate reparation to African nations and to the descendants of Africans for the damage caused by the slave trade and the practice of slavery, the Government spokesman in the House of Lords, Lord Chesham, stated:

. . . we all agree that slavery was shameful. Indeed, my right honourable friend the Prime Minister, speaking in Cape Town in September 1994, described slavery as a moral outrage. No one can feel proud about the traffic in human beings, a traffic which is still taking place today, as many noble Lords have said, in various parts of the world, including Africa. Indeed, one of the worst aspects of the slavery of which we read today is the encompassment of child prostitution with it. The Government totally deplore that slavery. I can assure the noble and learned Lord, Lord Wilberforce, and my noble friend Lord Gisborough that the Government are doing whatever they can to see that it is stopped wherever it occurs.

I turn now to the Atlantic slave trade. Attributing responsibility for that is difficult; it is not straightforward. Slavery existed in Africa for centuries before outsiders began to engage in the trade, and continued after they had stopped. Far more people were enslaved internally in Africa than were ever exported across the Atlantic. The first outside slave traders were in fact North African Arabs, plying across the Sahara. That took place at least some seven or eight centuries before the first Europeans began to practise the trade. The Atlantic trade first began by tapping that long-standing trans-Saharan slave trade to North Africa. In East Africa, the trade was almost entirely in the hands of Arabs from Oman and the Gulf. Nor, as has been mentioned, is slavery a monopoly of Africa: it existed in the Greek and Roman empires, and in many other parts of the world.

At the height of the transatlantic slave trade, considerable numbers of African slavers and middlemen were involved. African rulers could open and close the market at will, at a time when European penetration of Africa was limited. Traders made their own arrangements with African rulers for slaves, supplied by fellow Africans, and had to pay gifts and taxes to various African rulers along the West African coast. African societies often had control of the slaves until they were loaded on to European ships. That is supported by a large body of academic research.

To claim that the Atlantic slave trade was imposed by Western nations on powerless African communities is to deny Africa's political history. African leaders were themselves active participants with the capacity to determine how trade with Europe developed. Many of the highly impressive African Kingdoms and empires in West Africa were built on the foundations of slavery, such as the Asante kingdom in present-day Ghana.

Africans, Arabs and Europeans participated in the slave trade. Responsibility for British involvement in the transatlantic slave trade does not rest on the shoulders of the British Government. British participation in the trade was not conducted by the Government but by individual traders and companies. After the abolition of the slave trade in 1807, the Royal Navy played an honourable part in suppressing the transatlantic slave trade by maintaining naval patrols off the West African coast. British also drew up anti-slavery treaties with African leaders in an attempt to suppress the slave trade. As was written in the Chronicle of Abuju, written in Hausa by the two brothers of the Emir of Abuja in 1945, 'when the British came, those men who had been earning a rich living by this trade saw their prosperity vanish, and they became poor men'.

The case for reparations for slavery rests on the premise that the effects of slavery are still being felt on Africans now living in Africa and the Diaspora. There is no evidence of that. Current historical research has revised the thinking on the numbers involved in the Atlantic trade and it effects on demography and depopulation. The main areas of slaving, for example, in the Niger delta and Benin, are now among the most densely populated parts of Africa. The majority of slaves exported were male and not female, and this has less impact on demography due to the widespread practice of polygamy. A comparison with Europe illustrates that the economic long-term effects of the Atlantic slave trade are often exaggerated. Emigration from southern Europe, particularly from Italy, to the New World between 1880 and 1914 is estimated at about 30 million. The total of the Atlantic slave trade over a far greater period is now generally accepted to number between 20 million and 25 million.

Mention has been made of the growing support for the campaign for reparations for slavery. However, African leaders increasingly accept that many of the economic problems have arisen from policies pursued since independence. As former Nigerian head of state General Obasanjo said in 1991 at the Africa Leadership Forum Conference in Nigeria: 'the major responsibility of our present impasse must be placed squarely on the shoulders of our leaders'. General Obasanjo is currently detained in Nigeria.

. . .

I touched earlier on the responsibility for slavery. I wish to return to that. Arabs, Europeans, Americans and Africans were all directly involved in the trade, but even if it could be decided to whom the bill should be sent, to whom should any proceeds go? Which Africans would benefit and how? Which descendants of slaves living in America, the Caribbean, or the UK should benefit? To whom, incidentally, should the UK send the bill for the naval squadrons that patrolled the waters of West Africa for half a century to prevent the Spaniards, Brazilians and others from slaving long after we had abolished it?

We should remember also the large percentage of slaves who were prisoners of war in ethnic clashes who would otherwise just have been killed.

. . .

Comment has been made about international precedents. In May 1991 in Lagos Chief Anyaoku, Secretary General of the Commonwealth, devoted an entire speech to the legacy of slavery. However, he stated that, although the moral case was strong, there was no precedent for reparations outside the post-war settlement. The fact that reparations for war crimes have been paid in this century—for example, Germany, Japan and Iraq—is a red herring. It provides no historic parallel. They were among the terms for peace imposed at once by victors in the wars upon vanquished governments and could be precisely catalogued.

The noble Lord, Lord Gifford, mentioned the Queen's apology to the Maoris. Her Majesty's apology to a New Zealand Maori tribe for the killings and seizure of land that it suffered under Queen Victoria was at the instigation of her New Zealand Ministers; in other words, the New Zealand Government, which is constitutionally distinct from the British Government. It was not a personal apology from the Queen. It was an acknowledgement of the breach of the treaty signed in 1840. The situation is therefore entirely different. It was not a question of slavery but one of the possession of land resulting from war.

(HL Debs., vol. 570, cols. 1056–9: 14 March 1996)

The Permanent Representative of the UK to the United Nations in New York, Sir John Weston, addressed the following letter, dated 21 May 1996, to the President of the Security Council:

I have the honour to refer to the letter of 10 April 1996 to your predecessor as president of the Security Council from the Permanent Representative of the Libyan Arab Jamahiriya to the United Nations (S/1996/269). The letter refers to two newspaper articles about a documentary programme shown recently on British television. Woman Police Constable Yvonne Fletcher was murdered on 17 April 1984 outside the Libyan diplomatic mission in St. James' Square, London, by shots from a gun fired from a window of that mission. The television programme contained speculation that the shots might have come from else-where in the Square. The Libyan letter treats the speculations in the programme as fact. The truth is as follows.

Following the murder of Constable Fletcher, the Libyan Arab Jamahiriya refused to cooperate in a criminal investigation or to allow its diplomatic mission to be searched. Instead it proposed that a Libyan mission of inquiry should come to the United Kingdom, and that any Libyan found to be implicated should be put on trial in the Libyan Arab Jamahiriya. The United Kingdom regarded this as a totally inadequate response to the killing of a British citizen carried out in broad daylight on the streets of London, and accordingly broke off diplomatic relations with the Libyan Arab Jamahiriya. At the inquest held by a coroner, the evidence given led to the jury deciding that Constable Fletcher was unlawfully killed by a bullet coming from one of two first floor windows at the front of the Libyan People's Bureau.

The Libyan Government has maintained its refusal to accept responsibility for the actions of Libyan officials, to tender an apology or pay compensation to Constable Fletcher's family. In 1991 the United Kingdom Police Dependents' Trust received a cheque for £250,000 from the Libyan Police syndicate in connection with the murder, but the Trust declined to accept it.

. . .

(S/1996/360)

In reply to the question 'if UK dependent nations are bound to abide by international conventions to which the UK has signed up; and what responsibility is held by which UK authorities for ensuring that they adhere to such conventions', the Minister of State, FCO, wrote:

The UK dependent territories are bound to abide by only those international conventions that the UK, in consultation with the territories in question, has extended to them.

The Government bear international responsibility for ensuring that the dependent territories comply with the obligations of those international conventions which apply to them.

(HC Debs., vol. 281, WA, col. 540: 17 July 1996)

In the course of a debate in the UN Security Council on 26 July 1996, the UK Permanent Representative, Sir John Weston, stated:

The Security Council is about to vote on a draft resolution which makes clear this Council's condemnation of the use of weapons against civil aircraft in flight. That is why my delegation will be voting in favour of the draft resolution. The United Kingdom would like to take this opportunity to express its deep condolences to the families of those who were killed on 24 February 1996.

In the Council President's statement of 27 February 1996, the Council strongly deplored the shooting down by the Cuban Air Force of two civil aircraft on 24 February and requested the International Civil Aviation Organization (ICAO) to investigate this incident and to report its findings to the Security Council. The United Kingdom strongly supports the draft resolution's endorsement of the ICAO report and resolution. And I think it is fair in the context of this afternoon's discussion to remind ourselves of what some of the conclusions of that report are.

Conclusion 3.12 is that the first aircraft was destroyed by an air-to-air missile fired by a Cuban MiG-29 aircraft. Conclusion 3.13 is that the second aircraft was destroyed by an air-to-air missile fired by a Cuban MiG-29 military aircraft. Conclusion 3.18 is that means other than interception were available to Cuba, but had not been utilized. Conclusion 3.19 is that during the interceptions no attempt was made to guide them away or instruct them to effect a landing at a designated aerodrome. Conclusion 3.20 is that the standard procedures for manoeuvering and signals by the military interceptor aircraft were not followed. Conclusion 3.22 is that the rule of customary international law that States must refrain from resorting to the use of weapons, as codified in article 3 bis of the Chicago Convention, apply irrespective of whether or not such aircraft is within the territorial airspace of that State.

There can be no doubt that Cuba has contravened principles of international law in using force against civil aircraft and in not following established international procedures on interception of such aircraft. The message in this draft resolution is clear. Such incidents are unacceptable to the international community.

There is an obligation on all States to comply with the provisions of international law and the standards and recommended practices set down in the Chicago Convention and its annexes, and to cooperate fully with the International Civil Aviation Organization. The United Kingdom looks to all States to abide by their obligations in this regard.

. . .

The purpose of this draft resolution is firstly to draw attention to the illegal use of weapons in this incident.

. . .

In taking action this day, the Security Council is doing no more than upholding the principles of international law and fulfilling its responsibilities to safeguard international peace and security. It is with this in mind that I commend the draft resolution to colleagues in this Council, and that is why we shall vote for it ourselves.

(S/PV.3683, pp.15–16)

On 7 November 1996, the UK representative, Professor I. Brownlie, made a statement to the Sixth Committee of the UN General Assembly discussing the report of the International Law Commission. In the course of this statement he said:

Let me begin with 'State crimes'. One approaches this concept with mixed feelings, knowing how controversial it has been since it was first put forward by the Special Rapporteur in 1976.

The United Kingdom has of course expressed views at previous sessions on the proposed distinction between State delicts and 'State crimes', views that varied from the cautious to the outright sceptical. So there is a natural sense of disappointment at seeing the corresponding Articles still there in the Commission's project. We acknowledge that differing views have been voiced by Governments in these debates. But we are quite clear that the concept of 'State crime' has not gained the broad international acceptance that would be required for the introduction into the law of a new concept with such wide-ranging consequences.

That is not to say, however, that we criticise the Commission in any way for attempting to work the consequences out. The whole essence of propounding a concept of 'crimes' distinct from delicts is that different consequences follow in each case. As the Commission says in the current Report, 'The effect of the introduction of Article 19 of Part One has been to recognise a category of wrongful acts to which, because of their seriousness, special consequences should attach. Whether that category is called "crimes"' (the Commission itself puts the term in quotation marks) 'is immaterial in the sense that, however termed, special consequences should attach: otherwise, there is no point in distinguishing this category from other internationally wrongful acts.'

The late Professor Ago said the same when first putting the idea forward 20 years ago. But he made it plain that in his concept, the commission of a 'State crime' should be visited by the application of punitive measures, including sanctions, over and above the obligation to make reparation. He went further still in acknowledging that a severe regime of that kind did not yet exist in the international system, but he hoped that the adoption of his draft would hasten its arrival. 20 years on we can judge whether it has.

The Commission's very difficulty in working out what the legal consequences of a 'State crime' might be serves powerfully to reinforce our view that the concept itself lacks an adequate juridical basis and should not be retained. The consequences stipulated for, moreover, call into question the relevance and acceptability of the concept.

In this context it is important to appreciate the extent to which the concept of State criminality remains inchoate and lacking the modalities of implementation.

It is one thing to punish members of a Government or a high command for breaches of international criminal law on the basis of individual criminal responsibility. It is quite another thing to set out to punish a collectivity like a State, which means punishing its population and its economy. Punitive measures of that kind would raise major political, social and moral problems.

(Text provided by the FCO)

In the course of a speech to the UN General Assembly on 12 November 1996 on the subject of US political relations with Cuba, the UK Permanent Representative to the UN in New York, Sir John Weston, made the following observation in the name of the EU:

We have also seen the shooting down of the two Hermanos al Rescate aircraft, in violation of international law, and with complete disregard for the right to live.

(Text provided by the FCO)

Speaking on 12 November 1996 in the Sixth Committee of the UN General Assembly discussing the report of the work of the International Law Commission, the UK representative, Sir Franklin Berman, stated in respect of that part of the report dealing with the topic of international liability for injurious consequences arising out of acts not prohibited by international law:

Mr Chairman, on many of the items reported this year, the Commission has come up with fresh insights. Not alas here. The report goes to prove what many of us have suspected for some years, and voiced in these debates, that the topic is hollow at its core. Despite all the efforts of Ambassador Barboza and the working group he chaired, what the citizens of the host country would call the giveaway appears in article 3 of the draft in its report. It may well be that, as the Commission proposes, '[t]he freedom of States to carry on or permit activities in their territory or otherwise under their jurisdiction or control is not unlimited.' It may well be that this freedom is subject to the general, as well as to the specific, obligations stated in the next sentence. But that is simply another way of saying, as we already know, that *sic utere tuo ut alienum non laedas* is a substantive rule of customary international law, and it follows from that without further demonstration that breach of that substantive obligation may entail liability according to the normal rules of State responsibility. From this my delegation draws two conclusions. The first is that, while the provisions on prevention are useful, they are not in themselves fit material for a legal code. The second is that the provisions on liability beg so many questions that we could not support them even if we had no separate draft on State responsibility. To these must be added a third conclusion, in the light of the terms of this year's report, that to add in the additional category of cases tentatively mentioned in draft article 1(b) would be to make an already bad situation disastrously worse. In short, we are now reluctantly confirmed in the view that to maintain this topic in being would be an unfair and unreasonable burden to impose on the incoming Commission. It should be set aside.

(Text provided by the FCO; see also A/C.6/51/SR.38, p. 6)

Part Eleven: II. A. 5. *Responsibility—responsible entities—States—matters excluding responsibility*

In the course of a debate on 23 October 1995 in the UN Human Rights Committee on the subject of the Special Report of the UK in respect of Hong Kong, the UK representative, Mr H. Steel, stated:

A number of members of the Committee had . . . raised the question of his Government's continuing responsibility after 30 June 1997, as distinct from its continuing interest and *locus standi*. While he would not speculate as to what his Government could or would do if it felt after 30 June 1997 that a situation was arising which was not in accordance with the Joint Declaration he saw considerable difficulty in the proposition that a State retained legal responsibility in respect of a territory over which it no longer had sovereignty, when the territory and consequent responsibility had in fact passed to another State.

(CCPR/C/SR. 1536, p. 3)

Part Eleven: II. A. 6. *Responsibility—responsible entities—States—reparation and other remedies*

The following provisions appear in the Agreement for the Promotion and Protection of Investments, signed on 3 July 1996 by the Governments of the UK and Slovenia but not yet in force:

ARTICLE 4

Compensation for Losses

(1) Nationals or companies of one Contracting Party whose investments in the territory of the other Contracting Party suffer losses owing to war or other armed conflict, revolution, a state of national emergency, revolt, insurrection or riot in the territory of the latter Contracting Party shall be accorded by the latter

Contracting Party treatment, as regards restitution, indemnification, compensation or other settlement, no less favourable than that which the latter Contracting Party accords to its own nationals or companies or to nationals or companies of any third State. Resulting payments shall be freely transferable.

(2) Without prejudice to paragraph (1) of this Article, nationals and companies of one Contracting Party who in any of the situations referred to in that paragraph suffer losses in the territory of the other Contracting Party resulting from:

  (a) requisitioning of their property by its forces or authorities, or
  (b) destruction of their property by its forces or authorities, which was not caused in combat action or was not required by the necessity of the situation,

shall be accorded restitution or adequate compensation. Resulting payments shall be freely transferable.

ARTICLE 5

Expropriation

(1) Investments of nationals or companies of either Contracting Party shall not be nationalised, expropriated or subjected to measures having effect equivalent to nationalisation or expropriation (hereinafter referred to as 'expropriation') in the territory of the other Contracting Party except for a public purpose related to the internal needs of that Party on a non-discriminatory basis and against prompt, adequate and effective compensation. Such compensation shall amount to the genuine value of the investment expropriated immediately before the expropriation or before the impending expropriation became public knowledge, whichever is the earlier, shall include interest at a normal commercial rate until the date of payment, shall be made without delay, be effectively realizable and be freely transferable. The national or company affected shall have a right, under the law of the Contracting Party making the expropriation, to prompt review, by a judicial or other independent authority of that Party, of his or its case and of the valuation of his or its investment in accordance with the principles set out in this paragraph.

(2) Where a Contracting Party expropriates the assets of a company which is incorporated or constituted under the law in force in any part of its own territory, and in which nationals or companies of the other Contracting Party own shares, it shall ensure that the provisions of paragraph (1) of this Article are applied to the extent necessary to guarantee prompt, adequate and effective compensation in respect of their investment to such nationals or companies of the other Contracting Party who are owners of those shares.

(Cm 3496)

The following appendix was annexed to an FCO publication, *Nazi Gold: Information from the British Archives*, issued in September 1996 (second revised edition January 1997):

TRIPARTITE COMMISSION FOR THE RESTITUTION OF MONETARY GOLD

The Establishment of the Commission

The Commission had it origins in the Paris Conference on Reparation of 1945 attended by the Representatives of the Governments of Albania, Australia, Belgium, Canada, Czechoslovakia, Denmark, Egypt, France, Greece, India, Luxembourg, New Zealand, the Netherlands, Norway, South Africa, the UK the USA and Yugoslavia. An Agreement on Reparation was signed on 14 January 1946. Austria, Italy and Poland later also subsequently adhered to the arrangement for the restitution of monetary gold set out in Part III of the Agreement, entitled 'Restitution of Monetary Gold'. This provided that monetary gold looted by Germany and recovered by the Allied Forces, and monetary gold recovered from third countries, should be pooled and distributed to claimant countries in proportion to their losses.

The British, French and US Governments became the instrument for verifying claims and distributing the gold, and on 27 September 1946 established the Tripartite Commission for the Restitution of Monetary Gold, to which the three governments each appointed a Commissioner.

For the sake of convenience, the Commission was established in Brussels, co-located with the Inter-Allied Reparation Agency (IARA). The first Commissioners were also the three governments' Commissioners to the IARA, though the commission was constitutionally separate from and independent of the Agency. The status of the Commission as a recognised international organisation was acknowledged in a Belgian law of 1 August 1952, retroactive to 27 September 1946.

The Gold Pool

By the middle of 1948 a considerable quantity of looted monetary gold had been taken into custody by the Allied authorities or identified as having been deposited in third countries. By July of that year, a total of about 306,343 kg of gold in bars and coins had been deposited with the Federal Reserve Bank of New York or the Bank of England or was held at the Foreign Exchange Depository in Frankfurt by the Military Government. The grand total available to the gold pool rose further, to about 336,890 kg by December 1974 (worth about US$ 4.18 bn at current prices).

Claims

On 13 March 1947, the Commission issued a questionnaire to potential claimant countries seeking information which would allow it to make awards from the gold pool on a proportionate basis. Claims were duly submitted by Albania, Austria, Belgium, Czechoslovakia, Greece, Italy, Luxembourg, the Netherlands, Poland and Yugoslavia. They totalled about 735,548 kg, but the total of claims validated in due course after detailed examination by the Tripartite Commission amounted to about 514,060 kg, which was nevertheless considerably more than the total amount of gold recovered by the Western Allies for the gold pool.

The Adjudications

With the help of seconded banking and financial experts, the Commission examined the claims, put queries to certain claimant countries, and obtained further evidence from them. As the amount of gold retrieved by the Allies at the end of the Second World War fell far short of the total claims by the various governments, it was decided that each claimant government would, by the end of the process of restitution, receive approximately 64% of their claim. The drafting of adjudication of claims began in 1952; by 1958, 10 adjudications had been signed by the Commissioners on behalf of their governments; the eleventh, for Czechoslovakia, was signed in 1982. (Poland received two adjudications: for pre-war Poland and Danzig.)

The Preliminary Distribution of Gold

It became clear by the middle of 1947 that there was an urgent need to distribute some of the gold to meet the critical requirements of claimant governments; it was therefore decided by the three member governments of the Commission that a preliminary distribution of gold should be made before the totality of claims could be considered and adjudicated upon. Accordingly rough calculations were made by the Commission of the amounts of gold likely to be attributed in due course to each claimant government and between October 1947 and November 1950 a total of about 266,210 kg of gold (worth about US$ 3.31 bn at current prices) was distributed to Austria, Belgium, Czechoslovakia, Italy, Luxembourg, the Netherlands and Yugoslavia. The distribution of the share allocated to Albania was delayed because of a counter-claim by Italy to most of the gold in question. No preliminary distribution was made to Greece because the amount of the Greek claim was very small. Poland did not participate in the preliminary distribution because it was a late adherent to the Paris Agreement and its claim was not properly formulated until 1950.

The Second and Quasi-final Distribution of Gold

Following the finalisation of the Commission's adjudications, a second, quasi-final distribution of gold took place. Between 1958 and 1982, a total of about 58,016 kg (worth about US$ 720.5 m at current prices) was distributed to Austria, Belgium, Greece, Italy, Luxembourg, Yugoslavia, the Netherlands, Poland and Czechoslovakia.

The distribution of gold to Albania was delayed by a number of factors, among them the existence of claims against Albania by the three member governments, all of which were resolved by late 1995/early 1996. Arrangements for the distribution to Albania are now being made.

The Winding up of the Commission

Once Albania has received its preliminary and quasi-final shares, the Commission will be able to carry out the final share-out of the remaining gold (approximately 5,500 kg, worth approximately US$ 74.5 m at current prices). When the preliminary and quasi-final shares were distributed, allocations were rounded down to the nearest 50 kg of gold. The claimant countries will therefore receive, as their final share of the pool, the difference between their individual allocations and the actual amounts they have received so far; plus their share of the residual gold pool. The Commission is also addressing the question of final shares to the Czech Republic and Slovakia and to the successor states of the former Yugoslavia; this should not delay the final distribution to the other claimant countries. Once the final distribution is complete, the Commission will be wound up.

The Accountability of the Commission

The three Commissioners are instructed by, and report to, their respective governments, who are in turn accountable to their Parliaments. (The Paris Agreement of 1946 does not impose any formal requirement on the three governments to report back to the signatories of the Paris Agreement or to the claimant Governments.) The proceedings of the Commission have from the outset been confidential to the member governments because of the sensitivity of the adjudication of competing claims and of international movements of monetary gold. Information about the Commission has, however, been provided from time to time as a result of Parliamentary Questions,[1] in a Parliamentary debate in July 1987 and in the FCO archives, as detailed in the FCO History Note No. 11, 'Nazi Gold: Information from the British Archives'. The Commission will provide a Final Report to the three member governments when its work is complete.

The Gold held on behalf of the Commission in the Bank of England

This currently amounts to about 5, 100 kg. It is stored by the Bank of England for a nominal charge, which the Commission pays from its sterling account with the Bank. Neither the Bank of England nor HMG receive any benefit from the gold. The value of the gold has fluctuated over the years as the price of gold has changed. It is currently about £40.5 m (US$ 63 m).

(Foreign and Commonwealth Office, September 1996)

The following question was asked:

To ask the Secretary of State for Foreign and Commonwealth Affairs if he will make a statement on the progress in negotiations with the Albanian Government regarding an outstanding claim for compensation arising from the Corfu incident and the return of the Albanian gold?

In reply, the Minister of State, FCO, wrote:

---

[1] *Hansard* 17 May 1984 Columns 232–233, 24 April 1985 Columns 1118–1120, 25 April 1985 Column 507, 12 March 1986 Columnn 515, 3 November 1986 Column 307, 26 January 1987 Columns 42–43, 10 April 1987 Column 431, 19 March 1990 Column 451, 12 March 1991 Columns 433 and 434, 12 March 1992 Column 624.

The Secretary-General of the tripartite gold commission met in London on 29 October with representatives of the Government of Albania to conclude the transfer of gold from the tripartite gold commission to Albania. At the same time, the Government of Albania settled the British Government's claim for compensation for the Corfu channel incident.

(HC Debs., vol. 284, WA, col. *224*: 31 October 1996)

In reply to a question, the Minister of State, FCO, wrote in part:

Compensation for former prisoners of war was legally settled in the 1951 San Francisco peace treaty. This provided for the proceeds of Japanese assets held by the allies to be used for reparations.

(HC Debs., vol. 285, WA, col. *459*: 19 October 1996)

On 29 October 1996, an FCO spokesman drew attention to the following statement by the Secretary General of the Tripartite Gold Commission:

The Secretary General of the Tripartite Gold Commission met in London today with representatives of the Government of Albania to conclude the transfer of gold from the Tripartite Gold Commission to the Government of Albania.

This is the last major single share of the Commission's gold pool to be settled. The Commission will now proceed with preparations for the final distribution of the remaining gold in the pool to the claimant governments.

The FCO spokesman then added:

The UK is pleased that the gold held by the Tripartite Gold Commission is now to return to Albania. The matters remaining in dispute between the UK and Albania have now been settled.

This is a historic day for Albania and for our bilateral relationship. It marks the end of our dispute on this issue with the previous regime.

The FCO provided the following background note:

BACKGROUND NOTE ON ALBANIAN GOLD

Gold worth approximately £13 million (US$ 19 million) on today's markets has been held in the Bank of England on behalf of the Tripartite (US/French/UK) Gold Commission (TGC) since World War II. The Nazis looted Albanian gold from the National Bank of Albania in 1945. The TGC could not distribute gold to Albania, until the Governments of Britain, United States and France agreed. In 1991, after settlement of the Corfu Channel Incident whereby the Albanians promised to pay us US$ 2 million, we lifted our block on the return of the gold. The Americans lifted their hold in 1995 subsequent to the settlement of certain outstanding claims with the Government of Albania. After the French gave their agreement for the restitution of the gold to Albania in February 1996, the TGC began the legal procedures for the distribution of the gold to Albania.

Corfu Channel Incident

On 22 October 1946 Royal Navy warships were exercising their right of innocent passage in Albanian waters between Albania and the Greek island of Corfu. While heading north, just off Sarande, the destroyers Saumarez and Volage ran into an undeclared minefield and were seriously damaged. Forty four men lost their lives and the Saumarez had to be scrapped. In 1949 the International Court of Justice ruled that Albania should pay the UK £843,947 in compensation. Agreement was reached with the Albanian Government in 1992 to settle the UK claim with $2 million. The payment of this amount will take place simultaneously with the restitution of the gold

(Text provided by the FCO)

Part Eleven: II. A. 7. (a). (ii). *Responsibility—responsible entities— States—procedure—diplomatic and consular protection—exhaustion of local remedies*

(See also Part Three: I. A. 2., above)

In the course of a debate on the subject of Mr Paul Grecian, a United Kingdom national arrested on an Interpol extradition warrant in South Africa on charges of breaching United States arms export control legislation and bank fraud, the Minister of State, FCO, Mr Jeremy Hanley, stated:

As to whether the United Kingdom authorities should demand Mr. Grecian's release, it is contrary to international practice for official intervention to be made in cases before foreign courts which are still sub judice and until all local legal procedures have been completed. Consideration is then given to such intervention if there are prima facie grounds for believing that there has been a miscarriage of justice. Since his arrest, Mr. Grecian has received, and will continue to receive, full consular support from our staff in South Africa. The same support would be extended to any British citizen in Mr. Paul Grecian's situation.

(HC Debs., vol. 273, col. 550: 7 March 1996)

Part Eleven: II. D. *Responsibility—responsible entities—individuals, including corporations*

(See also Part One: II. D. 3, above)

The following question was asked of Her Majesty's Government:

Whether they agree that crimes against humanity, as defined in Article 3 of the Statute of the International Tribunal for Rwanda, and violations of Article 3 common to the Geneva Conventions and of Additional Protocol II, are crimes of universal jurisdiction, and if so, what arrangements they have made, together with other states, for the collection of witness statements and other evidence, preparatory to bringing charges against Saddam Hussain and his principal lieutenants for these crimes, and in particular for the mass murder by chemical weapons of over 5,000 men, women and children in the town of Halabja on 17th March 1988?

The Minister of State, FCO, wrote in reply:

The article of the four Geneva Conventions of 1949 providing for the prosecution by all parties or persons alleged to have committed grave breaches of the conventions do not cover breaches of Common Article 3. Additional Protocol 2 to the Geneva Conventions does not contain any provisions for the prosecution of grave breaches. As regards crimes against humanity, there is no international agreement providing for universal jurisdiction over such crimes, though it is proposed that they should form one of the categories of crimes over which the proposed International Criminal Court should have jurisdiction. We are aware that certain organisations are collecting and assessing information relating to events in Halabja in March 1988.

(HL Debs., vol. 571, *WA* 2: 1 April 1996)

Speaking on 28 October 1996 in the Sixth Committee of the UN General Assembly considering the establishment of an International Criminal Court, the representative of Ireland, on behalf of the European Union, stated:

At the commencement of both of the sessions of the Preparatory Committee, in March-April and August of this year, the European Union issued statements indicating what it regarded as the fundamental considerations underlying the establishment of an international criminal court. It wishes to repeat those considerations before this Committee as we begin our examination of this topic.

The European Union accordingly reiterates the following summary of its views:
— A permanent international criminal court should be established.
— The Court should be an independent institution with the widest participation of States in its Statute, and closely linked to the United Nations.
— The Court should be complementary to national systems of justice, and this principle of complementarity should be duly reflected in the Statute.
— The jurisdiction of the Court should be limited to the most serious offences of concern to the international community and there should be certainty as to the crimes which fall within its jurisdiction.
— The Statute of the Court should also contain provisions on the general rules of criminal law to be applied by the Court.
— The Court should have proper standards of due process to protect the rights of the accused.
— The Statute of the Court should provide for the protection of witnesses and victims.
— The Statute of the Court should provide for states parties' obligations to cooperate with the Court in an effective and speedy manner in the field of transfer of individuals, taking into account the existing structures of judicial cooperation.

— The Court will have an important role in deterring serious crimes of concern to the international community, including serious violations of international humanitarian law, and in ensuring that those responsible for such crimes are brought to justice.

(Text provided by the FCO)

Part Twelve: I. *Pacific settlement of disputes—the concept of an international dispute*

In the course of a speech, the Minister of State, FCO, Sir Nicholas Bonsor, observed:

. . . in the dispute between Greece and Turkey over the small and uninhabitable island of Imia, the question of sovereignty has not been resolved. It is for the parties to the dispute to resolve it peacefully between themselves.

(HC Debs., vol. 271, col. 321: 7 February 1996)

In reply to a question on the same subject, the Minister of State, FCO, wrote:

. . . my hon. Friend the Member for Upminster (Sir N. Bonsor) observed in his oral answer on 7 February 1996, *Official Report*, columns 321–23, that the Greek and Turkish Governments take different positions on sovereignty over the island of Imia. We warmly welcome expressions by both sides of determination to deal with the issue by peaceful means. This must be right. It is important that it is done in accordance with international law.

(HC Debs., vol. 271, WA, col. *489*: 13 February 1996)

In reply to a later question on the same subject, the Minister of State wrote:

The two sides do not agree on the question precisely because they take different views of the relevance of international documents concerned. The 1923 treaty of Lausanne, two agreements of 1932, and the 1947 Paris treaty of peace with Italy are among these.

(Ibid., vol. 272, WA, col. *346*: 26 February 1996)

Part Twelve: II. A. *Pacific settlement of disputes—modes of settlement— negotiation*

In the course of a press interview given on 3 January 1996, the Secretary of State for Foreign and Commonwealth Affairs, Mr Malcolm Rifkind, stated:

Clearly any long term agreement with regard to the use of the resource of the Caspian Sea cannot proceed unless there is genuine agreement between all the littoral States. It is therefore important that not only for Russia and Iran, but also for the other countries that share the coastline of the Caspian Sea to try and reach agreement on the outstanding question of jurisdiction over any oil exploitation. Any prospect for agreement has to be based on sound international legal principles, but will also be facilitated if there is a political will to reach an early agreement so that these economic opportunities can be realised.

(Text provided by the FCO)

Part Twelve: II. D. *Pacific settlement of disputes—modes of settlement—good offices*

(See also Part Twelve: II. G. 1. (item of 5 November 1996), below)

In reply to a question on the subject of Her Majesty's Government's policy towards Kashmir, the Minister of State, FCO, wrote:

We continue to believe that the best way forward on Kashmir should involve simultaneous progress on dialogue between India and Pakistan as provided for under the 1972 Simla agreement; an improvement in human rights in Kashmir and a genuine political process there; and a clear cessation of external support for violence in Kashmir. We stand ready to offer our good offices to help resolve the dispute if both sides so wish.

(HC Debs., vol. 269, WA., col. *247*: 10 January 1996)

The following question was asked of Her Majesty's Government:

Whether in view of the current dispute between Eritrea and the Yemen over the Hanish islands, they accept that the United Kingdom as the former colonial power in the region, has some responsibility for the dispute; what protection they are offering to any British trading interests that may remain in the region; and what steps they are taking to promote a peaceful settlement of the dispute?

In reply, the Government spokesman in the House of Lords wrote:

Her Majesty's Government do not consider they have responsibility for the dispute. The 1923 Treaty of Lausanne provides for the future of the islands to be settled by the parties concerned. We support efforts by the French Government and others to help resolve the dispute, and have made clear we are willing to provide access for both sides to historical documents in our possession. We continue to ensure that British shipping and aviation are kept informed of developments in the area.

(HL Debs., vol. 570, *WA 141*: 27 March 1996)

Part Twelve: II. G. *Peaceful settlement of disputes—modes of settlement—arbitration*

In reply to the question what steps were Her Majesty's Government taking to assist in preventing the rise of conflict between Greece and Turkey, the Minister of State, FCO, stated:

We are encouraging both sides to eschew provocative actions or statements and look for ways of developing constructive dialogue. We have suggested to both that, on the specific question of Imia, the best way forward must be to submit the dispute to arbitration.

(HC Debs., vol. 273, WA, col. 255: 6 March 1996)

In reply to a question asking, *inter alia*, 'why [Her Majesty's Government] are unwilling publicly to acknowledge Greece's international border with Turkey', the Government spokesman in the House of Lords wrote:

The precise demarcation of the border between Greece and Turkey involves judgments on the complex international legal background to maritime boundaries in the Aegean. The matter is one for the parties to sort out in accordance with international law. The best way to proceed must be to submit the dispute to arbitration. We regularly discuss tensions in the Aegean with the United States.

(HL Debs., vol. 571, *WA 19*: 3 April 1996)

Part Twelve: II. G. 1. *Pacific settlement of disputes—modes of settlement—arbitration—arbitral tribunals and commissions*

The following provisions appear in the Agreement between the Governments of the UK and the Republic of Slovenia for the Promotion and Protection of Investments, signed on 3 July 1996 but not yet in force:

ARTICLE 8

Settlement of Disputes between an Investor and a Host State

(1) Disputes between a national or company of one Contracting Party and the other Contracting Party concerning an obligation of the latter under this Agreement in relation to an investment of the former which have not been amicably settled shall, after a period of three months from written notification of a claim, be submitted to international arbitration if the national or company concerned so wishes.
(2) Where the dispute is referred to international arbitration, the national or company and the Contracting Party concerned in the dispute may agree to refer the dispute either to:

  (a) the International Centre for the Settlement of Investment Disputes (having regard to the provisions, where applicable, of the Convention on the Settlement of Investment Disputes between States and Nationals of other States, opened for signature at Washington DC on 18 March 1965 and the Additional Facility for the Administration of Conciliation, Arbitration and Fact-Finding Proceedings); or
  (b) the Court of Arbitration of the International Chamber of Commerce; or

(c) an international arbitrator or *ad hoc* arbitration tribunal to be appointed by a special agreement or established under the Arbitration Rules of the United Nations Commission on International Trade Law.

If after a period of three months from written notification of the claim there is no agreement to one of the above alternative procedures, the dispute shall at the request in writing of the national or company concerned be submitted to arbitration under the Arbitration Rules of the United Nations Commission on International Trade Law as then in force. The parties to the dispute may agree in writing to modify these Rules.

ARTICLE 9

Disputes between the Contracting Parties

(1) Disputes between the Contracting Parties concerning the interpretation or application of this Agreement should, if possible, be settled through the diplomatic channel.

(2) If a dispute between the Contracting Parties cannot thus be settled, it shall upon the request of either Contracting Party be submitted to an arbitral tribunal.

(3) Such an arbitral tribunal shall be constituted for each individual case in the following way. Within two months of the receipt of the request for arbitration, each Contracting Party shall appoint one member of the tribunal. Those two members shall then select a national of a third State who on approval by the two Contracting Parties shall be appointed Chairman of the tribunal. The Chairman shall be appointed within two months from the date of appointment of the other two members.

(4) If within the periods specified in paragraph (3) of this Article the necessary appointments have not been made, either Contracting Party may, in the absence of any other agreement, invite the President of the International Court of Justice to make any necessary appointments. If the President is a national of either Contracting Party or if he is otherwise prevented from discharging the said function, the Vice-President shall be invited to make the necessary appointments. If the Vice-President is a national of either Contracting Party or if he too is prevented from discharging the said function, the Member of the International Court of Justice next in seniority who is not a national of either Contracting Party shall be invited to make the necessary appointments.

(5) The arbitral tribunal shall reach its decision by a majority of votes. Such decision shall be binding on both Contracting Parties. Each Contracting Party shall bear the cost of its own member of the tribunal and of its representation in the arbitral proceedings; the cost of the Chairman and the remaining costs shall be borne in equal parts by the Contracting Parties. The tribunal may, however, in its decision direct that a higher proportion of costs shall be borne by one of the two Contracting Parties, and this award shall be binding on both Contracting Parties. The tribunal shall determine its own procedure.

(Cm 3496)

At a press conference held at Sana'a, Yemen, on 5 November 1996, the

Secretary of State for Foreign and Commonwealth Affairs, Mr Malcolm Rifkind, stated:

I very much welcome the agreement that has been reached between Yemen and Eritrea—that they should go to arbitration. We are delighted that the Arbitral Tribunal will be hearing and discussing these matters in London, in the United Kingdom. And we have indicated that the British Royal Navy will be able to provide expert help in hydrography that will assist the work of the Tribunal.

(Text provided by the FCO)

Part Twelve: II. H. 1. *Pacific settlement of disputes—modes of settlement—judicial settlement—the International Court of Justice*

(See also Part Six: I. B. (item of 20 March 1996), Part Eight: II. A. (item of 6 September 1996) and Part Nine: IX. (item of 31 October 1996), above)

The following Presidency statement on behalf of the EU was made on 20 February 1996:

The European Union, deeply concerned about recurrent episodes which imperil internal peace and regional stability in Africa, as well as about border disputes which threaten to pave the way to countless territorial claims, while deploring the recourse to the use of military force by the parties concerned, expresses its apprehension regarding the dispute between Cameroon and Nigeria in the Bakassi peninsula as well as its concern about the signs of renewed military confrontation registered since 3 February 1996.

The Union invites the parties confronting one another to abstain from all military intervention and abide by international law and particularly by the charter of the United Nations and expresses its wish that a peaceful solution be found to the dispute through recourse to the International Court of Justice.

The European Union requests the parties to revert to the positions that they held prior to the appeal to the Court of Justice.

(*Bulletin of the European Union*, 1996–1/2, p. 79)

Speaking in the UN General Assembly on 24 September 1996, the Secretary of State for Foreign and Commonwealth Affairs, Mr Malcolm Rifkind, stated:

The International Court of Justice has performed ground breaking work in settling disputes between States, and I am proud that the United Kingdom has always been among the States that accept its compulsory jurisdiction. I hope that others will join us in pledging both moral and material support to the International Court. The more who accept that international law must be the foundation of international relations, the safer we shall all be.

(A/51/PV.6, p. 17)

In a press release issued on 20 December 1996, the Secretary of State for Foreign and Commonwealth Affairs, Mr Malcolm Rifkind, referred to the Sino-British Joint Declaration of 1984 (the JD) and continued:

The present electoral arrangements in Hong Kong are entirely consistent with the Joint Declaration. Independent legal experts confirmed this in evidence to the House of Commons Foreign Affairs Committee in 1994. Our proposals commanded strong public support in Hong Kong, as was shown by opinion polls and record levels of voter registration and turn-out. Hong Kong's stability and prosperity have been enhanced, not damaged, by a legislature elected on an open and fair basis. There is no justification for China to replace a legislature elected openly and fairly by more than one million Hong Kong people. This will be a serious set-back for the development of representative government in Hong Kong foreseen in the JD and China's Basic Law for the Hong Kong Special Administrative Region (the BL). China should be prepared to trust Hong Kong people with the measure of democracy we have introduced. There is no basis for a provisional legislature in the JD or the BL. Common sense suggests that a body chosen by a hand-picked 'electorate' of 400 is not, in any reasonable sense, a 'legislature constituted by elections', as required by paragraph 49 of the JD. We take an equally serious view of China's plan to have a provisional legislature start operating six months before the handover. All the tasks China apparently has in mind for a provisional legislature before the handover can and should be accomplished by others, notably the Chief Executive (designate) and his team. China has solemnly committed itself in the JD to cooperating with British administration of Hong Kong until the handover, in the interest of maintaining and preserving Hong Kong's prosperity and stability (JD30). After the handover China will continue to be bound by its promise that the legislature of the Hong Kong Special Administrative Region will be constituted by elections. A provisional legislature composed on the basis proposed by China cannot meet this promise. China thus has a clear duty to return as soon as possible to unambiguous implementation of the JD and to minimise the damage which a provisional legislature may cause. We are therefore calling on China, in the interests of Hong Kong,—first, in accordance with its JD commitment to cooperate with British administration of Hong Kong, strictly to honour the undertaking given me by the Chinese Foreign Minister, Vice Premier Qian Qichen, in April this year that 'the PL will not assume its functions before 1 July 1997'; and—second, to ensure that the Government of the Hong Kong Special Administrative Region takes steps as soon as possible after the handover to replace the provisional legislature with a substantive legislature constituted by genuine elections in the sense in which any reasonable person would understand that term. If China were seriously to argue that its action was consistent with its JD commitments, we would be willing to join China in submitting the question to independent legal settlement, for example to the International Court of Justice. We should also welcome the views of respected international independent legal institutions on the matter.

(Text provided by the FCO)

Part Thirteen: I. B. *Coercion and counter-measures short of the use of force—unilateral acts—non-forcible counter-measures*

On 7 November 1996, the UK representative, Professor I. Brownlie, made a statement to the Sixth Committee of the UN General Assembly discussing the report of the International Law Commission. Speaking of draft articles prepared by the Commission, he stated:

Let me pass now to the second issue: the appropriateness of the provisions on counter-measures. The United Kingdom delegation explained its basic position on this matter in a written paper circulated last year which contained comments on the provisional draft Articles dealing with counter-measures adopted to date. In the present state of international organisation, the right of an injured State to have recourse to counter-measures is both necessary and unavoidable.

. . .

All in all, it seems better to adhere to the more general limitation that counter-measures are recognised as a legitimate measure of last resort, but subject to a criterion of necessity. These guiding principles could be spelled out more directly in the draft.

(Text provided by the FCO)

Part Thirteen: II. A. *Coercion and counter-measures short of the use of force—collective measures—regime of the UN*

The United Nations Arms Embargoes (Dependent Territories) Order 1995 (Statutory Instruments 1995, No. 1032), which came into force on 16 May 1995, was accompanied by the following explanatory note:

This Order, made under the United Nations Act 1946, applies to each of the territories specified in Schedule 1. It imposes restrictions pursuant to decisions of the Security Council of the United Nations in resolution 713 (1991) of 25th September 1991, which provided for States to 'implement a general and complete embargo on all deliveries of weapons and military equipment' to the former Yugoslavia, and in resolution 733 (1992) of 23rd January 1992, resolution 788 (1992) of 19th November 1992 and resolution 918 (1994) of 17th May 1994, which made similar provision in relation to Somalia, Liberia and Rwanda respectively.

In reply to questions, the Government Minister in the House of Lords wrote:

Sanctions against Libya cannot be evaluated in terms of value for money. The aim of sanctions is to ensure that Libya complies with its international obligations. In any case British exports to Libya rose 15 per cent. in 1995.

It is misleading to evaluate the United Nations sanctions against Iraq in terms of their impact on the price of oil. The aim of United Nations sanctions is to ensure that Iraq complies with its international obligations under relevant United Nations Security Council Resolutions and that it cannot again threaten regional security. The maintenance of international peace and security is very much in our interests.

(HL Debs., vol. 569, *WA 67–8*: 20 February 1996)

The following notice, dated 27 February 1996, was issued by the FCO:

UNITED NATIONS ACT 1946

The Serbia and Montenegro (United Nations Prohibition of Flights) Order 1992 (No. 1304)

The Serbia and Montenegro (United Nations Sanctions) Order 1992 (No. 1302)

The Serbia and Montenegro (United Nations Sanctions) (Channel Islands) Order 1992 (No. 1308)

The Serbia and Montenegro (United Nations Sanctions) Order 1993 (No. 1188)

The Serbia and Montenegro (United Nations Sanctions) (Channel Islands) Order 1993 (No. 1253)

The Serbia and Montenegro (United Nations Sanctions) (Isle of Man) Order 1993 (No. 1254)

The Former Yugoslavia (United Nations Sanctions) Order 1994 (No. 2673)

The Former Yugoslavia (United Nations Sanctions) (Channel Islands) Order 1994 (No. 2675)

In his Notice of the 24th November 1995, the Secretary of State for Foreign and Commonwealth Affairs gave notice that, by resolution 1022 (1995) adopted on 22nd November 1995, the Security Council of the United Nations had decided to suspend indefinitely the operation of the measures imposed by resolutions 757 (1992), 820 (1993) 942 (1994) and other relevant resolutions, which imposed certain measures in relation to Serbia and Montenegro and the United Nations Protected Areas of the Republic of Croatia, with the exception that certain assets frozen or impounded pursuant to resolutions 757 (1992) and 820 (1993) shall remain frozen or impounded as provided in paragraph 5 of resolution 1022 (1995).

Pursuant to the provisions of Article 1(2) of the abovementioned Orders, the Secretary of State hereby gives notice that the suspension is extended, with effect from 27th February 1996, to the measures imposed by the said resolution in relation to the areas of Bosnia and Herzegovina controlled by the Bosnian Serb forces.

By resolution 1022 (1995) the Security Council further decided that, on the occurrence of certain events specified in the resolution, (a) the measures would be automatically reimposed, or (b) the measures would be cancelled. In either of these cases a further notice will be issued.

By resolution 1022 (1995) the Security Council further decides that States shall continue to ensure that there shall be no claim in connection with the performance of any contract or other transaction where such performance was affected by the measures imposed by the resolutions referred to above and related resolutions.

In accordance with the provisions of the said Article 1(2), the operation of the above-mentioned Orders was therefore suspended indefinitely with effect from 27 February 1996 in respect of the measures imposed in relation to the areas of Bosnia and Herzegovina controlled by the Bosnia Serb forces.

(*The London Gazette*, 1996, p. 3180)

In reply to a question asking for a list of the Security Council resolutions which preclude the release of interest from frozen Iraqi assets in the UK in order to produce money to compensate claimants, the Minister of State, FCO, wrote:

None of the United Nations Security Council resolutions concerning Iraq provide for the interest on funds in frozen Iraqi accounts in the United Kingdom to be made available by the Government to meet the claims of UK nationals against Iraq.

As required by the provisions of UNSCR 778, all funds in the UK representing the proceeds of the sale of Iraqi petroleum or petroleum products, paid for on or after 6 August 1990, have been transferred to the United Nations' escrow account provided for in UNSCRs 706 and 712. Under SCR 778, sequestrated funds are net of any amounts needed to meet third party rights over such funds existing at the time of its adoption. Funds in the UN escrow account are available to the UN Compensation Commission—UNCC—for meeting the costs of compensation arising out of the Gulf war. They are also available for meeting the costs of UN activities and humanitarian relief. The relevant UNSCRs do not make provision for the Government to have access to these funds or interest on them for the purpose of meeting claims by UK nationals against Iraq other than through the mechanism of the UNCC.

(HC Debs., vol. 273, WA, col. *392*: 8 March 1996)

The United Nations (International Tribunals) (Former Yugoslavia) Order 1996 (Statutory Instruments 1996, No. 716), which came into force on 15 March 1996, has the following explanatory note attached to it:

This Order makes provision as respects the United Kingdom to implement a resolution of the Security Council of the United Nations relating to the former Yugoslavia.

The Order has effect for the purpose of enabling the United Kingdom to co-operate with the International Tribunal for the Prosecution of Persons Responsible for Serious Violations of International Humanitarian Law Committed in the Territory of the Former Yugoslavia since 1991 established by Resolution 827 (1993) of the Security Council of the United Nations ('International Tribunal') in the investigation and prosecution of persons accused of committing International Tribunal crimes and the punishment of persons convicted of such crimes.

The United Nations (International Tribunals) (Rwanda) Order 1996 (Statutory Instruments 1996, No. 1296), which entered into force on 17 May 1996, has the following explanatory note attached to it:

This Order makes provision as respects the United Kingdom to implement a resolution of the Security Council of the United Nations relating to Rwanda.

The Order has effect for the purpose of enabling the United Kingdom to co-operate with the International Criminal Tribunal for the Prosecution of Persons Responsible for Genocide and Other Serious Violations of International Humanitarian Law Committed in the Territory of Rwanda and Rwandan citizens responsible for genocide and other such violations committed in the territory of neighbouring states, between 1 January 1994 and 31 December 1994, established by resolution 955(1994) of the Security Council of the United Nations ('International Tribunal') in the investigation and prosecution of persons accused of committing international tribunal crimes and the punishment of persons convicted of such crimes.

In a press statement issued on 20 May 1996, an FCO spokesman observed:

United Nations Security Council Resolution 1054 required UN members to reduce significantly the number and the level of staff at Sudanese diplomatic missions and restrict or control the movement of those who remain; and to take steps to restrict the entry into or transit through their territory of members and officials of the government of Sudan and members of its armed forces. We have, therefore, decided to expel three Sudanese diplomats, including a Minister-Counsellor. We have also decided to refuse to grant visas to those specified in the resolution and to require notification of journeys by Sudanese Embassy staff outside the Greater London area.

The Sudanese Ambassador was summoned to the FCO today and told of the decision by a senior official. The diplomats would have one month in which to leave London. Travel by the remaining Sudanese diplomats outside the London area would in future be subject to prior notification.

There would be no justification for retaliation against implementation of UN sanctions. The resolution was the result of concern at Sudanese complicity in acts of terrorism.

(Text provided by the FCO)

Speaking in exercise of a right of reply in the UN General Assembly on 1 October 1996, the UK representative, Mr Hollis, referred to the 'consistent failure of the Libyan Government to comply fully with Security Council resolutions 731(1992), 748(1992) and 883(1993)'. He continued:

Compliance with Security Council resolutions under Chapter VII is an obligation of all State Members of the United Nations. The United Kingdom seeks no more, and no less, than that Libya demonstrates its respect for the United Nations and the international community by complying fully with the relevant resolutions. It is not for Libya to try to negotiate with the Security Council about its obligations under Chapter VII of the Charter. These obligations are clearly set out in the resolution. So-called compromises offered by the Libyans, and referred to in the Libyan representative's speech, are not acceptable.

(A/51/PV.17, p. 28)

In a press statement issued on 12 June 1996, an FCO spokesman remarked in part:

We deplore Iraq's obstruction of UNSCOM inspection teams, contrary to their obligations under relevant Security Council resolutions.

(Text provided by the FCO)

In reply to a question, the Minister of State, FCO, wrote:

On 18 June, the UN Security Council confirmed that the UN arms embargo on former Yugoslavia was terminated in accordance with UN Security Council resolution 1021. The Government have decided that, taking into account the overall situation in the states of the former Yugoslavia and the paramount importance of ensuring the safety of British and other troops deployed in Bosnia and Herzegovina and Croatia, applications for arms export licenses will be dealt with on the following basis:
   (a) for Slovenia and the Former Yugoslavia Republic of Macedonia, applications for licences to export military equipment listed in group 1 of part III of schedule 1 to the Export of Goods (Control) Order 1994 and dual use equipment will be considered on a case-by-case basis;
   (b) for Bosnia and Herzegovina, Croatia and the Federal Republic of Yugoslavia, our policy is not to allow the export of military equipment listed in group 1 of part III of schedule 1 to the Export of Goods (Control) Order of 1994 during the period of the NATO-led implementation force's deployment. Within this context, applications for export licences will continue to be considered on a case-by-case basis, as will applications for export of dual use goods.
   The EU as a whole has adopted a common position along these lines. We will keep this policy under review, particularly in light of progress in implementing the peace agreement for Bosnia and Herzegovina.

(HC Debs., vol. 281, WA, col. 358: 15 July 1996)

The United Nations Arms Embargoes (Former Yugoslavia) (Amendment) Order 1996 (Statutory Instruments 1996, No. 1629), which came into force on 30 July 1996, has the following explanatory note attached to it:

This Order, made under the United Nations Act 1946, amends the United Nations Arms Embargoes (Liberia, Somalia and the Former Yugoslavia) Order 1993 by revoking the restrictions contained therein on the delivery and supply of arms and related materiel to the territories of the former Yugoslavia. The Order implements the decision of the Security Council of the United Nations, in a resolution adopted on 22nd November 1995, to terminate the arms embargo in respect of the territories of the former Yugoslavia. In addition, the opportunity has been taken to bring the definition of 'prohibited goods' into line with recent legislation and to take account of the termination of the United Nations Operation in Somalia II.

The United Nations Arms Embargoes (Somalia, Liberia and Rwanda) (Isle of Man) Order (Statutory Instruments 1996, No. 3153), which entered into force on 21 December 1996, was accompanied by the following explanatory note:

This Order, made under the United Nations Act 1946, gives effect in the Isle of Man to the imposition of restrictions pursuant to decisions of the Security Council of the United Nations in Resolution No. 733 of 23rd January 1992 which provided for States to 'implement a general and complete embargo on all deliveries of weapons and military equipment' in relation to Somalia, Resolution No. 788 of 19th November 1992 which made similar provision in relation to Liberia, and Resolution No. 918 of 17th May 1994 which made similar provision in relation to Rwanda.

The United Nations Arms Embargoes (Somalia, Liberia and Rwanda) (Channel Islands) Order 1996 (Statutory Instruments 1996, No. 3154), which came into force on 21 December 1996, was accompanied by the following explanatory note:

This Order, made under the United Nations Act 1946, gives effect in the Channel Islands to the imposition of restrictions pursuant to decisions of the Security Council of the United Nations in Resolution No. 733 of 23rd January 1992 which provided for States to 'implement a general and complete embargo on all deliveries of weapons and military equipment' in relation to Somalia, Resolution No. 788 of 19th November 1992 which made similar provision in relation to Liberia, and Resolution No. 918 of 17th May 1994 which made similar provision in relation to Rwanda.

Part Thirteen: II. B. *Coercion and counter-measures short of the use of force—collective measures—outside the UN*

In reply to a request to list those members of the Nigerian Government who are prohibited from entry to the UK, the Minister of State, FCO, wrote:

In accordance with the common position adopted by the European Union on 4 December, all members of the Federal Executive Council, the provisional Ruling Council, serving members of the military and security forces, and their families shall be refused entry to the United Kingdom.

(HC Debs., vol. 269, WA, col. *486*: 16 January 1996)

In reply to the question 'whether it is in accordance with international law or World Trade Organisation rules for one country to declare economic sanctions on another without the approval of the UN Security Council', the Minister of State, FCO, wrote:

Whether economic sanctions are permissible under international law in the absence of a UN Security Council Resolution depends on all the circumstances. Within the context of the World Trade Organisation, GATT Articles XX and XXI allow action to be taken by a member against another member in the cases set out in those articles.

(HL Debs., vol. 568, *WA 86*: 25 January 1996)

In reply to a question, the Parliamentary Under-Secretary of State, Department of Trade and Industry, wrote:

At the end of last year, the European Union decided to strengthen its measures against the military regime in response to adverse developments in Nigeria. Among these measures was strengthening of the existing restrictions on the sale of military equipment, though there was no agreement to extend these measures to existing contracts and therefore export licences which were issued against those contracts were not revoked.

So far as future exports are concerned, in common with arms embargoes against other countries, the embargo against Nigeria will include all military, security and para-military goods and arms, ammunition and related material which is listed in group 1 of part III of schedule 1 to the Export of Goods (Control) Order 1994, available from HMSO. The rules do not distinguish between items intended for the military and for the police, nor has any exception been allowed for international peacekeeping operations in which the Nigerians might be involved.

(HC Debs., vol. 272, WA, col. *231*: 22 February 1996)

In reply to a question, the Minister of State, FCO, wrote:

At the recent General Affairs Council in Luxembourg, Ministers adopted an EU common position on Burma, which imposes the following measures on the ruling State Law and Order Restoration Council—SLORC:

> ban on entry visas for senior members of the SLORC and their families:

> ban on entry visas for senior members of the military or the security forces who formulate, implement or benefit from policies that impede Burma's transition to democracy, and their families;

> suspension of high-level bilateral governmental visits to Burma (Ministers and officials at level of political director and above).

(HC Debs., vol. 284, WA, col. *533*: 6 November 1996)

Part Fourteen: I. B. 6. *War and other uses of force—international war and armed conflict—the laws of war and armed conflict—humanitarian law*

In reply to the question whether the use of shells containing 3-inch steel darts (*fléchettes*) contravenes international humanitarian law, the Government spokesman in the House of Lords wrote in part:

Whether the use of *fléchette* rounds contravenes international humanitarian law depends on the circumstances of each case. We deplore the use of such weapons where they are excessively injurious or have indiscriminate effects, in particular where they cause casualties among the civilian population or a neutral force such as UNIFIL.

(HL Debs., vol. 569, *WA* 7: 5 February 1996)

In reply to the question 'whether [Her Majesty's Government] will propose to the relevant international fora that Common Article 3 of the Geneva Convention applies to the armed conflict widespread in Turkey since 1984', the Minister of State, FCO, Baroness Chalker, stated:

My Lords, whether a state of internal armed conflict for the purpose of Common Article 3 of the Geneva Conventions exists at any given time is a question of fact to be determined in the light of all the circumstances. It is not a matter for other governments to propose or dispose. We will continue to urge the Turkish Government to take a multi-faceted approach to the conflict in the south east.

(HL Debs., vol. 576, col. 931: 10 December 1996)

Part Fourteen: I. B. 7. *War and other uses of force—international war and armed conflict—the laws of war and armed conflict—belligerent occupation*

In the course of a debate in the House of Lords on the subject of East Jerusalem, the Government spokesman, Lord Chesham, observed:

Our position is that all settlements in occupied territory are illegal and are an obstacle to peace. We have raised the issue repeatedly with the Israeli Government.

(HL Debs., vol. 568, col. 257: 11 January 1996)

In the course of answering an oral question on the subject of the Middle East peace process, the Minister of State, FCO, Mr Jeremy Hanley, referred to the coming visit to Hebron of the Secretary of State for Foreign and Commonwealth Affairs and continued:

He will state firmly to the Israelis our position on Israeli settlements in the occupied territories. Under the fourth Geneva Convention, all settlements in the occupied territories are illegal and an obstacle to peace.

(HC Debs., vol. 284, col. 635: 30 October 1996)

During a press conference given at Hebron on 3 November 1996 by the Secretary of State for Foreign and Commonwealth Affairs, Mr Malcolm Rifkind remarked:

I am asked about the question of settlements. The British Government believe that all the Israeli settlements, the Jewish settlements, in the Occupied Territories are illegal and therefore should not continue.

(Text provided by the FCO)

Part Fourteen: I. B. 9. *War and other uses of force—international war and armed conflict—the laws of war and armed conflict—nuclear, bacteriological and chemical weapons*

In reply to a question, the Minister of State, FCO, wrote:

The Outer Space Treaty does not specifically prohibit the possession or use of anti-satellite weapons. The United Kingdom is not a party to the Anti-Ballistic Missile Treaty and it is therefore not for Her Majesty's Government to comment on its interpretation.

(HL Debs., vol. 568, *WA 85*: 25 January 1996)

In reply to the question 'what assessment [the Secretary of State] has made of allegations that the United Kingdom breached its obligations in regard to article II of the nuclear non-proliferation treaty in trade with Iraq since 1979', the Minister of State, FCO, wrote:

Article II of the nuclear non-proliferation treaty confers obligations on non-nuclear weapon states party to the treaty not to obtain or manufacture nuclear weapons or other nuclear explosive devices, or seek or receive any assistance in their manufacture. The United Kingdom is a nuclear-weapon state and the obligations under article II of the treaty are therefore not directly relevant.

(HC Debs., vol. 272, WA, col. *558*: 28 February 1996)

In a statement issued on 10 April 1996, an FCO spokesman observed:

The British Government will sign Protocols I and II to the African Nuclear-Weapons-Free Zone Treaty (Treaty of Pelindaba) at the signing ceremony in Cairo on 11 April.

Following the extension of the Non-Proliferation Treaty in 1995 and our signature in March this year of the Protocols to the Treaty of Rarotonga (South Pacific), our support for the Treaty of Pelindaba further demonstrates our commitment to nuclear non-proliferation and to the objectives set out in the Document on Principles and Objectives for nuclear non-proliferation and disarmament adopted at the Nuclear Non-Proliferation Treaty Review and Extension Conference in 1995.

Taken with our signature of the Protocols to the Treaty of Rarotonga it also underlines our wish to see a permanent end to nuclear testing and early conclusion of the Comprehensive Test Ban Treaty.

(Text provided by the FCO)

In reply to a question, the Minister of State, FCO, wrote:

The UK signed, subject to ratification, protocols 1 and 2 to the African nuclear weapons free zone treaty on 11 April. Parties to protocol 1 undertake not to use or threaten to use nuclear weapons against parties to the treaty. On signature we stated that we would not be bound by this undertaking if a state party to the treaty attacked us in alliance with a nuclear weapon state, or was in breach of its own non-proliferation obligations under the treaty. Our statement also noted that compliance with international agreements to prevent the proliferation of weapons of mass destruction is vital to the maintenance of world security.

(HC Debs., vol. 279, WA, col. *40*: 10 June 1996)

In reply to a question, the Minister of State, FCO, wrote:

The Latin America Nuclear Weapon Free Zone (NWFZ) was established in 1967 by the Treaty of Tlatelolco; the South Pacific Nuclear Free Zone in 1985 (Treaty of Rarotonga); the South East Asian NWFZ in 1995 (Treaty of Bangkok); and the African NWFZ in April 1996 (Treaty of Pelindaba).

Other possible NWFZs which have been subject to recent UNGA resolutions include zones in South Asia and the Middle East. In line with the Principles and Objectives document agreed at the 1995 NPT Review and Extension Conference, the UK supports the establishment of nuclear weapon free zones on the basis of arrangements freely arrived at among the states concerned.

Under the existing NWFZ treaties, signatories within the zones undertake not to develop, manufacture, acquire or possess nuclear weapons and those Nuclear Weapon States which have ratified the relevant protocols undertake not to use or threaten to use nuclear explosive devices against them. All five Nuclear Weapon States have ratified the relevant protocols to the Treaty of Tlatelolco and signed those to the Treaty of Rarotonga. The UK, US, France and China have signed the relevant protocols to the Treaty of Pelindaba. In adhering to these protocols, the UK has made clear that we will not be bound by our undertaking in the case of an invasion or other attack on us, our dependent territories, our allies or a state to which we have a security commitment which has been carried out or sustained by a party to one of the treaties in association or alliance with a Nuclear Weapon State. France has stated that the protocols will not undermine its right to self defence as recognised in Article 51 of the UN Charter.

(HL Debs., vol. 573, *WA 93*: 2 July 1996)

In a letter dated 16 September 1996 addressed to Mr David Hanson MP, the Minister of State, FCO, Mr David Davis, wrote:

Thank you for your letter of 3 September to Nicholas Bonsor, about the opinion given recently by the International Court of Justice (ICJ) on the legality of the threat or use of nuclear weapons.

As you may be aware, the UK argued before the ICJ that this issue was not suitable for judicial determination,. We also argued that the use of nuclear weapons is not prohibited *per se* under international law and that the legality of any such use would depend upon all the circumstances of the case. We remain of that view.

The Court's Opinion is long and complex and we are of course studying it. But we note that, amongst other things, the Court concluded by a large majority that there is in international law no comprehensive and universal prohibition of the threat or use of nuclear weapons as such. We also note that on the key point of whether the use or threat of use of nuclear weapons would be unlawful in all circumstances, the Court concluded that it was unable to offer a definitive opinion.

We do not believe that the Opinion gives rise to any new factors affecting the fundamentals of UK and NATO defence policy, including the continuing importance of nuclear deterrence in maintaining peace and stability in Europe. Nor do we believe that the Court's opinion imposes any new disarmament obligations on us.

(Text provided by the FCO)

Speaking in the UN General Assembly on 24 September 1996, the Secretary of State of Foreign and Commonwealth Affairs, Mr Malcolm Rifkind, stated:

The world is safer today too with the historic signature of the Comprehensive Nuclear-Test-Ban Treaty. Earlier this morning I had the privilege of signing the Treaty for the United Kingdom. . . . It is the sovereign right of every State to decide whether or not to be bound by international agreements. But it is our firm conviction that this Treaty is in the interest of all, and I urge all States to give it their full support.

(A/51/PV.6, p. 17)

The following question was asked of Her Majesty's Government:

Whether they agree with the Opinion of the International Court of Justice that 'in view of the unique characteristics of nuclear weapons, their destructive capacity and capacity to cause untold human suffering and damage for generations to come, their use in fact seems scarcely reconcilable with respect for the law applicable in armed conflict . . . the threat or use of nuclear weapons would generally be contrary to the rules of international law', and if so whether they will move a Motion to that effect in the United Nations?

In reply, the Minister of State, Baroness Chalker, stated:

. . . we consider that the Opinion, taken as a whole, does not give rise to any new factors affecting the fundamentals of UK and NATO defence policies. Nuclear deterrence continues to be important in maintaining peace and stability in Europe.

In reply to a further question, the Minister stated:

. . . the judgment is extremely complicated. On different aspects of the judgment different groups joined together. I mentioned the large majority which found that in international law there is no comprehensive and universal prohibition of the use or threat of nuclear weapons as such. I do not have the exact break-down of who divided which way on that. What is clear is what I said in my original Answer; that is, that the Opinion must be read as a whole. There is no way in which picking out the bits that appeal to one or other noble Lord or one country or another represents a proper use either of the ICJ or of proper judicial determination. Therefore, the Opinion as a whole must be judged. It is extremely varied, and it is right that this country should proceed in the manner I described in response to the noble Lord . . . .

(HL Debs., vol. 575, cols. 436–8 *passim*; 31 October 1996)

The Minister of State, FCO, Mr David Davis, issued the following statement on 1 November 1996:

I warmly welcome 65th ratification of the Chemical Weapons Convention (CWC). This means CWC will definitely enter into force in 6 months time. This is a milestone in international arms control efforts. The CWC is the first multilateral treaty to impose a complete ban on an entire class of weapons and establish a verification regime to monitor compliance.

(Text provided by the FCO)

Part Fourteen: III. *War and other uses of force—self-defence*

(See also Part Fourteen: I. B. 9. (item of 2 July 1996), above)

In the course of his reply to an oral question on the subject of human rights in Indonesia, the Minister of State, FCO, Mr Jeremy Hanley, remarked:

As for arms to Indonesia, or any defence equipment, under article 51 of the United Nations Charter all sovereign states enjoy the right to self-defence.

(HC Debs., vol. 284, col. 644; 30 October 1996)

APPENDICES

I. MULTILATERAL AGREEMENTS SIGNED BY THE UNITED KINGDOM IN 1996[1]

Title	Place and Date	UK Signature	Text[2]
Amendments to Annex IV of the Convention on the Conservation of European Wildlife and Natural Habitats, done at Berne on 19.9.1979	Strasbourg, 24.3.1995		TS No. 39 (1996) (Cm 3227)
International Rubber Agreement	Geneva, 3.4–28.12.1995	22.12.1995	Misc. No. 27 (1996) (Cm 3468)
Amendments to the Operating Agreement relating to the International Telecommunications Satellite Organization (INTELSAT), done at Washington on 20.8.1971	Singapore, 4–7.4.1995		TS No. 101 (1996) (Cm 3478)
Amendment to Article 20, Paragraph 1 of the Convention on the Elimination of All Forms of Discrimination against Women	New York, 22.5.1995		Misc. No. 15 (1996) (Cm 3286)
Agreement among the States Parties to the North Atlantic Treaty and the Other States Participating in the Partnership for Peace regarding the Status of their Forces	Brussels, 19.6.1995	7.3.1996	Misc. No. 12 (1996) (Cm 3237)

[1] Information supplied by the Foreign and Commonwealth Office. The table includes some agreements signed by the United Kingdom before 1996, where information was not previously available. The information is correct as at January 1997, although in some cases information available since that time has been included.

[2] Publication is in various series of UK Command Papers, including Miscellaneous Series (Misc.) and Treaty Series (TS.) Cm = Command Paper number.

Title	Place and Date	UK Signature	Text
Amendment to the Operating Agreement of the European Telecommunications Satellite Organization (EUTELSAT)	7.7.1995		
1995 Amendments to the Annex to the International Convention on Standards of Training, Certification and Watchkeeping for Seafarers, 1978, with Final Act	London, 7.7.1995		
Amendments to the Agreement on the Conservation of Bats in Europe	Bristol, 18-20.7.1995	18.7.1995	Misc. No. 7 (1996) (Cm 3155)
Protocol on the Authentic Quinquelingual Text of the Convention on International Civil Aviation, done at Chicago on 7.12.1944	Montreal, 29.9.1995	29.9.1995	Misc. No. 21 (1996) (Cm 3341)
Protocol relating to an Amendment to the Convention on International Civil Aviation (Chicago, 7.12.1944)	Montreal, 29.9.1995	29.9.1995	Misc. No. 20 (1996) (Cm 3340)
Amendment to the Schedule of Fees annexed to the Regulations under the Patent Co-operation Treaty (PCT) done at Washington on 19.6.1970	Geneva, 3.10.1995		TS No. 40 (1996) (Cm 3236)
Agreement for the Implementation of the Provisions of the United Nations Convention on the Law of the Sea of 10.12.1982 relating to the Conservation and Management of Straddling	New York, 4.12.1995– 4.12.1996	27.6.1996	Misc. No. 12 (1995) (Cm 3125)

Title	Place and Date	UK Signature	Text
Fish Stocks and Highly Migratory Fish Stocks	New York, 4.12.1995– 4.12.1996	27.6.1996	Misc. No. 12 (1995) (Cm 3125)
Amendments to Appendices II and III of the Convention on the Conservation of European Wildlife and Natural Habitats, done at Bern on 19.9.1979	Strasbourg, 26.1.1996		TS No. 41 (1996) (Cm 3244)
Protocols I, II and III to the African Nuclear Free Zone Treaty (The Treaty of Pelindaba) [The United Kingdom is not a signatory to the Treaty]	Cairo, 11.4.1996	11.4.1996	Misc. No. 29 (1996) (Cm 3498)
Protocol of 1996 to amend the Convention on Limitation of Liability for Maritime Claims, 1976	London, 2.5.1996	16.10.1996	
International Convention on Liability and Compensation for Damage in connection with the Carriage of Hazardous and Noxious Substances by Sea	London, 3.5.1996	16.10.1996	
Protocol on Prohibitions or Restrictions on the Use of Mines, Booby-Traps and Other Devices as amended on 3.5.1996 (Protocol II as amended), annexed to the Convention on Prohibitions or Restrictions on the Use of Certain Conventional Weapons which may be Deemed to be Excessively Injurious or to have Indiscriminate Effects	Geneva, 3.5.1996		

Title	Place and Date	UK Signature	Text
Annex A to the Final Document of the First Conference to Review the Operation of the Treaty on Conventional Armed Forces in Europe and the Concluding Act of the Negotiation on Personnel Strength	Vienna, 15-31.5.1996		
Appendix to the Anti-Doping Convention	Strasbourg, 30-31.5.1996		
Agreement concerning Specific Stability Requirements for Ro-Ro Passenger Ships undertaking Regular Scheduled International Voyages between or to or from Designated Ports in North West Europe and the Baltic Sea	Stockholm, 1.7.–30.9.1996	1.7.1996	
Agreement concerning Home Work (ILO Convention No. 177), with Recommendation	Geneva, 20.6.1996		
Amendments to the Schedule to the International Whaling Convention, 1946	Aberdeen, 28.6.1996		
Agreement on the Conservation of African-Eurasian Migratory Waterbirds	The Hague, 15.8.1996	23.9.1996	Misc. No. 26 (1996) (Cm 3482)
Comprehensive Nuclear-Test-Ban Treaty with Annexes and Protocol	New York, 10.9.1996	24.9.1996	

II. EUROPEAN COMMUNITIES AGREEMENTS SIGNED BY THE UNITED KINGDOM IN 1996[1]

Title	Place and Date	UK Signature	Text[2]
European Agreement establishing an Association between the European Communities and their Member States, of the one part, and the Republic of Lithuania, of the other part, including Exchanges of Letters and Protocols with Declarations and Final Act	Luxembourg, 12.6.1995	12.6.1995	EC No. 10 (1996) (Cm 3228)
Convention drawn up on the Basis of Article K.3 of the Treaty on European Union on the Use of Information Technology for Customs Purposes	Brussels, 26.7.1995	26.7.1995	EC No. 18 (1996) (Cm 3460)
Protocol to the Fourth ACP-EC Convention of Lomé Consequent on the Accession of the Republic of Austria, the Republic of Finland and the Kingdom of Sweden to the European Union	Mauritius, 4.11.1995	4.11.1995	EC No. 12 (1996) (Cm 3284)
Agreement Amending the Fourth ACP-EC Convention of Lomé, with Final Act	Mauritius, 4.11.1995	4.11.1995	EC No. 14 (1996) (Cm 3278)
Euro-Mediterranean Agreement establishing an Association between the European Communities and their Member States,	Brussels, 20.11.1995	20.11.1995	EC No. 11 (1996) (Cm 3239)

---

[1] Information supplied by the Foreign and Commonwealth Office. The table includes some agreements signed by the United Kingdom before 1996, where information was not previously available. The information is correct as at January 1997, although in some cases information available since that time has been included.

[2] Publication is in the European Communities Series of UK Command Papers (EC). Cm = Command Paper number.

Title	Place and Date	UK Signature	Text
of the one part, and the State of Israel, of the other part, including Protocols with Exchange of Letters, Declarations and Final Act	Brussels, 20.11.1995	20.11.1995	EC No. 11 (1996) (Cm 3239)
Inter-regional Framework Co-operation Agreement between the European Community and its Member States, of the one part, and the Southern Common Market and its Party States, of the other part, with Exchange of Letters	Madrid, 15.12.1995	15.12.1995	EC No. 15 (1996) (Cm 3342)
Internal Agreement between the Representatives of the Governments of the Member States, meeting within the Council, on the Financing and Administration of Community Aid under the Second Financial Protocol to the Fourth ACP-EC Convention	Brussels, 20.12.1995	20.12.1995	EC No. 13 (1996) (Cm 3292)
Convention on the Accession of the Republic of Austria, the Republic of Finland and the Kingdom of Sweden to the Convention on the Elimination of Double Taxation in Connection with the Adjustment of Profits of Associated Enterprises, with Minutes of Signing	Brussels, 21.12.1995	21.12.1995	
Euro-Mediterranean Agreement establishing an Association between the European Communities and their Member States, of the one part, and the	Brussels, 26.2.1996	26.2.1996	

Title	Place and Date	UK Signature	Text
Kingdom of Morocco, of the other part, with Final Act	Brussels, 26.2.1996	26.2.1996	
Partnership and Co-operation Agreement establishing a Partnership between the European Communities and their Member States, of the one part, and the Republic of Georgia, of the other part, with Final Act	Luxembourg, 22.4.1996	22.4.1996	EC No. 21 (1996) Cm 3472)
Partnership and Co-operation Agreement establishing a Partnership between the European Communities and their Member States, of the one part, and the Republic of Armenia, of the other part, with Final Act	Luxembourg, 22.4.1996	22.4.1996	EC No. 16 (1996) (Cm 3452)
Partnership and Co-operation Agreement establishing a Partnership between the European Communities and their Member States, of the one part, and the Republic of Azerbaijan, of the other part, with Final Act	Luxembourg, 22.4.1996	22.4.1996	EC No. 19 (1996) (Cm 3456)
Europe Agreement establishing an Association between the European Communities and their Member States, acting within the Framework of the European Union, of the one part, and the Republic of Slovenia, of the other part, with Final Act	Luxembourg, 10.6.1996	10.6.1996	
Framework Cooperation Agreement leading ultimately to the Establishment of and Political and Economic	Florence, 21.6.1996	21.6.1996	EC No. 1 (1997) (Cm 3511)

Title	Place and Date	UK Signature	Text
Association between the European Community and its Member States, of the one part, and the Republic of Chile, of the other part, with Minutes of Signing	Florence, 21.6.1996	21.6.1996	EC No. 1 (1997) (Cm 3511)
Partnership and Co-operation Agreement establishing a Partnership between the European Communities and their Member States, of the one part, and the Republic of Uzbekistan, of the other part, with Final Act	Florence, 21.6.1996	21.6.1996	EC No. 20 (1996) (Cm 3463)
Additional Protocol to the Europe Agreement establishing an Association between the European Communities and their Member States, of the one part, and Romania, of the other part	Brussels, 30.6.1996	30.6.1996	EC No. 1 (1996) (Cm 3081)
Protocol drawn up on the basis of Article K.3 of the Treaty on European Union to the Convention on the Protection of the European Communities' Financial Interests	Dublin, 27.9.1996	27.9.1996	
Convention drawn up on the basis of Article K.3 of the Treaty on European Union relating to Extradition between the Member States of the European Union	Dublin, 27.9.1996	27.9.1996	

Title	Place and Date	UK Signature	Text
Protocol drawn up on the basis of Article K.3 of the Treaty on European Union on the Interpretation, by way of preliminary rulings, by the Court of Justice of the European Communities of the Convention on the Protection of the European Communities' Financial Interests, with Declaration	Brussels, 29.11.1996	29.11.1996	

III. Bilateral Agreements Signed by the United Kingdom in 1996[1]

Country and Title	Place and Date	Text[2]
ALGERIA		
Exchange of Notes concerning Certain Commercial Debts (UK/ Algeria Debt Agreement No. 2 (1995))	Algiers, 18.2.1996	TS No. 77 (1996) (Cm 3352)
ARGENTINA		
Convention for the Avoidance of Double Taxation and the Prevention of Fiscal Evasion with respect to Taxes on Income and Capital, with Protocol	Buenos Aires, 3.1.1996	
AZERBAIJAN		
Agreement for the Promotion and Protection of Investments	Baku, 4.1.1996	TS No. 19 (1997) (Cm 3576)
BOLIVIA		
Exchange of Notes concering Certain Commercial Debts (UK/ Bolivia Debt Agreement No. 6 (1995))	London, 10/25.6.1996	
BRAZIL		
Exchange of Notes concering the UK/Brazil Debt Rescheduling Agreement (No. 1) 1996	Brasilia, 31.1.1996	TS No. 37 (1996) (Cm 3235)
Exchange of Notes concering the UK/Brazil Debt Rescheduling Agreement (No. 2) 1996	Brasilia, 31.1.1996	TS No. 38 (1996) (Cm 3227)
CHILE		
Agreement for the Promotion and Protection of Investments, with Protocol	Santiago, 8.1.1996	

---

[1] Information supplied by the Foreign and Commonwealth Office. The table includes some agreements signed by the United Kingdom before 1996, where information was not previously available. The information is correct as at January 1997, although in some cases information available since that time has been included.

[2] Publication is in various series of UK Command Papers, including Miscellaneous Series (Misc.) and Treaty Series (TS). Cm = Command Paper number.

Country and Title	Place and Date	Text
CHINA (PEOPLE'S REPUBLIC OF)		
Exchange of Notes concerning Liability for Damage during the Launch Stage of the Apstar-IA and Apstar-IIR Satellites	Peking, 5/6.2.1996	TS No. 52 (1996) (Cm 3274)
Agreement concerning Maritime Transport	London, 17.7.1996	TS No. 91 (1996) (Cm 3454)
Protocol amending the Agreement for the Reciprocal Avoidance of Double Taxation and the Prevention of Fiscal Evasion with respect to Taxes on Income and Capital Gains	Peking, 2.9.1996	
Exchange of Notes concerning the Establishment of a Consulate-General of each Country in the other at Guangzhou and Edinburgh	Peking, 2.9.1996	TS No. 100 (1996) (Cm 3477)
Exchange of Notes concerning the Establishment of a British Consulate-General in Hong Kong	Peking, 26.9.1996	
COTE D'IVOIRE		
Exchange of Notes concerning the UK/Côte d'Ivoire Restrospective Terms Agreement 1996	London, 8.1.1996	
CROATIA		
Agreement concerning Air Services	Zagreb, 21.2.1996	
Agreement on Co-operation in the Fields of Culture, Education and Science	Zagreb, 21.2.1996	Croatia No. 1 (1996) (Cm 3376)
Exchange of Notes concerning Certain Commercial Debts (UK/ Croatia Debt Agreement No. 1 (1995))	Zagreb, 1/4.4.1996	TS No. 11 (1997) (Cm 3543)
CZECH REPUBLIC		
Exchange of Notes regarding the Interpretation of the Consular Convention between the Government of the UK and the Government of the Czechoslovak	London, 4.7/5.11.1996	TS No. 5 (1997) (Cm 3509)

Country and Title	*Place and Date*	*Text*
Socialist Republic, done at Prague on 3.4.1975, for the purposes of Paragraph 3, Article 31 of the 1969 Vienna Convention on the Law of Treaties, concerning Honorary Consuls and Honorary Consular Posts of the Czech Republic in the UK	London, 4.7/5.11.1996	TS No. 5 (1997) (Cm 3509)

DENMARK

Exchange of Notes terminating the Extension of the Convention for the Avoidance of Double Taxation and the Prevention of Fiscal Evasion with respect to Taxes on Income, done at London on 27.3.1950, to the Faroe Islands by an Exchange of Notes on 31.10.1960	London, 28.3/25.6.1996	
Protocol to Amend the Convention for the Avoidance of Double Taxation and the Prevention of Fiscal Evasion with respect to Taxes on Income and on Capital Gains, signed at Copenhagen on 11.11.1980, as amended by the Protocol signed at London on 1.7.1991, with Exchange of Notes	London, 15.10.1996	

DOMINICAN REPUBLIC

Agreement on Maritime Delimitation concerning the Delimitation of the Maritime Boundary between the Dominican Republic and the Turks and Caicos Islands	Santo Domingo, 2.8.1996	Dominican Republic No. 1 (1996) (Cm 3461)

ECUADOR

Exchange of Notes concerning the UK/Ecuador Debt ODA Rescheduling Agreement 1995	London, 8.11.1995	TS No. 43 (1996) (Cm 3247)

Country and Title	Place and Date	Text
ESTONIA		
Agreement on Co-operation in the Fields of Education, Science and Culture	Tallinn, 18.7.1996	TS No. 98 (1996) (Cm 3475)
FINLAND		
Exchange of Notes concerning the Extension of the European Convention on Extradition to Certain Dependent Territories	Helsinki, 6.5/5.7.1996	
Protocol to Amend the Convention for the Reciprocal Avoidance of Double Taxation and the Prevention of Fiscal Evasion with respect to Taxes on Income and on Capital, signed at London on 17.7.1969, as amended by the Protocols signed at London on 17.5.1973, 16.11.1979, 1.10.1985 and 26.9.1991, with Exchange of Notes	Helsinki, 31.7.1996	
FRANCE		
Agreement on Maritime Delimitation concerning Anguilla, on the one hand, and Saint Martin and Saint Barthelemy, on the other	London, 27.6.1996	TS No. 29 (1997) (Cm 3654)
Agreement on Maritime Delimitation concerning Montserrat and Guadeloupe	London, 27.6.1996	TS No. 28 (1997) (Cm 3653)
GABON		
Exchange of Notes concerning Certain Commercial Debts (UK/ Gabon Debt Agreement No. 5 (1995))	Yaounde/ Libreville, 30.7/20.9.1996	
GUINEA		
Exchange of Notes concerning Certain Commercial Debts (The UK/Guinea Debt Agreement No. 5 (1995))	Dakar/ Conakry, 8.12.1995/ 12.2.1996	TS No. 65 (1996) (Cm 3311)

Country and Title	Place and Date	Text
HUNGARY		
Exchange of Notes concerning the Extension of the European Convention on Extradition to Certain Dependent Territories	Budapest, 15.8.1995/ 24.6.1996	
Agreement on International Road Passenger Transport	London, 4.11.1996	
ISRAEL		
Exchange of Notes concerning the Extension of the European Convention on Extradition to Certain Dependent Territories	Tel Aviv, 14.2.1996	
JAMAICA		
Convention on Social Security	London, 12.11.1996	TS No. 32 (1997) (Cm 3666)
KOREA REPUBLIC OF		
Exchange of Notes concerning an Amendment to the Air Services Agreement, done at Seoul on 5.3.1984	Seoul, 11.9.1996	TS No. 12 (1997) (Cm 3544)
Convention for the Avoidance of Double Taxation and the Prevention of Fiscal Evasion with respect to Taxes on Income and on Capital Gains, with Exchange of Notes	Seoul, 25.10.1996	TS No. 10 (1997) (Cm 3530)
LATVIA		
Convention for the Avoidance of Double Taxation and the Prevention of Fiscal Evasion with respect to Taxes on Income and on Capital Gains, with Exchange of Notes	London, 8.5.1996	TS No. 23 (1997) (Cm 3592)
LITHUANIA		
Agreement on Co-operation in the Fields of Culture, Education and Science	Vilnius, 8.11.1996	
MACEDONIA (FORMER YUGOSLAV REPUBLIC OF)		
Agreement on International Road Transport	Skopje, 18.6.1996	Macedonia No. 1 (1996) (Cm 3484)

Country and Title	Place and Date	Text
MALAYSIA		
Agreement for the Avoidance of Double Taxation and the Prevention of Fiscal Evasion with respect to Taxes on Income	Kuala Lumpur, 10.12.1996	
MALDIVES		
Agreement concerning Air Services	Malé, 20.1.1996	TS No. 46 (1996) (Cm 3256)
MEXICO		
Agreement concerning Mutual Assistance in the Investigation, Restraint and Confiscation of the Proceeds and Instruments of Crime other than Drug Trafficking	Mexico City, 26.2.1996	TS No. 79 (1996) (Cm 3358)
MISCELLANEOUS		
Headquarters Agreement with the International Oil Pollution Compensation Fund 1992	London, 30.5.1996	TS No. 78 (1996) (Cm 3354)
MOLDOVA		
Agreement for the Promotion and Protection of Investments	London, 19.3.1996	Moldova No. 1 (1996) (Cm 3255)
Agreement on International Road Transport	London, 15.10.1996	
MONGOLIA		
Convention for the Avoidance of Double Taxation and the Prevention of Fiscal Evasion with respect to Taxes on Income and Capital	London, 23.4.1996	
Agreement on Co-operation in the Fields of Education, Science and Culture	London, 23.4.1996	TS No. 68 (1996) (Cm 3333)
NICARAGUA		
Agreement for the Promotion and Protection of Investments	Managua, 4.12.1996	
NORWAY		
Exchange of Notes concerning the Export of Uranium to Norway	Oslo, 6.6/2.7.1995	TS No. 97 (1995) (Cm 3111)

Country and Title	*Place and Date*	*Text*
Exchange of Notes concerning the Extension of the European Convention on Extradition to the British Dependent Territories	Oslo, 29.6/7.7.1995	
Exchange of Notes concerning the Export of Uranium to Norway	Oslo, 26.1/5.2.1996	TS No. 71 (1996) (Cm 3334)

PERU

Exchange of Notes concerning Certain Commercial Debts (UK/ Peru Debt Agreement No. 5 (1996))	Lima, 4.11.1996	

POLAND

Exchange of Notes concerning the Extension of the European Convention on Extradition to Certain Dependent Territories	Warsaw, 1/25.3.1996	

ROMANIA

Agreement concerning the Restraint and Confiscation of the Proceeds and Instruments of Crime	Bucharest, 14.11.1995	

RUSSIAN FEDERATION

Exchange of Notes concerning the UK/Russia Debt Agreement No. 3 (1995)	London, 21/26.2.1996	TS No. 59 (1996) (Cm 3287)
Agreement on Science and Technology Cooperation	Moscow, 28.5.1996	TS No. 88 (1996) (Cm 3434)
Agreement on Co-operation in the Peaceful Uses of Nuclear Energy	London, 3.9.1996	TS No. 107 (1996) (Cm 3500)
Agreement on the Design and Construction of Embassy Buildings in London and Moscow, with Annexes	London, 15.10.1996	TS No. 2 (1997) (Cm 3503)
Agreement concerning the Leases of New Embassy Premises in Moscow and London, with Annexes	London, 15.10.1996	TS No. 1 (1997) (Cm 3502)

Country and Title	Place and Date	Text
SENEGAL		
Exchange of Notes concerning Certain Commercial Debts (The UK/Senegal Debt Agreement No. 11 (1995))	Dakar, 9.10/ 13.11.1995	
SIERRA LEONE		
Exchange of Notes concerning Certain Commercial Debts (UK/ Sierra Leone Debt Agreement No. 7 (1996))	Freetown, 26.6/15.7.1996	TS No. 97 (1996) (Cm 3474)
SLOVENIA		
Agreement for the Promotion and Protection of Investments	Ljubljana, 3.7.1996	
SWITZERLAND		
Exchange of Notes concerning the Extension of the European Convention on Extradition to Certain Dependent Territories	Berne, 9/26.1.1996	
Exchange of Notes concerning the Proposed Export by British Nuclear Fuels Plc to the Nordostschweizerische Kraftwerke AG of Dottingen, Switzerland of 12 Mixed Oxide Fuel Assemblies for the Purpose of Electricity Generation	Berne, 4/9.10.1995	TS No. 63 (1996) (Cm 3294)
TOGO		
Exchange of Notes concerning Certain Commercial Debts (UK/ Togo Debt Agreement No. 10 (1995))	Lomé, 20.9/ 25.10.1995	TS No. 64 (1996) (Cm 3312)
UGANDA		
Exchange of Notes concerning Certain Commercial Debts (UK/ Uganda Debt Agreement No. 6 (1995))	Kampala, 28.2.1996	TS No. 80 (1996) (Cm 3377)
UKRAINE		
Exchange of Notes concerning the Termination of the Agreement between the Government of the UK and the Government of the Union of Soviet Socialist Republics concerning the Mutual	Kiev, 13.10.1995/ 29.3.1996	TS No. 94 (1996) (Cm 3462)

Country and Title	Place and Date	Text
Abolition of Consular Fees on Visas, done at Moscow on 13.4.1964	Kiev, 13.10.1995/ 29.3.1996	TS No. 94 (1996) (Cm 3462)
Agreement concerning the Restraint and Confiscation of the Proceeds and Instruments of Criminal Activity other than Drug Trafficking	Kiev, 18.4.1996	Ukraine No. 3 (1996) (Cm 3382)
Agreement concerning Mutual Assistance in Relation to Drug Trafficking	Kiev, 18.4.1996	Ukraine No. 2 (1996) (Cm 3375)

UNITED STATES OF AMERICA

Exchange of Notes concerning the Agreement on the Annex on Intellectual Property Rights of 29.11.1995	Washington, 29.11.1995	TS No. 89 (1996) (Cm 3435)
Agreement for Promotion of Aviation Safety	London, 20.12.1995	TS No. 32 (1996) (Cm 3193)
Supplementary Agreement amending the Agreement on Social Security with Supplementary Administrative Agreement	London, 6.6.1996	United States No. 2 (1996) (Cm 3374)
Supplementary Administrative Agreement amending the Administrative Agreement for the Implementation of the Agreement on Social Security	London, 6.6.1996	
Exchange of Notes further amending the Agreement concerning the Investigation of Drug Trafficking Offences and the Seizure and Forfeiture of Proceeds and Instrumentalities of Drug Trafficking done at London on 9.2.1988, as amended by the Exchange of Notes of 6.1.1994	London, 19.6/ 29.7.1996	TS No. 82 (1996) (Cm 3380)

Country and Title	Place and Date	Text
VENEZUELA		
Convention for the Avoidance of Double Taxation and the Prevention of Fiscal Evasion with respect to Taxes on Income and Capital Gains, with Exchange of Notes	Caracas, 11.3.1996	TS No. 18 (1997) (Cm 3570)

IV. United Kingdom Legislation During 1996 Concerning Matters of International Law[1]

The Asylum and Immigration Act (1996 c. 49) amends and supplements the Immigration Act 1971 and the Asylum and Immigration Appeals Act 1993. It makes new provision for appeals by, and removal to safe third countries of, asylum seekers; creates new offences in relation to immigration; and regulates the entitlement to housing and social security benefits of persons subject to immigration control. (See Part Four: VI., above.)

The Chemical Weapons Act (1996 c. 6) implements the United Kingdom's obligations under the Convention on the Prohibition of the Development, Production, Stockpiling and Use of Chemical Weapons and on their Destruction, 1993. It creates offences in relation to the use, development, production and possession of chemical weapons, and empowers the Secretary of State to authorise the removal and destruction of chemical weapons and the destruction of premises or equipment for the production of chemical weapons. It provides for inspections to be made in accordance with the Convention and for the enjoyment of certain of the privileges and immunities of diplomatic agents by members of inspection teams and observers. (See UKMIL 1995, pp. 605–6.)

The Civil Aviation (Amendment) Act (1996 c. 39) amends the Civil Aviation Act 1982 so as to provide for the prosecution of persons committing offences on foreign aircraft while in flight to the United Kingdom. (See Parts Eight: II. D. and Ten: II. A. 2., above).

The Hong Kong Economic and Trade Office Act (1996 c. 63) provides for the application of certain of the privileges and immunities contained in the Vienna Convention on Consular Relations, 1963, in relation to any economic and trade office established in the United Kingdom by the Government of the Hong Kong Special Administrative Region.

The Hong Kong (War Wives and Widows) Act (1996 c. 41) provides for the acquisition of British citizenship by certain women resident in Hong Kong whose late or former husbands served in defence of Hong Kong during the Second World War.

---

[1] Compiled by C. A. Hopkins.

TABLE OF CASES[1]

---

[1] The figures in heavier type indicate the pages on which cases are reviewed.

INDEX